Contents

Handbook of Urban Education

The *Handbook of Urban Education* comes at a time when urban schools and the communities they serve are experiencing ferocious attacks. We need research to defend the promise of equal educational opportunity in a just society, and the contributions to this volume do just that.

—Lois Weiner, Professor of Elementary and Secondary Education, New Jersey City University

Milner and Lomotey have assembled a dream team of scholars to effectively map the urban education terrain . . . This is a must read for all who are committed to access, equity, and social justice for ALL of America's youth.

—Maisha T. Winn, Susan J. Cellmer Chair in English Education Department of Curriculum and Instruction University of Wisconsin-Madison

As opposed to searching for the "one silver bullet" solution to school reform, the *Handbook of Urban Education* takes a comprehensive approach to the challenges facing urban education, examining both schools and communities and their interrelationships. The authors succeed admirably in summarizing complex research in a way that contributes to practical solutions to our most pressing social justice concerns. This volume is the "go to" place for scholars and urban educators looking for research to inform action.

—Mark R. Warren, Associate Professor of Public Policy and Public Affairs, University of Massachusetts Boston

This handbook is a must-read for teacher educators, policymakers, practitioners, and community activists who are committed to advancing educational equity for our nation's most disadvantaged and underserved youth.

—Dorinda Carter Andrews, Associate Professor of Teacher Education, Michigan State University

From considerations of culturally responsive education to discussions of school choice and descriptions of successful family outreach efforts, this *Handbook* provides as comprehensive a landscape of urban education as has ever been available.

—Sonia Nieto, Professor Emerita, University of Massachusetts, from the Afterword

At this moment in history, we witness a stunning consensus among educators, parents, students and communities, demanding a moratorium on school closings, on high stakes testing and on zero tolerance discipline policies. We understand all of these neo-liberal "de-forms" have systematically assaulted schools serving Black and Latino low income children, immigrants and struggling families, and extracted corporate profits dedicated to colonizing public education and undermining a multi-racial engaged public sphere. As the state invests in surveillance and criminalization of Black and Brown communities, we witness "target practice" on the backs of poor children—quotas on tests, on stop and frisk, on corporate profits. We know what we are against and what we are up against.

The *Handbook of Urban Education* marinates in critique and moves to action, offering a much needed blueprint-in-motion for mobilizing toward justice. Cultivated in the soil of critique and desire, speaking in voices of evidence and outrage and nurtured through an understanding of history and the present assault on and gentrification of urban education, the volume speaks through a dialect of Critical Race Theory to invite us to widen our educational imaginations for racial justice, labor justice and educational justice as three threads in a braided lifeline to a very different tomorrow.

—Michelle Fine, Distinguished Professor of Psychology and Urban Education,
The Graduate Center of the City University of New York

Handbook of Urban Education

Edited by
H. Richard Milner IV & Kofi Lomotey

NEW YORK AND LONDON

First published 2014
by Routledge
711 Third Avenue, New York, NY 10017

and by Routledge
2 Park Square, Milton Park, Abingdon, Oxon OX14 4RN

Routledge is an imprint of the Taylor & Francis Group, an informa business

Library of Congress Cataloging-in-Publication Data

Handbook of urban education / edited by H. Richard Milner IV, Kofi Lomotey.
pages cm
Includes bibliographical references and index.
1. Urban schools—United States. 2. Education, Urban—Social aspects—United States. 3. Education—Research. I. Milner IV, H. Richard. II. Lomotey, Kofi.
LC5131.H355 2013
370.9173′2—dc23
2013038553

ISBN: 978-0-415-63476-2 (hbk)
ISBN: 978-0-415-63477-9 (pbk)
ISBN: 978-0-203-09428-0 (ebk)

Typeset in Bembo
by Apex CoVantage, LLC

Dedications

HRM

For Anna Grace and Elise Faith

KL

For Shawnjua, Juba and Mbeja

Foreword

Linda Darling-Hammond

This Handbook is an extraordinary piece of work: thoughtful, comprehensive, and multifaceted, it provides multiple lenses on urban contexts and issues affecting children, teaching, schools, and communities in cities. The organization of the volume is like the concentric circles that ripple out from a stone dropped into a pond: from the individual student at the center to a broader sociological look at the school and community; from a focus on classroom teaching to a concern for leadership and administration, curriculum, and policy. Informed by some of the nation's leading scholars and researchers, the reader is led to think deeply about how individuals and groups are constructed and treated by social forces and institutions, as well as how these institutions are shaped by the adults and children they attract and serve.

This volume forces us to consider what urban education means in the U.S. context today. On its face, "urban" denotes a densely populated area, generally created as a hub of commerce and transport, and often—as a consequence—a location where people have come from many other places, representing diverse geographic and, increasingly, linguistic, ethnic, and racial origins. The intermingling of peoples, customs, and ideas often brings a cosmopolitan edge to cities that distinguishes their institutions and their people. Cities in some countries are more economically and educationally advantaged than many other communities, and are especially desirable places to live, work, and study.

This is certainly true of many cities in the United States. However, in contemporary U.S. society, "urban" has often come to connote places where the changing economy has left many families behind, where poverty and segregation are concentrated, and where severely under-resourced schools struggle to meet the increasingly intense needs of their students and families. Many of the chapters in this Handbook deal with these issues, as they affect children psychologically, physically, socially, emotionally, and academically.

As the U.S. safety net has become increasingly tattered, more children in cities lack more basic supports—housing, health care, and food security—than in any other industrialized nation. In many U.S. cities, the confluence of these concerns can be so intense as to constitute what Gloria Ladson-Billings has called "aggressive neglect" of children, as rates of severe poverty have grown to levels not seen since the Great Depression.

Furthermore, whereas other high-achieving nations fund schools centrally and equally, the United States spends much more on the education of affluent children than it does on poor children, with wealthy suburbs often spending twice what central cities can, and three times what poor rural areas can afford. Both segregation of schools and inequality in funding have increased in many states over the last two decades, leaving a growing share of African American and Latino students in highly segregated apartheid schools that lack qualified teachers, up-to-date textbooks and materials, libraries, science labs and computers, and safe, adequate facilities.

A school-to-prison pipeline operates at full force in many of these communities, where far too many young people join the growing ranks of inmates in what the *New York Times* recently dubbed our "prison nation," which incarcerates more people than any other country in the world. With 5% of the world's population, we have 25% of the world's inmates, at a cost of more than $50 billion annually to taxpayers and untold costs in human tragedy. States that would not spend $10,000 a year to ensure adequate education for young children of color in poorly funded city schools later spend over $30,000 a year to keep them in jail.

This situation is not inevitable. During the years following *Brown v. Board of Education*, when desegregation and school finance reform efforts were launched, and when the Great Society's War on Poverty increased investments in low-income communities, substantial gains were made in equalizing both educational inputs and outcomes. Childhood poverty was reduced to levels more than one-third what they are today. Investments were made in urban education through federal grants for desegregation, magnet schools, community schools, pipelines of well-qualified teachers, school funding reforms, and higher education assistance.

These investments paid off in measurable ways. By the mid-1970s, urban schools spent as much as suburban schools, and paid their teachers as well; perennial teacher shortages had nearly ended; and gaps in educational attainment had closed substantially. Federally funded curriculum investments transformed teaching in many schools. Innovative schools flourished, especially in the cities. Large gains in Black students' performance throughout the 1970s and early 1980s cut the literacy achievement gap by half in just 15 years. For a brief period in the mid-1970s, Black and Hispanic students attended college at rates comparable to Whites, the only time this has happened before or since. Ironically, had this rate of progress been continued, the achievement gap would have been fully closed by the beginning of the 21st century.

Unfortunately, reforms and budget cuts during the Reagan years undid much of this work, cutting the federal education budget in half, ending most aid to cities and most supports for teacher recruitment and training, while also slashing health and human service budgets and shifting costs to the states. This caused states to reduce equalization aid to schools in order to pick up other social service costs.

The Reagan era introduced a new theory of reform focused on outcomes rather than inputs—that is, high-stakes testing without investing—that drove most policy initiatives. The situation in many urban (and rural) schools deteriorated over the decades. Drops in real per-pupil expenditures accompanied tax cuts and growing enrollments. Meanwhile student needs grew with immigration, concentrated poverty and homelessness, and increased numbers of students requiring second-language instruction and special educational services. Although some federal support to high-need schools and districts was restored during the 1990s, it was not enough to fully recoup the earlier losses, and after 2000, inequality grew once again.

Since the 1980s, national investments have tipped heavily toward incarceration rather education. As the number of prisoners has quadrupled since 1980, state budgets for corrections grew by over 900%, three times faster than funds for education. The strong relationship between undereducation, unemployment, and incarceration has created a vicious cycle, as lack of adequate investment in education increasingly funds prisons that now compete with the funding available for education. Today, at least five states spend more on corrections than they spend on public colleges and universities, and some, like California, are decreasing slots in their higher education systems as other nations are aggressively increasing theirs.

As this volume documents, the "cures" embodied in recent policies are often worse than the cause, leading to test-based incentive systems that push struggling students out of school; punish professionals who choose to work in these locations; and close or privatize public schools in high-need communities, further gutting the opportunities families have available. With federal requirements to identify and close schools where test scores are low, contemporary education policy has reintroduced the prospect of redlining: the once-common practice in which banks would draw a red line on a map—often along a natural barrier like a highway or river—to designate neighborhoods where they would not invest. Stigmatized and denied access to loans and other resources, redlined communities, populated by African Americans and other people of color, often became places that lacked businesses, jobs, grocery stores and other services, and thus could not retain a thriving middle class. Redlining produced and reinforced a vicious cycle of decline for which urban residents themselves were typically blamed.

If privatization and abandonment characterize the future of urban public education, the American dream of education as the great equalizer will have been punctured, perhaps irreparably, for generations to come.

This Handbook represents a deep awareness of the issues that face children, educators, families, and public officials in urban communities. Many of its authors have experience on the ground in urban schools as well as in long study of their realities, contexts, and possibilities. Across the chapters, they present a sophisticated appreciation of how children learn in different contexts; how teaching unfolds and can be more effective; how organizations behave and respond to obstacles, supports, and incentives; and how policy strategies that respond to this knowledge could make a genuine difference for the future of urban education in the United States—and, for that matter, around the world. I hope, for the sake of our children and our nation, that this volume will be widely read, appreciated, and acted upon.

Linda Darling-Hammond
Stanford University
May 18, 2013

Introduction

H. Richard Milner IV & Kofi Lomotey

Is urban education a discipline or a subfield to other academic domains? If it is a distinct field of inquiry and practice, then what do we know about it—and what more do we need to know in order to advance it? If urban education is not a freestanding field, then what is it, and what insights can we garner from those who study aspects of it to contribute to larger scholarly discourses and, more importantly, to support, through practice, students who attend urban schools? These questions, related to the identity of urban education, shape the motivation for this *Handbook*. Education is not the only scholarly area that has failed to well define and conceptualize "urban." Identity challenges in the conceptualization of urban are prevalent in other domains such as sociology, anthropology, public policy, economics, geography, environmental studies, and political science as well (see, for example, Frey & Zimmer, 2001; Kottis, 1972; Munasinghe, 1998; Rueff, 2012; Sayer, 1984).

To define, name, construct, and advance the identity of urban education as a field or subfield, we have brought together many leading scholars in U.S. urban education. An aim of the volume is for these scholars to conceptualize and name our collective reality. Contributors were challenged to construct and deconstruct what urban education is, can be, and should be. Critical race theorists note a central principle of the critical legal studies movement (Crenshaw, Gotanda, Peller & Thomas, 1995) was for scholars, in general, and scholars of color in particular, to name and construct their own reality in order to shape discourse, knowledge, and practice. We utilize this principle striving for this volume to assist newer as well as seasoned researchers, theorists, policy makers, and practitioners in elevating and strengthening their work and also in constructing a path to overhaul ineffective practices. In some combination, the contributors to this volume all focus on the following aspects in defining and conceptualizing urban education: (1) *the size* of the city in which schools are located: dense, large, metropolitan areas; (2) *the students* in the schools: a wide range of student diversity, including racial, ethnic, religious, language, and socioeconomic; and (3) *the resources:* the amount and number of resources available in a school, such as technology and financial structures through federal programs as well as property taxes.

Due to structural and systemic inequities (Anyon, 2005; Haberman, 2000; Kozol, 1991, 2005; MacLeod, 1995), the 6.9 million students (Council of the Great City Schools, 2013)[1] in urban environments are the most underserved in the United States. We see structural and systemic inequities as well as other challenges in urban education associated with underperformance of students as those practitioners and policy makers must address and solve but also as ones that researchers and theorists should be on the frontlines of interrogating to inform practice.

Challenges in urban schools are caused by factors both inside and outside of school (see Milner, 2013; Noguera & Wells, 2011). For instance, inadequate teaching practices, inadequate funding, poor administrative decisions, underdeveloped counseling and psychological services as well as curricular opportunities that are unchallenging for and unresponsive to students are all inside-of-school factors that urban schools need to address. Outside-of-school factors such as family income, parental educational level, family structure, and student home living conditions all seem to play a role in students' experiences inside of school.

Students whose first language is not English, those living in poverty, and children of color disproportionately receive and experience the most disturbing educational experiences across the United States and in urban schools in particular. For example, poverty seems to be a pervasive social problem that can have a lasting influence on students in urban communities and schools. However, the rate of children/people of color living in poverty is astounding. Adapted from Munin (2012); Simms, Fortuny, and Henderson (2009), Table 1 demonstrates the disproportionate representation of White, Black, and Hispanic (Brown) low-income families in the United States. In Munin's words:

> In an equitable society, if Whites constitute 65% of the total population, they should also make up 65% of those in the low-income bracket. But this group is actually 23.6 percentage points lower in representation in the low-income family category. Conversely, Blacks make up a larger percentage than their overall size in the low-income population by 9.8 percentage points. The same is true for Hispanics, who constitute a greater share of the low-income group compared to their population size by 14.6 percentage points. (pp. 4–5)

Table 1 Low-Income Families by Race Adapted from Munin (2012), Simms, Fortuny, and Henderson (2009)

Race	*Percentage of Low-Income Families*	*Percentage of U.S. Population*
White	42%	65.6%
Black	22%	12.2%
Hispanic/Brown	30%	15.4%
Total Percentage for Black and Brown	52%	27.6%

In this way, scholarship and practices need to address race and poverty in terms of how they intersect and manifest independently inside and outside of school. Rather than perceiving students and their families as inferior or deficient because they live in poverty, for instance, the point is to identify, study, and address structural forms of inequity that do not serve students well in education and beyond.

Based in part on what we call an *identity crisis in urban education*, we chose to produce this volume because of what we conceive as

- a sporadic, disconnected, multidimensional knowledge base in urban education;
- an absence of a coherent assessment of needs, challenges, problems, and solutions in urban education;
- the nonexistence of a consistent definition or conceptualization of the concept, urban education;
- an underdevelopment of research and theoretical tools to analyze and improve urban education; and
- a significant disconnect between research and practice in urban education.

It is difficult to consider urban education a field or even as a subfield without a more disciplined identity framing of "urban" educational research, theory, policy, practice, and praxis. In this volume we address some of these challenges and encourage readers to address these broader challenges in their work.

A Crisis

At least two levels of crisis are prevalent in urban education. One crisis concerns micro-level practices and programs that inadequately address the needs of students in urban schools. For many years, researchers have studied the various dimensions of this crisis in urban schools. They have looked at factors related to teaching, including teacher preparation, teacher attitudes, teacher qualifications, and more (Delpit, 2012; Kozol, 1991; Warren, 2005; Zhou, 2003). The leadership of principals has been explored (Blank, 1987; Hallinger & Heck, 1996; Wallace Foundation, 2013) and student characteristics and needs have also been addressed. These student characteristics have included—but have not been limited to—factors related to family background and student motivation (Jeynes, 2007; Noguera, 2001; Stewart, 2008). What we know is that the answers to solving a school-level crisis are not singularly dimensional but are in fact multidimensional and quite complex.

A second crisis is broader and addresses the failure of research, theory, and policy to make significant strides in impacting urban schools. From our review and analyses of the existing literature on urban education, research and policy span several different areas. These areas include school choice, common core standards, alternative routes into teaching, scripted curriculum mandates, and pay for performance. We attempt to address both the breadth and depth of the range of scholarship available in the education field in order to *capture* urban education. In an attempt to capture the breadth of available knowledge in urban education, this volume addresses seven general areas. Below we list these areas and provide the reader with questions representative of those addressed in each section and also those that need further exploration to advance urban education. In this way, we chart a research agenda to encourage researchers to design studies in order to address the questions below.

- Psychology, Health, and Human Development
  - What psychological factors shape the experiences and practices of students and teachers in urban environments?
  - How do psychological and health factors impact the achievement of students in urban schools?
  - What psychological issues do students in urban schools face and how can they be addressed?
  - In what ways might human development intersect with student learning, motivation and interactions in urban schools?
  - How can teachers, administrators, counselors, and parents support the psychological, health, and human development of students?
- Sociological Perspectives
  - How do societal factors contribute to—or detract from—efforts to educate students in urban schools?
  - How do social forces support and/or hinder student resilience inside and outside of school?
  - In what ways do socially constructed categories such as race and sexual orientation contribute to students' experiences in schools?
  - How can teachers, administrators, counselors, and parents support students to navigate and negotiate sociological factors to succeed in political and academic environments?

- Families and Communities
  - o What roles, historically and contemporarily, do parents, families, and communities play in the education of students in urban schools?
  - o What is the role of families and communities in enabling English-language learners to be successful in urban schools?
  - o What is the intersected nature of language, race, and class on family and community involvement in schools?
  - o How can urban schools build on and from the assets of families and communities in their practices?
- Teacher Education and Special Education
  - o How can we improve the preparation of teachers in general and special education teachers in particular?
  - o What knowledge, skills, attitudes, dispositions, and practices are essential for urban teacher/special education?
  - o What unique challenges and needs do students in urban schools face that need to be addressed in teacher preparation and in P–12 special education?
- Leadership, Administration, and Leaders
  - o How effective are urban school systems in selecting principals to lead their schools? How might their efforts be improved?
  - o Is the professional development of principals adequate in meeting the needs of today's students in urban schools?
  - o How do preparation programs support effective urban administrators?
- Curriculum and Instruction
  - o Why are culturally relevant and culturally responsive teaching practices effective in urban schools?
  - o To what extent should teachers in urban schools consider the influence of hip hop in the teaching/learning process?
  - o What do we know about subject matter–specific curriculum and instruction in urban schools?
- Policy and Reform
  - o How do historical movements and policies influence urban schools and urban education?
  - o What do we know about the benefits and evolving nature of school choice and other reform efforts in urban schools?
  - o How do policy and reform shape discourse and practice in urban education and urban schools?

We are suggesting that researchers situate their work building from the areas above so that we are able to more systematically construct knowledge and move urban education forward.

Absence of Critical Assessment

Despite the plethora of research that has been conducted over the years that spans the areas outlined above, little has been provided in the way of a *critical* assessment of the challenges we face in urban schools and urban education. While, as a collective in urban education, we have insufficiently analyzed these challenges, we have also spent too little time highlighting strategies that have been shown to be effective in urban schools. We are not suggesting that so-called best or promising practices can be replicated without consideration of context. What we are suggesting is that too little effort has been made in exploring the successes that have been achieved in some urban schools to determine the applicability and transferability of those strategies in other urban contexts. An important contribution of this volume is the critical assessment that opens the door for additional exploratory as well as theory-testing studies looking at the applicability of these best practices and much more. Heretofore, research and theory related to urban education in the areas outlined above have provided important insights. However, the overall body of work is disparate at best; this volume provides a critical assessment of what is available.

Conceptualizing "Gaps"

Rather than conceive of gaps solely related to "achievement" disparities between White students and Black and Brown children, we believe that we need to address gaps in the work we do to build a more robust knowledge base in urban education to chart a course that will benefit students and practitioners in urban ecologies. Several gaps exist that urban education needs to address.

- *Definitional Gap:* Research has failed to provide a comprehensive, uniform definition of urban education. For example, when a researcher discusses policy in urban schools, it is useful to have a definition of the concept so others may look at the work in the context of previous work on that topic to advance what is known about the topic for/in urban education.
- *Historical Gap:* Researchers rarely provide a historical context—or even a contemporary one—in urban education scholarship and practice. It is often difficult to compare otherwise similar studies when historical framing is not provided or varies considerably across studies. In short, there is not a concrete historical storyline of scholarly work and practice in urban education.
- *Methodological Gap:* Research methods used to study urban education vary substantially across and between studies. Our critique here is that researchers too often do not draw from and build on previously used methodological frameworks to advance knowledge. Replicating studies can assist us in generalizing and transferring findings through consistent, rigorous methods.
- *Theoretical Gap:* Many published studies in urban education are a-theoretical or borderline a-theoretical, providing little or no theoretical basis or theory building in their analysis. The lack of theory consistency makes it difficult to draw from and build on theory to advance urban education.
- *Theory-to-Practice Gap:* Few coherent, consistent practical suggestions are provided to advance the work of practitioners in urban schools or even in the preparation of teachers, superintendents, principals, and counselors. When research-based strategies and suggestions are made about practice in the existing scholarship, they are often disconnected from recommendations from other published work.
- *Policy Gap:* Too often there is insufficient communication between and among practitioners, policy makers, and researchers. In part because of this limited communication, the necessary concerted efforts required to develop and implement useful policies do not materialize.

Addressing the Gaps

Each of the contributions in this volume offers (1) a definition of urban education as it relates to the particular area of interest being considered, (2) a historical context for the discussion, (3) knowledge about what we know about the particular area of interest as it relates to urban education based on the existing literature, and (4) a charting of a course for the future, through the provision of an explicit implications section addressing research, practice, theory, policy, and/or praxis.

In the first section of this volume, the contributors address aspects of psychology, health, and human development related to urban education. They consider how these factors impact the overall development and ultimately the academic, physical, psychological, social, and emotional success of students in urban schools. Tate, Hamilton, Jones, Robertson, Macrander, Schultz, and Thorne-Wallington compellingly offer an extensive discussion of urban youth and mental illness and present a comprehensive assessment of intervention strategies. King, Akua, and Russell consider the impact of culture on urban education. They offer striking illustrations of academic and cultural excellence in urban education, while rightfully emphasizing the importance of culture in providing excellence in urban education. Hodge and Vigo-Valentin artfully discuss the association between health promotion and life circumstances of students in urban schools. They stress the importance of communities, families, and urban schools, focusing on the health, nutrition, and physical activity of students both inside and outside of school.

The four contributions in Section II are devoted to sociological perspectives and their significance in urban schools and education. The contributors consider factors in society that impact the success of urban school students. O'Connor, Mueller, and Neal consider the resilience—or lack thereof—of students in urban schools. They skillfully contextualize risk factors that impact these students. Easton-Brooks ponders the clash between home culture and school culture in urban centers in light of racial differences (i.e., large numbers of students of color and similarly large numbers of White teachers). He importantly considers the benefits of same-race teachers for urban students and effectively demonstrates the benefits of same-race teachers and students on student academic performance. Noguera confronts, head-on, the underachievement of African American male students in urban schools. He passionately stresses that traditional reforms have not helped and that a focus on what he calls a "safety net," drawing on the social contexts and strengths of communities, is necessary. Noguera provides an historical context for the educational experiences of African American male students in urban schools. In another important work in this section, Blackburn and McCready adeptly consider LGBTQQ people and some of the challenges (e.g., homophobia and transphobia) they encounter in urban schools. Emphasizing the undertheorizing of these issues, the authors provide an historical context for these challenges in part through the use of vivid and powerful illustrations.

In the three chapters in the third section, the importance of families and communities is considered. Jeynes offers a broad historical assessment of parental involvement in urban schools. He astutely discusses the development of research that addresses the significance of parental involvement in student success. Boutte and Johnson fervidly posit that parental involvement is essential, yet minimal, in too many urban schools. They pose and address 10 essential questions related to this quagmire. Iddings, Combs, and Moll discuss the critically important challenges faced by the growing number of English-language learners in urban schools. They adroitly build on and from the perspective that schools need to work with families to address the needs of English-language learners in order to improve students' experiences in schools.

Section IV of this volume deals with teacher education and special education. The importance of this section is evident given the well-known and longstanding importance of teachers in the teaching/learning process and the inadequate preparation that many teachers receive for work in urban schools. Howard and Milner dissect the field of teacher education as it relates to urban schools. They effectively address key changes related to knowledge construction that must be addressed if teachers are going to facilitate a turnaround in the massive underachievement of large numbers of urban school students. Toshalis looks at teacher education programs wherein attempts are made to encourage and prepare students to teach in their own urban communities. He compellingly discusses the utility of these programs as well as the various models employed. Lamenting the underachievement of Latina/o students in urban schools and the historic failure of reform efforts to help, Irizarry and Welton hopefully ponder the implications of these students doing research on their own educational experiences. Drawing upon data from a study, the authors demonstrate the value of student engagement in participatory action research. This chapter has implications not only for teacher education grounded in the voices of urban, English-language learners but also for participatory action research as a useful framework for this work. Tefera, Thorius, and Artiles take a look at the role of teachers in the disproportionate placement of students of color in special education. Offering worthwhile strategies for improvement, they explore the reasons for this gross overrepresentation and look at aspects of teacher preparation that may affect these circumstances. Blanchett, with a useful historical perspective, considers special education and its particular impact on African American students in urban schools. She offers valuable insights into ways we can counter the historic disproportionality in the placement of African American students in special education.

The authors in Section V address leadership practices, administration, and leaders themselves. Most researchers, practitioners, and policy makers acknowledge that school leaders and leadership are essential in establishing and maintaining a culture of academic excellence through such efforts as facilitating a culturally responsive environment and stressing a commitment to student success. Crow and Scribner contend that the changing nature of urban schools calls for a shift in the type of leadership displayed by urban school principals. The singular focus on the "technocratic" approach, they argue, is not appropriate today for leaders in these schools. Transformational leadership, they argue forcefully, must appear more prominently in the training of leaders. Bogotch, Nesmith, Smith, and Gaines address the biased nature of the selection of principals. In the interest of the educational success of students in urban schools, they effectively argue for a reconsideration of the way principals are selected. The idea of "fit," they stress, is more political than anything else. In a review of the relevant research conducted in the past 25 years, Lomotey and Lowery explore the leadership of Black principals in urban schools. In their comprehensive review, they look at gender differences, differences in elementary and secondary school leadership, and qualities of Black principals in effective schools.

Section VI addresses curriculum and instruction. Within this section, several topics are considered, including culturally relevant and responsive teaching, math, literacy, and the significance of hip hop in the teaching and learning process. Gay discusses the importance of culturally responsive teaching practices in urban schools. She skillfully examines the importance of such a focus, and how it can be accomplished by building from models of programs and practices already in existence. Martin and Larnell effectively describe how urban mathematics education was addressed in the past and how it is currently constructed. They consider the challenges of—and approaches to—urban math education and powerfully argue for a rethinking of the way it is addressed to benefit students in these schools. Kirkland explores the learning of literacy in urban schools. He ponders the question, "What is literacy?" He argues efficiently that we should rethink or reframe our conception of literacy. He discusses the significance of the social interactions of urban youth in their acquisition of literacy. Yasin deliberately and keenly describes hip hop culture as a vehicle for negotiating life and urban school experiences across multiple subject matter areas. In describing the history of hip hop, he defines it as a discourse, a source of motivation, and as a teaching and learning vehicle.

The authors in the last section of the volume focus on issues of policy and reform. Indeed, reform movements are plentiful in urban education. In her own inimitable way, Ladson-Billings looks at historic and contemporary legal barriers to equitable education for students in urban schools. Using critical race theory (CRT) as her analytical framework, she argues that these barriers contribute significantly to the underachievement of selected groups of students in urban schools. Berends methodically addresses the evolution of school choice initiatives as an effort at reform. Drawing from current data, he describes this evolution and makes suggestions for future research. The jury is still out, he finds, with regard to the effectiveness of these models. Dixson, Royal, and Henry, using Philadelphia, Chicago, and New Orleans for illustrative purposes, discuss school reform in the United States. More particularly, they artfully address how school reform in the nation has impacted the power of teacher unions and school boards and the number of charter schools in urban districts. Looking at several local and national studies of charter schools, Chapman tactfully chronicles the growth of these institutions. She notes the limitations of these studies and, in the context of four stated initial goals of charter schools, she also explores their impact on achievement. Heilig, Khalifa, and Tillman acknowledge the persistence of the underachievement of Black and Brown students in urban schools despite numerous efforts at reform. Using a postcolonial theory framework, they deftly address reform in U.S. education, focusing on high-stakes testing.

Conclusion

In this *Handbook*, we offer readers a typology of issues related to urban education and an assessment of the research that has been done. Moreover, we provide an assessment of where we have been, where we are, and where we are (and need to be) heading. The contributors offer substantive suggestions that are germane to future efforts of researchers, theorists, practitioners, and policy makers.

What we have compiled is a resource for seasoned scholars, as well as a helpful overview for newcomers to urban education and for laypeople. Research and clinical faculty, graduate students, and advanced undergraduate students in (urban) education, policy, multicultural education, curriculum and instruction, leadership and policy, and teacher education will likely find this volume useful as they ponder the challenges in contemporary (urban) education. In addition, practitioners in P–12 institutions (teachers, counselors, and administrators) and educational policy makers at the local, state, and federal levels will find the *Handbook* valuable.

As coeditors, we are indebted to the scholars who contributed; they are thoughtful, experienced, and knowledgeable about the challenges facing urban schools and the children who attend them as well as urban education in general. Moreover, they understand the rich resources in urban schools and communities, and they help readers understand these assets. In their writings herein, they have, indubitably, made a significant step in critically assessing and addressing the identity of urban education, crises in urban education, and macro-level gaps that persist in urban education. As we continue to seek ways to improve upon the educational experiences of the millions of students in urban centers, we are comforted knowing that these and other "long distance runners" continue tilling the fields, addressing the questions and helping us to uncover the solutions to improving the life chances of all students in urban environments.

Note

1. For our purposes here, urban schools are defined as those in cities with more than 250,000 people and with student enrollments exceeding 35,000 (Council of the Great City Schools, 2013).

References

Anyon, J. (2005). *Radical possibilities: Public policy, urban education, and a new social movement.* New York, NY: Routledge.

Blank, R.K. (1987). The role of principal as leader: Analysis of variation in leadership of urban high schools. *Journal of Educational Research, 81*(2), 69–80.

Council of the Great City Schools. (2013). *Fact Book.* www.cgsc.org/Page/72

Crenshaw, K., Gotanda, N., Peller, G., & Thomas, K. (Eds.). (1995). *Critical race theory: The key writings that formed the movement.* New York, NY: New Press.

Delpit, L. (2012). *"Multiplication is for white": Raising expectations for other people's children.* New York, NY: The New Press.

Frey, W.H., & Zimmer, Z. (2001). Defining the city. In Ronan Paddison (Ed.), *Handbook of urban studies* (pp. 14–35). London: Sage Publications.

Haberman, M. (2000). Urban schools: Day camps or custodial centers? *Phi Delta Kappan, 82*(3), 203–208.

Hallinger, P., & Heck, R.H. (1996). Reassessing the principal's role in school effectiveness: A review of empirical research, 1980–1995. *Educational Administration Quarterly, 32*(1), 5–44.

Jeynes, W.H. (2007). The relationship between parental involvement and urban secondary school student achievement. *Urban Education, 42*(1), 82–110.

Kottis, G.C. (1972). Problems of defining an urban economy. *Planning Outlook, 12*(1–2), 9–16.

Kozol, J. (1991). *Savage inequalities: Children in America's schools.* New York, NY: Crown.

Kozol, J. (2005). *The shame of a nation: The return of apartheid schooling in America.* New York, NY: Crown.

MacLeod, J. (1995). *Social reproduction in theoretical perspective. Ain't no makin it: Aspirations and attainment in a low-income neighborhood.* San Francisco, CA: Westview Press.

Milner, H.R. (2013). Analyzing poverty, learning, and teaching through a critical race theory lens. *Review of Research in Education, 37*(1),1–53.

Munasinghe, H. (1998). Towards a conceptual framework for the conservation of urban heritage. *Buitt-Environment-Sri Lanka, 9*(1), 1–4.

Munin, A. (2012). *Color by number: Understanding racism through facts and stats on children.* Sterling, VA: Stylus.

Noguera, P. (2001). Transforming urban education through investments in the social capital of parents. In S. Saegert, J.P. Thompson, & M.R. Warren (Eds.), *Social capital and poor communities* (n.p.). New York, NY: Russell Sage Foundation.

Noguera, P.A., & Wells, L. (2011). The politics of school reform: A broader and bolder approach for Newark. *Berkeley Review of Education, 2*(1), 5–25.

Rueff, B.T. (2012). Spring focus on sustainability and the environment: Characterization study of urban cohousing communities. *Journal of Undergraduate Studies.* Retrieved from http://ufdc.ufl.edu/UF00091523/00621

Sayer, A. (1984). Defining the urban. *GeoJournal, 9*(3), 279–285.

Simms, M.C., Fortuny, K., & Henderson, E. (2009). *Racial and ethnic disparities among low-income families.* New York, NY: Urban Institute.

Stewart, E.B. (2008). School structural characteristics, student effort, peer associations, and parental involvement. *Education and Urban Society, 40*(2), 179–204.

Wallace Foundation. (2013). *Districts matter: Cultivating the principals urban schools need.* New York, NY: Author.

Warren, M.R. (2005). Communities and schools: A new view of urban education reform. *Harvard Educational Review, 75*(2), 133–173.

Zhou, M. (2003). Urban education: Challenges in educating culturally diverse children. *Teachers College Record, 105*(2), 208–225.

Acknowledgements

Rich acknowledges the uncompromising support and love of his family, especially his wife, Shelley, parents Henry and Barbara, sister, Tanya, and in-laws, Dick and Margaret. Your commitment to the work, call, and responsibility placed on his life is demonstrated in not only what you say but what you do. Thank you for loving him, reminding him of his responsibilities to improve the human condition, and pushing him to keep fighting for equity. He is better because of you.

Kofi acknowledges his two grandchildren, Ayanna and Isaiah, both of whom are too young to appreciate this work now. However, it is his hope that this work—along with other stimuli—will inspire them to develop a thirst for reading and knowledge accumulation and a desire to contribute to changing the circumstances that will surround them as they grow up in the United States and in this world.

Co-Editors

H. Richard Milner IV is the Helen Faison Endowed Chair in Urban Education, Professor of Education, and Director of the Center for Urban Education at the University of Pittsburgh. He also holds academic appointments (by courtesy) in Africana Studies and Social Work at the University of Pittsburgh and is Editor-in-Chief of *Urban Education*. Professor Milner's research, teaching, and policy interests concern urban (teacher) education, English education, and the sociology of education. He has published several books, journal articles, and book chapters. His most recent authored book, published in 2010 by Harvard Education Press, is *Start Where You Are but Don't Stay There: Understanding Diversity, Opportunity Gaps, and Teaching in Today's Classrooms*. Previously, Professor Milner was Associate Professor of Education at Vanderbilt University. He and his wife, Shelley, are the parents of twin daughters, Anna and Elise.

Kofi Lomotey is the Chancellor John Bardo and Deborah Bardo Distinguished Professor in Educational Leadership at Western Carolina University in Cullowhee, NC. His research interests include urban schools, African American students in higher education, African American principals in elementary schools, and independent African-centered schools. He is the editor of the *Sage Encyclopedia of African American Education,* a two-volume, 1,200-page publication. For 19 years, Lomotey served as the editor of the journal, *Urban Education*. He and his wife, A. Nahuja, are the parents of three and grandparents of two.

Contributors

Chike Akua is a doctoral candidate in Education Policy Studies at Georgia State University and holds a Master's of Education with a concentration in School Counseling from Clark Atlanta University. He is a nationally recognized trainer and author of 10 books.

Alfredo J. Artiles is the Ryan C. Harris Memorial Endowed Professor of Special Education at Arizona State University. His scholarship examines the consequences of educational inequities related to the intersections of disability, race, social class, gender, and language.

Mark Berends is Professor of Sociology at the University of Notre Dame, where he also directs the Center for Research on Educational Opportunity (CREO) and the Center for Research on Educational Policy (CREP). His main fields of interest are sociology of education, school and schooling effects, and test score gaps among racial-ethnic and socioeconomic groups. He is currently examining organizational and instructional differences in charter, private, and traditional public schools. His latest books are *Examining Gaps in Mathematics Achievement Among Racial-Ethnic Groups, 1972–1992* (2005, RAND), *Charter School Outcomes* (2008, National Center on School Choice), *Handbook of Research on School Choice* (2009, Routledge), and *School Choice and School Improvement* (2011, Harvard Education Press).

Mollie Blackburn is Associate Professor of Teaching and Learning at Ohio State University, where she co-coordinates the Sexuality Studies program. She is the author of *Interrupting Hate: Homophobia in Schools and What Literacy Can Do About It* and the co-editor of *Acting Out!: Combating Homophobia Through Teacher Activism,* among other related publications, including articles in *Reading Research Quarterly, Theory Into Practice, English Journal,* and the *Journal of Gay and Lesbian Issues in Education.* Her scholarship has received the Queer Studies special interest group of the American Educational Research Association's award for a body of work, among others.

Wanda J. Blanchett is Dean of the School of Education and Ewing Marion Kauffman/Missouri Endowed Chair in Teacher Education at the University of Missouri, Kansas City. She has published numerous scholarly articles and presented extensively at annual conferences of the American Educational Research Association and the American Association of Colleges of Teacher Education. Dr. Blanchett's research focuses on issues of inequity including urban teacher preparation; issues of race, class, culture, and gender; disproportionate representation of students of color in special education; severe disabilities; and issues of sexuality for students with disabilities.

Ira Bogotch is Professor of Educational Leadership at Florida Atlantic University. In the 1990s, while at the University of New Orleans, Ira facilitated the development of leadership standards in the state of Louisiana. He is the associate editor of the *International Journal of Leadership in Education* and co-editor of the forthcoming *International Handbook on Educational Leadership and Social (In)Justice*. For the past few years, he has been working with educators in Malaysia, Scotland, and Australia as well as in Southeast Florida.

Gloria Swindler Boutte is the Department Chair and the Yvonne and Schuyler Moore Child Advocacy Distinguished Chair for the Department of Instruction and Teacher Education at the University of South Carolina. Dr. Boutte's scholarship, teaching, and service focus on equity pedagogies and teaching for social justice. She is the author of two books: *Multicultural Education: Raising Consciousness* (1999) and *Resounding Voices: School Experiences of People From Diverse Ethnic Backgrounds* (2002). She has received over $1,700,000 in grants and has published over 75 articles. She has presented her scholarship on curriculum, instruction, and diversity issues nationally and internationally. Dr. Boutte is the founder of a statewide Center of Excellence for the Education and Equity of African American Students (CEEEAAS). As a Freedom Scholar whose focus is on teaching for liberation, her goal is to help educators view teaching culturally and linguistically diverse students as rewarding and exhilarating.

Thandeka K. Chapman's work focuses on schooling outcomes of desegregation policies in urban and suburban districts. She conducts research with teachers and students in urban and racially diverse settings to examine and resolve the ways in which institutional racism is manifested in school climate, curriculum, adult and student relationships, and school policies. Under the umbrella of research in urban and racially diverse settings, Dr. Chapman also researches teaching and learning writing in secondary classrooms. She employs her research findings to assist districts and traditional and charter schools in alleviating barriers to student learning, and developing policies, teaching practices, and curricula that better serve the social and academic needs of all students.

Mary Carol Combs is Professor in the Department of Teaching, Language and Sociocultural Studies, University of Arizona. Her research interests include bilingual education, English as a second language (ESL) methods, sheltered content instruction, language policy and education law, language activism, and indigenous language revitalization and development. She is the former director of the Washington, DC–based English Plus Information Clearinghouse, a national clearinghouse on language rights and public policy. She remains active in national networks concerned with policy developments in the education of English-language learners.

Gary M. Crow is Professor and Department Chair in the Department of Educational Leadership and Policy Studies at Indiana University. His research interests include school leadership and school reform, leadership development, and professional identities. Crow is currently conducting research on successful school principals and professional identities of urban school leaders in reform contexts. His most recent book is *The Principalship: New Roles in a Professional Learning Community* (with Joe Matthews, published in 2009 by Allyn and Bacon). He is also a co-editor of the *International Handbook on the Preparation and Development of School Leaders* (2008) and the *Handbook of Research on the Education of School Leaders* (2009). Crow is a past president of the University Council for Educational Administration.

Adrienne D. Dixson (MA, Educational Studies, University of Michigan–Ann Arbor; PhD, Multicultural Education and Curriculum Studies, University of Wisconsin–Madison) is Associate Professor of Critical Race Theory and Education in the Department of Education Policy,

Organization and Leadership in the College of Education at the University of Illinois at Urbana-Champaign. A former public school teacher in pre-Katrina New Orleans, Dr. Dixson's research examines school reform and school choice policies in urban schooling contexts particularly as they manifest in the urban south.

Donald Easton-Brooks is the Dean in the Colleges of Education and Business at Eastern Oregon University. His research is on the impact of educational policy and social factors on students in urban and ethnically diverse communities. He has published several articles and book chapters on this topic. Dr. Easton-Brooks' work has been cited nationally and internationally. His work on educational policy has been cited in letters to senators, the U.S. Secretary of Education, and educational initiatives in Africa and Australia. He has consulted with local, state, national agencies on issues related to urban education and teacher quality.

Frank Gaines is a PhD candidate in Educational Leadership at Florida Atlantic University. He is an Intern Principal at a large urban high school in Southeast Florida in his 22nd year, the last 11 as an administrator in urban middle and high schools. His lifelong commitment has been in correcting the inequitable distribution of educational, social, political, and economic opportunities for students of color. His dissertation in progress, "Creating Urban High Schools of Opportunity for Students," aims to build a model to overcome roadblocks to success and opportunities in tight urban spaces.

Geneva Gay is Professor of Education at the University of Washington, Seattle, where she teaches courses in general curriculum theory and multicultural education. Her particular areas of interest are intersections among race, ethnicity, culture, teaching, and learning for students of color in urban schools. In her work these interests are coded as culturally responsive teaching, and actualized within the contexts of curriculum development, teacher preparation, and instructional practice in K–12 classrooms. She endeavors to demonstrate what culturally responsive teaching means conceptually and operationally, and its feasibility as a tool for improving the academic, cultural, social, civic, and personal achievement of students of color.

Christopher Hamilton is a Lynne Cooper Harvey Fellow in American Culture Studies, a Fellow of the Center for New Institutional Social Sciences and a doctoral student in the Department of Education at Washington University in St. Louis. His research interests include the political economy of urban education, the intergenerational transmission of socioeconomic and health disparities, and applications of Geographic Information Systems (GIS) in education research. Currently, he is examining school discipline policies and practices, mental health services, and the interinstitutional relationship between schools and the juvenile justice system.

Julian Vasquez Heilig is an award-winning researcher and teacher. He is currently Associate Professor of Educational Policy and Planning and African and African Diaspora Studies (by courtesy) at the University of Texas at Austin. He is also a Faculty Affiliate of the Center for Mexican American Studies and the Warfield Center for African and African American Studies at the University of Texas at Austin. His current research includes quantitatively examining how high-stakes testing and accountability-based reforms and incentive systems impact urban minority students. Additionally, his qualitative work considers the mechanisms by which student achievement and progress occur in relation to specific NCLB-inspired accountability policies in districts and schools for students of different kinds. Julian's research interests also include issues of access, diversity, and equity in higher education. He obtained his PhD in Education

Administration and Policy Analysis and a Master's in Sociology from Stanford University. He also holds a Master's of Higher Education and a Bachelor's of History and Psychology from the University of Michigan. He blogs at Cloaking Inequity.

Kevin Lawrence Henry, Jr., was born and raised in New Orleans, Louisiana. Kevin is currently a graduate student in the Department of Curriculum and Instruction at the University of Wisconsin–Madison. His research interests examine educational reform with a particular emphasis on charter schools; educational law; resilience in urban educational contexts; and critical race theory in education.

Samuel R. Hodge is Professor in the Department of Human Sciences at Ohio State University, where he received a doctoral degree in physical education and research methodology. His scholarship focuses on diversity, disability, and social justice in education and sport.

Tyrone C. Howard is Professor at the University of California, Los Angeles in the Graduate School of Education and Information Studies' Urban Schooling Division. He is the Faculty Director of Center X, and the Founder and Director of the UCLA Black Male Institute. Professor Howard's research is primarily concerned with race, culture, access, and the academic achievement of youth in urban schools.

Ana Christina DaSilva Iddings is Associate Professor of Language, Literacy, and Culture—Early Childhood at the University of Arizona. Her research interests are second-language learning in elementary schools, immigration and equity in education, and the preparation and professional development of teachers to work with young English language learners and their families.

Jason G. Irizarry is Associate Professor in the Department of Teacher Education and Curriculum Studies and Director of Urban Education in the College of Education at the University of Massachusetts-Amherst. A former middle school teacher in New York City, his research focuses on urban teacher recruitment, preparation, and retention with an emphasis on increasing the number of teachers of color, culturally responsive pedagogy, youth participatory action research, and Latino/a students in U.S. schools. A central focus of his work involves promoting the academic achievement of youth in urban schools by addressing issues associated with teacher education. Manuscripts documenting the findings of his research have been published or accepted for publication in a variety of peer-reviewed journals in the field including the *American Educational Research Journal*, *Teachers College Record*, *Education and Urban Society*, *Multicultural Perspectives*, the *Journal of Latinos and Education*, *Teaching and Teacher Education*, and the *Centro Journal of Puerto Rican Studies* and others appearing as chapters in various books. His book, *The Latinization of U.S. Schools: Successful Teaching and Learning in Shifting Cultural Contexts* (Paradigm Publishers, 2011), was recently awarded the Phillip C. Chin Book Award from the National Association for Multicultural Education.

William Jeynes is Professor of Education at California State University, Long Beach and a Senior Fellow at the Witherspoon Institute in Princeton, New Jersey. He graduated first in his class at Harvard University. He was the architect of the Korean economic and education stimulus package that helped it emerge from the 1997–1998 Asian economic crisis. Dr. Jeynes often speaks for and works with government leaders at the White House and in various U.S. government departments. He has conducted a number of meta-analyses on parental involvement that have gained a great deal of attention in the academic and government communities. He has over 120 academic publications, including 10 books.

George L. Johnson, Jr., is Assistant Professor and Academic Coordinator of the Special Education Program at South Carolina State University. For the past 5 years, Dr. Johnson's scholarship, teaching, and service have focused on equity pedagogies, teaching for social justice, and critical race theory in education with an emphasis on culturally and linguistically diverse students. Dr. Johnson has been both Principal and Co-Investigator of grants totaling in excess of $300,000 and has authored or coauthored six articles and a book review and two monographs. Additionally, he has presented nationally and internationally on special education and disproportionality and diversity issues.

Brittni D. Jones is a Chancellor's Graduate Fellow at Washington University in St. Louis where she is completing doctoral studies in the Department of Education in Arts and Sciences. She earned a BA in Biology, *summa cum laude,* from Fisk University, where she was also inducted into the Phi Beta Kappa Society. Her research interests include broadly the social contexts of education and the development of adolescents in urban communities. Her more specific areas of interest are the social determinants of attainment in science, technology, engineering, and mathematics (STEM) and the relationship between STEM understanding and health outcomes.

Muhammad Khalifa is Assistant Professor in the Department of Educational Administration at Michigan State University. He has worked as a public school teacher and administrator in Detroit. His research focuses on culturally responsive leadership in urban schools and demonstrates the necessity of school leaders to enact a nuanced school leadership unique to the sensibilities and histories of the local community. He also has served school leaders in a number of international locations in Asia, the Middle East, and Africa. He has recently been helping urban school leaders with conducting equity audits in local school districts.

Joyce E. King holds the Benjamin E. Mays Endowed Chair for Urban Teaching, Learning and Leadership and is Professor of Educational Policy Studies at Georgia State University.

David E. Kirkland is a transdisciplinary scholar of language, literacy, and urban education. He has received many awards for his work including a NAEd/Spencer Foundation Postdoctoral Fellowship Award, Ford Foundation Postdoctoral Fellowship Award, NCTE Cultivating New Voices Fellowship Award, 2006 AERA Division G Dissertation Award, among many others. His most recent articles include " 'Books Like Clothes': Engaging Young Black Men With Reading," " 'Black Skin, White Masks': Normalizing Whiteness and the Trouble With the Achievement Gap," and "We Real Cool: Examining Black Males and Literacy." He recently completed his fourth book, *A Search Past Silence: The Literacies of Black Males* (2013).

Gloria Ladson-Billings is the Kellner Family Chair of Urban Education in the Department of Curriculum and Instruction and faculty affiliate in the Departments of Educational Policy Studies and Afro American Studies at the University of Wisconsin–Madison.

Gregory Vincent Larnell is Assistant Professor in the Department of Curriculum and Instruction in the College of Education at the University of Illinois at Chicago. Specializing in mathematics education, his research interests center on the intersection of mathematics learning experience, identity, and race and equity. His current research focuses on the experiences of

African American students enrolled in remedial mathematics courses amid the transition to college. As a former doctoral fellow of the National Science Foundation, he has also conducted and collaborated on extensive research of contemporary mathematics curricula.

Kendra Lowery has a PhD in education from the Department of Educational Leadership and Policy Analysis (ELPA) at the University of Wisconsin–Madison. Her dissertation research focused on what the experiences of some of the earliest hired African American administrators in desegregated northern school districts can teach us about how race and gender influence individual and group problem-solving processes within organizations. She spent 15 years as a high school teacher and is currently an assistant principal at Sennett Middle School in Madison.

Ashley Macrander is a Lynne Cooper Harvey Fellow at Washington University in St. Louis where she is completing doctoral studies in the Department of Education in Arts and Sciences. Her research interests include comparative international social policy and tertiary education, more broadly. Specifically, she is interested in the role of race and other ecological determinants of higher education access in South Africa, as well as among the multiracial student population in the United States.

Danny Bernard Martin is Professor of Education and Mathematics at the University of Illinois at Chicago. His research focuses on understanding the salience of race and identity in Black learners' mathematical experiences. He is author of *Mathematics Success and Failure Among African Youth* (2000, Erlbaum), editor of *Mathematics Teaching, Learning, and Liberation in the Lives of Black Children* (2009, Routledge), and co-editor of *The Brilliance of Black Children in Mathematics: Beyond the Numbers and Toward New Discourse* (2013, Information Age).

Lance T. McCready is Associate Professor of Urban Education and Director of the Centre for Urban Schooling in the Department of Curriculum, Teaching and Learning at Ontario Institute for Studies in Education, University of Toronto (OISE/UT). His research program focuses on the education, health, and well-being of urban youth, in particular young Black men and boys and queer youth of color.

Luis C. Moll is Professor in the Language, Reading and Culture Program of the Department of Teaching, Learning and Sociocultural Studies, College of Education, University of Arizona. He was awarded his PhD (1978) in Educational Psychology/Early Childhood Development from the University of California, Los Angeles. Prior to his current position, he was an Assistant Research Psychologist at the Laboratory of Comparative Human Cognition of the University of California, San Diego. His main research interest is the connection among culture, psychology, and education, especially as it relates to the education of Latino children in the United States.

Jennifer Mueller is Associate Professor and Early Childhood Education Program Chair in the Department of Curriculum and Instruction, University of Wisconsin–Milwaukee. Her research focuses on identity in teacher education and preparation of teachers for urban schools.

Alaina Neal is a doctoral student in the Department of Educational Studies in the School of Education at the University of Michigan. Her developing research agenda focuses on the racial identity and schooling experiences of Black girls.

Leo Nesmith is a PhD candidate in educational leadership at Florida Atlantic University. He is also a public school principal in a large urban school district in Southeast Florida. His research interests are in urban education, social and racial equity, diversity, critical race theory, school leaders, educational leadership, and exceptional student education. He is currently finalizing his dissertation study titled, "The Vestiges of *Brown:* An Analysis of the Placements of African American Principals in Florida Public Schools (2010–2011)."

Pedro A. Noguera is the Peter L. Agnew Professor of Education at New York University. He holds tenured faculty appointments in the Departments of Teaching and Learning and Humanities and Social Sciences at the Steinhardt School of Culture, Education and Development at NYU. He is also the Executive Director of the Metropolitan Center for Urban Education and the Co-Director of the Institute for the Study of Globalization and Education in Metropolitan Settings (IGEMS). Dr. Noguera is the author of seven books and over 150 articles and monographs. His most recent books are *Creating the Opportunity to Learn* with A. Wade Boykin (2011, ASCD) and *Invisible No More: Understanding and Responding to the Disenfranchisement of Latino Males* with A. Hurtado and E. Fergus (2011, Routledge). Dr. Noguera appears as a regular commentator on educational issues on CNN, National Public Radio, and other national news outlets. He serves on the boards of numerous national and local organizations including the Economic Policy Institute and *The Nation* Magazine. In 2009 he was appointed by the Governor of New York to serve as a Trustee for the State University of New York (SUNY).

Carla O'Connor is Arthur F. Thurnau Professor and Associate Dean of Academic Affairs in the School of Education at the University of Michigan. Her disciplinary emphasis is sociology of education and she has expertise in the areas of Black achievement, urban education, and ethnographic methods.

W. Brett Robertson is a doctoral candidate in Education and Lynne Cooper Harvey Fellow in American Culture Studies at Washington University in St. Louis. His research examines the impacts of school choice on racial and socioeconomic stratification at multiple spatial scales. He is interested in using statistical methodologies such as hierarchical linear modeling, longitudinal modeling, and spatial statistics to describe these effects in space and time. Current projects include "Mapping the Profit Motive," a comparison of the geographic distribution, student population characteristics, and academic outcomes in charter schools run by for-profit and non-profit educational management organizations.

Camika Royal has been a teacher, teacher coach, and administrator for urban schools since 1999. She has also taught at Lincoln University, Temple University, and Ursinus College. Her doctoral research focused on the experiences of Black educators within the political landscape in the School District of Philadelphia from 1967 through 2007. Her research interests include urban educators, the sociopolitical context of school reform, and critical race theory.

LaToya Russell is a doctoral candidate in Education Policy Studies from Georgia State University and holds a Master's of Education Leadership, Politics and Advocacy from New York University.

Lyndsie Schultz is a doctoral student in the Department of Education in Arts and Sciences at Washington University in St. Louis. Combining her previous experience in television media production with interests in education reform, she is building a scholarly agenda focused on the new media literacy, social contexts of literacy in elementary schools, and education policy.

Samantha Paredes Scribner is Assistant Professor in Educational Leadership and Policy Studies at Indiana University-Purdue University Indianapolis (IUPUI). Her research and teaching focus on the organizational and political dynamics within and around urban K–12 schools, the policy contexts of these dynamics, and the consequences of leadership practices for various constituents of urban school communities. She is currently investigating the ways in which schools (and leaders) in urban settings, serving high percentages of ethno-linguistically and racially diverse students and families, navigate current reform context, and the implications of their actions on educational equity and social justice. Her recent work focuses on Latino immigrant school-family engagement and urban principal professional identity.

Scott V. Smith recently defended his PhD dissertation in Educational Leadership at Florida Atlantic University. It was titled, "The Concept of Fit: Intersections in Educational Leadership." Although Scott was born and raised in rural Indiana, he is currently a lead teacher at a large suburban public high school in Southeast Florida. Prior to becoming an educator, Scott earned an MBA at Purdue University and worked as an executive in the engineering and finance industries for more than a decade.

William F. Tate IV is the Edward Mallinckrodt Distinguished University Professor in Arts and Sciences at Washington University in St. Louis. He is a faculty scholar and member of the advisory council of the Institute for Public Health at the university. His past professional activities include serving as the President of the American Educational Research Association. Tate is a Fellow of the association and the recipient of a presidential citation for his contributions to theory and methods associated with research on opportunity to learn and social disparities. His research interests include psychiatric epidemiology and the use of geospatial applications in education, health, and human development.

Adai Tefera is a postdoctoral scholar at the Equity Alliance at Arizona State University's Mary Lou Fulton Teacher's College. Her research focuses on the intended and unintended consequences of high-stakes education policies on students of color labeled with disabilities.

Kathleen King Thorius is Assistant Professor of Special Education in Indiana University's School of Education and Principal Investigator for the Great Lakes Equity Center: a regional Equity Assistance Center. Dr. Thorius's work focuses on racial and linguistic disproportionality in special education, inclusive education, response to intervention, and addressing educational equity through teacher learning. Her research explores how systemic factors, including policy and teacher learning opportunities, mediate educator practices and shape opportunities to learn of underrepresented students, particularly with disabilities. Dr. Thorius has a strong record of facilitating equity-focused professional learning with state departments of education, districts, and professional organizations.

Elizabeth Thorne-Wallington is a doctoral student in the Department of Education in Arts and Sciences at Washington University in St. Louis. Her research interests include social contexts of literacy, new media literacy, applications of GIS in literacy, and policy studies in education. Currently, she is examining neighborhood effects on literacy achievement using geographically weighted regression models.

Linda C. Tillman is Professor in the Educational Leadership Program at the University of North Carolina–Chapel Hill. She is a former Vice President of Division A (Administration, Organization, and Leadership) of the American Educational Research Association and the former Associate Director of Graduate Student Development for the University Council for Educational Administration (UCEA). She has published in numerous peer-reviewed journals and is the Editor-in-Chief of the *Sage Handbook of African American Education,* the first comprehensive collection of scholarship written by African American scholars and leaders on the education of African Americans; co-editor (with Len Foster) of *African American Perspectives on Schools: Building a Culture of Empowerment;* and co-editor (with James Scheurich) of *Handbook of Research on Educational Leadership for Diversity and Equity.* Her research interests include African Americans in K–20 education and culturally sensitive research approaches.

Eric Toshalis has served urban education as a middle and high school teacher, coach, mentor teacher, union president, community activist, youth mentor, teacher educator, curriculum developer, author, consultant, and researcher. Eric received his BA, teaching credential, and Master of Education from the University of California, Santa Barbara, a master's degree from Harvard Divinity School, and a doctorate from the Harvard Graduate School of Education. He is the coauthor of *Understanding Youth: Adolescent Development for Educators* (2006, Harvard Education Press), and his forthcoming book, *Make Me: Understanding and Engaging Student Resistance in the Classroom* (Harvard Education Press, 2014).

Alexander Vigo-Valentín is Assistant Professor in the Department of Kinesiology at Towson University. He received a PhD in Physical Education Teacher Education from Ohio State University. Dr. Vigo-Valentín examines physical activity behaviors and opportunities in school settings, especially among Hispanic adolescents. He also focuses on school physical activity and physical education policies.

Anjalé DeVawn Welton is Assistant Professor in the Department of Education, Policy, Organization and Leadership at the University of Illinois at Urbana-Champaign. Welton's scholarship primarily examines the educational opportunity structures of students of color from low socioeconomic backgrounds. Welton examines how institutional and social structures shape the connections students of color make to educational resources, navigate school, and ultimately matriculate to postsecondary education. Other research areas include problematizing the politics of race and diversity in school reform and improvement, underrepresented groups (persons of color and women), navigating the pipeline to academia, and youth of color voice and leadership. Her professional experiences include coordinator of a leadership and empowerment program for urban youth, a facilitator of an urban education teacher preparation program, and a teacher in large urban districts.

Jon A. Yasin is Professor of English and Linguistics at Bergen Community College in Paramus, New Jersey. Yasin was Le Responsable D'Animation Rurale in N'gabou, Senegal, West Africa, for two years. He taught Linguistics at the Boston State Campus of the University of Massachusetts, and subsequently, was a founding faculty member at Roxbury Community College in Boston. From 1981 through 1988, Yasin was Professor of Linguistics at the United Arab Emirates University in Al Ain, Abu Dhabi. He was the Director of the University of Islam School #11 for three years and after its reorganization, Convener of the Board of the Clara Muhammad School for two years. Currently, he serves on the National Education Council for the Clara Muhammad Schools. Yasin was a King Fellow at Northeastern University, a Fellow with the National

Academy of Education, and a Mid Careers Fellow at Princeton University. His undergraduate studies were completed at California State University at Hayward. He received the MPA from the Kennedy School at Harvard University, the MEd from Northeastern University, the PhD from Indiana University of Pennsylvania, and the EdD from Teachers College, Columbia University. Yasin's research interests include Hip Hop and youth culture, history of the Muslim schools in America, and African American vernacular English. Over the years, he has coauthored a book and published various articles on these topics.

Section I

Psychology, Health, and Human Development

1

Serving Vulnerable Children and Youth in the Urban Context

William F. Tate IV, Christopher Hamilton, Brittni D. Jones, W. Brett Robertson, Ashley Macrander, Lyndsie Schultz & Elizabeth Thorne-Wallington

The task of providing appropriate interventions for vulnerable children and youth in urban communities is a major challenge in national and international contexts (Yeakey, 2012). Fortunately, a growing scientific literature focused on the sociological and epidemiological study of child and adolescent mental disorder and learning trajectories has developed where community and neighborhood environments are examined for their predictive influence (Spencer, Tinsley, Dupree, & Fegley, 2012). An emerging set of studies within this larger effort has attempted to understand better the role of multilevel pathways to child and adolescent education outcomes, criminal behavior, psychiatric disorders, and prosocial behavior among urban youth. However, this literature is disjointed, with few conceptual or linguistic bridges afforded to scholars in the field of education interested in better understanding the complex ecology of youth development in the urban context. The purpose of this chapter is to provide a synthetic review of three distinct literatures—youth mental health, juvenile justice, and special education—with a specific aim to help clarify classifications across these fields as part of an effort to understand better how youth service providers and educators might strategically support the development and learning outcomes of urban youth experiencing mental disorder.[1] The review is in part an examination of the influence of neighborhood and other social conditions in urban communities on a narrowly focused area of youth development. We recognize that historically the fields being examined have treated geographic context as a distal factor or have ignored geographic influences altogether.

Over the past 20 years there has been a renewed interest in the effects of geospatial factors and social contexts on growth, development, and health—including child and adolescent mental health. Our review is narrowly focused on this emerging literature, as its aim is to illustrate selected points of intersection in these literatures that support cooperative services across youth providers in urban communities. Why is it important to focus on urban youth? One reason is the relationship between perception and youth policy. Edwards (2010) argued that the legal regulation of youth is built on a dichotomous perspective. Typically, children are held unaccountable for their choices. For example, they do not have the ability to contract in the law. They are not legally sanctioned to vote, serve in the military, or make their own health decisions. However, Edwards argued there is a retreat from the child-adult dichotomy in legal policy toward youths' criminal conduct. More specifically, affluent and privileged children are often granted the assumption of infancy and not held accountable for their behavior, while poor and minority youth are characterized as adults. Too often poor and minority youth are viewed as not needing care, support, and education in order to transition to healthy productive adulthood. This perspective is uniquely problematic for urban youth, as they reside in communities that are perceived as locations that support degenerative behavior. For example, the demographer Douglas Massey (2009), in an analysis describing the growing geographic concentration of affluence and poverty in urban communities throughout the world, argued that these contrasting ecologies would breed opposing peer subcultures among rich and poor youths.

The growing concentration of poor and minority youth living in urban communities is perceived as being a part of an oppositional subculture. This perception supports a narrative that aligns with subjecting members of this subculture to adult treatment in the criminal justice system, rather than appropriate supports in the human service and education sectors. This paradigm is reflected in school disciplinary practices. Racial disparities abound in school disciplinary procedures and outcomes (e.g., suspensions and expulsions) and in the demographics of the juvenile justice system (Wilf, 2012). According to the National Mental Health Association (2004), White juvenile offenders are more likely to have previously received mental health services than are African American offenders. Youth of color who do receive treatment are often underserved by mental health systems. African American youth, for example, are more likely to be diagnosed with severe mental disorders, often considered less treatable. Compared to White youth, African American youth are two to three times more likely to be hospitalized for psychiatric reasons, "suggesting that prevention and early intervention services may be less available to African American youth" (National Mental Health Association, 2004, p. 11). Additionally, the report notes, "African American adolescents (particularly males) are more likely to be referred to the juvenile justice system rather than to the treatment system" (p. 11).

Our current systems of youth-serving organizations operate politically and pragmatically in a fashion that is influenced by stereotypic thinking about youth. Spencer et al. (2012) argued that stereotypes about minority and economically impoverished youths' development are attributable primarily to the belief that these children and adolescents are responsible for creating their own physical surroundings, social context, and psychological conditions. In sum, this type of stereotypic thinking characterizes privilege as earned and disadvantage as volitional. Artiles (2011) argued that research associated with youth assigned to schools, psychological support services, and special education programming should attend to the temporal, spatial, and sociocultural dimensions of youth experiences. His recommendation is in response to evidence suggesting that this approach might more accurately capture the nature of youth development while informing the response of society.

Mental disorder prevalence rates within the juvenile justice system point to the need for interdisciplinary efforts between researchers focused on youth development and organizations interested in intervening on the developmental pathways of urban youth. Failure to do so has dire social and individual consequences. For example, one study of male detainees in Cook County (Chicago) jails estimated the prevalence of mental disorders there was two to three times higher than in the general population (Teplin, 1990). The largest mental institution in the United States is the Los Angeles County Jail (Montague, 2008). According to one report (National Public Radio, 2011), the three largest inpatient psychiatric facilities in the United States are jails in urban communities: Los Angeles County, Rikers Island (New York City), and Cook County (Chicago). An epidemiological study of 822 inmates in five jails (three in New York and two in Maryland) using the Structured Clinical Interview for *Diagnostic and Statistical Manual of Mental Disorders,* 4th ed. (*DSM-IV;* American Psychiatric Association, 2000) to estimate the existence of serious mental illness—that is, schizophrenia, schizophrenia spectrum disorder, schizoaffective disorder, bipolar disorder, brief psychotic disorder, delusional disorder, and psychotic disorders not otherwise specified—found a total of 16.6% of the prisoners met criteria for one of these diagnoses in the previous month, with the rate among women (31%) being much higher than that among men (14.5%) (Steadman, Osher, Robbins, Case, & Samuels, 2009). This estimate is consistent with higher rates of mental illness among women described in other jail and prison surveys.

The current state of affairs in adult prisons is arguably linked to earlier developmental pathways experienced by youth. Each year from 1985 to 2010, the juvenile courts processed at least 1.1 million youth for delinquency cases (Puzzanchera & Kang, 2013). Juvenile court referrals will place many youth with mental disorders as well as learning disabilities into the adult criminal justice system. A National Center for Mental Health and Juvenile Justice (NCMHJJ) study conducted by Shufelt and Cocozza (2006) reported that the majority (70.4%) of youth in the juvenile justice system meets criteria for at least one mental health disorder. This finding is consistent with earlier studies of mental health prevalence estimates from juvenile justice research (e.g., Teplin, Abran, McClelland, Dulcan, & Mericle, 2002). In addition, the NCMHJJ study found that youth in contact with the juvenile justice system experience high rates of disorder across the types of mental health disorders—disruptive disorders (46.5%), substance use disorders (46.2%), anxiety disorders (34.4%), and mood disorders (18.3%). Over 60% of youth met criteria for three or more diagnoses.

The chapter is organized into five sections. The first section is a review of child and adolescent mental health disorders. It includes a discussion of the conceptual and linguistic challenges associated with youth mental health and securing related psychosocial supports. The second major section is a brief review of emerging literature that examines the school-to-prison pipeline debate. The third major section examines individual, family, school, and community interventions. The purpose of the section is to highlight effective strategies to support vulnerable youth. Similarly, the next major section is a discussion of ecological interventions designed for juvenile offenders or students at risk of contact with the juvenile justice system. The final section is a charge for urban educators and youth providers.

Child and Adolescent Mental Disorder: What We Know

In this chapter, we will review epidemiological evidence that estimates age-of-onset and prevalence rates of psychiatric disorders in order to better understand the need for new interventions. These studies may help explain why some youth entrusted to the juvenile justice system will require appropriate mental health services during their period of care.

Kessler and colleagues (2005) argued that the lifetime prevalence and age-of-onset distributions of *DSM-IV* disorders was understudied. To address this void, they estimated lifetime *DSM-IV* anxiety, mood, impulse-control, and substance use disorders using the fully structured World Mental Health Survey version of the Composite International Diagnostic Interview. The interview was completed as part of the National Comorbidity Survey Replication (NCS-R). The NCS-R is a nationally representative survey of English-speaking household residents aged 18 years and older in coterminous United States (n = 9,282). While earlier surveys and results reported high lifetime prevalence and general early age-of-onset distributions of most *DSM-III* and *DSM-III-R* disorders, it would be inappropriate to assume similar findings would continue for *DSM-IV* disorders because of the greater point of emphasis on clinically significant distress in *DSM-IV* than in earlier editions. Kessler et al. (2005) estimated that the most prevalent lifetime disorders were major depression disorder (16.6%), alcohol abuse (13.0%), and specific phobia (12.5%). Anxiety disorders were estimated as the most prevalent class of disorders (28.8%), followed by impulse-control disorders (24.8%), mood disorders (20.8%), and substance use disorder (14.6%). According to the survey estimates, the lifetime prevalence of any disorder was 46.4%, while 27.7% of participants had two or more lifetime disorders and 17.3% had three or more.

Kessler and colleagues (2005) reported two patterns in the disorder onset distributions. First, the median age of onset (i.e., 50th percentile on the age-of-onset distribution) was 14 years. In addition, the second pattern indicated that the median age-of-onset was earlier for anxiety disorders and impulse-control disorder—age 11 years. In comparison, the age-of-onset for substance use disorder and mood disorder was 20 years and 30 years, respectively. A limitation for the purposes of this chapter in Kessler and colleagues' study is the absence of a geospatial approach. The study did include a number of socio-demographic predicators. For example, females had significantly higher risk than did males of anxiety and mood disorders. Males had a significantly higher risk than females of impulse-control and substance use disorders. Also, non-Hispanic Blacks and Hispanics had a significantly lower risk than did non-Hispanic Whites of anxiety, mood, and substance use disorders (the latter among non-Hispanic Blacks only). Low educational attainment was a risk factor for substance use disorders. In light of the disorder onset distributions reported by Kessler and colleagues (2005), we examine the area of emotional disturbance and juvenile justice. This examination provides some insight into the need for conceptual and linguistic bridges across the fields of youth mental health, juvenile justice, and special education.

Emotional Disturbance: Linguistic Bridge Building

According to the National Dissemination Center for Children with Disabilities (2010, p. 2), children who have an emotional disturbance may exhibit the following characteristics and behaviors:

- Hyperactivity (short attention span, impulsiveness);
- Aggression or self-injurious behavior (acting out, fighting);
- Withdrawal (not interacting socially with others, excessive fear or anxiety);
- Immaturity (inappropriate crying, temper tantrums, poor coping skills); and
- Learning difficulties (academically performing below grade level).

The National Dissemination Center for Children with Disabilities (2010, p. 1) states that "emotional disturbance" can be viewed as an "umbrella term for a number of different mental disorders" including the following: anxiety disorders, bipolar disorder, conduct disorder, eating disorders, obsessive-compulsive disorder, and psychotic disorders. Mental disorders, generally, must meet the formal diagnostic criteria for disorders outlined in *DSM-IV*, the official diagnostic manual published by the American Psychiatric Association. However, the definition used by the U.S. Department of Education is not always easily mapped onto diagnostic categories of mental disorders. Nonetheless, and complicating our efforts in this chapter, these psychiatric categories are used in prevalence studies by researchers examining schools and the juvenile justice system. Definitional mismatch potentially affects both interinstitutional research and those youth receiving services across multiple service areas.

Definitions. Emotional disturbance (ED) is useful as an analytic category in education research because it is codified as part of the Individual with Disabilities Education Act (IDEA), the federal law that governs how early intervention, special education, and other services are provided to qualifying infants, toddlers, children, and youth with disabilities (ages birth–21). The U.S. Department of Education determines eligibility for some special education services under IDEA based on the IDEA definition of emotional disturbance. The IDEA (2004) defines emotional disturbance as follows:

(i) Emotional disturbance means a condition exhibiting one or more of the following characteristics over a long period of time and to a marked degree that adversely affects a child's educational performance:

(A) An inability to learn that cannot be explained by intellectual, sensory, or health factors.
(B) An inability to build or maintain satisfactory interpersonal relationships with peers and teachers.
(C) Inappropriate types of behavior or feelings under normal circumstances.
(D) A general pervasive mood of unhappiness or depression.
(E) A tendency to develop physical symptoms or fears associated with personal or school problems.

(Code of Federal Regulations, Title 34, §300.8(c)(4)(i))

(ii) Emotional disturbance includes schizophrenia. The term does not apply to children who are socially maladjusted, unless it is determined that they have an emotional disturbance under paragraph (c)(4)(i) of this section.

(Code of Federal Regulations, Title 34, §300.8(c)(4)(ii))

Defining emotional disturbance is fraught with problems and contention that can make assessment and intervention difficult. Other federal agencies and professional associations offer similar, but functionally distinct, definitions of emotional disturbance. Under IDEA, exhibiting one of the characteristics contained in the definition is sufficient to qualify for services, but only if it is experienced "over a long period of time" and "to a marked degree that adversely affects a child's educational performance." Both of these conditions serve to clarify identification of ED among populations (children and youth) for whom short periods of conditions consistent with the ED definition may be quite common. At the same time, such definitional constraints may serve to exclude some youth in need of special services. Notably, not all of the disorders associated with children in the *DSM-IV* are considered disabilities under the IDEA. Mood disorders and conduct disorders, for example, would not count as disabilities unless they adversely affect educational performance over a long period of time.

Despite definitional differences and various methodological shortcomings of numerous studies, it is possible to provide a general range of the prevalence of mental health disorders among the general youth population and the population of youth in the juvenile justice system. Analyzing nationally representative data from the National Health Interview Survey, Simpson et al. (2008) identified emotional and behavioral problems among parents' greatest concerns for their children. The study found that in 2005–2006, 17.6% of boys' and 11.2% of girls' parents talked to health care providers or school staff about such problems. Overall, the parents of 8.3 million children aged 4–17 (14.5%) talked to school staff or health care providers about concerns regarding their child's emotional or behavioral challenges. About 5% of children were prescribed medication. Eighty-nine percent of medication recommendations addressed symptoms associated with ADHD. Five percent of the children received treatment other than medication. Boys were prescribed medication at nearly twice the rate of girls (6.6% to 3.4%, respectively). Of those who received treatment, almost 60% of the children were treated in a private mental health practice, clinic, or center; nearly 40% received treatment at their school.

To better understand the epidemiological evidence and the importance of linguistic bridge building, a review of another study is instructive. Merikangas et al. (2010) provided lifetime prevalence results for a nationally representative sample of American youth (n = 10,123) ages

13–18. Their findings, based on face-to-face interview data from the National Comorbidity Survey—Adolescent Supplement, suggest high prevalence rates for an array of *DSM-IV* categories that may qualify as "emotional disturbance" under the federal IDEA law. Anxiety disorders were present in 31.9% of surveyed youth, followed by behavioral disorders (19.1%), mood disorders (14.3%), and substance abuse disorders (11.4%). Forty percent of those that met criteria for one disorder also met criteria for at least one other disorder. Nearly one in four or five (22.2%) U.S. youth meets criteria for a severely impairing disorder. Median onset ages for anxiety disorders were 6 years, 11 years for behavioral disorders, 13 years for mood disorders, and 15 years for substance abuse disorders. The study highlights the need for early prevention and intervention, as many adult disorders likely first emerge in childhood or adolescence. However, there is a unique challenge to addressing this problem space. Recent shifts in how schools respond to youths' developmental challenges present an obstacle and an opportunity for rethinking policy.

School-to-Prison Pipeline

Researchers, lawyers, and other stakeholders increasingly turn to the metaphor of a *school-to-prison pipeline* to describe a process through which students are pushed out of public schools and correspondingly funneled into the juvenile justice and criminal justice systems (e.g., Kim, Losen, & Hewitt, 2010; Wald & Losen, 2003; Yeakey, 2003). Convinced that the pipeline is in operation well before schooling starts due to differential early childhood experiences shaped by race and poverty, especially unequal access to health care and mental health care services, the Children's Defense Fund refers to a "cradle" to prison pipeline (Edelman, 2007).

Several indicators capture the concerns about youth transitioning from school to prison. Suspension risk for all students has grown since the early 1970s (from 3.7% in 1973 to 6.9% in 2006), but the rate of increase has been greatest for Black students. It is important to note that levels of school violence have remained stable or decreased since 1985 (American Psychological Association Zero Tolerance Task Force, 2008). In 1973 the Black/White gap for suspension risk was three percentage points (6% vs. 3.1%, respectively); by 2006 the gap was over 10 points (15% vs. 4.8%, respectively) (Losen & Skiba, 2010). In other words, the racial gap in the use of exclusionary discipline has grown, as zero tolerance policies have been implemented throughout the nation. This gap is not explained by socioeconomic factors and Black students do not engage in or receive referrals for serious disruptive behaviors or violence at a higher rate than do their White peers (American Psychological Association Zero Tolerance Task Force, 2008; Skiba et al., 2002). A gender gap across racial demographic groups exists as well—28.3% of Black males and 18% of Black females were suspended in 2006; 16.3% of Hispanic males were suspended compared to 8.5% of Hispanic females; for White students, 10% of males and 4% of females were suspended; the average of the overall sample in the study was 11.2% in 2006 (Losen & Skiba, 2010).

The 2009–2010 Civil Rights Data Collection (CRDC) survey conducted by the U.S. Department of Education Office for Civil Rights (OCR) covered approximately 85% of the nation's students. The OCR reports African American students constitute 18% of students in the CRDC sample, but a third of the students suspended once, nearly half of those suspended more than once, and over a third of students expelled (U.S. Department of Education, Office for Civil Rights, 2012). Nationwide, compared to White students, Black students are 3.5 times more likely to be suspended or expelled. In districts with more than 50,000 students, Black and Hispanic students accounted for over 70% of school-related arrests or referrals to law enforcement. Boys were more likely to be suspended or expelled than were girls, but racial disparities existed within gender groups as well. Twelve percent of students in the sample had a disability (under IDEA or Section 504). Thirteen percent of students with a disability covered under IDEA received one or more out-of-school suspensions compared to 6% for non-IDEA students.

School-level policies and practices, most notably the widespread adoption of zero tolerance discipline policies, are often cited as the regulatory framework supporting the school-to-prison pipeline. In addition, there is a profound mental health crisis in America's schools and a tremendous need gap for mental health services across the developmental pathways of our most vulnerable youth. Limited access to mental health services for urban youth, especially those who are impoverished and/or racial minorities, may contribute significantly to the pipeline. Suspension, expulsion, and being arrested at school have all been linked to poor academic performance, school dropout, and other poor psychosocial outcomes (Advancement Project, 2010; Balfanz, Spiridakis, Curran Neild, & Legters, 2003). The National Center for Education Statistics found that students suspended three or more times were five times more likely to drop out or graduate late than were students never suspended (New York Civil Liberties Union, 2011). In addition, dropouts have been found to be eight times more likely to be incarcerated than are students who finish high school (Advancement Project, 2010). The high prevalence rates for mental health disorders among juvenile offenders, coupled with evidence that most youth involved in the justice system have been suspended or expelled from school prior to incarceration, indicates that far too many urban youth with treatable mental illnesses have unmet developmental and educational needs (Leone & Weinberg, 2010).

A review of zero tolerance policies by a task force convened by the American Psychological Association (APA) found that despite 20 years of implementation, zero tolerance policies do not appear to create safe or productive schools; in fact, these policies may be developmentally inappropriate as psychological interventions because youth, "Particularly before the age of 15 . . . appear to display psychosocial immaturity in at least four areas: poor resistance to peer influence . . . attitudes toward and perception of risk . . . future orientation . . . , and impulse control . . . " (American Psychological Association Zero Tolerance Task Force, 2008, p. 855). Youth with mental disorders, especially those exhibiting externalizing behaviors at school, face a heightened risk for exclusionary discipline even though isolation may lead to further problems. "Zero tolerance policies may create, enhance, or accelerate negative mental health outcomes for youth by creating increases in student alienation, anxiety, rejection, and breaking of healthy adult bonds" (p. 856). According to the American Academy of Pediatrics (2003), when youth are not in school they are more likely to engage in risky or criminal behaviors such as fighting, carrying a weapon, using drugs and alcohol, and having sex. Suicidal thoughts and behaviors may be likely as well. The same study found that suspended or expelled students are rarely referred to substance abuse counseling or mental health services while completing their punishment outside of school.

According to a report by the Justice Policy Institute (2009), the juvenile justice system is overburdened and over the last 20 years has expanded both by the number of cases processed as well as the range of cases the courts are willing to hear. Much of this is related to school policy. To illustrate, the report points out that the number of school-based referrals to law enforcement grew 71% in Denver between 2000–2004. Likewise, in four of five states examined by Krezmien, Leone, Zablocki, and Wells (2010), the share of juvenile court referrals from schools increased from 1995 to 2004. The Advancement Project (2010) reports that school-based arrests almost tripled in Pennsylvania from 1999–2000 to 2006–2007 (4,563 to 12,918). The same report highlights substantial and increased budget allocations for security and policing in schools. For example, in New York City, the budget for police and security in schools rose to over $221 million in 2008, an increase of more than 65% since 2002, which "has resulted in the police department's school safety division being larger than the entire police force of Washington D.C., Detroit, Boston, and Las Vegas" (Advancement Project, 2010, p. 16). Maintaining holding facilities for approximately

90,000 incarcerated young people nationwide costs an average of $88,000 per person per year. That amounted to $5.7 billion in 2007 (Justice Policy Institute, 2009).

Cost-benefit research indicates that correcting school misbehavior through exclusionary discipline and the juvenile justice system is not cost-effective. The American Psychological Association Zero Tolerance Task Force (2008) concluded that "there is a strong body of evidence showing that preventing or treating delinquency and school failure are more cost effective than doing nothing or paying welfare and prison costs incurred by undereducated and alienated youth" (p. 856). Once a youth has been arrested, the chance of future arrests increases. Youth who have been imprisoned have higher recidivism rates than do youth offenders who did not face imprisonment (Justice Policy Institute, 2009). Delinquency is a normal part of young male development for many youth and most youth offenders "age out" of criminal behavior by adulthood on their own; punitive action appears to delay this process and possibly lead to continued criminality (Redding, Sevin Goldstein, & Heilbrun, 2005). Effective intervention and treatment to keep youth in school can reduce the costs of the pipeline—costs that "begin well before the children enter prison and extend well after their release, with gang activity, recidivism, and unemployment" (Osher, Quinn, Poirier, & Rutherford, 2003, p. 91).

Individual, Family, School, and Community Interventions

Research highlights the relationship between the precipitous decline of a youth's mental health status and the likelihood that he or she will be involved in the juvenile justice system (Foster, Qaseem, & Connor, 2004). The converse is true as well: youth within juvenile correctional facilities are likely to suffer from mental health disturbances. As such, it is imperative to investigate how mental health services support prevention and intervention within this dyadic relationship. The purpose of this section is to review what the field is learning about individual, family, school, and community supports. This is not an exhaustive review; rather the intent is to provide a review of selected research studies focused on preventive measures or interventions with the potential to disrupt the school-to-prison pipeline.

Individual Therapeutic Interventions. The brief review of research presented here aims to describe the effects of a small number of therapeutic intervention strategies on promoting prosocial outcomes and reducing antisocial behaviors among those youth who have mental health disturbances and are at risk for engagement in delinquent behavior or are already in the care of juvenile justice authorities. Children with severe mental health disturbances often manifest their disordered psychology through aggressive behaviors (Nitkowski, Petermann, Buttner, Krause-Leipoldt, & Petermann, 2009). Oppositional defiant disorder (ODD) and conduct disorder (CD) are two delinquent manifestations of aggression and both disorders are prevalent among 5- to 15-year-olds, as well as youth found in child welfare systems (Nitkowski et al., 2009). These disorders are viewed as a part of the ED category of IDEA.

Nitkowski and fellow researchers (2009) sought to investigate whether psychotherapeutic interventions among children with aggressive behaviors in child welfare systems could not only decrease aggressive and delinquent behavior, but also increase prosocial behaviors. The study included 24 children aged 7–11years, recruited from a single child welfare institution in Germany (Nitkowski et al., 2009). Participants in the experimental study were divided into two groups (an intervention and wait-list control group) (Nitkowski et al., 2009). Each group included at least five children diagnosed with ODD, one child with CD, and six children with both ODD and CD (Nitkowski et al., 2009). The intervention in the study was exposure to Training with Aggressive Children (TAC), a cognitive-behavioral therapy developed by two of the researchers, which consists of individual and group therapy sessions where children learn to "analyze conflicts in more detail" and "correct their distorted perception of social processes" (Nitkowski et al., 2009, p. 479). Also, children from both the intervention and control groups participated in the child welfare program.

Nitkowski and his fellow researchers (2009) found that cognitive-behavioral therapy (like the TAC), in addition to a child welfare program, leads to reduced aggressive and delinquent behavior. Moreover, early introduction of the cognitive-behavioral therapy into the child welfare program leads to increased prosocial behaviors. The study was limited, however, by a small sample size and the possibility of group differences at pretest that would inevitably reduce group comparability.

Trupin, Stewart, Beach, and Boesky (2002) conducted a similar experimental study in which they utilized Dialectical Behavioural Therapy (DBT) as a treatment intervention for female offenders incarcerated at a State of Washington juvenile rehabilitation administration facility. DBT has functioned as an effective therapeutic approach for adult women with borderline personality disorder; therefore, the likelihood for successful application to female juvenile offenders who suffer from similar mental health disturbances guided this study (Trupin et al., 2002). DBT utilizes "skills training, problem solving, and validation to enable patients to reduce self-destructive, impulsive, and aggressive behaviours" (p. 121).

Participants in the study were recruited from three treatment cottages at the Washington facility. One cottage was a mental health treatment unit; the second, a general population unit (DBT was implemented at these two sites); and the third was a general population unit that served as the comparison site—treatment at this site continued as usual (Trupin et al., 2002). Twenty-two participants were recruited from the mental health unit, 23 participants from the general population unit that received the DBT intervention, and 15 from the general population unit that served as the comparison group. Additionally, records from 30 other female offenders served as a baseline comparison for offense and mental health screen measures. Composite variables of youth behavior problems and the punitive actions of the Washington facility staff were created, Community Risk Assessment Scores (a measure used for placement and security level) were assessed at participant intake and during a 90-day follow-up, and data from the Massachusetts Youth Screening Instrument (a measure of youth mental health symptoms) were collected at participant intake and during a 90-day follow-up as well.

Trupin and his fellow researchers (2002) found that among a population of female juvenile offenders who exhibit the types of para-suicidal and aggressive behaviors that DBT targets, the therapeutic intervention can be successful in reducing behavioral problems and increasing staff's use of therapeutic rather than punitive responses. The positive response to the introduction of DBT at the Washington facility resulted in female juvenile offenders (in the mental health unit) having greater access to drug and alcohol rehabilitation services, as well as employment opportunities.

A second strategy for addressing the needs of children and adolescents with mental health disturbances in the juvenile justice system, beyond differing therapeutic intervention methods, is to establish a system of care delivery among the multiple agencies serving this population (Foster et al., 2004). A system of care is an integrated and coordinated method of addressing the mental health needs of youth across the community, rather than within a single agency. This approach frames mental health as a public health priority and focuses on keeping youth with emotional and behavioral problems out of the juvenile justice system.

Foster et al. (2004) analyzed data from a longitudinal study of Stark County and 66 other communities in Ohio that participated in an evaluation of the "Children's Program"—the

Comprehensive Community Mental Health Services for Children and Their Families Program. Three of the participating systems of care sites were matched as part of a quasi-experimental study in order to examine comparison communities. Foster et al. (2004) utilized the resultant data from one pair (Stark County and Mahoning County) to identify whether "the system of care can eliminate or delay involvement in juvenile justice among youths receiving mental health services" (p. 860). The study sample included 449 African American and Hispanic youth aged 6–17 years who had emotional and behavioral problems and were utilizing mental health services. The data were gathered from two sites: the management information systems of mental health services centers and juvenile justice systems in the two Ohio communities, and were studied utilizing the Cox proportional hazards model. Covariates used in the analysis included a site indicator, a pre–post indicator related to study entry, an interaction between these two variables, as well as several covariates related to child and family characteristics (age, race, mental health status, family structure, caregiver education level, etc.). The findings indicated that the systems of care approach to delivering mental health services to youth "can reduce or delay entry into the juvenile justice system as well as recidivism among those who have been involved in the system" (p. 864). This relationship was stronger for those children or adolescents who were engaged in more serious offenses. The study suggests there is a link between addressing the individual therapeutic needs of delinquent youth and the encouragement of prosocial behavior or delay of engagement in antisocial behavior. However, obtaining data from only two Ohio communities was a study limitation and led the researchers to suggest replication in other communities with differing research methodologies, including randomized experimentation.

Family and Peer Group Interventions. Interventions targeting the family and peer group represent another opportunity to influence the life course of vulnerable children and youth positively. We review several studies that illustrate the potential of interventions associated with family and peer groups. Here, we have not included an exhaustive list of studies; rather, we demonstrate the potential of this type of intervention.

The Nurse-Family Partnership (NFP) promotes children's and their families' long-term healthy development (Olds, 2008). The program enrolls primarily low-income women who have never given birth. Nurses visit participants' homes several times through the end of the second trimester of pregnancy. Visits from nurses were associated, particularly for poor, single women, with children's improved neuro-psychological development and functioning through adolescence. According to economic analyses, the NFP saves families $17,000 and most significantly benefits families experiencing greater risk of poverty and associated social problems.

Whereas the study describing the NFP focused on the prenatal period, other evaluations have examined interventions during the first five years of life. Ippen, Harris, Van Horn, & Lieberman (2011) reanalyzed data from a randomized controlled trial (RCT) to estimate the effectiveness of child-parent psychotherapy (CPP) for children who had been exposed differentially to domestic violence. In the original study, researchers recruited 75 ethnically diverse children aged 3–5 years and their mothers to participate. For approximately one hour, mother-child pairs participated in weekly CPP sessions with clinicians for 50 weeks. High-risk children who received CPP experienced greater reductions in post-traumatic stress disorder (PTSD), depression-related symptoms, and total behavioral problems. For PTSD and for symptoms of depression, effect sizes were large ($d > 1$); for total behavioral problems, they were medium. Six months after treatment ended, high-risk children who received CPP continued to demonstrate fewer total behavioral problems. The findings suggest that including the parent as an integral participant in the child's treatment may be effective for young children exposed to multiple risks. Methodological limitations of the study included, among others, the small size of the sample and reliance on maternal reports.

Other experimental studies have examined the long-term effects of preventive programs for children who have entered school. In a single-site RCT, the Montreal Longitudinal-Experimental Study enrolled disruptive boys aged 7–9 years from socioeconomically disadvantaged neighborhoods (Tremblay, Pagani-Kurtz, Masse, Vitaro, & Pihl, 1995). In addition to a school-based component for their sons, parents participated in a home-based training program for two years. The parent sessions each lasted less than an hour and taught parents skills to manage family crises, monitor behavior, discipline effectively, and reinforce positive behaviors. Boys were invited, but not required, to attend parent sessions. To determine long-term effectiveness in preventing delinquency, researchers followed participants for six years after treatment. Relative to those in the control group, participants in the program reported significantly fewer delinquent behaviors yearly from ages 10–15. Researchers noted the relatively small number of participants receiving the treatment as one limitation of the study.

School as Prevention and Intervention. Numerous studies have established the importance of schools in predicting and preventing juvenile delinquency. A number of studies have examined risk and protective factors. Ellonen (2008) used data from the Finnish Self-Report Delinquency Study and, using a multilevel logistic regression analysis, found that social control, defined as an individual's bond to society, determines boys' delinquent behavior. Ellonen found that boys who attended schools having a high rate of school-level social control were at a lower risk of engaging in delinquent behavior than were boys who attended schools with lower levels of social control.

Payne (2008) examined similar factors, by using multilevel analysis to examine communal school organization and school bonding. Communal school organization refers to the organization of a school as a community. School bonding is the student's bond to the school community. Similar to Ellonen (2008), Payne found that the social organization of a school influences an individual student's involvement in delinquency. Students who attended more communally organized schools were less likely to engage in delinquency than were students who attended less communally organized schools.

Beyond social factors, other studies have found risk factors exhibited by students that predict later delinquency. Henry, Knight, and Thornberry (2012), using data from the Rochester Youth Development Study, found that the school disengagement warning index was robustly related to dropout, delinquency, and problem substance use. This index was calculated from school district records from each student's 9th and 10th school years, and is the sum of binary risk indicators, including test scores, attendance, failing grades, suspension, and grade retention. Similarly, Hallfors, Cho, Brodish, Flewelling, and Khatapoush (2006) found that GPA and attendance records were predictors for substance use, emotional problems, and delinquency. The authors concluded that GPA and attendance could be used to identify students who were at risk.

In addition to these risk factors, Tobler, Komro, Dabroski, Aveyard, and Markham (2011) examined whether schools achieving better than expected educational outcomes reduced the risk of delinquency. Using data from a longitudinal group-randomized control trial of an alcohol preventative intervention for racial/ethnic minority youth, the authors employed multilevel regression to examine the influence of the schools' value-added status on each student's drug use and delinquency outcome in the 8th grade. Value-added education was associated with lower incidence of recurrent alcohol, cigarette, and marijuana use and delinquent behaviors in the 8th grade when considering initial risk behavior. The authors concluded that while this study did have limitations, these findings suggest that value-added education may break the strong link between social disadvantage and drug use and delinquency among adolescents.

Beyond research of risk and protective factors and the more general role schools play in influencing juvenile delinquency, there are also a number of studies that examine the efficacy and effects of particular school-based programs. First, using data from the Chicago Longitudinal Study, Mann and Reynolds (2006) examined the role of preschool intervention in a juvenile delinquency (arrests) prediction model. Using a quasi-experimental design, data from a cohort of approximately 1,400 preschool children from high-poverty neighborhoods in Chicago involved in the Chicago Child-Parent Center (CPC) Program were compiled and compared with data from a control group. Students in the CPC Program received up to six years of preschool and after-school programming. Mann and Reynolds (2006) gathered data consisting of incidents of juvenile delinquency, preschool participation, kindergarten word achievement, grade retention, classroom behavior, special education placements, amount of parental involvement, incidents of child maltreatment, peer social skills, number of school moves, and magnet school enrollment. Students who had at least one year of preschool were 40–50% less likely to engage in juvenile delinquency up to 12 years later. Despite the promising results, there were several limitations to the study. The researchers acknowledged that they were constrained by available data, as well by the model specifications. In addition, the data obtained was from 1985 through 1997—prior to a welfare reform designed to enable more mothers to work.

Other programs focused on specific behavioral changes related to later delinquency. Klevens, Martinez, Le, Rojas, Duque, and Tovar (2009) evaluated a universal, low-cost classroom management strategy that was combined with parent training to assess the impact upon aggressive and antisocial behavior in young children in a resource-poor setting in Colombia, South America. Twelve schools (a total of 2,491 students) were randomly assigned into one of three groups: teacher-only intervention, parent and teacher intervention, and control. Teachers using the National Longitudinal Survey of Children and Youth prior to and following intervention measured aggression and prosocial behaviors. One of the researchers trained the teachers on how to use the scales from the survey. While multivariate analysis showed a significant difference in change of behavior between both intervention groups and the control group, it was most likely due to the control group increasing in aggression, while the intervention groups remained constant; neither group decreased in aggression.

The Metropolitan Area Child Study Research Group also examined methods designed to reduce aggression and promote protective factors in their eight-year prevention program (Eron et al., 2002). Using a universal intervention in two urban contexts (city urban poor and urban poor with more resources), the researchers randomly assigned 16 schools to one of three interventions: social-cognitive classroom curriculum (Level A); classroom enhancement plus 2-year small group training for high-risk children (Level B); and general enhancement, small-group training, and 1-year family intervention (Level C). Intervention was provided to cohorts during early elementary, late elementary, or both. The researchers found that Level C intervention significantly reduced aggressive behavior in high-risk children, but only in poor urban communities with more resources. None of the interventions reduced aggression when given only in late-elementary school.

In sum, there is evidence suggesting that schools provide an opportunity for prevention and intervention strategies targeting vulnerable urban youth. The evidence indicates that early interventions were successful at reducing aggressive behaviors and juvenile delinquency. However, interventions staged prior to middle of elementary school, about third grade, were particularly successful.

Prevention and Intervention in Community. There is a body of scholarship that has investigated the effectiveness of community-based preventative measures and interventions on urban youth. Why is this important? Turner, Hartman, and Bishop (2007) found that biosocial indicators predict life-course-persistent offending only for people of color in disadvantaged neighborhoods. In other words, simply living in a highly segregated low-income community is a significant risk factor. Disadvantaged people of color reside in neighborhoods that are "ecologically distinct" from those in which poor Whites reside that increases the negative impacts of individual-level deficits and family disadvantage.

Molnar, Cerda, Roberts, and Buka (2008) used data from the Project on Human Development in Chicago Neighborhoods on 2,226 ethnically diverse, urban youths, their caregivers, and the 80 neighborhoods in which they resided and found that neighborhood risk factors could be moderated by living in a neighborhood with a higher concentration of organizations or services serving young people and adults. Sampson, Raudenbush, and Earls (1997) found that collective efficacy, defined as social cohesion among neighbors combined with their willingness to intervene on behalf of the common good, is linked to reduced violence, based on the results of a 1995 survey of 8,782 residents of 343 neighborhoods in Chicago, Illinois. Multilevel analyses showed that a measure of collective efficacy yields high reliability and is associated with reductions in violence. Associations of concentrated disadvantage and residential instability with violence are largely mediated by collective efficacy, indicating that collective efficacy can mediate the risks youth face in high-poverty neighborhoods.

While we are learning about the importance of the lived experience of juveniles in communities, there is a growing body of research that is focused on the effectiveness of community-based interventions. Welsh, Jenkins, and Harris (1999) described the outcomes of community-based delinquency prevention programs in Harrisburg and Philadelphia. The evaluated intervention was focused around developing and supporting a formal coalition of neighborhood organizations providing trainings, workshops, and recreation and followed 191 youth over three years (1992–1995). The major objective was to reduce rates of arrest and re-arrest for clients; programs also attempted to reduce major risk factors such as educational failure, dropout, and truancy. Measurement based on levels of program attendance (control, low and high) showed that the program was successful in reducing recidivism (50.6% recidivism for the control group, 41.3% for the low-attendance group, and 25.8% for the high-attendance group); however, effects on school outcomes were generally weak.

Another strategy designed to improve living conditions for youth includes social policy designed to assist families in moving to different communities. A federally funded research demonstration, Moving to Opportunity, was part of a randomized control trial that moved families from high-poverty to low-poverty neighborhoods in seven U.S. cities between 1994 and 2006. Johnson's (2012) synthetic review of analyses of Moving to Opportunity found that the educational benefits of moving families was limited and short-lived in all but one location, due to problems with thresholds of replication, cultural discontinuities, educational policy mismatches, and a lack of understanding of neighborhood mechanisms. Jackson et al. (2009) synthesized 22 separate evaluations and reviews of Moving to Opportunity. Their review focused on the mental health outcomes of families who moved, as well as the mechanisms through which moving influenced mental health. Their review suggested that even when moves are voluntary, as they were in Moving to Opportunity, there are potentially negative mental health outcomes from these types of social interventions. The study concludes with the recommendation that directing resources toward the improvement of existing communities is a better way to improve mental health outcomes for all community residents.

One demonstration project aimed to inform the feasibility of improving existing communities is the Promise Neighborhood effort. Komro, Flay, and Biglan (2011) detail the Promise Neighborhoods Research Consortium's approach to developing a comprehensive theoretical scientific framework for the promotion of child health and development within distressed high-poverty neighborhoods. They describe a model of child and adolescent developmental outcomes and define a comprehensive intervention framework to bring about a significant increase in the proportion of young people in high-poverty neighborhoods who will develop successfully. Based on a synthesis of research from diverse fields, Komro et al. designed the Creating Nurturing Environments framework to guide community-wide efforts to improve child outcomes and reduce health and educational inequalities through provision of comprehensive, wraparound services to residents. In this way, they see neighborhood-level interventions as capable of moderating individual- and family-level risk factors. Unfortunately, at this time, there is little data on outcomes associated with "Promise Neighborhood" interventions.

Ecological Interventions for Juvenile Offenders

Thus far the review has largely focused on prevention research related to specific institutional and contextual settings (e.g., family, school, or community) relevant to the lives of youth. Increasingly, however, researchers point to the need for interinstitutional interventions rooted in a holistic approach to young people's complex social ecologies. This section examines research on effective interventions with juvenile offenders. Common elements of effective interventions include the following: a focus on addressing risk factors (e.g., harmful family, school, and peer effects), a rehabilitative rather than punitive orientation, skill and behavioral interventions, and institutionalized support to maintain treatment fidelity. Improving family interactions and providing adult caretakers with skills to effectively supervise youth appear to be the most important interventions, whereas the least successful interventions are punitive or use fear to dissuade delinquency (Greenwood, 2008). Unfortunately, although over 1,000,000 American youth come into contact with the juvenile justice system each year, only 5% are treated with evidence-based interventions (Greenwood, 2008). Most juvenile offenders receive interventions through the courts, which do not have a strong base of empirical support or may even contribute to anti-social behaviors and recidivism. A general consensus exists among researchers, for example, that typical court involvement whether through probation or residential placement, does not appear to work (Greenwood, 2008; Henggeler & Schoenwald, 2011).

One review of literature suggests there are approximately a dozen "proven" delinquency interventions with less robust research findings pointing to another 20 to 30 "promising" interventions that need additional study (Greenwood, 2008). This section focuses on three interventions that have been shown to be effective in reducing recidivism among juvenile offenders: Multisystemic Therapy, Functional Family Therapy, and Multidimensional Treatment Foster Care. These are the only three community-based interventions for juvenile offenders that meet the stringent standards of program effectiveness as part of the Blueprints for Violence Prevention initiative that was developed by the Center for the Study and Prevention of Violence at the University of Colorado–Boulder and supported by the Office of Juvenile Justice and Delinquency Prevention, U.S. Department of Justice (Mihalic, Fagan, Irwin, Ballard, & Elliott, 2004). The Blueprints selection criteria are as follows: evidence of deterrent effect with a strong research design, sustained effect, and multiple site replication. Analysis of mediating factors and costs versus benefits are also considered. Further, in a recent meta-analysis the three programs reviewed in this section were also found to produce larger effect sizes than typically estimated in studies of programs of this type (Greenwood, 2008).

Multisystemic Therapy. Multisystemic Therapy (MST) "is an intensive family-and community-based treatment program that focuses on the entire world of chronic and violent juvenile offenders—their homes and families, schools and teachers, neighborhoods and friends" (Multisystemic

Therapy, 2012). Typically, over a period of four months, the therapist works with the family to identify the strengths of the family system and develop caregiving practices that foster effective familial control and keep the young person focused on school or work. Treatment is intensive; therapists are available to families around the clock for emergencies and, in turn, work a reduced caseload. Schools, faith communities, peer groups, and other community stakeholders are engaged to foster social support and accountability. In this family therapy context, the youth participate in an evidence-based clinical treatment such as cognitive-behavioral therapy to develop prosocial goals and behaviors. Finally, quality assurance and fidelity to the treatment design are maintained via a strict therapeutic protocol and regular expert oversight.

For adolescents who have had some contact with the juvenile justice system, several studies have analyzed the impact of interventions targeting them and their families. In one of the longest follow-up studies of serious juvenile offenders, Schaeffer and Borduin (2005) examined the effects of MST. Focusing on all environmental systems that impact chronic and violent juvenile offenders, MST targets participants' homes and families, schools and teachers, and neighborhoods and friends. An average of 13.7 years later, Schaeffer and Borduin tracked the long-term criminal activity of 176 serious adolescent offenders who had received either MST or individual therapy (IT) in an RCT. Compared to those who received IT, participants of MST had significantly lower rates of recidivism. In addition, participants of MST had 54% fewer arrests and 57% fewer days of confinement in adult detention facilities than did those who received IT. Sawyer and Borduin (2011) conducted a 21.9-year follow-up study of the MST cohort. Their findings suggest that positive treatment effects on serious and minor criminal behaviors, as measured by felony recidivism and misdemeanor offending, respectively, extended as far as young adulthood. Relying upon official records of arrests during the follow-up may have underestimated the actual number of crimes committed by the offenders.

Another MST study found that long-term re-arrest rates are reduced by 25–70%, while out-of-home placements are reduced by 47–64% (Mihalic et al., 2004). MST has been found to improve the function of the family and the mental health status of youth (Mihalic et al., 2004). The first randomized clinical trial conducted independent of MST developers found a significant reduction in the likelihood of re-arrest at 18 months post-treatment (Timmons-Mitchell, Bender, Kishna, & Mitchell, 2006). At six months post-treatment, researchers found an improvement across four areas of functioning (home, school, community, emotions) among youth randomly assigned to MST compared to the control group who received treatment as usual through the court system. Importantly, this study was conducted in a community setting and, thus, contributes to the literature highlighting the gap between the findings of efficacy studies and effectiveness studies in the research literature on MST (Timmons-Mitchell et al., 2006). Consistent with prior research, this study found that while MST participation reduced recidivism, the magnitude of the reduction was smaller than the effect sizes reported in efficacy studies.

Other studies point to the sustainability of the MST treatment effect. Henggeler, Clingempeel, Brondino, & Pickrel (2002) examined the four-year outcomes of 80 (out of an original 118) substance-abusing juvenile offenders who participated in a randomized clinical trial comparing MST with usual community services. The study measured criminal behavior, illicit drug use, and psychiatric symptoms using a multimethod assessment tool (self-report, biological, and archival measures). Findings indicated a significant long-term reduction in aggressive criminal activity (0.15 vs. 0.57 convictions per year) but not for property crimes. Illicit drug use findings were mixed, but MST participants had a significantly lower rate of marijuana use. The results did not indicate a sustainable treatment effect for psychiatric symptoms. Schaeffer and Borduin (2005) compared the long-term criminal activity of 176 youths who had received either MST or individual therapy in a randomized clinical trial. At an average of 13.7 years (range = 10.2–15.9) after treatment (average age 28.8 years), recidivism rates for the MST participants (50%) were significantly lower than for those who received individual therapy (81%). Moreover, compared to the individual therapy group, MST participants had less than half the number of arrests and less than half the number of days of confinement in adult facilities.

Another study estimated that the typical average cost per participant of MST is about $4,743 (Aos, Phipps, Barnoski, & Lieb, 2001). According to the analysis, taxpayers gain approximately $31,661 in subsequent criminal justice cost-savings for each participant. Moreover, including the benefits to victims of crime increased the expected net present value to $131,918 per participant. These values equate to a benefit-to-cost ratio of $28.33 for every dollar spent. Overall, evidence exists that MST may be an effective long-term treatment for juvenile offenders and those with substance abuse problems.

Functional Family Therapy. Like MST, Functional Family Therapy (FFT) targets youth ages 10–18 who are at serious risk of delinquency due to conduct disorder and/or substance abuse. Risk and protective factors are addressed at both the individual level and at the level of the youth's ecosystem with an ultimate goal of inducing lasting behavioral change across ecosystemic settings. The program is "strength based" with a relational approach to therapy: the focus is on developing the unique strengths of individual youth and their families by improving emotional connections and developing problem-solving and communication skills, thereby enhancing the function of the family system and the ability of adult caretakers to provide structure and guidance. FFT usually takes place over a period of 3–4 months with an average of 12 sessions and is usually delivered in home settings by individual therapists under the direct supervision of other more experienced therapists. Research on FFT has documented its effectiveness across numerous youth populations and settings and with a wide variety of service providers. Reductions in youth re-offending (between 25–60%) have been demonstrated in controlled comparison follow-up studies at 1, 3, and 5 years (Mihalic et al., 2004).

Multidimensional Treatment Foster Care. Multidimensional Treatment Foster Care (MTFC) is designed as an alternative for youth who have received an out-of-home placement (e.g., residential treatment, incarceration, and hospitalization) for an extended period. Separate MTFC programs exist for children ages 3–6, 7–11, and youth ages 12–17. In this model, foster families are trained to take one youth (who does not pose a serious threat to themselves or others) into their home on a short-term basis (around 7 months). These families are paid more than traditional foster parents and are trained to provide intensive levels of support and consistent behavior management in a therapeutic living environment. Case management teams support the foster parents through daily phone calls and weekly group support meetings. Youth receive weekly social and behavioral skills–focused therapy in addition to close academic monitoring and support. In the MTFC home, youth receive positive reinforcement for prosocial behaviors and predictable consequences for violating expectations. As youth adapt to new behavioral norms in the MTFC home, structure and adult supervision are gradually reduced and youth gain limited access to free time and peers. Biological families also receive family therapy to support healthy reintegration into the home.

A 12-month follow-up demonstrated that MTFC participants had significantly fewer arrests (an average of 2.6 vs. 5.4) than did a control group that participated in a traditional residential group home placement (Mihalic et al., 2004). MTFC youth were also found to spend fewer days in custody than were youth in other community-based programs. And after treatment, significantly fewer were ever incarcerated (Mihalic et al., 2004). Eddy, Whaley, and Chamberlain (2004) collected follow-up data for a period of 2 years on a group of 79 adolescent male juvenile offenders assigned to either MTFC or to a services-as-usual group home care (GC) as part of a randomized clinical trial. MTFC youth were significantly less likely to commit violent offenses than youth placed in a traditional group home. During the study's duration, 24% of the GC youth had two or more criminal referrals for violent offenses compared to only 5% of MTFC participants. Rates of self-reported violent offending were also 4–9 times lower for MTFC youth.

In sum, family-based interventions that are coordinated across the primary institutions that constitute a youth's social ecology have large and sustainable effects in addition to replicable implementation strategies. Interinstitutional ecological interventions provide a way to improve mental health outcomes while reducing criminal behavior and improving school outcomes—thus disrupting the school-to-prison pipeline. Building linguistic bridges and institutional cooperation among families, schools, courts, health care providers, and other social service agencies represent a real opportunity to improve urban education going forward.

Implications for Urban Education

It has been established using empirical methods that criminal justice sanctions imposed on urban school children have educational consequences (Kirk & Sampson, 2013). Specifically, juvenile arrest has a direct effect on later high school dropout and college enrollment for urban adolescents with otherwise similar residential, school, family, peer, and individual characteristics. Urban school leaders should not ignore this pattern. A foundational challenge for helping vulnerable youth is designing effective coordination and partnerships between urban school districts, researchers, and human service agencies. Part of this challenge includes addressing confidentiality while building common language, sharing data, and integrating information systems, but agencies are seeking solutions. Building robust interagency coordination focused on youth in need of support should be a central aim of every urban school district in the United States.

One effort in the very early stages of development is happening in St. Louis. A cooperative agreement between the St. Louis Public School District and Juvenile Court Judge Jimmie Edwards has resulted in a school specifically designed to meet the developmental needs of troubled youth. The juvenile court provides youth supervision, support services, and secures community partners, while the school district provides teachers, transportation, and building maintenance.[2] In this case, the cooperative agreement allows the school district to focus on instruction and school operations without sacrificing the developmental supports required to successfully educate youth in need of targeted psychological and social interventions. Specifically, the Juvenile Court is positioned to secure the type of evidence-based treatments discussed earlier and to closely monitor academic progress. While the arrangements may vary across urban school districts and jurisdictions, the focus should be similar—building developmental pathways to support urban youth.

The field has developed sufficiently robust strategies to support vulnerable youth at risk of antisocial behavior. The challenge is not about treatment effectiveness or how to implement an intervention. Unfortunately, too often it comes down to questions of costs, priority, or will. Rather than relying on a school-to-prison pipeline, long term for individuals and society, we need to develop a common language and set of supports that youth providers can access early in the life course of children and adolescents. Vulnerable youth should not be left to the streets.

Notes

1. Cooper's (2010) taxonomy of literature reviews informs the conceptualization of this chapter. He argues that focus, goals, perspective, coverage, organization, and audience characterize research reviews. Each characteristic shapes the review. In this chapter, we will review research findings, practices, and applications related to vulnerable youth in urban communities. While we attend less to theories and research method, they are

included in some cases to inform arguments. With respect to goals, we aim to bridge linguistically multiple research literatures. We espouse a particular perspective and make no attempt to appear neutral on this front. More specifically, we view linguistic bridge building about effective practice with at-risk youth in the research community as an important frame to support integrated services and opportunity structures for vulnerable children in practice. Our strategy for coverage is representative.

2. The general partners and community partners are listed at http://www.courts.mo.gov/hosted/circuit22/blewett_school_01.htm#General_Partners

References

Advancement Project. (2010). *Test, punish, and push out: How "zero tolerance" and high-stakes testing funnel youth into the school-to-prison pipeline.* Washington, DC: Author.

American Academy of Pediatrics. (2003). Policy statement: Out of school suspension and expulsion. *Pediatrics, 112,* 1206–1209.

American Psychiatric Association. (2000). *Diagnostic and statistical manual of mental disorders* (4th ed.). Arlington, VA: Author.

American Psychological Association Zero Tolerance Task Force. (2008). Are zero tolerance policies effective in the schools? An evidentiary review and recommendations. *American Psychologist, 63,* 852–862.

Aos, S., Phipps, P., Barnoski, R., & Lieb, R.C. (2001). *The comparative costs and benefits of programs to reduce crime.* Olympia, WA: Washington State Institute for Public Policy.

Artiles, A.J. (2011). Toward an interdisciplinary understanding of educational equity and difference: The case of the racialization of ability. *Educational Researcher, 40,* 431–445.

Balfanz, R., Spiridakis, K., Curran Neild, R., & Legters, N. (2003). High poverty secondary schools and the juvenile justice system: How neither helps the other and how that could change. *New Directions for Youth Development, 99,* 71–89.

Cooper, H. (2010). Research synthesis and meta-analysis: A step-by-step approach (4th ed.). Los Angeles, CA: Sage.

Eddy, M.J., Whaley, R.B., & Chamberlain, P. (2004). The prevention of violent behavior by chronic and serious male juvenile offenders: A two-year follow-up of a randomized trial. *Journal of Emotional and Behavioral Disorders, 12,* 2–8.

Edelman, M.W. (2007, July). The cradle to prison pipeline: An American health crisis. *Preventing Chronic Disease, 4*(3). Retrieved from http://www.cdc.gov/pcd/issues/2007/jul/07_0038.htm

Edwards, M.C. (2010). Understanding adolescence: A policy perspective. In D.P. Phillips, M.C. Edwards, & M.B. Spencer (Eds.), *Adolescence development during a global era* (pp. 477–498). London, UK: Academic Press.

Ellonen, N. (2008). Adolescent delinquency and social control in Finnish schools: A multilevel analysis. *Journal of Scandinavian Studies in Criminology and Crime Prevention, 9,* 47–64.

Eron, L., Huesman, R., Spindler, A., Guerra, N., Henry, D., Tolan, P., & VanAcker, R. (2002). A cognitive-ecological approach to preventing aggression in urban settings: Initial outcomes for high-risk children. *Journal of Consulting and Clinical Psychology, 70,* 179–194.

Foster, E.M., Qaseem, A., & Connor, T. (2004). Can better mental health services reduce the risk of juvenile justice system involvement? *American Journal of Public Health, 94,* 859–865.

Greenwood, P. (2008). Prevention and intervention programs for juvenile offenders. *The Future of Children, 18*(2), 185–210.

Hallfors, D., Cho, H., Brodish, P., Flewelling, R., & Khatapoush, S. (2006). Identifying high school students "at risk" for substance use and other behavioral problems: Implications for prevention. *Substance Use & Misuse, 41,* 1–15.

Henggeler, S.W., Clingempeel, W.G., Brondino, M.J., & Pickrel, S.G. (2002). Four-year follow-up of multisystemic therapy with substance-abusing and substance-dependent juvenile offenders. *Journal of the American Academy of Child & Adolescent Psychiatry, 41,* 868–874.

Henggeler, S.W., & Schoenwald, S.J. (2011). Evidence-based interventions for juvenile offenders and juvenile justice policies that support them. *Social Policy Report, 25*(1), 1–20.

Henry, K., Knight, K., & Thornberry, T. (2012). School disengagement as a predictor of dropout, delinquency, and problem substance use during adolescence and early adulthood. *Journal of Youth Adolescence, 41,* 156–166.

Individuals with Disabilities Education Act, 20 U.S.C. § 1400 (2004).

Ippen, C.G., Harris, W.W., Van Horn, P., & Lieberman, A.F. (2011). Traumatic and stressful events in early childhood: Can treatment help those at highest risk? *Child Abuse & Neglect, 35,* 504–513.

Jackson, L., Langille, L., Lyons, R., Hughes, J., Martin, D., & Winstanley, V. (2009). Does moving from a high-poverty to lower-poverty neighborhood improve mental health? A realist review of "Moving to Opportunity." *Health and Place, 15,* 961–970.

Johnson, O. (2012). Relocation programs, opportunities to learn, and the complications of conversion. *Review of Educational Research, 82,* 131–178.

Justice Policy Institute. (2009). *The costs of confinement: Why good juvenile justice policies make good fiscal sense.* Washington, DC: Author.

Kessler, R.C., Berglund, P., Demler, O., Jin, R., Merikangas, K.R., & Walters, E.E. (2005). Lifetime prevalence and age-of-onset distributions of *DSM-IV* disorders in the National Comorbidity Survey Replication. *Archives of General Psychiatry, 62,* 593–602.

Kim, C., Losen, D., & Hewitt, D. (2010). *The school-to-prison pipeline: Structuring legal reform.* New York, NY: New York University Press.

Kirk, D.S., & Sampson, R.J. (2013). Juvenile arrest and collateral educational damage in the transition to adulthood. *Sociology of Education, 86,* 36–62.

Klevens, J., Martinez, J., Le, B., Rojas, C., Duque, A., & Tovar, R. (2009). Evaluation of two interventions to reduce aggressive and antisocial behavior in first and second graders in a resource-poor setting. *International Journal of Educational Research, 48,* 307–319.

Komro, K., Flay, B., & Biglan, A. (2011). Creating nurturing environments: A science-based framework for promoting child health and development within high-poverty neighborhoods. *Clinical Family Psychological Review, 14,* 111–134.

Krezmien, M.P., Leone, P.E., Zablocki, M.S., & Wells, C.S. (2010). Juvenile court referrals and the public schools: Nature and extent of the practice in five states. *Journal of Contemporary Criminal Justice, 26,* 273–293.

Leone, P., & Weinberg, L. (2010). *Addressing the unmet educational needs of children and youth in the juvenile justice and child welfare systems.* Washington, DC: Center for Juvenile Justice Reform, Georgetown University.

Losen, D., & Skiba, R. (2010). *Suspended education: Urban middle schools in crisis.* Montgomery, AL: Southern Poverty Law Center.

Mann, E., & Reynolds, A. (2006). Early intervention and juvenile delinquency prevention: Evidence from the Chicago Longitudinal Study. *Social Work Research, 30,* 153–167.

Massey, D.S. (2009). The age of extremes: Concentrated affluence and poverty in the twenty-first century. In H.P. Hynes & R. Lopez (Eds.), *Urban health: Readings in the social, built, and physical environments of U.S. cities* (pp. 5–36). Sudbury, MA: Jones and Bartlett.

Merikangas, K. R., He, J. P., Burstein, M., Swanson, S. A., Avenevoli, S. Cui, L. Benjet, C., Georgiades, K., & Swendsen, J. (2010). Lifetime prevalence of mental disorders in US adolescents: Results from the national comorbidity study-adolescent supplement (NCS-A). *Journal of the American Academy of Child and Adolescent Psychiatry, 49,* 980–989.

Mihalic, S., Fagan, A., Irwin, K., Ballard, D., & Elliot, D. (2004). *Blueprints for violence prevention.* Boulder, CO: Center for the Study and Prevention of Violence, University of Colorado–Boulder.

Molnar, B., Cerda, M., Roberts, A., & Buka, S. (2008). Effects of neighborhood resources on aggressive and delinquent behaviors among urban youths. *American Journal of Public Health, 98,* 1086-1093.

Montague, R. (2008, August 13). Inside the nation's largest mental institution. *NPR.* Retrieved from http://www.npr.org/templates/story/story.php?storyId=93581736.

Multisystemic Therapy. (2012). Retrieved from http://mstservices.com/

National Dissemination Center for Children With Disabilities. (2010). *Emotional disturbance* (Disability Fact Sheet #5). Washington, DC: Author.

National Mental Health Association. (2004). *Mental health treatment for youth in the juvenile justice system: A compendium of promising practices.* Alexandria, VA: Author.

National Public Radio. (2011, September 4). *Nation's jails struggle with mentally ill prisoners.* Retrieved from http://www.npr.org/2011/09/04/140167676/nations-jails-struggle-with-mentally-ill-prisoners

New York Civil Liberties Union. (2011). *Education interrupted: The growing use of suspension in New York City's public schools.* New York, NY: Author.

Nitkowski, D., Petermann, F., Buttner, P., Krause-Leipoldt, C., & Petermann, U. (2009). Behavior modification of aggressive children in child welfare: Evaluation of a combined intervention program. *Behavior Modification, 33,* 474–492.

Olds, D.L. (2008). Preventing child maltreatment and crime with prenatal and infancy support of parents: The nurse-family partnership. *Journal of Scandinavian Studies in Criminology & Crime Prevention, 9*(Suppl. 1), 2–24.

Osher, D.M., Quinn, M.M., Poirier, J.M., & Rutherford, R.B. (2003). Deconstructing the pipeline: Using efficacy, effectiveness, and cost-benefit data to reduce minority youth incarceration. *New Directions for Youth Development, 99,* 91–120.

Payne, A. (2008). A multilevel analysis of the relationships among communal school organization, student bonding, and delinquency. *Journal of Research in Crime and Delinquency, 45,* 429–455.

Puzzanchera, C., & Kang, W. (2013). *Easy access to juvenile court statistics: 1985–2010.* Retrieved June 29, 2013 from http://ojjdp.gov/ojstatbb/ezajcs/asp/process.asp

Redding, R.E., Sevin Goldstein, N.E., & Heilbrun, K. (2005). Juvenile delinquency: Past and present. In K. Heilbrun, N.E.S. Goldstein, & R.E. Redding (Eds.), *Juvenile delinquency: Prevention, assessment, and intervention* (pp. 45–66). Oxford: Oxford University Press.

Sampson, R., Raudenbush, S., & Earls, F. (1997). Neighborhood and violent crime: A multilevel study of collective efficacy. *Science, 277,* 918–924.

Sawyer, A.M., & Borduin, C.M. (2011). Effects of multisystemic therapy through midlife: A 21.9-year follow-up to a randomized clinical trial with serious and violent juvenile offenders. *Journal of Consulting and Clinical Psychology, 79,* 643–652.

Schaeffer, C.M., & Borduin, C.M. (2005). Long-term follow-up to a randomized clinical trial of multisystemic therapy with serious and violent juvenile offenders. *Journal of Consulting and Clinical Psychology, 73,* 445-453.

Shufelt, J.L., & Cocozza, J.J. (2006, June). *Youth with mental health disorders in the juvenile justice system: Results from a multi-state prevalence study.* Delmar, NY: National Center for Mental Health and Juvenile Justice.

Simpson, G., Cohen, R. A., Pastor, P. N., & Reuben, C. A. (2008). *Use of mental health services in the past 12 months by children aged 4–17 years: United States, 2005–2006* (NCHS data brief, No. 8). Hyattsville, MD: National Center for Health Statistics, Centers for Disease Control and Prevention.

Skiba, R.J., Michael, R.S., Nardo, A.C., & Peterson, R. (2002). The color of discipline: Sources of racial and gender disproportionality in school punishment. *Urban Review, 34,* 317–342.

Spencer, M.B., Tinsley, B., Dupree, D., & Fegley, S. (2012). Maximizing culturally and contextually sensitive assessment strategies in developmental and educational research. In W.F. Tate (Ed.), *Research on schools, neighborhoods, and communities: Toward civic responsibility* (pp. 299–325). Lanham, MD: Rowman & Littlefield.

Steadman, H.J., Osher, F.C., Robbins, P.C., Case, B., & Samuels, S. (2009). Prevalence of serious mental illness among jail inmates. *Psychiatric Services, 60,* 761–765.

Teplin, L.A. (1990). The prevalence of severe mental disorder among male urban jail detainees: Comparison with the Epidemiologic Catchment Area Program. *American Journal of Public Health, 80,* 663–669.

Teplin, L., Abran, K., McClelland, G., Dulcan, M., & Mericle, A. (2002). Psychiatric disorders in youth in juvenile detention. *Archives of General Psychiatry, 59,* 1133–1143.

Timmons-Mitchell, J., Bender, M.B., Kishna, M.A., & Mitchell, C.C. (2006). An independent effectiveness trial of multisystemic therapy with juvenile justice youth. *Journal of Clinical Child & Adolescent Psychology, 35,* 227–236.

Tobler, A.L., Komro, K.A., Dabroski, A., Aveyard, P., & Markham, W.A. (2011). Preventing the link between SES and high-risk behaviors: "Value-added" education, drug use and delinquency in high-risk, urban schools. *Prevention Science, 12,* 211–221.

Tremblay, R.E., Pagani-Kurtz, L., Masse, L.C., Vitaro, F., & Pihl, R.O. (1995). A bimodal preventive intervention for disruptive kindergarten boys: Its impact through mid-adolescence. *Journal of Consulting and Clinical Psychology, 63,* 560–568.

Trupin, E.W., Stewart, D.G., Beach, B., & Boesky, L. (2002). Effectiveness of a dialectical behaviour therapy program for incarcerated female juvenile offenders. *Child and Adolescent Mental Health, 7,* 121–127.

Turner, M., Hartman, J., & Bishop, D. (2007). The effects of prenatal problems, family functioning, and neighborhood disadvantage in predicting life-course-persistent offending. *Criminal Justice and Behavior, 34,* 1241–1261.

U.S. Department of Education, Office for Civil Rights. (2012). *Data summary of 2009–2010 CRDC Survey.* Washington, DC: Author. Retrieved from http://ocrdata.ed.gov/DataSummary

Wald, J., & Losen, D.J. (2003). Defining and redirecting a school-to-prison pipeline. *New Directions for Youth Development, 99,* 9–15.

Welsh, W., Jenkins, P., & Harris, P. (1999). Reducing minority overrepresentation in juvenile justice: Results of community-based delinquency prevention in Harrisburg. *Journal of Research in Crime and Delinquency, 36,* 87–110.

Wilf, R. (2012, March 3). *Disparities in school discipline move students of color toward prison.* Washington, DC: Center for American Progress. Retrieved from http://www.americanprogress.org/issues/2012/03/school_discipline_disparities.html

Yeakey, C.C. (2003). From classrooms to cellblocks: African American juveniles in the justice system. In C.C. Yeakey & R.D. Henderson (Eds.), *Surmounting all odds: Education, opportunity, and society in the new millennium* (pp. 191–214). Greenwich, CT: Information Age Publishing.

Yeakey, C.C. (Ed.). (2012). *Living on the boundaries: Urban marginality in national and international contexts.* Bingley, UK: Emerald Press.

2

Liberating Urban Education for Human Freedom

Joyce E. King, Chike Akua & LaToya Russell

Introduction

In 1907 Edgar Gardner Murphy, the head of the Southern Education Board, wrote to Wallace Buttrick, executive officer of the General Education Board: "There is not only no chance to help the situation of the Negro educationally, but it is steadily growing worse, and their schools, upon every sort of pretext, are being hampered and impoverished where they are not actually abandoned" (White, 2002, p. 89).[1] While education for Black people in the north was not faring much better then (or now), and has certainly advanced beyond the post-Reconstruction nadir Murphy reported, 150 years after our "emancipation," African Americans' aspirations for social, political, and economic justice by means of liberating education remain largely unfulfilled. In 1997 nearly a century after Murphy's dismal admission, Murrell observed that "African-American children as a group" were still being "horribly served" in major underresourced urban school systems. Today, after more than 60 years of integration, the conditions of Black education that Murrell described have further deteriorated:

> . . . African American children, particularly males, fare dramatically less well than their European-American counterparts. They are disproportionately expelled, suspended, and relegated to special programs for the emotionally disturbed, learning disabled, and mentally retarded. They have dramatically higher drop-out rates, yet dramatically lower grade point averages and rates of matriculation. Half as many young African-American men go to college than a decade ago. (Murrell, 1997, p. 23)

Moreover, women are now the fastest-growing prison population including a disproportionate number of Black women and girls (Meares, 2011; Ravoira & Patino, 2011; Winn, 2011). In fact, Black education, particularly in urban schools, remains a question of our survival as a people. Whether urban education should actually enable Black students to develop not only academically but also to be conscious and committed to this sense of "peoplehood" continues to be contested (Ravitch, 1990, 2010).

This chapter presents an interpretive discussion of representative research and scholarship selected to illuminate important linkages between academic and cultural excellence in urban education and the role of culture and consciousness as a foundation for liberating urban education for human freedom (National Alliance of Black School Educators [NABSE], 1984). Research and scholarship focused solely on the underachievement of Black students in comparison to Whites and Asians in urban schools—the so-called achievement gap—typically fail to consider the positive role racial/ethnic group identity (e.g., cultural ways of being) and socialization can play with regard to student achievement. Hilliard and Sizemore argued in the NABSE Task Force Report (1984) that for African American students academic excellence cannot be achieved without cultural excellence:

> African American children must be given the opportunity to experience an appropriate cultural education which gives them an intimate knowledge of and which honors and respects the history and culture of our people . . . [This means] preparing students for self-knowledge and to become a contributing problem-solving member of his or her own community and in the wider world as well. No child can be ignorant of or lack respect for his or her own unique cultural group and meet others in the world on an equal footing. (NABSE, 1984, p. 23)

Thus, the focus of this chapter is the importance of consciousness as an alternative to miseducation, hypernationalism, and assimilation. The chapter begins with examples of deficit thinking in selected explanatory frameworks regarding inequity in urban education, then considers what the research says concerning identity, achievement, and cultural well-being in scholarship on transformative curriculum and pedagogy interventions, culturally grounded African consciousness, and an African cultural understanding of excellence in urban education. The chapter ends with a brief discussion of implications for liberating urban education theory, research, policy, and practice for human freedom.

Explanatory Frameworks and Ideological Assaults on Cultural Blackness

Integration was expected to "fix" the problem of Black students' "low-achievement." In "Straight Talk About School Desegregation Problems," Hilliard (1978) noted:

> It must be remembered that the present day push for "integrated education" had its roots in the general belief that the education white children got was quality education, and that if only Afro-American and other cultural groups could be present when this quality education was offered, they would be better off than under segregation. (p. 100)

Integration was thus not an attempt to merge cultures, or even to accommodate cultural differences, but an assimilation effort in which Black culture was considered detrimental and students' ways of knowing and being were considered deficits, and consequently, given prevailing assumptions about the superiority of the White "race" and the inferiority of Black people, it was thought that for Black students to achieve on par with White students they would need to adapt to and exhibit the cultural norms of the dominant group.

However, urban schools have become more racially concentrated and more oppressive for Black students who have not fully adopted the dominant culture's norms (Delpit, 2012). As Black cultural styles "remain dominant" and pervade Black students' ways of knowing and being, their academic underachievement persists and constitutes a national crisis (Carter, 2008b; King, 2010).[2] Despite numerous (but flawed) attempts to "include" content about diverse "others" in the curriculum, not only what is taught but also how, contributes to the pervasive elevation of Euro-American culture as the norm (Buras, 2008; Swartz, 2009; Wynter, 1992/2012). School curricula and pedagogy convey the idea that to have a quality education one must become a Europhile, in the arts, music, literature, history and the behavioral sciences, as well as math and science (Boutté & Strickland, 2008).

It is our contention that research frameworks that ignore this reality and explain inequity in urban education by focusing primarily on and defining "Black-White" (and Latino/a) outcome disparities only in terms of an "achievement gap" rather than as the failure of integration or in terms of the survival of Africans in America *as a people* reflect dysconscious deficit thinking that implicitly accepts categories of racial hierarchy as normative (King & Akua, 2012). Dysconsciousness, as compared to critical consciousness, "is an uncritical . . . habit of mind that justifies inequity and exploitation by accepting the existing order of things as given" (King, 1991, p. 135). For instance, the importance of a (positive) role for culture (not to be conflated with racialized "culture of poverty" explanations) in education remains underinvestigated. Yet, culture continues to be a battleground for educators and political leaders, as Blackness has been condemned as intellectually and morally inferior (King, 2011), criminalized (Muhammad, 2010), and nihilated as "Nigger chaos" (Wynter, 1984).[3] Such normalized negations of what Wynter referred to as "conceptual blackness" within this society's cultural model of race illustrate what race actually does. As an ideological form of knowledge, race denigrates African peoples' heritage and cultural ways of knowing and being (King, 2006). Nevertheless, Black students (like students from other historically dominated groups) are being taught and tested on a way of being that supports neither their identity nor their development as African people. As Hilliard (1978) stated, the problem is:

> The very knowledge base which we pass on to our children and the conceptual tools for dealing with that knowledge base have themselves been colonized. We live with the legacy of those years reflected in our curricula, textbooks, school organization, and into our training programs for educators. (p. 103)

Attention to how the curriculum contributes not only to outcome inequity but also how school knowledge and pedagogy undermine the academic and cultural excellence of Black students, as well as their agency and self-determination, should replace the present preoccupation with racialized performance gaps. Since Woodson's (1933) seminal work, *The Miseducation of the Negro,* scholars have continued to call for curricula designed to educate all American children within a knowledge base that is not grounded solely in Eurocentric ideals.

Research and writing on the achievement gap, then, leads to the conclusion that Black students' underachievement is a consequence not only of societal inequalities (e.g., underresourced and inadequately staffed urban schools) but is also a result of self-imposed or internalized pressures that undermine students' achievement (Whaley & Noël, 2012). One such explanation, the "acting white" hypothesis, proposed by Fordham and Ogbu (1986), is grounded in cultural ecological theory. Ogbu and Simons (1998) suggested that involuntary (or nonimmigrant "caste-like") minorities (who have been conquered, colonized, or enslaved) are less economically successful than voluntary minorities; these groups usually experience greater and more persistent cultural and language difficulties and do less well in school, so the theory goes, because they link academic achievement or activities related to academic achievement to assimilation efforts, that is, to "acting white." According to Ogbu and Simons (1998), "What the students reject that hurt their academic performance are 'White' attitudes and behaviors conducive to making good grades" (n.p.). This theoretical approach has had an enormous impact on teachers' thinking about teaching and learning in urban schools and in teacher preparation.

Steele's research on "stereotype threat" is another explanatory framework within which the problems of urban education are posed. This research program has focused on the sense of threat that can arise when one knows that he or she can possibly be judged or treated negatively on the basis of a negative stereotype about one's group (Steele, 1992, 1997; Steele & Aronson, 1995). Stereotype threat requires that an individual be highly identified with a domain, that the individual believe he or she is being evaluated, and that the self-concept be implicated in that evaluation (Goff, Steele, & Davies, 2008). In experimental studies Steele and his colleagues have found that negative stereotypes about African American intellectual abilities impede Black student performance on standardized tests—a condition he called "stereotype threat." Steele developed the theory that a stereotype threat—the threat of being perceived in terms of a negative stereotype or the fear of poor performance confirming that stereotype—can be powerful enough to shape the intellectual performance and academic identities of entire groups of people. According to Steele, everyone experiences "stereotype threat" because we are all members of some group about which negative stereotypes exist. When capable Black college students fail to perform as well as their White counterparts, the explanation often has less to do with preparation or ability than with the threat of stereotypes about their capacity to succeed (Steele, 2003).

Murrell (2009) offers an explanatory framework regarding Black student's achievement that differs markedly from the explanations Ogbu and Steele provide: It is the "dynamic interplay between racial identity and academic identity" (p. 90). Murrell's framework contradicts the assumption that African American students' underperformance, as indicated in achievement gap data, is a consequence of their "disidentification with education and schooling" (Murrell, p. 90). Murrell's explanation of academic identity development among African American learners identifies three levels of social identity development: (1) the intrapersonal identity development process, (2) the interpersonal identity development process of social identification, and (3) the transpersonal identity process of individuals gaining the agency to improvise their own expressions of self in dynamic interaction with others who may attempt to ascribe unwanted and ego-degrading projections to the individual. In this framework, Murrell uses situated-mediated identity theory to explain that educational attainment is much less a matter of an individual's disidentification with school and more a matter of the school context's disidentification with the student (Murrell, 2009, p. 97). Murrell concludes that to be both African American and a school achiever means that developing a healthy (i.e., ego-integrated) racial identity is not an option but a necessity.

The intent of this chapter is to go beyond explanatory frameworks, which in effect ascribe deficits to Black students and their families and communities, by pinpointing the elements of deficit-thinking that inform these research perspectives (Dudley-Marling & Lucas, 2009). In contrast, for example, Ladson-Billings (2006) emphasizes the importance of recognizing that there is an "educational debt"—not an achievement gap. Other researchers use the language of "opportunity gap" (Darling-Hammond, 2010; Milner, 2012). Hilliard (2003) suggested the achievement gap not be discussed in terms of "minority" students' performance versus European American students' performance as normative, but as a gap between African American students' performance and levels of excellence expected of them. Hilliard noted in culturally affirming socio-educational contexts:

> Many of the same students, supposedly debilitated by their avoidance of "acting white," damaged by "rumors of inferiority," or avoiding intellectual work because of peer pressure, have been turned around virtually in an instant to dominate chess tournaments, to become fierce competitors in street law programs, to become writers, mathematicians, and the like. (Hilliard, 2003, p. 147)

Indeed, much of the current debate over the "test score gap" places the blame for disparate educational outcomes on attitudes and cultural norms inherent in the families and communities of Black students (Anderson, 2004). Hilliard's observations are worth citing further:

> We should not begin with a search for student deficiencies as the explanation for their academic failure or success. Language and cultural diversity, poverty, crime and drug-ridden neighborhoods, single-parent mostly female-headed households may determine opportunity to learn, not capacity to learn. (Hilliard, 2003, p. 147)

Deficit approaches to teaching and learning, firmly in place in educational research and scholarship prior to and during the 1960s and 1970s that remain in what has come to be known as "urban education," have included the expectation that students will shed their cultural identities, subjectivities, and language in order to be academically successful (Kinloch, 2010; Kynard, 2013; Thomas, 2010). Valenzuela (1999) described this expectation and associated practices as "subtractive schooling" in a study of immigrant and U.S.-born Mexican youth in a Texas high school. This expectation incorporates a view of the languages, literacies, and cultural ways of being of many historically marginalized students as deficiencies to be overcome through cultural assimilation as a prerequisite to learning the legitimized or normative dominant language, literacy, and cultural ways of schooling (Paris, 2012). The dominant language, literacy, and cultural practices demanded in urban schools align with White, middle-class norms that position languages and literacies outside those norms as inferior and unworthy, that is, as obstacles to learning in U.S. schools and to effective functioning in society. Simply put, the goal of deficit approaches is to eradicate the linguistic, literate, and cultural practices many of these students bring from their homes and communities in order to replace them with what is viewed as superior cultural capital (P. Carter, 2003; Heath, 1989). In contrast to such deficit-oriented explanatory frameworks, the research discussed in the next section addresses identity and achievement within a cultural well-being framework.

What the Research Says About Identity, Achievement, and Cultural Well-Being

In "the struggle for identity in today's school" Fraser (2000) situated the requirement of cultural assimilation within "the politics of recognition" or the "identity model." Fraser continues, "one becomes an individual subject only by virtue of recognizing, and being recognized by, another subject" (p. 2). Suggesting that this lack of recognition or "omission" of African-centered education (e.g., that permits African Americans to see themselves in the curriculum and processes of schooling) from the discussion of the achievement gap is to deny that Black students have a place in American society. Such denial in the education system situates Black students as unimportant in America. This lack of recognition ultimately leads them to struggle for a group identity—for a sense of belonging that is a primary need of all people.

Recognition from others is thus essential to the development of a sense of self. To be denied recognition or to be misrecognized is to suffer both a distortion of one's relation to one's self and an injury to one's identity. Fraser's point merits quoting at length:

> The proponents of politics of recognition contend that to belong to a group that is devalued by the dominant culture is to be misrecognized. As a result of repeated encounters with the stigmatizing gaze of a culturally dominant other, members internalize negative self-images. The politics of recognition aims to repair this negative image by proposing that members of misrecognized groups reject such images in favor of self-representations of their own making—which, publicly asserted, will gain the respect and esteem of society at large. The result, when successful, is 'recognition': an undistorted relation to oneself. (Fraser, 2000, p. 2)

The denial of recognition in education distorts the self-perception of Black students and denies them a collective group identity. If there is no information or history to draw from, then students have no platform on which to connect. Taylor (1994) argued that "due recognition is not just a courtesy we owe people, it is a vital human need." While identity and culture are recognized and formed in the home, the constant opposition from the education system to their positive identity formation is an assault on Black students and their ability to negotiate the racism in society.

While understanding the sociocultural contexts in which Black students learn in urban education settings enables educators to better meet their academic needs, research also indicates that equally in-depth examinations of how Black students construct aspects of their identities can serve this purpose as well. An increased understanding of Black students' attitudes about race, awareness of racism in society, and their understanding of the utility of schooling for academic, social, and economic mobility can help educators identify and embody curricula and pedagogical practices that foster not only academic achievement but also Black students' healthy, positive identity construction and personal development (D. Carter, 2008b). If Black students are not offered positive images and accounts of history to identify with in school, they are left with alienating negative images that can undermine their ability to achieve academic and cultural excellence without the self-abnegation of rejecting African American cultural ways of being (King & Wilson, 1990). Such "subtractive schooling" also alienates parents and community members in the process.

Students of African ancestry who internalize the concept of White superiority/Black inferiority, for example, are "prisoners" of a myth (belief structure) that will ultimately warp their self-image, subvert their self-esteem, undermine their self-worth, stifle their self-motivation, and dim their prospects for high-level achievement. In order to address Black students' need for affirming identity formation, educators must acknowledge their culture, heritage, and ways of knowing and being. For instance, Spencer, Noll, Stoltzfris, & Harpalani (2001) found that high self-esteem was related to high academic performance, "high Eurocentricity" was associated with low achievement, and "proactive Afrocentricity," or a positive sense of self as an African American, was related to high achievement (Whaley & Noël, 2012). In addition, Oyserman, Gant, and Ager (1995) suggested that racial centrality (the degree to which an individual values race as a core part of his or her self-concept) is related to higher academic achievement (Ford & Harris, 1997; Sellers, Smith, Shelton, Rowley, & Chavous, 1998). Racial centrality is similar to the construct of connectedness Oyserman et al. (1995) investigated. This study found that Black adolescents describe a sense of self as part of Black familialism and kin networks. The sense of connectedness to the Black community provides a sense of meaning and purpose and ties the self to strategies for school achievement.

According to Stevenson, Best, Cassidy, and McCabe (2003), racial socialization "represents different processes whereby families, peers and caring communities prepare youth to survive in a world hostile to racial difference" (p. 43). McAdoo (2002) defined racial socialization as "the process by which the parents shape their children's attitudes about race and show the children how they fit into the context of race in their society" (p. 50). A growing body of research in several disciplines (child development, counseling psychology, Black psychology, social work, and youth development) indicates various ways in which racial socialization, that is to say, culture-based parenting, actually supports Black students' academic and social development (Graham & Anderson, 2008; King, 2008; Wakefield & Hudley, 2007; Wang & Huguley, 2012). In addition to research on racial, ethnic, and cultural socialization through which Black youth acquire values, identity, and social and survival competence, Majors and Ansari (2009) discussed "cultural community practices as urban classroom resources" in curriculum design work, such as Lee's (2007) Cultural Modeling Project and Majors's (2003) application of "Shoptalk" discourse as pedagogical approaches that are both "race-conscious and equity-oriented" and that attempt to "de-normalize the dominant group experience" in "community social spaces" (p. 107). This extant scholarship reports positive academic impacts of culturally responsive approaches and "pedagogical supports that are cultural in nature" linked to students' "cultural socialization" (Majors & Ansari, 2009) and racial (ethnic) identification (e.g., Altschul, Oyserman & Bybee, 2006; Bowman & Howard, 1985; Chavous, Bernat, Schmeelk-Cone, Caldwell, Kohn-Wood & Zimmerman, 2003; Davis, Aronson, & Salinas, 2006; Hilliard, 2003; Lee, 2007; Lewis, Sullivan, & Bybee, 2006, 2012; Nasir & Hand, 2005; Oyserman, Harrison, & Bybee, 2001; Oyserman, Kemmelmeier, Fryberg, & Hart-Johnson, 2003; Smith-Maddox, 1998). Research within this paradigm is consistent with a cultural well-being framework advanced in both international human rights policy and an influential Conference on College Composition and Communication 1974 policy statement, "Students' Right to Their Own Language" (SRTOL).[4] An alternative to deficit theorizing, this cultural well-being paradigm also extends to research on African-ancestry populations in other diaspora contexts such as Canada and the Caribbean (Herrero, 2006; Hudicourt-Barnes, 2003).

In a study of academically successful Black students, D. Carter (2008b) found that their "critical race consciousness and pride in being members of the Black community were two elements that enabled them to develop strategies for succeeding in the school context and pursuing their future goals" (p. 20). Likewise, Graham and Anderson (2008) provide evidence that positively embracing their "blackness" is associated with Black males' higher academic achievement and resilience. These researchers found that in the absence of culturally relevant curriculum content, socialization rooted in Black cultural ideals (e.g., respect for ancestors' struggles) and parental/community support can encourage a strong group identity that in turn encourages academic success. In addition to racial socialization and positive identification with Black culture, researchers also find that critical racism awareness and a collective cultural orientation can serve as protective cultural assets for academic success and personal resilience (Bowman & Howard, 1985; Thomas, Davidson, & McAdoo, 2008).

From this perspective, a strong cultural or racial-ethnic identity among African American youth encourages academic success in ways that are mutually reinforcing. Thus, D. Carter (2008b) calls for a "combination of a positive racial identity, critical race consciousness and a pragmatic attitude about the utility of schooling that can enable Black students to *persist* in school." In addition, notes Carter:

> In all cases, their persistence may not lead to high academic performance. Thus, one might conclude that the combination of these three concepts is necessary—but not entirely sufficient—as a recipe for high academic achievement among Black students. Nonetheless, these ingredients prove helpful for increased academic success for these adolescents. (p. 16)

The next section includes examples of transformative curriculum and pedagogy interventions that are needed in urban schools to liberate urban education and, given societal racism, "to heal a people" (Murrell, 1997).

Transformative Curriculum and Pedagogy Interventions

Thomas, Davidson, and McAdoo (2008) implemented a school-based intervention for Black high school girls that included an African American history component, a focus on cultural unity and values, as well as academic explorations. This youth development intervention demonstrates that such a culturally relevant "strengths based" intervention can promote ethnic identity, a collectivist orientation, racism awareness, and youth activism that can protect

Black girls from the adverse effects of racism. The school curriculum needs to recognize and to address Black students' need to develop a positive self-perspective to be educated to become agents of change rather than acquiesce to oppressive schooling that ensures the status quo. In this regard Shujaa's distinction between education and schooling is illuminating: "Schooling is a process intended to perpetuate and maintain the society's existing power relations and the institutional structures that support those arrangements" (Shujaa, 1994, p. 15). And as Mabie (2000) posited:

> Those who have studied worldwide liberation struggles know that the manipulation of information, including propaganda and disinformation, are primary tactics employed in the domination process. Oppressive populations change the true human record through the denial of the very reality of the total human experience, even their own. African-centered means . . . reversing that order and reclaiming the right, responsibility, and authority to name oneself and to identify with one's heritage. (n.p.)

As King (2004) noted, this understanding of liberating education is rooted in the Black intellectual tradition that is well represented in the work of DuBois, Woodson (1933), and others who stress the importance of preserving African American cultural originality and identity. In his introduction to a collection of essays on the education of Black people, Aptheker (1973), DuBois's editor and biographer (a radical White historian in his own right), explained:

> DuBois saw education (to be truly education) as partisan and—given the realities of the social order—fundamentally subversive. Specifically, in this connection, he wrote as a Black man in the United States; in this sense he was concerned in the first place with the education of his people in the United States, and that education as part of the process of the liberation of his people. Thus, his writing on education—as on everything else—has a kind of national consciousness, a specific motivation which—while directed towards his people—at the same time and therefore was meant to serve all humanity. (p. xi)

Wynter (1992/2012), a Black Studies scholar, who describes herself as a "Woodsonian," proposed that Black alterity must play a role in abolishing the ideological metanarrative of race.[5]

On the other hand, it is precisely this form of identity (and consciousness) that orthodox scholarship and public discourse reject as racially "divisive." Minority students' embrace of a pan-ethnic identity (e.g., "Raza" or "Pan-African") is identified as a problem that blocks their academic and social advancement as well as societal cohesion or *e pluribus unum*. Actually, the problem is the basis of that cohesion. This assimilationist discourse, which is now represented in purportedly multicultural common core curriculum standards as "our shared history," and which targets African-centered education as "separatist" and antidemocratic (Buras, 2008; Ginwright, 2004; Merry & New, 2008; Ravitch, 1990), has persisted, most contentiously in the "culture wars" over the curriculum of the 1990s (King, 2004). African-centered schools have earned a reputation for outstanding academic and cultural excellence, including one established in Toronto, Canada, in 2008 that has garnered both high academic achievement scores as well as intense criticism along these same lines. Likewise, the Arizona legislature shut down Tucson's demonstrably effective K–12 Mexican American studies curriculum, which was designed to support students' pan-ethnic "Raza" identity and consciousness (Romero, 2011). Contrary to the evidence, the justification for Arizona's HB 2261 law that banned Mexican American studies is that this legislation prohibits "courses or classes that promote the overthrow of the United

States Government or promote resentment toward a race or class or people" (Thorne, 2012). This belief that curriculum that connects students to their heritages necessarily promotes racial resentment has not been the focus of any systematic research but it clearly affects education policy and the "problem" these policies frame.

The charge is consistent with the position Ravitch (1990) advanced in the early 1990s: "ethnic loyalties" ought to be rejected and curriculum from this perspective—in the case of African-centered education—is tantamount to "worshipping dead civilizations on foreign continents," or "filiopietism." Calling Ravitch "the most eloquent voice" of the multicultural "Inclusionists," Parrillo (2009) explains that Ravitch "envisioned the elimination of allegiance to any specific racial and/or ethnic group, with emphasis instead on our common humanity, our shared national identity, and our individual accomplishments" (p. 149). However, embracing "our common humanity" is obstructed by normative culture-systemic beliefs embedded in school knowledge and practice that assault cultural Blackness. Thus, multicultural education is problematic insofar as it only involves the peppering of people of color onto an essentially Eurocentric curriculum framework as if the basis of societal cohesion is uncritical accommodation with "essentialist" White supremacy racism (Frankenberg, 1993; Wynter, 1992/2012). This conception of national unity and "our common humanity" often refuses to recognize "unequal power in society and its effect on multicultural curriculum" (Karenga, 2002, p. 56).

In contrast, education, as defined by Murrell (1997): "should provide that center from which children learn to contest the destruction of black urban communities, to resist the assault on cultural blackness, and to sustain the struggle for true democracy" (p. 20). Murrell elaborated further: "Children need intellectual tools for developing critical consciousness in order to develop a robust racial identity as well as a sense of self-agency and self-determination" (p. 28). Describing this as "critical Africanist pedagogy," Murrell further explained that African American students in urban schools need to develop "the means to deconstruct and decode white supremacy as a *cultural phenomenon* as well as racism as cultural imperialism" (p. 29).

In a review of learning innovations that involve high school students-as-researchers "becoming critical" and supporting urban teacher development, King (2008) cited several examples that are innovative but not necessarily liberating, using Carter's description of critical race consciousness or Murrell's conception of critical Africanist pedagogy as a standard:

> Morrell (2004), Morrell and Collatos (2002), and Oakes et al. (2006) describe participatory social inquiry and organizing activities as learning opportunities that build communities of practice for pre-service and in-service teacher education, urban school reform, and community change using critical research methods. (King, 2008, p. 1111)

Also, according to Giroux (2013), within pedagogy learning is about "transforming knowledge as part of a more expansive struggle for *individual* rights and social justice" (p. 188, emphasis added). Thus, promoting students' identities as members of a racial-ethnic group is apparently not a priority task of critical pedagogy. Likewise, youth-centered engagement in community development, participatory evaluation (Sabo, 2003), and youth organizing for civic engagement (Ginwright, Noguera, & Cammarota, 2006) also lack a focus on critical Africanist (or Raza) consciousness or the "moral and spiritual center" Murrell articulated that is consistent with the nationalist ideal Black intellectuals like DuBois, Woodson, and others have articulated. There are possible exceptions such as the "race-cognizant" youth-organizing framework Aguilar-San Juan (2006) described:

> Youth of color, in particular, need to learn about their collective histories and cultures . . . But recognizing group cultures goes against the individualistic orientation of white, middle-class society and the prevailing "color-blind" approach to race and racism. (pp. 262–263)

In the 1990s teachers and researchers created community-based learning opportunities for racially marginalized students to study their own cultures and communities as ethnographers—a paradigm that takes students' group identity and consciousness into account (Egan-Robertson & Bloom, 1997; Mercado, 1997; Torres-Guzmán, Mercado, Quintero, & Viera, 1994). For example, Black and Indigenous students in Costa Rica produced reading texts for classroom use based on oral histories they completed focused on "reclaiming [their] indigenous cultures." Their inquiry addressed questions such as: "How can a diverse community of learners retain their individual and unique cultures against the encroachment of urban pressures and modernity?" (Montero-Sieburth, 1997, p. 220).

This is liberating content and pedagogy to the extent that students are enabled to successfully develop a personal and communal sense of self that ultimately leads to academic and cultural excellence versus what is deemed to be successful individual achievement in school measured solely by the standards of a Eurocentric system of education that ignores pan-ethnic subjectivities and the needs of historically marginalized communities. From this point of view African American children and others who have been subjected to racial domination need the opportunity to experience an appropriate cultural education that gives them an intimate knowledge of and that honors and respects their people's history and culture (Hanley & Noblit, 2009).

Policy attempts to establish more truthful (and valid) curricula have gained little traction in educational practice or among funders or researchers. In the last decade, however, state-level legislation in the United States such as Florida's Statute -1003.42(h), Title XLVIII of the Education Code, §"Required Instruction,"[6] as well as the Amistad Commissions established first in New Jersey (2002),[7] then Illinois (2004), and New York (2005), illustrate curriculum policies that require the teaching of African American history, particularly African enslavement, in public schools. Florida law emphasizes teaching about the African heritage *before* enslavement (e.g., "the history of African Americans, including the history of African peoples before the political conflicts that led to the development of slavery"). Likewise, a district-level policy in Philadelphia mandated African American history as a high school graduation requirement since the 1970s.[8] However, Traoré (2009) observes that Black Studies "intervention" is required because the mandate remains largely unfulfilled: "Many students of African descent still struggle to be reconnected to the rich African traditions from which they originated" (p. 663).

In a study of the effects of ethnic studies, Sleeter (2011) concludes there is considerable evidence that well-executed programs are associated with positive outcomes on a wide array of important social and academic indicators, including sense of agency, engagement, higher-order thinking, high school graduation, grades, motivation, and writing skills. Among 185 Latino/a eighth-graders whom Sleeter studied, those with higher grades tended to have *bicultural* identities. Both those students who showed *little* identification with their ethnicity and the handful of students who identified *only* with their culture of origin did worse than those students who identified with *both* Anglo and Mexican culture. Earlier studies of African American students showed similar results. Likewise, Payne (2012) found that reconnecting students to a more complex history of the civil rights movement restores their ancestors to them (p. 10). MacLeod (1991) provided an earlier example of engaging youth in actively studying the involvement of family members in the civil rights movement. From an African-centered perspective, however, as will be discussed below, the African American story does not begin with slavery (King, 1992).

If the dominant group insists on imposing, first, political control on other cultural groups and seeks also to impose ideological control, effectively denying the historicity of the group, denying the value of its cultural systems, that is when problems arise due to hegemony (Mabie, 2000). As Hilliard (1978) observed: "If elementary, secondary and post-secondary schools had mental liberation of all students as a goal for education, desegregation and integration in education would be achieved as a natural consequence of a non-exploitative, non-chauvanistic search for the truth" (p. 104). In a truly integrated culturally democratic system every student group's culture and heritage would be recognized and respected allowing them to form a positive (informed) self-perspective and sense of group belonging. However, in the current education system, the Eurocentric worldview that dominates in schools takes precedence over any other group's racial/ethnic identity and consciousness (Delpit, 1995; A. Lewis, 2003; Swartz, 2007).

Improving educational outcomes for urban students will mean implementing measures to address and oppose this hierarchy of identity. Accordingly, as Wellman (1977) observed, the existing social order cannot provide for unlimited (or equal) opportunity for Black people while maintaining racial privileges for Whites. Thus, elimination of the societal hierarchy is inevitable if the social order is to be reorganized; but before this can occur, the existing structural inequity must be recognized as such and actively struggled against (King, 1991). Participation in this struggle for social transformation requires liberating urban education: consciousness and forms of identity, including a communal view of the self, which are linked to the capacity for "critical studyin' " that are not likely to be available to Black students as school knowledge, curricula, and pedagogy in urban education settings are currently organized (King, 2006).

Scholars (and teachers) who equate equality with assimilation and color-blindness dismiss the importance of such heritage knowledge (King, 2006). Although research and practice show positive benefits of such identity development for Black student achievement, the way that schools normally teach about Africa and the Black experience institutionalizes a dangerously incomplete conception of what it means to be African and what it means to be human, which obstruct Black students' opportunities to identify with their heritage (King, 1992). Others are denied opportunities to grasp fully the implications for society of the degradation of Blackness and for their own well-being and to appreciate the deep wounds in their own identities and consciousness caused by the fictions of White supremacy racism (Asante, 2009a; Jensen, 2005). What is needed is serious investigation of the healing potential of transformative curriculum and pedagogy interventions, as Traoré (2009) documented in her research in the Philadelphia public schools: tensions between African American and African immigrant students dissipated when they learned together about their shared heritage.

Ladson-Billings (1994, 1995), the scholar most responsible for advancing the concept of culturally relevant pedagogy, maintains that this approach serves to empower students to be able to examine critically educational content and process and to ask what is the role of education in creating a truly democratic and multicultural society. It is instructive that a parent whom Ladson-Billings asked how to define success and how to identify successful teachers of African American students said: "I want him (the child) to hold his own in the classroom and not forget his own at home" (Ladson-Billings, 1997, p. 133). Culturally relevant pedagogy uses the students' culture as an asset to help them create meaning and understand the world. Thus, not only academic success, but also social and cultural excellence, are emphasized (Boutté, Kelly-Jackson, & Johnson, 2010; Milner, 2012).

Students in urban schools can also benefit from learning experiences that connect them with the heritages historically marginalized groups actually share. In fact, there are a number of intersections transformative curriculum research can explore, including Pacifica (Tonga, Samoa) activists who returned to New Zealand and founded the Polynesian Panthers after their experiences with members of the Black Panther Party in California (Anae, 2006), the African presence in Mexico (Hernández-Cuevas, 2004; Horne, 2005), the Black Indians of New Orleans (Kennedy & Harrison, 2010; King, 2011), and Asian Americans who participated in and identified with the Black freedom struggle (Boggs, 1988; Fujino, 2005, 2012; Kochiyama, 2004, see also, Kynard, 2007, p. 386, note 20). How would African American, Mexican American, and other Latin American students relate to each other if they knew the larger story of the African presence in Mexico and the Afro-Latino/a heritage in countries like Ecuador, Columbia, Costa Rica, Venezuela, among others (Moore, Sanders, & Moore, 1995; Teaching for Change, 1993; Kleymeyer, 1994)? How would Black students (U.S.- and Caribbean-born) treat Haitian immigrant students, if they knew the real story of the Haitian revolution (King, 2011)? How would White students and teachers appreciate their own antiracist heritage if they knew more about John Brown's collaboration with free African Americans (DuBois, 1909/2001)? Such questions are suggested by an interdisciplinary, critical Black Studies perspective and culturally grounded (Africanist) consciousness that is explored next.

Culturally Grounded (Africanist) Consciousness

An Afrocentric education approach, grounded in Black Studies scholarship that allows Black students to build a critical Black (Africanist) consciousness, that is, a pan-ethnic communal view of themselves, can ultimately allow each student to be a free thinker with the ability to question and examine the current hierarchy and forms of domination within which we live. According to Hotep (2008), here at the beginning of the 21st century, the cardinal task of the "Black thinker" is to break out of *conceptual incarceration* and *comfortable captivity*. The outcome for Black students is either internalizing the negative constructions of Blackness and the nonrecognition of themselves and their culture/heritage or developing a positive self and group perception and critical race consciousness that lead to affirming rather than nihilating conceptions of what it means to be Black/African American. Research suggests that these opposing self and group perceptions can be directly linked to students' academic outcomes (D. Carter, 2008a,b; P. Carter, 2008; Nasir, 2011; Nasir & Saxe, 2003; Whaley & Noël, 2012).

Nurturing the development of diaspora literacy (King, 1992), that is to say, a critical Black (Africanist) consciousness in African American children and adolescents, is a way to pass on the "cultural heritage of African-American achievement" (Murrell, 1997, p. 28). Another related approach is Perry's (2003) call for counternarratives. Perry posits that these narratives—oral and written—depict the historical significance of education for freedom that has long been central to the identity formation of Blacks as intellectuals. When parents, teachers, schools, and community members embrace the importance of these counternarratives, we begin to understand the role that racial caste-group status has played in the varying levels of academic performance for Black youth. What D. Carter (2008b) refers to as "critical race consciousness" is a counternarrative, because it "stands in opposition to the dominant society's notions about the intellectual capacity of African Americans, the role of learning in their lives, the meaning and purpose of school, and the power of their intellect" (p. 24).

Black students' ways of knowing and being include their linguistic, literate, and cultural practices. In order to develop a liberatory pedagogy that allows Black students to exist in this "space of being" (Grande, 2004) and, therefore, to develop a positive sense of self and community, Paris (2012) offers the term "culturally sustaining pedagogy" as an alternative that embodies some of the best past and present research and practice in the resource pedagogy tradition and as a term that supports the value of our multiethnic and multilingual present and future. The term *culturally sustaining* requires that our pedagogies be more than responsive or relevant to the cultural experiences and practices of young people—it requires that they support young people in sustaining the cultural and linguistic competence of their communities while simultaneously offering access to dominant cultural competence. Culturally sustaining pedagogy, then, has as its explicit goal supporting multilingualism and multiculturalism in practice and perspective for students and teachers. Expanding on Paris's conceptualization of culturally sustaining pedagogy, the following section of this chapter explicates an African cultural understanding of excellence in urban education. The point is to show that education can not only sustain the cultural competence students bring to school, but it can and should also be rooted in the liberating purpose of identity restoration and consciousness in order to free students of/from the current forms of oppression that hegemonic education enacts.

African Cultural Understanding of Excellence in Urban Education

African people introduced the world to its first understanding of educational excellence, which was situated within the culture (Nobles, 2008). In the Nile Valley of Africa, in Kemet (Egypt) we find humanity's first word relative to teaching and learning: *seba*. In the language of *medu netcher* (often referred to by the Greek term *hieroglyphics*) *seba* actually has three primary meanings: teach, door, and star (Obenga, 2002). Akua's observation is pertinent:

> It is in the construction and connotation of this word that we find the ancient African philosophy of education and it is this—the teacher opens the door to the universe so that the student may shine like a star. Seba came to refer also to the deep thought and wisdom of the wise and learned. The master teacher in ancient Kemet (Egypt) was referred to as a *Seba*. (Akua, 2012, p. 14)

Hilliard posed Kemetic concepts in education as fundamental to everyone's education.

> Ancient Kemet was a high-tech society. It required armies of educated people . . . The process of education was not seen primarily as a process of acquiring knowledge. It was seen as a process of transformation . . . disciplined study under the guidance of a master teacher was the single path to becoming a new person. The education system was an open admission system that was not tied to heredity. (Hilliard, 1997, pp. 122–123)

Moreover, Hilliard made clear that study and preparation for matriculation into the education process was viewed as initiation into the deep knowledge of the culture:

> The ultimate aim of Kemetic education was for the student to become godlike by acquiring ten virtues through the study of the seven liberating disciplines [later referred to as the Seven Liberal Arts]. The Ten Cardinal Virtues were as follows:
>
> 1. Control of thought
> 2. Control of action
> 3. Steadfastness of purpose
> 4. Identity with the spiritual life
> 5. Evidence of having a mission in life
> 6. Evidence of a call to spiritual orders
> 7. Freedom from resentment under persecution and wrong
> 8. Confidence in the power of the master as teacher
> 9. Confidence in one's own ability to learn
> 10. Readiness or preparation for initiation.

Hilliard also pointed out that when the history of Western education is truthfully deconstructed, altered African philosophical concepts emerge:

> It is well known to historians of philosophy that Plato was said to have spent 12 years as a student under African teachers in the Kemetic Mystery System. Plato took some of the virtues and left others. He took numbers one and two and called them justice. He took number three and called it fortitude. He took number four and called it temperance. He took numbers five and six and called them prudence. These are Plato's four Cardinal Virtues. What he left behind is as significant as what he decided to keep. . . . It is not because they are African, or even because they are ancient that we have reason to give serious consideration to these systems. It is because they were and are good and useful. (pp. 135–136)

This African cultural understanding of the essence and expression of the purpose of education could serve the world quite well today (Hotep, 2008). Purportedly, the great fear is that African-centered education and other approaches based in culture-centered knowledge will become hegemonic and oppressive as is the Eurocentric approach (King, 2004). This "presupposes that an African-centered education would simply be a Black version of Eurocentric education" (Shockley, 2008, p. 18). Because Afrocentric education is represented in this way, as was the case previously with both Negro history and Black history (King, 2004), it is important to emphasize Karenga's (1998) point that African-centered education "does not seek to deny or deform others' history and humanity, but to affirm, rescue, and reconstruct its own . . . " (p. 52).

Akua (2012) argued that an accurate reading of history shows the cultural wealth of African American students, which is not only their birthright but that also ought to be available to them as a basis for their identity development. However, as Akua contended, their identity has been stolen from them—a debt that is ignored in discussions of achievement and opportunity "gaps." Indeed, African American youth today are the carriers of Africa's cultural legacy that gave the world reading and writing, language and literature, architecture and engineering, agriculture and astronomy, mathematics and medicine, science and technology—and much more (Finch, 1998). Yet, these youth are bombarded with popular media images of themselves as "pimps, playas, criminals and thugs." While their embrace and reversal of this negating imagery can be interpreted as a form of resistance (but too often without critical Africanist consciousness or recognition of the damage done to their own humanity), these degenerate popular images place the worst of the cultural adaptations that (any) people make under conditions of oppression and dispossession in broad global circulation and implanted in the minds of educators obscuring the *best* of African people's culture and heritage.

That most urban school children (and their teachers) know little to nothing of their legacy with regard to African people's contributions to world civilization[9] is not happenstance but part and parcel of the way that schools "assault cultural Blackness"—denying Black children a positive collective identity. Clarke observed, "The task of Africans at home and abroad is to restore to their memory what slavery and colonization made them forget . . . in most of Africa, the job was so complete it was tantamount to a brain transplant" (Carruthers, 1999, p. xi). When urban education curricula are an anthology of White supremacy, it then becomes necessary to question, as Nobles observed, not only the content, but also the *intent* (Nobles, 1990). When we examine intent, what also becomes clear is there has been not only intentional "identity theft," the intended outcome is *identity replacement*. As Akbar (1998) emphasized, identity replacement produces the "alien identity." That is, African Americans have been strategically and systematically separated from the best of our culture and heritage in America's schools and scholars who have attempted to address this reality are admonished for engaging in narrow, "essentialist," "identity politics" (Gates, 1992; Ginwright, 2004; Giroux, 1992) and "ethnic cheerleading" (King, 1992).

Perhaps this is why Clarke (1991) noted with sober incisiveness: "The powerful will never educate the powerless to take their power from them" (p. 18). In addition, Clarke explained:

> Education has but one honorable purpose . . . to prepare the student to be a responsible handler of power. Any other type of education is a waste of time . . . All education must lead to some type of power . . . one has to have power in order to be a total human being. (p. 331)

For Akbar (1998) "the first function of education is to provide identity" (p. 1). This, then, suggests that in contrast to education as identity theft, liberating education is about *identity restoration* for human freedom. Identity restoration produces an authentic identity, one that includes character, culture, consciousness, and commitment. As Akua (2012) explained:

> The purpose of this identity restoration is twofold: for the resurrection of African people and the redemption of humanity. Identity restoration requires consciousness. When Black children are exposed to proper cultural and character development, a new mental and spiritual phenomenon emerges. We call it *consciousness.* Consciousness is "the expanded awareness of your place in the universe." Our children need their character and their culture to speak to their consciousness. When this happens, they will be transformed by the renewing of their minds. With this new consciousness comes a new *commitment*—a commitment to actively participate in the resurrection of African people and the redemption of Humanity. (p. 90)

Revered elder, the late Seba Baba Hannibal Afrik, also observed one of the dimensions of Africentric (i.e., Afrocentric) culture is consciousness, namely: (a) acceptance of the concept of pan-Afrikanism, which, in simple terms, recognizes that "We are an Afrikan people," (b) establishment of a relationship with our homeland Afrika and the diaspora, and (c) ensuring reverence for our ancestors. Together, these individual acceptances constitute collective consciousness, which is manifested in behavioral changes and positive action. However, "consciousness is more than mere acceptance, it is also response! It is action demonstrable and meaningful . . . " (Gallman, Ani, & Williams, 2004, p. 33). Afrik continued: consciousness is "a commitment to our destiny as a people. Every ethnic group has vested interests that ensure the survival of their group" (p. 33).

Another aspect of consciousness that liberating urban education for human freedom should make possible is an understanding of racialized class exploitation, as well as how race, culture, and ethnicity differ. For one thing, race is a Western cultural construct with no basis in scientific reality; it is a tool of hegemony deployed to conceptualize and dichotomize which people are ostensibly superior and those who are deemed inferior within the Western belief structure. Culture, as a "design for living," according to Nobles (1990), involves guiding beliefs and principles that contain the ways in which groups of people have chosen to live. Ani (1994) observed that culture is "ordered behavior" and Nobles stated that culture "makes cooperation natural." Finally, Hilliard (1997) explained ethnicity in relation to race and class, thusly:

> Before the problem of the education and socialization of African people can be approached, each African must make a fundamental decision. It is a decision to understand and uncompromisingly accept our African ethnicity. It is not a decision about race or class. Rather, it is a decision to recognize and accept not only our connection to the human family, but also our connection to a unique ethnic family with all of the responsibilities that come with that decision. Our survival as a people is connected to our unwavering identification as Africans. (p. 22)

Making the conscious connection to "our unwavering identification as Africans" possible is an essential task and standard of "success" within an African cultural understanding of educational excellence. While recognition of Black students' language, literacies, and cultural ways of being remain fundamental for their positive identity development and academic excellence, African language study is a neglected resource for cultural excellence, which should include deep knowledge of African culture. However, current policy that defines students' "success" and effective teaching practice in urban schools only in terms of standardized high-stakes tests of "common core" knowledge excludes any such consideration of cultural well-being or community-defined standards of liberating educational purpose as a criterion. Indeed, evidence of the success of African-centered education programs (in- and after-school) as well as parent education are neglected in the urban education reform agenda, models of best practice in prevailing policy and youth development approaches, as well as the professional preparation of urban school leaders and teachers (Belgrave, Reed, Plybon, Butler, Allison, & Davis, 2004; Herold, 2011; King, 2008; Lewis, Andrews, Gaska, Sullivan, Bybee, & Ellick, 2012; Potts, 2003; Payne, 2012; Thomas, Davidson, & McAdoo, 2008).

Implications of this cultural well-being paradigm for liberating urban education research, policy, and practice discussed below in the concluding section address the fundamental issue of the survival of African Americans as a people.

Implications: Liberating Urban Education Theory, Research, Policy, and Practice

If urban education is to be liberating in terms of African American people's survival, as a people, research, policy, and practice must be liberated from the privileging, hierarchical belief structure of race (Wynter, 2005). Educational efforts to overcome the negative impact of race should not deny Black students a conscious connection to their identity as Africans. The focus on the achievement gap as well as surreptitious assimilation expectations masquerading as "our" common core curriculum and "our" shared history must be replaced with a deeper appreciation of the role of culture in education drawing on the Black Studies intellectual tradition to inform research, policy, and practice. For instance, Karenga (2002) is correct to assert: "the established order cannot be left to define and impose its own version of multiculturalism" (p. 56).

In addition, theorizing within an achievement framework considers cultural identification among African American youth and their academic pursuits as mutually reinforcing components of their individual and transpersonal (academic) identity development (i.e., Murrell's third level). This African cultural understanding of educational excellence requires a focus on students' cultural well-being as a human right, which is typically neglected by researchers and practitioners working within explanatory frameworks, policy orientations, and curriculum and pedagogy paradigms that give primacy to the "disadvantages associated with how poverty affects children's ability to learn," their "dysfunctional families," or how to teach the nation's "common cultural heritage" (Ravitch, 2010). Excluded is any consideration regarding how representations of students' cultural heritage in the curriculum (and teacher preparation) might also disadvantage them and affect their academic engagement, opportunities to learn, and their development. This debt remains largely unrecognized in academic discourse within deficit explanations focused narrowly on achievement and opportunity "gaps" rather than analyses grounded in an achievement framework that emphasizes culture and identity as important resources for academic and cultural excellence. However, research by scholars of color, particularly along these lines, has been overlooked (Fu-Kiau, 1991; Hilliard, 1988; King, 2005; Murrell, 2006; Perry, 2003).

Another overlooked implication for research and practice is that transformative curriculum praxis and pedagogical inquiry for cultural well-being, in which Blackness is regarded as a source of strength, has potential to be used to address intergroup and intragroup relations among Asian, Black (African American, African, Caribbean), Pacifica, Native American as well as Latino/a students in urban schools. Such curriculum and pedagogy interventions necessarily include heritage knowledge that goes beyond engaging students in "becoming critical" by allowing them to identify with the struggles and successes of their ancestors (Graham & Anderson, 2008; King, 2006; Payne, 2012). When students are given the gift of consciousness and heritage knowledge, they can then thrive by understanding and appreciating all cultures while remaining rooted in their own. This simply suggests that students can acquire "the cultural codes required for school success while also recognizing the value of their own cultures" (D. Carter, 2008a, p. 469).[10]

Finally, there is an urgent need to broaden theory, research, and practice with regard to African American students' language rights beyond African American language and literacies as cultural ways of being and the forms of knowledge students hold (Lee, 2008). As Kynard (2007) observes, "identity is connected to language, culture and race" but Black students are routinely denied access to deep knowledge of their African linguistic cultural heritage (p. 111). Therefore, research is needed that not only focuses on ways students' home language and community intelligence can support their identity development, cultural subjectivities, and academic engagement, but also how curriculum and pedagogy (content and intent) can include "the imaginary of Africa as a place that would keep Black folks whole" (Kynard, 2007, p. 386, note 18). Thus, how might African language study contribute to students' critical race (Africanist) consciousness, which includes the ability to decode race and racism as cultural phenomena? For instance, African Americans studying the Songhoy language (of Mali, West Africa) experience liberating, healing knowledge: extremely positive meanings are associated with "Blackness" in this language compared to "Blackness" in English (and other Euro-languages) that are deeply implicated in what race does (King, 2008; Maiga, 2005). Furthermore, Hernández-Cuevas (2012) explains that beliefs about racial superiority/inferiority embedded in the Spanish language obstruct the identification of Afro-Mexicanos with their African heritage. "Names such as 'Casta,' 'Chilango,' 'Jarocho,' and 'Boshito,' all . . . refer to the lack of blood cleanliness of non-white persons" (n.p.). These are but a few of the research questions and implications for liberating urban education practice to be pursued, if as Nunn (2011) suggests: "Africans must resurrect and maintain their African culture . . . to eliminate their oppression in the United States" (p. 147).

In conclusion, cultural consciousness can liberate urban education allowing everyone to benefit from the critical insights and contributions African people have made to humanity and civilization. This is the path to human freedom. For in the end, to teach African American children using their culture as a bridge rather than a barrier is not about creating Black pride. Though Black pride is an unmistakable byproduct of heritage knowledge, as Hilliard advised:

> ... Our own cultural traditions provide ample answers to the basic human questions all must ask. We can start from our own African center in the creation of a future. Finally, we can once again share this humane, democratic, and deeply spiritual way of life with the world. (Hilliard, 1997, p. 39)

Notes

1. Both church-affiliated organizations were established by wealthy northern and southern White philanthropists, industrialists, planters, missionaries, and college presidents who participated in invitation-only conferences on "the Negro Question" beginning in the 1890s at Lake Mohonk, New York, and Capon Springs, West Virginia—to address the education of (and to control the destinies of) freedmen and women. "Negroes" were expressly excluded. See also: Lovell Pugh-Basset (2006), *Meeting of Their Minds to Control Ours: An Analysis of the 1890 & 1891 Mohonk Conferences on the Negro Question and the Creation of Selected Historically Black Colleges and Universities* (PhD dissertation), Temple University.
2. King (2011) presents example of ideological assaults on cultural Blackness in widely publicized rumors presented as fact—that in the aftermath of Hurricane Katrina young Black men in New Orleans were "raping babies," young girls, and elderly women. In fact, these young men were the real "first responders": They demonstrated what Karenga describes as "black cultural ideals" by organizing mothers with babies and the elderly to be rescued first—one of the highest expressions of Black people's cultural virtues (Asante, 2009b). The press also depicted Black men as "looters," while Whites in the same circumstances were said to have "found" food and other survival items.
3. As compared to arguments that Black culture is nihilistic (West, 1994), Wynter explained that Black culture has been (néantisé) nihilated (Wynter, 2006).
4. The United Nations Convention on the Rights of the Child, Article 30, states that where there are "ethnic, religious or linguistic minorities or persons of indigenous origin exist, a child belonging to such a minority or who is indigenous shall not be denied the right . . . to enjoy his or her own culture . . . " See: http://www2.ohchr.org/english/law/crc.htm. For further explication of the CCCC—SRTOL policy, see Kinloch (2010) and Kynard (2007, 2013).
5. Alterity: the "stigmatized category of Otherness" that enables the liminal perspective advantage that Blacks have as a result of the alter ego relation between conceptual Blackness and Whiteness. See Sylvia Wynter, 1997, pp. 13–14.
6. http://www.leg.state.fl.us/Statutes/index.cfm/Ch0499/index.cfm? App_mode=Display_Statute&Search_String=&URL=1000-1099/1003/Sections/1003.42.html Accessed Oct. 1, 2012.
7. See, for example, the New Jersey Amistad Commission and the American Institute for History Education online interactive textbook: http://njamistadcurriculum.org/. New York's Commission is "stalled." See http://www. bnyee.org/blackhistorynow.htm. The Illinois Amistad Commission is defunct.
8. While a systematic focus on school district reforms is beyond the scope of this chapter, worth mentioning is that African-centered immersion schools were established in Minneapolis in the early 1990s, Baltimore designated African-centered grade-level classrooms, and the Detroit Public Schools established the African-Centered Social Studies Department (Pollard & Ajirotutu, 2000).
9. Consider these scientifically documented examples: (1) The Ishango Bone found in northeastern Zaire is dated at 25,000 years old and contains markings that demonstrate ancient Africans' understanding of multiplication by doubling and prime numbers (Finch, 1998); (b) Ancient Africans invented papyrus, the world's first piece of paper (Browder, 1992); (c) The Ahmase Mathematics Papyrus is over 3,800 years old and known to be a copy of an older African text. It is the oldest mathematics textbook in the world with examples of algebra, trigonometry, sine, cosine, tangent, cotangent, square roots, area, circumference, volume, etc. (Obenga, 2004); (d) People came to West Africa's Songhoy Empire from Europe and the "Middle East" to be educated at the great universities of Djenné, Walata, Gao and Sankoré at Timbuktu and indigenous Songhoy writing existed long before the arrival of Arabs or Europeans in this region (Maiga, 2010). See also Van Sertima, 1983, 2001.
10. Consciousness refers to the "critical comprehension of the essential nature of society, its myths, and one's own interests" (King, 1992, p. 319). This understanding of consciousness is similar to Paulo Freire's conceptualization of conscientização or "conscientization": "a process in which people are encouraged to analyze their reality, to become more aware of the constraints on their lives, and to take action to transform the situation" (Brown, 1978, p. 20).

References

Aguilar-San Juan, Karin. (2006). Taking charge in Lake Wobegon: Youth, social justice, and antiracist organizing in the Twin Cities. In S. Ginwright, P. Noguera, & J. Cammarota (Eds.), *Beyond resistance! Youth activism and community change: New democratic possibilities for practice and policy for America's youth* (pp. 247–265). New York, NY: Routledge.

Akbar, Na'im. (1998). *Know thyself.* Tallahassee, FL: Mind Productions & Associates.

Akua, Chike. (2012). *Education for transformation: The keys to releasing the genius of African American students.* Conyers, GA: Imani Enterprises.

Altschul, Inna, Oyserman, Daphna, & Bybee, Deborah. (2006). Racial-ethnic identity in mid-adolescence: Content and change as predictors of academic achievement. *Child Development, 77*(5), 1155–1169.

Anae, Melani. (Ed.). (2006). *Polynesian Panthers.* Auckland, NZ: Reed Books.

Anderson, James. (2004). The historical context for understanding the test score gap. *Journal of Public Management and Social Policy, 10*(1), 1–15.

Ani, Marimba. (1994). *Yurugu: An African-centered critique of European cultural thought and behavior.* Trenton, NJ: African World Press.

Aptheker, Herbert. (Ed.). (1973). *The education of Black people: Ten critiques by W.E.B. DuBois, 1906–1960.* New York, NY: Monthly Review.

Asante, Molefi K. (2009a). *Erasing racism: The survival of the American nation.* New York, NY: Prometheus Books.

Asante, Molefi K. (2009b). *Maulana Karenga: An intellectual portrait.* Malden, MA: Polity Press.

Belgrave, Faye Z., Reed, Melba C., Plybon, Laura E., Butler, Deborah S., Allison, Kevin W., & Davis, Trina (2004). An evaluation of Sisters of Nia: A cultural program for African American girls. *Journal of Black Psychology, 30*(3), 329–343.

Boggs, Grace L. (1988). *Living for change: An autobiography.* Minneapolis: University of Minnesota Press.

Boutté, Gloria, Kelly-Jackson, Charlease, & Johnson, George Lee. (2010). Culturally relevant teaching in science classrooms: Addressing academic achievement, cultural competence, and critical consciousness. *International Journal of Multicultural Education, 12*(2), 1–20. Retrieved from http://ijme-journal.org/index.php/ijme/article/view/343/512

Boutté, Gloria, & Strickland, Jennifer. (2008). Making African American culture and history central to early childhood teaching and learning. *Journal of Negro Education, 77*(20), 131–142.

Bowman, Phillip J., & Howard, Cleopatra. (1985). Race-related socialization, motivation, and academic achievement: A study of Black youth in three-generation families. *Journal of the American Academy of Child Psychiatry, 24*(22), 1173–1182.

Browder, Anthony. (1992). *Nile Valley contributions to civilization.* Washington, DC: Institute of Karmic Guidance.

Brown, Cynthia Stokes. (1978). *Literacy in 30 hours: Paulo Freire's process in North East Brazil.* Chicago, IL: Alternative Schools Network.

Buras, Kristen L. (2008). *Rightist multiculturalism: Core lessons on neoconservative school reform.* New York, NY: Routledge.

Carruthers, Jacob. (1999). *Intellectual warfare.* Chicago, IL: Third World Press.

Carter, Dorinda J. (2008a). Achievement as resistance: The development of a critical race achievement ideology among Black achievers. *Harvard Educational Review, 78*(3), 466–497.

Carter, Dorinda J. (2008b, Winter-Spring). Cultivating a critical race consciousness for African American school success. *Educational Foundations, 22*(1–2), 11–28.

Carter, Prudence. (2003). "Black" cultural capital, status positioning, and schooling conflicts for low-income African American youth. *Social Problems, 50*(1), 136–155.

Carter, Prudence. (2008). *Keepin' it real: School success beyond black and white.* New York, NY: Oxford University Press.

Chavous, Tabbye M., Bernat, Debra H., Schmeelk-Cone, Karen, Caldwell, Cleopatra H., Kohn-Wood, Laura, & Zimmerman, Marc A. (2003). Racial identity and academic attainment among African American adolescents. *Child Development, 74*(3), 1076–1090.

Clarke, John H. (1991). *Notes for an African world revolution: Africans at the crossroads.* Trenton, NJ: Africa World Press.

Darling-Hammond, Linda. (2010). *The flat world and education: How America's commitment to equity will determine our future.* New York, NY: Teachers College Press.

Davis, Claytie, Aronson, Joshua, & Salinas, Moisese. (2006). Shades of threat: Racial identity as a moderator of stereotype threat. *Journal of Black Psychology, 32*(4), 399–417.

Delpit, Lisa. (1995). *Other people's children: Cultural conflict in the classroom.* New York, NY: New Press.

Delpit, Lisa. (2012). *"Multiplication is for white people": Raising expectations for other people's children.* New York, NY: New Press.

Dubois, W. E. B. (1909/2001). *John Brown.* New York, NY: Random House.

Dudley-Marling, Curt, & Lucas, Krista. (2009). Pathologizing the language and culture of poor children. *Language Arts, 86*(5), 362–370.

Egan-Robertson, Ann & Bloome, David. (Ed.). (1997). *Students as researchers of culture and language in their own communities.* New York, NY: Hampton Press.

Finch, Charles. (1998). *The star of deep beginnings: The African genesis of science and technology.* Atlanta, GA: Khenti Press.

Ford, Donna, & Harris, J.J. (1997). A study of the racial identity and achievement of black males and females. *Roeper Review, 20*(2), 105–110.

Fordham, Signithia, & Ogbu, John. (1986). Black students' school success: Coping with the "burden of 'acting white.' " *Urban Review, 18*(3), 176–206.

Frankenberg, Ruth. (1993). *White women, race matters: The social construction of whiteness.* Minneapolis, MN: University of Minnesota Press.

Fraser, Nancy. (2000, May–June). Rethinking recognition. *New Left Review.* Retrieved from http://newleftreview.org/II/3/nancy-fraser-rethinking-recognition

Fujino, Diane C. (2005). *Heartbeat of struggle: The revolutionary life of Yuri Kochiyama.* Minneapolis, MN: University of Minnesota Press.

Fujino, Diane C. (2012). *Samurai among the Panthers: Richard Aoki.* Minneapolis, MN: University of Minnesota Press.

Fu-Kiau, Kimbwadende Kia Bunseki. (1991). *Self-healing power and therapy.* New York, NY: Vantage Press.

Gallman, B., Ani, Marimba, & Williams, Obadele. (2004). *To be African: Essays by Africans in the process of Sankofa—returning to our source of power.* Atlanta, GA: M.A.A.T., Inc.

Gates, Henry L. (1992). *Loose canons: Notes on the culture wars.* New York, NY: Oxford University Press.

Ginwright, Shawn. (2004). *Black in school: Afrocentric reform, urban youth, and the promise of Hip-Hop culture.* New York, NY: Teachers College Press.

Ginwright, Shawn, Noguera, Pedro, & Cammarota, Julio (Eds.). (2006). *Beyond resistance! Youth activism and community change: New democratic possibilities for practice and policy for America's youth.* New York, NY: Routledge.

Giroux, Henry. (1992). *Border crossings: Cultural workers and the politics of education.* New York, NY: Routledge.

Giroux, Henry. (2013). *America's education deficit and the war on youth: Reform beyond electoral politics.* New York, NY: Monthly Review Press.

Goff, P.A., Steele, C.M., & Davies, P.G. (2008). The space between us: Stereotypes threat and distance in interracial contexts. *Journal of Personality and Social Psychology, 94,* 91–107.

Graham, Anthony, & Anderson, Kenneth A. (2008). "I have to be three steps ahead": Academically gifted African American male students in an urban high school on the tension between an ethnic and academic identity. *Urban Review, 40,* 472–499.

Grande, Sandy. (2004). *Red pedagogy: Native American social thought.* Lanham, MD: Rowman & Littlefield.

Hanley, Mary S., & Noblit, George. (2009). *Cultural responsiveness, racial identity and academic success: A review of the literature.* Pittsburgh, PA: The Heinz Endowments. Retrieved from http://www.heinz.org/UserFiles/Library/Culture-Report_FINAL.pdf

Heath, Shirley B. (1989). Oral and literate traditions of Black Americans living in poverty. *American Psychologist, 44*(2), 367–373.

Hernández-Cuevas, Marco Polo. (2004). *African Mexicans and the discourse on modern nation.* Lanham, MD: University Press of America.

Hernández-Cuevas, Marco Polo. (2012). Afro-Latin and the Negro Common: An interview with Dr. Marco Polo Hernández-Cuevas. Retrieved from http://www.racialicious.com/2012/09/05/afro-latin-and-the-negro-common-an-interview-with-dr-marco-polo-hernandez-cuevas/

Herold, Benjamin. (2011). "Why aren't African-centered charters running turnarounds?" *The Philadelphia Notebook, 18*(4). Retrieved from http://thenotebook.org/february-2011/113290/why-arent-african-centered-charters-running-turnarounds

Herrero, E. (2006). Using Dominican oral literature and discourse to support literacy learning among low-achieving students from the Dominican Republic. *International Journal of Bilingual Education and Bilingualism, 9*(1), 219–238.

Hilliard, Asa G. (1978). Straight talk about school desegregation problems. *Theory Into Practice, 17*(2), 100–106.

Hilliard, Asa G. (1988). Conceptual confusion and the persistence of group oppression. *Equity and Excellence in Education, 24*(3), 36–43.

Hilliard, Asa G. (1997). *SBA: The reawakening of the African mind.* Tallahassee, FL: Makare.

Hilliard, Asa G. (2003). No mystery: Closing the achievement gap between Africans and excellence. In T. Perry, C. Steele, & A.G. Hilliard (Eds.), *To be young, gifted and Black: Promoting high achievement among African-American students* (pp. 131–166). Boston, MA: Beacon Press.

Horne, Gerald. (2005). *Black and brown: African Americans and the Mexican Revolution, 1910–1920.* New York, NY: New York University Press.

Hotep, Uhuru. (2008). Intellectual Maroons: Architects of African sovereignty. *Journal of Pan African Studies, 2*(5), 3–19.

Hudicourt-Barnes, J. (2003). The use of argumentation in Haitian Creole science classrooms. *Harvard Educational Review, 73*(1), 73–93.

Jensen, Robert. (2005). *The heart of whiteness: Confronting, race, racism and white privilege.* San Francisco, CA: City Lights.

Karenga, Maulana. (1998): *Kwanzaa: A celebration of family, community, and culture.* Los Angeles, CA: University of Sankore Press.

Karenga, Maulana. (2002). *Introduction to Black Studies.* Los Angeles, CA: University of Sankore Press.

Kennedy, Al, & Harrison, Herreast. (2010). *Big Chief Harrison and the Mardi Gras Indians.* Gretna, LA: Pelican.

King, Joyce E. (1991). Dysconscious racism: Ideology, identity, and the miseducation of teachers. *Journal of Negro Education, 60*(2), 133–146.

King, Joyce E. (1992). Diaspora literacy and consciousness in the struggle against miseducation in the Black community. *Journal of Negro Education, 61*(3), 317–340.

King, Joyce E. (2004). Culture-centered knowledge: Black studies, curriculum transformation and social action. In J.A. Banks & C.M. Banks (Eds.), *The handbook of research on multicultural education* (rev. 2nd ed., pp. 349–378). San Francisco, CA: Jossey Bass.

King, Joyce E. (2005). *Black education: A transformative research and action agenda for the new century.* Mahwah, NJ: Lawrence Erlbaum Associates.

King, Joyce E. (2006). "If justice is our objective": Diaspora literacy, heritage knowledge and the praxis of critical studyin' for human freedom. In Arnetha Ball (Ed.), *With more deliberate speed: Achieving equity and excellence in education—Realizing the full potential of* Brown v. Board of Education (NSSE 105th Yearbook, Pt. 2, pp. 337–360). New York, NY: Ballinger.

King, Joyce E. (2008). Critical and qualitative research in teacher education: A Blues Epistemology for cultural well-being and a reason for knowing. In M. Cochran-Smith, S. Felman-Nemser, J. D. McIntyre, & K. E. Demers (Eds.), *Handbook of research on teacher education* (3rd ed., pp. 1094–1136). New York, NY: Routledge.

King, Joyce E. (2010). Mis-education or the development of critical race consciousness: Curriculum as heritage knowledge. In K.L. Buras, J. Randals, Ya Salaam, K., & Students at the Center (Eds.), *Pedagogy, policy and the privatized city: Stories of dispossession and defiance from New Orleans* (pp. 126–130). New York, NY: Teachers College Press.

King, Joyce E. (2011). "Who dat say (we) too depraved to be saved?" Re-membering Katrina/Haiti (and beyond): Critical studyin' for human freedom. *Harvard Educational Review, 81*(2), 343–370.

King, Joyce E., & Akua, Chike. (2012). Dysconscious racism and teacher education. In J.A. Banks (Ed.), *Encyclopedia of diversity in education* (pp. 723–726). Thousand Oaks, CA: Sage Publications.

King, Joyce E., & Wilson, Thomasyne L. (1990). Being the soul-freeing substance: The legacy of hope in Afro-humanity. *Journal of Education, 172*(2), 9–27.

Kinloch, Valerie. (2010). "To not be a traitor of Black English": Youth perceptions of language rights in an urban context. *Teachers College Record, 112*(1), 103–141.

Kleymeyer, Charles D. (1994). *Cultural expression and grassroots development: Cases from Latin America and the Caribbean.* Boulder, CO: Lynne Rienner.

Kochiyama, Yuri. (2004). *Passing it on!* Los Angeles, CA: UCLA Asian American Studies Center.

Kynard, Carmen. (2007). "I want to be African": In search of a Black radical tradition/African-American-vernacularized paradigm for "Students' Right to Their Own Language," critical literacy, and "class politics." *College English, 69,* 360–390.

Kynard, Carmen (2013). *Vernacular insurrections: Race, Black protest, and the new century in composition-literacies studies.* Albany, NY: SUNY Press.

Ladson-Billings, Gloria. (1994). *Dreamkeepers: Successful teachers of African American students.* San Francisco, CA: Jossey-Bass.

Ladson-Billings, Gloria. (1995). Toward a theory of culturally relevant pedagogy. *American Educational Research Journal, 32,* 465–491.

Ladson-Billings, Gloria. (1997). "I know why this doesn't feel empowering": A critical race analysis of critical pedagogy. In P. Freire, T. McKinnon, D. Macedo, & J. W. Fraser (Eds.), *Mentoring the mentor: Critical dialogue with Paulo Freire* (pp. 127–142). New York, NY: Peter Lang.

Ladson-Billings, Gloria. (2006). From the achievement gap to the education debt: Understanding achievement in US schools. *Educational Researcher, 35*(7), 3–12.

Lee, Carol. (2007). *Culture, literacy and learning: Taking bloom in the midst of the whirlwind.* New York, NY: Teachers College Press.

Lee, Carol. (2008). Synthesis of research on the role of culture in learning among African American youth: The contributions of Asa G. Hilliard, III. *Review of Educational Research, 78*(4), 797–827.

Lewis, Amanda. (2003). *Race in the schoolyard: Negotiating the color line in classrooms and communities.* New Brunswick, NJ: Rutgers University Press.

Lewis, Kelly M., Andrews, Emily, Gaska, Karie, Sullivan, Cris, Bybee, Deborah, & Ellick, Kecia L. (2012). Experimentally evaluating the impact of a school-based African-centered emancipatory intervention on the ethnic identity of African American adolescents. *Journal of Black Psychology, 38*(3), 259–289.

Lewis, Kelly M., Sullivan, Cris, & Bybee, Deborah. (2006). An experimental evaluation of a school-based emancipatory intervention to promote African American well-being and youth leadership. *Journal of Black Psychology, 32*(1), 3–28.

Mabie, G.E. (2000). Race, culture, and intelligence: An interview with Asa G. Hilliard III. *Educational Forum, 64*(3), 243–251.

MacLeod, Jay. (1991). Bridging street and school. *Journal of Negro Education, 60*(3), 260–275.

Maiga, Hassimi O. (2005). When the language of education is not the language of culture: The epistemology of systems of knowledge and pedagogy. In J.E. King (Ed.), *Black education: A transformative research and action agenda for the new century* (pp. 159–182). Mahwah, NJ: Lawrence Erlbaum Associates.

Maiga, Hassimi O. (2010). *Balancing writing history with oral tradition: The legacy of the Songhoy people.* New York, NY: Taylor & Francis.

Majors, Yolanda J. (2003). Shoptalk: Teaching and learning in an African American hair salon. *Mind, Culture and Activity, 10*(4), 289–310.

Majors, Yolanda J., & Ansari, Sana. (2009). Cultural community practices as urban classroom resources. In L.C. Tillman (Ed.), *The Sage handbook of African American education* (pp. 107–121). Thousand Oaks, CA: Sage Publications.

McAdoo, Hariette P. (2002). The village talks: Racial socialization of our children. In H.P. McAdoo (Ed.), *Black children: Social, educational and parental environments* (2nd ed., pp. 46–55). Thousand Oaks, CA: Sage Publications.

Meares, Christina Faye. (2011). *Disappearing acts: The mass incarceration of African American women* (master's thesis, Paper 9). Georgia State University, African-American Studies Department. Retrieved from http://digitalarchive.gsu.edu/aas_theses

Mercado, Carmen I. (1997). When young people from marginalized communities enter the world of ethnographic research: Scribing, planning, reflecting and sharing. In A. Egan-Robertson & D. Bloome (Eds.), *Students as researchers of culture and language in their own communities* (pp. 69–92). New York, NY: Hampton Press.

Merry, Michael S., & New, William. (2008, November). Constructing an authentic self: The challenges and promise of African-centered pedagogy. *American Journal of Education, 115*(1), 35–64.

Milner, H. Richard. (2012). Beyond a test score: Explaining opportunity gaps in educational practice. *Journal of Black Studies, 43*(6), 693–718.

Montero-Sieburth, Martha. (1997). Reclaiming indigenous cultures: Student-developed oral histories of Talamanca, Costa Rica. In A. Egan-Robertson & D. Bloome (Eds.), *Students as researchers of culture and language in their own communities* (pp. 217–241). New York, NY: Hampton Press.

Moore, Carlos, Sanders, Tanya R., & Moore, Shawna (Eds.). (1995). *African presence in the Americas.* Trenton, NJ: African World Press.

Morrell, Ernest. (2004). *Becoming critical researchers: Literacy and empowerment for urban youth.* New York, NY: Peter Lang.

Morrell, Ernest, & Collatos, A.M. (2002). Toward a critical teacher education: High school student sociologists as teacher educators. *Social Justice, 29*(4), 60–70.

Muhammad, Khalil G. (2010). *The condemnation of blackness: Race, crime, and the making of modern urban America.* Boston, MA: Harvard University Press.

Murrell, Peter C. (1997). Digging again the family wells: A Freirian literacy framework as emancipatory pedagogy for African American children. In P. Freire, T. McKinnon, D. Macedo, & J. W. Fraser (Eds.), *Mentoring the mentor: A critical dialogue with Paulo Freire* (pp. 19–58). New York, NY: Peter Lang.

Murrell, Peter C. (2006). Toward justice in urban education: A model of collaborative cultural inquiry in urban schools. *Equity and Excellence in Education, 39*(1), 81–90.

Murrell, Peter C. (2009). Identity, agency, and culture: Black achievement and educational attainment. In L.C. Tillman (Ed.), *The Sage handbook of African American education* (pp. 89–105). Thousand Oaks, CA: Sage Publications.

Nasir, Na'ilah. (2011). *Racialized identities: Race and achievement among African American youth.* Stanford, CA: Stanford University Press.

Nasir, Nai'lah, & Hand, Victoria. (2005). Exploring sociocultural perspectives on race, culture, and learning. *Review of Educational Research, 76*(4), 449–475.

Nasir, Na'ilah, & Saxe, Gregory. (2003). Ethnic and academic identities: A cultural practice perspective on emerging tensions and their management in the lives of minority students. *Educational Researcher, 32*, 14–18.

National Alliance of Black School Educators (NABSE). (1984). *Saving the African American Child.* Task Force Report. Washington, DC: Author.

Nobles, Wade W. (1990). The infusion of African and African American content: A question of content and intent. In A.G. Hilliard, L. Payton-Stewart, & L.O. Williams (Eds.), *Infusion of African and African American content in the school curriculum. Proceedings of the First National Conference, October 1989* (pp. 5–24). Morristown, NJ: Aaron Press.

Nobles, Wade W. (2008). *Per Âa* Asa Hilliard: The Great House of Black Light for educational excellence. *Review of Educational Research, 78*(3), 727–747.

Nunn, Kenneth B. (2011). The Black Nationalist cure to disproportionate minority contact. In N. Dowd (Ed.), *Justice for kids: Keeping kids out of the juvenile justice system* (pp. 135–156). New York, NY: New York University Press.

Oakes, Jeanie, Rogers, John, & Lipton, M. (2006). *Learning power: Organizing for education and justice.* New York, NY: Teachers College Press.

Obenga, Theophile. (2002). *Imhotep Magazine.* San Francisco, CA: San Francisco State University Press.

Obenga, Theophile. (2004). *African philosophy: The Pharaonic Period: 2780–330 BC.* Dakar, Senegal: Per Ankh.

Ogbu, John U., & Simons, H.D. (1998). Voluntary and involuntary minorities: A Cultural-Ecological Theory of School Performance with some implications for education. *Anthropology & Education Quarterly, 29*(2), 155–188.

Oyserman, Daphna, Gant, Larry, & Ager, Joel. (1995). A socially contextualized model of African American identity: Possible selves and school persistence. *Journal of Personality and Social Psychology, 69,* 1216–1232.

Oyserman, Daphna, Harrison, Kathy, & Bybee, Deborah. (2001). Can racial identity be promotive of academic efficacy? *International Journal of Behavioral Development, 25*(4), 379–385.

Oyserman, Daphna, Kemmelmeier, Marcus, Fryberg, Stephanie, Brosh, Hezi, & Hart-Johnson, Tamera. (2003). Racial-ethnic self-schemas. *Social Psychology Quarterly, 66*(4), 333–347.

Paris, Django. (2012). Culturally sustaining pedagogy: A needed change in stance, terminology, and practice. *Educational Researcher, 41*(3), 93–97.

Parrillo, Vincent N. (2009). Is multiculturalism a threat? Chapter 9 in *Diversity in America* (3rd ed., pp. 147–165). Thousand Oaks, CA: Sage Publications.

Payne, Charles M. (2012). Countering the master narratives: The "why?" of education for liberation. Chicago, IL: Annenberg Institute for School Reform. Retrieved from http://www.annenberginstitute.org/VUE/wp-content/pdf/VUE34_Payne.pdf

Perry, Theresa. (2003). Up from the parched earth: Toward a theory of African American achievement. In T. Perry, C. Steele, & A.G. Hilliard (Eds.), *To be young, gifted and Black: Promoting high achievement among African-American students* (pp. 1–107). Boston, MA: Beacon Press.

Pollard, Diane S., & Ajirotutu, Cheryl S. (Eds.). (2000). *African-centered schooling in theory and practice.* Westport, CT: Bergin & Garvey.

Potts, Richard G. (2003). Emancipatory prevention versus school-based prevention in African American communities. *American Journal of Community Psychology, 31*(1–2), 173–183.

Ravitch, Diane. (1990). Diversity and democracy. *American Educator, 14*(1), 16–20 *ff.*

Ravitch, Diane. (2010). *The death and life of the great American school system: How testing and choice are undermining education.* New York, NY: Basic Books.

Ravoira, Lawanda, & Patino, Vanessa. (2011). Girl matters: Unfinished work. In N. Dowd (Ed.), *Justice for kids: Keeping kids out of the juvenile justice system* (pp. 157–179). New York, NY: New York University Press.

Romero, Augustine. (2011). The hypocrisy of racism: Arizona's movement toward state-sanctioned apartheid. *Journal of Educational Controversy, 6*(1). Retrieved from http://www.wce.wwu.edu/Resources/CEP/eJournal/v006n001/a013.shtml

Sabo, Kim. (2003 Summer). Youth participatory evaluation: A field in the making. *New Directions for Evaluation, 98.* Theme Issue.

Sellers, Robert M., Smith, Mia A., Shelton, J. Nicole, Rowley, Stephanie A.J., & Chavous, Tabbye M. (1998). Multidimensional model of racial identity: A reconceptualization of African American racial identity. *Personality and Social Psychology Review, 2*(1), 18–39.

Shockley, Kmt. (2008). *The miseducation of Black children.* Chicago, IL: African American Images.

Shujaa, Mwalimu. (1994). *Too much schooling, too little education: A paradox of Black life in White societies.* Trenton, NJ: Africa World Press.

Sleeter, Christine. (2011). *The academic and social value of ethnic studies: A research review.* Washington, DC: National Education Association.

Smith-Maddox, Renee. (1998). Defining culture as a dimension of academic achievement: Implications for a culturally responsive curriculum, instruction and assessment. *Journal of Negro Education, 67*(3), 302–317.

Spencer, Margaret B., Noll, Elizabeth, Stoltzfris, Jill, & Harpalani, Vinay. (2001). Identity and school adjustment: Revisiting the "acting White" assumption. *Educational Psychologist, 36,* 21–30.

Steele, Claude M. (1992, April). Race and the schooling of Black Americans. *Atlantic Monthly, 269,* 68–78.

Steele, Claude M. (1997). A threat in the air: How stereotypes shape intellectual identity and performance. *American Psychologist, 52,* 613–629.

Steele, Claude M. (2003). Stereotype threat and student achievement. In T. Perry, C. Steele, & A.G. Hilliard (Eds.), *To be young, gifted and Black: Promoting high achievement among African-American students* (pp. 109–130). Boston, MA: Beacon Press.

Steele, Claude M., & Aronson, Jay. (1995). Stereotype threat and the intellectual test performance of African Americans. *Journal of Personality and Social Psychology, 69,* 797–811.

Stevenson, Howard C., Best, Garland, Cassidy, Elaine F., & McCabe, Delores. (2003). Remembering culture: The roots of culturally relevant anger. In H.C. Stevenson (Ed.), *Playing with anger: Teaching coping skills to African American adolescent boys through athletics and culture* (pp. 21–54). Westport, CT: Greenwood Press.

Swartz, Ellen. (2007). Emancipatory narratives: Rewriting the master script in the school and curriculum. *Journal of Negro Education, 3*(2), 173–186.

Swartz, Ellen. (2009). Diversity: Gatekeeping knowledge and maintaining inequalities. *Review of Educational Research, 79*(2), 1044–1083.

Taylor, Charles. (1994). *Multiculturalism: Examining the politics of recognition.* Princeton, NJ: Princeton University Press.

Teaching for Change. (1993). *Collective memory: The African presence in Latin America—A Study Guide on the Maroon Community of Esmeraldas, Ecuador.* Washington, DC: NECA (Network of Educators on the Americas).

Thomas, Oseela, Davidson, William, & McAdoo, Harriette P. (2008). An evaluation study of the Young Empowered Sisters (YES!) program: Promoting cultural assets among African American adolescent girls through a culturally relevant school-based intervention. *Journal of Black Psychology, 34*(3), 281–308.

Thomas, P.L. (2010). The Payne of addressing race and poverty in public education: Utopian accountability and deficit assumptions of middle-class America. *Souls: A Critical Journal of Black Politics, Culture, and Society, 12*(30), 262–283.

Thorne, Ashley. (2012, May 13). Arizona ends divisive Chicano studies in schools. *National Association of Scholars Newsletter.* Retrieved from http://www.nas.org/polArticles.cfm?doc_id_1321

Torres-Guzmán, Maria E., Mercado, Carmen I., Quintero, Anna H., & Viera, Diana R. (1994). Teaching and learning in Puerto Rican/Latino collaboratives: Implications for teacher education. In E.R. Hollins, J.E. King, & W.C. Hayman (Eds.), *Teaching diverse populations: Formulating a knowledge base* (pp. 105–128). Albany, NY: State University of New York Press.

Traoré, Rosemary. (2009). More than 30 years later: Intervention for African American Studies required. *Journal of Black Studies, 38*(4), 663–678.

Valenzuela, Angela. (1999). *Subtractive schooling: U.S.-Mexican youth and the politics of caring.* Albany, NY: State University of New York Press.

Van Sertima, Ivan. (Ed.). (1983). *Blacks in science: Ancient and modern.* Piscataway, NJ: Transaction Books.

Van Sertima, Ivan. (2001). *Blacks in science: Ancient and Modern.* New Brunswick, NJ: Transaction.

Wakefield, W. David, & Hudley, Cynthia. (2007). Ethnic and racial identity and adolescent well-being. *Theory Into Practice, 46*(2), 147–154.

Wang, Ming-Te, & Huguley, James P. (2012). Parental racial socialization as a moderator of the effects of racial discrimination on education success among African American adolescents. *Child Development, 83*(5), 1716–1731.

Wellman, David. (1977). *Portraits of white racism*. Cambridge, MA: Cambridge University Press.

West, Cornell. (1994). *Race matters*. New York, NY: Vintage Books.

Whaley, Arthur L., & Noël, La Tonya. (2012). Sociocultural theories, academic achievement, and African American adolescents in a multicultural context: A review of the cultural incompatibility perspective. *Journal of Negro Education, 81*(1), 25–38.

White, Ronald C., Jr. (2002). *Liberty and justice for all: Racial reform and the social gospel (1877–1925)*. Louisville, KY: Westminster John Knox Press.

Winn, Maisha T. (2011). *Girl time: Literacy, justice and the school-to-prison pipeline*. New York, NY: Teachers College Press.

Woodson, Carter G. (2000). *The miseducation of the Negro*. Chicago, IL: African American Images. (Original work published in 1933).

Wynter, Sylvia. (1984). The ceremony must be found. *Boundary/2, 12*(3)/*13*(1), 19–61.

Wynter, Sylvia. (1992/2012). "*Do not call us Negroes.*" *How multicultural textbooks perpetuate racism*. San Francisco, CA: Aspire Books.

Wynter, Sylvia. (1997). Alterity. In C.A. Grant & G. Ladson-Billings (Eds.), *Dictionary of multicultural education* (pp. 13–14). Phoenix, AZ: Oryx Press.

Wynter, Sylvia. (2005). Race and our biocentric belief system: An interview with Sylvia Wynter. In J.E. King (Ed.), *Black education: A transformative research and action agenda for the new century* (pp. 361–366). Mahwah, NJ: Routledge.

Wynter, Sylvia. (2006). On how we mistook the map for the territory, and re-imprisoned ourselves in our unbearable wrongness of being, of désêtre: Black Studies toward the Human Project. In L.R. Gordon & J.A. Gordon (Eds.), *Not only the master's tools: African American Studies in theory and practice* (pp. 85–106). Boulder, CO: Paradigm.

3

Health, Nutrition, and Physical Activity

Samuel R. Hodge & Alexander Vigo-Valentín

Introduction

Over 40 years ago, education historian Lawrence A. Cremin (1970) defined education as "the deliberate, systematic, and sustained effort to transmit, evoke, or acquire knowledge, attitudes, values, skills, or sensibilities, as well as any outcomes of that effort" (as cited by Franklin, 2003, p. 153). Our conceptualization of urban education is captured in the preceding quote as well as in Banks (2006) description of the general purpose of education in a democratic society. Specifically, he asserted that:

> Education in a democratic society should help students acquire the knowledge, attitudes, and skills needed to become productive workers within society as well as develop the commitment, attitudes, and skills to work to make our nation and the world just places in which to live and work. We should educate students to be effective citizens of their cultural communities, the nation, and the world. (Banks, 2006, p. 145)

Historically and contemporarily situated, the preceding quotes provide an appropriate start to our discussion on health, nutrition, and physical activity through the medium of physical education for youth in urban schools and communities.

Traditional physical education is instruction in (a) physical and motor fitness; (b) fundamental motor skills and patterns; and (c) skills in aquatics, dance, and individual and group games and sports including intramural and lifetime sports (Hodge, Lieberman, & Murata, 2012). In urban schools, physical education teachers tend to focus instruction on physical fitness, activity-related content knowledge and skill, personal and social skill development, and fundamental motor skill development (Hodges Kulinna, McCaughtry, Cothran, & Martin, 2006). There is a long, dynamic and rich history of physical education in the United States with an increasing focus on health, nutrition, and physical activity.

Historical Account and Current Emphasis

The history[1] of physical education in the United States progresses from a focus on gymnastics and calisthenics for schools in the 1800s, through a transition to a focus on sport, games, and dance at the beginning of the 20th century (Vlček, 2011). Political and militaristic influence associated with war (World Wars I and II, as well the Korean and Vietnam Wars) shifted the emphasis to physical fitness and exercise in response to concerns about fitness levels of military personnel and American citizens in general (Jurkechová, Vlček, & Bartík, 2011; Vlček, 2011). Since the mid-1960s, the benefits of physical activity have been widely published. For example, Hein and Ryan (1960) discussed the importance of physical activity in an article titled, "The Contributions of Physical Activity to Human Well-being." In the 1970s and 1980s, school physical education programs were dominated by curricular[2] innovations such as adventure education, cooperative learning, movement education, social responsibility models, sport education, and more as well as activities for the inclusion of students with disabilities (Hodge et al., 2012; Vlček, 2011). Economic recessions and concerns about program quality in the 1980s and 1990s contributed to cutbacks in many school physical education programs characterized by reductions in the amount of time students spend in physical education classes (Vlček, 2011). In contrast, the publication of the National Standards for Physical Education by the National Association for Sport and Physical Education (NASPE, 1995, 2004) has influenced the development of physical education curricula, instruction, and assessment. Its mission "is to enhance knowledge, improve professional practice, and increase support for high quality physical education, sport, and physical activity programs" (NASPE, 2013, p. 1). Likewise the organizers of the 2005 World Summit on Physical Education called for stronger international status of physical education in school politics and in daily school function as integral to education and to human and social development (Hodge et al., 2012).

In today's physical education programs, students are encouraged to live a physically active life through skillful movement, recreation and leisure, and sports. Physical education programs should promote knowledge, social development, skill acquisition and improvement, regular physical activity, and participation in healthy activities, including games, sports, leisure, and recreational activities (Hodge et al., 2012). All youth should be physically active daily for good health and wellness because this constitutes an important component of a healthy lifestyle. This must also include healthy dietary choices and habits. However, despite results published in credible reports from various scientific communities (i.e., health, medical, educational, and governmental) about the need for and benefits of physical activity and proper nutrition, many youth do not engage in physical activity regularly and have poor dietary habits, particularly those living in rural and urban communities (Centers for Disease Control & Prevention [CDC], 2006a). There is continued need for research in the public interest that is theoretically[3] sound regarding the health, nutrition, and physical activity behaviors of youth in urban schools and communities.

Demography and Urban Schools

Though confounded, most nations worldwide have established ethnic/racial categories (Carter & Fenton, 2009). Specific to the United States, there are several "categories denoting race and ethnicity . . . in accordance with the 1997 Office of Management and Budget (OMB) standard classification scheme" (Aud et al., 2012, p. vii). In this scheme, the designation of Hispanic is an ethnicity category, not a race category (Aud et al., 2012). The terms used to identify race/ethnic categories are American Indian/Alaska Native, Asian/Pacific Islander, Black (not Hispanic), Hispanic (not White), White (not Hispanic), and Two or more races (Aud et al., 2012). These broad categories are far from perfect, however, as there are many different groups with their own socio-cultural heritages, languages, traditions, and lifestyles within each category (e.g., African American, Italian American, Mexican American, Puerto Rican, and many more).

Today, Black and Hispanic residents are the two largest race/ethnic minority groups in the United States. The U.S. Census Bureau reports that 30% of the total population is either Black (16%) or Hispanic (17%). In 2009–2010 at public schools, much higher percentages of Hispanic (37%), Black (37%), and American Indian/Alaska Native (29%) attended high-poverty schools (i.e., highest quartile of schools in the state in terms of poverty) than Asian/Pacific Islander (12%) and White (6%) students (Aud et al., 2012). These schools are often in rural and urban areas.

The term *urban* typically denotes major cities and metropolitan areas. Common to large urban communities are school districts with high-poverty and low-performing schools. This includes those defined as persistently lowest-achieving schools (U.S. Department of Education, 2013). Many problems epitomize high-poverty urban schools. Common problems include budget deficits, equipment/supply shortages, inadequate school facilities, overcrowded classes, high percentages of poor (including White) and mostly Black and Hispanic students who tend to perform lower on standardized tests compared to White peers within suburban districts. In fact, White students are more likely to attend schools in suburban and rural areas and less likely to attend schools in high-poverty urban communities (Aud et al., 2012).

Educational disparities persist in these schools, which include persistently low-achieving schools. Those identified as *persistently lowest-achieving schools* are defined as among the lowest-achieving 5% of Title I schools or a high school that has had a graduation rate of less than 60% over multiple years (U.S. Department of Education, 2013). Although between 1990 and 2010, high school dropout rates declined for Black, Hispanic, and White students, rates were typically much higher for Black and Hispanic students compared to Asian/Pacific Islander and White students (Aud et al. 2012). This means that although there have been improvements in such factors as high school graduation rates for Black and Hispanic students, large gaps still exist between them and the academic achievement of Asian/Pacific Islander and White students, particularly in urban schools (Swanson, 2009). In addition to the aforementioned educational and economic issues and problems, the health of youth in urban communities is of concern (Skala, Springer, Sharma, & Hoelscher, 2012; Sweeney, Glaser, & Tedeschi, 2007).

It is well accepted by educational, health, and medical professionals that physical activity and proper nutrition are essential to the health and wellness of youth (U.S. Department of Health and Human Services, 2008; Strong et al., 2005). However, most youth do not meet the national guidelines of at least 60 minutes of moderate to vigorous physical activity daily (Lounsbery, McKenzie, Morrow, Monnat, & Holt, 2013; Troiano et al., 2007). This is true for youths with disabilities in urban communities also (Ortiz-Castillo, 2011). These issues are "particularly relevant given the recent increases in obesity and its associated problems, including high blood pressure, elevated cholesterol, and Type 2 diabetes, which disproportionately affect minority and socio-economically disadvantaged children" (Lounsbery et al., 2013, p. S141).

Health, Nutrition, and Physical Activity

The research literature[4] suggests that education, health and medical, legislative, and governmental entities should position themselves strategically to act as a team in addressing health priorities (Blanchett, Mumford, & Beachum, 2005). Andrade and Dean (2008) explained that through the 20th century health, medical, and related professionals worldwide mostly focused their attention on attending to societal issues such as the world wars and the polio epidemic. For the past 50 years, however, there has been more attention given globally to health issues linked to lifestyle such as heart diseases, smoking-related diseases, hypertension, stroke, obesity, diabetes, and cancer (Andrade & Dean, 2008).

Health Crisis in Urban America

The aforementioned health issues can reduce life expectancy. There are racial/ethnic disparities in morbidity and mortality rates and these differences have negative consequences particularly for the poor, Black, and Hispanic populations (Heron, 2012; Keppel, Pearcy, & Heron, 2010; Miniño & Murphy, 2012). For example, national mortality data reveal that in 2001 "Black men and women had the highest death rates from all causes combined and from many specific causes at nearly all levels of education, and the largest average life years lost before age 65 years" (Jemal et al., 2008, p. 1). Yet for more than 30 years, reducing racial/ethnic disparities in mortality rates has been a part of the national health agenda (Keppel et al., 2010). Even so, disparities in mortality between racial/ethnic groups persist (Keppel et al., 2010; Miniño & Murphy, 2012). Higher mortality rates are also associated with low educational success and other indicators of poverty and low income (Jemal et al., 2008). Tellingly, and emblematic of life circumstances (e.g., poverty and food deserts) and lifestyle decisions and behaviors (e.g., poor eating habits), cardiovascular diseases and diabetes are among the top five causes of death for Black and Hispanic Americans (U.S. Department of Health and Human Services, 2010a, b).

For school-age youth, asthma (a chronic respiratory disease) is a major health issue, which disproportionately affects students of color in urban communities and adversely affects their quality of life and school experiences (Basch, 2011a). In fact, experiencing an asthmatic attack is the leading cause of absenteeism across school contexts (Krenitsky-Korn, 2011). Students with asthma are more likely to miss school, perform less well academically, and participate less in school activities compared to peers without asthma (Basch, 2011a; Krenitsky-Korn, 2011). From an analysis of national health statistics, Basch (2011a) reported that "poor urban minority children not only have higher rates of asthma and more severe forms of the disease, but are much less likely to receive contiguous high-quality medical care and to consistently use appropriate, efficacious medications" (p. 607). He explained that such youth are more likely to experience severe asthma that influences their quality of life negatively including lowering their motivation and ability to learn in school. Disability and poor health also adversely affects physical activity levels (Ortiz-Castillo, 2011). For example, a youth with severe asthma finds difficulty in breathing, and, consequently is less likely to be physically active, but more likely to spend greater amounts of screen time such as watching television and playing computer/video games (Conn, Hernandez, Puthoor, Fagnano, & Halterman, 2009).

There is a cyclical pattern in that those in poor health and/or have disabilities are more likely to be physically inactive, which contributes to overweight and obesity status, and this body status adversely affects health. David L. Katz, Editor-in-Chief of the journal, *Childhood Obesity,* argued that "obesity is on the causal pathway to every major chronic disease that plagues modern societies. Obesity is the major driver of diabetes trends around the globe, and the reason that what was once adult-onset diabetes was transformed into type 2 diabetes, a condition afflicting youth now all too routinely" (Katz, 2013, p. 1). Lifestyle-related health issues such as those identified here can be addressed effectively through education, proper nutrition, and regular physical activity for meaningful health benefits (Andrade & Dean, 2008).

Nutrition and Physical Activity in Urban America

There is reason for concern regarding the food choices of families who reside in urban communities, particularly those who are poor, including White, but mostly Black and Hispanic youth (Fisher, Arreola, Birch, & Rolls, 2007; Zive, Berry, Sallis, Frank, & Nader, 2002). For instance, studies reveal that as the consumption of soft drinks, fruit drinks, and fried foods has increased considerably in the past 30 years or so, the consumption of healthier foods, such as fruits, vegetables, and milk has decreased for adolescents (Malik, Schulze, & Hu, 2006). Youths in urban communities tend to have a high consumption of fat, sodium, cholesterol, and total daily caloric intake (Sweeney et al., 2007). Both Black and Hispanic youth tend to regularly consume sweetened juices and soft drinks and this increases their risk of being overweight or obese, which has negative consequences to health and wellness (Malik et al., 2006; Tanasescu, Ferris, Himmelgreen, Rodriguez, & Pérez-Escamilla, 2000; Vigo-Valentín, Hodge, & Kozub, 2011).

There is also concern about physical inactivity among residents in urban communities, particularly for Black and Hispanic groups and persons with disabilities (CDC, 2006a; Ewing, Schmid, Killingsworth, Zlot, & Raudenbush, 2003; Ortiz-Castillo, 2011). Black and Hispanic youth are less likely to participate in organized or leisure-time physical activity compared to White peers (Annesi, Faigenbaum, Westcott, & Smith, 2008; Basch, 2011b; CDC, 2012). However, Floyd, Spengler, Maddock, Gobster, and Suau (2008) found that moderate and vigorous forms of physical activity were higher with unorganized activities such as walking in a city park. Linked to physical inactivity, Black youth have both the highest prevalence and increase of overweight and obesity (Annesi et al., 2008). Black and Hispanic girls are at higher risk for overweight and obesity compared to White girls of their age (Basch, 2011b; Gordon-Larsen et al., 2004; Harris, Gordon-Larsen, Chantala, & Udry, 2006). This is because socio-cultural and environmental factors play a major role in childhood obesity among these populations (Barr-Anderson, Adams-Wynn, DiSantis, & Kumanyika, 2013). For example, culturally influenced dietary habits (e.g., consumption of sweet snacks and carbonated beverages), and high amounts of screen time and other sedentary behaviors, influence Black and Hispanic girls' weight status (Barr-Anderson et al., 2013; Thompson et al., 2003). Youth who are overweight or obese are more likely to become adults who are overweight or obese (Dowda et al., 2004). This trend may occur across generations within families. Predictably, and troubling as well, research indicates that even 2- to 5-year-old children with excessive body weight are likely to become obese adults (U.S. Department of Health and Human Services, 2010c).

Physical activity behaviors are influenced by cultural; environmental; hereditary (e.g., adiposity or body fat); psychosocial (e.g., self-efficacy, support of parents and peer groups); and individual (e.g., sports, physical fitness goals) factors (Choh et al., 2008; Pérusse, Tremblay, LeBlanc, Bouchard, 1989; Saunders et al., 1997). In regard to environmental factors, African American boys and girls in urban spaces typically have less access to programs, facilities, and safe and attractive areas for play (Annesi et al., 2008). Moreover, crime has been cited as a barrier to physical activity, particularly among those living in rural and urban communities (McGinn, Evenson, Herring, Huston, & Rodriguez, 2008). Nonetheless, youth residing in urban areas with high levels of incivility and crime are "more likely to walk to school, in spite of lower levels of perceived safety" (Rossen et al., 2011, p. 262). Reasoned efforts should be directed at reducing these youths' exposure to dangers in these communities by constructing safe routes to and from school (Rossen et al., 2011).

It is well accepted that daily physical activity during childhood and adolescence is beneficial to health. Common benefits include "lower adiposity, improved cardiovascular health and fitness, reduced symptoms of depression and anxiety, greater global self-concept and esteem, and better academic performance" (Rossen et al., 2011, p. 262). In contrast, a lack of regular physical activity combined with poor dietary habits lead to health conditions associated with overweight and obesity status. A wealth of research confirms that a strong association exists between overweight and obesity of youth and an increased risk of various chronic diseases such as asthma, cardiovascular diseases, hypertension, and diabetes (Galal, Fahmy, Lashine, Abdel-Fattah, & Galal, 2011; Olshansky et al., 2012; Peeters et al., 2003; Sinha et al., 2011). Dietary habits such as the consumption of healthy foods (e.g., fruits and vegetables) as opposed to unhealthy foods (e.g., sugary snacks) are major factors that influence the health status of youth in urban communities. Likewise, time spent participating in sedentary activities rather than moderate to vigorous physical activities can adversely impact youths' health and wellness including whether they will become overweight or obese.

Childhood Overweight and Obesity

The prevalence of childhood obesity has increased markedly in the last three decades (Ogden, Carroll, Curtin, Lamb, & Flegal, 2010; Wang & Beydoun, 2007) and is a public health issue. U.S. Surgeon General, Regina M. Benjamin, exclaimed,

> Our nation stands at a crossroads. Today's epidemic of overweight and obesity threatens the historic progress we have made in increasing American's quality and years of healthy life. Two-third of adults and nearly one in three children are overweight or obese. In addition, many racial and ethnic groups and geographic regions of the United States are disproportionately affected. The sobering impact of these numbers is reflected in the nation's concurrent epidemics of diabetes, heart disease, and other chronic diseases. If we do not reverse these trends, researchers warn that many of our children—our most precious resource—will be seriously afflicted in early adulthood with medical conditions such as diabetes and heart disease. This future is unacceptable. (U.S. Department of Health and Human Services, 2010c, p. 1)

It is estimated that about one third of youth are either overweight or obese (Ogden et al., 2010). In high school, about 30% of the students are either overweight or obese (CDC, 2011a). Those who are obese during childhood are predisposed to experience a decline in life expectancy along with health-related ailments and socio-psychological issues (Galal et al., 2011; Olshansky et al., 2012; Peeters et al., 2003; Sinha et al., 2011). Different factors including culture, ethnicity, and socioeconomics influence the likelihood of youth becoming overweight or obese (Caprio et al., 2008; Harris et al., 2006; Wang & Beydoun, 2007).

Troubling disparities in childhood obesity exist between groups from ethnically and socioculturally diverse backgrounds. In particular, the prevalence of overweight and obesity among and between Black and Hispanic adolescents is significantly higher compared to their White peers (Crawford, Story, Wang, Ritchie, & Sabry, 2001). Less than half of Black and Hispanic adolescents attending high school are physically active for at least 60 minutes most days of the week (CDC, 2011b). In today's society, many youth would rather spend time watching television and engaged in other sedentary activities (e.g., computer/video games) instead of being physically active (Gordon-Larsen, Adair, & Popkin, 2002). This occurs more now than in past years because of today's lifestyles that are influenced by increased access to technological innovations such as computer/video games (Amusa, Toriola, & Goon, 2012).

It is no surprise therefore that increases in obesity rates in recent years have contributed to health concerns (Flegal, Carroll, Ogden, & Curtin, 2010). The national obesity rate is 36% and is estimated to reach 50% by the year 2030 (Dionise & Pompa, 2012). *Obesity* is a chronic disease defined as a range of weight that is greater than what is considered healthy for a given height (Flegal et al., 2010). It compromises health because a disproportionate amount of body fat relative to lean body mass raises the likelihood of certain diseases (RAND Corporation, 2004). The RAND Corporation (2004) presented the following findings about obesity:

- Obesity in the U.S. population has increased steadily over the last two decades.
- Severe obesity is increasing the fastest.
- Obesity is linked to rising health care costs more than either smoking or drinking.
- The health effects associated with overweight and obese youth can also lead to an increase in morbidity in adulthood.

There are many different methods to assess body composition such as underwater (hydrostatic) weighing, bioelectric impedance, skinfold thickness, waist-to-hip ratio, body mass index (BMI), and more (Fogelholm & van Marken Lichtenbelt, 1997). BMI has become a widely accepted measure in estimating body composition. BMI is calculated as a person's weight in kilograms divided by height in meters squared (kg/m^2). It is a statistical measure of a person's weight-to-height ratio. For adults, a BMI of $\geq 30kg/m^2$ is labeled as obese and morbidly obese is defined as BMI $\geq 40kg/m^2$. For youth and adolescents ages 2–20 years, BMI classifications (e.g., normal, overweight) take into consideration age and gender.

The CDC defines *obese* as at or above the 95th percentile of BMI for one's age. Further it defines *overweight* as between the 85th and 95th percentile of BMI. Youths with a high BMI "are more likely than those with a normal BMI to have insulin resistance (which can lead to diabetes), high blood pressure, and unhealthy levels of fats and other lipids" (U.S. Department of Health and Human Services, 2010c, p. 2). In addition to physical ailments, youth who are overweight or obese may also face social stigmas and psychological difficulties (U.S. Department of Health and Human Services, 2010c).

Obesity and Disability

There is a causal relationship between obesity and disability. Researchers have reported that at all ages obesity plays a major role in disability. For example, research indicates there is "a positive association between increased adiposity, frequently measured as . . . BMI or waist circumference . . . , and physical disability as defined by impairments in performing activities of daily living" (Wong et al., 2012, p. 710). In most cases, a person who is excessively overweight or obese is likely to have other health-related issues, such as asthma, diabetes, high blood pressure, and high cholesterol as well as limited mobility. This contemporary phenomenon is known as *mobility disability*. It is the condition in which movement decreases as obesity increases and it is becoming increasingly prevalent. Obesity can negatively affect an individual's ability to perform activities of daily living, including many forms of physical activity and can decrease quality of life. For youth who are morbidly obese, active movement alone (e.g., running in the gym) can be difficult. In addition, youth who are obese may face social stigmas and potential ridicule (e.g., bullying at school) that are associated with their weight status.

Students who are morbidly obese may require accommodations to their education program, as mandated in Public Law 108–446, the Individuals with Disabilities Education Improvement Act (IDEA, 2004). The disability category, *Other Health Impairments,* is defined as limited strength, vitality, or alertness caused by chronic or acute health problems that adversely affect educational performance (IDEA, 2004). A student who is obese may qualify for special education services under this category. If the student qualifies for special education services, then an Individualized Education Program (IEP) and/or Individualized Health Plan must be written to address his or her health concerns and educational programming. Before participating in physical education, the student will need a comprehensive medical exam, thorough evaluation, and an IEP developed. A high-quality physical education program is beneficial to youth who are less competent movers and those who are obese. The IEP team should provide input into a student's overall individualized program and the physical education teacher works with the student at a pace that is comfortable and nonthreatening to her or his psychological safety.

It is clear that from the 1970s to today obesity rates have increased continuously for both female and male youth alike. Between 1971 and 2000, the prevalence of obesity quadrupled (i.e., changed from 4% to 16%) in the United States for youth ages 6 to 11 years old and more than doubled (i.e., changed from 6% to over 15%) among youth ages 12 to 19 years old. Overall, about 16% to 19% of youth (ages 6 to 19 years old) are overweight. Of particular concern, Black, Hispanic, and American Indian youth tend to be overweight and obese more so than White youth. For example, Hispanic youth are at over 25% and Black females are at 23%. Further over 39% of American Indian youth, including Native Alaskans ages 5 to 18 years old, are overweight or obese. If obesity trends for youth continue to ascend at current rates, obesity will soon become a *pandemic*. A pandemic is defined as an epidemic occurring over a wide geographic area and affecting an unusually high proportion of the population. Many factors contribute to childhood obesity and some are modifiable and others are not.

Most factors linked to obesity-related health issues are modifiable such as physical inactivity, sedentary lifestyles, and poor eating habits. On the other hand, nonmodifiable causes are usually not under a person's control but still may affect her or his ability and will to manage weight and health, such as socioeconomic status, environment, and genetics. Next, we briefly discuss both modifiable and nonmodifiable factors.

Modifiable Factors

Typically, modifiable causes of overweight/obesity status are under the control of the individual and are associated with lifestyle choices and behaviors, cultural norms, and family values and influences. These causes are therefore modifiable through education and lifestyle changes such as increased exercise and informed life choices. As such, engaging youth in healthy experiences (e.g., bicycling) may affect their attitude and behavior toward healthier lifestyles. In fact, most factors associated with obesity-related conditions are modifiable. Next, we present examples of modifiable lifestyle choices and behaviors with reference to pertinent research.

Physical inactivity—the lack of regular physical activity (exercise) correlates with an increase in overweight and obesity rates throughout the United States and is now identified as the fourth-leading risk factor for mortality worldwide (World Health Organization, 2010). Logically as physical education teachers encourage and demonstrate physically active lifestyles for their students, combined with parental support and role modeling, students may increase (modify) their physical activity behaviors (Hodge et al., 2012). It is also important to mention that habits of physical inactivity develop early on in a child's life and may persist into adulthood and perpetuate continued physical inactivity (Dowda et al., 2004). Physical inactivity is further exacerbated for individuals with disabilities (Ortiz-Castillo, 2011).

Empirical studies confirm that most adults with disabilities do not participate in any leisure-time physical activity compared to adults with no disabilities (Rimmer, Riley, Wang, Rauworth, & Jurkowski, 2004). Likewise youths with disabilities participate in physical activity less so compared to peers without disabilities (Ortiz-Castillo, 2011). In that, they tend to be less physically active, have lower levels of fitness, and higher rates of obesity than peers without disabilities (Rimmer et al., 2004; Rimmer & Rowland, 2008; U.S. Department of Health and Human Services,

2000). It is reported that youths with physical disabilities (e.g., cerebral palsy, muscular dystrophy) have lifestyles that are more sedentary compared to peers without disabilities or those with other types of disabilities such as hearing impairments (Imms, 2008; Longmuir & Bar-Or, 2000). It is important for physical education teachers to encourage and promote regular daily physical activity for students with and without disabilities. This should be augmented with the support and encouragement of parents at home and in the community. Further, physical education teachers should promote physical activity beyond the school setting. For example, physical education teachers in concert with health professionals can provide advice and serve as leaders in the conceptualization, development, implementation, and evaluation phases of urban health promotion programs, especially for those programs intending to increase physical activity behaviors (Lawson, 2005).

Sedentary behavior—a high percentage of youth are less active compared to those of past generations. Today's youth tend to watch television (TV), sit at a computer, play video games, and engage in similar behaviors at high rates that take up time that could be used for physical activity. Watching TV is the most prevalent (75% of youths) sedentary pursuit and is a predictor of overweight/obesity. Gordon-Larsen and colleagues (2004) found that African American: (a) caregivers (mothers/grandmothers) controlled the quality rather than quantity of TV that their daughters or granddaughters watched; (b) caregivers were generally unaware of the amount of TV their daughters/granddaughters watched; (c) daughters/granddaughters preferred sedentary behavior (i.e., TV viewing) rather than physical activity; (d) mothers/grandmothers perceived TV as filling an important role as that of safe and affordable child supervision; and (e) mothers/grandmothers were poor role models for a physically active lifestyle, and acknowledge their own low motivation to be physically active. Of course, African American parents care deeply about their children's health and wellness. However, they often face barriers to supporting healthy eating and physical activity for themselves and their children. In general, research indicates that personal (e.g., time constraints and fatigue); social (e.g., lack of family support); community (e.g., limited access to, and expense of recreational facilities); and environmental (e.g., lack of safety, unlit sidewalks for exercising at night, and lack of safe bicycling and walking trails) factors tend to adversely affect the physical activity levels of African American adults; which in turn, influence their children (Bopp et al., 2007). It is noteworthy to mention that research indicates for each additional hour of TV watching by youth there is a 2% increase in the prevalence of obesity (Kohl & Hobbs, 1998). There is a positive link between the amount of TV viewing and the consumption of sweets and snacks as well (Tanasescu et al., 2000).

Poor eating habits—overconsumption of high-calorie foods increases a person's risk of becoming overweight or obese; it also increases the risk of other health-related conditions (e.g., high cholesterol, high blood pressure, and diabetes). This means that poor dietary choices and habits combined with physical inactivity results in high risks and problems associated with excessive weight gain and obesity status (Hodge et al., 2012). Poor dietary behaviors include high consumption of soda and sweetened drinks, as well as high-fat and fried food. Instead, youth should consume higher portions of fruits and vegetables in their diet. According to the CDC (2011b), Black and Hispanic youth tend to consume fewer proportions of fruits, salads, and vegetables compared with their White peers. In general, parents' dietary habits influence their children's food choices (Morello, Madanat, Crespo, Lemus, & Elder, 2012). Further, there is a negative association between unhealthy eating behaviors and screen time among ethnic minority youth (Sisson, Shay, Broyles, & Leyva, 2012).

Urban schools should provide students with health information, including discourse about dietary choices and behaviors, and implement culturally responsive physical education programs that promote healthy living (Vigo-Valentín et al., 2011). Culturally responsive physical education programs are designed to recognize students' socio-cultural norms, life experiences, and other relevant factors to facilitate meaningful learning experiences that lead to healthier lifestyles (Timken & Watson, 2010). To advance such a program, teachers must accept that: (a) all students can achieve educational success, (b) they are part of and have obligations to serve their local communities, (c) they are responsible for creating positive learning experiences that help motivate students to learn, and (d) each student brings life experiences that can enhance the overall learning context (Hastie, Martin, & Buchanan, 2013).

Nonmodifiable Factors

There are also nonmodifiable factors that influence a person's health. Socioeconomic and environmental factors as well as genetics are considered nonmodifiable factors. These are factors that are not under an individual's direct control (Hodge et al., 2012).

Socioeconomic status—can have a significant influence on health and wellness within families and across multiple generations. Socioeconomic status is defined as the position of a family or an individual on a scale that measures such factors as education, income, occupation, and place of residence. Poverty has negative consequences for health and health care services in rural and urban environments (Peterson & Litaker, 2010; Salgado de Snyder et al., 2011). Data from the National Center for Education Statistics show that Black and Hispanic youths are much more likely to live in poverty than are White and Asian youth (Aud et al. 2012). National data indicate that the "percentage of Black children living in poor households varied from 41 percent in 1990, to 32 percent in 2000 and 34 percent in 2006. Since 2007, this percentage has steadily increased from 31 percent to 37 percent in 2011" (Aud et al., 2012, p. 28). In addition to educational disparities, lower socioeconomic status can have a significant impact on obesity and obesity-related ailments and conditions within families.

Increasingly common in urban communities are overweight and obese youth. National trend data for the past 50 years show overweight and obesity of youth has increased steadily in the United States (Crespo & Arbesman, 2003). Tellingly, Black, Hispanic, and American Indian youth are more likely to be overweight or obese compared to White peers (Wechsler, McKenna, Lee, & Dietz, 2004). In addition to concerns about their physical health, youth who are overweight or obese may struggle with social and psychological issues. It is not uncommon for youth who are overweight or obese to be targets of relentless teasing with fat jokes, bullying, and even threats with bodily harm (Li, Rukavina, & Wright, 2012). These youth may turn to unhealthy snacks as a source of comforting. Taken together, physical inactivity, poor dietary habits, and childhood obesity appear to have an adverse effect on academic performance (Datar, Sturm, & Magnabosco, 2004; Li et al., 2012). More forcefully, Basch (2011b) said, "physical inactivity is highly and disproportionately prevalent among school-aged urban minority youth, has a negative impact on academic achievement through its effects on cognition" (p. 626). Poor eating habits combined with low levels of physical activity are cause for concern with many students in urban schools. Schools should provide students with information on proper nutrition and making good dietary choices to promote healthier lifestyles (Hodge et al. 2012).

Environment—the built environment can contribute to an increase or decrease in obesity rates. For instance, urban neighborhoods that include commercial and retail stores, recreational destinations, and interconnectivity between places may provide increased access to physical activity opportunities and thereby help decrease obesity rates. For some families, however, their physical activity behaviors are hindered by concerns about safety in the communities in which they live. Parents may be reluctant to send their children outside to play—or even let them walk to school—if the community is unsafe. Contrasting this, King et al. (2006) found that those (mostly Black and White women) perceiving the community as generally safe reported more minutes of moderate to vigorous physical activity compared with those reporting their community as less safe.

It is troubling, yet reality, that youth in urban cities are likely to witness or even engage in high-risk behaviors such as smoking cigarettes, drinking alcohol beverages, or using illegal drugs (Atav & Spencer, 2002). They have limited access to healthier food choices as well, which can contribute to weight gain (Galvez et al., 2009). High-poverty communities are often food deserts, in which healthy, reasonably priced food is unavailable within walking distance or on a bus route. Instead convenience stores, fast-food restaurants, and liquor stores are very accessible within urban perimeters (Galvez et al., 2009; Hearst, Fulkerson, Maldonado-Molina, Perry, & Komro, 2007; Lucan, Barg, & Long, 2010). Disconcerting as well, access to quality health care services is limited in these areas (Harris & Mueller, 2013).

Genetics—a greater risk of obesity has been found in youth of obese/overweight parents. Empirical studies indicate that genetic heredity (e.g., adiposity or body fat) accounts for obesity in 25–40% of individuals who experience it, and researchers believe that some youth are predisposed to overweight or obesity status. In addition to environmental, social, and economic factors, it is argued that genetic factors also influence physical activity behaviors (Choh et al., 2008; Pérusse et al., 1989). Choh et al. (2008) asserted that sport and leisure physical activity are significantly influenced by genetic factors such as adiposity. There also appear to be strong associations between adiposity, obesity, and health conditions such as asthma (Fenger et al., 2012). Genetic predispositions toward behavioral tendencies such as physical activity versus inactivity require additional empirical analyses. In some cases, however, individuals may need medication to stabilize and control health conditions such as asthma.

Physical Education in Urban America

In urban schools, physical education teachers are responsible for helping students from economically, ethnically, culturally, and linguistically diverse communities become physically literate. But it is not uncommon for students to experience inadequate and marginalized physical education programs at urban schools (Ward & O'Sullivan, 2006). Commonly, physical education teachers in urban schools face such issues as (a) poor facilities and equipment shortages; (b) disruptive, disengaged, and defiant students; and (c) inadequate professional preparation and unsupportive administrators (McCaughtry, Barnard, Martin, Shen, & Hodges Kulinna, 2006). These challenges tend to adversely affect the quality of physical education programs in urban schools. Not surprisingly, there is strong advocacy for addressing urban challenges. This must include reevaluation of school physical education policies and practices to help address health and wellness issues linked to sedentary lifestyles, poor nutrition, and limited physical activity (Lounsbery et al., 2013).

Physical education advocacy is also given in the 2012 *Shape of the Nation Report,* which was released jointly by the NASPE and the American Heart Association. NASPE's position is "that every child in the U.S. deserves a quality physical education and needs physical activity, whether that activity occurs within a formal program or is outside the classroom at recess, through intramurals or in recreational play" (NASPE and American Heart Association, 2012, p. 3). Recently, First Lady Michele Obama launched the *Let's Move!—Active School* initiative to promote a higher level of physical activity in schools through physical education and active engagement before, during, and after school (www.letsmove.gov). Further, the enactment of Goals 2000: Educate America Act (Public Law 103–227) promotes a comprehensive approach to education. Of particular relevancy here, Goal Three of the Educate America Act specifies that all students will have access to physical education and health education to ensure they are fit and healthy (U.S. Congress, 1994). For that purpose and more, physical education teachers should structure their curricula and pedagogies around national standards. NASPE (2004) provides six national standards for physical education. These standards and essential components of a comprehensive physical education program are presented in Table 3.1.

Table 3.1 NASPE Content Standards and Essential Components of a Comprehensive Physical Education (PE) Program

*NASPE Content Standards**	
Standard 1	Demonstrates competency in motor skills and movement patterns needed to perform a variety of physical activities.
Standard 2	Demonstrates understanding of movement concepts, principles, strategies, and tactics as they apply to the learning and performance of physical activities.
Standard 3	Participates regularly in physical activity.
Standard 4	Achieves and maintains a health-enhancing level of physical fitness.
Standard 5	Exhibits responsible personal and social behavior that respects self and others in physical activity settings.
Standard 6	Values physical activity for health, enjoyment, challenge, self-expression, and/or social interaction.
*Components of a Comprehensive PE Program***	
Component 1	Is organized around content standards that offer direction and continuity to instruction and evaluation.
Component 2	Is student centered and based on the developmental urges, cultures, tendencies, and interests of students.
Component 3	Has physical activity and motor-skill development at its core.
Component 4	Teaches management skills and self-discipline.
Component 5	Emphasizes inclusion of all students.
Component 6	Emphasizes instruction focused on the process of learning rather than performance outcomes.
Component 7	Teaches lifetime activities that students can use to promote their health and personal values.
Component 8	Teaches cooperative and responsibility skills and helps students develop sensitivity to multiple diversities.

*Taken from NASPE (2004, p. iv). **Adapted from Darst and Pangrazi (2006, p. 2).

Most states mandate that students at all school levels must take some type of physical education. Still, there is considerable variability across school districts for time (minutes) required in physical education per week at the different school levels (NASPE and American Heart Association, 2012). More effort is needed to ensure that students are enrolled in physical education rather than being exempted from it simply because they participate in athletic events or they are members of a school's marching band as is common today. The enactment of the Local School Wellness Policy (U.S. Department of Agriculture, 2011) encourages schools to include supplementary nutrition and physical activity opportunities for students. In a survey study, which included the East, Midwest, and West regions of the United States, Lounsbery et al. (2013) found that elementary schools provide about 63 minutes per week of physical education with a range of 30 to 250 minutes per week. Nationally, across all 50 states and the District of Columbia, the required minutes per week of physical education ranges from 0 to 150 minutes or more at the elementary level, 0 to 225 minutes or more at the middle/junior high school level, and 0 to 225 minutes or more at the high school level (NASPE and American Heart Association, 2012). Physical education programs should more consistently provide students with opportunities and ample time for physical activity through a variety of experiences.

The need for regular moderate to vigorous physical activity for all youth in the *Healthy People 2010* and *2020* reports (CDC, 2006a; U.S. Department of Health and Human Services, 2000, 2010b) provide strong advocacy as well for physical education. The reports specify that regular moderate to vigorous physical activity can benefit all individuals and that physical activity can enhance stamina, muscular strength, and quality of life by improving the ability to perform activities of daily living. This is especially important for youth with low fitness levels. Physical activity experiences should be provided in physical education programs by culturally competent teachers. Culturally competent teachers can more justly serve students in urban schools. Yet physical education teachers have self-reported low to modest levels of cultural competency in working in diverse settings (Harrison, Carson, & Burden, 2010). As findings from studies confirm, physical education teachers generally value student diversity, but tend to struggle or fail to implement culturally responsive pedagogies (Columna, Foley, & Lytle, 2010; Harrison et al., 2010). Harrison and colleagues (2010) asserted that to ensure equitable opportunity for student success, "it is important to prepare teachers by requiring a broad base of cultural knowledge and culturally responsive teaching strategies" (p. 194). For instance, it is important that teacher candidates have opportunities for student teaching at urban schools to identify issues, address problems, reflect, and think critically about what cultural competency means in teaching students from diverse communities (Columna et al., 2010; Harrison et al., 2010).

School-Wide Considerations

Urban schools should address health, nutrition, and physical activity issues to benefit students and their communities. This starts as basic as critically reflecting on the types of foods they serve, the amount of physical activity they provide, and how they build awareness of healthy eating habits and the importance of increased physical activity for all students. To those aims, comprehensive school health and physical education programs are necessary. Table 3.2 presents strategies that schools might implement in promoting proper dietary habits and ensuring students participate in moderate to vigorous physical activity daily.

Physical education teachers should also reflect on their pedagogies in working with students who are overweight or obese, including those with mobility disability and/or who have other disabling health conditions such as severe asthma.

Table 3.2 Coordinated School Health and Physical Education Programs to Combat Obesity

Programmatic Strategies
1 Implement a coordinated school health program. A coordinated school health program integrates eight components to improve students' health awareness and behaviors: (a) health education; (b) physical education; (c) health services; (d) nutrition services; (e) counseling, psychological and social services; (f) health school environment; (g) health promotion for staff; and (h) family and community involvement.
2 Designate a school health coordinator to direct and monitor nutritional values and foods sources and to work collaboratively with the physical educators to ensure that health-related physical activity and fitness programs are provided and strengthened.
3 Assess the school's health policies and programs and develop a plan for improvement.
4 Implement a quality health promotion program for school staff.
5 Implement a high-quality course of study in health education.
6 Implement a high-quality course of study in physical education. For students with disabilities and those who are obese, a caring, nurturing, and supportive physical education teacher can increase their motivation to become physically active.
7 Implement quality school meals and work to ensure that students have access to appealing, healthy choices in foods and beverages outside of the school meals program.
8 Educate students and their families about physical activity and nutrition.

Note: Adapted from Hodge et al. (2012) and Wechsler, McKenna, Lee, and Dietz (2004).

Teaching Considerations

For a student who is obese with severe asthma, for example, not all moderate to vigorous physical activities (e.g., distance running) are suitable (Hodge et al., 2012). Excess body weight, physical illness, and social and psychological factors such as poor self-image are barriers to healthy living. In such cases, an individualized health and physical education plan should be implemented (Hodge et al., 2012). Before creating such a plan, a medical exam is necessary to determine if other health-related conditions are present such as diabetes and/or high blood pressure. The CDC (2006b) has identified strategies for schools and districts to consider in supporting students with asthma within a coordinated school health program. This document is available at www.cdc.gov/HealthyYouth/asthma/pdf/strategies.pdf. Moreover, students who are obese should generally avoid contraindicated activities such as (a) lifting their own weight in such activities as chinning and rope climbing, (b) lifting heavy weights, (c) partner tumbling stunts, and (d) excessive running (Hodge et al., 2012).

In teaching youth who are obese, physical education teachers must have an awareness and competence in promoting physical activity, proper diet management and nutrition, and behavior modification. *Healthy People 2020* guidelines recommend that students engage in at least 60 minutes of moderate to vigorous physical activity daily (U.S. Department of Health and Human Services, 2010b). However, with students who are obese such a recommendation must be approached with reasonable caution. One consideration is using an individualized physical education program with such students. Hodge and colleagues (2012) insisted that such a "program should address burning fat, increasing energy expenditure, and even weight loss management" (p. 233). However, prolonged fasting to lose weight and excessive caloric restrictions are not advisable for youth because poor eating habits are established during childhood. Not only are these approaches psychologically stressful, but also they can adversely affect growth and the youth's beliefs about proper eating behaviors. In all cases, consideration and respect must be afforded families and their youth who fast because of religious reasons, however. A balanced diet with moderate caloric restriction, especially reduced dietary fat intake, is important to addressing obesity status. Important dietary guidelines are provided by the U.S. Department of Agriculture and can be found at www.choosemyplate.gov.

For a student who has limited mobility and health concerns due to excessive weight, a behavior modification plan is an important consideration as well. Chambliss (2004) proposed the following four-phase approach to behavioral modification for combating overweight/obesity:

1. Phase I (*Assessment*) provides the foundation for a safe and personalized intervention. Such assessment and evaluation includes medical and psychiatric history, energy balance, and psychosocial factors.
2. Phase II is the *acute phase of treatment* involving multiple treatment modalities as determined by the evaluation of student needs and attributes. The acute phase promotes a reduced-calorie diet, exercise, and behavioral skills training.
3. Phase III is the *transition phase* in which the student is given greater responsibility for his/her goals and treatment plan in preparation for the final phase. The student develops long-term strategies, focuses on the relapse prevention, and development of long-term caloric and exercise goals.
4. Phase IV (*Maintenance*) occurs when behaviors are incorporated as a lifestyle; weight management depends on continued application of eating and physical activity behaviors; implement acute phase strategies if the student regains weight. (pp. 143–145)

The proportion of youth in urban dwellings, particularly poor, and mostly Black and Hispanic, who are overweight or obese and physically inactive is a national health concern. In a recent editorial, Katz (2013) phrased it quite well that obesity is "always a proxy measure and, for that matter, health is a proxy measure, too. Health only matters because it changes the quality of our lives. It is really living that matters. Healthy people live better. Healthy people have more fun!" (p. 2).

Conclusion

Health and physical education professionals as change agents can promote the enactment and implementation of school policies that enhance culturally relevant opportunities for students to live healthier. Urban schools and communities need health and physical activity programs designed for youth to participate in before, during, and after school hours. Programs that reinforce proper dietary habits and physical activity during recess, lunch, and after school will also increase the likelihood of youth engaging in physical activities regularly, while reducing the risks of overweight and obesity.

Notes

1. In this chapter, we give only a brief account of historical milestones. Many other scholars have discussed in greater detail key historical events in the profession (Jurkechová, Vlček, & Bartík, 2011; Kelly & Melograno, 2004; Lumpkin, 2011; Massengale & Swanson, 1997; Siedentop, 2006; Vlček, 2011; Zeigler, 2005).
2. For informed discourse about these and other models used in physical education, we recommend: Lund and Tannehill's (2010) book, *Standards-Based Physical Education Curriculum Development;* and Dyson, Griffin, and Hastie's (2004) article, "Sport Education, Tactical Games, and Cooperative Learning: Theoretical and Pedagogical Considerations."

3. Many theories situate research and practice in physical education, physical activity, and health. These include the social-cognitive model, the transtheoretical model, theory of planned behavior, and social ecological approaches. For informed dialogue about these theoretical models, we recommend works by Ajzen (1991), Bandura (1986), Cardinal, Engels, and Zhu (1998), Foley et al. (2008), Golden and Earp (2012), Langille and Rodgers (2010), Marcus and Simkin (1994), Wang, Castelli, Liu, Bian, and Tan (2010).
4. Scholarly works cited in this chapter were selected based on their relevancy and informed discourse with priority given to up-to-date research associated with health, nutrition, and physical activity in the United States, and in particular, given to urban populations and areas.

References

Ajzen, I. (1991). The theory of planned behavior. *Organizational Behavior and Human Decision Process, 50,* 179–211.

Amusa, L.O., Toriola, A.L., & Goon, D.T. (2012). Youth, physical activity and leisure education: Need for a paradigm shift. *African Journal for Physical, Health Education, Recreation and Dance, 18*(4:2), 992–1006.

Andrade, A.D., & Dean, E. (2008). Aligning physical therapy practice with Brazil's leading health priorities: A "call to action" in the 21st century. Direcionando a prática da Fisioterapia com as principais prioridades de Saúde no Brasil: Uma "chamada para ação" no Século XXI. *Revista Brasileira de Fisioterapia, 12*(4), 260–267.

Annesi, J.J., Faigenbaum, A.D., Westcott, W.L., & Smith, A.E. (2008). Relations of self-appraisal and mood changes with voluntary physical activity changes in African American preadolescents in an after-school care intervention. *Journal of Sports Science and Medicine,* 7, 260–268.

Atav, S., & Spencer, G.A. (2002). Health risk behaviors among adolescents attending rural, suburban, and urban schools: A comparative study. *Family & Community Health, 25*(2), 53–64.

Aud, S., Hussar, W., Johnson, F., Kena, G., Roth, E., Manning, E., Wang, X., & Zhang, J. (2012). *The Condition of Education 2012* (NCES 2012–045). United States Department of Education, National Center for Education Statistics. Washington, DC. Retrieved from http://nces.ed.gov/pubsearch

Bandura, A. (1986). *Social foundations of thought and actions: A social-cognitive theory.* Englewood Cliffs, NJ: Prentice-Hall.

Banks, J.A. (2006). Democracy, diversity, and social justice: Educating citizens for the public interest in a global age. In G. Ladson-Billings, & W.F. Tate (Eds.), *Education research in the public interest: Social justice, action, and policy* (pp. 141–157). New York, NY: Teachers College Press.

Barr-Anderson, D.J., Adams-Wynn, A.W., DiSantis, K.I., & Kumanyika, S. (2013). Family-focused physical activity, diet and obesity interventions in African-American girls: A systematic review. *Obesity Reviews, 14*(1), 29–51.

Basch, C.E. (2011a). Asthma and the achievement gap among urban minority youth. *Journal of School Health, 81*(10), 606–613.

Basch, C.E. (2011b). Physical activity and the achievement gap among urban minority youth. *Journal of School Health, 81*(10), 626–634.

Blanchett, W.J., Mumford, V., & Beachum, F. (2005). Urban school failure and disproportionality in a post-*Brown* era: Benign neglect of the constitutional rights of students of color. *Remedial and Special Education, 26*(2), 70–81.

Bopp, M., Lattimore, D., Wilcox, S., Laken, M., McClorin, L., Swinton, R., Gethers, O., & Bryant, D. (2007). Understanding physical activity participation in members of an African American church: A qualitative study. *Health Education Research, 22*(6), 815–826.

Caprio, S., Daniels, S.R., Drewnowski, A., Kaufman, F.R., Palinkas, L.A., Rosenbloom, A.L., & Schwimmer, J.B. (2008). *Influence of race, ethnicity, and culture on childhood obesity: Implications for prevention and treatment* (Vol. 16, pp. 2566–2577). Presented at the Obesity Conference (Silver Spring, MD). doi:10.1038/oby.2008.398

Cardinal, B.J., Engels, H.J., & Zhu, W. (1998). Application of the transtheoretical model of behavior change to preadolescents' physical activity and exercise behavior. *Pediatric Exercise Science, 10,* 69–80.

Carter, B., & Fenton, S. (2009). Not thinking ethnicity: A critique of the ethnicity paradigm in an over-ethnicised sociology. *Journal for the Theory of Social Behaviour, 40*(1), 1–18.

Centers for Disease Control and Prevention. (2006a). *Disability and health state chartbook: Profiles of health for adults with disabilities.* Atlanta, GA: Author.

Centers for Disease Control and Prevention. (2006b). *Strategies for addressing asthma within a coordinated school health program, with updated resources.* Atlanta, GA: Centers for Disease Control and Prevention, National Center for Chronic Disease Prevention and Health Promotion. Retrieved from http://www.cdc.gov/

Centers for Disease Control and Prevention. (2011a). *Dietary behaviors.* Retrieved from http://www.cdc.gov/

Centers for Disease Control and Prevention. (2011b). *How much physical activity do children need?* Retrieved from http://www.cdc.gov/

Centers for Disease Control and Prevention. (2012). *U.S. physical activity statistics: 2008 state demographic data comparison.* Retrieved from http://www.cdc.gov/

Chambliss, H.O. (2004). Behavioral approaches to obesity treatment. *Quest, 56,* 142–149.

Choh, A.C., Demerath, E.W., Lee, M., Williams, K.D., Towne, B., Siervogel, R.M., Cole, S.A., & Czerwinski, S.A. (2008). Genetic analysis of self-reported physical activity and adiposity: The Southwest Ohio Family Study. *Public Health Nutrition, 12*(8), 1052–1060.

Columna, L., Foley, J.T., & Lytle, R.K. (2010). Physical education teachers' and teacher candidates' attitudes toward cultural pluralism. *Journal of Teaching in Physical Education, 29,* 295–311.

Conn, K.M., Hernandez, T., Puthoor, P., Fagnano, M., & Halterman, J.S. (2009). Screen time use among urban children with asthma. *Academic Pediatrics, 9*(1), 60–63.

Crawford, P.B., Story, M., Wang, M.C., Ritchie, L.D., & Sabry, Z.I. (2001). Ethnic issues in the epidemiology of childhood obesity. *Pediatric Clinics of North America, 48*(4), 855–878.

Cremin, L.A. (1970). *American education: The colonial experience, 1607–1783.* New York, NY: Harper & Row.

Crespo, C.J., & Arbesman, J. (2003). Obesity in the United States. *Physician and Sports Medicine, 31*(11), 486–490.

Darst, P.W., & Pangrazi, R.P. (2006). *Dynamic physical education for secondary school students* (5th ed.). San Francisco, CA: Pearson Education.

Datar, A., Sturm, R., & Magnabosco, J.L. (2004). Childhood overweight and academic performance: National Study of Kindergartners and First-Graders. *Obesity Research, 12*(1), 58–68.

Dionise, J., & Pompa, F. (2012, September 19). Obesity on the rise. A new study projects that the national obesity rate is headed higher for every state. *USA Today,* 1A.

Dowda, M., Pate, R.R., Felton, G., Saunders, T., Ward, D., & Dishman, R.K. (2004). Physical activities and sedentary pursuits in African Americans and Caucasian girls. *Research Quarterly for Exercise and Sport, 75*(4), 352–360.

Dyson, B., Griffin, L.L., & Hastie, P. (2004). Sport education, tactical games, and cooperative learning: Theoretical and pedagogical considerations. *Quest, 56,* 226–240.

Ewing, R., Schmid, T., Killingsworth, R., Zlot, A., & Raudenbush, S. (2003). Relationship between urban sprawl and physical activity, obesity, and morbidity. *American Journal of Health Promotion, 18,* 47–57.

Fenger, R.V., Gonzalez-Quintela, A., Vidal, C., Gude, F., Husemoen, L.L., Aadahl, M., Berg, N.D., & Linneberg, A. (2012). Exploring the obesity-asthma link: Do all types of adiposity increase the risk of asthma? *Clinical & Experimental Allergy, 42,* 1237–1245.

Fisher, J.O., Arreola, A., Birch, L.L., & Rolls, B.J. (2007). Portion size effects on daily energy intake in low-income Hispanic and African American children and their mothers. *American Journal of Clinical Nutrition, 86,* 1709–1716.

Flegal, K.M., Carroll, M.D., Ogden, C.L., & Curtin, L.R. (2010). Prevalence and trends in obesity among U.S. adults, 1999–2008. *Journal of the American Medical Association, 303*(3), 235–241.

Floyd, M.F., Spengler, J.O., Maddock, J.E., Gobster, P.H., & Suau, L. (2008). Environmental and social correlates of physical activity in neighborhood parks: An observational study in Tampa and Chicago. *Leisure Sciences, 30,* 360–375.

Fogelholm, M., & van Marken Lichtenbelt, W. (1997). Comparison of body composition methods: A literature analysis. *European Journal of Clinical Nutrition, 51,* 495–503.

Foley, L., Prapavessis, H., Maddison, R., Burke, S., McGowan, E., & Gillanders, L. (2008). Predicting physical activity intention and behavior in school-age children. *Pediatric Exercise Science, 20,* 342–356.

Franklin, V.P. (2003). Education in urban communities in the United States: Exploring the legacy of Lawrence A. Cremin. *Paedagogica Historica, 39*(1/2), 153–163.

Galal, O., Fahmy, S., Lashine, S., Abdel-Fattah, N., & Galal, M. (2011). Systemic hypertension and associated factors in school adolescents. *International Journal of Collaborative Research on Internal Medicine & Public Health, 3*(2), 167–176.

Galvez, M.P., Hong, L., Choi, E., Liao, L., Godhold, J., & Brenner, B. (2009). Childhood obesity and neighborhood food-store availability in an inner-city community. *Academic Pediatrics, 9*(5), 339–343.

Golden, S.D., & Earp, J.A.L. (2012). Social ecological approaches to individuals and their contexts: Twenty years of health education and behavior health promotion interventions. *Health Education & Behavior, 39*(3), 364–372.

Gordon-Larsen, P., Adair, L.S., & Popkin, B.M. (2002). Ethnic differences in physical activity and inactivity patterns and overweight status. *Obesity Research, 10*(3), 141–149.

Gordon-Larsen, P., Griffiths, P., Bentley, M.E., Ward, D.S., Kelsey, K., Shields, K., & Ammerman, A. (2004). Barriers to physical activity: Qualitative data on caregiver–daughter perceptions and practices. *American Journal of Preventive Medicine, 27*(3), 218–223.

Harris, J.K., & Mueller, N.L. (2013). Policy activity and policy adoption in rural, suburban, and urban local health departments. *Journal of Public Health Management and Practice, 19*(2), E1–E8.

Harris, K.M., Gordon-Larsen, P., Chantala, K., & Udry, J.R. (2006). Longitudinal trends in race/ethnic disparities in leading health indicators from adolescence to young adulthood. *Archives of Pediatrics & Adolescent Medicine, 160*(1), 74–81.

Harrison, L., Jr., Carson, R.L., & Burden, J., Jr. (2010). Physical education teachers' cultural competency. *Journal of Teaching in Physical Education, 29,* 184–198.

Hastie, P.A., Martin, E., & Buchanan, A.M. (2013). Stepping out of the norm: An examination of praxis for a culturally-relevant pedagogy for African-American children. *Journal of Curriculum Studies, 38*(3), 293–306.

Hearst, M.O., Fulkerson, J.A., Maldonado-Molina, M.M., Perry, C.L., & Komro, K.A. (2007). Who needs liquor stores when parents will do? The importance of social sources of alcohol among young urban teens. *Preventive Medicine, 44*(6), 471–476.

Hein, F.V., & Ryan, A.J. (1960). The contributions of physical activity to physical health. *Research Quarterly, 31*(2), 263–285.

Heron, M. (2012). Deaths: Leading causes for 2009. *National Vital Statistics Reports, 61*(7). Hyattsville, MD: National Center for Health Statistics.

Hodge, S.R., Lieberman, L.J., & Murata, N.M. (2012). *Essentials of teaching adapted physical education: Diversity, culture, and inclusion.* Scottsdale, AZ: Holcomb Hathaway.

Hodges Kulinna, P., McCaughtry, N., Cothran, D., & Martin, J. (2006). What do urban/inner-city physical education teachers teach? A contextual analysis of one elementary/primary school district. *Physical Education and Sport Pedagogy, 11*(1), 45–68.

Imms, C. (2008). Children with cerebral palsy participate: A review of the literature. *Disability and Rehabilitation, 30,* 1867–1884. doi:10.1080/09638280701673542

Individuals with Disabilities Education Improvement Act. (2004). Public Law 108–446, 118 STAT. 2647 [H.R. 1350], December 3, 2004.

Jemal, A., Thun, M.J., Ward, E.E., Henley, J., Cokkinides, V.E., & Murray, T.E. (2008). Mortality from leading causes by education and race in the United States, 2001. *American Journal of Preventive Medicine, 34*(1), 1–8.

Jurkechová, M., Vlček, P., & Bartík, P. (2011). Development of school physical education in Slovakia and in the USA. *Acta Facultatis Educationis Physicae Universitatis Comenianae, 51*(1), 17–30.

Katz, D.L. (2013). Childhood obesity trends in 2013: Mind, matter, and message. *Childhood Obesity, 9*(1), 1–2.

Kelly, L., & Melograno, V. (2004). *Developing the physical education curriculum: An achievement based approach*. Champaign, IL: Human Kinetics.

Keppel, K.G., Pearcy, J.N., & Heron, M.P. (2010). Is there progress toward eliminating racial/ethnic disparities in the leading causes of death? *Public Health Reports, 125,* 689–697.

King, A.C., Toobert, D., Ahn, D., Resnicow, K., Coday, M., Riebe, D., Garber, C.E., Hurtz, S., Morton, J., & Sallis, J.F. (2006). Perceived environments as physical activity correlates and moderators of intervention in five studies. *American Journal of Health Promotion, 21*(1), 21–35.

Kohl, H.W., & Hobbs, K.E. (1998). Development of physical activity behaviors among children and adolescents. *Pediatrics, 101*(3) Supplement, 549–554.

Krenitsky-Korn, S. (2011). High school students with asthma: Attitudes about school health, absenteeism, and its impact on academic achievement. *Pediatric Nursing, 37*(2), 61–68.

Langille, J.D., & Rodgers, W.M. (2010). Exploring the influence of a social ecological model on school-based physical activity. *Health Education & Behavior, 37*(6), 879–894.

Lawson, H.A. (2005). Empowering people, facilitating community development, and contributing to sustainable development: The social work of sport, exercise, and physical education programs. *Sport, Education and Society, 10*(1), 135–160.

Li, W., Rukavina, P., & Wright, P. (2012). Coping against weight-related teasing among adolescents perceived to be overweight or obese in urban physical education. *Journal of Teaching in Physical Education, 31,* 182–199.

Longmuir, P.E., & Bar-Or, O. (2000). Factors influencing the physical activity levels of youth with physical and sensory disabilities. *Adapted Physical Activity Quarterly, 17,* 40–54.

Lounsbery, M.F., McKenzie, T.L., Morrow, J.R., Jr., Monnat, S.M., & Holt, K.A. (2013). District and school physical education policies: Implications for physical education and recess time. *Annals of Behavior Medicine, 45*(Suppl. 1), S131–S141.

Lucan, S.C., Barg, F.K., & Long, J.A. (2010). Promoters and barriers to fruit, vegetable, and fast-food consumption among urban, low-income African Americans—A qualitative approach. *American Journal of Public Health, 100*(4), 631–635.

Lumpkin, A. (2011). *Introduction to physical education, exercise science, and sport studies.* New York, NY: McGraw-Hill.

Lund, J., & Tannehill, D. (Eds.). (2010). *Standards-based physical education curriculum development* (2nd ed.). Sudbury, MA: Jones and Bartlett.

Malik, V.S., Schulze, M.B., & Hu, F.B. (2006). Intake of sugar-sweetened beverages and weight gain: A systemic review. *American Journal of Clinical Nutrition, 84,* 274–288.

Marcus, B.H., & Simkin, L.R. (1994). The transtheoretical model: Applications to exercise behavior. *Medicine and Science in Sports and Exercise, 26,* 1400–1404.

Massengale, J., & Swanson, R. (Eds.). (1997). *The history of exercise and sport science.* Champaign, IL: Human Kinetics.

McCaughtry, N., Barnard, S., Martin, J., Shen, B., & Hodges Kulinna, P. (2006). Teachers' perspectives on the challenges of teaching physical education in urban schools: The student emotional filter. *Research Quarterly for Exercise and Sport,* 77(4), 486–497.

McGinn, A.P., Evenson, K.R., Herring, A.H., Huston, S.L., & Rodriguez, D.A. (2008). The association of perceived and objectively measured crime with physical activity: A cross-sectional analysis. *Journal of Physical Activity and Health, 5,* 117–131.

Miniño, A., & Murphy, S. (2012). *Death in the United States, 2010.* NCHS Data Brief, No 99. Hyattsville, MD: National Center for Health Statistics.

Morello, M.I., Madanat, H., Crespo, N.C., Lemus, H., & Elder, J. (2012). Associations among parent acculturation, child BMI, and child fruit and vegetable consumption in a Hispanic sample. *Journal of Immigrant and Minority Health, 14*(6), 1023–1029.

National Association for Sport and Physical Education. (1995). *Moving into the future: National standards for physical education—A guide to content and assessment*. Reston, VA: Author.

National Association for Sport and Physical Education. (2004). *Moving into the future: National standards for physical education* (2nd ed.). Reston, VA: Author.

National Association for Sport and Physical Education. (2013). *NASPE strategic plan 2010–2012*. American Alliance for Health, Physical Education, Recreation and Dance. Retrieved from http://www.aahperd.org/naspe/

National Association for Sport and Physical Education and American Heart Association. (2012). *2012 Shape of the Nation Report: Status of physical education in the USA*. Reston, VA: American Alliance for Health, Physical Education, Recreation and Dance.

Ogden, C.L., Carroll, M.D., Curtin, L.R., Lamb, M.M., & Flegal, K.M. (2010). Prevalence of high body mass index in US children and adolescents, 2007–2008. *Journal of the American Medical Association, 303*(3), 242–249.

Olshansky, S. J., Passaro, D. J., Hershow, R. C., Layden, J., Carnes, B. A., Brody, J., Hayflick, L., Butler, R. N., Allison, D. B., & Ludwig, D. S. (2012). A potential decline in life expectancy in the United States in the 21st century. *New England Journal of Medicine, 352*(11), 1138–1145.

Ortiz-Castillo, E. (2011). *The physical activity patterns and factors influencing physical activity participation among adolescents with physical disabilities in urban communities* (Unpublished doctoral dissertation). The Ohio State University, Columbus.

Peeters, A., Barendregt, J. J., Willekens, F., Mackenbach, J. P., Mamun, A. A., & Bonneux, L. (2003). Obesity in adulthood and its consequences for life expectancy: A life-table analysis. *Annals of Internal Medicine, 138*(1), 24–32.

Pérusse, L., Tremblay, A., LeBlanc, C., & Bouchard, C. (1989). Genetic and environmental influences on level of habitual physical activity and exercise participation. *American Journal of Epidemiology, 129*(5), 1012–1022.

Peterson, L.E., & Litaker, D.G. (2010). County-level poverty is equally associated with unmet health care needs in rural and urban settings. *Journal of Rural Health, 26*, 373–382.

RAND Corporation. (2004). *Obesity and disability: The shape of things to come*. Retrieved from http://www.rand.org/pubs/research_briefs/RB9043/index/html

Rimmer, J.H., Riley, B., Wang, E., Rauworth, A., & Jurkowski, J. (2004). Physical activity participation among persons with disabilities: Barriers and facilitators. *American Journal of Preventive Medicine, 26*, 419–425.

Rimmer, J.H., & Rowland, J.L. (2008). Physical activity for youth with disabilities: A critical need in an underserved population. *Developmental Neurorehabilitation, 11*, 141–148.

Rossen, L.M., Pollack, K.M., Curriero, F.C., Shields, T.M., Smart, M.J., Furr-Holden, C.D.M., & Cooley-Strickland, M. (2011). Neighborhood incivilities, perceived neighborhood safety, and walking to school among urban-dwelling children. *Journal of Physical Activity and Health, 8*, 262–271.

Salgado de Snyder, V.N., Friel, S., Fotso, J.C., Khadr, Z., Meresman, S., Monge, P., & Patil-Deshmukh, A. (2011). Social conditions and urban health inequities: Realities, challenges and opportunities to transform the urban landscape through research and action. *Journal of Urban Health: Bulletin of the New York Academy of Medicine, 88*(6), 1183–1193.

Saunders, R.P., Pate, R.R., Felton, G., Dowda, M., Weinrich, M.C., Ward, D.S., Parsons, M.A., & Baranowski, T. (1997). Development of questionnaires to measure psychosocial influences on children's physical activity. *Preventive Medicine, 26*, 241–247.

Siedentop, D. (2006). *Introduction to physical education, fitness, and sport* (5th ed.). New York, NY: McGraw-Hill.

Sinha, R., Fisch, G., Teague, B., Tamborlane, W. V., Banyas, B., Allen, K., Savoye, M., Rieger, V., Taksali, S., Barbetta, G., Sherwin, R. S., & Caprio, S. (2011). Prevalence of impaired glucose tolerance among children and adolescents with marked obesity. *New England Journal of Medicine, 346*(11), 802–810.

Sisson, S.B., Shay, C.M., Broyles, S.T., & Leyva, M. (2012). Television-viewing time and dietary quality among U.S. children and adults. *American Journal of Preventive Medicine, 43*(2), 196–200.

Skala, K.A., Springer, A.E., Sharma, S.V., Hoelscher, D.M., & Kelder, S.H. (2012). Environmental characteristics and student physical activity in PE class: Findings from two large urban areas of Texas. *Journal of Physical Activity and Health, 9*(4), 481–491.

Strong, W. B., Malina, R. M., Blimkie, C. J. R., Daniels, S. R., Dishman, R. K., Gutin, B., Hergenroeder, A. C., Must, A., Nixon, P. A., Pivarnik, J. M., Rowland, T., Trost, S., & Trudeau, F. (2005). Evidence based physical activity for school-age youth. *Journal of Pediatrics, 146,* 732–737.

Swanson, C.B. (2009). *Cities in crisis 2009—Closing the graduation gap: Educational and economic conditions in America's largest cities.* Editorial Projects in Education Research Center. Bethesda, MD: Editorial Projects in Education, Inc.

Sweeney, N.M., Glaser, D., & Tedeschi, C. (2007). The eating and physical activity habits of inner-city adolescents. *Journal of Pediatric Health Care, 21,* 13–21.

Tanasescu, M., Ferris, A.M., Himmelgreen, D.A., Rodriguez, N., & Pérez-Escamilla, R. (2000). Biobehavioral factors are associated with obesity in Puerto Rican children. *Journal of Nutrition, 130,* 1734–1742.

Thompson, V.J., Baranowski, T., Cullen, K.W., Rittenberry, L., Baranowski, J., Taylor, W.C., & Nicklas, T. (2003). Influences on diet and physical activity among middle-class African American 8- to 10-year-old girls at risk of becoming obese. *Journal of Nutrition Education & Behavior, 35*(3), 115–123.

Timken, G.L., & Watson, D. (2010). Teaching all kids: Valuing students through culturally responsive and inclusive practice. In J. Lund & D. Tannehill (Eds.), *Standards-based physical education curriculum development* (2nd ed., pp. 122–153). Sudbury, MA: Jones and Bartlett.

Troiano, R.P., Berrigan, D., Dodd, K.W., Masse, L.C., Tilert, T., & McDowell, M. (2007). Physical activity in the United States measured by accelerometer. *Medicine & Science in Sports & Exercise, 40*(1), 181–188.

United States Congress. (1994). Goals 2000: Educate America Act (PL 103–227). Washington, DC: United States Congress.

United States Department of Agriculture. (2011). *Child nutrition reauthorization 2010: Local school wellness policies.* Retrieved from http://www.fns.usda.gov/cnd/Governance/Policy-Memos/2011/SP42–2011_os.pdf

United States Department of Education, Office of Special Education and Rehabilitative Services, Office of Special Education Programs. (2013). *Fiscal year 2013: Application for new grants under the Individuals with Disabilities Education Act (IDEA).* Washington, DC: Author.

United States Department of Health and Human Services. (2000). *Healthy people 2010: Understanding and improving health.* Washington, DC: U.S. Government Printing Office.

United States Department of Health and Human Services. (2008). *Physical activity guidelines for Americans.* Washington, DC: U.S. Government Printing Office.

United States Department of Health and Human Services. (2010a). *Dietary guidelines for Americans.* Retrieved from www.dietaryguidelines.gov

United States Department of Health and Human Services. (2010b). *Healthy people 2020: Improving the health of Americans.* Washington, DC: U.S. Government Printing Office.

United States Department of Health and Human Services. (2010c). *The Surgeon General's Vision for a Healthy and Fit Nation.* Rockville, MD: U.S. Department of Health and Human Services, Office of the Surgeon General.

Vigo-Valentín, A., Hodge, S.R., & Kozub, F.M. (2011). Adolescents' dietary habits, physical activity patterns, and weight status in Puerto Rico. *Childhood Obesity,* 7(6), 488–494.

Vlček, P. (2011). A comparison of physical education (PE) development in the Czech Republic, Germany, and the USA—A historical perspective. *Acta Universitatis Palackianae Olomucensis Gymnica, 41*(1), 51–59.

Wang, J., Castelli, D.M., Liu, W., Bian, W., & Tan, J. (2010). Re-conceptualizing physical education programs from an ecological perspective. *Asian Journal of Exercise & Sports Science,* 7(1), 43–53.

Wang, Y., & Beydoun, M.A. (2007). The obesity epidemic in the United States—Gender, age, socioeconomic, racial/ethnic, and geographic characteristics: A systematic review and meta-regression analysis. *Epidemiologic Reviews, 29*(1), 6–28.

Ward, P., & O'Sullivan, M. (2006). The context of urban settings. *Journal of Teaching in Physical Education, 25,* 348–362.

Wechsler, H., McKenna, M.L., Lee, S.M., & Dietz, W.H. (2004). Overweight among children and adolescents. *National Association of State Boards of Education, 5*(2), 4–12.

Wong, E., Stevenson, C., Backholer, K., Mannan, H., Pasupathi, K., Hodge, A., Freak-Poli, R., & Peeters, A. (2012). Adiposity measures as predictors of long-term physical disability. *Annals of Epidemiology, 22,* 710–716.

World Health Organization. (2010). *Global recommendations on physical activity for health.* Retrieved from http://whqlibdoc.who.int/publications/2010/9789241599979_eng.pdf

Zeigler, E. (2005). *History and status of American physical education and educational sport.* Victoria, BC: Trafford.

Zive, M.M., Berry, C.C., Sallis, J.F., Frank, G.C., & Nader, P.R. (2002). Tracking dietary intake in white and Mexican-American children from age 4 to 12 years. *Journal of the American Dietetic Association, 102,* 683–689.

Section II
Sociological Perspectives

4
Student Resilience in Urban America

Carla O'Connor, Jennifer Mueller & Alaina Neal

Scholars have characterized individuals as "resilient" when these individuals have succeeded despite risk and adversity (Masten, 2001; Schoon & Bynner, 2003; Werner & Smith, 1992). But how have scholars specifically made sense of resilience when the subject of study was school-aged children growing up in urban America? Our answer to this question constitutes the substance of this chapter. In addressing this question, we delineate how scholars have defined the success of urban youth designated as resilient and by implication what constitutes poor or maladaptive outcomes on the part of these youth. We also delineate how scholars have defined adversity (or risk) in urban contexts.

In documenting how scholars have characterized urban risk and resilience, we make evident how notions of risk and resilience have shifted over time and we illuminate the assumptions that undergird these shifting characterizations. We conclude the chapter by analyzing the promise and limitations of contemporary notions of urban student resilience as a referent for directing future research, and reconceptualizing student resilience in urban America. We discuss the implications for policy and practice that follow from our analysis. Our discussion begins by reporting on the origin of resilience as a concept and how these early examinations of resilience framed considerations of student resilience in urban settings.[1]

The Origin and Development of (Urban) Resilience as a Concept

Founded in the field of psychology, the earliest research on resilience treated resilience as a mundane social phenomenon that occurred under unremarkable circumstances and was evidenced in response to everyday challenges. The tenor of this early work is well illustrated by that of Lois Barclay Murphy and her colleagues who sought in the 1950s and 1960s to document among preschool children "sequences of behavior" that demonstrated "a loss of children's normal level of functioning and recovery to that level," and also examined "what babies and children did to prevent distress and disturbance," including "coping with all kinds of ordinary obstacles and challenges" (Murphy, 1974, pp. 85–86).

Beginning in the 1970s, psychologists and psychiatrists began studying resilience systematically, alternatively referring to resilient youth as invulnerable, invincible, or stress resistant.[2] In contrast to the work of Murphy and her colleagues, this work, which solidified resilience as a field of study, emphasized how resilience emerged under profound circumstances and in response to atypical challenges (Anthony, 1974; Garmezy, 1971, 1974; Murphy, 1974; Murphy & Moriarty, 1976; Rutter, 1979). Focusing first on the children of schizophrenics, scholars sought to understand why some of these children "remained inviolate to psychopathology" despite evidence that their parentage increased their statistical likelihood of experiencing mental disorder and other maladaptive outcomes (Garmezy, 1971, p. 101). And, like previous studies of resilience, this work was pursued under the "fundamental assumption that understanding how individuals overcome challenges to development and recover from trauma will reveal processes of adaptation that can guide intervention efforts with others at risk" (Masten, 1994, p. 3).

Scholars were similarly invested in studying individuals who had presumably defied the negative outcomes associated with perinatal (e.g., premature birth), psychosocial (e.g., childhood trauma, parental abuse and neglect), and environmental hazards (e.g., poverty; crime-ridden or violent neighborhoods; economic depression; institutional or foster care) (Masten, 1994, 2001; Maton, 2005; Werner & Smith, 1992). Much of this work was concerned with advancing theory on the etiology of psychopathologies and the generation of interventions aimed at protecting those believed to be most vulnerable to psychopathology (Cowen, Wyman, Work, & Iker, 1995; Luthar, 2006; Masten 2007).

Considerations of environmental hazards additionally yielded examinations of individuals who seemed insusceptible to or had been protected not only from psychological but especially social pathologies (e.g., delinquency, criminality) and evidenced productive mainstream or conventional outcomes (e.g., competitive academic achievement; high school and college completion; gainful employment) (e.g., Brooks-Gunn, Duncan, & Aber, 1997; Elder, 1974; Elder, van Nguyen, & Caspi 1985; Werner & Smith, 1982).[3] The study of environmental hazards gave way to the study of resilience in urban contexts.

As was the case with previous indices of risk, the presumed riskiness of urban environments was partly a statistical artifact. That is, urban residence was presumed "risky" in and of itself, due to the statuses and experiences that were more concentrated among urban populations (e.g., poverty, single-parent-headed households; being of African or Latino descent) and statistically correlated with negative life outcomes within and outside of school (e.g., low levels of academic achievement and educational attainment, high teenage pregnancy rates). By implication, resilient urban residents and the school-aged students amongst them did not evidence the undesired outcomes that provided the referent of the investigation. Instead, these students evidenced the positive pole of these outcomes (e.g., experienced high as opposed to low achievement; graduated from rather than dropped out of high school; had children as adults rather than as adolescents).

But to make full sense of how a statistical outcome gets rendered as negative versus positive or low versus high, we must simultaneously recognize the extent to which resilience is an "inferential concept" that rests on two key judgments (Masten, 2001). There is judgment with regard to what constitutes a good outcome; and this judgment is determined against a normative referent by which some outcome is assessed as good. Second, the good outcome must be evidenced against circumstances that are judged to derail its prospective manifestation (Masten, 1994, 2001). Here too there is a referent against which circumstances are judged as risky or as having the potential to derail good outcomes. For urban populations, the normative, although implicit, referent for both judgments is suburban (read White, middle-class) populations (DeHaan, Hawley, & Deal, 2013).

As such, when calculating the risk of urban contexts, researchers have relied on their own or other scholars' calculations of a broad range of social and educational statistics (e.g., crime, unemployment, graduation, and dropout rates) that distinguish suburban and urban settings at the aggregate level and situate urban (including schools) within closer proximity to the undesirable pole of these statistics compared to suburban settings. Otherwise, researchers have focused on Black, Brown, and economically disadvantaged youth who disproportionately reside in urban settings, and again relied on aggregate statistics in comparing them (again often implicitly) with middle class and white youth who disproportionately reside in suburban settings. Similar to the urban-suburban comparisons, Black, Brown, and economically disadvantaged youth were situated within closer proximity to the undesirable pole of the statistics under study compared to their White, middle-class peers. As per scholars' reliance on actuarially based and normatively framed predictors of "bad" outcomes, urban settings and the presumed risks that inhered therein were consigned to sweeping negative characterizations that we delineate below.

Prevailing Characterizations of Urban "Risk"

Researchers have commonly conflated urban life with a life of poverty. As per this conflation, researchers then offered a host of other problems and dysfunctions that correlated with poverty status (and, thus, defined urban life). For example, in setting the stage for their examinations of resilience in urban environments, some scholars have described "widespread poverty, low socioeconomic status, and large percentages of parents with low levels of education" as "endemic" to urban communities (Samel, Sondergeld, Fischer, & Patterson, 2011, p. 96). Other scholars similarly emphasized that the "worst social and economic conditions exist" in urban contexts and indicated that "high levels of crime, unemployment, drug dependency, broken families, illegitimacy rates, density of liquor stores, and concentrated poverty describe the critical status of students who are currently living in our nation's inner-city neighborhoods" (Waxman & Huang, 1996, p. 93). Others, still, reduced urban life to one of youth violence, gang warfare, and drug use/trafficking, (e.g., Cunningham & Swanson, 2010; O'Donnell, Schwab-Stone, & Muyeed, 2002). Reported as a "pervasive condition" of urban settings, poverty and its correlates were said to compromise the academic, social, and psychological development of urban youth (Kanevsky, Corkee & Frangikiser, 2008, p. 453).

As evidenced above, many of these correlates were analyzed at the level of the family or household. Thus the research assumed that the status, structure, and/or culture of the families residing in urban contexts compromised development (Brooks-Gunn, Duncan, & Aber, 1997; Finn & Rock, 1997; Garbarino, 1995; Wyman et al., 1999). The scholarship emphasized the extent to which urban students disproportionately grew up in single-parent-headed households and with adults who had achieved low levels of education, had low-skilled, low-waged jobs or were unemployed. Scholars presumed that these demographic characteristics led not only to heightened stress within families but to family dynamics and parenting practices that impinged on these families' capacities to raise academically successful children who were also socially and psychologically competent and, thereby, resilient (Belle, 1982; Belle, Flay, & Paikoff, 2002; Gorman-Smith, Tolan, & Henry, 2000; Kim-Cohen, Moffitt, Caspi, & Taylor, 2004; Prelow & Loukas, 2003; Smokowski, Reynolds, & Bezruczko, 1999; Sosa 2012). (Also see O'Connor and Fernandez [2006] for an extended discussion on how scholars have otherwise linked poverty at the family level to compromised human development.)

Within the resilience literature, "urban" and the associated economic deprivations and "problems" were simultaneously conflated with the experience of Black and Brown people in that studies that foregrounded the experience of *urban* students who were resilient almost exclusively discussed the experience of students who were of African and Latino descent (e.g., Reis, Colbert, & Herbert, 2005; Ripple & Luthar, 2000; Shin, Daly, & Vera, 2007; Tiet, Huizinga, & Byrnes, 2010). As per these conflations, pernicious boundaries were drawn between urban contexts (Black, Brown, and economically disadvantaged) and the suburban contexts (White and middle class) that provided the normative comparison.[4] The notion of "risk" was therefore portrayed as inhering not only in urban environments, but in those persons who signified urban life. As such, much of the work on the resilience of urban students focused on their presumptive at-risk status as low-income youth of color rather than on the context-specific risks these youth may have experienced in their urban neighborhoods and schools (e.g., Morales, 2010; Ripple & Luthar, 2000 Shin et al., 2007; Waxman, Padrón, Shin, & Rivera, 2008).

Relying first on a range of classifications that signaled poverty and/or Black and Brown identities (e.g., Black, African American, Latino, minority, English Language Learner, low SES, disadvantaged), researchers subsequently reported on the depressed outcomes of these students relative to White and/or middle-class students and those residing in suburban contexts (i.e., via discussions of a range of racial achievement gaps) (Plunkett, Henry, Houltberg, Sands, & Abarca-Mortenson, 2008; Ripple & Luthar, 2000; Rivera & Waxman, 2011; Shin et al., 2007; Waxman et al., 2008). They then attributed these depressed outcomes to the prospective risks encountered by these populations overall as opposed to the actual risks encountered by those featured in their study. In other words, without examining whether the students in their study were actually at risk, they summarily deemed them at-risk as per previously documented inequities in educational and social outcomes. To provide one example, in establishing the context for their study of resilient Mexican American youth in Los Angeles, Plunkett et al. (2008) explained that "Mexican-origin adolescents are at increased vulnerability for education risk . . . [as they] often encounter . . . educational systems developed for other ethnic groups, negative stereotypes, discrimination, identity issues, and poverty" (p. 335). Plunkett and his colleagues did not, however, analyze how these prospective risks specifically materialized either in Los Angeles or in the schools their participants attended. As such, Plunkett and his colleagues, as is the case for many resilience researchers, decontextualized risk and stripped it of empirical and analytical specificity.

Despite the tendency of Plunkett et al. and others to treat risk as an amorphous social category rather than confirm the actual risks to which their participants may have been exposed, it is important to consider that urban students can find themselves surrounded by a host of environmental risks. Some urban youth do live and attend schools in neighborhoods that are violent and suffer under gang warfare and drug trafficking. Urban contexts also do have disproportionate shares of underresourced neighborhoods and schools, and residents living in poverty. But evidence of these social problems does not mean that these problems are always and everywhere operating in urban settings. Nor is it the case that all urban youth are similarly exposed to these social problems; and, as such, the risk for negative outcomes must be differentiated within urban populations. Researchers have, nevertheless, reduced urban contexts to a sweeping constellation of negative social conditions that presumably establish "formidable impediments to healthy development" (Gorman-Smith, Tolan & Henry, 2010, p. 137). Accordingly, estimations of urban risk were forwarded with the presumption that the less-than-optimal academic outcomes evidenced by urban schools and students was a function of the pathologies that plagued these environments.

Many urban students, nevertheless, demonstrate academic outcomes and indices of development that defy the statistical predictions and the accordant taken-for-granted "pathologies" that have, at least in the literature, defined their at-risk status. It is these students who have been characterized as resilient.

Prevailing Characterizations of Urban Student Resilience

Who Counts as Resilient?

In defining who among urban students (read Black, Brown, and economically disadvantaged youth residing in urban contexts or attending urban schools) is resilient, researchers have relied on a range of traditional indices of academic performance. Scholars have defined as resilient students who achieved high grades or ranked competitively in their graduating class (Gonzalez & Padilla, 1997; Miller & MacIntosh, 1999; Morales, 2010; O'Connor, 1997); scored well on standardized tests (Borman & Overman, 2004; Shumow, Vandell, & Posner, 1999; Smokowski et al., 1999; Waxman et al., 2008); enrolled in college preparatory courses or gifted programs (Ford, 1994; Reis et al., 2005); and received academic awards or honors (Reis et al., 2005). Resilient youth also were described as having completed high school (Luthar, Cicchetti, & Becker, 2000), qualified for college admission, accumulated college credits, and matriculated to and/or completed college (Floyd, 1996; Morales, 2000; O'Connor, 2002).

Scholars have also defined resilient students in terms of their social and behavioral accommodation to school norms and expectations, and included students who had regular as opposed to poor school attendance (e.g., Waxman et al., 2008) and those whose teachers evaluated them favorably in terms of their work habits, peer relations, and compliance with classroom and school regulations (Luthar, Cichetti, & Becker 2000; Waxman et al., 2008). Urban students were also sometimes characterized as resilient when they demonstrated accommodations to broader societal norms and included students who either avoided peers who were delinquent or avoided delinquent or antisocial behaviors themselves (e.g., vandalism, drug use or abuse, gang involvement, and physical violence or aggression) (Miller & MacIntosh, 1999; O'Donnell, Schwab-Stone, & Muyeed, 2002; Smokowski et al., 1999; Tiet et al., 2010).

In short, across a wide range of studies, resilient urban youth were variously described as not only being academically talented and achieving in school, but as also working hard in school, making nice with peers, following school and teacher rules, being sufficiently social with teachers but not too social with peers, and avoiding delinquency directly or by approximation. Such behaviors were also offered as evidence of resilient students' positive social-psychological development.

Resilience as a Process Rather Than as an Individual Trait

Having defined some urban students as resilient as per the aforementioned measures, researchers sought to identify the source of this resilience. Early on, scholars attributed resilience to a static set of inherent traits, natural abilities, or personal temperaments (Baldwin et al., 1993). Consequently, resilient individuals were variously described as intelligent, confident, optimistic, motivated, goal directed, and efficacious (Anthony 1987; Masten, 1994; Werner & Smith, 1992; Worland, Weeks, & Janes, 1987). Researchers indicated that these individual-level characteristics either operated passively in that they facilitated an individual's capacity to withstand stress, trauma, or adversity (Condly, 2006); or operated actively in that they influenced an individual's capacity to alter his or her environment so as to minimize his or her overall or everyday exposure to stress, trauma, or adversity (Scarr & McCartney, 1983). For example, researchers discussed how some characteristics made those designated as resilient attractive to others (e.g., teachers, parents, school counselors) who then intervened in their lives in helpful ways (Masten, 1994; Werner & Smith, 1982, 1992). Whether operating passively or actively, these characteristics were classified as *protective factors* as they mitigated risk—allowing for healthy development where risk conditions would have otherwise "predicted" poor outcomes (Rutter, 1990).

Current literature continues to describe resilient urban students in terms of individual-level characteristics (Cunningham & Swanson, 2010) but instead of rendering these characteristics as traits (Benard, 2004), researchers have increasingly illuminated how these resilience-promoting characteristics emerge as a consequence of social processes—particularly those that inhere in families and peer groups. As an example, Morales (2010) attributed the motivation of the resilient urban low-income and minority students in his study to their having parents who had sacrificed time, money, or energy in proactive efforts aimed at helping their children avoid their neighborhood schools, which they anticipated would limit their children's educational opportunities. Morales (2010) explained that in recalling the parents' initiative and sacrifice, the students felt obligated to persist through college.

While the research of Morales and others (e.g., Connell, Spencer, & Aber, 1994; Tiet et al., 2010) showed how protective factors can grow resilience-enhancing characteristics or personal qualities, other research revealed mechanisms by which protective factors actually buffered youth against risk and adversity (e.g., Domínguez & Watkins, 2003; Fried & Chapman, 2012; Jarrett, 1994). For example, research by Jarrett and Jefferson (2003) documented the range of parenting strategies low-income mothers invoked to ensure their children's positive development by buffering them against the violence and negative peer influences in the neighborhood (i.e., "monitoring," "cautionary warnings," "danger management," "chaperonage," and "confinement"). In terms of mechanisms by which peer groups as opposed to parents can enhance youth development and promote resilience, Reis et al. (2005) reported that the resilient youth in their study had friends who refused to let them falter—providing pep talks, encouragement, and academic assistance when the participants experienced academic challenges or missteps.

The work of Reis et al. (2005), Jarrett and Jefferson (2003), and Morales (2010) are all ethnographic in nature and are better suited to revealing the mechanisms by which protective factors (such as positive peer groups or supportive parents) affect the process of resilience. However, much of the work on resilience—including that on urban student resilience—relies on survey research, which is not well suited to illuminating the processes that are at play in the production of resilience. Consequently, much of the research on resilient urban youth, as is the case for research on resilient youth overall, has offered a long and consistent list of protective factors that correlate with resilience; and as per the limits of the methodology, researchers have speculated about the process of resilience absent empirical specification. These protective factors included:

- having parents (e.g., Benard, 1991; Li, Nussbaum, & Richards, 2007; Masten, Best, & Garmezy, 1990; Reynolds, 1998; Rutter, 1990; Wang, Haertel, & Walberg, 1994) and teachers (e.g., O'Conner, Mason, & Mennis, 2012; Stanton-Salazar, 2001; Wang et al., 1994; Werner & Smith, 1982) with whom they feel connected and who extend high expectations and social support;
- positive and pro-social peer groups (Klem & Connell, 2004; Shin, Daly, & Vera, 2007); and
- involvement in extracurricular activities (Braddock, Royster, Winfield, & Hawkins, 1991; Hawkins & Mulkey, 2005).

Despite the empirical challenges involved in specifying the mechanisms by which protective factors influenced "unpredicted" social and educational outcomes, the field as a whole now generally takes for granted that resilience should be treated as a process as opposed to a trait or personal quality (DeHaan et al., 2013; Luthar et al., 2000; Masten, 2001; Morrison et al., 2006; O'Connor, 2002; Spencer, 2005; Spencer et al., 2006). Resting upon this assumption, scholars have rendered resilience a complex social phenomenon by attending to its situated-ness and dynamism.

Resilience as a Dynamic and Situated Social Phenomenon

Researchers currently recognize that the dynamism of resilience is demonstrated as per the finding that the very characteristics that promote resilience in regard to one dimension or a set of outcomes may function as a liability in relation to a different dimension or set of outcomes. For example, some scholars have indicated that the very skills or dispositions that incline some low-income urban students toward academic success might leave them more social-psychologically vulnerable—noting that the cognitive resources that support academic success may also increase youths' recognition of and sensitivity to stressors that might inhere in their environment—compromising, in turn, the young people's social psychological health (e.g., they might find themselves emotionally stressed and depressed) (Luthar, 1991; Condly, 2006).

A similar dynamism is also evident in terms of how racial identity can operate as both a protective factor and a risk factor (e.g., Miller and Macintosh, 1999; Sellers, 2012; Sellers, Chavous, & Cooke, 1998; Shin et al., 2007). For example, researchers have shown that Black students with a strong racial identity demonstrate greater awareness of racial inequities and discrimination (Fordham, 1993; Sellers, 2012; Sellers & Shelton, 2003)—compromising, in turn, the achievement motivation of some (e.g., Fordham, 1993; Fordham & Ogbu, 1986) and the inclination of others to experience stress and depressive symptoms under low levels of discrimination (Sellers, 2012). However, O'Connor (1997) found that with a developed sense of Black collective agency African American students evidenced effort optimism and persisted in school despite an acute recognition of racial inequalities. And Sellers (2012) demonstrated that under high levels of discrimination students with a strong racial identity experienced less stress and depressive symptoms compared to same race peers who believed that Blacks were positively regarded in the public domain. Shin et al. (2007) alternatively illuminated how a strong racial identity protected " 'at-risk' adolescents from being led astray by the variety of negative pressures that they may be exposed to" (p. 381).

These aforementioned findings also illuminate the extent to which resilience is, in part, a function of subjectivity. That is, the impact of environmental stressors (e.g., poverty, racial discrimination), while having clear material effects on a wide variety of educational and social outcomes, also draw their effects from whether and to what extent the stressors are recognized as such. Thus, the perception of risk, rather than its objective or consensus designation, can also place individuals at risk for depressed outcomes (Gordon & Song, 1994). Some risks or stressors are not in fact psychologically debilitating precisely because the subject under study does not perceive them as stressors. Importantly, however, even when there are no apparent debilitating psychological effects, these same risks can still, in objective terms, compromise an individual's academic and social achievements.[5] The capacity for a particular characteristic to induce as well as compromise success as a function of subjectivity or as consequence of the referent against which it is analyzed makes transparent the extent to which resilience is "situational in its operation" (Condly, 2006, p. 225). To further emphasize the situated-ness of resilience, Condly points out that "what is considered risk or resilience in one culture or context may be the norm or rebellion in another" (Condly, 2006, p. 226).

The situated-ness and dynamism of resilience has been otherwise recognized as per scholars having documented the extent to which resilience varies over the life course. As Braddock et al. (1991) noted more than 20 years ago, "neither academic resilience nor academic resignation emerges at a specific point in time but rather over time as opportunities for capturing students' interests and for nurturing persistence are cultivated or lost" (p. 114). Other scholars have noted that students who were designated as resilient in their studies may have previously demonstrated low achievement (Reis et al., 2005). Bottrell (2009) additionally cautioned that individuals can simultaneously demonstrate behaviors and intentions that have been attributed to both resilient and nonresilient students despite the tendency in the literature to dichotomize pro-social and delinquent peer groups, marking the former as resilient and the latter as not resilient. In her study of at-risk girls, she found that the girls and the peer networks in which they were embedded revealed *both* "pro-social [i.e. strong friendship bonds; practical social support systems; problem solving resources] and delinquent [i.e., school suspensions; "troublesome" school behavior; drug use] elements that challenge[d] stereotypes of disadvantaged young people as threatening or deficient" and consequently ,"fixed notions of resilience and young people's reinscription within categories of resilient *or* deficit youth" (Bottrell, 2009, pp. 477–478; our emphasis).

The Structuring of Resilience

In addition to making transparent the extent to which the dynamism of resilience reflects iterative, and in-situ processes of adaptation, researchers have prompted considerations of how resilience can vary across historical time and physical and institutional spaces (O'Connor, 2002; O'Connor, Fernandez, and Girard, 2007). Although very little of this research has been conducted under the auspices of resilience research per se, these investigations do operate under the key premise of resilience research in that they revealed and sought to explain the emergence of competitive achievement in places where it would not be predicted statistically.

Consequently, research on effective schools (Delpit, 2003; Hill, 2008; McDonough, 1997; Morgan, 2012; Morris, 2004; Sizemore, 1988; Wang, Haertel, & Walberg, 1990), and on effective, value-added, and culturally responsive teachers (Han & Thomas, 2010; Ladson-Billings, 2009; Love & Kruger, 2005; Slavin, 1996; Sosa & Gomez, 2012; Wang et al., 1990) all evidenced considerable academic success and engagement among populations designated at-risk for depressed academic outcomes.[6] In a complementary fashion, the children and families of the Harlem Zone boasted more positive outcomes than would be predicted absent this neighborhood-level intervention and coordination of services (Dobbie & Fryer, 2009); and the Comer Project before that demonstrated that whole-school–level interventions that included the integration and empowerment of families could enhance positive youth development in underserved and underperforming urban schools (Haynes, 2007). These findings indicated that resilience does not only operate at the individual level but can also function as a collective property; a property that could be structured per institutionalized and systemic opportunities. Within the field of resilience research, O'Connor (2002) revealed the historical specificity of these institutionalized practices and systems of opportunity, finding that the feasibility of and the mechanisms by which individuals persevered academically—despite risk—were partly a function of the structured opportunities (e.g., resources, institutionalized supports, social changes, and specific political events) that were differentially available from one historical period to the next.

In contemplating how schools might specifically structure resilience, Condly (2006) noted:

> children spend a great deal of time in school. If the schools are resource poor, short on qualified staff, and/or exist in dangerous neighborhoods, then the development of resilience is likely to be hampered. On the other hand, because schools are places in which children spend so much time, they are ideal locations for the implementation of programs designed to support children and assist them in overcoming environmental stressors. (p. 229)

Despite the promise of schools to affect resilience, this promise remains underanalyzed in resilience research. Sometimes this underanalysis has been a function of researchers' tendency to focus on the attributes of schools rather than on the processes by which these attributes impacted positive outcomes. Thus, while resilience research has examined how schools can work to produce resilience, the focus of the analyses emphasized the characteristics that distinguished these effective schools (e.g. caring teachers, an orderly environment, high expectations, improved home-school partnerships, and meaningful student engagement). Thus, as was the case for the early examinations of individual-level resilience, the characteristics that coincided with resilience in these schools dwarfed systematic and empirical attention to the processes by which these characteristics produced positive academic outcomes.

Other times, the underanalysis of the resilience-enhancing capacity of schools is a function of a disproportionate focus on the composition of the student body and the presumed risks students carried into school with them (Valenzuela, 1999). For example, in explaining how the resilience of the disadvantaged youth in his study was partly due to the students having attended out-of-zone schools (i.e., Catholic or magnet high schools), Morales (2010) offered that these schools facilitated access to "new and different cultures, peoples, values, and norms" and simultaneously "separated the students . . . from negative aspects of their immediate communities" (p. 170). Left unanalyzed was the prospect that these out-of-zone schools provided greater educational opportunities than the in-zone schools; and that these enhanced opportunities supported, in turn, the students' academic engagement and achievement. Research on Catholic schools, magnet schools, and gifted programs support this likelihood as Black, Brown, and economically disadvantaged youth in these educational settings have been shown to outstrip the performance of their peers in less selective schools as per the higher academic standards and more conducive instructional climates often associated with these selective settings (e.g., Bryk, Lee, & Holland, 1993; Coates, Perkins, Vietze, Cruz, & Park, 2003; Cobb, Bifulco, & Bell, 2009).

The extent to which enhanced learning opportunities may dwarf the effects of peer composition and influence is further evidenced by Plunkett et al. (2008). These scholars found that academic support from friends was least important in explaining academic outcomes, while teacher academic support was the most salient predictor of academic outcomes. Similarly, Borman and Overman (2004) found that the effect of peer-group composition (at least at the elementary school level) was less powerful than previously advanced and was particularly less powerful than characteristics of the effective schools models. Importantly, this study also found that the resilience of low-income Black students was more dependent on attending an effective school than was the resilience of economically disadvantaged White students.

The extent to which school effects may be particularly powerful for students of color (Coleman et al., 1966)[7], and the capacity with which teachers can powerfully affect student engagement and learning above and beyond curriculum resources and student background, has long been documented (Barr & Dreeben, 1983). Within the province of resilience research, however, Waxman and colleagues provided the most compelling findings on this front (Waxman et al., 2008; Rivera & Waxman, 2011). Most of their research focused on the behavioral differences between resilient and nonresilient Hispanic students attending mostly urban schools. As per their observations, they found that on average the students designated as resilient were more attentive in the classroom, were more apt to interact with teachers for instructional purposes, and were less apt to create disruptions or interact with peers for social purposes. The behaviors between resilient and nonresilient students were, however, indistinguishable in the few classrooms where teachers departed from the modal pattern of instruction, which was characterized by "whole-class instruction with students working in teacher-assigned activities and generally in a passive manner" (Waxman et al., 2008, p. 28). In the few classrooms where Waxman and colleagues observed dynamic student-teacher interactions and where instructional opportunities were authentic and culturally responsive, nonresilient students no longer appeared bored or reluctant to participate and appeared as motivated and engaged as their resilient peers.

The findings of this study are especially impressive in light of how students were designated as resilient. All students came from families of low SES and/or lived with a single relative or guardian. Resilient and nonresilient students were distinguished as per teachers' assessments of how they differed on test scores, attendance, quality of daily work, and motivation—with resilient students performing more competitively on each of these measures. The fact that the instructional climate and demands of select classrooms appeared to "wash out" the effects of these at-risk statuses requires us to question the designation of students as being "at-risk" (where risk functions as a human quality). Given these findings it is more appropriate to examine how schools and/or particular classrooms may "place" children at risk (in which case risk functions as a structured status).

Summary and Implications of Extant Conceptualizations of Urban Student Resilience

Over time, scholars have increasingly recognized resilience—including urban student resilience—as a complex and dynamic phenomenon. Having largely abandoned the notion that resilience is a static personal trait that establishes an individual's capacity to either withstand or alter his or her exposure to risk, scholars have explored the protective factors and accordant social processes that mitigate risk and cultivate resilience. Researchers have simultaneously illuminated the situated-ness of resilience and the extent to which the resilience-promoting capacity of individual-level characteristics is bound to the contextual demands or outcomes under study. These analyses have highlighted how the same characteristics can promote resilience in relation to some set outcomes while determining an individual's vulnerability in relation to another set of outcomes. Accordingly, researchers have decried fixed notions of resilience that reify hard distinctions between those who are and who are not resilient as at any moment in time a single individual is marked by a wide variety of skills, dispositions, and characteristics—some of which enhance and others of which constrain the likelihood of positive outcomes depending on the circumstances at hand.

Researchers have simultaneously designated the objective (or material) and subjective dimensions of resilience. Scholars have also indicated the extent to which an individual's experience with resilience varies over the life course as a consequence of accumulated and lost opportunities and the particular constellation of resources that are available at particular historical moments. More recently, they have examined resilience as a collective characteristic and illuminated how resilience can be structured as per the institutionalized opportunities that are differentially evidenced across time and space—with some compelling evidence of how schools and classrooms can structure and nurture the resilience of urban students.

While scholars have been conceiving of resilience with ever-increasing sophistication, efforts to demarcate the complexity of urban environments (and by implication the risks that inhere therein) have paled in comparison. This imbalance is theoretically problematic. As previously indicated by O'Connor (2002), although the concepts of risk, constraint, opportunity, and resilience are analytically distinct, they converge in the real world. That is, in creating opportunity (whether through the provision of resources, the institutionalization of supports, or the structuring of access), we mitigate constraints on life chances and opportunities and, thereby, reduce risk. Alternatively, in limiting access to opportunity, constraints are magnified and impinge on life chances. Given the interdependence of risk and resilience in the real world, the mis-specification and underanalysis of the risks that inhere in urban environments means that we have stopped short of fully conceptualizing the process of resilience as it unfolds for urban students.

Reanalyzing Urban Risk as a Starting Point for Reconceptualizing Urban Student Resilience

As previously discussed, resilience research has tended to homogenize and pathologize life in urban areas. In turn, this literature has regularly overlooked the extant resources in urban environments and by implication the "possible sources of protective factors for predicting resilience in diverse groups of color" (Spencer, 2005, p. 822), including among the very children and families who often reside in urban environments. Wang and Gordon (1994) noted that "U.S. cities are a startling juxtaposition between the despairing and the hopeful, between disorganization and restorative potential. Alongside the poverty and the unemployment, the street fights and drug deals, are a wealth of cultural, economic, educational and social resources" (p. ix). In reconceptualizing risk and resilience in urban education, it is essential to emphasize that like suburban centers,[8] urban centers are variegated as are the experiences of the individuals that reside therein.

Despite this variation in urban life, "urban" has come to signify life in the "inner" city, with many researchers using the terms *urban* and *inner-city* interchangeably. Gorman-Smith et al. (2010) remind us that the inner-city should be treated as a historically and sociologically distinct social space that is found within urban centers but is not synonymous with urban life. Inner-city is more appropriately applied to those areas of the city that struggle under concentrated poverty as per deindustrialization (Wilson, 1987), a constellation of historical discriminatory housing practices and policies (Massey & Denton, 1993), continued economic decline (Wilson, 1996), and persistent job discrimination (Pager, 2007). According to Wilson (1987), individuals living under these conditions constitute the "urban underclass" who are socially isolated from a wide range of public/social services, mainstream resources, social networks, and occupational opportunities. As per histories of racial discrimination in the job and housing market, this underclass is disproportionately represented by minorities and especially by persons of African descent (Massey & Denton, 1993; Pager, 2007).

It is equally important to note that variation exists even within areas of concentrated poverty as per varying levels of social disorganization. According to Sampson and Groves (1989), social disorganization, "in general terms . . . refers to the inability of a community structure to realize the common values of its residents and maintain effective social controls" (p. 777). Communities with high levels of social disorganization lack adequate informal (e.g., friendship ties) and formal (e.g., organizational participation) networks that might be effectively deployed to achieve shared values and redress local problems (Kornhauser 1978; Sampson & Groves, 1989; Shaw and McKay, 1942). Measured by levels of concentrated poverty, density of single-parent households, the degree of residential mobility, and extant crime rates, neighborhoods evidence different levels of social disorganization (Tiet et al., 2010). Consequently, while some urban neighborhoods suffer under concentrated poverty and social disorganization, others do not. Urban youths' experiences are thereby differentiated by such variation in neighborhoods.

Urban students' experiences also differ within neighborhoods. Thus in the study of urban student resilience, scholars have increasingly sought to document the extent to which the youths in their study actually experience in their day-to-day lives the stressors that have been associated with urban centers (Miller, Webster, & MacIntosh, 2002; Wyman et al., 1999). For example, Miller and his colleagues have relied on their urban hassles scale to assess students' experiences with a range of hassles that may coincide with but are not determined by urban contexts (e.g., having to take different routes home to keep safe; feeling pressured by friends to join a gang; worrying that someone will try to take your belongings; feeling pressured to carry a weapon for protection; working to help pay bills at home; nervous about gunshots/sirens at night) (Miller et al., 2002). Although the items on this scale should not be interpreted as the province of life in urban contexts, the need for the scale indicates that these experiences do not mark the experiences of all urban youth or all urban neighborhoods.

In terms of variegated school experiences, we know that, broadly, urban school systems have historically experienced grave decline, though these systems had been previously hailed for the rigor of their instruction and had once been recognized as being among the best in the nation and even the world (Mirel, 1999; Saatcioglu & Rury, 2012). However, even within these now low-performing districts, there exist successful schools where children are thriving. Some of the best high schools in the United States are still found in urban centers (*New York Times,* 2012; *US News and World Report,* 2012). And while over time, low-income and Black and Brown students have had reduced access to these specialized public institutions (*New York Times,* 2012), there are also a host of "open access" urban schools that have been hailed for their capacity to produce high achievement among otherwise marginalized students (*Newsweek,* 2010). Although schools of this kind might be uncommon in urban centers, urban youth who have the fortune of attending them are on some dimensions less at-risk than their peers who attend urban schools that feature low academic standards and low-quality instruction. Brown and Black youth who are living in poverty and are attending these specialized urban schools may, nevertheless, be placed at some risk in these same environments as per evidence of the race and class stratification that has been documented in desegregated and specialized schools (Ascher, 1986; Gerstl-Pepin, 2002; Southworth & Mickelson, 2007). Whatever the scenario, the evidence, degree, and nature of risk varies across and within urban schools—requiring differential (or sometimes no) adaptations on the part of youth to exhibit performances and norms of behavior that have been traditionally offered as indices of resilience.

It is critical that we distinguish who is actually at-risk in urban contexts and how they have been placed at risk. The reliance on statistical and amorphous designations of risk increases the prospect that researchers may inadvertently seek to explain resilience using as their referent the experiences of respondents who may have never been at risk for negative outcomes whether as a consequence of the neighborhoods in which they resided, the schools they attended, and/or their day-to-day experiences. In these instances researchers would be explaining the processes and pathways by which urban youth experience productive social and academic outcomes (a subject that is in and of itself worthy of investigation) rather than the processes by which they defied the odds of achieving these outcomes.

A more deliberate focus on the experience of successful students who live in neighborhoods or attend schools that are defined as more risky must be approached with caution, however. Such a focus may inadvertently deny the extent to which pro-social and productive behaviors and outcomes reflect normal as opposed to exceptional experiences in urban contexts. Thus to define as resilient youth who are not engaged in delinquent or violent activities is to ignore the fact that most low SES students are not delinquent and that their lack of involvement in violence is actually normative even if there is greater evidence of violence in the communities in which they reside. Similarly, to define as resilient students who have good grades, are positively oriented toward school, and expect to graduate high school is to ignore the fact that these experiences and dispositions are also normative among urban populations (Catterall, 1998). Consequently, we need to consider, as Murphy (1974) did some 50-plus years ago, that resilience is everywhere normative and constitutes what Masten (2001) more recently described as "ordinary magic." As such, resilience rather than deviance constitutes the norm in urban communities including in high-poverty and socially disorganized neighborhoods.

As importantly, under conditions where students and their families are experiencing stressors outside of school, the likelihood is that they have developed some coping strategies that could be built upon to scaffold academic success. In part, scholars are blinded to these prospective scaffolds for learning because the field of resilience has traditionally relied on a host of indices that situate low-income Black and Brown youth as deficient. McCubbin and McCubbin (2013) specifically noted that the "dependence on Western, white, middle class measures" has been coupled with the "conspicuous absence of metrics grounded in the ethnic and cultural dynamics and processes of the populations being studied" (p. 176). The consequence has been that resilience researchers remain fettered in their understanding of the differing ways "ethnic" families (McCubbin and McCubbin's term) may cope and be resilient within the family unit and the resources, capacities, and skills that develop as per these adaptations.

Accordantly, there is no attendant identification or framing of indices that would simultaneously make evident the resources and capacities extant in the neighborhoods in which some Black and Brown youth reside and would by comparison situate White, middle-class populations as lacking. As such, urban youth are inappropriately normed against a referent whereby their prospective resilience or their resilience-enhancing skills or capacities are rendered invisible at best, and more often are situated as deviant or dysfunctional. At the same time, the prospect that White, middle-class, and suburban populations may be in need of remediation in order to compensate for their own deficiencies and for the purpose of building their resilience goes unanalyzed. To provide a powerful example of how the skills and capacities of economically disadvantaged youth might be underanalyzed or pathologized and the skills and capacities of middle-class youth might be inflated as per the privileging of a middle-class normative referent, we need only consider Lareau's (2002) examination of the "cultural logics" that distinguish the child rearing of middle-class families from that of poor and working-class families.

Lareau (2002) evaluated as productive the child-rearing logic of middle-class families that cultivated children's sense of power and efficacy as it inclined children to presume that individuals and institutions should be responsive to them and should accommodate their individual needs. However, we might otherwise frame this inclination as deviant and dysfunctional, as this inclination might alternatively signal a profound sense of entitlement likely to work against these youths' orientation to take up and support practices aimed at developing the collective good over personal advantage. Of course, our presumption here is that the collective good is the superior commitment.

In comparison, Lareau found that the child-rearing logic of low-income and working-class families that provided children more leeway in coordinating their time, absent adult intervention, compromised the development of skills evidenced by middle-class children. Absent a middle-class referent, however, we might also readily imagine that the opportunity provided low-income and working-class youth to define and coordinate their free time may have also cultivated their self-sufficiency, peer leadership and mediation, independence, resourcefulness, flexibility, and spontaneity in ways that would be unmatched by the more structured lives of their middle-class peers. In order to consider, much less assess, this prospect requires that we look for the potential resources rather than the potential deficiencies extant in marginalized communities.

To provide a school-based example of how the skills and capacities of urban youth might be rendered invisible, deficient, or deviant as per a White, middle-class normative referent, we might consider research on Black and Brown preschoolers in urban settings who are dual-language learners (e.g., Bialystok, 2001; Poulin-Dubois, Blaye, Coutya, & Bialystok, 2011). As children whose first language is not English they would be situated as deficient relative to monolingual English speakers and at educational risk as per actuarially based predictors for poor outcomes in school. These children, however, demonstrated several attributes that primed them for academic success. They evidenced higher levels of executive functioning (working memory, inhibitory control, suppressing interference, mental flexibility), were more adaptive in their thinking, and evidenced higher levels of social/emotional development—advantages that were reaped precisely *because* they were emerging bilinguals (Bialystok, 1999; Bialystok, 2001; Bialystok, Craik, & Ryan, 2006). However, Espinosa (2008) evidenced that these advantaged statuses washed out as children progressed through school unless realized as positive and adaptive such that they were invoked by teachers and schools as instructional resources.

The failure to identify and build upon instructionally the strengths and assets that Black, Brown, and economically disadvantaged urban youth bring to school may be especially dire for youth residing in neighborhoods suffering under high levels of social disorganization. These youth may be particularly placed at risk by schools as per the findings of Johnson's (2012) study of the achievement gains and losses of these youth during periods where they have greater exposure to the ecological curriculum (summer months) compared to their receipt of school instruction during the academic year ("directed development").

The prevailing notion is that low SES students tend to gain as much or more than socio-economically advantaged students in reading and math during periods of directed development, and the extant gaps in achievement between low-income and middle-class youth are primarily a function of out-of- school learning opportunities afforded to middle-class youth during the summer months. Moreover, the summer loss on the part of low-income youth has been shown to be at the heart of racial gaps in achievement as summer gains and losses were a function of social class differences and did not vary much according to race when poverty status was controlled (Downey, von Hippel, & Broh, 2004; Entwisle & Alexander, 1992). In studying the experience of students in neighborhoods with high levels of social disorganization, Johnson (2012), however, found that achievement gaps grew during the academic year as Black and Hispanic students actually experienced greater losses in reading and math during periods of directed development.

Conclusion

Taken in total, our review of the research literature on urban student resilience reveals an imbalance in the evolution of the concepts of resilience and risk. While researchers have increasingly explored the dynamism and complexity of resilience as a social phenomenon, they have reduced urban risk to a static and undifferentiated social status. Situating White, middle-class suburbs as the normative frame of reference, urban contexts are imagined as Black and Brown and have been reduced to that of poverty and pathology. The homogenizing and pathologizing of urban contexts impairs precise calculations of where, why, and how some urban youth find themselves at risk and the role that schools (and not just neighborhoods) play in the structuring of that risk. This sweeping pathologization simultaneously denies the assets and resources extant in urban communities and those that are especially found among the Black, Brown, and economically disadvantaged youth who reside therein, and might be capitalized upon for the purpose of teaching and learning. Some of these assets and resources may in fact be founded in the processes by which these youth and their families have coped productively with the specific risks they may have encountered.

Conversely, the simultaneous casting of White, middle-class suburban environments and the families therein as universally protective and supportive circumscribes our capacity to examine where and how these children find themselves at risk and how we might intervene in their lives to facilitate resilience. On this point we need only consider recent news events, and the fact that some of the most heinous massacres in U.S. history (i.e., at Sandy Hook Elementary and less recently at Columbine High School) have occurred in the very settings and by the very children who have provided the normative referent by which the educational and psycho-social health of urban students have been negatively evaluated (Allen & Blackden, 2012; Caleb, 2012; Obmascik, 1999).

Leadbeater, Dodgen, and Solarz (2010) indicated that we need to move from a focus on "individuals' and families' capacities for adaptive functioning in contexts of adversity towards the systems and institutional responses that build on or serve to challenge these capacities" (p. 48). Building educational systems for resilience would require us to evaluate all school children as potentially at risk, to define that risk precisely, and to identify and then invoke these same children's assets and resources in the interest of developing differentiated academic pathways by which resilience might be cultivated. This, of course, means that educational policy makers and practitioners will need support in identifying, framing, and capitalizing upon the differentiated ways of being and the accordant resources and assets that are brought to school by children and youth of all backgrounds (Sosa & Gomez, 2012).

Notes

1. As our chapter focuses on the resilience of urban students, we began our literature review by identifying research that illuminated the resilience of urban students or the resilience of students who resided or attended schools in urban centers. To do this, we relied on the following search engines (i.e., Proquest, ERIC, and JSTOR) and searched for literature using three categories of search terms. That is, terms that captured (1) studies conducted in urban settings (i.e., urban, disadvantaged, impoverished, poverty, or inner-city); (2) research conducted on students, schools, and education (i.e., education, schooling, achievement or academic success); and (3) research on resilience (i.e., resilient, resilience, educational resilience, resilience [psychology]). We applied these search terms in various combinations and from the universe of articles identified via this search process, we selected for analysis those articles in which (1) the concept of or experience with resilience was explicitly under study; and (2) the article empirically or conceptually examined urban schools or the experience of students who attended urban schools or lived in urban neighborhoods. This process produced a working bibliography of over 125 articles, which we supplemented with literature that examined resilience writ large.
2. The race of study participants and subjects of scholarly interest often went unspecified in publications printed during the 1970s. In describing participants, researchers usually limited considerations to social class background as per the presumption that economic hardship posed a predominant risk to positive human development and adaptation (e.g., Anthony, 1974; Elder, 1974; Garmezy, 1971). Researchers thereby designed studies in which participants were either selected on the basis of experiencing economic hardship or were purposely avoided due to their low-income status (Lyman, 1984). When the race of the participants was designated in these early studies, the participants were identified as White. When left undesignated an examination of the longitudinal data sets upon which some resilience researchers relied indicated that the participants were wholly or mostly White (e.g., see Watt, Anthony, Wynne, & Rolf [1984] for an overview of several of these longitudinal studies).
3. Sociologists did not use resilience as part of their nomenclature or as a conceptual referent. However, as per their considerations of ecological development, they examined how neighborhoods and the degree of social disorganization evidenced therein influenced children's academic and social development.
4. The conflation of urban, dysfunction, and the status and experience of Black and Brown people—both in the imaginations of researchers and the general public—is a common and previously documented phenomenon (Kelley, 1998; Leonardo & Hunter, 2007).
5. For example, African American and Latino students may experience less day-to-day stress in the absence of recognizing historical and contemporary forms of institutionalized and everyday racism that impinge on their likelihood of accessing equitable educational opportunities. Absent such recognition and the consequent psychological strain, these students' opportunities to learn would be, nevertheless, compromised by these systemic inequities (see Ladson-Billings [2006] discussion of the educational debt owed Black and Brown people).
6. The effective schools literature designates a specific field of research and we reference here literature from this field as well as that research not included in this field but, nevertheless, reported on schools that produced unanticipated positive outcomes among marginalized youth.
7. Although the Coleman report is usually cited as evidence that student background trumps school effects, the report simultaneously found that the demonstrated school effects, even if dwarfed by student background, were more powerful for Blacks.

8. Suburban contexts vary not only in their economic viability but in the racial and socioeconomic demographics of the residents—with an increasing number of suburban contexts reflecting the same risk factors that have been traditionally associated with urban contexts (e.g., high rates of crime, underemployment and unemployment, depressed levels of academic achievement and attainment) (Hall & Lee, 2010; Murphy, 2007).

References

Allen, N., & Blackden, R. (2012). Massacre at Sandy Hook leaves 20 children dead. *The Daily Telegraph*. Retrieved from http://search.proquest.com.proxy.lib.umich.edu/docview/1238442675?accountid=14667

Anthony, E.J. (1974). The syndrome of the psychologically invulnerable child. In E.J. Anthony & C. Koupernik (Eds.), *The child in his family: Children at psychiatric risk* (pp. 529–545). New York, NY: John Wiley & Sons.

Anthony, E.J. (1987). Risk, vulnerability, and resilience: An overview. In E.J. Anthony and B.J. Cohler (Eds.), *The invulnerable child* (pp. 3–48). New York, NY: Guilford Press.

Ascher, C. (1986). Creating racial integration in a desegregated magnet school. ERIC/CUE Digest, Number 29. Retrieved from http://search.proquest.com.proxy.lib.umich.edu/docview/63312963?accountid=14667

Baldwin, A.L., Baldwin, C.P., Kasser, T., Zax, M., Sameroff, A., & Seifer, R. (1993). Contextual risk and resiliency during late adolescence. *Development and Psychopathology, 5,* 741–741.

Barr, R., & Dreeben, R. (1983). *How schools work.* Chicago, IL: University of Chicago Press.

Belle, C.C., Flay, B., & Paikoff, R.L. (2002). Strategies for healthy behavior change. In J. Carrington (Ed.), *The health behavioral change imperative: Theory, education, and practice in diverse populations* (pp. 17–39). New York, NY: Kluwer Academic/Plenum.

Belle, D.E. (1982). The impact of poverty on social networks and supports. *Marriage and Family Review, 5,* 89–103.

Benard, B. (1991). *Fostering resiliency in kids: Protective factors in the family, school, and community.* Portland, OR: Northwest Regional Educational Laboratory, U.S. Department of Education.

Benard, B. (2004). *Resiliency: What have we learned.* Danvers, MA: West End.

Bialystok, E. (1999). Cognitive complexity and attentional control in the bilingual mind. *Child Development, 70*(3), 636–644.

Bialystok, E. (2001). *Bilingualism in development: Language, literacy, and cognition.* Cambridge, UK: Cambridge University Press.

Bialystok, E., Craik, F., & Ryan, J. (2006). Executive control in a modified antisaccade task: Effects of aging and bilingualism. *Journal of Experimental Psychology: Learning, Memory and Cognition, 32*(6), 1341–1354.

Borman, G.D., & Overman, L.T. (2004). Academic resilience in mathematics among poor and minority students. *Elementary School Journal, 104*(3), 178–195.

Bottrell, D. (2009). Dealing with disadvantage: Resilience and social capital of young people's networks. *Youth and Society, 40*(4), 476–501.

Braddock, J.H., Royster, D.A., Winfield, L.F., & Hawkins, R. (1991). Bouncing back: Sports and academic resilience among African-American males. *Education and Urban Society, 24,* 113–131.

Brooks-Gunn, J., Duncan, G.J., & Aber, J.L. (1997). *Neighborhood poverty: Context and consequences for children.* New York, NY: Russell Sage Foundation.

Bryk, A., Lee, V., & Holland, P. (1993). *Catholic schools and the common good.* Cambridge, MA: Harvard University Press.

Caleb, I. (2012). World in shock over massacre at Sandy Hook. *Wales on Sunday.* Retrieved from http://search.proquest.com.proxy.lib.umich.edu/docview/1238819028?accountid=14667

Catterall, J.S. (1998). Risk and resilience in student transitions to high school. *American Journal of Education, 106*(2), 302–333.

Coates, D., Perkins, T., Vietze, P., Cruz, M., & Park, S. (2003). *Teaching thinking to culturally diverse, high ability, high school students: A triarchic approach.* Storrs, CT: National Research Center on the Gifted and Talented.

Cobb, C., Bifulco, R., & Bell, C. (2009). *Evaluation of Connecticut's interdistrict magnet schools.* Stanford, CA: Center for Education Policy Analysis.

Coleman, J.S., Campbell, E.Q., Hobson, C.J., McPartland, J., Mood, A., Weinfeld, F.D., & York, R.L. (1966). *Equality of educational opportunity.* Washington, DC: U.S. Department of Health, Education, and Welfare.

Condly, S.J. (2006) Resilience in children: A review of literature with implications for education. *Urban Education, 41,* 211–236.

Connell, J.P., Spencer, M.B., & Aber, J.L. (1994). Educational risk and resilience in African American youth: Context, self, action, and outcomes in school. *Child Development, 65*(2), 493–506.

Cowen, E.L., Wyman, P.A., Work, W.C., & Iker, M.R. (1995). A preventive intervention for enhancing resilience among highly stressed urban children. *Journal of Primary Prevention, 15*(3), 247–260.

Cunningham, M., & Swanson, D.P. (2010). Educational resilience in African American adolescents. *Journal of Negro Education, 79*(4), 473–487.

DeHaan, L.G., Hawley, D.R, & Deal, J.E. (2013). Operationalizing family resilience as process: Proposed methodological strategies. In D.S. Becvar (Ed.), *Handbook of family resilience* (pp. 17–29). New York, NY: Springer.

Delpit, L. (2003). Dewitt Wallace–Reader's Digest Distinguished Lecture—Educators as "seed people" growing a new future. *Educational Researcher,* 7(32), 14–21.

Dobbie, W., & Fryer, R. (2009). *Are high quality schools enough to close the achievement gap?: Evidence from a social experiment in Harlem.* Working Paper No.15473. Cambridge, MA: National Bureau of Economic Research.

Dominguez, S., & Watkins, C. (2003). Creating networks for survival and mobility: Social capital among African-American and Latin-American low-income mothers. *Social Problems, 50*(1), 111–135.

Downey, D.B., von Hippel, P.T., & Broh, B.A. (2004). Are schools the great equalizer? Cognitive inequality during the summer months and the school year. *American Sociological Review, 69*(5), 613–635.

Elder, G.H. (1974). *Children of the Great Depression: Social change in life experience.* Chicago, IL: University of Chicago Press.

Elder, G.H., van Nguyen, T., & Caspi, A. (1985). Linking family hardship to children's lives. *Child Development, 56,* 361–375.

Entwisle, D.R., & Alexander, K.L. (1992). Summer setback: Race, poverty, school composition and mathematics achievement in the first two years of school. *American Sociological Review, 57*(1), 72–84.

Espinosa, L. (2008). *Challenging common myths about young English language learners.* Policy Brief #8. Foundation for Child Development. New York, NY.

Finn, J.D., & Rock, D.A. (1997). Academic success among students at risk for school failure. *Journal of Applied Psychology, 82*(2), 221–234.

Floyd, C. (1996). Achieving despite the odds: A study of resilience among a group of African American high school seniors. *Journal of Negro Education, 65*(2), 181–189.

Ford, D. (1994). Nurturing resilience in gifted Black youth. *Roeper Review, 17,* 80–86.

Fordham, S. (1993). "Those loud Black girls": (Black) women, silence, and gender "passing" in the academy. *Anthropology & Education Quarterly, 24*(1), 3–32.

Fordham, S., & Ogbu, J. (1986). Black students' school success: Coping with the "burden of 'acting white.'" *Urban Review, 18*(3), 176–206.

Fried, L., & Chapman, E. (2012). An investigation into the capacity of student motivation and emotion regulation strategies to predict engagement and resilience in the middle school classroom. *Australian Educational Researcher, 39*(3), 295–311.

Garbarino, J. (1995). *Raising children in a socially toxic environment.* San Francisco, CA: Jossey-Bass.

Garmezy, N. (1971). Vulnerability research and the issue of primary prevention. *American Journal of Orthopsychiatry, 41,* 101–116.

Garmezy, N. (1974). The study of competence in children at risk for severe psychopathology. *Children at Psychiatric Risk, 3,* 77–97.

Gerstl-Pepin, C. (2002). Magnet schools: A retrospective case study of segregation. *High School Journal, 85*(3), 47–52.

Gonzalez, R., & Padilla, A.M. (1997). The academic resilience of Mexican American high school students. *Hispanic Journal of Behavioral Sciences, 19,* 301–317.

Gordon, E.W., & Song, L.D. (1994). Variations in the experience of resilience. In M.C. Wang & E.W. Gordon (Eds.), *Educational resilience in inner-city America: Challenges and prospects* (pp. 27–43). Hillsdale, NJ: Lawrence Erlbaum Associates.

Gorman-Smith, D., Tolan, P.H., & Henry, D.B. (2000). A developmental-ecological model of family functioning to patterns of delinquency. *Journal of Quantitative Criminology, 16*(2), 169–198.

Gorman-Smith, D., Tolan, P., & Henry, D. (2010). Promoting resilience in the inner city: Families as a venue for protection, support, and opportunity. In R.D. Peters, B. Leadbeater, & R.J. McMahon (Eds.), *Resilience in children, families, and communities* (pp. 137–155). New York, NY: Kluwer Academic/Plenum.

Hall, M., & Lee, B. (2010). How diverse are suburbs? *Urban Studies, 47*(3), 3–28.

Han, H.S., & Thomas, M.S. (2010). No child misunderstood: Enhancing early childhood teachers' multicultural responsiveness to the social competence of diverse children. *Early Childhood Education Journal, 37,* 469–476.

Hawkins, R., & Mulkey, L.M. (2005). Athletic investment and academic resilience in a national sample of African American females and males in the middle grades. *Education and Urban Society, 38*(1), 62–88.

Haynes, N. (2007). The comer school development program: A pioneering approach to improving social, emotional and academic competence. In R. Bar-On, J.G. Maree, & M. Elias (Eds.), *Educating people to be emotionally intelligent* (pp. 95–107). Westport, CT: Praeger.

Hill, L.D. (2008). School strategies and the "college-linking" process: Reconsidering the effects of high schools on college enrollment. *Sociology of Education, 81*(1), 53–76.

Jarrett, R.L. (1994). Living poor: Family life among single parent, African-American women. *Social Problems, 41,* 30–49.

Jarrett, R.L., & Jefferson, S.R. (2003). "A good mother got to fight for her kids": Maternal management strategies in a high-risk, African-American neighborhood. *Journal of Children and Poverty, 9*(1), 21–39.

Johnson, O. (2012). A systematic review of neighborhood and institutional relationships related to education. *Education and Urban Society, 44*(4), 477–511.

Kanevsky, L., Corke, M., & Frangkiser, L. (2008). The academic resilience and psychosocial characteristics of inner-city English learners in a museum-based school program. *Education and Urban Society, 40*(4), 452–475.

Kelly, R.D. (1998). *"Yo' mama's disfunktional!"*: Fighting the culture wars in urban America. Boston, MA: Beacon Press.

Kim-Cohen, J., Moffitt, T.E., Caspi, A., & Taylor, A. (2004). Genetic and environmental processes in young children's resilience and vulnerability to socioeconomic deprivation. *Child Development, 75*(3), 651–668.

Klem, A.M., & Connell, J.P. (2004). Relationships matter: Linking teacher support to student engagement. *Journal of School Health, 74,* 262–273.

Kornhauser, Ruth. (1978). *Social sources of delinquency.* Chicago, IL: University of Chicago Press.

Ladson-Billings, G. (2006). From the achievement gap to the education debt: Understanding achievement in U.S. schools. *Educational Researcher, 35*(7), 3–12.

Ladson-Billings, G. (2009). *The dreamkeepers: Successful teachers of African American children.* San Francisco, CA: John Wiley & Sons.

Lareau, A. (2002). Invisible inequality: Social class and childrearing in black families and white families. *American Sociological Review, 67*(5), 747–776.

Leadbeater, B., Dodgen, D., & Solarz, A. (2010). The resilience revolution: A paradigm shift for research and policy?. In R.D. Peters, B. Leadbeater, & R.J. McMahon (Eds.), *Resilience in children, families, and communities* (pp. 47–61). New York, NY: Kluwer Academic/Plenum.

Leonardo, Z., & Hunter, M. (2007). Imagining the urban: The politics of race, class, and schooling. In W.T. Pink and G.W. Noblit (Eds.), *International handbook of urban education,* vol. 19 (pp. 779–802). Dordrecht, The Netherlands: Springer International Handbooks of Education.

Li, S.T., Nussbaum, K.M., & Richards, M.H. (2007). Risk and protective factors for urban African-American youth. *American Journal of Community Psychology, 39*(1), 21–35.

Love, A., & Kruger, A. (2005). Teacher beliefs and student achievement in urban schools serving African American students. *Journal of Educational Research, 99*(2), 87–98.

Luthar , S.S. (1991). Vulnerability and resilience: A study of high-risk adolescents. *Child Development, 62*(3), 600–616.

Luthar, S.S. (2006). Resilience in development: A synthesis of research across five decades. In D. Cicchetti & D.J. Cohen (Eds.), *Risk, disorder, and adaptation* (Vol. 3, pp. 739–795). New York, NY: John Wiley & Sons.

Luthar, S.S., Cicchetti, D., & Becker, B. (2000). The construct of resilience: A critical evaluation and guidelines for future work. *Child Development, 71,* 543–562.

Luthar, S.S., Doernberger, C.H., & Zigler, E. (1993). Resilience is not a unidimensional construct: Insights from a prospective study of inner-city adolescents. *Development and Psychopathology, 5*(4), 703–717.

Lyman, W. (1984). The University of Rochester Child and Family Study: Overview of research plan. In N.F. Watt, E.J. Anthony, L.C. Wynne, & J.E. Rolf (Eds.), *Children at risk for schizophrenia: A longitudinal perspective* (pp. 335–347). New York, NY: Cambridge University Press.

Massey, D., & Denton, N. (1993). *American apartheid: Segregation and the making of the underclass.* Cambridge, MA: Harvard University Press.

Masten, A.S. (1994). Resilience in individual development: Successful adaptation despite risk and adversity. In M. Wang & E. Gordon (Eds.), *Risk and resilience in inner-city America: Challenges and prospects* (pp. 3–25). Hillsdale, NJ: Lawrence Erlbaum Associates.

Masten, A.S. (2001). Ordinary magic: Resilience process in development. *American Psychologist, 56,* 227–238.

Masten, A.S. (2007). Resilience in developing systems: Progress and promise as the fourth wave rises. *Development and Psychopathology, 19,* 921–930.

Masten, A.S., Best, K.M., & Garmezy, N. (1990). Resilience and development: Contributions from the study of children who overcome adversity. *Development and Psychopathology, 2*(4), 425–444.

Maton, K.I. (2005). The social transformation of environments and the promotion of resilience in children. In R.D. Peters, B. Leadbeater, & R.J. McMahon (Eds.), *Resilience in children, families, and communities* (pp. 119–135). New York, NY: Kluwer Academic/Plenum.

McCubbin, L.D., & McCubbin, H.I. (2013). Resilience in ethnic family systems: A relational theory for research and practice. In D.S. Becvar (Eds.), *Handbook of family resilience* (pp. 175–195). New York, NY: Springer.

McDonough, P. (1997). *Choosing colleges: How social class and schools structure opportunity.* Albany, NY: State University of New York Press.

Miller, D., & MacIntosh, R. (1999). Promoting resilience in urban African American adolescents: Racial socialization and identity as protective factors. *Social Work Research, 3,* 159–169.

Miller, D.B., Webster, S.E., & MacIntosh, R. (2002). What's there and what's not: Measuring daily hassles in urban African American adolescents. *Research on Social Work Practice, 12*(3), 375–388.

Mirel, J. (1999). *The rise and fall of an urban school system: Detroit, 1907–81.* Ann Arbor, MI: University of Michigan Press.

Morales, E.E. (2000). A contextual understanding of the process of educational resilience: High achieving Dominican American students and the "resilience cycle." *Innovative Higher Education, 25,* 7–22.

Morales, E.E. (2010). Linking strengths: Identifying and exploring protective factor clusters in academically resilient low-socioeconomic urban students of color. *Roeper Review, 32*(3), 164–175.

Morgan, H. (2012). Poverty-stricken schools: What we can learn from the rest of the world and from successful schools in economically disadvantaged areas in the US. *Education, 133*(2), 291–297.

Morris, J.E. (2004). Can anything good come from Nazareth? Race, class, and African American schooling and community in the urban south and Midwest. *American Educational Research Journal, 41*(1), 69–112.

Morrison, G. M., Brown, M., D'Incau, B., O'Farrell, S. L., Furlong, M. J. (2006). Understanding resilience in educational trajectories: Implications for protective possibilities. *Psychology in the Schools*, 43, 1, 19–31.

Murphy, A.K. (2007). The suburban ghetto: The legacy of Herbert Gans in understanding the experience of poverty in recently impoverished American suburbs. *City and Community, 6*(1), 21–37.

Murphy, L.B. (1974). Coping, vulnerability, and resilience in childhood. In G.V. Coelho, D.A. Hamburg, & J.E. Adams (Eds.), *Coping and adaptation* (pp. 69–100). New York, NY: Basic Books.

Murphy, L.B., & Moriarty, A.E. (1976). *Vulnerability, coping, and growth: From infancy to adolescence.* New Haven, CT: Yale University Press.

New York Times. (2012). Editorial—The exclusive eight. Retrieved from http://www.nytimes.com/2012/10/17/opinion/the-exclusive-eight-high-schools.html?ref=stuyvesanthighschool&_r=0

Newsweek. (2010). America's best high schools: The List, #17 Preuss UCSD. Retrieved from http://www.newsweek.com/content/newsweek/feature/2010/americas-best-high-schools/list.html

Obmascik, M. (1999, April 21). High school massacre: Columbine bloodbath leaves up to 25 dead. *Denver Post.* Retrieved from http://search.proquest.com.proxy.lib.umich.edu/docview/410629524?accountid=14667

O'Conner, J., Mason, M., & Mennis, J. (2012). Valuing but not liking school: Revisiting the relationship between school attitudes and substance use among urban youth. *Education and Urban Society, 44*(6), 672–687.

O'Connor, C. (1997). Dispositions toward (collective) struggle and educational resilience in the inner city: A case analysis of six African-American high school students. *American Educational Research Journal, 34,* 593–629.

O'Connor, C. (2002). Black women beating the odds from one generation to the next: How the changing dynamics of constraint and opportunity affect the process of educational resilience. *American Educational Research Journal, 39*(4), 855–903.

O'Connor, C., & Fernandez, S.D. (2006). Race, class, and disproportionality: Reevaluating the relationship between poverty and special education placement. *Educational Researcher, 35*(6), 6–11.

O'Connor, C., Fernandez, S.D., & Girard, B. (2007). The meaning of "Blackness": How Black students differentially align race and achievement across time and space. In A. Fuligni (Ed.), *Contesting stereotypes and creating identities* (pp. 183–208). New York, NY: Sage.

O'Donnell, D.A., Schwab-Stone, M.E., & Muyeed, A.Z. (2002). Multidimensional resilience in urban children exposed to community violence. *Child Development, 73,* 1265–1282.

Pager, D. (2007). Marked: Race, crime, and finding work in an era of mass incarceration. Chicago, IL: University of Chicago Press.

Plunkett, S., Henry, C., Houltberg, B., Sands, T., & Abarca-Mortenson, S. (2008). Academic support by significant others and educational resilience in Mexican-origin ninth grade students from intact families. *Journal of Early Adolescence, 28*(3), 333–355.

Poulin-Dubois, D., Blaye, A., Coutya, J., & Bialystok, E. (2011). The effects of bilingualism on toddlers' executive functioning. *Journal of Experimental Child Psychology, 108*(3), 567–569.

Prelow, H.M., & Loukas, A. (2003). The role of resource, protective, and risk factors on academic achievement-related outcomes of economically disadvantaged Latino youth. *Journal of Community Psychology, 31,* 513–529.

Reis, S.M., Colbert, R., & Herbert, T.P. (2005). Understanding resilience in diverse, talented students in an urban high school. *Roeper Review, 27,* 110–115.

Reynolds, A.J. (1998). Resilience among black urban youth: Prevalence, intervention, effects, and mechanisms of influence. *American Journal of Orthopsychiatry, 68*(1), 84–100.

Ripple, C., & Luthar, S. (2000). Academic risk among inner city adolescents: The role of personal attributes. *Journal of School Psychology, 38*(3), 277–298.

Rivera, H.H., & Waxman, H.C. (2011). Resilient and nonresilient Hispanic English language learners' attitudes toward their classroom learning environment in mathematics. *Journal of Education for Students Placed at Risk, 16,* 185–200.
Rutter, M. (1979). Protective factors in children's responses to stress and disadvantage. In M.W. Kent & J.E. Rolf (Eds.), *Primary prevention of psychopathology. Vol. 3, Social competence in children* (pp. 49–74). Hanover, NH: University Press of New England.
Rutter, M. (1990). Psychosocial resilience and protective mechanisms. In J. Rolf, A.S. Masten, D. Cicchetti, K.H. Nuechterlein, & S. Weintraub (Eds.), *Risk and protective factors in the development of psychopathology* (pp. 181–214). New York: Cambridge University Press.
Saatcioglu, A., & Rury, J.L. (2012). Education and the changing metropolitan organization of inequality: A multilevel analysis of secondary attainment in the United States, 1940–1980. *Historical Methods: A Journal of Quantitative and Interdisciplinary History, 45*(1), 21–40.
Samel, A.N., Sondergeld, T.A., Fischer, J.M., & Patterson, N.C. (2011). The secondary school pipeline: Longitudinal indicators of resilience and resistance in urban schools under reform. *High School Journal, 94*(3), 95–118.
Sampson, R.J., & Groves, W.B. (1989). Community structure and crime: Testing social-disorganization theory. *American Journal of Sociology, 94*(4), 774–802.
Scarr, S., & McCartney, K. (1983). How people make their own environments. A theory of genotype environment effects. *Child Development, 54*(2), 424–435.
Schoon, I., & Bynner, J. (2003). Risk and resilience in the life course: Implications for interventions and social policies. *Journal of Youth Studies, 6*(1), 21–31.
Sellers, R.M. (2012, July 22–July 27). *Racial identity matters: The role of race, risk, and resilience in the psychological well-being of African American youth.* Paper presented at the 2012 meeting of the International Congress of Psychology, Cape Town, South Africa.
Sellers, R.M., Chavous, T.M., & Cooke, D.Y. (1998). Racial ideology and racial centrality as predictors of African American college students' academic performance. *Journal of Black Psychology, 24*(1), 8–27.
Sellers, R.M., & Shelton, J.N. (2003). The role of racial identity in perceived racial discrimination. *Journal of Personality and Social Psychology, 84*(5), 1079–1092.
Shaw, C., & McKay, H. (1942). *Juvenile delinquency and urban areas.* Chicago, IL: University of Chicago Press.
Shin, R., Daly, B. & Vera, E. (2007). The relationships of peer norms, ethnic identity and peer support to school engagement in urban youth. *Professional School Counseling, 10*(4), 379–388.
Shumow, L., Vandell, D.L., & Posner, J. (1999). Risk and resilience in the urban neighborhood: Predictors of academic performance among low-income elementary school children. *Merrill-Palmer Quarterly, 45*(2), 309–331.
Sizemore, B. (1988). The Madison elementary school: A turnaround case. *Journal of Negro Education, 57*(3), 243–266.
Slavin, R.E. (1996). Success for all: A summary of research. *Journal of Education for Students Placed at Risk, 1*(1), 41–76.
Smokowski, P.R., Reynolds, A.J., & Bezruczko, N. (1999). Resilience and protective factors in adolescence: An autobiographical perspective from disadvantaged youth. *Journal of Psychology, 37*(4), 425–448.
Sosa, T. (2012). Showing up, remaining engaged and partaking as students: Resilience among students of Mexican descent. *Journal of Latinos and Education, 11*(1), 32–46.
Sosa, T., & Gomez, K. (2012). Positioning urban teachers as effective: Their discourse on students. *Education and Urban Society, 44*(5), 590–608.
Southworth, S., & Mickelson, R.A. (2007). The interactive effects of race, gender and school composition on college track placement. *Social Forces, 86*(2), 497–523.
Spencer, M. (2005). Crafting identities and accessing opportunities post-*Brown*. *American Psychologist, 60*(8), 821–830.

Spencer, M., Harpalani, V., Cassidy, E., Jacobs, C., Donde, S., Goss, T., Miller, M.-M., Charles, N., & Wilson, S. (2006). Understanding vulnerability and resilience from a normative development perspective: Implications for racially and ethnically diverse youth. In D. Chicchetti and E. Cohen (Eds.), *Handbook of developmental psychopathology* (Vol. 1, pp. 627–672). Hoboken, NJ: John Wiley & Sons.

Stanton-Salazar, R. D. (2001). *Manufacturing hope and despair: The school and kin support networks of U.S.-Mexican youth.* New York, NY: Teachers College Press.

Stanton-Salazar, R.D., & Spino, S.U. (2000). The network orientations of highly resilient urban minority youth: A network-analytic account of minority socializations and its educational implications. *Urban Review, 32,* 227–261.

Tiet, Q.Q., Huizinga, D., & Byrnes, H.F. (2010). Predictors of resilience among inner-city youths. *Journal of Child and Family Studies, 19,* 360–378.

US News and World Report. (2012). Best high schools: Magnet schools. Retrieved from http://www.usnews.com/education/best-high-schools/national-rankings/magnet-school-rankings

Valenzuela, A. (1999). *Subtractive schooling: U.S.-Mexican youth and the politics of caring.* Albany, NY: State University of New York Press.

Wang, M.C., & Gordon, E.W. (1994). *Educational resilience in inner-city America: Challenges and prospects* (pp. 27–43). Hillsdale, NJ: Lawrence Erlbaum Associates.

Wang, M.C., Haertel, G.D., & Walberg, H.J. (1990). What influences learning? A content analysis of the review literature. *Journal of Education Research, 84*(1), 30–43.

Wang, M.C., Haertel, G.D., & Walberg, H.J. (1994). Educational resilience in inner cities. In M.C. Wang & E.W. Gordon (Eds.), *Educational resilience in inner-city America: Challenges and prospects* (pp. 45–72). Hillsdale, NJ: Lawrence Erlbaum Associates.

Watt, N.F., Anthony, E.J., Wynne, L.C., & Rolf, J.E. (1984). *Children at risk for schizophrenia: A longitudinal perspective.* New York, NY: Cambridge University Press.

Waxman, H.C., & Huang, S.Y.L. (1996). Motivation and learning environment differences in inner-city middle school students. *Journal of Educational Research, 90*(2), 93–102.

Waxman, H.C., Padrón, Y.N., Shin, J.Y., & Rivera, H.H. (2008). Closing the achievement gap within reading and mathematics by fostering Hispanic students' educational resilience. *International Journal of Social Sciences, 3*(1), 24–34.

Werner, E.E., & Smith, R.S. (1982). *Vulnerable but invincible: A longitudinal study of resilient children and youth.* New York, NY: McGraw-Hill.

Werner, E.E. & Smith, R.S. (1992). *Overcoming the odds: High risk children from birth to adulthood.* Ithaca, NY: Cornell University Press.

Wilson, W. J. (1987). *The truly disadvantaged: The inner-city, the underclass, and public policy.* Chicago, IL: University of Chicago Press.

Wilson, W.J. (1996). *When work disappears: The world of the urban poor.* New York, NY: Alfred A. Knopf.

Worland, J., Weeks, D.G., & Janes, C.L. (1987). Predicting mental health in children at risk. In E.J. Anthony & B.J. Cohler (Eds.), *The invulnerable child* (pp. 185–210). New York, NY: Guilford Press.

Wyman, P.A., Cowen, E.L., Work, W.C., Hoyt-Meyers, L., Magnus, K.B., & Fagen, D.B. (1999). Caregiving and developmental factors differentiating young at-risk urban children showing resilient versus stress-affected outcomes: A replication and extension. *Child Development, 70*(3), 645–659.

5

Ethnic-Matching in Urban Schools

Donald Easton-Brooks

As the field of education views the landscape of urban schools over the past few decades, the evidence shows that many ethnic minority students[1] are generationally not hitting or exceeding satisfactory academic benchmarks. While there are a number of approaches, policies, and research on strategies designed to help ethnic minority students become more successful in urban schools, research has been clear on the need for a greater connection or continuity between home culture and school culture (Ledlow, 1992; Reed-Danahay, 2000; St. Germaine, 1995). Within a system heavily populated by ethnic minority students and nonethnic minority teachers, developing connections or building continuity between school and home cultures can be challenging and in turn can contribute to the dismal outcomes we see among some ethnic minorities in urban school settings.

Researchers (Banks, 1996; Easton-Brooks, Lewis, & Zhang, 2010; Foster, 1990, 1997; Gay, 2000; Holmes, 1990; Irvine & Irvine, 1983; Ladson-Billings, 1994; Lewis, 2006; Lynn, 2006; Milner, 2006; Ogbu, 2003; Shipp, 1999) have argued that diversifying the teacher education profession can open up opportunities to discuss the challenges of connecting diverse home cultures with school culture, as well as assisting in effective policies for promoting better school environments and outcomes for students. Further, some researchers and policy makers hold to the fact that schools and teachers account for less than 10% of the changes in the academic outcomes of students, with factors outside of the school accounting for roughly 90% of the difference in the academic outcomes of students (Easton-Brooks & Davis, 2009; Hanushek, Kain, & Rivkin, 2002). However, in this chapter, I present evidence that shows that if students are in schools with teachers of their same ethnicity, this process can account for or explain up to 17% of the difference in academic outcomes of ethnic minority students.

As this chapter will also point out, an issue facing U.S. public and urban schools is in the changing demographics of the U.S., urban, and public school population, with an increased number of nonethnic minority teachers and ethnic minority students entering public classrooms. Another issue pointed out in this chapter is the need for increasing the retention of ethnic minority teachers. The chapter will also present the impact of ethnic-matching on the outcomes of ethnic minority students, as well as studies validating the reason ethnic-matching has an impact on the academic achievement scores of ethnic minority students. This chapter will conclude with summarizing the findings of ethnic-matching for ethnic minority students as well as suggesting strategies designed to aid in diversifying public and urban schools.

Trends in Population Shifts in the United States

As we explore the impact of ethnic-matching, it is important to consider the changing trend in the U.S. population. A most recent U.S. Census (2006) report shows that over a span of two decades, the U.S. ethnic landscape has changed considerably, as the rate of ethnic minorities in the United States has grown at a rate dwarfing the growth of European Americans. U.S. Census data have shown that between 1980 and 2005, Asian/Pacific Islanders grew 260%, Spanish-speakers grew 192%, Native Americans grew 68%, and African Americans grew 39%. In comparison, European Americans grew 10%. The U.S. Census Bureau predicts that by 2020, the U.S. ethnic minority population will increase by 32 percent, meaning that ethnic minorities will make up 39% of the total U.S. population.

Further, a 2011 U.S. Census report concluded that between 2010 and 2050 this trend would continue. What is interesting to note is that while U.S. Census shows that 79.5% of the U.S. population is White (this percentage includes those of Hispanic descent), Table 5.1 shows that White non-Hispanic people make up 64.7% of the U.S. population. The table also shows an increase in the rate of Asian and Hispanic/Latinos and a slight increase in non-Hispanic Whites and African Americans over the next 40 years. This matches the data shown in Table 5.2. The table shows that between 1990 and 2011, there has been a noticeable increase in the birth of Hispanic/ Latinos and Asian American populations (65% and 56%, respectfully) and a decrease in the White non-Hispanic, African American, and Native American populations (between 18 to 12%). These findings suggest that not only are we seeing a change in the ethnic make-up of the U.S. population, we are also seeing a possible major linguistic influence on the U.S. population.

Similar to the national growth in ethnic minorities, U.S. public schools have also experienced an increase in this population. During a 10-year span (1993 to 2003), the public school ethnic minority population increased 7%, with Spanish-speakers and Asian students representing the largest increase in history. In 2004, ethnic minorities made up 42% of U.S. public school enrollments. Other data show that four out of ten students in U.S. schools are ethnic minority students (U.S. Department of Education, 2006). Still, Ingersoll and May (2011) found that between

Table 5.1 U.S. Census Population Projections (2010–2050)

Demographics	*2010*	*2050*
Non-Hispanic Whites	64.7%	46.3%
Hispanics/Latinos (of any race)	16.0%	30.2%
African Americans	12.9%	13.0%
Asian Americans	4.6%	7.8%

Source: Vincent and Velkoff (2010).

Table 5.2 Birth Rates (1990 to 2011)

Ethnic Groups	*1990*	*2011*	*Change*
White Non-Hispanic	2,626,500	2,150,926	–18%
African American	661,701	583,079	–12%
Hispanic/Latino	595,073	912,290	+65%
Asian American	141,635	253,864	+56%
Native American	39,051	46,536	–16%

Source: U.S. National Center for Health Statistics (2012).

1988 and 2008 the number of ethnic minority students in public schools increased 73% while White students decreased by 2%. It is predicted that by 2026, ethnic minorities will represent 70% of the public school population.

Data also show that in 2004, inner-city urban schools had a growth of 9%, with ethnic minorities representing 65% of the population. Also of importance, urban fringe public[2] schools saw an increase of 5%, 2% less than the national average. Ethnic minority students represent 37% of the urban fringe public school population. Spanish-speakers make up the largest percent of growth in ethnic minorities in both inner-city urban and urban fringe public schools.

The Trend of Ethnic Minority Teachers in Public Schools

While there is a belief that there is a decline in the number of ethnic minority teachers in U.S. public schools, recent studies have shown that this is not necessarily the case. When the data are examined at a glance, research (Ingersoll & May, 2011) shows that elementary public schools are made up of 41% ethnic minority students, secondary schools are made up of 31% ethnic minority students, and only 16% of public schools are staffed by ethnic minority teachers. However, surprisingly, from the nationally representative Schools and Staffing Survey (SASS) and the Teacher Follow-up Survey (TFS), studies (Bireda & Chait, 2011; Boser, 2011; Ingersoll and May, 2011) found that while the gap between percentage of ethnic minority students and ethnic minority teachers exists, since the late 1980s, the number of European American teachers has decreased while the number of ethnic minority teachers increased. Ingersoll and May (2011) found that while the number of nonethnic minority teachers increased 41%, the number of ethnic minority teachers increased 96%. These findings show that the growth in the number of ethnic minority teachers has more than doubled the growth in nonethnic minority teachers. The authors also found that during this time, the number of ethnic minority teachers has almost doubled and the growth in ethnic minority teachers has been greater than the growth of ethnic minority students. While these findings show that there is a notable increase in the percentage of ethnic minority teachers over a two-decade span, ethnic minority teachers still only make up 16.5% of the public school teaching population. Therefore, the gap between students and ethnic minority teachers is still considerably large. Further, these findings vary by demographic groups. For instance, prior to 1978, African American teachers represented 12% of the teacher workforce. In the 2003–2004 academic year, African American teachers represented 7% of the teacher workforce.

Findings (Bireda & Chait, 2011; Boser, 2011; Ingersoll and May, 2011) also show that the growth of ethnic minority teachers even doubled the growth rate of nonethnic minority teachers. Bireda and Chait attribute this increase to programs such as Teach for America, the New Teacher Project-Fellowship Program, the Urban Teacher Enhancement Program, the North Carolina Teaching Fellows Scholarship Program, and Teacher Tomorrow in Oakland. Findings (Bireda & Chait, 2011; Boser, 2011) found that more than a quarter of African American and Spanish-speaking teachers come through alternative licensure programs, compared to 11% of White teachers.

While there has been some movement toward reducing the gap between ethnic minority students and teachers, Boser (2011) has shown that there are some strong spots and weak spots in reducing this gap. Using SASS data, Boser developed a teacher diversity gap index ([TDI], p. 2), which ranks states on the percentage point difference between ethnic minority teachers and students. I then pull data from the achievement test score gap, by state, between Spanish-speakers and European American students; and African American and European American students from the National Assessment of Educational Progress (NAEP) dataset. I then ran a Pearson correlation to determine if there was a correlation between the TDI and the achievement gap for each group in reading and mathematics at 8th grade. I found that there was a significant correlation on all measures ranging between $r = .46$ to .77. These findings suggest that as the gap in the teacher/student diversity increases, the state achievement score gap for Spanish-speakers and African American students increases significantly.

What was noticed in the Boser study was that there were four states (Vermont 4%, Maine 4%, West Virginia 4%, and New Hampshire 6%) with a less than 10% gap between students and teachers. However, these states (Vermont 6%, Maine 6%, West Virginia 7%, and New Hampshire 8%) have the lowest ethnic minority population in the country. To further understand the impact of the findings from the TDI, I ran a Pearson correlation between the TDI and the percentage of ethnic minorities (PEMS) who reside in a state. The findings showed a significantly strong positive correlation ($r = .73, p < .01$) between the TDI and PEMS. These findings suggest that the greater the percentage of ethnic minorities in a state, the higher the gap between ethnic minority teachers and students. I then created a similar index (State Teacher Diversity Index [STDI]) by subtracting the PEMS from the TDI. For instance, Minnesota had a TDI of 21 and a PEMS of 17. Therefore, the STDI for Minnesota was –4. These findings suggest that the difference in the relationship between ethnic minority teachers and students is 4% greater than the percentage of minorities in the state.

I then ran a Pearson correlation on the STDI and the 8th grade reading achievement gap scores of African Americans and European American students. I found a significant negative correlation ($r = -47, p = .002$). These findings suggest that those states with a low STDI score are associated with having a high reading achievement gap score between African American and European American students. In other words, if the difference in the percentage of ethnic minority teachers and students is greater than the percentage of minorities in the state (indicated by a low STDI), the state will have a significantly higher reading achievement gap between African American and European American students than those states with a higher STDI (difference in percentage of ethnic minority teachers and students is lower than the percentage of minorities in the state). In summarizing these findings, there is a significant association between states with lower gaps between their diverse teachers and students and the achievement score gaps.

Related to ethnic minority teachers in the field, studies (Bireda & Chait, 2011; Boser, 2011; Ingersoll and May, 2011) show that these teachers are primarily employed in public schools serving high-poverty, high-ethnic minority, and urban student populations. Their findings show that ethnic minority teachers are two to three times more likely than nonethnic minority teachers to work in schools with students from families and communities with high stress factors. In turn, nonethnic minority teachers are more likely to leave schools with a higher percentage of ethnic minority students when these schools have high poverty or are in urban communities.

Related to ethnic minority teachers retention, Ingersoll and May (2011) found that over the past 20 years, ethnic minority teachers transferred from school to school or left the profession at a higher rate than their European American counterparts, at statistically significant levels. The gap in the turnover rate has grown over a 20-year span. For instance, in the 1987–1988 academic year, there was a 0.7% difference in the turnover rate between ethnic minority teachers and nonethnic minority teachers. In three academic years (1994–1995, 2004–2005, and 2008–2009), there was a 3 to 4% difference in the turnover rate between ethnic minority teachers and nonethnic minority teachers. Salary could be one of the contributing factors to transfers and turnover; as Boser (2011) found, 63% of African American and 54% of Spanish-speaking teachers were not satisfied with their pay compared to 48% of White teachers.

Given that ethnic minority teachers are often more employed in high-needs schools, the researchers found factors such as salaries, classroom resources, and professional development opportunities had little to do with these teachers leaving the classroom. While Ingersoll and May (2011) found that 35% of the ethnic minority teachers who left the profession return, they found that faculty decision making and the degree of individual instructional autonomy were the most influential factors for ethnic minority teachers leaving the classroom. These findings simply present that ethnic minority teachers, whose input is more valued, tend to stay in the classroom at a higher rate than those teachers whose input is less valued. The pressing point of these findings is that ethnic minority teachers are electing to teach in schools with higher populations of ethnic minority students who are in high-challenging schools. This desire to teach in these schools may come from their desire to impact the change in the lives of ethnic minority students (Milner, 2006). However, what these teachers may be finding is the value in standardized test and test scores outweigh the need for connecting with students at a more humanistic or cultural level. Further, Boser (2011) found that ethnic minority teachers were less satisfied with the way their school was run in comparison to White teachers.

These findings show that despite the gap between ethnic minority teachers and ethnic minority students, the effort to recruit ethnic minority teachers is greater than in previous decades. However, it seems that keeping or retaining ethnic minority teachers has become a new challenge. With this challenge, research has shown that there is a tremendous need for an increasingly diverse teacher population. Research (Dee, 2004; Easton-Brooks et al., 2010; Eddy & Easton-Brooks, 2011) has shown that when matched with a teacher of the same ethnicity, elementary-level ethnic minority students performed higher on academic achievement tests than those ethnic minority students who are not taught by ethnic minority teachers.

Ethnic-Matching Outcomes

While this chapter focuses on ethnic-matching in the field of education, this topic is not exclusive to the field of education. In fields outside of education, researchers have found that ethnic-matching is a beneficial practice. Researchers have shown that ethnic-matching in the workplace (Elliott & Smith, 2001; Field & Caetano, 2010; Flicker, Waldron, Turner, Brody, & Hops, 2008) reduces tension in work environments. Research (Campbell & Campbell, 2007) has also shown that in a higher education environment, ethnic-matching mentoring between faculty and students increases the GPA, number of units completed, and retention rate by the end of students' first year in college. The findings also show that these students stay on campus to pursue graduate studies and complete teaching credentials at a higher rate than those not mentored by the same ethnic mentors. Further, research (Cabral & Smith, 2011; Shin, Chow, Camacho-Gonsalves, Levy, Allen, & Leff, 2005) in the counseling and therapeutic field has also found ethnic-matching to produce desirable outcomes.

However, research on ethnic-matching in the field of education is limited. Of the 151 articles and 20 books on the topic of ethnic-matching found, 5 articles focus on ethnic-matching in education, with 2 centered on urban education. Additionally, 4 of these studies are limited to examining the effects of ethnic-matching between African American students and teachers in elementary school. It is critical that the field of education take a closer look at the impact of ethnic-matching on the academic outcomes of all ethnic minority students. It cannot be assumed that the findings associated with African American students will be representative of all minority students. Below are a few quantitative research studies, which point out the impact of ethnic-matching and the critical need for the field of education to explore more quantitative studies on ethnic-matching among various other ethnic minority populations.

In 2004, Dee's study on teachers, race, and student achievement examined the impact of ethnic-matching between African American teachers and African American students, and between European American teachers and European American students. In the study, Dee used longitudinal data from Tennessee's Project STAR. The data were collected on students entering kindergarten in 1985 and follow-up data were collected over the next 3 years. Given the limited number of Spanish-speakers, Asian, and Native American participants, Dee was only able to examine teacher/student ethnic-matching on the African American and European American populations.

Dee's study examined the effects of teacher/student ethnic-matching based on students' scores on the Stanford Achievement Tests (SAT) in math and reading. The findings in this study indicated that test scores among African American and European American students were higher for those assigned to a teacher of their own ethnicity. The findings showed that smaller class size, being female, and free lunch eligibility also made a difference in achievement scores of students in a classroom with a teacher of their same ethnicity (see Table 5.3).

While the data above do not suggest a significant difference between having a teacher of the same ethnicity or not, in a regression analysis, Dee found a statistically significant association between ethnic-matching, small class size, free/reduced lunch eligibility, and mathematics scores, with scores increasing at least 3.2 percentile points higher. In other interesting findings, Dee found that in the urban schools, 97% of the students were African American, while 50% of the teachers were African American. This percentage gives more emphasis to the findings in Table 5.1, which suggest that these ethnic minority teachers had a greater impact on achievement scores among ethnic minority students. Similar cross-sectional studies showed that the reading skills (Hanushek, 1992) and the mathematics achievement (Clewell, Puma, & McKay, 2005) of African American students increased when an African American teacher was teaching these students.

Further findings by Dee showed that African American students were significantly less likely to have a teacher of their own ethnicity, which is not surprising given the low teacher/student ratio between African American teachers and African American students. Further, students eligible for free/reduced lunch were also significantly less likely to have a teacher of their own ethnicity. More notably, the study found that students assigned to a teacher of their own ethnicity were associated with higher achievement scores in both mathematics and reading. Kindergarten students with a teacher of their own ethnicity scored 3.6 percentile points higher in mathematics.

Table 5.3 Project STAR K–3 Data

Student Variables	*European American Students*		*African American Students*	
	Teacher of Own Race	*Teacher of Other Race*	*Teacher of Own Race*	*Teacher of Other Race*
Mathematics scores	56.7 (27.8)	50.0 (28.5)	40.7 (27.6)	37.6 (26.7)
Reading scores	56.9 (28.0)	51.5 (28.9)	39.9 (26.1)	37.6 (26.5)
Small class	0.31 (0.46)	0.29 (0.45)	0.30 (0.46)	0.27 (0.44)
Female students	0.48 (0.50)	0.48 (0.50)	0.50 (0.50)	0.49 (0.50)
Free lunch				
Sample Size	15,033	922	3,542	4,386

Source: Dee (2004, p. 198)

Clewell et al. (2005) presented one of the few studies on ethnic-matching on a non-African American student of color population. While African Americans were included in their study, the researchers focused on Spanish-speaking students. Their findings showed an increase in the reading and mathematics scores of African American and Spanish-speaking elementary students at 4th and 6th grade when taught by a teacher of their same ethnicity. For those Spanish-speaking students who were taught by a Spanish-speaking teacher of the same ethnicity, their mathematics scores at 4th and 6th grade were higher than those Spanish-speaking students who were not taught by a teacher of their same ethnicity. In reading, those Spanish-speaking students taught by a Spanish-speaking teacher of the same ethnicity scored higher than Spanish-speaking students who were not taught by a teacher of their same ethnicity.

While Dee's (2004) and Clewell et al.'s (2005) studies cannot be generalized to the entire U.S. population, these studies presented foundational findings for which factors to further examine ethnic-matching among teachers and ethnic minority students. Studies that follow these studies focus more on the long-term effects of ethnic-matching on the academic achievement of ethnic minority students. These studies on the long-term effects are more interested in the academic growth of ethnic minority students who were taught by an ethnic minority teacher.

In one longitudinal study, Zhang (2007) used the Early Childhood Longitudinal Study—Kindergarten (ECLS-K) dataset to explore the long-term effects of ethnic-matching on ethnic minority students. Zhang used this national dataset to study the effects of ethnic-matching on African American students from the beginning of kindergarten through the end of kindergarten. Zhang found that by the end of kindergarten, African American students do not necessarily benefit from having an African American teacher. However, the study is not a true longitudinal study in that longitudinal studies are traditionally designed around at least three data points. Additionally, at the time of her study, the ECLS-K data were limited to kindergarten data. In a follow-up study, Easton-Brooks et al. (2010) used the Early Childhood Longitudinal Study—Kindergarten through Fifth Grade (ECLS-K-5) data to again examine the long-term effect of ethnic-matching. However, the study was limited to African American students for two reasons: (1) the proportion of Asian and Native American teachers and students were limited in the dataset, and (2) it was difficult to determine if Spanish-speaking students in the study received language assistance associated with the possibility of limited English proficiency.

The researchers of this study used a two-level hierarchal linear model (HLM), which allowed them to examine the effects of ethnic-matching on the reading test scores and reading test score growth of students between kindergarten and 5th grade. To best understand the effects of teachers on the test scores of students, the researchers used value-added modeling (VAM) techniques (Ballou, Sanders, & Wright, 2004; Callender, 2004; McCaffrey, Lockwood, Koretz, Louis, & Hamilton, 2004; Sanders, Saxton, & Horn, 1997; Webster & Mendro, 1997). Researchers such as Rubin, Stuart, and Zanutto (2004) presented VAM as a technique for understanding how much of the change in student performance over time can be attributed to differences associated with the teacher. This approach accounted for approximately 60%–61% of the reliable variance in reading growth (Rowan, Correnti, & Miller, 2002).

Using VAM to determine the effectiveness of the classroom teacher, the researchers removed external variables that could confound the findings. The researchers removed students who were in special education as identified by those students with an Individualized Evaluation Plan (IEP) on file at any of the assessment points because such students were likely to receive instruction from multiple teachers, confounding the attribution of test score growth to a principal classroom teacher. Students who attended private schools or who transferred between schools at any of the assessment points were also eliminated from this study to avoid confounding teacher and school effects. Also excluded from this study were students who were not first-time kindergarteners or who were retained in kindergarten.

Other than issues related to confounding factors associated with these variables, participants who were removed from the study were based on a number of other important reasons. For instance, African American students, as well as other ethnic minority groups, often have a higher rate of having an IEP and transfer between schools at a higher rate than European American students. Therefore, removing or controlling for these factors allowed the researchers to eliminate those external factors that may have a greater effect on the achievement scores of African American students but not on the achievement scores of European American students. The researchers designed a study to examine the effects of ethnically matched teachers on a general population of students who experience less impact from external factors that can have a direct impact on academic achievement. This approach was conducive to specifically focusing on the effects of the classroom teacher.

Similar to Dee's study, 53% of the African American students in the Easton-Brooks et al. (2010) study had an African American teacher between kindergarten and 5th grade. In this national representative sample, only 26% of the African American students in schools with a minority population less than 50% had at least one African American teacher. In comparison, 61% of students in schools with a minority population above 50% had at least one African American teacher between kindergarten and 5th grade. Of those students living in a family in poverty, 65% had an African American teacher.

The study presented a partially conditional (model 2, see Table 5.4) and two fully conditional models (models 3 & 4, see Table 5.4). The first model (2) examined if having an African American teacher increased the reading achievement scores of African American students at kindergarten and their growth in reading achievement over time. The study found that African American students who had at least one African American teacher between kindergarten and 5th grade scored 1.50 points higher in reading than those students who did not have at least one African American teacher during this same time. While the student may not have had an African American teacher in kindergarten, a hypothesis is that even being exposed to an African American teacher in the school could have had an indirect effect on a student's achievement. However, there is no evidence to support this hypothesis. This model also showed that, for African American students who had at least one African American teacher between kindergarten and 5th grade, reading scores increased 1.75 points per year. Further, those students with at least one African American teacher scored at least 7 points higher in reading than African American students who did not have an African American teacher by the time these students completed 5th grade. This model accounted for 3% of the variance or difference in the growth of scores over time, meaning that the ethnic-matching variable explains 3% of the change in scores over time. While this is a small percentage, it is worth noting that ethnic-matching does account for some significant change in the reading achievement scores of students over time.

The next model (model 3) explained the effects of gender, the family social economic status (SES), and percentage of minorities in the school on reading achievement scores of African American students with an African American teacher. The findings show that having some exposure to an African American teacher had a significant effect on gender, with African American females scoring 2.31 points higher at kindergarten than males. Also, students in families with higher SES scored 4.41 higher than students in lower SES families, and the gap increased 4.18 points each year. These findings suggest that by 5h grade African American students with an African American teacher from a family with a high SES will score at least 16 points higher than African American students with an African American teacher from a family with a lower SES.

Table 5.4 Unconditional, Partial, and Conditional Model for Ethnic-Matching on Reading Achievement Scores

	Fully Unconditional		*Partially Conditional*		*Fully Conditional*			
	Model 1 (n = 1,207)		*Model 2 (n = 1,207)*		*Model 3 (n = 637)*		*Model 4 (n = 570)*	
	Est.	*S.E.*	*Est.*	*S.E.*	*Est.*	*S.E.*	*Est.*	*S.E.*
Intercept								
	36.75***	0.31	37.54***	0.44				
Intercept					35.10***	1.44	35.78***	1.06
Teacher's Ethnicity	–	–	–1.50**	0.60	–	–	–	–
Gender	–	–	–	–	2.31***	0.80	0.92	0.88
SES	–	–	–	–	4.41***	0.86	4.44***	0.88
% of Minorities	–	–	–	–	–2.05	1.38	–1.24	1.01
Random error	130.12***	9.29	129.51***	6.36	108.27***	7.51	140.55***	14.30
Slope								
	27.17***	0.38	28.10***	0.47				
Intercept					25.59***	1.02	27.06***	0.86
Teacher's Ethnicity	–	–	–1.75***	0.41	–	–	–	–
Gender	–	–	–	–	1.39	.054	1.26**	1.26
SES	–	–	–	–	4.18***	0.59	1.86**	3.24
% of Minorities	–	–	–	–	–0.63	0.93	–0.64	2.13
Random error	34.85***	2.18	33.97***	2.21	31.90***	2.84	29.42***	2.81

Note: * = p < .05; ** = p < .01, *** = p < .001. Easton-Brooks et al. (2010, p. 236).

Source: From Easton-Brooks et al. (2010, p. 236).

The variables in this model (i.e., having at least one African American teacher, gender, SES, and percentage of minorities in schools) explained 17% of the variance or difference in scores at the start of kindergarten and 8% of the difference in reading scores over time.

The last model (model 4) examined the effects of gender, the family social economic status (SES), and percentage of minorities in the school on reading of African American students who did not have at least one African American teacher between kindergarten and 5th grade. The model showed that those African American students in families with a higher SES and who did not have an African American teacher scored significantly higher at kindergarten (4.44 points), and the gap increased significantly by 1.86 points per year. However, there was not an effect of gender or percentage of minorities in the school on this population. It is important to note that having no exposure to an African American teacher combined with SES accounted for the highest percent of the variance or difference in the growth in reading between kindergarten and 5th grade (16%). However, a combined 25% of the variance or difference in scores was explained by having exposure to an African American teacher, gender, the family social economic status (SES), and percentage of ethnic minorities in the school.

While the study by Easton-Brooks et al. (2010) focused on the effects of ethnic-matching and reading achievement scores, Eddy and Easton-Brooks (2011) argued that the study focused on reading content and suggested that the relationship between the teachers and students language/ethnic dialect may have influenced the association between reading outcomes and ethnic-matching. The belief is that the interactions between teachers and students can be motivated by familiarity associated with cultural engagement. Delpit (1995) found that the usage of language and language styles (i.e., grammar and syntax, discourse style and interaction patterns, and behavioral norms) encourages the interaction between teachers and students of the same ethnicity. This familiarity can serve as a tool for helping teachers connect with the students in their classrooms. Further, Eddy and Easton-Brooks (2011) suggested that parents/guardians contribute more to the early reading development of children and focus less on early mathematics development. Therefore, schoolteachers teach most of the mathematics skills developed by young children. Furthermore, unlike reading, where cultural language can be used to provide meaning of words in context, the interpretation of mathematics constructs from a cultural framework can propose instructional difficulties. Therefore the researchers questioned whether ethnic-matching in a nonlanguage-related subject matter such as mathematics would show a significant long-term effect on student outcomes.

Table 5.5 Unconditional, Partial, and Conditional Model for Ethnic-Matching on Mathematics Achievement Scores

	Fully Unconditional		*Partially Conditional*		*Fully Conditional*			
	Model 1 (n = 1,200)		*Model 2 (n = 1,200)*		*Model 3 (n = 633)*		*Model 4 (n = 570)*	
	Est.	*S.E.*	*Est.*	*S.E.*	*Est.*	*S.E.*	*Est.*	*S.E.*
Intercept								
Intercept	27.85***	0.25	28.61***	0.37	28.31***	1.32	30.45***	0.92
Teacher's Ethnicity	–	–	–1.44**	0.50	–	–	–	–
Gender	–	–	–	–	0.66	0.68	–0.08	0.73
School Poverty	–	–	–	–	1.09	0.77	–1.24	0.96
% of Minorities	–	–	–	–	–3.01**	1.18	–2.14**	0.80
Community Setting					1.20	0.70	0.16	0.75
Random error	77.01***	4.27	76.42***	4.26	72.76***	5.62	76.04***	6.32
Slope								
Intercept	11.83***	0.10	12.18***	0.14	12.16***	0.49	13.03***	0.35
Teacher's Ethnicity	–	–	–0.64***	0.19	–	–	–	–
Gender	–	–	–	–	–0.22	0.26	–0.45	0.28
School Poverty	–	–	–	–	–0.43	0.30	–0.49	0.35
% of Minorities	–	–	–	–	–0.63***	0.93	–0.30***	0.31
Community Setting					0.87	0.26	–0.65	0.28
Random error	7.43***	0.46	7.31***	0.46	7.07***	0.59	6.83***	0.68

Note: * = p < .05; ** = p < .01, *** = p < .001. Eddy and Easton-Brooks (2011, p 1290)

Source: From Eddy and Easton-Brooks (2011, p. 1290).

Eddy and Easton-Brooks (2011) replicated the study by Easton-Brooks et al. (2010) (see Table 5.5). However, they used mathematics achievement scores in place of reading achievement scores. The researchers were able to conclude that African American students with at least one African American teacher did perform better in mathematics than African American students who did not have an African American teacher between kindergarten and 5th grade. Their findings showed that students who were exposed to at least one African American teacher scored significantly (1.44 points) higher on the mathematics achievement test at the end of kindergarten than students who were not exposed to an African American teacher between kindergarten and 5th grade. In addition, by the end of 5th grade, the growth in the mathematics scores of these students was at least 0.64 points higher than those students not exposed to an African American teacher between kindergarten and fifth grade. Different from the study by Easton-Brooks et al. (2010), this study found that the percentage of ethnic minorities in the school had a significant effect on mathematics scores. For instance, those African American students schools with a lower percentage of ethnic minorities and who had at least one African American teacher scored a significant 3.01 points higher than African American students with a lower percentage of ethnic minorities and who had at least one African American teacher. Additionally, the gap in the students' scores increased significantly .63 points per year. This model accounted for 6% of the difference in scores at kindergarten and 5% of the difference in the growth in scores over time. While these findings may not be surprising, the findings suggested that from those African American students in schools with a low percentage of minority students, having at least one African American teacher in the school has a significant impact on the mathematics scores of these students.

Validation on the Impact of Ethnic-Matching for Ethnic Minority Students

The quantitative studies presented above show the statistical impact of ethnic-matching. However, prior to the line of quantitative research, qualitative researchers (Foster, 1994, 1995, 1997; Henry, 1998; Ladson-Billings, 1994; Lewis, 2006; Milner, 2006; Milner & Howard, 2004; Ogbu, 2003; Shipp, 1999) have demonstrated a strong connection between culture and knowledge related to ethnic minority teachers when linked to the learning and instruction of ethnic minority students. The rationale backing these researchers is in understanding the differences between the home culture and school culture of students (Banks, 1996; Gay, 2000; Milner, 2007; Nieto, 2000). Some researchers (Foster, 1990, 1997; Holmes, 1990; Irvine & Irvine, 1983; Ladson-Billings, 1994; Lewis, 2006; Lynn, 2006; Milner, 2006; Ogbu, 2003; Shipp, 1999) suggested that ethnic minority teachers are better able to bridge the gap between home and school cultures of students. While others (Casteel, 1998; Ehrenberg, Goldhaber, & Brewer, 1995; Ferguson, 1998; Zimmerman, Khoury, Vega, Gil, & Warheit, 1995) have also found that the teachers tend to evaluate the academic outcomes of students of their own ethnicity more favorably than students of other ethnic groups. This can relate to cultural similarities that may exist between teachers and students.

These cultural similarities could be associated with the perceptions teachers have of the ability of students to learn. For instance, Dee (2004) found that if a student was not matched by both ethnicity and gender, the student was more likely to be perceived as disruptive by the teacher. Rimm-Kaufman and Pianta (2000) proposed that when describing students, nonethnic minority teachers tend to describe ethnic minority students as having a hard time following directions, as being immature, and coming from disorganized homes. Similar findings (Ainsworth-Darnell & Downey, 1998; Ehrenberg et al., 1995; Ferguson, 1998; Irvin, 1990) showed that nonethnic minority teachers rated the academic performance of ethnic minority students less favorably than ethnic minority teachers. Meier, Stewart, and England (1989) further described that ethnic minority students were suspended, expelled, or placed in special education classes less when they attended schools with a large proportion of ethnic minority teachers than when they attended schools with a smaller proportion of ethnic minority teachers.

The findings presented in the proceeding paragraphs suggest that the perception and experience of ethnic minority teachers and ethnic minority students are notably different than the perception and experience of nonethnic minority teachers and ethnic minority students. Further the findings in the proceeding paragraphs have led to the conceptual theory that ethnic-matching has a positive impact on the academic success of ethnic minority students. In return, this conceptual theory has led to the development of essential frameworks for understanding the impact of ethnic minority teachers on the academic outcomes of ethnic minority students and culturally relevant teaching practice.

This chapter is not meant to suggest that the solution for dealing with the challenges facing ethnic minority students in public schools, particularly urban public schools, is simply to hire more ethnic minority teachers to work directly with ethnic minority students. Rather, the findings presented here show that there is a significant connection between teachers and ethnic minority students. As Milner (2006) proposed, researchers and educators should strive to determine which attributes held by successful ethnic minority teachers can help train all teachers on successful strategies for working with ethnic minority students.

Conclusion

As presented in this chapter, having an ethnic minority teacher can have a significant influence on the achievement of ethnic minority students. As the various findings from the study by Easton-Brooks et al. (2010) and Eddy and Easton-Brooks (2011) show, having an African American teacher, at some level, explained the difference in the achievement scores of African American students. In addition, research by others indicates that the expectation of ethnic minority teachers provided students with a more healthy school experience (Casteel, 1998; Ehrenberg et al., 1995; Ferguson, 1998; Zimmerman et al., 1995).

However, research on the effects of ethnic-matching still has a long way to go. For instance, more studies are needed to understand the effect of ethnic-matching on populations of color besides African Americans. A limitation to this line of inquiry is the effects of certified teachers on the academic outcomes of ethnic minority students. For instance, Easton-Brooks and Davis (2009) found that when African American students interact with certified teachers, the reading test scores of African Americans increase significantly over time. Future studies on ethnic-matching should examine the effects of certified teachers or teacher quality (Darling-Hammond, 2000) on the academic outcomes of ethnic minority students. Also important is the influence of male ethnic minority teachers on the academic outcomes of ethnic minority students, especially male ethnic minority students (Lynn, 1999, 2002, 2006; Milner, 2007).

Further, Milner (2006) proposed that researchers should determine which attributes held by successful ethnic minority teachers can be used to help train nonethnic minority teachers to successfully work with ethnic minority students. This approach is a valuable alternative. However, increasing the number of ethnic minority teachers will benefit all students and the U.S. educational system. In short, evidence would suggest that ethnic minority teachers benefit all students, not just ethnic minority students (Easton-Brooks et al., 2010; Milner, 2006). A challenge in increasing the number of ethnic minority teachers resides in the fact that less than 10% of college ethnic minority students elect education as their major. Most of these students go into fields such as business and social science (Dickson, 2010; Porter & Umbach, 2006). These students elect not to go into the field of education because of expanded opportunities for ethnic minorities, low teacher salaries, rigorous testing standards in schools and more demanding certification and licensing requirements, and social perception of the teaching profession (Easton-Brooks, et al., 2010; Lewis, 2006). Based on these challenges, it will take the efforts of colleges/universities and school districts to recruit, retain, and graduate more ethnic minority teachers. Lewis (2006) proposed strategies for recruiting African American teachers, which could be followed to recruit other groups of ethnic minority teachers. The proposed approach is as follows: (1) collaboration with communities, (2) faculty mentors, (3) refinement of entrance requirements, (4) college and school collaboration, (5) academic supports, and (6) collaborations with community colleges. While these recommendations were based on the recruitment of African American males, the feelings here is that these strategies should also be used in the recruitment of all preservice ethnic minority teachers. Boser (2011) recommendations include (1) increasing federal oversight of and increased accountability for teacher preparation programs, and (2) creating statewide initiatives to fund teacher preparation programs aimed at ethnic minority teachers. In addition, efforts also should be made by policy makers to increase salaries and/or incentives to entice qualified ethnic minority teachers to the field of education.

There are also areas beyond higher education that are key in the recruitment and retention of ethnic minority teachers. Based on their findings, Easton-Brooks et al. (2010) recommended that school district human resources offices, school administrators (principals), and teacher education programs work on efforts to recruit and retain ethnic minority teachers. To improve the academic achievement of ethnic minority students, it is critical that human resources officials at the school district level further examine data and findings on ethnic-matching and utilize the findings to improve current school practices. While Ingersoll and May (2011) demonstrated the increase in ethnic minority teachers over the past two decades, it is important that human resources departments continue their efforts in recruiting ethnic minority teachers, and develop strategies for improving the retention of ethnic minority teachers. In continuing efforts to recruit ethnic minority teachers, human resources departments should attend selected job fairs at Historically Black Colleges and Universities (HBCUs), which produce the largest percentage of African American teachers (Lewis, 2006), and Hispanic Serving Institutions (HSI). Also, key relationships need to be formed with these colleges and universities to recruit the best and the brightest, especially in high-needs areas such as mathematics, science, and special education in urban schools.

In direct relationships with schools, principals play a key role in solving this dilemma as well. Principals, particularly those looking for teachers in high-needs areas, should work closely with school district hiring officials to diversify, recruit, hire, and retain qualified ethnic minority teachers. In most situations, the principal has the final decision-making authority on what teachers will be hired at the local school site.

In conclusion, the chapter presents evidence that ethnic-matching is an effective strategy for increasing the academic outcomes among ethnic minority students. And while ethnic minority teachers are attracted to those schools with a larger percent of minorities in the schools with greater needs, it is critical that all invested partners work together to develop effective strategies for retaining ethnic minority teachers. As various ethnically diverse teachers enter the field of education, more research on this topic is needed, especially related to populations in which languages other than English is a significant part of a student's culture. Further, while the percent of ethnic minority teachers is increasing, the field of education still employs heavily European American teachers. Therefore, it is important that we assess the attributes of ethnic minority teachers to assist in training all teachers, especially as we witness the ethnic change in public and urban schools as a result of shifts in the U.S. population in general.

Notes

1. The term *ethnic minority* refers to a category of people whose ethnic origin is different from that of the U.S. ethnic majority. The term ethnic minority can extend to all people of ethnic minority origin including those of migrant, indigenous, and nomadic communities. Related to urban education as described in this chapter, the term refers to the three main ethnic minority groups in the United States (African American, Mexican, and Native American). The definition is in association with the generational academic gap between these ethnic minority students and majority White students.
2. Fringe is the transitional zone where the urban and rural connects, which includes suburban areas.

References

Ainsworth-Darnell, J. W., & Downey, D. B. (1998). Assessing the oppositional culture explanation for racial/ethnic differences in school performance. *American Sociological Review 63*, 536–553.

Ballou, D., Sanders, W., & Wright, P. (2004). Controlling for student background in value-added assessment of teachers. *Journal of Educational and Behavioral Statistics, 29*(1), 37–65.

Banks, J. (1996). *Multicultural education, transformative knowledge, and action: Historical and contemporary perspectives.* New York, NY: Teachers College Press.

Bireda, S., & Chait, R. (2011). *Increasing teacher diversity: Strategies to improve the teacher workforce.* Washington, DC: Center for American Progress. Retrieved from http://www.americanprogress.org/wp-content/uploads/issues/2011/11/pdf/chait_diversity.pdf

Boser, U. (2011). *Teacher diversity matters: A state-by-state analysis of teachers of color.* Washington, DC: Center for American Progress. Retrieved from http://www.americanprogress.org/wp-content/uploads/issues/2011/11/pdf/teacher_diversity.pdf

Cabral, R.R., & Smith, T.B. (2011). Racial/ethnic matching of clients and therapists in mental health services: A meta-analytic review of preferences, perceptions, and outcomes. *Journal of Counseling Psychology, 58*(4), 537–554.

Callender, J. (2004). Value-added assessment. *Journal of Educational and Behavioral Statistics, 29*(1), 5.

Campbell, T.A., & Campbell, D.E. (2007). Outcomes of mentoring at-risk college students: Gender and ethnic matching effects. *Mentoring & Tutoring: Partnership in Learning, 15*(2), 135–148.

Casteel, C.A. (1998). Teacher–student interactions and race in integrated classrooms. *Journal of Educational Research, 92,* 115–120.

Clewell, B.C., Puma, M.J., & McKay, S.A. (2005, April). *Does it matter if my teacher looks like me? The impact of teacher race and ethnicity on student academic achievement.* Paper presented at the Annual Meeting of the American Educational Research Association, Montreal, Canada.

Darling-Hammond, L. (2000). Teacher quality and student achievement: A review of state policy evidence. *Educational Policy Analysis Archives, 8*(1). Retrieved from http://epaa.asu.edu/epaa/v8n1/

Dee, T.S. (2004). Teachers, race, and student achievement in a randomized experiment. *Review of Economics and Statistics, 86*(1), 195–210.

Delpit, L. (1995). *Other people's children: Cultural conflict in the classroom.* New York, NY: New Press.

Dickson, L. (2010). Race and gender differences in college major choice. *The Annals of the American Academy of Political and Social Science, 627*(1), 108–124. doi:10.1177/0002716209348747

Easton-Brooks, D., & Davis, A. (2009). Teacher qualification and the achievement gap in early primary grades. *Education Policy Analysis Archives, 17*(15), 1-19.

Easton-Brooks, D., Lewis, C., & Zhang, Y. (2010). Ethnic-matching: The influence of African American teachers on the reading scores of African American students. *National Journal of Urban Education & Practice, 3,* 230–243.

Eddy, C., & Easton-Brooks, D. (2011). Ethnic matching, school placement, and mathematics achievement of African American students from kindergarten through fifth grade. *Urban Education, 46*(6), 1280–1299.

Ehrenberg, R.G., Goldhaber, D.D., & Brewer, D.J. (1995). Do teachers' race, gender, and ethnicity matter? Evidence from the National Educational Longitudinal Study of 1998. *Industrial and Labor Relations Review, 48*(3), 547–561.

Elliott, J.R., & Smith, R.A. (2001, May 1). Ethnic matching of supervisors to subordinate work groups: Findings on "Bottom-up" ascription and social closure. *Social Problems, 48*(2), 258–276.

Ferguson, R.F. (1998). Teachers' perceptions and expectations and the African American–White test score gap. In C. Jencks & M. Phillips (Eds.), *The Black-White test score gap* (pp. 273–317). Washington, DC: Brookings Institution Press.

Field, C., & Caetano, R. (2010). The role of ethnic matching between patient and provider on the effectiveness of brief alcohol interventions with Hispanics. *Alcoholism: Clinical and Experimental Research, 34,* 262–271.

Flicker, S.M., Waldron, H.B., Turner, C.W., Brody, J.L., & Hops, H. (2008). Ethnic matching and treatment outcome with Hispanic and Anglo substance-abusing adolescents in family therapy. *Journal of Family Psychology, 22*(3), 439–447.

Foster, M. (1990). The politics of race: Through the eyes of African-American teachers. *Journal of Education, 172,* 123–141.

Foster, M. (1994). Effective Black teachers: A literature review. In E.R. Hollins, J.E. King, & W.C. Hayman (Eds.), *Teaching diverse populations: Formulating a knowledge base* (pp. 225–241). Albany, NY: State University of New York Press.

Foster, M. (1995). African American teachers and culturally relevant pedagogy. In J. Banks & C.A. McGee Banks (Eds.), *Handbook of research on multicultural education* (pp. 570–581). New York, NY: Macmillan.

Foster, M. (1997). *Black teachers on teaching.* New York, NY: New Press.

Gay, G. (2000). *Culturally, responsive teaching: Theory, research and practice.* New York, NY: Teachers College Press.

Hanushek, K. (1992). The trade-off between child quantity and quality. *Journal of Political Economy, 100,* 84–117.

Hanushek, E.A., Kain, J.F., & Rivkin, S.G. (2002). Inferring program effects for specialized populations: Does special education raise achievement for students with disabilities? *Review of Economics and Statistics, 84*(4), 584–599.

Henry, A. (1998). *Taking back control: African Canadian women teachers' lives and practice.* Albany, NY: State University of New York Press.

Holmes, B.J. (1990). New strategies are needed to produce minority teachers. In A. Dorman (Ed.), *Recruiting and retaining minority teachers.* (Guest Commentary). Policy Brief No. 8. Oak Brook, IL: North Central Regional Educational Laboratory.

Ingersoll, R., & May, H. (2011). *Recruitment, retention, and the minority teacher shortage.* Philadelphia, PA: Consortium for Policy Research in Education, University of Pennsylvania and Center for Educational Research in the Interest of Underserved Students, University of California, Santa Cruz.

Irvin, J.J. (1990). *Black students and school failure: Policies, practices, and prescriptions.* Westport, CT: Greenwood Press.

Irvine, R.W., & Irvine, J.J. (1983). The impact of the desegregation process on the education of black students: Key variables. *The Journal of Negro Education, 52*(4), 410-422.

Ladson-Billings, G. (1994). *The dreamkeepers: Successful teachers of African American children.* San Francisco, CA: Jossey-Bass.

Ledlow, S. (1992). Is cultural discontinuity an adequate explanation for dropping out? *Journal of American Indian Education, 31*(3), 21–36.

Lewis, C.W. (2006). African American male teachers in public schools: An examination of three urban school districts. *Teacher College Record, 108*(2), 224–245.

Lynn, M. (1999). Toward a critical race pedagogy: A research note. *Urban Education, 33,* 606–626.

Lynn, M. (2002). Critical race theory and the perspectives of Black men teachers in the Los Angeles Public Schools. *Equity & Excellence in Education, 35,* 87–92.

Lynn, M. (2006). Education for the community: Exploring the culturally relevant practices of Black male teachers. *Teacher College Record, 108,* 2497–2522.

McCaffrey, D.F., Lockwood, J.R., Koretz, D., Louis, T.A., & Hamilton, L. (2004). Models for value-added modeling for teacher effects. *Journal of Educational and Behavioral Statistics, 29*(1), 67–101.

Meier, K.J., Stewart, J., & England, R.E. (1989). *Race, class, and education: The politics of second generation discrimination.* Madison, WI: University of Wisconsin Press.

Milner, H.R. (2006). The promise of Black teachers' success with Black students. *Educational Foundations, 20*(3–4), 89–104.

Milner, H.R. (2007). African American males in urban schools: No excuses teach and empower. *Theory Into Practice, 46*(3), 239–246.

Milner, H.R., & Howard, T.C. (2004). Black teachers, Black students, Black communities and *Brown:* Perspectives and insights from experts. *Journal of Negro Education, 73*(3), 285–297.

Nieto, S. (2000). *Affirming diversity: The sociopolitical context of multicultural education* (3rd ed.). New York, NY: Longman.

Ogbu, J. (2003). *Black American students in an affluent suburb: A study of academic disengagement.* Mahwah, NJ: Lawrence Erlbaum Associates.

Porter, S.R., & Umbach, P.D. (2006). College major choice: An analysis of Person-Environment Fit. *Research in Higher Education, 47*(4), 429–449.

Reed-Danahay, D. (2000). Habitus and cultural identity: Home/school relationships in rural France. In B.A.U. Levinson, K.M. Borman, M. Eisenhart, M. Foster, & A.E. Fox (Eds.), *Schooling the symbolic animal: Social and cultural dimensions of education* (pp. 223–236). Lanham, MD: Rowman & Littlefield.

Rimm-Kaufman, S.E., & Pianta, R.C. (2000). An ecological perspective on the transition to kindergarten: A theoretical framework to guide empirical research. *Journal of Applied Developmental Psychology, 21,* 491–511.

Rowan, B., Correnti, R., & Miller, R. J. (2002). What large-scale, survey research tells us about teacher effects on student achievement: Insights from the prospects study of elementary schools. *Teachers College Record, 104*(8), 1525–1567.

Rubin, D.B., Stuart, E.A., & Zanutto, E.L. (2004). A potential outcomes view of value-added assessment in education. *Journal of Educational and Behavioral Statistics, 29,* 103–116.

Sanders, W.L., Saxton, A., & Horn, S. (1997). The Tennessee value-added assessment system: A quantitative, outcomes-based approach to educational assessment. In J. Millman (Ed.), *Grading teachers, grading schools: Is student achievement a valid measure?* (pp. 138–162). Thousand Oaks, CA: Corwin Press.

Shin, S.M., Chow, C., Camacho-Gonsalves, T., Levy, R.J., Allen, I.E., & Leff, H.S. (2005). A meta-analytic review of racial-ethnic matching for African American and Caucasian American clients and clinicians. *Journal of Counseling Psychology, 52*(1), 45–56.

Shipp, V.H. (1999). Factors influencing the career choices of African American collegians: Implications for minority teacher recruitment. *Journal of Negro Education, 68*(3), 343–351.

St. Germaine, R. (1995). BIA schools complete first step of reform effort. *Journal of American Indian Education, 35*(1), 30–38.

U.S. Census Bureau. (2006). *Statistical Abstract of the United States: 2006* (126th ed.). Washington, DC: U.S. Government Printing Office.

U.S. Department of Education, National Center for Education Statistics. (2006). *The condition of education 2006 (NCES 2006–071).* Washington, DC: U.S. Government Printing Office.

U.S. National Center for Health Statistics. (2012). Births: Final Data for 1990, Vol. 58, No. 24, August 2012.

Vincent, G.K., & Velkoff, A.V. (2010). The next four decades, the older population in the United States: 2010 to 2050, current population reports, P25-1138. Washington, DC: U.S. Census Bureau.

Webster, W.J., & Mendro, R.L. (1997). The Dallas value-added accountability system. In J. Millman (Ed.), *Grading teachers, grading schools: Is student achievement a valid measure?* (pp. 81–99). Thousand Oaks, CA: Corwin Press.

Zhang, Y. (2007). *Effects of teacher-student ethnic matching on kindergarteners' academic achievement and on teachers' ratings of kindergarteners' academic performance* (Doctoral dissertation, University of Virginia). Retrieved from Dissertations & Theses: A&I database. (Publication No. AAT 3260656)

Zimmerman, R.S., Khoury, E.L., Vega, W.A., Gil, A.G., & Warheit, G.J. (1995). Teacher and parent perceptions of behavior problems among a sample of African American, Hispanic, and non-Hispanic White students. *American Journal of Community Psychology, 23*(2), 181–198.

6

Urban Schools and the Black Male "Challenge"

Pedro A. Noguera

On all of the indicators of academic achievement, educational attainment, and school success, African American males are noticeably distinguished from other segments of the American population by their consistent clustering in categories associated with failure (Noguera, 2008; Schott Foundation, 2010a). This tends to be the case at schools throughout the United States but the problems are most acute in urban schools and districts where poverty is concentrated and students are racially segregated. In such schools, African American males are typically more likely than students in other groups to be cited for behavior problems and their achievement patterns are characterized by indicators associated with risk and failure—low test scores in reading and math, low graduation rates, high rates of referral to special education, and high dropout rates (Boykin & Noguera, 2011).

The academic and social challenges confronting African American males are often compounded by the fact that many are enrolled in chronically underperforming schools. In such schools the academic performance of all students tends to have been low for so long that failure is often "normalized" and an air of complacency and indifference about academic outcomes often takes hold among students and staff (Payne, 1984). These are the schools that Education Secretary Arne Duncan has described as "dropout factories" (Gonzalez, 2010) and author Ray Rist once described as "factories for failure" (1972). More often than not, such schools are located in distressed neighborhoods where poverty is concentrated, crime rates are high, and jobs are scarce. These are the neighborhoods that sociologist William Julius Wilson described as "truly disadvantaged" because they were marginalized by deindustrialization and the flight of capital (Wilson, 1987).

In much of the literature on school failure, there has been relatively little attention paid to the ways in which the challenges rooted in urban neighborhoods impact the performance of students and schools (Bowen, Bowen, & Ware, 2002; Noguera, 2003). This is also the case with respect to the public policies that in recent years have been used to guide and shape the direction of school reform. Consistently, education policies have been adopted and reforms have been carried out without sufficient attention to how they must interact with the social and economic conditions present within economically depressed urban communities. Since the adoption of No Child Left Behind (NCLB), school reform has become the primary national strategy used to combat poverty as other antipoverty policies have become less politically viable (Noguera, 2003; Rothstein, 2004).

There is very little evidence to support the notion that schools alone can counter the effects of poverty on children, and there is ample evidence that when the basic social needs of children are unaddressed, the academic challenges they face tend to become more severe. Nonetheless, the decontextualized approach to school reform that began with NCLB (Rothstein calls it "the schools alone approach") has persisted even though there is ample evidence that it has failed as a strategy for improving the most disadvantaged schools (Payne, 2008). As I will show in the pages ahead, the persistent failure of urban school reform has also contributed to the educational crisis confronting Black male students. Rather than schools serving as essential elements of a community's support system for children, they are more frequently the settings where the problems facing African American male students emerge and worsen over time.

A recent study conducted by Anthony Bryk and his colleagues at the Consortium for School Improvement at the University of Chicago found that 10 years of intensive reform that included the closure of "failing" schools, massive investments in technology and professional development for educators, and the creation of new "innovative" school models did little to improve the quality of schools in Chicago's poorest neighborhoods. Bryk and his colleagues found that problems related to poverty—crime, substance abuse, child neglect, unmet health needs, housing shortages, interpersonal violence, and so forth—were largely ignored by the reform policies pursued in Chicago, and consequently they had limited impact upon the improvement of urban schools (Bryk et al., 2010). The Chicago case mirrors patterns observed in cities throughout the United States where education policy has focused on raising academic standards and increasing accountability but largely ignored the social and economic conditions that impact school environments and learning opportunities for students (Miner, 2013). As a consequence of this narrow approach and these omissions, urban school reform in the United States has been characterized by persistent failure.

The academic challenges confronting African American male students are directly related to the unfulfilled promise of school reform (Noguera, 2003, 2011).

The inability of urban schools to respond to the complex environmental challenges confronting the communities they serve has exacerbated the challenges confronting African American males because the problems they face are not simply school-based (Anderson, 1990; Majors & Billson, 1992). While the data show that African American males are vastly overrepresented among students who are suspended and subjected to discipline referrals, who are placed and referred to special education, who are most likely to drop out of school, and who lag on most indicators of African American performance (Schott Foundation, 2012a), close reading of the data also reveals that harmful environmental conditions (e.g., high rates of neighborhood violence, drug trafficking, and unemployment) contribute to negative academic and social outcomes (Greenberg & Schneider, 1994; Smitherman, 1977). There is also growing evidence that school failure and punitive approaches to school discipline are contributing to juvenile crime (Kim, Losen, & Hewitt 2010) and the emergence of a school-to-prison pipeline (Alexander, 2010). The term is more than merely a metaphor. There is growing evidence that the inability of schools to meet the needs of African American male students is contributing to the steady increase in their presence in the criminal justice system (Advancement Project, 2012).

A vast amount of evidence from decades of social science research suggests that by ignoring the social context of schooling and the unmet social, psychological, and emotional needs of children in high-poverty urban areas, it will not be possible to produce sustained school improvement or higher levels of academic achievement for inner city youth generally (Barton & Coley, 2010) and Black males specifically (Noguera, 2008). Schools are inextricably linked to the social and economic environment where they are located, and the factors that influence child development—health, nutrition, safety, emotional support, among others—invariably influence learning and achievement (Noguera, 2003). For young African American males who are more likely than any other group to be subjected to a broad array of negative stereotypes and risks outside of school, including homicide and other forms of interpersonal violence, police harassment, arrest, and incarceration (Noguera, 2008), it is clear that a new approach to education is needed.

In the pages ahead I show how the problems confronting high-poverty urban areas have overwhelmed schools and compounded the difficulties confronting African American males. Drawing on research carried out at schools in New York City between the years 2008–2010, I show how neighborhood conditions have compounded the challenges facing African American males and the schools they attend. A disproportionate number of these are chronically under-performing schools, and in such schools, the evidence suggests that raising the achievement of African American males is extremely difficult because the schools lack the capacity to meet their academic and social needs. The empirical evidence that I present shows that altering the academic trajectories of African American males so that they are on track to go to college at the time they enter high school may be nearly impossible unless effective intervention strategies are implemented in elementary and middle schools. In the final pages, I describe some of the interventions that are being utilized in schools that are succeeding in promoting academic success for African American males in the hope that educators and policy makers can learn from these examples.

The goal of this chapter is to make the case that greater progress in supporting African American males can be achieved on a larger scale through a different approach, one that I and others have described as a broader and bolder approach to school reform (Noguera & Wells, 2011). It is an approach that focuses on developing a social safety net for children and schools and that draws upon the strengths and resources of local communities to meet their needs. In so doing, I hope to demonstrate to educators and policy makers what it might take to develop schools that can successfully mitigate the effects of poverty and simultaneously meet the academic and social needs of African American males.

The Pipeline Crisis

One of the reasons why dropout and failure rates for low-income Black (and in many cases Latino males, see *Invisible No More: Understanding the Disenfranchisement of Latino Men and Boys* by Noguera et al., 2011) is so high is because they are more likely to reside in marginalized communities. Numerous studies have shown that where poverty is concentrated, the underground economy flourishes and problems such as drug trafficking, gangs, and violence become pervasive (Bowen et al., 2002; Greenberg & Schneider, 1994). In such areas the pull of the "streets" tends to be strong and the ability of families and schools to counter these harmful influences is often limited (Anderson, 1990). Not surprisingly, schools in such communities are influenced and often overwhelmed by the problems present within the community. Unless a concerted effort is made to counter these negative effects, their presence often contributes to the development of dysfunctional school cultures where relationships between educators and students are often weak and strained due to a lack of trust (Bryk et al., 2010; Payne, 2008). Such schools frequently experience a lack of stability in leadership due in part to high turnover among superintendents and principals (Balfanz & Byrnes, 2006), and an unwillingness among teachers to collaborate and to take responsibility for learning outcomes (Payne, 1984; Boykin & Noguera, 2011). Lack of discipline and motivation among students in turn contributes to a lack of order and safety. When such conditions exist simultaneously a "perfect storm" for failure is created. The school environment simply does not support effective teaching and learning, and failure for large numbers of students invariably becomes more likely (Maeroff, 1989; Payne, 1984, 2008; Noguera, 2003).

In school systems where such conditions prevail, what can be termed a pipeline crisis frequently emerges. By pipeline I am referring to a disruption in what would otherwise be the *normal* progression of students from elementary, to middle, to high school, and eventually college. Such a progression is presumed to be the norm for schools that serve middle-class children. However, for low-income children, especially Black males who reside in economically depressed urban areas, there is frequently a break down at various points along the metaphorical pipeline. Rather than a smooth transition from one grade to the next, or from one school to the next, a certain number of students are lost at each stage. For a variety of reasons that I have discussed elsewhere (Noguera, 2003; Noguera, 2008), failure rates are generally highest for African American males (Schott Foundation, 2012a). Black male students typically are clustered in categories associated with academic failure across the educational pipeline. Understanding how school dysfunction and neighborhood distress contribute to school failure and the development of a pipeline crisis is critical for devising interventions.

In 2009, the Metropolitan Center for Urban Education that I direct at New York University[1] and the Center for Research on Fathers, Children and Family Well-Being (CRFCFW) led by Professor Ron Mincy at Columbia University collaborated on a study of the educational pathways of Black males in public schools (K–12) in New York City. The goal of the research was to better understand the ways Black male students navigate New York City schools in order to determine which factors contribute to their educational progress and how. Our goal was to produce a nuanced analysis of the educational pipeline for Black males that did more than merely confirm what we already knew—that large numbers of Black males were failing in school. We wanted to know when patterns of academic trouble began to emerge and what were the school conditions most associated with high rates of failure. We thought the best way to address these questions was to generate empirical research that could provide a clear and accurate portrait of the educational experience of Black male students over time. Our research started with the assumption that educational experiences of Black males are not monolithic and that uncovering how factors related to school, community, family, and peer groups influenced performance might be important for devising interventions that could succeed in altering academic and social outcomes.

To carry out this research we used Hierarchical Linear Models to examine the growth in math proficiency scores on standardized examinations. We also used Latent Class Growth Models (LCGM) to examine how trajectories in math proficiency levels cluster around common patterns. The research made it possible for us to observe variations in the educational trajectories of young Black males who were in 4th grade in 1998 and were expected to graduate in 2007. We focused specifically on the early years—from elementary school through middle school in order to gain an understanding of how the Black males in our sample were progressing in school. The initial sample consisted of 11,803 Black males who were in the system between fall 1998 and fall 2003 or who entered the system during that time period. Because we sought to track the students from elementary school through high school, we decided to narrow our sample of students to those who were present in the system beginning in 1998 (expected 4th grade) and for whom we had performance data over the time period of interest. We decided to focus on math performance because some of the students in our sample were English Language Learners and during this time period, they were not required to take the same state or city English Language Arts exam as native speakers of English. In order to study the relationship between individual students and the schools they attended over time, we only included students whom we could link to the schools in the study.

Our central research question was: "What are the patterns of educational trajectories for Black males in New York City Schools?" To make this determination, first we examined patterns among trajectory groupings of students within the cohort utilizing several statistical procedures. After this analysis we linked the trajectories we observed to the schools they attended, exploring and comparing the factors within and across the different types of groupings. From there we examined how the trajectories we observed were related to the characteristics of the middle schools that the students attended. This allowed us to observe how different types of schools influenced academic performance in their first year in high school (as measured by course credit completion). Finally, we used our analysis of trajectories to identify the critical points of intervention so that policies and programs could be designed to reinforce the pathways that positively influence academic outcomes for Black male students. Our goal was to use this analysis to answer the question, "What are the points of intervention where we can effect change in academic and social outcomes?" We did this so that targeted education policies and practical interventions could be devised specifically to address the needs of Black male students.

In our analysis we looked closely at student proficiency levels on the state math exam, and we found an acute downward trend in proficiency levels between 1999 and 2003. Overall, in 1999, 43% of the sample obtained a score that was within the proficiency or high-proficiency level (level 3 or level 4). However, by 2003, this percentage decreased by 17%, with only 26% of the students in the sample obtaining proficiency or above. Most notable was the change in performance for the students in the sample who were the highest performers in 1999. While 7.7% of the students in the sample obtained advanced proficiency (level 4) on the math exam in 1999, in 2003 the percentage had decreased dramatically to just 1.9% of the total sample (see Figure 6.1).

After including all of the theoretically relevant variables, we found that the 4th-grade standardized math scores of students who received subsidized lunch and students who had been retained at least one grade level were *substantially lower* on average compared to other students across New York State. Standardized scores of special education students in the cohort showed a modest upward trend, while the standardized math scores of mobile students (students who had transferred to another school before completing elementary, middle, or high school) showed a somewhat larger downward trend. Finally, the average math scores of the classmates of the Black male students in the sample was the only variable that had a significant association with the growth of their standardized math scores. That is, Black male students who attended schools with higher-performing students had higher scores that those who attended schools with lower performers. This suggests that putting Black male students in more challenging learning environments where they are surrounded by academically motivated peers may be the best way to increase math proficiency (and possibly literacy) over time. This was an important finding because school enrollment is one of the only variables that we discovered waspotentially amenable to policy manipulation in New York City. However, we also understood that many of the public schools in our study were located in neighborhoods characterized by extremely high levels of racial and socioeconomic isolation. In such communities, finding ways to increase diversity in school enrollment will not be easy.

Our second analysis sought to determine if the academic achievement of the Black males in our sample clustered into common performance trajectory groupings in the five years prior to their entry into high school (expected 4th—8th grade). In further exploring the limited trend between 1999 and 2003, we observed six performance trajectory patterns emerging among our sample. By 2003, three-quarters of the students in the sample performed below proficiency levels (Level 1 or 2)—73.2% and were not on track for college. Approximately 25% of the sample maintained relatively flat trajectories at the proficiency level with slight declines in performance over time. This finding is consistent with research that has found that performance gaps tend to be rigid or to even widen over time (see Jencks & Phillips, 1998 for an example).

Interestingly, we observed that two of the below-proficiency trajectory groupings—to which about one-quarter of our sample were assigned—"changed tracks" during the middle school years, either downward or upward. This suggests that middle school can be a place where significant growth or decline in math proficiency can occur. The declining math performer

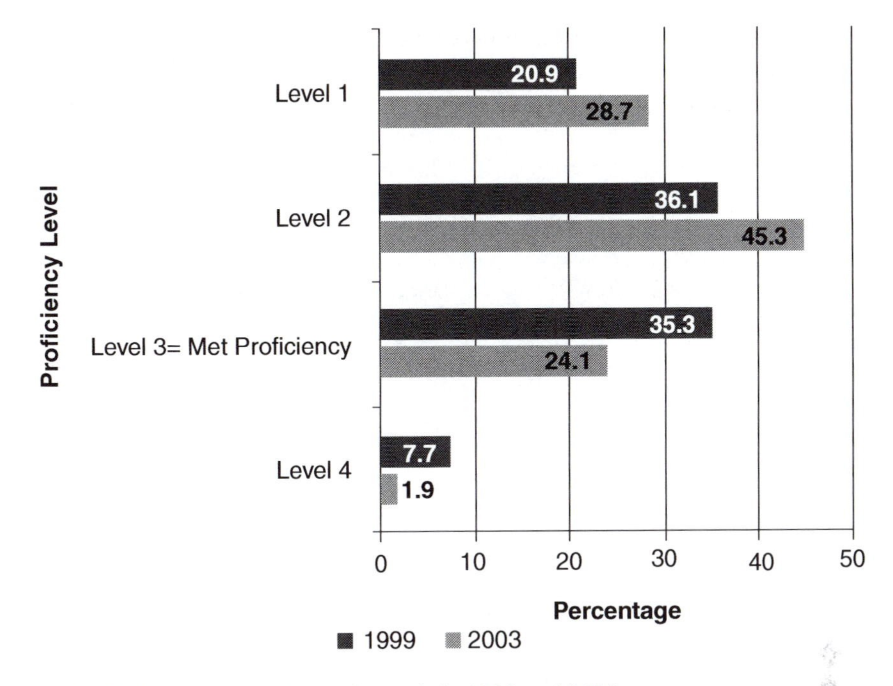

Figure 6.1 Math proficiency levels of sample in 1999 and 2003.

trajectory grouping took a particularly steep fall in the middle school years and, alternatively and most surprisingly, the improving math performance trajectory grouping that started between the persistently low and declining group made strong gains in middle school. This finding led us to seek additional information on the schools these students attended.

In our final analysis we examined the extent to which trajectory groupings combined with middle school characteristics (where the twists and turns happened) predicted how well students performed during their first year of high school. We found that patterns of performance on the math exam in elementary and middle school years continued into their first year of high school, as measured by the number of courses they passed in 9th grade. We found that for the 25% who were performing at proficiency by the 8th grade the majority managed to remain at proficiency into high school if they attended one of the high-performing high schools that the study identified.

In addition, we discovered that some of the variables that provided insights into the academic performance of individual students were unique predictors of whether or not a student was on track and still in the college pipeline by the 9th grade. Primary among these was credit completion. Regardless of their proficiency level, students who did not have sufficient credits to advance to the 10th grade were at greater risk of not being on track to graduate from high school (See Table 6.1). Not surprisingly, 9th-grade course completion was significantly lower for students assigned to the declining performance cluster than for students assigned to all other performance clusters. Course completion rates were also lower for students who were classified as learning disabled. Similarly, the kinds of schools the students entered played a role in how some groupings performed in high school. Middle school characteristics were correlated with whether or not a student was in the lowest-performing cluster and the improving cluster on performance. Again, students who attended middle schools where fewer schoolmates qualified for subsidized lunch and a greater number of schoolmates obtained higher math scores on standardized exams also completed more courses in the 9th grade.

Table 6.1 Selected Student Characteristics—Four Persistent Trajectories

	Below Math Proficiency				*At or Above Math Proficiency*			
	Persistently Low Math Performers		*Almost Proficient Math Performers*		*Proficient Math Performers*		*High Math Performers*	
	N	%	N	%	N	%	N	%
Total in Trajectory Grouping	998	15.5	2468	35.1	1437	20.4	424	6.0
Foreign Born	64	6.4	231	9.4	143	10.0	55	13.0
Qualified for Free Lunch*	928	93.0	2197	89.0	1239	86.2	344	81.1
Referred for Special Education Services**	444	44.5	363	14.7	106	7.4	9	2.1
% Students Transferred > 2 Between Y1–First Year of HS	191	19.1	316	21.8	153	10.7	35	8.3
Middle School and High School of Entry Are the Same	19	1.9	41	1.7	37	2.6	8	1.9
No. of Failing Schools Attended***	341	39.2	615	24.9	225	15.7	50	11.8

* Percentage of students in the sample who qualified for free or reduced-cost lunch

** Percentage of students in the sample who were designated as learning disabled and qualified for educational services

*** Number of schools attended by students in the sample that were designated as failing by the NY Department of Education. Schools regarded as "failing" in New York City received an "F" on the school report card by the department.

As a result of our analyses, the research team was able to generate the following findings and make the following recommendations:

- Provide intensive targeted academic support to 2nd to 5th grade students who are not performing at grade level. Several studies have shown that if these students can enter middle school performing at the proficiency level or higher, they will be substantially more likely to be on track for college (Balfanz & Byrnes, 2006). Intervening with strong academic support is easier and more cost effective during the elementary school years as opposed to waiting to provide remedial support in middle or high school.
- For middle school students who are not able to attend one of the high-performing schools we found it would be important for schools to provide intensive case management, tutoring both during and after school, and mentoring during the middle school years. The research is very strong in showing that students who enter 9th grade at proficiency are more likely to remain on track for college during high school (Balfanz, R. and Herzog, L. 2005; Pierce & Vandell, 1999). Other research has shown that schools can utilize the following indicators:irregular attendance, referrals for disruptive behavior, non- submission of homework, and academic difficulties in the classroom, to trigger for more deliberate interventions (Balfanz & Herzog, 2005).
- The data clearly show that students who had access to high-quality, diverse middle schools were more likely to perform on a higher level and to remain on track for college throughout high school. While it may be difficult to expand access and reduce the racial and socioeconomic isolation of the most academically vulnerable students because most reside in geographically isolated, economically marginal communities, a concerted effort must be made to improve school options in these neighborhoods. I will expand on this point later.

- The research also showed that the higher-performing schools had strategies in place to recruit and retain cohorts of teachers with a record of effectiveness in high-need schools. While this might seem like an obvious goal to embrace it is important to acknowledge that structural and procedural obstacles have often made it difficult for school districts to control the placement of teachers in high-need schools. There is no evidence to support the practice of assigning the least-experienced teachers to such schools as an intervention strategy.

As we probed the data further to uncover the relationship between school enrollment and long-term academic performance, we began noticing a distinct pattern—all of the high-performing schools for African American boys were located outside of the low-income neighborhoods where the most disadvantaged students resided. For example, in Brooklyn neighborhoods such as Brownsville, Bedford Stuyvesant, East New York, and Bushwick, there were very few middle schools that had received either an A or a B on their school ratings (Schott Foundation, 2012a). In effect this means that unless students in these geographically isolated and economically depressed areas are able to gain access to superior middle schools in other parts of the city, their chance of entering 9th grade proficient and on track for college was substantially reduced.

A recent report by Norman Fruchter, entitled "Is Demography Destiny?" (2012), illustrates this point powerfully. The disturbing correlation between college readiness and neighborhoods in Brooklyn reveals a disturbingly consistent pattern. With such low rates of college readiness among all students in these Brooklyn neighborhoods, it is clear that Black male students, who typically cluster at the lowest levels, are at a tremendous disadvantage simply because of where their families live (See Table 6.2).

Table 6.3 illustrates this pattern further by illustrating the relationship between ability levels for students and their status at the time they graduated or left high school. These data reinforce the importance of intervening during elementary or middle schools if we are to increase high school graduation rates and college attendance.

Another important finding from the trajectory study was the effect of access to after-school and other out-of-school time (OST) programs on academic outcomes for Black male students. Consistently we found that when students had access to such supports there was a positive impact on their academic performance. The research showed that the students who were most

Table 6.2

Neighborhood	*% College Ready*	*% of Student Population Black/Latino*
East New York	12	96
Ocean Hill	12	99
North Baychester	12	93
Edenwald	12	93
Melrose	12	103
Hunt's Point	12	103
East Tremont	12	98
Mount Hope	11	98
Bathgate	11	95
Brownsville	11	100
Crotona Park	11	99

Table 6.3 Selected Student Descriptive Outcomes by Trajectory Clusters

*Final Deposition Fall, 2007**	*Persistently Low Math Performers*		*Almost Proficient Math Performers*		*Proficient Math Performers*		*High Math Performers*		*Improving Math Performers*		*Declining Math Performers*	
	N	*%*	*N*	*%*	*N*	*%*	*N*	*%*	*N*	*%*	*N*	*%*
Graduated With Regents/HR diploma	26	2.6	685	27.7	802	55.8	343	80.9	137	14	49	6.7
Graduated With Local Diploma	183	18.3	616	25	297	14.5	23	5.4	284	29	141	19.2
Graduated With IEP Diploma	46	4.1	4	0.2	0	0	0	0	8	0.8	5	0.7
GED	15	1.5	92	3.7	53	3.7	14	3.3	21	2.1	16	2.2
Still Attending in Fall 2007	497	49.8	810	32.8	291	20.3	39	9.2	373	38.1	370	50.5
Dropped out of School	236	26.4	261	29.2	83	5.8	5	1.2	156	15.9	152	20.7

* These were categories we created based upon a student's academic performance over time.

likely to experience improvements in academic performance, or to at least remain the same over time, were more likely to have participated in an OST program. Further research from our study revealed that the most effective of these programs were academic in nature and focused on providing tutoring, mentoring, college advising, or some other form of educational enrichment. Our research confirms what has been found in several national studies. Over the last two decades, there have been several studies documenting the benefits of participation in out-of-school time activities on student performance (Lauver, 2004). Participation has been associated with higher (more, or improved) school attendance, higher academic achievement as measured by performance on standardized tests, and the adoption of positive attitudes toward school and schoolwork (Pettit, Laird, Bates, & Dodge, 1997; Pierce & Vandell, 1999; Posner & Vandell, 1994, 1999). Studies have also shown a strong link between OST participation and homework completion, aspirations for college, work habits, and interpersonal skills (Hofferth & Jankuniene, 2001). In addition to the demonstrated benefits, studies have shown that participation in OST activities is linked to decreases in negative behaviors such as juvenile arrests, drug activity, and teenage pregnancy (Mason-Dixon Pulling and Research, 2002; National Institute on Out-of-School Time (NIOST), 2004; Patten & Robertson, 2001).

Our research showed that Black boys benefited considerably from OST activities and that these activities had numerous benefits, including improved social and emotional development, health and wellness outcomes, and were linked to college enrollment. Our findings are supported by a number of related studies that have also found positive association between OST participation and academic outcomes (Cooper, Valentine, Nye, & Lindsay, 1999; Gardner, Roth, & Brooks-Gunn, 2008; Hansen, Larson, & Dworkin, 2003; Lauer et al., 2006; NIOST, 2004; Peck, Roeser, Zarrett, & Eccles, 2008; Roffman, Pagano, & Hirsch 2001).

Acting on What We Know

Like their counterparts in other large urban areas, Black male students in New York City exhibit a wide variety of hardships and disadvantages that suggest their educational needs are not being met. The general pattern is that in nearly every category associated with academic failure, Black males are overrepresented and in categories associated with academic success they are dramatically underrepresented. In February 2010 it was reported that less than 5% of the students admitted to the New York's gifted programs and most selective high schools were Black males, and only seven Black males were admitted to prestigious Stuyvesant High School for the fall of 2010 (Santos, F. Feb. 5, 2012). Despite numerous reform initiatives carried out in New York City over the last several years, reforms that have resulted in a steady increase in graduation and college attendance rates for most students in the city, there has been very little evidence of progress for Black or Latino males. In 2006, the four-year graduation rate for Black males in New York City was only 26% (Schott Foundation, 2012b), while the overall rate was 66% (Fruchter, 2012). Nationally, while from 1973 to 1977 there was a steady increase in Black male enrollment in college, since 1977 there has been a sharp and continuous decline (Carnoy, 1996; National Research Council, 1989).

The findings from this research demonstrate that race and gender-neutral approaches to solving the problems confronting African American male students are unlikely to be successful because of the unique ways in which they are exacerbated by the interaction between school and neighborhood conditions. For this reason interventions and reforms must be designed to address the particular challenges facing schools located in neighborhoods where economic hardships are greatest and social problems are most severe. Most important, this research demonstrates that there is a need for public policies, school reform strategies, and supplemental interventions that consciously and specifically are implemented in an integrated manner to address the needs of Black male youth.

A New Reform Agenda: Ignoring the Past and the Present

With the financial backing of hedge fund managers and the Gates and Broad Foundations, a new orthodoxy over what constitutes legitimate education reform has emerged. Led by Joel Klein, the former Chancellor of New York City, Michelle Rhee, the former Chancellor of Washington, D.C., and Joe Williams of Democrats for Education Reform, this new crop of reformers has argued that "bad teaching" rather than poverty is the primary cause of failure in urban schools. They argue that in order to improve urban public schools, power must be taken away from unions and others who defend the "status quo," and charter schools should be used to replace failing public schools. Claiming to oppose treating poverty as an excuse for low achievement, Klein and his allies in the Education Equity Project (EEP) wrote the following in the April 9, 2010, edition of the *Washington Post:*

> In the debate over how to fix American public education, many believe that schools alone cannot overcome the impact that economic disadvantage has on a child, that life outcomes are fixed by poverty and family circumstances, and that education doesn't work until other problems are solved. This theory is, in some ways, comforting for educators.... Problem is, the theory is wrong. It's hard to know but plenty of evidence demonstrates that schools can make an enormous difference despite the challenges presented by poverty and family background. (p.23)

Such assertions may seem encouraging because they suggest that these advocates reject the notion that certain students (especially those who are poor and non-White) are inherently less capable of learning, a perspective that was widespread in the United States for most of its history (Boykin & Noguera, 2011). However, there is also a bit of naïveté inherent in the views of those who would suggest that poverty is an issue that can be ignored, as well as some degree of callous indifference. In 2012, child poverty rates were at their highest level in 60 years (22% of all children in the United States come from families with incomes that fall below the poverty line) and the number of children who arrive at school with basic unmet needs (including hunger) has risen dramatically.

In such a context, "no excuses"—the name given to many of the reform strategies embraced by this new crop of neoliberal policy advocates—constitutes more than merely an educational strategy. The ideas of these reformers have power and influence. They have been embraced by several of the major foundations that are funding current reform efforts and the U.S. Department of Education. Their influence and reach has led to a common set of strategies being embraced by states (particularly since the enactment of Race to the Top) and large urban districts across the country. These are the types of reforms that were first introduced in Chicago when the public schools were under the leadership of U.S. Education Secretary Arne Duncan. They include shutting down "failing schools," evaluating teachers by scores students receive on standardized tests and releasing the results in newspapers, and allowing private for-profit organizations to assume control of public schools.

The evidence from Chicago, New York, and several other cities is clear: The reforms are not producing the improvement in public schools that was promised. For African American males, the results may be even more damaging given the fact that incarceration and dropout rates remain high, while employment rates and college attainment rates remain low. Over 12 years after the enactment of No Child Left Behind (NCLB), dropout rates for African American and Latino males in many American cities remain high, well above 50% (Schott Foundation, 2012a). This includes cities such as New York, Austin, and Miami where graduation rates have been rising (Fergus & Noguera, 2010; Gonzalez, 2010; Schott Foundation, 2012b). As the data presented in this paper illustrate, it is important to recognize that the problems confronting Black males are not exclusively limited to the challenges they confront in school. In the labor market, the health care system and in government, Black males are often at a tremendous disadvantage. The situation confronting Black males is particularly critical in the criminal justice system. As legal scholar Michele Alexander has noted, for the last 30 years the United States has embarked on a policy of "mass incarceration." This is occurring on a scale that is almost unparalleled in human history (Alexander, 2010). As prison populations throughout the United States have increased dramatically over the last 30 years, overwhelmingly, Black men have borne the brunt of the drive to incarcerate. There are now more Black men ensnared by the criminal justice system—in prison, on probation, in county jails, or on parole—than any other racial or ethnic group, and more than all others combined. Of the more than 6,000,000 persons across the United States held in prison, more than 50% are Black men, and in several states, the percentage of the incarcerated that are Black males is substantially higher (Alexander, 2010).

Equally troubling is the fact that school is often the place where the process of socializing Black males for entry into the criminal justice system begins. As recent studies by the Schott Foundation and the U.S. Department of Education have shown, Black males are more likely than any other segment of the population to be subjected to harsh forms of school discipline (Annie E. Casey Foundation, 2011). Typically, this involves some form of exclusion for multiple days for even minor behavior infractions. Children who are not in school, or who are subjected to arrest for minor violations of school rules, are more likely to enter the criminal justice system and commence a life entangled with court orders, probation officers, and in many cases, periods of incarceration (Losen & Orfield, 2002).

Learning From Schools That Work

In 2009, the Metropolitan Center for Urban Education conducted a study on dropout rates among Black and Latino males in New York City. The results were disturbing. Although official graduation rates in New York City have been rising since 2002, and are now over 65%, we found that less than 40% of Black and Latino males were graduating, and fewer than 30% were graduating with a Regents diploma, the certification used to determine college readiness. However, during the course of our study we also identified over 20 high schools in New York City where the graduation rate for Black and Latino males was over 80%. We were surprised both by the number of schools that were achieving at this level and by the fact that the knowledge educators had gained about how to serve this population was not being shared widely among schools throughout New York City.

We began studying these schools to learn more about the practices they relied upon to obtain such impressive results. We were encouraged to find that many of the practices and policies we had endorsed in our earlier trajectory study—mentoring, the use of after-school tutorials, leadership development, among others—were being embraced by these schools. For example, at schools like Frederick Douglass Academy and Thurgood Marshall in Harlem, there was a deliberate effort to place students in academically rigorous courses such as physics and advanced placement writing that would prepare them for college. At Eagle Academy, an all-male public school in the South Bronx, a partnership with a community organization called One Hundred Black Men made it possible to provide each student with a mentor. A strong induction program for 9th graders, a comprehensive college counseling program, and extensive outreach to parents also made it possible for Eagle Academy to create a positive learning culture that promoted student success.

At these schools and others, high graduation rates have been the norm for several years. It is important to note that these schools serve students from low-income backgrounds and who come from some of the most troubled and disadvantaged neighborhoods in New York City. These schools have found ways to create school cultures that are able to counter the influence of gangs, promote healthy social and emotional development, and affirm the importance of learning. Our research in these schools has shown us that strong, positive relationships between teachers and students are critical ingredients for their success. Equally important is the need to provide personalized learning supports with mentors, counseling, and services that make it possible for schools to intervene early and effectively when problems arise. Not surprisingly, these schools have strong and effective school leaders, but that does not mean they are authoritarian and intimidating. On the contrary, students report that principals like David Banks at Eagle Academy and Tim King at Urban Prep in Chicago (another urban high school with high graduation rates) are regarded more like big brothers and father figures. These are safe schools where students feel they can be themselves, where the peer culture reinforces the value of learning, and where character, ethics, and moral development are far more important than rigid discipline policies.

It is important to note that while some of these high-performing schools are all-male, others are co-educational. Schools like Thurgood Marshall have developed a mentoring program specifically for male 9th graders who are paired with high-performing female seniors. The school's principal realized that if girls are better at school than boys in many cases, why not have them model success for their younger male peers? Similarly, former principal Juan Mendez at Enterprise, Business and Technology High School in Williamsburg, Brooklyn, learned early on that counseling and a strong focus on career internships that lead to real job opportunities could keep his young men engaged.

Education is an important arena for interventions because there is ample evidence that individuals with higher levels of educational attainment are more likely to be employed, to earn higher salaries, to live longer, healthier lives, and to stay out of prison. Moreover, it is likely that if more Black males had access to high-quality education in preschool and K–12, many of the hardships they confront later in life might be averted. However, even as we focus on addressing the educational needs of African American males we must also recognize that factors that are external to schools, namely, parental support, peer influences, housing, crime, and public health, also have an impact on the development and academic success of African American males. Children do not exist in a vacuum and neither do the schools they attend. More often than not, environmental conditions present in the local context have an impact on the performance of schools and on child development. For this reason, what is needed is an integrated and holistic policy—an approach to supporting Black males and the schools they attend that makes it possible to develop a safety net through a system of buffers and supports. There is good reason to believe that such a system would make success for African American males more likely.

It is important to keep in mind that our schools need help in meeting the needs of those they serve, especially those who are most vulnerable in American society. Black and Latino males are among those who are most vulnerable but there is no reason that support systems cannot be developed to counter the obstacles and threats they face. For this to happen we must address the issue with a sense of urgency and treat it as an *American problem,* rather than as a problem that only those who directly experience it in the Black community should be concerned about. The continued failure of so many young men not only increases the likelihood that many will end up in prison, permanently unemployed, or dead at an early age, but that our society will increasingly accept such conditions as normal and even acceptable. The more that happens, the more our entire society will be endangered by its complacency and its tolerance for failure.

Note

1. The Metropolitan Center for Urban Education at New York University specializes in research and technical assistance to urban schools throughout the United States, http://steinhardt.nyu.edu/metrocenter/about/. I have served as the Executive Director of the Metro Center since 2003.

References

Advancement Project. (2012). Ending the Schoolhouse to Jailhouse Track. Washington, DC: Advancement Project.

Alexander, M. (2010). *The new Jim Crow: Mass incarceration in an era of colorblindness.* New York, NY: New Press.

Anderson, E. (1990). *Street wise: Race, class and change in an urban community.* Chicago, IL: University of Chicago Press.

Annie E. Casey Foundation. (2011). *No place for kids: The case for reducing juvenile incarceration.* Baltimore, MD: Author.

Balfanz, R., & Byrnes, V. (2006). Closing the achievement gap in high-poverty middle schools: Enablers and constraints. *Journal of Education for Students Placed at Risk, 11,* 143–159.

Balfanz, R., & Herzog, L. (2005, March). *Keeping the middle grades students on track to graduation: Initial analysis and implications.* Paper presented at the second Regional Middle Grades Symposium, Philadelphia, PA.

Barton, P., & Coley, R. (2010). *The black-white achievement gap: When progress stopped.* Princeton, NJ: Education Testing Service.

Bowen, N.K., Bowen, G.L., & Ware, W. (2002). Neighborhood social disorganization, families, and the educational behavior of adolescents. *Journal of Adolescent Research, 17,* 468–489.

Boykin, A. W. & Noguera, P. (2011). Creating the opportunity to learn: Moving from research to practice to close the achievement gap. Washington, DC: ASCD.

Bryk, A. S., Sebring, P. B., Allensworth, E., Luppescu, S., & Easton, J. Q. (2010). *Organizing schools for improvement: Lessons from Chicago.* Chicago, IL: University of Chicago Press.

Carnoy, M. (1996). *Faded dreams: The politics and economics of race in the United States.* Cambridge, UK: Cambridge University Press.

Cooper, H., Valentine, J.C., Nye, B., & Lindsay, J.J. (1999). Relationships between five after-school activities and academic achievement. *Journal of Educational Psychology, 91*(2), 369–378.

Fergus, E., & Noguera, P. (2010). Doing what it takes to prepare Black and Latino males in college. In C. Edley & J. Ruiz (Eds.), *Changing places: How communities will improve the health of boys of color* (pp. 23–49). Berkeley, CA: University of California Press.

Fruchter, N. (2012). *Is demography destiny?* New York, NY: Annenberg Foundation.

Gardner, M., Roth, J., & Brooks-Gunn, J. (2008). Adolescents' participation in organized activities and developmental success 2 and 8 years after high school: Do sponsorship, duration, and intensity matter? *Developmental Psychology, 44*(3), 814–830.

Gonzalez, J. (2010, May 25). High school dropout rate is cited as key obstacle to Obama education goals. *Chronicle of Higher Education.* Retrieved from http://chronicle.com [p. 16]

Greenberg, M., & Schneider, D. (1994). Young Black males is the answer, but what was the question? *Social Science Medicine, 39*(2), 37–62.

Hansen, D.M., Larson, R.W., & Dworkin, J.B. (2003). What adolescents learn in organized youth activities: A survey of self-reported developmental experiences. *Journal of Research on Adolescence, 13*(1), 25–55.

Hofferth, S., & Jankuniene, Z. (2001). Life after school. *Educational Leadership, 58*(7), 19–23.

Jencks, C., & Phillips, M. (1998). *The Black-White test scores gap.* Washington, DC: Brookings Institution Press.

Kim, C., Losen, D., & Hewett, D. (2010). *The school-to-prison pipeline: Structuring legal reform.* New York, NY: New York University Press.

Klein, J.I., Lomax, M., & Murguia, J. (2010). Poverty is not the issue. *Washington Post,* April 9.

Lauver, S. (2004). Attracting and sustaining youth participation in after school programs. *The Evaluation Exchange, 10*(1), 4–5.

Lauer, P., Akiba, M., Wilkerson, S., Apthorp, H., Snow, D., & Martin-Glen, M. (2006). Out of school time programs: A meta-analysis of effects for at-risk students. *Review of Educational Research, 76,* 275–313.

Losen, D., & Orfield, G. (2002). *Racial inequality in special education.* Cambridge, MA: Harvard Education Press.

Maeroff, G. (1989) "Whithered hopes and stillborn dreams: The dismal panorama of inner-city schools." *Phi Delta Kappan, 69,* 632–638.

Majors, R., & Billson, M. (1992). *Cool pose: The dilemmas of Black manhood in America.* New York, NY: Simon and Schuster.

Mason-Dixon Pulling and Research. (2002). New York state survey of teens. Retrieved October 12, 2008, from http://www.fightercrime.org/ny/teenpoll

Miner, Barbara. (2013). *Lessons from the heartland: A turbulent half-century of public education in an iconic American city.* New York, NY: New Press.

National Institute on Out-of-School Time (NIOST). (2004). *Making the case: A fact sheet on children and youth in out-of-school time.* Wellesley, MA: Wellesley College, Center for Research on Women. Retrieved from http://www.niost.org

National Research Council. (1989). *A common destiny: Blacks and American society.* Washington, DC: National Academies Press.

Noguera, P. (2003). *City schools and the American dream: Reclaiming the promise of public education.* New York, NY: Teachers College Press.

Noguera, P. (2008). *The trouble with black boys and other reflections on race, equity and the future of public education.* San Francisco, CA: John Wiley and Sons.

Noguera, P., & Wells, L. (2011). The politics of school reform: A broader and bolder approach to school reform in Newark. *Berkeley Review of Education, 2*(1), 5–25.

Noguera, P., Hurtado, A., & E. Fergus. (2011). Understanding and responding to the disenfranchisement of Latino men and boys. New York, NY: Routledge.

Patten, P., & Robertson, A.S. (2001). *Violence prevention resource guide for parents.* Washington, DC: ERIC Clearinghouse on Elementary and Early Childhood Education.

Payne, C. (1984). *Getting what we ask for: The ambiguity of success and failure in urban education.* Santa Barbara, CA. Greenwood Publishing Group.

Payne, C. (2008). *So much reform so little change: The persistence of failure in urban schools.* Cambridge, MA: Harvard Education Press.

Peck, S.C., Roeser, R.W., Zarrett, N., & Eccles, J.S. (2008). Exploring the roles of extracurricular activity quantity and quality in the educational resilience of vulnerable adolescents: Variable- and pattern-centered approaches. *Journal of Social Issues, 64*(1), 135–155.

Pettit, G., Laird, R., Bates, J., & Dodge, K. (1997). Patterns of after school care in middle childhood: Risk factors and developmental outcomes. *Merrill-Palmer Quarterly, 43,* 515–538.

Pierce, K.M., & Vandell, D.L. (1999). *Safe haven program evaluation.* Madison, WI: University of Wisconsin Center for Educational Research.

Posner, J. K. & Vandell, D. L. (1994). Low-income children's after-school care: Are there beneficial effects of after-school programs? *Child Development, 65*(2), 440–456.

Posner, J.K., & Vandell, D.L. (1999). After-school activities and the development of low-income children: A longitudinal study. *Developmental Psychology, 35*(3), 868–879.

Rist, Ray C. (1972). *The urban school: A factory for failure.* Cambridge, MA: MIT Press.

Roffman, J.G., Pagano, M.E., & Hirsch, B.J. (2001). Youth functioning and experiences in inner-city after-school programs among age, gender, and race groups. *Journal of Child and Family Studies, 10*(1), 85–100.

Rothstein, R. (2004). Out of balance: Our understanding of how schools affect society and how society affects schools. *Spencer Foundation 30th Anniversary Essay.* Chicago, IL: Spencer Foundation.

Santos, F. (2012). To be black at Stuyvesant High School. *New York Times*, February 25.

Schott Foundation. (2012a). *The urgency of now.* Cambridge, MA. Retrieved from www.blackboysreport.org

Schott Foundation. (2012b). *The rotten apple: Education redlining in New York City.* Cambridge, MA: Author.

Smitherman, G. (1977). *Talkin' and testifyin': The language of Black America.* Boston: Houghton Mifflin.

7

Lesbian, Gay, Bisexual, Transgender, Queer, and Questioning People and Issues in Urban Education

Mollie V. Blackburn & Lance T. McCready

In an effort to explore lesbian, gay, bisexual, transgender, queer, and questioning (LGBTQQ) people and issues in education, we begin by articulating a conceptual framework that delineates our understanding of pertinent dynamics and offer a historical overview of LGBTQQ people and issues in urban education. We then discuss the current urban education landscape, with a particular focus on prominent themes in the literature: homophobia, academic performance, and activism. We conclude with a consideration of directions for future work; this conclusion revisits concerns raised in our conceptual framework.

Conceptual Framework

LGBTQQ people and issues in urban education tend to be undertheorized with respect to the social, cultural, economic, and political dynamics that create and maintain the boundaries of urban space, which includes youth-serving institutions in the city, including but not limited to schools. Therefore, we first provide a conceptual framework for the chapter that takes into account the ways politics of resource distribution, immigration, cultural pluralism and multiculturalism, segregation and gentrification, to name a few dynamics, shape urban space and therefore are related to LGBTQQ people and issues in urban education. We argue that using a conceptual framework intended to problematize and theorize urban space opens up new possibilities for understanding the complexity of LGBTQQ people served by, and issues taken up in, schools and organizations that serve LGBTQQ youth.

Perhaps the best way to start a consideration of LGBTQQ people and issues in urban education is to consider the term *urban* itself. Urban has come to connote many different things, of course, but at its most essential level, it denotes meaning about physical and imaginary space. Physically, cities are defined by spatial relationships. Population density, the geographic arrangement of districts with different functional activities, and residential status hierarchies are just a few of the more obvious socio-spatial dimensions of city life (Rury & Mirel, 1997). Because schools are so often defined by their immediate social environment, the social geography of cities and their larger metropolitan regions exerts a telling effect on urban education. The most well-resourced schools, for example, are often located in the most affluent neighborhoods. Underperforming schools tend to be located in poor or low-income communities (Kozol, 1992; Lipman, 2008, 2005). Thus the first step in developing a framework for LGBTQQ people and issues in urban education is to consider the social, political, economic forces that shape cities themselves. One could ask the following: What are the spatial relationships that have shaped the existing conceptions of LGBTQQ people and issues in urban education? What are the factors shaping the larger social and political environment of lives of LGBTQQ people in the city? What are the differences between LGBTQQ people and issues in urban education in different cities noted by observers over the years? What are the forces of historical change that have affected LGBTQQ youth programs in urban schools, and how has the research community thought about them, if at all?

It seems many of the crises affecting LGBTQQ people and issues in urban education for the past several decades parallel a larger set of developments in many dimensions of urban life. For example, large census metropolitan areas in North America are increasingly characterized by growing ethnic and racial diversity and coupled with increasing income polarization (Abu-Lughod, 1999; Badcock, 1997; Marcuse & van Kempen, 2000; Wilkinson, 2010). This is evident in both gay-straight alliances (GSAs) and alternative schools for LGBTQQ youth, both of which we discuss later in this chapter. Take, for example, the GSA that McCready (2010) studied. He found that a racially diverse secondary school in Northern California boasted a GSA that unintentionally excluded students of color. He found that the race-class housing dynamics in the surrounding neighborhood and community paralleled achievement and engagement patterns in the school, including extracurricular activities, and, even more specifically, the GSA. That is to say, students who were more privileged in terms of race and class were more likely to take advantage of the GSA, making it a less viable resource for poor and working-class students of color. This is just one example of how the challenges facing LGBTQQ people in urban education are related to polarizing forces of race and class in cities themselves.

The work of researchers, educators, and policy makers, locally and nationally, in both metropolitan and rural locales is related to LGBTQQ people and issues in urban education. Practitioners in these areas need to understand and be prepared to address multiple social and cultural issues that intersect with sexual and gender identities and discrimination. This necessitates an intersectional analysis. Intersectionality can be defined as a theory to analyze how social and cultural categories of identity and oppression are interconnected.

Historical Overview

We offer this historical overview with an awareness that the extant scholarship on the topic privileges White people and *cisgender* people, or "individuals who have a match between the gender they were assigned at birth, their bodies, and their personal identity" (Schilt & Westbrook, 2009, p. 461), particularly men. Although we work to disrupt such privileging in our discussion of the current landscape, it is worth keeping this limitation in mind when reflecting on the history of LGBTQQ people and issues in urban education. Also, throughout this historical overview, we reference other social movements in the United States in order to provide a frame of reference for the ones of focus in this chapter, that is, those focused on LGBTQQ people and issues in urban education.

We can trace teachers who experienced and acted on same-sex desire all the way back to Plato and Socrates (Rofes, 1985). We can trace social movements related to homosexuality in cities in the United States back to the early 20th century (Jagose, 1996). However, because we are interested in LGBTQQ people and issues in U.S. urban education, it is worth looking back to mid-20th century. It was during this time, in 1954, that the case of *Brown versus Board of Education of Topeka, Kansas* determined that separate schools for White people and people of color were inherently unequal and therefore banned racial segregation of schools. It was also when Rosa Parks started the Montgomery Bus Boycott, in 1955. In other words, the civil rights movement in the United States was gaining considerable momentum. Also during this time, there was a "growing visibility of homosexual communities in urban areas around the country" (Blount, 2005, p. 854). This prominence provoked a "virulent backlash movement" (Blount, 2005, p. 854) within education, which resulted in suspicion of teachers who were not married. If suspicions of these teachers' homosexuality were even vaguely confirmed, they were forced out of classrooms and schools (Graves, 2009). According to Lugg (2005), "Historically, formal education policies have generally either ignored lesbian, gay, bisexual, and transgender (LGBT) youth and personnel or targeted them as a problem that needed to be repressed or eliminated" (p. 293). Therefore, schools, even urban schools, were not welcoming places for LGBTQQ people.

This, however, changed by the late 1960s. Recall that by this time, the celebrated March on Washington for Jobs and Freedom, when Dr. Martin Luther King, Jr. gave his famous "I Have a Dream" speech, had happened, in 1963. It is worth noting in this context, though, that Bayard Rustin, the chief organizer of the March, was hardly recognized for his efforts because of being a gay man. During this time, teachers who self-identified as homosexuals had "experienced so much frustration with social sanctions that passivity and self-destruction eventually gave way to resistance. . . . LGBT teachers began fighting back" (Blount, 2005, p. 854). They began, by the late 1960s, filing lawsuits to allow them to keep their jobs, and although the trailblazers in this area were not successful in getting their jobs back, "their cases established legal precedent making such dismissals more difficult" (Blount, 2005, p. 854).

In the 1970s, community-based programs for sexual minority youth, or youth whose sexual identities differ from those of the majority or, more plainly, youth who are not straight, began forming in some cities (Clare & James, 2005). Around this time, LGBTQQ activists improved schools "simply by being open about their sexual orientations and gender identities. For many, the presence of openly identified LGBT individuals helped to alleviate fears of being the only one" (Hayes, Herriott, & Rice, 2005, p. 234). LGBT experiences started to be made visible in curriculum around this time as well (Hayes, Herriott, & Rice, 2005, p. 235), in part because of the increasing visibility of LGBTQQ people. With respect to students, the first GSA can be traced to a group of students at New York City's George Washington High School who in 1972 founded the first school-based gay group on record in the United States (Johnson, 2007). It is also worth noting that in 1973, the American Psychological Association determined that homosexuality was no longer a mental disorder.

The 1980s, however, brought the AIDS epidemic and thus gay health issues to the fore (Blount, 2005; Hayes, Herriott, & Rice, 2005). Although this brought increased attention to gay people and topics, it did so, again, in ways that raised suspicions and fears. Countering this was the ongoing LGBT activism, which, in 1988, pushed the National Education Association to pass a "resolution favoring the development and implementation of school counseling that supported the unique needs of LGBT and questioning students—as opposed to more traditional counseling that strictly urged heterosexual conformity" (Blount, 2005, p. 855).

Advocacy organizations, like the national organization GLSEN, or Gay Lesbian Straight Education Network, and local gay-straight-alliances began to bring LGBTQQ people together with allies to make schools better places for LGBTQQ people (Blount, 2005).

More recently, LGBT-based secondary schools or classrooms have been established.

> These programs tend to be established in urban communities where the number of LGBT youth and the pressures on them have risen to levels that require separate, safe learning environments. (Clare & James, 2005, p. 755)

Such progress offers great hope for LGBTQQ people in urban education, but this progress comes with significant challenges as well, which we discuss below, throughout the various aspects of the current landscape.

Current Landscape

LGBTQQ people and issues in schools are taken up more in the context of urban school communities compared to rural or school communities (McCready, 2007). There are advantages and challenges to this fact, which we discuss throughout our examination of the resources available. Prominent themes emerging from our review include homophobia and its academic impact, cultural and economic challenges, as well as student activism, and are therefore considered below.

Resources. LGBTQ people living in urban communities experience some real advantages that their rural and suburban counterparts do not. The "concentration of population and the presence of alternative subcultures in urban areas, give LGBT youth more opportunities for existence and protection" (Lomine, 2005, p. 308). This concentration also provides more opportunities to establish "networks with other LGBT families" (Hulsebosch, 2005, p. 603). Moreover, in cities, LGBTQ people are more likely to find spiritual support in the form of "support groups within mainstream denominations, which assist youth in finding LGBT-positive perspectives and theologies, as well as inclusive religious groups" (Horne & Biss, 2005, p. 824). There are also more community-based organizations that cater to LGBTQ people in cities compared to rural communities (Bell & Binnie, 2004; Bieschke, 2005; Clare & James, 2005). Consider, for examples, the Hetrick Martin Institute in New York, the Attic Youth Center in Philadelphia, Kaleidoscope Youth Center in Columbus, Ohio, ROSMY in Richmond, Virginia, among many others.

LGBTQ-specific services are more prevalent in some urban schools, too. Some services are offered at schools, but outside of official curricula, such as Los Angeles's Project 10 (Uribe, 1995) and gay-straight alliances (GSAs) (i.e., Lee, 2002). Moreover, some cities, like Toronto, Ontario, San Francisco, California, and Columbus, Ohio, for example, have GSA networks that include multiple high school programs. Still, not every middle and high school in census metropolitan areas has a GSA (Kosciw, Diaz, & Greytak, 2008), and they should. Not because they meet the needs of all LGBTQQ students but because

> LGBT students in schools with GSAs are less likely to hear biased language, such as homophobic remarks, are less likely to feel unsafe in school because of their sexual orientation and gender expression, and are less likely to miss days of school because they are afraid to go. (GLSEN, 2007, p. 3)

Thus, GSAs are important for all schools to have, including urban ones.

In addition, there is evidence of teachers' and administrators' efforts to combat heterosexism and homophobia in urban classrooms, schools, and districts (i.e., Cohen & Chasnoff, 1997), including through greater curricular exposure to LGBTQ content (Asher, 2005). Some learn to do this through training efforts, consider NEA's National Training on Safety, Bias, and LGBT Issues (http://www.nea.org/home/Training-Program-GLBT-Issues.html); others learn to do this through teacher inquiry groups, such as the teachers in *Acting Out! Combating Homophobia Through Teacher Activism* (Blackburn, Clark, Kenney, & Smith, 2009); others learn to do it in their teacher preparation programs (Clark, 2010); still others learn to do this through their own trial and error. Overall, though, it seems urban educators, as a group, continue to have mixed reactions to the idea of the mandatory inclusion of antihomophobia in their social justice work. Urban educators in North America may privilege race, class, ethnicity, immigration, and citizenship differences in their efforts to address power, privilege, and discrimination in schools (McCaskell, 2005). There are, however, a few schools in the United States designed specifically to provide a safe and supportive academic environment for lesbian, gay, bisexual, transgender, and questioning (LGBTQ)[1] youth, such as the Harvey Milk School in New York City and the Alliance School in Milwaukee, Wisconsin (Clare & James, 2005). The Harvey Milk School, for example, is described, indeed advertised, as a "public school where some of the city's most at-risk youth—those who are gay, lesbian, bisexual, transgender, and questioning (LGBTQ)—could learn without the threat of physical violence and emotional harm they faced in a traditional educational environment" (http://www.hmi.org/page.aspx?pid=230). The Alliance School advertises as a "safe place for students regardless of sexuality, identity, appearance, ability or beliefs" (http://www5.milwaukee.k12.wi.us/school/selections/alliance-school/), and while this may seem more ambiguous, its commitments are made clear in a variety of ways, including an image of a gender creative adolescent. Moreover, in the Great Schools website, there are reviews by stakeholders, like this one by a parent:

> This school has a zero tolerance policy towards bullying. It is one of the few safe places in MPS for kids who are different, whether that be in beliefs, appearance, ability, or any of the numerous other arbitrary standards that kids use as an excuse to pick on one another. It gives these students acceptance, and allows them to not only try, but to actually succeed. My child went from failing to a 4.0 GPA, because he felt safe and accepted, and was able to concentrate on his work, rather than on escaping the bullies at his old school. (http://www.greatschools.org/wisconsin/milwaukee/3525-Alliance-School-Of-Milwaukee/?tab=reviews)

Although these schools raise the question of shouldn't all schools be safe for LGBTQQ students, which of course they should be, in the meantime, they offer an alternative for LGBTQQ students, at least in those cities.

Given these resources and services, one might assume that urban communities and schools are meeting the needs of queer youth, especially in comparison to suburban and rural locales. In fact, the Gay, Lesbian and Straight Education Network's (GLSEN) recent national school climate survey (Kosciw et al., 2008) suggested "students in small town and rural schools were less likely to have access to LGBT-related resources and supports than students in urban and suburban schools" (p. 94). The experiences of queer urban youth, however, suggest a more complicated story.

Homophobia. Even with the rich resources to support gay life available in many urban communities, youth in cities across the United States continue to report school environments rife with homophobia. Such environments are the result of verbal and physical abuse enacted by homophobic students and the perpetuation of such abuse by the failure of adults in schools to address such abuse. These environments are exacerbated by adults in schools who overtly exhibit homophobia.

Table 7.1 Characteristics of Participants' Schools

	Sexual Orientation	*Gender Expression*
Verbal Harassment	84.6%	63.7%
Physical Harassment	40.1%	27.25
Physical Assault	18.8%	12.5%

Source: From Kosciw, Greytak, Diaz, & Bartkiewicz (2010).

That homophobic students verbally and physically abuse LGBTQ youth in U.S. schools is well documented by the 2010 GLSEN study (Kosciw, Greytak, Diaz, & Bartkiewicz, 2010) that found 84.6% of LGBT students experience verbal harassment because of their sexual orientation and 63.7% because of their gender expression (p. xvi). It also found that 40.1% of LGBT students report having been physically harassed because of their sexual orientation and 27.2% because of their gender expression. Moreover, 18.8% of this population reported being physically assaulted because of their sexual orientation and 12.5% because of their gender expression (p. xvi). It is worth noting, though, that the GLSEN study is not limited to urban schools; only 30.1% of LGBTQ students who responded to the GLSEN survey characterize their schools as urban (p. 11).

To illustrate that such homophobic abuses are occurring in urban schools, we turn to accounts captured by qualitative studies, in part as a complement to such quantitative studies as the GLSEN school climate surveys, but also to hone in on the experiences of urban youth, something that is not a goal of these larger-scale studies. For example, in the Bay Area, which is renowned for being "queer-friendly," David, who was a Black gay male, said, "'people used to think I was a girl and I used to get teased a lot because of that. . . . People eventually started throwing things at me and shit'" (McCready, 2004a, pp. 138–139). Somkiat, a gay student who attended a racially diverse Midwestern city school and was not "out" (openly gay), described his daily experience this way:

> Everyday they make fun of me and stuff. They call me gay and faggot and stuff. And, when I'm in class people, guys don't want to sit by me because they think I'm going to touch them and whatever. . . . When I'm late for class, I really don't want to go in because I'm scared [that] when I walk in they'll make fun of me. They always do that. My teacher, she sees it too. She always talks to me after class is up. . . . I feel like there's nobody there to protect me. (Ngo, 2003, p. 118)

The personal impact of Somkiat's classmates' homophobia is compounded by the teacher's lack of action. Talking to Somkiat after class instead of interrupting the harassment on the spot sends the message that, as Somkiat reasons, the teacher does not view herself as someone whose job it is to publicly advocate for her LGBTQQ students.

Dylan, an out[2] gay student in Atlanta, Georgia, experienced homophobia like Somkiat, only it was made worse by school officials' failure to address the hatred:

> One day in the parking lot outside his school, six students surrounded [Dylan] and threw a lasso around his neck, saying, "Let's tie the faggot to the back of the truck." . . . The school took no action to discipline Dylan's harassers. Instead, school officials told him not to discuss his sexual orientation with other students. . . . After the lasso incident, the harassment and

> violence intensified. . . . "It gave permission for a whole new level of physical stuff to occur." (Human Rights Watch, 2001, p. 1)

Parents and/or guardians of LGBT students may also feel conflicted about confronting school officials about homophobia their children experience in school, especially if they believe that, based on their ethnic, racial, or religious identifications, homosexuality is a cultural abomination. Amina, a South Asian queer-identified student in Toronto reported that

> Boyfriends, sex, and sexual orientation were topics not even on the radar. And if I did bring them up, I was set for another good yelling because they defined the pinnacle of Westernized Evil . . . My father made a comment that he believed that being gay was a symptom of being exposed to Western culture. As far as he was concerned, Muslims could not be gay. If a Muslim was gay, well then he/she was just not really Muslim. (Planned Parenthood Toronto, 2004, p. 14)

The tendency of school officials to fail to address homophobic abuse is also documented by GLSEN's school climate survey (Kosciw et al., 2008). According to this report, when LGBT students told school staff about "incidents of victimization, students most commonly said that no action was taken" (p. 41). Although this finding was more pronounced for suburban, small town, and rural schools, even in urban schools, only "21.7% of students . . . said that school staff intervened most of the time or always when hearing homophobic remarks" (p. 71).

Moreover, GLSEN found that 59.7% of LGBT youth reported hearing homophobic language and 67.7% reported hearing biased language about gender expression from teachers or other school staff. Although this statistic was not analyzed by GLSEN according to locale, and the dynamic has not been the focus of qualitative studies of LGBTQ youth in urban schools, that urban school officials exhibit overt homophobia has been captured in newspapers. For example, Marion Bolden, the superintendent of Newark Public Schools, made the executive decision to blackout a photo of Andre Jackson, a senior, kissing his boyfriend in the school yearbook. Ms. Bolden said she thought the photo was "suggestive" while Jackson said, "I didn't intend to say 'Oh hey look at me, I'm gay.' It was just a picture showing my emotion, saying that I'm happy you know. It was to look back on as a memory" ("Gay Pair," 2007). In Memphis, Tennessee principal Daphne Beasley went as far as to make a list of student couples to see who was engaging in "public displays of affection," and when she came across the names of two gay male students, she "outed them" or disclosed their sexual identity to their parents. One of the outed students, Nicholas (last name omitted), said it was "frightening to see a list with my name on it where not just other teachers could see, but students as well . . . I really feel that my personal privacy was invaded. I mean, Principal Beasley called my mother and outed me to my mother!" (Friedman, 2008). Although Bolden and Beasley seem to err in opposite directions, both could have served their students better if they had more nuanced understandings of their students' (dis)comfort with their sexual identities. In other words, if Bolden were comfortable with same-gender affection, she would not have felt the need to conceal an image of two young men kissing, and if Beasley knew more about the experiences of LGBTQQ students, she would have known that outing them to their parents sometimes results in those young people having their familial support, both emotional and financial, withdrawn from them, and would never out a student to his or her parents or guardians.

Overall, it seems LGBTQ youth experience homophobia in urban schools from students and staff, and school staff do not excel, relative to their nonurban counterparts, at addressing the abuse. This is made even more significant by the fact that such abuse impacts the academic performance of this population (Meyer, 2008).

Academic Impact. That homophobic school climates negatively impact the scholastic achievement of LGBTQQ youth and supportive school climates have the opposite effect are both documented by GLSEN's school climate survey (Kosciw et al., 2008). With respect to homophobic school climates hindering academic achievement, this study found that:

> the reported grade point average of students who were more frequently harassed because of their sexual orientation or gender expression was significantly lower than for students who were less often harassed. For example, the grade point average for students who were frequently physically harassed because of their sexual orientation or gender expression was almost half a grade lower than for other students (2.8 versus 2.4). (p. 84)

In terms of supportive school climates strengthening academic achievement, the same study found:

> Students who were out to all students and staff at their school reported a greater sense of belonging to their school community than those who were not out . . . [and] having a greater sense of belonging to one's school is related to greater academic motivation and effort as well as higher academic achievement. (p. 89)

Again, these findings are not uniquely pertinent to urban students. (As a reminder: approximately one-third of survey respondents described their schools as urban.) The following accounts, however, are focused on students in schools in cities, and they highlight the former dynamic, that is, homophobic schools hinder the academic achievement of LGBTQ students.

Teddy in San Francisco and Kira in Philadelphia both reported being good students before coming to know themselves and/or being known as not-straight. Teddy, a Filipina-American, Catholic student, withdrew from school when she came to understand herself as lesbian her junior year. She was not out to anyone else, but she struggled with internalized homophobia:

> I loved school. I excelled academically until high school. . . . However, in my third year, my grades dropped dramatically, I stopped going to classes for weeks at a time, and I just barely graduated. What changed? I realized I was a lesbian in my junior year. I was depressed and withdrew from interacting with my friends from school. Mostly, I would skip class to spend my days in a park alone with a book or my guitar. Although there were a few on-campus resources for queer youth, they were never announced publicly and I never knew of them. I never told anyone I was lesbian until I was twenty. (Consolacion, 2001, p. 84)

Whereas Teddy's educational success was hindered by her internalized homophobia, Kira, a self-described biracial, working-class dyke, raised by an African American foster mother, was a strong student whose schooling was thwarted by homophobia. Kira attended a magnet high school for the arts in Philadelphia, the type of school depicted as safe for queer teens in popular media such as the Hollywood film *Fame*. For Kira, however, it was difficult to find a peer group, and the isolation brought on by not having friends eventually caused her to leave school:

> I had friends that just stopped talking to me and never explained why. . . . I didn't really care that I didn't have any more friends. I just wouldn't, I just wouldn't go to school. . . . It's really hard to sit at a lunch table if you don't talk to anybody. . . . When you go to the same school for four years, and then, your senior year, you're alone, you're just like,

> "ok," so you don't go to lunch, then, eventually, you just don't go to school. (Blackburn, 2003, para. 43)

As these voices of queer youth in urban schools reveal, homophobia negatively affects academic performance.

Cultural and Economic Challenges. On the one hand, the neighborhoods and communities that constitute metropolitan areas tend to be more racially and ethnically diverse than rural communities (Holloway, Wright, & Ellis, 2012). They also tend to have more programs and services for LGBTQ youth, even if not located in schools. On the other hand, at the same time that metropolitan areas are becoming more racially and ethnically diverse, they are becoming less economically diverse, leading to income polarization (Badcock, 1997; Wilkinson, 2010). In other words, it is increasingly difficult for working and middle-class families to live comfortably in the core cities. Cities are becoming places for the extreme haves and have nots: the poor, who tend to be racial minorities, and the wealthy, who tend to be White and members of some Asian ethnic groups. The conditions of ethnoracial diversity and income inequality in metropolitan areas present unique cultural and economic challenges for LGBTQ youth.

Concerns include having to endure multiple forms of hatred, to cultivate multiple marginalized identities, and to negotiate multiple understandings of sexuality. Human Rights Watch, for example, found that "harassment against LGBTQ students of color is prevalent and is usually combined with racial and ethnic harassment" (Baez, 2005, p. 389). So, oftentimes, an urban LGBTQ youth needs to "cultivate both a sexual identity and an ethnic identity," "resolve any conflicts" between his or her "ethnic reference group and to a gay community," and "negotiate any stigmas and discrimination encountered because of the interconnections of homophobia, racism, and sexism" (Savin-Williams (1998) as cited by Pallotta-Chiarolli, 2005, p. 304). In addition to increased biases and multiple identity negotiations, there is, among urban LGBTQ people, specifically immigrant populations, the issue of navigating different and sometimes competing notion of sexuality. So, for example, immigrant communities often comprise "nonwhite, nonnative speakers of English who understand their sexual identity from a non-Western or at the very least dual cultural frame of reference" (McCready, 2005, p. 879). For example, in some African and South Asian countries homosexuality is illegal. Non-Western languages may or may not have specific words for nonheterosexual identities that connote the same meanings as the Western sense of "gay," "lesbian," "bisexual," or "transgender."

In addition to cultural challenges, there are economic constraints. There is the massive resegregation of public schools, for example, which is due, in part, to segregated housing patterns and the waning commitment of the federal government to enforce court-ordered desegregation in the 21st century. Essentially what this means is a return to neighborhood schools in urban communities that are racially segregated, and in most cases, areas of concentrated poverty as well. Urban LGBTQ youth who attend segregated schools in poor communities are likely to face a host of problems, related to the structure and organization of these schools. Racially segregated schools in communities where the median family income is below average are less likely to have programs specifically aimed at LGBTQ youth; there simply are not enough economic resources to support such efforts (McCready, 2005).

Public schools with a weaker residential tax base may attempt to maximize their resources through specialized courses or curricula such as magnet schools and international baccalaureate programs that are attractive to middle-class families (Clotfelter, 2004). In most cases, students with academic potential come from families with more economic, social, and cultural capital. Several national census studies indicate that in racially diverse communities, these families tend to be White or Asian. In such environments, Black and Latino students tend to be placed in lower-tracked classes where work or "getting a job" is emphasized over issues of college attendance or sexual identity (Kozol, 1992).

Another economic challenge facing LGBTQQ urban youth is homelessness (Cruz, 2008). LGBTQQ youth from rural and suburban communities migrate to cities in search of intimate relationships, programs, and services for sexual minorities. However, there are not enough programs and services for all youth who identify as sexual minorities, and most that do exist are located in or near the "gay ghettos" or neighborhoods with LGBTQ nightclubs and community centers. Most youth who migrate to cities, where the standard of living is more expensive than rural or suburban communities, find it difficult to sustain employment with a salary that pays for housing, food, and transportation. Most jobs available to youth with a high school diploma or less are part-time and in the service industry (department store, coffee shop, fast food, and so forth). Moreover, these jobs are competitive and subject to the whims of the market. In the absence of economically stable support networks and viable employment, LGBTQQ youth in urban environments are at risk for engaging in sex work (for money) or substance abuse (drugs, alcohol) to temporarily escape the economic and cultural challenges they face.

It is imperative to balance a look at all of these significant challenges with a look at student activism in order to avoid misunderstanding LGBTQQ urban youth only as victims rather than as complex people who are sometimes victims but also, other times, agents who assert themselves and demand their rights even in the face of such challenges.

Activism. Despite the challenging cultural and economic conditions of urban environments, we found that LGBTQ youth have an amazing capacity to make a difference and affect social change in both large and small ways (Quinn, 2007), within and beyond school walls (Rodriguez, 1998). Recall, for example, the first school-based gay group on record in the United States was at a high school in New York (Johnson, 2007). Queer youth in urban schools continue this activism today through professional development, official curricula, and GSAs.

David, for example, designed professional development sessions on meeting the needs of queer students. When he returned to his Bay Area high school he parlayed his experience working at a local queer youth center into antihomophobia workshops and panel presentations for administrators. He said, "'To be able to sit up in front of the administrators and talk about my experiences was really something. After that I became even more vocal in classrooms, voicing my opinion'" (McCready, 2001, p. 50).

Queer youth also find ways to make space to assert themselves and work against homophobia within the official curricula of schools. Justine, a middle-class, lesbian, African American student at the same urban magnet high school that Kira attended, brought a lesbian love poem from the queer youth center where she spent time and photos from a lesbian history book of her own to school for a class project (Blackburn, 2002–2003). Thus, she found ways to "make space" within the parameters of her curricula by including materials and information about herself as a lesbian, which in turn educated her classmates and teachers about the lives of queer people.

Another way queer students in urban schools engage in antihomophobia work is through GSAs. Lee's (2002) study of a GSA in Salt Lake City captures youth voices naming several benefits of their GSA with safety being one the most important. For example, Erin, who is implicitly identified as lesbian when she refers to the gay community as her community, said, "'I personally feel a lot less scared, because of the group. Because we have numbers now. Because we are visible'" (p. 21). Erin, among others, also reported improved relationships with "'administrators, teachers, family and peers'" (p. 18) as a result of their participation in the GSA. She said, "'I feel more willing to identify with a diversity of people at school. Now I feel rooted in who I am. I can go talk to other people. I don't need to wimp out'" (p. 18). In addition to feeling safer and sharing better relationships with people at school, and perhaps because of these things, the students in the GSA asserted that their academic performance improved as a result of their participation in the club. For example, Kelli, a lesbian, said:

> I faced a lot of harassment being one of the only "out" students at East High School before the club. And I was terrified to go to school. I avoided going to school. I failed most of my classes my freshman through junior year. My senior year I attended regularly and held down the best GPA I've had since I've been in school. (p. 17)

The experiences of young people in Salt Lake City suggest that GSAs hold tremendous promise as organizations that support the development of queer youth in schools. This finding is supported by GLSEN's 2008 school climate survey (Kosciw et al., 2008).

However, there is a growing number of studies of GSAs that suggest that queer youth who attend urban schools in non-White, multiracial, poor, and working-class communities experience difficulty starting and/or accessing their schools' GSAs. For example, McCready's (2004b) study of Project 10, which functioned as a GSA at a Bay Area high school, revealed the shortcomings of this club when it came to meeting the needs of queer students of color. Jamal and David both described the club as inaccessible because it was "under surveillance by their heterosexual Black peers" (p. 42). "Jamal believed these dynamics were particularly evident when students read the daily Bulletin announcing school-wide events, including Project 10" (p. 42). When Jamal was in predominantly White classes, Project 10 announcements would be read aloud with little event, but when a similar announcement was read in predominantly Black classes, Jamal said,

> they would skip over it like the club did not exist. They would either speak through it, or it was just treated differently than the other club announcements. . . . [T]here was a running joke at school, like people wanted to go and see who actually went to the club. . . . Like you don't want to be seen walking up to the third floor on the day that Project 10 is meeting. (p. 43)

Even when a student of color, like David, endured the scrutiny to attend a Project 10 meeting, he felt alienated and excluded. He called the group "a select group of White girls. . . . just teatime for a few lesbians and their friends. . . . I went two consecutive weeks and then I stopped going because it wasn't doing anything for me. There's nothing there for me" (p. 45). The combination of David's Black peers skipping over the Project 10 meeting announcement, in a sense ignoring the fact that some Black students may want to attend a social/support group for LGBTQQ students, and the fact that mostly "White girls" participated in the group, alienated David and made him feel like such a group could not possibly serve his personal and/or social needs. Because of these dynamics, which McCready theorizes stem from racial segregation and the normalization of Whiteness, the GSA, at least at this school, failed to meet the needs of queer students of color.

Quinn's study of queer girls of color starting a GSA at an all-girls public charter middle and high school in Chicago points to different, though equally troubling, social and cultural dynamics related to leadership and participation (Quinn, 2007). The group started in order to create formally a space for socializing and support:

> At first we used to just . . . talk to a counselor . . . 'cause everybody was pretty much in the closet, and . . . just we only knew who was gay or not. . . . And then after that, it seemed like somebody thought of a GSA. And then from then on, it just snowballed. (p. 35)

When parents heard about the GSA from their children, some organized to oppose the group because they believed it was immoral, students in middle school were too young to hear about the group, and it might cause them to question their sexuality. School administrators initially dismissed objections to the GSA; however, as the controversy unfolded, flyers announcing GSA activities were defaced and removed from the school's bulletin boards, the pressure on administration became too great and the GSA was disbanded. Although the group was reinstated a year later, Quinn notes that at this school,

> lesbian students claimed both cultural and sexual specificity by acting as loud black and often masculine girls. They rejected conformity to norms of leadership valued in the school and society—both raced and gendered—when they acted assertively and collectively to start the GSA. (p. 42)

In this way, these girls challenged the notion that GSAs are for White girls and troubled the idea of what school leaders can look and be like. Both the McCready and the Quinn studies point to the complicated and ongoing nature of activism, particularly as it pertains to LGBTQQ students in urban schools.

In addition to efforts in schools, young urban LGBTQQ people are also leading the way in efforts to make change outside of schools. Consider, for example, the New York–based organization, FIERCE, which is an acronym for Fabulous Independent Educated Radicals for Community Empowerment (n.d.). It was founded by LGBTQ youth of color in 2000, and strives to

> develop politically conscious leaders who are invested in improving [themselves] and [their] communities through youth-led campaigns, leadership development programs, and cultural expression through arts and media. FIERCE is dedicated to cultivating the next generation of social justice movement leaders who are dedicated to ending all forms of oppression. (http://www.fiercenyc.org/index.php?s=84)

Such activism by LGBTQQ youth of color living in urban environments can serve as a model for urban educators who want to cultivate leadership among LGBTQ youth of color and make urban environments more relevant to and inclusive of their experiences. In other words, teachers might follow the lead of these students by educating other teachers about the needs of LGBTQQ students, of inserting LGBTQQ people and topics in curricula, and initiating and supporting extracurricular supports for LGBTQQ people (see, for example, the activist teachers in Blackburn et al., 2009).

Directions for Future Work

McCready (2007) posited that equity and social justice work related LGBTQQ people can be stymied by practitioners' ambivalence about the "relevance of anti-homophobia to their social justice work in urban schools" (p. 74). So, this obstacle must be overcome and the opportunity to grapple with the complicated notion of intersectionality should be embraced.

In terms of research, an intersectional approach requires strategies that locate LGBTQQ people and issues in urban education in relation to the sociocultural, political, economic contexts of metropolitan areas. The research literature on urban education has tended to focus on the problems of low-status minority groups, the complexity of urban school systems, and the financing and governance of such systems (Gordon, 2003). Among urban educators in the United States, race-gender gaps (or disparities by race and gender) in achievement, discipline, and participation are considered most pressing (Lopez, 2003; Noguera, 2008). Researchers might consider, for example, how do LGBTQQ people in urban education experience these gaps?

Quantitative researchers using surveys and psychometric instruments need to include measures for LGBTQQ people's perception of urban communities and schools, so that these constructs can be used to predict education outcomes in relation to sexual identity. In this way, researchers can see how urban school communities are related to academic achievement and engagement (see Battle & Barnes, 2010).

Qualitative researchers have a range of approaches at their disposal to better understand the relationship between urban contexts and school engagement of LGBTQQ people. For example, through a case study of Black gay male students' experience of marginalization using ethnographic methods, McCready (2010) learned that gay and gender nonconforming Black male students narrated their experiences in ways that were both similar to and different from the dominant discourse of Black male student marginalization in the school. One student in particular challenged the heteronormative, hypermasculine performance standards of the African dance program by wearing hair extensions and mimicking the movements of female dancers. Such performances of identity, McCready argued, are gay and gender nonconforming Black male students' way of "making space" in the social and cultural climate of the school where hypermasculinity and heterosexuality are viewed as the norm among Black male students (McCready, 2010). This and other stories of marginalization and empowerment point to the need for urban educators to devise more complex identity development models that take into account the ways LGBTQQ students' gender and sexuality identities evolve in relation to the social context of urban communities and schools. In addition, the experiences of gay and gender nonconforming Black male students offer another way of looking at the complex relationship between LGBTQQ students' identities and participation in urban school programs that are defined by race and class.

In theorizing the notion of *making space,* McCready (2007) pointed to three conceptual tools that hold the possibility for different kinds of practices and interventions. *Feminist intersectional perspectives* or "intersectionality" helps urban educators uncover multiple identities and reveal different types of marginalization that occur among Black students (see Collins, 2000). The concept of *multiple masculinities* provides a framework for understanding how Black male students' gender identities are constantly being built, negotiated, and maintained (see Connell, 1996). Moreover, multiple masculinities call attention to the existence of nonhegemonic masculinities (masculinities that are subordinated, or repressed) like those of gay and gender nonconforming Black male students. What seems to prevent urban educators from considering the critical possibilities of nonhegemonic masculinities is the ways these forms of masculinity, which can be embodied by boys, girls, men and/or women, disrupt the societal norms of sex, gender, and sexuality and by extension, race, class, and ethnicity. One reason why some educators might be reluctant to show and discuss video of cultural icon James Baldwin in the 1970s is that he was unapologetically effeminate, which disrupted the dominant representation of Black men as heterosexual and hypermasculine at the time (Reid-Pharr, 1996). Thus, antihomophobia education is a crucial conceptual tool for urban educators who want to address intragroup marginalization based on gender and sexuality. Antihomophobia education is both dynamic and volatile because it invites students and educators to confront and negotiate a range of complex and contradictory subject positions associated with politics, gender identity, and sexuality (see Robinson, Ferfolja, & Goldstein, 2004).

In terms of policy development, this may mean, for example, ensuring confidentiality so that students whose family values emphasize heterosexuality and gender normativity are not made more vulnerable by reporting abuse. Trainings of teachers should include education about particular populations in the school and the stances taken on homosexuality and gender expression within these populations. In other words, notions of right and wrong should be rejected and replaced with complicated ideas that recognize multiplicity and variability within the school community. Resources should be available in the languages spoken by the various student populations within the school, and they should represent diverse peoples and communities. Curricular materials should be similarly representative, and extracurricular efforts, such as GSAs, should be recognized both for what they do and do not accomplish in urban schools. When GSAs prove to inadequately serve the school's populations, for example, alternatives should be generated from students and facilitated, indeed nurtured, by adults in the school. Such representation, recognition, and accommodation should be both policy and practice. Moreover, intersectionality should be viewed not as a burden but as a rich opportunity in terms of shaping policy and providing training, resources, and curricular and extracurricular supports.

One of the most exciting tasks for 21st century educators, researchers, and policy makers in urban education is to develop comprehensive approaches to their work, approaches that take into account how the social, cultural, and economic dynamics of the city affect LGBTQQ people in urban education. A good example of curriculum and policy work is the Respect Campaign (RC) launched by Out for Equity in eight Saint Paul, Minnesota, schools. RC was a two-year project including 12 schools that served to "identify obstacles to a respectful school climate, develop a vision for positive change, chart and implement a course of action and evaluate success" (Horowitz & Itzkowitz, 2007, p. 3). The project reveals an understanding that students in urban schools face multiple forms of oppression and discrimination that can make school feel unsafe. Based on this understanding, RC helped urban educators develop a multidimensional framework of a healthy school climate, one that addresses issues of homophobia and heterosexism, but also takes into account oppression and discrimination based on race, ethnicity, class, gender, and religion. Such work provides an example of an approach that seems to better meet the needs of LGBTQQ people in urban education.

Conclusion

LGBTQQ people and issues are taken up more in urban education than in any other educational context in the forms of social networks, resources, and supports, in and out of school. Still, even in these contexts, homophobia and transphobia exist significantly enough to impact negatively LGBTQQ students' academic achievement. Moreover, there are some cultural and economic challenges that impact urban LGBTQQ students more than their suburban and rural counterparts. Meeting and exceeding these challenges demands a conceptual framework designed to bring social, cultural, economic, and political dynamics to the fore. Such a framework invites understandings of LGBTQQ people in all of their complexity and intersectionality, including but not limited to identities shaped by race, ethnicity, socioeconomic class, nationality, religion, and citizenship—understandings that are imperative in urban education.

Notes

1. Here we use LGBTQ instead of LGBTQQ in an effort to honor the language used by these schools.
2. *Out* here means that this student self-identifies as gay, so he is out to himself, but also that others, including but not limited to his classmates, teachers, and administrators, know he identifies in this way. The term, used in this way, comes from the idea of being *out* of the metaphorical closet that one is said to be *in* when a person is LGBTQQ but doesn't self-identify in that way yet and/or doesn't reveal that identity to anyone else. Later we use the term *outed*. This means that someone other than the LGBTQQ person reveals the person's LGBTQQ identity.

References

Abu-Lughod, J.L. (1999). *New York, Chicago, Los Angeles: America's global cities.* Minneapolis, MN: University of Minnesota Press.

Asher, N. (2005). Curriculum, antibias. In J.T. Sears (Ed.), *Youth, education, and sexualities: An international encyclopedia* (pp. 227–229). Westport, CT: Greenwood Press.

Badcock, B. (1997). *Restructuring and spatial polarization in cities.* Thousand Oaks, CA: Sage Publications.

Baez, B. (2005). Harassment. In J.T. Sears (Ed.), *Youth, education, and sexualities: An international encyclopedia* (pp. 388–391). Westport, CT: Greenwood Press.

Battle, J., & Barnes, S.L. (2010). *Black sexualities: Probing powers, passions, practices, and policies.* New Brunswick, NJ: Rutgers University Press.

Bell, D., & Binnie, J. (2004). Authenticating queer space: Citizenship, urbanism and governance. *Urban Studies, 41*(9), 1807–1820.

Bieschke, K.J. (2005). Counseling. In J.T. Sears (Ed.), *Youth, education, and sexualities: An international encyclopedia* (pp. 210–211). Westport, CT: Greenwood Press.

Blackburn, M.V. (2002–2003). Disrupting the (hetero)normative: Exploring literacy performances and identity work with queer youth. *Journal of Adolescent & Adult Literacy, 46*(4), 312–324.

Blackburn, M.V. (2003). Losing, finding, and making space for activism through literacy performances and identity work. *Penn GSE Perspectives on Urban Education, 2*(1). Retrieved from http://www.urbanedjournal.org/articles/article0008.html

Blackburn, M.V., Clark, C.T., Kenney, L.M., & Smith, J .M. (2009). *Acting out! Combating homophobia through teacher activism.* New York, NY: Teachers College Press.

Blount, J. (2005). Teachers, LGBT and history. In J.T. Sears (Ed.), *Youth, education, and sexualities: An international encyclopedia* (pp. 853–856). Westport, CT: Greenwood Press.

Clare, M.M., & James, S.E. (2005). Secondary schools. LGBT. In J.T. Sears (Ed.), *Youth, education, and sexualities: An international encyclopedia* (pp. 754–759). Westport, CT: Greenwood Press.

Clark, C. T. (2010). Preparing LGBTQ-Allies and combating homophobia in teacher education. *Teaching and Teacher Education, 26*(3), 704-713.

Clotfelter, C.T. (2004). *After* Brown: *The rise and retreat of school desegregation.* Princeton, NJ: Princeton University Press.

Cohen, H.S. (Producer), & Chasnoff, D. (Producer & Director). (1997). *It's elementary: Talking about gay issues in school* [film]. (Available from Women's Educational Media, San Francisco, CA).

Collins, P.H. (2000). *Black feminist thought: Knowledge, consciousness, and the politics of empowerment* (rev. 10th anniversary ed.). New York, NY: Routledge.

Connell, R.W. (1996). Teaching the boys: New research on masculinity, and gender strategies for schools. *Teachers College Record, Winter, 98*(2), 206–235.

Consolacion, T. (2001). Where I am today. In K. Kumashiro (Ed.), *Troubling intersections of race and sexuality: Queer students of color and anti-oppressive education* (pp. 83–85). Lanham, MD: Rowman and Littlefield.

Cruz, C. (2008). Notes on immigration, youth, and ethnographic silence. *Theory Into Practice, 47*(1), 67–73.

Fabulous Independent Educated Radicals for Community Empowerment (FIERCE). (n.d.). Retrieved from http://www.fiercenyc.org/index.php?s=84

Friedman, E. (2008, May 2). Principal allegedly outs gay students. *ABC News.* Retrieved from http://abcnews.go.com/US/Story?id=4773381&page=1

Gay, Lesbian and Straight Education Network (GLSEN). (2007). *Gay-Straight Alliances: Creating safer schools for LGBT students and their allies.* (GLSEN Research Brief). New York, NY: Author.

Gay Pair's Photo Blacked out of Yearbook. (2007, June 22). *The Star Ledger.* Retrieved from http://www.nj.com/news/index.ssf/2007/06/gay_pairs_photo_blacked_out_of_1.html

Gordon, E.W. (2003). Urban education. *Teachers College Record, 105*(2), 189–207.

Graves, K. (2009). *And they were wonderful teachers: Florida's purge of gay and lesbian teachers.* Champaign, IL: University of Illinois Press.

Hayes, J.P., Herriott, T.K., & Rice, P.J. (2005). Curriculum, higher education. In J.T. Sears (Ed.), *Youth, education, and sexualities: An international encyclopedia* (pp. 233–236). Westport, CT: Greenwood Press.

Holloway, S.R., Wright, R., & Ellis, M. (2012). The racially fragmented city? Neighborhood racial segregation and diversity jointly considered. *Professional Geographer, 64*(1), 63–82. doi:10.1080/00330124.2011.585080

Horne, S.G., & Biss, W.J. (2005). Spirituality. In J.T. Sears (Ed.), *Youth, education, and sexualities: An international encyclopedia* (pp. 824–828). Westport, CT: Greenwood Press.

Horowitz, A., & Itzkowitz, M. (2007, October). Out for equity middle school project. *Out for Equity,* 1, 3, 4, 10.

Hulsebosch, P. (2005). Parents, LGBT. In J.T. Sears (Ed.), *Youth, education, and sexualities: An international encyclopedia* (pp. 601–605). Westport, CT: Greenwood Press.

Human Rights Watch. (2001). *Hatred in the hallways: Violence and discrimination against lesbian, gay, bisexual, and transgender students in U.S. schools.* New York, NY: Author.

Jagose, A. (1996). *Queer theory: An introduction.* New York, NY: New York University Press.

Johnson, D. (2007). "This is political!" Negotiating the legacies of the first school-based gay youth group. *Children, Youth and Environments, 17*(2), 380–387.

Kosciw, J.G.. Diaz, E.M., & Greytak, E.A. (2008). *The 2007 National School Climate Survey: The experiences of lesbian, gay, bisexual, and transgender youth in our nation's schools.* New York, NY: Gay, Lesbian and Straight Education Network.

Kosciw, J.G., Greytak, E.A., Diaz, E.M., & Bartkiewicz, M.J. (2010). *The 2009 National School Climate Survey: The experiences of lesbian, gay, bisexual and transgender youth in our nation's schools.* New York, NY: Gay, Lesbian and Straight Education Network.

Kozol, J. (1992). *Savage inequalities: Children in America's schools* (1st Harper Perennial ed.). New York, NY: HarperPerennial.

Lee, C. (2002, February/March). The impact of belonging to a high school gay/straight alliance. *High School Journal,* 13–26.

Lipman, P. (2005). Metropolitan regions: New geographies of inequality in education: The Chicago metro region case. *Globalisation, Societies and Education, 3*(2), 141–164. doi:10.1080/14767720500166902

Lipman, P. (2008). Mixed-income schools and housing: Advancing the neoliberal urban agenda. *Journal of Education Policy, 23*(2), 119–134.

Lomine, L.L. (2005). Europe. LGBT youth and issues in. In J.T. Sears (Ed.), *Youth, education, and sexualities: An international encyclopedia* (pp. 307–311). Westport, CT: Greenwood Press.

Lopez, N. (2003). *Hopeful girls, troubled boys: Race and gender disparity in urban education.* New York, NY: Routledge.

Lugg, C.A. (2005). Educational policies. In J.T. Sears (Ed.), *Youth, education, and sexualities: An international encyclopedia* (pp. 293–296). Westport, CT: Greenwood Press.

Marcuse P., & van Kempen, R. (2000). *Globalizing cities: A new spatial order?* London, UK: Blackwell.

McCaskell, T. (2005). *Race to equity: Disrupting educational inequality.* Toronto, Canada: Between the Lines.

McCready, L.T. (2001). When fitting in isn't an option, or, Why Black queer males at a California high school stay away from Project 10. In K. Kumashiro (Ed.), *Troubling intersections of race and sexuality: Queer students of color and anti-oppressive education* (pp. 37–53). Lanham, MD: Rowman and Littlefield.

McCready, L.T. (2004a). Understanding the marginalization of gay and gender non-conforming Black male students. In M.V. Blackburn & R. Donelson (Eds.), Sexual identities and schooling [Special issue]. *Theory Into Practice, 43*(2), 136–143.

McCready, L. (2004b). Some challenges facing queer youth programs in urban high schools: Racial segregation and de-normalizing whiteness. *Journal of Gay and Lesbian Issues in Education, 1*(3), 37–51.

McCready, L.T. (2005). Urban youth and schools. In J.T. Sears (Ed.), *Youth, sexualities, and education: An international encyclopedia* (pp. 877–881). Westport, CT: Greenwood Press.

McCready, L.T. (2007). Queer urban education: Curriculum and pedagogy for LGBTQI youth in the city. *Journal of Curriculum and Pedagogy, 4*(2), 71–77.

McCready, L.T. (2010). Black queer bodies, Afrocentric reform and masculine anxiety. *International Journal of Critical Pedagogy, 3*(1), 52–67.

Meyer, E. (2008). Gendered harassment in secondary schools: Understanding teachers' (non) interventions. *Gender and Education, 20*(6), 555–570.

Ngo, B. (2003). Citing discourses: Making sense of homophobia and heteronormativity at Dynamic High School. *Equity and Excellence in Education, 36,* 115–124.

Noguera, P. (2008). *The trouble with black boys: Essays on race, equity, and the future of public education* (1st ed.). San Francisco, CA: Jossey-Bass.

Pallotta-Chiarolli, M. (2005). Ethnic identity. In J.T. Sears (Ed.), *Youth, education, and sexualities: An international encyclopedia* (pp. 303–306). Westport, CT: Greenwood Press.

Planned Parenthood Toronto. (2004). *Hear me out.* Toronto, Canada: Second Story Press.

Quinn, T.M. (2007). "You make me erect!": Queer girls of color negotiating heteronormative leadership at an urban all-girls' public school. *Journal of Gay and Lesbian Issues in Education, 4*(3), 31–47.

Reid-Pharr, R. (1996). Tearing the goat's flesh: Homosexuality, abjection and the production of a late twentieth-century black masculinity. *Studies in the Novel, 28*(3), 372–394.

Robinson, K.H., Ferfolja, T., & Goldstein, T. (2004). Editorial: Anti-homophobia teacher education [Special issue]. *Teaching Education, 15*(1), 3–8.

Rodriguez, N. (1998). (Queer) youth as political and pedagogical. In W.F. Pinar (Ed.), *Queer theory in education.* (pp. 173–185). Mahwah, NJ: Lawrence Erlbaum Associates.

Rofes, E. (1985). *Plato, Socrates, and guys like me.* Boston, MA: Alyson.

Rury, J.L., & Mirel, J.E. (1997). The political economy of urban education. *Review of Research in Education, 22,* 49–110.

Schilt, K., & Westbrook, L. (2009). Doing gender, doing heteronormativity: "Gender normals," transgender people, and the social maintenance of heterosexuality. *Gender & Society, 23*(4), 440–464.

Uribe, V. (1995). A school-based outreach to gay and lesbian youth. In G. Unks (Ed.), *The gay teenager* (pp. 203–210). New York, NY: Routledge.

Wilkinson, R.G. (2010). In K. Pickett (Ed.), *The spirit level: Why greater equality makes societies stronger.* New York, NY: Bloomsbury Press.

Section III
Family and Community

8

Parent Involvement for Urban Students and Youth of Color

William Jeynes

Parental involvement is one of the hottest topics in educational circles. Concurrently, urban students are probably the group most studied by educational researchers. Unquestionably, understanding the dynamics of this involvement in urban students is one of the most important quests in the social sciences today. This chapter traces: (1) the historical development of parental involvement among urban children in the United States from colonial times until present; (2) the growth of research in parental and community engagement among urban youth; (3) what the body of research indicates about the importance of parental involvement in relation to being a key to raising academic outcomes in the cities; and (4) how the body of research in this discipline can help parents, teachers, and communities become more effective in educating children.

The chapter addresses not only the extent to which parental involvement is or is not associated with higher scholastic outcomes, but also what components of this engagement are the most salient. The chapter distinguishes between what expressions of voluntary parental involvement are most important, but also examines what components of parental involvement programs have the greatest impact. School strategies that best attract mothers and fathers to become active in schools are also investigated. Suggestions for further research in this field are also propounded.

The Historical Development of Parental Involvement Among Urban Children in the United States From Colonial Times Until Present

Parental involvement has been a practice by healthy American families since the nation's founding. One must not think that this concept was an unknown construct before the burgeoning of the social sciences. Some of America's earliest European settlers, especially the Puritans, were strong believers in the primacy of parental involvement (McClellan & Reese, 1988). As one might imagine, the Puritans generally did not use the words *parental involvement*. Nevertheless, their family emphasis, evening joint reading sessions, and their emphasis on the father exhibiting the spiritual qualities of the Heavenly Father all exemplified a profound commitment to parental involvement (Hiner, 1988; McClellan & Reese, 1988). Among African Americans, especially those enslaved in the South, in the absence of educational support by most of the owners of enslaved Africans, the role of parents was especially salient in securing the intellectual and spiritual development of children. Immigrants, especially those of color, faced unique challenges coming to a new land and because of this, mothers and fathers played a particularly important role in the educational and moral preparation of their children (Jeynes, 2007a). Given that parental engagement is actually a practice that goes back to the nation's founding, what researchers are simply doing is calling Americans to practice again a lifestyle and set of priorities that previously has been interwoven into the fabric of American life, but due to the demands of modern society, diverse concepts of family life, and a variety of other factors have been neglected or deemphasized (Jeynes, 2007a).

Two major reasons why parental involvement was so apparent in Puritan homes included their educational emphasis and their belief that a strong bond between the home, the church, and the family was a prerequisite for children's overall success (Gangel & Benson, 1983; Hiner, 1988; McClellan & Reese, 1988). One of the chief mottos of the Puritans was the biblical declaration, "You shall know the truth and the truth will set you free" (NIV Bible, John 8:32). The Puritans influenced the early American education system more than any of the other settlers from Europe. They established the nation's first secondary school (Boston Latin) and its first college (Harvard), and passed the first compulsory education laws (Fraser, 2001; Rippa, 1997). The Puritan emphasis on parental involvement influenced family practices and schooling for centuries (Gangel & Benson, 1983; Hiner, 1988; Rippa, 1997).

William Bradford, the primary governor in the early years of the Puritan Massachusetts settlement, was a strong believer in supporting "an intelligent gospel" (Bartlett, 1978). In 1642 the Massachusetts legislature passed a law requiring that the head of every household teach all the children in one's home, both male and female (Hiner, 1988). This law is often referred to as the Massachusetts Compulsory School Law. This was a call for parents all across the Massachusetts Commonwealth to teach their children how to read. Cubberley (1920, p. 354) noted the significance of the 1642 law when he stated that, "for the first time in the English-speaking world, a legislative body representing the State ordered that all children should be taught to read."

The Puritans, as well as the Pilgrims before them, asserted that children could reach their highest potential in school if the family, church, and school all worked together in partnership, in what one might call a "holy triad" (Gangel & Benson, 1983; Hiner, 1988; McClellan & Reese, 1988). Consistent with this belief, Puritan teachers visited the homes of their students before the school year began to build a relationship with the family and to obtain insight into the strengths and weaknesses of the child and learn just how they could help the child maximize his or her potential (Gangel & Benson, 1983; Jeynes, 2006, 2007a). So prominent and vital was this practice in the United States that several East Asian countries adopted it when American educators and missionaries helped these nations develop their own systems of education in the mid- to late 1800s (Amano, 1990; Hood, 2001; Shimizu, 1992). For many American settlers not only was parental involvement indispensable, but it was the cornerstone of efficacious instruction.

The Home. The Puritans asserted that the home was the primary place of schooling and maturing (McClellan & Reese, 1988). They affirmed that if the home environment was not in order, even if the child attended the finest church and school, the child would not develop into a properly educated individual. The colonists maintained that the home was where the academic training given at school and the spiritual training given at church were applied to the child's daily experience (McClellan & Reese, 1988). During the colonial period, particularly among the Puritans, the father was much more involved in the raising of the children than one tends to witness in modern society (McClellan & Reese, 1988). Part of this paternal involvement emanated from the Christian concept of the Trinity: the Heavenly Father, the Son, and the Holy Spirit. Many colonists believed that children formed a loving and holy image of the Heavenly Father based on seeing these attributes manifested in their earthly father (Jeynes, 2007a; McClellan & Reese, 1988; Willison, 1966).

Most Puritan and Pilgrim families, particularly those living in the more urbanized settings, held family devotionals in which they would study the Bible and pray together as a family. This practice served the purpose of encouraging spiritual and academic development and not only included studying the Bible, but also reading the newspaper and classic books (Hiner, 1988). They believed that knowledge, however, needed to be founded in spiritual wisdom. Otherwise, the increased knowledge could be injudiciously used and could create much harm. Ironically Martin Luther King declared this same belief, when he gave speeches in the 20h century (King, 1998). The Puritans maintained a balance between parental discipline and encouragement when they educated their children. Cotton Mather said, "We are not wise for our children, if we do not greatly encourage them" (Mather, 1708, p. 30).

The Church and the School. The church's purpose in schooling was to train the colonists regarding the teachings of the Bible and how to be compassionate and righteous godly people. The church was also the administrative hub for nearly all of a community's schooling of the young (Johnson, 1997). The Puritans believed that the most vital function of the school was to promote the development of righteous individuals (Clarke, 1730). The Puritans believed that in terms of teaching children, the family was the center (Hiner, 1988). It was absolutely essential for teachers to engage parents in the schooling of their children (Hiner, 1988; Morgan, 1986). The significance of the Puritan emphasis on parental participation and the "holy triad" was profound because it was embraced by many of the colonies, and eventually, by a large portion of the nation (Hiner, 1988; Morgan, 1986).

Other Pre–Revolutionary War Parental Involvement Practices

Schooling in Maryland and the Southern states was more of a family matter than even in New England. One should note that essentially all of the early settlers on the East Coast, and African Americans throughout the nation as well, believed that it was primarily the responsibility of the family to educate children. This is especially significant because through the 1700s and 1800s, the East was the most urbanized section of the country. As a result of possessing this orientation, most families in these areas either taught their children themselves or hired tutors to do the instruction (Urban & Wagoner, 2000).

Parental Involvement in the Late 18th and 19th Centuries

The United States had a myriad of its early post–Revolutionary War leaders promote the importance of parental engagement in urban learning (Blinderman, 1976; Webster, 1793, 1834). Benjamin Rush was an educator and was regarded as the nation's foremost physician (Blinderman, 1976; Lewy, 1996; Urban & Wagoner, 2000). Rush claimed that families needed to be well educated in order to efficaciously instruct their children (Blinderman, 1976; Rush, 1786a 1786b). On this basis, Rush emphasized that schooling for females was essential for the instruction of America's youth (Blinderman, 1976; Rush, 1786a, 1786b). Rush declared that parental involvement was especially salient in order to foster virtue in children, which most educators of the era believed stood as the key component of instruction (Blinderman, 1976; Rush, 1786a, 1786b). Noah Webster, who many nicknamed America's schoolmaster, maintained similar views to Rush's, asserting that parental involvement was key to maximizing a child's development both morally and academically (Webster, 1793, 1834).

In the early 19th century, DeWitt Clinton and Joseph Lancaster arose as two of the most prominent educators in the country (Bourne, 1870; Cornog, 1998; Cubberley, 1920; Fitzpatrick,

1969). DeWitt Clinton served as president of the New York Free School Society, a system of private schools that offered schooling with school fees on a sliding scale so that a myriad of children could be schooled at no charge (Bourne, 1870; Cornog, 1998; Cubberley, 1920; Fitzpatrick, 1969). Joseph Lancaster propounded the most popular model for operating these schools (Bourne, 1870; Cornog, 1998). Lancaster and Clinton maintained that if parents and schools worked as partners, they could have an influence on the character development of children in particular (Bourne, 1870; Cornog, 1998; Kaestle, 1973). Clinton apparently thought this partnership was effective because after decades of serving as head of the New York Free School Society he declared in a speech: "Of the many thousands who have been instructed in our free schools in the City of New York, there is not a single instance known of anyone being convicted of a crime" (quoted in Fitzpatrick, 1969, p. 54). The development of charity schools was important for children of color as well, because most freed African Americans and other people of color also received their education in charity schools (Jeynes, 2007a).

The leaders of the common- or public-school movement also understood the key contribution that parental involvement made, although not all Americans interpreted this to be the case (Downs, 1975; Gutek, 1968). Many parents felt that the common schools would usurp their power as the primary providers of tutelage (Downs, 1975; Gutek, 1968). Over time, however, one individual was especially helpful to Horace Mann and Henry Barnard in convincing parents that common school teachers could be trusted—a Swiss man named Johann Pestalozzi (1746–1827) (1898, 1916). Pestalozzi discussed what is often called the maternal role of the schools. That is, he opined that the teacher should in many respects function like a mother away from home (Pestalozzi, 1898, 1916). This was appealing to many parents who were less trusting of public school teachers than they were of private school teachers, because the latter they usually already knew through church and their community. According to Pestalozzi, educators should seek to be sensitive to parental concerns such as these and only then could they hope to maximize parental trust and activity (Downs, 1978; Lilley, 1967; Ulich, 1957, 1968).

Horace Mann also asserted that the schools had a responsibility to uphold the moral values of parents and society at large (Mann, 1849). Mann (1849) believed that it was important for schools to especially partner with parents in moral education, which he believed to be the most important function of school instruction. Mann was concerned about the potential of teachers emphasizing only academics, at the expense of partnering with parents to teach moral education. Mann stated, "The more I see of our present civilization and of the only remedies for its evils, the more I dread intellectual eminence when separated from virtue. We are in a sick world, for whose maladies, the knowledge of truth, and obedience to it, are the only healing" (quoted in Filler, 1965). Mann believed that only with parents and teachers working together could this goal be realized.

Friedrich Froebel's founding of the kindergarten was also a salient event in the historical development of urban parental engagement. Although industrial progress was changing society, Froebel opined that this transformation was also resulting in a growing number of components in society becoming more interconnected. Consequently, parents and teachers needed to work harmoniously to reach common goals (Downs 1978, Lilley, 1967). Froebel believed that it was essential for the school not to dictate to the parents what the orientation of early childhood schools would be (Downs, 1978; Lilley, 1967; Ulich, 1957, 1968). Froebel contended that the level of parental involvement had a considerable impact on child development (Downs, 1978; Lilley, 1967; Ulich, 1957, 1968). He frequently observed that there existed a considerable variation in schoolchildren's academic abilities, even at a young age, and that this was largely due to the degree that parents interacted with and trained their children (Downs, 1978; Lilley, 1967). Froebel believed that to the extent that kindergarten teachers supported parental values and worked cooperatively with them, family members would possess a greater tendency to participate in school-related activities.

The Role of Parental Involvement Declines

To be sure, the rise of the common schools increased the partnership between parents and teachers in a number of respects; the incipient development of industrialization was causing the balance of power in that relationship to change (Cubberley, 1920; Cremin, 1977; Rury, 2002). Family members were retreating somewhat from their earlier role of taking the initiative in the training and schooling of their children. The populace was increasingly aware of this trend and felt ambivalent about the school taking on a larger role in the inculcation of children. Some people thought that the school leaders were usurping some of the roles of education that best rested in the home (Downs, 1975; Gutek, 1968). Horace Mann and other common school leaders emphasized the importance of parental involvement and of schools partnering with the student's family. Nevertheless, Mann also emphasized the need for parents to view teachers as professionals, at a level Americans had never before witnessed (Mann, 1957). Mann supported legislation that extended the role of the state in emphasizing the educational and psychological welfare of children (Gatto, 2001). The legislation spawned a fledgling distrust that numerous Americans possessed for the chief proponents of the common school movement (Gatto, 2001).

Mann's belief that parents view urban teachers as professionals was probably needed in some ways, but prior to this time parents regarded teaching as a ministry (Gatto, 2001). The growing emphasis on professionalism detracted from this view (Gatto, 2001; Peressini, 1998). Mann (1849) also emphasized recruiting female teachers rather than male teachers, because he believed they were less likely than men to be alcoholics and therefore would serve as superior moral examples for children. This orientation, together with the male teacher losses due to the Civil War, caused females to become and remain the majority of teachers by the end of the war (Elsbree, 1939; Jeynes, 2007a). In fact, as the years passed, females would become the overwhelming majority of the elementary school teaching force to such an extent that this may have hampered the academic advancement of urban males, particularly those of color, from the 1970s until present (Ogbu, 1992, 1993).

The common school movement and the changes taking place in society sewed some of the seeds of decreased parental involvement in the 19th century. Nevertheless, the overwhelming number of American parents was still actively participating in their children's education throughout the 19th century (Husband & O'Loughlin, 2004; Jeynes, 2011b, 2012a). As the United States became the world's foremost industrial power around 1900, many fathers, in particular, worked outside the home (Husband & O'Loughlin, 2004; Rury, 2002). This was a major step to parental involvement becoming more difficult (Husband & O'Loughlin, 2004; Jeynes, 2003a; 2005, 2007b; Rury, 2002). The influence of industrialization accelerated with the emergence of educational philosopher, John Dewey (1859–1952). Dewey (1915, 1990) not only opined that industrialization did have an impact, he averred that it *should* have an impact (Lawson & Lean, 1964). Dewey (1915, 1964, 1990) claimed that two realities must have an effect on teaching. First, people in society were becoming more specialized and therefore teachers should become the schooling specialists and replace parents as the primary educational influence. Second, Dewey (1964) stated that industrialization was eroding the primacy of the family and that it was the responsibility of the schools to assume some of the responsibilities that had previously been reserved for the family (Dewey, 1964). In Dewey's view, this trend was happening all around the world (Dewey, 1964). Therefore, it was the school's responsibility to increase the authority of its role and execute some of the same functions previously reserved for the family (Dewey, 1964). Dewey's approach was likely well meaning, but the result was to relegate the position of parents as instructors to a patent secondary level (1915, 1964, 1990).

Equally salient to Dewey's ideas was the fact that many Americans accepted the validity of these assertions (Dewey, 1964; Egan, 2002; Martin, 2002). What they may not have understood nor anticipated, however, is that Dewey (1902, 1964, 1978) also asserted that teachers should not have an obligation to support the present values of parents (Egan, 2002). Rather, he declared that instructors should teach in order to help children to think for themselves (1902, 1964, 1978). Indubitably this perspective often caused consternation among parents, who felt that this exhortation undermined the spirit of partnership that had long existed between parents and teachers (Egan, 2002; Horne, 1923, 1931, 1932). With the forces of industrialization and Dewey's interpretation of those forces at work, although many teachers recognized the value of parental involvement as a concept, often they viewed parental engagement as parental meddling (Horne, 1923, 1931, 1932; Peressini, 1998).

The Changing Nature of the American Family

In spite of the fact that the changes of the late 19th and early 20th century had caused some deterioration in the level of parental involvement, by the 1940s, most families were strongly involved in their children's education (Pong, Dronkers, & Hampden-Thompson, 2003). Starting in 1963, however, the American divorce rate began to surge, after being in slight decline during the 1948–1962 period (U.S. Census Bureau, 2001). Moreover, married women were entering the workforce in record numbers (U.S. Census Bureau, 2001). What this meant is that not only were fathers frequently away from the home, but mothers were as well (McLanahan & Sandefur, 1994). The divorce rate then commenced to rise for 17 consecutive years and concurrently the infamous SAT score decline took place during precisely the same 1963–1980 period (Wirtz, 1977). Although there are some people who claim that these two concurrent trends are merely coincidental, most social scientists believe there is a relationship (McLanahan & Sandefur, 1994; Wirtz, 1977). In 1977 the College Board, the developers of the SAT, also concluded that there was a relationship (Wirtz, 1977).

In addition, from the 1960s to the 1980s, a broad line of research also arose indicating that the deterioration of the family influences juvenile behavioral outcomes. Youth from one-parent homes are considerably more likely to end up in prison than children from two-parent homes (U.S. Department of Justice, 1999). Children from one-parent homes have a greater tendency to take illegal drugs, alcohol, and cigarettes than do children from two-parent homes (CBS News, 1994). According to the College Board panel, the surge in marital dissolution meant that parents were spending less time teaching their children than before. According to the *Metropolitan Life Survey of the American Teacher,* teachers in the late 1980s listed "having parents spend much more time with their children in support of school and teachers" as the number one step that would "help a lot to improve education." In fact, 84% of the teachers questioned viewed this as very important (U.S. Department of Education, 2005). All of these historical developments in mind help catapult parental involvement to a central place of concern in the minds of myriad Americans.

The Growth of Research in Parental and Community Engagement Among Urban Youth

The growth of research in the discipline of parental and community involvement among urban students is profoundly important for a variety of reasons and this is why studies that have been done in this area have attracted so much attention (Jeynes, 1999, 2002a). First, problems that arise in urban areas are often a precursor of what will likely soon occur in the nation at large (Jeynes, 1999, 2002a; Raikes, 2005). There is a plethora of reasons for this trend, but it is undeniable that in the world at-large urban trends tend to predict national trends (Goldstein, Candau, & Clarkek, 2004; Janta, Goetz, & Shelley, 2004; Kakaraparthi & Kockelman, 2011). Second, urban areas are nearly always the business centers of industrialized nations and therefore they can influence the nation's economy considerably more than other areas of the country (Goldstein et al., 2004; Janta et al., 2004; Kakaraparthi & Kockelman, 2011). It is very difficult for a city to enhance its rate of economic growth if it is muddled in the moral mire of surging murder rates, gang violence, and organized crime (Davalos, Chavez, & Guardiola, 2005; Jeynes, 2002a). Third, urban areas in the United States are more likely to be ethnically diverse and may provide the most accurate window into trends that are developing in an increasingly diverse United States (Janta et al., 2004; Kakaraparthi & Kockelman, 2011). Fourth, as the populations of the larger cities and nations steadily increase, urban trends may emerge as the best indicators of future trends in society as a whole (Janta et al., 2004; Kakaraparthi & Kockelman, 2011; Sharma et al., 2007).

Urban parental and community involvement research grew as an offspring of other types of family studies that existed previously (Jeynes, 2003a, 2010a). The two primary "parents" of parental involvement research were family structure and family functioning analysis (Jeynes, 2005, 2007b). As one examines the development of parental engagement research in retrospect, it only seems logical that academic inquiry into the effects of a child's family structure would lead to parental engagement research. This is the case because it is likely that family structure and functioning are the two primary contributors that determine the level of involvement that exist in a given family.

The prominence of the structural aspect is axiomatic because it is patent that mothers and fathers cannot participate in a child's education if they are absent, have passed away, or were never really in the household to begin with; engagement becomes difficult if not impossible (Jeynes, 2002a, 2003b). Urban family involvement is more likely to transpire when a mother and father are present to offer their support and assistance (Brooks & Goldstein, 2001; Burgos, 2003; Jeynes, 2003a). Generally, the farther one departs from the two biological parent intact family structure, the greater an impact there is on the academic, psychological, and behavioral outcomes of the children (Kwan, 2010; Kwan & Ip, 2009; Thomas, 2009). Determining the extent of the effects of parental absence depends largely on two factors: first, the number of family structure transitions that a given child has endured and second, the amount of exposure the child generally has to the parent in terms of time and accessibility (Jeynes, 2006, 2010b; Strous, 2007).

An example of these principles is that a child who is from a divorced remarried family structure on average has more depressed levels of achievement, psychological, and behavior measures than a child from a single-parent divorced family, because the youth in the divorced and remarried parental family structure has not only experienced the challenge of having one's parents divorce but has experienced the additional adjustment of having to adapt to a person who is from outside the household joining in residence with the custodial family members (Jeynes, 1999, 2003b, 2006; Kwan & Ip, 2009; Riggio, 2004). To be sure, there are exceptions to these principles, but on average these are the effects of parental family structure (Jeynes, 1999, 2003b; Kwan, 2010; Thomas, 2009). In addition to the number of transitions being a major consideration, it is also vital to understand that children do better in virtually every aspect of their lives if they have greater access to their parents as opposed to when such access is unusual (Kim, 2011; Riggio, 2004; Wolfinger, Kowlaleski-Jones, & Ken, 2003). For centuries it has been understood that children originating from such family structures on average experience lower levels of parental involvement than do their counterparts in families with both fathers and mothers present. For example, humankind has acknowledged that losing one's father in warfare was a development that had severe consequences for the welfare of children (Jeynes, 2007a; Shenk & Scelza, 2012).

Beginning in the 1960s other family structures became more common, such as never married single-parent families and cohabitation, that had even greater average downward effects on the access that youth would typically have to their parents, as well as the number of family transitions a child would have to endure (Boggs & Pollard, 2003; Thornton & Young-DeMarco, 2001). These developments further hastened the growth of the study of parental and community involvement (Jeynes, 2003a, 2005, 2007b). Studies arose, in part, out of the intuitive assertions of scholars, leaders, and the general public that not only was there a strong connection between family involvement and the structure of home life, but also that parents, who were cognizant of some of the challenges their children had in terms of transitions, would try to compensate for those challenges by becoming more engaged. The idea behind this additional participation is that at least some of the disadvantage of a child experiencing a new family structure could be alleviated with intense parental effort (Moon & Lee, 2009; Stewart & Menning, 2009). The fact that family structure concerns sparked interest in parental involvement for more than one reason helped ensure that research in this field would mature rapidly (Moon & Lee, 2009; Stewart & Menning, 2009).

How Research on Family Functioning Yielded as an Interest in Parental Involvement

Family functioning also influences the level of parental involvement. Research also indicates that although coming from a two biological parent intact family is more conducive to experiencing high levels of mother and father engagement than is coming from a single-parent family structure, originating from this environment does not guarantee that mothers and fathers will be involved (Jeynes, 1999, 2003a, 2003b; Pong et al., 2003; Rodgers & Rose, 2002).

There are prominent tangible external indicators that suggest that a household is more or less functional (Moon & Lee, 2009; Pong et al., 2003; Rodgers & Rose, 2002; Thornton & Young-DeMarco, 2001). For example, the likelihood that a father or mother is engaged in illegal drug abuse, nicotine addiction, alcoholism, promiscuous and disloyal sexual behavior, and similar behaviors, is often indicative of dysfunctional behavior and tends to exert a downward pressure on parental engagement (Jeynes, 2002b). Fathers and mothers who are engaged in marital unfaithfulness affairs are likely to be less available to help their children and, in fact, are likely to be less concerned about tending to certain needs of their children because they are fulfilling certain selfish drives (Wallerstein & Lewis, 1998).

Over the years, sociologists, psychologists, and family scientists have investigated the effects of family functioning on children. Moreover, a myriad of social scientists has noted that there is also a distinct relationship, on average, between healthy family functioning and whether the nuptial union remains intact. In other words, marital dissolution is often a direct consequence of unhealthy family interactions and attitudes. Beyond this, however, these social scientists have also been interested in examining the underlying factors that cause such destructive parental behaviors (Kim, 2011). When the social sciences were at a more fledgling stage, theorists relied on Freudian concepts to guide their examinations (Crews, 1998; Salkind, 2006). As methodological inquiry matured, however, an increasing number of theorists and psychologists have dismissed the majority of Freudian theories, asserting that they may have reflected Freud's own personal psychological problems more than they constituted any coherent theory (Crews, 1998; Doinick, 1998; Salkind, 2006). In the mid-20th century researchers more commonly employed a behaviorist perspective to explain family functioning. This strategy tended to produce results that were considerably more accurate than those based on Freudian paradigms, but sometimes caused academics to reach rigid conclusions because they did not sufficiently represent internal realities that enabled academics to procure insight into the inner workings of human emotions and thought (Jeynes, 2006).

Following the first 70 years of the 20th century, social scientists propounded more sophisticated rubrics to help explain the levels of functionality apparent in a variety of families. Some of these models, such as Baumrind's (1971) descriptions of rearing styles, that is, authoritarian, authoritative, and permissive, examined the family within the largely closed environs of the household. Other researchers averred that these typologies were too insular, given the illimitable influences of the broader social environment. These social scientists preferred to incorporate the most sophisticated and complete description of societal functioning that was possible. They posited that only within this prodigious model could family functioning truly be understood. In this context, myriad researchers esteemed the approach of Urie Bronfenbrenner of Cornell University. Bronfenbrenner's (1979) multidimensional and multilevel approach, called Ecological Systems Theory, launched a more inclusive approach that appeared to render previous approaches almost unfathomably simplistic. Bronfenbrenner's paradigm was also attractive because it appeared to most faithfully reflect the prevailing understanding of the general public. The general public never totally embraced Freudian psychology, which appeared to run contrary to many people's notions of common sense. Freudian concepts such as the Oedipus and Electra complexes seemed aberrant to some of the most notable leaders of urban communities, such as African American ministers, schoolteachers, and political representatives (Doinick, 1998; Jeynes, 2002a). They opined that Freud's declarations reduced humans to pure animals with the most baleful and barbaric motivations. Some even asserted that Freud's theories caused people to classify entire races as possessing too much "id," which both spawned and reinforced racial stereotypes (Doinick, 1998; Fromkin, 1973). In their view, Freud's conceptualization of humans seemed totally devoid of integrity and any trace of the divine touch (Bronfenbrenner, 1979). As an increasing number of family-structure and family-functioning studies became published, the pattern of results became undeniable. The research highlighted the fact that household realities were some of the factors most likely to influence youth academically and psychologically as well (Epstein, 2001; Wallerstein & Lewis, 1998).

Current Urban Education Landscape and What We Know About the Topic

There is an increasing appreciation of the truth that parental involvement and community engagement in the schooling of young people are highly related to academic outcomes. Most fair-minded scholars, political leaders, and members of the general public now acknowledge this relationship (Henderson & Mapp, 2002; Lee & Bowen, 2006). To be sure, the understanding of this relationship is nothing more than a recognition of the obvious (Jeynes, 2003a, 2005, 2007b). Nevertheless, this step was a key development that enabled the current inquiries to take place into the components of parental involvement that are most likely to enhance the educational outcomes of urban youth. The fact that research has headed in this direction is helping teachers, parents, and administrators.

Social scientists have posited a number of theories and orientations to best help families enhance the scholastic outcomes of their children. Some of these theorists have propounded economic theories and solutions, asserting that the best policies involve making certain families and communities have material resources to help their children (Rothstein, 2004). However, recent studies indicate that money must not be a substitute for the physical presence of parents. Other theorists are engaged in a debate about whether school-based solutions or individual-based solutions are most helpful for children (Gregory, Nygreen, & Moran, 2006). To be sure, both emphases are needed, but increasingly social scientists realize that if one focuses only on school-based solutions, students are more likely to fall behind their counterparts in education and in life as a whole. Research has consistently indicated that variables outside the school, particularly in the family, have a greater impact on educational outcomes than school-based variables (Coleman 1966).

It is this new emphasis on attempting to determine the most important facets of parental involvement that is one of the most important developments in the study of parental and community contributions in urban areas. This emphasis was possible because of the utilization of a statistical approach called a meta-analysis. A meta-analysis statistically combines all the relevant existing studies on a given subject in order to determine the aggregated results of said research. In this case, over 1,000 studies are initially considered for the meta-analysis, but only 100–200 of these studies contain sufficient quantitative data to be included in the various meta-analyses that have been undertaken that examine parental involvement. The orientation of focusing on specific components of parental involvement is especially helpful for a number of reasons: (a) it enables academic information about the general effects of parental involvement to have more practical implications that can enhance the scholastic outcomes of urban children and youth of color (Jeynes, 2003a, 2005, 2007b); (b) it can empower parents and teachers to take specific actions to raise youth achievement and alleviate the achievement gap (Lee & Bowen, 2006); and (c) it can enable the academic community to catch up to where most parents and teachers live. That is, most people are cognizant of the fact that family engagement can help raise the scholastic outcomes of children. What they are generally not aware of, however, is what components of parental involvement are the most ameliorative (Jeynes, 2003a; 2005, 2007b).

There is a growing body of research that is providing insight into the extent to which parental participation is helpful to urban children and also to youth of color, who are disproportionately likely to reside in urban areas (Jeynes, 1999, 2003b; Lee & Bowen, 2006). There is even some encouraging findings that suggest that the positive effects of parental involvement may be even greater for African American and Hispanic children than they are for their White and Asian American counterparts (Jeynes, 2003a). As salient as these findings are, it is difficult to determine precisely why the effects of parenting would be greater for African American and Hispanic children than it would be for others. There are several potential explanations. One hypothesis is that to the extent to which fathers and mothers of color are, on average, less likely to be involved in the schooling of their children than are parents in other groups, the positive influence of when these family members are involved might be greater than would normally be the case (Jeynes, 2003a). A second hypothesis is that because African American and Hispanic children are more likely to be in a single-parent family, when the children are from a two-parent family the effects are greater than is the case in a White or Asian American family (McLanahan & Sandefur, 1994). A third possibility is that when African American and Hispanic parents become involved the level of intensity of their engagement, on average, is greater than for other groups. One possible reason for this possibility is that they may be aware of the fact that often there are fewer nonparental supports (e.g., economic supports) for children of color and therefore mothers and fathers are wise if they attempt to compensate for that fact.

The second truth that the research community knows is that the subtle aspects of parental engagement may have more of an impact on urban student achievement than more overt expressions of mother and father engagement (Jeynes, 2005, 2006, 2007b). Expressions of parental engagement such as maintaining high expectations and practicing a combination of a loving and structured home environment actually had a much stronger association with student academic outcomes than did some of the more overt expressions of parental involvement (Jeynes, 2003b, 2005, 2007b). Positive and consistent communication between parents and their children also was a salient aspect of subtle communications that had a strong association with the scholastic outcome of youth (Jeynes, 2003b, 2005, 2007b). The results of such research do not indicate that more overt expressions of parental participation are impotent, but rather that contrary to common past hypotheses the most salient types of parental involvement are subtle (Jeynes, 2003b, 2006, 2007b). These types of parental engagement are not typically the components that teachers and parents most frequently practice (Jeynes, 2003b, 2006, 2007b). These advances mean that in order for schools and families to produce the most efficacious parental involvement programs they must rethink family practices in education (Jeynes, 2012a). One vital implication of this fact at the school level is that teachers need to be cognizant of these facts so that they can direct parents to practice the most efficacious kinds of engagement. Most mothers and fathers want to be involved in their children's schooling, but are not informed about how they can most productively participate. They frequently look to teachers to provide that guidance and it is important that instructors be able to supply that information. There are few more vital services that educators can provide than this one.

Third, an increasing number of studies are examining the effects of mother and father involvement at very young ages (Burgos, 2003; Downer, 2005; Downer, Campos, McWayne, & Gartner, 2010). This includes not only elementary school age children, but also preschool age children (Burgos, 2003; Downer, 2005; Downer et al., 2010). Meta-analyses do suggest that the effects of parental involvement, albeit significant at the high school level, are particularly strong at the elementary school level (Jeynes, 2005, 2007b). This and similar findings have encouraged others to hypothesize that if during the typical schooling years parental engagement appears to have more influence when children are younger, is it not consistent to think that if one chooses to determine and divulge the trends that exist at even younger years, the influence of mothers and fathers might be even greater (Burgos, 2003; Downer et al., 2010; Fagan, Newash, & Schloesser, 2000)? There is a growing body of research that suggests that family activity in the lives of children, and particularly that of the father, yields positive academic and behavioral outcomes in the lives of preschool children (Karther, 2002; Rimm-Kaufman, 2005).

Fourth, research on reducing the achievement gap is becoming increasingly clear indicating that educators, acting without the active support of families and local communities, can only reduce the gap to a certain degree (Lee & Bowen, 2006). It is becoming increasingly patent that one of the reasons that academic research has tended to post rather disappointing results regarding bridging the achievement gap originates with the fact that social scientists tend to view the solutions to various problems within the confines of their particular disciplines (Jeynes, 2010a, 2011a; Lee & Bowen, 2006). That is, sociologists tend to look at sociological solutions to problems, psychologists gravitate to examining psychological answers, educators tend to focus on educational resolutions, economists emphasize economic remedies, and so forth (Jeynes, 2011b, 2012a, 2012b). Recent research on the achievement gap suggests that a combination of these factors will yield the most puissant results in terms of reducing the achievement gap (Jeynes, 2010a). At the classroom level, it is vital that educators appreciate the fact that there is only a limited amount of progress that they can make with their students if they do not partner with mothers and fathers in schooling children. Teachers may have educational expertise, but they need the knowledge that parents have of their children in order to maximize their instructional effectiveness.

Fifth, social scientists are increasingly looking at the intergenerational transmission of mother and father involvement (Belsky, 2005; Downer et al., 2010). That is, family science studies indicate that youth, when they become adults, often act on the family behavior that their mothers, fathers, and others have set before them (Belsky, 2005). Typically, then, young parents often display similar behavior and attitude patterns toward their children to that which they received in their youth, when raised in their homes (Belsky, 2005; Downer et al., 2010).

Sixth, practitioners are attempting to weave parental involvement programs more and more into school-based and government-based programs. Admittedly, research indicates that voluntary parental involvement is more effective than are these types of programs (Jeynes, 2012a; Slavin &

Madden, 2006). Nevertheless, recent research suggests that parental involvement programs can contribute to higher academic outcomes among urban students (Jeynes, 2012b; Slavin & Madden, 2006). And it appears likely that these programs—whether they be church-based, school-based, Head Start, or community-based programs—can effectively supplement voluntary parental involvement (Jeynes, 2012b; Slavin & Madden, 2006).

Seventh, increasingly social scientists are recognizing that it is not just a matter of a need to have higher levels of parental engagement in urban children's lives, but specifically there is an underestimated value that comes when fathers become involved in their children's education (Raikes, 2005). Hence, particularly by the late 1990s a new line of father involvement studies arose as a new and specific outgrowth of the parental emphasis social science discipline (Karther, 2002). Academics realized that as ameliorative as family participation was, much of the level of that participation is determined by the availability of the mother and the father (Raikes, 2005). And naturally, much of that availability is dependent on whether these individuals reside in the home (Karther, 2002). Given that nearly 90% of the time that a parent is absent from the home it is the father who is not present, theorists realize that there is a real need to determine the effects of proactive fatherhood specifically, more than merely proactive parenthood. Father absence is particularly a problem in urban communities and among African American and Hispanic families (McLanahan & Sandefur, 1994). As much as the United States, as a nation, has made reducing the socioeconomic and racial achievement gap its top priority over the last 50 years, if this goal is to become reality, both mothers and fathers need to be involved (Jeynes, 2010b).

The research results that highlight the effects of the family in influencing student outcomes is a healthy reminder to teachers that they cannot regard themselves as the educational specialists in much the same way that those on an assembly line cannot be viewed this way. Fortunately, an increasing number of educators now embrace the notion that they need the help of parents and local communities in order to help children become all that they can be and in order to overcome the achievement gap (Epstein, 2001; Henderson & Mapp, 2002; Mapp, Johnson, Strickland, & Meza, 2010).

Direction for Future Work (and Needs) in the Field of Urban Education

One trend that clearly appears in place is that over the last 10 or 15 years, research on the effects of parental and community engagement for urban students has become considerably more sophisticated than it was before (Stewart & Menning, 2009). Two of the areas of greatest progress during this period have been first in recognizing that a multidisciplinary approach to resolving the socioeconomic and racial achievement has some real promise; and second, identifying the various components of parental engagement that most help urban students. The fact that a host of factors have the potential to reduce the achievement gap is quite noteworthy. It confirms the notion that the existence of this gap has psychological, economic, educational, family-based, and sociological elements (Jeynes, 2010a). Based on this research, it appears that previous studies have underestimated the place of religious faith and parental involvement and family structure in reducing the achievement gap (Jeynes, 2010a). Each of these variables highlights the salience of the family. Family structure is important not only in its own right, but because the level of possible parental involvement is often dictated by family structure (Stewart & Menning, 2009). In addition, mothers and fathers also often play a major role in guiding their children into their religious faith and moral conviction (Jeynes, 1999). But beyond these more salient factors, it appears that there are variables within the context of a full gamut of disciplines that can act to raise urban student achievement, especially at the family and community level.

And the more social scientists are able to draw from these variables, the more educational outcomes for urban children and children of color will rise. With these breakthroughs in mind, the next step is for researchers to better understand why it is that certain factors impact urban student outcomes more than others. Then once this is determined policy makers can develop elaborate means of conquering the achievement gap.

A second area of further inquiry is to undertake additional studies to assess how the subtle aspects of parental engagement work with urban youth and children of color. The fact that social scientists are beginning to appreciate that subtle aspects of parental involvement are the most important has special ramifications. The most vital of these is that the whole notion of what constitutes the most efficacious components of family involvement will have to be rethought and readministered. Just how large a role the subtle aspects of parental involvement are is particularly important for urban children and youth of color, because there is a rising body of evidence that suggests that over the last three decades social scientists have been underestimating the extent of parental involvement among these specific demographic categories (Jeynes, 2010b, 2011a). The reason for this is that over the years a variety of researchers have noted that low-SES and racial minority fathers and mothers have had, on average, lower levels of overt expressions of involvement than other parents. With the rise of research that examines the subtle aspects of engagement, however, what is now becoming evident is that the parents from these backgrounds tend to express their participation subtly, in such ways as through parental expectations, style, and communication (Jeynes, 2010b, 2011b). In terms of these more subtle manifestations, it appears that these parents tend to do just as well as parents from other groups. Ironically, to whatever extent it is now apparent that the subtle expressions of parental involvement are actually the most important, it would now appear that urban and racial minority fathers and mothers are considerably more involved than was previously assumed (Jeynes, 2010b, 2011b).

The findings presented in the previous paragraph make it clear that researchers need to fully investigate the extent to which the practice of parental engagement in the homes of urban and racial minority students is quite different than what is witnessed in other contexts. Given that the salience of subtle expressions of involvement has only been appreciated recently in the academic community, the reality is that social scientists have a real dearth of knowledge regarding how these more subtle acts of family participation differ across a variety of settings.

Conclusion

There is no question that parental involvement and community factors have played major roles in urban achievement. This is evident by examining the historical role of such involvement, as well as the rise of research on this topic. There is also no question as to the importance of applying what social scientists know about urban education today, especially as it applies to children of color, because what happens in the cities today will likely presage what happens in much of the nation in the future. It should especially be noted that recent breakthroughs in appreciating the place of subtle acts of parental involvement are helping social scientists to better appreciate that a myriad of urban parents already are heavily involved in their children's schooling and if educators and society at large can better draw from these strengths, countless children in urban areas will benefit.

References

Amano, I. (1990). *Education and examination in modern Japan*. Tokyo, Japan: University of Tokyo Press.

Bartlett, R. M. (1978). *The faith of the pilgrims*. New York, NY: United Church Press.

Baumrind, D. (1971). Current patterns of parental authority. *Developmental Psychology, 4*(1), 1–103.

Belsky, J. (2005). Intergenerational transmission of warm-sensitive-stimulating parenting: A prospective study of mothers and fathers of 3-year-olds. *Child Development, 76,* 77–93.

Blinderman, A. (1976). *Three early champions of education: Benjamin Franklin, Benjamin Rush, and Noah Webster.* Bloomington, IN: Phi Delta Kappan Educational Foundation.

Boggs, C., & Pollard, T. (2003). Postmodern cinema and the demise of the family. *Journal of American Culture, 26*(4), 445–463.

Bourne, W. O. (1870). *History of the public school society.* New York, NY: Wood.

Bronfenbrenner, U. (1979). *The ecology of human development.* Cambridge, MA: Harvard University Press.

Brooks, R. B. & Goldstein, S. (2001). *Raising resilient children: Fostering strength, hope, and optimism in your child.* Lincolnwood, IL: Contemporary Books.

Burgos, L. (2003). The effect of the father-child relationship on the social conduct of 2 1/2 year old children in preschool. *European Journal of Psychology of Education, 18,* 136–155.

CBS News. (1994). WBBM radio. Chicago, IL, August 28, 1994.

Clarke, J. (1730). John Clarke's classical program of studies. In Wilson Smith (Ed.). (1973). *Theories of education in early America* (pp. 38–45). Indianapolis, IN: Bobbs-Merrill.

Coleman, J. S. (1966). *Equality of educational opportunity.* Washington, DC: U.S. Department of Health, Education and Welfare.

Cornog, E. (1998). *The birth of empire: DeWitt Clinton and the American experience, 1769–1828.* New York, NY: Oxford University Press.

Cremin, L.A. (1977). *Traditions of American education.* New York, NY: Basic Books.

Crews, F.C. (1998). *Unauthorized Freud: Doubters confront a legend.* New York, NY: Viking.

Cubberley, E. (1920). *The history of education.* Boston, MA: Houghton Mifflin.

Davalos, D.B., Chavez, E.L., & Guardiola, R.J. (2005). Effects of perceived parental school support and family communication on delinquent behaviors in Latinos and white non-Latinos. *Cultural Diversity & Ethnic Minority Psychology, 11*(1), 57–68.

Dewey, J. (1902). *The child and the curriculum.* Chicago, IL: University of Chicago Press.

Dewey, J. (1915). *The school and society.* Chicago, IL: University of Chicago Press.

Dewey, J. (1964). *John Dewey's impressions of Soviet Russia and the revolutionary world: Mexico-China-Turkey, 1929.* New York, NY: Teachers College Press.

Dewey, J. (1990). *The school and society/The child and the curriculum.* Chicago, IL: University of Chicago Press.

Doinick, E. (1998). *Madness on the couch: Blaming the victim in the heyday of psychoanalysis.* New York, NY: Simon & Schuster.

Downer, J.T. (2005). African American father involvement and preschool children's school readiness. *Early Education and Development, 12,* 23–45.

Downer, J., Campos, R., McWayne, C., & Gartner, T. (2010). Father involvement and children's early learning: A critical review of published empirical work from the past fifteen years. In W. Jeynes (Ed.), *Family factors and the educational success of children* (pp. 64–105). New York, NY: Routledge.

Downs, R. B. (1975). *Heinrich Pestalozzi: Father of modern pedagogy.* Boston, MA: Twayne.

Downs, R.B. (1978). *Friedrich Froebel.* Boston, MA: Twayne.

Egan, K. (2002). *Getting it wrong from the beginning.* New Haven, CT: Yale University Press.

Elsbree, W. (1939). *The American teacher: Evolution of a profession in a democracy.* New York, NY: American Book Company.

Epstein, J. (2001). *School, family, and community partnerships.* Boulder, CO: Westview Press.

Fagan, J., Newash, N., & Schloesser, A. (2000). Female caregivers' perceptions of fathers' and significant adult males' involvement with their Head Start children. *Families in Society, 81,* 186–196.

Filler, L. (1965). *Horace Mann on the crisis in education.* Yellow Springs, OH: Antioch Press.

Fitzpatrick, E.A. (1969). *The educational views and influence of DeWitt Clinton.* New York, NY: Arno Press.

Fraser, J.W. (2001). *The school in the United States.* Boston, MA: McGraw-Hill.

Fromkin, V. (1973). *Speech errors as linguistic evidence.* The Hague, Netherlands: Mouton.

Gangel, K.O., & Benson, W.S. (1983). *Christian education: Its history and philosophy.* Chicago, IL: Moody.

Gatto, J.T. (2001). *The underground history of American schooling.* New York, NY: Oxford Village Press.

Goldstein, N.C., Candau, J.T., & Clarkek, K.C. (2004). Approaches to simulating the march of bricks & mortar. *Computers, Environment & Urban Systems, 28*(1/2), 125–147.

Gregory, A., Nygreen, K., & Moran, D. (2006). The discipline gap and the normalization of failure. In P.A. Noguera & J.Y. Wing (Eds.), *Unfinished business: Closing the racial achievement gap in our schools.* San Francisco, CA: Jossey-Bass.

Gutek, G.L. (1968). *Pestalozzi and education.* New York, NY: Random House.

Henderson, A.T., & Mapp, K.L. (2002). *A new wave of evidence: The impact of school, family, and community connections on student achievement.* Austin, TX: Southwest Educational Development Laboratory.

Hiner, N.R. (1988). The cry of Sodom enquired into: Educational analysis in seventeenth century New England. In B.E. McClellan and W.J. Reese (Eds.), *The social history of American education.* (pp. 3–22). Urbana, IL: University of Illinois Press.

Holy Bible, NIV Version. (1978). Grand Rapids, MI: Zondervan.

Hood, C. (2001). *Japanese education reform: Nakasone's legacy.* London, UK: Routledge.

Horne, H.H. (1923). *Idealism in education or first principles of making men and women.* New York, NY: Macmillan.

Horne, H.H. (1931). *This new education.* New York, NY: Abingdon.

Horne, H.H. (1932). *The democratic philosophy of education: Companion to Dewey's democracy and education.* New York, NY: Macmillan.

Husband, J. & O'Loughlin, J. (2004). *Daily life in the industrial United States, 1870–1900.* Westport, CT: Greenwood.

Janta, C.A., Goetz, S.J., & Shelley, M.K. (2004). Using the SLEUTH urban growth model to simulate the impacts of future policy scenarios on urban land use in the Baltimore-Washington metropolitan area. *Environment & Planning, 31*(2), 251–271.

Jeynes, W. (1999). The effects of religious commitment on the academic achievement of black and Hispanic children. *Urban Education, 34*(4), 458–479.

Jeynes, W. (2002a). *Divorce, family structure, and the academic success of children.* Binghamton, NY: Haworth Press.

Jeynes, W. (2002b). The relationship between the consumption of various drugs by adolescents and their academic achievement. *American Journal of Drug and Alcohol Abuse, 28*(1), 1–21.

Jeynes, W. (2003a). A meta-analysis: The effects of parental involvement on minority children's academic achievement. *Education & Urban Society, 35*(2), 202–218.

Jeynes, W. (2003b). The effects of black and Hispanic twelfth graders living in intact families and being religious on their academic achievement. *Urban Education, 38*(1), 35–57.

Jeynes, W. (2005). A meta-analysis of the relation of parental involvement to urban elementary school student academic achievement. *Urban Education, 40*(3), 237–269.

Jeynes, W. (2006). Standardized tests and the true meaning of kindergarten and preschool. *Teachers College Record, 108*(10), 1937–1959.

Jeynes, W. (2007a). *American educational history: School, society & the common good.* Thousand Oaks, CA: Sage Publications.

Jeynes, W. (2007b). The relationship between parental involvement and urban secondary school student academic achievement: A meta-analysis. *Urban Education, 42*(1), 82–110.

Jeynes, W. (2010a). Religiosity, religious schools, and their relationship with the achievement gap: A research synthesis and meta-analysis. *Journal of Negro Education, 79*(3), 263–279.

Jeynes, W. (2010b). The salience of the subtle aspects of parental involvement and encouraging that involvement: Implications for school-based programs. *Teachers College Record, 112*(3), 747–774.

Jeynes, W. (2011a). Fostering parental involvement among some of the students who need it the most. *Phi Delta Kappan, 93*(3), 38–39.

Jeynes, W. (2011b). *Parental involvement and academic success.* New York, NY: Taylor & Francis/Routledge.

Jeynes, W. (2012a). A meta-analysis of the efficacy of different types of parental involvement programs for urban students. *Urban Education, 47*(4), 706–742.

Jeynes, W. (2012b). Reaching out to make a difference. *Phi Delta Kappan, 93*(6), 80.

Johnson, P. (1997). *A history of the American people.* New York, NY: Harper Collins.

Kaestle, C. (1973). *Joseph Lancaster & the monitorial school movement.* New York, NY: Teachers College Press.

Kakaraparthi, S.K., & Kockelman, K.M. (2011). Application of UrbanSim to the Austin, Texas region. *Journal of Urban Planning & Development, 137*(3), 238–247.

Karther, D. (2002). Fathers with low literacy and their young children. *Reading Teacher, 5,* 184–193.

Kim, H.S. (2011). Consequences of parental divorce for child development. *American Sociological Review, 76*(3), 487–511.

King, M.L. (1998). *The autobiography of Martin Luther King.* C. Carson (Ed.). New York, NY: Warner.

Kwan, Y. (2010). Life satisfaction and self-assessed health among adolescents in Hong Kong. *Journal of Happiness Studies, 11*(3), 383–393.

Kwan, Y., & Ip, W. (2009). Adolescent health in Hong Kong: Disturbing socio-demographic correlates. *Social Indicators Research, 91*(2), 259–268.

Lawson, D., & Lean, A.E. (1964). *John Dewey and the world view.* Carbondale, IL: Southern Illinois University Press.

Lee, J. & Bowen, N. K. (2006). Parent involvement, cultural capital, and the achievement gap among elementary school children. *American Educational Research Journal, 43,* 193-218.

Lewy, G. (1996). *Why America needs religion.* Grand Rapids, MI: Eerdmanns.

Lilley, I. M. (1967). *Friedrich Froebel: A selection from his writings.* Cambridge, UK: Cambridge University Press.

Mann, H. (1849). *Twelfth annual report.* Boston, MA: Dutton & Wentworth.

Mann, H. (1957). *The republic and the school: Horace Mann on the education of free men.* New York, NY: Teachers College, Columbia University.

Mapp, K.L., Johnson, V.R., Strickland, C.S., & Meza, C. (2010). High school family centers: Transformative spaces linking schools and families in support of student learning. In W. Jeynes (Ed.), *Family factors and the educational success of children* (pp. 336–366). New York, NY: Routledge.

Martin, J. (2002). *The education of John Dewey: A biography.* New York, NY: Columbia University Press.

Mather, C. (1708). "A master in our Israel." In Wilson Smith (Ed.). (1973). *Theories of education in early America* (pp. 9–24). Indianapolis, IN: Bobbs-Merrill.

McClellan, E.B., & Reese, W.J. (1988). *The social history of American education.* Urbana, IL: University of Illinois Press.

McLanahan, S., & Sandefur, G. (1994). *Growing up with a single parent: What hurts, what helps.* Cambridge, MA: Harvard University Press.

Moon, S.S., & Lee, J. (2009). Multiple predictors of Asian American children's school achievement. *Early Education & Development, 20*(1), 129–147.

Morgan, J. (1986). *Godly learning: Puritan attitudes towards religion, learning, and education.* New York, NY: Cambridge University Press.

Ogbu, J.U. (1992). Adaptation to minority status and impact on school success. *Theory Into Practice, 31,* 287–295.

Ogbu, J.U. (1993). Differences in cultural frame of reference. *International Journal of Behavioral Development, 16,* 483–506.

Peressini, D. D. (1998). The portrayal of parents in the school mathematics reform literature: Locating the context for parental involvement. *Journal for Research in Mathematics Education, 29*(5), 555–582.

Pestalozzi, J. (1898). *How Gertrude teaches her children: An attempt to help mothers to teach their own children and an account of the method.* (Lucy Hoilland & Francis Turner, Trans.). Syracuse, NY: Bardeen.

Pestalozzi, J. (1916). How a child is led to God through maternal love. In J.A. Green (Ed.), *Pestalozzi's educational writings* (pp. 3–32). London: Edward Arnold.

Pong, S., Dronkers, J., & Hampden-Thompson, G. (2003). Family policies and children's school achievement in single- versus two-parent families. *Journal of Marriage & the Family, 65,* 681–699.

Raikes, H.H. (2005). Father involvement in early Head Start programs. *Fathering, 3,* 29–58.

Riggio, H.R. (2004). Parental marital conflict and divorce parent-child relationships, social support, and relationship anxiety in young adulthood. *Personal Relationships, 11*(1), 99–114.

Rimm-Kaufman, S.E. (2005). Father-school communication in preschool and kindergarten. *School Psychology Review, 34,* 287–308.

Rippa, S.A. (1997). *Education in a free society.* White Plains, NY: Longman.

Rodgers, K.B., & Rose, H.A. (2002). Risk and resiliency factors among adolescents who experience marital transitions. *Journal of Marriage & the Family, 64,* 1024–1037.

Rothstein, R. (2004). *Class and schools: Using social, economic, and educational reform to close the black-white achievement gap.* New York, NY: Columbia University.

Rury, J.L. (2002). *Education and social change: Themes in the history of American schooling.* Mahwah, NJ: Lawrence Erlbaum Associates.

Rush, B. (1786a). *A plan for the establishment of public schools and the diffusion of knowledge in Pennsylvania.* Philadelphia: n.p.

Rush, B. Benjamin Rush letter to Richard Price, May 25, 1786. In L.H. Butterfield (Ed.). (1951). *Letters of Benjamin Rush, Vol. 1* (pp. 388–389). Princeton, NJ: Princeton University Press.

Salkind, N.J. (2006). *Encyclopedia of human development.* Thousand Oaks, CA: Sage Publications.

Sharma, H.P., Matsui, E.C., Eggleston, P.A., Hansel, N.N., Curtin-Brosnan, J., & Dietta, G.B. (2007). Does current asthma control predict future care among black preschool-aged-inner-city children? *Pediatrics, 120*(5), 1174–1218.

Shenk, M.K., & Scelza, B.A. (2012). Paternal investments and status-related child outcomes: Timing of father's death affects offspring success. *Journal of Biosocial Science, 44*(5), 549–569.

Shimizu, K. (1992). Shido: Education and selection in Japanese middle school. *Comparative Education, 28*(2), 114–125.

Slavin, R., & Madden, N. (2006). Reducing the gap: Success for all and the achievement of African American students. *Journal of Negro Education, 75*(3), 389–400.

Smith, W. (1973). *Theories of education in early America.* Indianapolis, IN: Bobbs-Merrill.

Stewart, S.D., & Menning, C.L. (2009). Family structure, nonresident father involvement, and adolescent eating patterns. *Journal of Adolescent Health, 45*(2), 193–201.

Strous, M. (2007). Post-divorce relocation: The best interests of the child? *South African Journal of Psychology, 37,* 223–244.

Thomas, K. (2009). Parental characteristics and the schooling progress of the children of immigrant and U.S.-born blacks. *Demography, 46*(3), 513–534.

Thornton, A., & Young-DeMarco, L. (2001). Four decades of trends in attitudes toward family issues in the United States: The1960s through the 1990s. *Journal of Marriage & Family, 63*(4), 1009–1037.

Ulich, R. (1957). *Three thousand years of educational wisdom.* Cambridge, MA: Harvard University Press.

Ulich, R. (1968). *A history of religious education.* New York, NY: New York University Press.

Urban, W., & Wagoner, J. (2000). *American education: A history.* Boston, MA: McGraw-Hill.

U.S. Census Bureau. (2001). *Census 2000.* Washington D.C.: U.S. Census Bureau.

U.S. Department of Education. (2005). *Digest of education statistics.* Washington, DC: Author.

U.S. Department of Justice. (1999). *Age-specific arrest rate and race-specific arrest rates for selected offenses, 1965–1998.* Washington, DC: Author.

Wallerstein, J.S., & Lewis, J. (1998). The long-term impact of divorce on children: A first report from a 25-year study. *Family and Conciliation Courts Review, 36*(3), 368–383.

Webster, N. (1793). *Effects of slavery on morals and industry.* Hartford, CT: Hudson & Goodwin.

Webster, N. (1834). *Value of the Bible, and the excellence of the Christian religion: For use of families and schools.* New Haven, CT: Durrie & Peck.

Willison, G.F. (1966). *Saints and strangers.* London, UK: Longmans.

Wirtz, W. (1977). *On further examination.* New York, NY: College Entrance Examination Board.

Wolfinger, N.H., Kowlaleski-Jones, L., & Ken, R. (2003). Double impact: What sibling data can tell us about the long-term negative effects of parental divorce. *Biodemography & Social Biology, 50*(1/2), 58–76.

9

Community and Family Involvement in Urban Schools

Gloria Swindler Boutte & George L. Johnson, Jr.

Introduction

Dialogue about parent involvement is pervasive in schools, policy circles, and in the voluminous body of research which extends over several decades. Virtually all educators, in suburban, urban, and rural school settings alike, theoretically support the notion that parent involvement is an essential element in students' success in school. Educational policies in recent decades have included mandates for parent involvement (e.g., *Goals 2000, No Child Left Behind, 2001*). Yet, despite the existence of such pervasive and well-intentioned practices and policies, the long-standing trend of low parent involvement in urban schools has remained stagnant (Bowers & Griffin, 2011).

An all-too-familiar mantra in urban circles is that student achievement would improve and disciplinary problems would be reduced if parents were more involved. The heavy focus on parent involvement to increase student achievement has been viewed by some as an attempt to shift the responsibility for student academic achievement from schools to families (Bowers & Griffin, 2011; Graue & Benson, 2001). Therefore, a guiding premise of this chapter is that in collaboration with families and community members, educators must begin the complex work of re-visioning the involvement of parents, families, and communities from the current dominant deficit narrative to one of collaboration, promise, and hope. Understanding that schools and homes/communities are not dichotomous in terms of the roles that each plays in the academic and social success of urban students and also acknowledging that the current state of affairs is mutually frustrating to educators, parents, families, and communities alike, several critical questions guided our thinking and analysis of the literature that is presented in this chapter.[1] Since the questions are overlapping and inherent in the literature, we present them first and will not necessarily explicitly address each one in turn. They serve as a preview of the complex issues that have collectively been raised in the extant literature.

1. What should be the purpose of urban parent, family, and community development efforts? How does a parent involvement function differently in urban versus rural or suburban contexts? Do parent involvement efforts need to have different outcomes for different contexts in their own right rather than comparative, universal approaches?

2. How can we move the school practices with urban parents, families, and communities forward by using existing research to build new definitions of collaborative involvement models? In other words, given the wealth of existing research, how can we engage educators, parents, families, and communities in utilizing that research to generate more effective practices in ways that advocate on behalf of urban students?
3. What transformations are necessary in urban school settings to better meet the needs of families and communities? What models exist? What processes, models have been shown to be most helpful for urban school/home collaborations? How do we create and maintain a "dialogue of collaboration" (Madison, 2005)? In what ways do traditional parent involvement models oppress urban parents by reifying societal biases and ideologies (Snell, Miguel, & East, 2009)?
4. What does it mean to advocate for and with urban parents, families, and communities? What knowledge is necessary for educators to possess in order to advocate effectively for urban parents, families, and communities?
5. How can educators do a more effective job of connecting school content to the lived experiences of urban communities and families so that students are engaged and the content is relevant? What are the existing familial and community funds of knowledge, resources, and wisdom that educators can learn about and *from?* Who are the "sages" in urban communities that educators can enlist to advocate on behalf of urban students?
6. How can urban schools initiate and/or facilitate collaborative grassroots efforts among parents and families in urban communities? How can existing grassroots groups coalesce in a focused manner to improve urban schools? What roles can urban youth play in this process?
7. How can we support educators in their commitment and knowledge base on parent, family, and community development? What models and processes work best for ongoing professional development for P–12 educators and teacher educators?
8. While educators express that we value parent involvement, how does this manifest itself in meaningful parent and community involvement?
9. How can dynamic and fluid models of parent involvement be developed and sustained?
10. What do urban parents think about parent involvement in schools? How can researchers and educators go beyond examining if parent programs work to examining *whom they work for, why do they work,* or *why do parents get involved or not* (Barton, Drake, Perez, St. Louis, & George, 2004)?

As these questions suggest, there is a longstanding and sustainable body of literature which seeks to figure out how best to address the "problem" of low parent and community involvement in urban and other settings. At the onset, we recognize that even the best parent, family, and community involvement efforts are not a panacea for the deeply rooted underlying issues facing urban schools. We acknowledge the complexity of the issue but, at the same time, will focus on the role that parent, family, and urban involvement can play (in concert with other efforts) in the process of improving urban schools. We readily admit that such involvement is a complex and sometimes adversarial process. While we concur that parent and community involvement are important factors in the academic and social outcomes for students, conceptualizing parents as the key problem makes it unlikely that authentic and sustainable solutions will emerge or that visionary and transformative models of parent, family, and community involvement will be developed by schools. The realization becomes more pronounced since parents and communities are rarely consulted in any structural or sustainable way (Boutte & Hill, 2006; Long, Volk, Baines, & Tisdale, 2013).

In our analysis, glaringly missing are the voices, perspectives, and input of the very people who educators hope to involve—the parents, families, and community members themselves. At the same time, we do not intend to romanticize or essentialize urban parents, families, and communities. We acknowledge that there are areas of improvement that can be made by parents, families, and communities. We readily concede that there is tremendous variation (e.g., ethnicity, geographic differences) among these populations and contexts as well. In an effort to offer a targeted versus global response, our goal is to focus on the role that schools and educators at all levels can play in the process. This does not mean that we focus only on school-*centered* or -initiated efforts but that emphasis will be placed on positionalities of school officials as they develop and sustain involvement efforts that are informed by and collaboratively developed with parents, families, and community members.

This chapter is divided into four major sections. First, we begin with a discussion of how parent, family, and community involvement are defined. Second, we provide a historical account of how parent involvement literature developed over the decades. Here we will give an overview of three major paradigms used in studies that emerged from our review of literature. Third, we discuss what we know about the topic from the extant literature. To do this, we summarize overall findings and then distinguish between deficit- and strengths-based studies. Fourth, we chart a course for further development in the field as well as probe educational implications.

Throughout each section, our discussion is conceptually guided by extrapolating from one of King's (2005) *Principles for Black Education,* which examines possible ways of responding to and resolving problems. While these principles were focused on Black education, they also serve as a useful heuristic that can be extrapolated to other cultural groups such as urban families and communities (which also tend to be heavily African American and Latino American) (Lewis, James, Hancock, & Hill-Jackson, 2008; U.S. Department of Education, 2007–2008b). Hence, we assume that suggested solutions that have been presented in the academic literature to address the problem of low levels of urban parent, family, and community involvement (historically and currently) have likely used one of three modes of responses to the existing landscape: (1) *Adaptation*—Urban schools seeking to address the low involvement levels of culturally and linguistically diverse parents, families, and communities have adopted practices and policies that they deemed useful or that have been put forth as *best practices,* which were typically based on traditional conceptions of parent involvement. In this case, schools typically would adapt their parent and family involvement practices to fit with new or existing policies and mandates; (2) *Improvisation*—Urban schools using this response pattern to demands for increased parent, family, and community involvement have typically substituted or improvised on suggested *best practices* policies and practices to make them more sensitive and responsive to the needs of urban schools; (3) *Resistance*—Though this response goes against the trends, there are schools which have resisted parent, family, and community involvement strategies which they viewed as being destructive and not in the best interests of urban students, parents, families, and communities. While each of these modes of responses are understandable and influenced by factors such as contexts, cultures, current policies, and other factors, schools seeking to address the needs of urban parents, families, and communities may find it useful to *resist* and to transform "traditional" parent involvement models as will be discussed later in this chapter.

Definition of Urban Parent, Family, and Community Involvement

For the purposes of this chapter, parental involvement is defined as "parental participation in the educational processes and experiences of their children" (Jeynes, 2007). We selected this definition because it is used prominently in research studies and theoretical works. We view parent involvement as part of a triad—parent/family/community and use parent and family involvement synonymously at times. We recognize all configurations of caregivers/parents/guardians to include single, married, dual, same sex, transgendered, extended, cohabitating, biological, adopted, foster, teenage, and so forth. We consider both traditional and nontraditional parent involvement efforts and approaches.

> The traditional definition of parental involvement includes activities in the school and at home. Parental involvement can take many forms, such as volunteering at the school, communicating with teachers, assisting with homework, and attending school events such as performances or parent-teacher conferences . . . However, viewed through this lens, African American and Latino families demonstrate low rates of parental involvement . . . Tradition definitions of parent involvement require investments of time and money from parents, and those who may not be able to provide these resources are deemed uninvolved. (Bowers & Griffin, 2011, p. 78)

As noted by Bowers and Griffin (2011), traditional definitions of parent involvement often overlook activities such as providing nurturance and care for children, talking and engaging in other activities, and providing moral, spiritual, and cultural values. Additionally, traditional definitions of parent involvement tend not to give attention to ways that urban parents deliberately involve themselves in their children's education (Jackson & Remillard, 2005; Volk & Long, 2005). We recognize the need to broaden the definition since, even with best intent, most traditional parent involvement models are school-initiated and -centered and are not truly bidirectional. While there are some efforts to learn about families and to develop and sustain relationships with them (e.g., Morris, 2004), few seek to learn *from* them (Boutte & Hill, 2006). We found that traditional parent involvement approaches have tended to be overly prescriptive, narrowly defined, and contrived. Most have used the same general (Eurocentric) approaches regardless of the cultural backgrounds or unique aspects of families and communities (Bowers & Griffin, 2011). This does not suggest intentional insensitivity nor is it intended to dichotomize traditional versus more culturally and context-responsive models since there are definite overlaps, but is intended to point out limitations of traditional versus more culturally responsive models as shown in Table 9.1.

Engagement in schooling has been complicated and difficult for culturally and linguistically diverse students because of historical, institutional, and cultural factors (Perry, Steele, & Hilliard, 2003; Williams, Pemberton, & Dyce, 2012). While collaboration between families and schools is crucial for engaging urban learners, barriers to meaningful engagement include institutionalized racism and classism and cultural disconnection between schools and families (Boutte, 2012; Lewis et al., 2008). Despite barriers and pervasive deficit views surrounding parent involvement, urban parents (like other parents) want their children to achieve academically (LeFevre & Shaw, 2012; Ramirez, 2003; Williams et al., 2012).

Most of the research on parent involvement has focused generically on parents rather than on urban parent involvement (Jeynes, 2007). Hence, there is a need to define and tease out what urban parent involvement should look like. We use the term *urban* to refer to schools and communities that have high population density (actual numbers vary and are idiosyncratic to a particular area) in a particular geologic area. According to the U.S. Department of Education (2007–2008a), there are nearly 26,000 urban schools in the United States, constituting 26 percent of all public elementary and secondary schools. These schools are typically geologically located in places designated as "urban" centers, often labeled as high-poverty schools—schools with more than 40 percent of students receiving free/reduced lunch, enroll large numbers of students

Table 9.1 Summary of Traditional Versus Culturally and Context-Responsive Parent Involvement Models

Traditional	*Culturally and Context Responsive*
Heavily based on Eurocentric norms and ways of knowing	Attempts to be culturally responsive for particular demographics of families
Unidirectional (information flows one way: from school to home)	Bidirectional (invites and welcomes family-initiated communication, policy input, etc.); parents as partners; involvement in decision making; relationship-building; mutual engagement; parents involves in leadership roles)
Narrow and mono-cultural definitions of parent involvement (e.g., in terms of what constitutes caring, communication styles, family configurations or specifications for how academics should be supported such as limited to reading bedtime stories versus other forms of literacy experiences)	Elastic, fluid definitions (polyliterate efforts are recognized, respected, and built on); multidimensional focus. Definitions of parent involvement build from knowledge and appreciation of multiple ways to support and care for students at home
Efforts to learn *about* families	Efforts to learn about, with, *and* from families
Few, if any, attempts to learn about the community or attempts are largely in-school based.	Intentional efforts to learn about the community through engagement in communities.
Primarily contrived activities (PTA meetings, open house, weekly reports, School Improvement plans)	Integrated; ongoing; systemic; living policies and actions (e.g., use of social media, texting, educators teaching adult education classes at school for parents)
Preset policies—polices are already in place with no input from families.	Generative policies—some policies may already be in place, but they are flexible enough to allow for input from families and can be changed.
Curriculum may be designed on a "one size fits all" cultural model often starting with that students *do not* know.	Curriculum is dynamic and tailored to the strengths and needs of students because teachers know families and communities; curriculum starts with what students *do* know.
Home and community visits are based on unexamined, inaccurate and often deficit assumptions resulting from limited involvement in unfamiliar communities	Home and community visits are based on strength-based assumptions learned through firsthand relationships *in* communities.
Few collaborative discussions with parents to gain their insights and construct concrete ways to promote success for all students. For example, discussions around making sure that more students are prepared to qualify for Advanced Placements classes and programs. This would help parents to understand the depth of the issues beyond their own children	Families and community members are integral to school discussions about issues such as curriculum, testing, suspensions, expulsions, special education and gifted placements, coursework, disciplinary measures, etc.

Source: Constructed by the authors based on a summary of the literature.

of color, and increasingly high proportions of English Language Learners (Boutte, 2012). The overview of literature that is presented in the next section on the historical and current account of urban parent and community development will show that not much has changed over the past few decades.

Historical Account of Urban Parent, Family, and Community Involvement

For this review of literature, we surveyed studies and conceptual works that we found to be most relevant to the topic and that were published from 1990 to the present date. These articles were generated from an initial, focused search on parent involvement using the keywords: urban, African American, Latino American, poor, parent involvement, parent engagement, community, school, and family. Some of the articles in the final set of 54 were works that we found particularly relevant when they were referenced in initial articles or were ones that we were familiar with. The list of 54 readings can be found in Table 9.2. Consistently, but not surprising, most of the studies did not seek the input and understandings of the parents, families, and communities in an inductive or sustained manner. Many did administer surveys to parents using preset questions and response choices.

In an effort to maintain the integrity of critical questions raised at the beginning of this chapter, we paid particular attention to studies in which serious attempts were made to capture the voices and worldviews of urban parents, families, students, and/or community members rather than to research the phenomenon without involving the very people they intend to "help." We found it useful to think about the paradigms in which most studies were situated because we realized that the underlying assumptions that researchers make about the nature of parent involvement (and implications) were important and drove the conception of the studies. After examining the literature, three broad paradigms were evident based on our interpretation of the underlying paradigms. We recognize that there may be other categories or other authors may classify them differently than we did. This paradigmatic approach was useful in making sense of the focus and goals of the existing research. While recognizing that each paradigm has strengths, below we explain limits of two of the paradigms (positivistic and ecological) and why we believe that critical paradigm best complements urban parent involvement efforts. We concede that parts of the paradigms may overlap and are not dichotomous.

> *The question is not what you look at, but what you see.*
>
> Henry David Thoreau (as cited in Delpit & Dowdy, 2002, p. 143)

Using well-known and sometimes competing paradigms to explain how different schools of thought view the same problem (low levels of parent involvement) through distinctly different lenses, we provide brief descriptions of positivistic, ecological, and critical schools of thought about parent involvement. While current research is still guided by all three paradigms and all have advanced from thinking about parents/families as passive *subjects* to study to regarding them as *participants* who have active roles in the research process, critical paradigms by design regard parents as *partners* or *collaborators* who jointly engage in the research process and who may even take the study in a direction not anticipated by the researcher.

1. *Positivistic*—As a rule, research in this paradigm seeks to identify observable "facts" which are measurable. Viewing knowledge as objective, researchers are guided by deductive logic, hypothesis testing, and the like. This approach often seeks to find universal or generalizable patterns of behavior (Cannella, 1997). The positivistic tradition with a heavy focus on quantitative data analyses dominated educational studies for decades and although other paradigms have increased tremendously since the 1980s, tensions still exist between the quantitative and qualitative approaches (Lichtman, 2010).

Table 9.2 Readings by Paradigms (Positivistic, Ecological, and Critical)

Positivistic	*Ecological*	*Critical*
1. Bauch, P., & Goldring, E. (2000)	1. Barton, A. C., et al. (2004)	1. Boutte, G. S., & Hill, E. (2006)
2. Bowers, H. A., & Griffin, D. (2011)	2. Cabrera, N., Beeghly, M., & Eisenberg, N. (2012)	2. Howard, T. C., & Reynolds, R. (2008)
3. Desimone, L. (1999)	3. Cabrera, N., & Bradley, R. (2012)	3. Lewis, C. W., et al., (2008)
4. Grolnick, W., & Slowiaczek, M. (1994)	4. Chrispeels, J. (1996)	4. Snell, P., et al. (2009)
5. Hayes, D. (2011)	5. Cole-Henderson (2000)	5. Volk, D., & Long, S. (2005)
6. Hayes, D. (2012)	6. Day-Vines, N., & Day-Hairston, B. (2005)	
7. Hayes, D., & Cunningham, M. (2003)	7. De Gaetano, Y. (2007)	
8. Hill, N., & Craft, S. (2003)	8. Epstein, J. L. (2010)	
9. Jeynes, W. (2003)	9. Evans, A., et al. (2012)	
10. Jeynes, W. (2005)	10. Fredericks, J., & Simpkins, S. (2012)	
11. Jeynes, W. H. (2005)	11. Galindo, R., & Medina, C. (2009)	
12. Jeynes, W. H. (2007)	12. Garcia Coll, C., et al. (1996)	
13. Lee, J., & Bowen, N. (2006)	13. Giles, C. (2006)	
14. McWayne, C., et al., (2004)	14. Hill, N., & Taylor, L. (2004)	
15. Overstreet, S., et al., (2005)	15. Ingram, M., et al. (2007)	
16. Paulson, S. (1994)	16. Jackson, K., & Remillard, J. T. (2005)	
17. Paulson, S., & Sputa, C. (1996)	17. Kenyon, D., & Hanson, J. (2012)	
18. Reynolds, A. (1992)	18. Kirshner, B., & Ginwright, S. (2012)	
19. Slaughter-Defoe, D., & Rubin, H. (2001)	19. Knight, G., & Carlo, G. (2012)	
20. Taylor, L., Hinton, I., & Wilson, M. (1995)	20. Li-Grining, C. (2012)	
21. Wong, S., & Hughes, J. (2006)	21. Mannan, G., & Blackwell, J. (1992)	
22. Yan, W. (2000)	22. McBride, B., & Len, H. (1996)	
23. Zhou, Q., et al. (2012)	23. Mesman, J., et al., (2012)	
	24. Neblett, E., Rivas-Drake, D., & Umana-Taylor, A. (2012)	
	25. Smrekar, C., & Cohen-Vogel, L. (2001)	
	26. Williams, J., et al. (2012)	

The studies that we classified as positivistic did not involve parents in a substantive way. That is, few, if any, attempts were made to understand the voices, perspectives, and lived experiences of families and communities. A particular limitation as it applies to studying urban parent involvement is that these studies did not focus on or acknowledge structural inequities that affect families and communities. Some of these studies do consider issues of race as a moderating variable, use it as a comparative factor (e.g., Black versus White parents), and some even statistically *control* for the effects of race (Steinberg & Fletcher, 1998). We agree with Steinberg and Fletcher (1998) who wisely raised the question, *What does it mean to control for a person's ethnic background since this is a key part of the person's identity?*

In the studies that we reviewed, the analysis was often on the level of the individual—focusing on the child or parent as the level of analysis—which inadvertently problematizes parents. The intent here is not to disparage these types of studies or to imply that some aspects of this paradigm cannot be useful for studying urban parent involvement. We note that we have also engaged in similar work earlier in our career (Boutte & Samuels, 1992) but found it necessary to use other paradigms which engaged parents, families, and community members. We viewed this as a move from learning *about* to learning *with and from* the parents. In other words, we wanted intentionally subjective methods which may answer questions such as: What do we still not know? Whose voices are missing? How can we probe deeper?

2. Ecological—Ecological theories have been used to explain the complex issues surrounding parent involvement and school achievement. Most of the studies reviewed using ecological models employed qualitative methods (e.g., Giles, 2006; Jackson & Remillard, 2005; Smrekar & Cohen-Vogel, 2001) or some conceptual works (e.g., Barton et al., 2004; Epstein, 2010; Hill & Taylor, 2004). Typically, the studies viewed home settings from a strengths-based (versus deficit) approach. Research opting for this paradigm normally attempts to take a comprehensive approach by focusing holistically on parents in relation to their environments. Hence, ecological or systems theories focus on family, friends, school, community, and the school as important influences on an individual's life (Bronfenbrenner, 1979, 2004). The importance of these variables should be considered when addressing programs and strategies for schools. Ecological approaches also consider situations or contexts that surround parents' decision to participate in an event, including their relationships with other individuals, the history of the event, and the resources available (Barton et al., 2004). This paradigm recognizes that factors outside students' control may affect students' experiences, but is typically silent on structural issues of race or class.

One widely used Ecological theory which is cited often in the extant literature is Bronfenbrenner's (2004) model, which proposes that development is influenced by five environmental systems.

a) microsystem—The home, the school, the community, parents, and peers are examples of microsystems in which the child is directly involved. Because children spend large amounts of time in these contexts, they are influenced heavily by what happens there.
b) mesosystem—In addition to looking at how mircosystems operate independently, mesosystems or relationships between various contexts and systems are important to consider. Systems that have strong connections work better and benefit the child more than those that do not. Therefore, strong and functional home/school connections are important.
c) exosystem—Exosystems include social settings that do not directly involve children, but nevertheless affect their experiences in immediate settings—for example, formal organizations such as families' workplaces, health services, social welfare services, mass

media, legal services, policies. For example, *No Child Left Behind* mandates regarding regular school attendance can affect parent-child and student-teacher interactions.

d) macrosystem—Cultural values, laws, customs, and resources that are reflective of the general society in which children live are examples of macrosystems. For example, the current focus on school accountability has changed the overall ideology about the role of schools and may be related to schools feeling added pressure to produce test results which show that all students are progressing adequately. This tension, in turn, often results in schools placing additional pressure and blame on families. Frequently, it also interferes with high-quality instruction and student achievement because teachers are pressured to "teach to the test." Interestingly, researchers using this paradigm do not typically address two key aspects of the U.S. and world macroculture—racism and classism. Ironically, these two types of oppression undergird many of the problems faced by urban families (Boutte, 2012).

e) chronosystem—Chronosystems include the temporal dimensions or constant changes in life events. Many of the studies reviewed mentioned that urban parents, parents of color, and/or parents from low socioeconomic backgrounds may have historically had negative experiences with schools which could impede their willingness to participate in school activities. Understanding this historical piece would be useful for school officials as would understanding the history (and currency) of how school segregation affects schooling—that is, effectively relegating urban students to low-resourced settings. While comprehensive in their conceptualization and thinking about systems that affect the child, most of the ecological parent involvement studies have advocated more of the same traditional parent involvement (with a few that we would label *nonsubstantive* add-ons). Even though most researchers acknowledge the urban families' strengths (and some of the challenges), the parent involvement programs and methods tend to be pretty school-centric.

3. *Critical*—This paradigm unapologetically acknowledges that researchers and educators are value-laden individuals who bring certain assumptions, ideologies, and biases to the research process. The studies reviewed in this paradigm primarily used qualitative methods. This paradigm seeks to eliminate false consciousness by provoking research participants to critique and question the conditions of their lives. It openly addresses issues of power and seeks to facilitate the emancipation of groups that have been historically oppressed—that is, urban students and families. Studies that we classified as *critical* included feminists, interpretive, race-specific, race-centered, praxis-oriented, critical ethnographic, and Freieran participatory—to name a few. Researchers who use critical theories which actively address structural inequities as their conceptual framework or method of analysis also hold agents (teachers, administrators) responsible for the Black/White, Black/Latino achievement gap (Lewis et al., 2008). Hence, schools are called on to critically consider what may be done in their educational spaces to improve the educational outcomes of urban students. This can be done in collaboration with families, but does not absolve schools from the process—even in difficult situations like urban schools and communities.

As noted by Lewis et al. (2008), any serious attempts to address issues of achievement should be approached from multiple theoretical perspectives and paradigms. We are not suggesting that critical theoretical approaches are "silver bullets" but do think that this paradigm lends itself to the most promise because it outwardly addressed structural issues of racism and classism; attempts to propose, make, and sustain structural changes in schools, policies, and communities; and seeks guidance, leadership, input, and collaboration from the families and community members. Other scholars who tend to approach issues from positivistic and ecological paradigms also acknowledge a need to broaden paradigms to consider the specific needs of urban parents and educational institutions in the U.S. schooling system (Slaughter-Defoe & Rubin, 2001). As previously mentioned, the paradigms converge and diverge on some points. Likewise, the research designs used for this work are likely to be diverse: quantitative, qualitative, or mixed methodology. However, as will be discussed later, deficit conceptions of parent involvement are damaging and counterproductive and will not advance the purpose of improving student outcomes via working with families and communities.

What We Know About Parent and Community Involvement—Summary of the Literature

It is not a revelation that parents who engage in traditional parenting involvement activities (e.g., actively promote learning in the home, have direct and regular contact with school) are likely to have children who achieve at higher rates academically in school, drop out at lower rates, and a host of other positive academic and social outcomes (Howard & Reynolds, 2008; McWayne, Hampton, Fantuzzo, Cohen, & Sekino, 2004). Parent involvement has also be shown to relate to improved student behavior, lower absenteeism, increased self-esteem, and more positive attitudes toward school (Hayes, 2012; Snell et al., 2009). Overwhelmingly, research has demonstrated this point. For example, using two separate meta-analyses which canvassed 42 studies focusing on elementary students (Jeynes, 2005) as well as 52 studies which focused on secondary students (Jeynes, 2007) to determine the influence of parental involvement on the educational outcomes of *urban students,* Jeynes (2005, 2007, respectively) concluded that the overall effect of parent involvement was significant for both elementary and secondary school children. The positive effects of parental involvement held for children of color and White children.

Conceptually, it should not be surprising that there is also a relationship between how children are perceived by educators and levels and types of parent involvement (Howard & Reynolds, 2008). That is, parents who are actively involved in schools are likely to have children who achieve at higher levels than parents who are not actively involved in school. Intuitively and from experience, we know that educators are likely to positively perceive children whose parents are active and present in school. And while not downplaying the importance of this role, *it is important that urban schools figure out how to equitably respond to students whose parents may not be actively involved in school (in ways that are apparent or recognized by schools).* That is, school officials will have to question, "What needs to be done differently and with respect for parents who do not participate in traditional ways? How can schools ensure that these children's and families' needs are not marginalized?"

While the vast majority of studies have found positive influences of parent involvement, the literature was mixed. For example, some studies have shown no significant relationships between parent involvement and children's achievement (Gauvain, Savage, & McCollum, 2000; Hayes, 2011, 2012; Mattingly, Prislin, McKenzie, Rodriguez, & Kayzar, 2002; Sheldon, 2002). Closer scrutiny of this literature shed light on these mixed findings (McWayne et al., 2004). First, as previously noted, different paradigms, theoretical and conceptual frameworks, and variables have been studied. Second, various studies have focused on different aspects of parent involvement. Such isolated items may not be representative of the broader, more comprehensive conceptualizations of parent involvement. Third, the studies have included children of various ages, ethnicities, and socioeconomic statuses, and, thus, yielded different results.

A theme that was apparent in the literature was the evolving need to *engage* parents as collaborators and to move away from deficit perceptions. Below we distinguish between deficit- and strengths-based studies.

Deficit Conceptions of Parent Involvement

> When beginning teachers come into minority communities, many are unable to understand the students' home language, social interaction patterns, histories, and cultures. Thus they cannot truly educate the students. Their perceptions of deficiency and competence are socially and culturally constructed. Without greater exposure to the students' culture teachers lack the tools with which to make sense of much that transpires in the classroom.
>
> (Ladson-Billings, 1994, p. 134)

There is a need for ongoing and systematic focus on demonstrating that "urban" and "deficit" are not synonymous (Milner, 2008; Picower, 2009). When parent involvement is viewed from a deficit perspective, parents are often blamed for the academic and social problems that students have. They are assumed to have little knowledge or cultural capital to advocate on behalf of their children and parental involvement is often limited to school-sanctioned/school-initiated activities (Howard & Reynolds, 2008). One dominant narrative that recurred in the literature about causes of the Black-White/Latino-White achievement gap was that it is largely due to familial, community, and cultural deficiencies (De Gaetano, 2007; Lewis et al., 2008; Volk & Long, 2005). Hence, it is not surprising to learn that many earlier parent involvement efforts were referred to as *interventions* since the intent was to intervene and correct parenting styles and beliefs, while not honoring existing parental values, beliefs, voices, and perspectives.

We stress that what we refer to as deficit conceptions are not intended to convey the idea that these were intentionally malicious. Rather, the assumptions of the paradigm from which they were conceived are often written from the perspective of White, middle-class viewpoints and norms and, by default, malign other cultural perspectives. Consider the following quote from a well-circulated statement regarding Developmentally Appropriate Practice (National Association for the Education of Young Children, 2009):

> Behind these disparities in school-related performance lie dramatic differences in children's early experiences and access to good programs and schools. Often there is also a mismatch between the "school" culture and children's cultural backgrounds. A prime difference in children's early experience is in their exposure to language, which is fundamental in literacy development and indeed in all areas of thinking and learning. On average, children growing up in low- income families have dramatically less rich experience with language in their homes than do middle-class children. They hear far fewer words and are engaged in fewer extended conversations. By 36 months of age, substantial socioeconomic disparities already exist in vocabulary knowledge, to name one area. (National Association for the Education of Young Children, 2009, p. 2)

The assumptions guiding this well-intentioned approach imply that certain parenting types are preferred. This approach overlooks familial strengths that may not fit narrow definitions of parent involvement. A summary of some of the assumptions are below (Mallory & New, 1994, pp. 20–21).

- The belief that some cultural practices are preferable (and others, if not "deficient," certainly less desirable)
- The focus on individuals (children and family members) in an effort to rectify social ills
- The intent to provide children with experiences they are not likely to get at home
- The commitment to share with parents the knowledge that they ostensibly lack

- Defining dominant cultural practices as normal, positive, and universally applicable
- Claiming that it is incumbent upon those who are knowledgeable about "child development knowledge" to impart this knowledge to parents (thereby setting up a "we/they" relationship based on the privileged position of the profession)
- Focusing too narrowly on children and their families

Guided by these deficit-based assumptions, parental involvement policies typically employ a one-size-fits-all framework which does not address the needs of culturally and linguistically diverse (CLD) families and which treats all parents as if they have the same needs or the same experiences. For example, assuming that authoritative parenting styles are preferred to authoritarian or permissive parenting styles disregards research which indicate that context and culture mediate which parenting styles work best. Such approaches are fueled by unacknowledged structural racism (De Gaetano, 2007) and can disparage parenting styles of Asian and African American families who tend to use authoritarian parenting styles or Native Americans who tend to use permissive parenting styles (Zhou et al., 2012). In essence, studies and parent involvement programs which assume deficit stances unintentionally position schools as expert and do not acknowledge the strengths that parents have.

Strengths-Based Parent Involvement

One of the most widely referenced strengths-based parent involvement model is Epstein's (1996, 2010) model which has a six-category typology. The influence of this model on parent involvement is evidenced by the constant references to Epstein's work in nearly all of the 42 studies that we read—even a few which were using a critical stance. Epstein's (1996, 2010; Epstein & Dauber, 1991) model provides a framework that schools can use in developing programs to encourage relationships with parents and includes: (1) parenting—helping families establish supportive home environments; (2) communicating—designing effective school-to-home and home-to-school communications; (3) volunteering—recruiting and organizing parental help and support; (4) learning at home—providing information and ideas to families about how to help students at home; (5) decision making—including parents in school decisions and developing parent leaders and representatives; and (6) collaborating with the community—identifying and integrating resources and services from the community. All six of these categories have the goal of improving students' academic achievement (Epstein, 2010). While Epstein's typology validates efforts made by parents in the home and educators in school, the types of home/school connections identified privilege the school's role in determining "what counts" as parent involvement. Additionally, there is no evidence that "this characterization of parent involvement begins with exploration into what parents are already doing for their children, in ways visible and invisible to the school" (Jackson & Remillard, 2005, p. 53). As one study concluded, "The Epstein Model may not fully capture how parents are or want to be involved in their children's education, indicating that new ways of working with parents in high-minority, high poverty schools are warranted" (Bowers & Griffin, 2011, p. 85).

Other promising strengths-based parent and community involvement models encourage educators to look for existing strengths and sources of wisdom in urban families and communities (Boutte & Hill, 2006; Moll, 2000). These approaches suggest that if educators look using strengths-based lenses, they would notice that urban students who "misbehave" and "underperform" in school behave quite differently in their home and community contexts—for example, the children are able to sit through (and be involved in) three hours of religious services. Here, it is noted that the differences lie, in part, in differential expectations and relevance of activities (Boutte & Hill, 2006).

Schools that wish to effectively engage parents, families, and communities must position themselves as learners and be willing and open to learning *from* urban families and communities. This necessarily must be a dialogic process (and not an antidialogic one like most of the traditional parent involvement approaches which do not consult families). Educators will have to be positioned to see the existing *funds of knowledge* (defined as knowledge, resources, and competencies that families and communities members have because of their lived experiences) that urban families hold (Moll, 2000). For example, Boutte and Johnson (2012) noted that African American children's homes are often filled with multiliteracies that escape the notice of schools such as complex oral narratives, songs, music, and digital literacies.

Suggesting that educators must examine their positionality as they enter homes and communities of urban families does not mean that we should romanticize these settings and not recognize the challenges that exist. It means that the challenges have to be factored into the equation with the explicit expectation that there are also numerous strengths which have allowed families to improvise, survive, and succeed against many odds. This strength can be extrapolated to parent involvement efforts. So instead of viewing families as "struggling," perhaps it is useful for educators to think of the struggles that they are facing in their schools and how to circumvent and transcend these. In collaboration with others who do this work, urban educators who desire to have successful family and community involvement must begin the work of re-visioning it from the dominant deficit narrative to one of promise and hope.

Charting a Course for Future Developments in Parent and Community Involvement

So a larger question on which this chapter begs is, "Can we change the social order of schools?" Speaking to this question, Smrekar and Cohen-Vogel (2001) commented,

> These patterns of communication are lodged in an established social order that suggests that school personnel possess a certain body of knowledge and expertise. This social order is a product of human activity; that is, the social order defining family–school interactions comes into being as parents and school officials take action, interpret that action, and share with others their interpretations. (p. 92)

That said, since the existing social order was socially constructed, it can be socially deconstructed and transformed. There are exemplars of urban schools succeeding despite incredible odds. These are encouraging and provide insights into competencies that are effective. For instance, Morris's (2004) account of his three-year involvement with African American, low-income urban elementary schools—one in St. Louis, Missouri, and the other in Atlanta, Georgia—represent an example of this. Despite racial and social class inequalities which undermined their schools, the educators and family members collectively worked to meet the children's social and educational needs. Morris concluded that the interpersonal relationships between the teachers and families as well as the teachers' valuing and building on African American culture were essential elements of the schools' success over time. Unlike many educators who teach urban youth, teachers in both schools were connected—culturally, psychologically, and proximally—to the children in the school. Hence, they understood the children's lives beyond school. Distinct from many urban schools, most of the teachers remained at the school and were highly committed to the children's academic and social achievements. Such examples represent only a preview of the large range of promising possibilities in urban schools. These efforts should be amplified and emulated as we ask what can these exemplars teach us. We end with recommendations which can be useful for charting the course for urban parent and community education.

Recommendations for Moving Forward

> The education of any people should begin with the people themselves, but Negroes thus trained have been dreaming about the ancients of Europe and about those who have tried to imitate them.
>
> (Woodson, 1933/1990, p. 32)

As the quote intimates, we must begin by entering into dialogue with urban parents. Simultaneously drawing from DuBois's timeless question, "How does it feel to be a problem?" (DuBois, 1903/1990, p. 7), and the recommendation that the solutions that we seek may lie in part with the families themselves, leads us to conclude that families must have spaces to express what and how they think parent-school involvement may look like as well as their thoughts about what it feels like to be positioned as *the problem*. Educators must seek to understand and build on existing funds of knowledge in urban communities. The following recommendations and questions should direct readers regarding next steps and considerations. Although they were conceived and generated based on key implications from the present review of the literature on urban schools, they are not germane to urban school parents, families, and communities and may be extrapolated to other geologic and cultural groups (e.g., rural families and communities). Returning to King's (2005) three modes of responses—adaptation, improvisation, and resistance, the following suggestions are made in the spirit of resisting traditional parent, family, and community involvement efforts which do not seem to be effective in lieu of activities and strategies that: (1) are more responsive to the needs of families and communities; (2) involve structural and sustainable changes; and (3) are open to evolution and dynamism.

- Connecting School Content to Urban Communities—A guiding question that educators may ask is, "How can I connect school content to urban communities so that students are engaged by (feel connected to) the lesson?" This is a complicated task because some of the funds of knowledge that are found in homes and communities may readily connect to adults, but not children (Moll, 2000). Hence, educators would be advised to carefully investigate daily routines that *children* engage in (Lee, 2008). Even this task is daunting as discretion must be used regarding which aspects of children's and families lives are private and which are open to sharing.
- Exploring Existing Resources—Educators should sensitively and critically explore existing resources, "sages," and sources of wisdom that are available in urban communities (Boutte & Hill, 2006). Schools can support efforts and abilities of parents and community elders to work with youth to develop effective strategies for encouraging high student achievement (King, 2005). For example, while some families may not be readily available to participate in "traditional" parent involvement activities when it is expected, there may be other willing and connected community members who may be able to participate on behalf of the child (e.g., ministers, barbers, Big Brothers, college students, sorority or fraternity members). A description of a community exploration activity is found in Boutte (1999) that can be adapted for educators to use to find out more about communities. Perhaps schools could enlist the assistance of local institutions which would be willing to sponsor an advocate.
- Welcoming Parents—Schools must find out ways to welcome parents in schools and classrooms. How are parents treated when they call and visit schools? Are training programs in place to provide guidance to parents who want to volunteer in classrooms? Is there planning time for teachers and parents to jointly plan for this? What specific skills do parents have that can be shared with schools? Are there parents/guardians/advocates who can tutor students? If so, training, guidance, and support must be provided for this.

- Building Collaborative Communities—Schools should engage in collaborative community building—creating opportunities for effective community teachers to share their knowledge with teachers in urban schools.

Educators can immerse themselves in communities by volunteering in neighborhoods—for example, teaching adult education or sharing a skill. Teachers can also engage students and themselves in service learning activities beyond the typical missionary-type, one-time (Thanksgiving or Christmas) per-year food or clothing drive. An excellent example of this can be found in Cowhey's (2006) book, *Black Ants and Buddhists: Thinking Critically and Teaching Differently in the Primary Grades.* Other examples include:

- Planning to spend *extensive* time in settings where students congregate (e.g., church, barbershops, restaurants) and reflecting on what was learned that can be used as a bridge.
- Extensively studying aspects of children's and families' culture (e.g., via magazines, television shows, social and religious organizations, music, humor—that is, what makes them laugh).
- *Integrating* (not superficially adding) "liberation literature" (which celebrates the cultural strengths of families and communities) into classrooms (in consultation with parents and administrators). This suggestion is a very advanced one because of endemic racism and many families may not perceive themselves as oppressed. For more information on liberation literature, see Jackson and Boutte (2009).
- Making Structural Changes—Principal leaders must engage in a series of structural changes at their schools (Giles, 2006). In order to get buy-in, parents and teachers must co-plan ways to best advocate for their school and to change policies that will benefit families (e.g., planning time for teachers to organize parent volunteers in classrooms). Dialogue with school board members should be ongoing, keeping the larger goal of student achievement as the goal. Having exemplary models to share will be useful.
- Using Social Media—Schools can think of ways they may better use social media to communicate with parents—e.g., texting reminders about school and board meetings.
- Locating and Using Existing Resources—There is no need to recreate what already exists. Educators must seek out existing and promising, transformative models of family and community development which are flexible, elastic, generative, responsive to community needs, and dialogic. Such models will be mutually beneficial to schools and home. The process of involving parents should not be thought of as being free of conflicts so conflicts should be anticipated and worked through with the understanding that most family and community members want to support schools. Part of the conflict will involve both schools and homes/ communities getting past misconceptions and fear so it will not be an overnight process and student achievement is not likely to be instantaneous.
- Addressing Issues on Multiple Fronts—Simultaneously address issues on multiple fronts such as curriculum development, professional development for teachers, teacher and parent expectations, and community needs.
- Going Beyond Traditional Parent Involvement Activities—Go beyond regular School Improvement Council (where a written plan of action is developed, but rarely including structural changes) meetings, Parent Open Houses, and the like. Parents should be able to co-develop the agenda for Parent Meetings and add and lead agenda items. Authentic dialogue about school expectations and perceptions should occur.
- Making Structural Changes—Parent-school-community collaborations should be mutually beneficial to all involved. Because we are interconnected, it is impossible to "save" a child without saving the family or community. Hence, interactions should bidirectional, authentic,

goal-oriented. Parents should be involved in policy making and advocacy efforts. There is also a need for parent networks (Howard & Reynolds, 2008).

Special Education Individual Education programs (IEP) meetings which require parent involvement by law should go beyond superficial parent input in which educators are positioned as the experts.

Teacher Education programs must substantively change the content and experiences that prospective and practicing teachers are receiving about urban parent and community involvement (Sewell, 2012).

Efforts to involve youth will be important. How can schools engage in community organizing with adolescents to plan actions and protests against underperforming urban schools (Kirshner & Ginwright, 2012; Perry, Moses, Wynne, Cortes, & Delpit, 2010)?

As we chart a course for urban parent and community involvement, it should be a deliberate, systemic, collaborative, explorative, and empowering process that connects parents/families to schools. The process should be validating and should contextualize their experiences within the broader community and political realms. The ultimate goal is to elevate the voices of parents/families who have been excluded from the school (Snell et al., 2009).

Conclusion

> Teachers are often simultaneously perpetrators and victims, with little control over planning time, class time, or broader school policies—and much less over the unemployment, hopelessness, and other "savage inequalities" that help shape our children's lives.
>
> (Au, Bigelow, & Karp, 2007, p. x)

As we conclude, we reiterate that the intent is not to vilify schools, educators, or researchers since all have the mutual goal of improving parent and community involvement. Yet, the reality is that both educators and families have distinct roles in some ways. This chapter was written from the perspective of what educators need to do in our spaces and how we may rethink our efforts toward the logical, ethical, and policy mandates to engage families and communities. This is a massive undertaking and current thinking and trends will not change overnight since they are also deeply embedded in societal structures. While multiple avenues and trajectories exist, educators should go beyond the simple rejection of deficit perspectives which assume that urban students enter school culturally deprived or disadvantaged because of deficiencies in their homes and communities. Some of the answers to the questions posed at the beginning of this chapter have been embedded within. Others are rhetorical in some ways, provoking and prompting thoughtful actions. We do know, however, that current approaches are failing miserably in engaging the very people we seek to help.

Note

1. Unless otherwise noted by citations, some of these questions are adapted from a concept paper written by Dr. Susi Long and Dr. Gloria Boutte as part of an advocacy agenda on behalf of children who have been marginalized. Dr. Long and Dr. Boutte hold the Yvonne and Schulyer Moore Child Advocacy Chair at the University of South Carolina. Some of the questions that are not referenced were devised by the authors after reviewing the literature and are based on reflections of areas of need in research and practices around urban parent, family, and community development.

References

Au, W., Bigelow, B., & Karp, S. (2007). Introduction: Creating classrooms for equity and social justice. In W. Au, B. Bigelow, & S. Karp (Eds.), *Rethinking our classrooms: Teaching for equity and justice* (2nd ed., Vol. 1, x–xi). Milwaukee, WI: Rethinking Schools.

Barton, A.C., Drake, C., Perez, J.G., St. Louis, K., & George, M. (2004). Ecologies of parental engagement in urban education. *Educational Researcher, 33*(4), 3–12.

Bauch, P., & Goldring, E. (2000). Teacher work context and parent involvement in urban high schools of choice. *Educational Research and Evaluation: An International Journal on Theory and Practice, 6*(1), 1–23.

Boutte, G. (1999). *Multicultural Issues: Raising Consciousness.* Atlanta, GA: Wadsworth.

Boutte, G.S. (2012). Urban schools: Challenges and possibilities for early childhood and elementary education. *Urban Education, 47*(2), 515–550.

Boutte, G.S., & Hill, E. (2006). African American communities: Implications for educators. *New Educator, 2,* 311–329.

Boutte, G.S., & Johnson, G. (2012). Do educators see and honor biliteracy and bidialectalism in African American language speakers? Apprehensions and reflections of two grandparents/professional educators. *Early Childhood Education Journal.* doi:10.1007/s10643–012–0538–5

Boutte, G.S., & Samuels, V.D. (1992). Home and school: Bridging the gap in education. *National Association of Laboratory School Journal, XVI*(3), 8–29.

Bowers, H.A., & Griffin, D. (2011). Can the Epstein model of parental involvement work in a high-minority, high-poverty elementary school? A case study. *ASCA Professional School Counseling, 15*(2), 77–87.

Bronfenbrenner, U. (1979). *The ecology of human development: Experiments by nature and design.* Cambridge, MA: Harvard University Press.

Bronfenbrenner, U. (2004). *Making human beings human.* Thousand Oaks, CA: Sage Publications.

Cabrera, N., Beeghly, M., & Eisenberg, N. (2012). Positive development of minority children: Introduction to the special issue. *Child Development Perspectives, 6*(3), 207–209.

Cabrera, N., & Bradley, R. (2012). Latino fathers and their children. *Child Development Perspectives, 6*(3), 232–238.

Cannella, G.S. (1997). *Deconstructing early childhood education. Social justice and revolution.* New York, NY: Peter Lang.

Chrispeels, J. (1996). Effective schools and home-school community partnership roles: A framework for parent involvement. *School Effectiveness and School Improvement, 7*(4), 297–323.

Cole-Henderson, B. (2000). Organizational characteristics of schools that successfully serve low-income urban African American students. *Journal of Education for Students Placed at Risk, 5*(1-2), 77–91.

Cowhey, M. (2006). *Black ants and Buddhists: Thinking critically and teaching differently in the primary grades.* Portland, ME: Sternhouse.

Day-Vines, N., & Day-Hairston, B. (2005). Culturally congruent strategies for addressing the behavioral needs of urban, African American male adolescents. *Professional School Counseling, 8*(3), 236–243.

De Gaetano, Y. (2007). The role of culture in engaging Latino parents' involvement in school. *Urban Education, 42*(2), 145–162.

Delpit, L., & Dowdy, J.K. (2002). *The skin that we speak: Thoughts on language and culture in the classroom.* New York, NY: New Press.

Desimone, L. (1999). Linking parent involvement with student achievement: Do race and income matter? *Journal of Education Research, 93*(1), 11–30.

DuBois, W. E. B. (1903/1990). *The souls of Black folk.* New York, NY: First Vintage Books/The Library of America Edition.

Epstein, J.L. (1996). Perspectives and previews on research and policy for school, family, and community partnerships. In A. Booth & J.F. Dunn (Eds.), *Family-school links: How do they affect educational outcomes?* (pp. 209–246). Mahwah, NJ: Lawrence Erlbaum Associates.

Epstein, J.L. (2010). School/family/community partnerships. Caring for the children we share. *Phi Delta Kappan, 92*(3), 81–96.

Epstein, J.L., & Dauber, S.L. (1991). School programs and teacher practices of parent involvement in inner-city elementary and middle schools. *Elementary School Journal, 91*(3), 289–305.

Evans, A., Banerjee, M., Meyer, R., Aldans, A., Foust, M., & Rowley, S. (2012). Racial socialization as a mechanism for positive development among African American youth. *Child Development Perspectives, 6*(3), 251–257.

Fredericks, J., & Simpkins, S. (2012). Promoting positive youth development through organized after school activities: Taking a closer look at participation of ethnic minority youth. *Child Development Perspectives, 6*(3), 280–287.

Galindo, R., & Medina, C. (2009). Cultural appropriation, performance, and agency in Mexicana parent involvement. *Journal of Latinos and Education, 8*(4), 312–331.

Garcia Coll, C., Lamberty, G., Jenkins, R., McAdoo, H., Crnic, K., Wasik, B., & Garcia, H. (1996). An integrative model for the study of developmental competencies in minority children. *Child Development, 67*(5),1891–1914.

Gauvain, M., Savage, S., & McCollum, D. (2000). Reading at home and at school in the primary grades: Cultural and social influences. *Early Education & Development, 11,* 447–463.

Giles, C. (2006). Transformational leadership in challenging urban elementary schools: A role for parent involvement? *Leadership and Policy in Schools, 5*(3), 257–282.

Graue, M.E., & Benson, B.A. (2001). Children, parents, and schools. In J.C. Westman (Ed.), *Parenthood in America* (pp. 158–163). Madison, WI: University of Wisconsin Press.

Grolnick, W., & Slowiaczek, M. (1994). Parents' involvement in children's schooling: A multidimensional conceptualization and motivation model. *Child Development, 65*(1), 237–252.

Hayes, D. (2011). Predicting parental involvement. *High School Journal, 94,* 154–166.

Hayes, D. (2012). Parental involvement and achievement outcomes in African American adolescents. *Journal of Comparative Family Studies, 43*(4), 567–582.

Hayes, D., & Cunningham, M. (2003). Family and school environments working together to impact academic achievement in African American adolescents. In C.C. Yeakey, & R. Henderson (Eds.), *Surmounting all odds: Education, opportunity and society in the new millennium* (pp. 107–123). Greenwich, CT: Information Age.

Hill, N., & Craft, S. (2003). Parent-school involvement and school performance: Mediated pathways among socioeconomically comparable African American and Euro-American families. *Journal of Educational Psychology, 95*(1), 74–83.

Hill, N., & Taylor, L. (2004). Parental school involvement and children's academic achievement. Pragmatics and issues. *Current Directions in Psychological Science, 13*(4),161–164.

Howard, T.C., & Reynolds, R. (2008). Examining parent involvement in reversing the underachievement of African American students in middle-class schools. *Education Foundations, 22*(1), 79–98.

Ingram, M., Wolfe, R., & Lieberman, J. (2007). The role of parents in high-achieving schools serving low-income, at-risk populations. *Education and Urban Society, 39*(4), 479–496.

Jackson, K., & Remillard, J.T. (2005). Rethinking parent involvement: African American mothers construct their roles in the mathematics education of their children. *School Community Journal, 15*(1), 51–73.

Jackson, T., & Boutte, G. (2009). Liberation literature: Positive cultural messages in children's and adolescent literature at freedom schools. *Language Arts, 87*(2),108–116.

Jeynes, W. (2003). The effects of black and Hispanic 12th graders living in intact families and being religious on their academic achievement. *Urban Education, 38*(1), 35–57.

Jeynes, W. (2005). The effects of parental involvement on the academic achievement of African American youth. *Journal of Negro Education, 74*(3), 260–274.

Jeynes, W.H. (2005). A meta-analysis of the relation of parental involvement to urban elementary school student academic achievement. *Urban Education, 40*(3), 237–269.

Jeynes, W.H. (2007). The relationship between parental involvement and urban secondary school student academic achievement. A meta-analysis. *Urban Education, 42*(1), 82–110.

Kenyon, D., & Hanson, J. (2012). Incorporating traditional culture into positive youth development programs with American Indian/Alaska native youth. *Child Development Perspectives, 6*(3), 272–279.

King, J. E. (2005). *Black education. A transformative research and action agenda for the new century.* New York: Routledge.

Kirshner, B., & Ginwright, S. (2012). Youth organizing as a developmental context for Latino and African American youth. *Child Development Perspectives, 6*(3), 288–294.

Knight, G., & Carlo, G. (2012). Prosocial development among Mexican American youth. *Child Development Perspectives, 6*(3), 258–263.

Ladson-Billings, G. (1994). *The dreamkeepers: Successful teachers of African American children.* San Francisco, CA: Jossey-Bass.

Lee, C.D. (2008). The centrality of culture to the scientific study of learning and development: How an ecological framework in education research facilitates civic responsibility. *Educational Researcher, 37*(5), 267–279.

Lee, J., & Bowen, N. (2006). Parent involvement, cultural capital, and the achievement gap among elementary school children. *American Educational Research Journal, 43*(2), 193–218.

LeFevre, A.L., & Shaw, T.V. (2012). Latino parent involvement and school success: Longitudinal effects of formal and informal support. *Education and Urban Society, 44*(6), 707–723.

Lewis, C.W., James, M., Hancock, S., & Hill-Jackson, V. (2008). Framing African American students' success and failure in urban settings: A typology for change. *Urban Education, 43*(2), 127–153.

Lichtman, M. (2010). *Qualitative research in education. A user's guide (2nd ed.).* Los Angeles, CA: Sage.

Li-Grining, C. (2012). The role of cultural factors in the development of Latino preschoolers' self-regulation. *Child Development Perspectives, 6*(3), 210–217.

Long, S., Volk, D., Tisdale, C., Baines, J. (2013). "We've been doing it your way long enough": Syncretism as a critical process. *Journal of Early Childhood Literacy.* doi:10.1177/1468798412466403

Madison, S. (2005). *Critical ethnography: Method, ethics, and performance.* Thousand Oaks, CA: Sage Publications.

Mallory, B., & New, R.S. (1994). *Diversity and developmentally appropriate practices. Challenges for early childhood education.* New York, NY: Teachers College Press.

Mannan, G., & Blackwell, J. (1992). Parent involvement: Barriers and opportunities. *Urban Review, 24*(3), 219–226.

Mattingly, D.J., Prislin, R., McKenzie, T.L., Rodriguez, J.L., & Kayzar, B. (2002). Evaluating evaluations: The case of parental involvement programs. *Review of Educational Research, 72*(4), 549–576.

McBride, B., & Len, H. (1996). Parental involvement in prekindergarten at-risk programs: Multiple perspectives. *Journal of Education for Students Placed at Risk, 1*(4), 349–372.

McWayne, C., Hampton, V., Fantuzzo, J., Cohen, H.L., & Sekino, Y. (2004). A multivariate examination of parent involvement and the social and academic competencies of urban kindergarten children. *Psychology in the Schools, 41*(3), 363–377.

Mesman, J., Van IJzendoorn, M., & Bakermans-Kranenburg., M.J. (2012). Unequal in opportunity in process: Parental sensitivity promotes positive child development in ethnic minority families. *Child Development Perspectives, 6*(3), 239–250.

Milner, H.R. (2008). Disrupting deficit notions of difference: Counter-narratives of teachers and community in urban education. *Teaching and Teacher Education, 24*(6), 1573–1598.

Moll, L. (2000). The diversity of schooling: A cultural-historical approach. In M. Reyes & J. Halcon (Eds.), *The best for our children: Critical perspectives on literacy for Latino students* (pp. 29–47). New York, NY: Teachers College Press.

Morris, J.E. (2004). Can anything good come from Nazareth? Race, class, and African-American schooling and community in the urban South and Midwest. *American Educational Research Journal, 41*(1), 69–112.

National Association for the Education of Young Children. (2009). *Developmentally appropriate practice in early childhood programs serving children from birth through age 8. Position Statement.* Retrieved from http://www.naeyc.org/files/naeyc/file/positions/PSDAP.pdf/

Neblett, E., Rivas-Drake, D., & Umana-Taylor, A. (2012). The promise of racial and ethnic protective factors in promoting ethnic minority youth development. *Child Development Perspectives, 6*(3), 295–303.

Overstreet, S., Devine, J., Bevans, K., & Efreom, Y. (2005). Predicting parental involvement in children's schooling within an economically disadvantaged African American sample. *Psychology in the Schools, 42*(1), 101–111.

Paulson, S. (1994). Relations of parenting style and parental involvement with ninth-grade students' achievement. *Journal of Early Adolescence, 14*(2), 250–267.

Paulson, S., & Sputa, C. (1996). Patterns of parenting during adolescence: Perceptions of adolescents and parents. *Adolescence, 31*(122), 369–381.

Perry, T., Moses, R.P., Wynne, J.T., Cortes, E., Jr., & Delpit, L. (2010). *Quality education as a constitutional right.* Boston, MA: Beacon Press.

Perry, T., Steele, C., & Hilliard, A. III. (2003). *Young, gifted, and Black: Promoting high achievement among African-American students.* Boston, MA: Beacon Press.

Picower, B. (2009). The unexamined Whiteness of teaching: How White teachers maintain and enact dominant racial ideologies. *Race Ethnicity and Education, 12*(2), 197–215.

Ramirez, A. Y. F. (2003). Dismay and disappointment: Parental involvement of Latino immigrant parents. *Urban Review, 35*(2), 93–110.

Reynolds, A. (1992). Comparing measures of parental involvement and their effects on academic achievement. *Early Childhood Research Quarterly,* 7(3), 441–462.

Sewell, T. (2012). Are we adequately preparing teachers to partner with families? *Early Childhood Education Journal, 40,* 259–263. doi:10.1007/s10643-011-0503-8

Sheldon, S.B. (2002). Parents' social networks and beliefs as predictors of parent involvement. *Elementary School Journal, 102*(4), 301–316.

Slaughter-Defoe, D.T., & Rubin, H.H. (2001). A longitudinal case study of Head Start eligible children: Implications for urban education. *Educational Psychologist, 36*(1), 31–44.

Smrekar, C., & Cohen-Vogel, L. (2001). The voices of parents: Rethinking the intersection of family and school. *Peabody Journal of Education, 76*(2), 75–100.

Snell, P., Miguel, N., & East, J. (2009). Changing directions: Participatory action research as a parent involvement strategy. *Educational Action Research, 17*(2), 239–258.

Steinberg, L., & Fletcher, A.C. (1998). Data analytic strategies in research on ethnic minority youth. In V.C. McLoyd & L. Steinberg (Eds.), *Studying minority adolescents* (pp. 279–294). Mahwah, NJ: Lawrence Erlbaum Associates.

Taylor, L., Hinton, I., & Wilson, M. (1995). Parental influences on academic performance in African-American students. *Journal of Child and Family Studies, 4*(3), 293–302.

U.S. Department of Education, National Center for Education Statistics, Common Core of Data (CCD). (2007–2008a). *Public Elementary/Secondary School Universe Survey.* Retrieved from http://nces.ed.gov/surveys/ruraled/tables/a.1.a.-2.asp?refer=urban

U.S. Department of Education, National Center for Education Statistics, Common Core of Data (CCD). (2007–2008b). *Public Elementary/Secondary School Universe Survey, Table B.1.b.-1. Number and percentage distribution of public elementary and secondary students, by race/ethnicity and locale: 2007–08.* Retrieved from http://nces.ed.gov/surveys/ruraled/tables/b.1.b.-1.asp?refer=urban

Volk, D., & Long, S. (2005). Challenging myths of the deficit perspective: Honoring children's literacy resources. *Young Children, 60*(6), 12–19.

Williams, J., Tolan, P., Durkee, M., Francois, A., & Anderson, R. (2012). Integrating racial and ethnic identity research into developmental understanding of adolescents. *Child Development Perspectives, 6*(3), 304–311.

Williams, T.M., Pemberton, K.D., & Dyce, C.M. (2012). Engagement without judgment: Building effective school, family, and community partnerships for African American learners. A primer for teachers and administrators. *African American Learners, 1*(2). Retrieved from https://isaac.wayne.edu/research/journal/article.php?newsletter=133&article=1899

Wong, S., & Hughes, J. (2006). Ethnicity and language contributions to dimensions of parent involvement. *School Psychology Review, 35*(4), 645–622.

Woodson, C.G. (1933/1990). *The mis-education of the Negro.* Trenton, NJ: Africa World Press.

Yan, W. (2000). Successful African American students: The role of parental involvement. *Journal of Negro Education, 68*(1), 5–22.

Zhou, Q., Tao, A., Chen, S.H., Main, A., Lee, E., Ly, J., Hua, M., & Li, X. (2012). Asset and protective factors for Asian American children's mental health adjustment. *Child Development Perspective, 6*(3), 312–319.

10

English Language Learners and Partnerships With Families, Communities, Teacher Preparation, and Schools

Ana Christina DaSilva Iddings, Mary Carol Combs & Luis C. Moll

Students designated as English language learners (ELLs) are a rapidly growing population in urban contexts (Milner, 2012; Moore, 2012). More than 5 million ELLs from all over the world attend public schools in the United States and they speak at least 460 different languages (Kindler, 2002, in Rios-Aguilar & Gandara, 2012). It has been estimated, however, that between 80% and 89% of all English language learners speak Spanish as their home or heritage language (Goldenberg & Coleman, 2010; Gándara & Hopkins, 2010). These students are often immigrants or are born to immigrant parents and are mostly Latinos (Pew Hispanic Center, 2011). In this chapter, we address the partnerships between Latino immigrant families, teachers, community members, and university faculty toward the education of ELLs. We engage the concept of *funds of knowledge* (Moll, Amanti, Neff, & Gonzalez, 1992) to illuminate relationships between these students' cultural, social, and linguistic repertoires and the institutional context of schools. In addition, we utilize Freire's (1970) concept of *praxis* (awareness and action) as we pay particular attention to power relations as related to the literacy education of ELLs in contexts where historically underserved populations are educated. In so doing, we problematize educational ideologies, embodied in educational policies and school practices that can produce dialectical tensions between local household, community knowledge, and institutional structures. For example, the adoption of certain educational approaches or school rules and consequences about using first language and literacy during classroom instruction, reductive pedagogy, inadequate assessment tools can potentially pose such a tension. Alternatively, we advocate for an ecological view of learning and a comprehensive approach to the education of ELLs that begins with teacher education programs centering on the resources families and communities bring to the classroom.

Grounded in the theoretical concepts cited above and on empirical examples, we aim to contribute to the refinement of current understandings regarding the learning and teaching of ELLs as situated across classroom, family, and community contexts that are continuously changing. Our analysis challenges narrow conceptions of learning context (e.g., home or school sites) as bounded/contained physical places, implicit comparisons of ELLs with monolingual English speakers as the standard, static views of immigrant families' funds of knowledge, and limited attention to the teachers' role in promoting the agency, identities, and strategic actions of ELLs across contexts.

Funds of Knowledge

The research on "funds of knowledge," brought forth over 20 years ago, was mainly concerned with the literacy education of Latino,[1] mostly Mexican American, children in the U.S. Southwest (e.g., Moll, 1990; Vélez-Ibáñez & Greenberg, 1992). In this work, teachers as co-researchers collaborated using ethnographic-like household observations and interviews with household members. Importantly, this research advanced a "sociocultural" orientation in education, seeking to build strategically on the experiences, resources, and knowledge of families and children, especially those from low-income neighborhoods (e.g., Hogg, 2011).

From this perspective, families, especially those in the working class, have been characterized by the practices they have developed and knowledge they have produced and acquired in the living of their lives. The social history of families, and their productive or labor activities in both the primary and secondary sector of the economy, are particularly relevant to educational contexts and teachers because they reveal experiences (e.g., in farming, construction, gardening, household maintenance, or secretarial work) that generate much of the knowledge household members may possess, display, elaborate, or share with others. This knowledge may develop through their participation in social networks, often with kin, through which such funds of knowledge may be exchanged in addressing some of life's necessities. As Moll, Soto-Santiago, and Schwartz (in press) further explained:

> one might help a neighbor fix a car, because one has the required knowledge and experience as an auto mechanic, and the neighbor incurs an obligation to reciprocate and help paint one's house, a task that is within his or her areas of expertise. (p. 23)

The authors note that these forms of reciprocal exchange are not of cash for labor as in commercial transactions; instead, it is an exchange in another currency, that of funds of knowledge. One could argue, then, that funds of knowledge in a particular household or in a network of households may form part of a broader (nonmonetary) household economy (Moll, Soto-Santiago, & Schwartz, in press).

Thus this type of research, especially if conducted in collaboration with teachers, provides one with an opportunity to (a) initiate relations of trust—or *confianza*—with families to enable discussion of their practices and funds of knowledge; (b) document families' lived experiences and knowledge that may prove useful in defining households as having ample intellectual resources or assets that may be valuable for instruction; and (c) establish discursive settings with teachers to prepare them theoretically, methodologically, and analytically to do the research, and to assess the utility of the findings for classroom practice (González, Moll, & Amanti, 2005, p. 213). In other words, their study shows that the knowledge base one can accrue through this approach to households can be treated pedagogically as cultural resources for teaching and learning in schools. It represents an opportunity for teachers to identify and establish the "educational capital" of families often assumed to be lacking any such resources, and to leverage this capital in the classroom.

Many subsequent studies in different parts of the world have pointed to the usefulness of the funds of knowledge concept, especially when working with students and families of diverse backgrounds. Kenner's (2004, 2005) work with immigrant children growing up in London, for example, serves as a heeding call for the use of home language/culture as resources for schooling situations and for reconsiderations of monolingual and Anglocentric practices in schools that continuously undermine the learning capabilities of immigrant students. Drury's (2007) study confirms the findings of an ever-growing corpus of empirical data making evident the importance of reconciling the complex realities of children's home and school experiences, and of harnessing resources from home contexts in order to foster children's literacy learning. Also along those lines, scholars advocate for educational approaches that help us identify and situate ELLs' literacy practices within their specific households, schools, and communities and that focus on the dynamic and mutual relationships between learners and surrounding contexts (DaSilva Iddings, Combs, & Moll, 2012; Ovando & Combs, 2012). With a basis on a close understanding of these interrelationships, pedagogical and social action toward more equitable education for ELLs are possible.

Extending the notions of funds of knowledge and praxis, scholars also argue for the rupture of prevalent institutional patterns of exclusion of minority populations from schools and call for (a) an increased understanding and respect for the values, needs, and aspirations of immigrant families; (b) a greater understanding about immigrant households as places that contain valuable knowledge and experiences that foster and support the literacy development of young children (as opposed to common misconceptions about immigrant homes as places from which children need to be rescued); and (c) a growing awareness that literacy is fundamentally related to cultural identity, and shaped by ethnicity, primary language, and social class (see DaSilva Iddings, 2009 for a review of this literature). Specifically in relation to literacy practices Dworin (2011) adds that in addition to understanding them as constituted within specific contexts, such as homes, schools, worksites, and communities, educators must also consider the *conditions* [emphasis added] in which literacy practices occur, including the broader social and ideological issues.

Ideology and Action in the Literacy Education of ELLs: The Concept of Praxis

When discussing literacy teaching and learning for populations that have been historically underserved, the Brazilian educator Paulo Freire is often invoked. According to Freire (1970), literacy education can provide the knowledge, dispositions, and skills for the redistribution of power and income in a given society. However, for the educator, literacy is not merely a series of skills to be taught, but rather a social condition that empowers individuals. Under these circumstances, becoming literate does not simply imply learning how to read and write, but also involves a deep understanding of one's own history within the world. In other words, literacy according to Freire, develops not only through reading the word, but also through reading the world—both the world of nature and the social world of people as created through material objects, institutions, practices, and other phenomena (in Roberts, 2000). Thus, following Freire, literacy does not develop as a sequential, lock-step, "cause-and-effect" relationship, but as complex process of constant, multilayered interaction between human beings and the world. From this point of view, "consciousness" and the "world" are inextricably connected. In addition, according to this perspective, the relationship between consciousness and the world is intrinsically dialectical and such an approach demands that social phenomena and problems be understood not in abstract isolation but as lived experiences. In this way, Freire and Macedo (1996) was concerned with the dialectical unity between consciousness (knowledge/theory) and action that results in the creation of something new—this is the idea of *praxis.*

Freire's pedagogical approach is therefore consistent with this principle. He warned that the goal of teaching is not to transfer knowledge, but instead, to stimulate the learners' epistemological curiosity (or the willingness to know and to think about one's own reality), to disrupt common sense with new viewpoints, to help learners to take as strange that which has become naturalized. In this way, the learners' new forms of understanding are constructed or amplified, new interpretations of reality are made available, and change becomes possible. Freire's approach is situated in the learners' life experiences and empirical knowledge, which are taken as starting points for understanding the world, acting on it, and transforming it. Situating literacy activity in the lived experience of ELLs and their families/communities, and understanding it in light of a funds of knowledge perspective, opens up a series of possibilities. For example, educators can approach praxis by examining curriculum and reshaping practices in ways that provide a critical lens for ELLs and their families and teachers to reconsider the limiting educational circumstances, and therefore, the social conditions that constrain, and often can even prevent, opportunities for learning.

By utilizing a funds of knowledge framework (Gonzalez et al., 2005) and the concept of praxis (Freire & Macedo, 1996), we aim to delineate a much-needed more equitable approach to urban education and to the education of ELLs whereby learning is constituted within the specific practices of a variety of social contexts such as home, schools, and communities that are ever changing. In addition, we propose that taking into full consideration the relationships among these various learning contexts is necessary in order to envision new possibilities for praxis. However, we point out that equitable approaches to urban education need to be advanced in tandem with critical examinations of ideological issues surrounding deficit-oriented language policies and the prevalent educational programs that continue to disadvantage ELLs.

Language Policies Guiding the Education of English Language Learners

Numerous federal policies, acts, and mandates have attempted to address the educational needs of linguistically diverse students. In 1970 the federal Office for Civil Rights (OCR) issued a memorandum which declared a violation of civil rights law if: (a) students are excluded from effective participation in school because of their inability to speak and understand the language of instruction; (b) students are inappropriately assigned to special education classes because of their lack of English skills; (c) programs for students whose English is less than proficient are not designed to teach them English as soon as possible; or (d) parents whose English is limited do not receive school notices or other information in a language they can understand. This memorandum led to the 1974 Supreme Court decision in *Lau v. Nichols* that if English learners did not understand the language of instruction, their education could in no way be "meaningful" (*Lau v. Nichols,* 414 US 563 (1974). The case also strengthened Title VI of the 1964 Civil Rights Act, which forbids discrimination on the basis of national origin by institutions that receive federal funding—like schools and school districts.

Education policy for English language learners is also guided by two related legal developments. The first is the Equal Educational Opportunities Act (EEOA) of 1974, which requires school districts to take "appropriate action to overcome language barriers that impede equal participation by its students in its instructional programs" (Title 20 U.S.C. § 1703[f]). What "appropriate action" actually meant was clarified in *Castañeda v. Pickard,* a 1981 5th Circuit Court decision that created an analytical framework for determining whether or not school districts helped English language learners overcome language barriers. The so-called Castañeda Test is still used to evaluate school district compliance with the EEOA. It is composed of three parts: sound theory, reasonable implementation, and verifiable results (Combs, 2012):

- *Theory:* The district must be "pursuing a program informed by an educational theory recognized as sound by some experts in the field, or at least, deemed a legitimate experimental strategy."
- *Implementation:* The programs and practices of the school district must be "reasonably calculated to implement effectively the educational theory adopted by the school."

- *Results:* The program must "produce results indicating that the language barriers confronting students are actually being overcome."

The federal No Child Left Behind Act (2001) has issued provisions focusing on promoting English acquisition and helping English language learners meet content standards by holding school districts accountable for the academic progress as well as the attainment of English for students with limited English proficiency (LEP). However, despite federal efforts to "level the playing field" for English language learners, according to the National Assessment for Educational Progress (NAEP) (National Center for Education Statistics, 2009), these students continue to underachieve in American schools. Reports for the 2009–2010 academic year claim that 71% of all assessed 8th-grade English language learners achieved below basic levels, 24% scored at basic levels, and only 4% scored at proficient levels in reading standardized assessments.

No Child Left Behind (NCLB) has played a significant role on the preservation of hegemonic ideologies about English as the only or the principal language in school contexts. Similarly, print-based literacy, or *academic literacy,* is most emphasized and valued in schools. These reductionist conceptions (Menken, 2008; Menken & García, 2010; Reyes & Kleyn, 2010) of language and literacy can undermine ELLs' linguistic resources and discourage their bilingualism or biliteracy development at school and in the society at large. In addition, the hegemony of English in educational settings has become institutionalized through antibilingual, English Only education initiatives in Arizona, California, and Massachusetts and reified through Official English laws in 31 states (Crawford, 2008; U.S. English, n.d.). Regrettably, these language policies have guided institutional educational models for ELLs and thus have curtailed what counts as resources for learning and prevented teachers and students from building on the ample linguistic and cultural affordances in their environments. In addition, with few exceptions, these policies impose a top-down approach to the education of English in the form of English-only or English-mostly instruction and scripted or regimented reading programs. These kinds of instruction and prescribed reading programs as a rule pay little attention to the intellectual development of students, and more to a presumed need to accelerate the speed of English acquisition. Also, the development of deep understandings about family literacy practices and histories is often taken as irrelevant to academic achievement or school learning, and students' funds of knowledge figure rarely in the curriculum. Additionally, in many cases teachers have little or no substantive professional preparation in teaching ELLs (Crawford & Krashen, 2008; Moll, 2002). Without the proper supports, ELLs are placed in deficit situations and are unable (or rather, not permitted) to utilize their most valuable linguistic, social, and cultural resources. In order to counteract these detrimental elements for ELL schooling, we recommend that we begin by educating prospective teachers to work effectively with ELLs and their families and communities in efforts to achieve a paradigm shift from deficit perspectives to a pedagogy of possibilities through the application of the concepts of funds of knowledge and praxis.

Forging Partnerships for Change in Teacher Education for ELLs

Although teacher preparation programs recognize the need to better prepare preservice teachers to work in urban contexts (Amatea, Cholewa, & Mixon, 2012; Nieto, 1992; Sleeter, 2001), many approaches taken by universities to better prepare future teachers to work with ELLs have stopped short of their goals (Voltz, Collins, Patterson, & Sims, 2008).

The traditional or isolated approach provides teacher candidates with a specific course on alternative methods of teaching ELLs and overcoming social stereotypes. Although more research is necessary to determine the best ways to prepare preservice teachers to work with the linguistically diverse, many recent studies point to the importance of field experiences in urban contexts as the key to provide preservice teachers with opportunities to develop authentic perceptions of the challenges and possibilities when teaching students from diverse language backgrounds (Onore & Gildin, 2010; Waddell, 2011; Zeichner, 2010).

Therefore, in view of the arguments we have delineated here regarding the teaching and learning of ELLs, we provide an example of a teacher education program that has as a goal the improvement of early childhood education and early childhood teacher education for ELLs, paying particular attention to the literacy development of these students, their families, and communities. The Community as Resources in Early Childhood Teacher Education Project (CREATE, n.d.) (www.createarizona.org) has aimed to design an early childhood teacher education curriculum vis-à-vis a professional development program and home visits in order to foster collaborations between family and community members, teachers in the respective partnering schools, preservice teachers, university professors, and researchers. Moreover, the goal has been to create opportunities for a new platform of action, a space for interaction among multiple stakeholders, to promote literacy and to inform curricula (both in the teacher preparation program and in the partner preschools), pedagogy, and to establish meaningful relationships among the different realms of communities. In order to do that, the primary investigators for the project closely examined the university curriculum, carefully mapped the syllabi for every course in the program for course objectives and assignments, interviewed the instructors of all courses as well as the students in relation to their goals for the program and for the individual courses in order to ensure a coherent focus on funds of knowledge (and deepening of this concept) in all courses across the four semesters in the program.

The new curriculum required consistent home visits, family and community interactions as part of the field experiences and as an integral part of their course work every semester—a minimum of 12 home visits. In addition, preservice teachers, together with family members, were required to co-design and co-implement school and community functions for families in a variety of formats. An example of such an effort was the creation of a Family Welcome Center—a designated space inside our partnering schools where various types of formal and informal literacy activities took place for ELLs and their families. The activities aimed to (a) recognize ELLs' cultural backgrounds; (b) build on their family's linguistic and literate histories; (c) promote social interactions and community leadership among parents; and (d) develop common classroom and home literacy practices. In keeping with these goals, the texts used for the purposes of developing literacy for students and their participating family members were derived from their oral narratives and were concerned with their lives in their homeland as well as their routines in daily life in the new culture (see also DaSilva Iddings, 2009, p. 308).

Overall, the CREATE program redesign focused on providing multiple opportunities for early childhood educators, community and family members to enter into dialogue and explore together ways to attend to diverse linguistic, social, cultural, and community backgrounds of the children. This home visit program allowed the preservice teachers to build relationships with students' families beyond the walls of the classroom and to develop close understandings about their respective funds of knowledge and literacy practices (Reyes & DaSilva Iddings, 2012). These new understandings were then leveraged as resources for learning in order to enhance the literacy development of ELLs. Our primary purpose in designing these visits was to counter a still prevalent ideology that ELLs and their families are somehow literacy deficient or that they lack resources (i.e., a deficit-oriented perspective). Our research shows that by and large the preservice teachers we interviewed (about 100 over three years) were able to break stereotypes, although in spite of all efforts, some (about 17%) remained intractable in their beliefs.

In addition, as part of our CREATE project, we engaged in teacher professional development programs in the various school districts where preserveice teachers were placed for their practicum experiences. These professional development series were inspired by Freire's (1970) notions of critical pedagogy and emergent methologies. During the monthly sessions we worked with family members, cooperating teachers, teacher assistants, preservice teachers, university professors, researchers, and our community liasons to engage in dialogue regarding specific challenges or issues based on empirical evidence from the teachers' practicing classrooms and/or the home visits. We then employed recursive inquiry-driven cycles to study literacy practices in the various contexts as a means to learn about ELL literacy development. The goal of the professional development was to arrive at literacy practices that bridged different contexts, and create a literature-based preschool curriculum that reflected the lived histories of the families and communities that came to the school.

Conclusion

In this chapter, we have proposed that a funds of knowledge approach is central to the concerns of urban education as the enrollment of ELLs continues to grow in urban areas. We argue further that a close understanding of students and their families' literacy practices, and of the dynamic and evolving living histories that produce and/or transform such practices, is essential if we are to take seriously the literacy education of these students.

In these ways, we have advocated for a paradigm change that departs from a deficit-oriented view of students, to a view of education that emphasizes the cultural and intellectual resources of ELLs, especially in terms of how the students use literacy. We have posed that there is a need to follow the threads of ELLs' literacy practices beyond the walls of the classroom and break through the hegemony of English that perpetuates power relations between home or community knowledge and institutional ways of knowing. We have proposed that educators must examine ELLs' literacy learning across classrooms, schools, districts, families, and communities so to understand how these students construct literacy knowledge and how they use this knowledge across contexts. We have also pointed out that it is important to consider the flow of information between the social spaces of home-school-community literacy practices in order to understand literacy learning as a multifaceted and dynamic (i.e., not static) process. Overall, in this chapter, we have aimed to illuminate some useful theoretical constructs as applied to the literacy education of ELLs and to exemplify their practices in order to contribute to new understandings and new actions for the improvement of their education. We believe that the policies that guide the experiences that these students have in schools need to be fundamentally changed in order to counteract the prevalent deficit orientation toward ELLs. In addition, we pose that the education of ELLs needs to be addressed comprehensively, starting from the ways we educate teachers, to support these students in meaningful literacy activities. We note that it is important to keep in mind that these students are acquiring learning biographies that index the identities they develop as literate members of society.

Note

1. *Latino* is a generic designation for any population of Latin American descent; we will use it interchangeably with the term *Hispanic* throughout this chapter.

References

Amatea, E.S., Cholewa, B., & Mixon, K.A. (2012). Influencing preservice teachers' attitudes about working with low-income and/or ethnic minority families. *Urban Education, 47*(4), 801–834.

Castañeda v. Pickard, 648 F. 2d 989 (1981).

Combs, M.C. (2012). Everything on its head: How Arizona's Structured English Immersion policy re-invents theory and practice. In M.B. Arias & C. Faltis (Eds.), *Implementing educational language policy in Arizona* (pp. 59–85). Bristol, UK: Multilingual Matters.

Community as Resources in Early Childhood Teacher Education (CREATE). (n.d.). Retrieved from www.createarizona.org

Crawford, J. (2008). *Advocating for English learners*. Clevedon, UK: Multilingual Matters.

Crawford, J., & Krashen, S. (2008). *English learners in American classrooms*. New York, NY: Scholastic.

DaSilva Iddings, A.C. (2009). Bridging home and school literacy practices and empowering families of recent immigrant children: A sociocultural approach. *Theory Into Practice, 48*(4), 304–312.

DaSilva Iddings, A.C., Combs, M.C., & Moll, L.C. (2012). In the arid zone: Drying out resources for English Language Learners through policy and practice. *Urban Education, 47*(2), 495–514.

Drury, R. (2007). *Young bilingual learners at home and school: Researching multilingual voices*. Stoke-on-Trent, UK: Trenthan Books.

Dworin, J. (2011). Listening to graduates of a K-12 bilingual program: Language ideologies and literacy practices of former bilingual students. *Education and Learning Research Journal, 5,* 104–126.

Equal Educational Opportunities Act of 1974, Pub. L. No. (93–380), 88 Stat. 514 (1974).

Freire, P. (1970). *Pedagogy of the oppressed*. New York, NY: Herder and Herder.

Freire, P., & Macedo, D.P. (1996). *Letters to Cristina: Reflections on my life and work*. New York, NY: Routledge.

Gándara, P., & Hopkins, M. (2010). *Forbidden language: English learners and restrictive language policies*. New York, NY: Teachers College Press.

González, N., Moll, L.C., & Amanti, K. (2005). *Funds of knowledge: Theorizing practices in households, communities, and classrooms*. Mahwah, NJ: Lawrence Erlbaum Associates.

Goldenberg, C., & Coleman, R. (2010). *Promoting academic achievement among English learners: A guide to the research*. Thousand Oaks, CA: SAGE.

Hogg, L. (2011). Funds of knowledge: An investigation of coherence within the literature. *Teaching and Teaching Education, 27,* 666–677.

Kenner, C. (2004). *Becoming biliterate: Young children learning different writing systems*. Stoke-on-Trent, UK: Trentham Books.

Kenner, C. (2005). Bilingual families as literacy eco-systems. *Early Years: An International Journal of Research and Development, 25*(3), 283–298.

Kindler, A.L. (2002). *Survey of the states' limited English proficient students and available educational programs and services 1999–2000 summary report*. Washington, DC: National Clearinghouse for English Language Acquisition and Language Instruction Education Programs (NCELA). Retrieved from http://www.ncela.gwu.edu

Lau v. Nichols. (1974). Retrieved from http://www.stanford.edu/~kenro/LAU/IAPolicy/IA1aLauvNichols.htm

Menken, K. (2008). *English learners left behind: Standardized testing as language policy*. Clevedon, UK: Multilingual Matters.

Menken, K., & García, O. (2010). *Negotiating language policies in schools: Educators as policymakers*. New York, NY: Routledge.

Milner, H.R. (2012). But what is urban education? *Urban Education, 47*(3), 556–561.

Moll, L. C. (1990). *Vygotsky and education*. Cambridge, UK: Cambridge University Press.

Moll, L. (2002). The concept of educational sovereignty. *Penn GSE Perspectives on Urban Education, 1*(2), 1–11.

Moll, L., Amanti, C., Neff, D., & Gonzalez, N. (1992). Funds of knowledge for teaching: Using a qualitative approach to connect homes and classrooms. *Theory Into Practice, 31*(2), 132–140.

Moll, L., Soto-Santiago, S., & Schwartz, L. (in press). Funds of Knowledge in changing communities.

Moore, J.R. (2012). Urban education's core challenges: How racial and socioeconomic segregation and poverty help create a culture of low expectations and achievement in urban schools. *International Journal of Humanities & Social Science, 3*(13), 149–157.

National Center for Education Statistics. (2009). *National Assessment of Educational Progress: An overview of NAEP.* Washington, DC: National Center for Education Statistics, Institute of Education Sciences, U.S. Department of Education.

Nieto, S. (1992). *Affirming diversity: The sociopolitical context of multicultural education.* New York, NY: Longman.

No Child Left Behind (NCLB). (n.d.). U.S. Department of Education. Retrieved from http://www.ed.gov/nclb/landing.jhtml

Onore, C., & Gildin, B. (2010). Preparing urban teachers as public professionals through a university-community partnership. *Teacher Education Quarterly, 37*(3), 27–44.

Ovando, C.J., & Combs, M.C. (2012). *Bilingual and ESL classrooms* (5th ed.). New York, NY: McGraw-Hill.

Pew Hispanic Center. (2011). *The new Latino: The context and consequences of rapid population growth.* Washington, DC: Author.

Reyes, I., & DaSilva Iddings, A.C. (2012, December). *Pre-service teachers' perspectives on the language and literacy development of pre-school English language learners through home visits.* San Diego, CA: Literacy Research Association (LRA).

Reyes, S.A., & Kleyn, T. (2010). *Teaching in 2 languages: A guide for K–12 bilingual educators.* Thousand Oaks, CA: Corwin Press.

Rios-Aguilar, C., & Gandara, P. (2012). (Re)conceptualizing and (re)evaluating language policies for English language learners: The case of Arizona. *Language Policy, 11*, 1–5.

Roberts, P. (2000). *Education, literacy, and humanization: Exploring the work of Paulo Freire.* Westport, CT: Bergin & Garvey.

Sleeter, C.E. (2001, January 1). Preparing teachers for culturally diverse schools: Research and the overwhelming presence of Whiteness. *Journal of Teacher Education, 52*(2), 94–106.

U.S. English. Retrieved January 3, 2012 from http://www.us-english.org/view/13

Vélez-Ibáñez, C.G., & Greenberg, J.B. (1992, December 1). Formation and transformation of funds of knowledge among U.S.-Mexican households. *Anthropology & Education Quarterly, 23*(4), 313–335.

Voltz, D.L., Collins, L., Patterson, J., & Sims, M.J. (2008, March 1). Chapter 2: Preparing urban educators for the twenty-first century. *Action in Teacher Education, 29,* 25–40.

Waddell, J. (2011). Crossing borders without leaving town: The impact of cultural immersion on the perceptions of teacher education candidates. *Issues in Teacher Education, 20*(2), 23–36.

Zeichner, K. (2010). Rethinking the connections between campus courses and field experiences in college- and university-based teacher education. *Journal of Teacher Education, 61,* 89–99.

Section IV

Teacher Education and Special Education

11

Teacher Preparation for Urban Schools

Tyrone C. Howard & H. Richard Milner IV

The changing demographic texture of the United States has resulted in unprecedented diversity in schools. In particular, urban schools and communities have witnessed these shifts for some time. As a country that has celebrated in theory its diversity, the United States has seen its urban communities often serve as the hallmark of the ethnic, socioeconomic, racial, cultural, and linguistic diversity that the United States purports makes it unique. The paradox in this current state of affairs is that while urban schools and communities have witnessed the type of diversity that the United States supposedly cherishes, the manner in which children in urban schools have been served has been far from ideal (Delpit, 2012; Howard, 2010; Ladson-Billings, 2006). In fact, although one might argue that schools in U.S. society are diverse, a closer examination of racial and ethnic trends in urban schools demonstrates less diversity as many schools are resegregating (Boger & Orfield, 2005). A perusal of the professional literature would reveal that low-income, and children of color (namely African American and Latino American—the populations most present in urban schools) perform far below their high-income and White peers on standardized tests (Barton & Coley, 2010; Chubb & Loveless, 2002; Jencks & Phillips, 1998; Pino & Smith, 2004).

Our purpose in this chapter is to interrogate some of the core challenges that are currently being encountered by urban schools and concurrently researchers, theorists, practitioners and policy makers in urban education. When it comes to examining the academic outcomes of many students in urban schools, the evidence has been overwhelming that teachers can make the single biggest influence within schools on students' academic outcomes (Darling-Hammond, 2010; Milner, 2010). In this chapter, we consider the following questions based on an examination of teacher education literature.

- What knowledge do teachers in urban schools need to be successful?
- Are teachers adequately being prepared to work in urban schools?
- What steps need to be taken at the in-service and preservice levels to ensure that teachers who are entering, or currently in, urban schools, are equipped with the necessary knowledge, skills, and dispositions for practice to service all students effectively?

The literature regarding teacher preparation/education and urban education is not well developed. For instance, in our recent search (December 2012) of academic databases, a relatively small number of refereed articles emerged. Using keywords "urban education" and "teacher education" (which also included "urban education" and "teacher preparation"), 13 articles were found in Google Scholar, 6 in ERIC, and 10 in PsycINFO. A search for "urban teacher education" yielded eight articles in Google Scholar, 21 in ERIC, and 10 in PsycINFO. A search for the combined "urban education" and "diversity" resulted in 13 articles in Google Scholar, 7 in ERIC, and 9 in PsycINFO. In this chapter, we concentrate on literature that succinctly focused on teachers' subject matter knowledge, pedagogical content knowledge, as well as racial and cultural knowledge to explain essential aspects of preparing teachers to teach in urban schools. This literature was reviewed and conceptualized because teachers' knowledge emerged as an essential element in their development for teachers in urban sociopolitical contexts. Moreover, we draw from these areas because they are evident in the literature in responding to the guiding questions above. We will frame this chapter with an explicit stance on the need for more direct calls for rethinking the manner in which teachers are prepared to teach and work in urban schools. Our synthesis of the aforementioned knowledge represents the focus of our discussion and is where we transition our focus after a look at the changing face of urban schools and defining urban education. We conclude with a discussion of broad challenges that need to be considered by researchers, theorists, policy makers, and practitioners to move the field of teacher education forward in the preparation of teachers for urban education.

In short, teachers are not being well prepared to teach in urban schools across the United States, which is directly connected to their performance in these schools (Darling-Hammond, 2010; Sleeter, 2001). Indeed, a growing number of scholars have made the claim that one of the most significant steps that can be taken to improve urban schools is to ensure that all student have access to highly qualified, and skillfully trained teachers (Cornbleth, 2008; Howard, 2010; Milner, 2005). We contend that a one-size-fits-all approach to teacher preparation has not adequately served all students well—namely, children in urban schools. If there is to be improved outcomes in urban schools, teachers need to be prepared in a manner that allows them to acquire the essential knowledge, skills, and dispositions that are uniquely situated for work in urban schools; anything less than this will reify the chronic failure of schools to educate students (Irvine, 1990) in urban schools, with ill-prepared teachers being one of the major culprits bringing about this reality.

Changing Face of a Nation and Schools

Over the past two decades, the United States has experienced unprecedented demographic transformation. According to demographers, the types of racial, ethnic, and cultural increases witnessed in large urban cities such as Los Angeles, New York, Miami, and Chicago are now engulfing other cities across the nation (Banks, 2007). The changing demographics nationally have given public schools and teacher education the arduous task of providing a high-quality education to an increasingly different student population than that which existed a decade ago, much less several decades ago. More concerning than the changing demographics in the nation's schools are the persistent underachievement rates of students who come from culturally diverse and low-income backgrounds (Howard, 2010; Jencks & Phillips, 1998). Researchers have uncovered a litany of data that reveal that many students in urban schools continue to disproportionately underachieve in comparison to their counterparts in suburban schools (Jencks & Phillips, 1998; Johnson & Viadero, 2000; Orfield, 2004). These disturbing realities have led to a call to examine the manner in which teachers are prepared to meet the complex challenges that await them in the nation's schools in general and urban schools in particular.

There are currently over 1,400 teacher education programs across the United States. As the student population has changed, the number of teachers who are close to retirement has increased dramatically, which has prompted many researchers to examine the impending "teacher shortage" that appears inevitable (Buckley, Schneider, & Shang, 2004), especially in mathematics and science (Vasquez Heilig & Jez, 2010). While teacher education programs have sought to provide hard-to-staff school districts with more qualified teachers, a more disconcerting factor has been the high rate of teacher attrition in many urban school districts (Darling-Hammond, 2010). Research has shown that approximately one-third of all beginning teachers leave the profession within the first four years (Benner, 2000; Rowan, Correntti, & Richard, 2002), and as many as 50% of teachers leave during this time period in urban schools (Zeichner, 2010). Many teachers are underprepared to meet the complexities and demands common in urban schools that contribute to their decisions to leave the profession (Milner, 2012a; Weiner, 2006). Thus, while many teacher education accrediting agencies have continued to place an emphasis on teacher preparation programs to meet various diversity standards, it goes without question that many believe that preparation in most teacher training programs falls terribly short in this area.

In response to the high turnover rate of teachers in urban schools, a number of scholars have made the call for revising teacher education (Cochran-Smith, 1995, 2004; Irvine, 2009; Ladson-Billings, 1999), others have called for curricular reform in teacher education in a manner which pays special attention to multicultural and social justice–oriented approaches to preparing teachers (Banks, 2001; Gay, 2000; Irvine, 2009; Nieto, 2004), while some have suggested a more radical altering of the political and economic structures in the United States that influence schools and the teachers and students who occupy those spaces (Anyon, 2005; Giroux, 1992). While each of these areas merits further investigation and undoubtedly has implications for the current and future educational climate, the focus of this work is on the preparation of teachers who are being prepared to work in urban schools. Before engaging in an informed discussion of teacher preparation for urban schools, it is essential to bring clarity to the concept "urban schools."

Defining Urban Education

Typically educational researchers and practitioners when using the term *urban* offer it as a euphemism for Black, Brown, and poor students. Others associate the term *urban* with large districts, being near a center city, or other characteristics that run the gamut that would include chronic school failure, limited parental engagement, teacher apathy, and high administrative turnover.

Milner (2012b) offered a typological framework in a quest to help clarify urban. He described three types of urban districts. The first is *urban intensive,* which refers to large cities in which schools are located. The size and density of a particular community makes these environments unique. Cities such as Los Angeles and New York, with populations in excess of 1 million people, provide a layer of intensity in that sometimes limited resources are expected to service an immense number of students in schools and the surrounding city. What sets these cities apart from other cities is their size—the density of them. These environments would be considered intensive because of the sheer number of people in the city and consequently the schools. In these cities, the infrastructure and large numbers of people can make it difficult to provide necessary and adequate resources to the large numbers of people who need them. In sum, urban intensive speaks to the size and density of a particular locale; the broader environments, outside of school factors such as housing, poverty, and transportation, are directly connected to what happens inside of the school.

A second type of urban Milner described is *urban emergent,* wherein schools and districts are in large cities but typically have populations smaller than 1 million people; nonetheless, these cities are fraught with many of the same challenges as urban intensive schools, but not on the same scale. Finally, Milner conceptualized *urban characteristic* as a third dimension of the framework where districts are not necessarily located in or even near large cities but can be located in suburban or rural areas. Yet, these communities are beginning to experience some of the shifts and realities seen in much larger districts—increasingly diverse populations, increases in the number of immigrant families and students, and those from lower socioeconomic backgrounds. These points are salient within our argument, because the idea is that in many instances, teacher education programs are preparing teachers for classrooms that no longer exist. It is common for teachers to report that they wish to teach in rural or suburban districts, and these teachers believe their decision shields them from challenges teachers face in urban emergent and urban intensive environments (Milner, 2010, 2012a).

The realities of large, growing cities and districts is that there is a need to rethink the manner in which teachers are equipped to work with students who possess a wide array of academic, linguistic, psychological, social, and emotional needs. In many ways, all teachers are seeing some, if not many, of the characteristics that are seen in urban intensive schools, even in urban emergent and urban characteristic contexts. Hence, the need to be explicit about preparing teachers within an urban framework is more critical now than ever before, and all teachers should be prepared to teach within an urban framework because they may indeed teach in urban-like settings.

Several areas emerged as essential to understanding and preparing teachers to teach in urban classrooms. We focus on knowledge—what teachers know and *should know*—in this chapter, although we realize that teacher knowledge is only part of a much more complex and dynamic process of learning and being able to teach in urban environments. The areas we cover below are subject matter knowledge, pedagogical content knowledge, as well as racial and cultural knowledge. We conclude with a discussion of broad challenges that need to be addressed to move the field of teacher education forward in the preparation of teachers for urban schools and education.

Subject Matter Knowledge

Amidst the ongoing debates regarding the professionalization of teaching, the roles of varying governing bodies over certification, and the essential skills needed to teach, subject matter and pedagogical knowledge have consistently emerged as important areas of teacher knowledge (Cochran-Smith, Feiman-Nemser, McIntyre, & Demers, 2008; Shulman, 1987) and consequently practice (Milner, 2010). The importance of subject matter knowledge has been part of the discourse regarding teacher preparation and a characteristic of effective teaching for at least the last two centuries (Darling-Hammond & Bransford, 2005). The claim has always been straightforward and transparent—teachers should have a deep knowledge of the subject areas (e.g., mathematics, language arts, social studies, history, science, art, physical education) that they teach (Shulman, 1987; Munby, Russell, & Martin, 2001; Wilson, Shulman, & Richert, 1987) in order to be effective with their students. More important, a litany of research has revealed that teachers who have strong background knowledge in their content areas are more comfortable in their command of content, feel more efficacious, are better equipped to help lower-performing students, and typically have higher outcomes than their counterparts who do not have deeper levels of subject matter knowledge (Darling-Hammond, 2000; Goldhaber & Brewer, 2000). The U.S. Department of Education and the American Board for the Certification of Teacher Excellence (2003) both advocate that mastery of subject matter knowledge and verbal ability are the only empirically supported characteristics of high-quality teachers.

An increasing amount of research has been dedicated to examining the influence subject matter knowledge has on teacher effectiveness and student learning, and the findings from these studies have been mixed. Floden and Meniketti (2005) provided an exhaustive review of the correlations between subject matter and teacher effectiveness. Their findings revealed that the mere exposure to subject matter alone does not ensure high levels of teacher effectiveness. In short, Floden and Menikettti argued that additional empirical research is needed, but what they were clear about was that teachers' mastery of subject matter combined with the ability to convey content could improve teaching and learning.

The area where there appears to be the most empirical research is in the field of secondary mathematics, where a positive association between the study of math and learning of math by students was found in several studies (see Wenglinksy, 2002, Wilson, Floden, & Ferrini-Mundy, 2001; Wilson & Floden, 2003). Monk (1994), using data from the Longitudinal Study of American Youth, found that the amount of college coursework that math and science teachers have taken in their subject matter areas was positively related to student achievement gains. Similar research by Begle (1979) and Goldhaber and Brewer (2000) also found that content area expertise makes a difference in student learning. However, in the areas of English and social studies, there is limited research showing a relationship between subject matter knowledge and student learning.

Given the significant attention to subject matter knowledge that teachers are supposed to have in order to be successful, a number of states have taken steps to ensure teacher candidates have adequate amounts of subject matter knowledge before entering the classroom. Assessment measures such as *Praxis I,* which measures basic skills in reading, writing, and mathematics, in addition to licensure, and *Praxis II,* which assesses subject-specific content knowledge, as well as general and subject-specific teaching skills that candidates need before beginning teaching, are a step in the right direction in terms of ensuring that all teachers are prepared with the subject matter knowledge necessary for success in the P–12 classroom. In addition to assessments such as the *Praxis I and II,* many states require additional subject matter exams. In California, for example, teacher candidates are required to pass the California Subject Exam for Teachers (CSET), which is mandated by the California Commission on Teaching Credentialing. The purpose is to provide an additional layer of subject matter proficiency for teachers in training.

At the national level, in an attempt to establish criteria for teaching excellence, the National Board for Professional Teaching Standards (NBPTS) also stressed the importance of subject matter knowledge for teaching. Established in 1987, the NBPTS sought to advance the quality of teaching and learning in U.S. schools through a rigorous certification process. NBPTS certification requires teachers to possess a repertoire of instructional strategies coupled with content mastery to help all students maximize learning. National Board Certification is based on five core propositions that teachers must show through mastery:

1. Teachers are committed to students and their learning
2. Teachers know the subjects they teach and how to teach those subjects to students
3. Teachers are responsible for managing and monitoring student learning
4. Teachers think systematically about their practice and learn from experience
5. Teachers are members of learning communities.

While researchers continue to evaluate the intricacies of how teachers' mastery of subject matter knowledge contributes to learning outcomes across all subject matter, what is clear is that students who attend urban schools are more likely to have teachers who do not have subject matter mastery, and are less likely to have national board certified teachers (Howard & Aleman, 2008; Roza & Hill, 2004). A broad message here is that this lack of knowledge likely correlates with ineffective teachers that, in turn, results in less than admirable results on standardized test scores for students in urban sociopolitical contexts. It is painstakingly clear that one of the most critical steps that can be taken to reform urban schools is to ensure that every student has access to highly trained teachers, and an essential teacher characteristic is mastery of subject matter content. Darling-Hammond (2010) called for the creation of

> a high quality, nationally available teacher performance assessment for beginning teachers, measuring actual skill in the content areas, [that] would contribute to this effort to raise the bar dramatically on the quality of preparation. In states that have already used them, these assessments have been strong levers for improving preparation and mentoring, as well as determining teachers' competence. (p. 315)

In addition to the fact that teachers in urban contexts are the least likely to have strong mastery in their subject matter area, increasing subject matter knowledge may not be enough in the grand scheme of preparing teachers to be effective in urban classrooms. Some researchers, teacher educators, policy makers, teachers, and principals believe that subject matter expertise is the only real important contributor to student and teacher success. However, Haberman (1995), building from 40 years of research on teachers of urban and high-poverty students, explained that while it is essential for teachers to know their content/subject matter, this is insufficient for the kind of work necessary to be successful in urban and high-poverty schools. He maintained that many teachers fail in high-poverty urban environments because they do not have the ability to connect with students and build relationships with them so that students are willing to participate in learning. In this way, subject matter knowledge is necessary but is insufficient in meeting the needs of students living in urban environments.

Pedagogical Content Knowledge

Although some research has shown that mastery of subject matter is the most essential aspect of effective teaching, others contend that the mere knowledge of subject matter alone is insufficient for teachers to work in schools in general and urban schools in particular (Haberman, 1995; Milner, 2010). Equally essential, we have found from our own work and our review of the extant literature, is teachers' ability to teach that subject matter to students. Methods or approaches to teaching—pedagogy—are equally as important as subject matter knowledge. This includes breadth and depth in the critical concepts, themes, and skills most germane to the subject, which would allow the content to be presented in a multitude of ways (Grossman, Schoenfeld, & Lee, 2005). Each of the major areas of study—English, language arts, mathematics, social studies, and science—has established essential content standards that embody central concepts of the discipline, and each area stresses content and process as part of the mastery of the subject. Some research has shown while teachers who have majored in the area they are teaching are more likely to increase student achievement (Monk, 1994; Monk & King, 1994), teachers who have a rich, deep, or organizationally clear concept of their subject area in a manner suitable for teaching may be more effective in teaching that material to students (Ball & Bass, 2000; Ma, 1999). Any discussion of core skills for teaching in urban schools should pay careful attention to the importance of how content is delivered or made accessible to learners. During the early part of the 20th century, the issue of pedagogy, or instructional approaches, became increasingly common in discussions of teacher training and was considered an important attribute of effective teaching. Shulman (1986) helped to advance the thinking on pedagogical content knowledge:

> The most regularly taught topics in one's subject area, the most useful forms of representations of those ideas, the most powerful analogies, illustrations, examples, explanations, and demonstrations, in a word, ways of representing and formulating the subject that makes it

> comprehensible to others. Pedagogical content knowledge also includes an understanding of what makes the learning of specific topics easy or difficult; the conceptions and preconceptions that students of different ages and backgrounds bring with them to the learning of those most frequently taught topics and lessons. (pp. 9–10)

Shulman's notion of pedagogical content knowledge was predicated on the contention that subject matter and pedagogy were often treated as two distinct, separate domains. He suggested instead that the intersection of the two concepts provided a clear blending of how they could be organized in a manner that makes learning more accessible to learners. Although Shulman dramatically influenced thinking in the field regarding pedagogical content knowledge, he was not the first to discuss the importance of the role of pedagogy. John Dewey (1897) suggested that the educational process "has two sides—one psychological and one sociological; and that neither can be subordinated to the other or neglected without evil results following" (p. 78). Drawing on Dewey's and Shulman's ideas, teacher educators across the United States have made a more concerted effort for training programs to emphasize the role of subject matter, pedagogy, and the pedagogical content knowledge nexus. Some have contended, however, that the shift to pedagogical content knowledge has come at the expense of the necessary emphasis on content knowledge (Ball & McDiarmid, 1990).

More than a decade ago, Ball (1990) found that the mathematics teachers in her study were not acquiring the necessary content knowledge in teacher education programs. Ball reminded us that the subject matter [knowledge] preparation

> of teachers is rarely the focus of any phase of teacher education. Instead, everyone is willing to assume that it [the learning of content/subject matter] will happen somewhere else: prior to college, in liberal arts classes, from teaching. (p. 465)

Not focusing on subject matter knowledge in teacher education programs points to a "danger," as Ball described it, that teacher education programs need to take seriously and responsibly. Today, perhaps even more than ever in the past, teacher education programs must provide prospective teachers with subject matter knowledge in addition to the pedagogical knowledge necessary to meet the needs of a culturally diverse student population and particularly in urban contexts.

Reynolds (1995) discovered some similar findings around the void of knowledge acquired among teachers in teacher education programs. That is, while Ball found that teacher education students did not receive the necessary subject matter experience and instruction in teacher education programs, Reynolds found that students—future teachers—were not receiving the necessary pedagogical knowledge to make meaningful instructional decisions as they worked to meet the needs of "differences" among students. Reynolds explained that prospective and beginning teachers had

> difficulty seeing the pedagogical implications of student differences, even though they may be able to detect overt differences among students. Thus, they are unable to tailor materials and instruction to individuals, which results in lessons that are only superficially appropriate for the subject matter and students. (p. 216)

Several decades later, the problem is not necessarily that prospective and beginning teachers seem to continue experiencing "difficulty [in] seeing the pedagogical implications of student differences." But rather, it seems that teacher education programs and prospective teachers are still struggling to help students work through these difficulties—especially with an eye toward student diversity in particular locations (e.g., urban environments).

Helping teachers develop knowledge is an essential aspect to preparing them to teach in urban classrooms. We have focused on teachers' subject matter knowledge and pedagogical knowledge. Although the established literature in these two areas mentions outside-of-school factors and other critical aspects of urban education such as race, socioeconomic status, and language, this literature does not provide a wide and compelling look at the need to help teachers develop cultural knowledge—knowledge about and tools to learn about the cultural background, characteristics, and experiences of their students. Indeed, teachers need to know a range of information—from how to best organize their classroom to maximize student learning to how to best handle discipline problems when they present themselves in the classroom. Teachers need to know their subject matter, how to teach it, and they need to understand the contextual idiosyncrasies as they work to teach that content.

Racial and Cultural Knowledge

A third dimension of knowledge necessary for successful teaching and learning in urban contexts is racial and cultural knowledge. The idea that race and culture should be an integral part to the education of teachers is not new and was conceptualized by pioneers in education through their scholarship (DuBois, 1903; Woodson, 1933). In addition, for several decades, research related to race, racism, and culture have been prevalent in teacher education (Cochran-Smith, 1995; Foster, 1997; King, 1991; Ladson-Billings, 1999; Shujaa, 1994). In its simplest conceptions, research has suggested that teachers need to build knowledge about and be aware of the racial and cultural background of students in order to address the range of needs students bring to school.

Accomplishing this racial and cultural form of knowledge construction in teacher education has been extremely complex—perhaps more difficult than that of subject matter and pedagogical content knowledge. For instance, Cochran-Smith (1995) maintained that she had

> become *certain only of uncertainty* [our emphasis added] about how and what to say, whom and what to have student teachers read and write, and about who can teach whom, who can speak for or to whom, and who has the right to speak at all about the possibilities and pitfalls of promoting a discourse about race and teaching. (p. 546)

Where race and racism were concerned, much of Cochran-Smith's concerns focused on the curriculum in teacher education and how to develop curricula and related experiences that can successfully prepare students for life in the P–12 classroom and also how to study these issues.

Student responses to cultural and racialized curricula experiences in teacher education vary. For instance, Milner and Smithey (2003), consistent with Cochran-Smith's (1995) research, found student responses to race-central discussions, assignments, and activities on a classroom level ranged from students' being receptive to them and reporting new levels of insights and consciousness[1] for their P–12 student needs, to students' being resentful and not understanding why or how such foci are necessary. Brown's (2004) explanation of the lack of interest, growth, and understanding among teachers in developing racial and cultural knowledge is consistent with the research of Banks (1995) and Irvine (1992). Brown insisted,

> Resentment is frequently reflected on teacher evaluations, whereas resistance is apparent in inadequate pre-class preparation, reluctance to engage in class discussions and activities, and a lack of commitment to required cross-cultural interactions and research. (p. 326)

A critical element in supporting teachers in developing racial and cultural knowledge concerns teachers' inability to connect with students and to construct curriculum and instructional practices consistent with the needs of all learners (Gay, 2010; Howard, 2010). Racial and cultural congruence and incongruence often were used as frames to discuss the complexities embedded in preparing teachers to meet the needs of *all* students in urban schools (Irvine, 2003; Milner, 2010). In other words, because White teachers and students of color, in certain ways, possess different racialized and cultural experiences and repertoires of knowledge and knowing, both inside and outside the classroom, racial and cultural incongruence may serve as a roadblock for academic and social success in the classroom (Irvine, 2003). However, as Gay (2000) explained, "similar ethnicity between students and teachers may be potentially beneficial, but it is not a guarantee of pedagogical effectiveness" (p. 205). Hence, teachers from any ethnic, cultural, or racial background can be successful with any group of students when the teachers possess (or have the skills to acquire) the knowledge, attitudes, dispositions, and beliefs necessary to meet the needs of their students (Ladson-Billings, 2009; Milner, 2010).

Building racial and cultural knowledge about their students requires that teachers attend to their own deep-rooted beliefs, ideologies, and values. A growing number of scholars have called for greater attention to be given to the political values, ideologies, and beliefs that teachers bring to the classroom in order to understand them in relation to their students (Duncan-Andrade, 2009; Gay, 2010; Howard, 2003, 2010; Ladson-Billings, 2009; Milner, 2010). Moll and Arnot-Hopffer (2005), for example, explained the need for teachers to have "ideological clarity" about the work they do, and to recognize that teaching is always a political endeavor (Anyon, 2005). They stressed that ideological clarity requires that teachers have an awareness of the political economy in which urban schools operate, recognize the extensive cultural capital that students bring to the classroom, and know how to take advantage of the rich array of cultural, social, and community resources that reside within their classrooms and within the students that they teach. They make a call for helping teachers develop sociocultural competence if they are to be effective working in urban schools.

Grounded in the building of racial and cultural knowledge, there is a need to have a deep understanding of the sociopolitical context of urban communities, how they have changed over time, and the larger historical set of factors that continue to influence them. Much of the understanding of critical consciousness emerged from the concepts of critical pedagogy, and critical educational theorists. Critical educational theorists clearly advocate that teachers must first understand that schools are sociopolitical spaces (Anyon, 1988). Moreover, critical theorists in education assert that schools are spaces where social hierarchies and social practices are reified through curriculum, policy, pedagogy, daily interaction, discipline, and punishment. Because all school practices are embedded in these larger institutional social structures, many critical theorists see educational institutions as prime contributors to ideological hegemony (Anyon, 1988; Giroux, 1988; Macedo, 2000; McCarthy & Crichlow, 1993; McClaren, 2003), and a critical aspect to teachers building racial and cultural knowledge lies in their ability to understand these issues. Duncan-Andrade and Morrell (2008) went one step further and maintained:

> Let us begin by rethinking the position that urban schools are failing. Given the overwhelming body of evidence that reveals decades of funding and structural inequalities between schools in high- and low-income communities . . . it is illogical to compare schools across these communities and then decry urban schools as failures. When one set of schools is given the resources necessary to succeed and another group of schools is not, we have predetermined winners and losers. In this scenario, failure is not actually the result of failing. . . . On the one hand, urban schools are producing academic failure at alarming rates;

> at the same time, they are doing this inside a systematic structural design that essentially predetermines their failure. Urban schools are not broken; they are doing exactly what they are designed to do. (p. 1)

Part of developing a racial and cultural knowledge with the goal of critical consciousness is centered on the idea of recognizing the complexities of urban schools, their too often chronic underperformance, and inept organizational systems that reinforce existing class structures (Spring, 2006).

Milner (2003) explained that it is important for teacher education programs to be able to help teachers facilitate difficult dialogue across racial and cultural differences, which is a key component of critical consciousness. Moreover, he maintained that given the racial and cultural dynamics that are ever present in urban classrooms, teachers who do not possess the ability to pose tough questions would have a challenging time becoming effective teachers in culturally and racially diverse schools, particularly urban schools. Ullucci and Beatty (2011) called for an explicit dialogue with White preservice teachers in particular around race and Whiteness. They offered a framework steeped in the tenets of color consciousness that interrogates individualism, meritocracy, Whiteness, and neutrality. They reported that such a framework is desperately needed with White preservice teachers because

> Students frequently resist these lines of conversation, creating intellectual roadblocks that in a domino-like way stymie further talk about culturally relevant teaching, critical pedagogy, and equitable schooling in general. When students enact a color-blind perspective, it automatically challenges the legitimacy of our work. Why do students need a course on race and education if they have decided race plays *no role in education?* (p. 1196)

Bigelow (1995) supported the idea of incorporating a more transformative approach to teaching and learning, and argued that introducing critical pedagogy, where students (teachers) learn to critique injustices in the larger world, encourages students to view the world with a critical lens so that they can learn to ask "why?" and "what can we do about it?" (pp. 292, 304). Moreover, Bigelow observed that a critical pedagogy curriculum

> should examine past and present times when people worked together to challenge injustices; include meetings with real individuals and organizations who[/that] actively work towards a more egalitarian society; and empower students themselves to see themselves as capable of joining together to change the world and create a more equal and humane society. (p. 303)

Pedagogical approaches and instructional strategies are common in the teacher education literature regarding the building of cultural and racial knowledge among teachers. As Irvine (2009) has explained, the curriculum of teacher education needs to be drastically and radically reformed in order to meet the needs of culturally diverse learners, Milner (2010) offered several constructs and principles essential for inclusion in any teacher education program committed to helping teachers build racial and cultural knowledge. The framework encompassed five interrelated tenets essential in building racial and cultural knowledge: colorblindness, cultural conflicts, meritocracy, deficit mindsets and low expectations, as well as context-neutral mindsets and practices. In short, the idea is for this framework to serve as a guide for teacher education programs interested in helping students disrupt previously conceived notions and simultaneously build a cultural and racial knowledge base essential for practice in urban and highly diverse schools.

A summary of the literature on subject matter and pedagogical knowledge suggests there is a need for additional research. This research does show that subject matter makes a difference in teacher knowledge, but it is essential to develop a better understanding of how teachers' subject matter proficiency plays out across all subject matters, and across grade levels. In an era of standardized testing, and increasing restriction on teacher certification, the field of teacher education can benefit from additional inquiry into how, why, and in what ways content and pedagogy inform teacher knowledge, and subsequently their practices and student outcomes. It is also vital for work on this topic given explicit attention to the levels of mastery currently held by teachers in urban schools. At a time when teachers in urban school are often given highly scripted curricula, and seemingly rendering pedagogy meaningless, it is imperative to see how teachers modify and in some cases subvert calls for restrictive curriculum.

The need to build and understand racial and cultural knowledge is equally as important as subject matter and pedagogy. Yet, there is a need for more research evaluating the influence of teachers' racial and cultural knowledge on student outcomes, students' social and emotional well-being, and their overall development. We also need to know more about the relationship of teachers' racial and cultural knowledge to their practices—what they do and do not do. What is clear from a summary of the work on race and culture in teacher education is that a stronger call for recognizing, understanding, and implementing racial and cultural knowledge is emerging. Yet, what is lacking is empirically based assessment that looks at teacher education programs that explicitly address this topic, as well as any longitudinal inquires that assess how students fare with teachers who do or do not possess and utilize this information.

Challenges in Teacher Education for Urban Education

We conclude this chapter with several areas that need serious attention in order to advance the field of teacher education for urban schools and urban education. The three aspects of knowledge discussed above (subject matter knowledge, pedagogical knowledge, and racial and cultural knowledge) need to continue being investigated and understood along with effective practices to better meet the needs of teachers for students in urban environments. However, it is difficult to advance the field related to these dimensions of knowledge as well as in other areas due to broader problems that need to be addressed. Cochran-Smith and Zeichner (2005) provided a compelling, more developed, synthesis of some of the critiques below specific to teacher education. In teacher education for urban education, we face

- an *epistemological issue:* it is difficult to study teacher education for urban schools because it is not clear what teacher education programs are covering them, whether traditional or nontraditional. How do we know what we know in the field regarding urban education and what worldviews are privileged over others in our studies of teacher preparation for urban schools?
- a *discourse dissonance* issue: related to epistemology, it is difficult to build a strong knowledge base because there is not a consistent and common vocabulary in teacher education (Cochran-Smith & Zeichner, 2005) for urban schools. The varied constructs that different teacher education researchers and programs employ in their studies and program structures and outcomes make it difficult to draw logical connections between and among studies. Cochran-Smith and Zeichner (2005) reported the difficulty in expanding the knowledge base in teacher education because of the inconsistency of language used among and between researchers. In this way, it is difficult to build knowledge about the preparation of teachers for urban education because of the variation of discourse used in the field.

- *a theoretical issue:* it is difficult to build theory about teacher education for urban schools because the literature and knowledge base is so scattered. The theoretical issue is at least threefold: What relevant and useful analytic tools are, could be, and should be employed to explain teacher education practices for/in urban schools? How do we build theoretical knowledge *from the ground up* to conceptualize practices in teacher education for urban schools? And how do we theorize about urban education in P–12 urban classrooms/contexts for teacher education?
- *a practice issue:* it is unclear how practices, such as student teaching and practicum experiences, are carried out across and between different teacher education programs. Moreover, at present, there is no way to gauge the links between what teachers are learning in teacher education and their actual practices (in P–12 urban schools) with students.
- *a racial demographic issue:* the racial demographic of teacher educators is also a concern that needs to be addressed in thinking about what gets covered in teacher education programs, especially because students of color in urban contexts are too often on the margins of teaching and learning. Some teacher educators are underprepared themselves to prepare teachers to teach for diversity and equity (Merryfield, 2000). We need to be concerned about the racial demography of teacher educators. It is wrong to assume that teacher educators are committed, capable, or prepared automatically to prepare teachers to meet the complex needs of students in P–12 urban environments; it certainly cannot be assumed that they are committed philosophically, theoretically, practically, or empirically to develop, enact, and study a curriculum that is consistent with the needs of students in urban schools, for example. Figures 11.1 and 11.2 summarize racial demographic realities of teacher educators.

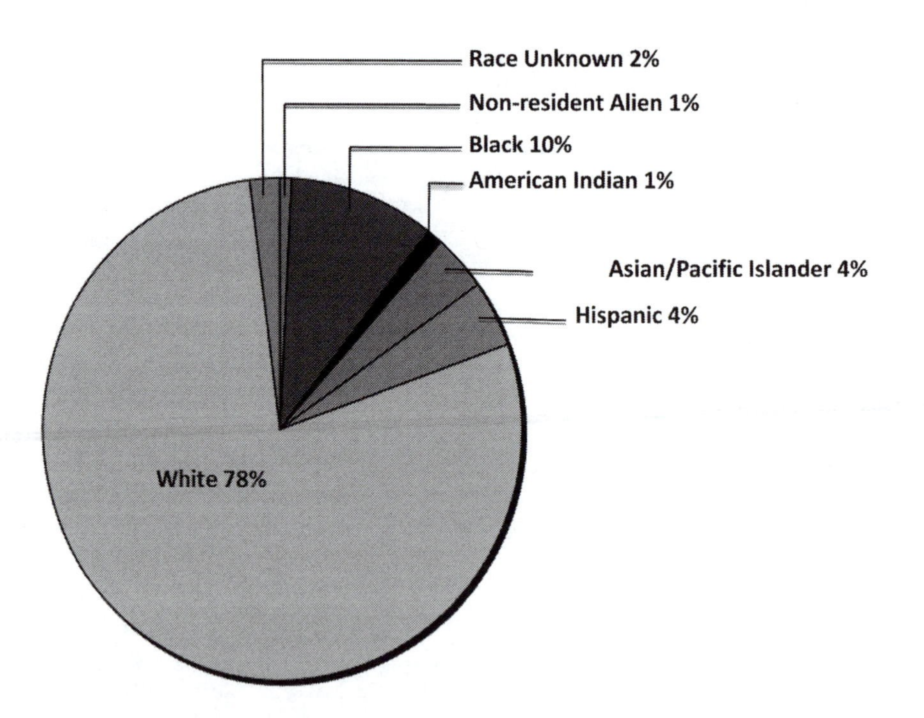

Figure 11.1 An emerging picture of the teacher preparation pipeline race and ethnicity of full-time faculty in professional education programs, Fall 2007. Adapted from Ludwig, Kirshstein, Sidana, Ardila-Rey, & Bae (2010).

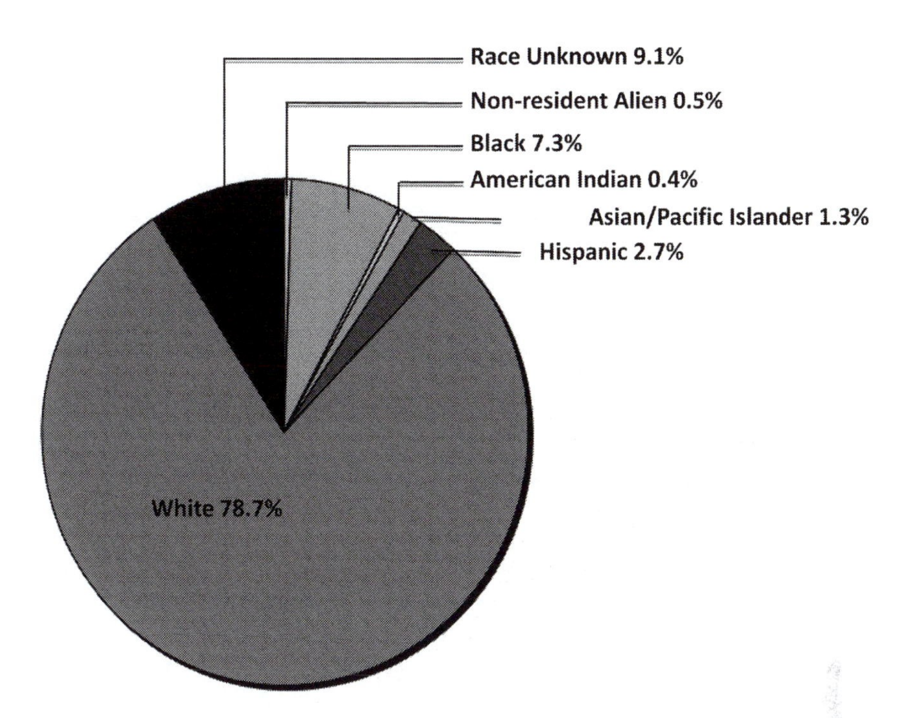

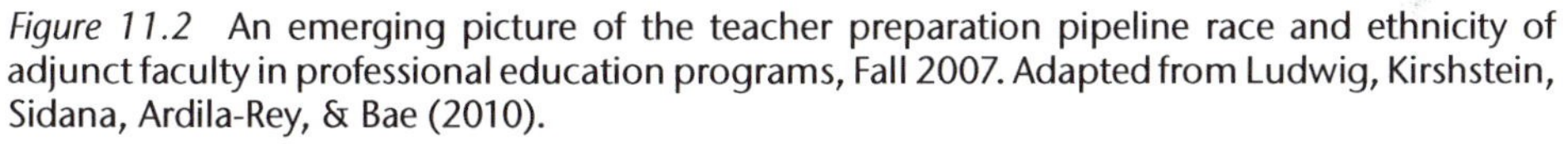

Figure 11.2 An emerging picture of the teacher preparation pipeline race and ethnicity of adjunct faculty in professional education programs, Fall 2007. Adapted from Ludwig, Kirshstein, Sidana, Ardila-Rey, & Bae (2010).

The racial demographic information above is representative of both full-time and adjunct faculty in teacher education programs. We have included racial demographic data of adjunct faculty in addition to full-time faculty, considering the fact that a representative number of teacher education programs across the United States rely on adjunct instructors to teach in teacher education. The idea here is that having a more racially diverse cadre of teacher educators could potentially benefit the preparation of teachers as they work to prepare teachers for racially diverse students in urban schools.

- *a research issue:* ultimately and collectively, these epistemological, discourse construction, theoretical, and practice issues can make it difficult to meaningfully study teacher education for urban schools. How do we study teacher education for urban schools in a way that allows us to deepen and broaden our knowledge about theory, research, policy, and practice? Pondering this question requires that we negotiate and navigate our knowledge construction in both teacher education and urban education. How can we build research agendas and trajectories that deeply and meaningfully allow us to know more about, theorize more sophisticatedly about, and develop practices that contribute to sustainable and productive *urban* teacher education programs?

Conclusions and Implications

The research literature suggests that what teachers know and believe impact what P–12 students have the opportunity to learn in school. In a sense, knowledge is practice in that what teachers know or come to know influences what happens in the classroom—the curriculum and instructional decisions teachers make, how they interact with students, how they manage the classroom, and how they assess students' learning and progress. Theory related to teachers' knowledge and its place and importance are well established (see, for instance, Carter, 1990; Clark & Peterson, 1986; Shulman, 1987). There has been, on some level, an evolution of sorts as we think about what is central and salient knowledge for teachers in public schools; that is, Shulman's (1987) work pointed to the necessity of teachers' subject matter knowledge and pedagogical content knowledge. Other researchers (Ball & Tyson, 2011; Ladson-Billings, 1999; Sleeter, 2001) have also stressed the necessity for teachers to develop racial and cultural knowledge in learning to teach. How best to help teachers develop these multiple layers of knowledge has long been a struggle for teacher education programs and is not an easy task. Perhaps the struggles that teacher education programs are facing stem from the peculiar, multifaceted nature of teaching and learning to teach. Moreover, the struggles that teacher education faces in preparing teachers to teach all students effectively (especially in urban environments) is, we argue, also a function of much broader challenges in teacher education such as discourse problems, research problems, and demographic problems. Essentially, the skill of linking theory to practice, connecting practice to theory, and the conceptual change that is necessary for teachers to move from novice to expert in an era of reform are complicated issues that require some serious rethinking. However, to address these matters in substantive ways in teacher education requires that, as a field, we address broader challenges that can allow us to advance what we know (theoretically and conceptually) and how we know it (empirically and epistemologically) in the field.

Note

1. Clearly, it is not enough for teachers in teacher education to learn about race and to develop expanded insights about racism in teacher education classrooms. These issues must also be considered in field placements, such as student teaching and practicum opportunities.

References

American Board for the Certification of Teacher Excellence. (2003). *American Board for the Certification of Teacher Excellence: Promoting teacher quality—impacting student learning.* Available from http://www.abcte.org

Anyon, J. (1988). Schools as agencies of social legitimation. In W. Pinar (Ed.), *Contemporary curriculum discourses* (pp. 175–200). Scottsdale, AZ: Gorsuch Scarisbrick.

Anyon, J. (2005). *Radical possibilities.* New York, NY: Routledge.

Ball, A.F., & Tyson, C.A. (Eds.). (2011). *Studying diversity in teacher education.* Lanham, MD: Rowman & Littlefield and the American Educational Research Association.

Ball, D.L. (1990). The mathematical understandings that prospective teachers bring to teacher education. *Elementary School Journal, 90*(4), 449–466.

Ball, D.L., & Bass, H. (2000). Interweaving content and pedagogy in teaching and learning to teach: Knowing and using mathematics. In J. Boaler (Ed.), *Multiple perspectives on the teaching and learning of mathematics* (pp. 83–104). Westport, CT: Able.

Ball, D.L., &. McDiarmid, G.W. (1990). The subject matter preparation of teachers. In R. Houston (Ed.), *Handbook of research on teacher education* (pp. 437–449). New York, NY: Macmillan.

Banks, J.A. (1995). Multicultural education: Historical development, dimensions, and practice. In J.A. Banks & C.A. McGee Banks (Eds.), *Handbook of research on multicultural education* (pp. 3–24). New York, NY: Simon & Schuster.

Banks, J.A. (2001). Citizenship education and diversity: Implications for teacher education. *Journal of Teacher Education, 52*(5), 5–16.

Banks, J.A. (2004). Multicultural education: Historical development, dimensions, and practice. In J.A. Banks & C.A.M. Banks (Eds.), *Handbook of research on multicultural education* (2nd. ed) (pp. 3–24). San Francisco: John Wiley & Sons..

Banks, J.A. (2007). *An introduction to multicultural education* (4th ed.). Boston, MA: Pearson Allyn & Bacon.

Barton, P.E., & Coley, R.J. (2010). *The black-white achievement gap: When progress stopped.* Princeton, NJ: Educational Testing Services.

Begle, E.G. (1979). *Critical variables in mathematics education: Findings from a survey of the empirical literature.* Washington, DC: Mathematical Association of America.

Benner, A.D. (2000). *The cost of teacher turnover.* Austin, TX: Texas Center for Educational Research. Retrieved from http://www.sbec.state.tx.us/SBECOnline/txbess/turnoverrpt.pdf

Bigelow, B. (1995). Inside the classroom: Social vision and critical pedagogy. In W. Ayers & P. Ford (Eds.), *City kids, city teachers: Reports from the front row* (pp. 292–304). New York, NY: New Press.

Boger, J.C., & Orfield, G. (2005). *School resegregation: Must the South turn back?* Chapel Hill, NC: University of North Carolina Press.

Brown, E.L. (2004). What precipitates change in cultural diversity awareness during a multicultural course: The message or the method? *Journal of Teacher Education, 55*(4), 325–340.

Buckley, J., Schneider, M., & Shang, Y. (2004). *The effects of school facility quality on teacher retention in urban school districts.* Washington, DC: NationalClearinghouse for Educational Facilities. Retrieved from http://www.edfacilities.org/pubs/teacherretention.pdf

Carter, K. (1990). Teachers' knowledge and learning to teach. In M.C. Wittrock (Ed.), *Handbook of research on teaching* (pp. 291–310). New York, NY: Macmillan.

Chubb, J.E., & Loveless, T. (Eds.). (2002). *Bridging the achievement gap.* Washington, DC: Brookings Institution Press.

Clark, C.M., & Peterson, P.L. (1986). Teachers' thought processes. In M.C. Wittrock (Ed.), *Handbook of research on teaching* (pp. 255–296). New York, NY: Macmillan.

Cochran-Smith, M. (1995). Color-blindness and basket making are not the answers: Confronting dilemmas of race, culture, and language diversity in teacher education. *American Educational Research Journal, 32,* 493–522.

Cochran-Smith, M. (2004). The problem of teacher education [Editorial]. *Journal of Teacher Education, 55,* 295–299.

Cochran-Smith, M., Feiman-Nemser, S., McIntyre, D., & Demers, K. (Eds.). (2008). *Handbook of research on teacher education* (3rd ed.). New York, NY: Routledge.

Cochran-Smith, M., & Zeichner, K. (Eds.). (2005). *Studying teacher education.* Mahwah, NJ: Lawrence Erlbaum Associates.

Cornbleth, C. (2008). *Diversity and the new teachers: Learning from experience in urban schools.* New York, NY: Teachers College Press.

Darling-Hammond, H. (2000). Teacher quality and student achievement: A review of state policy evidence. *Education Policy Analysis Archives, 8*(1). Retrieved from http://epaa.asu.edu/epaa/v8n1

Darling-Hammond, L. (2010). *The flat world and education: How America's commitment to equity will determine our future.* New York, NY: Teachers College Press.

Darling-Hammond, L., & Bransford, J. (Eds.). (2005). *Preparing teachers for a changing world.* San Francisco, CA: Jossey-Bass.

Delpit, L. (2012). *Multiplication is for white people: Raising expectations for other people's children.* New York, NY: New Press.

Dewey, J. (1897). My pedagogic creed. *School Journal, LIV*(3), 77–80.

DuBois, W. E. B. (1903). *The souls of Black folks.* New York, NY: Fawcett.

Duncan-Andrade, J. M. R. (2009). Note to educators: Hope required when growing roses in concrete. *Harvard Educational Review, 79*(2), 1–13.

Duncan-Andrade, J. M. R., & Morrell, E. (2008). *The art of critical pedagogy.* New York, NY: Peter Lang.

Floden, R., & Meniketti, M. (2005). Research on the effects of coursework in the arts and sciences and in the foundations of education. In M. Cochran-Smith & K. Zeichner (Eds.), *Studying teacher education* (pp. 261–308). Mahwah, NJ: Lawrence Erlbaum Associates.

Foster, M. (1997). *Black teachers on teaching.* New York, NY: New Press.

Gay, G. (2000). *Culturally responsive teaching.* New York, NY: Teachers College Press.

Gay, G. (2010). *Culturally responsive teaching: Theory, research, and practice* (2nd ed.). New York, NY: Teachers College Press.

Giroux, H. (1988). Border pedagogy in the age of postmodernism. *Journal of Education, 170*(3), 162–181.

Giroux, H. (1992). *Border crossings: Cultural workers and the politics of education.* New York, NY: Routledge.

Goldhaber, D.D., & Brewer, D.J. (2000). Does teacher certification matter? High school teacher certification status and student achievement. *Education Evaluation and Policy Analysis, 22*(2), 129–145.

Grossman, P.L., Schoenfeld, A., & Lee, C.D. (2005). Teaching subject matter. In L. Darling-Hammond & J. Bransford (Eds.), *Preparing teachers for a changing world* (pp. 201–231). San Francisco, CA: Jossey Bass.

Haberman, M. (1995). *Star teachers of children in poverty.* West Lafayette, IN: Kappa Delta Pi.

Howard, T.C. (2003). Culturally relevant pedagogy: Ingredients for critical teacher reflection. *Theory Into Practice, 42*(3), 195–202.

Howard, T.C. (2010). *Why race and culture matters: Closing the achievement gap in America's classrooms.* New York, NY: Teachers College Press.

Howard, T.C., & Aleman, G.R. (2008). Teacher capacity for diverse learners: What do teachers need to know? In M.C. Smith, S. Feiman-Nemser, D.J. McIntyre, & K.E. Demers (Eds.), *Handbook of research on teacher education* (pp. 157–174). New York, NY: Routledge.

Irvine, J.J. (1990). *Black students and school failure: Policies, practices and prescriptions.* New York, NY: Greenwood Press.

Irvine, J.J. (1992). Making teacher education culturally responsive. In M.E. Dilworth (Ed.), *Diversity in teacher education* (pp. 779–792). San Francisco, CA: Jossey-Bass.

Irvine, J.J. (2003). *Educating teachers for diversity: Seeing with a cultural eye.* New York, NY: Teachers College Press.

Irvine, J.J. (2009). *The caring behaviors of African American teachers.* Paper presented at the Annual Meeting of the American Educational Research Association, San Diego, CA.

Jencks, C., & Phillips, M. (Eds.). (1998). *The black-white test score gap.* Washington, DC: Brookings Institution Press.

Johnson, R.C., & Viadero, D. (2000, March 15). Unmet promise: Raising minority achievement. *Education Week, 19*(27), 1, 18–19.

King, J.E. (1991). Dysconscious racism: Ideology, identity, and the miseducation of teachers. *Journal of Negro Education, 60*(2), 133–146.

Ladson-Billings, G. (1999). Preparing teachers for diversity: Historical perspectives, current trends, and future directions. In L. Darling-Hammond & G. Sykes (Eds.), *Teaching as the learning profession. Handbook of policy and practice* (pp. 86–123). San Francisco, CA: Jossey-Bass.

Ladson-Billings, G. (2006). From the achievement gap to the education debt: Understanding achievement in U.S. schools. *Educational Researcher, 35*(7), 3–12.

Ladson-Billings (2009). *The dreamkeepers: Successful teachers of African American children* (2nd ed.). San Francisco, CA: Jossey-Bass.

Ludwig, M., Kirshstein, R., Sidana, A., Ardila-Rey, A., & Bae, Y. (2010). *An emerging picture of the teacher preparation pipeline: A report by the American Association of Colleges for Teacher Education and the American Institutes for Research for release at the briefing: Teacher preparation: Who needs it? What the numbers say.* Washington, DC: American Association of Colleges for Teacher Education and American Institutes for Research.

Ma, L. (1999). *Knowing and teaching elementary mathematics: Teachers' understating of fundamental mathematics in China and the United States.* Mahway, NJ: Lawrence Erlbaum Associates.

Macedo, D. (2000). *Chomsky on miseducation.* New York, NY: Rowan & Littlefield.

McCarthy, C., & Crichlow, W. (1993). Introduction: Theories of identity, theories of representation, theories of race. In C. McCarthy & W. Crichlow (Eds.), *Race, identity, and representation in education*. New York, NY: Routledge.

McClaren, P. (2003). *Life in schools: An introduction to critical pedagogy in the foundations of education* (4th ed.). New York, NY: Addison Wesley Longman.

Merryfield, M.M. (2000). Why aren't teachers being prepared to teach for diversity, equity, and global interconnectedness? A study of lived experiences in the making of multicultural and global educators. *Teaching and Teacher Education, 16*, 429–443.

Milner, H.R. (2003). Reflection, racial competence, and critical pedagogy: How do we prepare pre-service teacher to pose tough questions? *Race Ethnicity and Education, 6*(2), 193–208.

Milner, H.R. (2005). Stability and change in prospective teachers' beliefs and decisions about diversity and learning to teach. *Teaching and Teacher Education, 21*(7), 767–786.

Milner, H.R. (2010). *Start where you are, but don't stay there*. Cambridge, MA: Harvard Education Press.

Milner, H.R. (2012a). Challenges in teacher education for urban education. *Urban Education, 47*(4), 700–705.

Milner, H. R. (2012b). But what is urban education? *Urban Education, 47*(3), 556–561.

Milner, H.R. & Smithey, M. (2003). How teacher educators created a course curriculum to challenge and enhance preservice teachers' thinking and experience with diversity. *Teaching Education, 14*(3), 293–305.

Moll, L. C., & Arnot-Hopffer, E. (2005). Sociocultural competence in teacher education. *Journal of Teacher Education, 56*(3), 242–247.

Monk, D.H. (1994). Subject area preparation of secondary mathematics and science teachers and student achievement. *Economics of Education Review, 13*(2), 125–145.

Monk, D.H., & King, J. (1994). Multilevel teacher resource effects on pupil performance in secondary mathematics and science: The role of teacher subject matter preparation. In R.G. Ehrenberg (Ed.), *Contemporary policy issues: Choices and consequences in education* (pp. 29–58). Ithaca, NY: ILR Press.

Munby, H., Russell, T., & Martin, A.K. (2001). Teachers' knowledge and how it develops. In V. Richardson (Ed.), *Handbook of research on teaching* (4th ed., pp. 877–905). Washington, DC: American Educational Research Association.

Nieto, S. (2004). Affirming diversity. *The sociopolitical context of multicultural education*. Boston, MA: Pearson.

Orfield, G. (2004). *Dropouts in America*. Cambridge, MA: Harvard Education Press.

Pino, N.W., & Smith, W.L. (2004). African American students, the academic ethic, and GPA. *Journal of Black Studies, 35*(1), 113–131.

Reynolds, A. (1995). The knowledge base for beginning teachers: Education professionals' expectations versus research findings on learning to teach. *Elementary School Journal*, 95(3) 199–221.

Rowan, B.R., Correnti, R. & Richard, R.J. (2002). *What large-scale survey research tells us about teacher effects on student achievement*. Philadelphia, PA: Consortium for Policy Research in Education, University of Pennsylvania. Retrieved from http://www.cpre.org/Publications./rjr51.pdf

Roza, M., & Hill, P. (2004). How within-district spending inequities help some schools to fail. In D. Ravitch (Ed.), *Brookings Papers on Education Policy* (pp. 201–218). Washington, DC: Brookings Institution Press.

Shujaa, M.J. (1994). *Too much schooling, too little education: A paradox of Black life in White societies*. Trenton, NJ: Africa World Press.

Shulman, L.S. (1986). Those who understand: Knowledge growth in teaching. *Educational Researcher, 15*(2), 4–14.

Shulman, L.S. (1987). Knowledge and teaching: Foundations of the new reform. *Harvard Educational Review, 15*(2), 4–14.

Sleeter, C.E. (2001). Epistemological diversity in research on preservice teacher preparation for historically underserved children. *Review of Research in Education, 25*, 209–250.

Spring, J. (2006). *Deculturalization and the struggle for equity: A brief history of the education of dominated cultures in the United States*. Columbus, OH: McGraw-Hill Higher Education.

Ullucci, K., & Beatty, D. (2011). Exposing color blindness/grounding color consciousness: Challenges for teacher education. *Urban Education, 46,* 1195–1225.

Vasquez Heilig, J., & Jez, S.J. (2010). *Teach for America: A review of the evidence.* Boulder, CO and Tempe, AZ: Education and the Public Interest Center & Education Policy Research Unit. Retrieved from http://epicpolicy.org/publication/teach-for-america

Weiner, L. (2006). *Urban teaching: The essentials.* New York, NY: Teachers College Press.

Wenglinsky, H. (2002). How schools matter: The link between teacher classroom practices and student academic performance. *Education Policy Analysis Archives, 10*(12). Retrieved from http://epaa.Asu.edu/epaa/v10n12?

Wilson, S., Shulman, L., & Richert, A. (1987). "150 different ways of knowing": Representations of knowledge in teaching. In J. Calderhead (Ed.), *Exploring teachers' thinking* (pp. 104–123). Eastbourne, UK: Cassell.

Wilson, S.M., & Floden, R.E. (2003). *Creating effective teachers—concise answers for hard questions: An addendum to the report Teacher Preparation Research: Current knowledge, gaps, and recommendations.* Washington, DC: ERIC Clearinghouse on Teaching and Teacher Education.

Wilson, S.M., Floden, R.E., & Ferrini-Mundy, J. (2001). *Teacher preparation research: Current knowledge, gaps, and recommendations.* Seattle, WA: Center for the Study of Teaching and Policy.

Woodson, C.G. (1933). *The mis-education of the Negro.* Washington, DC: Associated Publishers.

Zeichner, K. (2010). Rethinking the connections between campus-based courses and field experiences in college and university-based teacher education. *Journal of Teacher Education, 89*(11), 89–99.

12

Grow Your Own Teachers for Urban Education

Eric Toshalis

Introduction

Those of us working in P–12 education and teacher preparation are by now quite used to the relentless "sky is falling" assessments of our public school classrooms. Our teaching, research, advocacy, and policy making seem to play out against a dreary backdrop of disturbing "achievement gaps," alarming dropout rates, staggering teacher attrition statistics, vast cultural misunderstandings, enormous budget shortfalls, and decaying infrastructures. But such assertions—heartbreakingly accurate though they may be—often eclipse the pioneering success stories that counteract some of these problems. Preferring to dwell on our forest of dysfunction, we sometimes miss those trees of innovation.

Seeking to participate in a reversal of this trend, I review in this chapter the creation and expansion of "grow your own" (GYO) teacher education programs in the United States and focus specifically on those that serve urban settings. GYO programs are designed to recruit, support, and prepare educators to return to teach in the communities from which they spring. In many cases, they represent the end product of legislatures,' districts,' universities,' and communities' collaborative efforts to create and sustain a youth-centered, culturally responsive, multitalented, and locally accountable teacher workforce. GYO programs tend to target four separate groups for recruitment: middle or high school aged youth, postservice military veterans, paraprofessional educators, and mid-career transitioning professionals. In this chapter, I focus solely on those programs aimed at preparing middle and high school students for careers in education because it is those programs that most capture the whole span of urban teacher development, from the aspirations of youth to the induction of professionals. As I will show, these "pipeline" programs (Sleeter & Milner, 2011) offer not only rigor, relevance, responsiveness, and reform, but also that priceless component that is so critical to successful urban education: hope.

This chapter is organized around the answers to three questions:

1. What problems in urban education do GYO programs seek to remedy?
2. What models for secondary GYO teacher education programs have been developed in the United States, and what commonalities and differences exist among these models?
3. What do the answers to these questions suggest about the most promising future directions in GYO program development?

Surveying various policies, curricula, organizational structures, and institutional collaborations across numerous states, this chapter characterizes both longstanding and emerging trends found in research literature and in state, district, and school program documentation. By providing an overview of the field, the treatment is intended to highlight the potential for GYO programs to remedy multiple ills in urban education and the teacher preparation pipeline in hopes that greater attention will be focused on GYO programs and increased dedication of resources to them may follow.

Grow Your Own Programs: One Solution to Many Challenges in Urban Education

GYO programs provide solutions to a variety of problems associated with urban education. In this section, the focus is primarily on the extent to which GYO programs address the need for: (1) approaches that ameliorate drop-out/push-out factors, address the developmental needs of marginalized youth, and reduce the various "achievement gaps"; (2) policies that reduce teacher burnout and attrition and address disparities in the distribution of highly qualified educators; (3) recruitment, training, and induction programs capable of producing culturally responsive teachers; and (4) methods of teacher education that avoid the liabilities of fast-track teacher education programs.

Because GYO programs' structures and processes differ depending on the school, district, state, and the nature of partnerships with institutions of higher education, there is no single standardized version to which we might refer here. During the last decade of school reform in which uniformity of process and outcome is often an implicit if not explicit goal, the plurality of GYO programs may be mistakenly cast as a deficit. In the rush to standardize and "scale up" successes in urban education, the expectation that all will adhere to a norm is often assumed, but in this case that assumption is problematized. The diversity of GYO programs—indeed, their *lack* of uniformity—is a key aspect of their success. GYO programs represent unique if not idiosyncratic responses to homogenizing educational mandates in that they each emerge from and attempt to respond first to localized contexts more than national directives. That said, it is clear GYO programs do in fact address numerous macro-level trends in urban education and teacher education. In this way, GYO programs think globally but work locally. This section offers a brief survey of those trends to help contextualize the extent to which GYO programs, in all their diversity, often directly ameliorate some of the most pernicious problems in urban education.

GYO Programs Promote Academic Achievement, Ameliorate "Push-Out" Factors, and Reduce "Achievement Gaps"

GYO programs capitalize on an array of key findings from adolescent psycho-social developmental research. Studies demonstrate that in order to succeed academically and behave prosocially, youth need to belong (Baumeister & Leary, 1995; Chhuon & Wallace, 2012), to discern a purpose (Damon, Menon, & Bronk, 2003, #4979; Kerpelman, Eryigit, & Stephens, 2008; Strayhorn, 2009), and to formulate an identity that is affirmed by peers and significant adult figures (Erikson, 1968; Helms, 1990; Marcia, 1980; Nakkula & Toshalis, 2006; Rodriguez, 2008; Tatum, 1999; Ward, 1989). These needs are specifically addressed in many GYO programs in their use of cohort models, vocational discernment processes, and identity affirmations as both members and future leaders of educational communities. Abundant research in the field of achievement motivation suggests that academic work is often most productive when it is aligned with students' intrinsic motivators (Reeve, 2006; Ryan & Deci, 2000; Toshalis & Nakkula, 2012; Wentzel, 2005) and experiencing a sense of belonging and purpose are among the most powerful internally held motivators a student can possess (Demanet & Van Houtte, 2012; Singh, Chang, & Dika, 2010; Van Ryzin, Gravely, & Roseth, 2009). Achievement motivation is also enhanced by relevancy in curricula such that students can see how they are being prepared for a future they desire and are provided with a viable school-to-career pathway (Kerckhoff, 2002; Museus, Harper, & Nichols, 2010; Orr, 2009; Skorikov & Vondracek, 2007). When GYO programs name students as college bound and headed for a profession, they teach youth that they do not have to sever ties with home in order to be academically and vocationally successful. This forward-looking trajectory coupled with an ongoing community rootedness can be tremendously motivating for those youth who feel marginalized by "subtractive" schooling experiences (Chun & Dickson, 2011; Conchas, Oseguera, & Vigil, 2012; Gándara & Rumberger, 2009; Harris, 2011; Menken & Kleyn, 2010; Suárez-Orozco & Suárez-Orozco, 2009; Umaña-Taylor et al., 2008; Valenzuela, 1999) that too often focus on perceived student deficits rather than build on their assets. However, when an educator identifies a teenager as someone with the potential to contribute to and even lead a community, that educator sends profound messages that convey a sense of trust, confidence, and hope. In fact, one study has shown that the greatest predictor of students' active consideration of "teaching as a career is simply whether or not other individuals have discussed this possibility with them" (Page & Page, 1984), which further supports the powerful influence teaches can have on students' vocational decision making when students are understood in terms of their gifts rather than their deficiencies. When teachers encourage and prepare youth to become their future colleagues and serve the community they call home, future aspirations, achievement motivation, academic performance, social and cultural capital all can be greatly enhanced.

GYO Programs Reduce Teacher Attrition and Address Disparities in Distribution

GYO programs are often created, in part, as vocational schools designed to provide underserved youth specific pathways into college and educational professions. That they serve youth is ideal, but such programs also promise to help solve the problems of teacher distribution and attrition. Multiple studies have demonstrated that new teachers tend to gravitate toward those settings that most mirror or are geographically closest to the ones they attended when they were students (Boyd, Lankford, Loeb, & Wyckoff, 2005; Darling-Hammond, 2004; Storm, 2009, 2011; Strong, 2005). Given the predominantly White, middle-class, and female teacher workforce, this leads to a skewed distribution of teachers that overstock suburban districts and understaff urban and rural ones. Such skewing is pervasive across the landscape of public education. It is projected that by the year 2020, 48% of the nation's school-aged children will be students of color (Milner, 2003, p. 197), increasing to 56% by the year 2050 (Easter et al., 1999, p. 205). While student populations are becoming more diverse, however, a full 86% of all elementary and secondary teachers remain White. The percentage of so-called racial minority teachers has shrunk to an all-time low of 5%, with a full 42% of all public schools in the United States possessing no "minority" teachers whatsoever (Franklin, 2003, p. 7). By targeting students of color, first-generation college attendees, and those from households struggling with poverty, GYO programs are poised to reverse these trends.

Likewise, considerable research investigating the so-called achievement gaps (Ferguson, 2003; Haberman, 2003; Hatt, 2007; Rushton & Jensen, 2005) points to the inequitable distribution of talent among the teacher workforce as a key factor in disproportionate failure rates among minoritized and poor students. As Haycock (2001) observes, "students in high poverty schools are more likely than other students to be taught by teachers without even a minor in the subjects they teach" and "only about half the teachers in schools with 90 percent or greater minority enrollments meet even their states' minimum requirements to teach those subjects" (p. 10). By recruiting teachers from a school's surrounding community and preparing them in traditional postbaccalaureate programs, GYO programs are well positioned to reverse the "achievement gap" by first recognizing it as a personnel problem—as a "teaching gap," per se.

Related to teacher distribution is the issue of teacher attrition. Teacher "burnout" has been linked to a variety of factors, not the least of which is cultural misunderstanding between teachers and students who do not share the same or even similar backgrounds (Haberman, 2005; Palmer, 2007; Weiner, 2003). Haberman (2005) explained that teachers often leave the profession "because they cannot connect with the students and it is a continuous, draining hassle for them to keep students on task. In a very short period, leavers are emotionally and physically exhausted from struggling against resisting students for six hours every day" (p. 162). He later added this observation: "The fact that most teachers are [W]hite and that most stress and burnout occurs in schools serving predominantly diverse children in poverty is highly significant. So too is the fact that the highest attrition rates for new teachers is in schools serving minority populations" (2005, p. 168). Each of these factors is directly addressed if not ameliorated by many GYO programs' emphasis on preparing teachers to serve in the communities they most understand—their own.

GYO Programs Produce Culturally Responsive Teachers

Variously conceived, culturally responsive teaching (Bondy, Ross, Gallingane, & Hambacher, 2006; Borjian & Padilla, 2010; DiAngelo & Sensoy, 2010; Gay, 2000; Milner, 2010; Santamaria, 2009; Sensoy & DiAngelo, 2012; Sleeter, 2012; Villegas & Lucas, 2002; Ware, 2006; Weinstein, Curran, & Tomlinson-Clarke, 2003) is largely understood as an essential component of successful urban education in the 21st century. To understand youth, families, communities, and schools, educators must explicitly and implicitly recognize the salience of race, ethnicity, socioeconomic status, linguistic heritage, and culture (among other categories) in everyday classroom interactions. For teachers who differ from their students in any one of these respects, learning how to appreciate and orient toward (rather than avoid or dismiss) such differences can be a tremendously difficult task on top of already full lesson-writing, test-giving, and paper-grading workloads. To address this situation, researchers have argued that it may be best to focus our efforts not on trying to teach privileged teachers how to do this work, but rather to focus more of our efforts on recruiting, preparing, and sustaining teachers who come from *within* the communities where such teachers are most needed (Education Commission of the States, 2003; Hill & Gillette, 2005; Irizarry, 2007; Villegas & Lucas, 2002; Zeichner, 2003). Studies repeatedly underscore the difficulties associated with learning culturally responsive teaching methods and how they are often a make-or-break situation in postbaccalaureate teacher education programs where preservice teachers of privilege sometimes struggle to extricate themselves from deficit modes of thinking and injurious pedagogies that blame the victims of social inequity rather than interrogate the structures that perpetuate injustice (see, for example: Aveling, 2004; Case & Hemmings, 2005; Daniel, 2009; de Freitas, 2005; DiAngelo & Sensoy, 2012; Gallavan, 2005; Grant & Gillette, 2006; Hytten & Warren, 2003, #30131; Maher & Tetreault, 2009; Marx, 2004; Marx & Pennington, 2003; Sleeter, 2001; Toshalis, 2011; Ullucci & Battey, 2011). Left unaddressed, these tendencies can contribute to alienating and oppressive climates in schools that may further marginalize already minoritized students. But, these trends can be reduced if not eliminated when members of urban communities become teachers within these communities.

Synthesizing decades of research on the quality and preparedness of those seeking to become educators in urban settings, Martin Haberman lists a "set of background factors which are predictive of what kind of people will be effective and remain in schools serving diverse students in poverty" (2010, n.p.), factors that are directly addressed in GYO urban education programs. (For an exhaustive list of these factors, see Haberman, 2010.) Though Haberman warns the attributes he conceptualizes "do not guarantee success as an urban teacher," he does contend that "they raise the probability that individuals with these attributes will succeed and remain." As will be evident in the analysis below, the necessity to *learn* how to be culturally responsive and community accountable is provided naturally in GYO programs simply because the teachers-in-training are already longstanding members of the community they intend to serve.

GYO Programs Address Problems Created by Fast-Track Teacher Preparation

To fill teacher vacancies due to attrition, retirement, and population growth, many states and districts have resorted to a host of alternative certification programs designed to make the pathway into the classroom simpler, shorter, or both. The research suggests that many of these programs, Teach for America chief among them, may overaccelerate teacher preparation, deprofessionalize teaching, underappreciate the time required to develop an adequate pedagogical skill set, perpetuate problematic "save the savage" models of service, and create a revolving door of educators who are rarely capable of understanding, much less meeting, the unique needs of underserved urban communities (Achinstein et al., 2010; Darling-Hammond, 2008; Darling-Hammond, Holtzman, Gatlin, & Heilig, 2005; Falk, 2012; Guarino, Santibañez, & Daley, 2006; Kumashiro, 2010; Labaree, 2010; Ladson-Billings, 1999; Peske & Haycock, 2006; Schonfeld & Feinman, 2012; Veltri, 2008). Such programs may indeed fill vacancies in school staffing, but they often perpetuate problems due to faculty turnover and the lack of sustained pedagogical talent and the accumulation of institutional memory. In contradistinction, recent scholarship evaluating an array of alternative certification programs suggests that given "the proper mix of candidates' backgrounds, program supports, and school placement" some nontraditional models of teacher preparation "can produce new teachers who are effective starting on the first day of school" (Humphrey, Wechsler, & Hough, 2008, p. 39). Many GYO programs represent this "proper mix" by targeting recruitment in underserved communities then supporting students through college and in credential programs where field placements are established in home communities (see, for example, the ITRP, SCCTR, AHSTP, and UTAP programs described below).

Though many alternative certification programs shorten the distance from college graduation to full-time classroom teaching and accelerate the pace of preparation for nontraditional, mid-career transitioning professionals, GYO programs typically seek the opposite. Taking the long view that frames quality teacher preparation as a lengthy process involving the slow cultivation of content proficiency, context sensitivity, community embeddedness, and age- and culturally appropriate practices, many GYO programs commit to teachers the way many schools want teachers to commit to their communities—for the long haul.

Models of Secondary-Level Grow Your Own Programs

Though the need for widespread, rigorous, and well-supported GYO programs may be most pronounced now, the idea to structure secondary vocational education and teacher preparation in this manner is anything but new. Two decades ago, the DeWitt Wallace/Reader's Digest Fund commissioned a study by Recruiting New Teachers, entitled *Teaching's Next Generation: A National Study of Precollegiate Teacher Recruitment* (1993). It remains the most comprehensive study of youth-oriented GYO programs to date. Using data gathered nationwide and summarizing multiple components such as program objectives and student representation, origins in legislative action or school-university partnerships, national distribution and localized density, diversity of structure and curricula, and what were then emerging data on evaluation, effectiveness, and replication, the paper provides an invaluable snapshot of the GYO movement nearly two decades ago. Though this study identified more than 200 programs across the nation (many of which still exist), the need for an updated accounting is clear when one considers Phi Delta Kappa's Future Educators Association (FEA), the organization to which many GYO programs now belong, which currently lists a total of 442 chapters dispersed across 40 states (FEA, 2012, http://www.futureeducators.org/ about/chapters.htm). To systematically compare such programs (and countless others not captured by FEA's membership) so that patterns can be discerned in how they are structured, implemented, and evaluated would require a vast dataset beyond the scope of this chapter. However, significant developments since the *Teaching's Next Generation* report are worth noting, and it to those items that this analysis now turns.

To generate a representative cross-sectional view of the contemporary context of GYO programs, I chose to limit the number of analyzed components (see listing below). Because I narrowed my focus to urban programs that prepare middle and high school aged youth for careers in education, this analysis does not include programs that target paraprofessional educators, mid-career transitioning professionals, or soldiers transitioning out of military service, though such programs are key contributors to the development of a diverse and culturally responsive professional educator workforce. As stated above, I am restricting my analysis to youth-oriented programs because they most capture the whole span of urban teacher development, from the germination of career aspirations to the induction into the profession. Using the Recruiting New Teachers original report (1993) to help set the scope of the search, I have focused my analysis on five broad areas both because they effectively characterize the current state of the field and because the information was readily available from institutional or online sources. These five areas are:

1. state legislation and/or district-level policies that created such programs;
2. funding sources that support program and scholarship development;
3. recruitment and retention efforts that specifically target secondary students interested in teaching, and any data on their relative success or failure;
4. curricula that have been developed or used to prepare youth for careers in teaching;
5. delegation of responsibilities and distribution of accountability among state, district, university, school, and community officials.

After retrieving relevant documents directly from institutions and/or from online sources, I compared and contrasted the above characteristics of each program. Data were drawn primarily from texts of legislation or initiatives passed by state or district governing bodies, online descriptions of program components and pathways, website explanations, curricular materials, funding and budget reports, recruitment documents, and scholarship details. Secondary sources from newspaper articles, periodicals, and journal articles were used to contextualize descriptions found from the above sources, and I conducted several in-person interviews at a GYO program near where I lived. After gathering all data, I generated a broad cross-sectional assessment of GYO programs nationwide and noted the areas of greatest consistency and variance.

Analysis and Findings

At least 11 states now support GYO programs with varying levels of legislative, financial, and institutional commitment, and there are dozens—perhaps hundreds—of localized programs that exist outside of state funding structures. According to South Carolina's Center for Educator

Recruitment, Retention, and Advancement (CERRA), 33 states beyond South Carolina have implemented or infused its Teacher Cadet Program curriculum into their future teacher programs (CERRA, n.d., http://www.teachercadets.com/training.aspx) though the extent of this implementation and infusion is unclear. The Future Educators Association (FEA) reports that at the beginning of 2012 they had "over 11,000 members . . . 30% of whom were from historically underrepresented populations in the teaching workforce" (FEA, 2012, http://www.futureeducators.org/about/history-21st-century.htm). As mentioned above, the FEA's website lists over 400 active chapters dispersed across 40 states (FEA, 2012, http://www.futureeducators.org/ about/chapters.htm) with some states like California, North Carolina, and Nevada having only a few chapters while states like Virginia, Arizona, and New Jersey have 40 or more. These figures suggest that GYO programs have become deeply integrated into some states' overall education and teacher preparation systems while they have yet to even materialize in other states.

Beyond these figures, it is difficult to ascertain the precise number of up-and-running GYO programs in the nation. Programs such as dedicated GYO academies or magnets, after-school clubs, summer courses or camps, and structured tutoring or service learning opportunities all provide vital on-ramps to educational careers, but the idiosyncrasies and scale of their design make them difficult to find, much less compare. Consequently, in this analysis, which is concerned primarily with the extent to which GYO programs target and ultimately serve urban schools, I focus largely on those GYO components found in dedicated academies (i.e., "schools-within-schools" that are typically housed within comprehensive public schools) and magnets (theme-based public schools dedicated to educational careers) as opposed to less-intensive pipeline programs that involve only college visits, conferences and speaker series, and/or tutoring opportunities (Sleeter & Milner, 2011, p. 86). In Figure 12.1, I depict the range of GYO programs nationwide, with the shaded areas indicating where this analysis concentrated.

After investigating the content and design of scores of programs nationwide, I opted to limit my scan to programs that target secondary-level students (as opposed to school-based paraprofessionals,

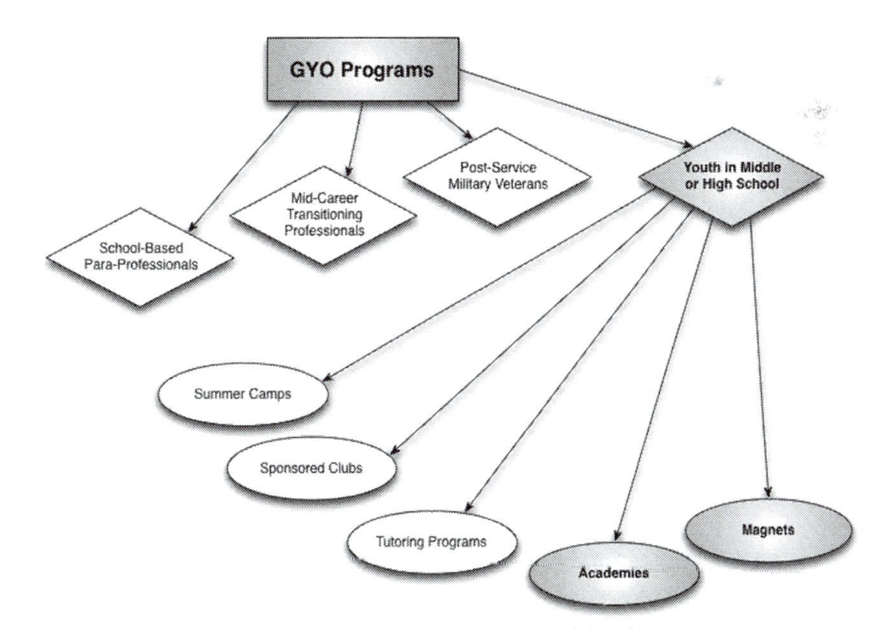

Figure 12.1 A Taxonomy of GYO Programs

mid-career transitioning professionals, or postservice military veterans) in public school settings and I used the search criteria above to identify specific components of those programs that would yield illuminating comparisons. In doing so, I discerned six main areas of consistency and six areas where the programs most varied.

Areas of Consistency

The first area of consistency is the stated purposes of the GYO programs. Promotional brochures, websites, program descriptions, legislative language, and officials quoted in newspaper articles frequently cite the same set of goals that motivate officials to create and sustain their GYO programs. Though they are phrased in a variety of forms, they generally include the following:

- To supply local schools with high-quality teachers who know firsthand the challenges and resources of their community;
- To expand the pool of teachers from underrepresented minorities;
- To prepare culturally responsive and bilingual/bicultural educators to serve the unique needs of a particular region;
- To prepare students to succeed in college, especially students of color from lower socioeconomic backgrounds;
- To stimulate interest in teaching as a career;
- To reduce teacher attrition;
- To recruit and retain science, mathematics, and special education teachers;
- To create public school advocates.

All programs that constitute this study did not endorse all of these goals, but taken as a group, each of the above was prevalent across those surveyed. Together, they suggest that the purpose of GYO programs cannot be reduced solely to a teacher pipeline issue, nor can it be reduced to college preparation or culturally responsive education. Each of these general goals is intimately linked with the others.

For example, the mission statement of Wichita Public Schools' Grow Your Own Teacher (GYOT) program is:

> To increase representation of people of diverse backgrounds at all levels of education in the Wichita Public Schools. GYOT will assist in the development of teachers who reflect the demographics of the community, with a goal of creating an educational system that is sensitive to the needs of all students. (Wichita Public Schools, n.d., http://hr.usd259.org/modules/groups/group_pages.phtml?gid=1505366&nid=127180&sessionid=)

The Mesa Grow Your Own Teachers Program (MGYO) in Arizona states its purposes as follows:

> Teacher recruitment and selection in American public schools is increasingly a cause for concern. Nationwide, principals and administrators who hire teachers confront a shortage in key subject areas like special education, science, and bilingual education. Some regions of the country have an adequate supply of teachers in most subject areas, but school administrators across the country are concerned about the quality of the teacher candidates available to shape our children's future. These two problems of teacher supply and quality are paramount when you consider that the caliber of the teacher as the single most influential variable that we can control in affecting student success in our schools.

> The "Mesa Grow Your Own Teachers" Program (MGYO) is designed to address both of these concerns, in addition to meeting other key objectives.... The premise behind MGYO is straightforward; if we can target promising prospective teachers from among our own students before they graduate, support them in their post secondary training, and ensure that their preparation is compatible with and will enhance Mesa's ability to serve the youngsters in our schools, then we will significantly enrich the pool of teacher candidates available to MPS in the future. (Mesa Public Schools, n.d., http://www.mpsaz.org/guidance/diversity_programs/teachers_program/)

Similarly, the Jefferson County Schools in Louisville, Kentucky, intend to "provide middle and high school students with opportunities to explore teaching/education as a career option [and to help] students gain an understanding of the multi-faceted nature of the education field and the role of the teacher," as well as supply "an exploratory venue for minority students in order to increase the pool of minority educators in Kentucky" (Jefferson County Public Schools, n.d., http://www.jefferson.k12.ky.us/schools/middle/noe/FEA.html; for a detailed analysis of Jefferson County's GYO program, see Storm, 2009). Programs like these explicitly recognize the multi-faceted value of GYO programs and the extent to which they benefit both current and future students in diverse and often underresourced urban schools.

Some GYO programs link the purposes above and direct them into more activist stances in teacher preparation. Organizers of the Paterson Teachers for Tomorrow (PT4T) program in New Jersey, for example, take a more culturally responsive if not critical approach. According to Hill and Gillette (2005), the PT4T program seeks to "challenge, overcome, and change oppressive schooling experiences by questioning and eventually acting upon policies and practices and in public schools that do not lead to equitable access and outcomes" (p. 45). Likewise, the Illinois Grow Your Own Teachers initiative summarizes recent scholarship from Villegas and Irvine (2010) to underscore the value of its program's emphasis on the diversification of the teaching force. At the top of the homepage, it presents the following:

> Policy makers argue for more teachers of color in American classrooms for three major reasons:
>
> 1. Teachers of color produce better academic results for students, notably students of color.
> 2. Teachers of color provide positive effects on teaching and the classroom.
> 3. Teachers of color provide needed teachers in hard-to-staff schools. (GYOT, 2012, http://www.growyourownteachers.org/)

Examples such as these illustrate that a consistency of goals across programs is generalizable only at the meta-level. This may be due to the fact that each GYO organization typically emerges from a specific set of circumstances, drawing from a unique assembly of individuals, and using a distinctive arrangement of assumptions that target local contexts. Though the lack of a nationally unifying set of goals and purposes may stretch the generalizability of these comparisons, the diversity of expression across these programs suggests a common commitment to local responsiveness which may be read, in this era of mandated standardization and forced adherence to the Common Core, as a strength more than a limitation.

Another area of consistency across GYO programs is the prevalence of school-university partnerships. Though few states have created legislation to mandate such alliances, school districts and institutions of higher education have frequently collaborated to facilitate their construction (Hirsch, 2001, p. 8) by using preexisting state funds, writing grants, or creating novel interagency affiliations. In California, for example, there are 33 "partnership academies" supported by state grants in which high schools are required to link up with nearby universities to offer internships, course credit, field trips, research opportunities, and curricular enhancements (full list available at http://www.cde.ca.gov/ci/gs/hs/cpagen.asp). In Arizona, the Mesa Public School District's Grow Your Own Teachers Program partners with Mesa Community College's two separate campuses, Chandler-Gilbert Community College, Arizona State University, Polytech, and Arizona State University, Tempe (Mesa Public Schools, n.d.). The Los Angeles Unified School District collaborated with the California State University system and its multiple Los Angeles–area campuses to create the In-House Teacher Recruitment Program (ITRP). The ITRP is supported by 14 different Teacher Career Academies throughout greater Los Angeles in which "students are prepared for college with a university outreach component that includes many field trips to college campuses and an overview of the path to college . . . [and] are offered scholarships to help pay for their education while they study to become teachers" (LAUSD Career Ladder Office, n.d.). Such partnerships abound in GYO programs since the needs of teacher credentialing institutions of higher education and the school districts that eventually employ their graduates often can be better realized through combined efforts and shared resources. Clarification of and preparation for the many pathways into teaching is often facilitated by interinstitutional cooperation, especially given the confusing and ever-changing array of subject area tests, state-mandated forms, course requirements, program constraints, evaluation instruments, and logged hours each candidate must produce. In short, when GYO programs result from the collaboration of district and university officials, they help demonstrate to the future teacher how to get from high school, to college, to graduate school, and into a job.

A third area of consistency across GYO programs is the use of curricula that targets the intellectual and vocational needs of secondary students learning to become teachers. According to Berrigan and Schwartz (2000), these curricula "cover much of the same material that college-level education departments cover: learning theory, classroom management, multiculturalism, child development, and assessment" (p. 6), and some programs actually provide college credit for courses taken at the high school level. Perhaps the most widely adopted and historically successful curriculum specifically constructed for GYO programs is the one the South Carolina Center for Teacher Recruitment's (SCCTR) created for its Teacher Cadet Program. The *Experiencing Education* curriculum was developed for the Teacher Cadet Program in 1986 and is in its 10th edition. It progresses through four scaffolded investigations, from "Experiencing the Learner," to "Experiencing the Profession," then onto "Experiencing the Classroom," and concluding with "Experiencing Education" (CERRA, 2009). The SCCTR offers a ProTeam Program designed to interest middle school students "in the education profession before they become 'turned off' to the possibility of a career in teaching" (CERRA, n.d.). It also holds a weeklong institute for Black male high school freshmen and another for rising high school seniors interested in teaching (Center for Public Information, n.d.). According to the National Conference of State Legislatures, 18 states currently offer programs and curricula that directly replicate South Carolina's Teacher Cadet Program (National Conference of State Legislatures, n.d.). Some, like Virginia, have adapted its *Experiencing Education* curriculum by producing extensive supplements that are specifically designed to address their state's history and populations (see http://www.cteresource.org/TFTfinalWebFiles/index.html for examples). School officials in Broward County, Florida, produced their own three-part curriculum entitled *Exploratory Teaching, I-III* that extends throughout four years of high school experiences in their Urban Teacher Academy Program (Cech, 2005; Teaching and Leadership Center, n.d.). To prepare secondary students for educational careers, district officials in Mesa, Arizona, have created a junior high *Teens 'n' Teaching* curriculum as well as a high school *Teachers 'n' Training* course (Mesa Public Schools, n.d.). In Houston, Texas, the Austin High School for Teaching Professions (AHSTP) has developed a four-year progression of experiences that weaves coursework with tutoring, internships, and after-school activities (Stephen F. Austin High School, 2009). In each of these examples, the GYO programs have recognized the need for curricula aimed at the unique requirements of educators who teach about teaching and students who learn about learning.

A fourth area of consistency across surveyed programs is the frequent existence of internships or field placements designed to provide "hands-on" experiences for youth who intend to pursue careers in education. Just as the clinical component is crucial to adult teacher preparation programs, providing site-specific experiences in real-life classrooms under the mentorship of seasoned educators, youth-oriented GYO programs also benefit from structured opportunities to experiment, apply, and develop one's pedagogical talents. For these reasons and more, GYO programs routinely incorporate field placements into their organizational and curricula structures. Such precollege internship experiences are typically provided at local elementary or middle schools, and some even place juniors and seniors in freshman or sophomore classrooms as teacher's aides. The range of experiences offered to students often include guest lecturing, tutoring, class observation, and mentorship activities (Recruiting New Teachers, 1993, p. 34). In the Teaching and Educational Careers Academy at Pacifica High School in Oxnard, California (part of the California Partnership Academy system), students spend a few days per week of their 11th-grade elective child development course at a nearby elementary school where they assist teachers, supervise small group work, and present lessons attuned to the developmental needs of the age group they serve (McFadyen, 2008). At the AHSTP in Houston, Texas, students proceed through the following experiences:

> Ninth grade students at AHSTP are given an opportunity to assist classroom teachers on a regular basis. Sophomores & juniors participate in a Big Brother/Big Sister program, and the Franklin Project, tutoring elementary school students. This sequential approach prepares AHSTP students for their senior year and the Educational Internship Course. Here students are assigned to teachers in one of five HISD schools and work 1½ or 2 hours a day as a student intern. (Stephen F. Austin High School, 2009)

In a *Teacher Magazine* article about the success of Broward County's Urban Teacher Academy Program (UTAP), the author recounts a teacher's assessment of what such internships do for sometimes reluctant future teachers:

> "The [teenage] boys are always more reluctant at first," she says quietly. But once they experience what it's like to teach someone something, she adds, smiling, they're hooked. Even on days they're not feeling well and would ordinarily miss school, "they'll drag themselves out of bed to make sure to get here." (Cech, 2005, p. 40)

One teacher in the AHSTP reported, "My students' grades went up, discipline problems decreased, and attendance improved. On the days when the high school students were to be at the elementary school, I usually had 100 percent attendance" (Bonner, 1999). Results such as these indicate the power of GYO programs to motivate and engage students to invest not just in their own academic potential but in others' too.

A fifth area of consistency can be seen in GYO programs' tendency to include college readiness activities as part of their curricular offerings. Since many GYO programs target students who are traditionally underrepresented on college campuses nationwide, significant efforts are frequently devoted to preparing not just good teachers, but good students. Summarizing national research, Hill and Gillette (2005) echo the aims of many GYO programs when they suggest several "key factors that tend to increase student persistence and success in college," especially for those "first generation college students and students of color from low-income families." Those factors are:

> academic preparation, including pre-college programs, social integration, and personal connections on campus; a close connection to the institution, including living on campus and club participation; financial aid; and support including programs that provide mentoring and tutoring services. (Hill & Gillette, 2005, p. 46)

GYO programs in South Carolina, Arizona, Florida, and North Carolina (among others) all specify college readiness as a core component of their approach. Through test preparation, GPA tracking, college visits, guest speakers, financial aid workshops, study skill development, and math/writing remediation, GYO programs specifically address the need for *student* preparation as much as teacher preparation. Given how important achievement motivation (Brophy, 2010; Eccles & Wigfield, 2002; Suárez-Orozco, Pimentel, & Martin, 2009; Van Ryzin et al., 2009; Wigfield & Eccles, 2002), future aspirations (Garg, Kauppi, Lewko, & Urajnik, 2002; La Guardia, 2009; Museus et al., 2010; Strayhorn, 2009), and the ability to envision school-to-career pathways (Finn, 1989; Glover & Marshall, 1993; Kerckhoff, 2002; Skorikov & Vondracek, 2007; Steinberg, Cushman, & Riordan, 1999; Zarrett & Eccles, 2006) are to adolescent school engagement, GYO programs represent an ideal combination of academic and vocational opportunities, particularly for marginalized students.

The last GYO program component that demonstrated consistency across various sites is the use of scholarships and forgivable loans to entice and sustain future teachers. According to Hirsch (2001), as of 2001, 27 states

> offer college scholarships, forgivable loans, or tuition assistance to recruit more high quality teachers and to motivate teachers to serve in shortage areas. . . . Programs in 11 states specifically target academically talented candidates who are required to commit a designated number of years to teaching in K-12 schools. (p. 8)

Another study found that 31 states "make loans that college students do not need to repay if they teach for a specified time after graduation" (Recruiting New Teachers, 1993, p. 21). One state, North Carolina, instituted its Teaching Fellows Program in 1986 and currently offers 500 scholarships per year to 18 college campuses in the state. Each scholarship of $6,500 per year for four years is awarded to high-achieving North Carolina high school seniors who agree to teach for four years after graduating college in one of the state's public or U.S. government schools. If the recipient cannot repay the scholarship through service, the loan is repaid to the state with interest (see http://www.teachingfellows.org/ for details). Florida supports its GYO graduates similarly, through its Teacher Fellowship Program. It provides a "2+2" prepaid scholarship that covers tuition for 60 hours at a community college plus 60 hours of tuition or its equivalent value at one of the nearby participating universities. Upon graduation from the accredited teaching program at the university and receiving the required certification to teach in Florida, the Fellow is guaranteed a full-time teaching position in Broward County Schools. In return, the Fellow agrees to teach in the district one year for each year the Fellow received the scholarship (see http://www.coe.fau.edu/tlc/content/programs-btf-description.htm for details). Virginia and Kansas offer similar programs, and California bundles Perkins and Stafford loans with its Assumption Program of Loans for Education (APLE). In this program, the state assumes up to $11,000 in educational loans as long as the recipient completes four consecutive years of full-time teaching in a designated teacher-shortage field in an eligible California K–12 public school. APLE participants who teach in mathematics, science, or special education may receive both the basic $11,000 and up to $1,000 of additional loan forgiveness during each of four years, and another $1,000 of benefits may be received in each of the four years by those who teach mathematics, science, or special education in a school ranked in the lowest 20 percentile of the state's Academic Performance Index, resulting in a maximum of $19,000 in loan assumption benefits (see http://aple.csusuccess.org/about2 for details). Because many state universities have had to drastically increase their tuitions to offset declines in revenue (e.g., the California State University System raised its tuition over 383% in the decade between 2001 and 2011 [California State University, 2012]), it is more important than ever to attend to the severe costs associated with becoming a teacher. GYO programs are well served by financial incentives that defray or remove costs associated with higher education, thereby allowing those low-income and often underserved students a chance at becoming teachers in the neighborhood they call home.

Areas of Variance

A detailed investigation of how GYO programs vary across states, counties, districts, schools, and communities is beyond the scope of this chapter, but a few remarks about major areas of difference are appropriate. As with any policy initiatives outside of federal control or funding, states vary greatly in their financial and legislative commitments to GYO programs. The Illinois state legislature passed the Grow Your Own Teacher Education Act in 2004, and the program received its first appropriations in 2005, later receiving federal 501(c)(3) status (GrowYourOwnIllinois, n.d.). Other than South Carolina's level of commitment, I could find no other states that have dedicated this level of support to GYO programs. California has its 33 partnership academies and Illinois, New Jersey, Virginia, and South Carolina, for example, each support GYO programs throughout their respective states, but how that support is given and in what amounts varies from state to state, and year by year.

If GYO programs are financially supported, it is often through private foundations. Such is the case with Broward County's UTAP program in Florida and the PT4T Program in Paterson, New Jersey. Recognizing the logic and value of such programs, universities and secondary schools are sometimes able to leverage their influence and social networks to convince funders of the merits of the GYO approach. During the current economic crisis as states must decide which social programs to downsize or cut altogether, it is likely that private sources of support will need to be sought and secured with increasing regularity. Due to their wide-ranging effects and the fact that they leverage preexisting interinstitutional collaboration, GYO programs offer some of the best ways for funders interested in positively affecting urban education to achieve the most long-term impact with the least expenditure.

Another area of significant variety is the existence of instructor training. Few programs match South Carolina's for its comprehensiveness, and that includes its commitment to supporting the educators who teach the GYO courses. For those teaching in or administering its Teacher Cadet Program, a three-day foundational training course is mandated. According to its website, this training

> focuses on the knowledge, skills, and understandings critical to those who work with beginning teachers . . . [and] is guided by the belief that learning to teach is a career-long developmental process that involves continuous cycle of planning, teaching, and reflecting. At the heart of this work is the mentor's ability to respond to each new teacher's individual developmental and contextual needs and to promote the ongoing examination of classroom practice. (CERRA, n.d.)

South Carolina's Teacher Cadet training includes the following exhaustive list of topics:

- State and National Teacher Attrition
- SC Induction and Mentoring Guidelines
- Mentor Selection and Assignments
- Initial and Advanced Trainings
- Professional Development
- Incentives
- Variety of Teachers Supported
- Creating a Vision for Teaching
- Defining Mentoring Roles
- Identifying New Teachers Needs
- Understanding the Attitudinal Phases of New Teacher Development
- Building an Effective Mentoring Relationship
- Selecting Support Strategies
- Establishing an Environment for Professional Growth
- Developing the Language and Behavior of Support
- Highlighting the Role of Professional Standards in Mentoring
- Assessing the Beginning Teacher's Level of Practice

Such commitments, however, are rare. Outside of South Carolina, when there are identified curricula that a particular GYO program uses, it is often unclear how much the instructors are supported to learn and use it. In the case of Oxnard's TECA program, for example, the faculty create their own courses, find their own texts, and adapt whatever materials they can find amid countless other teaching tasks each week (McFadyen, 2008). As with all pedagogical and curricular innovations, it is critical that teachers be supported in learning the content before being expected to teach it, and that significant professional development opportunities exist to sustain that learning over time.

Despite the common goals of GYO programs enumerated above—namely, to produce talented teachers from and for the communities that need them the most—there is considerable variance in employment guarantees upon successful completion of program requirements. Expressed as a binary, either the program promises a job or it does not. Few do, it turns out. Of all the programs examined, only Broward County's UTAP in Florida guarantees its graduates a teaching position in the district upon successful completion of a state-accredited credential program. While there are surely multiple barriers to such guarantees that arise from collective bargaining agreements, budgetary limitations, and fluctuations in vacancies by school and subject area (to name a few), it takes no stretch of the imagination to predict, especially in this economy, that GYO graduates would be relieved to know that their years of work were actually leading toward (not just hoping for) a teaching position in their community of origin. In addition, the guarantee of a job at the end of a long and expensive professional preparation is likely crucial for those students who may be the first in their family to attend college and whose relatives depend on them to stay local and contribute to the extended family's resources, as is often the case with many youth in low-income, urban settings.

Lastly, GYO programs display a wide variety of criteria for admission and matriculation. Required grade-point averages range from 2.5 to 4.0 on weighted and nonweighted scales. Some programs require essays, interviews, and recommendations, while others require merely that the proper enrollment forms be submitted on time. Threshold units in specific content areas needed for admission to college are often adopted as the minimal requirements in GYO programs, but many adopt additional requirements that exceed them. SAT scores are either required or not, and if so, adhere to different minimum values depending on the program. As with pathways into teaching, there seems to be an array of requirements to enter and complete GYO programs. Though this makes cross-program comparison difficult, it is to be expected as each program caters its design to fit the unique needs of its students, schools, and communities. As stated above, amid rampant standardization and forced curricular uniformity, this diversity may be understood as a strength more than a weakness.

Grow Your Own Programs: Promising Direction for Future Work in Urban Education

The 1993 study entitled *Teaching's Next Generation,* while broad and detailed, depicts the GYO movement in an era long since past. Since that time, No Child Left Behind, Race to the Top, the charter school explosion, the privatization movement, changing national and regional demographics, anti-immigrant or English-only referenda, expanding alternative teacher certification programs, and countless new or revised federal and state regulations have changed the face of public education and teacher preparation in this country. Though GYO programs seemed to have largely weathered these storms and may have even expanded in the process, current trends make it clear that GYO programs merit greater attention and dedication of resources. That teacher shortages still exist, cultural mismatches between the teacher workforce and the student population continue, and the rationale for the preparation of culturally responsive teachers remains, all suggest that GYO programs are as urgently needed today as they were nearly two decades ago. To begin to suggest how that need may be met, two primary implications are suggested by this study.

The first is that there is a need for a national clearinghouse or organization to chronicle, support, network, and share the variety of GYO approaches, structures, funding opportunities, successes, and challenges found nationwide. Such an organization could sponsor research, analyze best practices, produce newsletters, manage a website, host regional or national gatherings, issue press releases, convene a think tank, and it could gather data on participants at each step of the pipeline to inform future decision making. At the very least, such an organization could bring together the leaders of and participants in GYO programs to combine efforts and distribute curricula. Those that were successful at leveraging community, university, and foundation support to garner commitments from their state legislatures or departments of education could share their process, while those that have created or innovated their courses or internships could work with those just beginning to build their programs or strengthen existing ones. Such an organization could fund research that would lead to peer-reviewed publication and distribution of findings in mainstream media, thereby attracting the attention of directors of nonprofit organizations and/or local education funds, both of which have proven adept at shifting public opinion regarding matters pertaining to public schooling. If such a national organization were created, policy makers too might be involved and eventually convinced of the efficacy and fiscal value of GYO programs, and this could lead to the drafting of legislation to further develop the field. As GYO programs continue to expand and diversify, it would be of enormous utility to those involved to have a single organizational source for insights and assistance.

As a second implication, I offer this observation: to adequately evaluate the success of GYO programs, the research needs to move from the anecdotal to the empirical. Longitudinal data that constellates participants' college success, credential program matriculation, their eventual placement in a teaching position, longevity in that position, their ability to successfully promote academic achievement in their classrooms, and their capacity to produce meaningful reform in schools need to be gathered and analyzed. Other data such as parent and principal satisfaction, student ratings, subsequent professional or academic development (additional credentials received, degrees awarded, and so forth), and extracurricular involvement might also be included to give an overall picture of a GYO graduate's relative level of success as a teacher for a given community. Absent such studies, we do not know conclusively whether GYO programs and all the efforts and funds devoted to them are truly successful.

Conclusions

Public education and teacher preparation are popularly perceived to be at a crossroads. Amid growing concern with school and teacher accountability, increasing pressure to privatize schools and deprofessionalize teaching, and a seemingly ever-widening set of "achievement gaps," there are clear demographic trends suggesting the need for culturally responsive educators capable of reaching and teaching all students, especially those who are minoritized by their schooling experiences. A lack of racial/ethnic/linguistic diversity within the teaching force persists (despite an increasingly diverse student population), and unsustainable trends in teacher attrition continue, which is why many public schools are struggling to identify, prepare, and retain teachers who demonstrate the capacity to meet the needs of their particular students. Seeking to answer the question "How can schools prepare students for academic and vocational success while they simultaneously support and retain those teachers who often know best how to do such work in a multicultural setting?" GYO programs, in all their variety and similarity, are ideally suited to respond to these trends.

For GYO programs to flourish, however, officials from multiple sectors must collaborate to articulate a young adult's pathway from middle and high school, to college, to credential program, to gainful employment in a home district. In such a case, interdisciplinary collaboration and data-driven decision making are not theoretical possibilities but instead are essential "do-or-die" practices. Working across institutional and paradigmatic boundaries, legislators, district officials, university researchers, P–12 teachers, and community members have put inclusivity and collegiality at the core of their work when creating GYO programs. By observing whose knowledge is valued and whose is displaced when the demographics of the teacher workforce fail to represent the diversity within the student body, those creating GYO programs typically seek coalitions more than mandates when making decisions. Rather than insulating their efforts from outside influence or isolating their programs within small geographies or institutions, GYO officials frequently create alliances among key stakeholders and amass information from multiple sources to safeguard the stability and longevity of their programs. Thus, GYO programs illuminate the tremendous value of an interdisciplinary approach that musters empirical, institutional, linguistic, racial, ethnic, and cultural resources to inspire the minds of today's youth.

For these reasons and more, GYO programs are a promising if not enduring development in teacher education. Because they directly address many of the most troubling contemporary issues in urban education and teacher preparation, GYO programs deserve continued recognition and increased dedication of support. As a form of alternative certification that strengthens rather than weakens teacher preparation, GYO programs are built on a solid foundation of lived commitments to culturally responsive teaching, underserved students, and locally accountable school reform. The innovations, outcomes, and forms of collaboration each with their tremendous successes have long established the merits of the approach. What remains is a coordinated and well-funded effort to expand and integrate GYO programs in urban settings where its impact is most needed. In short, if we are to "grow our own," we must *own* the fact that it takes a village, a community, a district, a university, and a state to *grow* a good teacher.

References

Achinstein, B., Ogawa, R.T., Sexton, D., & Freitas, C. (2010). Retaining teachers of color: A pressing problem and a potential strategy for 'hard-to-staff' schools. *Review of Educational Research, 80*(1), 71-107. doi: 10.3102/0034654309355994

Aveling, N. (2004). Being the descendant of colonialists: White identity in context. *Race Ethnicity and Education, 7*(1), 57–71. doi:10.1080/1361332042000187306

Baumeister, R.F., & Leary, M.R. (1995). The need to belong: Desire for interpersonal attachments as a fundamental human motivation. *Psychological Bulletin, 117*(3), 497–529. doi:10.1037/0033–2909.117.3.497

Berrigan, A., & Schwartz, S. (2000). *Urban teacher academy project toolkit: A guide to developing high school teaching career academies.* Washington, DC: Council of Great City Schools. Retrieved from ERIC Document Reproduction Service No. ED449246.

Bondy, E., Ross, D.D., Gallingane, C., & Hambacher, E. (2006). *Creating environments of success and resilience: Culturally responsive classroom management and more.* Proceedings from Annual Meeting of the American Educational Research Association, San Francisco, CA.

Bonner, D. (1999). Austin High School for Teaching Professions and the "fully functioning person." Retrieved from http://www.ascd.org/publications/books/199031/chapters/Austin-High-School-for-Teaching-Professions-and-the-%E2%80%9CFully-Functioning-Person%E2%80%9D.aspx

Borjian, A., & Padilla, A. (2010). Voices from Mexico: How American teachers can meet the needs of Mexican immigrant students. *Urban Review, 42*(4), 316–328. doi:10.1007/s11256–009–0135–0

Boyd, D., Lankford, H., Loeb, S., & Wyckoff, J. (2005). The draw of home: How teachers' preferences for proximity disadvantage urban schools. *Journal of Policy Analysis and Management, 24*(1), 113–132. doi:10.1002/pam.20072

Brophy, J.E. (2010). *Motivating students to learn* (3rd ed.). New York, NY: Routledge.

California State University. (2012). *Financial aid and tuition rates: Historical tuition rates.* Retrieved from http://www.calstate.edu/budget/fybudget/2012–2013/documentation/13-historical-suf-rates.shtml

Case, K.A., & Hemmings, A. (2005). Distancing strategies: White women preservice teachers and antiracist curriculum. *Urban Education, 40*(6), 606–626. doi:10.1177/0042085905281396

Cech, S.J. (2005). Homegrown. *Teacher Magazine, 16*(6), 37–40.

Center for Educator Recruitment, Retention, & Advancement (CERRA). (2009). *Experiencing education curriculum.* Retrieved from http://www.teachercadets.com/previewchaps.aspx

Center for Educator Recruitment, Retention, & Advancement (CERRA). (n.d.). *ProTeam Program: A middle school teacher recruitment program.* Retrieved from http://www.cerra.org/proTeam

Center for Educator Recruitment, Retention, & Advancement (CERRA). (n.d.). *South Carolina Foundations in Mentoring: A training for those who work with beginning teachers.* Retrieved from http://www.cerra.org/teacherLeaders

Center for Public Information. (n.d.). *Wanted: Good teachers.* Retrieved from http://www.centerforpubliceducation.org/site/c.kjJXJ5MPIwE/b.4626569/k.6655/Wanted_Good_teachers.htm#Before

Chhuon, V., & Wallace, T.L. (2012). Creating connectedness through being known: Fulfilling the need to belong in U.S. high schools. *Youth & Society.* doi:10.1177/0044118X11436188

Chun, H., & Dickson, G. (2011). A psychoecological model of academic performance among Hispanic adolescents. *Journal of Youth and Adolescence, 40*(12), 1581–1594. doi:10.1007/s10964–011–9640-z

Conchas, G., Oseguera, L., & Vigil, J. (2012). Acculturation and school success: Understanding the variability of Mexican American youth adaptation across urban and suburban contexts. *Urban Review, 44*(4), 401–422. doi:10.1007/s11256–012–0197–2

Damon, W., Menon, J., & Bronk, K.C. (2003). The development of purpose during adolescence. *Applied Developmental Science, 7*(3), 119–128. doi:10.1207/S1532480XADS0703_2

Daniel, B.-J. (2009). Conversations on race in teacher education cohorts. *Teaching Education, 20,* 175–188. doi:10.1080/10476210902730497

Darling-Hammond, L. (2004). Inequality and the right to learn: Access to qualified teachers in California's public schools. *Teachers College Record, 106*(10), 1936–1966. doi:10.1111/j.1467–9620.2004.00422.x

Darling-Hammond, L. (2008). A future worthy of teaching for America. *Phi Delta Kappan, 89*(10), 730–735. Retrieved from http://www.kappanmagazine.org/content/89/10/730.short

Darling-Hammond, L., Holtzman, D.J., Gatlin, S.J., & Heilig, J.V. (2005). Does teacher preparation matter? Evidence about teacher certification, Teach for America, and teacher effectiveness. *Education Policy Analysis Archives, 13*(42), 1–51. Retrieved from http://www.nctq.org/nctq/research/1114011196655.pdf

de Freitas, E. (2005). Pre-service teachers and the re-inscription of Whiteness: Disrupting dominant cultural codes through textual analysis. *Teaching Education, 16*(2), 151–164. doi:10.1080/10476210500122725

Demanet, J., & Van Houtte, M. (2012). School belonging and school misconduct: The differing role of teacher and peer attachment. *Journal of Youth and Adolescence, 41*(4), 499–514. doi:10.1007/s10964–011–9674–2

DiAngelo, R., & Sensoy, Ö. (2010). "OK, I get it! Now tell me how to do it!": Why we can't just tell you how to do critical multicultural education. *Multicultural Perspectives, 12*(2), 97–102. doi:10.1080/15210960.2010.481199

DiAngelo, R., & Sensoy, Ö. (2012). Getting slammed: White depictions of race discussions as arenas of violence. *Race Ethnicity and Education*. Advance online publication. 26 pp. doi:10.1080/13613324.2012.674023

Easter, L. M., Shultz, E. L., Neyhart, T. K., & Reck, U. M.. (1999). Weighty perceptions: A study of the attitudes and beliefs of preservice teacher education students regarding diversity and urban education. *Urban Review, 31*(2), 205–220. doi:10.1023/A:1023287608741

Eccles, J.S., & Wigfield, A. (2002). Motivational beliefs, values, and goals. *Annual Review of Psychology, 53*(1), 109–132. doi:10.1146/annurev.psych.53.100901.135153

Education Commission of the States. (2003). Recruiting teachers of color: A program overview. Retrieved from http://www.ecs.org/teachingquality/

Erikson, E.H. (1968). *Identity, youth, and crisis.* New York, NY: W.W. Norton.

Falk, B. (2012). Ending the revolving door of teachers entering and leaving the teaching profession. *New Educator, 8*(2), 105–108. doi:10.1080/1547688X.2012.670565

Ferguson, R.F. (2003). Teachers' perceptions and expectations and the Black-White test score gap. *Urban Education, 38*(4), 460–507. doi:10.1177/0042085903038004006

Finn, J.D. (1989). Withdrawing from school. *Review of Educational Research, 59*(2), 117–142. Retrieved from http://www.jstor.org/stable/1170412

Franklin, T. (2003). "I teach who I am, I am who I teach": Understanding difference through the eyes of a teacher. Paper presented at the Alumni of Color Conference, Harvard Graduate School of Education. Cambridge, MA.

Future Educators Association. (2012). *About FEA*. Retrieved from http://www.futureeducators.org/about/docs/Factsheet_gen.pdf

Gallavan, N. P. (2005). Helping teachers unpack their "invisible knapsacks." *Multicultural Education, 13*(1), 36–39. Retrieved from http://www.freepatentsonline.com/article/Multicultural-Education/137921591.html

Gándara, P., & Rumberger, R.W. (2009). Immigration, language, and education: How does language policy structure opportunity? *Teachers College Record, 111*(3), 750–782. Retrieved from http://www.tcrecord.org/Content.asp?contentid=15343

Garg, R., Kauppi, C., Lewko, J., & Urajnik, D. (2002). A structural model of educational aspirations. *Journal of Career Development, 29*(2), 87–108. doi:10.1023/A:1019964119690

Gay, G. (2000). *Culturally responsive teaching: Theory, research, and practice.* New York, NY: Teachers College Press.

Glover, R.W., & Marshall, R. (1993). Improving the school-to-work transition of American adolescents. *Teachers College Record, 94*(3), 588–610.

Grant, C.A., & Gillette, M. (2006). A candid talk to teacher educators about effectively preparing teachers who can teach everyone's children. *Journal of Teacher Education, 57*(3), 292–299. doi:10.1177/0022487105285894

GrowYourOwnTeachers (2012). Retrieved from http://www.growyourownteachers.org/

GrowYourOwnIllinois. (n.d.). *About Grow Your Own Illinois*. Retrieved from http://www.growyourownteachers.org/AboutUs/index.htm

Guarino, C.M., Santibañez, L., & Daley, G.A. (2006). Teacher recruitment and retention: A review of the recent empirical literature. *Review of Educational Research, 76*(2), 173–208. doi:10.3102/00346543076002173

Haberman, M. (2003). Can teacher education close the achievement gap? In D.M. McInerney & S.V. Etten (Eds.), *Sociocultural influences and teacher education programs* (pp. 1–14). Greenwich, CT: Information Age.

Haberman, M. (2005). Teacher burnout in black and white. *New Educator, 1*(3), 153–175. doi:10.1080/15476880590966303

Haberman, M. (2010). *Selecting and preparing urban teachers*. Retrieved from http://www.educationnews.org/ed_reports/40638.html

Harris, A.L. (2011). *Kids don't want to fail: Oppositional culture and Black students' academic achievement*. Cambridge, MA: Harvard University Press.

Hatt, B. (2007). Street smarts vs. book smarts: The figured world of smartness in the lives of marginalized, urban youth. *Urban Review, 39*(2), 145–166. doi:10.1007/s11256-007-0047-9

Haycock, K. (2001). Closing the achievement gap. *Educational Leadership, 58*(6), 6–11.

Helms, J.E. (1990). *Black and White racial identity: Theory, research, and practice*. Westport, CT: Greenwood Press.

Hill, D.A., & Gillette, M.D. (2005). Teachers for tomorrow in urban schools: Recruiting and supporting the pipeline. *Multicultural Perspectives, 7*(3), 42–50. doi:10.1207/s15327892mcp0703_8

Hirsch, E. (2001). *Teacher recruitment: Staffing classrooms with quality teachers*. Denver, CO: State Higher Education Executive Officers. Retrieved from www.sheeo.org

Humphrey, D.C., Wechsler, M.E., & Hough, H.J. (2008). Characteristics of effective teacher certification programs. *Teachers College Record, 110*(4), 1–63.

Hytten, K., & Warren, J. (2003). Engaging whiteness: How racial power gets reified in education. *International Journal of Qualitative Studies in Education, 16*(1), 65–89. doi:10.1080/0951839032000033509a

Irizarry, J.G. (2007). "Home-growing" teachers of color: Lessons learned from a town-gown partnership. *Teacher Education Quarterly, 34*(4), 87–102. Retrieved from EbscoHost.

Kerckhoff, A.C. (2002). The transition from school to work. In J.T. Mortimer & R. Larson (Eds.), *The changing adolescent experience: Societal trends and the transition to adulthood* (pp. 52–87). Cambridge, UK: Cambridge University Press.

Kerpelman, J., Eryigit, S., & Stephens, C. (2008). African American adolescents' future education orientation: Associations with self-efficacy, ethnic identity, and perceived parental support. *Journal of Youth and Adolescence, 37*(8), 997–1008. doi:10.1007/s10964-007-9201-7

Kumashiro, K.K. (2010). Seeing the bigger picture: Troubling movements to end teacher education. *Journal of Teacher Education, 61*(1–2), 56–65. doi:10.1177/0022487109347318

Labaree, D.F. (2010). Teach for America and teacher ed: Heads they win, tails we lose. *Journal of Teacher Education, 61*(1–2), 48–55. doi:10.1177/0022487109347317

Ladson-Billings, G. (1999). Preparing teachers for diverse student populations: A critical race theory perspective. *Review of Research in Education, 24,* 211–247.

La Guardia, J.G. (2009). Developing who I am: A self-determination theory approach to the establishment of healthy identities. *Educational Psychologist, 44*(2), 90–104. doi:10.1080/00461520902832350

LAUSD Career Ladder Office. (n.d.). TCAs—*Teacher Career Academies*. Retrieved from http://www.teachinla.com/ladder/ProgramsandServices/TeacherCareerAcademiesTCAs/tabid/88/Default.aspx

Maher, F.A., & Tetreault, M. K. T. (2009). Learning in the dark: How assumptions of whiteness shape classroom knowledge. *Harvard Educational Review, 67*(2), 321–350.

Marcia, J.E. (1980). Identity in adolescence. In J. Adelson (Ed.), *Handbook of adolescent psychology* (pp. 159–187). New York, NY: John Wiley.

Marx, S. (2004). Regarding whiteness: Exploring and intervening in the effects of White racism in teacher education. *Equity & Excellence in Education, 37,* 31–43. doi:10.1080/10665680490422089

Marx, S., & Pennington, J. (2003). Pedagogies of critical race theory: Experimentations with white pre-service teachers. *Qualitative Studies in Education, 16*(1), 91–110. doi:10.1080/0951839022000036381

McFadyen, I. (2008, April 9). Personal communication with the Director of the Teaching and Educational Careers Academy at Pacifica High School in Oxnard, CA.

Menken, K., & Kleyn, T. (2010). The long-term impact of subtractive schooling in the educational experiences of secondary English language learners. *International Journal of Bilingual Education & Bilingualism, 13*(4), 399–417. doi:10.1080/13670050903370143

Mesa Public Schools. (n.d.). *Grow Your Own Teacher Program: An overview.* Retrieved from http://www.mpsaz.org/mgyo/overview.html

Milner, H.R. (2003). Reflection, racial competence, and critical pedagogy: How do we prepare pre-service teachers to pose tough questions? *Race Ethnicity and Education, 6*(2), 193–208. doi:10.1080/13613320308200

Milner, H.R. (2010). *Start where you are but don't stay there: Understanding diversity, opportunity gaps, and teaching in today's classrooms.* Cambridge, MA: Harvard Education Press.

Museus, S.D., Harper, S.R., & Nichols, A.H. (2010). Racial differences in the formation of postsecondary educational expectations: A structural model. *Teachers College Record, 112*(3), 811–842. Retrieved from http://www.tcrecord.org/Content.asp?ContentID=15890

Nakkula, M.J., & Toshalis, E. (2006). *Understanding youth: Adolescent development for educators.* Cambridge, MA: Harvard Education Press.

National Conference of State Legislatures. (n.d.). *Education Program: Teacher recruitment.* Retrieved from http://www.ncsl.org/programs/educ/trecru.htm

Orr, M.T. (2009). Transitions to college: An in-depth look at the selected influences of demographics, development, and policy. *Teachers College Record, 111*(10), 2311–2319. Retrieved from http://www.tcrecord.org/Content.asp?ContentID=15712

Page, J.A., & Page, F.M., Jr. (1984). High school senior perceptions of teaching as a career opportunity. Paper presented at the annual meeting of the American Educational Research Association, New Orleans. Retrieved from http://www.eric.ed.gov/ERICWebPortal/detail?accno=ED241534

Palmer, K. (2007). Why teachers quit. *Teacher Magazine, 18*(6), 45.

Peske, H.G., & Haycock, K. (2006). Teaching inequality: How poor and minority students are shortchanged on teacher quality: A report and recommendations by the Education Trust. *Education Trust.* Retrieved from http://eric.ed.gov/ERICWebPortal/recordDetail?accno=ED494820

Recruiting New Teachers, Inc. (1993). *Teaching's next generation: A national study of precollegiate teacher recruitment.* Report No. ISBN-884139–01–9. Retrieved from ERIC Document Reproduction Service No. ED364523.

Reeve, J. (2006). Extrinsic rewards and inner motivation. In C.M. Evertson & C.S. Weinstein (Eds.), *Handbook of classroom management: Research, practice, and contemporary issues* (pp. 645–664). Mahwah, NJ: Lawrence Erlbaum Associates.

Rodríguez, L. (2008). Struggling to recognize their existence: Examining student-adult relationships in the urban high school context. *Urban Review, 40*(4), 436–453. doi:10.1007/s11256–008–0091–0

Rushton, J.P., & Jensen, A.R. (2005). Thirty years of research on race differences in cognitive ability. *Psychology, Public Policy, and Law, 11*(2), 235–294. doi:10.1037/1076–8971.11.2.235

Ryan, R.M., & Deci, E.L. (2000). Self-determination theory and the facilitation of intrinsic motivation, social development, and well-being. *American Psychologist, 55*(1), 68–78. doi:10.1037/0003–066X.55.1.68

Santamaria, L.J. (2009). Culturally responsive differentiated instruction: Narrowing gaps between best pedagogical practices benefiting all learners. *Teachers College Record, 111*(1), 214–247. Retrieved from http://www.tcrecord.org/Content.asp?ContentID=15210

Schonfeld, I.S., & Feinman, S.J. (2012). Difficulties of alternatively certified teachers. *Education and Urban Society, 44*(3), 215–246. doi:10.1177/0013124510392570

Sensoy, Ö., & DiAngelo, R.J. (2012). *Is everyone really equal?: An introduction to key concepts in social justice education.* New York, NY: Teachers College Press.

Singh, K., Chang, M., & Dika, S. (2010). Ethnicity, self-concept, and school belonging: Effects on school engagement. *Educational Research for Policy and Practice, 9,* 159–175. doi:10.1007/s10671–010–9087–0

Skorikov, V., & Vondracek, F.W. (2007). Positive career orientation as an inhibitor of adolescent problem behaviour. *Journal of Adolescence, 30*(1), 131–146. doi:10.1016/j.adolescence.2006.02.004

Sleeter, C.E. (2001). Preparing teachers for culturally diverse schools. *Journal of Teacher Education, 52*(2), 94–106. doi:10.1177/0022487101052002002

Sleeter, C.E. (2012). Confronting the marginalization of culturally responsive pedagogy. *Urban Education, 47*(3), 562–584. Retrieved from http://uex.sagepub.com/content/47/3/562.abstract

Sleeter, C. E., & Milner, H. R. (2011). Researching successful efforts in teacher education to diversify teachers. In A. F. Ball & C. A. Tyson (Eds.), *Studying diversity in teacher education* (pp. 81-103). Lanham, MD: Rowman & Littlefield.

Steinberg, A., Cushman, K., & Riordan, R.C. (1999). *Schooling for the real world: The essential guide to rigorous and relevant learning.* San Francisco, CA: Jossey-Bass.

Stephen F. Austin High School. (2009). *Austin High School for Teaching Professions.* Retrieved from http://hs.houstonisd.org/AustinHS/specialprograms/magnetprogram.htm

Storm, J. (2009). Raising teachers. *EDge, 4*(5), 3–15. Retrieved from EbscoHost.

Storm, J. (2011). Raising teachers [Blog post]. Retrieved from http://www.pdkintl.org/blog/category/raisingteachers/

Strayhorn, T.L. (2009). Different folks, different hopes: The educational aspirations of Black males in urban, suburban, and rural high schools. *Urban Education, 44*(6), 710–731. doi:10.1177/0042085908322705

Strong, M. (2005). Teacher induction, mentoring, and retention: A summary of the research. *New Educator, 1,* 181–198. doi:10.1080/15476880590966295

Suárez-Orozco, C., Pimentel, A., & Martin, M. (2009). The significance of relationships: Academic engagement and achievement among newcomer immigrant youth. *Teachers College Record, 111*(3), 712–749. Retrieved from http://www.tcrecord.org/Content.asp?contentid=15342

Suárez-Orozco, C., & Suárez-Orozco, M. (2009). Educating Latino immigrant students in the twenty-first century: Principles for the Obama administration. *Harvard Educational Review, 79*(2), 327–401. Retrieved from http://her.hepg.org/index/231151762p82213u.pdf

Tatum, B.D. (1999). *"Why are all the Black kids sitting together in the cafeteria?" and other conversations about race.* New York, NY: Basic Books.

Teaching and Leadership Center. (n.d.). *Urban Teacher Academy Program (UTAP).* Retrieved from http://www.coe.fau.edu/tlc/content/programs-uabc-utap.htm

Toshalis, E. (2011). The rhetoric of care: Preservice teacher discourses that depoliticize, deflect, and deceive. *The Urban Review, 44*(1), 1–35. doi: 10.1007/s11256-011-0177-y

Toshalis, E., & Nakkula, M.J. (2012). *Motivation, engagement and student voice.* Retrieved from http://www.studentsatthecenter.org/sites/scl.dl-dev.com/files/Motivation%20Engagement%20Student%20Voice_0.pdf

Ullucci, K., & Battey, D. (2011). Exposing color blindness/grounding color consciousness. *Urban Education, 46*(6), 1195–1225. doi:10.1177/0042085911413150

Umaña-Taylor, A. J., Vargas-Chanes, D., Garcia, C. D., & Gonzales-Backen, M. (2008). A longitudinal examination of Latino adolescents' ethnic identity, coping with discrimination, and self-esteem. *Journal of Early Adolescence, 28*(1), 16–50. doi:10.1177/0272431607308666

Valenzuela, A. (1999). *Subtractive schooling: U.S.-Mexican youth and the politics of caring.* Albany, NY: State University of New York Press.

Van Ryzin, M., Gravely, A., & Roseth, C. (2009). Autonomy, belongingness, and engagement in school as contributors to adolescent psychological well-being. *Journal of Youth and Adolescence, 38*(1), 1–12. doi: 10.1007/s10964-007-9257-4

Veltri, B.T. (2008). Teaching or service? The site-based realities of Teach for America teachers in poor, urban schools. *Education and Urban Society, 40*(5), 511–542. doi:10.1177/0013124508319281

Villegas, A., & Irvine, J. J. (2010). Diversifying the teaching force: An examination of major arguments. *The Urban Review, 42*(3), 175-192. doi: 10.1007/s11256-010-0150-1

Villegas, A.M., & Lucas, T. (2002). Preparing culturally responsive teachers: Rethinking the curriculum. *Journal of Teacher Education, 53*(1), 20–32. doi:10.1177/0022487102053001003

Ward, J.V. (1989). Racial identity formation and transformation. In C. Gilligan, N.P. Lyons, & T. J. Hammer (Eds.), *Making connections: The relational worlds of adolescent girls at Emma Willard School* (pp. 215–232). New York, NY: Troy.

Ware, F. (2006). Warm demander pedagogy: Culturally responsive teaching that supports a culture of achievement for African American students. *Urban Education, 41*(4), 427–456. doi:10.1177/0042085906289710

Weiner, L. (2003). Why is classroom management so vexing to urban teachers? *Theory Into Practice, 42*(4), 305–312. doi:10.1207/s15430421tip4204_7

Weinstein, C., Curran, M., & Tomlinson-Clarke, S. (2003). Culturally responsive classroom management: Awareness into action. *Theory Into Practice, 42*(4), 269–276. doi:10.1207/s15430421tip4204_2

Wentzel, K.R. (2005). Peer relationships, motivation, and academic performance at school. In A. Elliot & C. Dweck (Eds.), *Handbook of competence and motivation* (pp. 279–296). New York, NY: Guilford Press.

Wichita Public Schools. (n.d.). *Wichita Public Schools Human Resources.* Retrieved from http://www.usd259.com/employees/humanresources/grow/default.htm

Wigfield, A., & Eccles, J.S. (2002). *Development of achievement motivation.* San Diego, CA: Academic Press.

Zarrett, N., & Eccles, J. (2006). The passage to adulthood: Challenges of late adolescence. *New Directions for Youth Development, 111,* 13–28. doi:10.1002/yd.179

Zeichner, K.M. (2003). The adequacies and inadequacies of three current strategies to recruit, prepare, and retain the best teachers for all students. *Teachers College Record, 105*(3), 490–519. doi:10.1111/1467-9620.00248

13

Latina/o Youth as Educational Researchers

Implications for Teaching and Learning in Urban Schools

Jason G. Irizarry & Anjalé DeVawn Welton

The discourse of school reform has become commonplace in popular parlance, as policy makers and educators have applied free-market business principles such as "choice" and "vouchers" to purportedly improve educational opportunities for young people, especially in urban communities that have been historically underserved by schools. However, these school reform efforts have largely been top-down and misguided, often excluding the participation of youth and families as meaningful partners in policy decisions. Similarly, the preparation of teachers is rarely, if ever, informed by the urban communities many of these teachers will eventually serve. As a result, many educators are unprepared to meet the challenges of working in urban schools and teaching across lines of cultural, racial, linguistic, and socioeconomic difference (Milner, 2010; Sleeter, 2001; Talbert-Johnson, 2006).

If urban youth were trained as researchers, given the opportunity to collect and analyze data regarding the educational experiences and outcomes for students like themselves, what would they say? What recommendations would they offer to improve the quality of teaching and learning in their schools? Drawing from data collected as part of an ethnographic study of Latina/o high school students involved in a participatory action research project, this chapter aims to address these questions. Framing urban school reform within the context of Latinization—rapid demographic shifts in the population of Latinas/os in the United States and the subsequent responses in policy and practice—this chapter critically examines Latina/o students' critiques and recommendations for improving the educational experiences for students in urban schools. After offering an overview of how school reform efforts often ignore the perspectives of communities of color, we describe the methods used to collect and analyze the data emanating from the larger ethnographic study of which these data are a part and discuss the theoretical frameworks that inform our research. The chapter concludes with a discussion of the importance and absolute necessity for meaningfully including urban youth in efforts aimed at improving teaching and learning in urban schools.

Urban School Reform and the Suppression of Student Voice

Educational policies seem to be in a proverbial déjà vu. Even though countless studies have provided empirical evidence to suggest that standardization and market-driven reforms such as high-stakes accountability, school turnaround and reconstitution policies, school choice, and privatization/corporate management of schools do not improve student achievement and promote sustainable change (Hursh, 2007; Lipman, 2004, 2011; Scott, 2011; Trujillo, 2012), federal and local government agencies have continued to authorize, and at times require, urban districts to engage in these problematic reform efforts (Hursh, 2007 Scott, 2011). Even suburban districts have increasingly confronted similar hegemonic policies as they have become responsible for the education of students of color who have had a growing presence in those districts. In fact, suburban school districts have experienced unprecedented growth among students of color and students from lower socioeconomic circumstances in recent years (Frankenberg & Orfield, 2012; Holme, Welton, & Diem, 2012). Despite these demographic trends, school reform initiatives primarily target urban districts and schools, as "reformers" seek to develop and implement remedies to address the seemingly intractable issue of academic underachievement. For the most part, policy makers and legislators who move these reform initiatives forward are not part of the communities where these policy and pedagogical changes will be made. For example, even though Latinas/os represent approximately 13% of the U.S. population and more than 20% of students attending schools, fewer than 2% of all elected and appointed officials are Latina/o (Irizarry, 2011). In short, Latinas/os, the largest and one of the fastest-growing "minoritized" groups in the United States, are rarely in a position to lead urban school reform efforts and rarely have a welcomed voice in this process.

While the underlying policy intentions of school reform initiatives such as No Child Left Behind (NCLB) and Race to the Top are to increase student achievement, these policies fail to address the structural inequalities that are largely responsible for the differential outcomes between urban and suburban schools and between students of color and White students (Duncan-Andrade & Morrell, 2008; Leonardo, 2007). Instead these policies situate urban schools and students of color as the source of school maladies (Leonardo, 2007; Valencia, Valenzuela, Sloan, & Foley, 2001). Furthermore, policies driven by high-stakes accountability measures often force schools to solve a complex problem, such as the so-called achievement gap, with prescriptive monitoring of subgroups (racially/ethnically minoritized students, children from lower socioeconomic strata, special education students, and "English Language Learners") that are overwhelmingly represented by students of color (Leonardo, 2007; Pollock, 2004). Policies that enforce regulatory student achievement data monitoring can obscure the role that schools and other social institutions play in reproducing racial and economic inequities, positioning students and families as the "problem" and solely responsible for the pessimistic academic outcomes that often characterize urban schools (Irizarry, 2011; Pollock, 2004; Valencia et al., 2001). Oversimplified and deficit-based understandings of the root causes of educational inequities often overshadow any critical analyses of the underlying causes of disparities in achievement among groups (Milner, 2010, 2012). If unexamined, the achievement gap discourse can result in White students being viewed as more intelligent and worth investing time in, while students of color internalize the negative messages about them, discouraging their aspirations and academic performance (Irizarry, 2011; Kirkland, 2010; Valencia, 1997).

The abovementioned neoliberal approaches to eradicate the achievement gap have egregious implications for Latina/o youth. Numerous scholars have placed urban school reform on trial by documenting ways in which these policies and practices are largely subtractive, repressing Latina/o students' cultural, linguistic identities and opportunities to learn (Antrop-Gonzalez, 2011; Irizarry, 2011; Valenzuela, 1999). Furthermore, when Latina/o students are the target of teacher and administrators' deficit perceptions and attitudes, they become further disconnected from academic life as schools are then no longer a site of support but one of "institutional neglect and abuse" (Gonzalez, Stoner, & Jovel, 2003, p. 153; Irizarry, 2011; Kimura-Walsh, Yamamura, Griffin, & Allen, 2009; Valencia, 1997; Valenzuela, 1999). Thus, these inequitable policies, structures, and practices largely explain why Latina/o youth and their Black peers are typically taught by inexperienced teachers (Jerald, Haycock, & Wilkins, 2009), recipients of harsh disciplinary sanctions (Brown, 2007), are overrepresented in the lowest academic tracks (Solórzano & Ornelas, 2002), have significantly lower chances of completing high school within four years (Balfanz & Legters, 2004), and receive limited resources and supports to matriculate to college (Gonzalez et al., 2003, Irizarry, 2012; Valadez, 2008).

Restrictive school reform policies and the bureaucratic structures and practices that proceed them have a deleterious impact on the overall school culture and climate, which in turn negatively impacts Latina/o youth's level of connectedness and engagement in school (Patterson, Hale, & Stessman, 2007; Valenzuela, 1999). Latina/o youth currently have the highest dropout rates among any racial/ethnic group (Rumberger & Rodriquez, 2011), and research shows that their decisions to leave school commonly stem from an uncaring school culture where they are alienated, relatively unknown, and invisible to teachers and administration (Rodriguez, 2008). However, antagonistic structures and school personnel's negative attitudes toward Latina/o youth also precipitate a student's decision to leave school. For example, Latina/o youth who are relegated to the lowest track classes are often conscious of the limited rigor and low expectations set for them in these classes, and thus resort to frequent absenteeism as a form of resistance to school boredom (Brown & Rodriguez, 2009; Cammarota, 2004; Welton, 2011). Also, teacher inattentiveness to a student's academic needs and struggles can lead to disengagement and a student's decision to permanently exit school (Brown & Rodriguez, 2009). According to Fine (1991), schools tend to ignore and silence any discussions that aim to raise consciousness regarding inequities in schooling. Students who resist school-sponsored silencing are considered adversarial and are pushed out of school through a number of exclusionary tactics, especially disciplinary infractions (Fine, 1991).

School cultures that are subtractive, as opposed to additive, enforce heavy surveillance of Latina/o youth, police expression of their cultural and linguistic identities, and make limited efforts to affirm their identities in the curriculum (Irizarry, 2011; Valenzuela, 1999). Research has shown that Latina/o youth are rightfully apprehensive about embedding themselves in school academics and social networks because they feel schools are racially and structurally antagonistic environments that generally promote White, middle-class norms (Valadez, 2008). Even though Latina/o youth are the majority in many urban schools, they are still most often taught by predominately White teachers from middle-class backgrounds who are typically unprepared to teach and relate to Latina/o youth and their identities (Irizarry, 2011). Teacher preparation programs are still limited in training and discussions related to culturally responsive and race conscious approaches, and consequently White teachers commonly default to asserting their identity, which is primarily Eurocentric and rooted in Whiteness, as the school norm (Raible & Irizarry, 2007; Milner, 2010; Sleeter, 2001). According to research Latina/o youth's experiences with teacher racial bias and racial discrimination in school are highly correlated with their disengagement and decision to drop out of school (Katz, 1999; Wayman, 2002). In order to survive school, Latina/o youth learn to navigate White dominant structures, while maintaining some semblance of their personal cultural identities (Valadez, 2008; Yosso, 2005).

Presently, educational policies in the U.S. context are colorblind by design. As stated earlier in this chapter, NCLB aims to rectify the achievement gap but with race-neutral, deficit-oriented approaches that attempt to fix the student, not the broken system as a whole. However, while colorblind policies are subtler in their efforts to sustain the racial order, a new wave of policies are more deliberate in their assault on Latina/o youth. The state of Arizona has garnered national media attention and critical discourse for two xenophobic policies passed in 2010: SB 1070, the anti-immigration law (Foxen, 2010; Lacayo, 2011; Oboler, 2010), and HB 2281, the anti-intellectual Ethnic studies in K–12 law (Oboler, 2010; Patel Stevens & Stovall, 2011). SB 1070, the anti-immigration law in Arizona, adds to the burden of racial profiling and police surveillance experienced by Latina/o youths in schools across the country (Foxen, 2010).

Substantial scholarship has documented the policy processes of both SB 1070 and HB 2281 and critical scholars contend that both policies are the epitome of "systemic racism ground in white racial hegemony and social institutions serving white interests" (Clark & Reed, 2010, p. 38) and are "continuations of past racial policies aimed at the reifying of the White nation state" (Patel Stevens & Stovall, 2011, p. 297). Since SB 1070's inception, 31 other states attempted to pass a similar law, and only one state, Utah, was successful (Lacayo, 2011). The policy "fuels anti-immigrant sentiment" forcing undocumented persons to live in the "shadow of society" (Irizarry, 2011, p. 109–110). According to the National Council of La Raza in 2007 small-scale raids (homes and neighborhood businesses) impacted approximately 125,000 undocumented youth, generating fear, isolation, and psychological trauma for undocumented youth (NCLR, 2007). Unfortunately, supporters of the passage of SB 1070 have been linked to the prison industry, as increased criminalization of immigrants means potential profit for the private prison system (Lacayo, 2011).

Arizona's HB 2281 prohibits any public or charter school from implementing programs or courses that promote resentment toward a race or class of people, are specific to an ethnic group, promotes ethnic solidarity instead of promoting individuals, and discusses or promotes overthrowing the U.S. government (Kunnie, 2010). HB 2281 gives Arizona's state education agency the legal grounds to investigate school districts that may be out of compliance in ceasing and desisting their ethnic studies programs, and districts that fail to comply are at risk of receiving the ultimate sentence—a 10% loss of their state funding each year they do not comply (Otero & Cammarota, 2011). In January 2012 Tuscan Unified School District (TUSD) was labeled by the Arizona Department of Education as out of compliance with HB 2281, and immediately after this ruling the TUSD school board voted to eliminate the Mexican American studies classes and related books (Herbert, 2012).

While the abovementioned policies deter the promotion of Latina/o youth's cultural identities, at least three states—Arizona, California, and Massachusetts—have passed laws that impede students' linguistic identities. All three states' policies place emphasis on English instruction, not the use of a student's native language, to facilitate the process of learning English. Furthermore, these policies mandate rapid English language acquisition, giving language minority students only one year in some form of sheltered English immersion setting before transitioning to an English only classroom (Gándara & Baca, 2008). The rapid time in which English language learners are expected to acquire academic English is counter to research that has conclusively found that academic English language acquisition takes between 4 to 7 years (Gándara & Baca, 2008). California's Proposition 227 has contributed minimally to no gains in the achievement of English Language Learners in California. Even with much contestation from the policy, scholarly, and local school communities, these subtractive language policies still remain. Latina/o youth are impacted the most by these "English only" policies as they represent nearly 80% of the U.S. English learner population (Gándara & Rumberger, 2009).

Finally, the policing of Latina/o youth in school has long-lasting implications for their future beyond the schoolhouse. The overrepresentation of students of color in special education and exclusionary discipline practices fuel the prison industrial complex and what is now called the school-to-prison pipeline (Kim, Losen, & Hewitt, 2010; Raible & Irizarry, 2010). Educators' emphasis on classroom management and control is a major contributor to the school-to-prison pipeline phenomenon. Also, in the last 20 years nationwide spending for prisons has gone up by 127%, but there was only a 21% increase in spending for higher education (Pew Research

Center, 2010. Linkages between school disciplinary sanctions and the criminal detention of youth also fuel the pipeline. In general students of color are more likely than their White counterparts to be referred to disciplinary alternative programs, and Latina/o youth specifically are three times more likely to be arrested in school than their White peers (Kim et al., 2010). Furthermore, even though children of color (specifically Latina/o youth & their Black peers) represent over a third of the school population, they represent just shy of 70% of youth detained in the criminal justice system (Kim et al., 2010). These statistics for youth mirror incarceration rates for adults of color in the U.S. prison system. Currently Latinas/os and African Americans combined represent approximately a quarter of the U.S. population, but three-fourths of adults incarcerated in the U.S. prison system (Raible & Irizarry, 2010).

School reform efforts have failed to provide equitable schooling experiences for Latina/o youths (Gándara & Contreras, 2009), and those in power who are responsible for these policies unequivocally send a message to Latina/o youth that they do not have a right to an education (Welton, 2011). Therefore, we should give recognition to Latina/o youth by considering the ways in which they are "often stigmatized, pathologized, and criminalized in society and within various institutions that are intended to serve them" (Rodriguez, 2012; p. 4). Persistent educational inequities and failed attempts at school reform make it clear that educational scholars, school leaders, and policy makers who shape policies and practices have not advocated enough for Latina/o youth and other groups of young people equally underserved by schools (Welton, 2011). Adults are largely responsible for shaping the school structures that Latina/o youth must navigate, and for this reason adults must take responsibility for and acknowledge the unequal conditions and structures Latina/o youth face in school (Rodriguez, 2012).

In order to counter the many ways in which school reform efforts suppress their identities, Latina/o youth must be given opportunities in school spaces and curriculum to engage in critical thinking and dialogue that enable them to deconstruct the politics of school reform. Engaging in political critique also gives Latina/o youth the opportunity to reclaim their voice and affirm their identities (Irizarry, 2009; Rodriguez, 2012). Because of their growing numbers in schools—currently accounting for approximately one in every four students in U.S. schools—one can convincingly argue that Latina/o youth are most impacted by the current school reform agenda. As primary targets of school reform, the perspectives of Latina/o youth should be included in these debates. To that end, the first author, Irizarry, created a research collaborative with Latina/o youth aimed at inserting their heretofore silenced voices into the conversation on how to improve urban schooling. In what follows we discuss the students' research project and findings in further detail.

Methods

Genuinely concerned by the lack of academic success experienced by so many Latina/o youth and in an effort to remain connected to urban schools and communities, especially those serving Latina/o students, the first author returned to the secondary-school classroom and offered a course on action research at Rana High School (RHS), a pseudonym, between 2008 and 2010. The class was embedded in a larger multigenerational research collaborative called Project FUERTE (Future Urban Educators conducting Research to transform Teacher Education). High school student researchers worked with Irizarry and a small cadre of graduate students to critically examine the educational experiences of and outcomes for Latina/o youths and to develop empirically based recommendations for the preparation of teachers, both preservice and inservice, to work with Latina/o youths (see Irizarry, 2011). It was our belief that inserting the brilliant, yet often silenced voices of Latina/o youth into the debates regarding the academic achievement in urban schools would challenge these problematic school reform discourses and inform the personal and professional development of educators, hopefully resulting in changes in policy and pedagogy that might lead to improved learning opportunities for Latina/o students and other groups who have been historically underserved by urban schools. During the two-year period in which Project FUERTE included students from RHS (the previous year the project was located at a different urban high school), Irizarry simultaneously conducted a multiyear ethnographic study of the Project FUERTE participants. The data shared in this chapter stem from the ethnography.

Participants and Setting

The cohort of participants consisted of seven students from RHS, a comprehensive high school located in the northeastern United States and serving approximately 1,000 students. As did about half of all RHS students, the participants identified themselves as Latina/o, with five self-identifying as Puerto Rican and two as Mexican American. Six of the seven students were juniors at RHS at the outset of the project, and one was a senior. They varied in age from 15 to 18 at the inception of the study. Three of the students had (im)migrated to the mainland United States, two coming with their families from Mexico as young children and one moving from Puerto Rico as a 14-year-old. The remaining participants had completed all of their formal education up to that point in Rana City schools. All of the students articulated a desire to attend college, but only two were enrolled in college-prep courses, such as Algebra 1 and 2, that are prerequisites for admission into four-year institutions of higher education.

Reflective of the demographic shifts occurring in many communities across the United States, RHS was experiencing a surge in its Latina/o population, and the majority of teachers, administrators, and professional staff were unprepared to meet the needs of these students. As part of one of the lowest-performing and most economically depressed districts in the state, the school was under increased pressure to improve student performance and graduation rates while also under significant economic constraints. The official annual dropout rate of the school for the year the study began was 4.1%, but a more nuanced look at the data reveals that less than half of all Latina/o students who entered the school as 9th graders were enrolled in the 12th grade four years later.

Data Collection and Analysis

Throughout the two years of data collection and analysis, a primary goal of the study was to understand how Latina/o youth experienced school within the contexts of Latinization and increased pressures on schools to meet accountability standards. Comments offered through formal interviews, class discussions, written assignments, and research presentations addressed an array of issues impacting the educational experiences and outcomes for Latina/o youth (see Irizarry, 2011).

As part of the formal structure of the course the research team met twice a week for two consecutive academic years, spanning the students' 11th- and 12th-grade years and moving through high school graduation. These class meetings represent only a small fraction of the time spent together, as the research collaborative often convened outside of the traditional school day, including after school, weekends, and during school vacations to contribute to the work of Project FUERTE. Over the two-year period, the research team had spent more than 400 hours together, which, in addition to fostering important, mutually enriching relationships, also led to the development of a large data set. Field notes were made after most class periods and out-of-school meetings. Student presentations were recorded on video and analyzed to provide another layer of data that directly spoke to how the participants made meaning of their experiences in school and the recommendations they forwarded for improving them. In addition, each student was formally interviewed six times over the two-year period, using a standard format for phenomenological interviews (Seidman, 2006). Each interview was transcribed and, along with field notes, presentations, and student work products, served as the primary data for this study.

Ethnographic methods (Carspecken, 1995) were employed to critically examine the ways that the sociopolitical context in which the youth were embedded shaped the opportunity structure available to them and their daily experiences navigating school and the meaning they assigned to them. Also illuminated through this process were the ways the seemingly benign guise of school and state efforts to close gaps in achievement between Latina/o and White students negatively informed the educational experiences of Latina/o students in ways that further alienated them from school. Culling themes that emerged from the data collected during the course of the ethnography, a grounded theory approach to data analysis was employed (Corbin & Strauss, 2008).

Congruent with this method, key themes were identified through a process of constant comparison (Corbin & Strauss, 2008) to identify and test for the robustness of various themes. Finally, student participants were consulted and given an opportunity to offer insights at every step in the process from data collection through analysis and presentation of the findings, allowing for triangulation of the data and findings.

Theoretical Framework

The stories documented here are not completely unique to this particular school or community but rather are reflective of the context in which millions of Latinas/os in urban schools are educated (see Murillo, 2010; Pedraza & Rivera, 2005). Schools do not exist in a vacuum. The education of Latina/o youth is influenced by larger societal forces, including institutional racism and other forms of oppression. For the purposes of this chapter, we locate the experiences of the students within the context of Latinization, which includes efforts to assert and preserve Latina/o identities in the face of pressures to assimilate, shed one's identity, and adopt Anglo cultural norms. The responses to Latinization are evidenced not only through the students' experiences with Eurocentric curricula, the painful impact of budget cuts on already struggling communities, and culturally insensitive educators, documented in what follows, but also clearly demonstrated in national discourses and public policy regarding immigration, bilingual education, and ethnic studies, all the target of recent legislation aimed at curbing opportunity for Latina/o communities.

To better understand the role of race/ethnicity in the lives of Latina/o youth as they tried to successfully navigate school within the context of efforts to curtail or contain Latinization, we employed Latina/o Critical Race Theory (CRT generally, and LatCrit specifically) as an analytical tool. The use of LatCrit as a theoretical lens is especially appropriate given the centrality of race and racism in the students' experiences. The theory centralizes race in analyses but also focuses on the intersection of race with other variables and identity characteristics, including language, (im)migration status, ethnicity, and culture (Delgado & Stefancic, 2001), that were manifested throughout the study. Consistent with the tenets of LatCrit, the subaltern voices of Latina/o youth in this chapter provide a counternarrative (Solórzano & Yosso, 2002) to popular color/culture-blind and purportedly race-neutral approaches to school reform, highlighting the value, if not necessity, for including urban youth more actively in the study of urban schooling and how to improve it.

Findings: Books, Budgets, and Blancos

Consistent with the goals of participatory action research, the student-researchers were active in every phase of the project, from developing the research questions and methods to answering them, to data collection, analysis, and dissemination of the findings. To initiate the development of our research questions, the students were encouraged to voice all of the issues related to their schooling that upset them or caused them concern. As you can imagine, responses ranged from critiques of cafeteria food and unclean restrooms to larger structural issues such as what students perceived to be the disproportionate application of discipline policies and the groups' interests and concerns about a lack of access to academically rigorous learning experiences that would prepare them for what they referred to as the "real world." The topics the students believed to be most salient were grouped into three themes: Books, Budget Cuts, and Blancos. The first, Books, refers to issues of access to academically rigorous and culturally responsive curriculum. Budget cuts speak to the impact of economic hardships that have swept the country recently and the adverse impact they have on schools like RHS located in communities that were already experiencing significant economic challenges. Finally, Blancos, speaks to "the overwhelming presence of whiteness" (Sleeter, 2001) that characterized the culture of the school the students attended. All of these themes are discussed in more detail below.

Books

While significant lip service is given in policy forums and school reform efforts to raising academic standards, many Latina/o students in urban schools still struggle to gain access to quality learning experiences that prepare them for higher education and beyond. President Barack Obama recently established a goal for the United States to once again have the highest proportion of college graduates of any industrialized nation by 2020 (Carey, 2009). Given the rapidly growing number of Latinas/os in U.S. urban schools, if half of all Latinas/os continue not to graduate from high school (National Center for Educational Statistics, 2012), and if many of those who do graduate are not prepared to go to college (Greene & Winters, 2005), the country will never be able to reach this goal. Because of the economic and social implications of academic underachievement, one can easily argue that the future success of the country is predicated in large part on the academic success of Latina/o youth.

Based on the students' experiences, it seems like the goal of raising standards as a means for improving achievement and access to higher education is elusive at best. The students began their participation in the research collaborative as 11th graders. During one of the first meetings of the group we discussed their college aspirations and the eligibility requirements for successful candidates for four-year institutions of higher education in their state. Within minutes it became obvious that the majority of the students were not taking courses that would put them in a position to attend a bachelor's degree–granting institution upon graduation. The following is an excerpt of the discussion culled from field notes that highlights the moment when many of the students became more fully aware that their aspirations to attend college might be severely compromised by the course of study established for them by counselors and teachers:

IRIZARRY: You need to have Algebra 1 and 2 to attend most four-year colleges in the country.

MULTIPLE VOICES: I haven't taken that. What do you mean? That's hard. If I am not in it now, when can I take it?

IRIZARRY: What Math classes have you taken, if you are not taking Algebra?

TAÍNA:	Consumer Math. I am in Consumer Math with Mr. Smith.
NATASHA:	Yeah, me too . . . Consumer Math.
ALBERTO:	I don't have any Math right now. I took that class (Consumer Math) already. I have some free periods . . . you know study halls and stuff but no Math right now. Is that bad?
JASMINE:	That Algebra is too hard. Like seriously hard I heard.
RAMÓN:	That's for the White kids . . . the smart kids.
MULTIPLE VOICES:	(Snickering) Yeah, that's true. Yup.
IRIZARRY:	Is that why you haven't taken Algebra? Is it your choice?
CARMEN:	Basically, Guidance has screwed us.
TAÍNA:	Yup. That's how they do. They don't want us to make it. Yup. That's messed up. I want to go to college, but do they care? No.
CARMEN:	Seriously? Like seriously? They make the schedule. They tell you what to take.

After coming to the personal realization that, almost without exception, the students were not being scheduled into classes, such as Algebra 1 and 2, necessary to position them as viable candidates for higher education, the conversation shifted to speak to the more institutional aspects of marginalization through the highly racialized practice of academic tracking, or sorting students into particular classes based on their perceived ability levels. Also referred to as academic apartheid (see Akom, 2003), referencing the highly racialized aspects of it, tracking is a practice that often limits opportunities for youth from historically marginalized communities and contributes to the social reproductive function of schooling. That is, schools that serve students from lower socioeconomic strata and youth of color often provide them a poor-quality education, potentially limiting their life choices (MacLeod, 2005; Noguera, 2001; Duncan-Andrade & Morrell, 2008).

As a result of a poor-quality education, many students are unprepared to meet the rigors of higher education and often lack the skills essential to survive in an increasingly knowledge-based society. Consequently, as social reproductive theory suggests, they remain stuck in a cycle of poverty. Schools that serve middle-class and upper-class kids typically offer them a higher-quality education than they offer students attending schools in communities that are economically disadvantaged to ensure that they have the knowledge and skills necessary to progress onto college and secure jobs that help them stay in the middle and upper classes. Because class and race are interrelated variables—people of color are overrepresented in the lower socioeconomic strata—social reproduction takes on a racial as well as economic tenor.

As the students became increasingly aware of the social reproductive function of schooling through their work in the research collaborative, they shifted their gaze from solely implicating individual students for a lack of school success to critically examining how the system of public education, and particularly how opportunities were structured at their school, portended for them academic and professional trajectories that were drastically different than those they had imagined for themselves. Part of their study of tracking in their school involved looking at the racial/ethnic composition of classes at various levels of rigor (i.e., Advanced Placement, College Prep, and Fundamentals). Their findings were consistent with the research literature and suggested that Latina/o students were significantly underrepresented in "college-prep" courses and overrepresented in the least academically rigorous, basic-level courses in their school (see Irizarry, 2011). As their understandings of institutional oppression became more sophisticated, they moved from solely critiquing academic apartheid to also forward suggestions for restructuring schools so that they work in the best interest of all students. Carmen's critical analysis provide a poignant summary of the student researchers' recommendations relative to tracking and underscores the dire necessity to engage young people more actively in the process of school reform. As she noted, instead of tapping into the potential of Carmen and other Latina/o students of her generation, the racialized practice of tracking is used as a mechanism of control to prevent Latinas/os, the largest group of minoritized people in the United States and the emerging majority in schools, from obtaining the education necessary to assume leadership positions and shape policy.

> before I was in this class, I didn't think nothing of the fact that I was getting taught less than the other students. I mean, I knew it was there, but I wasn't really thinking—I never thought—"Oh, I can do something to change this," you know? And now that we're in this class . . . it dawns on me every single time that we've already started change because people are talking. As Latinas/os are becoming the majority, if things stay the way they are, we are not getting the education we need to be President of the United States or just even to go to college and be whatever you want. Things are bad for us now. Just look at this school as an example. We can make it better but we can do more if we get a good education and college degrees and jobs that put us in a spot to change it.

Throughout history, U.S. social institutions, such as schools, have been imbued with the stain of institutional racism. Tracking students of color into classes that hinder them from meeting their personal goals and fail to help them develop the skills necessary to have choices in an increasingly knowledge-based economy is a present-day manifestation of institutional forms of oppression based on race, class, and other target identities. As the voices of the student researchers in this study demonstrated, this highly racialized practice can alienate young people from school, depress their aspirations, and potentially lead to a pessimistic fate, as students have few employment options beyond the low-wage service sector of the economy (see Cammarota, 2008). Critical race theory suggests that the policies and practices such as tracking that serve to limit educational opportunity are not randomly applied, nor are the pessimistic academic and social outcomes seen in these communities an unintended consequence. The student researchers implored educators and policy makers to critically analyze the deleterious impact of tracking and other school reform policies. Moreover, their emic perspectives remind us of the "community cultural wealth" (Yosso, 2005)—forms of cultural capital that are rarely acknowledged by schools—that exist in their communities and the potential utility to leverage this knowledge base to inform meaningful school reform efforts.

Budget Cuts

Rana High School was located in one of the most economically disadvantaged communities in the state. During the recent recession many states cut back on the funding provided to schools to help balance budgets. While budget cuts hurt all schools, the student researchers suggested that they have a disproportionately adverse impact on schools in communities that were already struggling economically. For example, as part of their research they spoke with administrators who revealed some of the budget constraints under which they were forced to operate. In this particular setting, budget cuts resulted in the loss of teachers, and additional fees were put in place for students wanting to participate in the athletics program, and several sports teams were cut. The students found that the school cafeteria ran out of food several times a month, leaving many students without access to nourishment during the day. Another consequence of budget restrictions was that the school was no longer able to provide calculators and other learning resources to students. Understandably, all of these school-based responses to budget cuts have a negative impact on students who come from families with limited economic resources.

Commenting on the cumulative impact of budget cuts on their school and other schools serving Latina/o youth dealing with similar circumstances, as well as school funding patterns in the state, Jasmine offered the following critique:

> The [school] funding stuff that we read, that was like Whoa. You never really think about it. Kids who live in poor communities, like with less money, they have less money going into their school. That seems wrong. It should be equal, more equal. This small state has more than like 150 school districts. Basically everybody only looks after their own. Kids in [suburban schools] don't have to worry about getting calculators or paying for sports and stuff. We do and it isn't fair. Schools should have what they need so that we have a real chance in life.

While the local impact of budget cuts are worthy of study, it is important to locate these choices within a larger system of inequitable school funding. The budget cuts that the students rightfully lament are reflective of larger racialized processes at work where a predominantly older, White voting populace is positioned to vote on school budgets and other services for an increasingly non-White student body. The racial/ethnic and generational patterns are evident in recent school budget elections. In 2010, the second year of the study, school operating budgets were not approved in many communities with large percentages of students of color and sizable populations of older Whites, including the community where my student co-researchers attended school, where the budget was voted down three times before passing. These voting patterns support the findings from a 2007 study conducted by the Population Reference Bureau, which found that states in which the majority of voters were White and whose public schools served a majority of students of color often spend less on education than states in which the racial/ethnic texture of the voting population was more congruent with that of the students (Cohn, 2007). These trends highlight the power of a large, predominantly older, White electorate to shape public policy that will undoubtedly affect the opportunity structure for an increasingly Brown school-aged population.

While it is important to recognize the value of providing quality educational opportunities to students of color for themselves and their communities, improving the quality of schooling for minoritized students is also in the best interests of White people. That is, if students of color continue to underachieve at alarming rates in schools, they will not be able to obtain the jobs necessary to "pay if forward" for the entitlements enjoyed by older generations. More than just an economic benefit, the educational marginalization of Latina/o students and other students of color also means the country will continue to lose out on the resources, broadly defined, of an entire generation. Perhaps approaches to school reform might be more likely to improve the plight of urban schools if policy makers understood "interest convergence," a concept within critical race theory that suggests that racism will end only when Whites see that it is in their best interests to end it (see Bell, 1980; Milner, 2008).

Blancos

The third area of focus for the student researchers was the pervasive nature of Whiteness within their schooling. The curriculum, according to their analysis, was Eurocentric, failing to include the perspectives and contributions of People of Color. The racialized nature of tracking and the disproportionate application of school discipline policies, among other data points, provided further evidence of the marginalization of students of color and the privilege afforded White students (Irizarry, 2011). When examined collectively, these policies and practices speak to how the cultural frames of reference, histories, and experiences of Whites were framed as "normal" while those of people of color are positioned as deviant or abnormal (Leonardo, 2007; Sleeter, 2001). Race-based privileges, such as access to college-prep courses, receiving the benefit of the doubt from teachers, seeing yourself reflected in the curriculum, often remain invisible and unchallenged. Moreover, while the denial or restriction of educational opportunity can result in people of color internalizing the negative perceptions about themselves that abound in society, they can also reinscribe a feeling of superiority among Whites who view the rewards they reap from Whiteness and White privilege as stemming solely from merit and hard work. Thus, Whiteness as a construct reinscribes White supremacy and allows racialized aspects of the policies and practices cited throughout this chapter to go unexamined. During one of their working group meetings, the student researchers identified and critiqued the ways that Whiteness informs the culture of their school.

CARMEN: Look at the books and everything in this school. It is like all White. We [Latinas/os] are here, too, but you wouldn't know it by looking at the posters on the wall, the books, the [daily morning] announcements always done by White kids . . .

ALBERTO: They kill the Spanish names, yo. Then they always be laughing and stuff.

TAÍNA: You feel it, but until now I didn't really put it all together. It is all White even though like half or more of the kids here are Latina/o. It is like they are holding up the model—the White.

CARMEN: The Principals, Guidance, all the teachers, like are all White. Only like the cafeteria staff has Latinas/os. Everything around is White. Everything around us reminds us that we are not White. Right.

SEVERAL STUDENTS: Yup.

In the contexts of this school, and in most schools across the United States, Whites are most often taught by White teachers, learn more about White people than about any other group, get to learn using their dominant language, and teachers build on their cultural frames of reference. When communities of color ask for the same, they are portrayed as separatist or un-American, as is the case in the attack on the ethnic studies program in Tucson, Arizona. The students experienced a similar backlash, documented in this commentary offered by Tamara during one of the group's research presentations transcribed from my field notes.

> We just want to learn more about stuff that we like, that we are interested in. We are not saying take all of the so-called "classic books" (using air quotes to emphasize her point) should all be thrown out. We just also want to be introduced . . . to read books written by Latinas/os and other authors. We want teachers who look like us, who come from our neighborhoods, who know us. Is that asking too much? I don't think so.

The student researchers emphasized the need for increased attention to issues of racial/ethnic and linguistic diversity within their schooling experience. Because of the pervasive nature of Whiteness, many of the student participants felt alienated from school. Those that remained hopeful about the potential of schooling to help them meet their goals were ill prepared to pursue their dreams of higher education because as a result of their academic and social marginalization within the school, they were ultimately unprepared to meet the rigors of higher education. Their critique of Whiteness should not be confused with a critique of all White teachers. There were several White teachers with whom the students developed important relationships, and additional research regarding White teachers who are particularly successful working with students of color is also needed. Nevertheless, despite these individual relationships, the school was structured in ways that ultimately alienated and underserved Latina/o students.

Latina/o Youth as Educational Researchers

This chapter has explored three primary areas of concern that emerged from a youth participatory action research project in which the perspectives and interests of Latina/o students were centered. Using CRT and LatCrit to critically analyze the pervasiveness of race and racism in the educational experiences of Latina/o youth navigating schools within the context of Latinization, this chapter highlights how culturally unresponsive curricula, financial constraints, and a school culture dominated by Whiteness—captured by the students in the thematic categories Books, Budget Cuts, and Blancos—served to marginalize Latina/o youth. Based on these findings, in what follows we briefly outline three implications for educators and policy makers seeking to improve the educational experiences and outcomes for students of color in urban schools.

First, because of the important emic perspectives they bring to the process, youth need to be included more meaningfully in the process of school reform and teacher education. Urban youth of color, the schools they attend, and their communities are typically positioned as pathological or in need of control (Leonardo, 2007). Furthermore, despite failed top-down policy solutions to closing the so-called achievement gap, educational policy makers continue to default to high-stakes and market-driven approaches that aim for rapid results to a problem that is actually more complex in nature (Hursh, 2007; Lipman, 2011; Welton, 2011). Rarely, if ever, are they included as equal partners in school reform efforts. Most often, school reform policies target urban schools without ever consulting the students and families the institutions serve. Without the perspectives of youth of color we can never really know anything about their schooling experiences or respond appropriately to meet their educational needs.

The work of the student researchers and some of their insights shared in this chapter demonstrate the insider perspectives that are necessary to create real changes in urban schools. The issues that were most salient for the students were not test scores or the need for higher standards. Rather, they focused on the quality and rigor of the curriculum and the need to address issues of diversity in the curriculum and within the faculty and staff. They reject the meritocracy myth that suggests that students who try the hardest experience the highest level of academic success, and they replace that dominant narrative with a more race- and culture-conscious counternarrative that reveals how urban youth are being underserved by their schools. Reforms that do not listen to and honor the perspectives of urban youth will not motivate the types of substantive changes that are needed in urban education. Thus, because youth of color are researching issues that impact their educational trajectories, they can provide unique context-specific solutions that policy makers who examine these issues from a distance are unable to address.

The research about the impact of teachers of color highlights the many benefits of a more diverse teaching force. Several studies, for example, have argued that the academic struggles of Latina/o students are connected, at least in part, to the dearth of Latina/o/a teachers and other school personnel who may be better equipped to meet the needs of this group (Becket, 1998; Monzó & Rueda, 2001; Villegas & Clewell, 1998). Others have suggested that there are significant academic and social benefits to having a more diverse teaching force (Dee, 2004; Zirkel,

2002). As noted above, the students spoke to the stifling presence of Whiteness within their school and how the lack of racial/ethnic diversity among the faculty and staff served to reinscribe the culture of the school, which they experienced as often hostile and oppressive. Increasing diversity in all aspects of school life, especially among the faculty and administrative ranks where people of color are woefully underrepresented, would, in the estimation of the students, go a long way to improve students' experiences and outcomes.

The point, however, is not solely to increase the presence of people of color in the teaching profession, although proportionate representation is a laudable goal. Rather, all teachers need to be trained in ways that allow them to disrupt the status quo and make the changes the students whose voices are included in this chapter advocate for. Engaging youth in research on urban schooling and engaging them in the development of recommendations to improve it can potentially help contribute to creating communities of practice (Mitra, 2005) consisting of cadres of critical educators committed to transforming urban schools.

Finally, the students' voices passionately underscore the immediate need for authentic reform in urban schools. In their estimation, they experience school reform as trying to change students and their academic outcomes without seriously considering the factors that actually lead to the need for reform in the first place. That is, students—particularly students of color—are often constructed as the problem to be fixed. The students in this study urge us to shift the focus onto the institutions that educate them. If we are ever to improve urban schools and provide all students with a quality education that prepares them for higher education and beyond, we need to reposition youth—from problems to be fixed to researchers with invaluable perspectives—support them, and heed their advice.

References

Akom, Antwi A. (2003). Reexamining resistance as oppositional behavior: The nation of Islam and the creation of a black achievement ideology. *Sociology of Education, 76*(4), 305–325.

Antrop-Gonzalez, R. (2011). *Schools as radical sanctuaries: Decolonizing urban education through the eyes of youth of color and their teachers.* Charlotte, NC: Information Age Publishing.

Balfanz, R., & Legters, N. (2004). *Locating the dropout crisis.* Baltimore, MD: Johns Hopkins University Center for Social Organization of Schools.

Becket, D.R. (1998). Increasing the number of Latino and Navajo teachers in hard-to-staff schools. *Journal of Teacher Education, 49,* 196–205.

Bell, D. A. (1980). *Brown v. Board of Education* and the interest convergence dilemma. *Harvard Law Review, 93,* 518–533.

Brown, T.M. (2007). Lost and turned out: Academic, social, and emotional experiences of students excluded from school. *Urban Education, 42*(5), 432–455.

Brown, T.M., & Rodriguez, L.F. (2009). School and the co-construction of dropout. *International Journal of Qualitative Studies in Education, 22*(2), 221–242.

Cammarota, J. (2004). The gendered and racialized pathways of Latina and Latina/o youth: Different resistances in the urban context. *Anthropology and Education Quarterly, 35*(1), 53–74.

Cammarota, J. (2008). *Sueños Americanos: Barrio youth negotiate social and cultural identities.* Tucson, AZ: University of Arizona Press.

Carey, K. (2009, June 11). On accountability: Achieving President Obama's college completion goal. *Diverse Issues in Higher Education.* Retrieved from http://diverseeducation.com/artman/publish/article_12633.shtml

Carspecken, P.F. (1995). *Critical ethnography in educational research: A theoretical and practical guide.* New York, NY: Routledge.

Clark, A.D., & Reed, T.D. (2010). A future we wish to see: Racialized communities studies after white racial anxiety and resentment. *Black Scholar, 40*(4), 37–49.

Cohn, D. (2007). *The divergent paths of baby boomers and immigrants.* Washington, DC: Population Reference Bureau.

Corbin, J., & Strauss, A. (2008). *Basics of qualitative research: Techniques and procedures for developing grounded theory* (3rd ed.). Thousand Oaks, CA: Sage Publications.

Dee, T. (2004). Teachers, race, and student achievement in a randomized experiment. *Review of Economics and Statistics, 86,* 195–210.

Delgado, R., & Stefancic, J. (2001). *Critical race theory: An introduction.* New York, NY: New York University Press.

Duncan-Andrade, J., & Morrell, E. (2008). *The art of critical pedagogy: The promise of moving from theory to practice in urban schools.* New York, NY: Peter Lang.

Fine, M. (1991). *Framing dropouts: Notes on the politics of an urban high school.* Albany, NY: State University of New York Press.

Foxen, P. (2010). *Speaking out: Latino youth on discrimination in the United States.* Washington, DC: National Council of La Raza.

Frankenberg, E., & Orfield, G. (2012). *The resegregation of suburban schools: A hidden crisis in American education.* Cambridge, MA: Harvard Education Press.

Gándara, P., & Baca, G. (2008). NCLB and California's English language learners: The perfect storm. *Language Policy, 7,* 201–216.

Gándara, P., & Contreras, F. (2009). *The Latino education crisis: The consequences of failed social policies.* Cambridge, MA: Harvard Education Press.

Gándara, P., & Rumberger, R.W. (2009). Immigration, language, and education: How does language policy structure opportunity? *Teachers College Record, 111*(3), 750–782.

Gonzalez, K.P., Stoner, C., & Jovel, J.E. (2003). Examining the role of social capital in access to college for Latinas: Toward a college opportunity framework. *Journal of Hispanic Higher Education, 2*(1), 146–170.

Greene, J.P., & Winters, M. (2005). *Public high school graduation and college readiness: 1991–2002.* New York, NY: Manhattan Institute for Policy Research.

Herbert, M. (2012, March). Tucson grapples with ethnic studies ban. *District administration.* Retrieved from http://www.districtadministration.com/article/tucson-grapples-ethnic-studies-ban

Holme, J.J., Welton, A., & Diem, S. (2012). Pursuing "separate but equal" in suburban San Antonio: A case study of Southern Independent School District. In E. Frankenberg & G. Orfield (Eds.), *The resegregation of suburban schools: A hidden crisis in American education* (pp. 45–67). Cambridge, MA: Harvard Education Press.

Hursh, D. (2007, September). Assessing No Child Left Behind and the rise of neoliberal policies. *American Educational Research Journal, 44*(3), 493–518.

Irizarry, J.G. (2009). Reinvigorating multicultural education through youth participatory action research. *Multicultural Perspectives, 11*(4), 194–199.

Irizarry, J.G. (2011). *The Latinization of U.S. schools: Successful teaching and learning in shifting cultural contexts.* Boulder, CO: Paradigm.

Irizarry, J. G. (2012). Los Caminos: Latino/a youth forging pathways into higher education. *Journal of Hispanics in Higher Education, 11*(3), 291–309.

Jerald, C.D., Haycock, K., & Wilkins, A. (2009). *Fighting for quality and equality, too. How state policymakers can ensure the drive to improve teacher quality doesn't just trickle down to poor and minority children.* Washington, DC: Education Trust.

Katz, S.R. (1999). Teaching in tensions: Latino immigrant youth, their teachers and the structures of schooling. *Teachers College Record, 100*(4), 809–840.

Kim, C.Y., Losen, D.J., & Hewitt, D.T. (2010). *The school-to-prison pipeline: Structuring legal reform.* New York, NY: New York University Press.

Kimura-Walsh, E., Yamamura, E.K., Griffin, K.A., & Allen, W.R. (2009). Achieving the college dream?: Examining disparities in access to college information among high achieving and non-high achieving Latina students. *Journal of Hispanic Higher Education, 8*(3), 298–315.

Kirkland, D. (2010). "Black skin, White masks": Normalizing Whiteness and the trouble with the achievement gap. *Teachers College Record.* Retrieved from http://www.tcrecord.org/Content.asp?ContentId=16116

Kunnie, J. (2010). Apartheid in Arizona: HB 2281and Arizona's denial of human rights of peoples of color. *Black Scholar, 40*(4), 16–26.

Lacayo, A.E. (2011). *One year later: A look at SB 1070 and copy cat legislation.* Washington, DC: National Council of La Raza.

Leonardo, Z. (2007). The war on schools: NCLB, nation creation and the educational construction of whiteness. *Race Ethnicity and Education, 10*(3), 261–278.

Lipman, P. (2004). *High stakes education: Inequality, globalization, and urban school reform.* New York, NY: Routledge.

Lipman, P. (2011). *The new political economy of urban education: Neoliberalism, race, and the right to the city.* New York, NY: Routledge.

MacLeod, J. (2005). *Ain't no makin' it: Aspirations and attainment in a low-income neighborhood.* Boulder, CO: Westview Press.

Milner, H.R. (2008). Critical race theory and interest convergence as analytic tools in teacher education policies and practices. *Journal of Teacher Education, 59*(4), 332–346.

Milner, H.R. (2010). *Start where you are, but don't stay there: Understanding diversity, opportunity gaps, and teaching in today's classrooms.* Cambridge, MA: Harvard Education Press.

Milner, H.R. (2012). Beyond a test score: Explaining opportunity gaps in educational practice. *Journal of Black Studies, 43*(6), 693–718.

Mitra, D.L. (2005). Adults advising youth. Leading while getting out of the way. *Educational Administration Quarterly, 41*(3), 520–553.

Monzó, L.D., & Rueda, R. (2001). *Sociocultural factors in social relationships: Examining Latino teachers' and paraeducators' interactions with Latino students.* Research Report 9. Santa Cruz, CA: Center for Research on Education, Diversity, and Excellence.

Murillo, E. (Ed.). (2010). *Handbook of Latinos and education: Research, theory and practice.* Mahwah, NJ: Lawrence Erlbaum Associates.

National Center for Educational Statistics. (2012). *Digest of educational statistics 2012.* Washington, DC: U.S. Department of Education.

National Council of La Raza. (2007). *Paying the price: The impact of immigration raids on America's children.* Retrieved from http://lideres.nclr.org/content/article/detail/3301/

Noguera, P.A. (2001). Racial politics and the elusive quest for excellence and equity in education. *Education and Urban Society, 34*(1), 18–41.

Oboler, S. (2010). On race, racial profiling and states of mind(lessness). *Latino Studies, 8*(2), 149–155.

Otero, L.R., & Cammarota, J. (2011). Notes from the ethnic studies home front: Student protests, texting, and the subtexts of oppression. *International Journal of Qualitative Studies in Education, 24*(5), 639–648.

Patel Stevens, L., & Stovall, D.O. (2011). Critical literacy for xenophobia: A wake-up call. *Journal of Adolescent and Adult Literacy, 54*(4), 295–298.

Patterson, J.A., Hale, D., & Stessman, M. (2007). Cultural contradictions and school leaving: A case study of an urban high school. *High School Journal, 91*(2), 1–15.

Pedraza, P., & Rivera, M. (2005). *Latino education: An agenda for community action research.* Mahwah, NJ: Lawrence Erlbaum Associates.

Pew Research Center. (2010). *Time lost: The high cost, low return of longer prison terms.* Retrieved from http://www.pewstates.org/research/reports/time-served-85899394616

Pollock, M. (2004). Race wrestling: Struggling strategically with race in educational research and practice. *American Journal of Education, 111*(1), 25–67.

Raible, J. & Irizarry, J.G. (2007). Transracialized selves and the emergence of post-white teacher identities. *Race, Ethnicity, and Education, 10*(2), 177–198.

Raible, J., & Irizarry, J.G. (2010). Redirecting the teacher's gaze: Teacher education, youth surveillance and the school-to-prison pipeline. *Teacher and Teacher Education, 26,* 1196–1203.

Rodriguez, L.F. (2008). "Teachers know you can do more": Manufacturing deliberate cultures of success for urban high school students. *Educational Policy, 22,* 758–780.

Rodriguez, L.F. (2012). "Everybody grieves, but still nobody sees": Toward a praxis of recognition for Latina/o students in U.S. schools. *Teachers College Record,* ID No. 010302. Retrieved from http://www.tcrecord.org/Content.asp?ContentId=010302.

Rumberger, R.W., & Rodriguez, G.M. (2011). Chicano dropouts: An update of research and policy issues. In R.R. Valencia (Ed.), *Chicano school failure and success: Past, present, and future* (3rd ed., pp. 101–116). New York, NY: RoutledgeFalmer.

Scott, J.T. (2011). Market-driven education reform and the racial politics of advocacy. *Peabody Journal of Education, 86,* 580–599.

Seidman, I. (2006). *Interviewing as qualitative research: A guide for researchers in education and the social sciences* (3rd ed.). New York, NY: Teachers College Press.

Sleeter, C.E. (2001). *Culture, difference and power.* New York, NY: Teachers College Press.

Solórzano, D.G., & Ornelas, A. (2002). A critical race analysis of advanced placement classes: A case of educational inequality. *Journal of Latinos and Education, 1*(4), 215–229.

Solórzano, D.G., & Yosso, T.J. (2002). A critical race counterstory of affirmative action in higher education. *Equity and Excellence in Education, 35*(2), 155–168.

Talbert-Johnson, C. (2006). Preparing highly qualified teacher candidates for urban schools: The importance of dispositions. *Education and Urban Society, 39*(1), 147–160.

Trujillo, T. (2012). The paradoxical logic of school turnarounds: A Catch-22. *Teachers College Record,* ID No. 16797. Retrieved from http://www.tcrecord.org/Content.asp?ContentId=16797

Valadez, J.R. (2008). Shaping the educational decisions of Mexican immigrant high school students. *American Educational Research Journal, 45*(4), 834–860.

Valencia, R.R. (1997). *The evolution of deficit thinking: Educational thought and practice.* Bristol, PA: Taylor and Francis.

Valencia, R.R., Valenzuela, A., Sloan, K., & Foley, D.E. (2001). Let's treat the cause, not the symptoms: Equity and accountability in Texas revisited. *Phi Delta Kappan, 83*(4), 318–321.

Valenzuela, A. (1999). *Subtractive schooling: US-Mexican youth and the politics of caring.* Albany, NY: State University of New York Press.

Villegas, A.M., & Clewell, B.C. (1998). Increasing the number of teachers of color for urban schools. *Education and Urban Society, 31*(1), 42–61.

Wayman, J.C. (2002). Student perceptions of teacher ethnic bias: A comparison of Mexican American and non-Latino White dropouts and students. *High School Journal, 85*(1), 27–37.

Welton, A. (2011). The courage to critique policies and practices from within: Youth participatory action research as critical policy analysis. A response to "Buscando la Libertad: Latino youths in search of freedom in school." *Democracy and Education, 19*(1), Article 11.

Yosso, T.J. (2005). Whose culture has capital? A critical race theory discussion of community cultural wealth. *Race Ethnicity and Education, 8*(1), 69–91.

Zirkel, S. (2002). Is there a place for me? Role models and achievement among White students and students of color. *Teachers College Record, 104,* 357–376.

14

Teacher Influences in the Racialization of Disabilities

Adai Tefera, Kathleen King Thorius & Alfredo J. Artiles

The disproportionate representation of racial minorities in special education, particularly in urban schools,[1] is an enduring educational equity problem in the United States and beyond (Artiles, Kozleski, & Waitoller, 2011).[2] The problem is multilayered and defies linear and univariate explanations. Nevertheless, teacher influences have been recurrently mentioned in this work. We provide in this chapter a critical sociocultural and sociopolitical perspective regarding teacher influences in the racialization of disabilities. We critique how teacher influences have been studied in this literature and broaden the analysis to include considerations of teacher quality, particularly within the context of current education policy and teacher learning. Although teacher quality has been identified as an influence in the educational failure of racial minority students and current teacher evaluation systems are being implemented to improve quality, we argue that narrow definitions of what constitutes a highly qualified or effective teacher disregards the role of structural inequalities, and insufficiently emphasizes teachers' preparation to engage with learners from diverse backgrounds, including students of color, students with disabilities, English learners, and those students who are at the intersection of multiple labels. This is particularly evident in urban schools, and thus, research on the racialization of disability cannot afford to ignore these forces.

In their discussion of disproportionality and creating culturally responsive educational systems, Klingner et al. (2005) argue, "[i]t is imperative to understand the ideological premises and histories leading to the ratification of the policies that guide educators' work." We therefore contend that given the current focus on the evaluation of teachers to improve teacher quality and learning, discussions include a critical examination of the ideological influences guiding these policies and practices and its potential consequences on racial disproportionality in special education. We also examine sociocultural contexts, particularly inequitable structural barriers that continue to go unaddressed despite nominal calls for equitable reform within the current neoliberal context. To date, education research focused on the sociopolitical context, specifically neoliberal influences, and teachers have been minimal (for exceptions, see, Sleeter, 2008; Weiner, 2007; Zeichner, 2010), with even fewer researchers focused on the intersection of neoliberalism and racial disproportionality in special education (Berhanu, 2010).

Overview of the Racialization of Disabilities

The advent of the civil rights movement for racial minorities propelled significant social changes for other marginalized groups, including disabled children and youth that culminated in the passage of the Individuals with Disabilities Education Act in 1975. This federal legislation significantly expanded educational access and opportunities for this population. A formal service delivery system was built and personnel preparation programs were launched across all geographical regions of the United States. Indeed, these changes marked a consequential response to longstanding injustices for people with disabilities (Artiles, Trent, & Palmer, 2004).

Notwithstanding the advances afforded by these historical developments in the education of disabled learners, special education has also been construed as a source of inequities for racial minority students. Specifically, researchers and parents of racial minorities have raised questions and sued school districts due to the disproportionate representation of these learners in the so-called subjective or high-incidence disabilities—that is, learning disabilities, intellectual disabilities, and emotional/behavioral disorders. Key legal cases include *Diana v. California State Board of Education* and *Larry P. v. Riles* in the 1970s. Furthermore, Dunn's (1968) reflections published in a widely cited journal article, and two reports published by the National Research Council (Donovan & Cross, 2002; Heller, Holtzman, & Messick, 1982) demonstrate the importance of this issue, particularly in the last 30 years. The disabilities under consideration are described as "mild" or "high incidence" because they constitute about two-thirds of the population with disabilities. These disability categories are also called "subjective" because clinical decision making or professional judgment is at the core of the diagnosis process.

The term *disproportionate representation* is associated with over- and under-representation in diagnostic categories. The former, overrepresentation, is the most studied in this research area. Disproportionate representation refers to disability identification patterns that are mediated by learners' traits such as race, social class, language background, or gender. Disproportionate representation has been defined as "unequal proportions of culturally diverse students in special education programs" (Artiles & Trent, 2000, p. 514). African American and American Indian students are the most persistently affected by mild disability overrepresentation at the national level. Other racial groups can be over- or under-represented at the regional, state, city, or district levels. Disproportionality is highly consequential since it is entangled with other barriers that deepen inequities for racial minority students, which include school suspensions, expulsions, and dropouts (Losen, 2011; Skiba, Michael, Nardo, & Peterson, 2000; Skiba et al., 2011).

It is interesting to note that although the overrepresentation of racial minority students has been discussed, debated, and reviewed since the late 1960s, the bulk of the studies have been published in the last 10 years (Waitoller et al., 2010). A complex web of findings characterizes this literature. To wit:

- Donovan and Cross reported in 2002 that, at the national level, African Americans were 2.35 times more likely than White peers to receive an [intellectual disability] diagnosis. Native Americans were 24% more likely than their peers to receive a [learning disability] label. African Americans were 59% more likely than their counterparts to be identified as [emotionally/behaviorally disordered].
- The [intellectual disability] category increased by 400% between 1948 and 1966; it was the largest disability group in 1975. [Learning disability] prevalence has grown by over 200% since 1975.

- Boys represent about 80% of the [emotionally/behaviorally disordered] population, 70% of [learning disabled] students, and 60% of students with [intellectual disabilities]. Poor students are disproportionately represented in these categories.
- After students are placed in special education, academic performance remains low, the risk for dropout and juvenile justice placement increases, and access to college is limited compared with that of their nondisabled peers; in adulthood this population tends to stay in low-paying jobs. White students with disabilities tend to do better than their racial minority peers.
- Racial minority students have more limited access to related services and are placed in more segregated programs than their White peers with the same disability diagnosis.
- Poverty is associated with disability status; however, race is a significant predictor of disability diagnosis after controlling for poverty. Poverty moderates the risk for disability diagnosis in complex ways, depending on school or community poverty levels, student race and gender, disability category, and school location (Artiles, 2011, p. 432).

An important insight from analyses of this problem is that special education embodies a paradox in which resources, access, and opportunities are made available to disabled individuals, while discrimination, barriers, and marginalization may also arise for other minority groups identified with these labels. How do researchers explain this complex problem? Is there consensus about the explanations advanced thus far? We address briefly these issues in the next section.

A Problem in Search of Explanations

Two explanations have dominated the disproportionality research to date, namely a sociodemographic thesis and a professional practice account (Waitoller et al., 2010).[3] The former is represented in studies that examine the influence of student, school, and community sociodemographic traits on disability diagnosis or special education placement risks. Poverty (of students or urban communities) figures prominently in this research (see, for example, Skiba et al., 2008). Although child poverty is associated with disability prevalence, researchers have also shown that student race makes a significant and independent contribution to the probability of disability diagnosis (Skiba et al., 2005).

The second explanation raises the question as to whether professional practices, ranging from pre-referral, referral, assessment, and teams' diagnostic decisions, influence or mediate the disproportionate representation of racial minorities in special education. Research grounded in this perspective constitutes about two-thirds of the empirical studies published in scientific journals between 1968 and 2006.

We focus in this chapter on the second explanation, not only because of the number of studies produced, but also because of the critical role, we argue, teachers play in students' education. As we know, teachers are one of the most influential forces in determining students' educational outcomes (Harris & Sass, 2011; Kane & Staiger, 2008; Rivkin, Hanushek, & Kane, 2005). We therefore address the roles of macro factors that affect teacher labor—that is, education policies on accountability and teacher evaluation—along with professional practices in the racialization of disability. Our focus fills an important gap for disproportionality research that examines professional practices, particularly in the role of how teachers have been framed in problematic ways. More specifically, this line of disproportionality research has centered on individual teachers as the unit of analysis to determine whether variables such as teacher beliefs or (racial, gender, social class) biases determine or are associated with decisions to refer or place minority students in special education. We find a number of substantial limitations in these studies that merit a reframing of the ways in which teacher influences have been examined in this literature.

First, many of these studies are based on simulation methodologies[4] that offer only a glimpse on the complexities under which teachers think, make decisions, and act in classrooms and schools. Second, studies about teacher influences on disproportionality seemingly assume that teacher decisions and actions are directly caused by cognitive variables, hence, ignoring the considerable force of sociocultural and sociopolitical contexts, both distal and proximal in the processes and outcomes of classroom life and teacher labor. Third, the work lives of teachers in urban schools vary dramatically from the conditions under which teachers labor in suburban and rural environments. Teachers face unique barriers in urban contexts that are often associated with structural disadvantages related to factors such as school funding, class size, the nature of the curriculum and assessment technologies, and institutional climate (Artiles, 2011). In addition, teacher quality in urban schools that are largely populated by low-income, minority students is lower, as reflected in indicators such as certification status and experience level. We argue that how these structural conditions affect the probabilities for disability identification ought to be explored more systematically and deeply. Fourth, and related to the previous point, teachers are not passive agents merely reacting to the contextual and structural conditions of their workplaces. Indeed, teachers are consistently engaged in learning on the job about subject matter, pedagogy, assessment, their own students, and other aspects of school practices. This vision of professional learning also raises questions about the definitions of teacher quality that have been favored in recent educational reforms and policies. Unfortunately, this vision of teacher learning has not been used as a prism to document the precursors, mediators, and structural correlates of disproportionate representation.

The purpose of this chapter, therefore, is to make the case for the systematic study of previously ignored, yet highly consequential, forces in the creation, maintenance, and reproduction of the racialization of disabilities. For this purpose, we outline the current sociopolitical landscape of teacher quality and learning, examine the potential unintended consequences of how a narrow focus on what constitutes teacher quality may contribute to disproportionality in special education, overlooking the influence of structural inequalities and growing cultural and linguistic diversity. We end the chapter with a framework for teacher learning in urban educational systems with the explicit aim to disrupt disproportionality.

The Sociopolitical Landscape of Teacher Quality

Recent education policies, from the No Child Left Behind Act (NCLB) which includes the provision that every student has a highly qualified teacher (U.S. Department of Education, 2004, to recent NCLB state waivers which focus on developing highly effective teachers (U.S. Department of Education, 2011), have steadily remained focused on teachers as the conduit for improved student outcomes. Darling-Hammond (2003, 2005) argues that the definitional work of what it means to have a highly qualified teacher is not trivial. Through the adoption and implementation of these education policies what has remained constant in the current sociopolitical climate is the influence of neoliberalism, which has been exemplified in the continued emphasis on choice, standards, and competition in schools (Apple, 2001; Harvey, 2005; Hursh & Martina, 2003; Sleeter, 2008; Zeichner, 2010). A defining characteristic of neoliberalism in education is an abiding faith in the market to dictate the education process over a commitment to social outcomes, including a rearticulation of equity to mean standards and choice determined by free market ideals (Apple, 2001). Like many policies, the current focus on teacher quality has the potential of leading to both intended and unintended consequences and an exposure to contradictions, particularly as it relates to so-called subgroups of students; that is, students of color, students in special education, English learners (ELs), and students attending high-poverty schools.

Potential Unintended Consequences of Current Education Policy on Urban Special Education Teachers and Their Students

When the Elementary and Secondary Education Act (ESEA) was reauthorized in 2001, becoming the No Child Left Behind Act (NCLB), many, including those in the civil rights community, hailed the law as a major advancement for historically marginalized students, including students with disabilities. While many perceived the law to be an initial feat given that words of "equity" and "accountability" were infused throughout the NCLB law, 10 years later many lessons have been learned regarding both the law's successes and failures. Evidence of the unintended and often negative consequences related to NCLB is numerous, particularly in whether the law has aptly served those students that have been historically marginalized (Darling-Hammond, 2007; Heilig, 2011; Lipman, 2006; Valenzuela, Prieto, & Hamilton, 2008).

One of the main critiques of the law has been the looming 2014 deadline for 100 percent of students to be proficient in reading and math, and because of this deadline, the growing number of schools that have been deemed failing due to schools' inability to meet adequate yearly progress (AYP). With Congress unable to reach an agreement to reauthorize ESEA, the U.S. Department of Education decided in 2011 to grant states flexibility by allowing them to apply for ESEA state waivers. Three primary areas of focus the Department of Education articulates in the waiver application include: (1) college and career readiness; (2) state-developed accountability; and (3) supporting effective instruction and leadership (U.S. Department of Education, 2011). While discussions of teacher quality have changed since the passage of NCLB, ambiguity persists regarding new teacher evaluation systems, particularly around how students who are arguably in the most need of high-quality teachers, will be affected. For example, how will students in special education, especially students of color, and students attending high-poverty schools, be affected by the evolving definition of teacher quality? We should also remember that these accountability policies are converging at the local level with federal policies to reduce disproportionality, and policies that offer additional resources for struggling learners, such as Response to Intervention (RTI). A perverse unintended consequence of this convergence of policies, which intended to address equity concerns in the first place, is that disproportionate numbers of racial minority students continue to be placed in special education, while their educational performance remains below proficiency levels. This is happening with no policy consequences since this state of affairs is shaped in part by gaming strategies used by state and local actors (Artiles, 2011).

Nearly all of the ESEA state waivers that have been granted thus far have included teacher evaluation systems, many of which are determined by complex value-added models (VAM). VAM for teacher effectiveness includes the use of quantitative methods to measure changes in student scores from one year to the next, while taking into consideration the ability, racial, linguistic, and income characteristics of students (Sanders, 2000). However, in a recent study conducted by Newton et al. (2010), a number of problems regarding the reliability and validity of VAM in schools, particularly for students in special education, culturally and linguistically diverse students, and students attending high-poverty schools. For example, when Newton, Darling-Hammond, Haertel, & Thomas (2010) examined VAM in five school districts, they found extreme variability and instability. Specifically, after examining teachers' VAM scores over a two-year period they found that 70–80% of teachers did not have the same ratings in the second year as their first year. In fact, 20–45% of teachers scoring in the bottom 20% of rankings in their first year moved to the top part of the distribution the following year.

Significantly, Darling-Hammond, Amrein-Beardsley, Haertel, & Rothstein (2011) emphasized that while VAMs aim to statistically "control for" student characteristics such as ability, race, income, and language, it is not uncommon for a teacher to go from being ranked in the lowest category one year to the highest category the next year, due simply to a change in the classroom demographics or the number of students from diverse racial, linguistic, and income backgrounds. A great deal of concern exists, as a result, regarding the lack of stability of teacher evaluations based on VAM (Amrein-Beardsley, 2010) and the potential of fewer teachers being willing to teach students in special education, English Learners, and students attending high-poverty schools. Given this evidence, questions arise regarding the consequences of current teacher evaluation models for students. For example, will the instability of VAM scores lead to a reduction in the number of teachers interested in teaching special education, particularly in urban schools serving majority students of color? What consequences will teacher evaluations have on quality, preparation, special education prereferral and referral rates, and ultimately disproportionality in schools?

Structural Inequalities and Teacher Quality

Part of the challenge with current education policy is that while it aims to improve teacher effectiveness and student outcomes, it continues to negate the larger context in which schools, teachers, students, and school leaders are situated. The shortage of special educators in schools, for example, is pervasive throughout the United States and is an even more acute problem in poor, urban schools (McLeskey, Tyler, & Flippin, 2003). In fact, nearly 11% of those providing special education and related services are not fully certified, resulting in just over 700,000 students receiving instruction from teachers who were not deemed highly qualified (Shealey, McHatton, & Farmer, 2009). Most alarming is the fact that these shortages are most severe in high-poverty schools serving a majority of students of color, which are compounded even further by high teacher turnover rates (Ingersoll, 2002; Shealey et al., 2009). Already existing teacher shortages in special education may be further exacerbated by current teacher evaluation systems in states.

An additional issue that has gone unaddressed in current discussions of teacher quality is the number of teachers that are without certification and/or enrolled in alternative certification programs, and the propensity with which these teachers attend urban, high-poverty schools with greater numbers of students of color. According to Darling-Hammond and Sykes (2003), teacher certification can serve as a proxy for teachers' knowledge of the subject area they are teaching.

Currently, however, in the United States there has been an explosion in the number of teachers in alternative certification programs with some parts of the country having as many teachers entering the field through alternative certification programs as traditional teacher preparation programs (Zeichner, 2010). The consequence of which must not be overlooked, particularly given that many teachers are entering the classroom with little knowledge or experience teaching and managing classrooms (Grossman & Loeb, 2008; Harry, Klingner, Cramer, & Sturges, 2007). Highly troubling is that schools with the largest numbers of underprepared teachers, that is, teachers that do not have certification or novice teachers, continue to serve mostly students of color who are frequently taught by temporary, underprepared teachers throughout their time in schools (Darling-Hammond & Sykes, 2003; Donovan & Cross, 2002; Peske & Haycock, 2006). This is significant given that teachers without the adequate preparation to effectively manage their classroom may be more likely to refer students to special education (Harry & Klingner, 2006).

Furthermore, little is being done to address the persistent problem of inequitable funding practices and loopholes that affect the working conditions, recruitment, and retention efforts of teachers (Darling-Hammond, 2005). In a report on school funding practices nationwide, Adamson and Darling-Hammond (2011) point out that the highest-spending school districts spend on average nearly 10 times more than the lowest-spending districts. The authors argue that greater resources for instructional supports and teacher salaries impact the quality of teachers.

According to Sleeter (2008), "teacher education's generally weak response to the urgent need to improve the quality of teaching in historically underserved communities—who stand to benefit most from strengthened teaching—greatly contributes to the irrelevance with which it is increasingly seen in the U.S." (p. 1948). As a consequence, we have seen an explosion in the number of alternative certification programs in recent years (Feistritzer, 2011). However, ensuring that teachers, both special and general educators, are equipped to teach and engage with our rapidly diversifying student population is critical. This is particularly important given the growing number of teachers receiving training through alternative certification programs, many of which may or may not be providing training on how to teach and engage with culturally and linguistically diverse learners, particularly those in special education.

Addressing Cultural and Linguistic Diversity and Multiculturalism in Education

As previously noted, disproportionate representation of students of color in special education is greater in high-incidence categories of disability, which are more subjectively determined than low-incidence categories of disability (Donovan & Cross, 2002; Sullivan & Artiles, 2011). Elsewhere, Artiles (2011) emphasized that while poverty is one of the most commonly cited reasons for the disproportionate number of students of color in special education, race also affects the likelihood of a student to be labeled with a disability (Skiba et al., 2005). Given that schools in the United States often function based on cultural values and norms that are increasingly dissimilar to the growing number of students from culturally and linguistically diverse backgrounds (Benner, 1998), many teacher education programs have adopted multicultural or social justice teacher offerings. However, Sleeter (2008) argues that the current sociopolitical landscape has influenced the move "away from explicit multicultural, equity-oriented teacher preparation, and toward preparing teachers as technicians to implement measures school districts are taking to raise student test scores" (p. 1952).

This may be particularly problematic given the substantial discontinuities between the cultural traits and background experiences of teachers and students in urban schools. Many teachers either belong or adhere to the values of the White, middle class, while the majority of students in urban schools come from low-income racial and linguistic-minority backgrounds. Therefore, it is not uncommon for teachers to perceive personality, behavior, and social competence to be more important than students' academic abilities, thus affecting how teachers react to students, particularly students of color (Gay, 2002). But teacher perceptions, beliefs, and potential biases are not exclusively rooted in the psyche. There are explicitly deficit-oriented tropes and images about minority students circulating in popular culture, educational research, and historical accounts of educational performance that mediate teacher understandings of these learners. In other words, we cannot reduce this issue to a personal matter in which there are biased or unbiased professionals that cause disproportionate placement patterns in special education. Thus, teacher decisions to refer students to special education is a phenomenon that should be studied as shaped by individual, historical, and institutional forces. Evidence to date based on such framing is nonexistent.

With this in mind, it remains critical that teacher preparation programs and notions of quality expand to include teachers' adequate preparation to engage with students from diverse backgrounds by unpacking, questioning, and critically examining the various ways privilege and power may influence the disproportionate representation of students of color in special education (Trent, Artiles, Fitchett-Bazemore, McDaniel, & Coleman, 2002). To this end, the subsequent section offers a framework for teacher learning in urban contexts, with the explicit aim of mitigating racial disproportionality in special education, particularly within the current sociopolitical climate.

A Framework for Teacher Learning in Urban Educational Systems

Teacher learning, or the development of in-service teachers' knowledge and skills through professional development opportunities, remains a key mechanism for improving teachers' practice. Yet, 13 years after Wilson and Berne's (1999) substantive review of the literature, definitions and goals of teacher learning continue to be situated at the intersection of neoliberal sociopolitical forces that shape definitions and assessments of teacher quality and student achievement.

The Sociopolitical Landscape of Teacher Learning

Contemporary teacher learning approaches emphasize measurement of teacher quality on the basis of content-knowledge measured by tests, sometimes utilized to circumvent a need for university teacher preparation programs necessary for licensure (Sleeter, 2008), as well as student performance on high-stakes assessments. As public education becomes gradually influenced by neoliberalism, transformed into a means to accomplish global capitalism, districts are increasingly relying on scripted curricula and pedagogies aligned with state standards and related government-mandated high-stakes tests (Margolis, 2006). Within these contexts, teacher learning is often viewed as a mechanism for ensuring federal and state polices are enacted locally (Coburn & Stein, 2006), and related professional development is focused on ensuring teacher compliance with such policies (Lieberman & Mace, 2010). That is, teacher learning is both coordinated with and situated within the current policy implementation context, and as a result, in-service teachers are being professionally socialized as technicians knowledgeable of state-adopted learning standards and who are able to implement standardized curricula with fidelity, primarily assessed by student performance on high-stakes tests; this is particularly the case in urban educational systems (Lieberman & Mace, 2010).

Teacher Learning in Urban Systems

Within urban educational settings, concerns with equity in student opportunities and outcomes abound due to a higher likelihood of underresourced schools (Kozol, 1992), complex and dense bureaucracies (Milner, 2006), and the presence of educators who do not represent the racial, ethnic, linguistic, and socioeconomic backgrounds of their students (Strizek, Pittsonberger, Riordan, Lyter, & Orlofsky, 2006). Consequently, the convergences and intersections of difference that exist in urban schools provide additional political, cultural, and organizational context within which teacher learning takes place, while mediating the content, process, and desired outcomes of such learning (Thorius & Scribner, in press).

Urban educational systems necessitate specific content and processes for teacher learning, shaped by "explorations of identity and sociocultural, political, and economic histories of urban systems and schools, as well as individual and cultural views about difference" (Thorius & Scribner, in press). Beyond commitments to acknowledging and building on the resources of their students, urban teachers must demonstrate theoretical knowledge of teaching and learning that in turn informs their practice, as well as flexibility and responsiveness in solving problems, collecting and interpreting data, and reflecting on their own practice and professional growth (Cochran-Smith, Davis, & Fries, 2004).

In a synthesis of recent research on teacher learning, Thorius and Scribner (in press) presented several intersecting features of urban teacher learning that result in improvements in practice and that, in turn, improve student outcomes and address unequal access to resources and power in urban schools and surrounding communities. The first of these arenas draws from a large body of research on teacher learning over the past two decades; the situated nature of teacher learning centered on the study of everyday practice (Lieberman & Mace, 2010; Stoll, Bolam, McMahon, Wallace, & Thomas, 2006; Wilson & Berne, 1999) is grounded in theory that adult learning is facilitated when embedded within the communities in which they practice (Donovan, Bransford, & Pellegrino, 1999; Lave & Wenger, 1990), and allows adult learners to collaboratively examine authentic problems of practice (Hord, Roussin, & Sommers, 2010; McLauglin & Talbert, 2010).

Relatedly, teacher learning in urban schools also attends to the unique sociopolitical features of urban spaces including the strengths of diverse resources and experiences of students and their families, as well as the challenges associated with the structural effects of poverty (Lareau, 2011), to inform and shape the content and desired outcomes of such learning. This means that teachers examine student progress and outcomes in light of the structural and situational forces of the communities within which they live, and the associated impact on why and how students and their families approach formal educational experiences.

A final arena for urban teacher learning is an explicit inquiry into the historical legacies of inequitable opportunities to learn particularly for students of color, students with disabilities, and English Learners. This seldom-taught inquiry (Milner, 2003) also includes teachers' engagement in critical reflections on their own identity toward understanding the roles of their cultural memberships and experiences in mediating their beliefs about teaching, learning, students, families, and communities (Thorius & Scribner, in press). This represents a shift from merely focusing attention on improving existing systemic operations that only peripherally addresses the improvement of outcomes for marginalized students toward advancements in systemic organization centered on the achievement of equitable outcomes for historically underserved students (Kozleski & Artiles, 2011). As applied, such inquiry may include educators' critical reflection on their explanations for why certain students struggle academically, and thus are referred for special education eligibility consideration, with a focus on explanations that avoid examination of the quality of general education curriculum and instruction.

Urban Teacher Learning to Address the Disproportionality of Historically Underserved Students in Special Education

There is perhaps no issue more illustrative of the impact of macro and local contexts on student outcomes in urban educational settings than that of the disproportionate representation of students of color in special education (Artiles, 2011; Teese, Lamb, & Duru-Bellat, 2007). Teacher learning focused on addressing the complex issues that position disproportionality as a miner's canary (Waitoller et al., 2010) in urban schools provides teachers with an opportunity for exploring macro sociopolitical forces such as the meritocratic values of a capitalist economy, as well as the connection between such forces and the social and institutional patterns of policies, practices, and belief systems within urban schools that create conditions for disproportionality to exist. Now, we shift to put forth three distinct recommendations for application of the arenas in this framework for in-service urban teacher learning to the elimination of disproportionality in an urban local school setting.

Provide a Space for Situated, Collaborative, and Authentic Examination of Disproportionality

Just as the examination of data in the form of student work is a central feature of teacher learning that can lead to improvements in teacher practice and improved student outcomes (Fernandez, Cannon, & Chokshi, 2003), examination of local data is a useful tool in teacher learning aimed at eliminating disproportionality. However, forms of data must move beyond the quantification of disproportionality, which alone do not provide insight into the reasons why such disproportionality exists. Without examination of other forms of data educators may reproduce deficit-based explanations for disproportionality (see Waitoller et al., 2010) as stemming primarily from factors over which educators have no control: students' experiences in relation to income, race, ethnicity, national origin, and primary language. While the possibilities for which data are collected and explored are myriad, areas for consideration include the ways in which observation of curriculum and instruction in the general education classroom are (or are not) considered in special education eligibility determination decisions, review of reasons for teachers' written requests for assistance to child study or building-based multitiered intervention teams, and examination of video-recorded dialogue during lessons between teachers and students, all with an eye on the role of general education curriculum and instruction on the creation of culturally responsive opportunities to learn. The collective nature of this examination requires that educators' not only collect their own data, but also share and reflect upon these data in coordination with their colleagues over time.

Examine the Sociopolitical Landscapes Contributing to Disproportionality

Urban teacher learning aimed at eliminating disproportionality requires teachers to identify and interpret both intended and unintended consequences of the multiple, and often conflicting, policy demands that focus teachers' attention toward standardized practice, often at the expense of curriculum and instruction that is responsive to diverse students' lived experiences. Providing teachers a space to critically analyze disproportionality within a larger sociopolitical context provides a much-needed perspective that shifts attention away from the oversimplification of teachers as being those in need of improvement to a more contextual understanding of the ways in which policies are influenced and mediated by larger sociopolitical forces that often contribute to inequitable outcomes. This includes policies that support the tracking and grouping of students by ability and language proficiency, as well as school and district discipline and attendance procedures.

Explicit Inquires Into Disproportionality and Related Critical Reflections on Identity and Practice

As part of the process described in the preceding paragraph, teachers are able to actively engage the ethical dilemmas of practice these policies pose, and the assumptions about urban students and families these policies represent, while developing ways to counter through practice the policies that contribute to disproportionality and other forms of inequity (see, for example, El-Haj, 2003). Further, teachers also examine the consequences of their own racial and other demographic markers of identity and related beliefs, values, and experiences, facilitated through reflective questioning strategies. For example, Kohli (2009) calls on teacher education preparation programs to provide a space for teachers to engage in critical race reflections by utilizing their own personal histories and experiences to challenge racism and other forms of oppression in schools. More specifically, as Milner (2003) suggests, teachers may reflect on the relationships between their own racialized educational experiences and how they understand those of their students. This suggestion has implications for educators' questioning the intersections of race and disability by asking themselves, "How might my racial experiences, as well as those of my struggling students, contribute to my beliefs about their need for special education?"

The preceding recommendations for in-service teachers require that federal and state policy structures, school districts, and professional development are committed to and deliberate about recognizing and addressing racial disproportionality. We recognize that doing so requires a prioritization of resources to provide teachers with ongoing professional learning opportunities that include consistent mentoring, in order to ameliorate disproportionality. Specifically, professional development should be embedded within teachers' daily work, develop teachers' capacity for critical race reflections on practice, and feature examination of classroom and school data not only on student achievement and discipline, but also on special education referral rates, teacher-student interactions, and other locally determined sources which may indicate disparate patterns in student access, participation, and outcomes.

Conclusion

In this chapter we argue for the systematic study of the forces that create, maintain, and reproduce the racialization of disabilities beyond individual-level factors. To this end, we examined the current sociocultural and sociopolitical landscape of teacher quality and learning, and the ways in which narrow definitions of quality overlook structural inequality, potentially contributing to disproportionality in special education. Ensuring that notions of teacher quality and effectiveness expand to include not only the ability to teach students valuable academic skills, but to do so in ways that respect and honor students' cultural and linguistic backgrounds, is an important piece that current policy has overlooked. Because of the seeming convergence of the increasingly diverse student population and the growing number of teachers going through both traditional and alternative certification programs, it is important that definitions of teacher quality expand to include the ability to engage with and teach students from diverse racial, ability, and linguistic backgrounds. Given that the current sociopolitical climate and focus on teacher evaluations does little if anything to address these issues, in this chapter we offer a framework for teacher learning in urban educational systems with the explicit aim of disrupting racial disproportionality in special education.

Notes

Authors' note: Address correspondence to Adai Tefera at atefera@asu.edu. The first author is grateful for the support of an Office of Special Education Programs' Leadership Grant #H325D080027. The second author acknowledges the support of the Great Lakes Equity Center, under the Office of Elementary and Secondary Education's grant #S004D110021. The third author acknowledges the support of the Equity Alliance at Arizona State University. Funding agencies' endorsement of the ideas expressed in this manuscript should not be inferred.

1. The Office of Management and Budget (2000) defines an urban school as one that is located in a metropolitan statistical area that has a population of 250,000 people or more. More specifically, urban schools are often underresourced with respect to teachers, technology, and books, and also serve the most diverse learners, including students of color, students with disabilities, English Language Learners, and students from low-income families, at higher rates than rural and suburban schools.
2. Although there is evidence that disproportionate representation is also observed in suburban or low-poverty schools, the bulk of the literature on this topic has focused on urban schools and low-income racial minority students (Waitoller, Artiles, & Cheney, 2010).
3. A third explanation has been identified in the literature—studies focused on what was described as socio-historical contexts, specifically on "the role of race and power in shaping this problem, including the structural nature of race" (Waitoller et al., 2010, p. 36)—though only two studies were published in peer-refereed journals based on this paradigm between 1968 and 2006 (Waitoller et al., 2010).
4. Researchers present hypothetical scenarios, vignettes, or cases to practitioners and prompt them to make decisions such as referrals, diagnoses, or assessments of student performance and/or behaviors.

References

Adamson, F., & Darling-Hammond, L. (2011). Addressing the inequitable distribution of teachers: What it will take to get qualified, effective teachers in all communities. Stanford Center for Opportunity Policy in Education. Retrieved from http://edpolicy.stanford.edu/sites/default/files/publications/addressing-inequitable-distribution-teachers-what-it-will-take-get-qualified-effective-teachers-all-_1.pdf

Amrein-Beardsley, A. (2010). Methodological concerns about the education value-added assessment system. *Educational Researcher, 2,* 65–75.

Apple, M. (2001). *Educating the "right" way: Markets, standards, God, and inequality.* New York, NY: Routledge.

Artiles, A.J. (2011). Toward an interdisciplinary understanding of educational equity and difference: The case of the racialization of ability. *Educational Researcher, 40,* 431–445.

Artiles, A.J., Kozleski, E., & Waitoller, F. (Eds.). (2011). *Inclusive education: Examining equity on five continents.* Cambridge, MA: Harvard Education Press.

Artiles, A.J., Kozleski, E.B., Trent, S.C., Osher, D., & Ortiz, A. (2010). Justifying and explaining disproportionality, 1968–2008: A critique of underlying views of culture. *Council for Exceptional Children, 76,* 279–299.

Artiles, A.J., & Trent, S.C. (2000). Representation of culturally/linguistically diverse students. In C.R. Reynolds, & E. Fletcher-Jantzen (Eds.), *Encyclopedia of special education, Vol. 1* (2nd ed., pp. 513–517). New York, NY: John Wiley & Sons.

Artiles, A.J., Trent, S.C., & Palmer, J. (2004). Culturally diverse students in special education: Legacies and prospects. In J.A. Banks & C.M. Banks (Eds.), *Handbook of research on multicultural education* (2nd ed., pp. 716–735). San Francisco, CA: Jossey-Bass.

Benner, S. (1998). *Special education issues within the context of American society.* Belmont, CA: Wadsworth.

Berhanu, G. (2010). Even in Sweden? Excluding the included: Some reflections on the consequences of new policies on educational processes and outcomes, and equity in education. *International Journal of Special Education, 25,* 148–159.

Coburn, C.E. & Stein, M.K. (2006). Communities of practice theory and the role of teacher professional community in policy implementation. In M.I. Honig (Ed.), *New directions in education policy implementation: Confronting complexity* (pp. 25–46). Albany, NY: State University of New York Press.

Cochran-Smith, M., Davis, D., & Fries, K. (2004). Multicultural teacher education: Research, practice, and policy. In J. Banks (Ed.), *Handbook of research on multicultural education* (3rd ed., pp. 931–975). San Francisco, CA: Jossey-Bass.

Darling-Hammond, L. (2005). *Preparing teachers for a changing world: What teachers should learn and be able to do.* San Francisco, CA: Jossey-Bass.

Darling-Hammond, L. (2007). Race, inequality and educational accountability: The irony of "No child left behind." *Race Ethnicity and Education, 10,* 245–260.

Darling-Hammond, L., Amrein-Beardsley, A., Haertel, H.E., & Rothstein, J. (2011). Getting teacher evaluation right: A background paper for policymakers. Capitol Hill research briefing held by the American Educational Research Association and the National Academy of Education, Washington, DC.

Darling-Hammond, L., & Sykes, G. (2003). A national teacher supply policy for education: The right way to meet the "highly qualified teacher" challenge. *Education Policy Analysis Archives, 11.* Retrieved from http://epaa.asu/epaa/v11n33/

Diana v. California State Board of Education, Civil Action No. C-7037RFP (N. D. Cal. Jan. 7, 1970 & June 18, 1973).

Donovan, M.S., Bransford, J.D., & Pellegrino, J.W. (1999). *How people learn: Bridging research and practice.* Washington, DC: National Academies Press.

Donovan, M.S., & Cross, C.T. (Eds.). (2002). *Minority students in special and gifted education.* Washington, DC: National Academies Press.

Dunn, L. (1968). Special education for the mildly retarded: Is much of it justifiable? *Exceptional Children, 35,* 5–22.

El-Haj, T.R.A. (2003). Practicing for equity from the standpoint of the particular: Exploring the work of one urban teacher network. *Teachers College Record, 105,* 817–845.

Feistritzer, E. (2011). *Profile of teachers in the U.S. in 2011.* Washington, DC: National Center for Education Information.

Fernandez, C., Cannon, J., & Chokshi, S. (2003). A U.S.-Japan lesson study collaborative reveals critical lenses for examining practice. *Teaching and Teacher Education, 19,* 171–185.

Gay, G. (2002). Culturally responsive teaching for teachers in special education for ethnically diverse students: Setting the stage. *Qualitative Studies in Education, 15*(6), 613–629.

Grossman, P., & Loeb, S. (Eds). (2008). *Taking stock: An examination of alternative certification.* Cambridge, MA: Harvard Education Press.

Harris, D.N., & Sass, T.R. (2011). Teacher training, teacher quality and student achievement. *Journal of Public Economics, 95,* 798–812.

Harry, B., & Klingner, J. (2006). *Why are so many minority students in special education? Understanding race and disability in schools.* New York, NY: Teachers College Columbia University.

Harry, B., Klingner, J., Cramer, E., & Sturges, K. (2007). *Case studies of minority student placement in special education.* New York, NY: Teachers College Press.

Harvey, D. (2005). *A brief history of neoliberalism.* New York, NY: Oxford University Press.

Heilig, J. (2011). Understanding the interaction between high-stakes graduation tests and English learners. *Teachers College Record, 113,* 1–25.

Heller, K.A., Holtzman, W.H., & Messick, S. (Eds.). (1982). *Placing children in special education: A strategy for equity.* Washington, DC: National Academies Press.

Hord, S.M., Roussin, J.L., & Sommers, W.A. (2010). *Guiding professional learning communities: Inspiration, challenge, surprise, and meaning.* Thousand Oaks, CA: Corwin Press.

Hursh, D., & Martina, C. (2003). Neoliberalism and schooling in the U.S.: How state and federal government education policies perpetuate inequality. *Journal of Critical Educational Policy Studies, 1*(2). Retrieved from http://www.jceps.com/?pageID=article&articleID=12

Ingersoll, R. (2002). The teacher shortage: A case of wrong diagnosis and wrong prescription. *NASSP Bulletin, 86,* 16–31.

Kane, T., & Staiger, D. (2008). *Estimating teacher impacts on student achievement: An experimental evaluation* (NBER Working Paper No. 14607). Cambridge, MA: National Bureau of Economic Research.

Klingner, J.K., Artiles, A.J., Klozleski, E., Harry, B., Zion, S., Tate, W., Duran, W., & Riley, D. (2005). Addressing the disproportionate representation of culturally and linguistically diverse students in special education through culturally responsive educational systems. *Education Policy Analysis Archives, 13.* Retrieved from http://epaa.asu.edu/epaa/v13n38/

Kohli, R. (2009). Critical race reflections: Valuing the experiences of teachers of color in teacher education. *Race Ethnicity and Education, 12,* 235–251.

Kozleski, E.B., & Artiles, A.J. (2011). Technical assistance as inquiry: Using activity theory methods to engage equity in educational practice communities. In G. Canella & S. Steinberg (Eds.), *Critical Qualitative Research Reader* (pp. 408–419). New York, NY: Peter Lang.

Kozol, J. (1992). *Savage inequities.* New York, NY: HarperCollins.

Lareau, A. (2011). *Unequal childhoods: Class, race, and family life. Second edition with an update a decade later.* Berkeley, CA: University of California Press.

Larry P. v. Riles. (1979). C-71-2270, FRP. Dist. Ct.

Lave, J., & Wenger, E.C. (1990). *Situated learning: Legitimate peripheral participation.* Palo Alto, CA, Institute for Research on Learning.

Lieberman, A., & Mace, D.P. (2010). Making practice public: Teacher learning in the 21st century. *Journal of Teacher Education, 61,* 77–88.

Lipman, P. (2006). The politics of education accountability in a post-9/11 world. *Cultural Studies Critical Methodologies, 6,* 52–72.

Losen, D. (2011). *Discipline policies, successful schools, and racial justice.* Boulder, CO: National Education Policy Center. Retrieved from http://nepc.colorado.edu/publication/discipline-policies

Margolis, J. (2006). New teachers, high-stakes diversity, and the performance-based conundrum. *Urban Review, 38,* 27–44.

McLaughlin, M.W., & Talbert, J. (2010). *Professional communities and the work of high school teaching.* Chicago, IL: University of Chicago Press.

McLeskey, J., Tyler, N., & Flippin, S. (2003). *The supply of and demand for special education teachers: A review of research regarding the nature of the chronic shortage of special education.* Gainesville, FL: Center for Personnel Studies in Special Education.

Milner, H.R. (2003). Teacher reflection and race in cultural contexts: History, meanings, and methods in teaching. *Theory Into Practice, 42,* 173–180.

Milner, H.R. (2006). Preservice teachers' learning about cultural and racial diversity: Implications for urban education. *Urban Education, 41*(4), 343–375.

Newton, X., Darling-Hammond, L., Haertel, E., & Thomas, E. (2010). Value-added modeling of teacher effectiveness: An exploration of stability across models and contexts. *Educational Policy Analysis Archives, 18.* Retrieved from http://epaa.asu.edu/ojs/article/view/810

Office of Management and Budget. (2000). Standards for defining metropolitan and micropolitan statistical areas. Notice. *Federal Register* (65) No. 249. National Center for Education Statistics. Retrieved from http://nces.ed.gov/surveys/urbaned/page2.asp

Peske, H.G., & Haycock, K. (2006). *Teaching inequity: How poor and minority students are shortchanged on teacher quality.* Washington, DC: Education Trust.

Rivkin, S.G., Hanushek, E.A., & Kane, J.F. (2005). Teachers, schools, and academic achievement. *Econometrica, 73*(2), 417–458.

Sanders, W. (2000). Value-added assessment from student achievement data: Opportunities and hurdles. *Journal of Personnel Evaluation and Behavioral Statistics, 29,* 103–116.

Shealey, M.W., McHatton, P.A., & Farmer, J. (2009). What does "highly qualified" mean for urban special educators? *Urban Education, 44,* 410–426.

Skiba, R.J., Horner, R.H., Chung, C.G., Raush, M.K., & May, S.L., & Tobin, T. (2011). Race is not neutral: A national investigation of African American and Latino disproportionality in school discipline. *School Psychology, 40,* 85–107.

Skiba, R., Michael, R., Nardo, A., & Peterson, R. (2000). *The color of discipline.* Bloomington, IN: Indiana Education Policy Center. Policy Research Report #SRS1.

Skiba, R.J., Poloni-Staudinger, L., Simmons, A.B., Feggings-Azziz, R., & Chung, C.G. (2005). Unproven links of poverty: Can poverty explain ethnic disproportionality in special education? *Journal of Special Education, 39,* 130–144.

Skiba, R.J., Simmons, A.B., Ritter, S., Gibb, A.C., Rausch, M.K., Cuadrado, J., & Chung, C. G. (2008). Achieving equity in special education: History, status, and current challenges. *Council for Exceptional Children, 74,* 264–288.

Sleeter, C.E. (2008). Equity, democracy, and neoliberal assaults on teacher education. *Teaching and Teacher Education, 54,* 1947–1957.

Stoll, L., Bolam, R., McMahon, A., Wallace, M., & Thomas, S. (2006). Professional learning communities: A review of the literature. *Journal of Educational Change,* 7(4), 221–258.

Strizek, G.A., Pittsonberger, J.L., Riordan, K.E., Lyter, D.M., & Orlofsky, G.F. (2006). *Characteristics of schools, districts, teachers, principals, and school libraries in the United States: 2003–04 schools and staffing survey (NCES 2006–313 Revised).* U.S. Department of Education, National Center for Education Statistics. Washington, DC: U.S. Government Printing Office.

Sullivan, L.A., & Artiles, J.A. (2011). Theorizing racial inequity in special education: Applying structural inequity theory to disproportionality. *Urban Education, 46,* 1526–1552.

Teese, R., Lamb, S., & Duru-Bellat, M. (Eds.). (2007). *International studies in educational inequality, theory, and policy* (Vols. 1–3). New York, NY: Springer.

Thorius, K.A.K., & Scribner, S.M.P. (in press). Teacher learning in urban schools. In E.B. Kozleski & K.A.K. Thorius (Eds.), *Ability, equity, and culture: The search for the holy grail in urban education reform.* New York, NY: Teachers College Press.

Trent, S.C., Artiles, A.J., Fitchett-Bazemore, K., McDaniel, L., & Coleman, A. (2002). Addressing theory, ethics, power, and privilege in inclusion research and practice. *Teacher Education and Special Education, 25,* 11–22.

U.S. Department of Education. (2011). *ESEA flexibility request.* Retrieved from http://www2.ed.gov/policy/eseaflex/ga.pdf

U.S. Department of Education. (2004). New No Child Left Behind flexibility: Highly qualified teachers. Fact Sheet. Retrieved from http://www2.ed.gov/nclb/methods/teachers/hqtflexibility.pdf

Valenzuela, A., Prieto, L., & Hamilton, M. (2008). No Child Left Behind (NCLB) and minority youth: What the qualitative evidence suggests. *Anthropology and Education Quarterly, 38,* 1–8.

Waitoller, F., Artiles, A.J., & Cheney, D. (2010). The miner's canary: A review of overrepresentation research and explanations. *Journal of Special Education, 44,* 29–49.

Weiner, L. (2007). A lethal threat to teacher education. *Journal of Teacher Education, 58,* 274–286.

Wilson, S., & Berne, J. (1999). Teacher learning and the acquisition of professional knowledge: An examination of research on contemporary professional development. *Review of Research in Education, 24,* 173–209.

Zeichner, K. (2010). Competition, economic rationalization, increased surveillance, and attacks on diversity: Neo-liberalism and the transformation of teacher education in the U.S. *Teaching and Teacher Education, 26,* 1544–1552.

15

African American Students and Other Students of Color in Special Education

Wanda J. Blanchett

We find ourselves in a very sad education dilemma where many African American and other students of color still are being denied the promise of *Brown*. Although we no longer have "Jim Crow Laws" and *White Only* signs legally and visibly posted that prevent African American and other students of color from attending schools attended by their White peers, make no mistake about it—we still have unexplained educational disparities on the basis of race, social class, and perceived ability and segregated schools in 21st-century America. In many respects, today's American public schools are remarkably different in terms of the student demographics from Jim Crow and court-ordered desegregation era schools, but yet they still bear some undeniable similarities in terms of equity and access. For example, in stark contrast to historic public school data trends, in 2010 White students constituted 50% or less of the public school enrollment in 12 states along with District of Columbia (Aud et al., 2012). Also, in 2010, African American students were the majority student populations in both the District of Columbia and the state of Mississippi (Aud et al., 2012). Similarly, Hispanic students were the majority student population in Arizona, California, New Mexico, and Texas. Across all states and territories, the District of Columbia boasted the highest percentage of African American students at 77% and New Mexico the highest percentage of Hispanics at 59% (Aud et al., 2012). During the 2009–2010 school year, English Language Learners (ELL) accounted for an average of 14% of the U.S. public school population. In our larger urban cities, ELL students constitute up to 18% of the student population (p. 30). Despite enrollment of students of color at an all-time high, the teaching force is still overwhelmingly White and female; and more important, the American educational system seems to lack the will and courage to appropriately educate these diverse students. Failure to design and deliver instruction that meets the educational needs of students of color in general education is directly related to the problem of disproportionate representation of students of color in special education. Research has shown that when students do not perform well academically, do not behave according to teachers' cultural expectations, when teachers do not know what to do with students due to cultural mismatch, and if they are African American students, teachers are more likely to refer them for special education (Williams, 2008).

It is well documented that African American and other students of color are at the greatest risk of being referred for and placed in the judgment or high-incident disability categories of learning disabilities, intellectual disabilities, and emotional disturbance. Once placed in special education, African American and other students of color are most often the very students who spend the majority of their school day in segregated special education settings with limited access to the general education classroom, nondisabled peers, and a rigorous curriculum while their White middle-class peers with the same disability labels are placed in inclusive education or general education settings. It seems that regardless of whether African American and other students of color are in regular American public school classrooms or in special education programs and classrooms, they are the very students most likely to receive their education in low-performing, high-poverty, and segregated settings. It seems that the more racially/ethnically and linguistically diverse American public schools become, the more troublesome the educational disparities, disproportionality, and the reality and depth of our education dilemma. Instead of taking more prudent and courageous steps to ensure the future of America's greatest natural resource—namely its children—by educating all of them well so that they are prepared to excel and compete in a highly technological globally diverse society, we seem to be regressing.

As we prepare to both commemorate and celebrate the 60th anniversary of *Brown,* it is quite evident that the American educational system is only working well for a fraction of the students it is charged with serving—not for all, and especially, not for African American and other students of color, poor children, and students labeled as having disabilities. Since the field of urban education is concerned with the inequitable treatment of students in urban settings, a disproportionate percentage of whom are African American and other students of color, and since one of the greatest threats to receiving an equitable education in American public schools for African American students is disproportionate placement in special education, it seems most natural that urban education and critical special educators would unite in the fight to eradicate disproportionality and all other forms of educational inequity. This chapter discusses (1) the original purpose of the American educational system, (2) the current context of African American and other students of color in the American educational system, (3) the original purpose of special education, (4) an historical account of the problem of disproportionate placement of African American and other students of color in special education, (5) what we know about disproportionality and years of educational inequity, and (6) what is needed to continue the fight to eradicate the disproportionate placement of African American and other students of color (particularly those in urban settings) in special education.

The Original Purpose of the American Educational System

To start to understand and comprehend potentially why the American public educational system seems to only work well for a few privileged children and families, we must more fully understand its original purpose and intent (Zion & Blanchett, 2011). Historically, American public schools were designed for the purpose of serving the dual role of controlling and sorting children deemed problematic or undesirable by society (Applied Research Center, 2006). In 1779, Thomas Jefferson proposed a two-track educational system, with one track for the laborer and one for the learned. This system would allow a very small number to advance from lower to upper classes, by "raking a few geniuses from the rubbish" (Applied Research Center, 2006). In 1805, the New York Public School Society was founded and developed a model of schooling that focused on obedience and discipline in response to what factory owners needed in workers. In 1851, the first compulsory education law was passed, with the goal of "ensuring that the children of poor immigrants get 'civilized' and learn obedience and restraint, so they make good workers and don't contribute to social upheaval" (Applied Research Center, 2006). Our public schools have long been used as an instrument of segregation and forced assimilation, beginning with laws that forbade enslaved Africans to learn to read, removed Native American students from their homes and placed them in boarding schools, outlawed the use of languages other than English in public school classrooms, and criminalized children who did not attend school (Gatto, 2005). Further, beginning in 1896 with *Plessy v. Ferguson,* the law authorized the notion of separate but equal, legitimized segregation in U.S. society, and allowed for continued segregation of African American students in public education. It is possible to argue that schools have come a long way since their initial establishment. After all, there is *Brown v. Board of Education,* which eliminated segregation based on race, the school choice movement, which created an array of charter school choices for families who can access them, and the disability rights movement, which ensured a free and appropriate education in public school settings—and yet, we seem to be no closer to closing the racial equity gaps in our education system (Berlak, 2007). Our American public education system was developed with a set of purposes, explicitly stated in law and public policy, to control and sort students according to the needs of the state (Zion & Blanchett, 2011). Joel Springs (2005), in *American Education,* named three purposes of schooling: (1) the political goal of educating future citizens to participate in a democratic republic, (2) the social goal of controlling the behaviors of the masses, and (3) the economic goal of socializing workers into industry. Our educational system was initiated, and refined, to meet these needs. Although current policies have moved from the notion of control and sorting into rhetoric about the provision of equitable opportunities and outcomes for all, it seems no surprise that reform efforts, particularly those aimed at providing an equitable education for students of color, all poor children, students with disabilities, and students in urban settings are not working. This reality does beg the question of is it possible that the American public education system has not worked to the benefit of African American and other students of color because it was not designed with them in mind? Additionally, have we been trying to fix a system that appears to be broken at its very foundation? Even if the answer to these questions is "yes," given the globally diverse context in which we live, I contend that the American public school system must now figure out how to serve well students it was not designed to serve.

African American Students and Other Students of Color in the American Educational System

While the student body in American public schools is more diverse today than at any other point in American history, African American and other students of color continue to attend schools where the retention and graduation rates lag significantly behind those of schools attended by White and Asian students. Additionally, African American and other students of color are more likely than their White and Asian peers to attend schools classified as "low-performing" and it seems that retention and graduation rates and whether a school is labeled low- or high-performing or low- or high-poverty are related to the racial/ethnic makeup of the majority student population. For instance, in high schools where more than 50% of the students are White, 16% were classified as low-retention schools. However, in high schools where African American students constituted more than 50%, 67% of high schools were low-retention. Similarly, in high schools where Hispanics represented 50% or more, 48% were designated as low-retention schools. The data also illustrated that 39% of high schools with 50% or more White students reportedly retained 91–150% of students (Aud et al., 2012). In contrast, high schools that served more than 50% of Hispanic and African American students retained 13% and 8%, respectively. It also appears that higher percentages of African American (37%), Hispanic (37%), and American Indian/Alaska Native students (29%) attended schools classified as high-poverty schools when compared to Asian/Pacific Islander (12%) and White students (6%). Given the above data, it is not altogether surprising that Asian/Pacific Islander (37%) and White (34%) students are more likely to attend low-poverty schools when compared to American Indian/Alaska Native (12%), Hispanic (12%), and African American students (8%). Although the general education disparities between African American and other students of color and their White and Asian peers cause serious reasons for concern, the field of urban education and urban education researchers should be equally concerned about the fact that special education has become a new form of segregation in American schools.

The Original Purpose of Special Education in the American Educational System

Since its formal establishment in 1975 by the All Handicapped Children Act [later renamed the Individuals with Disabilities Education Improvement Act (IDEA)], the field of special education has undergone several progressive philosophical changes with most of them occurring over the last couple of decades. Special education is a fairly new field that is still evolving. When initially conceptualized in theory, special education was conceived to provide support and training for students who were perceived as a challenge for the general education system, including African American students and other students of color, students with disabilities, and students impacted by the intersection of race/ethnicity and disability (Blanchett, 2009). Students who were eligible received specialized services such as individualized instruction, tutoring, and other forms of intervention to assist them in reaching their potential. Once students' needs were either met and/or appropriate strategies or modifications implemented, they would return to general education settings (Blanchett & Shealey, 2005).

In those early years, as special education theory evolved and resulted in actual educational practice, it became very clear that many students with disabilities were being educated in segregated, self-contained settings with little to no exposure or access to their nondisabled peers (Blanchett & Shealey, 2005; Blanchett, 2009). More important, these students did not have access to the same curricula content as their nondisabled peers. As a result, many were not living up to their potential and often exited public schools with insufficient skills to gain meaningful employment and to participate in all aspects of adult life. These revelations led to the initiation of several longitudinal studies designed to examine the postschool outcomes of students with disabilities and to compare their postschool outcomes to their in-school experiences and learning opportunities (Blackorby & Wagner, 1996). The findings of these studies suggested that special education theory and practice was not robust enough to prepare individuals with disabilities for life after school. Specifically, these studies revealed that students with disabilities often lack the social skills, life skills, basic academic skills, and employment training to participate in all aspects of adult life (Blackorby & Wagner, 1996). To prevent students with disabilities from continuing to experience such dismal postschool outcomes, disability rights advocates called for the reform of special education to address these shortcomings.

Although the 1980s gave birth to many special education reform ideas, the most radical of the special education reform ideas was the theory of inclusion (Blanchett, 2009). Full inclusion called for providing all special education services to students with disabilities in the general education context without removing students from the classroom. Advocates of inclusion have been very successful in rightfully arguing that incorporating these students into general education classrooms is consistent with the concept of normalization, the disability rights movement, the major tenets of the civil rights movement, the promise of *Brown,* and the equitable thing to do(Blanchett & Shealey, 2005; Blanchett, 2009). Moreover, research suggests that the benefits of inclusion are significant for all students. Students with disabilities who are included in general education classrooms have higher levels of social skills, are more accepted by their nondisabled peers, and have greater exposure to the general education curriculum. According to the U.S. Department of Education in 2011, the majority of students with disabilities are now included in general education classrooms for the majority or some portion of their school day. This represents a significant increase in their access to general education and integrated classrooms and is a radical shift from early special education theory and practice.

Without question, the field of special education has evolved considerably since its inception. For almost 50 years, the field has been in the midst of change, most of which has been aimed at moving away from a deficit model (Artiles, Kozleski, Trent, Osher, & Ortiz, 2010; Blanchett, 2009), humanizing educational interventions, practices, and obtaining better long-term results. The calls for accountability in general education have been amplified due in part to the assertion in the report from the President's Commission on Excellence in Special Education that, "children placed in special education were general education students first" (President's Commission on Excellence in Special Education, 2002). This represented a shift from simply advocating for and providing access to physical facilities to including such students in state and district assessments, working to ensure access to the general education curriculum, and holding states accountable for educating student labeled as having disabilities. However, the field continues to be entrenched in debate over the legitimacy of continuing to place some students with disabilities in self-contained settings, the level of access to the general education curriculum afforded to students in those settings, what constitutes a highly qualified special education teacher, and how the field might effectively address longstanding teacher shortages and a lack of diversity in the teaching force. In recent years, the debate has been extended to how the field might address the needs of racially, ethnically, and linguistically diverse learners receiving special education services.

Historical Account of the Problem of Disproportionate Placement of African American and Other Students of Color in Special Education

As I have noted elsewhere (2009), it is ironic that shortly after the courts ordered schools to desegregate and began enforcing desegregation plans in the years following the *Brown* decision, it became evident that significant percentages of African American children and Mexican American students in New York and California, respectively, were being labeled as mildly mentally retarded and placed in segregated self-contained classrooms (Dunn, 1968; Mercer 1973). In his work with poor inner-city students in New York, Dunn noted that African American students' representation in programs for students identified as having mild mental retardation exceeded rates that would be expected given their relative size in the general population of school-aged children compared to White students. Specifically, Dunn called attention to the fact that African American children were labeled as mildly mentally retarded and their White peers were not labeled at all, even when the White children evidenced more significant levels of mental retardation than the African American students (Blanchett, 2009). Mercer (1973) noted similar patterns in California among Mexican American students who were new immigrants and English-language learners or nonspeakers. The work of these researchers and others was the basis for *Larry P. v. Riles,* which helped to end the use of intelligence tests as the sole basis for determining special education eligibility, and played a role in securing some of the safeguards guaranteed by IDEA today (Blanchett, 2009). Additionally, this research provided the legal basis for parents and advocates to challenge special education referral, evaluation, and placement decision making and eventually led to the establishment of several national committees to study the disproportionate representation of African American and other students of color in special education. During the last several decades we have seen the Harvard Civil Rights Project play an ongoing role in studying this issue, two

National Academy of Science (NAS) studies commissioned, and the development of a lengthy list of recommendations for addressing this issue introduced by Dunn and Mercer. In recent years, we even have witnessed the U.S. Department of Education, Office of Special Education Programs (OSEP) confirm the problem of disproportionality and employ its own reporting mechanisms to disaggregate and report special education prevalence, risk ratio/index, placement, and outcome data on the basis of race/ethnicity. However, despite all of these notable efforts, overrepresentation and disproportionate representation of African American and other students of color has persisted for more than 44 years. The initial concerns related to disproportionality were centered on African Americans' and Mexican Americans' placement in mild mental retardation classrooms at disproportionate rates. However, as other socially constructed disabilities categories (e.g., Learning Disabilities, Emotional and Behavioral Disabilities) have been developed and incorporated into legislation, similar trends of disproportionality have been associated with them as well. More important, the American educational system and our society have not missed any opportunity to use special education to continue a sorting system for children on the basis of race, ethnicity, culture, and social class and to resegregate students of color.

These realities are very disheartening because in both its original and subsequent conceptualization, special education was not conceived as a place or location, but rather a service delivery structure (Blanchett & Shealey, 2005; Blanchett, 2009). However, for many African American students, "special education has too often been a place—a place to segregate minorities and students with disabilities" (Civil Rights Project, 2001). African American students and other students of color labeled as having disabilities have had a number of experiences in the American special education system that raise concerns. Among the concerns most frequently cited by researchers are (a) the persistent problem of disproportionate representation of African American and other students of color in special education, (b) the historical practice of placing African American students with disabilities into the most segregated instead of inclusive or general education settings, (c) the lack of culturally responsive instructional practices and educational services in both general and special education classrooms, and (d) the significant shortage of fully credentialed special education teachers, including teachers of color. In the early definition of overrepresentation and disproportionality, disproportionality was said to exist when a specific group's representation in special education as a whole and/or in specific disability categories exceeded its representation in the general school population or in the special education program (Harry & Anderson, 1995). However, in recent years, disproportionality has been determined using risk indexes on the basis of race/ethnicity. Although students served under IDEA are representative of all racial/ethnic, cultural, linguistic, and social class backgrounds, African American and other students of color are disproportionately represented and at risk for being labeled in the judgment or high-incidence disability categories of intellectual disabilities, specific learning disabilities, and emotional disturbance disabilities categories. For example, in 2006, of the percentage of all students receiving special education services across all disability categories by racial/ethnic groups, American Indian/Alaska Native students had the largest risk index at 13.86%, followed by African American students at 12.22%, White at 8.52%, and Hispanic students at 8.41% (U.S. Department of Education, 2011). American Indian/Alaska Native, African American, and Hispanic students have the highest risk ratio for LD (the risk of identification in comparison to White students) with risk ratios of 1.81, 1.46, and 1.19, respectively, compared to White students at 0.77 and Asian/Pacific Islander students at 0.39 (U.S. Department of Education, 2011). Although the category of intellectual disabilities is much smaller than that of LD and only accounts for 8.6% of all students ages 6–21 who receive special education services under IDEA, with a risk ratio of 2.75, African American students have the greatest risk ratio for being identified and labeled as having an intellectual disability and White students' risk ratio is 0.63.

Therefore, African American students are more than two times more likely to be identified and placed in special education for an intellectual disability when compared to their White peers. Similarly, the category of emotional disturbance or emotional and behavioral disabilities is a small disability category representing only 7.5% of all the 6- to 21-year-olds who receive special education services but, despite its relative size, African American students are disproportionately represented. With a risk ratio of 2.28 African American students also have the greatest risk ratio for being identified and served in the intellectual disabilities category when compared to all other racial/ethnic groups with American Indian/Alaska Native at 1.63, Whites 0.85, Hispanics 0.55, and Asian/Pacific Islander 0.26. These realities have made some researchers and educators (e.g., Artiles & Trent, 1994; Patton, 1998) question the identification and placement practices that have resulted in so many children of color in special education, and some (Blanchett, 2006) have even asserted that racism and White privilege is indeed at work here to produce these otherwise unexplainable risks.

What We Know About Disproportionality and Years of Educational Inequity

Without question, the passage and implementation of IDEA has astonishingly improved the educational services and benefits for students with disabilities. Currently, more than 6,081,890 children are federally guaranteed access to a free and appropriate public education in the least restrictive environment with a number of legal and procedural safeguards including due process, parental involvement, and individualized education plans (Blanchett, Mumford, & Beachum, 2005). Although we still struggle to be responsive to the educational needs of students with disabilities, today more are educated in general education classrooms with their nondisabled peers and attend postsecondary school than at any other point in American history. In addition, they are living in fully integrated communities and participating in competitive employment at much higher rates. For many parents, particularly African American parents, the passage of IDEA meant that their children were finally going to gain access to both integrated schools that were inclusive and reflective of our larger society in terms of race/ethnicity and their children with disabilities were going to be afforded a free and appropriate public education in the least restrictive environment (Blanchett, 2009).

Despite these astonishing benefits and opportunities afforded many students with disabilities, the benefits of special education have not been equitably distributed on the basis of race and social class. While few would argue against the significant positive changes in special education service delivery brought about as a result of the passage of IDEA, the positive benefits of special education have not been equitably distributed (Losen & Orfield, 2002). African American children with disabilities have not received schooling opportunities comparable to those experienced by their White peers. Segregation on the basis of race, poverty, disability/perceived disability, the intersection of race with disability/perceived disability and poverty, and the intersection of race and poverty is still a pervasive problem in our American educational system as a whole and in special education programs in particular (Blanchett, 2009). What African American parents did not know but history would later prove is that segregation would not end with either the decision in the *Brown* case, with the dismantling of Jim Crow laws, with court-ordered desegregation, or with the passage of IDEA. Their children would not attend integrated schools and those with disabilities would not have the access to the general education curriculum and their peers without disabilities that they had hoped.

Shockingly, even though IDEA has made it possible for students with disabilities to be educated in general education classroom settings, African American students are still more likely than any other group of students to be segregated and not placed in general education classrooms to the extent of other racial/ethnic groups labeled as having disabilities. For instance, in 2006, 95% of all students with disabilities were educated in general education classrooms for some portion of their day with "At least 50 percent of the students in each of the racial/ethnic groups except for the black group," with only 44.8% of African American students placed inside the regular classroom 80% or more of their school day (U.S. Department of Education, 2011, p. 61). White students were the most likely to be educated in the regular classroom for most of the school day (57.7%) (U.S. Department of Education, 2011, p. 61). African American (24%) and Asian (24.4%) students were the groups of students most likely to be inside the regular classroom for less than 40% of the day. Additionally, African American students were more likely to be educated in other environments (6.4%) than any other racial/ethnic group (U.S. Department of Education, 2011). These "other environments include separate school, residential facility, homebound/hospital environment, correctional facility and parentally placed in private school" (p. 61). These placement trends highlight the inequities associated with special education placements on the basis of race, as well as the need for educators making placement decisions to work hard to ensure that all students have equitable opportunities to be educated in the general education setting and with their nondisabled peers. Students in urban settings, a disproportionate number of whom are students of color and poor students, regardless of their race, would not have access to the same quality of schooling as their peers in suburban areas and/or those from middle- and upper-class social economic levels. For the last decade or more, researchers (Orfield, Kucsera, & Siegel-Hawley, 2012; Orfield & Lee, 2007) have documented the resegregation of African American students in urban schools as well as across the South, and of Hispanic students across the country regardless of where they attend school. These studies suggest that segregation would raise its ugly head again, but this time under the guise of urban education and special education.

Despite the intent and promise of the historic *Brown* decision, White privilege and racism have resulted in at least four subsystems of American public schooling as a whole (Blanchett, 2006). The first is a general education system for children who are (a) disproportionately White, and (b) perceived to be *normal* or without disabilities. These students often attend schools where teachers are highly educated and credentialed, meaning that the teachers were not hired with emergency licenses and often hold a master's or higher degree in the subject area that they teach (Blanchett et al., 2005; Robinson & Grant-Thomas, 2004). More important, these students are exposed to a rigorous college-preparatory curriculum, including advanced placement classes, travel abroad programs, access to three or more foreign-language programs, the latest technology, and state-of-the-art science labs (Brantlinger, 2003).

The second subsystem in the American educational system is a general education system for children who are (a) disproportionately African American or of color (Orfield & Lee, 2004), and (b) perceived to be normal or without disabilities. These students are likely to attend schools that are deemed high-poverty and that have high turnover of teaching and instructional staff, a high number of less experienced, uncertified, or provisionally licensed teachers, subpar facilities and learning resources, limited or no access to technology, one or no foreign-language programs, few educational specialists (e.g., in math, science, or reading), few advanced classes, and no travel abroad programs (Kozol, 1992; Orfield et al., 2012; Orfield & Lee, 2004). Siegel-Hawley & Frankenberg (2012) described these schools in the South as being "defined by double isolation by both race and poverty" (p. 1).

The third subsystem in American education is a special education system for children who are (a) disproportionately White, and (b) perceived as having disabilities. These children may be prejudicially perceived by some as *not normal* but may be of varying ability, some requiring no supports to excel academically and to participate in all facets of life, and some requiring extensive, ongoing support just to maintain life and certainly to acquire academic skills. These students are more likely to be fully included in general education classes at the schools described above in the first subsystem, meaning that all of their educational supports—such as special education services, physical therapy, speech and language therapy, and occupational therapy—are provided in the context of the general education curriculum. These students are not pulled out or segregated from their nondisabled peers for services (LeRoy & Kulik, 2003; U.S. Department of Education, 2011). Many of them graduate from high school with a "regular" high school diploma; typically they are the students with disabilities who go on to postsecondary education (Aud et al., 2012; U.S. Department of Education, 2011).

The fourth and final educational subsystem is the special education system for children who are (a) disproportionately African American, and (b) identified as having disabilities. These children may be prejudicially perceived by some as not normal and, like their White peers described in the third system, may be of varying ability. However, unlike their White peers, they often are excluded from inclusive education programs and the general education curriculum (LeRoy & Kulik, 2003; U.S. Department of Education, 2011). They tend to spend 40% or less of their school day in general education classes, meaning that they may spend 60% or their entire day in segregated special education placements with some of these students even spending their entire school day in separate classrooms or separate schools (U.S. Department of Education, 2011). They also are more likely to have uncertified or provisionally licensed teachers and to graduate with a certificate of attendance or completion rather than a high school diploma (Blanchett, 2010; Chamberlain, 2005).

What Is Needed to Continue the Fight to Eradicate the Disproportionate Placement of African American and Other Students of Color in Special Education?

In this chapter, I have primarily focused on the problem of the disproportionate placement of African American and other students of color in special education and tried to illustrate how this practice results in inequitable educational opportunities and outcomes for these students; the larger issue is the reality that the American educational system is not working for many African American and other students of color, especially those in urban settings, regardless of whether they are educated in general or special education classrooms. The failure of the American educational system to serve African American and other students of color well, especially those in urban settings, and the longstanding problem of disproportionality among the 6- to 21-year-old student population have been well documented in the professional literature in both general and special education. However, the research and theories offered as to why the problem exists, what factors contribute to it, and how to eradicate it are mixed and can be summarized into at least three thematic categories, including the (1) historical, cultural, and racial bias and White privilege in the American education system and in the special education referral and placement process that negatively impacts African American and other students of color; (2) lack of sufficient teacher preparation to effectively prepare educators to meet the needs of diverse students as illustrated by a sociocultural, linguistic, and socioeconomic mismatch between general education teachers and students of color; and (3) disproportionate predisposition of African Americans to poverty and all of the negative issues (e.g., health disparities, low birth weights, limited access to health care including prenatal care) associated with it that result in 6- to 21-year-old African American and other students of color being disproportionally referred and placed in special education. Now that the field has moved away from denying that disproportionality exists, this last hypothesis has prompted some researchers to conclude that maybe too much emphasis has been placed on the first two themes mentioned above and, in doing so, we have ignored the obvious—the impact of poverty. Recently, in their study, Morgan, Farkas, Hillemeier, & Maczuga (2012) sought to examine if and to what extent African American and other students of color and their families are disproportionally represented in special education early intervention services or early childhood special education since they are indeed disproportionately served in the 6- to 21-year-old high-incidence disability categories. The findings of this study illustrated that African American students and their families are underrepresented in early intervention or early childhood special education so many do not access these services prior to entering the PK–12 educational system. According to the authors, the lack of referral for early intervention and early childhood special education services that are designed to provide services to decrease the likelihood of the need for and possible intensity of future special education services might contribute to, "The many disparities reported for racial-ethnic minorities in adult health, education, and general well-being resulting in part from their earlier systematic lack of access to early intervention and early childhood special education services before school entry" (Morgan et al., 2012, p. 341). This finding is disturbing because it suggests that despite policy initiatives being implemented to eradicate disproportionality through the provision of early intervention services that many White families clearly are accessing, the students and families that may need these services the most to prevent the need for or intensity of special education services later are not accessing these services. Among the possible explanations offered as to why African American and other students of color might not be participating in early intervention services at a rate that would be expected included not having access to health care—since physicians often make referrals for early intervention services (Morgan et al., 2012), cultural differences in how parents view child development and disability issues, and cultural, linguistic, and socioeconomic obstacles in accessing early intervention services (Blanchett, Klingner, & Harry, 2009).

Given that the problem of disproportionality has persisted for more than four decades, it is clear that what we have done to try to eradicate it is not working. Therefore, to continue the fight and gain even more progress to finally eradicate the disproportionate placement of African American and other students of color in special education, it seems critically important that urban education, multicultural education, and critical special education unite in this fight. Like the failure of public education for students in urban settings, disproportionate placement of African American and other students of color in special education seems to be linked to the fact that the American educational system from its formation was never designed to educate students of color or students labeled as having disabilities. In fact, to extend rights and privileges associated with the American educational system to both African American and other students of color and to students with disabilities required sustained litigation and subsequent federal mandates so these two groups are already tied together as marginalized populations in pursuit of the failed promises of *Brown*. Despite this fact, the journey toward educational equity has itself been largely segregated with urban education, multicultural education, and critical special education scholars largely working in their own disciplines to address issues as there is no intersection between them. Therefore, the relationships between urban education, multicultural education, and special education have been at a minimum "complex" as stated by Irvine (2012) with scholars in special education drawing upon the extensive body of literature generated in urban education and multicultural education to frame special education equity issues and to advocate on behalf of the students and their families negatively impacted by disproportionality. Additionally, the fields of urban education and multicultural education have been invaluable to critical, urban, and multicultural special education scholars as they have fought for special education services to reflect best practices in urban and multicultural education. In contrast, only in a few instances (e.g., Gay, 2010; Hilliard, 1992; Irvine, 2012; Sleeter, 1987) have urban and multicultural education scholars concerned themselves with the plight and reality of African American and other students of color who are disproportionately referred for and placed in special education's most segregated placements. The fact that Irvine examined, "The complexity of the relationship between multicultural education and special education from an African American perspective by exploring areas of divergence and conflict between multicultural education and special education" (p. 268) in the *Journal of Teacher Education* has laid the foundation for renewed collaboration and the generation of possible solutions. Among the key areas of divergence and conflict cited by Irvine were disproportionate representation, cultural misunderstandings that influence the referral and placement process, tensions between home and school, and competition for limited resources in schools. In addition to offering the above areas of divergence and conflict, Irvine (2012) also called for special education teacher preparation programs to include culturally responsive pedagogy to better prepare special education teachers to meet the needs of students whom they often feel ill prepared to serve. While I agree that we can and should improve special education teacher preparation programs so that African American and other students of color who really do require special education services provided by special education teachers have access to teachers who practice culturally responsive pedagogy, we cannot let general education off the hook for educating all children. As I have noted (2009), general education has yet to assume responsibility for educating all of its students including African American and other students of color, poor students regardless of their race/ethnicity, students in urban settings, and students labeled as having disabilities. Therefore, in addition to focusing on helping special educators become more effective, if we can better equip general education teachers to serve all students (even students who stretch them) without referring them for special education services unnecessarily, and support students who truly have disabilities in the regular education classroom without placing them in segregated settings, we will move closer to eradicating disproportionality. General education teachers are overwhelmingly the ones referring students for special education. The problem of disproportionality long has been viewed by many as the problem of special education and not the problem of education as a whole. Despite the persistent nature of the challenge before us, if those of us who consider ourselves urban education, multicultural education, and critical special education scholars recognize disproportionality as an equity issue and work together, we can improve the quality of education offered all students, especially African American and other students of color in urban settings. In doing so, we also will make great progress toward eradicating disproportionately. As is often the risk with any longstanding and persistent problem or issue, the longer the problem continues, the more complacent and tired we become of fighting it with seemingly little success. To mount a valiant fight to ensure that the American educational system works for all students once and for all and to eradicate disproportionality will require a departure from business as usual. It will require reform in terms of how we view the problem of disproportionality and who is responsible for eradicating it, and how we prepare educators—all with implications for future educational research and theories. To move toward eradicating disproportionality demands that we work collaboratively to address this longstanding issue across and within disciplines dedicated to equity issues to move us toward a more socially just society by:

1. Owning the problem of the failure of the American educational system to serve all students well, including African American and other students of color, students in urban settings, students who are poor, and students labeled as having disabilities as a society and united body of equity scholars.
2. Continuing to fight for the dismantling of the four subsystems of the American educational system in favor of a single unified education system that equitably serves all students in truly integrated learning environments with all of the resources (e.g., highly prepared and

fully credentialed socially conscious and multicultural teachers; state-of-the-art and rigorous curriculum, labs, and technology) required for successful outcomes.

3. Rethinking how we prepare general education teachers (regardless of their backgrounds) so that we truly are preparing teachers to teach all students, including African American and other students of color, students in urban settings, students labeled as having disabilities, students who live in poverty, and students who are impacted by the intersection of all of these issues from a social justice and multicultural perspective.
4. Combining general and special education teacher education programs into a single teacher preparation program that is grounded in best practices in urban education, multicultural education, social justice, and critical special education versus continuing to develop and offer segregated teacher preparation programs in which general and special education teachers are prepared in isolation of each other.
5. Ensuring that when special education services are indeed needed, special education teachers are thoroughly prepared in culturally responsive pedagogy and comfortable delivering special education services that are culturally responsive.

In addition to the above-suggested reforms, we also must advance educational research and theory to address disproportionality. To move closer to eradicating the problem of disproportionality, future educational research and theory must seek to:

1. Thoroughly understand the complexity of the intersection of race/ethnicity, socioeconomic class, culture, linguistic, and perceived ability or disability and how they impact the in-school and postschool experiences and outcomes of African American and other students of color.
2. Completely understand what prevents African American and other families of color from accessing early intervention or early childhood special education services including further examining racial, cultural, socioeconomic, linguistic, and societal barriers and obstacles.
3. Develop and advance educational research aimed at moving us toward theories and models of educational practice designed to meet the needs of all diverse learners and that are grounded in an awareness of and appreciation for the complex intersection of race/ethnicity, socioeconomic class, culture, linguistic, and perceived ability or disability.
4. Develop and advance educational research aimed at moving us toward theories and models of educational service delivery and parental self-advocacy designed to help African American and other families of color become even more aware of the sequence of normal child development, recognize abnormal child development, and seek federally provided early intervention services.
5. Conduct and disseminate educational research and theories aimed at developing better models for equipping the medical field and early intervention service providers to offer culturally responsive early intervention services to African American and other families of color.

In conclusion, contrary to historical beliefs, the problem of disproportionality is not simply a special education issue; disproportionality is an equity issue. Therefore, it is a societal issue and most assuredly, it is an urban education and multicultural education issue and only can be eradicated if we all join forces in conducting and disseminating educational research from which bold and visionary theories are to be derived. Yes, this problem has been documented since at least 1968 and seems resistant to change but, despite this reality, "I don't feel no ways tired" as we must be more determined than ever to continue the fight to eradicate the disproportionate placement of African American and other students of color in special education.

References

Applied Research Center. (2006). *Historical timeline of education in the United States.* Retrieved from http://www.arc.org/content/view/100/48/

Artiles, A. J., & Trent, S. C. (1994). Overrepresentation of minority students in special education: A continuing debate. *The Journal of Special Education, 27*, 410–437.

Artiles, A.J., Kozleski, E.B., Trent, S.C., Osher, D., & Ortiz, A. (2010). Justifying and explaining disproportionality, 1968–2008: A critique of underlying views of culture. *Exceptional Children, 76*(3), 279–299.

Aud, S., Hussar, W., Johnson, F., Kena, G., Roth, E., Manning, E., Wang, X., & Zhang, J. (2012). *The Condition of Education 2012* (NCES 2012–045). U.S. Department of Education, National Center for Education Statistics. Washington, DC. Retrieved from http://nces.ed.gov/pubsearch

Berlak, H. (2007). Race and the achievement gap. *Rethinking Schools, 15*(4). Retrieved from http://www.rethinkingschools.org/archive/15_04/Race154.shtml

Blackorby, J., & Wagner, M. (1996). Longitudinal post-school outcomes of youth with disabilities: Findings from the National Longitudinal Transition Study. *Exceptional Children, 62*(5), 399–413.

Blanchett, W.J. (2006). Disproportionate representation of African Americans in special education: Acknowledging the role of White privilege and racism. *Educational Researcher, 35*(6), 24–28.

Blanchett, W.J. (2009). A retrospective examination of urban education: From *Brown* to the resegregation of African Americans in special education—it is time to "go for broke." *Urban Education, 44*(4), 370–388.

Blanchett, W. J., Klingner, J., & Harry, B. (2009). The intersection of race, culture, language and disability: Implications for urban education. *Urban Education, 44*(4), 389–409.

Blanchett, W.J. (2010). Telling it like it is: The role of race, class, & culture in the perpetuation of learning disability as a privileged category for the White middle class. *Disability Studies Quarterly, 30*(2). Retrieved from http://dsq-sds.org/article/view/1233/1280

Blanchett, W.J., Mumford, V., & Beachum, F. (2005). Urban school failure and disproportionality in a post-*Brown* era: Benign neglect of students of color's constitutional rights. *Remedial and Special Education, 26*(2), 70–81.

Blanchett, W.J., & Shealey, M.W. (2005). The forgotten ones: African American students with disabilities in the wake of *Brown*. In D.N. Byrne (Ed.), Brown v. Board of Education: *Its Impact on Public Education 1954–2005*. Thurgood Marshall Scholarship Fund. Brooklyn, NY: Word for Word.

Brantlinger, E. (2003). *Dividing classes: How the middle class negotiates and rationalizes school advantage.* New York, NY: RoutledgeFalmer.

Chamberlain, S.P. (2005). Issues of overrepresentation and educational equity for culturally and linguistically diverse students. *Intervention in School and Clinic, 41*, 110–113.

Civil Rights Project, The. (2001). *Discrimination in special education*. Cambridge, MA: The Civil Rights Project, Harvard University.

Dunn, L.M. (1968). Special education for the mildly retarded: Is much of it justifiable? *Exceptional Children, 35*, 5–22.

Gatto, J. (2005). *Dumbing us down: The hidden curriculum of compulsory schooling.* Gabriola Island, British Columbia: New Society.

Gay, G. (2010). *Culturally responsive teaching: Theory, research, and practice* (2nd ed.). New York, NY: Teachers College Press.

Harry, B., & Anderson, M.G. (1995). The disproportionate placement of African American males in special education programs: A critique of the process. *Journal of Negro Education, 63*(4), 602–619.

Hilliard, A.G. (1992). Behavioral style, culture, and teaching and learning. *Journal of Negro Education, 61*(3), 370–377.

Individuals with Disabilities Education Improvement Act of 2004 (IDEA 2004) H.R.1350. Retrieved from http://thomas.loc.gov/cgi-bin/query/z?c108:h.1350.enr

Irvine, J.J. (2012). Complex relationships between multicultural education and special education: An African American perspective. *Journal of Teacher Education, 63*(4), 268–274.

Kozol, J. (1992). *Savage inequalities.* New York, NY: HarperCollins.

Larry P. v. Riles. (1979). C-71–2270, FR.P. Dist. Ct.

LeRoy, B., & Kulik, N. (2003). "Who's there?" Students in inclusive education settings. *TASH Connections, 29*(19), 26–28.

Losen, D.J., & Orfield, G. (2002). *Racial inequity in special education.* Cambridge, MA: Harvard Education Press.

Mercer, J.R. (1973). *Labeling the mentally retarded.* Berkeley, CA: University of California Press.

Morgan, P.L., Farkas, G., Hillemeier, M.M., & Maczuga, S. (2012). Are minority children disproportionately represented in early intervention and early childhood special education? *Educational Researcher, 41*(9), 339–351.

Orfield, G., Kucsera, J., & Siegel-Hawley, G. (2012). E pluribus ... separation: Deepening double segregation for more students. *The Civil Rights Project,* UCLA. Retrieved from http://civilrightsproject.ucla.edu/research/k-12-education/integration-and-diversity/mlk-national/e-pluribus ... separation-deepening-double-segregation-for-more-students/orfield_ePluribus_executive_2012.pdf

Orfield, G. & Lee, C. (2007). Historic Reversals, Accelerating Resegregation, and the Need for New Integration Strategies. The Civil Right Project, UCLA. Retrieved from http://civilrightsproject.ucla.edu/research/k-12-education/integration-and-diversity/historic-reversals-accelerating-resegregation-and-the-need-for-new-integration-strategies-1/orfield-historic-reversals-accelerating.pdf

Orfield, G., & Lee, C. (2004). Brown *at 50: King's Dream or Plessy's Nightmare?* Cambridge, MA: The Civil Rights Project, Harvard University.

Patton, J. M. (1998). The disproportionate representation of African Americans in special education: Looking behind the curtain for understanding and possible solutions. *The Journal of Special Education,* 32, 25–31.

President's Commission on Excellence in Special Education. (2002). *President's Commission on Excellence in Special Education report: A new era: Revitalizing special education for children and their families.* Washington, DC: Author.

Robinson, L., & Grant-Thomas, A. (2004). *Race, place, and home: A civil rights and metropolitan opportunity agenda.* Cambridge, MA: The Civil Rights Project, Harvard University.

Sleeter, C.E. (1987). Why is there learning disabilities? A critical analysis of the birth of the field with its social context. In T.S. Popkewitz (Ed.), *The foundations of the school subjects* (pp. 210–237). London, UK: Palmer Press.

Seigel-Hawley, G., & Frankenberg, E. (2012). *Southern slippage: Growing school segregation in the most desegregated region of the country.* Los Angeles, CA: The Civil Rights Project, UCLA.

Springs, J. (2005). *American education.* New York, NY: McGraw-Hill.

U.S. Department of Education, Office of Special Education and Rehabilitative Services, Office of Special Education Programs. (2011). *30th annual report to Congress on the implementation of the Individuals with Disabilities Education Act, 2008.* Washington, DC: Author.

Williams, E.R. (2008). Unnecessary and unjustified: African-American parental perceptions of special education. *Educational Forum, 71*(3), 250–261.

Zion, S., & Blanchett, W.J. (2011). [Re] conceptualizing inclusion: Can critical race theory and interest convergence be utilized to achieve inclusion and equity for African American students? *Teachers College Record, 113*(10), 2186–2205.

Section V

Leadership, Administration, and Leaders

16

Professional Identities of Urban School Principals

Gary M. Crow & Samantha Paredes Scribner

Introduction

This chapter focuses on the leadership of urban schools, how its uniqueness and complexity have created the need for a different type of leader and a new way to think about the practice and preparation of these leaders. The importance of leadership has been well established. The discourse in education, in fact, has moved from a focus on management to one of leadership (Earley & Weindling, 2004), in part because of the finding that the effect of leadership on student learning is small but nevertheless significant (Leithwood & Louis, 2012). The importance of leadership, however, must be connected to the role context plays in leadership practice and effectiveness. Hallinger and colleagues (1996) stated, "Researchers have given inadequate attention to the influence that the organizational context exerts on educational administrators" (p. 529). Day et al. (2011) pointed to research connecting leadership effects with features from school, teacher, leader, student, district, and national contexts. Urban contexts are a particularly salient influence on the practice of school leadership.

Recently, more attention has been paid to the various elements of leadership. In addition to the overt behaviors of leaders, researchers in multiple international contexts have demonstrated that dispositions, values, and beliefs make a difference in the motivation and practice of leadership (Day & Leithwood, 2007). However, a popular response to the recent emphasis on the role and importance of urban school leaders has been the technocratic approach, in which job skills and competencies become the central, sometimes exclusive, focus. Unquestionably, skills and competencies, such as the use of data for instructional decision making, are critical for the success of these urban leaders. A lack of skills prevents leaders from being effective instructional and transformational leaders. However, the exclusive focus on skills and competencies ignores the role that values, beliefs, and identities play in shaping the practices of school leaders. In spite of the research on school leadership that emphasizes elements reflecting substantive complexity, for example, setting direction, developing people, and redesigning the organization (Leithwood, Louis, Anderson, & Wahlstrom, 2004; Louis, Leithwood, Wahlstrom, & Anderson, 2010; and Day et al., 2011), the trend in preparation programs has been toward the development of technical skills rather than role identities (Hargreaves, 2009) that motivate and inform substantively complex work. In the United States some states are using the standards developed by the Interstate

School Leaders Licensure Consortium (ISLLC) to create certification examinations and preparation programs that emphasize a multitude of technical skills. In the UK, Peter Gronn (2003) drew a similar conclusion about the National Professional Qualification for Headship (NPQH) examination.

> As providers in a highly competitive training market, the temptation for some university programmes to concentrate solely on the learning of model answers and finding ways of making students test-proficient, in order to satisfy accreditation and assessment requirements for certification and license, may prove difficult to resist. (p. 25)

An overemphasis on a technocratic orientation runs the risk of urban school leaders becoming skilled technicians with insufficient focus on transformational leadership. Lumby and English (2009) argued that this technocratic trend in the preparation and expectations of urban leaders "evades and miniaturizes the performance of leadership" (p. 95). Rather than ignoring the technical skills and competencies or focusing solely on them, these authors suggest that they need "to be decentered and seen as an adjunct to the more crucial endeavor, i.e., to confront the meaning of the leader's role, script and performance and how these relate to the identity construction of self, students, and the wider school community" (p. 112).

We begin with a review of the literature on the unique dimensions of urban school leadership highlighting dimensions that reflect the substantive complexity of the role. Contemporary policy and preparation have tended either to ignore this complexity or to respond to it with a catalogue of skills and competencies that reinforce a technocratic perspective. To understand this critique and to propose a remedy, we next review research on identity theory that emphasizes the role that identity plays in leadership practice and explore the elements of professional identity. In this review we illustrate how identity theory informs an understanding of urban school leaders' practices. We provide a critique of and balance to the technocratic perspective in ways that acknowledge the uniqueness and complexity of urban school leadership but provide a direction for practice, preparation, and research. The final section of the chapter describes implications for practice, preparation, and research to emphasize the uniqueness and complexity of urban school leadership and to reform leadership development for this critical group of school leaders.

Before discussing the literature on urban school leadership, it seems appropriate to indicate how we narrowed down the vast literature on this subject. Certainly there is a large volume of research and conceptual treatment of urban education in general and urban leadership in particular, as illustrated by, for example, the extensive and long-term presence of work published in *Urban Education,* as well as other journals. We have narrowed this vast literature to focus on studies that acknowledge the complexity of urban education leadership but take a more asset-based, rather than deficit-based, perspective. We primarily considered literature that is more contemporary—1990s and 2000s—and chose literature that takes a more systemic and critical view of urban education.

Unique Dimensions of Urban School Leadership

The organizational, cultural, and political dimensions of urban public education make urban school leadership an undeniably unique and complex endeavor. Public schools in cities across the United States are characterized by linguistic, ethnic, and socioeconomic diversity—high concentrations of poverty in the face of, in many cases, newly gentrified communities, and relentless accountability pressures on urban public schools amid broadening inducements in urban centers to establish school choice policies. Here, we focus on three dimensions, defined broadly, to draw attention to the unique demands urban contexts place on school leaders. First, we discuss the literature that highlights organizational complexities that urban school leaders negotiate on a daily basis. Second, we explore the political dimensions, especially as they relate to policy demands in urban schools. Finally, we review literature that highlights leadership practices focused on equity and social justice. While there may be other ways to organize a review of the literature, we argue that these three areas represent critical aspects of what is known about urban school leadership practice, and by extension, what it means to be an urban school leader. By highlighting the complex, political, and moral dimensions of urban educational leadership, we also expose the limitations of viewing effective and ethical leadership practice as technocratic. In fact, the relational and political themes in this review indicate the need to account for the ways that leaders integrate their values, beliefs, and identities into their leadership practice.

Complexity

The complex nature of urban school leadership can be attributed to many things. First, urban schools are socioeconomically, linguistically, racially and/or ethnically diverse organizations. In such settings, where the student and family demographics represent high concentrations of poverty, speakers of languages other than English, communities of color, and often varying citizenship statuses, school leaders are faced with an array of perspectives, instructional needs, resource demands, prejudices, and intersecting histories of oppression. As Noguera (1995) pointed out, "urban public schools are the only public agency charged with serving all young people regardless of whether they are homeless, undocumented, hungry or even sick " (p. 4). Additionally, families of color and urban poor are often met with a teaching and administrative staff that is often majority White and from middle-class backgrounds. Deficit views of students, reflecting wider deficit perspectives of urban communities in general, often prevail among urban leaders and teachers (Flessa, 2009). Policy makers help shape this by explaining the effects of urban decline and deindustrialization by blaming poor people on cultural and moral grounds, rather than accounting for the shifts in industry and capital, and the flight of middle-class residents (Noguera, 1995). Urban public schools persist in inner-city neighborhoods, despite shifts in urban economies, demographics, and policies. However, the capacities of urban schools to provide quality education have long been problematic and have grown more so in recent decades (Kozol, 1991, 2005). Unfortunately, Noguera's (1995) claim that urban school reform has typically decoupled school problems from wider urban development issues remains an issue that school leaders ignore at the peril of the education they are providing.

Given the prevalent mismatch of cultural experiences among students and school professional staff, including school leaders, scholars have argued for increased attention to the role of culture and a view of community histories that centers the experiences of communities of color in urban leadership practice (Beachum & McCray, 2011; Dantley, 2005; Lomotey, 1989, 1993; Murtadha & Watts, 2005; Tillman, 2005, 2004). To mitigate the persistent gap between school activities and the urban community contexts, scholars have argued for urban school reform that formally connects the school with its immediate community through linkages with community organizations (Sanders, 2003; Warren, 2005). Given the legacies of poverty and racism found in many urban communities, urban school improvement initiatives with any hope of sustainability should occur in tandem with community development initiatives (Noguera, 1995; Warren, 2005). Such linkages exist in different forms and seek different ends. For example, partnerships can provide social, economic, and health services to families; community organizations can bring cultural and social capital to the school, educating school personnel through asset-based perspectives of community members and histories; community groups can empower families and community members to make schools accountable and responsive to their community constituents; and finally, community-based partnerships can foster political coalitions who can advocate for school and community-based interests (Warren, 2005). Khalifa (2012) argued that the role of the urban school leader be defined in large part as that of a "community leader." This conception of school leadership introduces complexities that must be negotiated simultaneously with efforts to improve student achievement, ensure teacher quality, and in some cases, keep the school doors open. How, with whom, and to what ends school leaders make community connections can vary, and these choices undeniably influence (and are influenced by) the political, social, cultural, and material capital the school leader develops and directs toward educational programs and community engagement.

In addition to the community-based engagement and partnerships, urban school leaders are often also responsible for developing and sustaining external partnerships that are directly connected to externally funded school reform organizations. Honig (2009) pointed out that external organizations are playing an increasingly central role in the implementation of school reform in urban districts. In such cases, external agencies marshal reform implementation by acting as fiscal agents, providing human capital support, and/or evaluating or designing reform models. As external school reform "agents" become a growing sector in the "school improvement industry" (Rowan, 2006), school community relations becomes an ever more complex responsibility for school leaders. The work of the urban school leader involves significant negotiation of and attention to needs and interests originating outside the school walls. There is no question that urban principals have to attend to multiple constituencies and play multiple roles. In addition to the issues emerging in community and policy communities outside the school walls, urban school organizations present multiple responsibilities and spheres within and across which effective school leaders negotiate conflict, seek and accrue resources, and develop human and social capital in the interest of student learning. Goldring and her colleagues found in their study of urban principals that there were at least nine distinct categories of activities that occupied principals' time, including district duties, finance, professional growth, planning/goal setting, building operations, community relations, personnel issues, instructional leadership, and student affairs (Goldring, Huff, May, & Camburn, 2008). West and colleagues (2010) found that the work of urban school leadership has historically been characterized by expanding responsibilities and limited control over the unpredictability of events originating both within and outside the school walls. While district and community contexts may influence which roles are emphasized (Goldring et al., 2008), urban principals continue to juggle (and often struggle with) a wide array of responsibilities, often in response to unpredictable events, leaving little time for personal and professional activities (West, Peck, & Reitzug, 2010). Add to this, complexities introduced by developments in social media and technology, and the principals' tasks accelerate, multiply, and sometimes present public relations risks (West et al., 2010).

Perhaps one of the most pressing concerns for urban principals pertains to the professional development of teachers. Disproportionately high rates of teacher turnover occur in urban schools with its negative effect on school stability, instructional program, and professional development of in-service faculty, putting a strain on the instructional program, teacher collaboration, school morale, relational trust, and overall school improvement (Guin, 2004). Because teachers who often stay in urban schools tend to be less qualified than their counterparts in other districts (Guin, 2004; Lankford, Loeb, & Wyckoff, 2002), principals are faced with the persistent challenge of improving working conditions, developing in-service teachers, and recruiting new teachers. The intensification of accountability pressures, measured in publicized school "report cards" and threats of state "takeovers," has escalated the stakes of the urban principalship (West et al., 2010), often putting additional strains on the relational resources necessary for building trust among professional staff, students, and families.

The demands of and opportunities for school-community partnerships is a growing arena within which urban school leaders must navigate in order to raise material, human, social, political, and cultural resources for the schools they are leading. There is also increasing competition for student enrollments due to an increase in public charter schools and voucher policies that has put pressure on school leaders to "brand" schools as having a curricular theme or focus, with school reform initiatives holding both substantive and symbolic promise to school constituents. At the same time, urban school leaders are challenged by high rates of teacher turnover that compromise the development of instructional quality, organizational trust, teacher leaders, and school climates and cultures that foster authentic engagement of the school community. The complexity of urban school communities is undeniable, and its implications on leadership practice need to be consistently contextualized and untangled in order to do justice to the work transformative urban school leaders do. The cultural, historical, and organizational dimensions of urban schools make leading such schools a unique and complex endeavor. Additionally, attention to policies that affect urban development is becoming an imperative for urban school leadership development. Below we draw attention to literature that highlights educational policies and politics that have unique implications for urban school leadership.

Policy and Politics

Urban schools and school districts face increasingly intense accountability pressures with progressively threatening consequences for poor academic performance. More and more, urban school leaders and scholars of urban educational leadership are reporting that policies such as No Child Left Behind (NCLB) not only define a large part of principals' responsibilities, but they also shape principals' identities by becoming a powerful force in defining the means and ends of daily leadership practice (Lewis, 2010). The rewards and sanctions tied to NCLB, and the challenges of meeting Adequate Yearly Progress (AYP), press leaders to translate external mandates and pressures into reforms at the school level. Knapp and Feldman (2012) found that when urban school leaders across the United States were able to strengthen and sustain internal accountability systems while managing external pressures, they were able to translate pressures into resources for improving instructional practices within the school. Other cases illustrate how principals can implement NCLB requirements without sacrificing a multicultural approach to organizing and leading (Gardiner, Canfield-Davis, & Anderson, 2009). However, Spillane and his colleagues (2001), in their study of urban school district implementation of reforms in response to standards and accountability policies, found that school leaders distributed resources unequally across the instructional areas. Because there may be more pressure to resource instructional areas that are assessed on state achievement tests, urban schools struggling to meet AYP are especially at risk of narrowing the curricular offerings available for students.

In addition to the impact of accountability policies, urban leaders negotiate politics of school reform in the form of external school reform agents/organizations. The increasing presence of foundations and not-for-profit organizations and consortia of NPOs in urban school reforms, namely "small school reforms," documented by Honig (2009), introduce an additional layer of micropolitics. When external actors operated as insiders during the implementation process, providing design and pedagogical support, due to a match in the influence strategies among the organizations, the impact on institutional change was increased and the potential for building leadership capacity improved.

Yet, there is a disconnect between who governs urban districts and their constituencies. Urban districts are larger, and have higher concentrations of poverty and communities of color among the families they serve. However, school boards have historically not represented these constituencies in terms of class, ethnicity, or in the ratio of representatives (Iannaccone & Lutz, 1995). This legacy of disenfranchisement translates to potentially contentious school-community relations with which school leaders must contend. Given the new politics of charters and voucher legislations, school leaders are confronted with pressures to market to more affluent, often White, families who threaten to leave the district. Scribner and Nguyen (2011) found that these measures privilege interests of an elite group of families while eclipsing the interests and concerns of the majority student population, composed of families of color and immigrant families. Given a new political terrain driven by competition and neoliberal reforms espousing innovation and choice, the politics of disenfranchisement and advocacy for marginalized groups has receded from the mainstream reform rhetoric, while remaining a daily concern in urban schools. Dantley (2005) aptly argued, "Leadership in schools of urban, African American children cannot afford a learning environment where academic achievement is depoliticized or where they find themselves in school sites that ignore the political and cultural environment in which they are positioned" (p. 653).

Focus on Equity and Social Justice

The political and cultural realities of urban schools are reflected in an ever-increasing body of research on urban educational leadership, focusing on social justice, equity, and race. Scholars have documented that the stance an urban school leader takes on racial equity, and the policies and practices thus implemented, matter in efforts to combat low expectations of students of color. For example, Khalifa (2011) found that White teachers were more likely to "make deals" with Black students that resulted in academic disengagement; however, the school leader was instrumental in combatting this practice and requiring teachers to engage Black youth. The cultural differences among professional staff and students and families, coupled with the political disenfranchisement discussed above, exacerbate often already contentious school-community relations. The way principals view their role in relation to the community is significant in overcoming these issues. For example, when principals view themselves as not only school leaders, but also as community leaders, advocating on community issues, they and the school can come to be viewed as allies (Khalifa, 2012). This is echoed by Murtadha and Watts (2005), who argued that leadership of schools attended by African American children would be well informed by studying the legacy of Black community leaders, in particular Black women: "[B]ecause the issues [faced by Black constituents] were not only about formal education structures, access, and quality, community engagement was central to Black educational leadership" (Murtadha & Watts, 2005, p. 606).

African American scholars of educational leadership have made significant contributions to the knowledge base of educational leadership as it relates to issues of equity, teacher and leadership preparation and retention, culture, identity, ethics, and purpose (Beachum & McCray, 2011; Dantley, 2002, 2005; Gooden, 2005; Lomotey, 1993, 1989; Murtadha & Watts, 2005; Tillman, 2004, 2005). For example, Gooden (2005) found that when a principal shares and enacts cultural perspectives and practices reflected in the student body and school community, this could enable connections with and advocacy for community and student issues. Murtadha and Watts (2005) argued that scholars and leadership preparation programs would be well served by including stories of African American community, educational and civil rights activists. Accounts of women and men who fought for educational quality in their communities can provide educative and transformative models for interrogating and developing the purposes and impacts of educational leadership.

The literature on leadership in urban schools suggests that antiracist and social justice frameworks must be a part of educational leadership development. Dantley (2005) proposed prophetic pragmatism and spirituality frameworks for addressing persistent educational and social inequities. Some scholars argue for urban educational leadership guided by "Freirean dialogical tenets of love, faith, humility, hope, critical thinking and solidarity" (Miller, Brown, & Hopson, 2011, p. 1078). Furman (2012) also drew on Freire to develop a framework for social justice leadership as "praxis," emphasizing the role of reflection and action in socially just leadership practice. These perspectives emphasize the role of school leaders as agents of educational and social equity and justice. Given the cultural, political, and socioeconomic contexts of urban schools, urban principal preparation must address these dimensions of leadership practice.

Professional Identities of Urban School Leaders

The unique dimensions of urban school leadership identified in the previous section demonstrate the need to move beyond a technocratic approach that ignores values, beliefs, and identities. Our critique of this approach involves a closer examination of the literature on identity theory and how this literature informs a more balanced and complete view of the role and importance of urban school leaders. Although the roots of identity theory can be found in philosophy, sociology, and psychology, its application to leadership and to educational leadership has been considerably limited, based on a review of the literature. Only recently has identity theory gained attention in the literature on educational leadership (see, for example, Lumby & English, 2009; Ryan, 2007; Scribner & Crow, 2012). Moreover, the application to urban school principals is more rare, which is part of our reason for considering it in this chapter.

One reason we emphasize identity, in addition to arguing that there is a need to balance the technocratic perspective, is that identity affects the practice of urban school leadership. Identity provides the motivation for practice. "The energy, motivation, drive that makes roles actually work require that individuals identify with, internalize, and become the role" (Burke & Stets, 2009, p. 38). In urban schools facing state takeover or being labeled as so-called turnaround schools, effective principals possess an urgency in their motivation to make changes (Chicago Public Education Fund, 2008) and "create high performance expectations and motivate others" (Leithwood, Harris, & Strauss, 2010, p. 104). Possessing the skills to diagnose teaching and learning gaps is insufficient if it is not based on a sense of urgency and moral energy that these gaps need and ought to be closed. In addition, identity involves the lived experience within a professional community (Wenger, 1998). Identity affects practice because identities are constructed in relationships with others in the organization. As urban school leaders interact with teachers, students, parents, community members, and others, they develop and negotiate identities that are confirmed, disconfirmed, or revised by others, thus affecting how they practice leadership. Recognizing this negotiation of identity moves us away from heroic leadership practices to one in which leadership becomes a key element of the learning community. Practicing leadership in this way is enormously different from practicing urban leadership as if the urban leader is the only human and moral agent for change.

Understanding identity as lived experience also means that identity shapes and molds the roles leaders undertake. Identities differ from formal positions or roles in that identities are improvisational, emphasize human agency, and are dynamic in contrast to roles that are static, scripted, and deterministic (Ryan, 2007, p. 345). Wenger (1998) distinguished roles and identities further by stating, "One can design roles, but one cannot design the identities that will be constructed through these roles" (p. 229). "Institutions define roles, qualifications, and the distribution of authority—but unless institutional roles can find a realization as identities in practice, they are unlikely to connect with the conduct of everyday life" (pp. 244–245).

Rather than emphasize the techniques, skills, and competencies of urban school leadership, we argue that practice, preparation, and research need to examine and attend to the identities that are the lived experience of urban leadership. Being an effective urban leader certainly involves possessing skills, but without the identities to enact those skills in certain ways and with certain values and beliefs, an urban leader becomes a mere technician and automaton. In contrast, basing skills and competencies on identities that motivate and promote moral perspectives and that rely not only on individual abilities but community efforts and values provides the type of transformational leadership that can impact urban school settings.

Identity Theory

Our examination of the literature on identity theory is organized in terms of the roots of identity theory, the nature of identity, and the elements of identity. These inform our understanding of professional identity applied to urban school leadership. In reviewing the literature on identity, we illustrate various points with a case study of an urban high school principal and his identity construction. The specifics of the case, including the methodology, can be found in Scribner and Crow (2012).

Roots of Identity Theory

The roots of identity theory reach into the writings of both Kant and Hegel in terms of the philosophy of the subject. But more specifically, these roots can be found in the Chicago school of sociology through the influences of German formalism and American pragmatism (Barley, 1989). Through the writings of George Simmel and George Herbert Mead, the relationship between individuals and the social structure influenced the ways identity theory developed and the key elements of identity theory that we discuss in the following sections. Through Simmel the focus was on "social forms," which emphasized the repetition of patterns that influenced the "coherence and reproduction of bounded social worlds" (Barley, 1989, p. 42). Through Mead and other pragmatists, a complementary emphasis was highlighted in which individuals construct abstractions to make sense of the problems they face in the social world. Identities became one of the ways to understand this sensemaking process.

Burke and Stets (2009) emphasized that identity theory grew out of the symbolic interactionist perspective of Mead and other pragmatists. "Most symbolic interactionists would agree that we can best understand social behavior by focusing on individuals' definitions and interpretations of themselves, others, and their situations. By identifying the meanings that actors attributed to their surroundings by getting 'inside their head' and seeing the world from their perspective, we can understand why people do what they do" (Burke & Stets, 2009, p. 33). Two versions of symbolic interactionism, however, influenced identity theory. Burke and Stets (2009) refer to these versions as "traditional and structural." The traditional version viewed the social structure as always in flux, "in the process of being created and recreated through the interpretations, definitions, and actions of individuals in situations" (p. 34). The social structure only influences identities in terms of how individuals freely choose to define the situation. The structural version of symbolic interactionism viewed social structure as more "stable and durable" (Burke & Stets, p. 34), and therefore a more significant influence on identity construction. Burke and Stets emphasize that the social structure provides both constraints and opportunities for individual identity development.

In our discussion of the elements of identity theory we are influenced by Wenger (1998) who emphasized both individual and collective elements of identity construction. Wenger also argued that identity develops through participation in a community. This approach recognizes both human agency in constructing identities but also the influence of the social structure and culture of communities in constraining and facilitating that identity construction.

Nature of Identity

"An identity is the set of meanings that define who one is when one is an occupant of a particular role in society, a member of a particular group, or claims particular characteristics that identify him or her as a unique person" (Burke & Stets, 2009, p. 3). This definition of identity provides a broad perspective on identity that includes social identity (membership in a group), person identity (unique meanings that define an individual apart from roles and groups), and role identity (related to work). Individuals have multiple identities related to all three types. For example, an urban school leader may be a Latina mother who is a member of a particular church or civic organization. In this chapter we focus on role identity in terms of the "internalized meanings of a role that individuals apply to themselves" (Burke & Stets, 2009, p. 114). This definition, however, deemphasizes the ways the different types of identities—role, person, and group—interact and influence each other (Thoits & Virshup, 1997). For example, as Scribner and Crow (2012) found, the identities of a particular urban school leader were strongly influenced by his blue-collar background, his religious identity, his role as a father, his residence in the same urban neighborhood as the school, and his teaching background, as well as a number of role-related elements. Thus, while we focus on role identity, we acknowledge the overlap with other types of identities and recognize that individual urban school leaders bring multiple influences, including gender, race, class, experience, and organizational memberships, to bear on their leadership relationships and practices.

We have already noted Wenger's (1998) understanding of identity as "lived experience." This lived experience occurs as the individual participates within a community. "Identity is not merely a category, a personality trait, a role, or a label; it is more fundamentally an experience that involves participation and reification" (p. 163). While an individual urban school leader may be assigned the role or label of principal, this does not constitute her or his identity. Rather how the individual "lives" the role, constructs and internalizes meanings, and engages and participates with others determines the identities of the individual. This lived experience has both individual and collective elements. In fact, Wenger understood the nature of identity as the pivot between the individual and the collective. Identity and the development of identity is not a totally individualistic effort, although it does involve the meaning-making that individuals engage in as part of their work lives. In the same way, identity and its development is not totally determined by the social context, although it clearly involves the meanings that others attach to the individual's practices and enactment of the role. This two-fold perspective is critical for understanding urban school leaders who not only create their own meanings related to the role but also interact with teachers, students, parents, and community members in the confirming, disconfirming, and revising of identities. Scribner and Crow (2012) found that one urban school leader's identity as a rebel in which he positioned himself against the traditional perspective of the principal's role and the conformist view of relating to the district office was strongly confirmed and supported by his teachers.

Elements of Identity

Role identity has received some recent attention in the education literature; however, most of this has been about teachers' work rather than administrators' (Gee, 2001; Sachs, 2001). The time is appropriate to apply identity theory to the work of urban school leaders. Literature on identity from education, social psychology, and sociology has provided a more complex understanding of the elements of identity than had earlier literature. This recent literature maintains that identity is dynamic, multiple, contextual, developmental, and socially negotiated.

Dynamic. Historically, identity has been synonymous with self-concept and with the idea that this is a static condition once developed in adolescence and early adulthood. However, more recent research suggests that identity is dynamic. O'Connor (2008), in a study of teacher identities, emphasized this dynamic quality as "encompassing both an individual's professional philosophy and their (sic) public actions." "Professional identities are viewed as the means by which individual teachers negotiate and reflect on socially situated aspects of their role" (p. 118). This more active and engaged aspect of identity suggests that identities, far from being static, change throughout the individual's lived experience in the work setting. However, Burke and Stets (2009) maintained that identity is not in constant flux. Using symbolic interactionist perspectives, they argued that because there is a degree of constancy in organized groups and networks, individuals' responses seem to be somewhat focused rather than fragmented.

Wenger (1998) identified several dimensions that reflect this dynamic quality of identity: negotiated experiences, community membership, learning trajectory, nexus of multi-membership, and relation between the local and the global. Our discussion of the remaining four elements of identity reflects some of these dimensions.

Multiple (nexus of multi-memberships). Professional identities are multiple rather than single and have multiple meanings. These multiple meanings involve the various communities of practice in which leaders engage. For example, urban school leaders construct their identities not only in relation to the school or to groups such as teachers, but in relation to external communities and political entities. Scribner and Crow (2012) found in their case of an urban high school principal that he developed identities in relation to teachers, students, parents, supervisors, and community partners.

Wenger (1998) argued that our membership in any particular community is only part of our identity and our task becomes one of reconciling the identities that are constructed in these multiple communities of practice. Lumby and English (2009) acknowledged the multiple identities of school leaders but also recognized that these leaders struggle to construct a sense of self. Leaders create narratives in their relationships with others seeking to provide "a sense of coherence, worth, and belonging" (p. 95). "The self is neither unitary nor one-dimensional, but a combination of deep psychic strivings enveloped within any given socio-cultural context, at once specific but near universal. As such, it may have multiple identities (manifestations)" (p. 97).

Some scholars have attempted to categorize these multiple identities. For example, McCall and Simmons (1978) proposed two hierarchies of identities: prominence and salience. The first—prominence—is based on an idealized sense of self, that is, "how individuals like to see themselves given their ideals, desires, and what is central to them" (Burke & Stets, 2009, p. 40). An urban principal, for example, may see himself or herself as an instructional leader (Scribner & Crow, 2012), perhaps because of district and professional expectations, teaching background, rewards, or confirmation/support from teachers. The salience hierarchy (McCall & Simmons, 1978) includes identities that are more influenced by the situation and are called for at certain times but not others. In the Scribner and Crow (2012) study, the urban principal emphasized a rebel identity, which he felt was necessary given the chaos (state takeover) in the district as well as the value his teaching staff placed on his willingness to take risks to protect their instructional time and culture.

Contextual (community membership). These multiple identities are related to the multiple contexts or communities of practice in which the urban school leader interacts. Wenger (1998) maintained that identities are developed and enacted in communities of practice. He identified three elements of these communities: mutual engagement, in which we learn who we are as we interact in relationships with others; accountability to an enterprise, in which we develop a perspective that includes actions, choices, and values; and the negotiability of a repertoire, in which the history of practice presents events, references, memories, and experiences (pp. 152–153). The complex landscape in which urban school leaders work, including the demographic diversity, expanding responsibility, accountability demands, and cultural elements, creates not only multiple communities of practice but intense engagement and negotiation. In her study of women principals, Smulyan (2000) identified four types of contexts in which identities are relevant and negotiated. First, personal context involves the family and educational background and the career path to the principalship. Scribner and Crow (2012) found that the "father" identity was extremely salient for this urban principal because of his background, his educational career, and his current life circumstances. Second, the community context includes teachers and families in the school. In the Scribner and Crow study, the principal identified "teacher at heart," "sergeant," "rebel," and even "father" as identities related to the teachers; "one of them" and "mentor" related to the parents. Third, Smulyan (2000) identified the institutional context that includes power relationships and structural arrangements. In the Scribner and Crow study, the "rebel" identity was salient for this principal in dealing with the district context and chaos. Finally, the historical and social context influences the principal's identities. This context includes forces and norms, for example, the professional expectation of instructional leadership that is salient for most urban principals.

Developmental (learning trajectory). We have maintained that identities are dynamic rather than static. But they are also developmental, by which we mean an individual's identities do not come fully developed at once, but involve a learning trajectory in which they are adjusted, revised, eliminated, and so forth (Møller, 2005; Ryan, 2007). The temporal quality of identity and the "constant becoming" (Wenger, 1998, p. 154) means that identity development does not involve a fixed course or destination. Instead identity reflects a work in progress shaped by our efforts, our past, future, and present, and the negotiation with others in the communities of practice. Møller (2005) reflected Wenger's position about the learning trajectory of identity when she said, "Identity is temporally constructed in the process of shaping a learning trajectory consisting of both convergent and divergent trajectories. . . . It is not like a path that can be charted or foreseen. It is like a continuous motion—one that has a momentum of its own, but also opens to a field of influence" (p. 43). In the Scribner and Crow (2012) study, the urban high school principal's identities were adjusted over time as he spent more time in the school. Thus, while his personal background certainly influenced his identities in this urban environment, his interaction with teachers, students, and parents as well as the organizational changes within the school (e.g., newcomers) influenced adjustments and revisions.

An additional dimension of this temporal/developmental element is that individuals differ in terms of the ambiguity and/or certainty with which they view their identities. Certainly career stage makes a difference in terms of ambiguity or certainty. As socialization scholars acknowledge, role taking is more apparent at early career stages than role making (Hart, 1993). In addition, new institutional and societal expectations can influence the questioning of earlier identities and the promotion of others even at mid-career stages. For example, accountability and organizational demographics may influence urban school leaders to become less confident of particular identities that have seemed salient in the past. Moreover, this temporal element of identity development can involve not only self-identification but also self-dis-identification (McCall, 2003). In other words, identity development can include what an individual is not as well as what an individual is. In the Scribner and Crow (2012) study, the urban principal frequently described himself as "not like them," referring to more traditional or less innovative principals.

There are a variety of types of changes that influence this temporal element or developmental dimension of identity. Burke and Stets (2009, pp. 180–186) listed four sources of change: change in situation, identity conflicts, identity standard and behavior conflicts, and negotiation and the presence of others. For urban principals any of these sources are possible. For example, an urban principal's identity may change based on a critical number of faculty newcomers to the school, student demographic changes, or failure to meet Adequate Yearly Progress benchmarks. Urban leaders may also encounter changes related to identity conflicts, for example, role conflicts between urban neighborhood expectations and district expectations or between community partners and student needs (Scribner & Crow, 2012). In addition, the principal may encounter conflicts between staff perceptions of the principal and the principal's own identities.

Socially negotiated. An urban principal's identities are clearly not a solely individual matter because identities are socially constructed and negotiated in relationship with others in the organization. "Practice involves the negotiation of ways of being a person in that context" (Wenger, 1998, p. 149). Wenger further reminded us that identity is not just what we say about ourselves, the stories we tell, or what others say about us, although all of these are part of the process. At times the literature on urban school leaders suggests a heroic image in which the individual decides on her or his own what he or she will be and how he or she will be perceived. This perspective ignores the relational aspects of leadership and the nature of communities of practice in the urban school. Identities are formed through the social negotiation that takes place within the practice of the school/community. In the Scribner and Crow (2012) study, teachers on the whole confirmed the identities affirmed by the principal. However, in some instances, they took issue, for example, "father" identity with teachers, and even revised the identity. We doubt that these took place only during the interview. In fact, the principal described negotiations involving how "teacher at heart" had to be revised to consider the changing circumstances of the school and how the "rebel" identity was negotiated in light of teachers' fears of the principal losing his job by virtue of his rebellious response to district supervisors.

This social negotiation of identity, however, does not mean that the individual passively responds to the expectations and perspectives of the multiple audiences and contexts. The social negotiation is reciprocal involving all parties. In the case of the "teacher at heart" identity conflict mentioned in the Scribner and Crow (2012) case study, the principal took a strong position regarding the need to bring in different types of teachers whose characteristics may not have been particularly appealing to the current faculty at the outset.

These elements of identity and identity development can be helpful in understanding the urban school leader's role and for avoiding a technocratic bias that "evades and miniaturizes the performance of leadership" (Lumby & English, 2009, p. 95). Rather, identity theory provides a way to acknowledge and confront the complexity, politics, and moral dilemmas of the urban school leader's role.

Implications for Urban School Leadership

In this chapter we have maintained that the leadership of urban schools has become more intense and complex, involving organizational, political, and moral dimensions. We have also argued that the technocratic trend that emphasizes skills and competencies and ignores values, beliefs, and especially identities does not serve urban school leadership well. The type of substantive complexity necessary for the effective and transformative practice of urban school leadership calls for not only the recognition, but also the promotion, of reflective and critical identities to enhance this leadership. In this final section, we identify several implications of identity theory for the practice, preparation, and research of urban school leadership.

Implications for Practice

We have argued that the reflection and examination of a leader's identities is a richer way to understand and respond to the complexity of urban school leadership. For example, the increasing complexity of the role has emphasized more audiences and contexts for the practice of urban school leadership. Two particularly salient contexts involve the growing influence of external partners and communities as agents of reform (Goldring et al., 2008; Honig, 2009; Rowan, 2006). Urban school leaders develop identities that seek to make sense of the interactions with these diverse audiences. Rather than simply developing skills and competencies related to managing these audiences, urban school leaders' identities provide the motivation and drive to connect with these audiences and negotiate their resources for the school.

Urban school leaders also find themselves in the complex and sometimes unenviable position of having to reconcile different identities based on these audiences and contexts. Rather than finding a single identity that provides the perspective for engaging these diverse communities and partners, urban school principals have to socially negotiate in order to reconcile and balance perspectives. For example, external partners from business have an interest in contributing to the production of future workers. Communities have an interest in developing contributing citizens of the neighborhood. These perspectives, while not necessarily contradictory, may be expressed in different ways that put demands on the principal to negotiate and reconcile these expectations and different identities. For example, some urban principals have to reconcile the roles of salesperson and community leader (Khalifa, 2012; Scribner & Crow, 2012). Others are faced with reconciling reformer and community leader roles when advocacy for marginalized students and their families is ignored in the current competitive and neoliberal reforms (Dantley, 2005; Scribner & Nguyen, 2011).

The complex nature of urban school leadership also results in a broadening of communities and contexts. Smulyan's (2000) identification of four types of contexts (personal, community, institutional, and societal/historical) suggests that an urban principal must acknowledge a broader conception of the role than previously considered. For example, rather than being focused exclusively on the school, urban principals must acknowledge the community, institutional, and societal forces that impinge on urban students, their families, and the school itself, forces that include poverty, racism, and inequities.

Another element of complexity that affects urban school leaders is the rapidly changing, ever-evolving expectations and demands. We have identified accountability demands, political forces, and moral expectations, but few of these are static in how they confront the urban principal. The nature of work, which has become more substantively complex, especially for educators, requires that individuals be able to access data, rapidly use that data to inform decision making, and remain critical of data, problems, and solutions. But even more important is the urban principal's ability to be open to changing perspectives and critical understanding. A recognition of the dynamic nature of identities, how they evolve with changing contexts and demands, as well as the capacity to adjust, revise, and adapt identities, are essential for contemporary urban leaders. The day of developing your leadership style in a static way in which all problems are seen the same way and solved with the same tools is over. This dynamic view of identities produces, however, high anxiety for the individual urban school principal in the midst of intense, complex organizational, political, and moral contexts. This means that urban principals must have the capacity and the resources to deal with this type of identity conflict and anxiety.

Implications for Preparation

Traditional preparation programs for school leaders have been attacked from multiple fronts in the latest wave of reform. These programs are criticized for being overly theoretical, lacking sufficient field-based, clinical experiences, and neglecting to provide the skills and competencies necessary to respond to reforms, and more important, to the legitimate and critical needs of urban school students and schools (Levine, 2005). Although many of these criticisms are well founded, they typically have resulted in a misinformed, misdirected strategy for improving preparation. They have resulted in a technocratic approach that emphasizes the development of skills and competencies to the exclusion of values, beliefs, and identities. Ample research on successful school leaders has demonstrated that possessing only the skills without the dispositions, values, beliefs, and identities is not only shortsighted, but also ineffective for building and sustaining the type of change critically needed in complex urban environments (Day et al., 2011). Our discussion of the complex nature of urban school leadership and the elements of identity theory suggests several implications for more effective preparation programs for these urban leaders.

First, critical self-reflection becomes an essential component of effective preparation programs for urban school principals to recognize and develop identities that are multiple, dynamic, evolving, and socially negotiated. An unreflective accumulation of skills, regardless of how relevant, does not provide the motivation, drive, or perspective for using these skills in ethical, critical, and transformative ways to meet the complex needs of urban schools and students. Moreover, self-reflection does not come automatically or easily to many people. Effective preparation programs must build in experiences such as narratives, cases, and simulations, which provide the opportunities to engage in self-reflection regarding messy, difficult, and complex issues in schools. Such authentic engagement provides the opportunity for aspiring urban leaders to develop, negotiate, and critically question their identities.

Second, the multiple audiences to which urban principals must respond and negotiate their identities emphasize the need for preparation programs to help build capacity to recognize the importance of these audiences, to understand their values, resources, and expectations, and to develop a perspective on how to negotiate in building, revising, adapting identities for working with them. For example, urban principals whose identities primarily focus on being instructional leaders with the necessary data collection and monitoring may ignore the existence of a deficit perspective that weakens or severely damages working with parents and community members. A preparation program must help aspiring leaders develop the commitment and perspectives, as well as skills, they must have to negotiate identities necessary for the complex, multiple audiences of urban schools.

Third, preparation programs must develop strategies to prepare aspiring urban leaders to understand the need for and develop the capacity to engage in the evolving, dynamic nature of identity construction. Instead of the static view described earlier, in which preparation programs are designed to provide an unchanging set of skills and competencies, these programs must help new leaders create the capacity and commitment to adjust, revise, and critically evaluate their identities.

Implications for Research

The research on identity theory in education is only beginning and less has been done in terms of urban school leaders' identities (Lumby & English, 2009; Scribner & Crow, 2012). We propose three areas for research that should inform practice and preparation for urban school leaders.

First, research on how current reforms, accountability demands, and political forces are impinging on the identities of urban school leaders would provide empirical support to help in understanding how these forces are impacting the motivation, drive, and perspectives for change of these leaders. Although we have little information for comparison, gathering data from urban school leaders on their perspectives of how their role and identities have changed with various reform movements would inform policy making as well as preparation programs. For example, are reforms around teacher evaluation influencing the salience of certain identities and diminishing the prominence of others, for example, teacher at heart?

Second, communities impact the complexity of urban school leadership in various ways. Understanding how these community expectations, resources, and demographics influence the development of identities for urban leaders would be helpful in enriching our understanding of the social negotiations in which principals engage and inform preparation programs on how to build urban school leaders' capacity to work with and engage their communities. If, as research suggests (Day et al., 2011), context is critical for school leadership, we must understand how the multiple contexts in which urban principals interact influence the development, salience, and nature of their multiple identities.

Finally, we have focused exclusively in this chapter on role identity. However, there are two other types of identities—person and social (Burke & Stets, 2009). Urban school leaders' lives are not compartmentalized in such a way that their person and social identities do not impact their role identity. Research on how these three interact in the types and development of identities would provide a more complete and useful picture. For example, we have noted that in many urban schools, the race of the school staff and leadership does not reflect the race of the majority of students. Understanding how elements of person or social identity, such as race, gender, ethnicity, and social class, impact the kinds of role identities that become acceptable, salient, and negotiated is critical for urban leaders' own self-reflection as well as their practices with students, parents, and community members.

Conclusion

School leaders play a significant and urgently needed role within the complex political and moral contexts of urban schools. In order to play this role effectively and morally, they need not only the technical skills of leadership practice, but also the identities that motivate and energize their practice. It is essential that we move practice, preparation, and research on urban school leaders toward recognition of the importance of identity. Such recognition and examination should provide a richer and more nuanced picture of this critical role in urban education.

References

Barley, S.R. (1989). Careers, identities, and institutions: The legacy of the Chicago School of Sociology. In M.B. Arthur, D.T. Hall, & B.S. Lawrence (Eds.), *Handbook of career theory* (pp. 41–65). Cambridge, UK: Cambridge University Press.

Beachum, F.D., & McCray, C.R. (2011). *Cultural collision and collusion.* New York, NY: Peter Lang.

Burke, P.J., & Stets, J.E. (2009). *Identity theory.* New York, NY: Oxford University Press.

Chicago Public Education Fund. (2008). *School turnaround leaders: Competencies for success.* Chicago, IL: Author.

Dantley, M. E. (2002). Uprooting and replacing positivism, the melting pot, multiculturalism, and other impotent notions in educational leadership through an African American perspective. *Education and Urban Society, 34*(3), 334–352.

Dantley, M.E. (2005). African American spirituality and Cornel West's notions of prophetic pragmatism: Restructuring educational leadership in American urban schools. *Educational Administration Quarterly, 41*(4), 651–674.

Day, C., & Leithwood, K. (2007). *Successful principal leadership in times of change. An international perspective.* Dorchrecht, The Netherlands: Springer.

Day, C., Sammons, P., Leithwood, K., Hopkins, D., Gu, Q., Brown, E., & Ahtaridou, E. (2011). *Successful school leadership. Linking with learning and achievement.* Maidenhead, UK: Open University Press.

Earley, P., & Weindling, D. (2004). *Understanding school leadership.* London, UK: Paul Chapman.

Flessa, J. (2009). Urban school principals, deficit frameworks, and implications for leadership. *Journal of School Leadership, 19,* 334–370.

Furman, G. (2012). Social justice leadership as praxis: Developing capacities through preparation programs. *Educational Administration Quarterly, 48*(2), 191–229.

Gardiner, M.E., Canfield-Davis, K., & Anderson, K.L. (2009). Urban school principals and the 'No Child Left Behind' Act. *Urban Review, 4,* 141–160.

Gee, J.P. (2001). Identity as an analytic lens for research in education. In W.G. Secada (Ed.), *Review of research in education* (Vol. 25, pp. 99–125). Washington, DC: American Educational Research Association.

Goldring, E., Huff, J., May, H., & Camburn, E. (2008). School context and individual characteristics: What influences principal practice? *Journal of Educational Administration, 46,* 332–352.

Gooden, M.A. (2005). The role of an African American principal in an urban information technology high school. *Educational Administration Quarterly, 41*(4), 630–650.

Gronn, P. (2003). *The new work of educational leaders. Changing leadership practice in an era of school reform.* London, UK: Paul Chapman.

Guin, K. (2004). Chronic teacher turnover in urban elementary schools. *Education Policy Analysis Archives, 12*(42), Retrieved July 1, 2013 from http://epaa.asu.edu/epaa/v12n42/

Hallinger, P., Bickman, L., & Davis, K. (1996). School context, principal leadership, and student reading achievement. *The Elementary School Journal, 96*(5), 527–549.

Hargreaves, A. (2009). *The fourth way. The inspiring future for educational change.* Thousand Oaks, CA: Corwin Press.

Hart, A.W. (1993). *Principal succession: Establishing leadership in schools.* Albany, NY: State University of New York Press.

Honig, M. (2009). "External" organizations and the politics of urban educational leadership: The case of new small autonomous schools initiatives. *Peabody Journal of Education, 84,* 394–413.

Iannaccone, L., & Lutz, F.W. (1995). The crucible of democracy: The local arena. In J.D. Scribner & D.H. Layton (Eds.), *The Study of Educational Politics, the 1994 Commemorative Yearbook of the Politics of Education Association (1969–1994).* Philadelphia, PA: Falmer Press.

Khalifa, M. A. (2011). Teacher expectations and principal behavior: Responding to teacher acquiescence. *Urban Review, 43,* 702–727.

Khalifa, M.A. (2012). A re-new-ed paradigm in successful urban school leadership: Principal as community leader. *Educational Administration Quarterly, 48,* 424–467.

Knapp, M.S., & Feldman, S.B. (2012). Managing the intersection of internal and external accountability: Challenge for urban school leadership. *Journal of Educational Administration, 50*(5), 666–694.

Kozol, J. (1991). *Savage inequalities: Children in America's Schools.* New York, NY: Crown.

Kozol, J. (2005). *The shame of the nation: The restoration of apartheid schooling in America.* New York, NY: Crown.

Lankford, H., Loeb, S., & Wyckoff, J. (2002). Teacher sorting and the plight of urban schools: A descriptive analysis. *Educational Evaluation and Policy Analysis, 24*(1), 37–62.

Leithwood, K., Harris, A., & Strauss, T. (2010). *Leading school turnaround. How successful leaders transform low performing schools.* San Francisco, CA: Jossey-Bass.

Leithwood, K., & Louis, K.S. (2012). *Linking leadership to student learning.* San Francisco, CA: Jossey-Bass.

Leithwood, K., Louis, K.S., Andersen, S., & Wahlstrom, K. (2004). *How leadership influences student learning. Review of research.* Minneapolis, MN: Center for Applied Research, University of Minnesota.

Levine, A. (2005). *Educating school leaders.* Washington, DC: The Education Schools Project.

Lewis, A. L. (2010). *School leaders as both colonized and colonizers: Understanding professional identity in an era of no child left behind* (Doctoral Dissertation). Retrieved from Proquest Dissertations and Theses Database. (AAT 3430884).

Lomotey, K. (1989). African-American principals: School leadership and success. New York, NY: Greenwood Press.

Lomotey, K. (1993). African-American principals: Bureaucrat/administrators and ethno-humanists. *Urban Education, 27*(4), 395–412.

Louis, K., Leithwood, K., Wahlstrom, K., & Anderson, S. (2010). *Investigating the links to improved student learning.* Minneapolis, MN: Center for Applied Research, University of Minnesota.

Lumby, J., & English, F. (2009). From simplicism to complexity in leadership identity and preparation: Exploring the lineage and dark secrets. *International Journal of Leadership in Education, 12*(2), 95–114.

McCall, G. (2003). The me and the not me: Positive and negative poles of identity. In P.J. Burke, T.J. Owens, R.T. Serpe, & P.A. Thoits (Eds.), *Advances in identity theory and research* (pp. 11–26). New York, NY: Kluwer Academic/Plenum.

McCall, G., & Simmons, J. (1978). *Identities and interactions.* New York, NY: Free Press.

Miller, P. M., Brown, T., & Hopson, R. (2011). Centering love, hope, and trust in the community: transformative urban leadership informed by Paulo Freire. *Urban Education, 45*(5), 1078–1099.

Møller J. (2005). Old metaphors, new meanings: Being a woman principal. In C. Sugrue (Ed.), *Passionate principalship: Learning from life histories of school leaders* (pp. 42–57). Long, UK: Routledge Falmer.

Murtadha, K., & Watts, D.M. (2005). Linking the struggle for education and social justice: Historical perspectives of African American leadership in schools. *Educational Administration Quarterly, 41*(4), 591–608.

Noguera, P. (1995). Confronting the urban in urban school reform. *Urban Review, 28*(1), 1–19.

O'Connor, K.E. (2008). "You choose to care": Teachers, emotions and professional identity. *Teaching and Teacher Education, 24*(1), 117–126.

Rowan, B. (2006). The school improvement industry in the United States: Why educational change is both pervasive and ineffectual. In H.D. Meyer and B. Rowan (Eds.), *The New Institutionalism in Education.* Albany, NY: SUNY Press.

Ryan, J. (2007). Dialogue, identity, and inclusion: Administrators as mediators in diverse school contexts. *Journal of School Leadership, 17*(3), 340–369.

Sachs, J. (2001). Teacher professional identity: Competing discourses, competing outcomes. *Journal of Education Policy, 16*(2), 149–161.

Sanders, M. (2003). Community involvement in schools: From concept to practice. *Education and Urban Society, 35*(2), 161–180.

Scribner, S.P., & Crow, G.M. (2012). Employing professional identities: Case study of a high school principal in a reform setting. *Leadership and Policy in Schools, 11*(3), 243–274.

Scribner, S.M.P., & Nguyen, T.S. (2011). The construction of risk and threat in (and around) a diverse urban elementary school. Paper presented at the Annual Meeting of the University Council for Educational Administration, Pittsburgh, PA.

Smulyan, L. (2000). *Balancing acts. Women principals at work.* Albany, NY: State University of New York.

Spillane, J. P., Diamond, J.B., Walker, L.J., Halverson, R., & Jita, L. (2001). Urban school leadership for science instruction: Identifying and activating resources in an undervalued school subject. *Journal of Research in Science Teaching, 38*(8), 918–940.

Thoits, P., & Virshup, L. (1997). Me's and we's: Forms and functions of social identities. In R. Ashmore & L. Jussim (Eds.), *Self and identity: Fundamental issues* (pp. 106–133). New York, NY: Oxford University Press.

Tillman, L.C. (2004). African American principals and the legacy of *Brown*. *Review of Research in Education, 28,* 101–146.

Tillman, L.C. (2005). Mentoring new teachers: Implications for leadership practice in an urban school. *Educational Administration Quarterly, 41*(4), 609–629.

Warren, M. (2005). Communities and schools: A new view of urban education reform. *Harvard Education Review, 75*(2), 133–173.

Wenger, R. (1998). *Communities of practice: Learning, meaning, and identity.* Cambridge, UK: Cambridge University Press.

West, D.L., Peck, C., & Reitzug, U.C. (2010). Limited control and relentless accountability: Examining historical changes in urban school principal pressure. *Journal of School Leadership, 20,* 238–266.

17

Urban School Leadership and Fit[1]

Ira Bogotch, Leo Nesmith, Scott V. Smith & Frank Gaines

Introduction

The argument in this chapter proposes that we reconsider the dynamics of urban school leadership hiring practices. There may be no decisions more important than hiring and placing individuals to fill vacant positions,[2] whether it is a superintendent hiring school building principals or a principal hiring teachers (TNTP, 2012). Although much research attention has focused on questions related to teacher retention (Ingersoll, 2001), once educators earn tenure *within a school district,* they tend to remain in place as teachers and administrators until their retirement.[3] Therefore, personnel decisions affect individuals, individual schools, and school districts long term, which is critical for understanding the struggles necessary to bring about urban educational reforms and change processes (Fullan, 1993; Hord, Rutherford, Huling-Austin, & Hall, 1987).

"Fit derives from the continuing interaction that takes place between a leader, followers, and the culture in which they exist" (Duke & Iwanicki, 1992, p. 27). The conceptual framework of "fit" (Tooms, Lugg, & Bogotch, 2010) is used in this chapter as a sociopolitical justification for why and how individuals are recruited, selected, and placed in organizations. The term itself is expressed in the various phrases: "she/he was the best fit; she/he was a better fit; she/he was not a fit." These words are meant to end further discussion on the topic of hiring. For many, the terse non-explanation suffices, especially if the choice of individual confirms previously held biases and assumptions (e.g., such as affirmative action criteria or "role model theory"). For others, the deliberate vagueness of the term "fit" speaks to the politics of the school system and is an inadequate educational response.

We argue that there is more to the meanings of "fit" than just school system politics. That is, the impact of federal and state policies, the changing demographics in our nation's cities, a school's heritage and place in a community, and what educational researchers report as findings regarding personnel decisions, all combine and compete to influence policy makers and school administrators. The deliberate vagueness of the term "fit" allows for it to be used socially and politically by different political and professional constituencies who promote, in our opinion, contradictory goals for urban schools and public education. These competing interests seek to influence urban school reforms that logically emphasize different "fit" qualities in making personnel decisions. The position we take here is that any school leadership policy or action that frustrates deep discussions, honest explanations, and transparent debates ultimately undermines the legitimacy of public education—urban or otherwise—from within. For urban educators to reposition themselves in a national debate, the future of urban schools would need to be perceived as a "public good," rather than as a reform that benefits special interests or minority students alone.

Tooms et al. (2010) concluded that the way school districts use the explanation of "fit" is analogous to a watch with only an hour hand to tell time. After a while, the participants themselves forget that the watch is missing a minute hand. In other words, they get accustomed to telling "good enough" time, approximations that make realities acceptable, but never exact or excellent. If true, then we ought to consider the negative consequences of "fit" as mindsets and practices that perpetuate myths and limit opportunities for all principal candidates, especially African American principal candidates (Nesmith, 2012, 2013; Smith, 2013). Further, the lack of transparency attached to personnel functions casts a lingering cloud over urban school districts such that rumors and innuendos, including stereotypes, are perpetuated (Goffman, 1963).

The multiple perspectives of "fit" presented here include (1) compliance with federal, state, and district policies, (2) consequences of urban trends and municipal politics, (3) holding on to students' and communities' needs, and (4) reported findings from organizational and social science research. Each of these competing positions has clear implications regarding "who is a fit" and "who is not a fit" for leading urban schools. With respect to federal, state, and district policies, the meaning of fit is most closely associated with the system's goals, notably the raising of student test scores on standardized exams. The second dynamic related to urban trends investigates how city officials meet diverse needs of neighborhoods, whether those labeled "in transition," gentrified, immigrant, or ghetto. Third, within both large and midsize cities, there are specific Black school-communities that for historical reasons have remained "Historically Black"[4] in the post-*Brown* era. In such contexts, "fit" reflects a leadership disposition that is culturally responsive and relevant to today. Lastly, "fit" as described by social science researchers who study organizations, including schools, report empirical findings *as if* what participants say is important phenomenologically as a complete and orderly explanation of organizational realities. We question the validity of such findings, not only with respect to researchers' positing predictive models, but also with respect to policy makers', city officials', and community leaders' competing views of "fit."

The central issue is whether educators—at the federal, state, local, and school levels—have the political will to base personnel decisions on deep culturally responsive knowledge of students and their communities. What is required is a shift from defining "fit" solely in terms of individual qualities to a collective and responsible position of support for the success of communities who must learn to live together in urban settings. This responsibility extends to school leadership researchers who need to rethink their research designs, questions, methods, and evidence, which come typically from small samples and case study data. Urban students, their communities, as well as African American candidates for leadership, all deserve greater educational opportunities. In order to meet these objectives, researchers have to challenge conventional wisdom and entrenched traditional practices in studying and reporting not only on who is most qualified to lead urban schools, but how can diverse urban residents be successful.

Federal and State Policies

Since the 1990s, U.S. public education has moved more and more toward centralized control of educational governance. Public policy makers justify these educational reforms as necessary to address the nation's midrange rankings on international scales. In public education, we have moved from Goals 2000: Educate America Act (1994), to the passage of the 2001 No Child Left Behind Act (NCLB), to the 2009 Race to the Top (RTTP) competitive grant program.

The NCLB Act mandated that 100% of all children be proficient in mathematics and reading by 2014. Since Congress failed to reach agreement on the reauthorization of NCLB, states were offered the opportunity to apply for waivers. These waivers, if approved, require states to accept a national curriculum in mathematics and English language arts known as the Common Core Standards. States would also be required to evaluate teachers and principals based in large part on the test scores of their students. As of this writing, 45 states, the District of Columbia, four territories, and the Department of Defense Education Activity have adopted the Common Core State Standards (http://www.corestandards.org/in-the-states), indicating how punitive states view federal policies under NCLB.

Under NCLB, two remedies were available in schools that did not meet their Adequate Yearly Progress based on standardized test results: (1) school choice, whereby parents could move their children from a failing school; and (2) intervention options, including school closure, school restart (e.g., to be reopened as charters), school turnaround (e.g., assigning new principals and reevaluating the teaching staff/rehiring no more than 50%), or school transformation (e.g., similar, though less restrictive, to the turnaround option). Under NCLB, any school receiving a "failing" grade in two consecutive years was pressured to remove the school's principal as a precondition for state intervention—regardless of year-to-year student learning gains, community support, and/or the implementation of sustainable change initiatives.

The mandated reforms demand curricular and instructional alignment with standards, benchmarks, and annual standardized tests. Under the slogans of accountability, fairness, and "no excuses," this governance narrative essentially ignores contexts including the urban context. Accountability refers to both schools and students as either high or low performing in terms of letter grades or comparative rankings. When school district superintendents and principals align curriculum and instruction with the systems' apparatus, the meanings of "fit" serve the interests of systems' goals or the superintendents' agendas (Murphy, 2008). The criteria of fit, therefore, are based on selecting individuals who are judged to be loyal and dependable and who have the managerial skills to implement already developed and externally driven policies of curriculum and instruction. Fit reflects the superintendent's agenda that may or may not overlap with urban issues, students, parents, or communities. Because these administrative practices have to be justified in terms of RTTT turnaround—in low-performing schools—and student achievement measures of accountability, the vagueness ascribed to the meaning of "fit" serves these objectives without saying what it is intended to mean. In urban schools, "fit" is justified in terms of procedural fairness, due process, and research that support those aims. The political constituency served by top-down policies is clearly the system itself and "fit" is a matter of compliance, maintaining the system while rhetorically calling for turnaround school leadership and system reform.

City-Urban Intersections

There are 26 school districts (out of 13,592) in the United States with over 100,000 enrolled students. This translates to over 22,000 city schools, with 60% of the students in those schools qualifying for free and reduced lunch. In large cities across the country, the racial/ethnic composition of the dominant groups is first Hispanic with 33.4%, second Whites with 31.5%, and third African Americans with 26.4% (NCES.ed.gov/surveys/urbaned/enrollment.asp). These three demographic categories, however, do not fully explain urban demographic trends over the last 20 years.

The first noteworthy trend is the reduced number of African Americans living in our nation's cities. Black populations have been and continue to decline in cities like San Francisco, Chicago,

Atlanta, and Oakland. Even U.S. cities that had seen a rise in their Black populations from 1990 to 2000, such as Cleveland, Philadelphia, Dallas, and New Orleans, have experienced a drop in their Black populations (http://usatoday30.usatoday.com/news/nation/census/2011–03–22–1Ablacks22_ST_N.htm). So as working- and middle-class African Americans move to the suburbs or leave Northern, cold weather cities, the African Americans who remain in cities are fewer, poorer, and more isolated than just a decade ago. It also explains, in part, the resegregation of public schools in inner cities (Orfield & Lee, 2004).

The second demographic change is being driven by the phenomena of urban renewal, gentrification, and urban development, all of which can take place slowly or quickly. When it happens slowly, the neighborhood is referred to as "in transition." For example, today, in Brooklyn, New York, neighborhoods like Red Hook, Fort Greene, and Williamsburg reflect slow and quick transitions. There are streets today in Harlem with more White people living in converted upscale condominiums than Blacks as a result of gentrification.

Historically, the public policy of urban renewal was meant to revitalize U.S. cities. Instead, it too often separated families by driving six-lane highways through the heart of neighborhoods like historic Treme in New Orleans and elsewhere like in Miami. What does it matter if intact Black residential neighborhoods vanish? Cities need taxpayers to fund infrastructure, to pay property taxes to support local public schools. It is up to local politicians, strong mayors, city councils, and commissions to make decisions that benefit neighborhoods and cities. Too often these decisions come at the expense of the poor and powerless.

These demographic changes also raise issues regarding the growing distance between segregated neighborhoods and resegregated schools and the demographic and economic changes happening in our nation's and world's cities. Throughout the United States, wealth and income inequality is at an all-time high (Stiglitz, 2013). As the disparities of wealth continue to increase, as new urban homesteaders rediscover the benefits of living in cities, and as transitional neighborhoods provide inexpensive housing, our cities become even more hostile to the poor.

As pessimistic as these dynamics have been over the past decade, they also create opportunities for new dialogues regarding the public engagement between those historically isolated within inner cities and those seeking to make new lives in these same neighboring locales. Urban reformers are able to see a new urban future as a mutual convergence of interests, one not based primarily on race, but rather on economic and social opportunities afforded by living in urban environments.

The world's great cities as well as the great cities of the United States, many of which fall under Milner's (2012) category of urban intensive, are exciting places to reside in and to visit. Yet, each of these cities has inner-city schools with urban characteristics (Milner, 2012). The terms "city" and "urban" evoke contrasting images: the former ranges from entertainment, culinary delights, architectural wonders; while the latter evokes images of people in poverty, buildings with broken windows, and violent places where crime, drugs, and gangs rule. When the question turns to the "fit" for urban school leaders, its meaning shifts to creating the future of urban public schools in urban communities. The knowledge and skills needed will be based on the relationships between urban development and educational leadership going forward. In this dynamic and political context, "fit" is not about system maintenance, but rather it is directed to urban and community development, highlighting entrepreneurial qualities for school leaders. It also would require that school leaders have the capacity to build social networks across institutions and agencies and not focus exclusively on within-school district managerial variables.

New city homesteaders will insist upon world-class, big-city schools for which they are paying high tax dollars. It is up to today's urban school leadership to get out in front of the trends of gentrification and immigration to work for affordable housing and to make today's urban schools better for neighborhoods in transition. Within schools, urban leadership will have to balance short-term goals of raising test scores with having to assimilate all these diverse groups.

"Historically Black"

As Blacks migrated in large numbers into urban areas, Black educators "were almost invariably assigned to schools predominantly attended by Negroes" (Thompson, 1951, p. 136). Thompson noted that most Blacks willfully accepted the harsh conditions of *de jure* segregation just to obtain the few available teaching and administrative vacancies in all-Black schools. Thompson noted:

> [I]t was the almost universal practice to assign Negro personnel to schools predominantly attended by Negroes. Even as late as 1949, the Interracial Committee of Detroit in its study of the employment of Negro personnel . . . discovered that no Negroes were employed in administrative or supervisory positions; only one or two were teaching in high school; and the overwhelming majority were assigned to elementary schools predominantly attended by Negroes. (pp. 136–137)

Prior to the historic *Brown v. Board of Education of Topeka 347 U.S. 483 (1954)* ruling, many African American principals were well respected icons of their segregated schools and community, especially throughout the Jim Crow–led Southern states (Lomotey, 1987; Siddle Walker, 2000). They fulfilled various capacities such as instructional leaders, counselors, and positive mentors and role models. They also served as the main conduit between the needs of the school and community and the local school board (Siddle Walker, 2000). Essentially, African American principals were the central figure of schools during segregation.

Yet, for a period of two decades (1954–1975) immediately following the *Brown* ruling, Fultz (2004) explained that African American principals were systematically displaced and faced near extinction once their segregated Black schools were closed during desegregation. African American principals' value to many Black children was suddenly deemed "no longer needed" by many Southern White superintendents and school boards. "Invariably, the black principal has been desegregation's primary prey" (Hooker, 2000, p. 3).

Historically, Black principals have long served as positive role models for Black students (Tillman, 2004a, 2004b, 2008). Lomotey (1987, 1989) reviewed the positive effects Black principals have on the academic achievement of Black students and argued for increased Black leaders as role models for minority students. Lomotey (1987) described the connection a Black principal has with a Black student because of shared cultural backgrounds. He stated, "When two blacks interact or communicate, their shared beliefs and values suggest that homophily occurs, bringing about greater information usage, attitude formation, attitude change, and behavior change" (p. 175). Lomotey asserted that Blacks have a unique cultural history in America and typically react differently to situations than do members of other cultures. Therefore, Black principals identify with the needs of Black children better than principals of other races because "he or she would also consider the situation, understanding it in a way that a nonblack might not be able, given the different cultural basis of looking at the world" (p. 174).

Meier, Stewart, and England (1989) found the presence of Black school administrators within a district had the greatest influence on the recruitment and increased representation of Black teachers. Black administrators also serve as positive role models for Black teachers. Therefore, school districts that augment the representation of Black administrators would also ostensibly facilitate the increased presence of Black teachers.

Conversely, the lack of racial and cultural connections to serve as role models was called by Irvine (1990) a lack of "cultural synchronization" (p. 21). She explained that this cultural disconnect by White teachers often creates disharmony in the academic, behavioral, and emotional successes of Black students. Earlier, Irvine (1989) emphasized that Black teachers not only fulfill a strong pedagogical void in the education of Black children, but also serve as cultural advocates for them as well. In other words, "Black teachers are more likely than their white counterparts to be prepared to assume their role of cultural translator" (1989, p. 57).

Other scholars, notably Delgado (1995), Dilworth (1992), Frankenberg (2009), McCray, Wright, and Beachum (2007), and Sanchez, Thornton, and Usinger (2008), have argued for the need for minority administrators and teachers to serve as cross-cultural role models to promote diversity, as well as to foster racial awareness, understanding, and exposure of minorities to White students. According to Dilworth (1992), minority administrators and teachers play as equally important a role as cross-cultural role models for White students as they do in their functions as same-race role models for Black students.

Even though Frankenberg (2009), McCray et al. (2007), and Sanchez et al. (2008) acknowledged the positive contributions and impact African American school leaders and educators have on Black children, they also discussed various concerns regarding the perpetual placement of minority educational leaders and teachers as same race/cultural role models. McCray et al. (2007) explained African American (and other minority) principals are seldom given the opportunity to lead predominately White schools. Instead, they tend to be "in charge of schools that reflect the principal's ethnic and racial heritage" (p. 253). However, White principals are placed in all types of schools that may or may not have varied student racial diversity. According to McCray et al. (2007), the continued placement of African American and other minority principals under same race/cultural practices promotes "an underlying supposition within the field of education that minority principals should only be placed and can only lead schools with a heavy concentration of minority students" (p. 253). In other words, the assumptions would suggest African American principals are incapable of leading schools that are predominantly White, while White principals are capable and effective leaders in all types of schools regardless of the demographic composition of students.

Similarly, Sanchez et al. (2008) argued that "old patterns of segregation could be reestablished" (p. 5) if the placement of African American principals under same-race practices of role model theory continues, propagating contemporary *de facto* "exclusion" of African American principals in predominantly White schools as was the case for Black principal placements during *de jure* segregation of pre- and immediate post-*Brown* eras. Such placements would preclude cross-cultural opportunities for students and staff learning and interacting with individuals from other races. As Sanchez et al. (2008) contends, "all students must realize that leadership positions can be fulfilled by people of all races" (p. 5).

Irvine (1989) argued that minority students are in need of mentors (not role models) who are willing to challenge the policies and processes of school systems that do not fit the overall needs of their students. Along these lines, Delgado (1995) defined role model theory as an unassailable, moderate liberal affirmative action measure used to promote majoritarian purposes. He wrote that the majority group has always maintained the power to establish the standards of quality and merit. Minorities are ultimately expected to live up to certain standards established by the majority in order to truly benefit from affirmative action. Delgado wrote:

> You're hired (if you speak politely, have a neat haircut, and above all, can be trusted) not because of your accomplishments, but because of what others think you will do for them. If they hire you now and you are a good role model, things will be better in the next generation. (p. 357)

Delgado redefined "fit" in terms of qualities needed to advance minority schools. He described the all-too-common practices in which White institutions hire minorities based on their created definition(s) of "fit" simply to push their own goals rather than because minority applicants may meet or well exceed the qualifications for the job. Looking toward a not-too-distant future, Delgado postulated that Whites need assimilated minority role models to help mold the younger minority generations, enabling them to exhibit acceptable behaviors and work ethics to ensure the future labor market will not jeopardize their social security support. Specifically, "They must be taught to ask few questions, pay their taxes, and accept social obligations, even if imposed by persons who look different from them and who committed documented injustices on their ancestors" (p. 359). Delgado concluded that minorities must fit all of the images and behaviors that align with the majority's expectations of "fit." However, failure to meet the expectations turns them into poor role models and subjects them to the risk of being replaced by another minority aspirant.

The realities of "Historically Black" provide complex answers to social and political questions that all candidates for urban school leadership need to reflect upon and know if they wish to earn the trust of communities and students. Whereas the meaning of fit under federal and state mandates emphasizes the qualities of school management, loyalty, and dependability, and whereas the changing urban demographics and city-wide trends call for school administrators comfortable in political and diverse community settings, here, within the designation of "Historically Black," the meaning of fit turns inward to cultural responsiveness and sociological understandings related to city living. "Fit" becomes enmeshed with issues of advocacy and social justice as school leaders promote opportunities and success based on the needs of students and communities (Gaines, 2013). "Fit" as a culturally relevant set of knowledge and skills emerges in terms of (1) knowledge of America's racial history and how a child's heritage is related to classroom behaviors and academic success; (2) knowledge of the school and its surrounding communities and willingness to become an integral participant in those communities; (3) knowledge, skills, and dispositions to promote culturally relevant pedagogies and practices; (4) general knowledge of and interest in city-wide cultural activities; (4) capacity to enhance successful mentoring to teachers and provide students with diverse role models; (5) abilities to hire and motivate teachers to work successfully in urban schools, and the leader's (6) independence and willingness to advocate, when necessary, for community needs over those supported by the school system and state.

What's more is that in"Historically Black"majority-minority schools, students have the opportunity to see teachers as leaders who look like them.

> Does that make a difference? I'm not an advocate for separation, just an advocate for people being respected. But you have to know where you come from in order to know who you are and where you are going. The social studies teacher can ask you a question or she/he can bring to life the opportunity for voting, the opportunity for participating in student government, for becoming valedictorian, salutatorian, opportunities to be homecoming king, queen, to be leaders. For teachers to chair committees, lead clubs and be leaders. There are the many opportunities that create desires that I see emanating from this school. And I say, you must vote or you can kiss all of this good bye because we're going to be going backward. Don't waste that opportunity that's been given to you because somebody struggled to get you there. (Gaines, 2013, n.p.)

Urban school leaders know which teachers are passionate and caring, but for a number of reasons, there remain faculty who do not "fit" the needs of the students.

> We need passionate teachers to care about students. One of the problems is that sometimes teachers and administrators stay in the game too long. At one time, they were dynamic. They were great. They were outstanding. But things happen. They need to step aside. . . . Certain things the students find out about too late in their senior year. They're like "nobody told me." For instance, you need two years of a foreign language for most colleges and universities, and they're not put in those classes and so they don't figure it out until their senior year and so they can't go to a state university even with a 3.2 GPA because they don't have a foreign language. I've heard tons of heartbreaking stories like that. "Why didn't anybody ever tell me?. . . . [A]ll of that really poisons the whole process. (Gaines, 2013, n.p.)

There are professional-cultural tensions most obvious in "Historically Black" schools, subject matter teaching and standardized testing:

> I think we need to really start or go back to getting to know our kids beyond math, beyond English, beyond science. How can we kind of weave our way into their world to understand them? But yet, still be able to teach content of math, English and science.
>
> . . . [I]f anything I could put my spin on, it would be to give kids an opportunity to explore what's out there, whether it's taking field trips or whatever. The main thing is exposure. So yes, I would take testing away from the equation because what we are doing today is unlike any testing machine that we have ever seen. It has stripped the desire and the ability of many teachers to be creative in their classrooms. . . . If I could change anything, that would be it. Because then that would open the world for the students to get an opportunity to enjoy their experiences in school a little bit more. I think reducing the testing machine would have a huge impact right away. (Gaines, 2013, n.p.)

"Fit" as Cultural Relevance and Race

The cause of cultural relevance was not substantiated in a large urban district study of minority principals conducted by Weaver in 2009. Her primary research question was:" To what extent, if any, do principals of predominantly African American schools promote culturally relevant pedagogy and utilize culturally responsive leadership?" As a professional educator/developer and practitioner of Afro-centric methods, Weaver sought to find evidence and examples of how urban school leaders were using research on culturally responsive leadership and pedagogies with their schools' faculties. To authenticate her research methodologically, Weaver produced 10 vignettes reflecting the tenets of both critical/cultural pedagogies (Gay, 2000; Irvine, 2002; Ladson-Billings, 1995) and cultural relevant/responsive leadership (Beachum, Dentith, McCray, & Boyle, 2008). Weaver chose the vignette format so that principals could give their opinions about theoretical concepts with which they may not be familiar. Again, each of the vignettes was based on concepts of culturally relevant pedagogy (Ladson-Billings, 1995), culturally responsive teaching (Gay, 2000), culturally responsive urban school leadership (Johnson, 2006), and ethno-humanist leadership (Lomotey, 1993). These theoretical concepts assert a leadership style that takes into account the cultural backgrounds of students and uses the knowledge of these cultures to guide both leadership practices and shape teaching.

Weaver's thesis was premised on the cultural mismatch of African American students and standardized school curriculum, dominated more and more by standardized tests and testing. As a result, minority students, if not all students, become disengaged with not only the curriculum but also with the classroom pedagogies transmitting the subject matter content. In 2005, Dantley argued that

> Contemporary Black school principals continue to be constrained to position academics in a broader community context that imagines a brighter future for African American students. These principals in urban settings would do well to encourage teachers to practice culturally relevant pedagogy. These principals understand that students' achievement is curiously tied to sense of connectedness and purpose. (p. 661)

These assertions prompted Weaver to see if minority-majority race principals were encouraging their faculties in culturally relevant pedagogies. What she found was that principals had limited knowledge of the concepts of culturally relevant pedagogy and culturally responsive leadership. Moreover, they did not actively encourage teachers to utilize culturally relevant pedagogy as a means to improve the academic achievement of African American students. While the principals in her study expressed their sensitivity to culturally relevant theories and viewed them as potentially useful tools especially in managing of difficult students or the diffusing of problematic situations, their views did not translate into actions. Seeing the value of aligning culture with curriculum was, for whatever reasons, inadequate to change urban classroom practices. All the principals in Weaver's study were Black or Hispanic, thus, racially, they had the same or similar demographic "fit" as the students in their schools. As appointed urban school principals, they had met their school district's personnel criteria of "fit." That definition, however, did not include cultural relevance.

Competing Organizational and Social Science Theories of "Fit"

There is substantial empirical evidence to support the concept of "best fit" for an employee who looks the same and shares the same cultural values as other organizational members (Adkins & Caldwell, 2004; Judge & Cable, 1997). In public education, "teachers report their work is more difficult when they and their students do not share characteristics such as social expectations, race, ethnicity, and language" (Johnson & Birkeland, 2003, p. 584).

At the human level, Attraction-Selection-Attrition (ASA) (Schneider, 1987) and Role Model Theory (RMT) (Nesmith, 2013) are two particular social psychology theories relevant to judgments of "fit." The framework underlying Schneider's (1987) ASA model undergirds the hiring processes in how organizations attract, select, and retain their people. RMT is often promulgated and used as a hiring and placement practice to remedy structural inequities vis-à-vis race, gender, educational, and employment opportunities (e.g., affirmative action). Many passionately advocate and call for minority educators and leaders to serve as positive role models and mentors for students who share similar racial and cultural connections; many also urge the hiring of cross-cultural role models to meet the needs of all students regardless of race.

As researchers, our findings have to be based on reliable data and the validity of the evidence. With 49,000 Title I schools educating between 25 million students in those schools and 33.5 million in Title I programs (http://nces.ed.gov/surveys/urbaned/enrollment.asp), how should we assess the evidence we have from peer-reviewed studies? "What we know about how to transform chronically low-performing schools is driven primarily by case study analysis" (Barbour et al., 2010, p. 3). Although the literature on turnaround schools does not emphasize urban locations or urban problems, it is safe to assume a correlation between race, SES, and low performance on standardized tests. Still, the two most prominent empirical researchers on turnaround school leadership base their extensive findings on 16 and 31 case studies, respectively (Duke, 2008; Leithwood & Strauss, 2008). Both have acknowledged the methodological limitations and unit of analysis delimitations of their findings.

With respect to the topics of urban education, urban school leadership, turnaround school leadership, urban school district personnel functions, the range of questions associated with the politics and sociocultural dynamics of "fit" is broad. Sampling becomes a matter of judgment in terms of sample size and purposefulness.[5] From multiple research perspectives, it is safe to assume that what is said to be important to recruitment, selection, hiring, and placement may not be what is actually practiced or reported as being practiced.

As far as research evidence is concerned, urban education cannot rely primarily upon case study narratives of specific urban schools that are beating the odds. There have been and will always be outliers of success (Acker-Hocevar, Cruz-Jansen, & Williams, 2012; Jacobson & Bezzina, 2008; Leithwood, 2008). What we envision for urban education requires more than piecemeal one-school-at-a-time reforms or heroic turnaround school leaders; what is needed are systemic reforms based on socioeconomic and political commitments to make urban education a 21st-century reality. To do so will require increased funding for purposes of research only.

Operationalizing Fit in Urban Paradise School District

Based on the above discussions, it should not be surprising to learn that predictive models of "fit" such as one proposed by Smith (2013) was not confirmed by the data. Smith (2013) empirically operationalized "fit" in terms of three cluster variables: demographic fit, organizational fit, and group fit. Demographic fit refers to the person's gender and race/ethnicity in relationship to the context (Elfenbein & O'Reilly, 2007). Williams and O'Reilly (1998) reviewed more than 80 studies and found the most influential and salient demographic fit factors to be gender and the race/ethnicity of the candidates. The second variable, organizational fit, matches an individual's personality and expertise to the goals of the organization (Elfenbein & O'Reilly, 2007). It can also be stated as the relationship between the employee and the employer with respect to personality and past experiences. Each individual has a personality that may or may not match the duties and responsibilities of the different roles of any position. If a person wants to fit, he or she should behave in a manner befitting the perceived role by stakeholders. Lastly, group fit focuses on the relationships between the candidate and other stakeholders who wield influence within the organization (Elfenbein & O'Reilly, 2007). These relationships are person-to-person, or in small groups within the organization.

Smith (2013) examined how demographic, organizational, and group fit influenced the selection of assistant principal candidates in secondary school settings. He conducted his study in the Urban Paradise School District, one of the largest school districts in the United States. Its population totals 1.8 million over 1,205 square miles. Racially and ethnically, Urban Paradise is 48% White (non-Hispanic), 24% Black, 23% Hispanic, and 3% Asian. As with many urban districts in the Southeast, the demographics continue to change as new foreign-born immigrants—over 8%—coming from Jamaica, Haiti, Cuba, Columbia, Canada, and Brazil, mix with and replace previous generations of Italians, "Americans-Whites," Germans, and Irish. In 2009, the poverty rate in Urban Paradise was 12.9% overall, but at 20.4% for the Black population specifically.

Of the 197 applicants in Smith's study, only 39 were selected for administrative positions, leaving 158 not selected. Thus, Smith's first "fit" finding was that only 20% of candidates were selected over a five-year period to become administrators. As far as school districts are concerned, the approximately 20% who "fit" are said to be qualified, leaving the 80%—a significant number of whom are African Americans[6]—not selected with the labels "not a fit" or worse, unqualified. When spread out over a period of five years, the number of candidates selected for administrative positions at the secondary school level in Urban Paradise averaged around 8 per year. With respect to race and ethnicity, 24% of those selected were Hispanic, 16% were White, and 21% were Black candidates. Each of these percentages of selection by race and ethnicity was below the percentages of these populations throughout the district. While there was no statistically significant difference in selection across the three races, the results are skewed because there were twice as many Black candidates to choose from on the list. In other words, Black candidates were competing against other Black candidates in higher numbers for their 20% share of secondary school assistant principal positions.

The only "fit" measure that was statistically significant in predicting selection was the group fit variable. Smith (2013) operationalized the variable by the number of references a candidate received. That is, those who used only one recommendation at the principal and above levels were statistically less likely to be selected as school administrators. His findings, however, revealed a deeper meaning for group fit that he labeled networking and sponsorships. In other words, linked to the number of references was also where the candidate's sponsor was in the hierarchy of the school district and the candidate's own ability to circulate and network within the district.

Because "fit" is a high-stakes outcome, that is, a candidate is either selected or not, Smith (2013) offered conclusions in terms of both winners and losers from these district-level personnel processes. He stated that Black and Hispanic assistant principal candidates were winners because the district's list indicated candidates from these two demographic groups were selected at higher percentages and were more favored by hiring administrators than were White candidates. This judgment, however, needs to be put into a broader context, as the percentage of African Americans in the candidate pool was 50% while only 20% of all candidates regardless of race were selected. In other words, there were twice as many African American candidates who were "not selected." At best, this is a bittersweet outcome.

According to Smith, another group of winners were the individual schools where the assistant principal candidates worked. That is, all 197 assistant principal candidates did voluntary and not-so-voluntary work in order to fulfill the requirements of the assistant principal leadership-training program and to make themselves attractive as candidates. Many of these administrative projects were directed at improving student achievement and were completed at the school or district level *at no additional cost to the school district* that received the administrative support.

Each assistant principal candidate was highly encouraged to seek out any and all opportunities for gaining expertise in operations and curricula. They gained expertise through participating in programs or by doing "volunteer" hours. Many current secondary school administrators and assistant principals rely on aspiring assistant principals to "fill in" or share the responsibilities on many time-consuming administrative tasks. One selected assistant principal said it the best:

> [You] excuse yourself from pushing yourself almost to the edge of exhaustion. [Candidates need] to not only teach in the classroom, but also to get all the assistant principal experience you can. If you are not willing to push yourself like that, you have no business getting in this job.

Subsequently, many assistant principal candidates expressed frustration when they realized that they would never be selected; but that realization came only after years and years of actively, but unsuccessfully, pursuing a dream.

In sum, the whole of Urban Paradise School District wins when more educators are trained to take on leadership roles. Successful schools require leadership not only from the principal and the assistant principals, but also from the other employees, volunteers, parents, students, and associated stakeholders. Successful school districts distribute leadership throughout the organization. While the structures, responsibilities, and titles may be different, the concept of distributive leadership remains the same in successful organizations. Some of these leaders are given official titles or assigned specific duties, while many are not. Successful organizations need stakeholders, at all levels, to proactively take on leadership roles and "step up" when a "void" appears or opportunities become evident.

Those who have lost out in these personnel processes are most obviously those candidates who were not selected. We can assume that a percentage may exhibit decreased morale for being labeled as unqualified and unfit to become assistant principals. Some may regret having spent thousands of tuition dollars and investing hundreds of training hours at both the university and in the district. One aspiring assistant principal stated, "I was always led to believe that these jobs are already spoken for anyways." A selected assistant principal confirmed this belief when he shared, "They already know everything about you beforehand. It can be kind of skewed or manipulated a little bit, but when the interview comes it's pretty much set." At the same time, Smith (2013) found that in some instances the candidate's performance helped or hurt in subsequent interviews.

The results of the interviews confirmed subjective beliefs. A few interview participants indicated that they believed that the most qualified candidates were "passed over" or not selected because the school district preferred candidates with other demographic traits. One aspiring assistant principal shared his thoughts on this topic:

> It doesn't seem to me that it's always the most qualified person. They need someone to put in a category of whatever category your school is lacking to reflect the demographics or to have a more balanced kind of staff. When you look at who is being hired. If you look at the new AP's, they seem to be a big percentage of minorities and females.

We believe that the district's lack of transparency contributes to these persistent feelings that are shared by those selected and those not selected.

Another category of individuals who do not gain from the current personnel processes is the many mentors for these aspiring assistant principals. The Urban Paradise School District continues to train hundreds of candidates above and beyond the needs of a school district. Administrators spend a significant amount of time and effort to mentor, with less than a fifth who will ultimately become assistant principals. Thus, much time, effort, and resources are expended upon individuals who were never selected.

Placements in Urban Paradise School District

Smith (2013) found that many in Urban Paradise defined "fit" in terms of the practice of leadership team "balance."[7]

> You have to balance that out because there will be safety issues, there will be issues in the PE locker room and things like that. You've either got a male or a female, but you can't have all males or all females.

Another candidate commented:

> I think you want to have a balance in your administrative staff of men and women generally speaking. You can't have a guy search a girl for something, so you have to have that balance.

Based on 2008–2009 pilot research conducted in Urban Paradise, Nesmith (2012) found that as the minority student enrollment increased, so did the number of African American principals assigned to the school statewide (see next section), Nesmith found a positive Pearson Correlation value (r = .462) indicating that a moderately strong relationship existed between the

Table 17.1 2008–2009 Comparative Analysis of Assigned Principals Based on "African American Group Isolation" (Does not include charter schools data)

	Minority Students: 50%–59%	*Minority Students: 60%–69%*	*Minority Students: 70%–79%*	*Minority Students: 80%–89%*	*Minority Students: 90%–99%*
TOTALS	16	14	16	13	21
White	12	8	4	3	2
African American	3	3	11	10	19
Hispanic	1	3	1	0	0

percentage enrollment of African American students and the placements of African American principals (Table 17.1).

Nineteen out of the total of 21 principals assigned to schools with a minority student population of over 90% were African American.

Nesmith (2013) found that when African Americans are selected, they are placed in schools with predominantly minority student populations, most specifically, in schools with African American students. Moreover, as the percentage of minority students increased, so, too, did the African American principal placements. These results point to more limited vocational opportunities and career pathways for African American administrators, with many African Americans either (1) subject to intense oversight by state and district authorities, or (2) if not selected, labeled "not a fit" or unqualified.

Nesmith (2012), previously conducted interviews in Urban Paradise. One White principal stated:

> We know that we are not placed in predominantly Black schools. I'm certain a lot of it has to do with race. Seriously, how many of us are going to speak up about imbalance and unfairness? To do so means we will probably get assigned at very tough schools. It is not that we are better; it is just the way they choose to assign us.

An African American principal stated:

> First, I am happy to have a job. However, no one wants to openly acknowledge that we are always placed in the most challenging schools. It seems as though because we are black, only we can lead black schools, whereas they are only able to lead white schools because of their color. We have to deal with all of the pressures and expectations to quickly "fix" these schools.

Another African American principal stated:

> The feeling is that we [African Americans] are only good for to go into highly minority-populated schools. It is almost as if we are not "good enough" of doing an effective job in predominantly white schools as white principals. We work our behinds off under very tough conditions, but often get very little credit for the outstanding job we do. The irony is that we are told that "we know our kids best"; therefore, we can lead more effectively in minority schools. What is that? It [a high poverty, high need school] is a totally different world [from the world in which middle class African Americans are living] in these schools.

Table 17.2 Placement Breakdown of Principals Placed by Race for Schools With 10% and Less and 90% and Greater African American Student Enrollment

	10% and Less			*90% and Greater*		
	# of Principals	% of Principals	Proportion Within Race	# of Principals	% of Principals	Proportion Within Race
Non-AA	918	95.20	41.17	31	31.96	1.39
AA	46	4.80	9.68	66	68.04	13.89
Total	964	100		97	100	

Note: AA = African American

Nesmith (2013) then followed up his study of African American principal placements in Urban Paradise district by expanding his unit of analysis to the entire State of Paradise.

In the State of Paradise

The district of Urban Paradise is located inside the State of Paradise. The population of the state's 2,705 K–12 schools, excluding charters, in 2010–2011, included 475 African American principals or 17.5% of all principals (Table 17.2). Across the state, 16% of schools have over 50% African American students. Half of the state's African American principals were assigned to those schools. Only 5% of African American principals were in schools that had minority enrollments of less than 10%. And in schools with African American student enrollments of over 90%, African American principals led 68%.

Summary, Conclusions, and Implications

All of the candidates for school administration positions come to the interview table with very similar educational and professional backgrounds. Thus, every candidate in the administrative candidates' "pool" is qualified or else they would not be at the table. And yet, at the end of the interview process, when a candidate is not chosen, it is often said, mostly in informal conversations repeated again and again by top-level administrators and then again by researchers, that the nonselected candidates were "unqualified." The only official explanation (i.e., nonexplanation) for the district's personnel decision was that the candidate was not a fit.

Empirically, the findings indicated that of the three "fit" cluster variables, race predicted school placements (Nesmith, 2013), but not the initial selections from the lists of eligible candidates (Smith, 2013). With respect to group fit, it certainly mattered who supports/sponsors the candidate for selection. An indirect finding from Smith was the self-reported statements regarding the practice of building leadership teams that reflect diversity and balance by race and gender. However, Smith documented the social, political, and economic costs incurred to achieve a balance. That is, the current system of recruitment and selection is fraught with structural and social inefficiencies such that approximately 80% of all candidates, regardless of race or gender, who complete school leadership preparation programs are not selected for school administrative positions. Moreover, the candidate pools often have an overrepresentation of minority candidates from which to make their selections creating more conflict and tension. Among the many rumors perpetuated by "fit" is that district leaders already know who will be selected and placed at schools before committee interviews are held. Smith's data, however, indicated that all candidates, regardless of any "predetermined" outcome, could make a strong impression at the interview table that may have a positive effect on their future selection. However, all this seems like a high price to pay. Urban school districts and surrounding universities have historically argued the inequities of funding and can ill afford abuses and mismanagement of human capital. So while the make-up of candidate and committees meets the structural standards of fairness in a diverse society, what happens behind the scenes is costly and can be hurtful, if not also unethical. These personnel processes undermine the ability of the urban public school system to portray itself as a transparent "public good."

The major finding surrounding the placement of African American principals in African American schools limits their career opportunities to lead predominantly White or diverse schools. This limitation influences more than placement, however. That is, their urban school leadership is often constrained by federal- and state-level policies governing low-performing schools. Even in this era of accountability, school principals have discretionary authority and input to enhance student achievement as they are expected to serve as instructional leaders. For principals in low-performing or even failing schools, their administrative work is dictated to by district and state oversight with respect to the pace and rigor of curriculum that their teachers must follow. Should the short-term objectives of test scores improve, then the federal and state governments reverse their operations and move on to other failing schools, making the unsupported assumption that the school has been turned around. If principals are not able to raise their schools' test scores within a two- to three-year timeframe, they will be reassigned or demoted. These urban realities fall squarely on those selected and placed in the most isolated, lowest-performing schools. More often than not, those targeted individuals, depending on the city's demographics, are African Americans. In other words, as difficult as being a school principal is, the job today within the inner city is different and made more difficult because of today's educational accountability policies under both No Child Left Behind and Race to the Top.

Willingly or not, African American principals are more often tightly linked to federal, state, and local district policies, and thus affected by hiring decisions within this context. Whereas "fit" criteria vary across the different sociopolitical influences shaping urban education, within the sphere of top-down policies, leadership is defined as making short-term changes in order to turn a school around as defined by year-to-year increases in test scores. The dominant meaning of "fit" in this scenario revolves around compliance, system maintenance, loyalty, and dependability.

Yet, surrounding urban schools are other sociopolitical influences that come from changing demographics in students and the dynamics of local city politics. Trends indicate a decrease in the size of the population of African Americans in cities. While middle-class African Americans leave, those left behind are poorer and more isolated. The dynamics of immigration, diversity, and urban development, socially and economically, are transforming cities that, over time, will affect urban schools. The question we raised earlier was whether today's urban educators who were selected on the criteria of "fit" under federal and state policies would be able to negotiate the political dynamics of local politicians such as city mayors and new urban homesteaders. Urban reforms call for a school leader whose qualities of "fit" have to reflect the economic and political dynamics of our nation's cities in order to build political and community alliances.

Within "Historically Black" cultural contexts, role models, mentors, and cultural responsiveness present different dynamics in redefining "fit." As cities diversify, the school system's definition of "fit" promotes staying within one's racial community even as those very communities change in terms of social, economic, and political lifestyles. We cited literature extolling cultural relevance in leaders as well as studies questioning the relationship of race and cultural relevance (Weaver, 2009). Race alone does not reflect the varied talents of African American administrators nor where their placement would be most beneficial. The placement of an

African American in a predominantly African American school could reflect the same kinds of mismatches intellectually, professionally, and emotionally as would the hiring of any racial group member. That said, all students need mentors and role models, but what these terms mean has to now reflect the world in the 21st century.

Final Thoughts

Fit may begin with a person's heritage, but it should be extended to that person's core values, commitment, leadership style, and professional experiences with respect to curriculum and managerial operations. Unless we collectively rethink our criteria for fit, it is unlikely that change will take place systemically. But what would it take for today's urban superintendents to consider hiring individuals who will challenge standardization, annual standardized testing, and zero tolerance policies regarding "leaving the building" (to discover a world beyond street corners)? What will it take for superintendents and school boards to support personnel decisions based on culturally relevant pedagogies, connecting of curriculum to students' experiences and histories? How might the deliberateness and vagueness of fit be used to open new doors to change in terms of policies and personnel practices?

There was no empirical evidence found here to suggest that the various definitions of "fit" are interconnected. In fact, we labeled fit as those selected or not selected, as winners and losers. But unless urban school leaders learn how to bridge policy divides and ideological differences, it is unlikely that there will be any successful urban school reforms. If this rings true to readers, then the field of urban school leadership needs to become much more political, not less so.

As educational practitioners, urban leaders, and researchers, we can see that there is enough blame and finger pointing already. But if one group needs to be singled out for criticism, it is the profession of educational research. Researchers continue school-by-school, leader-by-leader approaches to studying urban schools without transforming practices to connect more closely to the needs of students and communities. The research literature cited to support hiring decisions based on the pillars of "fit" identified by Smith (2013) did not reflect an objective or predictive model for understanding within-school-district personnel practices.

As educational researchers, we embrace the complexities and contradictions in studying urban school leadership. The lack of support for a predictive model of "fit," however, does not lead us to call for better psychometrically designed instruments. Rather, the processes of fit are inherently political. Our call is for the competing interests to be publicly and transparently debated in order to bring content validity to the selection of urban school leaders, not construct validation methods. If we fail as educational leadership researchers, then the status quo of dominant discourses in federal and state policies, urban trends and demography, and the marginalizing of "Historically Black" will continue to play predominate roles in deciding the future for urban schools.

It is as if the unit of analysis of "fit" research designs is misplaced. We need to make sure that urban districts are ready to support school leaders for success that would involve shifting the responsibility of successful "fit" from the individual principal to the urban district's administration (Reyes-Guerra, 2012). As researchers, our advocacy is to make urban education perceived as a public good, and to lobby for sufficient resources for leadership preparation and development. What's wrong with "fit" currently is that in federal and state policies and in local city politics, it is not focused on the needs of students, but rather fit criteria meet the needs of superintendents and their administrations. It is about who is acceptable and who will carry out executive orders/mandates faithfully. It does not look for the *je ne sais quoi,* but instead for the known, predictable, and dependable.

Fit as a terse nonexplanation for the most important hiring decisions creates the wrong kinds of mental spaces. In fact, it hides and protects those who are already in place. The current use of "fit" also prevents an open and honest national dialogue on race and racism.

A dialogue on "fit" raises questions regarding the candidate's knowledge of histories of all racial and ethnic groups. Our role as educational leaders and educational leadership researchers is as role models and mentors to the next generation; and in urban contexts, in all unique contexts, we must learn to say what we mean rather than begin and end with the three-letter word "fit." As researchers, that means not reporting the nonexplanations of "fit" as if it defines who is qualified to lead an urban school without interrogating the competing influences from federal and state policies, urban communities, and the needs of urban students. Yes, urban school leaders ought to be dependable and loyal, but they must also be advocates for social justice, and knowledgeable on culturally responsive pedagogies to meet the needs of children. While fit may be political, it is also knowable, doable, and explainable.

Notes

1. The authors would like to thank Autumn Tooms Cypres for questioning "fit" politically, socially, and educationally, and for sharing her views on an earlier draft of this chapter.
2. Recruitment, selection, and placement are three early stages in the personnel functions of developing, evaluating, giving honest feedback, and retaining of quality educators.
3. Of the 3,380,300 public school teachers who were teaching during the 2007–2008 school year, 84.5% remained at the same school ("stayers"), 7.6% moved to a different school ("movers"), and 8.0% left the profession ("leavers") during the following year (Keigher & Cross, 2010).
4. While pre-K–12 schools do not have the official designation of "Historically Black," there remain many schools across the country that prior to desegregation were for Blacks only. While we have chosen to use Black and African American racial identities interchangeably, when referring to three of the schools in this study we will say "Historically Black."
5. Sampling limitations are almost endemic to educational research. For example, in one of our empirical studies, Smith (2013) identified that only 20% of his sample was selected to be school administrators, leaving 80% not selected. The 80% figure is based on a specific five-year period beginning in 2004 and ending in 2009. When the U.S. recession was felt by residents of Paradise School District (pseudonym), the demographics of both the district and the state were affected. Population growth ended and the pool of school administrator candidates closed in many school districts around the state. Vacancies were filled by reassigning administrators from school to school and reducing the size of the central office staff. Today, as we move further away from the recession and begin the retirement phase of Baby Boomers (who may or may not retire on the system's predicted schedule), it is unclear how this will affect the size of the eligible list, percentage of candidates selected and not selected.
6. There was an overrepresentation of African Americans in the eligible pool. That is, 50% of the pool was African American, even though they represented 26% of the district's population.
7. This finding was not tested empirically or confirmed by Smith or Nesmith or Gaines.

References

Acker-Hocevar, M., Cruz-Jansen, M., & Williams, C. (2012). *Leadership from the ground up: Effective schooling in traditionally low performing schools.* Charlotte, NC: Information Age.

Adkins, B., & Caldwell, D. (2004). Firm or subgroup culture: Where does fitting in matter most? *Journal of Organizational Behavior, 25*(8), 969–978. doi:10.1002/job.291

Barbour, C., Clifford, M., Corrigan-Halpern, P., Garcia, P., Maday-Karageorge, T., Meyer, C., Townsend, C., & Stewart, J. (2010, December). *A learning point: What experience from the field tells us about school leadership and turnaround.* Washington, D.C.. American Institutes for Research.

Beachum, F., Dentith, A., McCray, C., & Boyle, T. (2008). Havens of hope or the killing fields: The paradox of leadership, pedagogy, and relationships in an urban middle school. *Urban Education, 43*(2), 189–215.

Brown v. Board of Education of Topeka, Kansas, 347 U.S. 483(1954).

Common Core State Standards Initiative. (2012). http://www.corestandards.org/

Dantley, M. (2005). African American spirituality and Cornel West's notions of prophetic pragmatism: Restructuring educational leadership in American urban public schools. *Educational Administration Quarterly, 41*(4), 651–674.

Delgado, R. (1995). Affirmative action as a majoritarian device: Or, do you really want to be a role model? In R. Delgado (Ed.), *Critical race theory: The cutting edge* (pp. 355–361). Philadelphia, PA: Temple University Press.

Dilworth, M. (1992). *Diversity in teacher education*. San Francisco, CA: Jossey-Bass.

Duke, D. (2008). *Keys to sustaining successful school turnarounds*. Charlottesville, VA: Public Impact.

Duke, D., & Iwanicki, E. (1992). Principal assessment and the notion of "fit." *Peabody Journal of Education, 68*(1), 25–36.

Elfenbein, H.A., & O'Reilly, C.A. (2007). Fitting in: The effects of relational demography and person-culture fit on group process and performance. *Group Organization Management, 32*(1), 109–142. doi:10.1177/1059601106286882

Frankenberg, E. (2009). The demographic contexts of urban schools and districts. *Equity & Excellence in Education, 42*(3), 255–271.

Fullan, M. (1993). *Change forces: Probing the depth of educational reform*. New York, NY: Macmillan.

Fultz, M. (2004). The displacement of Black educators post-*Brown*: An overview and analysis. *History of Education Quarterly, 44*(1), 11–45.

Gaines, F. (2013). *Creating urban high schools of opportunity for students*. In progress, dissertation research, Florida Atlantic University, Boca Raton, FL.

Gay, G. (2000). *Culturally responsive teaching: Theory, research, and practice*. New York, NY: Teachers College Press.

Goffman, E. (1963). *Stigma: Notes on the management of spoiled identity*. New York, NY: Simon and Schuster.

Hooker, K. (2000). Superintendents' perceptions on the recruitment and selection of building level administrators. *Planning and Changing, 31*(3&4), 182–205.

Hord, S.M., Rutherford, W.L., Huling-Austin, L., & Hall, G.E. (1987). *Taking charge of change*. Alexandria, VA: Association for Supervision and Curriculum Development.

Ingersoll, R. (2001). Teacher turnover and teacher shortages. *American Educational Research Journal, 38*(3), 499–534.

Irvine, J. (1989). Beyond role models: An examination of cultural influences on the pedagogical perspectives of black teachers. *Peabody Journal of Education, 66*(4), 51–63.

Irvine, J. (1990). *Black students and school failure: Policies, practices, and prescriptions*. New York, NY: Praeger.

Irvine, J.J. (2002). *In search of wholeness: African American teachers and their culturally specific classroom practices*. New York, NY: Palgrave.

Jacobson, S., & Bezzina, C. (2008). The effects of leadership on student academic/affective achievement. In G. Crow, J. Lumby, & P. Pashiardis (Eds.), *International handbook on the preparation and development of school leaders*. Abingdon, UK: Routledge/Taylor & Francis.

Johnson, L. (2006). Making her community a better place to live: Culturally responsive urban school leadership in historical context. *Leadership and Policy in Schools, 5*, 19–36.

Johnson, S., & Birkeland, S. (2003). Pursuing a sense of success: New teachers explain their career decisions. *American Educational Research Journal, 40*(3), 581–617.

Judge, T.A., & Cable, D.M. (1997). Applicant personality, organizational culture, and organizational attraction. *Personnel Psychology, 50*(2), 359–394. doi:10.1111/j.1744–6570.1997.tb00912.x

Keigher, A., & Cross, F. (2010, August). *Teacher attrition and mobility: Results from the 2008–09 Teacher Follow-up Survey, First Look*. Washington, D.C.: Institute of Education Sciences, NCES, U.S. Department of Education.

Ladson-Billings, G. (1995). But that's just good teaching! The case for culturally relevant pedagogy. *Theory Into Practice, 34*(3), 159–165.

Leithwood, K. (2008). *A review of research on the characteristics of high-performing school districts.* Toronto, Canada: Final report prepared for the College of Alberta School Superintendents.

Leithwood, K., & Strauss, T. (2008). *Turnaround schools and the leadership they require.* Toronto, Canada: Canadian Education Association.

Lomotey, K. (1987). Black principals for black students. Some preliminary observations. *Urban Education, 22*(2), 173–181.

Lomotey, K. (1989). *African American principals: School leadership and success.* Westport, CT: Greenwood Press.

Lomotey, K. (1993). African-American principals: Bureaucrat/administrators and ethno-humanists. *Urban Education, 27*(4), 394–412.

McCray, C., Wright, J., & Beachum, F. (2007). Beyond *Brown:* Examining the perplexing plight of African American principals. *Journal of Instructional Psychology, 34*(4), 247–255.

Meier, K.J., Stewart, J., & England, R. (1989). *Race, class and education.* Madison, WI: University of Wisconsin Press.

Milner, R. (2012). But what is urban education? *Urban Education, 47*(3), 556–561.

Murphy, J. (2008). The place of leadership in turnaround schools: Insights from organizational recovery in the public and private sectors. *Journal of Educational Administration, 46*(1), 74–98.

Nesmith, L. (2012). *Using CRT to analyze inequalities in the placement of African American principals* (Unpublished manuscript).

Nesmith, L. (2013). *The vestiges of* Brown: *Analyzing the placements of African American principals in Florida Public Schools (2010–11).* Unpublished dissertation, Florida Atlantic University, Boca Raton, FL.

Orfield, G., & Lee, C. (2004). Brown *at 50: King's dream or Plessy's nightmare?* The Civil Rights Project, Harvard University. Retrieved from http://www.eric.ed.gov:80/PDFS/ED489168.pdf

Reyes-Guerra, D. (2012) Innovative school leadership preparation programs: How partnerships between districts and universities can address the learning needs of school leaders. Paper presented at the XVI International Educational Seminar APRENDO 2012, Santo Domingo, Dominican Republic.

Sanchez, J., Thornton, B., & Usinger, J. (2008, December). Promoting diversity in public education leadership. *NCPEA Publications, 3*(3), 1–10.

Schneider, B. (1987). The people make the place. *Personnel Psychology, 40,* 437–454.

Siddle Walker, V. (2000). Valued segregated schools for African American children in the South, 1935–1969: A review of common themes and characteristics. *Review of Educational Research, 70*(3), 253–285.

Smith, S. (2013). *The concept of fit: Intersections in educational leadership* (Unpublished doctoral dissertation). Florida Atlantic University, Boca Raton, FL.

Stiglitz, J. (2013, January 20). Inequality is holding back the recovery. *The New York Times,* Sunday Review, pp. 1, 8–9.

Thompson, C. (1951). Negro teachers and the elimination of segregated schools. *Journal of Negro Education, 20*(2), 135–139.

Tillman, L. (2004a). African American principals and the legacy of *Brown. Review of Research in Education, 28,* 101–146.

Tillman, L. (2004b). (Un)intended consequences? *Education and Urban Society, 36*(3), 280–303.

Tillman, L. (2008). The scholarship of Dr. Asa G. Hilliard, III: Implications for black principal leadership. *Review of Educational Research, 78*(3), 589–607.

TNTP. (2012). *The irreplaceables: Understanding the real retention crisis in America's urban schools.* Retrieved from http://tntp.org/assets/documents/TNTP_Irreplaceables_2012.pdf

Tooms, T., Lugg, C., & Bogotch, I. (2010). Rethinking the politics of fit. *Educational Administration Quarterly, 46*(1), 96–130.

Urban Education in America. (n.d.). National Center for Educational Statistics. http://nces.ed.gov/surveys/urbaned/

Weaver, T. (2009). *Principals' attitudes toward the use of culturally relevant pedagogy and culturally responsive leadership in predominantly African American schools* (Unpublished doctoral dissertation). Florida Atlantic University, Boca Raton, FL.

Williams, K.Y., & O'Reilly, C.A. (1998). Demography and diversity in organizations: A review of 40 years of research. In B. Staw & R. Sutton (Eds.), *Research in organizational behavior, 20* (pp. 77–140). Greenwich, CT: JAI Press.

18

Black Students, Urban Schools, and Black Principals

Leadership Practices That Reduce Disenfranchisement

Kofi Lomotey & Kendra Lowery

Introduction

Black students[1] underperform in U.S. urban schools.[2] The data are quite extensive documenting this truism (Barton & Coley, 2010; Delpit, 2012). The underachievement of Black students is a direct result of their persistent, pervasive, and disproportionate disenfranchisement[3] in urban schools. We define disenfranchisement in the U.S. educational context as the historical and systematic deprivation of access to quality education for Black students in urban schools. This disenfranchisement has come about as a result of societal and institutional concerted efforts over decades that have employed all of the structural scaffolding (e.g., housing, property taxes, deferred maintenance) on which to hang each discriminatory educational policy iteration.

The fundamental issue for Black students in urban schools is their underachievement, which is a result of their widescale disenfranchisement. Moreover, this disenfranchisement of Black students in urban schools can be addressed through the provision of a culturally responsive[4] educational experience facilitated in part by Black principals. Additionally, in this chapter we highlight the ways in which these culturally responsive practices are an important aspect of the ethno-humanist role identity of Black principals (Lomotey, 1993), which is discussed below. Research supports the notion of principals facilitating a culturally responsive educational experience (Gardiner & Enomoto, 2006; Lee, 2007). We analyze data from studies of Black principals in urban schools in part to attempt to determine how these leaders can assist in facilitating a culturally responsive educational experience for Black students. This approach is consistent with the work of Lenoar Foster (2005), who indicated that understanding the types of leadership characteristics displayed by Black principals will help researchers and leaders predict what environments will lead to greater Black student performance.

We begin by discussing the importance of Black principals for Black students. From there, we examine disenfranchisement and its sources. Next, we introduce the literature that we reviewed before offering an analysis of the research and discussing the implications of our review.

Black Principals for Black Students

For many years, researchers have posited that Black students experience increased franchisement and academic success in the presence of Black teachers. Similarly—and more recently—research has indicated that there is a benefit accrued to Black students when a Black principal is present (Kelley, 2012; Williams, 2012). In part because of a shared culture and common experiences, Black principals serve effectively as role models for Black students (Reitzug & Patterson, 1998; Tillman, 2004). In Lomotey's earlier work (1987, 1989a, 1993), he discussed the concept of homophily: the proclivity of people to fraternize and connect with like others. That is, "love of the same" or "Birds of a feather flock together." This phenomenon, we argue, is at play in the relationships established between Black educators (teachers and principals) and Black students in urban schools.

Lomotey's discussion of homophily in relation to the educational experiences of Black students is recalled in more recent studies wherein researchers have coined the terms *cultural relevance* or *cultural responsiveness* in discussing the educational experiences of Black students and other students in urban schools (Gay, 2010; Ladson-Billings, 2009). Such work speaks to the importance of the connection between the instructional programs in urban schools and the culture of Black students. Much of this recent work focuses on a culturally responsive educational environment for Black students facilitated by classroom teachers. Most recently, some researchers have looked at the role of the principal in establishing a culturally responsive environment for Black students in urban schools (L. Johnson, 2006; Lee, 2007).

Effects of Disenfranchisement

Black students have consistently underperformed as a result of the historic structural inequity and their disenfranchisement in U.S. urban schools. Every effort must be made to counteract the effects of this disenfranchisement so that these students can perform better academically. The condition of Black student disenfranchisement and its effects are at a crisis level. Black families and communities and the United States as a whole suffer because of this underutilization of a significant part of the national community. Too often Black students do not complete high school, cannot go on to college, and remain underemployed or unemployed because of their disenfranchisement and resultant underachievement in precollegiate institutions (Kuykendall, 1991; Lopez, 2011).

The terms *Black underachievement* and *culturally deprived* first came into prominence in the 1950s to describe the results of the disenfranchisement of Black students. Because of this historic disenfranchisement, it would be extremely difficult to identify a period of time in the history of the United States, or indeed to identify few, if any, regions, states, cities, or even school districts in the United States wherein large numbers of Black students have done well academically. This situation persists more than a decade into the 21st century. Data on the underperformance of Black students stand alone to highlight the significance of the under-education of these students.

Data from what is known as "the Schott Report" (2012) chronicled the failure of U.S. schools to adequately educate Black boys. In 2009–2010, the graduation rates for Black boys in New York, Washington, DC, and Ohio were 37%, 38%, and 45%, respectively; graduation rates for Black boys are less than 60% in 29 of the 49 states with sufficient data to analyze. Due in part to widescale disenfranchisement, no national, statewide, or local reform effort in the history of the United States—since it became legal to educate Blacks—has significantly benefitted the masses of Black students. Such efforts at reform have included increased funding, year-round schooling, desegregation, high expectations, increased parental involvement, private and/or charter schools, class size reductions, and much more. Nothing has successfully addressed the crisis—disenfranchisement—in Black education. This underperformance is a direct result of the historic disenfranchisement of large numbers of Black students in U.S. urban schools.

Sources of Disenfranchisement

On a societal level, race and racism still pervade U.S. society—and U.S. urban schools. Racism in U.S. society plays a key role in the disenfranchisement of Black students (Petitt, 2012). Our society is one in which people are discriminated against—in part—based upon their racial background. Along with other illegitimate forms of exclusion, racism continues to raise its ugly head throughout our society, including in schools. And in schools, Black students, more often than not, are the unfortunate recipients of the effects of racism.

Public policy and the availability of social services are significant sources of the disenfranchisement of Black students. Society reinforces the overrepresentation of drug abuse, crime, and incarceration that persists in the country's Black communities and this directly and indirectly impacts Black students in K–12 urban schools.

A myriad of challenges emanate from within urban schools that contribute to the crisis of Black student disenfranchisement (Hanushek & Rivkin, 2006). These impediments include teacher attitudes, teacher qualifications, principal leadership, cultural discontinuity, class size, number of Black teachers, and financial resources.

For more than 50 years, it has been known that the attitudes of teachers toward Black students contribute to these students' disenfranchisement and resultantly impact their performance (Ryan, 1970). In today's urban schools, many teachers still do not believe that Black students have the cranial capacity of their White peers (Delpit, 1995; Sledge & Morehead, 2006). Some researchers argue that Black students achieve less academic success because they are insufficiently challenged. This would be consistent with the work of Harber et al. (2012), who found that in U.S. urban schools Black children are challenged less than White students in similar situations. This insufficient challenging, we would argue, is one aspect of the disenfranchisement of Black students.

It is also true that the least qualified teachers are more often found in the lowest-performing urban schools in the United States. Researchers in one study (Gagnon & Mattingly, 2012) indicated that schools with larger percentages of Black students tend to have more teachers with little or no teaching experience. This is consistent with Delpit's work (2012), wherein she indicated that as the number of Black students increases in a district, the best teachers in that district—Black and White—tend to relocate away.

The degree of cultural responsiveness of the educational experience—often facilitated by the teacher—has an impact on student performance as do the number of students in the classroom, teacher race, and the level of funding available for the schools. Much research has been done demonstrating the benefits of increased funding in precollegiate education (Hanushek, 1997; Barnett & Ackerman, 2006).

In speaking about the disenfranchisement of Black students and its impact, Delpit (2012) suggests, "If we do not recognize the brilliance before us, we cannot help but carry out the stereotypic societal views that these children are somehow damaged goods and that they cannot be expected to succeed" (p. 5). If Delpit is correct, and we believe she is, the principal must take the lead in displaying confidence in students' ability, compassion for students' and their families, and commitment to students' education if there is to be any hope for addressing the effects of Black student disenfranchisement. In other words, the principal must help to facilitate a culturally responsive experience for Black students.

Our contention, again, is that Black students underperform in urban schools because of their historic disenfranchisement—which brings about their underachievement. This disenfranchisement can be addressed through the provision of a culturally responsive educational experience that can be facilitated in part by Black principals who exhibit the ethno-humanist role identity.

Ethno-Humanist Role Identity

Twenty years ago Lomotey (1993) coined the term *ethno-humanist* to describe one predominant role identity of Black principals.[5] The ethno-humanist role identity encompasses "commitment to the education of all students; confidence in the ability of all students to do well; and compassion for, and understanding of, all students and the communities in which they live" (p. 396). In discussing the ethno-humanist role identity, Lomotey said:

> In this role, principals identify with African-American students as a member of their culture. They argue that academic success is not enough. What is needed, these principals contend, is an education about one's culture, about life and about where these African-American students fit in the society and in the world. In essence, these leaders encourage African-American students to look at the world through an African-centered set of lenses that provides them with vision that is more focused, has a wider periphery and more depth. (p. 397)

The identification of this role identity was relevant some 20 years ago. More recently other researchers have employed this framework as an analytic tool in assessing the leadership of Black principals (Gooden, 2005; Tillman, 2009). A part of our analysis is focused on the question of the continuing relevance of this role identity because an important aspect of the ethno-humanist role identity is, in fact, a culturally responsive learning experience. Understanding the extent to which this role identity still exists will increase our understanding of the nature of culturally responsive educational experiences.

Research Questions

The specific research questions with which we are concerned in this chapter are:

1. What is known about the differences, if any, in the leadership of Black male principals and Black female principals in urban schools?
2. What is known about the differences, if any, in the leadership of Black elementary, middle, and high school principals in urban schools?
3. What is known about the leadership of Black principals in urban schools who are "successful"?
4. What is known about the extent to which Black principals in urban schools exhibit the ethno-humanist role identity?

The Review

Employing our findings, we summarized what is known about the leadership of Black principals in urban schools in order to frame the responses to our research questions. From there, we outlined the implications—for research, practice, and theory—of that knowledge for combatting the disenfranchisement of Black students and addressing their academic performance in today's urban schools.

The overwhelmingly large majority of the research on Black principal leadership in urban schools has been done in the past 25 years. Consequently, in our review, we focused on research published during the period from 1987 through 2012. Most of the research on principal leadership appears in dissertations and journals and we focused our search on these two sources. We sought to uncover studies of individuals or groups of Black principals who were leading in urban schools with Black students. We included one literature review (Foster, 2005) that focused on research on effective leadership practices of Black principals working with Black students in urban schools. We did not include other literature reviews (e.g., Tillman, 2004) that did not focus solely on the leadership characteristics of Black principals in predominantly Black urban schools. We only included studies that explored aspects of the relationship between Black principals and Black students. We uncovered a total of 31 studies: 17 emerged from journals and 14 were dissertations. All of the studies except 4 were qualitative, utilizing one or more of the following methods: interviews, case studies, focus groups, document review, and observations. One study used a mixed methods strategy and two studies were of an historical nature. (See Table 18.1). There was one literature review.

Table 18.1 Overview of Reviewed Studies

Author/Yr	*Source*	*Data*	*Sample*	*Findings*	*Additional Information*
Banks-Thompson (2006)	Dissertation	Case Study: observations, interviews, student focus groups, and document review	Two Black elementary school principals	Belief that all students can learn; relationship building focus; purpose and passion	Improving low-performing schools
Berry (2008)	Dissertation	Qualitative: interviews, observations, and focus group	Three Black female elementary school principals	God, data, student needs, teacher needs, parent needs, communication; church involvement	Critical spirituality
Bloom & Erlandson (2003)	Journal Article	Interviews, observations, and public records	Three Black female principals (two high school principals and one middle school principal)	Multiple sources of under-achievement, sociopolitical and historical context; tight-knit communities valuable; cultural consciousness	
Brown, & Beckett (2007)	Journal Article	Interviews	One Black male elementary/ middle school principal	Encouraged teachers to reach out; facilitated parent involvement; interest convergence (a tenet of critical race theory employed)	Communication barriers in a diverse community
Byrd (2009)	Dissertation	Case studies; interviews and focus group	Four (elementary, middle, high, and K–8) effective Black female principals	Mission-like responsibility to self, community, and children; community servants; Black female identity	Framework: Cross's four-stage theory of identity development: Nigrescense

(*Continued*)

Table 18.1 (Continued)

Author/Yr	*Source*	*Data*	*Sample*	*Findings*	*Additional Information*
Case (1997)	Journal Article	Observations and interviews	One Black female elementary school principal	Othermothering; commitment to Black students' education; awareness of student needs; firm expectations; gaining community respect	Focus on effective practices; Black ethic of care; caring about psycho-emotional needs; rooted in Black experience
Dean (2009)	Dissertation	Qualitative:	27 Black middle school principals	Self-reported exhibiting model; successful principals should network with each other	Exemplary leadership model: model, inspire, challenge process, enable others, and encourage Heart
Derrick (2009)	Dissertation	Qualitative (portraiture): interviews, observations, and focus groups	Two Black male high school principals	Mentoring has positive effect; self-esteem, self-confidence, and ambition positively impacted	No focus on race by anyone
Dillard (1995)	Journal Article	Case study: observations and interviews	One Black female high school principal	Keys for transformative leadership: leadership as interpretation and leadership as authentication (nurturing/ protecting)	Critical feminist theories of leadership; focus: effective schools and Black female principals' leadership; men's realities are not necessarily women's realities; understanding of leadership effectiveness necessitates inclusion of culture
Foster (2005)	Journal Article	Review of 13 studies	"Numerous"	Recognition of cultural norms, tying leaders to communities; recognition of race; help imperative	Interpersonal caring and institutional caring framework
Gooden (2005)	Journal Article	Case study, interviews, and document analysis	One Black male high school principal	Bureaucrat/ administrator and ethno-humanist roles. Ethno-humanist role critical for effectiveness	

(*Continued*)

Table 18.1 (Continued)

Author/Yr	*Source*	*Data*	*Sample*	*Findings*	*Additional Information*
Henderson (2008)	Dissertation	Survey, interviews, and focus group	Six Black male high school principals	Focus on culture of inclusion; love and support focus; self-respect and student-centeredness; commitment to academic success and life of students; community involvement; importance of inclusive and caring environment; belief that students can achieve; paternalistic role models; consistent and fair; concern for students' lives	Black principals develop extensive skills to deal with urban student academic success
Jefferson (2006)	Dissertation	Interviews	Six African American (five males and one female) high school principals	No changes due to NCLB; Involved all stakeholders; school autonomy & instruction key to academic success	Changes in Black principal leadership behaviors due to NCLB
Johnson, L. (2006)	Journal Article	Historical case study, primary and secondary sources	One Black female elementary school principal	Cultural responsive leadership: cultural knowledge and teaching and social justice focus	Important lesson for today's principals
Johnson, T. (2006)	Dissertation	Qualitative: document analysis, interviews, questionnaires, and surveys	12 Black principals	Neighborhood, community, background, district support, and family support influence their success	Early encouragement could increase pool; more Black principals could increase positive change voice in schools
Jones (2010)	Dissertation	Interviews	Six Black (5 high school and 1 elementary school) male principals; a retired principal and an assistant superintendent	Hat-switching, code-switching, and church as center; spirituality-influenced leadership through family values, relationship building, serving opportunities	Pastors and principals; spirituality important

(*Continued*)

Table 18.1 (Continued)

Author/Yr	*Source*	*Data*	*Sample*	*Findings*	*Additional Information*
Khalifa (2008)	Dissertation	Qualitative: observation, field notes, interviews, and document review	One Black male high school principal	Student and community relationships; earned trust and credibility and had rapport; challenged teachers	At-risk alternative school student success
Lee (2007)	Dissertation	Qualitative case study: interviews and observations	Three Black female elementary school principals	Promoted cultural responsiveness at classroom level only	Using culturally responsive learning environments to improve academic achievement: more of a focus on schoolwide and districtwide culturally relevant curriculum is needed
Loder (2005)	Journal Article	Qualitative: interviews, observations, and data sources	Five Black female (K–8 and high school) principals	Positive relations with families; conflict with managerial responsibilities (bureaucrat/administrator) and symbolic community responsibilities (ethno-humanist)	Othermothering; Black women practicing and viewing leadership
Lomotey (1993)	Journal Article	Interviews	Two Black female high school principals	Commitment, compassion, and confidence	Bureaucrat/administrator =schooling and ethno-humanist= education
Lomotey (1987)	Journal Article	Principal and teacher interviews	Three "more successful" Black (one female and two male) elementary school principals	Deep compassion for students	Premises: (1) Black principals positively impact Black student achievement; (2) homophily at play
Mack (2010)	Dissertation	Interviews, observations, field notes, and document review	Three Black women (two elementary school and one high school) principals	Democratic leadership style; developed teacher leaders; nurturing collaborators	Ethnicity impact on social climate; Black feminism, feminism, and CRT used

(*Continued*)

Table 18.1 (Continued)

Author/Yr	*Source*	*Data*	*Sample*	*Findings*	*Additional Information*
Miles Brown (2009)	Dissertation	Case study: interviews	Six (three elementary, two middle, and one high school) Black women principals	Five (intrinsic and personal qualities) themes: (1) call to leadership, (2) teamwork and collaboration with stakeholders, (3) community involvement, (4) beyond academics, and (5) spirituality	Impact of life on Black women principals' practice. These 5 qualities key to successful leadership
Miller (2011)	Dissertation	Interviews	One Black male high school principal	Autocratic, dogmatic, immoral, directive, intimidating, charismatic, and caring	Exploration of one principal's leadership style; controversial but successful
Morris (2004)	Journal Article	Qualitative: interviews, observations, and document analysis	Two Black elementary school principals (one male and one female)	Building cultural bridges between school and community; cultural and academic leaders; setting high academic standards	Schools that are successful in educating Black students; strong academic schools connected to families
Peters (2012)	Journal Article	Case study: interviews	Two Black female high school principals	(a) Lack of district support; (b) limited funding; (c) limited district follow-through, and (d) personal accountability; (1) caring, (2) experience, (3) dialog importance	Leadership creates effective schools; racially alike principals often selected because of a perceived ability to get along with students; Afrocentric feminist epistemology; district support critical
Pollard (1997)	Journal Article	Interviews	20 Black men (8) and women (12) elementary school principals	Three themes: (1) self-assertion, (2) ability confidence, and (3) special connection to Black students	Continuance of tradition of Black principals advocating for Black students
Randolph (2004)	Journal Article	Historical analysis of primary and secondary sources, oral histories, and interviews	Two Black elementary school principals: one male and one female	Confidence; role model, approachable; high expectations; community support and participation	All-Black school in Columbus, OH; historical leadership

(*Continued*)

Table 18.1 (Continued)

Author/Yr	*Source*	*Data*	*Sample*	*Findings*	*Additional Information*
Reed & Evans (2008)	Journal Article	Case study interviews and observations	One Black female principal in low-performing middle/high school	No othermothering; acted just like Whites	Significance of same-race principals, teachers, and students; Assumptions: (1) Black values and assumptions different from Whites, and (2) Black principals nurture; being Black is not enough to work effectively with Black students
Reitzug & Patterson (1998)	Journal Article	Observations, shadowing, interviews	One effective Black middle school female principal	(1) personal connection, (2) honor voice, (3) concern, (4) connecting to community, (5) seeing alternatives	Caring, empowering practices; empowerment through caring; (1) students a priority, (2) caring interactions, and (3) empowering students
Walker & Byas (2003)	Journal Article	Interviews, speeches, and document review	One effective Black male high school principal	Focus on achievement; community support; public communication/ marketing; community leader; exemplary leader; sought tight-knit community	

We analyzed the data from the studies in four ways. (See Table 18.2.) First, we looked at the research using a gender comparison. Some research has indicated a distinction between the leadership of men and women principals (Eagly & Johnson, 1990; Herndon, 2002). We sought to uncover any gender differences between the Black male principals and the Black women principals who were studied.

Second, we looked at comparisons between Black principals in urban elementary schools and Black principals in urban high schools. (There were too few studies of Black principals in urban middle schools.) The experiences within elementary schools are very different from those in high schools. This is true for students, teachers, and administrators. We sought to determine if these differences in experiences impact the leadership of Black principals in urban schools.

Third, looking at studies of effective principals, we sought to explore the characteristics of Black principals in urban schools who are successful in positively affecting the academic performance of Black students and resultantly addressing their disenfranchisement. Given the longstanding concern with regard to Black student disenfranchisement leading to the associated underachievement and the knowledge that the principal does make a difference (Sanchez,

Table 18.2 Summary of Types of Studies Reviewed: By Gender, School Type, and Success

Black Female Principals	*Black Male Principals*	*Elem. Schools*	*Middle Schools*	*High Schools*	*Mixed School Type*	*Effective/ Successful Principa*
(1) Berry	(1) Brown & Beckett	(1) Banks-Thompson	(1) Dean	(1) Derrick	(1) Bloom & Erlandson	(1) Banks-Thompson
(2) Bloom & Erlandson	(2) Derrick	(2) Berry	(2) Reitzug & Patterson	(2) Dillard	(2) Brown & Beckett	(2) Berry
(3) Byrd	(3) Gooden	(3) Case		(3) Gooden	(3) Byrd	(3) Byrd
(4) Case	(4) Henderson	(4) Johnson, L.		(4) Henderson	(4) Jones	(4) Dillard
(5) Dillard	(5) Jones	(5) Lee		(5) Jefferson	(5) Loder	(5) Foster (2005)
(6) Johnson, L.	(6) Khalifa	(6) Lomotey (1987)		(6) Khalifa	(6) Mack	(6) Henderson
(7) Lee	(7) Miller	(7) Morris		(7) Lomotey (1993)	(7) Miles Brown	(7) Khalifa
(8) Loder	(8) Walker & Byas	(8) Pollard		(8) Miller	(8) Reed & Evans	(8) Lee
(9) Lomotey (1993)		(9) Randolph		(9) Peters		(9) Lomotey (1987)
(10) Mack				(10) Walker & Bays		(10) Miller
(11) Miles Brown						(11) Morris
(12) Peters						(12) Randolph
(13) Reed & Evans						(13) Reitzug & Patterson
(14) Reitzug & Patterson						(14) Walker & Bays

Thornton, & Usinger, 2009; Williams, 2012), it seems clear that understanding the unique characteristics of Black principals who are successful would offer valuable insights.

Finally, using Lomotey's (1993) ethno-humanist role identity typology, we analyzed the studies to see if this role identity emerged. Again, the concern is the relationship between the ethno-humanist role identity and a culturally responsive educational environment. If we can learn more about this role identity, we may learn more about the function of Black principals in facilitating a culturally responsive learning environment and consequently have information necessary to address the longstanding intentional disenfranchisement of Black students.

Findings

Black Female Principals

Researchers in 14 studies focused on Black women principals (four in elementary schools, one in a middle school, three in high schools, and six in mixed school types). The studies were reported in nine journal articles and five dissertations. The four characteristics of the women principals

Table 18.3 Findings: By Principal Type

	Nurturing	*Community*	*Culture*	*Academics*	*Parents*
Women	X	X	X	X	–
Men	X	X	–	X	X
Elementary	X	X	X	X	–
High School	X	X	–	X	–
Successful	X	X	–	X	–

that were most prevalent included: (1) nurturing or developing caring and personal relationships with students, (2) a focus on community involvement or facilitating a mutually beneficial two-way relationship between community organizations and individuals and the school community, (3) an emphasis on a culturally responsive educational experience or stressing an academic experience that draws upon the culture of students to enhance their learning experience, and (4) a commitment to student academic performance or demonstrating a sincere concern for the academic success of their students. (See Table 18.3.)

The nurturing focus of these Black women principals took several forms. Mack (2010) spoke of the three Black female principals in her study as nurturing collaborators who each saw herself as "the matriarch of her educational community" (p. 98) and felt pressure to educate Black or minority children (p. 99). Peters (2012) described the two Black female high school principals in her study as caring. For example, both principals established a culture within their building of academic achievement for all students. Additionally, one of the principals "prided herself in the relationships she was able to develop with staff and students that helped strengthen her intent to improve the culture" (p. 32) of her school.

Reitzug and Patterson (1998) spoke of caring, empowering practices and of students being a priority for the Black female middle school principal in their study. Through their description of her actions, the authors showed how a principal's caring practices teach students how to care for each other and overcome messages of violence and negativity. The empowerment through caring exemplified in the principal's style was seen as effective because she helped students navigate their schooling by helping them solve problems, rather than by punishing them when they had conflicts at school.

Lomotey (1993), in his study of two Black female high school principals, described the compassion and commitment to education they had for their students. Berry (2008), in her study of three Black women elementary school principals, noted her subjects' commitment to addressing student needs. The principals felt that communication was essential to building relationships and emphasized the importance of "telling the truth in love" (p. 187).

Several researchers used the term *othermothering* to describe the nurturing role played by older Black women with younger Black children in their community. Case (1997, p. 36) notes that this othermothering is part of an "African American ethic of care," a term first used in relation to Black educators by Foster (1997). Case (1997) studied one Black woman elementary school principal and noted several "othermothering" characteristics including: (1) a strong connection to and sharing of oral history that shaped her commitment to educating Black children, (2) her awareness of the personal challenges her students faced along with the interventions she utilized to address these challenges, and (3) setting firm expectations for students that empower them.

Loder (2005), in her study of five Black women principals, described how the women felt they were called to "rebuild [their] communities through acts of nurturing, teaching, and leading" (p. 312).

Researchers also described the community involvement focus of these Black women leaders. Byrd (2009) explained this focus as mission-like, stating that the four women principals in his study viewed themselves as community servants. Reitzug and Patterson (1998) talked of the principal in their study seeking a connection to her community. The authors note, "Although Debbie Pressley was concerned with the 'healthy child' as an individual, her actions indicated that she was sensitive to the connectedness of the actions of individuals to the 'health' of others in the school community. Thus, in dealing with individuals, she was sensitive and nurturing but clearly communicated that there were limits" (p. 173).

Bloom and Erlandson (2003), in describing the three Black female principals in their study (two high school principals and one middle school principal), spoke of the importance of tight-knit communities in achieving high student performance. The three principals valued the legacy of tight-knit communities within the Black community and used a collective consciousness to create a vision for their school that included valuing the opportunity to give back to the community. Case (1997)—drawing on data from her study—spoke of the significance of principals gaining community support. Marguerite, the principal in Case's study, articulated the importance her mother taught her "of presenting yourself within and to the community" (p. 36).

Lomotey (1993) described compassion for students' communities as a quality shared by the principals in his study. He highlighted the statement of one principal, Ms. Scarlet, as the epitome of the ethno-humanist role that includes compassion: "I am interested in children learning and knowing information, but I think we need to have our children understand where we come from. Our people are able to deal with conflict, have an inner dignity and know how to cope with situations . . . I grew up learning that" (p. 408).

Loder (2005) talked of symbolic community responsibilities much in the way Lomotey described the ethno-humanist role identity of Black principals (1993). Loder found that the principals saw themselves as community rebuilders, nurturers, leaders, and teachers—or as "othermothers" (p. 312).

Miles Brown (2009) spoke of the importance of community involvement in discussing the commitment to social activism of the six Black women principals in her study. Finally, Berry (2008) acknowledged the importance of the church in the leadership of the principals in her study. Each of the principals was involved in a church activity that required their commitment to attend a church meeting at least once a week. Berry concluded that the principals, all of whom ascribed to a spiritual epistemology, were committed to supporting their community. They facilitated parent understanding of curriculum and promotion standards, and "expressed obligations to educate parents on community, city, and state services to improve their quality of life" (p. 185), and they "reported times when they have had to act as emotional support for their parents" (p. 185).

While the focus of this review was not on spirituality and its role in the leadership of Black principals, as illustrated above, it was discussed in some of the studies that we reviewed. Dantley (2010) discussed the notion of critical spirituality (a merging of critical theory and Black spirituality) composed of self-reflection, interpretation, creativity, and action. He argued that critical spirituality is important, particularly for urban school leaders, in that it enhances the ability of these leaders to be transformative; their spiritualty motivates their actions. He contended that they saw their school leadership as a form of ministry. In this review, Jones (2010), Miles Brown (2009), and Berry (2008) each addressed the significance of spirituality for Black principals in urban schools. This concept of spirituality in relationship to Black principal leadership did not appear in the literature as recently as 10 years ago.

Cultural responsiveness was also important to the Black women principals in this review. Miles Brown (2009) identified a willingness of the six women in her study to address the academic needs as well as the emotional development of their students. One principal stated, "You must know your students and help to give them the right tools and resources to succeed" (p. 92). Another principal noted, "We must help them [the students] to achieve academically, mentally, and socially within a school" (pp. 92–93).

Lee (2007) researched ways that urban elementary school principals promote culturally responsive learning environments "to improve the academic achievement of Black students" (p. 16). She found that the principals promoted cultural responsiveness in their schools by encouraging teachers to relate content to the culture of Black students, but concluded that student achievement would improve if culturally responsive activities were expanded throughout the district. L. Johnson (2006), in a case study of one Black woman elementary school principal, discussed the principal's culturally responsive leadership and the related significance of cultural knowledge and a social justice focus.

Several principals also exemplified the importance of principals' self-identification of race and gender in guiding their practice. Case (1997) discussed the importance of anchoring one's practices in the Black experience, noting that othermothering is a maternal action that is part of an "African American ethic of care" (p. 36). Bloom and Erlandson (2003) concluded that the three women principals in their study possessed a cultural consciousness about their heritage that guided their work in urban schools. Dillard (1995), in her case study of one Black female high school principal, used critical feminist theories to analyze the ways the principal's experiences helped to "(re)interpret the social and cultural nature of leadership" (p. 543). Dillard discussed the importance of including culture in one's efforts at effective leadership and argued that it is impossible to understand the effectiveness of leaders without taking their culture into account.

Byrd (2009) described the importance of Black female identity for Black women school leaders. Their Black female identity influenced their sense of "mission-like responsibility" (p. iv) to work in urban schools, their decision making, and a commitment to their communities. Peters (2012) addressed African-centered feminist epistemology and its impact on the leadership of Black principals. Both principals in the Peters study acknowledged that the intersection of their race, gender, and age impacted how they were perceived as school leaders, but that race was an advantage, while gender and age presented challenges. Mack (2010) spoke of her subjects' acknowledgment of the impact of their ethnicity on the social climate in their schools. The principals felt pressure to lead urban schools in order "to educate African American or minority children" (p. 99).

The fourth characteristic of the Black women principals in our review was commitment to student academic performance. Case (1997) referred to the commitment of the principal in her study to the education of Black students, awareness of student needs, and high expectations. Reitzug and Patterson (1998) spoke of the principal in their study making student success a priority. Lomotey (1993) referred to the commitment of the principals in his study to the education of Black students. Berry (2008) summarized the importance of the principals' critical spirituality which guides an ethic of caring with the following statement: "Our three principals of study create level playing fields so that children of color may secure educational and social capital with the end goal being that of college readiness" (p. 200).

In sum, the Black women principals in these 14 studies focused mostly on (1) providing a nurturing environment, (2) facilitating community involvement, (3) supplying a culturally responsive educational environment, and (4) a commitment to academic excellence for their students.

Black Male Principals

Eight of the studies focused on Black male principals (six in high schools and two unspecified). Four of the studies were dissertations and four were journal articles. The four qualities that were noted most often in these studies included (1) a focus on community involvement, (2) a parent involvement focus, (3) nurturing, and (4) a commitment to student academic performance. (See Table 18.3.)

These Black male principals shared a focus on community involvement. The eight male principals studied by Jones (2010)—all of whom were also religious leaders—built relationships with teachers, students, and the community: "In the participants' descriptions of the church, the church experience emerged as the center of their families and the communities where they lived" (p. 71). One principal stated that the "church was the foundation for the entire community and was attended by everyone" (p. 71). In a case study of one former Black male high school principal, Walker and Byas (2003) noted the principal's belief in the importance of community support, community leadership, and a tight-knit community.

Henderson (2008), in a study of six Black male high school principals, noted these leaders' focus on community involvement—what he termed, "collective involvement" (p. 129). Henderson delineated specific characteristics of this type of community involvement that the principals exhibited: (1) one principal held evening communication sessions with parents at a local church and YMCA, (2) they stressed the importance of connecting with churches and other community organizations that met the needs of students, and (3) they promoted "parental and family involvement as a critical element of a successful urban education environment" (p. 130).

Khalifa (2008), in a case study of one Black male high school principal, stressed this leader's focus on student and community relations. The principal developed relationships with students and the community that Khalifa identified as one factor in the school's success. The strategies included facilitating rap sessions with students and hosting Saturday community breakfasts. Additionally, the principal was able to earn trust and credibility and establish rapport with communities that were traditionally hostile and distant from traditional education institutions. The principal was able to address the educational needs of Black students in part through challenging teachers to do their best and through ensuring that the instructional program was geared to the needs of the students.

These principals also shared a belief in the importance of parental involvement. The Black male principal observed by Brown and Beckett (2007) emphasized the significance of facilitating parental involvement. Because the principal (who is also the lead author of the article) encouraged teachers to reach out to families in order to connect them to social service agencies, and also created opportunities for parents to be involved in school activities, particularly in the classroom, he allowed students to see their parents and teachers cooperating for a common purpose. Additionally, the principal facilitated discussion about discipline "between the city's disadvantaged African American community and its middle-class White community" (p. 25).

These male principals were also described as nurturing. Derrick (2009) in his study of two Black male principals uncovered the leaders' conviction that mentoring increased self-esteem, self-confidence, and ambition. Gooden (2005), in his case study of one Black male principal, noted the centrality of the "ethno-humanist" role identity of the principal as demonstrated by his commitment to the education of all of his students, and his compassion for understanding his Black students and their communities.

Henderson (2008) discussed the importance of a focus on love, support, student-centeredness, a caring environment, and concern for students' lives. The principals saw themselves as role models and operated out of a paternalistic framework when interacting with students. Miller (2011) described the Black male high school principal whom she observed as caring and charismatic.

Finally, the Black male principals whom these researchers observed were each committed to student academic performance. Walker and Byas (2003) noted their subject's focus on achievement. When the principal (Byas) resigned in 1968, standardized test scores had steadily increased and graduates of the school went on to attend elite universities across the country.

Henderson (2008) stressed the commitment of the principals in his study to the academic success of their students. Each principal expressed a belief in the ability of all of his or her students to succeed academically. One principal in the Henderson study stated that "everyone is capable of learning" and "every student is educable in something" (p. 131). Another principal stated that "all youngsters can learn," (p. 131), while another principal stated, "I strongly believe that every kid is worthwhile [sic] of an education" (p. 132). Khalifa (2008) stressed the principal's belief in his students' ability to excel academically by highlighting the principal's commitment to ensuring that instruction was designed to meet the needs of students, as well as his practice of challenging teachers to meet the needs of students.

The Black male principals in these eight studies emphasized (1) community and (2) parental involvement, (3) providing a nurturing environment for students, and (4) facilitating student academic success.

Black Middle School Principals

Only two of the studies that we reviewed focused solely on middle school principals. After conducting a quantitative study of the leadership behaviors of 27 principals for dissertation research, Dean (2009) concluded that principals should network with other principals in higher-performing schools to discuss leadership behaviors. Reitzug and Patterson (1998), in a journal article, highlighted the importance of community, connecting, concern, creativity, and respect. The principal's practice of "empowerment through caring" (p. 165) served as an example of principal actions that overcome the challenges of traditional controlling discipline strategies that are ineffective for urban students.

Black Elementary School Principals

Nine of the studies in our review focused on elementary school principals only. Three of the studies were in dissertations and the remaining six were published in journals. The four characteristics of these principals that emerged most often were (1) nurturing, (2) a commitment to student academic performance, (3) a focus on community involvement, and (4) an emphasis on a culturally responsive educational experience. (See Table 18.3.)

The evidence of a nurturing focus by these elementary school principals appeared in several of the studies. Banks-Thompson (2006), in a study of two Black elementary school principals, referred to the leaders' passion for building relationships with their students. Case (1997) used the term *othermothering,* and discussed awareness of student needs in describing the nurturing role of the principal in her study. For example, the principal stated that students "have to feel not only just your voice. They have to feel the warmth and caring that comes from you as a person" (p. 35). Lomotey (1987) described a deep compassion for students displayed by the Black elementary school principals in his study.

Pollard (1997), in her study of 20 Black elementary school principals, described their special connection to Black students. This was evident in the ways in which respondents related their own race, gender, and economic upbringing to the connection and empathy that they had for their students. Berry (2008) discussed the principals' passion for student learning that enabled them to focus on meeting student needs.

These elementary school principals also exhibited a commitment to student academic performance. Banks-Thompson (2006) concluded that students made academic progress when the principal operated out of a belief that all students can learn. Case (1997) explicitly referred to her subject's commitment to the education of Black students, awareness of student needs, and high expectations.

Lomotey (1987) posited that, in part because of homophily—a shared understanding between principal and students based on their common culture—Black principals aided Black students in increasing their academic performance. That is, communications were more effective between the Black students and Black principals because of their shared cultural traits that facilitated increased opportunities for learning. Morris (2004) described the high academic standards displayed by the two Black elementary school principals in his study. This included establishing high academic standards for their schools and referring to themselves as academic leaders—and acting accordingly.

Pollard (1997) described the confidence in the ability of Black students displayed by the principals in her study. The connections the principals created with their students formed the basis for "caring communication as a basis for demanding high standards of achievement and behavior from their students" (p. 366). In a study of two elementary school principals, Randolph (2004) described the high expectations that these leaders shared for their Black students, noting that the principals made sure that their schools "were among the best-performing schools on statewide standardized tests" (p. 94).

Community involvement was also important to these elementary school principals. Banks-Thompson (2006) focused on her subjects' reliance on relationship building. Drawing on data from her study, Case (1997) spoke on the importance of principals gaining community support. Morris (2004) described the role that the principals in his study played in building bridges between the schools and the surrounding communities: "The . . . educators did not wait for parents to initiate parental participation; they reached out and welcomed these parents into the school—an example of agency" (p. 89). Randolph (2004) described the leaders' emphasis on community support and participation. Berry (2008) talked about the principals' focus on the church in facilitating their leadership.

These principals exhibited an acknowledgment of the importance of a culturally responsive learning experience for students. Case (1997) discussed the importance of focusing one's practices in the Black experience thereby increasing opportunities for effective two-way communication with students. L. Johnson (2006) talked about the principal's cultural responsive leadership and the related significance of cultural knowledge and a social justice focus. Such a focus, Johnson argued, increases students' sense of ownership of the teaching-learning process and thereby increases their opportunities for academic success. Lee (2007) talked about the importance of culturally responsive curriculum for student performance. Here, the point is that, if students can see themselves in the curriculum, they are more likely to relate successfully with the curriculum content. Pollard (1997) described in her study the tradition of Black principals advocating for Black students, again emphasizing the importance of the cultural link between Black students and Black principals.

Like the Black women principals, the nine elementary school principals focused mostly on (1) providing a nurturing environment, (2) facilitating community involvement, (3) providing a culturally responsive educational environment, and (4) ensuring that students performed well academically.

Black High School Principals

The authors of 10 studies in our review considered the leadership of Black principals in urban high schools. Five of the studies were dissertations and five appeared in journals. The majority of the high school principals in these studies shared the following three characteristics: (1) commitment to student academic performance, (2) community involvement, and (3) nurturing. (See Table 18.3.)

Walker and Byas (2003) spoke of the student achievement focus of their subject principal. Lomotey (1993) observed a commitment to student success in his subject principals. Henderson

(2008) spoke of a commitment on the part of the principals in his study to student academic success as well as a belief in the ability of students to achieve.

In the area of community involvement, Walker and Byas (2003) discussed their principal's desire for a tight-knit community. Khalifa (2008) noted that the principal in his study focused on facilitating strong community relationships. Henderson (2008) alluded to community involvement as a focus of the principals in his study.

Nurturing was the third key characteristic of these Black urban high school principals. Peters (2012) discussed the caring nature of the two principals in her study. Miller (2011) described the principal in her study as charismatic and caring. Lomotey (1993) discussed the compassion displayed by the principals in his study. The principals in the Henderson (2008) study displayed a focus on love, inclusiveness, caring, and support for students, as well as a student-centeredness and concern for students' lives.

The Black high school principals in these 10 studies emphasized (1) ensuring academic success, (2) involving the larger community in school activities, and (3) offering a nurturing environment for students in their leadership.

Successful Black Principals

While the studies cited above focused on various aspects of Black principal leadership and the relationship between Black principals and Black students, 14 studies focused specifically on one or more Black principals who were considered to be "successful" in that by some measure their students were doing well academically or were improving substantially. Seven were journal articles and seven were dissertations. The three most common characteristics of these successful principals were (1) a focus on community involvement, (2) a commitment to student academic performance, and (3) nurturing. (See Table 18.3.)

Community involvement was one characteristic exhibited by the principals in these studies. Byrd (2009) talked about the principals in his study as community servants. Foster (2005) stressed the linkage between leadership and community for the principals in her literature review. These principals facilitated a caring environment and stressed concern for students' lives. Khalifa talked about the principal in his study focusing on student and community relationships.

Morris (2004) discussed the efforts of the two principals in his study at building cultural bridges between the school and community and connecting with families. Randolph (2004) described how the principals in her study stressed the importance of community support and parent and community participation. Reitzug and Patterson (1998) talked about the principal in their study stressing personal connections and connecting to communities. Walker and Byas (2003) talked about how the principal in their study stressed the importance of community support and how he sought to create a tight-knit community.

In illustrating a focus on commitment to the education of all students, Banks-Thompson (2006), in her study of two principals, referred to the principals in her study stressing relationship building and improving low-performing schools. Berry (2008), in her study of three principals, talked about the importance these women placed on student needs. Byrd (2009) described the mission-like sense of responsibility that the principals had in his study.

Foster (2005) spoke of the help imperative that the principals in the 13 studies that she reviewed felt with regard to their commitment to education. Henderson (2008) referred to the notion of a culture of inclusion and a commitment to academic success that the six principals in his study demonstrated. Khalifa (2008), in his qualitative study of one principal, spoke of how the principal in his study earned the trust and credibility of students, and in demonstrating their commitment to education, challenged teachers accordingly. Miller (2011) talked about the school principal in her study as autocratic, dogmatic, and directive—yet successful. These characteristics, Miller argued, reflected the principal's commitment to education. Randolph (2004) spoke of the high expectations that the two principals in her study displayed and described.

The principal in the Reitzug and Patterson study (1998) indicated unequivocally that, for her, students were the priority. Walker and Byas (2003), in their qualitative study of one principal, described the focus on achievement displayed by the principal (Byas) in their study.

These principals also demonstrated and articulated a nurturing attitude toward their students. Banks-Thompson (2006) and Henderson (2008) spoke of the principals in their studies demonstrating a belief that all students can learn. Dillard (1995) talked about how, for the principal in her case study, leadership and culture were linked and leadership meant nurturing and protecting students. Foster (2005) utilized an institutional and interpersonal caring framework in her study. Henderson (2008) described the love and support focus on the principals in his study. Lee (2007) talked about the focus of the three principals in her study on promoting cultural responsiveness at the classroom level. Lomotey (1987) highlighted the deep compassion for students displayed by the principals in his study and the significance of homophily in their relationships with their students. Miller (2011) described the charisma and caring characteristics of the principal in her study. The principal in the Reitzug and Patterson (1998) study also focused on caring and empowering practices, caring interactions, and empowering students. Randolph (2004) pointed out how the principals in her study stressed confidence in the abilities of their students.

Like the high school principals, the principals in successful environments concentrated on (1) ensuring academic success, (2) involving the larger community in school activities, and (3) offering a nurturing environment for students.

Conclusions

Gender

What is known about the differences, if any, in the leadership of Black male principals and Black female principals in urban schools? Previous research suggests that there are gender differences in the leadership of principals (Eagly & Johnson, 1990; Herndon, 2002). We sought to explore the possible existence of such differences in our comparison of Black women principals and Black male principals. The Black women principals in the studies that we reviewed valued nurturing, community involvement, and a culturally responsive educational experience, and they were committed to the academic success of their students. The Black men principals focused on nurturing, family values, and parental involvement, and they, too, were committed to the academic success of their students. Although both Black male and female principals valued nurturing, the nature of care by Black women was characterized by the gendered concept of "othermothering," which is rooted in African American female history and culture. While the end result of caring by Black men principals and Black women principals have similar effects of allowing students to see themselves as valuable human beings capable of learning, how the Black women principals and researchers characterize the nature of that care based on race and gender is significant.

The differences between the Black male principals and Black female principals in our review appear to be in the areas of community involvement, the importance of culture, family values, and parental involvement. The significant characteristics of Black women principals appeared to be their commitment to community involvement and a culturally responsive learning environment. Also, the Black men principals appeared to be committed to teaching family values and parental involvement, specifically, as distinguished from community involvement in general, more than the Black women principals. That is to say, the Black male principals focused more on being an example of leadership, while the women principals stressed being a part of the team and harnessing the energy of the school community members in order to be effective.

We suggest caution here in utilizing these findings. We are not suggesting that the Black men principals did not promote community involvement or a culturally responsive education. Nor are we suggesting that the Black women principals did not promote family values and parental involvement. We are merely reporting on the characteristics of these two sets of principals that seem most prominent given the data collected in each of these studies.

School Type

There were too few studies of Black middle school principals to include them in this analysis. (There were only two such studies.) Our review suggests that the most prominent characteristics of the Black elementary school principals were very similar to those of the Black high school principals. In each group, the principals valued nurturing and community involvement, and they were committed to student academic success. The one area of difference was cultural responsiveness in the educational experience. The Black elementary school principals appeared to focus on this more than did the high school principals. Here again we urge caution; the suggestion is not that the Black high school principals did not value a culturally responsive educational experience. What our review suggests is that they placed more of a focus on nurturing, community involvement, and student achievement. It is also likely that the strategies employed in demonstrating a focus on cultural responsiveness are different when comparing elementary and secondary schools.

The differences between Black male principals and Black female principals, and Black elementary school principals and Black high school principals, could also be explained by the research questions asked by the researchers. The way that the researchers asked questions and analyzed themes inevitably influenced the perceived characteristics of these principals. In short, perhaps in some instances the findings suggest more about what the researcher is looking for as opposed to what the principals actually do.

Successful Principals

Our review indicates that—like the Black high school principals—the Black successful principals valued nurturing, community involvement, and a commitment to student academic success.

The Ethno-Humanist Role Identity

The ethno-humanist role identity is related to addressing cultural goals. Each of the three predominant characteristics of the five groups of principals (Black women principals, Black men principals, Black elementary school principals, Black high school principals, and successful Black principals) in the studies that we reviewed is encompassed within the ethno-humanist role identity. Lomotey (1993) described the ethno-humanist role identity as entailing commitment to students' education, displaying confidence in students' abilities, and showing compassion for students and their communities. The three most prominent principal qualities in the present review were nurturing, a community focus, and a concentration on academics. Each of these is subsumed within Lomotey's ethno-humanist role identity. The nurturing is similar to compassion for students. A community focus is akin to showing compassion for students' communities, and a concentration on academics is related to displaying confidence in students' abilities.

The nurturing, compassion, caring focus in Lomotey's work and in the present review seems to be of particular relevance. That is, this characteristic appears to be very important for Black principals in their interactions with Black students in urban schools. Noddings (1992) discussed the importance of caring relationships between educators and students in bringing about trust, increased effort, and ultimately, student success. We would suggest that the nature of the increasing challenges within urban schools are such that perhaps Black principals are most often forced to focus on the ethno-humanist/caring aspect of their leadership.

Our review suggests that Black principals (be they women, men, in elementary schools, or in high schools) place a priority on their ethno-humanist role identity. They do this first by offering a nurturing/caring environment for their students, believing that such a focus benefits the students in their efforts to overcome their disenfranchisement and underachievement. These Black principals also share a belief that their students can be academically successful. This belief, no doubt, provides motivation, inspiration, and determination for these school leaders as they go about their daily routine. Finally, in their ethno-humanist role identity, the Black principals in the studies that we reviewed share a belief that the involvement of the larger community (i.e., churches, businesses, community people, and others) is critical for the success of the educational enterprise and they focus on this. We discuss the significance of these findings further in the following implications section.

Implications

While the 14 studies that focused specifically on successful principals each defined success differently, each defined it in a way that focused on student academic performance—a significant effect of the disenfranchisement that Black students experience. This suggests that the characteristics of nurturing, valuing community involvement, and being committed to student achievement are characteristics that researchers might focus on in attempting to better understand the key characteristics of environments wherein the disenfranchisement of Black students is effectively addressed and where Black students do well academically.

Given the suggestion that nurturing, a community involvement focus, and a commitment to student achievement appeared to be important/predominant characteristics of these effective Black principals, researchers might conduct studies in which they explore the nature of these characteristics and uncover the ways in which leaders display them. Qualitative studies as well as theory-testing studies might help to shed additional light on the significance of these characteristics.

Our findings present an opportunity to reflect upon the professional knowledge and experience gained over time by principals. The context in which a principal works is also of significance. Urban schools are different from rural and suburban schools—and the context differs from one urban school to another. These are issues that must be considered in future research and in administrator preparation programs.

Schools and colleges of education can benefit from the findings of this review. The findings suggest that successful Black principals are nurturing, are committed to community involvement, and believe that their students can overcome their disenfranchisement and be academically successful. Administrator preparation programs might emphasize the significance of principals providing a nurturing environment for students and provide opportunities for prospective administrators to develop or enhance their nurturing skills. Administrator training programs could also explore the notion of community involvement and encourage prospective administrators to employ efforts to increase community involvement in their schools. Finally, administrator-training programs can address the importance of self-reflection and help teachers to understand their relationship with their students. Only by doing this can administrators develop the confidence to aid all students in addressing their disenfranchisement and becoming academically successful.

We do not expect that efforts will be made to place Black principals at the helm in all predominantly Black urban schools—nor is it practical to do this. Moreover, the question still remains as to whether in fact Black students perform better academically with Black principals. We know little about the impact of White principals (or Hispanic principals or Asian principals or Native American principals) on Black students. We do not know if there is a set of unique characteristics held by *all* principals who are successful with Black students. This represents a potential area of study. Moreover, in light of the impracticality of staffing all predominantly Black schools with Black principals, there is a need to ensure that all principals in Black schools—regardless of their own racial background—possess the necessary skills to enable their students to combat their disenfranchisement and ultimately perform well academically.

In educational research we often look at "successful" educators or "successful" educational environments and attempt to determine how the success was achieved. In reality, the context matters. Who attends the school matters. The unique conditions of the school matter. Indeed, the experiences of the successful person matter. The biography of successful individuals cannot be duplicated, nor can the circumstances in which they have performed. Again, ethnographies, case studies, and other qualitative studies as well as quantitative theory-testing studies are called for.

Final Thoughts

We began by acknowledging the longstanding underperformance of Black students in urban schools. We argued that this underperformance is a byproduct of the longstanding and intentional disenfranchisement of Black students. We posited that, by focusing incorrectly on the underachievement, we lose sight of the real cause of this crisis. Importantly, we contended that this intentional disenfranchisement could be addressed with the establishment of a culturally responsive educational experience, which, we argued, could be facilitated in part by Black principals. Through our review we have suggested that the ethno-humanist role identity displayed by Black principals benefits Black students in regard to their academic performance. The principals in our review demonstrated a belief in the academic abilities of Black students. This is a key characteristic if we are to expect to aid these students in overcoming their disenfranchisement and perform better academically. These principals placed a focus on community involvement, because successfully addressing the negative school and societal factors that impact the disenfranchisement and underperformance of Black students necessitates a multipronged effort. The focus by the Black urban school principals in our study on nurturing, academic excellence, and community involvement in fact is a focus on bringing about a culturally responsive educational experience.

Our findings argue for (1) an increase in large-scale and small-scale qualitative and quantitative research on Black principals in urban schools, and (2) more Black principals. Additional work should be carried out utilizing the ethno-humanist role identity as we seek to increase our understanding of culturally responsive learning environments for Black students and for all students in urban schools. Increasing the number of Black principals—with a focus on the ethno-humanist role identity/culturally relevant education—could benefit Black students by reducing their disenfranchisement and improving their academic performance levels.

Notes

1. We use the term *Black* to refer to students (and people) of African descent living in the United States.
2. We borrow from Milner (2012) in defining urban schools as those schools that exist in large, dense metropolitan areas (population > 1,000,000). Milner refers to these schools as *urban intensive*.
3. We use the term *disenfranchisement* herein in describing the educational challenges faced by large numbers of Black students in urban schools to highlight the fact that these students are not primarily responsible for their status; forces beyond their control have foisted it upon them. While it is accurate to say that Black students underachieve, it is important to acknowledge that their widescale underachievement—and the related massive achievement gap—is primarily the result of intentional societal and institutional factors and not something intrinsic in Black students; we seek to avoid inadvertently and inaccurately blaming the victim.
4. We define a culturally responsive learning environment as an effective teaching/learning experience facilitated by educators who draw upon the culture of the student/learner, enabling them to "see themselves" in the curriculum (Gay, 2010; Lomotey, 1989b). As a result, students are more comfortable and feel as though they are active participants in the teaching/learning process. Many refer to this as a culturally relevant learning environment (Ladson-Billings, 2009).
5. Lomotey (1993) constructed two role identities that he observed in Black principals: the ethno-humanist role identity and the bureaucrat/administrator role identity. As we are concerned with culturally responsive learning environments herein, we focus in our analysis on the more closely aligned ethno-humanist role identity. The bureaucrat/administrator role identity focuses primarily on administrative tasks that the principal undertakes.

References

Banks-Thompson, J.E. (2006). *The impact of African American principal leadership on African American student achievement in low-performing elementary schools: A case study* (Unpublished doctoral dissertation). University of San Francisco, San Francisco, CA.

Barnett, W.S., & Ackerman, D.J. (2006). Costs, benefits, and long-term effects of early care and education programs: Recommendations and cautions for community developers. *Community Development, 37*(2), 86–100.

Barton, P.E., & Coley, R.J. (2010). *The black-white achievement gap: When progress stopped*. Policy Information Report. Princeton, NJ: Educational Testing Service.

Berry, S.D. (2008). *Principals of critical spirituality: African American females in elementary urban schools* (Unpublished doctoral dissertation). Texas A&M University, College Station, TX.

Bloom, C.M., & Erlandson, D.A. (2003). African American women principals in urban schools: Realities, (re)construction, and resolutions. *Educational Administration Quarterly, 39*(3), 339–369.

Brown, L.H., & Beckett, K.S. (2007). Building community in an urban school district: A case study of African American educational leadership. *School Community Journal, 17*(1), 7–32.

Byrd, C., Sr. (2009). *Voices of identity and responsibility: A description of the development of identity, using Cross' theory of Nigrescence, and the manifestation of responsibility among African American urban school principals* (Unpublished doctoral dissertation). Cardinal Stritch University, Milwaukee, WI.

Case, K.I. (1997). African American othermothering in the urban elementary school. *Urban Review, 29*(1), 25–39.

Dantley, M.E. (2010). Successful leadership in urban schools: Principals, and critical spirituality, a new approach to reform. *Journal of Negro Education, 79*(3), 214–219.

Dean, M. (2009). *A leadership behavior study of African American middle school principals in South Carolina* (Unpublished doctoral dissertation). South Carolina State University, Orangeburg, SC.

Delpit, L. (1995). *Other people's children: Cultural conflict in the classroom*. New York, NY: New Press.

Delpit, L. (2012). *"Multiplication is for white people": Raising expectations for other people's children*. New York, NY: New Press.

Derrick, L. (2009). *Exploring mentoring relationships between African American high school males and African American male principals* (Unpublished doctoral dissertation). Bowling Green State University, Bowling Green, OH.

Dillard, C.B. (1995). Leading with her life: An African American feminist (re)interpretation of leadership for an urban high school principal. *Educational Administration Quarterly, 31*(4), 539–563.

Eagly, A.H., & Johnson, B.T. (1990). Gender and leadership style: A meta-analysis. CHIP Documents. Paper 11. http://digitalcommons.uconn.edu/chip_docs/11

Foster, L. (2005). The practice of educational leadership in African American communities of learning: Context, scope, and meaning. *Educational Administration Quarterly, 41*(4), 689–700.

Foster, M. (1997). *Black teachers on teaching.* New York, NY: New Press.

Gagnon D., & Mattingly, M.J. (2012). *Beginning teachers are more common in rural, high-poverty, and racially diverse schools.* Issue Brief No. 53, Carsey Institute, University of New Hampshire, Durham, NH.

Gardiner, M.E., & Enomoto, E.K. (2006). Urban school principals and their role as multicultural leaders. *Urban Education, 41*(6), 560–584.

Gay, G. (2010). *Culturally responsive teaching: Theory, research, and practice.* New York, NY: Teachers College Press.

Gooden, M.A. (2005). The role of an African American principal in an urban information technology high school. *Educational Administration Quarterly, 41*(4), 630–650.

Hanushek, E.A. (1997). Assessing the effects of school resources on student performance: An update. *Educational Evaluation and Policy Analysis, 19*(2), 141–164.

Hanushek, E.A., & Rivkin, S.G. (2006). *School quality and the black-white achievement gap.* Working Paper No. 12651. Cambridge, MA: National Bureau of Economic Research.

Harber, K.G., Gorman, J.L., Gengaro, F.P., Butisingh, S., Tsang, W., & Ouellette, R. (2012). Students' race and teachers' social support affect the positive feedback bias in public schools. *Journal of Educational Psychology, 104*(4), 1149–1161.

Henderson, G. (2008). *Leadership experiences of male African-American secondary urban principals: The impact of beliefs, values and experiences on school leadership practices* (Unpublished doctoral dissertation). Cleveland State University, Cleveland, OH.

Herndon, J. D. (2002). *Gender differences in high school principals' leadership styles* (Unpublished doctoral dissertation). University of the Pacific, Stockton, CA.

Jefferson, J.T. (2006). *Changes in African American urban high school principals' leadership behavior in an era of No Child Left Behind* (Unpublished doctoral dissertation). Seton Hall University, South Orange, NJ.

Johnson, L. (2006). "Making her community a better place to live": Culturally responsive urban school leadership in historical context. *Leadership and Policy in Schools, 5*(1), 19–36.

Johnson, T. (2006). *A phenomenological study of African American educational leaders* (Unpublished doctoral dissertation). Walden University, Minneapolis, MN.

Jones, A.D. (2010). *Leadership and spirituality: The indivisible leadership of African American school administrators as pastors* (Unpublished doctoral dissertation). Iowa State University, Ames, IA.

Kelley, G. J. (2012). *How do principals' behaviors facilitate or inhibit the development of a culturally relevant learning community?* (Unpublished doctoral dissertation). Indiana State University, Terre Haute, IN.

Khalifa, M.A. (2008). *"Give me the worst of them, and I'll make them the best": An ethnographic study of a successful alternative school for at-risk African American children* (Unpublished doctoral dissertation). Michigan State University, East Lansing, MI.

Kuykendall, C. (1991). *Improving black student achievement by enhancing students' self image.* Chevy Chase, MD: Mid-Atlantic Equity Center.

Ladson-Billings, G. (2009). *The dreamkeepers: Successful teachers of African American children.* San Francisco, CA: John Wiley & Sons.

Lee, R. (2007). *How principals promote a culturally relevant learning environment to improve black student achievement in urban elementary schools* (Unpublished doctoral dissertation). Georgia Southern University, Statesboro, GA.

Loder, T.L. (2005). African American women principals' reflections on social change, community, othermothering, and Chicago public school reform. *Urban Education, 40*(3), 298–320.

Lomotey, K. (1987). Black principals for Black students: Some preliminary observations. *Urban Education, 22*(2), 173–181.

Lomotey, K. (1989a). *African-American principals: School leadership and success.* Westport, CT: Greenwood Press.

Lomotey, K. (1989b). Cultural diversity in the urban school: Implications for principals. *National Association of Secondary School Principals (NASSP) Bulletin, 73*(521), 81–85.

Lomotey, K. (1993). African American principals: Bureaucrat/administrators and ethno-humanists. *Urban Education, 27*(4), 395–412.

Lopez, R. (2011). The impact of involvement of African American parents on students' academic achievement. *Journal of Multiculturalism in Education, 7*(1), n.p.

Mack, Y.S. (2010). *Leading school improvement: African American women principals in urban educational settings* (Unpublished doctoral dissertation). University of Cincinnati, Cincinnati, OH.

Miles Brown, T.M. (2009). *The perceptions of African American women principals who have been influential in public education* (Unpublished doctoral dissertation). Robert Morris University, Moon Township, PA.

Miller, O.P. (2011). *A phenomenological case study of a principal leadership: The influence of Mr. Clark's leadership on students, teachers, and administrators at Eastside High School* (Unpublished doctoral dissertation). Georgia State University, Atlanta, GA.

Milner, H.R. (2012). But what is urban education? *Urban Education, 47*(3), 556–561.

Morris, J.E. (2004). Can anything good come from Nazareth? Race, class, and African American schooling and community in the urban south and Midwest. *American Educational Research Journal, 41*(1), 69–112.

Noddings, N. (1992). *The challenge to care in schools: An alternative approach to education.* New York, NY: Teachers College Press.

Peters, A.L. (2012). Leading through the challenge of change: African American women principals on small school reform. *International Journal of Qualitative Studies in Education, 25*(1), 23–38.

Petitt, J. (2012, February 12). Achievement gap: It's still about race; In American society, we can't avoid the fact that socioeconomic disparities are racial disparities. *The Baltimore Sun*, n.p.

Pollard, D.S. (1997). Race, gender, and educational leadership: Perspectives from African American principals. *Educational Policy, 11*(3), 353–374.

Randolph, A.W. (2004). The memories of an all-Black northern urban school: Good memories of leadership, teachers, and the curriculum. *Urban Education, 39*(6), 596–620.

Reed, L., & Evans, A. (2008). "What you see is [not always] what you get!" Dispelling race and gender leadership assumptions. *International Journal of Qualitative Studies in Education, 21*(5), 487–499.

Reitzug, U.C., & Patterson, J. (1998). "I'm not going to lose you!" Empowerment through caring in an urban principal's practice with students. *Urban Education, 33*(2), 150–181.

Ryan, W. (1970). *Blaming the victim.* (rev., updated ed.). New York, NY: Vintage Books.

Sanchez, J.E., Thornton, B., & Usinger, J. (2009). Increasing the ranks of minority principals. *Educational Leadership, 67*(2), n.p.

Schott Foundation for Public Education. (2012). *The urgency of now: The Schott 50 state report on public education and black males, 2012.* Retrieved from http://www.blackboysreport.org/urgency-of-now.pdf

Sledge, J.R., & Morehead, P. (2006, February). Tolerated failure or missed opportunities and potentials for teacher leadership in urban schools? *Current Issues in Education [On-line], 9*(3). Retrieved from http://cie.ed.asu.edu/volume9/number3/

Tillman, L. (2004). African American principals and the legacy of *Brown*. *Review of Research in Education, 28*(1), 101–146.

Tillman, L.C. (Ed.). (2009). *Sage Handbook of African American education.* Thousand Oaks, CA: Sage Publications.

Walker, V.S., & Byas, U. (2003). The architects of Black schooling in the segregated south: The case of one principal leader. *Journal of Curriculum and Supervision, 19*(1), 54–72.

Williams, I. (2012). Race and the principal pipeline: The prevalence of minority principals in light of a largely white teacher workforce. Unpublished manuscript.

Section VI
Curriculum and Instruction

19

Culturally Responsive Teaching Principles, Practices, and Effects

Geneva Gay

Persistent achievement disparities among students and enrollment patterns in urban schools demand serious consideration of culturally responsive teaching. Minimally, this consideration should examine why it is important to incorporate the cultural heritages, experiences, and perspectives of ethnically diverse students into educational programs and practices designed for them, how this can be accomplished in practice, and what consequences it generates. This discussion addresses these issues. It begins with a brief overview of the urban education context and why culturally responsive teaching is a good fit for it. This is followed by a summary of major assumptions, attributes, and principles of culturally responsive teaching. Third, some samples of culturally responsive programs and practices are examined. They target a variety of ethnic student populations, including African Americans, Asian/Pacific Islanders, Latino Americans, Native Americans, and Native Alaskans, and different levels of schooling (elementary, secondary, and college). In addition to describing the features of these practices, the results they accomplish in improving student achievement are presented. These achievements are academic, social, cultural, and personal.

Interest and involvement in culturally responsive teaching have increased significantly over the last 10 to 15 years. This growth is apparent, first, across all levels of education from elementary schools to colleges and universities; includes various disciplinary domains within education, including math, science, and technology; and involves areas of study beyond education, such as health care, social work, and business. Second, culturally responsive teaching is gaining international momentum in countries in Europe, Asia, Africa, and South America, as well as Canada, Australia, and New Zealand. A third indicator of the growing prominence of culturally responsive teaching is its expanding body of scholarship. A Google search listed 259,000 entries that included books, articles, book chapters, YouTube visuals, course descriptions, and professional development sessions. A search of the University of Washington libraries worldwide website produced over 1,400 entries. The first 56 of these were books and the next 120 were articles that included specific references to culturally responsive teaching in their titles, and were published between the mid-1990s and 2012. Undoubtedly, the content of some of these resources is tangential to the generally accepted conceptualizations of culturally responsive teaching. For example, some of the citations focus on linguistic and intellectual diversity, immigration, and special education, while issues of race, class, and ethnicity as they relate to facilitating learning are the primary concerns of culturally responsive teaching. Yet, the number of resources listed itself is noteworthy.

The Urban Context and Culturally Responsive Teaching

Although culturally responsive teaching is applicable to many different school contexts and student populations, those in urban centers are its primary targets of concern. The educational conditions of underachieving students of color provided the motivation for the beginning of culturally responsive teaching, and they continue to be its driving force. This is so because the school performance of these students is still far from adequate. Many students of color are not performing as well as they could in any school settings where teaching and learning are approached solely from the perspectives of Eurocentric values, assumptions, beliefs, and methodologies (Hawley & Nieto, 2010; Kozol, 2005; Tatum, 2007). However, the situation is the worst in urban schools with high concentrations of ethnically and culturally diverse student populations.

While the number of students of color in urban schools is increasing, their achievement is not keeping pace with these demographics. According to a 2010 report from the National Center for Education Statistics (NCES) on the characteristics of the 100 largest public school districts in the United States, Latino Americans and African Americans combined account for 63% of the student enrollments. The percentage per district ranged from 55% to 95%. With the exceptions of some Asian Americans (such as Japanese, Chinese, Koreans, and Taiwanese), students of color perform lower on all measures and indicators of achievement, including academic knowledge and skills, school persistence and completion, efficacy and agency, school discipline, and ethnic identity and cultural pride (NCES, 2012). The patterns of poor performance are comprehensive and consistent in that they prevail across time, location, schools, achievement type, and student demographics (www.centerforpubliceducation.org/).

National data on course-taking for 2008–2009 appeared to deviate somewhat from these trends. They indicated that all racial groups are taking more high-level math and science classes and advanced placement (AP) exams. However, the good news was not without qualification. The patterns of performance in these courses and exams were consistent with long-established ones in other performance areas, such as national and state academic achievement tests. Asian and European Americans consistently performed the highest in subjects tested (reading, math, science, U.S. History, geography, and civics), and African Americans the lowest on these measures of achievement across all grade levels assessed. Scores on the 2008 AP tests were illustrative of these trends. The highest possible score was 5.0, with 3.0 required to receive credit. The average scores by specific ethnic groups were 3.08 for Asian Americans, 2.96 for European Americans, 2.42 for Latino Americans, 2.39 for Native Americans and Alaskans, and 1.91 for African Americans (NCES, 2012). Other measures and indicators of school achievement follow similar patterns, with the lowest-performance records shared or traded among African Americans, Latinos, and Native/Alaskan Americans. For instance, even though high school dropout rates are declining for all ethnic groups, they are much higher for Latinos, and their graduation rates are significantly lower (64% in 2011) (http://www.centerforpubliceducation.org/).

These composite data indicate what some scholars have called school "resegregation" (Boger & Orfield, 2005; Darling-Hammond, 2010; Tatum, 2007), and the persistent and pervasive disparities in educational achievement. That is, U.S. school enrollments are concentrated by race, ethnicity, and economics, and students of color in urban areas are not receiving education comparable in quality to their peers in other residential locations (Center for Public Education, 2012).

Achieving educational equity and excellence for ethnically and racially marginalized students is the mission and mandate of culturally responsive teaching. This instructional technique is based on the premise that the underachievement of massive numbers of students of color is caused and perpetuated more by educational programs and practices that do not respect and reflect their cultures, perspectives, and experiences than their individual learning interests, motivation, and abilities (Gay, 2010b; Ladson-Billings, 2009; Lee, 2007; Valenzuela, 1999). Some fundamental changes need to occur in the education systems rather than blaming students and placing the burden of failure solely on them.

No one part of these systems alone can address the complexities of ethnic, racial, and cultural diversity in education adequately. However, classroom instruction plays a critical role. Much research conducted over the years shows that the interaction students have with teachers is a major determinant of their learning quality. Educational researchers and scholars (e.g., Au, 2006; Banks & Banks, 2004, 2012; Hollins, 1996; Pai, Alder, & Shadiow, 2006; Villegas & Lucas, 2002) also point out repeatedly that teaching and learning are sociocultural processes, and learning is more effective when there is a high level of congruence between teaching techniques and the cultural frames of reference of diverse students. For instance, Cohen and Lotan (2004, p. 737) explained, "The necessity of working with diversity is inseparable from the necessity to present intellectually challenging and grade appropriate content in such a way that students experience academic success." Asante (1991/1992) argued similarly in noting that cultural congruency between home and school engenders cultural respect, personal validation, and academic success for diverse students. These explanations support the idea that it is imperative for culturally responsive teaching to be a fundamental part of transforming urban education.

Another reason for making teaching and learning more inclusive of ethnic, racial, and cultural diversity is the demographic divide between students and teachers. It is an indisputable fact that urban students are increasingly racially, ethnically, and linguistically diverse and poor, while their teachers are overwhelmingly White, female, monolingual, and middle class. According to 2010 National Center for Education Statistics reports, in 70 of the 100 largest school districts of the United States (with student populations ranging from 47,000 to 982, 000) Latinos, African Americans, Asian/Pacific Islanders, Native Americans and Alaskans, and bi- or multiracial students constitute more than 50% of the total population, and in 35 that representation is from 75% to 95%. Comparatively, 84% of all public school teachers are European American (a decline from 91% in the late 1980s). Only 7% are African American, 7% are Latino American, and 2% are from other ethnic groups, including Asian/Pacific Islanders and Native American/Alaskans (Feistritzer, 2011). In addition to the disproportional numerical representation of teachers of color compared to students of color other troubling disparities that affect the quality of instructional opportunities and outcomes are apparent as well. For instance, teachers who work in schools with high populations of ethnically and racially diverse and poor students are less experienced and qualified than the national averages; many are not very confident about their preparation for and abilities to teach ethnically, racially, and linguistically diverse students; turnover rates are much higher in urban schools; funding in these schools is significantly lower and instructional resources fewer; and physical facilities are often outdated and/or dilapidated (Darling-Hammond, 2010; Kozol, 1991; Pang & Sablan, 1998). Cochran-Smith (2000, 2004) and Ladson-Billings (2011) attributed much of the high attrition rates among teachers in urban schools to inadequate preparation for teaching in culturally, socially, and ethnically diverse contexts, and what Chubbuck (2008) called "reality shock." That is, the imagined notions of many novices about teaching in urban schools are inconsistent with the complex actualities, As Ladson-Billings (2011, pp. 13–14) explained,

> classrooms are complex organisms. The students bring with them richly textured biographies that go beyond their racial and ethnic categorizations, and their teachers bring their own sets of complexities. Somewhere in the nexus of this humanity, we are charged with

> producing literate, numerate young citizens who are capable of learning more and faster than any generation that has preceded it. This is no small task. To address the challenge of teaching all students well, we must start with the talent pool from which we are drawing individuals who will take on this task. . . . Nearly all of them are European American, lower middle to middle income, English monolingual, suburbanites [who] may see urban teaching as noble and socially important, but it is "too hard" for them. Unfortunately, far too many of them will find themselves taking these "hard" jobs out of economic necessity, and their lack of preparedness will show and be a disservice to yet another generation of poor and disenfranchised students, their families, and their communities. Even among growing numbers of alternatively certified teachers who express a strong desire to teach in difficult-to-staff schools we find poorly prepared teachers who regularly depart—at an alarmingly high rate—from urban schools and classrooms serving poor children of color.

Because of differences in ethnicity, race, culture, and lived experiences students and teachers may not share many points of reference that can be used in urban classrooms to facilitate mastery of academic knowledge and skills. Furthermore, research indicates that curriculum content taught in schools does not give adequate treatment to the experiences and contributions of ethnically diverse groups and individuals (Loewen, 1995; Takaki, 2008). Thus, learning for African, Asian, Latino, and Native American students is compromised by cultural incompatibilities between them and their teachers, and instructional materials used in classrooms (Gay, 2010b).

The ethnic and racial diversity inherent in the urban context and the persistence and magnitude of low achievement demand some fundamentally different approaches to teaching students in urban schools. As Sullivan and A'Vant (2009) explained,

> Given that all demographic indicators suggest that the trend toward multi-cultural populations will only continue, the need to create systems that are responsive to student diversity is imperative. As a society, we cannot afford to undereducate such a substantial portion of students because of the negative implications both for their quality of life and their social contributions, among other things. Indeed, educational attainment is an important determinant of individuals' health, employment and earning potential, civic engagement, and socioeconomic status, all of which have powerful implications for the communities in which they reside. Developing and supporting equitable educational systems is the cornerstone to safeguarding the nation's social, civic, and economic future. (n.p.)

In a 1998 appeal for more teachers of color Richard Riley, then U.S. Secretary of Education, made some observations that were, in effect, an endorsement of culturally responsive teaching. He said,

> If we are to be responsive to the special demands and great opportunities of our nation's pluralistic make-up, . . . we need teachers who can relate to the lives of diverse students, and who can connect those students to a larger world and greater possibilities. . . . Teachers and students bring important cultural differences to the ways in which they think and learn. These differences are important, and they are part of the educational process. We should build on them as we educate ourselves and our children. (pp. 19–20)

Therefore, the nexus of culturally responsive teaching and urban demographics symbolizes the nature and challenge of U.S. ethnic reality and possibility. Urban schools and communities are the meeting grounds of the racial, cultural, and social diversity embodied in the nation's motto of *el pluribus unum*. Educators should embrace this diversity as normative of what is and generative of what can be for promoting equity and excellence in both schools and society at large for diverse individuals and groups. Culturally responsive teaching can facilitate the achievement of these goals.

Major Principles

Culturally responsive teaching uses the cultural orientations, heritages, and background experiences of students of color as referents and resources to improve their school achievement (Gay, 2002, 2010b; Howard, 2010; Ladson-Billings, 1995, 2009; Lee, 2007, 2009; Villegas & Lucas, 2002). Moll (1992), Moll and Gonzáles (2004), and Gonzáles, Moll, and Amanti (2005) called these social, cultural, and experiential resources "funds of knowledge" acquired in homes and communities, and explained how they should be used as leverage in teaching academic knowledge and skills. Shevalier and McKenzie (2012) equated culturally responsive teaching with a code of ethics for pedagogical thought and action. They reasoned that

> Culturally responsive teaching is neither simply about "what" or "how" nor solely an abstract, theoretical "why." It is really the nexus of "what," "how," and "why," and is, at its core, about ethics. It reflects *a system of moral principles* aligned with the interrelated components of a care-based education model. Each component recognizes that overall *rules of conduct* for the classroom arise through caring relationships that acknowledge, speak to, and develop *moral principles* in unique individuals. The ultimate goal and purpose of these interrelated components is to create and sustain *values relating to human conduct,* such that each individual reflects on and develops his or her actions as they pertain to *the rightness of certain actions* and *the goodness of motives and ends.* (p. 1100) (Emphases in original)

Culturally responsive teaching has two major pathways, with many different sites for change within each. One is primarily pedagogical in that it uses cultural knowledge about ethnically diverse students in teaching them school knowledge and skills. The other one is centered more in curriculum since it involves teaching all students more knowledge about the cultures, experiences, challenges, and accomplishments of racially and ethnically diverse groups. Elsewhere, I conceptualized this dual agenda as teaching *to and through* ethnic, racial, and cultural diversity (Gay, 2010a). "Through" is the goal of the first pathway, and "to" is the emphasis of the second. Some comments made by McCoy (2005) epitomized these two key aspects of culturally responsive teaching as they relate to Native Americans:

> We want our children to be educated Indians. We want them to know who they are—and we want their teachers and classmates to know who they are, too. We want our history, our art, our music, and our contributions included in the curriculum. We want our students to be held to high academic expectations, to be encouraged to enroll in Advanced Placement classes, and to be taught by adults who respect their potential and expect them to succeed. And, yes, we want our children to learn the skills they will need to get good jobs. . . . But, we know our students will only learn these skills in an educational system where our culture, our history, and our identity are respected rather than treated as a deviation from the norm. (p. B7)

The need for and intentions of culturally responsive teaching, or some facsimile of it, have been a part of the discourse on educating various racially and ethnically diverse student groups for many years. However, the nomenclature itself is relatively new, as is its increasing momentum in various disciplines, both nationally and internationally. For example, various kinds of ethnic-centric educational ideologies and practices that have occurred over the years include elements similar to culturally responsive teaching. Among these are ethnic groups' language schools, cultural arts and literature projects, street academies, Afrocentric education, and the cultural pride and racial uplift ideologies of early and mid-20th-century African Americans like Mary McLeod Bethune, Carter G. Woodson, James Baldwin, W.E.B. Dubois, Alain Locke, and Anna Julia Cooper.

Another significant and more directly related antecedent to culturally responsive teaching is multicultural education. In fact, some educators use the two interchangeably. However, Gay (2010b) suggested that while they are closely interrelated, there are some nuanced differences in their scopes and emphases. Multicultural education focuses primarily on *teaching content* (knowledge, values, issues, skills, perspectives, and concepts) *about* ethnic, racial, cultural, and social diversity (Banks & Banks, 2004, 2012; Bennett, 2010). Comparatively, and as characterized by Irvine (2003), Au (1993), Gay (2010b), Villegas and Lucas (2002), Tharp and Gallimore (1988), Ladson-Billings (2009), and Lee (2007), culturally responsive teaching emphasizes *teaching diverse students* through their own ethnic and racial identities, and experiential and cultural frames of reference.

In addition to classroom teaching other aspects of the educational enterprise are objects of culturally responsive reforms as well, including school leadership, counseling, classroom management, performance assessment, and research. Other professions such as social work, health care, religion, law, psychology, and the fine arts also are pursuing reasons and techniques for being culturally responsive to their constituencies. This expanding interest is indicative of growing recognition that the best quality performance opportunities provided for ethnically diverse clienteles are informed by and responsive to their cultural socialization and background experiences. These developments also suggest that culturally responsiveness is multidisciplinary and multidimensional, and offer a wide variety of implementation opportunities. Some scholars have described implications of these attributes as using multiple perspectives, multiple sources, and multiple techniques in examining issues of cultural diversity, and teaching ethnically diverse students (Banks & Banks, 2012; Bennett, 2010; Hollins, King, & Hayman, 1994).

A second major principle of cultural responsive teaching is building bridges for students and teachers to cross cultural borders. Contrary to conventional school practices that impose Eurocentric values and norms as the only standards of acceptability, or what Valenzuela (1999) calls subtractive schooling for students of color, culturally responsive teaching emphasizes students learning skills to function in multiple cultural settings, contexts, and systems. These include helping ethnically diverse students to be more proficient in their home or indigenous cultures, in mainstream culture, school culture (which is a variant of mainstream society culture), and other nonmainstream cultures. Functionally, this means students of color need to acquire cultural style shifting skills (Lee, 1993, 2007; Taylor, 1989; Wheeler & Swords, 2006), and teachers should facilitate these processes by being cultural brokers for them (Gentemann & Whitehead, 1983). Thus, developing multicultural competencies for both students and teachers is a major component of culturally responsive teaching.

A third guiding principle of culturally responsive teaching argues that race, ethnicity, and culture are inherent features of humanity and U.S. society, and they matter profoundly in teaching and learning. While their causes, meanings, and manifestations may be debatable, their existence is undeniable. As Hawley and Nieto (2010, p. 66), explained,

> when it comes to maximizing learning opportunities and outcomes for students from ethnically and racially diverse backgrounds, race and ethnicity matter . . . in two important ways. They affect how students respond to instruction and curriculum, and they influence teachers' assumptions about how students learn and how much students are capable of learning.

Pai, Adler, and Shadiow (2006), Erickson (2010), Spindler and Spindler (1994), and Gay and Kirkland (2003) suggested further that because culture influences how teachers and students think, believe, and behave, it is imperative for educators to understand its role in the design, implementation, and effects of curriculum and instruction for students and for themselves. Erickson (2010) added that

> everything in education relates to culture—to its acquisition, its transmission, and its invention. Culture is in us and all around us, just as the air we breathe. In its scope and distribution it is personal, familial, communal, institutional, societal, and global. Yet, . . . we do not think much about the structure and characteristics of culture as we use it, just as we do not think reflectively about any familiar tool in the midst of its use. (p. 35)

The taken-for-granted nature of culture, and the fact that nonmainstream cultures are not routinely and positively present in school procedures, programs, and practices underscore the importance of making cultural differences explicit in educating ethnically and racially diverse students. This is what culturally responsive teaching does. Consequently, teachers need to be multiculturally conscious and competent, as well as know how to "transform diversity into a pedagogical asset" (Moll & Gonzáles, 2004, p. 699).

A fourth principle of culturally responsive teaching is shifting the ideological and methodological axis in teaching underachieving students of color from problems to possibilities. Much of the discourse and praxis about closing the achievement gaps for students of color are grounded in pathological orientations toward ethnic, racial, and cultural diversity. That is, the reform efforts start with assumptions about what students of color do not have and cannot do, especially if they attend urban schools. The litany of deficits includes being poor, coming from a "broken family," not being motivated to learn, living in households that lack high levels of literacy stimulation, parents or guardians who are nonsupportive of school efforts, being nonnative speakers of English, and living in violent communities. A major fallacy is at play here—that failure indices are reasonable sites to launch reforms to improve the school success of students of color. Instead, it is more likely that success, not failure, generates subsequent success (Boykin, 2002; Hawley & Nieto, 2010). Precedents for this logic exist in other educational ideologies such as scaffolding, or building on students' prior knowledge and experiences, expanding horizons of learning, and zones of proximal development. Yet, many educators repeatedly fail to apply them to teaching low-achieving students of color, and seemingly without any concern for the double standards.

Culturally responsive teaching translates these general principles into practices within the contexts of ethnic, racial, and cultural diversity. It operates on assumptions that teachers' attitudes toward and beliefs about various kinds of diversity shape their instructional behaviors toward students from these backgrounds and identities. It is also true that students' beliefs and attitudes about their own and others' culture, ethnicity, and raciality can affect their learning behaviors either positively or negatively (Ayers, 2004; Bennett, 2010; Gay 2010a, 2010b; Nieto, 2005; Smith, Skarbek, & Hurst, 2005). Ayers (2004) illustrated the power of these relationships and the importance of their careful scrutiny as part of culturally responsive teaching in his observations that "we are, each of us, grounded in a context, . . . born in a race and place . . . [yet] race is unspeakable [and] we are rendered speechless" (pp. 65–66) by it. Nieto (2005, p. 217) added that the prevailing questionable attitudes teachers have toward ethnic and cultural diversity are understandable (although often intolerable) since they "pick up the same messages and misconceptions that we all do" (p. 217) from living in a racist society. Yet, teachers and students do not have to be voiceless about, prejudiced toward, or intimidated by ethnic, racial, and cultural diversity. They can learn to speak their thoughts about cultural diversity, scrutinize their related beliefs and behaviors, and transform them, both personally and professionally (Cochran-Smith, 2000; Gay, 2002, 2003; McLean Donaldson, 2001).

I proposed a series of critical reflection questions for teachers to ask of themselves regarding their beliefs about diversity, analyze how they are manifested in behavior and the consequences of them, and examine the feasibility of various alternations. Among them were: (1) What do I believe are the underlying causes of achievement difficulties of students from different ethnic backgrounds?; (2) Am I able and willing to articulate and critique these beliefs?; and (3) Can I detect specific beliefs about different ethnic groups embedded in my instructional programs and practices, and interpersonal relationships with students? (Gay, in press). Thus, developing reflective and reflexive critical cultural consciousness is a major aspect of preparation for effective culturally responsive teaching (Gay & Kirkland, 2003). To facilitate these examinations and transformations, culturally responsive teaching promotes ideological paradigms that focus on the strengths of diverse students rather than weaknesses, possibilities instead of problems, and institutional responsibilities instead of merely individual indictments. They are conveyed through such principles as incompatibility between the cultures of school and the communities of diverse students; power, productivity, and creativity in marginalized communities, families, and students; resilience of ethnically diverse people; and the positive benefits of affirming cultural diversity in teaching and learning (Banks & Banks, 2004, 2012; Bennett, 2010; Boykin, 2002; Gay 2010b; Grant & Sleeter, 2011).

Conceptual Attributes

Culturally responsive teaching gives practical meaning to equalizing educational opportunities for ethnically diverse students without them having to mimic mainstream European Americans, or repress and deny their own cultural heritages. It redefines equality as comparable quality rather than identical learning experiences for African, Asian, European, Latino, and Native Americans (Banks & Banks, 2004; Bennett, 2010; Gay, 2010b; Howard, 2010; Ladson-Billings, 2009; Lee, 2007, 2009). If, for example, the scientific contributions of Europeans Americans are considered significant and worthy enough to be taught in schools, then those of other ethnic groups should be taught as well. A similar position is taken on the processes of teaching and learning because students from different ethnic, cultural, and social backgrounds have different learning styles (Hollins et al., 1994; Ramírez & Castañeda, 1974; Shade, 1997). Although not all of this difference is attributed to cultural socialization, much of it is. Consequently, culturally responsive teachers are expected to use a variety of instructional techniques that reflect these differences.

Another important conceptual feature of culturally responsive teaching is its transformative nature. It is not enough to merely insert isolated and sporadic elements of ethnic, racial, and cultural diversity into existing school programs and practices. Instead, the cultural heritages and personal experiences of ethnically diverse students should be used routinely as instrumental tools in teaching and learning (Banks & Banks, 2004, 2012; Gay 2002, 2010b; Lipka, Mohatt & the Ciulistet Group, 1998; McCarty, 2002; Moll & González, 2004; Nieto & Bode, 2008). An essential part of this transformation is changing some of the long-held beliefs of educators about the role of racial, ethnic, and cultural diversity in teaching and learning. For example, traditional educational practices give high priority to individual initiative and meritocracy in learning, and use collaborative arrangements only as occasional alternatives. By comparison, students and teachers routinely working together in learning partnerships, groups, and communities, and exposing the hegemonic tendencies of mainstream schooling are habitual elements of culturally responsive teaching. Therefore, as Gay (2010b), Hollins (1996), Pang (2005), Lipka et al. (1998), Lipka, Yanez,

Andrew-Ihrke, and Adam (2009), Au (2006), and Irizarry (2011) suggested, pedagogical flexibility and plurality, and decentering mainstream assumptions about schooling, are fundamental features of culturally responsive teaching, and they require "considerable transformation" and "continuing responsibility" (Wlodkowski & Ginsberg, 1995, p. 286) on the part of teachers.

The transformative nature of culturally responsive teaching also exposes cultural biases embedded in what was once thought to be uncontestable objective knowledge taught in schools. It points out that because all knowledge is socially and culturally constructed, no one ethnic group has a monopoly on it, or can rightfully claim its version of "truth" is universal. Instead, the best way to come closer to teaching all students more accurately and effectively is to provide them with multiple cultural perspectives on knowledge claims made by different disciplines, scholars, and ethnic group experiences (Banks & Banks, 2004, 2012). Hence, academic English should not be taught as the only acceptable form of communication in *all* circumstances. Literary canons presented to students should comprise contributions from African, Asian, Latino, and Native American authors, as well as European Americans. Conceptual names for various developments in U.S. history and life that are inherently hegemonic, such as colonization, settlement, discovery, the Westward Movement, and referring to the United States as "America," are deconstructed and replaced with less Eurocentric privileging language. For example, "multidirectional populations dispersals" or "multiethnic diasporas" replace "the Westward Movement," and thus include the stories of historical and contemporary population distributions of many ethnic groups in the United States on a more egalitarian basis.

The ultimate goal of culturally responsive teaching is the liberation and empowerment of students from the most marginalized groups in urban schools through promoting equity and social justice in education. Equity and empowerment are multidimensional at both personal and academic levels. They include making cultural diversity more evident in the educational process *in intentional and systematic ways,* as well as validating its significance in the lives of individuals, groups, U.S. society at large, and the world. These emphases are designed to free ethnically diverse groups, their cultures, and their contributions from the shackles of invisibility, distortion, and denial that have been foisted upon them for too long.

Furthermore, culturally responsive teaching is a holistic enterprise. It encompasses more than merely transmitting content from textbooks and curriculum guides to students, or even learning new knowledge generated by scholars of color. It also involves a wide range of relationships between teachers and students, and students with students that are social, cultural, academic, moral, and political. Effective teachers of ethnically and racially diverse students must relate to them, simultaneously, as persons and as learners. This idea is illustrated by international and recent immigrant students in their references to teachers they work closely with as their academic mothers and fathers, and peers who are learning partners as their academic brothers and sisters. It also is embedded in the desire of African and Latino American students to establish personal bonds with teachers, and to create social contexts with each other as preludes to academic task performance (Howard 2010; Irizarry, 2011; Shade, 1997).

Another part of this holistic approach to teaching students of color is the need for teachers to be cultural brokers (Gentemann & Whitehead, 1983). Many students of color do not have the social and cultural capital required for school success. They may not know all of the unwritten rules, expectations, and protocols needed to maneuver well in school. Many do not have any significant others in their personal lives, such as older siblings, parents, other family members, or friends who were successful in school, and can pass on tips for doing so informally. As cultural brokers, teachers function as interpreters, negotiators, and advocates for these students and teach them how to navigate multiple cultural systems and contexts. Delpit (2006), Valenzuela (1999), and Howard (2010) explained this culturally responsive principle as ethnically diverse students acquiring the knowledge, skills, and codes (i.e., social and cultural capital) needed to participate fully in mainstream U.S. life while simultaneously maintaining and improving their own cultural expertise, and even constructing and using various degrees of cultural hybridity. Therefore, culturally responsive teaching is based on the belief that teaching and learning go beyond the academic and intellectual, as well as the boundaries of classrooms and schools, to helping students acquire knowledge and skills that serve multiple purposes in many different contexts.

Culturally Responsive Teaching Practice

Scholarship and research on culturally responsive teaching practice are not as extensive as its theory. This may be as much a function of availability as actuality. That is, more practice may be occurring, or at least some facsimile of it, than is being recorded in professional books and journal articles because teachers typically do not write about their classroom instruction. But all of the small body of praxis research and scholarship that does exist cannot be presented in its entirety here because of the focus limitations of this discussion. Since its emphasis is culturally responsive teaching within the context of urban education, only selected samples of practices in urban schools and/or primarily for students of color are presented.

According to Gay (2010b), Villegas and Lucas (2002), Ladson-Billings (2009), and Irvine (2003), culturally responsive teaching includes content, methodologies, relationships, and learning climates. But these components do not have to be distributed equally in any given practice event. Despite this variance, approaches to culturally responsive teaching practice can be organized into three categories based on their primary emphasis. These are (1) teaching content about ethnic, racial, and cultural diversity (i.e., curriculum), (2) using culturally diverse techniques to teach any knowledge and skills to ethnically diverse students (i.e., pedagogy), and (3) creating culturally responsive caring in and climates for learning. These approaches to practice are not mutually exclusive since each one includes some elements of the others. Differences among them are a matter of priority and degree of emphases. Unavoidably, content-based culturally responsive teaching practice includes some aspects of instruction, and climate and caring features are embedded in instruction and content. These categories of practice also are arbitrary and intended only to facilitate discussion, not to be perceived as immutable mandates. Furthermore, the sample practices described below are not intended to be representative of all conceivable possibilities. They are simply indicative of the kind of culturally responsive teaching that is actually occurring with different student populations in different educational locations, as opposed to the theorized and the imagined. In addition to illuminating theory, these practices are opportunities for educators to look critically at both theory and practice juxtaposed to each other, and improve the quality and further development of each.

Content-Based Culturally Responsive Teaching

Analyses of textbooks and other instructional materials indicate that the treatment of ethnic, racial, and cultural diversity has improved over time, but some problems persist. I (2010b, pp. 130–131) summarized some of these problems as follows:

> First, there is an imbalance across ethnic groups of color, with more attention given to African Americans and their experiences. Second, the content included about ethnic issues is rather bland, conservative, conformist, and "safe." . . . contentious issues and individuals are avoided, and the unpleasant sides of society and cultural diversity are either sanitized or bypassed entirely. Third, gender and social class disparities prevail within the representations

> of ethnic groups with preference given to males, the middle class, and events and experiences that are closely aligned with mainstream European American values, beliefs, and standards of behavior. Fourth, textbook discussions about ethnic groups and their concerns are not consistent across time, with contemporary issues being overshadowed by historical ones.

Many culturally responsive teaching practices address these concerns by providing content about different ethnic groups' heritages, cultures, and experiences that are more accurate and authentic. For example, the Multicultural Literacy Program (MLP) used literary texts written by and about different ethnic groups, including Native Americans, Asian Americans, African Americans, Latino Americans, and Native Hawaiians, to teach ethnically diverse K–8 graders multicultural knowledge and sensitivity, along with basic reading and writing skills (Diamond & Moore, 1995). The Webster Grove Writing Project used cultural texts to teach African American culture and literature, and improve the performance of African Americans in grades 6–12 on local district, state, and national writing assessments. It combined African American cultural traits such as personal narratives presented in conversational styles, storytelling, oral language interpretation, and dramatic speech with samples of African American literature in which the authors used similar techniques. Among the authors studied were Langston Hughes, Virginia Hamilton, Alice Walker, Richard Wright, Paul Lawrence Dunbar, and Nikki Giovanni (Krater, Zeni, & Cason, 1994).

McCarty (2002) and Lipka et al. (1998, 2009) described programs that teach indigenous knowledge, language, and cultural practices to Navajo and Alaskan Yup'ik children, respectively. The English-Navajo Language Arts Program is a bilingual/bicultural initiative located at the Navajo Nation's Rough Rock Demonstration School. Materials used for instruction were written by students and teachers themselves in consultation with community elders, and based on local Navajo cultural practices. For example, vocabulary lists and cultural memory stories provided by elders were the primary texts for teaching introductory classes in Navajo language and culture. As the students advanced through the grades, they became more actively involved in conducting oral histories and collecting community stories, and the community elders broadened their participation to include informal classroom teaching along with being cultural resources and consultants (McCarty, 2002).

Lipka and his Yup'ik colleagues used similar techniques in the Math in a Cultural Context (MCC) Project. Teams of university professors and researchers, mathematicians, Yup'ik teachers, and community elders have worked together for more than 20 years to compile information about daily activities in the lives of Alaskan Natives; to identify the math and science skills embedded in them; and to use these cultural texts in teaching school math. The motivations behind these curriculum creation processes, and how they operate in practice address concerns about diverse authentic voices and representations in culturally responsive teaching. Lipka et al. (2009, p. 266) explained them thusly:

> We do not attempt to teach elders' knowledge; elders are best equipped to teach their knowledge. However, what we try to accomplish is an authentic representation of both local and Western knowledge, bringing them together in a new way. . . . This is not necessarily the elders' knowledge nor necessarily typical Western pedagogy. It is an integration of Yup'ik everyday knowledge . . . with Western math and forms of pedagogy. . . . We do this through situating math knowledge in a context familiar to Alaskan students yet novel enough and different enough from national math curriculum to most likely increase students' motivation and access to the material. Thus, issues of culture, power, and creativity are weaved together . . . without losing sight of the critical importance of improving math learning.

The Math in a Cultural Context curriculum includes seven modules (Fish Racks, Star Navigation, Salmon Drying, Berry Picking, Parka Designs, Egg Island, and Smokehouse). These modules are used in 10 urban and rural school districts throughout Alaska. The achievement effects are positive for Yup'iks and students from a wide variety of other ethnic groups. According to Lipka et al. (2009, p. 260), "results consistently and repeatedly show that MCC's curriculum and professional development make a statistically significant difference when compared to comparable control group students using their district's adopted math curriculum."

The goal of the Algebra Project (Moses & Cobb, 2001; Moses, West, & Davis, 2009), which has been in existence since 1985, is to "raise the floor of mathematics literacy" (Moses et al., 2009, p. 242) for students of color performing in the lowest quartile on state and national achievement tests. Initially, it included only African Americans in one urban school but has since expanded to other ethnic groups in both urban and rural schools. The project now operates in school districts in 12 states. Like the Rough Rock English-Navajo Language Arts Program and the Math in a Cultural Context Project, the Transition Curriculum of the Algebra Project resulted from collaborations of multidisciplinary teams that included university mathematicians, Project staff, teacher educators, and classroom teachers. It uses local knowledge and sociocultural experiences in helping students to identify math concepts and skills embedded in activities and events they participate in on a daily basis, such as using public transportation and shopping. Scripted texts are included to model mathematical discourse, demonstrate how mathematics knowledge is constructed, and allow students to practice the language of the discipline as they converse with the mathematicians in the scripts. The project connects mastery of high-level pre-algebra, algebra, and geometry skills to promoting social justice and civil rights. The results show that across school sites and ethnic groups Algebra Project participants have higher test scores than their nonparticipating peers, and enroll more frequently in higher-level college preparatory mathematics courses (Moses et al., 2009). Another indicator of its success in the higher levels of participation in antiracist and social justice activities among graduates of the program (Moses & Cobb, 2001).

The curriculum of the Haskell Indian Nations University illustrates how culturally responsive teaching through content can be accomplished in higher education. This intertribal university is one of 34 federally recognized tribal colleges and universities (TCUs) located in 13 states. It enrolls students from 160 tribal groups (http://www.haskell.edu). The mission of Haskell University is to empower Native American and Native Alaskan scholars for leadership and service to Native communities and the world. This is accomplished by the university promoting "principles of sovereignty and self-determination through a culturally-based holistic lifelong learning environment that upholds . . . traditional American Indian/Alaskan Native cultural values of respect, cooperation, honesty, and responsibility" (http://www.haskell.edu). All students are required to take courses in American Indian/Native American cultural citizenship and contemporary issues, along with their areas of professional specialization. Options include Indian Law and Legislation, Tribal Sovereignty, Tribal Resources and Economic Development, and Indian poetry, art, music, and literature (http://www.haskell.edu).

In their review of culturally responsive education projects in several different Native American and Alaskan Native communities (including the Navajos, Yup'iks, Utes, and Hualapais), Deyhle and Comeau (2009) reported several results that are similar to culturally responsive curriculum projects involving other ethnic groups. In addition to teaching Native American students from their respective communities knowledge about and pride in their own ethnic groups' languages, heritages, and cultures, these techniques improve feelings of personal efficacy, academic achievement, and school persistence rates; recognize the significance of elders as mentors, instructors, and keepers of indigenous cultural knowledge; challenge the devaluing of indigenous knowledge and culture; alter historical claims of knowledge, authority, and power in education; and promote ethnic self-determination. In other words, these culturally responsive efforts lay important foundations for the educational, social, cultural, and political transformation of different Native American communities.

Pedagogy-Based Cultural Responsiveness

Approaches to culturally responsive teaching that are nested in the instructional dynamics of classrooms are more prominent and clearly constructed in research and practice than the content-based ones. They illuminate the conceptual ideas of teaching ethnically and racially diverse students *through* who they are, using cultural knowledge to inform instructional decisions and actions, and establishing congruency between classroom instructional techniques and the learning styles of different ethnic groups (Gay, 2010b; Lee, 2007; Shade, 1997; Shevalier & McKenzie, 2012; Tharp & Gallimore, 1988). Again space does not allow for a thorough discussion of all of the evidence that exists about the forms and effects of these approaches. Only a few examples are included to indicate patterns and trends.

One of the most impressive methods-based approaches to culturally responsive teaching was the Kamehameha Early Education Program (KEEP), a language arts project designed to improve the reading performance of underachieving Native Hawaiian students in the early elementary grades. It lasted for 24 years and accomplished its goal of improving performance on standardized tests from the 20th percentile to the 50th percentile. The results consistently exceeded this level. The project also increased motivation for, ownership of, and active engagement in learning, and the cultural pride and personal self-esteem of Native Hawaiian students. Throughout its duration a team of researchers and scholars worked with the KEEP teachers to help them understand Native Hawaiian culture, develop instructional techniques compatible with the cultural values and interactional styles, and to record the evolvement of the project. Some of these were Gallimore, Boggs, and Jordan (1974), Boggs, Watson-Gegeo, and McMillen (1985), Tharp and Gallimore (1988), and Au (1993). The intersection between Native Hawaiian cultural socialization and classroom practices generated teaching techniques such as activity centers, classroom communities of practice, cooperative learning, and frequent opportunities for students to engage in a form of cultural discourse and participation structures called "talk story" or "co-narration" (several people working collaboratively *in the moment* to create dialogue and construct meaning).

Lee (2001, 2007, 2009) created a technique she called cultural modeling to teach underachieving secondary school African Americans high-order literary interpretation and criticism skills. She combined cultural texts and affirmation of indigenous cultural competence with contrastive analysis to teach the students how to transfer skills from their social and cultural communicative practices into academic studies of literature. This was accomplished by first teaching students to analyze their own social discourse styles, and then identifying cultural attributes and literary techniques embedded in them such as irony, simile, analogical reasoning, figurative language, and metaphors. Second, they were taught how authors use these techniques in constructing various genres of literature. Third, the students were then taught to recognize parallels between how they talk on a daily basis and the writing techniques of different authors. To improve the interest appeal of the tasks Lee used books (i.e., "cultural texts") written by African American authors such as Zora Neale Hurston, Alice Walker, and Toni Morrison. Students' mastery of high-level literary techniques and understanding of their sociocultural discourse styles improved significantly.

In a later variation of this technique, the Cultural Modeling Narrative Project, with elementary African American students Lee wanted to determine if using familiar cultural rhetorical techniques and artifacts would improve narrative writing skills. Cultural data sets and scripts, such as lyrics of popular African American music and replicas of paintings by contemporary African American artists, were used to identify, analyze, and practice recognizing these techniques, and then converting them into the students' own self-composed narrative texts. The results validated the premise—students demonstrated more interest in and engagement with the cultural data sets used as learning prompts, and incorporated familiar cultural discourse features more fluidly and coherently into the narrative scripts they wrote (Lee, 2007; Lee, Rosenfeld, Mendenhall, Rivers, & Tynes, 2004). Data from KEEP, Cultural Modeling, the English-Navajo Language Arts Program, Math in a Cultural Context, and the Algebra Project confirmed the theory that the cultural funds of knowledge of ethnically and racially diverse students facilitate learning academic skills.

Culturally Responsive Teaching Through Caring and Climate

Ideologically, caring and climate are very viable and generally accepted avenues for culturally responsive teaching practice. But they are difficult to describe in actuality because they are so contextually and temporally specific, and deal with individual feelings and attitudes that can change from moment to moment. In explaining this paradox I noted,

> Caring is one of those things that most educators agree is important in working effectively with students, but they are hard-pressed to characterize it in actual practice, or to put a functional face on it that goes beyond feelings of empathy and emotional attachment. Feelings are important, but culturally responsive caring . . . is much more. It focuses on caring *for* not *about* the personal well-being and academic success of ethnically diverse students, with a clear understanding that the two are interrelated. While *caring about* conveys feelings of concern about one's state of being, *caring for* is active engagement in doing something to positively affect it. Thus, it encompasses a combination of concern, compassion, commitment, responsibility, and action. (Emphasis in original) (Gay, 2010b, p. 48)

A noteworthy example of how culturally responsive caring and climates facilitate learning for African American students is Historically Black Colleges and Universities (HBCUs). There are more than 100 HBCUs across 20 states, Washington, DC, and the Virgin Islands. Most of these institutions are located in the Southeastern region of the United States. Many of their students are first-generation college attendees from low socioeconomic backgrounds. Yet, these institutions have produced impressive legacies of success with African American students who do not meet admissions requirements at many predominately White institutions (PWIs), and are considered by some measures to be unlikely to complete college at all, not accomplish outstanding records of achievement in high-status professional careers and positions of leadership. Although HBCUs constitute only 3% of all U.S. institutions of higher education, they produce 20% of all undergraduate degrees earned by African Americans. Their graduate and professional studies records are even more impressive. HBCUs have produced 40% of all African American engineers; 75% of PhDs; 75% of military officers; 85% of federal judges; 50% of public school teachers; and 85% of African American physicians (Thurgood Marshall College Fund, n.d.). HBCUs vary in programmatic quality and success records but, generally, they graduate African Americans who are competitive in corporate, research, academic, governmental, and military arenas.

What accounts for this success? Allen (1992), Fleming (1991), Clay (2011), and the U.S. Commission on Civil Rights (2006) attributed much of it to caring and supportive relationships between students and faculty, and the validating cultural environments that exist on the campuses of HBCUs. According to Allen, achievement records are strong because students are surrounded by social and political involvement; expectations for high academic achievement; cultural affiliations; ethnic pride; and commitments to community services. The students also have more positive relationships with faculty, and experience strong feelings of personal engagement, institutional attachment, acceptance, and encouragement. Clay (2011) added that performance is high among African American students at HBCUs because academics are complemented with healthy social relationships and occur in environments replete with cultural heritage, cultural texts, and identity affirmation. Furthermore, African American students welcome and respond positively to the chance to live in a Black college community, to normalize Blackness, and to embrace the personal and cultural meaning of the upward mobility that college education enables.

These scholarly claims are confirmed by the personal experiences of alumni of Historically Black Colleges and Universities as evident by the informal conversations I had with 10 of them (Gay, 2010b). The individuals included males and females who attended different types of HBCUs (large and small, public and private; single gender and co-ed, religiously affiliated and secular) at different times and in different locations. All were involved in professional careers, and were either graduate students at predominately White institutions (PWIs) or had recently completed advanced degrees at the time the conversations occurred. Their explanations for why studying at HBCUS was effective for them included the following:

- There is a commitment to educating the whole person. This is evident in their promotion of intellectual knowledge and skills, personal self-esteem, psychosocial development, cultural competence, and economic productivity.
- Students are taught formally and through modeling that cultural, political, and civic responsibility comes with educational attainment.
- HBCUs promote and demonstrate the idea that college-educated African Americans are morally obligated to "give back" to less fortunate African American individuals and communities.
- HBCUS provide opportunities and assistance for African Americans students to clarify their ethnic identities, to know themselves, and to learn their cultures and heritages.
- These are places when African American students do not have to always be on the defensive and standing in readiness to resist racism and other attacks on their human dignity and worth, to be part of "the majority," and to be immersed in communities and legacies of success, respect, confidence, and productivity.
- HBCUS provide refuge, recovery, reconnection, and replenishing opportunities for African American students.
- HBCUs teach and model social, cultural, and professional etiquette and decorum, and demonstrate pride in and honor for African American racial identify, cultural heritage, and institutional affiliation (Gay, 2010b).

These comments affirmed Davis's (1998) observations that HBCUs are sites of African American cultural capital. By this he meant acquiring cultural knowledge, adhering to culturally acceptable values and behaviors, establishing cultural and academic connections, and communal identity and reciprocity are routine features of the education students who attend these institutions receive. They permeate the entire ecological setting from "the more explicit, direct instruction of proper etiquette and public social behavior, to the less obvious integration of African American literature and history in the curriculum" (Davis, 1998, p. 149). Therefore, HBCUs embody multiple aspects of the caring and climate components of culturally responsive teaching in their institutional ethos, instructional practices, daily campus life, and relationships among faculty and students.

Conclusion

The goal of culturally responsive teaching is to liberate ethnically and racially diverse students from the shackles of academic, social, personal, civic, and cultural underachievement. Its theoretical conceptualizations are quite comprehensive and compelling, but the body of research on its actual practice is still relatively small. However, the results of the actual studies are impressive and encouraging. Consistently across various types, locations, and student populations, culturally responsive teaching produces positive results in multiple domains, including improved academic performance on typically used measures of achievement such as standardized test scores, course-taking trends, and frequency and quality of engagement in learning tasks. Culturally responsive teaching also improves the ethnic pride, cultural affiliation, self-esteem, cultural competence, and personal efficacy and agency of students from various ethnic and racial backgrounds. All students also benefit from learning about other cultures as well as their own. These results are particularly striking for some of the most educationally and economically marginalized students—that is, those who are poor, of color, and attend urban schools.

Therefore, as the preceding discussion demonstrated, culturally responsive teaching contributes significantly to closing the achievement gaps for underserved student populations. While this is not an easy task, or a popular course of action to pursue, it is both pragmatically and pedagogically sound. Culturally responsive teaching is pragmatic because it is based on the fact that all students and teachers are cultural beings, and their cultural differences make a profound difference in teaching and learning. Consequently, it is a pedagogical mandate to evoke diverse cultural frames of reference in teaching diverse students of color, who are first and foremost human beings. Their humanity, culture, and education are inseparably connected rather than being mutual exclusive.

Culturally responsive teaching accepts this reality as an indisputable fact, and uses it as leverage in teaching diverse students to improve their achievement in multiple ways and on multiple levels. The extent to which it is institutionalized and implemented widely is the degree to which learning opportunities and outcomes will be transformed for African, Latino, Asian, and Native American students in urban schools and elsewhere. This is a challenging mandate but it can and must be done. The negative consequences of continuing to do otherwise are too great to take the risks for the students impacted directly and for society at large. Thus, culturally responsive teaching offers renewed hope, positive possibilities, and new directions to pursue in revitalizing, reenergizing, uplifting, and equalizing learning opportunities and outcomes for students of color in urban schools.

But, this hope and possibility need to be cultivated further, deliberately, and intentionally. Several avenues provide opportunities to do so in theory, research, and practice. Among them are the following:

- Because culture, the major ideological and operational anchor of culturally responsive teaching, is very complicated and strongly contested, more critical analyses and detailed descriptions are needed of how it operates for different ethnic groups generally, and in learning situations specifically.
- More conceptual clarifications are needed of the meanings of ideological principles of culturally responsive teaching in different referential contexts, such as for specific groups (i.e., Japanese Americans, Vietnamese Americans, East Indian Americans, etc.) within general ethnic categories (i.e., Asian Americans), and identifiers beyond race and ethnicity.
- More examinations of how culturally responsive teaching is affected by and influences within and across ethnic group differences by such variables as age, gender, and social class are needed.

- Explications of how concepts, principles, and techniques of culturally responsive teaching should be nuanced differently based on level of schooling, location of schools, and demographic compositions of classrooms are needed. For example, how do the challenges of and invitations for culturally responsive teaching differ in monoracial and multiracial learning environments?
- Explorations of how teachers' ethnic, racial, and gender identities, professional preparation, and years and locations of professional experience affect their understanding and implementation of culturally responsive teaching are needed.
- More explanations of and research on culturally responsiveness in domains of the educational enterprise other than classroom teaching, such as policy making; guidance and counseling; performance assessment of students and professional personnel; school administration and leadership; support services; school-family-community relationships; student-student interactions; and instructional resources, including textbooks and computer programs, are needed.
- More research on culturally responsive teaching in a wider range of subjects, and as implemented in regular classroom instruction instead of special projects, is also needed.
- Since culturally responsive teaching is a composite and comprehensive endeavor, more descriptive, theoretical, research, and practical details are needed on its different components, such as communication, learning climates, caring, relationships, and ethics.
- Despite its increasing popularity, significant resistance to culturally responsive teaching exists among classroom teachers and other educators. The causes and types of this resistance should be carefully scrutinized, and responsive strategies developed, implemented, and evaluated.
- More detailed explanations, with supportive research evidence, are needed on the effects of culturally responsive teaching on different types of achievement for different categories of students.

References

Allen, W. (1992). The color of success: African American college student outcomes at predominately White and historically Black public colleges and universities. *Harvard Educational Review, 62*(1), 26–44.

Asante, M.K. (1991/1992). Afrocentric curriculum. *Educational Leadership, 49*(4), 28–31.

Au, K.P. (1993). Literacy instruction in multicultural settings. Belmont, CA: Wadsworth/Thomson.

Au, K.H. (2006). *Multicultural issues and literacy achievement,* Mahwah, NJ: Lawrence Erlbaum Associates.

Ayers, W. (2004). *Teaching the personal and the political: Essays on hope and justice.* New York, NY: Teachers College Press.

Banks, J.A., & Banks, C.A.M. (Eds.). (2004). *Handbook of research on multicultural education* (2nd ed.). San Francisco, CA: Jossey-Bass.

Banks, J.A., & Banks, C.A.M. (Eds.). (2012). *Multicultural education: Issues and perspectives* (8th ed.). Hoboken, NJ: Wiley.

Bennett, C.I. (2010). *Comprehensive multicultural education: Theory and practice* (7th ed.). Boston, MA: Pearson/Allyn and Bacon.

Boger, J.C., & Orfield, G. (Eds.). (2005). *School resegregation: Must the South turn back?* Chapel Hill, NC: University of North Carolina Press.

Boggs, S.T., Watson-Gegeo, K., & McMillen, G. (1985). *Speaking, relating, and learning: A study of Native Hawaiian children at home and at school.* Norwood, NJ: Ablex.

Boykin, A.W. (2002). Talent development, deep cultural structure, and school reform: Implications for African American initiatives. In S.J. Denbo & L.M. Beaulieu (Eds.), *Improving schools for African American students: A reader for educational leaders* (pp. 81–94). Springfield, IL: Charles C. Thomas.

Center for Public Education. (2012). *The changing demographics of the United States and their schools.* Retrieved from http://www.centerforpubliceducation.org

Chubbuck, S.M. (2008). A novice teacher's beliefs about socially just teaching: Dialogue of many voices. *New Educator, 4*(4), 309–329.

Clay, P.L. (2011). Historically Black Colleges and Universities facing the future: A fresh look at challenges and opportunities. Retrieved from http://www.Fordfoundation.org/pdfs/Library/Facing-the-Future.pdf

Cochran-Smith, M. (2000). Blind vision: Unlearning racism in teacher education. *Harvard Educational Review, 70*(2), 157–190.

Cochran-Smith, M. (2004). Stayers, leavers, lovers, and dreamers: Insights about teacher education. *Journal of Teacher Education, 55*(5), 387–392.

Cohen, E.G., & Lotan, R.A. (2004). Equity in heterogeneous classrooms. In J.A. Banks & C.A.M. Banks (Eds.), *Handbook of research on multicultural education* (2nd ed., pp. 736–750). San Francisco, CA: Jossey-Bass.

Darling-Hammond, L. (2010). *The flat world and education: How America's commitment to equity will determine our future.* New York, NY: Teachers College Press.

Davis, J.E. (1998). Cultural capital and the role of historically Black colleges and universities in educational reproduction. In K. Freeman (Ed.), *African American culture and heritage in higher education research and practice* (pp. 143–153). Westport, CT: Praeger.

Delpit, L. (2006). *Other people's children: Cultural conflict in the classroom* (2nd ed.). New York, NY: W.W. Norton.

Deyhle, D., & Comeau K.G. (2009). Connecting the circle in American Indian education. In J.A. Banks (Ed.), *Routledge international companion to multicultural education* (pp. 265–275). New York, NY: Routledge.

Diamond, B.J., & Moore, M.A. (1995). *Multicultural literacy: Mirroring the reality of the classroom.* New York, NY: Longman.

Erickson, F. (2010). Culture in society and in educational practices. In J.A. Banks & C.A.M. Banks (Eds.), *Multicultural education: Issues and perspectives* (7th ed., pp. 33–56). Hoboken, NJ: Wiley.

Feistritzer, C.M. (2011). Profile of teachers in the U.S. Retrieved from http://www.edweek.org/media/pot2011final-blog-pdf

Fleming, J. (1991). *Blacks in college: A comparative study of students' success in Black and White institutions.* San Francisco, CA: Jossey-Bass.

Gallimore, R., Boggs, J.W., & Jordan, C. (1974). *Culture, behavior, and education: A study of Hawaiian-Americans.* Beverly Hills, CA: Sage Publications.

Gay, G. (2002). Preparing for culturally responsive teaching. *Journal of Teacher Education, 53*(2), 106–116.

Gay, G. (Ed.). (2003). *Becoming multicultural educators: Personal journey toward professional agency.* San Francisco, CA: Jossey-Bass.

Gay, G. (2010a). Acting on beliefs in teacher education for cultural diversity. *Journal of Teacher Education, 61*(1–2), 143–152.

Gay, G. (2010b). *Culturally responsive teaching: Theory, research, and practice* (2nd ed.). New York, NY: Teachers College Press.

Gay, G. (2013). Teaching to and through cultural diversity. *Curriculum Inquiry, 43*(1), 48–70.

Gay, G., & Kirkland, K. (2003). Developing cultural critical consciousness and self-reflection in preservice teacher education. *Theory Into Practice, 42*(3), 181–187.

Gentemann, K.M., & Whitehead, T.L. (1983). The cultural broker concept in bicultural education. *Journal of Negro Education, 52*(2), 118–129.

Gonzáles, N., Moll, L.C., & Amanti, C. (Eds.). (2005). *Funds of knowledge: Theorizing practices in households, communities, and classrooms*. Mahwah, NJ: Lawrence Erlbaum Associates.

Grant, C.A., & Sleeter, C.E. (2011). *Doing multicultural education for achievement and equity* (2nd ed.). New York, NY: Routledge.

Haskell Indian Nations University. (2013). Homepage. Retrieved from http://www.haskell.edu.

Hawley, W.D., & Nieto, S. (2010). Another inconvenient truth: Race and ethnicity matter. *Educational Leadership, 68*(3), 66–71.

Hollins, E.R. (1996). *Culture in school learning: Revealing the deep meaning.* Mahwah, NJ: Lawrence Erlbaum Associates.

Hollins, E.R., King, J.E., & Hayman, W.C. (Eds.). (1994). *Teaching diverse populations: Formulating a knowledge base.* Albany, NY: State University of New York Press.

Howard, T.C. (2010). *Why race and culture matter in schools: Closing the achievement gap in America's classrooms.* New York, NY: Teachers College Press.

Irizarry, J.G. (2011). *The Latinization of U.S. schools: Successful teaching and learning in shifting cultural contexts.* Boulder, CO: Paradigm.

Irvine, J.J. (2003). *Educating teachers for diversity: Seeing with a cultural eye.* New York, NY: Teachers College Press.

Kozol, J. (1991). *Savage inequalities: Children in America's schools.* New York, NY: Crown.

Kozol, J. (2005). *The shame of the nation: The restoration of apartheid schooling in America.* New York, NY: Crown.

Krater, J., Zeni, J., & Cason, N.D. (1994). *Mirror images: Teaching writing in black and white.* Portsmouth, NH: Heinemann.

Ladson-Billings, G. (1995). Toward a theory of culturally relevant pedagogy. *American Educational Research Journal, 32*(3), 465–491.

Ladson-Billings, G. (2009). *The dreamkeepers: Successful teachers for African American children* (2nd ed.). San Francisco, CA: Jossey-Bass.

Ladson-Billings, G. (2011). Is meeting the diverse needs of all students possible? *Kappa Delta Pi Record, 48*(1), 13–15.

Lee, C.D. (1993). *Signifying as a scaffold for literary interpretation: The pedagogical implications of an African American discourse genre.* Urbana, IL: National Council of Teachers of English.

Lee, C.D. (2001). Is October Brown Chinese? A cultural modeling activity system for underachieving students. *American Educational Research Journal, 38*(1), 97–142.

Lee, C.D. (2007). *Culture, literacy, and learning: Taking bloom in the midst of the whirlwind.* New York, NY: Teachers College Press.

Lee, C.D. (2009). Cultural influences on learning. In J.A. Banks (Ed.), *The Routledge international companion to multicultural education* (pp. 239–251). New York, NY: Routledge.

Lee, C.D., Rosenfeld, E., Mendenhall, R., Rivers, A., & Tynes, B. (2004). Cultural modeling as a frame for narrative writing. In C. Daiute & C. Lightfoot (Eds.), *Narrative analysis: Studying the development of individuals in society* (pp. 39–62). Thousand Oaks, CA: Sage Publications.

Lipka, J., Mohatt, G.V., & the Ciulistet Group. (1998). *Transforming the culture of schools: Yup'ik Eskimo Examples.* Mahwah, NJ: Lawrence Erlbaum Associates.

Lipka, J., Yanez, E., Andrew-Ihrke, D., & Adam, S. (2009). A two-way process for developing effective culturally based math: Examples from Math in a Cultural Context. In B. Greer, S. Mukhopadhyay, A.B. Powell, & S. Nelson-Barber (Eds.), *Culturally responsive mathematics education* (pp. 257–280). New York, NY: Routledge.

Loewen, J.W. (1995). *Lies my teacher told me: Everything your American History textbook got wrong.* New York, NY: New Press.

McCarty, T.L. (2002). *A place to be Navajo: Rough Rock and the struggle for self-determination in indigenous schooling.* Mahwah, NJ: Lawrence Erlbaum Associates.

McCoy, J. (2005, November 15). Education in Indian country. *The Seattle Times,* p. B7.

McLean Donaldson, K.B. (2001). *Shattering the denial: Protocols for the classroom and beyond.* Westport, CT: Bergin & Garvey.

Moll, L.C. (1992). Funds of knowledge for teaching: Using a qualitative approach to connect homes and classrooms. *Theory Into Practice, 31*(1), 132–141.

Moll, L.C., & González, N. (2004). Engaging life: A funds-of-knowledge approach to multicultural education. In J.A. Banks & C.A. McGee Banks (Eds.), *Handbook of research on multicultural education* (2nd ed., pp. 699–715). San Francisco, CA: Jossey-Bass.

Moses, R., & Cobb, C. (2001). *Radical equations: Math literacy and civil rights.* Boston, MA: Beacon Press.

Moses, R., West, M.M., & Davis, F.E. (2009). Culturally responsive mathematics education in the Algebra Project. In B. Greer, S. Mukhopadhyay, A.B. Powell, & S. Nelson-Barber (Eds.), *Culturally responsive mathematics education* (pp. 239–256). New York, NY: Routledge.

National Center for Education Statistics (NCES). (2010). *Characteristics of the 100 largest public elementary and secondary school districts in the United States: 2008–09*. Retrieved from nces.ed.gov/pubsearch

National Center for Education Statistics (NCES). (2012). *The condition of education*. Retrieved from http://www.nces.ed.org

Nieto, S. (Ed.). (2005). *Why we teach*. New York, NY: Teachers College Press.

Nieto, S., & Bode, P. (2008). *Affirming diversity: The sociopolitical context of multicultural education* (5th ed.). Boston, MA: Pearson/Allyn and Bacon.

Pai, Y., Adler, S.A., & Shadiow, L.A. (2006). *Cultural foundations of education* (4th ed.). Upper Saddle River, NJ: Merrill/Prentice Hall.

Pang, V.O. (2005). *Multicultural education: A caring-centered reflective approach* (2nd ed.). Boston, MA: McGraw-Hill.

Pang, V.O., & Sablan, V. (1998). Teacher efficacy: How do teachers feel about their abilities to teach African American students? In M. E. Dilworth (Ed.), *Being responsive to cultural differences: How teachers learn* (pp. 39–58). Washington, DC: American Association of Colleges for Teacher Education.

Ramírez, M., III, & Castañeda, A. (1974). *Cultural democracy, bicognitive development, and education*. New York, NY: Academic Press.

Riley, R.W. (1998). Our teachers should be excellent, and they should look like America. *Education and Urban Society, 31*(1), 18–29.

Shade, B.J. (Ed.). (1997). *Culture, style, and the educative process* (2nd ed.). Springfield, IL: Charles C. Thomas.

Shevalier, R., & McKenzie, B.A. (2012). Culturally responsive teaching as an ethics- and care-based approach to urban education. *Urban Education, 47*(6), 1086–1105.

Smith, R.L., Skarbek, D., & Hurst, J. (Eds.). (2005). *The passion of teaching: Dispositions in the schools*. Lanham, MD: Scarecrow Education.

Spindler, G., & Spindler, L. (Eds.). (1994). *Pathways to cultural awareness: Cultural therapy with teachers and students*. Thousand Oaks, CA: Corwin Press.

Sullivan, A.L., & A'Vant, E. (2009). The need for cultural responsiveness. *NASP Communiqué, 38*(3). Retrieved from http://www.nasponline.org/publications/cq/mocq383/cultural/responsive.aspx

Takaki, R.T. (2008). *A different mirror: A history of multicultural America* (2nd ed.). New York, NY: Bay Back Books/Little Brown.

Tatum, B.D. (2007). *Can we talk about race? And other conversations in an era of school resegregation*. Boston, MA: Beacon Press.

Taylor, H.U. (1989). *Standard English, Black English, and bidialectalism: A controversy*. New York, NY: Peter Lang.

Tharp, R.G., & Gallimore, R. (1988). *Rousing minds to life: Teaching, learning, and schooling in social context*. New York, NY: Cambridge University Press.

Thurgood Marshall College Fund. (n.d.). *About HBCUs*. Retrieved from http://thurgoodmarshallfund.net/about-tmcf/about-hbcus

U.S. Commission on Civil Rights. (2006). *The educational effectiveness of Historically Black Colleges and Universities*. Retrieved from http://www.usccr.gov/pubs/HBCU_webversion2.pdf

Valenzuela, A. (1999). *Subtractive schooling: U.S.-Mexican youth and the politics of caring*. Albany, NY: State University of New York Press.

Villegas, A.M., & Lucas, T. (2002). *Educating culturally responsive teachers: A coherent approach*. Albany, NY: State University of New York Press.

Wheeler, R.S., & Swords, R. (2006). *Code-switching: Teaching Standard English in urban classrooms*. Urbana, IL: National Council of Teachers of English.

Wlodkowski, R.J., & Ginsberg, M.B. (1995). *Diversity and motivation: Culturally responsive teaching*. San Francisco, CA: Jossey-Bass.

20

Urban Mathematics Education

Danny Bernard Martin & Gregory Vincent Larnell

In this chapter, we examine historical and contemporary conceptualizations and framings of *urban mathematics education* in research, policy, and practice within the U.S. context. We discuss the signifying roles that the term *urban* has played and could potentially play in characterizing an *urban* mathematics education. Focused attention is also given to how the "problems" of urban mathematics education have been conceptualized and framed and to the kinds of interventions that have been proposed to help alleviate these problems. Finally, we offer some reframings for the teaching and learning of mathematics in urban contexts that can help shift the discourse about and improve the experiences and outcomes of students who have been historically marginalized in mathematics education.

What Is Urban Mathematics Education?

In this section, we address the question of whether there is an identifiable domain characterized as *urban* mathematics education that differs in important ways or is different from mathematics education, more generally. If so, what features—theoretical, empirical, and ideological—characterize urban mathematics education? While our scholarly perspectives and orientations lead us to take the existence of an urban mathematics education enterprise for granted,[1] its theoretical and empirical robustness are not without debate (e.g., Gutiérrez, 2013; Matthews, 2008; Stinson, 2010; Tate, 2008; Walshaw, 2011). Therefore, it becomes important to unpack and discuss a range of relevant meanings for *urban* for the following purposes: (1) to circumscribe the conditions, inside and outside of mathematics education, that have given rise to the need for an urban-focused mathematics education, (2) to understand the *signifying*[2] roles that the term *urban* has played, currently plays, and could potentially play, in mathematics education research, policy, and practice, and (3) to discuss the potential of an urban mathematics education enterprise to positively impact mathematics practice in schools and children's mathematical development, especially those children who live and learn in urban contexts (Walshaw, 2011).

Because mathematics education is not a neutral enterprise, these conditions, significations, and potential necessarily implicate the values, ideologies, and power relations among its participants. They also reflect different and competing interpretations of human bodies, human experiences, human needs, spatial locations, and material conditions. Moreover, within the realm of power relations, an urban mathematics education enterprise may be simultaneously viewed by some as *supporting* one set of values and ideological orientations and *opposing* another set; welcomed as timely and necessary by some and dismissed or marginalized as irrelevant by others. Therefore, the assertion and existence of an *urban* mathematics education—as a constructed idea and as a knowledge-producing domain—vis-à-vis mathematics education are political acts (Walshaw, 2011).

As we will discuss later in the chapter, the emergence of an urban mathematics education enterprise—partly born out of what have been called the *social* (Lerman, 2000) and *sociopolitical* (Gutiérrez, 2013) moments in the evolution of mathematics education—is viewed by some as a necessary response to a long tradition of values, ideologies, and critical omissions that have characterized *mainstream* mathematics education (Gutiérrez, 2013; Lubienski & Bowen, 2000; Matthews, 2008; Parks & Schmeichel, 2012; Stinson, 2010). For example, Martin (2009b) offered the following characterization and critique:

> I distinguish *mainstream* mathematics education as that which has relied on traditional theories and models of teaching and learning (e.g., information processing, constructivism, situated cognition) and research approaches (race-neutral analyses, race-comparative approaches) developed primarily by white researchers and policy-makers to normalize the mathematical behavior of white children. Simultaneous to their use for normalization and generalization, these models have generated and validated conventional wisdoms about [children in other social categories] and mathematics. (p. 4)

Martin's characterization was nested in a larger call focused on "liberating the production of knowledge about African American children and mathematics," a call that included attending to the urban realities of many of these children and the impact of those realities on mathematics development. He argued that issues of race, class, gender, identity, and socialization, for example, needed to be studied differently than before—not only in relation to Black children but all children—in order to facilitate different interpretations of children's competencies and abilities. These different interpretations have the potential to serve as counternarratives to both discourses of deficiency (Stinson, 2006, 2009, 2010) and reifications and objectifications of Black children as mathematically illiterate (Martin, 2009a, 2009b, 2012). Martin also claimed that deficit-oriented knowledge production about Black children could only be sustained in certain kinds of ideological spaces and that *mainstream* mathematics is representative of such a space.

While Martin's characterizations and arguments grew out of a particular concern with knowledge production and practice in relation to Black children and mathematics, others (e.g., Matthews, 2008; Stinson, 2010; Tate, 2008; Walshaw, 2011) have posited that, more generally, an urban mathematics education offers the possibility of creating a different kind of space where the very meaning of urban can be troubled and where existing truths about urban conditions, urban students, urban schools, urban communities, and mathematics teaching and learning in different urban contexts can be challenged. Furthermore, research and commentary in this vein contend that urban mathematics education can be a site for illuminating the excellence and possibilities for building excellence that are usually rendered invisible by mainstream discourses (Matthews, 2008; e.g., Walker, 2012). Therefore, framing the aims and goals of an urban mathematics education and the production of knowledge thereof requires attention to the signifying role of the term *urban*.

Urban as a Signifier

We begin our unpacking of various conditions, significations, and potential for *urban* by first turning to discussions in the broader educational literature, acknowledging the dialectical and discursive relationships between education at large and mathematics education as a particular subdomain.

For example, historical and contemporary conditions impacting life in urban communities and schools—dual systems of schooling; racial segregation; liberal, neoliberal, and conservative school policies and reforms; disproportionate poverty; limited opportunity structure—extend into mathematics education. Similarly, mathematics education has been uniquely positioned in the school context as a determinant of educational and economic opportunity, and knowledge construction in the field continues to inform larger educational and societal discourses about children's competencies and abilities (Gutiérrez, 2008, 2013; Ladson-Billings, 1997; Martin, 2009a, 2009b; Secada, 1996; Weissglass, 2002).

One such discussion of the significations for urban was initiated by Leonardo and Hunter (2007), who, in their focus on the politics of race, class, and schooling, moved beyond a spatial theory of the urban context in favor of a theory of the *urban imagination* to argue that:

> the urban is socially and discursively constructed as a place, which is part of the dialectical creation of the urban as both a real and imagined space. The urban is real insofar as it is demarcated by zones, neighborhoods, and policies. However, it is imagined to the extent that it is replete with meaning, much of which contains contradictions as to exactly what the urban signifies. . . . As an imagined space, the urban is constructed through multiple and often contradicting meanings. These meanings are sites of contestation as to what the urban signifies in people's imagination. Consequently, the imagined aspect of the urban setting affects urban education because it socially and culturally constructs the people who live in it as well as their needs. (pp. 780–781)

Leonardo and Hunter (2007) described three ways that urban has been constructed in broader societal and educational discourses and imagination. They first noted how urban has been framed as "a sophisticated space where modernism expresses its advances in civil society through art and culture. In this case, being urban is a sign of being modern, of civilization itself" (p. 780). Yet, they also highlighted real contradictions in this "positive" connotation for urban, including the following:

- With respect to diversity, being urban usually connotes supporting the "right amount" of ethnic and racial difference, but not too much. Often tokenism stands in for real integration in order to preserve a certain image of the urban as a controlled place of difference.
- The increasing value of the signifier "urban" in education suggests that as the representation of diversity, urban people (read: students of color) are being recast in a "positive" light. Directly related to the meaning of urban, racial diversity is conscripted into a logic that co-opts it as a marker of cosmopolitanism, but with neither the reality nor the burden. Educators who deal with the urban are constructed as sophisticated, but the urban students and families themselves are not. (pp. 781–782)

The second characterization of urban noted by Leonardo and Hunter focused on urban contexts as "authentic places of identity for people of color. Both Whites and people of color construct the 'essential' or 'real' person of color as urban, usually born from the concrete activities and histories of the urban" (p. 780). Finally, they addressed the widely held perception of the urban context "as a pathological place marked by a profound disorganization, criminal character, and moral malaise . . . [and where] images of the underclass shine through the lens of the culture of poverty argument" (p. 780). Within this latter signification, the "urban problem" has been appropriated and reframed in educational discourse as the so-called achievement gap.

In our view, it is the third signification of urban described by Leonardo and Hunter that has emerged most strongly to inform the evolution of urban mathematics education research, policy, and practice, mainly for the purpose of (re-)generating a deficit-oriented, failure-focused master narrative about urban students, their schools, and their communities—as well as for generating success-focused counternarratives that draw on alternative epistemologies, ideologies, theories, and methods (Anderson & Tate, 2008; Berry, 2008; Ellington, 2006; English-Clarke, Slaughter-Defoe, & Martin, 2012; Gutiérrez, 2000, 2008, 2013; Larnell, 2011, under review; Martin, 2009a, 2009b, 2012; McGee & Martin, 2011a, 2011b; Noble, 2011; Secada, 1996; Stinson, 2006, 2009, 2010; Tate, 1994, 1995a, 1995b, 1996, 1997; Terry, 2011).

Building on this brief discussion of urban significations in the larger educational arena, we now turn to recent attempts to explicate *urban* mathematics education. Because a full review of the literature indexed by potential significations of urban mathematics education is beyond the scope of this chapter, the work that we highlight in the remainder of this chapter explicitly foregrounds urban significations of various types and the production of this work represents, in our view, watershed moments in the evolution of this domain. We recognize that such choices themselves can be viewed as political.

Despite the proposed impact of such watershed moments or "critical junctures" on the formulation of urban mathematics education (Gutiérrez, 2002, p. 145), there have been disproportionally infrequent publications of empirical and/or policy-oriented research that fit squarely within this category (Walker's [2012] recent text, *Building Mathematics Learning Communities: Improving Outcomes in Urban High Schools,* is a welcomed exception). As a result, our review[3] includes publications in which the primary and explicit focus was mathematics teaching, learning, educational research, or educational policy in urban spaces, but more often the review is informed by articles that tangentially meet this focus at the other points (e.g., urban education; equity, race, and racism; general educational policy; mathematics education, more broadly). From among the former group, our review includes or is informed by many of the influential and specifically urban-mathematics-education issues and projects that have emerged within the past few decades: for instance, William Tate's (1994, 1995a, 1995b, 1996, 2008) consistent calls to examine the significations of urban in mathematics education, opportunities to learn mathematics, and reform-oriented policy making and scholarship agendas (cf. Lipman, 2012); the QUASAR project as a forerunning, comprehensive urban mathematics education project (Silver, Smith, & Nelson, 1995); and Gutstein's (2003, 2006) more recent work to conceptualize mathematics teaching and learning for social justice in urban schools.

One of the most recent and significant developments in the construction and evolution of urban mathematics education was the launch of the *Journal of Urban Mathematics Education (JUME)* at Georgia State University. Launched on January 15, 2008, by five faculty members in the College of Education, the birth of the journal was characterized as "an unchartered quest to 'open up' within the mathematics education community a scholarly space that could honor—not marginalize—the professional work in the domain we characterized as *urban*" (Matthews, 2008, p. 1). The founders documented a need for this journal given that their reviews of top-tier journals in the field—including the flagship *Journal for Research in Mathematics Education (JRME)*—"revealed a suspicious absence of urban scholarship" (p. 1). Partly in response to this absence, the following mission statement was developed for *JUME: To foster a transformative global academic space in mathematics that embraces critical research, emancipatory pedagogy, and scholarship of engagement in urban communities.*

In the opening editorial of the first issue, co-founder and inaugural editor-in-chief, Lou Matthews (2008), noted the tensions that emerged in relation to this mission statement, including: (1) how to define urban in mathematics education, and (2) how they should orient themselves toward work in urban mathematics education. With respect to the former, the founders acknowledged that geographical location was insufficient to describe the complexities of urban conditions and mathematics education in the context of these conditions. Matthews stated that it was necessary to move beyond applying the term *urban* to human bodies; more specifically, as a deficit-oriented "umbrella term used indiscriminately to denote African American, Hispanic, immigrant, or low-income students" (Matthews, 2008, p. 2). Instead, they defined the urban domain as follows and suggested that all work in this domain attend to the complexities of this definition:

> Here, the view of the urban domain extends beyond the geographical context, into the lives of people within the multitude of cultural, social, and political spaces in which mathematics teaching and learning takes place. (p. 2)

With respect to the second concern of orienting work in the urban mathematics education domain, the founders noted their concerns about the invisibility of research focused on mathematics success and excellence in urban spaces, which could serve as a counternarrative to the longstanding preoccupation and focus on failure among some urban students (Gutiérrez, 2000, 2008, 2013; Leonard & Martin, 2013; Martin, 2000, 2009a, 2009b; Stinson, 2006, 2009; Tate, 1994, 1995a, 1995b, 1996; Téllez, Moschkovich, & Civil, 2011). Even while adopting an orientation focused on excellence, it was noted (Matthews, 2008) that:

> The reporting of excellence within the urban domain has been suspiciously underreported in top-tier mathematics education journals. The existence of this work outside of the espoused canons of mathematics education literature is cause for significant concern . . . [and] calls into question whether mathematics educators consider the urban domain as relevant engagement . . . or, even more ominous, whether our "major" scholarship is relevant for truly reforming urban practice. (p. 3)

In an essay titled *Putting the "Urban" in Mathematics Education Scholarship*—also published in the inaugural issue of *JUME*—William Tate (2008) continued the task of unpacking the potential for an urban mathematics education by issuing a "warning that developing and testing theories is central to making urban mathematics scholarship a visible research enterprise" (p. 5). Tate's caution was grounded in the observation that many education scholars, including those in mathematics education, ignore geospatial considerations related to urban cities and contexts. Tate suggested that theory-building and testing in relation to geospatial concerns could be modeled after, and perhaps incorporate theory and empirical methods from urban economics, urban sociology, urban politics, community psychology, and developmental sciences. These areas give explicit attention to urban forces that impact human development, social organization, economic capacity, education, and the geography of opportunity.

Working within a perspective that "problematizes impartial knowing, disinterested objectivity, and value neutrality" (p. 9), Walshaw (2011) argued for a postmodernist reframing of mathematics education that could address urban conditions and that could counter tendencies toward reification and generalization often found in mathematics education:

> mathematics education would be viewed, not in isolation, but head-on as a disciplinary endeavour situated at the interface of multiple and competing structures and processes . . . urban schooling would be interrogated as a construct, situated within institutions, historical moments, as well as social, cultural, and discursive spaces. Importantly, in this formulation,

> identities, social conditions, and political dimensions all become highly significant. These kinds of priorities run up against portrayals within mass-mediated and ideological constructions of the roles and functions of urban schools that often assume an essentialist character. (p. 9)

The characterizations and significations of urban described by Leonardo and Hunter (2007), more broadly, and discussed in the inaugural issue of the *Journal of Urban Mathematics Education,* as well as by Walshaw (2011), provide important lenses and perspectives that can be used to examine both historical and contemporary manifestations of urban mathematics education.

Research, Policy, and Practice in the Name of Urban Mathematics Education

In this section, we provide a broad overview of research, policy, and practice that have cloaked themselves under the cover of urban mathematics education during the last 50 years. We draw on Stinson and Bullock's (2012) useful characterization of the historical moments that have spanned this timeframe in mathematics education: (a) a process-product moment (1970s–) marked by the field's cognitive psychological orientations, increased attention to and attempts to measure student learning, and broadening use quantitative statistical inference to link classroom practices to student outcomes (p. 43); (b) an interpretivist-constructivist moment (1980s–) marked by the introduction of qualitative methodologies to go beyond prediction of teaching and learning events toward understanding them as social phenomena and constructivism as a means to interpret learning and guide teaching; (c) a social-turn moment (mid-1980s–), during which the importance of social factors, equity, discourse, and interactions is recognized and the "mathematics teaching-and-learning [dynamic] is understood within the sociocultural contexts in which it occurs . . . the situated context in which it is practiced . . . and the classroom context in which it is taken-as-shared" (p. 44); and most recently, (d) a sociopolitical turn moment (2000s–) foregrounding the relationships between mathematics teaching, learning, thinking on one hand, and issues related to identity and power on the other.

According to these scholars, "Each continuing moment . . . explores mathematics teaching and learning from different theoretical perspectives and employs different methodological procedures derived from a variety of academic disciplines" (Stinson, 2010, p. 5).[4] The latter two moments, in particular, have been concerned with issues of power, equity, social justice, and identity. Across all four moments, we discuss the significations and interpretations of urban that have emerged in each as well as how the "problems" of urban mathematics education have been defined and addressed.

Social Constraints and Affordances of an Emerging Urban Mathematics Education Enterprise: The Influence of Brown, Sputnik, and the Process-Product Moment (~1960–1970s)

Near the mid-20th century, a series of precedent-setting events circumscribed educational research and policy and together set a path toward later reform projects. The convergence of at least three specific events, we claim, is foundational to the emergence of an urban mathematics education enterprise, because they posed significant changes for the urban educational landscape and the role that school mathematics would assume therein: (1) the social and policy environment following the 1954 Supreme Court decision in the first case of *Brown v. Board of Education* (hereinafter referred to as *Brown*); (2) the nation's heightened attention to mathematics and science education in the wake of the 1957 Soviet Union launch of the first artificial

Earth-orbiting satellite, *Sputnik 1* (*Sputnik* hereinafter); and (3) the later (1960–1970s) and narrower process-product moment that predominated mathematics education research, policy, and practice (Stinson & Bullock, 2012).

In one of several past moments of perceived national crisis, the United States reacted to the Cold War–era launch of the *Sputnik* as if the event itself was an act of international conflict—spurring a thorough reexamination of American mathematics and science education (Schoenfeld, 2006). This connection between educational reform and global status was unmistakably related to an *exceptionalism* leitmotif[5] in which America's engagement with and technical superiority in relation to the rest of the world were hinged to students' proficiencies in mathematics and science. The most pressing problem of an emerging urban (i.e., advanced, modern) mathematics education was maintaining this superiority. The ensuing "new math" and subsequent "back-to-basics" reform movements helped to define the cognitive-positivist, process-product moment. These consecutive reform projects also unleashed shifting perspectives on school mathematics teaching and learning, undergirded by the question, "Who will do mathematics in service to the nation?" A common element of these reforms was to develop a form of mathematics education that would produce and nurture the "best and brightest." However, as we discuss later in this section, this quest was both constrained and informed by the social conditions, values, and ideologies of the day.

It is important to note that the exceptionalism narrative, at both the student level and the national-interest level, maps neatly onto a conceptualization of urban as a sophisticated space or, as interpreted through a *Sputnik*-era lens, a premier symbol of American production, modernism, and industrialism. This interpretation forges a special link between mathematics and urban education. As the nation sought to broaden participation in mathematics and science for international competitiveness in scientific production, the related "Who will do mathematics in service to the nation?" question was being renegotiated on both the national and international stages and was mitigated by the issue of "equal" access to education.

The product-process moment and post-*Sputnik* crisis also coincided with *Brown,* the landmark compilation of civil-rights era school desegregation cases. As an act of national agenda setting, *Brown* was crucial to developments in American education but, as Ladson-Billings (2004) argued, it has also contemporarily become an object of "uncritical devotion" and one that has "taken on a mythic quality that actually distorts the way many Americans have come to understand its genesis and function in the society" (pp. 3–4). At the same time that the United States sought to link mathematics education to exceptionalist interests, *Brown* compelled the nation (albeit with all deliberate speed) to also recognize that school desegregation was connected to larger political and foreign policy interests (Bell, 1980). As corroborated by the Justice Department (1954) in its amicus brief on *Brown,* the "United States is trying to prove to the people of the world, of every nationality, race and color, that a free democracy is the most civilized and secure form of government yet devised by man [*sic*]" (as cited by Ladson-Billings, 2004, p. 4).

Brown, Sputnik, the process-product moment, and the emergence of an urban mathematics education are intertwined inasmuch as the goal of broadening participation in mathematics and science would be connected to the nation's efforts to "confront its own credibility concerning Black people and their civil liberties" (ibid). As noted by Martin (2012):

> Although Cold War politics are put at the forefront of discussing the U.S. mathematics education reaction to Sputnik, a number of race-based considerations in the prevailing sociopolitical context are in order. Before and during the 1950's, the United States was in the midst of the new right racial project, characterized by overt Jim Crow racism and legal segregation. As a result, it could be argued that the new math movement to educate a

> generation of students who would help protect the U.S. from the Soviet intellectual threat did not include Blacks (or Native Americans, Chinese, Japanese, or Latinos). Just over a decade earlier, Black Americans were largely excluded from taking advantage of the GI Bill that helped many white males enroll in colleges and universities. And during the 1930s and 1940s, Black Americans, in particular, failed to benefit equitably from Roosevelt's New Deal, Social Security, or Truman's Fair Deal social programs (Katznelson, 2005). . . . An extended chronology of Civil Rights history surrounding the Sputnik era, including the death of Dr. Martin Luther King Jr. in 1968, would show that the new math reform project was not an anti-racist vessel in the sea of racial discord characterizing that time. With its emphasis on the "best and the brightest," it was just another mechanism for maintaining white (male) privilege. One chronology (Raimi, 2005) of the "prominent persons" involved in the political project of the new math movement identified mostly white males, from various backgrounds, as the key leaders and decision-makers of the movement, a finding that is common for white institutional spaces. If the nation had minimal will to integrate Black children into their schools and other public institutions or the voices of Blacks into its policy-making circles, it was certainly no more willing to integrate their needs into the mathematics education reforms of the day. (pp. 10–11)

These sentiments were echoed by Tate (1996), who stated, "the mathematics reform effort associated with Sputnik did little to address the concerns of [people] of color, who were often the residents of urban areas" (p. 373). Moreover, we would argue that the process-product research enterprise was characterized by the normalization of White children's thinking and learning, limiting the applicability of research findings and interventions to non-White children (Martin, 2009b).

The Interpretivist-Constructivist Moment (1980s–), A Nation at Risk, and the Resurgence of High-Modernist Reform: Urban Systemic Initiatives and the QUASAR Project as Exempla

Near the end of the product-process moment and by 1980, the theoretical preferences that integrated mathematics education and cognitive psychology were beginning to shift from traditional positivist roots (and postpositivist; Stinson & Bullock, 2012, p. 43). An interpretivist-constructivist moment had quickly emerged, presenting a new set of concerns for research and practice. Although theories of cognitive development continued to characterize much of the interpretivist-constructivist perspective (particularly building on the works of Piaget and van Hiele), there was also a focus on students' engagement with mathematical problem solving (e.g., Polya, 1957; Schoenfeld, 1985) and on the nature of "misconceptions, critical barriers, and epistemological obstacles" (Confrey & Kazak, 2006, p. 307). Still, some were concerned that the quick ascendancy of constructivism amid the successive waves of past reforms demonstrated a "tendency of the field to respond too quickly to fashions" (p. 306).

With respect to passing fashions, the shifting perspectives on mathematics teaching and learning coincided with a period during which the United States was declared "a nation at risk" (National Commission on Excellence in Education [NCEE], 1983). Explicitly extending the *Sputnik*-era exceptionalism narrative, the policy report, *A Nation at Risk,* called for numerous and specific changes in the nation's education enterprise aimed at combating mediocre educational performance. Among the report's findings, another concern emerged, one that went beyond matters "such as industry and commerce" to the "intellectual, moral, and spiritual strengths of our people" (p. 7). The NCEE was especially concerned that the diminishing quality of shared education would lead to inequities akin to those mentioned by Moses and Cobb (2001) nearly 20 years later, when they insisted that "individuals in our society who do not possess the levels of skill, literacy, and training essential to this new era will be effectively disenfranchised, not simply from the material rewards that accompany competent performance, but also from the chance to participate fully in our national life" (p. 7).

On the heels of *A Nation at Risk,* the National Research Council (NRC) (1989) produced its own report, titled *Everybody Counts,* which signaled the need for dramatic changes in U.S. mathematics education. This report, echoing *Sputnik*-era concerns about international competitiveness, contained an implicit call for attention to urban mathematics education. However, that implicit focus emerged most strongly in the "human resources" section of the document, which called for increased participation by minorities but only in light of fears about the decreasing numbers of White males.

One national response to this renewed warning was a set of systemic reform initiatives, some of which were sponsored by the National Science Foundation (NSF). Systemic reform (Smith & O'Day, 1991) or standards-based reform (Knapp, 1997; Senk & Thompson, 2003) pursues the goal of comprehensive and coordinated change by aligning the development and implementation of specific components of an educational system (e.g., curricula as texts and standards, assessment, teaching). Although the early focus of systemic reform was at the state level (e.g., California) during the mid-1980s, NSF began to target regional areas of the country for reform (rural before urban, however). Through the Urban Systemic Initiatives (USI) program, NSF funding was distributed to urban school districts with the highest concentrations of poverty among schoolchildren. Although USI projects differed from each other in terms of scope and scale and the systemic elements included, they were similar in their attentiveness to and philosophy toward alignment, effective teaching, and top-down policy activity (Knapp, 1997).

In terms of interventions focused on urban conditions and schools, the QUASAR project is an exemplum of this moment, as an interpretivist-constructivist-oriented and quasi-systemic mathematics education reform project specifically aimed at urban communities. According to its designers, QUASAR aimed to reveal the "intellectual bankruptcy of previous, deficit-based models of achievement" that prevailed during the process-product moment. The argument was that these perspectives were no longer sufficient, and they instead asserted, "all learners actively construct their own knowledge, even in intellectually complex domains such as mathematics" (Silver, Smith, & Nelson, 1995, p. 12). In this new view:

> the job of teachers and schools is to provide the support and materials in which each student not only refines and makes more mathematically sophisticated his or her own constructs and means of building knowledge but also appropriates uses of mathematical or general academic concepts, principles and processes contributed by others. (p. 11)

As an urban mathematics education project and one of the first of its kind, QUASAR was aligned with potentially contradicting significations of urban.[6] Corresponding to both the urban-as-sophisticated and urban-as-problematic significations, QUASAR was itself viewed as an "education reform project aimed at fostering and studying development and implementation of enhanced mathematics instructional programs for students attending middle schools in economically disadvantaged communities" (Silver et al., 1995, p. 10). Thus:

> QUASAR can be seen as part of broader set of efforts to create a society that offers opportunity to each of its members to be successful and to contribute to *the social and economic good.* Demographic trends indicate that continued underinvestment in the education of the

> poor, disproportionate numbers of whom are members of racial or ethnic minority groups, will exacerbate the current achievement gaps between groups in this society and between students in the United States and their counterparts in other industrialized countries. (Ibid, emphases added)

While the broad set of efforts associated with systemic reform aimed to contribute to both social and economic good, they marked the ascendency of a high-modernist agenda (Scott, 1998; cf. Greeno, 2003). High modernism separates the practice and activity of real contexts (e.g., mathematics classrooms) from the determination of (and from those who ultimately determine) the quality of that practice and activity. In terms of reform, high modernism offers a way to "characterize qualities of an activity that are highly valued" (Greeno, 2003, p. 304).

In the case of urban mathematics education, this translated into standards that were directly aligned to the work of urban mathematics teachers and that articulated highly valued learning, teaching, curriculum, and assessment practices. Alternatively, high-modernist reform emphasizes uniformity (e.g., fidelity of curricular implementation), which in some ways may "strip reality to the bare bones so that the rules will in fact explain more of the situation and provide a better guide to behavior. To the extent that this simplification can be imposed, those who make the rules *can* actually supply crucial guidance and instruction. This, at any rate, is what I take to be the inner logic of social, economic, and productive de-skilling" (Porter, 1995, as cited by Greeno, 2003, p. 309).

The Social-Turn Moment (Mid-1980s–), Sociocultural and Situated Perspectives, and Racial Achievement-Gap Concerns in Mathematics Education

> It is widely accepted today that as general research in mathematics education evolved during the 1960s and 1970s, psychological paradigms, methodologies, and research questions dominated the field. A few researchers then began to investigate factors related to the performance of under-represented and underachieving segments of the school population. These research foci opened the gate for the consideration of social factors as critical in understanding how they affected the outcomes of mathematics teaching. . . . In the 1980s and 1990s, mathematics education research witnessed a diversification of research thrusts and theoretical models coming from sociology, anthropology, and linguistics. (Atweh, Forgasz, & Nebres, 2001, p. ix)

The third moment in the evolution of an urban mathematics education, the "social turn," emerged as the field was experiencing momentous growth and increasing prominence, including the adoption of new theoretical frameworks (Lerman, 2000), the nascent standards movement, and the growing need for and "acute shortage" of mathematics education doctoral programs in the United States (Reys, 2000; Reys & Dossey, 2008). By "social," mathematics education scholars began to explore the utility of sociocultural perspectives, discourse analytic techniques, and "concepts such as 'communities of practice,' 'learning as participation/belonging,' and 'out-of-school mathematics' " to apply toward questions about mathematical thinking, teaching, policy, curriculum, and learning (Gutiérrez, 2013, p. 2). "As such," Gutiérrez noted "[the social turn] has opened doors for researchers to study classroom culture, participation structures, socialization processes, and teacher professional development in whole new ways" (ibid).

The moment also hinged on the landmark publication of the *Curriculum and Evaluation Standards for School Mathematics* (*Standards*) by the National Council of Teachers of Mathematics (NCTM, 1989). Around the time of the *Standards* publication (as a key artifact of high-modernist reform), the NCTM was widely recognized as the de facto flagship organization of the mathematics education enterprise (Berry, 2005).[7] The *Standards* were, in the words of the authors, "statements of criteria for excellence in order to produce change" (NCTM, 1989, p. 2). This proposed change, however, was itself a point of contention, with social issues being largely subsumed under the ongoing "math wars" between so-called reformers and traditionalists (Schoenfeld, 2004)—which verisimilarly centered on questions about and challenges to the universality of mathematics and its relationships to culture, democracy, and social mobility.

As a key period in the evolution of urban mathematics education, the social-turn moment was characterized also by its incorporation of sociocultural and situative perspectives (amidst increasing interdisciplinarity more generally; e.g., Cobb & Bowers, 1999; Greeno, 2003; Forman, 2003; Sfard, 1998), explicit but "parallel" attention to issues of equity and discourse (Gutiérrez, 2013; Herbel-Eisenmann, Chopin, Wagner, & Pimm, 2012), and recognition of access to school mathematics as a social filter (Matthews, 1983, 1984; Secada, Fennema, & Adajian, 1995). For instance, in "Needed: An Agenda for Equity in Mathematics Education," a special issue of the *Peabody Journal of Education,* Secada and Meyer (1989) acknowledge the then-emergent reforms (e.g., exemplified by the NCTM *Standards*), but they unequivocally affirm that "mathematics educators should be concerned that issues of educational equity have not appeared, have been raised only to be submerged under the rubric of excellence for all, or have been transformed into other kinds of issues" (p. 1; cf. Apple, 1992, 1995). The banner of the social turn was clear: "This state of affairs is [*sic*] in dire need of remedy" (Secada & Meyer, 1989, p. 1).

The social turn also included a limited attentiveness to issues of multiculturalism (e.g., Murtadha-Watts & D'Ambrosio, 1997; Sleeter, 1997). Early hints of an emerging, though not widely adopted, *critical* perspective, could be found, for example, in the scholarship of Tate (1994, 1995a, 1995b, 1996, 2002), who working from a perspective informed by Critical Race Theory, began advocating for culturally relevant pedagogy and attention to opportunity-to-learn issues. Tate was accompanied in this rare but growing critical slice of the social-turn movement by scholars such as Marilyn Frankenstein (1989, 1990, 1995) and Eric Gutstein (2003, 2006) who began to carve out a line of research that would come to focus on teaching mathematics for social justice.

Overall, the social turn differed considerably from past moments, taking "as its starting point a socially situated mathematics classroom—a classroom located in a wider social structure, one simultaneously constitutive of and constituted by social relations within it" (Adler, 2012, p. v.). This focus was evinced by the *Standards* themselves through new goals for students, including prominently featured notions like "opportunity for all" and "learning to communicate mathematically" (NCTM, 1989, pp. 4–6). With respect to the former, NCTM put forth the following perspective on mathematics education:

> The social injustices of past schooling practices can no longer be tolerated. . . . Mathematics has become a critical filter for employment and full participation in our society. We cannot afford to have the majority of our population mathematically illiterate: Equity has become an economic necessity. (p. 4)

This signature attentiveness to social aspects of mathematical thinking, learning, and teaching was complemented by national recognition of the distinct context of urban mathematics education. Through this lens, however, mathematics education reform was viewed as, and linked to, a deficit-oriented signification of urban. According to the report, *In the National Interest: The Federal Government in the Reform of K-12 Math and Science Education* (Carnegie Commission, 1991):

> The state of American education is therefore a reflection—indeed a *victim*—of the nation's social condition. With many children in impoverished urban communities facing inadequate

> educational stimulation and even basic nutrition at home, current financial, political, and institutional arrangements do not offer a means of escape from the spiral of despair. (As cited in Robinson, 1996, p. 382, emphasis added).

This baleful view of the needs of urban children and an urban mathematics education was in curious contrast to (and in potential tension with) social-turn scholars' sometimes accompanying commitments to equity and "opportunity for all." In many ways, the mixed rhetoric around urban-as-victim mapped onto imprecise conceptualizations of equity—most often, conflating it with equality or even enlightened self-interest (Secada, 1989), highlighted by the commodification of urban and minority students as workers whose skills are needed for economic and national security interests. Equity-as-equality and opportunity-for-all were later folded into and rebranded in mathematics-specific terms, most notably as "mathematics-for-all" (Martin, 2003).

In this spirit of math-for-all, the discourse around equity quickly became a discourse around the race-comparative *achievement gap perspective,* which reinforced and reified a racial hierarchy of mathematical ability, one that—without resistance from mainstream mathematics education researchers and policy makers—located African American, Latino, and Native American students at the bottom (Gutiérrez & Dixon-Román, 2011; Martin, 2009a, 2009b). This high-modernist, "project of legibility" (Scott, 1998) became a system in which "performance can be measured, records can be kept, and progress can be assessed in ways that can be understood from outside of the situation" (Greeno, 2003, p. 306). In this way, the problem of differential achievement became an object of research without an accompanying acknowledgement that such a "gaze" only stands to shed light on "issues of access and achievement from a dominant perspective (maintaining the status quo) with little concern for how students are constructed in the process, what additional skills are needed to negotiate the discursive spaces of education, and/or how power relations play out in learning" (Gutiérrez & Dixon-Román, 2011, pp. 21–22). Even research studies that foreground issues of equity, race, and identity could unwittingly support the broader, invidious achievement-gap perspective (e.g., Fuson, Smith, & Cicero, 1997).

The Sociopolitical Moment (2000s–): Getting Serious About Power, Identity, and Social Contexts of Mathematics Education[8]

As the social turn has proceeded with its spotlight on equity, sociocultural theories, discourses, and participation patterns, researchers have used these tools to reframe a variety of issues and problems within mathematics education. Some scholars, however, have begun to question openly the field's capacity to address issues of power and identity as they influence and are influenced by the mathematics education enterprise—including research methodologies and supporting researchers interested in "taking risks in this arena" (Gutiérrez, 2013, p. 1; cf. Stinson, 2010. Those risks involve a shifting away from and questioning some of the assumptions of the social turn—particularly its perspectives on equity-as-access and achievement–gap gazing. That questioning has led to the *sociopolitical* turn—sociopolitical because it regards "knowledge, power, and identity as interwoven and arising from (and constituted within) social discourses" (Gutiérrez, 2013, p. 4; See Figure 20.1). Research within this turn can be broadly characterized as a counternarrative to traditional perspectives that have constructed African American, Latino, Native American, and poor students as mathematically illiterate.

As a challenge to the sociopolitical turn, high-modernist reform and standardization (most recently reflected in the form the Common Core State Standards for School Mathematics), which "leave teachers with little room to reflect upon how such students are constructing themselves and being constructed with respect to mathematics" (Gutiérrez, 2013, pp. 1–2), continue

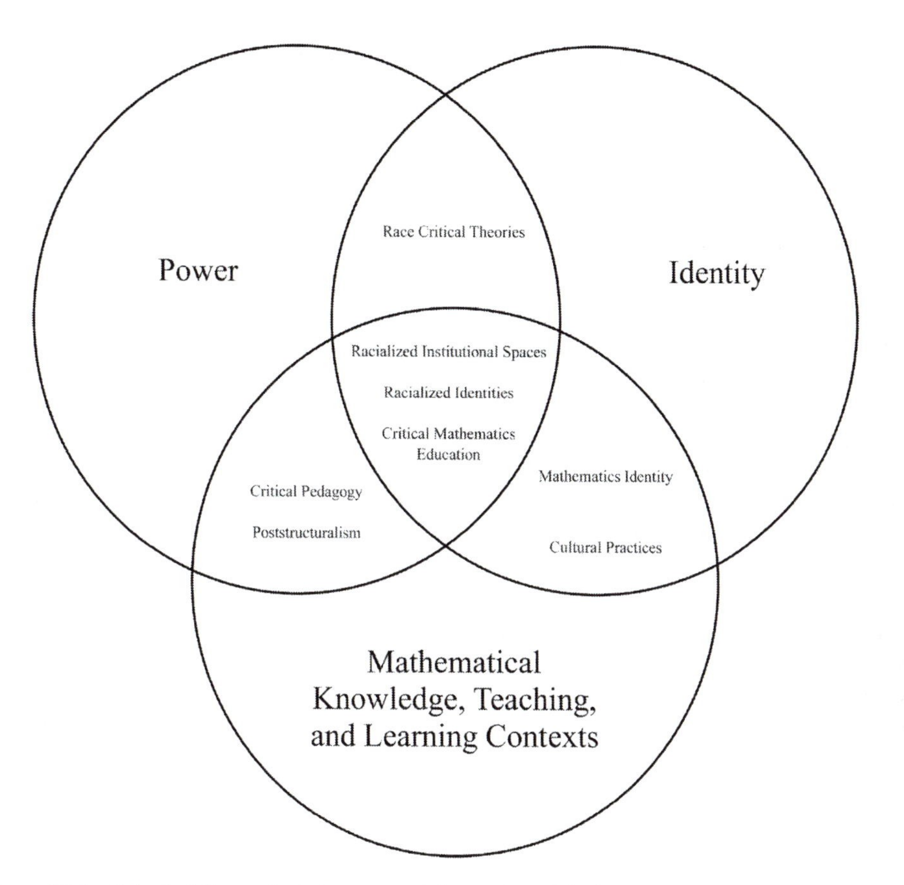

Figure 20.1 Selected theoretical elements of the sociopolitical-turning moment

to stifle the articulation of certain kinds of questions, such as "*why* this concept? *Who* benefits from students learning this concept? What is *missing* from the mathematics classroom because I am required to cover this concept? How are students' *identities* implicated in this focus?" (ibid). Alternatively, mainstream mathematics education scholars have attempted to question this turn by suggesting that the work being conducted is no longer *actual* research in mathematics education—for example, by asking "Where's the math?" (Heid, 2010; see Martin, Gholson, & Leonard, 2011 for a counterargument). However, we suggest that within the sociopolitical turn, a number of significant advancements have been made in relation to the evolution of an urban mathematics education, including:

(1) a focus on mathematics success and agency among urban students and the use of narrative-based methodologies that allow students to describe and explain their mathematics learning experiences (e.g., Berry, 2008; Ellington, 2006; Gutstein, 2006; Martin, 2000; McGee & Martin, 2011a, 2011b; Noble, 2011; Stinson, 2006, 2008, 2009; Terry, 2011);
(2) attention to the co-construction of students' multiple identities along with their mathematics identities; how those identities are used to position students relative to each other and to mathematics learning and teaching (e.g., DiME, 2007; Esmonde & Langer-Osuna, 2013; Hand, 2010; Horn, 2008; Jackson, 2009; Langer-Osuna, 2011; Nasir, 2002; Nasir & Shah, 2011; Spencer, 2009; Turner, Dominguez, Maldonado, & Empson, 2013);

(3) the utilization of race-critical perspectives including Critical Race Theory and LatCrit; postmodern perspectives; Freirian perspectives; and the deconstruction of mainstream mathematics education as an instantiation ofWhite institutional space (Berry, 2008; Gutiérrez, 2013; McGee & Martin, 2011a, 2001b; Stinson, 2006, 2008, 2009);
(4) the re-articulation of mathematics teaching and teaching for equity and social justice purposes (Aguirre, 2009; Bartell, 2013; Foote, 2010; Gonzalez, 2009; Gutstein, 2006; Hand, 2012; Leonard, 2008; Matthews, 2003, 2009; Wager & Stinson, 2012).

This list is by no means exhaustive. However, as urban mathematics education continues to develop and grow, advances in these areas provide a strong foundation from which to build. Research and policy emerging within the sociopolitical perspective has, for example, produced new understandings about mathematics success among African American and Latino learners; the configurations of power that emerge to marginalize some students and empower others in mathematics classroom contexts; the kinds of teaching practices that make mathematics culturally relevant to urban students; and begun to challenge the race-comparative approach as the exclusive mode for addressing equity and diversity issues in mathematics education.

Moreover, in the current context, the very nature of the mathematics education enterprise is subject to scrutiny (Martin, 2013; Valero & Zevenbergen, 2004; Walshaw, 2011). There has been an inward gaze that acknowledges that, as a knowledge-production enterprise, mathematics education, including urban mathematics education, is both a producer and consumer of prevailing meanings, discourses, and ideologies about urban students, urban conditions, and the teaching and learning of mathematics in urban contexts. In our view, an urban mathematics education should exist in order to counter deficit-oriented perspectives, question problematic significations and assumptions, provide alternative lenses through which to view students and urban contexts, and be reflective and reflexive enough to question its own assumptions. Moving forward, we offer some possibilities for continuing to build the urban mathematics education enterprise through research, policy, and practice.

Reframing Urban: What Can Urban Mathematics Education Become?

While our review of urban mathematics education was necessarily an incomplete one, it should be clear that various historical moments have served to create conditions, inside and outside of mathematics education, that require an *urban* mathematics education. These conditions, like the notion of urban itself, are not static. Nor are they isolated to the U.S. context. The changing nature of these conditions (and accompanying significations) and the processes that produce these conditions align with the notion of urban*ism* described by Lipman (2012) in her discussion of how "education policies, and their contestations, are intertwined with the radical economic, political, and spatial transformations of cities" (p. 8). In offering a vision for what urban mathematics might become, we first return to the concerns expressed by Tate (2008) earlier in this chapter. With attention to power, race, and identity, we propose that a theoretically and empirically rich urban mathematics education will need to take up geospatial concerns not only in local urban contexts but also with respect to global contexts, where urban as a signifier often connotes real divisions between the global North and the global South. How can our theorizing and empirical work in urban mathematics education help us to understand the simultaneous empowering and oppressive roles that mathematics plays within North and South contexts but also in maintaining North-South divisions in the first place? Moreover, how can we continue to bring to light the connections between urban mathematics education and global politics and projects (Martin, 2013)? For example, Cold War, *Sputnik*-era concerns about mathematics education in the United States were bookended and mitigated by civil rights realities and race-based societal ideologies that resulted in limited access to mathematics for Black Americans. The New Math reforms were not intended for Blacks despite reform-oriented rhetoric about educating the best and the brightest, rendering mathematics education a context where the contractions of democracy, access, and opportunity were put on display. More contemporary mathematics reforms have been bookended by the rise of neoliberalism in the 1980s, growing neoconservative and right-wing politics across the globe, post-911 politics in the United States, and the near collapse of global financial markets. How might urban mathematics education in the future be even more responsive to issues of access and opportunity in the context of such forces and global urbanism (Lipman, 2012)? In terms of knowledge production and the next iterations of urban mathematics education, we would argue for greater scholarly collaborations among scholars from global South and global North contexts. These collaborations would focus on explicating emerging urban conditions and explicating how mathematics education is put in service to sustaining or challenging those conditions.

We are not suggesting that urban mathematics education focus only on theorizing and critical analysis but that it also extend deeper into the realm of policy. This theory-to-policy demand represents a call for mathematics educators to not only help shape urban conditions but also propose solutions and interventions that those impacted by urban conditions take full advantage of mathematics so that they can change these conditions. For example, in the U.S. context, the sociopolitical turn (Gutiérrez, 2013) overlaps with the adoption of the Common Core State Standards for Mathematics. However, it could be argued that the insights on urban mathematics education gained from the sociopolitical had little impact on the development of these standards and may have little impact on their implementation. We believe that developing urban mathematics education policy based on robust, nondeficit significations of urban are needed as the field moves forward.

While we argue that knowledge production in urban mathematics education must ultimately influence mathematics education policy, we also believe that work in this area must continue to develop practice-based approaches—such as teaching mathematics for social justice (Gutstein, 2003, 2006)—that can impact the day-to-day experiences of students and teachers in classrooms. Yet, while teaching mathematics for social justice is among the most "critical" approaches to teaching mathematics, urban mathematics education scholars and practitioners must continue to flesh out this approach so that it is responsive to prevailing significations of urban and is able to generate significations that position urban mathematics education not simply as a counternarrative to mainstream ideology but that transform the entire field. In our view, this transformation is not simply about rearranging power relations and hierarchies inside and outside the field to produce new inequities but about realizing the potential of urban mathematics education to aid in the struggle against inequities.

Notes

1. We regard urban mathematics education not as wholly distinctive but as a more particular space in which different questions are raised and different theories are employed while maintaining a focus on mathematics teaching and learning and issues thereof.
2. In fact, *urban semiotics* is the study of meaning in urban form as generated by signs, symbols, and their social connotations.
3. To inform the review, we searched using commercial (e.g., Google Scholar) and institutional search engines for and through doctoral dissertations, policy documents, conference proceedings, peer reviewed books and handbooks (e.g., *Equity in Discourse for Mathematics Education; Mapping Equity and Quality in Mathematics Education; New Directions for Equity in Mathematics Education; A Research Companion to the Principles and Standards for School Mathematics*) and peer-reviewed articles from a diverse collection of scholarly

outlets, including *American Educational Research Journal; Educational Researcher; The Educational Forum; The High School Journal; Mathematical Thinking and Learning; Journal for Research in Mathematics Education; Journal of Negro Education; Journal of Urban Mathematics Education; The Mathematics Educator; Notices of the American Mathematical Society; Peabody Journal of Education; Review of Educational Research; Teachers College Record; Urban Education*).
4. As Stinson and Bullock do, we acknowledge that the use of rounded time markers to denote the bounds of these moments is necessarily imprecise, in some cases arbitrary, and possibly "misleading" (p. 43). We use these only as a way to characterize eras in theoretical and methodological developments in or points of inclusion into mathematics education research, policy, and/or practice.
5. This narrative, which has "historically referred to the perception that the United States differs qualitatively from other developed nations" (Koh, 2003), has also been viewed as "America's peculiar form of Eurocentrism" (Appleby, 1992, as cited in Ladson-Billings, 2004, p. 3).
6. Silver et al. (1995) describe the QUASAR project as "an educational reform project aimed at fostering and studying the development and implementation of enhanced mathematics instructional programs for students attending middle schools in economically disadvantaged communities" (p. 9).
7. Indeed, the Council's then-president indicated that the NCTM had taken the "helm" and proclaimed that, in reference to the *Standards,* "We [*sic*] realized that we could not sail our own ship without direction. We had to chart a new course" (Lindquist, 1993, p. 467).
8. See Apple's (1995) clarion call for mathematics education scholars to "take power seriously."

References

Adler, J. (2012). Discourse and equity: The simultaneous challenge of epistemological and social access. In B. Herbel-Eisenmann, J. Choppin, D. Wagner, & D. Pimm (Eds.), *Equity in discourse for mathematics education* (pp. v–vii). Dordrecht, Netherlands: Springer.

Aguirre, J. (2009). Privileging mathematics and equity in teacher education: Framework, counter-resistance strategies and reflections from a Latina mathematics educator. In B. Greer, S. Mukhopadhyay, S. Nelson-Barber, & A. Powell (Eds.), *Culturally responsive mathematics education* (pp. 295–319). New York, NY: Routledge.

Anderson, C. A., & Tate. W. F. (2008). Still separate, still unequal: Democratic access to mathematics in U.S. schools. In L. English (Ed.), *Handbook of international research in mathematics education,* 2nd ed. (pp. 299–318). New York, NY: Routledge.

Apple, M.W. (1992). Do the Standards go far enough? Power, policy, and practice in mathematics education. *Journal for Research in Mathematics Education, 23,* 412–431.

Apple, M.W. (1995). Taking power seriously: New directions in equity in mathematics education and beyond. In W.G. Secada, E. Fennema, & L.B. Adajian (Eds.), *New directions for equity in mathematics education* (pp. 329–348). New York, NY: Cambridge University Press.

Appleby, J. (1992). Rediscovering America's historic diversity: Beyond exceptionalism. *The Journal of American History, 79,* 419–431.

Atweh, B., Forgasz, H., & Nebres, B. (Eds.). (2001). *Sociocultural research on mathematics education: An international perspective.* Mahwah, NJ: Lawrence Erlbaum Associates.

Bartell, T.G. (2013). Learning to teach mathematics for social justice: Negotiating social justice and mathematical goals. *Journal for Research in Mathematics Education, 44*(1), 129–163.

Bell, D. (1980). *Brown v. Board of Education* and the interest-conversion dilemma. *Harvard Law Review, 93,* 518–533.

Berry, R.Q. (2005). Introduction: Building an infrastructure for equity in mathematics education. *The High School Journal, 88*(4), 1–5.

Berry, R.Q., III. (2008). Access to upper-level mathematics: The stories of successful African American middle school boys. *Journal for Research in Mathematics Education, 39*(5), 464–488.

Carnegie Commission. (1991, September). *In the national interest: The federal government in the reform of K-12 math and science education* (Report of Carnegie Commission on Science, Technology, and Government). New York, NY: Author.

Cobb, P., & Bowers, J. S. (1999). Cognitive and situated learning perspectives in theory and practice. *Educational Researcher, 28*(2), 4–15.

Confrey, J., & Kazak, S. (2006). A thirty-year reflection on constructivism in mathematics education in PME. In A. Gutiérrez & P. Boero (Eds.), *Handbook of research on the psychology of mathematics education: Past, present and future* (pp. 305–345). Boston, MA: Sense.

Diversity in Mathematics Education (DiME) Center for Learning and Teaching. (2007). Culture, race, power and mathematics education. In F. K. Lester (Ed.), *Second handbook of research on mathematics teaching and learning* (pp. 405–433). Charlotte, NC: Information Age.

Ellington, R. (2006). *Having their say: Eight high-achieving African-American undergraduate mathematics majors discuss their success and persistence in mathematics* (Unpublished doctoral dissertation). University of Maryland, College Park, MD.

English-Clarke, T., Slaughter-Defoe, D., & Martin, D. (2012). What does race have to do with math? Relationships between racial-mathematical socialization, mathematical identity, and racial identity. In D. Slaughter-Defoe (Ed.), *Racial stereotyping and child development* (pp. 55–79), Contributions to Human Development book series. Basel, Switzerland: Karger.

Esmonde, I. & Langer-Osuna, J. M. (2013). Power plays: How students in a small group negotiated mathematical discussions in hybrid spaces. *Journal for Research in Mathematics Education, 44*(1), 288–315.

Foote, M. Q. (Ed.) (2010). *Mathematics teaching & learning in K-12: Equity and professional development.* New York, NY: Palgrave Macmillan.

Forman, E.A. (2003). A sociocultural approach to mathematics reform: Speaking, inscribing, and doing mathematics within communities of practice. In J. Kilpatrick, W.G. Martin, & D. Schifter (Eds.), *A research companion to the Principles and Standards for School Mathematics* (pp. 333–352). Reston, VA: National Council of Teachers of Mathematics.

Frankenstein, M. (1989). *Relearning mathematics.* London, UK: Free Association Books.

Frankenstein, M. (1990). Incorporating race, gender, and class issues into a critical mathematical literacy curriculum. *Journal of Negro Education, 59,* 336–347.

Frankenstein, M. (1995). Equity in mathematics education: Class in the world outside the class. In W.G. Secada, E. Fennema, & L.B. Adajian (Eds.), *New directions for equity in mathematics education* (pp. 165–190). Cambridge, UK: Cambridge University Press.

Fuson, K.C., Smith, S.T., & Cicero, A.M.L. (1997). Supporting Latino first-graders' ten-structured thinking in urban classrooms. *Journal for Research in Mathematics Education, 28*(6), 738–766.

Gonzalez, L (2009). Teaching math for social justice: Reflections on a community of practice for high school teachers. *Journal of Urban Mathematics Education, 2*(1), 22–51.

Greeno, J.G. (2003). Situative research relevant to standards for school mathematics. In J. Kilpatrick, W.G. Martin, & D. Schifter (Eds.), *A research companion to the Principles and Standards for School Mathematics* (pp. 304–332). Reston, VA: National Council of Teachers of Mathematics.

Gutiérrez, R. (2000). Advancing African-American, urban youth in mathematics: Unpacking the success of one math department. *American Journal of Education, 109,* 63–111.

Gutiérrez, R. (2002). Enabling the practice of mathematics teachers in context: Toward a new equity research agenda. *Mathematical Thinking and Learning, 4*(2&3), 145–187.

Gutiérrez, R. (2008). A "gap-gazing" fetish in mathematics education? Problematizing research on the achievement gap. *Journal for Research in Mathematics Education, 39*(4), 357–364.

Gutiérrez, R. (2013). The sociopolitical turn in mathematics education. *Journal for Research in Mathematics Education, 44*(1), 37–68.

Gutiérrez, R., & Dixon-Román, E. (2011). Beyond gap gazing: How can thinking about education comprehensively help us (re)envision mathematics education? In B. Atweh, M. Graven, W. Secada, & P. Valero (Eds.), *Mapping equity and quality in mathematics education* (pp. 21–34). New York, NY: Springer.

Gutstein, E. (2003). Teaching and learning mathematics for social justice in an urban, Latino school. *Journal for Research in Mathematics Education, 34*(1), 37–73.

Gutstein, E. (2006). *Reading and writing the world with mathematics: Toward a pedagogy for social justice.* New York, NY: Routledge.

Hand, V.M. (2010). The co-construction of opposition in a low-track mathematics classroom. *American Educational Research Journal, 47*(1), 97–132.

Hand, V. M. (2012). Seeing power and culture in mathematics learning: Teacher noticing for equitable mathematics instruction. *Educational Studies in Mathematics, 80*, 233–247.

Heid, M.K. (2010). Where's the math (in mathematics education research)? *Journal for Research in Mathematics Education, 41*, 102–103.

Herbel-Eisenmann, B., Choppin, J., Wagner, D., & Pimm, D. (Eds.). (2012). *Equity in discourse for mathematics education.* Dordrecht, Netherlands: Springer.

Horn, I. S. (2008). Turnaround students in high school mathematics: Constructing identities of competence through mathematical worlds. *Mathematical Thinking and Learning, 10*(3), 201–239.

Jackson, K. (2009). The social construction of youth and mathematics: The case of a fifth grade classroom. In D.B. Martin (Ed.), *Mathematics teaching, learning, and liberation in the lives of Black children* (pp. 175–199). New York, NY: Routledge.

Katznelson, I. (2005). *When affirmative action was White: An untold history of racial inequality in twentieth-century America.* New York, NY: Norton.

Knapp, M.S. (1997). Between systemic reforms and the mathematics and science classroom: The dynamics of innovation, implementation, and professional learning. *Review of Educational Research, 67*(2), 227–266.

Koh, H.H. (2003). On American exceptionalism. *Stanford Law Review, 55*(5), 1479–1527.

Ladson-Billings, G. (1997). It doesn't add up: African American students' mathematics achievement. *Journal for Research in Mathematics Education, 28*(6), 697–708.

Ladson-Billings, G. (2004). Landing on the wrong note: The price we paid for *Brown. Educational Researcher, 33*(7), 3–13.

Langer-Osuna, J. M. (2011). How Brianna became bossy and Kofi came out smart: Understanding the trajectories of identity and engagement for two group leaders in a projects-based mathematics classroom. *The Canadian Journal for Science, Mathematics, and Technology Education, 11*(3), 207–225.

Larnell, G.V. (2011). *More than just skill: Mathematics identities, socialization, and remediation among African American undergraduates* (Doctoral dissertation). Retrieved from ProQuest/UMI (3465411).

Larnell, G.V. (under review). *More than just skill: Mathematics identities, inequities, and agency amid transitions to postsecondary mathematics.*

Leonard, J. (2008). *Culturally specific pedagogy in the mathematics classroom: Strategies for teachers and students.* New York, NY: Routledge.

Leonard, J., & Martin, D.B. (Eds.). (2013). *The brilliance of Black children in mathematics: Beyond the numbers and toward new discourse.* Charlotte, NC: Information Age.

Leonardo, Z., & Hunter, M. (2007). Imagining the urban: The politics of race, class, and schooling. In W.T. Pink & G.W. Noblit (Eds.), *International handbook of urban education* (pp. 779–802). New York, NY: Springer.

Lerman, S. (2000). The social turn in mathematics education research. In J. Boaler (Ed.), *Multiple perspectives on mathematics teaching and learning* (pp. 19–44). Westport, CT: Ablex.

Lindquist, M.M. (1993). President's report: Tides of change—Teachers at the helm. *Journal of Research in Mathematics Education, 24*(5),467–476.

Lipman, P. (2012). Neoliberal urbanism, race, and equity in mathematics education. *Journal of Urban Mathematics Education, 5*(2), 6–17.

Lubienski, S.T., & Bowen, A. (2000). Who's counting? A survey of mathematics education research 1982–1998. *Journal for Research in Mathematics Education, 31*, 626–633.

Martin, D.B. (2000). *Mathematics success and failure among African American youth: The roles of sociohistorical context, community forces, school influences, and individual agency.* Mahwah, NJ: Lawrence Erlbaum Associates.

Martin, D.B. (2003). Hidden assumptions and unaddressed questions in mathematics for all rhetoric. *The Mathematics Educator, 13*(2), 7–21.

Martin, D.B. (2009a). Researching race in mathematics education. *Teachers College Record, 111*(2), 295–338.

Martin, D.B. (2009b). Liberating the production of knowledge about African American children and mathematics. In D. Martin (Ed.), *Mathematics teaching, learning, and liberation in the lives of Black children* (pp. 3–38). London, UK: Routledge.

Martin, D.B. (2012). Learning mathematics while black. *Journal of Educational Foundations, 26*(1–2), 47–66.

Martin, D.B. (2013). Race, racial projects, and mathematics education. *Journal for Research in Mathematics Education, 44*(1), 316–333.

Martin, D.B., Gholson, M., & Leonard, J. (2011). Mathematics as gatekeeper: Power and privilege in the production of knowledge. *Journal of Urban Mathematics Education, 3*(2), 12–24.

Matthews, L.E. (2003). Babies overboard! The complexities of incorporation culturally relevant teaching into mathematics instruction. *Educational Studies in Mathematics, 53*(1), 61–82.

Matthews, L.E. (2009). "This little light of mine!" Entering voices of cultural relevancy into the mathematics teaching conversation. In D. B. Martin (Ed.) *Mathematics teaching, learning, and liberation in the lives of Black children* (pp. 63–87). London, UK: Routledge.

Matthews, L.E. (2008). Illuminating excellence: A movement of change within mathematics education. *Journal of Urban Mathematics Education, 1*(1), 1–4.

Matthews, W. (1983). Coloring the equation: Minorities and mathematics. *Journal for Research in Mathematics Education, 14*(1), 70–72.

Matthews, W. (1984). Influences on the learning and participation of minorities in mathematics. *Journal for Research in Mathematics Education, 15*(2), 84–95.

McGee, E. & Martin, D.B. (2011a). From the hood to being hooded: A case study of a Black male PhD. *Journal of African American Males in Education, 2*(1), 46–65.

McGee, E.O., & Martin, D.B. (2011b). "You would not believe what I have to go through to prove my intellectual value!": Stereotype management among academically successful Black mathematics and engineering students. *American Educational Research Journal, 48*(6), 1347–1389.

Moses, R.P., & Cobb, C. (2001). *Radical equations: Civil rights from Mississippi to the Algebra Project.* Boston, MA: Beacon Press.

Murtadha-Watts, K., & D'Ambrosio, B. (1997). A convergence of transformative multicultural and mathematics instruction? Dilemmas of group deliberations for curriculum change. *Journal for Research in Mathematics Education, 28*(6), 767–782.

Nasir, N. (2002). Identity, goals, and learning: Mathematics in cultural practice. *Mathematical Thinking and Learning, 2&3*, 213–248.

Nasir, N., & Shah, N. (2011). On defense: African American males making sense of racialized narratives in mathematics education. *Journal of African American Males in Education, 2*(1), 24–45.

National Commission on Excellence in Education. (1983). *A nation at risk: The imperative for educational reform.* Retrieved from http://datacenter.spps.org/uploads/SOTW_A_Nation_at_Risk_1983.pdf

National Council of Teachers of Mathematics. (1989). *Curriculum and evaluation standards for school mathematics.* Reston, VA: Author.

National Research Council. (1989). *Everybody counts: A report to the nation on the future of mathematics education.* Washington, DC: National Academies Press.

Noble. R. (2011). Mathematics self-efficacy and African American male students: An examination of models of success. *Journal of African American Males in Education, 2*(2), 188–213.

Parks, A. N., & Schmeichel, M. (2012). Obstacles to addressing race and ethnicity in the mathematics education literature. *Journal for Research in Mathematics Education, 43*, 238–252.

Polya, G. (1957). *How to solve it*. Princeton, NJ: Princeton University Press.

Porter, T. M. (1995). *Trust in numbers: The pursuit of objectivity in science and public life*. Princeton, NJ: Princeton University Press.

Raimi, R. (2005, August). *Brief chronology and dramatis personae of the new math*. Retrieved July 1, 2010 from http://www.math.rochester.edu/people/faculty/rarm/chron.html

Reys, R.E. (2000). Doctorates in mathematics education—An acute shortage. *Notices of the American Mathematical Society, 47*(10), 1267–1270.

Reys, R.E., & Dossey, J.A. (Eds.). (2008). *U.S. doctorates in mathematics education: Developing stewards of the discipline*. Providence, RI: American Mathematical Society; Washington, DC: In cooperation with Mathematical Association of America.

Robinson, S.P. (1996). With numeracy for all: Urban schools and the reform of mathematics education. *Urban Education, 30*(4), 379–394.

Schoenfeld, A.H. (1985). *Mathematical problem solving*. Orlando, FL: Academic Press.

Schoenfeld, A.H. (2004). The math wars. *Educational Policy, 18*(1), 253–286.

Schoenfeld, A.H. (2006). What doesn't work: The challenge and failure of the What Works Clearinghouse to conduct meaningful reviews of students of mathematics curricula. *Educational Researcher, 35*(2), 13–21.

Scott, J.C. (1998). *Seeing like a state: How certain schemes to improve the human condition have failed*. New Haven, CT: Yale University Press.

Secada, W.G. (1989). Agenda setting, enlightened self-interest, and equity in mathematics education. *Peabody Journal of Education, 66*(2), 22–56.

Secada, W. G. (1996). Urban students acquiring English and learning mathematics in the context of reform. *Urban Education, 30*, 422–448.

Secada, W.G., Fennema, E., & Adajian, L.B. (Eds.). (1995). *New directions for equity in mathematics education*. New York, NY: Cambridge University Press.

Secada, W.G., & Meyer, M. (1989). Needed: An agenda for equity in mathematics education. *Peabody Journal of Education, 66*, 1–5.

Senk, S.L., & Thompson, D.R. (Eds.). (2003). *Standards-based school mathematics curricula: What are they? What do students learn?* Mahwah, NJ: Lawrence Erlbaum Associates.

Sfard, A. (1998). On two metaphors for learning and the dangers of choosing just one. *Educational Researcher, 27*, 4–13.

Silver, E.A., Smith, M.S., & Nelson, B.S. (1995). The QUASAR Project: Equity concerns meet mathematics education reform in the middle school. In W.G. Secada, E. Fennema, & L.B. Adajian (Eds.), *New directions for equity in mathematics education* (pp. 9–56). New York, NY: Cambridge University Press.

Sleeter, C.E. (1997). Mathematics, multicultural education, and professional development. *Journal for Research in Mathematics Education, 28*(6), 680–696.

Smith, M.S. & O'Day, J. (1991). Systemic school reform. In S. Fuhrman & B. Malen (Eds.), *The politics of curriculum and testing* (pp. 233–267). Bristol, PA: Falmer Press.

Spencer, J. A. (2009). Identity at the crossroads: Understanding the practices and forces that shape African American success and struggle in mathematics. In D. B. Martin (Ed.), *Mathematics teaching, learning, and liberation in the lives of Black children* (pp. 200–230). New York, NY: Routledge.

Stinson, D.W. (2006). African American male adolescents, schooling (and mathematics): Deficiency, rejection, and achievement. *Review of Educational Research, 76*(4), 477–506.

Stinson, D.W. (2008). Negotiating sociocultural discourses: The counter-storytelling of academically (and mathematically) successful African American male students. *American Educational Research Journal, 45*(4), 975–1010.

Stinson, D.W. (2009). Negotiating sociocultural discourses: The counter-storytelling of academically and mathematically successful African American male students. In D. Martin (Ed.), *Mathematics teaching, learning, and liberation in the lives of Black children* (pp. 265–288). New York, NY: Routledge.

Stinson, D.W. (2010). How is that one particular statement appeared rather than another?: Opening a different space for different statements about urban mathematics education. *Journal of Urban Mathematics Education, 3*(2), 1–11.

Stinson, D.W., & Bullock, E.C. (2012). Critical postmodern theory in mathematics education research: A praxis of uncertainty. *Educational Studies in Mathematics, 80*(1–2), 41–55.

Tate, W.F. (1994). Mathematics standards and urban education: Is this the road to recovery? *Educational Forum, 58,* 380–390.

Tate, W. F. (1995a). School mathematics and African American students: Thinking seriously about opportunity-to-learn standards. *Educational Administrational Quarterly, 31*, 428–444.

Tate, W. F. (1995b). Race, retrenchment, and reform of school mathematics, *Phi Delta Kappan, 75*, 477–485.

Tate, W.F. (1996). Urban schools and mathematics reform: Implementing new standards. *Urban Education, 30*(4), 371–378.

Tate, W. F. (1997). Race, ethnicity, SES, gender, and language proficiency trends in mathematics achievement: An update. *Journal for Research in Mathematics Education, 28*, 652–680.

Tate, W.F. (2008). Putting the "urban" in mathematics education scholarship. *Journal of Urban Mathematics Education, 1*(1), 5–9.

Tate, W. F., & Rousseau, C. (2002). Access and opportunity: The political and social context of mathematics education. In L. English (Ed.), *International handbook of research in mathematics education* (pp. 271–300). Mahwah, NJ: Erlbaum.

Tellez, K., Moschkovich, J., & Civil, M. (Eds.). (2011). *Latinos/as and mathematics education: Research on learning and teaching in classrooms and communities*. Charlotte, NC: Information Age.

Terry, C.L., Sr. (2011). Mathematical counterstory and African American male students: Urban mathematics education from a critical race theory perspective. *Journal of Urban Mathematics Education, 4*(1), 23–49.

Turner, E. E., Dominguez, H., Maldonado, L., & Empson, S. B. (2013). English learners' participation in mathematical discussion: Shifting positionings, dynamic identities. *Journal for Research in Mathematics Education, 44*(1), 199–234.

Valero, P., & Zevenbergen, R. (Eds.) (2004). *Researching the socio-political dimensions of mathematics education: Issues of power in theory and methodology*. Boston, MA: Kluwer.

Wager, A., & Stinson, D. (Eds.). (2012). *Teaching mathematics for social justice: Conversations with educators*. Reston, VA: National Council of Teachers of Mathematics.

Walker, E.N. (2012). *Building mathematics learning communities: Improving outcomes in urban high schools.* New York, NY: Teachers College Press.

Walshaw, M. (2011). Positive possibilities of rethinking (urban) mathematics education within a postmodern frame. *Journal of Urban Mathematics Education, 4*(2), 7–14.

Weissglass, J. (2002). Inequity in mathematics education: Questions for educators. *Mathematics Educator, 12*(2), 34–43.

21
Urban Literacy Learning

David E. Kirkland

As part of my review for this chapter, I surveyed close to 2,000 articles, books, and chapters focused on urban literacy at the P–12 and/or postsecondary levels. This available literature is complex, focusing on issues that range from traditional language and literacy practices to more vernacular forms of literacy that embrace the spirit of the social turn in literacy research. The literature also suggests that some of the complexity surrounding literacy in urban literacy studies stems from the nature of literacy itself. While there are many competing definitions of literacy, scholarship on urban literacies suggests that there can be no single, "autonomous" definition of literacy (Street, 1995), for "what counts as literacy at a particular time and place depends on who has the power to define it" (Bloome, 1997, p. 107).

According to the literature, literacy is at an impasse, particularly in regard to urban literacy learning, as definitions of literacy continue to change and, therefore, elude scholars. We have seen over decades definitions of literacy that are constantly in flux, especially with the development of new technologies. Many in urban literacy studies now consider literacy to be the ability to locate, evaluate, use, and communicate using a wide range of resources including texts and visual, audio, and video sources (Alvermann, 2001; Morrell, 2008; Reinking, 1995; Winn, 2011). Further, definitions of literacy are shaped by the prevailing social and political trends of the time. Among these are different definitions formulated to meet the needs of state or religious institutions, and of those who oppose such institutions who link literacy to empowerment (Shor, 1992).

Another perspective widely cited in the literature with increasing frequency suggests that literacy is more than the acquisition of reading and writing skills. From this perspective, literacy is also a social practice or social currency (Bourdieu, 1977), and, as such, a key to social mobility and empowerment (Freire & Macedo, 1987; Gee 1991). The conception of literacy as socially practiced drives the critical and anthropological ideas (Erickson, 1984, 1987; Heath, 1983; Scribner & Cole, 1981; Street, 1984, 1995) that literacies are multiple, socially situated, and a fundamental consequence of power (Barton & Hamilton, 1998; Luke, 2004; New London Group, 1996). This conception pushes literacy scholars away from definitions of literacy as transcendent skills that can be taught in isolation, practiced, then transferred into other social contexts. Instead, acts of literacy are never neutral and are always embedded in symbolic social practices, in which members of a community seek to construct particular identities, relationships, or valued activities and objects.

By contrast, mainstream society and school classrooms have their own particular social practices in which literate acts are constructed by participants to achieve the valued ends of schooling (Dyson, 1993, 2003; Mahiri, 1998; Heath, 1983). Furthermore, school (or academic) literacy practices seldom reflect the literacy practices of historically oppressed groups (Heath, 1983; Morrell, 2004), and particularly those who exist in urban situations. This may be true for a variety of reasons (e.g., racism, classism, and other factors that play party to social neglect). However, it might also be true because too much remains unknown about literacy among disadvantaged populations. It is vital that urban youth find success in school in order to find success in society. Hence, there is an urgent need to better understand literacy practices from their perspectives so that educators can begin to rethink classroom literacy curriculum and instruction with them in mind.

This chapter has dual purposes: (1) to broadly frame literacy learning within urban contexts with respect to the scholarly literature, and (2) to illustrate where this framing of literacy needs expanding, especially as it pertains to urban contexts. Hence, just as rhythm through music takes on new meanings in the ears of different listeners, so too do literacies, which in the narratives of cities reveal themselves complexly both within and beyond the social limits ascribed to urban geographies. The larger point I wish to make in this chapter will illustrate urban literacies as complex and dialogic and fundamentally inclusive of the social lives of urban youth.

Urban Literacy Learning as a Social Process

In early studies of language in U.S. cities, scholars such as Smitherman (1977), Labov (1972), and Baugh (1983) relied heavily upon social and critical frameworks to underscore the operation of language within the lives of city residents. Their studies found that communication is not only a social act, but also a social process that invites the culture, history, and politics of the individual and the group into the communicative event (Gilyard, 1991). That is, these scholars found that language learning (as in communicative competence) develops through use, as interlocutors engage fully within situated linguistic contexts (i.e., discourse communities) and in the process become more expert users of particular linguistic varieties/codes.

The argument that these linguists, whom we now call sociolinguists, were making was that language in the city was influenced by *the city*—by the people in the city, their cultures, their histories, their motives and drives, their interactions, and so on. The idea that emerged was that language was, in particular, socially constructed and that its systems and rules emerged within a greater social context based almost exclusively upon social, historical, and cultural scripts written in the everyday lives of people interacting within valued and shared settings around meaningful activities and events (de Certeau, 1984; Lave & Wenger, 1992; Vygotsky, 1978). The idea of social language (Gee, 1996) was groundbreaking because it determined that languages (and by association literacy) nested in local environments. Hence, language variation (and, as we will see, situated literacies) could be explained by the nuances and uniquenesses of any particular environment, the political pulls that tug at it, and the common cultures that define it.

In this light, Smitherman (1999) argued that the often-unwritten languages (i.e., vernaculars) of people within cities (and primarily of urban Black people) had their own distinct characteristics. These characteristics, she explained, while often derided as "broken English" or "bad language" was in fact a unique codification, a language itself with unique—if not exclusive—rules that governed a particular type of social and cultural work. Many scholars such as Heath (1983), Dyson (1993), and Richardson (2002) have used elements of Smitherman's social approach to language to frame their articulations of urban literacies. For example, Heath (1983) drew upon Smitherman to explain how cultural differences accented the literacies of individuals from different communities. In so doing, she rejected the deficiency model that typically ignored, or worse vilified, the literacy practices of historical marginalized populations. Instead, she opted for a profit model that illustrated the politics of difference in relation to how literacy was valued in each community and revealed the economies of variation that marked the various worths of literacy within situated cultural markets.

Following the groundbreaking work of sociolinguists, literacy scholars such as Heath came to see literacy as social practice (Dyson, 1993; Vygotsky, 1978) and defined urban literacy learning within sociocultural literacy traditions (Heath, 1983; Scribner & Cole, 1981; Street, 1984). For urban literacy studies, the positioning of literacy as social practice has assumed greater urgency. Urban literacy scholars such as Hill (2009) and Irizarry (2011) have pointed out that, in our age of "accountability," pundits of culturally homogenized and standardized literacy curricula have invested a good deal of time, energy, and resources in the linguistic and cognitive dimensions of literacy that predate the social turn in language and literacy studies and dismiss the literacies most meaningful to urban youth. Hence, literacy policy in urban schools often fails to consider social context as critical to literacy learning (Kucer, 2001). In addition, federal and state governments through policies such as No Child Left Behind, Race to the Top, The Common Core State Standards have taken an overtly narrow stance in defining what counts as "scientifically based" literacy research. Too often, these narrow policy definitions and school-based enactments of literacy discount *literacies of social practice* and instead privilege *literacies of elite interests,* and usually to the detriment of the masses.

Literacy scholars have long critiqued the mismatch between literacy as we as a field are coming to understand it and literacy as it gets enacted in the public sphere, particularly in public policy. For example, Langer (1991) critiqued narrow definitions of literacy, contrasting "literacy as the act of reading and writing and literacy as ways of thinking" (p. 13). For Langer, "literacy can be viewed in a broader and educationally more productive way, as the ability to think and reason like a literate person, within a particular society" (p. 11). She argued:

> It is the culturally appropriate way of thinking, not the act of reading or writing, that is most important in the development of literacy. Literacy thinking manifests itself in different ways in oral and written language in different societies, and educators need to understand these ways of thinking if they are to build bridges and facilitate transitions among ways of thinking. (p. 13)

Limiting our understanding of literacy to language and cognition as gauged through experimental designs or as affixed to dominant traditions is to overlook the social and cultural nuances of literacy practices (Kucer, 2001). By contrast, urban literacy learning happens in the complexity not of the mind but in the interactions among space and purposes, individuals and tools. Morrell (2004), for example, argued that urban youth extended purposes of academic literacy in their everyday cultural productions in order to create meaningful opportunities to exist more fully human in relation to one another. In his participatory research study of urban youth, Morrell observed how literacy learning for urban youth involved dialogical sequences of popular textualizations—textualizations such as Hip Hop texts that, beyond school, mattered to urban youth in their understandings of the world. In this light, Morrell found that popular culture (including Hip Hop), new media, and sports played an important role in how the urban youth critically engaged in meaning-making processes in their own processes of becoming more conscious agents of literacy with greater command of their situations.

In her study of urban children, Dyson (2003) made observations similar to Morrell. The urban youth she studied constructed lives and learned literacy through the interplay of home and school, where items from popular culture, new media, and sports defined expanding fields of practice. For her part, Fisher (2003) explored "out-of-school" communities of practice (what she referred to as "African Diaporic Participatory Literacy Communities"), describing how literacy learning in two relatively sizable urban settings in California was leveraged in spaces such as bookstores and open-mic poetry venues. In a similar vein, Paris (2009), after examining a multiethnic community in Southern California, argued that urban youth tie their literacy learning to developing and complexly layered selves. In keeping with the studies of Morrell, Dyson, Fisher, and others, Paris maintained that urban literacy learning is a practice of pluralism where multiple social and cultural entities conspire in what Gutiérrez (2008) and others have termed a *third space* to format meaning and socially situated possibility within the porous boundaries of "multiethnic" urban communities.

Kinloch's (2010) examination of the changing faces of urban settings was far less celebratory. She argued that urban youth learn literacy in situations of hostility, cultural shift, and spatial mourning. In her study of a group of young men who use video cameras to record gentrification in their Harlem neighborhoods, Kinloch tied urban literacy learning to narratives of loss and remembrance. This theme holds true for Kirkland (2009) who examined the tattoos of a group of urban Black men. He argued that such young men used the tattoo needle to cope with loss and to aid memory in ways that sanctioned particular forms of healing in the midst of particular forms of despair.

These understandings of literacy learning—literacy learning as socially constructed—indeed problematizes narrow notions of literacy learning, notions that I argue work discursively to minimize what counts as literate performance and who counts as a literate person. The urban school-based and national and state policies surrounding literacy learning seem ineffectual in the face of urban literacy research. Heavily influenced by the social turn—a research orientation that looks beyond the individual to the cultural, historical, and political centers in which people live (Cushman, Kintgen, Kroll, & Rose, 2001)—urban literacy research suggests that social context is central to human development, as it has typically explored how the richness and complexity of the setting, its actors, their goals, and the cultural tools available in the setting interact to expand and shape how meanings are constructed (Kirkland, 2008; Lee & Smagorinsky, 2000). In this light, urban literacy learning can best be understood as a social process (where literacy itself is seen as a social practice) mediated by the use of cultural tools, particularly language, as people participate in culturally and historically valued activities.

Then, in addition to Langer's broad definition of literacy, a clearer picture of urban literacy learning is emerging within three broad theoretical perspectives—the ethnography of communication (Heath, 1983; Hymes, 1962), Vygotskian perspectives and cultural historical activity theory (Scribner & Cole, 1981), and the New Literacy Studies (Gee, 1996; New London Group, 1996; Street, 1995). As defined by Street (1995), these perspectives provide a "broader consideration of literacy as a social practice and in a cross-cultural perspective" (p. i). Unlike traditional views of literacy, which attempt to emphasize the differences between "literacy" and "orality" (the written word and the spoken one), and which put forward reading and writing as decontextualized technical skills, these perspectives on urban literacies can be briefly described as "integrated-social-cultural-political-historical" views (Gee, 1996, p. 122). These views situate urban literacies historically and politically and foreground issues of social interaction and cultural practices/production as well as resistances and relations of power (Barton & Hamilton, 1998; Heath, 1982, 1983; Lankshear & McLaren, 1993; Luke, 1988).

From a dialogic perspective (Bakhtin, 1981, 1986; Dyson, 2003), the notion of urban literacies is yet expanded again to include a multiplicity and diversity of voices—which in cities are many (Kirkland, 2010a). These voices, when socially considered within the streams of activity they facilitate, fold all human activity into complex unities of differences. In this way, urban literacy learning is influenced by a collaboration of personal and social aspects that define individuals and groups by class, gender, race, and so forth (Greene & Abt-Perkins, 2003). I have written extensively about urban literacy practices and the interaction among these social indices (Kirkland, 2011a, 2009, 2008), that in cities, literacy learning is linked dialogically—as in a more focused social act—to efforts of both individuals and groups to redress social inequities (Auerbach, 1993; Kirkland, 2010a; Morrell, 2008). Its purpose is to test ideas and thus determine what society should think and how people should live. Its characteristic forms are the expression, juxtaposition, or negotiation of our individual and our cultural differences.

Urban Literacy Learning and Its Complexities as a Dialogic Practice

Even as a social process, urban literacy learning must be thought of as more than interaction between individuals and individual participation in groups. There are other social factors that shape urban literacies and constructions of the "literate" individuals. Perhaps chief among them are race and gender and their constituent political exponents, sexism and racism.

Lopez (2001) defined race as "a group loosely bound together by historically contingent, socially significant elements of their morphology and/or ancestry . . . Neither an essence nor an illusion, [race] is an ongoing process of social and political struggle" (p. 193). Following Lopez's definition, race becomes a persistent factor in social practices, including literacy. As such, race raises critical questions about power and desire in the nature of literacy learning. To the issue, I agree with Gee (1990) that to "situate literacy in the individual person, rather than in the society of which that person is a member . . . obscures the multiple ways in which reading, writing, and language interrelate with the workings of power and desire in social life" (p. 27). In this regard, urban literacy learning is not only a social process; it is fundamentally a dialogic one that involves ongoing and delicate practices of negotiation.

Scholars such Delpit (1988), Purcell-Gates (2002), and others argue that learning literacy, or the learning of hidden rules and cultural codes of dominant culture, sanction struggle and regulate mobility. To be successful in school and society, urban youth, for example, must be able to function and move both within their own cultural communities and within the dominant society (Mahiri, 1998; Morrell, 2004; Ogbu, 1974, 1978; B. Tatum, 1992). From Delpit's (1988) perspective, non-Whites may find that their racial backgrounds may result in unequal and limited access to education and other resources that can facilitate social or economic progress (MacLeod, 1995; Rose, 1989). Due to their racial backgrounds, certain individuals are marginalized in society, and their cultures, languages, and moral codes frequently dismissed as inferior social practices, even in school settings (Delpit, 1988; Dyson, 2003; Smitherman, 1977). Individuals who are relegated to marginalized social positions consistently experience a lack of privilege and power. Therefore, they often internalize this experience (Ogbu, 1978), and internalized oppression, or believing that the self is somehow "less than" and "less worthy" than the other, results in lowered expectations in school and for life chances (Ferguson, 1998).

To more clearly illustrate this point, I use the example of urban African Americans, particularly Black males, who according to research internalize the oppression (i.e., self-hatred/disdain) taught through racism (Kirkland, 2010b; West, 1993). Researchers such as Kirkland (2010b) and A. Tatum (2008) have suggested that this internalization influences literacy learning by creating conditions through which literacy is (not) practiced. In a similar vein, Smitherman and van Dijk (1988) maintained, "Text and talk in many ways are constitutive of the social and political dimensions of structural racism in society" (p. 12). However, racism, discrimination based on race, in contemporary society is not always visible, particularly in urban settings (Greene & Abt-Perkins,

2003). As such, nascent forms of racism must be distinguished from the more blatant and overt manifestations in order to fully appreciate their impact on urban literacy learning—a literacy learning experience that takes place usually in fully racially heterogeneous settings.

In such settings, girls are typically more apt to read school texts than boys, as items such as gendered interests, performances of hypermasculinity, or exaggerated acts of maleness are intensified in city settings (Winn, 2011; Young, 2007). In the learning/making (and researching) of urban literacy, gender matters in relation to other important social factors such as race because it positions individuals in particular ways in relation to literacy. For example, Singh (1997) offered a nuanced notion of gender that considers the various mixings of an individual's social identity as important to urban literacy learning. That is, not only are urban literacies at once genderedly negotiated, they are also dependent upon and defined in relation to the political inflections of the self (raced or gendered) and, thus, the intersection of the gender marker with other relevant social identity markers, including social geographies.

While I emphasize the importance of race and gender here, I acknowledge that there are other important social issues to be raised within the dialogic tradition as the "multiple worlds" of city residents are put into conversation (Dyson, 1993). Heath (1983), for example, has maintained, "Opportunities, values, motivations, and resources available for communication in each community are influenced by that group's social history as well as by current environmental conditions" (pp. 6–7). As such, "social history" and social environment, or the contexts of literacy practice, play an important role in how literacy is negotiated to the point of learning.

In cities, the way one "learns" literacy and negotiates social space is shaped by and intermittently shapes her or his race, gender, and geographic context at once (Kinloch, 2010; Mahiri, 2004). Therefore, I not only assume that race, gender, and geographic context have much to do with how one learns literacy, I also contend that such factors are vital for understanding the workings of literacy within some dialogical sphere. As such, one wonders: How might we understand urban literacy learning with regard to the contexts of literacy practices and in relation to the societal constructs with which individuals and groups are associated? In order to understand its greater complexities, we must frame urban literacy learning in the complexities of the new urban literate and their literacies (Fisher, 2004).

Framing Urban Literacy Learning in the Complexities of Literacy

While there is a plethora of literature available on literacy as social practice, there is relatively little literature available on how urban youth learn (as opposed to practice) literacy. Notwithstanding, the literature that is available concerning urban youth literacy learning paints a disturbing picture that profiles gaps in achievement between poor urban youth and their more affluent counterparts (Jencks & Phillips, 1998). In this way, an achievement differential between urban and nonurban students has been well documented. While this difference has been widely discussed by researchers, educators have found little success in dealing with it (Kinloch, 2010). How, then, might we reframe the situations of literacy and achievement with respect to the differences between urban and nonurban youth?

We can take a cue from research on Black males. We know that young Black males in contemporary American society face major challenges to their development and well-being (Noguera, 2008). Like urban youth in relation to nonurban youth, Black males perform well below other students in basic subject areas (Reed, 1988). They are more likely to be remediated or placed into classes for students with learning disabilities than other students (Milofsky, 1974). They are suspended from school more often and for longer periods of time than other students (Noguera, 2008). Given only these examples, it is not surprising that there is an achievement differential between Black male students and other students. Not only are there achievement differences between them, the school experiences of Black males are vastly different from those of other students (Coleman et al., 1966; A. Ferguson, 2000).

Because of these differences, a growing body of literature on Black male school experiences has begun to show that being Black and male speaks almost definitively to issues of literacy achievement (Hunsander, 2002; Pollard, 1993). According to the National Assessment of Educational Progress (NAEP, 2012), nearly 70% of Black 4th-grade boys read below grade level, compared with 27% of White children. Even Hispanic and Asian 4th graders fared better on reading exams than Black males, although English is their second language. The point here is, by isolating the comparative variables, we only articulate narratives of lack to the peril of complexity when describing the urban literacy learning situation. Of course, all urban literacy learners are not Black males.

While there are many ways to explain why urban youth perform less well than more affluent youth on "literacy" tests, we know that one of the main reasons is because of language differences. As Smitherman (1977, 1999) and others (Foster, 2001; Hilliard, 1991) have shown, schools, and more specifically classrooms, penalize students who do speak or come from homes that speak the dominant dialect. From an early age, urban youth, particularly English learners, are confronted with a series of cultural and linguistic barriers that make it more challenging for them to achieve academic and social success (Kunjufu, 1985; Moss & Tilly, 1995; Noguera, 2001).

In thinking about the dilemmas facing urban youth, my interactions with a research participant known in my work as Shawn have been helpful (Kirkland, 2008). Based on my interactions with Shawn, I have been able to illustrate how the sociocultural battle that I was waging with literacy morphed into a political one. In this struggle, definitions of achievement, literacy, and even "the gap" were contested. By defining literacy in a way that does not consider the contributions and socio-symbolic practices of Black males like Shawn, I have argued that the idea of literacy in the official world has been constructed egregiously against them. In this way, the literacy agenda that state and national policies such No Child Left Behind (2001), Race to the Top (2011), and Common Core Standards endorse pose a unique social and educational threat to Black males (Kirkland, 2011b). Accordingly, Smith and Wilhelm (2002) warn, schools seem to be failing particular youth. They add, "while this failure may be rooted in a complex amalgam of issues . . . perceiving a problem of ANY group of students obligates us to try to understand it, so we can do something about it" (p. 3).

Beyond acknowledging the plight of urban literacy education, a critical question remains: How might we address important issues about literacy learning in urban contexts? As I will discuss later in this chapter using vignettes from Shawn's story for grounding examples, many urban youth are by far the most threatened demographic in our population both in school and out (Gibbs, 1988). As I have noted, this threat requires immediate attention because educational policies and literacy programs have failed and continue to fail to acknowledge the social dimensions of urban literacy learning. By extension, official spaces are being shaped in ways that, by situating literacy around unfamiliar social practices, both figuratively and literally, exclude many, if not most, urban youth from educational access. To deal with these threats, scholars must contend with society's flawed definitions of literacy and its comprehensive (mis)representation of urban youth.

The Statistics and the Problem of (Mis)representation

While they will never tell us much about literacy in the lives of urban youth, statistics will always work as a social mechanism, which attempts to describe some bounded phenomenon. In this way, statistics can be dangerous, as the pictures they paint are usually influenced by the hands of those who weld the pen. Nevertheless, statistical pictures can also be helpful. Given this, the portrait that statistics paint about urban youth, urban Black males in particular, and "literacy" gives us reason to be alarmed. For example, of our nation's youth, only 12% of urban Black males test proficiently in reading, as compared to 40% of other American youth (National Center for Education Statistics, 2011). Rosa A. Smith (2004), president of the Schott Foundation, relates these national data to other statistics that describe the multiple crises confronting urban youth. The Center for the Study of Social Policy (1993) reports that close to 40% of urban Black males will be jobless, either unemployed or incarcerated, by 2020. In addition to exorbitant jobless rates, the U.S. Department of Health and Human Services (2004) reports that young Black men (ages 10–14) have shown the largest increase in suicide rates since 1980 compared to other youth groups by sex and ethnicity, increasing 180%. Among 15- to 19-year-old Black males, rates (since 1980) have increased by 80% (Poussaint & Alexander, 2000). In addition, a Black male is twice as likely to die before the age of 45 as a White male (Roper, 1991; Spivak, Prothrow-Stith, & Hausman, 1988).

In education, Black males are at the bottom or near the bottom of all academic achievement categories and are grossly overrepresented among school suspensions, dropouts, and special education tracks (Noguera, 2008). Given the unbelievable magnitude of the situation, Smith (2004) describes the alarming situation of Black males in both schools and society as "catastrophic." In the foreword to a recent Schott Foundation study on Black male academic (under)achievement, Smith writes: "The facts that startled us [the Schott Foundation] the most—and defined new Schott work—were the alarming data on Black male students showing bleak under-achievement on every school related factor" (p. 2). But then again, there is more to Black male literacy learning than statistics.

Some might argue that Black males present the most extreme picture of urban youth. However, the issues they face are more or less reflected in the situations of all cities' kids. Particularly, the achievement differential, especially in literacy, between urban youth and other American youth suggests that schools have not clearly understood how to promote successful literacy learning among this population as a group. Moreover, the poor performances of many urban youth on national literacy assessments raise significant questions about the importance of social dimensions of literacy—including racism (Tatum, 1992) and gender politics (Thorne, 1993).

While the evidence clearly indicates that a troubling number of urban youth perform poorly on standardized measures of literacy proficiency, it would be naïve to assume that all urban youth are incapable of reading and writing in proficient ways. Rather, educators must attend to fundamental issues surrounding the social construction of literacy curricula and the social practice of literacy instruction at the secondary school level. Our collective failure to ameliorate such issues (i.e., injustice in the design of public education) prevents us from helping more urban youth achieve to their highest potential.

This explanation bears true in Shawn's case. Upon hearing the title of one of his raps ("Motherless Child"), I began to question some tenuous and unsettled explanations for racial differences in urban literacy achievement. Indeed, society functions as an arbiter of literacy through the ways it labels and represents (and misrepresents) individuals. In this way, Shawn was labeled by his school as an "illiterate." In its report to the school board, his high school's steering committee and improvement team cited Shawn as an example of "the many Black male students who are slipping through the cracks." According to the report,

> Deshawn Stevenson[1] is an example of the crisis, affecting our African American male students . . . many of [whom] cannot and do not read. Their test scores in writing are abysmal and worsening. . . . Hence, it is the obligation of the school to rectify this issue before we develop a population of illiterate Americans.

While literacy learning may be at issue here, there is another more crucial issue that deals with how schools label individuals as literate and illiterate. Labeling (and the labeled through "self-fulfilling prophesy" [Rist, 1970]) work to reinforce the valuations of a privileged class while obscuring the values and abilities of the oppressed (see Freire, 1970). For example, while looking through Shawn's school file, I caught a glimpse of a note written by Shawn's 10th-grade English teacher, who "feared" Shawn was illiterate. The note explained that Shawn "has trouble reading and shows difficulty expressing his thoughts on paper." But outside the classroom in the company of his friends and me, Shawn was always writing and was, perhaps, the most driven writer of the group.

The differences between my observations of Shawn and his teacher's observations of him concerned me. First, there were no signs to me that Shawn was even remotely illiterate, so why would she insinuate that he was? The only way that I could reconcile his teacher's conclusion (versus my own) was to assume that Shawn acted differently in the classroom than he did among his peers and me, or that Shawn's teacher did not know him like we did.

The other issue that stuck out to me deals with the politics of accommodating social norms. Research suggests that some urban youth accommodate inferior/marginal social roles at times as a way of protecting themselves from the punishment of discrimination or peer pressure. More or less, they comply with some school norms, even when those norms fail to match their social interests. By contrast, other less accommodating urban youth will find greater opposition in a racist structure than one who is seen as less threatening (hooks, 2004). Hence, researchers must never neglect the internal tensions faced by urban youth wanting to preserve senses of self. In addition, they must also acknowledge the systems of discrimination that influence the ways the youth may or may not perform in public spaces. Finally, they must understand that school literacy is used, not unproblematically, to interpret and label individuals like Shawn as "slow," "troubled," and, worst, (because of his resistance to the literate norms of schools and society) "illiterate."

The Problem of School

While the statistics may be disturbing, it is important to examine and not neglect the function of schools in manufacturing troubling perceptions of urban youth. In this way, A. Ferguson (2000) warned that statistics are misleading, and for many urban youth, schools might be threatening. As opposed to describing them as victims of illiteracy, Ferguson describes some urban youth as victims of the school. By taking an in-depth look into the school lives of a group of urban youth, Ferguson documents how schools create, shape, and regulate social identities, from tracking some students to be doctors to tracking others, particularly Black males, to be prisoners. She argues that the disciplinary system of schools and their practices of labeling and categorizing students construct urban youth as deviant and defiant.

Complicating school's role in constructing negative conceptions of urban youth (A. Ferguson, 2000) is the complexity of literacy and the limited nature of school literacy practices. Literacy is never stable or fixed, but is contingent and flexible, a practice that requires choice and selection. Why after 400 or 500 years, then, do we still read Shakespeare in classrooms? This question raises serious concerns as to who has ownership over classroom texts. While they have some ownership over the texts they read outside of classrooms, urban youth, in general, have limited ownership over texts read within classrooms.

Issues of authority and ownership of texts are not only important in understanding school's domination over classroom literacy learning. They are also important aspects of literacy learning in general. In her work on literacy, Au (1997) referred to children's ownership over texts [read or written] as influential to their sense of self-confidence and command of reading and writing. Building upon Au's work, Dahl and Freppon (1995) suggested that the desire to participate in literacy practices is connected to an attachment to and ownership of a given literacy task. Therefore, the story about a person's ability to read and write is always more complicated than what schools reveal.

Even though he could read and write, Shawn was labeled by his school as barely literate. In 3rd grade, his teacher identified him as "a struggling reader." Based on her assessment, Shawn received *Title I* support in reading. While he hasn't taken a reading assessment test since entering high school, Shawn's 7th-grade Michigan Educational Assessment Program (MEAP) scores bear out, at least numerically, the tension between Shawn's nonacademic and academic literate performances. According to his 7th-grade MEAP scores, Shawn ranked below 75% of Michigan students in reading.

In a recent conversation with me, Shawn expressed frustration with reading in school. To him, reading aloud was "scary," reading in school "boring," and "sometimes a chore." Even still, he admits, "I be reading stuff all the time at home . . . stuff that interest[s] me. It's not that I can't read; I don't like to [read] because the stuff they make you read [in school] ain't really important anyway." He continues by critiquing the school's emphasis on Shakespeare. According to Shawn, "What am I gonna do with Shakespeare? He ain't gon git me no job."

Since school literacy practices do not always reflect the cultural practices of all students, defining literacy solely along academic lines gives schools a potentially dangerous influence not only over what counts as literacy, but also over who counts as "literate." This leaves a considerable number of individuals, many of whom are young, urban Black males, powerless in a global economy that privileges credentials and labels produced by schools (Powell et al., 1985).

This isn't to say that multiple forms of illiteracy in America do not exist and should not be dealt with. Rather, as I have argued, labeling individuals "illiterate" is based not necessarily upon whether individuals can read or write, but upon ways that schools do and do not define literacy. As I have argued, schools' definitions of literacy are at best narrow and, perhaps worse, discriminatory. Since Heath (1983) has shown that school literacy is closely tied to the cultural practices of middle-class suburban Whites, defining illiteracy exclusively in relation to academic norms is not only myopic; it is fundamentally problematic.

Defining literacy in narrow ways has led researchers to make questionable linkages among "illiteracy," urban youth, and incarceration. These linkages are disturbing because they explain, in part, the school-to-prison pipeline in urban America. For structural reasons, some might argue that prisoners are not incarcerated simply because they have committed crimes or even because of personal dilemmas, political rifts, or social inequities. Instead, prisoners are unjustifiably incarcerated precisely because they lack access to the power codes of reading and writing, which in our society are defined in schools that reflect the culture of the elites (Anyon, 1981; Delpit, 1988; Kozol, 1985; Lareau, 1987).

Along these lines, Kozol (1985) made disturbing claims about illiteracy in his book *Illiterate America.* Since much of Kozol's argument about American illiteracy is based on a narrow, school-based notion of literacy, the complexities of literacy discussed earlier in this chapter may get lost in Kozol's analysis. Notwithstanding, Kozol's assertion that the prison population in the United States represents the highest concentration of adult illiterates is telling. Over 60% of those incarcerated and who have been labeled as functionally illiterate come from cities, and a large and growing number of those incarcerated represent isolated neighborhoods within these cities. While Kozol and others (hooks, 2004) relate the urban prison crisis to the American literacy crisis, scholars (A. Ferguson, 2000) interested in the ways that schools shape failure argue that schools (versus illiteracy) promote negative social outcomes for urban youth.

For example, hooks (2004) examined the role of the school in sanctioning "disengaged" and "prison-bound" urban Black males (pp. 40–41). According to her, "Educational systems fail to impart or inspire learning in black males of all ages" (p. 40). Schools, then, assist in the oppression of Black males, and the American "prison industrial complex" (see Davis, 2001) is just one manifestation of that oppression.

In response to the school's role in manufacturing urban youth oppression, scholars must consider issues beyond reading and writing as we continue to refine our definitions of literacy. We must also consider the ways in which schools and society sponsor oppression through their mechanistic control over how literacy is defined and disseminated in the public sphere. It is, therefore, not surprising that Kozol's idea of illiteracy gained national attention in the late 1980s, as it put literacy in the hands of elites (and illiteracy in sagging jeans and T-shirt). These conceptions of literacy, grounded in school authority, have helped to reinforce negative beliefs about urban youth.

The Problem of Media Discourses

(Mis)representations of urban youth and literacy raise some important scientific and sociological questions, especially with respect to intelligence and the role of the urban youth in civil society. Poor urban youth who like to read are often questioned (hooks, 2004, p. 40). It is not only those surrounding urban youth who buy into these stereotypes. Urban youth, themselves, also carry such ideological baggage. According to Madhubuti (quoted in hooks, 2004, p. 36),

> No one actually told men "you should hate yourself." However, the images, symbols, products, creations, promotions, and authorities of white America all very subtly and often quite openly taught me white supremacy, taught me to hate myself.

Indeed, there is a relationship between how one behaves and how one perceives herself or himself. Complicating this relationship are racist discourses funneled through the media surrounding urban youth and literacy. According to Smitherman and van Dijk (1988),

> [Discourses] are the means for the manufacture of an ethnic and racial, if not racist, consensus. In other words, discourse is not just a system or a signal of the problem of racism. It essentially reproduces and helps produce . . . racist cognitions and actions. (p. 18)

It would be, however, misleading to describe media discourses as acting in singular ways. According to Lankshear and Knobel (1997), "Discourses are dynamic, alive. Living in and through them is very much a process of constantly renegotiating them" (p. 96). Notwithstanding, the media discourses surrounding urban youth are overwhelmingly negative (Wilcox, 2005). For example, Wilcox (2005) argues that the majority of news stories featuring urban youth paint them in negative light, as criminal, social deviants, or lazy.

While media images of urban youth are rarely blatantly racist (Yosso, 2002), Smitherman and van Dijk (1988) explain:

> Our respected quality press will hardly print a blatantly racist article anymore . . . [but] . . . In everyday talk, underlying ethnic prejudices may indirectly appear in "innocent" stories . . . Although such stories claim to tell the "facts," describe how "they" did it (wrong) again, or generally imply that "they" are stupid, lazy, welfare-cheats, criminal, or lack motivation to learn, the storyteller may, at the same time, emphasize that he has nothing against "them," . . . Yet, the stories spreading quickly in families, schools, or neighborhoods, and occasionally greatly magnified by media reproduction, contribute to the fundamental communication and reproduction of racism in society. (p. 18)

In commenting on the role of the media and its proliferation of negative urban youth images, Smitherman and van Dijk (1988) contend:

> The forms of rhetoric and dramatization, their ability to focus and set public agenda [sic], and their news values do more than simply favor "negative" stories, or reflect what the elites, politicians, or institutions routinely communicate to them in press releases or interviews. The media do not passively report the facts, nor do they simply reflect the ethnocentric consensus; they help construct and reproduce it. They magnify the attitudes of the powerful few, and reinterpret and transmit this ideology to the powerless. (p. 23)

Our perceptions of urban youth and literacy are, thus, given to us not without bias. This does not mean that we are passive consumers of such ideas; it simply suggests that we have not been very active in countering them. In this way, Smitherman and van Dijk (1988) argue that attitudes in general, and prejudices in particular, are not individual aberrations, or pathological exceptions, but structurally rooted, shared social cognitions. The media in our information societies play the crucial role in presenting such dominant ideologies, if only by the failure to present alternative interpretations or counterideologies (p. 22).

Shawn's literacy story presents, for me, an alternative interpretation to the media narrative of urban youth as illiterates. Further, as I attempt to situate Shawn's story in the literature on urban youth and literacy, I realize that claims of urban youth illiteracy are not only misleading but threatening. As such, the true crisis that urban youth, such as Shawn, face deals more with power, authority, racism, and decentering than it does with reading and writing. In this way, literacy has been constituted unfairly, as study after study has suggested that urban youth often participate in unacknowledged literacy practices (e.g., rapping, tattooing, etc.) that kneel toward the bottom of the American literacy hierarchy. They are often overshadowed by the authority of the school or ignored or vilified in the exposure of media.

Both power and prejudice are always present in the contexts of literacy. According to Luke and Freebody (1997),

> the contexts of literacy events are not necessarily "level playing fields" where all learners have comparable access to resources, whether construed as access to representational systems and mediational means, linguistic knowledge, and cultural artifacts, or in terms of access to actual financial capital, institutional entry, and status. (p. 3)

Specifically, the "literate" and the "illiterate" are unfairly labeled. The events and activities that define them are "constitutive of and by material relations of discourse, power, and knowledge" (p. 3). Therefore, the image of the illiterate city kid deeply obscures the reality that many urban youth—who many believe are barely literate—are in some verifiable way highly literate. Notwithstanding, many urban youth are characteristically projected as less than literate and, at times, less than human. But as Freire (1970) suggests,

> These men [speaking specifically of Latin American men, but African American men certainly apply], illiterate or not, are, in fact, not marginal . . . They are not "beings outside of"; they are "beings for another." Therefore the solution to their problem is not to become "beings inside of," but men freeing themselves; for in reality they are not marginal to the structure, but oppressed men within it. Alienated men, they cannot overcome their dependency by "incorporation" into the very structure responsible for their dependency. There is no other road to humanization—theirs as well as everyone else's—but authentic transformation of the dehumanizing structure. (p. 339)

Using Freire's notion of "oppressed men," I contend that urban youth are structurally oppressed and dehumanized in a way that prevents their literate identities from being formally acknowledged. For this reason, many urban youth are looked upon as illiterate, not because they do not practice literacy, but because many have chosen to disregard the literacies they do practice. To report them as illiterates/low literates, which further sanctions their oppression, makes legitimate the dominant literacy practices of schools and the inaccurate projections of the media. The relationship between notions of literacy/illiteracy works to widen a socially maintained literacy gap. While much of my focus has been on Black males, we can infer the nature of literacy learning among other groups from them, as literacy learning among Black males parallels arguments about literacy learning more broadly across urban contexts (cf. Kinloch, 2010; Mahiri, 2004; Morrell, 2008; Winn, 2011).

Rethinking Urban Literacy Learning

Debates about urban literacy education are far from new, yet they are complex and not easily resolved. In this chapter, I have taken license from James Baldwin (2000) who in a rare collection of essays and memorable works published in 1985 described in a chapter titled "A Talk to Teachers" what he saw as one of the paradoxes of education: "that precisely at the point when you begin to develop a conscience, you must find yourself at war with your society" (p. 72). Baldwin did then what I have attempted to do here: frame education similar to how Freire (1970) defined literacy—as a consciousness-raising activity that motivates progressive action and resistance to the *status quo.* In keeping with Baldwin's and Freire's assertions of educational paradox better understood as critical social praxis, I have attempted to address how we in the field of urban education might consider literacy in line with a transformative project whose aim is the rearticulation of society on the basis of moral and political cues. In so doing, I have hoped to instigate and make visible the social fissures located in the contradictory social grammars of history. That is, precisely as urban youth learn powerful literacies, they are either deemed as a threat by the social elite or begin to see the ever-looming moral flaws of society and therefore resist society's definition/articulation of literacy.

Focusing close and careful attention to this paradox of literacy learning as it gets revealed in the scholarship of urban youth literacy practice, this chapter has provided an opportunity for reassessing the political, moral, and intellectual complexities of urban (literacy) education. This opportunity seems particularly important as much of urban education is intertwined with discourses/languages that both express and are exposed in volatile literacy artifacts produced by urban youth in response to issues ranging from racism, institutional violence, counteraesthetic urban realities, to sexism and neourban geographical occupation/colonization (also known as gentrification). Reflecting on these hypersymbolized systems that represent youth realities in urban spaces, youth literacy products, and how each gives us a way to reimagine urban education and youth resistances in official school settings, this chapter has finally insisted on a clear acknowledgment of the tensions in meaning that characterize urban education and the incredible instability formatting life and literacy learning in urban America.

Hence, the Discourse of urban literacy learning seems split between deficit descriptions (i.e., youth lacking literacy) and profit ones (i.e., youth possessing it). However, Discourses (as symbolic notions of being) act in no singular way. There are discourses that endorse and even help to foster the images of the illiterate city kid and those that challenge the image of the illiterate city kid. However, the purpose of this chapter has been to challenge the dominant image of urban youth lacking literacy and provide a counternarrative that not only expands our image of urban youth, but also our definitions of urban literacies. Urban youth such as Shawn are, indeed, literate yet in ways that we too often ignore, fail to privilege, or vilify.

A goal for urban literacy educators, then, should be to highlight educational inequities between urban youth and other Americans. Are students like Shawn that much different from other American youth? Dyson (1993) suggested that they are not and further maintains that the literacy gap is an aberration that reflects more accurately cultural derisions in our society than achievement ones. Hence, we must be careful when making sweeping claims about the literate capabilities of any group, especially urban youth, as these claims have historically worked negatively to reinforce dangerous assumptions about the cognitive and linguistic abilities of oppressed people.

Also factoring into educational inequity is the relationship between school and culture. As noted earlier, school literacy practices resemble greatly the literacy practices of middle-class suburban Whites. In this way, the academic literacy practices of middle-class suburban Whites help to produce more groups of middle-class suburban Whites. Conversely, our devaluing of urban literacies helps to produce more communities of devalued urban youth. Such cycles have profound implications for shaping society. For many urban youth the implications can be catastrophic, as young, urban men and women fill our street corners, our prisons, and, worse, our cemeteries.

Another goal of urban literacy educators should be to comment on the humanity of urban youth by locating their meanings and identities in their texts and textual understandings. As I listened to and re-read Shawn's "writings," I heard noises. But these noises were nothing like the rehearsed rumblings of readings performed in classrooms. These noises were peculiar, distinct, and even musical. They were poetry and spoken word—silent but loud. They were tattoos and tags and raps, all of which are communicative genres "rooted in the Black Oral Tradition of tonal semantics, narrativizing, signification/signifyin, the Dozens/playin the Dozens, Africanized syntax, and other communicative practices" (Smitherman, 1999, p. 269). Hence, Shawn's communicative performances were much like scholars communicative performances—traditional, bearing "traces" or "echoes" of cultures, societies, and histories past (Bakhtin, 1984; Derrida, 1976).

The literacies learned by urban youth constitute a collection of sounds which, all at once, sublimely reach backward and forward through both time and space, borrowing as it may the conjured reverberations of the past while supplying a new voice and a new perspective for our emerging future. Shawn's words are candescent, lively, and fresh. Yet, they are very much motivated by the appropriations, the deliberate borrowings, of old songs, catch phrases, and oral narratives, "reaccentuated" (Bakhtin, 1981) in both new and not-so-new ways. In this way, urban literacy learning is a dialogic practice that allows individuals, groups, and communities to add to history's multiplicity and diversity of voices. It describes current events, rendering old histories anew, giving established meanings new "accents."

By framing urban literacy learning within dialogic theory (Bakhtin, 1981; Dyson, 2003), which questions "the workings of power and desire in social life" (Gee, 1991, p. 39), I redefine literacies as dialogic practices (or practices based in language, interaction, and social transformation) mediated by the use of cultural/symbolic tools (e.g., language), which allow individuals and groups to participate in and negotiate community identities, shared relationships, historically valued activities. Following this definition of literacy, at least four important questions for enhancing urban literacy education and urban literacy research become apparent:

1. How might urban literacy educators and researchers expanded social conceptions of literacy by examining the intersection of multiple forms of oppression, including racism, sexism, and economic oppression, within texts produced by urban youth and across urban contexts?
2. How might urban literacy educators and researchers challenge linguistic and cognitive epistemologies of literacy and literacy reform that engender the thinking behind new millennium

educational reform initiatives such as NCLB, Race to the Top, and the Common Core State Standards?
3. How might urban literacy educators and researchers better rely upon qualitative empirical data to document, describe, and enhance literacy learning among urban youth?
4. Finally, how might urban literacy educators and researchers raise questions about literacy policy reflected in textbooks and classroom instruction, neither of which recognizes the complex literate existences of urban youth, such as the young people I have written about in this chapter?

By addressing these questions, future research in urban literacy education must refocus our thinking about urban literacy learning and challenge what counts as literacy and successful school-based literacy performance.

Note

1. All research participant names in this document are pseudonyms.

References

Alvermann, D.E. (2001). Reading adolescents' reading identities: Looking back to see ahead. *Journal of Adolescent & Adult Literacy, 44*(8), 676–690.
Anyon, J. (1981). Social class and school knowledge. *Curriculum Inquiry, 11,* 3–42.
Au, K.H. (1997). Ownership, literacy achievement, and students of diverse cultural backgrounds. In J.T. Guthrie & A. Wigfield (Eds.), *Reading engagement: Motivating readers through integrated instruction* (pp. 168–182). Newark, DE: International Reading Association.
Auerbach, E. (1993). Putting the *p* back in participatory. *TESOL Quarterly, 27*(3), 543–545.
Bakhtin, M.M. (1981). *The dialogical imagination.* Austin, TX: University of Texas Press.
Bakhtin, M.M. (1984). *Rabelais and his world.* Bloomington, IN: Indiana University Press.
Bakhtin, M.M. (1986). *Speech genres and other late essays.* Austin, TX: University of Texas Press.
Baldwin, J. (2000). A talk to teachers. In M.C. Brown II, & J.E. Davis (eds.), *Black sons to mothers: Compliments, critiques, and challenges for cultural workers in education* (pp. 123–131). New York, NY: Peter Lang Publishers.
Barton, D., & Hamilton, M. (1998). *Local literacies: Reading and writing in one community.* London, UK: Routledge.
Baugh, J. (1983). *Black street speech.* Austin, TX: University of Texas Press.
Bloome, D. (1997). This is literacy: Three challenges for teachers of reading and writing. *Australian Journal of Language and Literacy, 20,* 107–115.
Bourdieu, P. (1977). Cultural reproduction and social reproduction. In J. Karabel and A.H. Halsey (Eds.), *Power and ideology in education* (pp. 487–511). New York, NY: Oxford University Press.
Center for the Study of Social Policy. (1993). *Keeping pace with change: Black males and social policy.* Washington, DC: Author.
Coleman, J.S., Campbell, E.Q., Hobson, C.J., McPartland, J., Mood, A.M., Weinfeld, F.D., & York, R.L. (1966). *Equality of educational opportunity.* Washington, DC: U.S. Government Printing Office.
Cushman, E., Kintgen, E., Kroll, B.M., & Rose, M. (2001). *Literacy: A critical sourcebook.* Boston, MA: Bedford/St. Martins.
Dahl, K.L., & Freppon, P.A. (1995). A comparison of inner-city children's interpretations of reading and writing instruction in the early grades in skills-based and whole language classrooms. *Reading Research Quarterly, 30,* 50–74.
Davis, J.E. (2001). Black boys at school: Negotiating masculinities and race. In R. Majors (Ed.), *Educating our Black children: New directions and radical approaches* (pp. 169–182). London, UK: Routledge/Falmer.

de Certeau, M. (1984). *The practice of everyday life.* Berkeley, CA: University of California Press.

Delpit, L. 1988. The silenced dialogue: Power and pedagogy in educating other people's children. *Harvard Educational Review, 58,* 280–298.

Derrida, J. (1976). *Grammatology.* Baltimore, MD: Johns Hopkins University Press.

Dyson, A.H. (1993). *Social worlds of children learning to write in an urban primary.* New York, NY: Teachers College Press.

Dyson, A.H. (2003). *The brothers and sisters learn to write: Popular literacies in childhood and school cultures.* New York, NY: Teachers College Press.

Erickson, F. (1984). School literacy, reasoning, and civility: An anthropologist's perspective. *Review of Educational Research, 54*(4), 525–546.

Erickson, F. (1987). Transformation and school success: The politics and culture of educational achievement. *Anthropology and Education Quarterly, 18,* 335–356.

Ferguson, A.A. (2000). *Bad boys: Public schools in the making of Black masculinity.* Ann Arbor, MI: University of Michigan Press.

Ferguson, R. (1998). *Teachers' perceptions and expectations and the black-white test score gap.* In C. Jencks & M. Phillips (Eds.), *The Black-White test score gap* (pp. 273–317). Washington, DC: Brookings Institution.

Fisher, M.T. (2003). Open mics and open minds: Spoken word poetry in African Diaspora Participatory Literacy Communities. *Harvard Educational Review, 73*(3), 362–389.

Fisher, M.T. (2004). "The song is unfinished": The new literate and literary and their institutions. *Written Communication, 21*(3), 290–312.

Foster, M. (2001). *University of California report of Black student achievement.* Unpublished manuscript, Santa Barbara, CA: University of California, Santa Barbara.

Freire, P. 1970. *Pedagogy of the oppressed.* New York, NY: Continuum.

Freire, P., & Macedo, D. (1987). *Reading the word and the world.* Westport, CT: Bergin and Garvey.

Gee, J. (1990). *Social linguistics and literacies: Ideology in discourse.* London, UK: Taylor and Francis.

Gee, J. (1991). Socio-cultural approaches to literacy. *Annual Review of Applied Linguistics, 12,* 31–48.

Gee, J. (1996). *Social linguistics and literacies: Ideology in discourse* (2nd ed.). New York, NY: Falmer.

Gibbs, J.T. (1988). *Young, Black, and male in America: An endangered species.* New York, NY: Auburn House.

Gilyard, K. (1991). *Voices of the self: A study of language competence.* Detroit, MI: Wayne State University Press.

Greene, S., & Abt-Perkins, D. (2003). *Making race visible: Literacy research for cultural understanding.* New York, NY: Teachers College Press.

Gutiérrez, K.D. (2008). Developing a sociocritical literacy in the third space. *Reading Research Quarterly, 43*(2), 148–164.

Heath, S.B. (1982). Protean shapes in literacy events: Ever-shifting oral and literate traditions. In E. Cushman, E. Kingtgen, B. Kroll, & M. Rose (Eds.), *Literacy: A critical sourcebook* (pp. 443–466). Boston, MA: Bedford/St. Martins.

Heath, S.B. (1983). *Ways with words: Language, life and communication in communities and classrooms.* Cambridge, MA: Cambridge University Press.

Hill, M.L. (2009). *Beats, rhymes, and classroom life: Hip-hop pedagogy and the politics of identity.* New York, NY: Teachers College Press.

Hilliard, A. (1991). Do we have the will to educate all children? *Educational Leadership, 49*(1), 31–36.

hooks, b. (2004). *We real cool: Black men and masculinity.* New York, NY: Routledge.

Hunsander, P.D. (2002). Why boys fail: Unlearned literacy. *Education Digest, 68*(4), 29–31.

Hymes, D. (1962). The ethnography of communication. In T. Gladwin & W. Sturtevant (Eds.), *Anthropology and human behavior* (pp. 15–53). Washington, DC: Anthropological Society of Washington.

Irizarry, J.G. (2011). *The Latinization of US schools: Successful teaching and learning in shifting cultural contexts.* New York, NY: Paradigm.

Jencks, C., & Phillips, M. (Eds.). (1998). *The Black-White test score gap.* Washington, DC: Brookings Institution.

Kinloch, V. (2010). *Harlem on our minds: Place, race, and the literacies of urban youth.* New York, NY: Teachers College Press.

Kirkland, D.E. (2008). "The rose that grew from concrete": Postmodern Blackness and new English education. *English Journal, 97*(5), 69–75.

Kirkland, D.E. (2009). The skin we ink: Tattoos, literacy, and a new English education. *English Education, 41*(4), 375–395.

Kirkland, D.E. (2010a). English(es) in urban contexts: Politics, pluralism, and possibilities. *English Education, 42*(3), 293–306.

Kirkland, D.E. (2010b). 4 colored girls who considered suicide/when social networking was enuf: A Black feminist perspective on literacy online. In D.E. Alvermann (Ed.), *Adolescents' online literacies: Connecting classrooms, digital media, and popular culture* (pp. 71–90). New York, NY: Peter Lang.

Kirkland, D.E. (2011a). Books like clothes: Engaging young Black men with reading. *Journal of Adolescent & Adult Literacy, 55*(3), 199–208.

Kirkland, D.E. (2011b). Listening to echoes: Teaching young Black men literacy and the problem of ELA standards. *Language Arts, 88*(5), 373–380.

Kozol, J. (1985). *Illiterate America* (1st ed.). Garden City, NY: Anchor/Doubleday.

Kucer, S.B. (2001). *Dimensions of literacy: A conceptual base for teaching reading and writing in school settings.* Mahwah, NJ: Lawrence Erlbaum Associates.

Kunjufu, J. (1985). *Countering the conspiracy to destroy Black boys.* Chicago, IL: African American Images.

Labov, W. (1972). *Language in the inner city: Studies in the Black English vernacular.* Philadelphia, PA: University of Pennsylvania Press.

Langer, J. (1991). Literacy and schooling: A sociocognitive perspective. In E.H. Hiebert (Ed.), *Literacy for a diverse society: Perspectives, practices, and policies* (pp. 9–27). New York, NY: Teachers College Press.

Lankshear, C., & Knobel, M. (1997). Critical literacy and active citizenship. In S. Muspratt, A. Luke, & P. Freebody (eds.), *Constructing critical literacies.* Norwood, NJ: Hampton Press.

Lankshear, C., & McLaren, P. (Eds.). (1993). *Critical literacy: Politics, praxis, and the postmodern.* Albany, NY: State University of New York Press.

Lareau, A. (1987). Social class differences in family school relationships: The importance of cultural capital. *Sociology of Education, 60,* 73–85.

Lave, J., & Wenger, E. (1992). *Situated learning: Legitimate peripheral participation.* Cambridge, UK: Cambridge University Press.

Lee, C., & Smagorinsky, P. (2000). *Vygotskian perspectives on literacy research: Constructing meaning through collaborative inquiry.* New York, NY: Cambridge University Press.

Lopez, G. (2001). Re-visiting white racism in educational research: Critical race theory and the problem of method. *Educational Researcher, 30*(1), 29–33.

Luke, A. (1988). The non-neutrality of literacy instruction: A critical introduction. *Australian Journal of Reading, 11*(2), 79–83.

Luke, A. (2004). Teaching after the market: From commodity to cosmopolitan. *Teachers College Record, 106,* 1422–1443.

Luke, A., & Freebody, P. (1997). *Constructing critical literacies: Teaching and learning textual practice.* Cresskill, NJ: Hampton Press.

MacLeod, J. (1995). *Ain't no makin' it: Aspirations and attainment in a low-income neighborhood* (2nd ed. rev.). Boulder, CO: Westview Press.

Mahiri, J. (1998). *Shooting for excellence: African American and youth culture in new century schools.* New York, NY: Teachers College Press.

Mahiri, J. (2004). *What they don't learn in school: Literacy in the lives of urban youth.* New York, NY: Peter Lang Publishers.

Milofsky, C. (1974). Why special education isn't special. *Harvard Educational Review, 44*(4), 437–458.

Morrell, E. (2004). *Linking literacy and popular culture: Finding connections for lifelong learning.* Norwood, MA: Christopher-Gordon.

Morrell, E. (2008). *Critical literacy and urban youth: Pedagogies of access, dissent, and liberation.* New York, NY: Routledge.

Moss, P., & Tilly, C. (1995). *Raised hurdles for Black men: Evidence from interviews with employers.* New York, NY: Russell Sage.

National Assessment of Educational Progress. (2012). *The NAEP Reading Report Card.* Washington, DC: US Department of Education, Office of Educational Research and Improvement, National Center for Educational Statistics.

National Center for Education Statistics. (2011). *The Nation's Report Card: Reading 2011* (NCES 2012–457). Washington, DC: National Center for Education Statistics, Institute of Education Sciences, U.S. Department of Education.

New London Group. (1996). A pedagogy of multiliteracies: Designing social futures. *Harvard Education Review, 66*(1), 60–92.

No Child Left Behind Act. (2001). Retrieved from http://www2.ed.gov/policy/elsec/leg/esea02/107-110.pdf

Noguera, P.A. (2001). Racial politics and the elusive quest for equity and excellence in education. *Education and Urban Society, 34*(1), 27–42.

Noguera, P.A. (2008). *The trouble with Black boys: And other reflections on race, equity, and the future of public education.* San Francisco, CA: Jossey-Bass.

Ogbu, J. (1974). *The next generation.* New York, NY: Academic Press.

Ogbu, J. (1978). *Minority education and caste.* New York, NY: Academic Press.

Paris, D. (2009). "They're in my culture, they speak the same way": African American language in multiethnic high schools. *Harvard Educational Review, 79*(3), 428–448.

Pollard, D.S. (1993). Gender, achievement, and African American students' perceptions of their school experience. *Educational Psychologist, 23*(4), 294–303.

Poussaint, A., & Alexander, A. (2000). *Lay my burden down: Unraveling suicide and the mental health crisis among African Americans.* Boston, MA: Beacon Press.

Powell, A., Farrar, E., & Cohen, D. (1985). *The shopping mall high school: Winners and losers in the educational marketplace.* Boston, MA: Little Brown.

Purcell-Gates, V. (2002). " . . . As soon as she opened her mouth": Issues of language, literacy, and power. In L. Delpit & J.K. Dowdy (Eds.), *The skin that we speak: Thoughts on language and culture in the classroom* (pp. 121–144). New York, NY: New Press.

Race to the Top Act of 2011. (2011). Retrieved September 6, 2013 from http://www.govtrack.us/congress/bills/112/s844

Reed, R.J. (1988). Education and achievement of young Black males. In J.T. Gibbs (Ed.), *Young, Black and male in America: An endangered species* (pp. 37–96). Dover, MA: Auburn House.

Reinking, D. (1995). Reading and writing with computers: Literacy research in a post-typographic world. In K.A. Hinchman, D.J. Leu, and C.K. Kinzer (Eds.), *Perspectives on literacy research and practice* (pp. 17–33). Chicago, IL: National Reading Conference.

Richardson, E. (2002). *African American literacies.* New York, NY: Free Press.

Rist, R. (1970). Student social class and teacher expectations: The self-fulfilling prophesy in ghetto education. *Harvard Educational Review, 40,* 411–451.

Roper, W.L. (1991). The prevention of minority youth violence must begin despite risks and imperfect understanding. *Public Health Reports, 106*(3), 229–231.

Rose, M. (1989). *Lives on the boundary: The struggles and achievements of America's underprepared.* New York, NY: Free Press.

Scribner, S., & Cole, M. (1981). *The psychology of literacy.* Cambridge, MA: Harvard University Press.

Shor, I. (1992). *Empowering education: Critical teaching for social change.* Chicago, IL: University of Chicago Press.

Singh, P. (1997). Reading the silences within critical feminist theory: Response to Pam Gilbert. In A. Luke & P. Freebody (Eds.), *Constructing critical literacies: Teaching and learning textual practice.* Cresskill, NJ: Hampton Press.

Smith, M.W., & Wilhelm, Jeffrey D. (2002). "*Reading don't fix no Chevys*": *Literacy in the lives of young men.* Portsmouth, NH: Heinemann.

Smith, R.A. (2004). Foreword: When good people remain silent, bad things happen. In *Black boys: The litmus test for public school education* (p. 2). Cambridge, MA: The Schott Foundation for Public Education.

Smith, R.A. (2006). Foreword. In M. Holzman (Ed.), *Public education and Black male students: The 2006 State Report Card.* Cambridge, MA: Schott Foundation for Public Education.

Smitherman, G. (1977). *Talkin and testifyin: The language of Black America.* Detroit, MI: Wayne State University Press.

Smitherman, G. (1999). *Talkin that talk.* New York, NY: Routledge.

Smitherman, G., & van Dijk, T. (1988). *Discourse and discrimination.* Detroit, MI: Wayne State University Press.

Spivak, H., Prothrow-Stith, D., & Hausman, A. (1988). Dying is no accident: Adolescents, violence, and intentional injury. *Pediatric Clinics of North America, 35*(6), 1339–1347.

Street, B. (1984). *Literacy in theory and practice.* Cambridge, UK: Cambridge University Press.

Street, B. (1995). *Social literacies: Critical approaches to literacy in development, ethnography, and education.* London, UK: Longman.

Tatum, A.W. (2008). Toward a more anatomically complete model of literacy instruction: A focus on African American male adolescents and texts. *Harvard Educational Review, 78*(1), 155–182.

Tatum, B.D. (1992). Talking about race, learning about racism: The application of racial identity development theory in the classroom. *Harvard Educational Review, 62*(1), 1–24.

Thorne, B. (1993). *Gender play.* New Brunswick, NJ: Rutgers University Press.

U.S. Department of Health and Human Services and Administration on Children Youth and Families/Head Start Bureau. (Updated Summer 2004). Washington, DC: The Head Start Path to Positive Child Outcomes.

Vygotsky, L.S. (1978). *Mind in society* (M. Cole, V. John-Steiner, S. Scribner, & E. Souberman, Eds.). Cambridge, MA: Harvard University Press.

West, C. (1993). *Race matters.* Boston, MA: Beacon Press.

Wilcox, P. (2005). Beauty and the beast: Gendered and raced discourse in the news. *Social & Legal Studies, 14*(4), 515–532.

Winn, M.T. (2011). *Girl time: Literacy, justice, and the school-to-prison pipeline.* New York, NY: Teachers College Press.

Yosso, T.J. (2002). Critical race media literacy: Challenging deficit discourse about Chicanas/os. *Journal of Popular Film and Television, 30*(1), 52–62.

Young, V.A. (2007). *Your average nigga: Performing race, literacy, and masculinity.* Detroit, MI: Wayne State University Press.

22

Hip Hop Culture as a Teaching-Learning Tool in Urban Education

Jon A. Yasin

Introduction

As a freshman at Stanford University with an athletic scholarship, Wade C. was placed in a required calculus class. However, he had not studied the necessary prerequisite courses to successfully complete the calculus course. Because of his scholarship, the class was very important to Wade, so he studied very hard, did all of the homework, attended every class, and took every test; however, he failed each activity. Before the final examination, Wade asked another student in the course who was performing successfully, if they could study together for the final examination. After agreeing to study together, they went to the student's room and began composing a set of Hip Hop lyrics using the calculus equations and formulas as the content of the Hip Hop rhyme. They recorded the completed Hip Hop lyrics and sent a copy of the rhyme on a cassette tape to their professor. On receiving the Hip Hop rhyme, the professor telephoned Wade in his dorm room and told him that although he had worked hard, he had failed the other course activities. Moreover, she asked him to give her permission to use the taped rhyme with her other students, and told him that because of his efforts that she was certain he would pass the class.

Wade, a teacher in the Tucson, Arizona, school system, is an example of students, globally, who utilize elements of Hip Hop culture to negotiate features of their lives on a daily basis. Although there are many, the five primary elements of Hip Hop are taggin' [graffiti art]; deejayin' [playing and mixing recorded music]; emceein'/rhymin'/spittin'/flowin'/rappin' [reciting Hip Hop lyrics with music]; beat-boyin' and beat-girlin' [*break dancing* is a term created by the media]; and studyin' the knowledge of self. Rose (1994) defined Hip Hop as "a cultural form that attempts to negotiate the experiences of marginalization, brutally truncated opportunity and oppression within the cultural imperatives of African-American and Caribbean history, identity and community" (p. 21). These elements of Hip Hop are reconfigurations of certain African traditions maintained in the Diaspora for more than 400 years; moreover, since the late 1960s, having been used to successfully create a public space to communicate sensitivities of youths previously disenfranchised who had no public voice, these elements have been appropriated by youths internationally, although not universally. For example, a student from Albania wrote in a research paper on Jay-Z that because his family was extremely poor when they migrated to the United States, he and his siblings were ostracized and teased by children at school and in their community. He learned to cope with the bullying by listening to various Hip Hop rhymes by Jay-Z, noting how Jay-Z coped with the stresses of growing up in an impoverished area of Brooklyn, and thereby using Jay-Z as a role model. As another illustration, during the last presidential elections in Senegal, by rhyming about the differences between the candidates running for that office in their music, Hip Hop emcees were instrumental in bringing attention to corruption in the office of the incumbent president, ultimately causing his defeat.

Initially, a source of recreation and entertainment for urban youths, globally, youths now utilize Hip Hop elements for educational, mental health, political, and a variety of other purposes. Because Hip Hop is a generic component of their ways of life, people who interface with youths must understand the culture and should consider using it to benefit the youths and themselves. After a brief presentation of its history, Hip Hop as an integral feature of youth culture, as a motivational factor among youths, and as a teaching and learning tool for teachers shall be the focus of this discussion.

Urban Education

According to Howard Gardner (1999), formal education is associated, for the most part, with conventional school settings that provide study of "disciplines that reflect the culture's procedures for confronting questions about the physical, biological, and personal worlds" (pp. 28–29). Even though the United States is multicultural and multiethnic, the culture of schools has often been monolithic, reflecting only the culture of European Americans, because they represent the majority of policy makers, instructors, and students throughout the country, even though they are not always the majority in individual schools or school systems. This has resulted in many children from various cultures not achieving at their levels of potential. Carter G. Woodson identified this as a problem for African Americans in 1933 in *The Miseducation of the Negro.*

During the 1960s Civil Rights and Black Power Movements, this problem became a primary concern for many educators once again as African American students became the majority in certain urban schools, and an influx of other students of color into urban schools began. According to Gordon and Armour-Thomas (1992), frequent references from the 1960s through the 1980s were made about the educational problems of urban dwellers (p. 1459), and the term *urban education* was used to identify this issue; however, the field was not developed adequately. Furthermore, some 50 years after the Civil Rights and Black Power Movements, Milner (2009) wrote that still "there is not a static definition of urban education or urban contexts. Scholars define urban education in myriad ways" (pp. 124–125). He suggests urban education, to some, refers to inner-city schools and to others, those in urban metropolitan regions. In all probability, for certain policy makers and educators, *urban education* has been and is a pejorative coded "catch-all" term referring to the students of African ancestry, of Latino ancestry, from certain other non-European American ethnic groups, and in some instances, working-class and impoverished European Americans students, who attend schools in urban areas.

Any theory of urban education must focus on identifying the mismatch between the cultural ways of learning, teaching, and knowing that students of color bring with them into urban schools and such ways utilized in the dominant European American culture, which are widely existent in urban schools. In addition, to compensate for this mismatch, instructors of these diverse student populations must develop alternative teaching methods and learning activities to those traditionally utilized. These alternative methods must reflect certain procedures regarding teaching and learning within the cultural traditions of these students about the physical, biological, and personal worlds, not only those procedures of the majority European American culture.

Instructors must be versed in the early socialization practices of various cultures of the peoples of this country because early on children acquire cultural ways of thinking, learning, and teaching that they bring to the classroom on their first day of school. For example, Wade C., the student at Stanford, a Latino raised in an urban environment, having been socialized in Hip Hop culture early on, drew upon his knowledge of Hip Hop culture to study and to learn the necessary information for his mathematics course. Because of its prominence as an urban subculture in which children and adolescents participate globally, all teachers must be knowledgeable about Hip Hop culture, and they should employ aspects of it in the classroom as a "new way of teaching" (Emdin, 2010, pp. 6–7).

Hip Hop Culture

In 1967, during the height of the Civil Rights and Black Power Movements as many big cities were literally burning, with his family, Clive Campbell, at the age of 12, whom we now know as DJ Kool Herc, the father of Hip Hop, migrated to the United States from Jamaica. According to Herc, early on he was fascinated with the art of taggin', which Jeff Chang (2005) writes had its origins two years earlier in 1965, with an African American adolescent who wrote his moniker, cornbread, on various modes of public transportation around the city of Philadelphia, in an effort to impress Cynthia, a young girl, in whom he had a nonplatonic interest. cornbread's friend, top hat, brought that strange type of writing, the tag, to public spaces in New York City. Upon discovering it, a young Greek American bicycle messenger, appropriated and popularized this type of writing, leaving his moniker, taki 183, on subways and in every neighborhood where he made deliveries. A *tag* is like a signature; moreover, two other types of graffiti art are common to the Hip Hop community. A *throw-up* is a set of large bubble-like, colored-in letters, in metropolitan New York and other areas on the East Coast of the United States, while a large mural on buildings and other upright surfaces is a *scene*. These types of graf art might have different names in other parts of the country and the world, while, perhaps, communicating other types of specific messages local to that region. Interestingly, according to Miguel Sanchez (1999), a former tagger and student who resides in metropolitan New York City, the primary objective of the "writer," which taggers are also called, is to place his or her moniker in a location that is difficult to reach causing other writers to be envious and ponder how the tagger was able to gain access to that particular space.

Shortly after his arrival in the United States, Kool Herc developed a moniker, clyde as kool, and another person wrote his tag on the wall of the building in which Herc lived. Herc related that his father saw his tag the following morning and "beat my ass. My father is from the Caribbean and he does not play that shit" (personal communication, November 8, 2011). The beating dissuaded Herc from maintaining his interest in graf art and he began deejayin' with his father at parties for the Caribbean community. At home, Herc, however, influenced by the dance hall culture in Jamaica, amplified his father's speakers so the entire community could hear the music. While practicing his deejayin' skills, neighborhood youths gathered in the recreation room of the building and on the street to listen to the music emanating from Herc's room. In 1973, Herc's sister, Cindy, the mother of Hip Hop, wanted to celebrate the end of her summer job and needing additional money to buy school clothes, she persuaded him to organize a party in the recreation room of their building at 1520 Sedgewick Avenue, in the West Bronx section of New York City, now a national historic landmark. Kool Herc and Cindy employed taggers to make signs advertising the party in the community.

For the initial party, Kool Herc used the Jamaican dance hall culture format that included Kool Herc as deejay, using two turntables with amplified speakers to blend the music of one recording on one turntable into that of another on the second turntable. His friend, MC [emcee/mike controller] Coke La Rock, talked over the music on the microphone, welcoming those who came to the party, giving shout-outs to those dancing, and so forth. Wanting to attract adolescent females to the party, Herc charged them 25 cents, knowing that if the females came, the males would follow, so males were charged 50 cents. The party was a huge success and others soon followed, in addition to the free parties they gave in public spaces, anywhere they could hook up their equipment to utilize free electricity, from light poles in the streets, to parks and other places. Herc added beat boys [b-boys], Kevin and Keith, twins who had "power" moves in dance routines on the dance floor to specific musical recordings. Meanwhile, others studied Kool Herc, and while practicing their deejay skills, added crews like Herc's, and eventually, began giving their own parties.

At that time, the South Bronx community was populated heavily with African American, African Caribbean, and Latino families, primarily of Puerto Rican ancestry. There were 13 gangs in the South Bronx; nevertheless, Kool Herc had a rule that none of the gangs would rumble at his parties. There was no violence at any of Herc's parties, and ironically, he was the only one stabbed at one of his events, while interceding to curtail a dispute. Afrika Bambaataa, one of the other two pioneering deejays, known to many as Bam, was the leader of the Black Spades, one of the 13 notorious gangs in the area. Bam and those attending Herc's parties were interested in these contemporary art forms grounded in their traditional music and dance customs. Herc's absolute ban on violence at his parties, along with several other events that occurred, were the catalysts leading Bam to call a gang truce among all of the gangs, which is still in effect today! Hip Hop and those other events were motivating factors leading toward all 13 gangs forming the Universal Zulu Nation, which is now an international social activist organization.

Another catalyst for organizing the Zulu Nation was the popularity of the teachings of the Honorable Elijah Muhammad's Nation of Islam and the Black Muslims, which encouraged the people of the African Diaspora and the Latino community to study the knowledge of self, to research what caused them to be in the impoverished situation they were now in, and to do for the collective self by working to solve their own social and economic problems. The Nation of Islam at that time stressed transforming oneself to abstain from worldly vices—unhealthy goods and services, such as smoking cigarettes and patronizing gambling casinos—that generated much money and wealth for the country's rich power structure. Bam's relatives were a part of this movement. Simultaneously, President Lyndon Baines Johnson was forming the Great Society and J. Edgar Hoover, Director of the Federal Bureau of Investigation, was deciding who would participate in Johnson's Great Society.

Organizing the Counter-Intelligence Program, COINTELPRO, Hoover and the FBI sent spies and saboteurs to infiltrate the African American community in order to bring havoc to the many Civil Rights, Black Power, and grassroots community organizations that were working to gain legal civil and human rights denied them and to independently assume responsibility for their own destiny. Also, large amounts of heroin and cocaine were being dropped in the ghettos of New York City and other large cities. Disco, a new type of music, was being played on radio stations downtown, which many New York City youths living uptown in Harlem and other areas, did not like because it did not have the powerful uplifting and inspirational messages of the 1960s soul music, such as James Brown's "I'm Black and I'm Proud," nor the hard-driving funk music of Parliament/Funkadelic, and so forth. "Funk is a deliberate reaction to and a rejection of the traditional Western world's predilection for formality, pretense, and self-repression" (Vincent, 1996, pp. 3–4). In addition, the South Bronx was physically, socially, and economically torn apart with the construction of the Cross Bronx Expressway, built to accommodate commuters to New

York City, so they would not have to experience the impoverished conditions of the inner city. The minorities of the South Bronx were "Out of sight, out of mind!"

Hip Hop Culture's Contributions to Society

Because Hip Hop is now an international youth culture, DJ Afrika Bambaataa's grassroots, Hip Hop–based, Universal Zulu Nation, initially working to better the lives of the people of the Bronx who were suffering with the breakdown of their neighborhoods, some 40 years later has chapters around the globe, helping youths and others solve a plethora of social problems, which their governments and political leaders are not interested in addressing, for whatever reason. Solving gang violence is one of their specializations, which many law enforcement agencies have been apprised of, but, for some reason, they are reluctant to work with Zulu, which commands the respect of many youths, including gang bangers, because of the iconic DJ Afrika Bambaataa and others whom they know through Hip Hop culture. Interestingly, members of the Hip Hop community have commented that it is the duty of the police to *arrest,* so they are not interested in solving problems by other means. Furthermore, because of a variety of police policies, such as the stop and frisk policy of the NYC police and their many shootings of unarmed citizens, we are often told by youths around the country that the police are "just another gang, whose color is blue!" While discussing this comment with former policemen who are colleagues at the college from the Department of Criminal Justice, I have found that many have agreed. Members of Zulu and the Hip Hop community readily articulate how no individual or governmental agency has assisted them in solving certain survival problems, so they must find solutions for themselves. In fact, others often "blame the victims" and marginalize them.

In addition to the founding of Zulu, many other valuable outcomes and outgrowths of the advent of Hip Hop have been serendipitous. Other examples of Zulu's contributions include organizing and providing training in how to be grassroots activists. Trainees have assisted in organizing and developing such programs as "Turn off the Radio Thursdays," the campaign against negative, violent lyrics in rap music. For clarification, Hip Hop lyrics are described by many participants in the culture as emcees communicating positive uplifting messages. Hip Hop lyrics/rhymes are distinguished from spoken words/talk in other types of music because Hip Hop emcees pronounce each word syllable in time to the beat of the music (Yasin, 1997). According to these participants in Hip Hop culture, rap music, which is considered the bastard child of Hip Hop, is laced with profane language, communicates negative messages about life and women, and glorifies violence, and other forms of antisocial behavior. Such lyrics with profane language were not prevalent when Hip Hop music was introduced to mainstream society, nationally and internationally, in 1979, through its initial commercial recordings, first by Fatback and then, the more popular "Rapper's Delight" by the Sugar Hill Gang. Beginning with its introduction to mainstream America and the world, commercial rhymes, recorded and played on the radio, included such categories of themes as braggadocio; commentary on social and political events occurring in one's neighborhood, nationally, and internationally; comedic, and rhymes for partying. At that time, the majority of emcees were from the East Coast.

In 1991, however, NWA, Niggas with Attitudes, a group from Los Angeles, dropped the album, *Straight Outta Compton,* featuring the rhyme "F**k Tha Police" and others, all of which addressed legitimate social concerns of the 'hood, but that encoded profane language into the messages. Members of the group reported that they used such language to attract listeners' attention because this music genre was about 16 years old and they had just figured out how to rhyme. With enormous financial success of the album, the late Eazy E, the member of the group with the "street" background," met Jerry Heller (2006), an entertainment lawyer, who encouraged them to "push the envelope" on the themes of their rhymes and the language. In addition to the more profane language, NWA's later recordings included misogynistic messages, and lack of tolerance toward others, all of which culminated with the advent of antisocial messages common to what is known as "gangsta rap," a category of Hip Hop music that has become even more successful financially than its other categories.

Kitwana (2005) and others attribute the increased purchases of the music to suburban youth, primarily European American, buying Hip Hop music as of the early 1990s. Their attraction is "the standard ingredients of Hip Hop . . . brought about by Hip Hoppers' socialization in American society. The weight American society places on the acquisition of wealth and material possessions, patriarchy and the social construction of maleness, as a means of power and prestige, are factors in the production of the music, lyrics, expressive behaviors" and so forth (Richardson, 2003, p. 70). Hopefully, the Hip Hop community, with such leaders as Zulu Nation and other pioneers, will provide additional guidance and direction on this issue of types of messages communicated to children and youths in Hip Hop music, which has had a profound effect on popular culture and many youths' worldviews. The advent of this debate between pioneers and others celebrating the culture who believe that Hip Hop music must be about communicating positive uplifting messages versus those who create and participate in gangsta rap was the impetus for DJ Afrika Bambaataa to introduce the fifth element of Hip Hop, studyin' the knowledge of self, specifically, and gettin' an education, generally.

Serendipity accounts for the creation of jobs and other positive contributions that Hip Hop generated early on for marginalized youths in the African American, African Caribbean, and Latino neighborhoods of the West and South Bronx. Beginning with Herc's first party, in addition to the planners and performers—deejay, emcee, taggers, b boys and b girls, and so forth—from their community, cohorts were hired as security, cleaners, and to meet other needs. As others learned the elements and contributed to the creative growth and development of the elements, Hip Hop community members organized performance battles, where crews that included deejays, emcees, b boys and b girls, taggers, and handlers who acted as security for the crew, competed against other crews for a portion of the monies collected for entry into the event.

Organizers of these performance battles learned many fundamental skills of business, event planning, public relations with mainstream media, and so forth, as well, leading to employment in mainstream society. It was in preparation for one of these battles, in fact, where the third Hip Hop pioneering deejay, Grandmaster Flash, first influenced the emcees of his crew to pronounce each word syllable or word in time to the beat of the music, creating the act of rhyming and Hip Hop music, as we know it today. Previously, over the deejays' music, emcees had recited poetry, which has its own patterns of stressed and unstressed word syllables independent of the background music, in addition to engaging in other types of banter. DJ Grandmaster Flash, who attended a vocational high school in the Bronx, was an electronics student, who brought much of the contemporary technology at that time to deejayin', including many creative techniques on the turntables, while independently, "ironing out many of the problems" deejays had with mixing and blending music on the two turntables that they utilize.

The creativity of its participants has resulted in Hip Hop culture developing its own voice in mainstream society internationally. In addition to employing performers of Hip Hop elements to entertain—emcees, deejays, b boys and b girls, taggers—it is now necessary to employ their support staff: lawyers, accountants, managers and agents, and so forth. The Hip Hop community early on in its history influenced the fashion industry. During the 1980s, Hip Hop participants who were clothing designers created the label FUBU, For Us By Us, while various others from the Hip Hop community have continuously developed clothing lines, such as P. Diddy's Sean Jean line of clothing. Before members of the Hip Hop community entered the fashion world, the industry had appropriated Hip Hoppers' wardrobes, by designing, for example, the hugely popular oversized clothing for the larger society, which began with b boys and b girls buying clothing several sizes too large to cover padding on parts of their bodies to protect them from injury when they made certain moves, such as spins on their knees, on the dance floor (Melvin McLauren, personal communication, November 15, 1994).

Furthermore, various production studios, some with labels owned by participants in Hip Hop culture, produce, record, and distribute music of artists performing that genre of music. Companies, such as Hush Tours in New York City, provide bus and walking tours of the early sites where major events in Hip Hop occurred. Artists, like Jay-Z, who is part owner of the 40/40 Club in addition to the New York Nets basketball team, are now investing in various other types of business. Instances of Hip Hop's influence in the political world include the Hip Hop Caucus during the activities of the 2008 inauguration of President Barack Obama, and the Hip Hop Inauguration Ball in 2012. Mixing music on his turntables, DJ Cassidy was the only person providing music for the 2012 Democratic National Convention in Charlotte, North Carolina, from September 4 through September 6. During the 2012 presidential campaign, Jay-Z held a fund-raising event that raised $4 million for the democratic nominee, President Obama.

Moreover, on February 26, 2012, Ambassador Susan Rice and the United States Mission to the United Nations hosted the Conference on "Hip Hop and International Diplomacy: Is There a Bridge?" At that conference, the fourth Hip Hop world ambassador for the UN, a Ghanaian Hip Hop emcee among others, addressed the participants. In the field of mental health, because of the growing field of Hip Hop therapy, in 2011 Professor George Yancy and the Fordham University Graduate School of Social Work invited academicians, practitioners, students, and members of the Hip Hop community from around the world for a major conference on this field. Developed by professionals who are participants in Hip Hop, such therapy includes counseling children and young adults in educational institutions, as well (Howard, 2007). Kurtis Blow, a popular emcee of the early 1980s, now a minister has formed the Hip Hop Church, which has chapters throughout the United States. Christian/Gospel Hip Hop music has a large following. Traditions from African and other cultures, including art, music, talk, dance, and teaching and learning, having been reconfigured into Hip Hop culture, have had a profound effect in various ways on the major institutions and elements of society, globally.

Hip Hop as Youth Culture

Culture includes what one uses to assist that individual in successfully negotiating life and living situations in the world. Patterson (2000) writes that "culture . . . is a repertoire of socially transmitted and intra-generationally generated ideas about how to live and make judgments. . . . It is an information system with various levels of specificity" (p. 208). Values and beliefs are inherent in those ideas as part of that information system. Culture addresses what is appropriate formally and what is effective ecologically, according to Hunn (1989), who writes "culture is what one must know in order to act effectively in one's environment" (p. 145). Much of one's culture is acquired from one's parents, siblings, and extended family, beginning shortly after birth. As children grow and venture outside of the home, they begin to identify and to learn information that soon becomes important in order to live successfully in the environment outside of the home, including what others think about them as members of society, and how society treats them and their kind, including among other things, their race, ethnic group, religion, gender, socioeconomic status, and age group.

Race and ethnic group, socioeconomic class, and age group were common factors of the youths living in the South and West Bronx when Kool Herc began giving parties that spawned

Hip Hop culture. The participants, primarily of African American, African Caribbean, and Latino descent, were from working-class families, and in some cases families surviving below the poverty line. Being not of European American ancestry, young people in the West and South Bronx were *victims* of Hoover's COINTELPRO, *victims* of the drugs being brought into their working-class and impoverished community, *victims* of the loss of viable employment as the community was torn apart with the construction of the Cross Bronx Expressway causing businesses to have to relocate, and *victims* of racism, as some were subjected to disco music that played via the airways was redefining popular culture from the 1960s *spirit of change*. As victims, they experienced and continued to witness too many injustices against others because of such factors as race, ethnicity, and class.

One must remember that these pioneers of Hip Hop were born during the 1960s, witnessing the Decade of Terrorists Assassinations, when a large, yet still unknown number of leaders, such as Dr. Martin Luther King, Jr., El Hajj Malik Shabazz/Malcolm X, and others in the African Diasporic Civil Rights and Black Power Movements, as well as those in movements in the Latino and Native American communities were assassinated in an effort by the power structure to curtail the struggle by these peoples for their civil and human rights! (Yasin, 2009a). Many deaths of European Americans occurred as well, including the assassinations of President John Kennedy and his brother Robert, who had served as Senator from New York and United States Attorney General. While internalizing and exploring their cultural traditions, the young people of the Bronx who embraced Hip Hop culture began learning how to utilize this culture to negotiate such injustices and social problems as those cited above.

A primary difference between other inhabitants of the West and South Bronx and those embracing Hip Hop is that of age: the Hip Hoppers were adolescents and young adults! More than one half of a century ago, Parsons (1951) posited that adolescents are in the process of learning to function independently of their parents, so they depend on their peer group as a substitute for their parents. Thus, as the elements of Hip Hop culture were put in place by the creative genius of adolescents, these elements addressed interests and needs of adolescents and young adults! As an illustration, Cindy Campbell persuaded her brother, Kool Herc, to have a party because she wanted money to buy clothes for school. School is an institution that a majority of adolescents participate in throughout the world. Furthermore, adolescents and young adults embrace popular culture: music and contemporary dances generated for that music, movies, fashion, language, and so forth. Such features of youth culture, in fact, do represent an independence of parents and older generations.

These features of youth culture define what is happening in the world of these youths as they begin to struggle with clarifying their viewpoints of the world and how they ultimately define their perspectives of the world. For example, as youths, my parents' generation listened to the music of the Ink Spots, Duke Ellington, and Ella Fitzgerald, in addition to B.B. King, for instance, who sang about the hard times and difficulty of life in the African American community and world events of that time in "Why I Sing the Blues." After migrating from the southern United States to other states, my generation as teenagers listened to the poetry over drumming by the Last Poets and the music of John Coltrane and the Temptations because we were fighting for our civil and human rights as the Temptations, for example, captured those moments with "Run Away Child, Running Wild" and Aretha Franklin kept the goal of "R-E-S-P-E-C-T" before us.

Currently, two generations of the Hip Hop community celebrate the same genre of music, but many tend to have preferences for emcees from the decade within the generation in which they came of age as adolescents, directly identifying with the culture and life issues during that period in time. Examples are DJ Grandmaster Flash of the late 1970s with his Furious Five, Chuck D of Public Enemy of the late 1980s, Common Sense in the late 1990s, Eminem during the early 2000s, and Drake at the present time. Fasick (1984) reported in a study that adolescents hold views and values similar to their parents, and that their problems are attributed to more age segregation, which is very logical because of the issues that youths confront as adolescents and young adults. AIDS and random gun violence were not issues to be confronted during the 1960s, for example. So, many issues important to youths, today, vary from those of their parents and other adults. However, according to Steinberg (2008), adults worry about youth culture leading them to loose morals and changing values. Sometimes, foreign elements are introduced to youths, becoming catalysts for changes, positive and negative, made by youths. Witness COINTELPRO, which infiltrated a united, self-help, youth-oriented Black Panther Party for Self Defense, initiating whisper campaigns, for example, that resulted in members of the party distrusting each other.

Antisocial groups and the government introduce elements of youth culture, such as drugs, into the environments of youths, as well. Witness the crack cocaine epidemic of the 1980s, 1990s, and during the early years of the 21st century. During the 1990s, United States Congresswoman Maxine Waters of Los Angeles continuously charged elements of the U.S. government with being the suppliers of the cocaine in her congressional district, which later proved to be true. Interestingly, youth cultures most readily articulate their issues and problems in unique ways, as demonstrated by the group of Hip Hop artists under the direction of Chris Parker, KRS [Knowledge Reigns Supreme] ONE, who organized the Stop the Violence Movement, in the 1990s, which raised large sums of money, which they donated to the NAACP, Urban League, and other organizations to fight violence, the crack epidemic, and other critical issues. Those emcees recorded Hip Hop rhymes, made music videos, performed at benefits and held other events, and donated all monies raised to community organizations; however, the leaders in the organizations took the checks, thanked Chris/KRS-ONE, and never contacted him to collaborate with them toward working to solve those problems (personal communication, November 2, 2001). Chris, who was homeless, changed his plight in life because of his skills as a Hip Hop emcee. Now leader of the Temple of Hip Hop, he has successfully assisted many other youths in transforming their lives in many ways. Although Hip-Hop Education Project (H2ED) at the Metro Center for Urban Education at New York University's Steinhardt School has begun serious quantitative and qualitative work on Hip Hop and education (Diaz, Fergus, & Noguera, 2011), researchers must continue to study how this youth culture has assisted adolescents and young adults, such as KRS ONE, in such positive personal life transformations.

Hip Hop Culture as a Discourse

One feature of one's culture is that of language and other ways of communicating, which are initially acquired from contact with parents, siblings, one's extended family, and later, one's community. Various features of language have been exploited by participants in Hip Hop culture, such as the invention of new words, for example, *jiggy* [getting dressed up], by Jay-Z; phonetic spellings, for example, *catz;* and use of numbers to represent words, for example, 24/7/365, which refers to 24 hours a day, 7 days a week, 365 days a year, and means "usually" and "all of the time." Words from Hip Hop culture are now regular entries in the *Oxford English Dictionary.* Early on, children acquire words, then gradually, the dialect or dialects of the language or languages spoken in the home. A language has three major elements. The phonological system, the sound system of the language, includes the rules for which sounds are organized in meaningful units to speakers of a given language. Another primary element of a language is the syntax or system of grammar rules. The final language element is the lexicon or vocabulary words of the language. Children and adolescents learn to apply alternate rules of these elements of language, depending upon the person with whom they are communicating, which role they are playing, student, son or daughter, and so on.

Children, while acquiring language, learn a variation or dialect of the language, which is a variation of certain rules that have primary differences as a result of geography, socioeconomic status, and ethnicity/race. Examples include African American Vernacular English, Appalachian English, or Spanglish. Gee (1998) writes that "language . . . always comes attached to 'other stuff': to social relations, cultural models, power and politics, perspectives on experience, values and attitudes, as well as things and places in the world" (p. vii). As they grow into adolescence, teenagers take note of all of this, which is very important because they want to "fit in."

Not having learned other than vocabulary words of African American Vernacular English (AAVE) as a child growing up in the Laurel Heights section of San Francisco, I realized that as a teenager, in order to "hang out," I had to master the dialect, including AAVE's sound system and grammar in order to negotiate independently the now-gentrified Fillmore District, the African American community that was nearest to my home, as well as the other two in the city. Many youths still have similar experiences. This experience corroborates Gee's comment that much of "what we do with language . . . is create and act out different 'types of people' . . . by putting words, deeds, values, other people, and things together in integral combinations for specific times and places, and letting others do the same with us" (p. viii). In order to carry out one of our many roles, we need other people. For example, in the classroom, as the professor, I communicate in Edited American English, the accepted form of mainstream English in the academy with students, some of whom speak AAVE. However, privately in my office, as mentor/tutor/counselor/friend/parent, I regularly code switch with some students, bidialectal African Americans and many Latinos, who speak the dialect, as they may need to feel they are a part of the institution and have a right to be there. This creates a bond, early on allowing mentoring for success in the classroom and in the academy.

Bilingual colleagues, who speak Spanish, Russian, Korean, Haitian Creole, and other languages, use language in similar ways with students who speak the same languages. Many bidialectal people who speak two dialects of a language regularly code switch from one to the other dialect, *depending upon the situation,* whom they are conversing with, and *which role they are playing,* that is, teacher, husband, client, employee, and so forth. Bilingual speakers of two languages engage in code switching, as well.

The term *discourse* refers to any use of spoken or written language beyond the level of the sentence. Gee (1998) uses the term *Discourse* (with a capital D) to refer to the language used and a host of other things in any given situation (p. viii). According to Gee,

> Discourses . . . are ways of behaving, interacting, valuing, thinking, believing, speaking, and often reading and writing that are accepted as instantiations of particular roles (or "types of people") by specific *groups of people,* whether families of a certain sort, lawyers of a certain sort, bikers of a certain sort, business people of a certain sort, church members of a certain sort, African-Americans of a certain sort, women or men of a certain sort, and so on through a very long list. Discourses are ways of being "people like us." They are "ways of being in the world"; they are "forms of life." They are, thus, always and everywhere *social* and products of social histories. (p. vii; italics in original)

We acquire various primary Discourses early on and learn other Discourses using the primary Discourses we have acquired previously. As children, we learn to behave and talk a certain way with parents early on. This is one of our Discourses. If we have siblings, we learn to behave and talk with them in other ways than how we address our parents, which is another Discourse. For example, if a parent tells us to turn the light off, we will do it or explain why we still need it; in a different role, however, we might tell a sibling "no" or that he or she should turn it off themselves, as we throw something at him or her. These are primary Discourses, which Gee writes, "are those to which people are apprenticed early in life during their primary socialization as members of particular families within their sociocultural settings. Primary Discourses constitute first social identity, and something of a base within which we acquire or resist later Discourses. They form our initial taken-for-granted understandings of *who* we are and *who* people 'like us' are, as well as what sorts of things we ('people like us') do, value, and believe when we are not 'in public' " (p. 137). This is where our tolerance, acceptance, hatred, and so forth, of others begin, as well.

The language and elements of Hip Hop are a primary Discourse for the second generation of children and adolescents participating in Hip Hop culture, because it was introduced to them in their homes, in some cases by parents, by older siblings, by neighbors, by other children, and so forth. When Hip Hop was a generation old, in November 1993, during a presentation at the American Museum of Natural History in New York City, entitled "Talk in Music as an African Oral Tradition," upon playing the 1980 recording of "The Message" by DJ Grandmaster Flash and the Furious Five, several young Latino boys got up and began b boyin' in the aisles. These children, the oldest of whom was about eight years old, were not born when that first sociopolitical rhyme was popular. Talking with them and their parents after the program, we learned that the parents were b boys and b girls. Furthermore, they were teaching their children these dance skills. For these parents, things Hip Hop is a secondary Discourse, because they developed the skill of b boying' by using their primary Discourses as adolescents, during its initial development. However, for their children who were learning things Hip Hop as young children, Hip Hop is a part of their primary Discourses and they surely call on Hip Hop to learn secondary Discourses.

"Secondary Discourses are those to which people are apprenticed as part of their socializations within various local, state, and national groups and institutions outside early home and peer-group socialization—for example churches, gangs, schools, and offices. They constitute the recognizability and meaningfulness of our 'public' (more formal) acts" (Gee, 1998, p. 137). For the initial group who participated in the initial parties, battles, and other programs of Hip Hop, it is a secondary Discourse because they were adolescents when they first began creating and developing it and its elements, while using their primary Discourses to do so. His motivation to succeed in his calculus class—a condition for maintaining his scholarship at Stanford University—caused Wade to utilize Hip Hop culture, which, for him, was a primary Discourse that he began acquiring early on in life, in order to learn calculus, an aspect of a secondary Discourse for him, that of teaching and learning/schooling.

Hip Hop Culture as a Source of Motivation

Motivation, according to Bernstein and Nash (2005), includes influences that justify and explain the initiation, the direction, the intensity, and the persistence of behavior. Cindy, Kool Herc's sister, motivated to buy new school clothes, persuaded her brother to have a party with an entrance fee, in order to earn money to purchase these clothes. That is, Cindy's desire for new clothes initiated her persuasive rhetoric used with her brother, which resulted in Kool Herc's behavior that included organizing the party, an outgrowth of which was Hip Hop culture. Although there are four primary factors for human motivation—identified by Bernstein and Nash (2005) as biological, emotional, cognitive, and social—the two factors directing Cindy and her brother, initially, were cognitive and social. The cognitive factors of human motivation include a person's perception of the world, beliefs about what one can accomplish, and anticipation of how others will respond. Based on her experiences as an adolescent, Cindy perceived that adolescents and young adults enjoy music and dancing; also, she believed that her brother had the necessary skills to host a pay-for-entry party, and that neighborhood youths would respond by coming to the party to enjoy the music and to dance.

These factors generate certain behaviors, which a person will more likely carry out if one has confidence, which Cindy and Kool Herc probably gained as a result of observing that many neighborhood youths were listening when Herc was playing amplified music in his parents' apartment in the process of honing his deejayin' skills. Such cognitive factors caused Wade to continue studying calculus until he finally grasped the mathematical concepts after putting them into a rhyme that he had the skills to compose, leading him to have the confidence to send the rhyme to his professor, which ultimately would have a positive outcome.

Also, social factors for human motivation include one's reactions to other humans and other sociocultural forces. Sociocultural forces include humans whom an individual has expectations of and reciprocally, who have expectations of the individual. These include reciprocal relationships between the individual and parents, siblings, teachers, and friends, all of which motivate the individual in certain ways to engage in specific kinds of actions. Having new clothes for the beginning of the school year is a ritual among children and adolescents in the United States. They engage in admiring each other's new clothing, and Cindy wanted to be a part of that ritual, a motivating factor in encouraging Herc to organize his party. Moreover, inanimate objects, such as television and radio programs and Hip Hop rhymes and other types of music, motivate the individual to action, as well. The taggers' posters announcing Herc's party motivated youths to obtain the entrance fee and to attend the party. Artists wearing certain brands of clothes and shoes, such as Timberland, create a huge increase in the volume of clothing and shoes sold by the company. Various individuals hearing brand names in a Hip Hop rhyme that is pleasing to them feel certain emotions about the product (Bernstein and Nash, 2005), often resulting in desires for and purchasing the product. Sociocultural factors, such as family relationships, important to Wade, included demonstrating to his professor that he finally understood the necessary concepts to grasp the discipline of calculus.

What became Hip Hop culture was a valuable unexpected societal contribution, an outgrowth of Cindy's motivation to have money to buy new school clothes. Hip Hop emceein', for instance, was "born as a form of necessary speech. It provided young people, many of whom were from difficult and impoverished backgrounds, with a voice and a means of vivid expression" (Bradley & DuBois, 2010, p. xxxviii). The other elements of the culture, equally powerful, have provided creative participants of this youth culture with a much-needed public voice using the other necessary forms of expressive behavior, dance and art, making music, and so forth. Currently, because of their pervasiveness in society, these elements and Hip Hop culture early on become features of many children's primary Discourses, part of their first identity and their uses of language based upon whom they are interfacing with and communicating with at any given time. Their primary Discourses are used to learn other Discourses, secondary Discourses, including the Discourse of education and schooling, particularly, teaching and learning.

Hip Hop Culture as a Teaching and Learning Tool

Because many children, in urban schools and now, other settings, bring Hip Hop culture into the classroom as features of their primary Discourses, sincere teachers must consider using aspects of this culture as a tool in the teaching-learning process, for according to Gardner (1999), education should reflect the students' cultures' procedures in this process. Kozol and Anyon present poignant descriptions of how schools in urban areas have failed children, primarily of African

American and Latino origins, for various reasons, including ignoring their cultural procedures for learning and teaching. Kozol (2002)) in *Savage Inequalities* discusses the educational problems of children of color as a result of the unequal distribution of resources in urban schools. Anyon (2004) presented the hidden curriculum taught to children based on their parents' social class. In her ethnographic study of five different 5th-grade classrooms in five schools, each from a different socioeconomic class, Anyon presents examples of "how school knowledge and skills leading to social power and reward (e.g., medical, legal, managerial) all are made available to the advantaged social groups but are withheld from the working classes, to whom a more 'practical' curriculum is offered (e.g., manual skills, clerical knowledge)" (p. 195).

In the working-class schools, where parents are likely to be wage earners or salaried laborers, not owners of physical capital, decisions were made by teachers in an attempt to control classroom time and space, without any input by the children. Mechanical teaching methods requiring learning by rote memorization was what was expected of the children in both their written and oral work in the classroom. In some subject areas, the procedures presented to teach the children certain activities were fragmented and not complete, such as certain mathematics activities, and often the children were not given explanations about why the activities were assigned. These children are expected to be manual laborers. The middle-class schools were attended by children of parents whose relationship with the process of work and the process of product production is not always clear and in some cases exhibited contradictory characteristics. In these schools, it was important for such children to get the right answer in order to get a good grade.

Although one must follow directions in order to get the right answers, directions often call for some figuring, some choice, some decision making. Anyon found that in the middle-class schools, the learning activities usually did not require creativity. Control of students varied from easygoing to strict, but it often was based on rules and regulations with which the children were familiar. Performing well was stressed in order to receive other rewards, such as entrance into college or certain types of employment. The students in the affluent schools, where parents of students were professionals, were continuously expected to carry out creative work on an independent basis. When children needed to supply a correct answer, they were encouraged to decide on an answer after thinking about what they were being asked to do. Anyon provided an example where children were given a sheet to take home requesting their parents to fill in the number of cars they had, television sets owned, rooms in the house, and so forth. Then, each child had to figure out the average number of cars, and other kinds of possessions owned by the students' families in 5th grade. The emphasis was on expressing and illustrating ideas in certain subject areas. Control of the classes was by continuous negotiation. Children were obviously being "trained" to be entrepreneurs, scholars, creative artists, politicians, and to develop important critical thinking skills.

Anyon's description of learning activities, primarily based on rote memorization in classrooms for children of working-class parents, concurs with Kozol's (2002) description of the meager resources and learning aids provided in schools attended by poor children in the South Bronx, primarily Latino and of African descent. These schools were overcrowded, housed in poor facilities, and in some cases in buildings originally constructed for other purposes. One school was initially a roller skating rink! Another school had a capacity of 1,000 students, but had a student population of 1,550. And students had to share textbooks in some subject areas. Kozol writes, "[d]enial of 'the means of competition' is perhaps the single most consistent outcome of the education offered to poor children" (p. 113). Moreover, Anyon's findings on the classroom activities of children with affluent parents parallel Kozol's experiences while visiting schools in the affluent Riverdale section of the North Bronx. The external environment of the schools included trees and flowers, with a park nearby and a play area for children.

One school served about one half of the number of students served in the overcrowded school in the South Bronx. In this school, 130 students were of poor and either Latino or of African descent, many in special classes, while 700 were European American or Asian. Classrooms had small student populations and ample learning aids. This smaller-populated school, when provided with computers, was given the exact same number of computers as those given to the more crowded schools in the South Bronx, which provided students with less access time, if any, using the technology. In one affluent North Bronx school, one teacher had the same students from 1st grade through 3rd grade. During their 3rd-grade year, students with the most potential were identified and put into classes that followed a curriculum emphasizing reasoning and logic. "The planetarium, for instance, is employed not simply for the study of the universe as it exists. 'Children also are designing their own galaxies' " (Kozol, 2002, pp. 122–123). Interestingly, these schools in Kozol's study, located in the North and South Bronx, are both in District 10, under the same superintendent.

Such differences as allocation of resources, classroom instruction, access to technology, and so forth, surely result in an achievement gap. "By the end of fourth grade, African American, Latino, and poor children of all races are two years behind their wealthier, predominately white peers in reading and math. By eighth grade, they have slipped three years behind, and by 12th grade, four years behind" (Teachers College, 2005). This is not surprising when one confronts Anyon's "hidden curriculum" for the poor and working-class people, and when one confronts Kozol's "denial of the means of competition." When teachers prepare learning activities that rely solely upon rote memorization and do not rely upon negotiation and collaboration for control of the learning environment, what students bring to the classroom is not acknowledged, nor given any value.

Students bring language(s), dialects, their cultures—components of their primary Discourses—and other nonacademic elements into our classrooms daily (Yasin, 2009b, p. 270). Such "funds of knowledge," according to Moll and Greenberg (1990) would greatly benefit teachers if they understood them, and help them to provide positive learning experiences, by allowing the students to utilize the knowledge they have by associating it with what they are learning. Hip Hop elements are examples of students' funds of knowledge. Teachers' understanding of students' funds of knowledge would ameliorate the "two-way path from school to the community and from the community to school" (Heath, 1983, p. 125), which is vitally important if the learning process and information and skills, in a formal setting, such as school, are to be mastered by students. Knowledge that students bring to school with them informs Hip Hop's inherent educational value, which Diaz (2011) writes "derives from self-awareness, determination, and expression . . . [and] is founded on Hip-Hop pedagogy that procures alternative learning processes and multiple teaching and learning processes and praxis." Self-awareness, determination, and expression are all factors of motivation.

Some 20 years ago, a teacher in metropolitan Boston was not successful with her students learning their multiplication tables. One day, she left the classroom, and returned while they were reciting in unison the Hip Hop lyrics of a popular emcee at that time. Later, she decided to engage students in the upper grades, by giving them a list of the multiplication tables and having them write a Hip Hop rhyme incorporating the multiplication tables, and then, recording the rhyme, "Tough Times." She used Hip Hop, a cultural element from her students' funds of knowledge to develop learning materials for these students. The tape, once on sale, is no longer available. However, a variety of other materials are now available online by searching for "multiplication tables and Hip Hop." The students learned their tables, while one female student commented that she listened to the tape every night before sleeping, which was better than listening to the "boring teacher." For these students, Hip Hop was one of their primary Discourses learned at home and in their communities, which they used to learn a secondary

Discourse, multiplication tables. Alternative activities can be developed to have students practice such information, which they must memorize.

Several years ago, an article appeared in the *New York Daily News,* reporting that NASA, the National Aeronautics and Space Administration, had sent b boys and b girls to a school in the South Bronx to demonstrate concepts of physical science to students through dance. Emdin (2010), in one of the many teaching tools and techniques he presents, suggests that "in urban science classrooms, it is helpful to utilize places from the students' neighborhoods or locations from artists that are used in rap songs, as the examples to use in class" (p. 111).

In social science classes, Truesdale and Yasin (2012) inform us that teachers may rechannel students' classroom experiences through creative writing, assigning students the task of writing a Hip Hop rhyme, for example, to express a social, political, or economic position. This assignment encourages students to engage in written communication, expressing points of view that are academically, socially, and morally constructive. Truesdale uses these assignments with university students to assist them in developing research skills by finding expert support for information presented in the Hip Hop rhyme, which can be rewritten as a research paper. In the area of literature, Hill (2009) explains how he used Hip Hop lyrics for what was to be a literature course; students gravitated toward discussing lyrics of Hip Hop rhymes. Included in each class meeting were journal writing, journal sharing, group reading of the Hip Hop text, reader response activities, and a formal lesson and assignment, which included what the teachers wanted to discuss and teach.

Pough (2004) utilizes Hip Hop in the classroom to assist the student in exploring relationships and transformation of self. I invite Hip Hop emcees in writing classes to explain the writing process to students, why it is necessary to engage in research before writing, as well as the evils of academic dishonesty, at which they excel because they do not want others to "bite their rhymes," plagiarize their creative work. Often, the instructor has to explain some of the comments in academic English, but such students usually have the class's undivided attention. There are many, many additional types of materials and resources, which can be utilized to engage students, including having students produce and create elements of the culture themselves. Such activities motivate students because they bring confidence of knowing something about the learning activity and understanding teachers' expectations.

Conclusion

The use of Hip Hop culture as a teaching-learning tool can provide valuable guidance and direction toward developing the field of urban education because "[a] new wave of educators and cultural workers influenced by Hip-Hop culture, technology and globalization has emerged in recent years. The first wave began in the early 90s . . . [who] grew up with Hip-Hop. Today, . . . hundreds of teachers, artists, scholars, social workers, social entrepreneurs, and administrators . . . serve as an inter-generational cultural bridge" (Diaz et al., 2011). Diaz, Emdin, Pough, Truesdale, Hill, Howard, Bradley, DuBois, and Wade C. are examples of this new wave of educators who "live Hip Hop" and utilize it as a tool to assist children and youths in developing necessary academic skills for success in life. Hip Hop culture created a public space for voices to be heard that had been marginalized, but Duncan-Andrade and Morrell (2008) warn us that it is important to focus on academic skill development when utilizing critical pedagogy, as well. Hip Hop culture provides teachers with enough information to generate learning activities encouraging all students, especially urban students, to carry out creative work on an independent basis, as did the affluent students studied in Anyon's and Kozol's studies.

Gardner's (1993) work on multiple intelligences provides teachers with knowledge of how to identify nine factors, which can be considered some of Moll's funds of knowledge and strengths that students bring to the classroom, which can be used to assist them in developing other skills, as well as measuring their intelligence on individually centered constraints. Such issues should continue to be explored in Hip Hop courses offered in the academy, especially in the Hip Hop minor concentration program now offered at the University of Arizona and by the recipients of the Hip Hop Scholarships at the University of Wisconsin. Using Hip Hop culture and additional methods for teaching and learning in the classroom will force teachers to close their attitude gap (Kafele, 2012) about certain students and their cultures as they work to assist students in closing the achievement gap.

References

Anyon, J. (2004). Social class and the hidden curriculum of work. In G. Colombo, R. Cullen, & B. Lisle (Eds.), *Rereading America: Cultural contexts for critical thinking and writing* (6th ed., pp. 195–209). Boston, MA: Bedford/St. Martin's. (Original work published 1981).

Bernstein, D.A., & Nash, P.W. (2005). *Essentials of psychology* (3rd ed.). Boston, MA: Houghton Mifflin.

Bradley, A., & DuBois, A. (2010). *The anthology of rap.* New Haven, CT: Yale University Press.

Chang, J. (2005). *Can't stop, won't, stop: A history of the hip hop generation.* New York, NY: St. Martin's.

Diaz, M. (2011). *The world is yours: A brief history of hip-hop.* New York University Metro Center for Urban Education. Retrieved from http://steinhart.yu.edu./metrocenter/hiphopeducation

Diaz, M., Fergus, E., & Noguera, P. (2011). *Reimaging teaching and learning: A snapshot of hip hop education.* New York University Metro Center for Urban Education. Retrieved from http://steinhart.nyu.edu/metrocenter/hiphopeducation

Duncan-Andrade, J., & Morrell, E. (2008). *The art of critical pedagogy: The possibilities of moving from theory to practice in urban schools.* New York, NY: Peter Lang.

Emdin, C. (2010). *Urban science education for the hip-hop generation: Essential tools for the urban science educator and researcher.* Rotterdam, The Netherlands: Sense.

Fasick, F.A. (1984). Parents, peers, youth culture and autonomy in adolescence. *Adolescence, 19*(73), 143–157.

Gardner, H. (1993). *Frames of mind: Theories of multiple intelligences* (2nd ed.). London, UK: Fontana Press.

Gardner, H. (1999). *The disciplined mind: What all students should understand.* New York, NY: Simon & Schuster.

Gee, J.P. (1998). *Social linguistics and literacies: Ideology in discourses* (2nd ed.). London, UK: Falmer.

Gordon, E., & Armour-Thomas, E. (1992). Urban education. In M.C. Alkin (Ed.), *Encyclopedia of educational research* (6th ed.). (Vol. 3, pp. 1459–1470). New York, NY: MacMillan.

Heath, S.B. (1983). *Ways with words: Language, life and work in communities and classrooms.* Cambridge, UK: Cambridge University Press.

Heller, J. (2006). *Ruthless: A memoir.* New York, NY: Simon Spotlight Entertainment.

Hill, M.L. (2009). *Beats, rhymes, and classroom life: Hip-hop pedagogy and the politics of identity.* New York, NY: Teachers College Press.

Howard, N. (2007). *Hip hop as a counseling tool.* New York University Faculty Resource Network. Retrieved from http://www.nyu.ed/frn

Hunn, E.S. (1989). Ethnoecology: The relevance of cognitive anthropology for human ecology. In M.E. Frelich (Ed.), *The relevance of culture* (pp. 143–160). South Hadley, MA: Bergen & Garvey.

Kafele, B. (2012, February). *Closing teachers' attitude gaps toward their students.* Paper presented in honor of Black History Month at Bergen Community College, Paramus, NJ.

Kitwana, B. (2005). *Why white kids love hip-hop.* New York, NY: Basic Books.

Kozol, J. (2002). Savage inequalities. In L.G. Kirszner & S.R. Mandell (Eds.), *The Blair reader* (4th ed., pp. 112–124). Upper Saddle River, NJ: Prentice Hall.

Milner, H.R. (2009). Preparing teachers of African American students in urban schools. In L. Tillman (Ed.), *Sage handbook of African American education* (pp. 123–139). Los Angeles, CA: Sage Publications.

Moll, L.C., & Greenberg, (1990). Creating zones of possibilities: Combining social contexts for instruction. In L.C. Moll (Ed.), *Vygotsky and education* (pp. 319–348). Cambridge, UK: Cambridge University Press.

Parsons, T. (1951). *The social system*. Glencoe, IL: Free Press.

Patterson, O. (2000). Taking culture seriously: A framework and an Afro-American illustration. In L. Harrison & S.P. Huntington (Eds.), *Culture matters: How values shape human progress* (pp. 202–218). New York, NY: Basic Books.

Pough, G.D. (2004). *Check it while I wreck it: Black womanhood, hip-hop culture, and the sphere*. Boston, MA: Northern University Press.

Richardson, E. (2003). *African American literacies*. London, UK: Routledge.

Rose, T. (1994). *Black noise: Rap music and black culture in contemporary America*. Hanover, NH: Wesleyan University Press.

Sanchez, M. (March 1999). *Graffiti art in hip hop culture*. Paper presented at the Annual Conference on College Composition and Communication of the National Council of Teachers of English, Atlanta, GA.

Steinberg, L. (2008). *Adolescence*. New York, NY: McGraw-Hill.

Teachers College, Columbia University. (2005). *Academic achievement gap: Facts and figures*. Retrieved from http://www.tc.columbia.edu/news.htm

Truesdale, S., & Yasin, J.A. (2012). Revisiting cultural curriculum and marginalized youth: A critical pedagogy for educatin tha gangsta. *Journal of Arts and Humanities, 1*(3), 87–98.

Vincent, R. (1996). *Funk: The music, the people and the rhythm of the one*. New York, NY: St. Martin's Griffin.

Woodson, C. G. (2006). *The miseducation of the Negro*. San Diego, CA: The Book Tree.

Yasin, J.A. (1997). *In yo face! Rappin' beats comin' at you: A study of how language is mapped onto musical beats in rap music* (Unpublished doctoral dissertation). Teachers College, Columbia University, New York, NY.

Yasin, J.A. (2009a). Hip hop: A source of empowerment for African American male college students. In L. Tillman (Ed.), *Sage handbook of African American education* (pp. 283–296). Los Angeles, CA: Sage Publications.

Yasin, J.A. (2009b). Rockin' the classroom: Using hip hop as an educational tool. In J.A. Kleifgen & G.C. Bond (Eds.), *The language of Africa and the diaspora* (pp. 270–280). Bristol, UK: Multilingual Matters.

Section VII
Policy and Reform

23

Race, Research, and Urban Education

Gloria Ladson-Billings

In 1964 American artist Norman Rockwell painted what would become an icon of the civil rights movement, a painting entitled, "The Problem We All Live With." The painting is a depiction of Ruby Bridges, the 6-year-old African American girl who desegregated the New Orleans Parish Schools in 1960. In the painting, a brave little Black girl is seen striding between four federal marshals with her schoolbook and ruler in her hands and on the wall behind her are the heinous racial epithet and the remnants of a tomato that was tossed in her direction. In many ways this painting is emblematic of the experiences of racially minoritized[1] students over a long period of the nation's history and such a rendering persists today.

Throughout the literature on urban schooling and racial disparity, we encounter the terms *inequality* and *inequity*. In general, inequality refers to the condition of being unequal while inequity deals with questions of justice and fairness. Inequality exists. Some individuals, families, communities, and nations have more resources than others. This is a fact of the human condition. However, when some people (particularly in the same city, state, or nation) have less access to basic social services such as health, education, or decent housing, we have a condition of inequity. In qualitative research the terms *inequality* and *inequity* are sometimes used interchangeably. However, for the purpose of this chapter, I will use the term *inequity*.

This chapter uses a Critical Race Theory (CRT) framework to look at the way legal efforts have worked to both ensure and deny educational opportunities for students of color. While I will necessarily start with the landmark *Brown v. Board of Education* (1954) case, my intent is to focus on contemporary legal moves in education (e.g., state propositions, Supreme Court cases) as well as policy reforms that ostensibly propose to improve urban education but end up reinscribing inequality.

Introduction

Norman Rockwell was a beloved American artist credited with painting what the art world calls "Americana"—a style of painting designed to illustrate those things specific to America and reinscribe notions of American "exceptionalism." Typical Rockwell paintings showed scenes of barbershops and Fourth of July parades or Midwestern mothers baking apple pies. Rockwell's paintings regularly graced the covers of the *Saturday Evening Post* and provided the nation with the calm assurance that ours was a nation living true to its creed. Rockwell showed us the nation we believed ourselves to be.

However, in 1964 Rockwell could not ignore the reality of American life that was deeply flawed by the specter of race and the ways that Black Americans had little or no share in the Rockwellian images of the past. In this year Rockwell did a painting he titled, "The Problem We All Live With," that was a depiction of 6-year-old Ruby Bridges from New Orleans who was the first African American to desegregate New Orleans Parish Schools. So virulent were responses to the Bridges's family's decision to allow little Ruby attend New Orleans schools that she had to attend school protected by the National Guard. In the painting Ruby is center stage wearing a crisp pinafore and her hair in three pigtails. Ruby is walking between a set of federal marshals, but the painting does not include their faces. We see grey-suited White men with armbands declaring their missions. Only little Ruby is fully visible.

What I believe is especially significant about the painting is that Rockwell titled it, "The Problem We All Live With," as if to ensure that the viewers' response would not merely be one of pity toward Ruby but rather would hold everyone culpable for the insanity of the racial structures and inequality that we have constructed. Like an earlier argument about our education debt (Ladson-Billings, 2006), the Rockwell painting illustrates the collective responsibility we as citizens have toward addressing inequality and ongoing racism. Instead of mere individual responsibility, Rockwell chose a title that evokes the network of social obligation that makes us a nation of common purpose. For Rockwell, Ruby Bridges was not about the "White man's burden" or the "Black man's shame." She was the embodiment of the problem we all live with.

In this chapter I discuss the way schooling in the United States continues to uphold and reinforce racial inequality and how that inequality contributes to the achievement disparities extant in the nation's schools. I begin with a brief explanation of Critical Race Theory and its use in understanding inequality, followed by an examination of some of the legal cases, laws, and policies regarding education, and conclude with prospects for resolving "the problem we all live with."

Critical Race Theory as a Rubric for Understanding Inequality

Critical Race Theory (CRT) is more precisely a set of theories that argue that racism is normal, not aberrant in U.S. life (Delgado & Stefancic, 2001). Legal scholars proposed the notion of CRT after coming to the conclusion that even their more liberal White colleagues did not fully understand the incredible burden that race put upon people of color, despite advances in civil right rulings and legislation. Many liberal White legal scholars understood that the law and its application were unfair to a variety of people because of their status identities—that is, race, class, gender, sexuality, immigrant status, language use, or ability. Their solution to the built-in inequality of the law was to propose Critical Legal Studies (CLS) in workshops that analyzed legal scholarship and legal precedence. However, in the midst of one of the workshops, Black legal scholars recognized that even within this alternate space, issues of Black life and experience with the law continued to be marginalized (Crenshaw, 2011). Realization of this marginalization gave birth to Critical Race Theory—a place in legal scholarship where race would be central to analysis of inequality.

Early scholars in CRT include Derrick Bell (who is widely regarded as the "Father of Critical Race Theory"), Kimberly Crenshaw, Richard Delgado, Patricia Williams, Mari Matsuda, Charles Lawrence, III, Neil Gotanda, Cheryl Harris, Linda Greene, Gary Peller, Kendall Thomas, John O. Calmore, among others. They argued that traditional civil rights law's approach to addressing inequality through legislation and filing *amicus* briefs was too slow and ineffective to change the social and civil status of African Americans and other non-Whites. Indeed, CRT scholars argued that there are never civil rights laws enacted unless those laws also benefit Whites.

The major tenets of CRT include the following: racism as normal, not aberrant, and constitutive of the fabric of U.S. life and culture; much of reality is social constructed; storytelling or more accurately, counterstorytelling is a way for marginalized groups to address their marginalization; use of critical social science as a tool for analyzing inequality in the society; and interest convergence as a vehicle for moving civil rights agendas forward.

The belief that racism is normal is a difficult one for Americans to accept. Given a cultural narrative of never-ending progress and noble purpose, to suggest that racism is both a normative and predictable condition in the nation meets with denial and active resistance. Thus, those who point out the ongoing pattern and systemic nature of racism are discounted as malcontents or "racial opportunists." Critical race theorists identify "microagressions"(Sue, 2010) that speak to the daily racial indignities that people of color suffer. For instance, common everyday occurrences like being ignored by a merchant, challenged as to one's ability to pay, or being mistaken as a subordinate reflect the kinds of microagressions that people of color experience. For CRT scholars it is the accumulation of these events rather than the dramatic or tragic events (e.g., Trayvon Martin murder, Troy Davis execution).

The notion that much of reality is socially constructed is not a new one to social scientists. However, the primary research paradigms through which we do our work suggest a sense of reality through empirical verification. Legal scholars know that the work of American jurisprudence is about constructing a reality—to argue a case and a point of view. More pointedly, the very concept of race around which we organize most of our thinking about human beings is a social construction (Omi & Winant, 1994). Natural science refutes the existence of race but social science uses it as a primary organizing status category. Sociologists, psychologists, political scientists, and educationists all use race as a sense-making category while natural science points out that at the most basic biologic level—DNA and RNA are not racially distinguishable. Thus, race is not a helpful rubric for making most scientific decisions. It is important to note because some disease and genetic conditions appear more frequently in certain groups (e.g., sickle cell anemia, Tay Sachs disease, hypertension, or diabetes), there are ethical and moral challenges associated with treatment and insurance concerns. However, social science in the United States structures much of its work around the concept of race. In sociology we look at racial patterns in crime, incarceration, housing patterns, educational attainment, and other social conditions. Psychologists look at perceived racial differences in intelligence, giftedness, cognition, problem solving, and human development issues. Political scientists consider racial differences in voting patterns, political participation, and civic concerns. Thus, the tension between race as a social construct and race as a biological reality force scholars to deal with the shifting nature of knowledge and to question heretofore "epistemologically verified" notions of the social world.

Storytelling (or counterstorytelling) is an important tool for the CRT scholar. These stories can be fantastical (e.g., Derrick Bell's "Space traders") or realistic but what they have in common is that they are fictional tales designed to illustrate legal and/or moral dilemmas produced by the way laws, policies, and statutes are developed and implemented. The fantastical storytelling can take on the characteristics of the literary genre known as magical realism (Schroeder, 2004) commonly found in the literature of Latin America. Challengers to CRT point to storytelling as nonscientific, lacking rigor, and antithetical to the scholarly process. However, CRT scholars push back with claims that all scholars tell stories, especially legal scholars but that those stories may take the form of reports, logs, or descriptions of so-called empirical claims.

CRT scholars employ critical social science as a tool for analyzing racial situations and legal precedence. This means that their work starts from a place where inequity is assumed. That inequity might deal with race, class, gender, sexuality, disability, and so forth, and scholars like Bourdieu (1986), Foucault (2002), Fraser (2003), Freire (1970), or Gramsci (2011) can be instructive in providing an alternative vision of the social world—one that assumes the existence of inequality and the need to address it. I make this point about assumed inequity because much of the literature in the positivist-functionalist tradition makes no such assumption about *a priori* inequity. Thus, research done in the more positivist tradition may discuss issues of student or school-level achievement in generic ways that fail to take into account unequal starting points for individual students and/or school communities. For example, a study of advanced placement or honors course enrollment may not take into consideration the lack of such course offerings in most urban schools.

A final tenet of CRT that I will discuss includes an acceptance of the interest convergence principle. This notion was developed by Bell (1980a) to argue that Black social, economic, and civil concerns will only be addressed when they intersect or converge with those of Whites. Thus, even among our most cherished civil rights laws, CRT scholars uncover the way these laws also serve White interests. For example, the landmark *Brown v. Board of Education* (1954) decision is touted as one of the Supreme Court's finest moments. The ruling that "separate is inherently unequal" seemed on the surface to be a commitment to racial equality. Bell (1980a) and later Dudziak (1995) point out that despite the seeming civil rights meaning of the decision, it actually served as a foreign policy move during the Cold War to signal to nonaligned states that the United States provided fair and equal treatment under the law to its Black citizens. However, the proof of the proverbial pudding is the fact that more than 50 years past *Brown,* the majority of Black and Brown children attend deeply segregated schools. Even in those places where school desegregation was actually attempted, we see retrenchment from the law. Indeed, recent legal decisions (i.e., *Parents Involved in Community Schools v. Seattle School District No. 1*, 2007 and *Jefferson County Public Schools*, 2007) seemingly have turned *Brown* on its head to allow it to better serve the needs of White students.

Another example of interest convergence was evident in the 2008 presidential election. Although most U.S. voters voted along strict White/Non-White lines (i.e., Blacks, Latinos, and Asian Americans voted largely for President Obama and the majority of Whites voted for Senator McCain), enough White voters saw their own interests as aligned with Barack Obama to vote across the racial line. While many lauded the racial progress that the election signaled, as a CRT scholar, I would argue that the extant financial crisis made some White voters cast their lot with the Black candidate rather than chance the continuance of economic policies that landed the nation in the deep financial crisis of the time. However, in the recent 2012 election campaign, the racial divide was once again reinforced. Voters seemed unprepared for the slow pace of economic recovery primarily because they may not have been fully aware of the depth of the financial crisis and what the president was able to do to avoid a deeper recession and perhaps a depression. With continued high unemployment rates and a negative response to shoring up banks and major corporations like AIG and General Motors, many White voters seemed to have rejected Barack Obama as the answer to their financial woes. Why? Were White voters dissatisfied with President Obama's actions to meet their financial interests?

This is a necessarily brief discussion of CRT to provide a basic understanding of its tenets and how they can be applied to the analysis of racial inequity. In the remainder of the chapter I discuss specific legal cases, laws, and policies that contribute to ongoing inequity despite their expressed purpose to minimize or eradicate it.

Litigating the Way to Justice

The United States is the world's most litigious nation. Legislators, policy makers, pundits, and the general public lament the notion that everyone attempts to sue for any perceived offense. The proliferation of frivolous lawsuits might appear to minimize the importance of the law as a vehicle for social change. However, the law has been a primary vehicle for attempting to equalize educational opportunities. The seminal legal case in attempting to redress educational inequities is the *Brown v. Board of Education* (1954) case that was designed to eradicate separate and unequal schooling.[2]

Hess (2005) has argued the *Brown* decision is reified in the classroom. I contend that it also is reified in U.S. legal, political, and popular culture. On October 26, 1992, the U.S. Congress passed Public Law 102–525 establishing the Monroe Elementary School and its adjacent grounds in Topeka, Kansas, as a National Historic Site (the school was one of the segregated schools to which African American students were assigned). The National Archives and Records Administration (NARA) includes documents related to the case in its digital classroom, and the decision is a linchpin of much civil rights argumentation. *Brown* has taken on a mythic quality that actually distorts the way many Americans have come to understand its genesis and function in the society. Our tendency is to view *Brown* as a "natural" occurrence in the nation's steady march toward race relations' progress (Crenshaw, 1988). This notion of progress is coupled with a view of America as a nation endowed with inherent "goodness" and exceptionality. Of course, historians like Joyce Appleby (1992) challenge our view of this exceptionalism when she argued:

> Exceptionalism . . . is America's peculiar form of Eurocentrism. In the nation's critical first decades, it provided a way to explain the connection of the United States to Europe within a story about its geographic and political disconnection. But today, exceptionalism raises formidable obstacles to appreciating America's original and authentic diversity. . . . [O]ur peculiar form of Eurocentrism . . . created a national identity for the revolutionary generation . . . [and] foreclosed other ways of interpreting the meaning of the United States. It is to that foreclosure two centuries ago that we should now look to diagnose our present discomfort with calls for a multicultural understanding of the United States. (p. 420)

I want to suggest along with other critical race theorists (see Bell, 1980b; Dudziak, 1995) that the *Brown* decision was not the result of America as a good and altruistic nation but rather the result of the decision's particular historic and political context. This argument is not a new one, particularly to legal scholars, political scientists, and historians. However, it is one that has gained little or no currency in the education community as evidenced by the way *Brown* is taught in the nation's schools.

Again, I reference Hess (2005) who stated, "an object of uncritical devotion, *Brown* is most likely to be taught not simply as a correctly decided court case, but as an important symbol that continues to shape contemporary ideas about justice, equality, and the power of the Supreme Court" (p. 6). In an earlier article (Tate, Ladson-Billings, & Grant, 1993), colleagues and I raised questions about the Supreme Court's attempt to propose a mathematical solution (i.e., determine what constitutes segregation and desegregation by strict numbers) to complex social problems.

My argument here is that the case came at a moment in time where the Court had almost no other choice but to rule in favor of the plaintiffs. *Brown* is not just one case, but rather the accumulation of a series of cases over a more than 100-year period.[3] In 1849, Benjamin F. Roberts sued the city of Boston on behalf of his 5-year-old daughter, Sarah (Cushing, 1883). Sarah Roberts walked past five White elementary schools to a dilapidated elementary school for Black children. Initially Roberts attempted to enroll his daughter in one of the White schools. Failing this, he enlisted the legal support of Robert Morris, an African American attorney who recruited well-known White abolitionist Charles Sumner to join him on the case. Despite Sumner's attempt to leverage the Massachusetts Constitution by arguing that school segregation was discriminatory and harmful to *all* children, the court ruled in favor of the school committee.

Of course, the primary legal referent for *Brown* is the 1896 *Plessy v. Ferguson* case that *Brown* reversed. Homer Plessy was an African American who tested the Louisiana segregation law by riding in a train car reserved for Whites. The law stated that segregation was legal as long as the facilities maintained for Blacks were equal to those established for Whites. Plessy argued his case based on the 14th Amendment and its guarantee of equal protection. However, the U.S. Supreme Court upheld Judge Ferguson's ruling and in so doing, validated segregation throughout the nation. A number of subsequent challenges to the ruling failed to sway the court.

Although *Plessy* was concerned with a public accommodation, that is, transportation, later the National Association for the Advancement of Colored People (NAACP) would see equal education as the bigger, more significant prize. Thus, two cases in Delaware, *Belton v. Gebhart* and *Bulah v. Gebhart* (1952), started out as school transportation cases that the NAACP encouraged the plaintiffs to turn into school integration cases. The plaintiffs won limited local victories that did not have national impact. However, their cases would become a part of the larger *Brown* plea along with *Briggs v. Elliott,*[4] *Bolling v. Sharpe,*[5] and *Davis v. County School Board of Prince Edward County.*[6]

At the same time that parents were fighting for desegregated K–12 schools, activity at the college and professional school level was also heating up. In *McLaurin v. Oklahoma State Regents* (1950), the Supreme Court struck down University of Oklahoma rules that allowed a Black man to attend classes but fenced him off from the other students. On that same day, the Court ruled in *Sweatt v. Painter* (1950) that a makeshift law school that the state of Texas had created to avoid admitting Black students to the University of Texas Law School did not represent an equal facility as called for in *Plessy.*

One might think that the sheer volume of cases that the Court was hearing during this time made the reversal of *Plessy* seem inevitable. However, I want to suggest that the real catalyst for *Brown* is the larger sociopolitical context of the postwar era. However, there is no indication that the Eisenhower administration was enthusiastic about the ruling as evidenced in his letter to his friend retired Navy Captain, Swede Hazlett (October, 1954; retrieved electronically on 06/29/13 from http://docsteach.org/documents/186601/detail?menu=closed&page=8): "The segregation issue will, I think, become acute or tend to die out according to the character of the procedure orders that the Court will probably issue this winter. My own guess is that they will be very moderate and accord a maximum of initiative to the local courts" (p. 3). Thus, Eisenhower was counting on the power of state's rights to hold school segregation in check while the federal government could point to the ruling as an example of its commitment to equality.

Bell (1980b) pointed out that with the Cold War struggle to prevent the Soviets from spreading communism among emerging Third World peoples, the United States was compelled to address its own credibility issue concerning Black people and their civil liberties. The *amicus* brief filed in *Brown* by the U.S. Justice Department argued that desegregation was in the national interest in part due to foreign policy issues (Dudziak, 1995). The Justice Department argued (1954), "[t]he United States is trying to prove to the people of the world, of every nationality, race and color, that a free democracy is the most civilized and secure form of government yet devised by man" (*amicus curiae* at 6, 347 US 483). The brief also quoted Secretary of State Dean Acheson's letter to the attorney general in which Acheson wrote:

> During the past six years, the damage to our foreign relations attributable to [race discrimination] has become progressively greater. The United States is under constant attack in the foreign press, over foreign radio, and in such international bodies as the United Nations because of various practices of discrimination against minority groups in this country. . . . Soviet spokesmen regularly exploit this situation in propaganda against the United States. . . . Some of these attacks against us are based on falsehoods or distortion; but the undeniable

> existence of racial discrimination gives unfriendly governments the most effective kind of ammunition for their propaganda warfare. (cited in Layton, 2000, p. 116)

Dudziak (1995) pointed out that the continued legal segregation and racism that pervaded U.S. society created an embarrassing reality for U.S. foreign policy: "Newspapers throughout the world carried stories about discrimination against non-white visiting foreign dignitaries, as well as against American Blacks. At a time when the U.S. hoped to reshape the postwar world in its own image, the international attention given to racial segregation was troublesome and embarrassing" (p. 110). After all, Adolph Hitler had used the racial superiority argument to spread his Nazi ideology and the United States both through Jesse Owens's brilliant athletic demonstration in the 1938 Olympics and its triumph in World War II resolutely repudiated such thinking.

As I mentioned above, Bell (1980a, 1980b) concluded that what we have in the *Brown* decision is a prime example of what he called "interest convergence." In addition to the international embarrassment, Bell suggested that *Brown* provided "much needed assurance to American Blacks that the precepts of equality and freedom so heralded during World War II might yet be given meaning at home" (1980b, p. 96). However, dissident voices such as Paul Robeson's (cited in Bell, 1980b) asserted, "It is unthinkable . . . that American Negroes would go to war on behalf of those who have oppressed us for generations . . . against a country [the Soviet Union] which in one generation has raised our people to the full human dignity of mankind" (p. 96).

Bell (1980b) also suggested that *Brown* was championed by Whites who understood that the South could never make the economic transition from a "rural, plantation society to the sunbelt with all its potential and profit" (p. 96) unless it eradicated state-sponsored segregation. Thus, the *Brown* case could be positioned as serving White interests—improving the national image, quelling racial unrest, and stimulating the economy—as well as Black interests—improving the educational condition of Black children and promoting social mobility. It is this convergence of interests that made *Brown* feasible.

Despite all of the effort expended to litigate school desegregation and the seeming victory that the *Brown* decision represents, the empirical evidence suggests that African American (and Latino) students still attend, for the most part, deeply segregated schools. Several studies (Orfield & Yun, 1999; Frankenberg & Lee, 2002) indicate that the nation's schools are rapidly resegregating. We see a nation where public school enrollment reflects the country's growing diversity but Blacks and Latinos are more likely to be in racially isolated schools. This isolation is related in part to the differential birth rates in the White, Black, and Latino communities. But, when we look at the actual numbers, we see that fewer Whites live in major urban centers while Blacks and Latinos are concentrated in these areas. However, urban schools reflect a hypersegregation beyond that of their cities' overall population.

The Crescent City as National Model

Although it is dangerous to generalize from a single instance, the city of New Orleans is both an interesting and telling prototype on which to analyze urban education throughout the United States. And since this chapter is based on the Norman Rockwell painting of Ruby Bridges, "The Problem We All Live With," it seems a fitting exemplar for discussing what seems to be an intractable problem—underachievement and failure in the nation's urban schools. New Orleans also is a unique instance in that the city was completely decimated by the horrific Hurricane Katrina in late August 2005.

New Orleans is a city that lies below sea level—so low that residents are forced to bury their dead above ground. It sits at the mouth of the Mississippi River and on the shores of

Lake Pontchartrain. Located in the Deep South, New Orleans is a place with an almost tropical feel—hot, humid, and sticky. It is also a city that some may see as a place time forgot. It is an amazing mélange of its heritages—African, American Indian, French, and English—and one of the nation's greatest tourist towns. In the small area known as the French Quarter, people are encouraged to abandon conventions and inhibitions as they revel into the night drinking on Bourbon Street and sampling sumptuous concoctions like jambalya, shrimp etouffe, gumbo, bananas foster, and many other local dishes. New Orleans is also a place where human variation is finely codified and dissected. Because its first interactions with Europeans placed the entire area (later what would become the Louisiana Purchase covered territory as far north as Wisconsin) under French control, the French settlers subscribed to Napoleonic codes rather than British Common Law that was prevalent in the 13 British colonies.

Napoleonic codes meant that racial categories were specifically quantified. Under British Common Law if you "looked" Black and/or "lived" Black, you were assumed to be Black. Under Napoleonic codes, your Blackness was quantified. Being the offspring of two Black parents made you Black. Being the offspring of one Black parent and one White parent made you a "mulatto." One Black grandparent made you a "quadroon," and one Black great-grandparent made you an "octoroon." These quantifications gave us the "one-drop" rules that suggested one drop of "Black blood" declared one Black, regardless of phenotypical appearance and/or lifestyle. Thus, New Orleans, in addition to its Black-White racial divide, had groups of people known as "Creole," "Cajun," and "pase blanc" (or passing for White). Delineating these arcane racial distinctions is important because what little power Blacks exercised in the antebellum New Orleans came from these mestizo/creole classes.

New Orleans was a city very slow to educate its Black residents. Although public schools developed in the city about 1840, city leaders were so adamantly opposed to educating Black people that they passed a law making it illegal to teach slaves to read and prohibited all Blacks—slave and free—from attending public schools (DeVore & Logsdon, 1991). However, by the end of the Civil War about 40% of the city's Black population was literate and an unknown number of those known as "pase blanc" found their way into the public schools.

Despite efforts by the Catholic Church to provide free education for newly freed Blacks, resistance from the White community to educate Black children persisted. For a brief period following the Civil War, New Orleans became a model of school desegregation (DeVore & Logsdon, 1991) with the emergence of a few short-lived integrated schools. However, by the 1870s there was a return to strict school segregation and decades of woeful underfunding of Black schools. According to Carr (2013), "school officials decided in 1900 to limit public education for African Americans to grades one through five. By 1910, the city had sixty-eight schools for white students and only sixteen for black students, all of which were elementary schools" (p. 62).

Black community leaders fought valiantly to receive quality education over the next 40 years and the decision of the United States Supreme Court in the *Brown v. Board of Education* case in 1954 seemed a sweet reward. Unfortunately, the decision to fully test the law resulted in the nation's most rapid instance of White flight. Two schools, Frantz Elementary and McDonogh 19 Elementary, enrolled approximately 1,000 students in 1959. However, within hours of enrolling four Black girls, all of the White students at McDonogh left for other schools. At Franz, only two White students remained by the end of the week, and they were taught in a separate classroom from little Ruby Bridges, a six-year-old who would be taught alone in a classroom by the one White teacher (a Northerner) who was willing to teach her.

Desegregation did move forward in New Orleans over the succeeding decades, and the teaching staff also desegregated with the merger of the White and Black teachers' unions. By 1980 tens of thousands of White families had abandoned the Orleans Parish Schools for suburban and private schools. According to Carr (2013), New Orleans went from a city with nearly equal White and Black student populations to one with five times more Black students than White. By 2004 Orleans Parish Schools were 94% Black and just 3% White. When Hurricane Katrina hit, the Orleans Parish Schools were already embroiled in scandal, corruption, mismanagement, and academic failure. The hurricane's total destruction of the city, although tragic, provided the perfect opportunity to start over.

Reform on steroids: Major urban centers have been facing aspects similar to New Orleans Schools for many years. Cities like Chicago, Philadelphia, Baltimore, Detroit, Oakland, Houston, and St. Louis have been coping with White flight, shrinking tax bases, and academic failure. Each of these cities has struggled to maintain public support for its schools and has looked for ways to reform them. One strategy that played prominently among reform-minded school districts was to wrest control from school superintendents and to move toward mayoral control. Another strategy was to "get tough" on urban schools by stripping down the curriculum to "basics" such as reading and mathematics and to hold students to unreasonable academic standards, unaccompanied by opportunity to learn standards by providing fully qualified teachers, current textbooks and materials, and reasonable class size. A third strategy was to promote "innovation" via the expansion of privatization (through vouchers) and charter schools. A fourth strategy was to designate teachers (and especially their unions) as the villains and obstructionists to school reform (Weiner, 2012).

The primary prototype for school reform before Hurricane Katrina was Chicago. "CEO" Paul Vallas ran the school district and demanded that students pass tests at grades 3 and 8 before they could be promoted. Before long, great numbers of students were being retained, and it was clear that the system could not sustain the "standards" it set for itself. The next move was to create "small schools" that allegedly emanated from local community groups. To be fair, a number of these schools did emerge, most notably Social Justice High School,[7] but for the most part the guise of "local control" became a cover for expanding charter schools. From 2001 to 2008 Arne Duncan served as Chicago Public Schools' CEO and made some modest gains—moving the high school graduation rate from 43% to 55% and college-going rates from 44% to 50%. But even with these modest improvements, fewer than a third of the students who were freshmen in 2003 and graduated four years later enrolled in college. Many politicians, including former President Bill Clinton, praised Chicago's reform efforts. Chicago was serving as the model for urban school reform.

Chicago's role as the national model of urban school reform came to an abrupt halt in late August 2005 (August 23–30, 2005). When Hurricane Katrina hit all eyes turned toward New Orleans. How would the city (and indeed the nation) address the destruction that devastated every institution and social structure in the area? After the shock and dismay of losing virtually everything, the people of New Orleans were prepared to go about the business of rebuilding. One of the social institutions that had to be rebuilt was the schools. Many parents and community members eagerly welcomed the opportunity to start afresh. After all, Orleans Parish Schools were terrible *before* the storm. The silver lining of the storm was that it provided an opportunity to fix everything that was wrong with Orleans Parish Schools.

In the effort to remake the schools, city officials called on Paul Vallas—the same Paul Vallas who imposed draconian "reform" methods on Chicago and went on to do the same in Philadelphia. As superintendent of Philadelphia Public Schools, Vallas presided over the nation's largest experiment in privatized management of schools, with the management of over 40 schools turned over to outside for-profits, nonprofits, and universities beginning in Fall 2002. Although Vallas was touted as a reformer, his tenure in Philadelphia ended with his being accused of leaving the school district with a $73 million deficit.

Vallas left Philadelphia to head up the Recovery School District in New Orleans, and it was here that the entire neoliberal reform agenda got accelerated. New Orleans became a kind of school reform on steroids. By capitalizing on the collapse of the institutional and structural infrastructure wrought by Hurricane Katrina, Vallas and the neoliberals were able to quickly institute a new form of schooling that required less on the will of the public and more on the plans for privatization. Currently, New Orleans Schools are a patchwork of three governing agencies and five types of schools. The governing agencies are the Recovery School District (RSD), the Orleans Parish School Board (OPSB), and the Board of Elementary and Secondary Education (BESE). RSD administers both traditional public schools and charter schools. The OPSB administers both traditional public schools and charter schools, and BESE administers two charter schools. Some of the charter schools in the new school configuration are run by organizations like KIPP, First Line, and the University of New Orleans. New Orleans is known for employing alternatively certified teachers. However, according to the Louisiana State Department of Education, these teachers rarely stay in the district. The figures indicate that retention among Teach For America (TFA) teachers in the state is 0.04% while retention among traditionally prepared teachers is 40%. These examples reflect decisions about the schools that have been made with little or no input from the electorate. The lack of access to political input has been an ongoing pattern for Black and Latino communities and constitutes another aspect of education debt.

The move toward privatization and expansion of charter schools, like most issues regarding school reform, is a complex one. Privatization reflects an ideological position that treats schools like businesses and ignores their citizenship value and import (Ladson-Billings, 2004a). The other ideological position reflects the historical and traditional notion of the public school as "the common school"—the primary source for making students into citizens. Those who are fierce defenders of the current system *and* those who insist on privatization would be wise to consider ways that public schools can and should change while maintaining their core mission. That push for innovation is what spurred the charter school movement.

One of the more interesting points about charter schools is that it was Albert Shanker, head of the American Federation of Teachers, arguably the more militant of the two national teachers' unions, who first proposed them (Ravitch, 2010). Shanker endorsed charter schools as a way to get teachers out from under onerous regulations that he believed stifled teacher creativity and innovation. However, he insisted that the teachers' union and the local school district jointly approve charter schools. Shanker further believed that charter schools be used as a mechanism for helping the students who were failing to achieve success in traditional schools. Thus, urban students were the primary target of Shanker's proposal. Shanker believed that charter schools should collaborate and cooperate, not compete with, traditional public schools. In her new book, Delpit (2012) makes a similar point of critique. But, when Shanker realized that neoliberal forces were set to use charter schools as a vehicle for privatizing public schools, he turned against them. He could see the way that corporations and for-profit vendors intended to capitalize from poor urban communities' desire for academic excellence and realized he could no longer support them.

Today charter schools exist throughout the country. In first-ring suburbs where school districts are seeing an increasingly diverse school population, White middle-class families are using charter schools rules to avoid attending more racially diverse public schools. In cities like Milwaukee and Cleveland, neoliberals court Black and Latino families for both charter and voucher programs by playing on their desperation for educational opportunity. However, progressives see this as a power play to instantiate privatization and promote the destruction of public schools. Caught in the middle of this fight are poor, urban children and their families.

Finally, we are witnessing the vilification of teachers and their unions. A Forbes survey of professionals (Riper, 2006) found that teachers are among the highest-ranked professionals along with firefighters, doctors, scientists, and nurses. The 10 lowest-prestige professions were real estate agents/brokers, actors, bankers, accountants, entertainers, stockbrokers, journalists, union leaders, business executives, and athletes. The survey was not of the most highly paid professions because there seems to be something of an inverse relationship between prestige and money in this survey. But what is puzzling about the place of teachers on the high-prestige list is the sense that teachers have somehow become the new enemy. There has seemingly been a transformation of the teacher from hero to goat in the society and this transformation is rooted in two contradictory ideas about teaching that critics and reformers hold in their heads simultaneously—teachers are the source of the problem and teachers as the solution to the problem.

Although the primary focus of this chapter is on inequity and the structural concerns of urban schools, it is important to pay attention to the role of teachers in either maintaining or mitigating inequity in urban schools. Derrick Bell (1983) argued that the main problem with the *Brown* decision was that the plaintiffs never consulted teachers to determine what needed to happen inside of schools and classrooms to make the decision work. The NAACP lawyers were so preoccupied with providing opportunities for students that they forgot that the White teachers might work against those opportunities and the Black teachers would lose the meager opportunities they had (Fultz, 2004).

In an earlier article (Ladson-Billings 2004b) I pointed out how *Brown* devastated the Black teaching force. Almost 38,000 teachers in 17 Southern states lost their jobs between 1954 and 1965. In the post-*Brown* era very few Black teachers ever taught White students, and we can only speculate about the treatment Black students received from recalcitrant White teachers.

Today we recognize that there is an inverse relationship between the race of urban students and the race of their teachers. Most students, regardless of race or ethnicity, have White teachers. As we examine the discourse surrounding teachers in urban schools we must take up the contradictory narratives of "teacher as problem" and "teacher as solution."

Teachers as the Source of the Problem: In 1983 when then President Ronald Reagan's Commission on Excellence in Education published its report, *A Nation at Risk,* the American public was told that the primary problems with education in our country were the fragmented and weak curriculum, the lack of regular and standard assessments, the limited amount of time on task, and the teaching—particularly the preparation and those who select teaching as a profession (Commission on Excellence in Education, 1983). Out of the identification of that set of problems a more standards-based curriculum emerged, even a scripted one in some cases, constant standardized testing, the elimination of recess, and the paradox of increased teacher preparation requirements in traditional teacher education programs and the limited preparation for those who choose to go into teaching through alternative means.

It is popular to state the single most important aspect of a student's education is the teacher standing in his or her classroom. And most would agree teachers are extremely important in ensuring the quality of students' education. But in a knowledge economy where information comes from all directions and the ability to access that information is either helped or hindered by external forces, one cannot place the entire onus on teachers for educational success. If teachers are the sole variable, then the society must admit that it has put all of its best teachers in the suburbs and the worst ones in the cities and rural communities.

Could it be that teachers have been made to be the problem because they represent the low-hanging fruit? Talking about broad social policy seems too complex and the society has spent decades, indeed centuries, systematically disadvantaging entire groups of students. The easiest target becomes the teachers and their unions.

It is interesting to consider how the discourse about teachers now runs:

> Some fresh-faced but not very bright young people set out to teach. We place them in outdated, weak teacher preparation programs where they waste hours learning how to teach instead of learning more subject matter, and once they get out of school they head to school districts where the first thing they are asked to do is sign up with the union. After 2 or 3 years they earn tenure and now they have jobs for life. Because of their seniority they cannot be fired and some other young, enthusiastic, innovative new teachers certainly cannot replace them.

This has become a familiar narrative. Unfortunately, it is a poor approximation of the truth.

First, the problem of recruiting outstanding teacher candidates is a real one. Today's young people have many more career choices and those that offer the more lucrative remuneration also offer the most attractive preprofessional recruiting options. For example, when students at my own university are admitted into our engineering program, they often receive outstanding financial packages, summer internships, and job placement. Over at the education school we have few resources to offer prospective students. Our students pay their own way, go to school and work, and/or take out expensive education loans.

The issue of tenure is interesting. Teachers cannot give themselves tenure. Some administrator has to verify their competence. The job of the union is to ensure that dismissals are not arbitrary or capricious. A failure to "get rid of" a teacher generally reflects a failure to fully document performance (or nonperformance as the case may be). That part of the story seemingly has not made its way into the grand narrative on teachers. Finally, we must ask, who are these young, energetic teachers whom we are depriving of an opportunity to teach in favor of old, washed-up, tenured dinosaurs? They cannot be those not-so-bright, weak candidates with which we started the narrative. They must be the crew of alternatively certified teachers with a 6-week preparation program. Unfortunately, their track record is not nearly as good as some are claiming they are. In Louisiana they remain at a rate of about 4% compared to traditionally prepared teachers who stay at a rate of 40%. Neither number is adequate but the difference between 4 and 40 is startling, and we do know if a district constantly hires in brand-new teachers, it reduces its upfront costs because those people are hired at the first rung of the salary schedule.

It is also important to point out that no other professional field or industry would dream of pushing its most experienced people out of the door and expect to remain at the top. The best schools in our nation have incredible stability. At one of the successful urban schools I visited years ago when I was researching successful teachers of African American students (Ladson-Billings, 2009), I learned that the average teacher tenure there was 14 years. This new chant of let's do something about "last hired first fired" is a ploy that attempts to exploit the language of civil rights and make the public believe that teachers and their unions stand in the way of progress.

Teachers are no more the source of the problem than an umbrella is the cause of rain. No made-up story about bad old teachers and good young ones can change the social realities of students' lives. We, as a society, have to make a decision to make a commitment to care for the "least of these" before we can expect our students to reach their full potential not just as students but as citizens and human beings.

Teachers as the Solution: So if we cannot place all of the blame at the foot of teachers does that mean we can position teachers as the solution? I would argue that we cannot help but notice the same grand narrative that drives the notion of teacher as villain is at work when we decide that teachers are the heroes. The place where we most see this narrative at work is in Hollywood. Film depictions of teachers almost always carry the same storyline—the school is horrible, the administrator is horrible, the parents are horrible, and often the kids—especially those in urban environments—are horrible until one, spectacular teacher shows up and turns things around. This teacher is a loner and the only one who cares in the entire building. This teacher fights the administrator, the parents, and her other colleagues. Often this teacher has received minimal if any teacher preparation. Stories like *Dangerous Minds*, *Music of the Heart*, and *Freedom Writers* are examples of this genre.

In this narrative we have to see that the good teacher is the exception to the rule. This way we do not disturb the ongoing narrative of teacher inferiority. This narrative posits one lone teacher who is set down in an entirely dysfunctional school. Her colleagues are unprofessional and uncaring. Before she arrived no one exhibited any care or concern for the students. Her teacher colleagues, parents, and virtually every other adult have abandoned them. The other teachers think of them as unteachable "savages." Because of her superior morality this teacher is able to do what no other teacher has ever done. She persists where others gave up. She succeeds where others failed. And wait, she not only improves their academic lives, she improves their home lives. She gets recalcitrant parents to step up to their responsibilities. She challenges drug dealers and gang bangers. She is, in a word, the students' savior!

It is this unrealistic and simplistic portrait of the teacher that is plaguing the profession. If the teacher is not a superhero, then she or he cannot be seen as a good teacher. And, she or he certainly cannot be a superhero in concert with other teachers. She or he must distinguish herself or himself by being "not like the others." That characterization is especially troubling since it is one that African American achievers regularly confront. The notion that some are special, exceptional, and different from the others demeans the contributions of families, communities, and cultures in shaping individuals. Similarly, the set-apart teacher is used to condemn and discredit her or his colleagues. Her or his so-called exceptionality is used to reinforce the belief that others are just lazy or do not care. But as the public explores these narratives it quickly forgets that the exceptional teacher also had teachers. Someone assisted her or him along the way. She or he learned to teach from a combination of experience and careful guidance. Someone else helped her or him along the way.

Breaking Through the Prevailing Discourse

In work on effective teachers of African American students (Ladson-Billings, 2009), I learned that there are a number of outstanding teachers whom most of the public never hear about. They are not perfect, but they are especially effective in helping students achieve academically and develop positive cultural identities. Although they choose a variety of teaching strategies and approaches, they appear to have some other beliefs and dispositions in common that make them effective. Martin Haberman (1995) called them "star teachers." They are identified by a number of qualities that include the following:

Persistence: They are unwilling to give up on students—even the most oppositional or recalcitrant ones. They believe that in order to get results teachers have to stick with it—often long past any time others would. Most urban students who have not met with success will tell you that somewhere along the line, someone gave up on them.

Protecting Learners and Learning: Effective teachers recognize that the central enterprise of schooling is teaching and learning, so they avoid those things that detract from that mission.

They don't waste time on anything else because they know that what they have to offer students is different from anyone else in their lives.

Theory Into Practice: Effective teachers never talk about some aspect of education research as "too theoretical." Rather, they ask themselves, How do I put that theoretical idea into practice? If the theory says that punishment does not work but reward does, the effective teacher looks for ways to reward the behaviors she or he wants to see over and over again. She or he is testing the theory.

Professional-Personal Orientation to Students: Effective teachers know how to walk the fine line between familiarity and distance. They maintain their identity as the teacher—not the buddy, not the friend, or not the pal—but they know how and when to open up and share more personal moments with students. They exhibit a genuine interest in students' lives and are willing to let students in on some of their personal life, not for prurient or exhibitionist purposes but rather to connect with them in more meaningful ways.

Pedagogy to So-called At-Risk Students: I hesitate to use the term *at-risk* to describe students because it shifts the responsibility to the vulnerable. However, Haberman's point is that effective teachers have a planned strategy for dealing with the academic needs of students who are likely to struggle. They do not wait until they arrive in their classes to begin trying to figure out what to do, rather they start lining up scaffolding and bridging strategies so that those students recognize that they are full members of the classroom community from day one, and they are systematically helped along so they can get to grade-level performance.

Dealing With Bureaucracy: All institutions have bureaucracy, and all bureaucracies have ways of thwarting the true purpose of the institution. Unsuccessful teachers are thrown by the demands of the bureaucracy. They become frustrated with the paperwork, the policies, and the procedures. Effective teachers make strategic decisions about which part of the bureaucracy they will attend to. They realize that no one can be fully responsive to a bureaucracy and any attempt to do so takes away from so many other things they need to do.

Fallibility: Effective teachers are not afraid to admit that they make mistakes. By doing so they help students see their humanity. They also signal to students that they expect that they, too, will make mistakes. These teachers help students to use their mistakes as learning experiences rather than as a way to punish students.

Emotional and Physical Stamina: Good teaching requires good mental and physical health. The work is grueling—full days with energetic students, late afternoons and evenings of reviewing students' work and preparing for upcoming lessons—and it is never-ending. Spending 180 days or more a year with lots of children and youth means being regularly exposed to every germ and disease imaginable so effective teachers keep themselves in good health with strong immune systems. Effective teachers also have to maintain good mental and emotional health. Working with students can be a rollercoaster. Their life challenges find their way into the classroom and good teachers are empathetic without losing their main focus.

Organizational Ability: Good teachers know that teaching is a bit of a juggling act. So to keep all of the balls in the air, they have to be organized. They have a sense of how they want to structure learning and activities. While they may appreciate and invite spontaneity, they are not looking to create chaos. Their classrooms are places where students understand the importance of classroom rituals, routines, relationships, and rigor.

Effort Not Ability: One of the most powerful lessons I learned from outstanding teachers is the need to convey to students (and believe themselves) that the only thing that stands between them and excellence is effort. Effective teachers do not predetermine students' potential and help them realize if they are willing to put in more effort they will reap more rewards. Interesting, this effort not ability perspective is exactly what we see among our international competitors whose students perform at higher levels than our students. Unfortunately, far too many Americans (and this includes teachers) believe that some people are smart and some are not. In places like Japan or Singapore students learn that "smart" is something you become, not something you already are.

These are qualities I believe any teacher who wants to be a good teacher can learn and cultivate. He or she does not have to be a superman or superwoman to be this kind of teacher. Rather he or she has to be the kind of teacher who wants to be better. He or she has to be the kind of teacher who defends the profession in school and out. He or she has to be the kind of person who when asked what he or she does for a living is willing to say, "I do the hardest, most important work of a free society. I teach." He or she has to be willing to challenge his or her colleagues to work together to help struggling colleagues. He or she has to be willing to accept legitimate critique as a means of professional improvement, and he or she has to stand up against *ad hominem* attacks against teachers, no matter who levels those attacks.

Coda—But That's Just Good Teaching

The description of excellent teachers for urban children listed above often provokes skeptics to say, "But that's just good teaching." I agree. However, the question remains: "Why is so little of this teaching evident in urban classrooms serving African American and Latino students?" What is it about these students that does not allow the public and elected officials to make their education a priority? How is it that we can plot econometric models and recognize the large amount of human capital that we are wasting by not educating urban children adequately and still persist along the same path?

It may be cynical to suggest that we do not improve urban schools because we mistakenly believe that our real salvation resides in a return to a mythical time when schooling was unproblematic (Ladson-Billings, 1999). The narrative accompanying this false hope suggests that most students will be White, English-speaking, middle-class, and coming from two-parent households where one income is enough to provide for the family. Briefly, it is important to take apart each of those assumptions and describe why this vision of schooling in urban America cannot and will not exist. First, few urban communities will return to majority White ones. The demographics suggest that not only urban schools but suburban schools also will experience more racial and ethnic diversity for the foreseeable future. African American, Latino, Asian American, and immigrant students from all over the world will make up larger and larger proportions of the school-aged population.

The second flaw in the "return to Eden" narrative is the assumption that there was an idyllic time in public schools. From its creation the public school has been a site of contestation and concern (Tyack, 1974). Issues of segregation and exclusion have arisen along race, class, and gender lines. In our more recent history we have engaged in battles over whether public schools could or should serve students with disabilities. Schools have fought to exclude children who were HIV-positive or homeless or adjudicated.

The struggle for urban schools is about so much more than credentials and access to information. It is even about more than employment and economic security. In a democratic nation a free, quality public education remains the one best hope for ensuring that citizens are continually being made. Second-class education creates second-class citizens who are less likely to participate fully in the social and civic life of the society. Creating these second-class citizens only exacerbates the problem we all live with.

Notes

1. I use the term *minoritized* as it used by colleagues in the United Kingdom to symbolize the fact that people often do not see themselves as "minority group members," but the social structure of their society places them in these subordinate positions. Thus, rather than an adjective (i.e., minority), the more accurate term is a passive voice verb (i.e., minoritized).
2. This section on *Brown* was adapted from an earlier article (Ladson-Billings, 2004b).
3. The original Civil Rights Act of 1875 contained a school desegregation provision that was struck down before its passage. In 1883, the Supreme Court declared the act with its prohibition against discrimination in public accommodations unconstitutional.
4. This case was argued by Thurgood Marshall in South Carolina on May 17, 1950.
5. This case was filed in Washington, DC, by James Nabrit, Jr., on September 11, 1950.
6. This case was filed in Virginia by the NAACP on May 23, 1951.
7. Unfortunately, current Mayor Rahm Emanuel closed Social Justice High School without warning.

References

Appleby, J. (1992). Rediscovering America's historic diversity: Beyond exceptionalism. *Journal of American History, 79,* 419–431.

Bell, D. (1980a). *Brown v. Board of Education* and the interest-convergence dilemma. *Harvard Law Review, 93,* 518-533.

Bell, D. (1980b). *Brown* and the interest-convergence dilemma. In D. Bell (Ed.), *Shades of* Brown: *New perspectives on school desegregation* (pp. 90–106). New York, NY: Teachers College Press.

Bell, D. (1983). Time for the teachers: Putting educators back into the *Brown* remedy. *Journal of Negro Education, 52*(3), 290–301.

Bourdieu, P. (1986). The forms of capital. In J. Richardson (Ed.), *Handbook of theory and research for the sociology of education* (pp. 241–258). New York, NY: Greenwood.

Carr, S. (2013). *Hope against hope: Three schools, one city, and the struggle to educate America's children.* New York, NY: Bloomsbury Press.

Commission on Excellence in Education. (1983). A nation at risk: The imperative for education reform. Washington, DC: Author.

Crenshaw, K. (1988). Race, reform, and retrenchment: Transformation and legitimation in antidiscrimination law. *Harvard Law Review, 101,* 1331-1387.

Crenshaw, K. (2011). Twenty years of Critical Race Theory: Looking back to move forward. *Connecticut Law Review, 43*(5), 1253–1352.

Cushing, L. (1883). *Reports of cases argued and determined in the Supreme Judicial Court of Massachusetts, Vol. 5.* Boston, MA: Little, Brown & Co.

Delgado, R., & Stefancic, J. (2001). *Critical race theory: An introduction.* New York, NY: New York University Press.

Delpit, L. (2012). *Multiplication is for white people: Raising expectations for other people's children.* New York, NY: The New Press.

DeVore, D., & Logsdon, J. (1991). *Crescent City schools: Public education in New Orleans, 1841–1991.* Lafayette, LA: The Center for Louisiana Studies at the University of Southwestern Louisiana.

Dudziak, M. (1995). Desegregation as a cold war imperative. In R. Delgado (Ed.), *Critical race theory: The cutting edge* (pp.110–121). Philadelphia, PA: Temple University Press.

Foucault, M. (2002). *The archaeology of knowledge.* New York, NY: Routledge.

Frankenberg, E., & Lee, C. (2002). *Race in American public schools: Rapidly resegregating school districts.* Cambridge, MA: The Civil Rights Project, Harvard University.

Fraser, N. (2003). Mapping the radical imagination: Between redistribution and recognition. *Constellations, 12*(3), 295–307.

Freire, P. (1970). *Pedagogy of the oppressed.* New York, NY: Continuum.

Fultz, M. (2004). The displacement of Black educators post-*Brown:* An overview and analysis. *History of Education Quarterly, 44*(1), 11–45.

Gramsci, A. (2011). *Letters from prison, Vol. 1* (reprint). New York, NY: Columbia University Press.

Haberman, M. (1995). *Star teachers of children in poverty.* Indianapolis, IN: Kappa Delta Pi.

Hess, D. (2005). Moving beyond celebration: Challenging curricular orthodoxy in the teaching of *Brown* and its legacies. *Teachers College Record, 107*(9), 2046–2067.

Ladson-Billings, G. (1999). Preparing teachers for diversity: Historical perspectives, current trends, and future directions. In P. David Pearson & A. Iran-Najed (Eds.), *Review of research in education, Vol. 24* (pp. 211–247). Washington, DC: American Educational Research Association.

Ladson-Billings, G. (2004a). Differing conceptions of citizenship. In N. Noddings (Ed.), *Educating citizens for global awareness* (pp. 69–80). New York, NY: Teachers College Press.

Ladson-Billings, G. (2004b). Landing on the wrong note: The price we paid for *Brown. Educational Researcher, 33*(7), 3–13.

Ladson-Billings, G. (2006). From the achievement gap the education debt: Understanding achievement in U.S. schools. *Educational Researcher, 35*(7), 3–12.

Ladson-Billings, G. (2009). *The dreamkeepers: Successful teachers of African American children* (2nd ed.). San Francisco, CA: Jossey Bass.

Layton, A. S. (2000). International politics and civil rights policy in the United States, 1941–1960. Cambridge, UK: Cambridge University Press.

National Archives Experience. (1954). Letter from President Eisenhower to E. E. "Swede" Hazlett. Retrieved June 29, 2013 from http://docsteach.org/documents/186601/detail?menu=closed&page=8

Omi, M., & Winant, H. (1994). *Racial formation in the United States: From the 1960s to the 1990s* (2nd ed.). New York, NY: Routledge.

Orfield, G., & Yun, J. (1999). *Resegregation in American schools.* Cambridge, MA: The Civil Rights Project, Harvard University.

Ravitch, D. (2010). *The death and life of the great American school system: How testing and choice are undermining education.* New York, NY: Basic Books.

Riper, T.V. (2006). America's most admired professions. *Forbes.com.* Retrieved from http://www.forbes.com/2006/07/28/leadership-careers-jobs-cx_tvr_0728admired.html

Schroeder, S. (2004). *Rediscovering magical realism in the Americas.* Westport, CT: Praeger.

Sue, D.W. (2010). *Microaggressions in everyday life: Race, gender, and sexual orientation.* New York, NY: John Wiley.

Tate, W.F., Ladson-Billings, G., & Grant, C.A. (1993). The *Brown* decision revisited: Mathematizing social problems. *Educational Policy, 7,* 255–275.

Tyack, D. (1974). *The one best system: A history of American urban education.* Cambridge, MA: Harvard University Press.

Weiner, L. (2012). *The future of our schools: Teachers unions and social justice.* Chicago, IL: Haymarket Books.

Law Cases Cited

Belton v. Gebhart, 33 Del Ch 144, 87 A 2d 862 (1952)

Bolling v. Sharpe, 347 US 497 (1954)

Briggs v. Elliott, 342 US 350 (1952)

Brown v. Board of Education, 347 US 483 (1954)

*Bulah v. Gebhart, et al.*152, nos. 12-18, 33 Del. Chapt.144; 91A, 2nd 137 (1952)

Davis v. County School Board of Prince Edward County, VA Civil Action No. 1333 (1952)

Jefferson County Public Schools (with PICS) (2007)

McLaurin v. Oklahoma State Regents, 339 US 637 (1950)

Parents Involved in Community School v. Seattle School District No. 1, 551 US 701 (2007)

Plessy v. Ferguson, 163 US 537 (1896)

Sweatt v. Painter, 339 US 629 (1950)

United States Department of Justice. (1954). *Brief for the U.S. as Amicus Curiae at 6, Brown v. Board of Education* 347 U.S. 483

24

The Evolving Landscape of School Choice in the United States[1]

Mark Berends

Recent evidence from international comparisons reveals that students in the United States tend to compete well with those in other countries at younger ages (e.g., grade 4), but as U.S. students age, their academic achievement scores lag behind those of their international contemporaries. For instance, results from the Program for International Student Assessment (PISA), which administers assessments to nationally representative samples of 15-year-olds, reveals that the average reading score for U.S. students did not differ from the overall average across countries, but nine countries had higher average scores: including Shanghai, South Korea, Finland, Hong Kong, Singapore, Canada, New Zealand, Japan, and Australia (Fleischman, Hopstock, Pelczar, & Shelley, 2010).[2] Despite the many efforts in the United States to improve reading since 2000, student scores showed no measurable change in the 2009 PISA results. In mathematics, the 2009 PISA results show that among all participating OECD countries, 23 had higher average scores than the United States, 12 were similar, and 29 had lower average scores. In science, 18 countries had higher average scores than the United States.

Yet, these international scores obscure the test score inequalities in the United States. For example, if we examine the wealthiest schools or districts, the United States ranks near the top of the international comparisons (Gamoran, 2011). Moreover, the gap within the United States for students from wealthy versus poor families appears to be getting worse over time. As Reardon (2011) shows, the academic achievement gaps between children from high-income and low-income families has been growing over the past 50 years. For cohorts with more reliable data, the wealthy-poor achievement gap was 30% to 40% larger in 2001 compared with students born in the 1970s.

There is also an increasing percentage of high-poverty schools in the United States, a disproportionate number of which are located in central cities, typically enrolling a high percentage of African American and Latino students. The *2012 Condition of Education* defines a high-poverty school as one with more than 75% of students eligible for free or reduced-price lunches, and as of 2009–2010, about 19% of students in the United States attended a high-poverty school. Higher percentages of Latino students (37%) and African American students (37%) attend high-poverty schools compared with non-Hispanic White students (6%) (Aud et al., 2012). Moreover, the percentage of high-poverty schools has increased since 2000, now at 17% of schools compared with 12% a decade ago (Rowan, 2011).

There are myriad educational policies and reforms currently being implemented and examined in this nation to address these national and international challenges to help our students compete academically. There is no lack of data for educators, policy makers, and researchers to motivate their approaches, policies, and studies to address the nation's education problems.

One such set of policies has to do with school choice, which some argue is a notion becoming embedded in the public discourse (Berends, Cannata, & Goldring, 2011). The public may not understand the meaning of the many forms of school choice (i.e., charter schools, private schools, magnet schools, vouchers, tuition tax credits, inter- and intradistrict public school choice, virtual schools, and homeschooling), but the idea that parents should have some choice in the education of their children is deeply engrained in U.S. culture (Berends, Springer, Ballou, & Walberg, 2009). This is not to minimize significant debates over the past several decades about school choice and their impact on research, policy, and public opinion. Whether research and debates focus on the effects of vouchers or charter schools, these debates have not only been covered in national media outlets, but they have also propelled the research community to be transparent and careful in explaining methods, findings, interpretation, and policy implications—a significant development (Berends et al., 2011). The debates should continue, informed by research, to address whether school choice policies and their implementation have an impact on the learning opportunities of our nation's youth.

Federal policies have provided support for school choice over the past decade. For instance, the No Child Left Behind Act (NCLB) promoted choice for families if schools failed to make adequate progress over time. More recently, the Obama administration has called for an expansion of charter schools as part of the $4 billion Race to the Top program, which awards funding to states for school reforms related to adopting standards and assessments for college- and workplace-readiness, recruiting effective teachers and principals, building data systems to measure student progress and inform educators, turning around low-achieving schools, and expanding the number of charter schools (*Education Week,* 2013). As school choice options expand, public debate continues. Politicians scrutinize scholarship or voucher programs in cities and states—such as Washington, DC, Milwaukee, Florida, Ohio, and Indiana—while policy makers reexamine the role of school choice in postdesegregation school districts. The rigorous study of issues related to school choice is both timely and important for policy makers, practitioners, scholars, and families to understand what choice options are effective or not and the social context and conditions that promote or inhibit the effectiveness of school choice alternatives.

But how is the landscape of school choice changing? What does the research tell us about the effects of school choice policies? What theories inform the debates about school choice? This chapter focuses on these questions in terms of three of the popular school choice options that have been promoted to provide greater learning opportunities to students, particularly those in urban settings that lack high-quality options: charter public schools, vouchers, and education tax credit programs. *Charter schools* are government-funded public schools that are run under a charter by parents, educators, community groups, or private organizations to encourage school autonomy and innovation. *Vouchers or choice scholarships* provide parents the option of sending their children to the school of their choice, whether public or private, religious or nonreligious schools. With public funds usually spent by the district, vouchers are allocated to families for tuition payments, in part or perhaps in full. *Education tax credits* are provided to either corporations, individual families, or both. At the *corporate* level, businesses receive a state tax credit for making donations to nonprofit organizations called Scholarship Granting Organizations (SGOs), which use the donated money to fund private school scholarships for students. Anyone can start an SGO, and some establish certain income criteria for students to be eligible for scholarships. At the *individual* level, parents can receive a tax credit or tax deduction from state income taxes for approved educational expenses, which typically include private school tuition, books, supplies, computers, tutors, and transportation. Some programs have income restrictions for family eligibility or set the amount families can claim on their taxes.

Following are descriptions of how the landscape has changed over time, highlights of some key research findings, and suggestions for further research. Because these programs often target students in urban areas, it is important to understand the changing landscape and the research and theoretical basis for these policies. By *urban,* this chapter refers to students who attend schools in large cities (defined in the census as an urbanized area with a population of 250,000 or more), in mid-size cities (urban area with population between 100,000 and 250,000), or a small city in an urban area with a population of less than 100,000. For example, these school choice reforms are being implemented in large cities like Boston, Chicago, Miami, New York, and Los Angeles as well as cities like Cleveland, Milwaukee, and Indianapolis, and smaller cities like Ft. Wayne and South Bend, IN.

Charter Public Schools

Charter schools are public schools funded by the government, but they have a different governance structure compared with traditional public schools in that they are established under a charter by parents, educators, community groups, or private organizations to encourage school autonomy and innovation. In exchange for such autonomy and flexibility, charter schools are held accountable to current state and federal accountability standards, such as NCLB, which requires testing in certain grades and sets performance targets over time (overall and various subgroups). When a charter school has more students applying than there are seats available (i.e., oversubscription), the school is required to hold a lottery to select students for open seats at random.

Numbers and Composition

The first charter school appeared in 1992 in Minnesota after that state passed the first charter school law in 1991. Between the early 1990s and 2012, the number of schools has grown to 5,618, serving over 2.0 million students; leading states are California (984 charter schools), Arizona (530 charters), Florida (516), Ohio (357), and Texas (270) (National Alliance for Public Charter Schools, 2013). Much of this growth has occurred in the last decade, as shown in Figures 24.1 and 24.2. In the 1999–2000 school year, there were 1,542 charter schools serving 349,714 students, and in 2012, the number grew to 5,618 schools serving 2,050,168 students. Just over half of the charter schools are located in urban areas; about one-fifth are in suburban locales; the rest are in rural or small town areas. Thus, over the past 10 years or so, the number of charter schools has more than tripled. In part, this significant expansion is likely due to bipartisan support for charter schools at the federal, state, and local levels, but there are still many questions about what other factors have led to charter school expansion and the variability within and across states in charter school legislation, expansion, and implementation (Wong & Klopott, 2009; Wong & Shen, 2008).

Regarding the demographic characteristics of students in charter schools, there is concern about the racial-ethnic composition in terms of promoting social integration (Ladd, Fiske, & Ruijs 2011; Zimmer et al. 2009). Based on data from the National Alliance for Public Charter Schools, the percentage of charter public students who were White or Black declined, while the percentage of charter students who were Latino has increased significantly over time. For example, in 1999–2000 the percentage of charter students who were White was 41%, and this percentage declined to 36% in 2010–2011 (see Figure 24.3). The percentage of charter students who were African American declined from 32% in 1999–2000 to 29% in 2010–2011. By contrast, in 1999–2000, Latino students constituted 19% of the charter school population, but this percentage

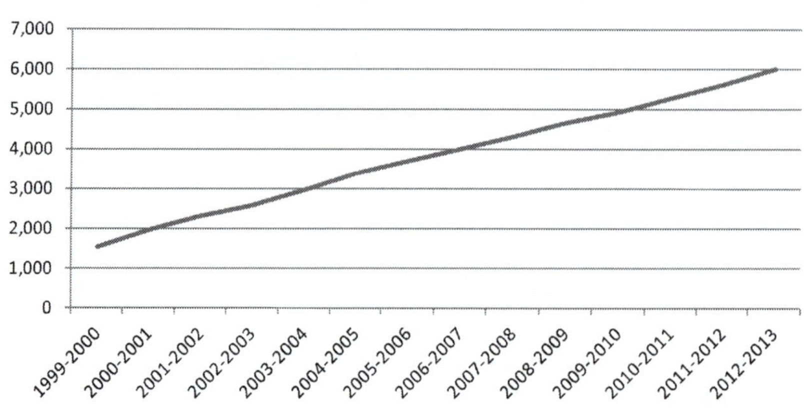

Figure 24.1 Total number of charter schools from 1999–2000 through 2012–2013. From National Alliance for Public Charter Schools (2013).

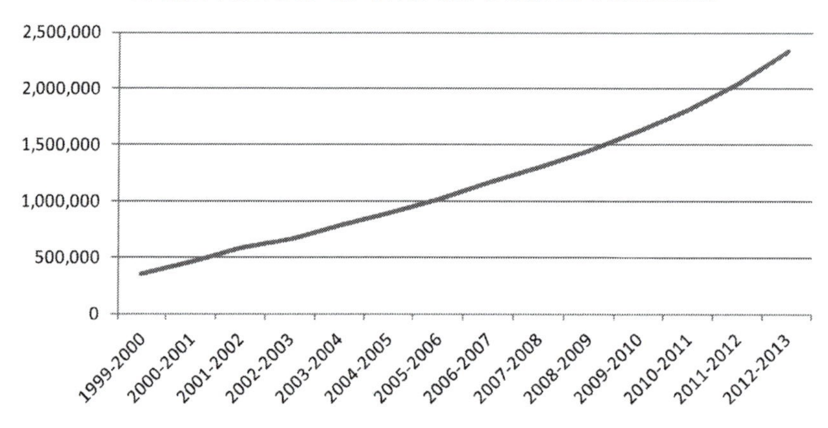

Figure 24.2 Total number of charter school students from 1999–2000 through 2012–2013. From National Alliance for Public Charter Schools (2013).

increased to 27% in 2010–2011. The percentage of charter students who classified themselves as Asian or some other racial-ethnic group remained relatively stable over this time period (about 3%). The changes in demographic characteristics over time is likely due to charter school expansion in states like California and Florida with large percentages of Latino students; between 1999–2000 and 2011–2012, the number of charter schools in Florida expanded from 113 to 515 and the number of charters in California expanded from 238 to 984 (National Alliance for Public Charter Schools, 2013).

Based on the most recent year with available data for public schools in the United States (2010–2011), the percentages of students by different racial-ethnic groups in traditional public

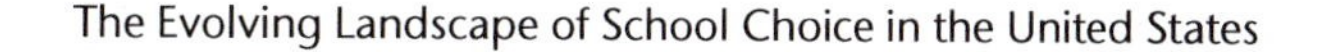

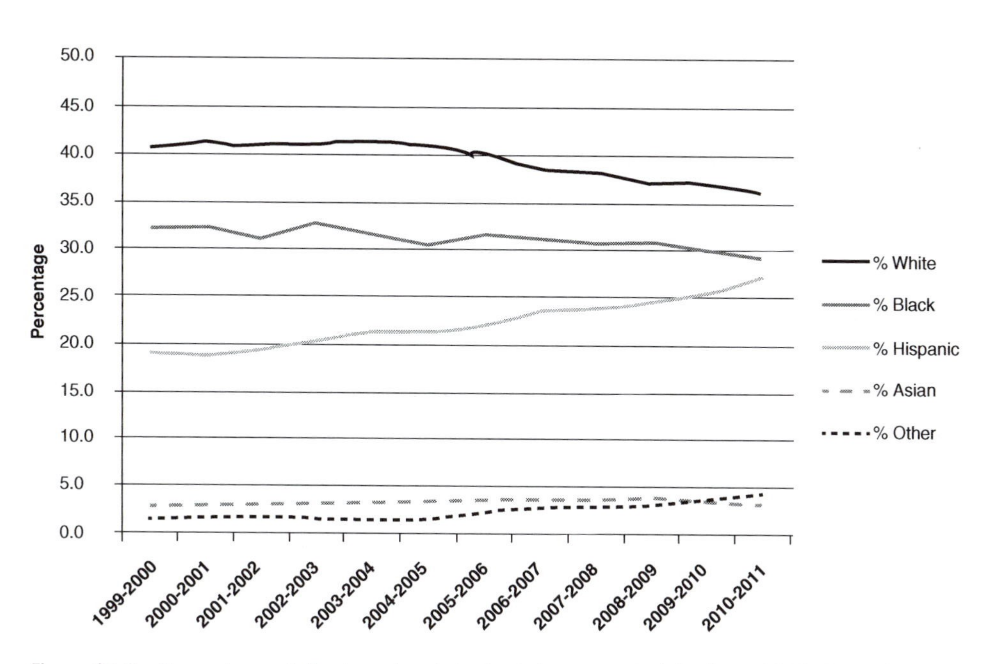

Figure 24.3 Percentage of charter school students by race-ethnicity from 1999–2000 through 2010–2011. From National Alliance for Public Charter Schools (2013).

schools were 57% White, 14% African American, 21% Latino, 3% Asian, and 5% from some other racial-ethnic group.[3] Thus, when compared to traditional public schools, the racial-ethnic composition of charter schools in 2010–2011 is disproportionately African American (29% vs. 14%) and Latino (27% vs. 21%); White students are underrepresented (36% vs. 57%). These compositional differences are due to many social factors within American society, not the least of which is that charter schools are predominately located in urban centers that have disproportionate numbers of students of color attending public schools, whether traditional or charter.

Over time, it also appears that the percentage of charter school students who are poor is increasing (see Figure 24.4). In the 1999–2000 school year, 27% of charter school students were eligible for free/reduced-price lunch, but this percentage has increased significantly over time—to 53% in 2010–2011 (which is somewhat higher when compared to 50% of the nation's students who are eligible for free/reduced-price lunch and attending traditional public schools).

Types of Charter Schools

In addition to the growth in numbers for charter schools and students, the last five years have seen significant growth in education management and charter management organizations (see Miron, Urschel, Aguilar, & Dailey, 2012). Charter management organizations (CMOs) are nonprofit organizations that operate like districts without borders in the sense that they run multiple charter schools as well as start new ones (e.g., KIPP, YES Prep, Green Dot Schools, Aspire). Educational management organizations (EMOs) are similar except that they are for profit (e.g., Imagine Schools, Academica, National Heritage Academies, and EdisonLearning Inc.).

Despite the national attention on EMOs and CMOs in the news media and even movies (e.g., *Waiting for Superman*), it is important to remember that over two-thirds of charter schools are freestanding and not affiliated with either CMOs or EMOs. Yet, the growth of CMOs is

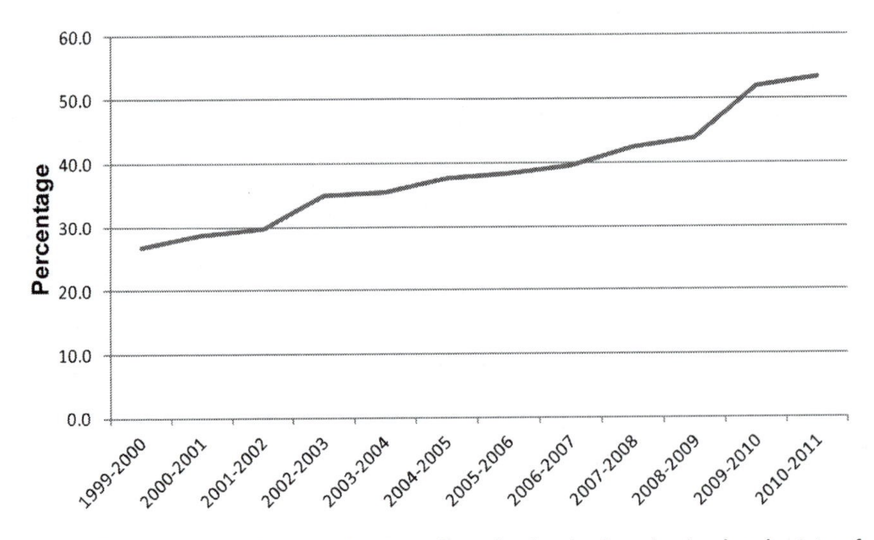

Figure 24.4 Percentage of charter school students by free/reduced-price lunch status from 1999–2000 through 2010–2011. From National Alliance for Public Charter Schools (2013).

noteworthy. As Figure 24.5 reveals, CMOs have increased in terms of the percentage of their share of the charter school sector from 11.5% in 2007–2008 to about 20% in 2010–2011. With this increase, there has been a slight drop in the percentage of charter schools that are freestanding, from 78% in 2007–2008 to 67.5% in 2010–2011. EMOs have remained relatively stable in terms of the percentage of charter schools, ranging between about 11–12% of all charter schools over this time period. As the charter sector has grown, so too have EMOs from 441 in 2007–2008 to 649 schools in 2010–2011.

Another aspect of the charter school landscape is that a large percentage of charter schools are newly started (start-up) rather than conventional public schools that converted to charter status (conversion). Over 90% of charter schools are start-up rather than conversion schools (see Figure 24.6). Since national data were available for start-up vis-à-vis conversion charter schools in 2009–2010, the number of conversion schools has remained relatively stable

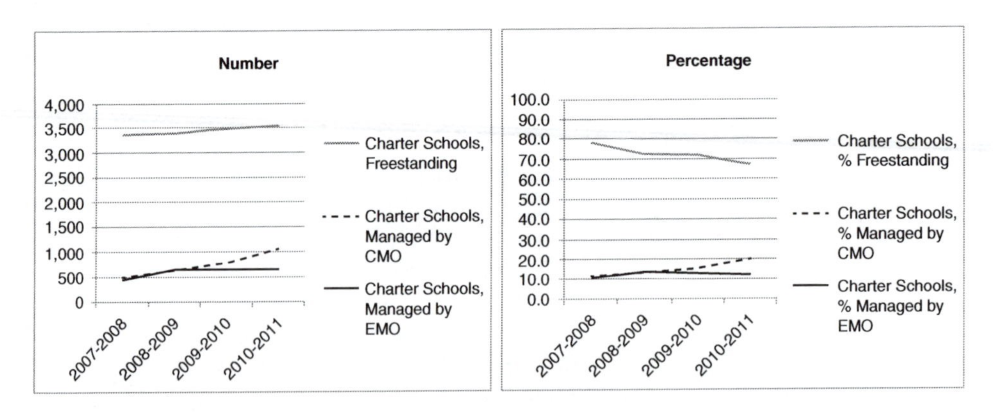

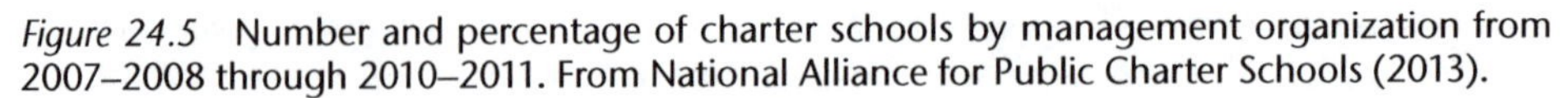
Figure 24.5 Number and percentage of charter schools by management organization from 2007–2008 through 2010–2011. From National Alliance for Public Charter Schools (2013).

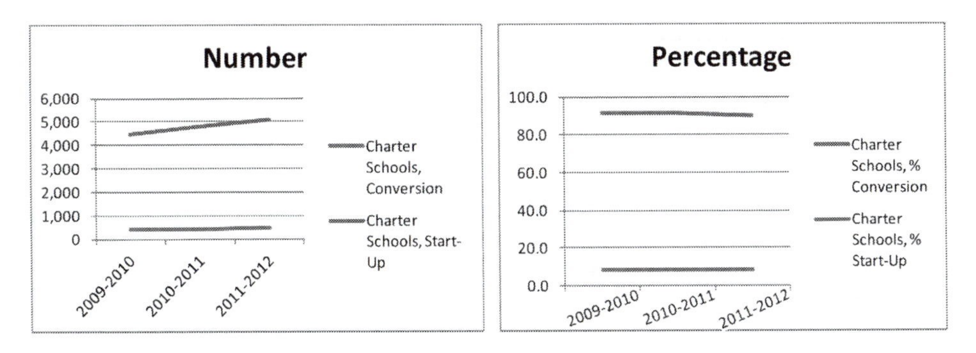

Figure 24.6 Number and percentage of charter schools by conversion/start-up from 2009–2010 through 2011–2012. From National Alliance for Public Charter Schools (2013).

(between 422 in 2009–2010 and 488 in 20011–2012), but the significant part of the charter school growth appears to be in the start-ups; in 2009–2010, there were 4,491 compared with 5,066 in 2011–2012.

With budget crises in pK–12 education, many states and districts are moving toward including online learning because of the cost savings. Because charter schools are granted autonomy and flexibility to be innovative, one might suspect that they have a competitive advantage in implementing online learning strategies and that virtual charter schools may be quite popular. Yet, at this point, virtual schools do not constitute a large percentage of all charter schools. Moreover, it is difficult to know whether charter schools are indeed more innovative in implementing online learning; more research needs to be done in this area whatever the sector (traditional public, charter public, or private) and whatever the level (elementary or secondary). In any case, at this point, the vast majority of charter schools are nonvirtual (92.4% in 2009–2010) compared with virtual charter schools (4.5% in 2009–2010) and a hybrid version that mixes virtual learning with in-classroom experiences (2.7% of all charter schools in 2009–2010) (see Figure 24.7).

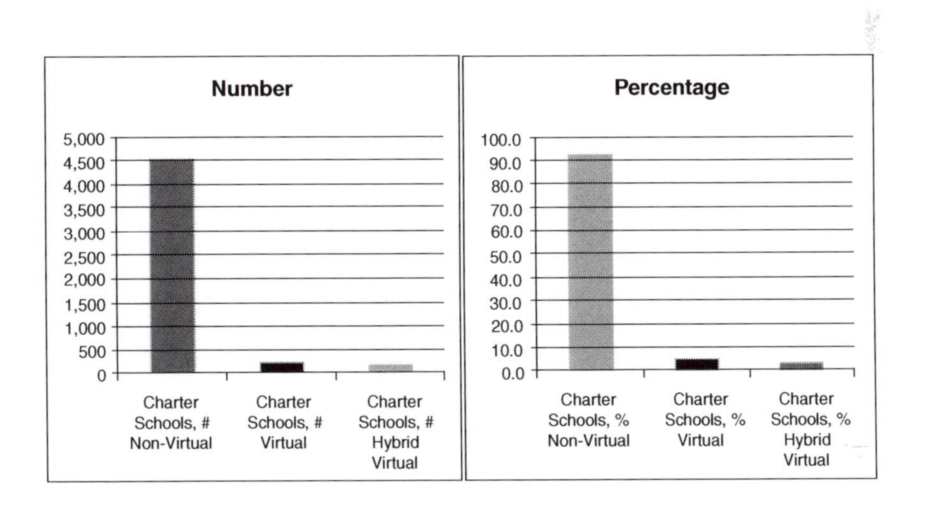

Figure 24.7 Number and percentage of charter schools by nonvirtual, virtual, and hybrid for 2009–2010. From National Alliance for Public Charter Schools (2013).

Choice Scholarships and Voucher Programs

Besides the changes in the charter school sector, another choice option is vouchers, or school choice scholarships, that provide parents with public funding to send their children to the school of their choice, which includes public or private schools (religious or nonreligious). These public vouchers are often means-tested and are allocated to families for tuition payments to pay for part or all of the tuition. Vouchers have also been highly contested and debated in educational policy, the media, and research communities. For instance, in studies in the 1990s of the Milwaukee voucher program, researchers disagreed about the effects of the program on student outcomes (see Berends et al., 2011). Although policy makers suspected that evaluation of the program would settle disputes about the effects of vouchers on students, the research findings instead were nuanced and mixed (for review, see Figlio, 2009; Zimmer & Bettinger, 2008).

Increase in Voucher Policy Actions

Despite the evidence, or lack thereof, the number of voucher bills passed by states and the number of states introducing voucher bills increased dramatically in the last few years. For example, Figure 24.8 shows the number of bills that have passed by state legislatures and the number of states introducing voucher bills between 2008 and 2011. In 2008, 19 bills passed; by 2011, that number increased to 63. In 2008, the number of states introducing voucher bills totaled 13 and increased to 33 in 2011. Both of these indicators reveal a dramatic increase over a short period of time.

Participation in Voucher Programs

In addition to the increase in the policy actions at the state level, the number of students participating in different voucher programs across the nation has increased significantly in the last decade—even though the total number of students receiving vouchers is a small fraction of the total number of students in the United States. Figure 24.9 shows some of the different voucher programs in the United States and the number of students participating in them; Table 24.1 is somewhat redundant

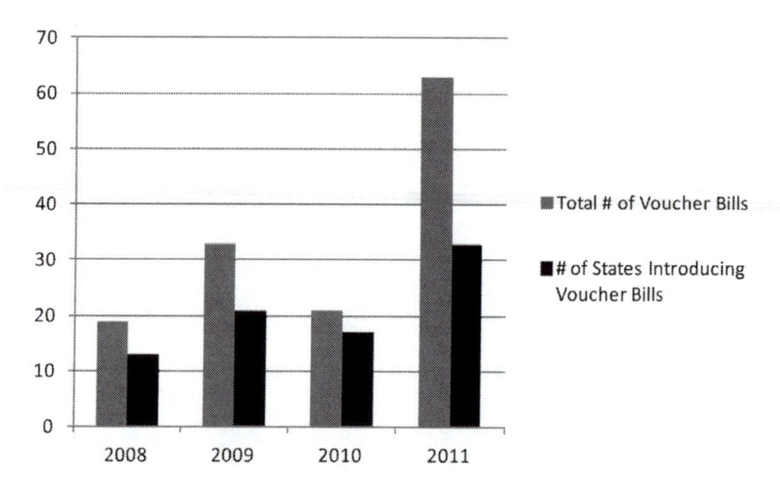

Figure 24.8 Number of voucher bills and states introducing voucher bills, 2008–2011. From Friedman Foundation for Educational Choice (2013).

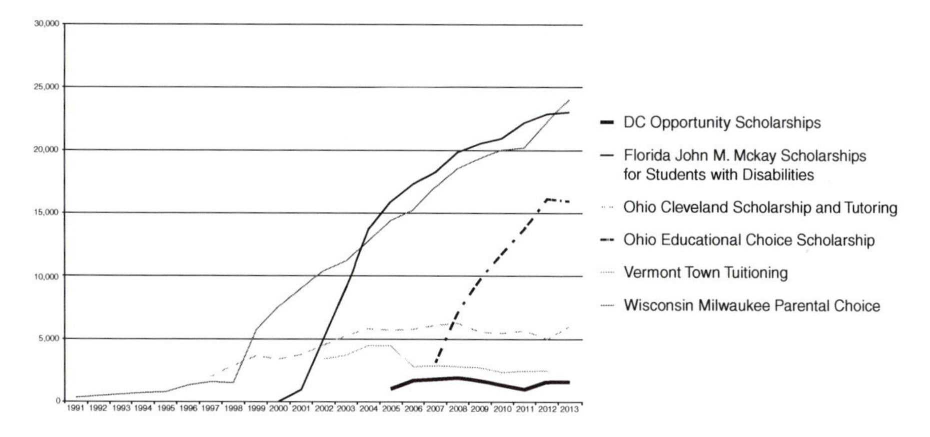

Figure 24.9 Number of students participating in selected voucher programs in the United States, 1991–2013. From Friedman Foundation for Educational Choice (2013).

with Figure 24.9, but shows the number of students participating in additional voucher programs as monitored by the Friedman Foundation for Educational Choice (2013). (For a description of these voucher programs and the urban locales in which they are being implemented, see http://www.edchoice.org/School-Choice/School-Choice-programs.aspx)

One of the more well-known voucher programs is the Milwaukee Parental Choice Program, which started in 1990. The program provides vouchers (capped at $6,442) to families earning up to 300% of the federal poverty level (about $69,000 for a family of four in 2012). In 1991, 337 Milwaukee students received a voucher; in 2013, 24,027 students received one. Another voucher program of note is Florida's John M. McKay Scholarships for Students With Disabilities, which started in 2000 with two students. These McKay Scholarships allow public school students with disabilities to receive vouchers to attend private or other public schools. As shown in Figure 24.9 and Table 24.1, this program has expanded to 23,011 students in 2013. Ohio launched its Educational Choice Scholarship Program in 2006 with 3,169 students, and now has expanded it to include 15,959 students. Ohio's students who are attending chronically low-performing schools are eligible for vouchers (called "EdChoice") to attend private schools; the cap on the number of vouchers is 60,000. A recent voucher program is Indiana's Choice Scholarship Program, which allows student in low- and middle-income families to receive vouchers to attend private schools.[4] Beginning in 2011–2012 with 3,919 students, the number of participating students increased to 9,324 students in 2012–2013. If the program withstands court challenges, it could be the largest in the United States.

Education Tax Credits

Another school choice option that has increased dramatically over the past decade is providing education tax credits to businesses and individuals. Parents can receive a tax credit or deduction for educational expenses (tuition, books, supplies, transportation), and businesses can receive a tax credit for making donations to nonprofits called Scholarship Granting Organizations (SGOs), which use the funds for private school student scholarships. Often education tax credits are seen as equivalent to vouchers in that they provide students with funds to attend private schools; it's the transfer mechanisms that differ. In addition, education tax credits have been seen as a more palatable way to get legislation passed in different states because of the controversies and debates

Table 24.1 Participation in Choice Scholarship (Voucher) Programs in the United States, 1991-2013. From Friedman Foundation for Educational Choice (2013)

PARTICIPATION BY PROGRAM	1991	1992	1993	1994	1995	1996	1997	1998	1999	2000	2001	2002	2003	2004	2005	2006	2007	2008	2009	2010	2011	2012	2013
Colorado Douglas County Choice Scholarship Pilot																						494	0
DC Opportunity Scholarship															1,027	1,716	1,805	1,930	1,714	1,322	1,017	1,615	1,584
Florida John M. McKay Scholarship for Students With Disabilities										2	970	5,013	9,130	13,739	15,910	17,300	18,273	19,852	20,530	20,926	22,198	22,861	23,011
Georgia Special Needs Scholarship																		899	1,596	2,068	2,529	2,965	3,227
Indiana Choice Scholarship																						3,919	9,324
Louisiana School Choice Pilot Program for Certain Students With Exceptionalities																						206	22
Louisiana Student Schol-arship for Educational Excellence																			624	1,194	1,678	1,912	4,944

Maine Town Tuitioning	n/a	n/a	n/a	n/a	n/a	n/a	n/a	n/a	n/a	n/a	n/a	n/a	n/a	n/a	n/a	n/a	n/a	n/a	n/a	4,808	5,438	8,818	n/a
Mississippi Dyslexia Therapy Scholarship																							42
Ohio Autism Scholarship															300	475	730	1,000	1,390	1,672	1,978	2,000	2,241
Ohio Cleveland Scholarship and Tutoring							1,994	2,914	3,674	3,404	3,797	4,523	5,281	5,887	5,710	5,813	6,116	6,272	5,562	5,476	5,697	5,030	6,001
Ohio Educational Choice Scholarship																	3,169	7,144	9,772	11,784	13,733	16,136	15,959
Ohio Jon Peterson Special Needs Scholarship																							1,342
Oklahoma Lindsey Nicole Henry Scholarships for Students With Disabilities																					6	135	169
Utah Carson Smith Special Needs Scholarship																107	340	548	582	602	624	679	714

(Continued)

Table 24.1 (Continued)

PARTICIPATION BY PROGRAM	1991	1992	1993	1994	1995	1996	1997	1998	1999	2000	2001	2002	2003	2004	2005	2006	2007	2008	2009	2010	2011	2012	2013
Vermont Town Tuitioning	n/a	n/a	n/a	n/a	n/a	n/a	n/a	n/a	n/a	n/a	n/a	3,437	3,752	4,511	4,495	2,808	2,900	2,785	2,718	2,370	2,469	2,501	n/a
Wisconsin Milwaukee Parental Choice	337	504	591	718	786	1,320	1,606	1,501	5,740	7,596	9,104	10,391	11,209	12,788	14,427	15,274	17,126	18,550	19,414	20,042	20,189	22,328	24,027
Wisconsin Racine Parental Private School Choice																						228	499
TOTAL PARTICIPATION	337	504	591	718	786	1,320	3,600	4,415	9,414	11,002	13,871	23,364	29,373	36,925	41,869	43,493	50,459	58,980	63,902	72,264	77,557	91,827	93,106

around vouchers and the direct provision of public funds to attend private schools. Education tax credits are a more indirect transfer of public funds.

Perhaps because education tax credits seem more acceptable in state legislatures and are not under scrutiny like voucher programs, there has been a great deal of policy activity at the state level since the 1980s, and certainly over the past few years (Huerta & d'Entremont, 2007; Schaeffer, 2009). For example, there were a total of 26 tax credit scholarship bills in 2008, and over a three-year period this number more than doubled to 53 in 2011 (see Figure 24.10).

As policy activity has increased, so too have the number of students participating in education tax credit programs throughout the United States. As shown in Figure 24.11, Florida's Tax

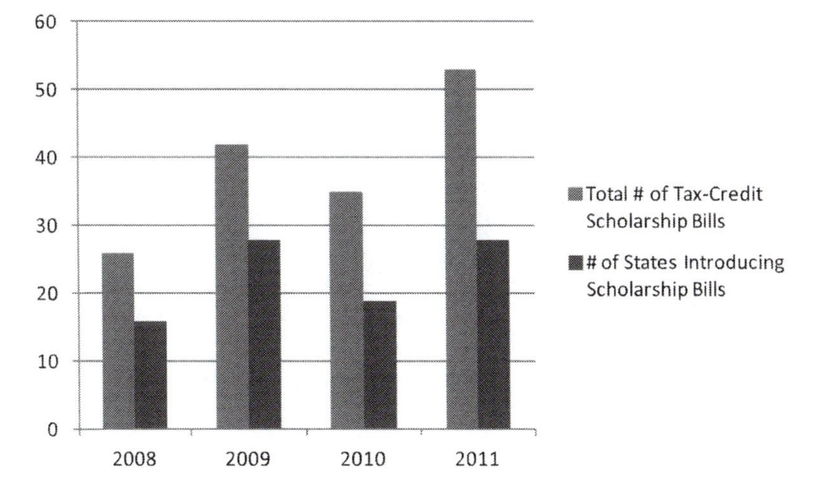

Figure 24.10 Number of tax credit scholarship bills and states introducing bills, 2008–2011. From Friedman Foundation for Educational Choice (2013).

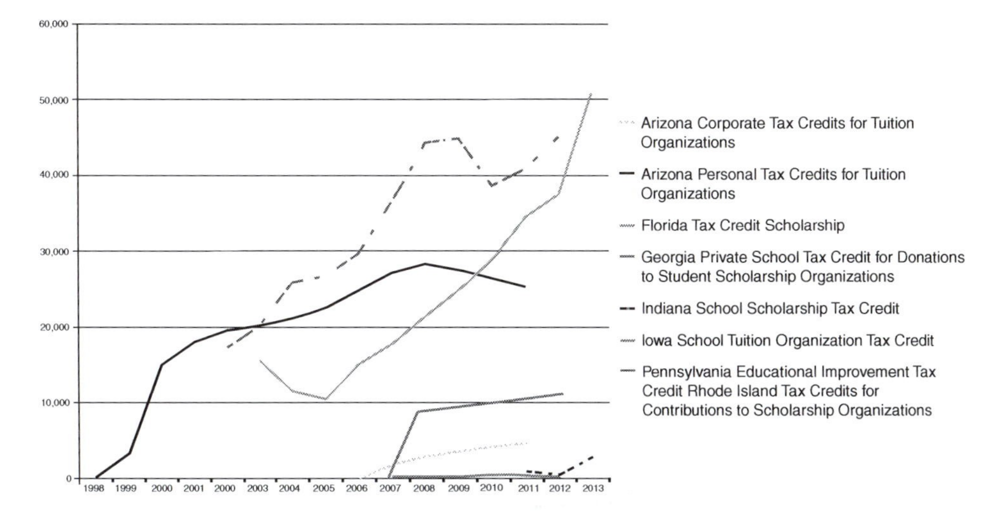

Figure 24.11 Number of students participating in selected education tax credit programs in the United States, 1998–2013. From Friedman Foundation for Educational Choice (2013).

Credit Scholarship Program—which provides a tax credit on corporate income taxes and insurance premium taxes for donation to SGOs that provide scholarships to low-income students, foster children, and funds for transportation to schools outside a student's district—had 15,585 students in 2003 and nearly 51,000 in 2013. Similarly, Pennsylvania's Educational Improvement Tax Credit expanded from 17,350 in 2002 to over 45,000 in 2012. Corporate contributions in Pennsylvania can go to SGOs to provide scholarships to students (eligible if their families make less than $75,000 in 2013) or to Educational Improvement Organizations, which are nonprofits that support innovative programs in public schools. In Arizona, one of the longer-standing tax credit programs is Personal Tax Credits for School Tuition Organizations, which provides a credit on individual income taxes for donation to SGOs. Individuals contributing to SGOs may claim a dollar-to-dollar credit up to $1,000 if the scholarships are for students leaving public schools to attend a private school.

What the Research Says About School Choice Effectiveness: A Brief Summary

Even though there has been a massive expansion of charter schools, voucher programs, and education tax credit programs in the last decade, what does the research have to say about the effects of these programs on students? In part, the argument for these choice programs is to allow low-income students at low-performing schools to attend a private school, presumably providing improved opportunities to learn. But as these programs have expanded, what does the research suggest? Are students performing better in schools of choice as measured by their test score gains relative to their traditional public school counterparts?

Unfortunately, the research appears to be less than conclusive—"unfortunate" because this provides fodder for continued debate at different levels of policy about whether or not to scale up these choice options. What is needed is more systematic research that looks at the educational trajectories of students in choice and nonchoice schools with data not only on test score gains and graduation rates, but other noncognitive measures of student outcomes (e.g., behavior, engagement, motivation, educational and occupational expectations). In addition, more systematic information needs to be gathered from the choice and nonchoice learning environments, including not only instructional conditions but also differences in the social organization of schools (see Berends, Goldring, Stein, & Cravens, 2010). What follows is a brief review of the research examining the effects of charter schools, vouchers, and education tax credits on student achievement. More thorough reviews are cited in the appropriate sections.

Research on Charter Schools

Although charter schools are the fastest-growing area of school choice, the evidence base is weak for scaling up charter school reform via federal policy and programs. For instance, some studies using randomized designs show modest effects on academic achievement gains for students in charter schools compared with those students who are not so enrolled (Abdulkadiroglu et al., 2009; Angrist et al., 2011; Dobbie & Fryer, 2011; Hoxby & Murarka, 2008; Hoxby, Murarka, & Kang, 2009). Other studies relying on broader samples of schools within a randomized design (Gleason, Clark, Tuttle, & Dwoyer, 2010) and those using quasi-experimental methods show mixed results for charter school effects on achievement (for a review see Betts & Tang, 2011; Center for Research on Education Outcomes [CREDO], 2009; Teasley, 2009).

Although it is important to understand that overall charter school studies show that effects on achievement are mixed (some positive, some negative, and some neutral), it is important to note that some studies have found significant and substantial positive effects of charter schools, particularly in urban areas where it has been difficult to implement meaning educational reforms.

For example, comparing students who won and lost charter school lotteries, Hoxby et al. (2009) found that charter students outscored the comparison group in both mathematics and English. The authors noted that students who attended charter schools in New York City over a longer period of time (e.g., kindergarten through 8th grade) matched the mathematics performance gains of their peers in affluent suburban schools—what they called the closing of the "Harlem-Scarsdale" achievement gap. Dobbie and Fryer (2011), who examined students who won and lost the charter school lotteries in the Harlem Children's Zone, found that the effects of charter elementary schools were large enough to close the racial achievement gap across subjects—that is, students gained about 0.20 of a standard deviation a year in both mathematics and English/Language Arts. Large effects of charter schools have also been found in Boston (Angrist et al., 2011).

Although studies of school choice shed some light on the main effects in different locales, they provide limited information about the schools as organizations and the conditions within them that may promote student achievement, particularly the curriculum and instruction that is most likely to affect student learning. Many researchers and policy makers advocate looking inside schools to better understand the conditions under which schools of choice have (or do not have) positive effects on achievement, pointing to the importance of detailed information about curriculum, instruction, organizational conditions that promote achievement, and teacher characteristics and qualifications (Berends, Watral, Teasley, & Nicotera, 2008; Berends et al., 2010; Betts & Loveless, 2005; Gill, Timpane, Ross, & Brewer, 2007; Zimmer & Buddin, 2007, 2008; Zimmer et al., 2003). To date, however, these calls to look at the organization of schooling within the charter sector have not been heeded, by and large—suggesting an important avenue for future research.

Research on School Vouchers

With the expansion in the number of voucher programs, the research addressing the effects of these programs has increased as well. However, the research portrays a mixed view of voucher impacts (Figlio, 2009; Peterson & Howell, 2006; Zimmer & Bettinger, 2008). The first study of a school voucher program in the United States was the official evaluation of the pioneering Milwaukee Parental Choice Program, 1990–1995 (see Witte, 2000). Subsequent work analyzed a portion of the data generated by that evaluation, and was reported in Greene, Peterson, and Du (1999) and Rouse (1998). These studies were different from Witte in their methodological approaches and, therefore, the findings reported differed. Based on regression models strengthened with Heckman selection corrections, the Witte work found generally no systematic differences on student achievement outcomes between voucher and public school students. The Greene et al. analysis was based on a subset of voucher participants who had won their voucher via a lottery system to a small number of oversubscribed private schools, finding positive achievement impacts associated with participation. Rouse employed a series of quasi-experimental approaches from student fixed effects and instrumental variable designs, finding no effect in reading but positive achievement impacts in math.

These differences between findings of positive and no achievement effects have since been reflected in other studies of voucher programs. For example, Greene (2001) found positive achievement impacts from an experimental analysis of the privately funded voucher program in Charlotte, a result generally supported by Cowen (2008) using more sophisticated statistical models. Howell, Wolf, Campbell, & Peterson's (2002) primary analysis of lottery-based privately funded programs in New York City, Washington, DC, and Dayton, Ohio, revealed positive student achievement outcomes for African American students, but not for the overall sample, a finding both confirmed (Barnard et al., 2003) and questioned (Krueger & Zhu, 2003) by subsequent analysts of the New York data. Studies of the Cleveland Scholarship Program similarly found both positive impacts for voucher students (Greene, Howell, & Peterson, 1999) and no significant differences (Metcalf et al., 2003), findings that differed due to study design and sample. Using a regression discontinuity approach on the statewide voucher system in Florida, Figlio and Hart (2011) found that the program generated statistically significant positive impacts on student reading achievement, at least for students near the income-eligibility ceiling. Witte, Cowen, Wolf, and Fleming (2012) reported that Milwaukee voucher students on average gained more than a matched sample of public school students in reading but not in math in the final year of that four-year evaluation. They noted that a new high-stakes testing policy may have been partly or wholly responsible for the voucher gains (see also Wolf, 2012).

The evaluation of the first federally funded voucher program in Washington, DC, relied on an experimental design based on scholarship lotteries (Wolf et al., 2010, 2011). The series of reports described significant achievement gains in reading in the third year of the evaluation but no significant reading impacts in other years, including the fourth and final year, or in math in any year. This same study revealed significant gains in voucher students' high school graduation rates. Cowen, Fleming, Witte, Wolf, & Kisida (2013) reported gains in educational attainment from the Milwaukee voucher program, both in terms of rates of high school graduation and four-year college enrollment. Recently, Chingos and Peterson (2012) found that African Americans who participated in the New York City privately funded voucher experiment enrolled in college at higher rates than the experimental control group, though there were no significant attainments effects of the program on the entire sample of students.

Similar to the research on charters, there have been very few studies that examined the specific learning conditions that students experienced in their schools of choice vis-à-vis comparable students in traditional public schools (Figlio, Goldhaber, Hannaway, & Rouse, in press; Zimmer & Bettinger, 2008). Although such studies are difficult to design and implement, more research is needed on school and classroom experiences to understand the conditions under which voucher programs provide more meaningful and substantive learning opportunities (or not).

Research on Education Tax Credits

The research on education tax credits is very limited (as mentioned by Belfield, 2001; Huerta & d'Entremont, 2007; Schaeffer, 2009; Zimmer & Bettinger, 2008), probably because education tax credits are often equated with vouchers. Similar to voucher programs, which in the end result in students transferring from the public to the private sector, more information is needed about the instructional practices and school organizational conditions that students using tax credits experience compared with their counterparts. Some questions that might further our understanding of tax credit effects include: Who chooses to apply and use a tax credit? What are the characteristics of students and their families receiving tax credits? To what schools do such students apply and attend? What are the learning opportunities in these schools vis-à-vis the schools that students attended before? What are the differences in the organizational and instructional conditions in the schools of destination (attending with vouchers) compared with schools of origin (where students attended previously)?

Theoretical Perspectives on School Choice

As school choice programs continue to expand, additional research will likely increase our understanding of the impact of choice options on families and students. As this research unfolds, it is important to keep in mind different theoretical frameworks that guide the research. Specifically, there are two competing theories about the possible impact of choice schools on teaching and learning and in school organizational conditions—market theory and institutional theory (Berends et al., 2010). Many reformers maintain that market style mechanisms of consumer choice and competition between autonomous schools will encourage diverse and innovative approaches to school organization, teaching, and learning (e.g., Chubb & Moe, 1990; Walberg, 2011; Walberg & Bast, 2003). The assumption is that as school choice undercuts bureaucratic political control of public education, it provides educators in schools of choice the opportunity and motivation to experiment with new organizational and instructional strategies to improve student achievement.

Proponents of choice argue that providing this freedom not only diversifies educational opportunities but also creates incentives for the improvement of traditional public schooling through increased market competition for services (Chubb & Moe, 1990; Friedman, 1962). In large part, this argument is about how market competition decreases the amount and influence of historical bureaucratic structures to increase the opportunities for parents and school staff to better relate to address parents' demands.

Some hold that privatization and school choice can bring about "creative destruction," borrowing from Joseph Schumpeter, who in the 1940s argued that entrepreneurs relied on radically new technologies—whether more effective, more efficient, or both—to promote economic progress and replace older technologies (Schumpeter 1942; Walberg, 2011). As the theory goes, such privatization and increased choice will lead to better outcomes, lower costs, and greater satisfaction of employees, parents, and students. According to Walberg (2011, p. 73), "market-based consumer-driven school choice seems the best hope for creative destruction of new technologies, the expansion of choice, competition, and diversity for substantial, sustained achievement improvement." Chubb and Moe (1990, p. 217) hold a similar position, calling choice a "revolutionary reform that introduces a new system of public education."

Critics of the market model, however, raise questions about the empirical validity of its key assumptions about parent-consumers (demand-side), schools (supply-side), and the products that a market in education would generate (Finnegan, 2007; Henig, 1999). From such criticism comes an alternative theory about the consequences of school choice: institutional theory. Stemming from broader organizational analysis, this *new institutionalism,* developed by John Meyer and colleagues over several decades (Meyer, 1977; Meyer & Rowan, 1977, 1978; Powell & DiMaggio, 1991; Scott & Meyer, 1994; Scott & Davis, 2007), characterizes schools as institutions with persistent patterns of social action that individuals take for granted.

Agreeing with market theorists that the bureaucratic form of schooling dominates the public school sector in the United States (and many other countries), institutional theorists take a different tack in their analysis of the education environment. For instance, the increase in bureaucratization of schools has led to an increase in rational coordination among the nested layers of the school—from the federal government to the state, districts, schools, and classrooms. According to institutional theorists such as Meyer and Rowan (1977, 1978), this bureaucratic, rational network has resulted in a system of categories or rules, called "ritual classifications," that define the actions of schools, teachers, students. Over time these ritual classifications become institutionalized and accepted as the norm for what constitutes a legitimate school and its activities (Bidwell & Kasarda, 1980). Institutional theorists refer to this as *isomorphism* and have documented its diffusion both in the United States and throughout the world (Bidwell & Dreeben, 2006; Meyer & Ramirez, 2000).

School compliance to ritual classifications is important for legitimacy—more important, according to institutional theorists—than maximizing efficiency and innovations of school operations (Meyer & Rowan, 1977; Scott & Meyer, 1994). In other words, schools adapt to their environments by adopting accepted rules and structures, leaving actual classroom instruction and learning relatively unexamined and unmonitored. Such loose coupling helps schools maintain their validity (Weick, 1976) and is further promoted by schools' logic of confidence that delegates instruction to teacher professionals who ultimately control what goes on inside their classrooms. It is the teachers who typically have made the choices about what to teach and how to teach it in their classrooms, a set of activities that until more recently, have been beyond the purview of principals, parents, and policy makers at the district and state levels (Elmore, 2007; Weick, 1976). With the implementation of NCLB over the past decade, states and districts have attempted to guide instruction in schools through high-states accountability, but even with specific instructional materials, it is the teachers in the classrooms and their relationships with students who are making choices about what to teach, how to teach, and how to learn (see Stecher & Vernez, 2010).

DiMaggio and Powell (1983) argue that there are different types of environmental pressures on organizations to make them more similar than different. These pressures include "coercive isomorphism," which stems from formal and informal pressures by organizations and groups on which the school depends (e.g., federal and state mandates under NCLB), "mimetic isomorphism," which stems from the adoption of similar structures and practices when facing uncertain tasks; and "normativeisomorphism," which stems primarily from professionalization of educators and professional networks.

When applied to school choice, institutional theory emphasizes that *all* schools operate within highly institutionalized environments, which define what counts as legitimate education. All types of schools, no matter the sector or organizational form, adopt rituals, norms, and myths to support their validity (Meyer & Rowan, 1977, 1978; Scott & Davis, 2007). Thus, even schools of choice pay attention to institutional rules such as teacher certification, curricular subject matter, instructional time, reasonable class size, and mostly age-based grade organization.

In short, institutional theorists argue that the institutional environment of American education is so strong that significant changes in instruction are likely to be rare or short-lived (see Elmore, 2007), and market theorists claim that increased choice will result in widespread autonomy promoting innovation, competition, and increased satisfaction and outcomes. Despite a couple of decades of school choice reform, researchers have not definitively supported market theory vis-à-vis institutional theory. The limited empirical research is mixed on improved and differentiated instruction and in-school organizational conditions, curriculum content, and pedagogy in schools of choice, supporting neither market nor institutional theories (see Berends et al., 2010; Lubienski, 2003; Preston, Goldring, Berends, & Cannata, 2012).

Future Research Possibilities

Thus, additional research is critical for understanding the various effects of school choice reforms, particularly as the landscape of choice reforms continues to expand in a dramatic fashion for students located in urban areas. Such research can make significant contributions to educational policy related to charter schools, vouchers, and education tax credits. As argued here, an important component of this future research should address questions that go beyond horse races between charter and noncharter students, voucher and nonvoucher students, and students benefiting from tax credits vis-à-vis those who do not. Rather, understanding the conditions under which these choice options are effective or not will help push policy debates forward. Such research will help research not merely accumulate in a fragmented number of studies, but cumulate to further systematic knowledge-building, revision of policies, within research and policy communities, so that there is systematic growth in our understanding of the policies and research (see Cohen, 2003). In the future, research is needed not only to inform the policy debates about school choice, but to examine the effects on those of most concern—students who have historically not had access to the resources and educational opportunities that lead to future educational and other adult attainments.

Notes

1. Thank you to Anna Nicotera, Senior Director of Research and Evaluation, National Alliance for Public Charter Schools, and Paul DiPerna, the Research Director at the Friedman Foundation for Educational Choice, for providing the data that are incorporated in this chapter. Thanks, too, to Ann Primus for her assistance and editing.
2. The Program for International Student Assessment (PISA) is coordinated by the Organization for Economic Cooperation and Development (OECD) and includes 65 participating countries. The PISA administers assessments in reading, mathematics, and science every three years to nationally representative samples of 15-year-old students in the participating countries. The assessments attempt to measure applied knowledge and literacy to address how well students nearing the end of compulsory schooling apply their knowledge to real-life situations.
3. These data come from the 2010–2011 Common Core Data, gathered by the U.S. Department of Education's National Center for Educational Statistics.
4. In 2012, eligibility requirements for the Indiana Choice Scholarship Program included the following: (1) students who are entering grades 1–12 must have attended a public school (included charter) for the preceding two semesters and who are from families earning up to 150% of the federal free/reduced-price lunch program ($63,964 for a family of 4 in 2013); (2) students who enroll in kindergarten; (3) students who previously received a tax-credit scholarship in the previous school year from a Scholarship Granting Organization; or (4) received a voucher in the prior school year under the voucher program.

References

Abdulkadiroglu, A., Angrist, J., Cohodes, S.R., Dynarski, S., Fullerton, J., Kane, T.J., & Pathak, P. (2009). *Informing the debate: Comparing Boston's charter, pilot, and traditional schools.* Boston, MA: Boston Foundation.

Angrist, J.D., Cohodes, S.R., Dynarski, S.M., Fullerton, J.B., Kane, T.J., Pathak, P.A., & Walters, C.R. (2011). *Student achievement in charter schools.* Boston, MA: Center for Educational Policy Research, Harvard University.

Aud, S., Hussar, W., Johnson, F., Kena, G., Roth, E., Manning, E., Wang, X., & Zhang, J. (2012). *The condition of education 2012* (NCES 2012–045). Washington, DC: U.S. Department of Education, National Center for Education Statistics. Retrieved from http://nces.ed.gov/pubsearch/

Barnard, J., Frangakis, C. E., Hill, J. L., & Rubin, D. B. (2003). Principal stratification approach to broken randomized experiments: A case study of school choice vouchers in New York City. *Journal of the American Statistical Association, 98*(42), 299–323.

Belfield, C.R. (2001). *Tuition tax credits: What do we know so far?* National Center for the Study of Privatization in Education Working Paper (www.ncspe.org). New York, NY: Teachers College.

Berends, M., Cannata, M., & Goldring, E.B. (Eds.). (2011). *School choice and school improvement.* Cambridge, MA: Harvard Education Press.

Berends, M., Goldring, E., Stein, M., & Cravens, X. (2010). Instructional conditions in charter schools and students' mathematics achievement gains. *American Journal of Education, 116*(3), 303–335.

Berends, M., Springer, M.G., Ballou, D., & Walberg, H.J. (Eds.). (2009). *Handbook of research on school choice.* New York, NY: Routledge.

Berends, M., Watral, C., Teasley, B., & Nicotera, A. (2008). Charter school effects on achievement: Where we are and where we're going. In M. Berends, M.G. Springer, & H.J. Walberg (Eds.), *Charter school outcomes* (pp. 243–267). New York, NY: Taylor & Francis.

Betts, J.R., & Loveless, T. (Eds.). (2005). *Getting choice right: Ensuring equity and efficiency in education policy.* Washington, DC: Brookings Institution Press.

Betts, J.R., & Tang, E. (2011). *The effect of charter schools on student achievement: A meta-analysis of the literature.* Seattle, WA: National Charter School Research Project, Center on Reinventing Public Education, University of Washington.

Bidwell, C.E., & Dreeben, R. (2006). Public and private education: Conceptualizing the distinction. In M.T. Hallinan (Ed.), *School sector and student outcomes* (pp. 9–37). Notre Dame, IN: University of Notre Dame Press.

Bidwell, C.E., & Kasarda, J.D. (1980). Conceptualizing and measuring the effects of school and schooling. *American Journal of Education, 88*(4), 401–430.

Center for Research on Education Outcomes (CREDO). (2009). *Multiple choice: Charter school performance in 16 states.* Stanford, CA: Author.

Chingos, M.M., & Peterson, P.E. (2012). *The effects of school vouchers on college enrollment: Experimental evidence from New York City.* Cambridge, MA: Harvard Kennedy School Program on Education Policy and Governance.

Chubb, J.E., & Moe, T.E. (1990). *Politics, markets, and America's schools.* Washington, DC: Brookings Institution Press.

Cohen, D. (2003). *Workshop on understanding and promoting knowledge accumulation in education: Tools and strategies for education research.* Washington, DC: National Academy of Sciences.

Cowen, J.M. (2008). School choice as a latent variable: Estimating the "Complier Average Causal Effect" of vouchers in Charlotte. *Policy Studies Journal, 36*(2), 301–315.

Cowen, J.M., Fleming, D.J., Witte, J.F., Wolf, P.J., & Kisida, B. (2013). School vouchers and student attainment: Evidence from a state-mandated study of Milwaukee's Parental Choice Program. *Policy Studies Journal, 41*(1), 147–168.

DiMaggio, P. J., & Powell, W. W. (1983). The iron cage revisited: Institutional isomorphism and collective rationality in organizational fields. *American Sociological Review, 48*(2), 147–160.

Dobbie, W., & Fryer, R.G. (2011). Are high quality schools enough to close the achievement gap? Evidence from a social experiment in Harlem. *American Economic Journal: Applied Economics, 3*(3), 158–187.

Education Week. (2013). *Obama's second term: What's ahead for education policy.* Bethesda, MD: Editorial Projects in Education.

Elmore, R. (2007). *School reform from the inside out: Policy, practice, and performance.* Boston, MA: Harvard Education Press.

Figlio, D.N. (2009). Voucher outcomes. In M. Berends, M.G. Springer, D. Ballou, & H.J. Walberg (Eds.), *Handbook of research on school choice* (pp. 321–337). New York, NY: Routledge.

Figlio, D.N., Goldhaber, D., Hannaway, J., & Rouse, C. (2013). Feeling the Florida heat? How low-performing schools respond to voucher and accountability pressure. *American Economic Journal: Economic Policy, 5*(2), 251–281.

Figlio, D.N., & Hart, C.M.D. (2011). Competitive effects of means-tested school vouchers. NBER Working Paper No. 16056. Cambridge, MA: National Bureau of Economic Research. Retrieved from http://www.nber.org/papers/w16056

Finnegan, K.S. (2007). Charter school autonomy: The mismatch between theory and practice. *Educational Policy, 21*(3), 503–526.

Fleischman, H.L., Hopstock, P.J., Pelczar, M.P., & Shelley, B.E. (2010). *Highlights from PISA 2009: Performance of U.S. 15-year old students in reading, mathematics, and science literacy in an international context (NCES 2011–004).* U.S. Department of Education, National Center for Education Statistics. Washington, DC: U.S. Government Printing Office.

Friedman, M. (1962). *Capitalism and freedom.* Chicago, IL: University of Chicago Press.

Friedman Foundation for Educational Choice. (2013). Retrieved from http://www.edchoice.org/

Gamoran, A. (October, 2011). The future of educational inequality: Will more accountability reduce the gaps? Paper presented at the CREO Seminar, University of Notre Dame, Notre Dame, IN.

Gill, B.P., Timpane, P.M., Ross, K.E., & Brewer, D.J. (2007). *Rhetoric versus reality: What we know and what we need to know about vouchers and charter schools.* Santa Monica, CA: RAND Corporation.

Gleason, P., Clark, M., Tuttle, C.C., & Dwoyer, E. (2010). *The evaluation of charter school impacts: Final report.* NCEE 2010–4029. Washington, DC: National Center for Education Evaluation and Regional Assistance,

Institute of Education Sciences, U.S. Department of Education. Retrieved from http://ies.ed.gov/ncee/pubs/20104029/pdf/20104029.pdf

Greene, J.P. (2001). Vouchers in Charlotte. *Education Matters, 1*(2), 55–60.

Greene, J.P., Howell, W.G., & Peterson, P.E. (1999). Lessons from the Cleveland Scholarship Program. In P.E. Peterson & B.C. Hassel (Eds.), *Learning from school choice* (pp. 357–394). Washington, DC: Brookings Institution Press.

Greene, J.P., Peterson, P.E., & Du, J. (1999). Effectiveness of school choice: The Milwaukee experiment. *Education and Urban Society, 31*(1), 190–213.

Henig, J. (1999). School choice outcomes. In S. Sugarman & F. Kemerer (Eds.), *School choice and social controversy* (pp. 68–106). Washington, DC: Brookings Institution Press.

Howell, W. G, Wolf, P.J., Campbell, D.E., & Peterson, P.E. (2002). School vouchers and academic performance: Results from three randomized field trials. *Journal of Policy Analysis and Management, 21*(2), 191–217.

Hoxby, C.M., & Murarka, S. (2008). Methods of assessing achievement of students in charter schools. In M. Berends, M.G. Springer, & H.J. Walberg (Eds.), *Charter school outcomes* (pp. 7–37). Mahweh, NJ: Taylor & Francis Group.

Hoxby, C.M., Murarka, S., & Kang, J. (2009). *How New York City's charter schools affect achievement.* Cambridge, MA: New York City Charter Schools Evaluation Project. Retrieved from http://www.nber.org/~schools/charterschoolseval/how_NYC_charter_schools_affect_achievement_sept2009.pdf

Huerta, L.A., & d'Entremont, C. (2007). Education tax credits in a post-Zelman era: Legal, political, and policy alternatives to vouchers? *Educational Policy, 21*(1), 73–109.

Krueger, A. B., & Zhu, P. (2003). Comment on "Principal stratification approach to broken randomized experiments: A case study of school choice vouchers in New York City." *Journal of the American Statistical Association, 98*(42), 314–318.

Ladd, H.F., Fiske, E.B., & Ruijs, N. (2011). Does parental choice foster segregated schools? In M. Berends, M. Cannata, & E.B. Goldring (Eds.), *School choice and school improvement* (pp. 233–253). Boston, MA: Harvard Education Press.

Lubienski, C. (2003). Innovation in education markets: Theory and evidence on the impact of competition and choice in charter schools. *American Educational Research Journal, 40*(2), 395–443.

Metcalf, K. K., West, S. D., Legan, N. A., Paul, K. M., & Boone, W. J. (2003). *Evaluation of the Cleveland scholarship and tutoring program, summary report 1998–2001.* Bloomington, IN: Indiana Center for Evaluation.

Meyer, J.W. (1977). The effects of education as an institution. *American Journal of Sociology, 83*(1), 55–77.

Meyer, J.W., & Ramirez, F. (2000). The world institutionalization of education. In J. Schriewer (Ed.), *Discourse formation in comparative education* (pp. 111–132). Frankfurt, Germany: Peter Lang.

Meyer, J.W., & Rowan, B. (1977). Institutionalized organizations: Formal structure as myth and ceremony. *American Journal of Sociology, 83*(2), 340–363.

Meyer, J.W., & Rowan, B. (1978). The structure of educational organizations. In M.W. Meyer & Associates (Eds.), *Environments and organizations* (pp. 78–109). San Francisco, CA: Jossey-Bass.

Miron, G., Urschel, J.L., Aguilar, M.A.Y., & Dailey, B. (2012). *Profiles of for-profit and nonprofit education management organizations.* Boulder, CO: National Education Policy Center.

National Alliance for Public Charter Schools. (2013). Retrieved from http://dashboard.publiccharters.org/dashboard/schools/page/overview/year/2012

Peterson, P.E., & Howell, W.G. (2006). *The education gap: Vouchers and urban schools.* Washington, DC: Brookings Institution Press.

Powell, W.W., & DiMaggio, P.J. (1991). *The new institutionalism in organizational analysis.* Chicago, IL: University of Chicago Press.

Preston, C., Goldring, E., Berends, M., & Cannata, M. (2012). School innovation in district context: Comparing traditional public schools and charter schools. *Economics of Education Review, 31*(2), 318–330.

Reardon, S.F. (2011). The widening academic achievement gap between the rich and the poor: New evidence and possible explanations. In G.J. Duncan & R.J. Murnane (Eds.), *Whither opportunity? Rising inequality, schools, and children's life chances* (pp. 91–115). New York, NY: Russell Sage Foundation.

Rouse, C.E. (1998). Private school vouchers and student achievement: An evaluation of the Milwaukee Parental Choice Program. *Quarterly Journal of Economics, 113*(2), 553–602.

Rowan, B. (2011). Intervening to improve the educational outcomes of students in poverty: Lessons from recent work in high-poverty schools. In G.J. Duncan & R.J. Murnane (Eds.), *Whither opportunity? Rising inequality, schools, and children's life chances* (pp. 523–537). New York, NY: Russell Sage Foundation.

Schaeffer, A.B. (2009). Education tax credits. In M. Berends, M.G. Springer, D. Ballou, & H.J. Walberg (Eds.), *Handbook of research on school choice* (pp. 593–613). New York, NY: Routledge.

Schumpeter, J.A. (1942). *Capitalism, socialism, and democracy.* New York, NY: Harper.

Scott, W.R., & Davis, G.F. (2007). *Organizations and organizing: Rational, natural and open system perspectives.* Englewood Cliffs, NJ: Prentice Hall.

Scott, W.R., & Meyer, J.W. (1994). *Institutional environments and organizations: Structural complexity and individualism.* Thousand Oaks, CA: Sage Publications.

Stecher, B.M., & Vernez, G. (2010). *Reauthorizing No Child Left Behind: Facts and recommendations.* Santa Monica, CA: RAND Corporation.

Teasley, B. (2009). Charter school outcomes. In M. Berends, M.G. Springer, D. Ballou, & H.J. Walberg (Eds.), *Handbook of research on school choice* (pp. 209–225). New York, NY: Routledge.

Walberg, H.J. (2011). *Tests, testing, and genuine school reform.* Stanford, CA: Hoover Institution Press.

Walberg, H.J., & Bast, J.L. (2003). *Education and capitalism: How overcoming our fear of markets and economics can improve America's schools.* Stanford, CA: Hoover Institution Press.

Weick, K.E. (1976). Educational organizations as loosely coupled systems. *Administrative Science Quarterly, 21*(1), 1–19.

Witte, J.F. (2000). *The market approach to education: An analysis of America's first voucher program.* Princeton, NJ: Princeton University Press.

Witte, J.F., Cowen, J.M., Wolf, P.J., & Fleming, D.J. (2012). *Milwaukee Parental Choice Program longitudinal educational growth study: Fifth year report.* Fayetteville, AR: University of Arkansas.

Wolf, P.J. (2012). *The comprehensive longitudinal evaluation of the Milwaukee Parental Choice Program: Summary of final reports.* Fayetteville, AR: University of Arkansas, School Choice Demonstration Project.

Wolf, P.J., Gutmann, B., Puma, M., Kisida, B., Rizzo, L., Eissa, N., & Carr, M. (2010). *Evaluation of the DC Opportunity Scholarship Program: Final Report* (NCEE 2010–4018). Washington, DC: National Center for Education Evaluation and Regional Assistance, Institute of Education Sciences, U.S. Department of Education.

Wolf, P.J., Kisida, B., Gutmann, G., Puma, M., Rizzo, L., & Eissa, N. (2011). School vouchers in the nation's capital. In M. Berends, M. Cannata, & E.B. Goldring (Eds.), *School choice and school improvement* (pp. 17–33). Boston, MA: Harvard Education Press.

Wong, K.K., & Klopott, S. (2009). Politics and governance in charter schools. In M. Berends, M.G. Springer, D. Ballou, & H.J. Walberg (Eds.), *Handbook of research on school choice* (pp. 115–135). New York, NY: Routledge.

Wong, K.K., & Shen, F.X. (2008). Charter law and charter operation: Re-examining the charter school marketplace. In M. Berends, M.G. Springer, & H.J. Walberg (Eds.), *Charter school outcomes* (pp. 131–161). New York, NY: Taylor & Francis.

Zimmer, Ron, & Bettinger, E.P. (2008). Beyond the rhetoric: Surveying the evidence on vouchers and tax credits. In H.F. Ladd & E.B. Fiske (Eds.), *Handbook of research in education finance and policy* (pp. 447–466). New York, NY: Routledge.

Zimmer, R., & Buddin, R. (2007). Getting inside the black box: Examining how the operations of charter schools affect performance. *Peabody Journal, 82*(2–3), 231–273.

Zimmer, R., & Buddin, R. (2008). Charter schools in California. In M. Berends, M.G. Springer, & H.J. Walberg (Eds.), *Charter school outcomes* (pp. 163–194). New York, NY: Taylor & Francis.

Zimmer, R., Buddin, R., Chau, D., Gill, B., Guarino, C., Hamilton, L., Krop, C., McCaffrey, D., Sandler, M., & Brewer, D. (2003). *Charter school operations and performance: Evidence from California*. Santa Monica, CA: RAND Corporation.

Zimmer, R., Gill, B., Booker, K., Lavertu, S., Sass, T. R., & Witte, J. (2009). *Charter schools in eight states: Effects on achievement, attainment, integration, and competition*. Santa Monica, CA: RAND Corporation.

25

School Reform and School Choice

Adrienne D. Dixson, Camika Royal &
Kevin Lawrence Henry, Jr.

School Reform and School Choice in Philadelphia, Chicago, and New Orleans

The 2012 teachers' strike in Chicago brought into sharp relief the contentious nature of school reform and public education policy in the United States. While most media reports focused primarily on the issues related to compensation and benefits and a very contentious evaluation system, the teachers were also concerned about curricular, pedagogical, and infrastructural issues that directly impacted the students in the Chicago Public Schools (Schools Students Deserve [SCSD] Report, 2012). The media rarely reported the range and scope of the issues that the Chicago Teachers' Union (CTU) raised that had a significant impact on their decision to strike, despite a change to the Illinois Educational Labor Relations Act (2011) that prohibited teachers from striking for issues other than compensation and benefits. Many of these concerns are related in large part to the ever-increasing number of charter schools, the closure of traditional schools, and dwindling budgets for public education.

The CTU strike also illustrates the unsettled nature of issues that have plagued public education since the inception of the common school. Historically, we have wrestled with four abiding questions: 1. Who gets to go to school? 2. What will students learn? 3. Who will pay for schools and public education? 4. Who makes decisions about public education? These questions are not abstracted from and very much impacted by issues of race, gender, class, national origin, linguistic background, physical and mental ability, and sexual identity.

In an attempt to answer those questions, the federal government, individual states, and local communities have designed and implemented a variety of policies or "reforms." While some reforms have been transformative, most have been met with significant resistance. The most sweeping reform legislation was the *Brown v. Board of Education* decision in 1954. One could argue that *Brown* not only ushered in considerable change, especially as it relates to school desegregation, but it has had the most significant impact on public school policy in the modern era. The decision certainly led to a number of other policies all aimed at providing educational equity particularly for students of color. Since *Brown,* school districts, especially urban school districts, have looked for ways to increase not only access to high-quality education for students of color, but to also raise their overall academic achievement. While most reforms still focus on "fixing the student," charter schools supporters argue that charter schools are a systemic and structural reform that will address issues of access and equity.

Using New Orleans, Philadelphia, and Chicago as case studies, this chapter examines the current reform movement that seeks to shrink traditional school boards, increase charter schools, and disempower teachers' unions. We examine the ways that education policies in these areas have been shaped by constituencies outside of the local contexts. In particular, we examine how these policies reflect a particular political ideology that in many ways exacerbates racial and educational inequity, a goal counter to what these constituencies presumably seek to address.

Defining Urban Education

We define urban education largely in geographic terms. That is, we understand urban education to reflect schools that are located in large, mid-sized and small cities. While we understand that the term *urban* often connotes a number of negative images, that is, poverty, crime, pollution, and dilapidated buildings, among others, we do not presume that urban communities are places of despair and disrepair. We recognize that far too often urban communities and in turn, schools that are located in urban communities, are impacted by a range of these issues; however, we view poverty, crime, and blight as symptomatic of larger sociopolitical issues and not reflective of the inherent nature of the communities and the people who live in them. Thus, we understand that popular perception of urban schools is that they are places that have significant populations of students of color who live in poverty. Indeed, for some, the term *urban* may in fact be a euphemism for African Americans. We do not hold the view that urban is code for African Americans, but recognize that far too many schools located in urban geographic spaces service students of color in general, especially those who live in poverty.

Research on School Reform

The educational reforms implemented in Philadelphia, Chicago, and New Orleans, though distinct, share elements that reflect part of the current larger apparatus of educational reform initiatives that reformers like Secretary of Education Arne Duncan, Michelle Rhee, Joel Klein, Wendy Kopp, Bill Gates, Eli Broad, the Walton Family, and a host of others, all endorse. The shrinkage of traditional school boards, the proliferation of charter schools, and the disempowerment of teachers' union are facets of a neoliberal approach to education that purports to remedy historical and current racial educational inequities; however, these "solutions" undermine those very efforts to the detriment of the constituencies the policies aims to assist. While the three cases covered in this chapter are shaped by local historical contexts, the form of the reforms in each city follows a similar pattern. Those similarities include the political nature of school reform, privatization of public education, and narrowly tailored accountability initiatives. Whereas we have separated these similarities into separate themes, they are not mutually exclusive and reflect the intersecting nature of racial and class disparities. Moreover, we argue that these broad themes are essential constitutive elements of neoliberal orientations to educational reform.

The Political Nature of School Reform

In each of the cases covered in this chapter, we discuss the political nature of education. In school reform initiatives, three dynamics play significant roles in how reformers implement the reforms: varied interests, coalitional work, and differential power relations. In addition to the reformers who operate at a national level with local representatives, a broadly based sector of actors that includes parents and teachers, to businesses and philanthropic groups, are also key to how the reforms are both implemented and received in their local contexts.

The Philadelphia and Chicago reforms became mired in legislative malaise and conflict where particular political positions and personalities forestalled reform efforts or challenged established reforms based on their ideological orientation or political persuasion (Lipman, 2011a; Useem, Christman, & Boyd, 2006). In the New Orleans case, the Louisiana legislature actively came together to alter legislation that changed the very nature of public schooling (Dixson, 2011). Moreover, the imprint of extra-educational actors in school reform initiatives is seen in each of the cases. It is not enough to say that extra-educational actors or interest groups are diverse. That is, mainstream media outlets and the general lay public often describe reform efforts as being successful because of the diversity of participants in public education reform, especially those who are not traditional educators, that is, philanthropists and corporations or grassroots organizations. It is the undue influence of the former that illustrates the exceptionally political nature of these reforms. It highlights the ways in which privilege, power, and prestige, or the lack thereof, becomes afforded to some. This is a political gesture as it not only deals with the distribution of resources and the ability to influence policy, but also suggests the ways in which educational reformers and their reforms, intentionally or unintentionally, render some voices mute (Dixson, 2011; Gold, Christman, & Herold, 2007; Lipman & Haines, 2007).

Interest groups like Teach for America, New Leaders for New Schools, the New Teacher Project, and others have entered the space of educational reform and positioned themselves as a balm for urban school issues especially as it relates to principals and teachers. This is especially true in New Orleans, although it is not unique to New Orleans. These reformers also bring actors from outside the local context to be the only "legitimate" sign and symbol of reform. Interest groups such as these offer support to the prevailing narrative that the public sphere is inherently "bad" and the private or nonpublic sphere is "good." The reworking of the public sphere and of the welfare state are indicative of the political nature of school reform as they operate in a larger matrix of neoliberal policies and practices.

Privatization

Each of the cases we analyze follows a similar pattern of wresting control of public schools from elected boards in favor of governance models that situate control in appointed boards and councils (Royal, 2012; Shipps, 1997; Wong, 2000). This is a significant change in schooling as it has the possibility to further remove the voices and perspectives of communities of color to the margin and to alter accountability mechanisms. The privatization or governance changes open spaces for "diverse providers" to enter these public spaces and allegedly "compete" with one another. The logic is to run schools and school systems more like private corporations (Lipman, 2011b) than democratic institutions. Schools that are deemed as failing are either closed or reconstituted as a charter school to be run by a variety of organizations—some for profit and others nonprofit.

In the case of the districts we analyzed, growth of these charter schools is often in response to a perceived disaster—either natural or otherwise.[1] Many charter schools have been wrought with controversy from nepotism, mismanagement, uncredentialed and inexperienced educators, and lack of oversight to the erasure of teacher's union protections such as collective bargaining for teachers and staff (Christianakis & Mora, 2011; United Teachers of New Orleans [UTNO]2007, 2010; Whitehorn, 2010). To be clear, charter schools are public schools. However, as illustrated by the work of many scholars, some charter schools are not divorced from the influence of neoliberal regimes that obfuscate social justice initiatives and undermine their democratic potential (Wells et al. 1999). Many charter schools, in their current iteration, rely so heavily on market discourse and systems of reasoning that democratic potential can be negligible (Buras, 2009; Dixson, 2011). Pernicious privatization schemes that reinforce a political economy of urban disinvestment and gentrification, to the chagrin of communities of color, venture philanthropy disconnected from community engagement and voice, as well as a particularized assault of teachers' unions without a critique of structural inequalities, situates charter schools as "enemies" of the communities in which they aim to "serve."

Accountability Initiatives

One element that holds and animates the impetus for privatization and the political nature of school reform are the high-stakes accountability measures. With the advent of high-stakes, and zero-sum standardized testing, particular possibilities for successful schools with thriving students and satisfied teachers becomes foreclosed. These accountability measures often highlight the achievement gap; yet they rarely address the education debt (Ladson-Billings, 2006). Because of student achievement issues illustrated in standardized testing via the high-stakes accountability policies, initiatives like statewide takeovers and the expansion of charter schools became the only tenable options for school improvement. Indeed, the shifting legislating of what constitutes success and failure made it possible to restructure New Orleans as an almost entirely charter district and fire its veteran teachers. These accountability practices lead to what appears, across the contexts we analyzed, as the abjection of students, teachers, and schools.

Modern Urban Schools

Almost immediately following the emergence of the Common School Movement, since the widespread inception of access to public education, there has been a persistent desire to reform education to train, assimilate, and socialize America's willing and unwilling immigrants so they may enter the workforce and contribute positively to American society (Cuban & Usdan, 2003; Ingersoll, 2003; Rury, 2005; Tyack, 1974; Tyack & Cuban, 1995). Derived from the Common School Movement, emerging during the industrial era of the 1800s, most school systems were created based on the notions of mass production and mass consumption, training the indigent, the immigrant, and African Americans in how to behave in American culture and society, preparing them for the roles society held for them (Rury, 2005; Tyack, 1974; Wilms, 2003). However, the structure of American public schools has not changed significantly over time because of systemic resistance and conflicts between various professional factions (Tyack & Cuban, 1995; Wilms, 2003). This is especially troubling for urban school systems in cities where concentrated poverty and racial/ethnic discord also influence how schooling is structured and implemented (Cuban & Usdan, 2003; Noguera, 2003). Rorrer, Skrla, and Scheurich (2008, p. 307) contended that school districts can be institutional actors if their goals are "to increase achievement and advance equity," but in spite of federal education legislation through the Elementary and Secondary Education Act (ESEA) in the 1960s, the repeal of federal money for local education in the 1980s, the *A Nation at Risk* and *A Nation Prepared* reports, and the No Child Left Behind Act (NCLB) of the new millennium, urban schools have persisted to be severely underfunded, understaffed, and struggling with student achievement stratified by race (Barton, 2004; Hilliard, 2003). They are teeming with students who often deal with these conditions at home and at school (Anyon, 2005; Kozol, 1991; Nieto, 2003; Noguera, 2003).

Low faith in public schools has led to disinvestment in public schooling; urban school districts often contain a stratified educational system with special-admission magnet schools, charter schools, and neighborhood, comprehensive schools (Gamoran, 1996; Saporito, 2003; Schneider

& Buckley, 2003; Tatum, 2007). Hilliard has written about the extreme pessimism with which some regard Black students in impoverished schools, and Rury wrote that most schools in urban districts are seen as the only option of those who cannot afford to send their children elsewhere (Hilliard, 2003; Rury, 2005). Because of these origins and current conditions, some continue to argue that public schooling was never intended to provide a transition for the populations they served beyond their social standing—that urban schools, in particular, were created for social reproduction of the White, wealthy power structure and, therefore, are not intended to be used for African Americans to transcend their social positions (e.g., Anderson, 1988; Fine, 1991; Watkins, 2001).

In addition to the structure of urban systems, other elements remain a challenge. Presently, many urban school districts are also becoming rapidly resegregated, in spite of desegregation attempts and lawsuits in the decades following *Brown* (Frankenberg & Lee, 2002; Orfield & Lee, 2007). Further, B.A. Jones (2005, p. 7) discussed that

> urban school systems have suffered from high teacher and administrator turnover; high student mobility; dilapidated building infrastructures; and woefully inadequate human, fiscal, and material resources to meet all of the needs of the diverse student populations. Additionally, urban school districts . . . are common targets of curriculum and governance experimentation.

Urban schools are notoriously difficult for students and their faculties; they are severely underfunded, understaffed, and struggling (Anyon, 2005; Kozol, 1991). Despite recent changes in student, educator, and school accountability, issues in teacher recruitment and retention remain for large urban school districts (Argue, Honeyman, & Shlay, 2006; Mac Iver & Vaughn, 2007; Neild, Useem, & Farley, 2005; Neild, Useem, Travers, & Lesnick, 2003; Useem, Offenberg, & Farley, 2007). Though district officials often know the types of efforts they believe would remedy these issues, because of chronic underfunding and other budgetary issues, such programs are often cut (Useem et al., 2007). Perhaps it is because of these conditions that Cuban and Usdan (2003) suggested that there is something uniquely distinct about being an urban educator that is different from working in suburban or rural schools. Working in urban schools is not for everyone. Indeed, according to Weiner (1999), students in urban schools may be so academically challenged that they need much more time and support than some teachers are willing to give since

> city teachers face the highest concentrations of students who desperately need education for economic mobility, but kids and teachers are sabotaged by the way urban schools are organized, funded, and run. The most subversive condition is constant pressure to deal with kids in a standardized, impersonal fashion. (p. 21)

Numerous works elucidate the need for urban educators to exude and operate from an "above and beyond/whatever it takes" ethos in order to be successful with their students (Du Four, 2004; Du Four, Eaker, & Karhanek, 2004; Nieto, 2003; Noguera, 2003; Matthews, 2009).

Modern Urban Education Reform

For almost as long as public schooling has existed in this nation, efforts to reform it, specifically in urban areas, have persisted (Cuban & Usdan, 2003; Tyack & Cuban, 1995). When upwardly mobile Americans flocked to the suburbs from the cities to escape the poverty and color within them after World War II, policy makers became concerned, again, for the education of the immigrants, racial minorities, and socioeconomically deficient city students left behind, which led to the creation of ESEA in 1965 as an element of the War on Poverty (Cuban & Usdan, 2003; Kantor, 1991). This was the first modern federal reform aimed at correcting educational disparities, though Rorrer et al. (2008) maintain, "educational institutions have successfully ensured inequity" (p. 328). From that legislation through the next 40 years, reforms replete with the rhetoric of improving the education available to Americans in public schools have abounded. For more than 40 years, the federal government, states, and local school districts have debated the best ways to improve what students learn and how they achieve (e.g., Ball, 2002; Gamoran, 1996; Kantor, 1991; Saporito, 2003; Schneider & Buckley, 2003). Hess (1998) contends that there has been a "policy churn" throughout this period regarding urban schools; politicians have cranked out education reforms to advance their political careers or based on the political climate, without ever having the intention of truly improving students' achievement, and ultimately, never doing so. Huge sums of money have been diverted toward school districts for this effort, with little change and even less success, having occurred in classrooms (Ball, 2002; Rorrer et al., 2008; Wellisch, MacQueen, Carriere, & Duck, 1978). Most school district reforms are symbolic political moves and have little impact on classrooms; they do not consult or invest the educators who actually implement the reforms (Anyon, 2005; Hess, 1998; Ingersoll, 2003; Wilms, 2003). Simultaneously, the public remains impatient and yearns to see immediate reform results, often not giving enough time to actually see change and improvement come to fruition (Boyd & Christman, 2003; Hess, 1998). Reform efforts have served to legitimize and/or condemn how urban school districts perform (Hess, 1998).

With the emergence of ESEA, the federal government demonstrated that it sought to attack poverty by increasing the funding provided to school districts to improve what students learn and how they achieve (Kantor, 1991; Kantor & Lowe, 1995). The best-known and notable element of ESEA legislation is likely Title I, which aimed to give educational aid to the children of impoverished families (Kantor & Lowe, 1995). Despite the flow of funds from the federal government to local school districts, these new federal policies were seen as interfering with local interests; the government's policies had to maintain balance between the concerns of opposing education and governance stakeholders (Kantor, 1991; Kantor & Lowe, 1995). Implementation of reform matters; therefore, governance and leadership are important, if not essential, elements in how urban schools operate, not just in the distribution of the federal monies and programs but also regarding how these programs are staffed and facilitated (Cuban & Usdan, 2003; Tyack, 1974; Tyack & Cuban, 1995; Wilms, 2003). In spite of the support they received from the federal government, some urban districts with high levels of poverty struggled to fully implement these reforms with fidelity (Rorrer et al., 2008).

Critics of the War on Poverty and the programs initiated through ESEA did not believe it had the positive impact they expected. Following suit, during the early 1980s, *A Nation at Risk* introduced the omnipresence of grossly underperforming public school students and teachers, substituting public school systems and their educators for poverty as the new national concern of political pundits, education policy makers, school stakeholders, and opinionated taxpayers alike (Cuban & Usdan, 2003). Kantor and Lowe (2004) have argued that *A Nation at Risk* decried a euphoric recall of what schooling once was but never actually existed; and Enderlin-Lampe (2002) has demonstrated that the blame-ridden, "coercive" reform initiatives of the 1980s, to which *A Nation at Risk* gave way, did not change how schools worked or how people perceived the schools. When district reform moved to decentralization, there was often little to no preparation for moving all levels of districts into this realm of operation (Enderlin-Lampe, 2002).

As education reform has moved toward greater accountability, the demand for increased student achievement, sound fiscal management, and excellent instruction, the NCLB Act of 2001 was created to ensure state standards, unified curricula, and the measurement of student learning by state-sanctioned, multiple-choice exams in an effort to ameliorate the underperformance of Black, Latino, and low-income students so that there is no difference between how these students achieve and how White, middle-class students achieve (Cuban & Usdan, 2003). NCLB aims to be "performance driven, test driven, measurable, and statistical" in order to evaluate how students, teachers, and schools perform and to make them do better (Lee, 2008). It assumes that if these educators are more invested in the outcomes produced by students, greater investment of educators will yield better instruction, more learning, and higher student test scores. This assumption lends itself to a leadership structure in schools whereby school administrators are more managers than educators (Wilms, 2003). This reform policy includes a system of punishments for chronic underperformance, such as publishing school performance rates, restructuring school staffs, removing school leadership, and the reallocation and/or withholding of federal funds, among other components (Vergari, 2007). Lipman (2004) has referred to this system of monitoring students' and schools' academic performances on these tests as spectacle and surveillance. Nieto (2003) argued that these reforms have become "mean-spirited and antagonistic" (p. 5). Many urban districts lament the continued underfunding of NCLB and even with these efforts at improving instruction for students, Ramanathan (2008) wrote, "there is little real indication that the law has made progress correcting the performance gap" (p. 306). Wong and Shen (2003) take issue with "underachieving urban school districts that have failed to improve, even after reform policies have been implemented" (p. 6). To some, Philadelphia could be considered one such district.

The School District of Philadelphia

Located in a "border state" and second-oldest in the nation, the School District of Philadelphia (SDP) was rife with endemic racism, almost since its inception in 1818, in its semisegregated schooling for Black students and its treatment of Black educators, so much so, that Franklin wrote that "in terms of its racial practices . . . Philadelphia should be considered a 'southern city' " (Foster, 1990; Franklin, 1979, p. 12). Separate schools for Black educators combined with hesitation to hire and promote them, low expectations and graduation rates for Black students, and a constantly weakening curriculum foretells the problematic way in which the Black citizens were viewed and the "detrimental policy practices" within SDP (Jones, 2005, p. 6). Despite modest improvements over time, school segregation in Philadelphia increased between 1954 and 1964, so much so, that in 1966, the Philadelphia branch of the NAACP petitioned the federal government not to fund the School District of Philadelphia until it integrated completely (Phillips, 2005). Employing the logic of *Brown,* the NAACP argued that Black students could not be well educated in single-race schools (Etheridge, 1979; Ladson-Billings, 2004; Phillips, 2005). Though busing students from overcrowded segregated schools was a solution to these issues, the mayor and city council president demanded an end to busing in 1964. A year later, the primary responsibility for fiscal management of the District and of the school board was given to the Philadelphia City Council (Cuban & Usdan, 2003; Phillips, 2005). Nationwide, mayors, school boards, and district leadership faced intense "political pressure to mediate interest-group competition since the 1960s," to manage ongoing crises (Wong & Shen, 2003, p. 5). Philly's first attempt at school reform revealed that "school policy is not apolitical, and thus any attempt at significant reform will have real winners and losers" (Birger, 1996, p. 169). In Philadelphia, the educational politics are racial, ethnic, and economic (Freire, 1970/2000; Nieto, 2003). Considering Philadelphia's racialized public education history, how reform gets enacted in this context matters.

Rorrer et al. (2008) advocated conducting research on districts that would examine the complexity and interrelatedness of districts' various components over time to capture the social, political, and economic contexts of districts. An examination of these elements in Philadelphia reveals its deep political entrenchment. Its politics are complicated by issues of race and insider-outsider tensions and are compounded by state politics and the national political landscape, to name a few. The politics within SDP were also influenced by the interpretation of the contemporary political narrative by the superintendent and his or her epistemological beliefs and ontological bent within that narrative. Politics and issues of power continually inhibit education reform within SDP. No educator is immune to the politics that plague and thwart attempts at reform in SDP. The politics are too entrenched. Some superintendents opt out of District leadership because they no longer want to deal with the politics (e.g., Constance Clayton: 1982–1993). Others are cajoled into departure because of political pressure (e.g., Mark Shedd: 1967–1971; Matthew Costanzo: 1972–1975; Michael Marcase: 1975–1982; and Arlene Ackerman: 2008–2011). Others know that they are leading an already anchored ship and they do their best to move the ship while they are there, knowing they will not stay and the ship will not likely move, despite their best efforts (e.g., David Hornbeck: 1994–2000 and Paul Vallas: 2002–2007). With them go the reforms they brought, creating a constant sense of doing and undoing in the District (Royal, 2012).

As of September 2011, SDP had approximately 146,000 students in 249 schools. The student population was 56% African American, 18% Hispanic/Latino, 14% White, 7% Asian/Pacific Islander, and 4% "Other"; 14% of the students are categorized as having learning disabilities; 80% of the students are considered economically disadvantaged (www.philasd.org).

School Reform in Philadelphia

Any attempt at school reform for Philadelphia's public schools has been thwarted and/or mired by political issues. By 1966, SDP had suffered 40 years of financial neglect and had been chronically underfunded (Birger, 1996; Franklin, 1979; Shedd Administration, 1971). The next year, the modern school reform movement for public schools began with Mark Shedd's arrival as the district's new superintendent. This effort at reform was short-lived, as Shedd's stay at the helm (1967–1971) was cut short due to lack of agreement on his reform methods, compounded by his political differences with the police chief-turned-mayor, Frank Rizzo (Birger, 1996; Countryman, 2006; PFT Teachers' Unit, 1971; Editorials & Comment: Children's Education, 1971; Editorials & Comment: Dr. Mark Shedd, 1971; Editorials & Comment: Parents and City Leaders, 1971; Royal, 2012). School reform in Philadelphia remained stalled during and shortly beyond Rizzo's tenure as mayor through the superintendencies of Matthew Costanzo (1972–1975) and Michael Marcase (1975–1982) (Royal, 2012). Education reform returned to SDP with the selection of Constance Clayton (1982–1993) as its superintendent. She was a district insider who had the support of educators, the Philadelphia Federation of Teachers (PFT), and Black political leaders. In her 11-year tenure, she standardized the curriculum, created a citywide testing program, managed a consistently balanced budget, secured an improved bond rating, and worked well with the PFT. She also brought political reform to SDP. In a system where political favors had been, historically, bought and sold and superintendents were beholden to various political entities, Clayton demanded the demonstration of merit in professional appointments. Still not immune to inter- and intraracial politics, she unexpectedly retired from her post in the summer of 1993.

David Hornbeck (1994–2000) succeeded Clayton, determined to reform SDP's culture and academic outcomes. Coming to Philadelphia by way of state-level education posts in Kentucky and Maryland, he advocated an accountability system tied to the pay of all SDP educators, including his own (Royal, 2012). His major reform plan was called "Children Achieving," which emphasized that all students can achieve at high levels (Boyd & Christman, 2003 Hornbeck, 1994; Hornbeck & Conner, 2009). He decentralized governance and management, shifting SDP's eight local districts to 22 clusters. The result was a lack of communication between SDP's Central Office and the clusters, and the administrators' union did not support the shift to clusters, nor did it support other important portions of "Children Achieving." This reform plan would cost more than $1 billion fully funded, and that full funding would only come at the behest of the state, which never came, perhaps due to Hornbeck's accusing the state of being racist in its funding process.[2] Throughout constant battles between Hornbeck and the state, calls came for Pennsylvania to assume control of Philadelphia's public schools. In 1998, Hornbeck threatened to close SDP before the school year ended if it did not get the money he sought from the state. Gov. Ridge retorted by pushing Act 46, which allowed for a state takeover of any district that did not complete at least 180 days of school. This fighting lasted two more years until Hornbeck resigned in summer 2000 (A Fine Legacy, 2000; Morgan, 2000; Useem, Christman, & Boyd, 2006). Paul Vallas (2002–2007) and Arlene Ackerman (2008–2011) brought their own versions of reform to SDP, as well, some of which remains, some of which has been undone due to the shifting prerogative of leadership and/or financial circumstances. The Philadelphia School Reform Commission next selected William Hite to be SDP's new superintendent. He began on October 1, 2012, intending to reform a desperate and distressed SDP.

From School Board to School Reform Commission

The 1990s talk of the state takeover of SDP resurrected chatter that started in 1981. At that time, incoming Mayor Green had campaigned on the promise to remove his predecessor's appointee from SDP's helm. However, when he realized the Rizzo-appointed BOE would not remove Marcase, Green began supporting state legislation to dissolve SDP's BOE. Some advocated for an elected school board so that all aspects of the city would be better represented. According to *The Philadelphia Tribune,*

> The mayor appointed Boards have gotten us in this mess. For the present, we can't see any light at the end of the tunnel. The community cannot afford to remain quiet any longer. The political cronies who run the schools will remain ever so present unless we, the people, force them out and revive the entire system if it isn't already too late. (Our Opinion, 1981)

Almost 20 years later, Hornbeck's battle with the state for funding resurrected the idea of state takeover of Philadelphia's schools.

In 2001, the state takeover of public schools made Philadelphia the first school district of its size to come under state control while simultaneously privatizing the management of many of its chronically underperforming schools (Useem et al., 2006; Royal, 2012). School takeover in Philadelphia was a political action, not one intended to save the schools from something other than governance with which some did not agree (State Might, 1998). The state's takeover of Philadelphia's public schools was about financial management and power, a demonstration of who was in charge. Under the previous configuration, the BOE had nine members who were appointed by the mayor and served six-year terms. The new School Reform Commission (SRC) would replace the long-standing Philadelphia School Board as the schools' governing body and would include five members. The legislation calls for the governor to appoint four members to the commission, but Gov. Schweiker appointed three and allowed Mayor Street two appointees to the first SRC (Boyd & Christman, 2003;

News In Brief, 2008; Toomer, 2006, July 14). The SRC officially replaced the School Board as of December 2001 (Brooks, 2002; Goss, 2001). With them, they brought a new structure that eliminated the superintendency, dividing the post among a Chief Executive Officer, a Chief Academic Officer, a Chief Financial Officer, and a Chief Operating Officer. School systems in major urban centers such as New York, Los Angeles, and Chicago were already using this model of governance. In January 2012, reeling from the extensive budget shortfall and dramatic exit of Arlene Ackerman from leading the district, the SRC created a position called the "Chief Recovery Officer," to lead the district and simultaneously serve as its Chief Financial Officer.

The Diverse Provider Model

A major reform the new SRC initiated for Philadelphia was the diverse provider model of schools. Govs. Ridge and Schweiker advocated market-based reforms for Philadelphia; the diverse provider model implemented by the SRC represented their preference. After Hornbeck left, Gov. Ridge paid Edison Schools Incorporated $2.7 million to conduct a three-month study of the condition of SDP. Edison proposed that it be responsible for the central office governance of SDP and that it take over 60 to 100 SDP schools (Useem, 2005). Informed by its study, the SRC identified 86 SDP schools as "low-performing" to get interventions from a "diverse provider model." While the District maintained control of 45 of those schools, the other 41 were managed by seven education management organizations at that time: Edison, Victory, Chancellor-Beacon (all from outside of Philadelphia and for-profit organizations); Foundations and Universal (both local and nonprofit organizations); and University of Pennsylvania and Temple University (Useem, 2005; Useem et al., 2006). Many of those schools have since returned to District control and/or have been converted into charter schools.

Charter school legislation had passed in the state legislature in June 1997 despite opposition from most Philadelphia Democratic lawmakers (Baer, 1997, June 12). That fall, the first four charter schools opened in Philadelphia, and by May 2000, Philadelphia had more than half of the state's charter schools with 14,000 students enrolled in them (Editorial: Charter Schools, 2000). By the spring of 2008, 65% of the state's charter schools were located in Philadelphia and its surrounding areas (Woodall, 2008). As of September 2011, there were 80 charter schools in Philadelphia educating 46,000 students (www.philasd.org).

Presently, more than a third of Philadelphia's charter schools are run by five education management organizations: Mastery Schools (11 schools), Universal Companies (6 schools), KIPP Philadelphia (4 schools), Aspira (4 schools), and Scholar Academies (3 schools). Mastery began in Philadelphia in 2001 with one location, adding one additional location in 2005, 2006, and 2007, but its growth heightened in 2010 as a result of Ackerman's Renaissance Schools Initiative, a reform plan in which existing schools would be converted to charters with the goal of improving academic outcomes.

Despite their rapid growth and expansion, charter schools in Philadelphia have not been without problems. In addition to one doubling as a nightclub that served alcohol, there have been accusations and federal investigations of charter schools across the city for fiscal mismanagement and malfeasance, nepotism in the form of contracts given and income and perks received, leadership with untenable qualifications (i.e., no college degree), fraud, and other ethical violations. Indeed to some, charter schools have become the new location for distribution and receipt of political favors and for those looking to line their pockets with easy money due to "little scrutiny," "scant oversight," and spotty retribution for noncompliance to state expectations (New Charter School Scandal, 2010; Woodall, 2008). In 1994 before charter schools existed in

Pennsylvania, *The Philadelphia Tribune* described student achievement as abysmally low, and it lamented that too many adults surrounding the system were looking for ways to milk SDP for its spoils instead of focusing on children and student achievement. It added that, "Aggravating low levels of achievement are adults inside and outside the system whose primary concern is not educating children but securing financial spoils from the School District in the form of fat salaries and contracts" (Editorial: Let's See, 1994). Charter schools and the diverse provider model were supposed to change that situation. In 2004, SDP was hailed by Department of Education Secretary Rod Paige for successfully blurring "the line between public and private" in its diverse provider model of schools, but Gold et al. (2007) argued diverse providers have become the very bureaucracy they were intended to disrupt. Furthermore, a 2011 Stanford University study demonstrated that, on average, the academic gains students made in Pennsylvania charter schools were less than those made in traditional public schools between 2007 and 2010 (Charter School Performance, 2011).

Despite these concerns, in April 2012, SDP's Chief Recovery Officer Thomas Knudsen proposed a plan created by the Boston Consulting Group that would close 60 SDP schools between 2013 and 2017 and would shift 40% of the district's students to charter schools. This was seen as a money-saving effort, not one intended to improve educational outcomes for Philadelphia's students. Since then, there have been protests and complaints of this plan with no word yet on how this situation will be resolved.

Outside Influence

There is an insider-outsider tension that exists in Philadelphia and SDP at all levels of engagement. The insider-outsider tension that was introduced during Shedd's administration became more apparent throughout the Hornbeck and Vallas administrations and Ackerman to a lesser extent. This tension refers to the relationship between people who are native to or familiar with an entity and those who are not. An insider is one who is from Philadelphia, was educated in its public schools, and/or has worked within SDP. An outsider is someone who may be from Philadelphia but was not educated in its public schools, may never have worked in SDP, or may not have ever lived in Philadelphia. Outsiders are perceived as not understanding the local context, whether that context is geographical or racial (Sutton, 1994). Shedd was an outsider. Costanzo, Marcase, and Clayton were all District insiders who had "risen through the ranks." Clayton was also an outsider, as she was the first Black person to lead the District that had only been led by White men (Royal, 2012). Since her 11-year tenure ended in 1993, there has not been another District insider to lead its schools. Hornbeck, Vallas, and Ackerman were all transplanted to Philadelphia from other locations. Of those three, only Hornbeck had previous experience with Philadelphia and Pennsylvania before assuming the leadership post there.

Importing outsiders to lead and impact SDP has been deliberate. After Clayton's retirement, choosing Hornbeck was not just about bringing an outsider to Philadelphia and to SDP, but it was choosing someone outside of education in the traditional sense. Hornbeck was an organizer, an advocate, and an education administrator at the state level. Whereas his bully pulpit approach outshined his value as an outsider, state and local business leaders sought another outsider with keen political skills to fill SDP's top spot. Former head of Chicago's public schools, Paul Vallas, was appointed Chief Executive Officer of SDP in 2002. Some Philadelphians credit Vallas with helping to heal political rifts between the city school system and the state left from years of dissonance, which were worsened during the Hornbeck era (Royal, 2012; Useem et al., 2006). Vallas was skillful in making powerful friends in high places. He made sure he got along with key people in the state legislature, and he built relationships with people on City Council (Royal, 2012).[3] However, his inability to get in front of the budget crisis in 2006—when it was found to be $21 million, then $70 million, then $73 million in arrears—led to his exit from SDP in 2007. Ackerman arrived to lead SDP after having run school systems in Washington, DC, and San Francisco. A career educator and Black woman, she was perceived as a racial and professional insider; geographically, she was an outsider. She quickly made people uncomfortable by eliminating the academic coach position from SDP, which had been filled with scores of veteran Philly educators. Her leadership style was viewed as steamroller-like, imposing reforms on educators instead of working with them (Graham & Woodall, 2010). In 2009, she used federal stimulus funds to support SDP's struggling budget, but when those funds were no longer available in 2011, and there was a budget gap speculation of up to $600 million, 2,700 SDP employees were laid off, many of them teachers. Her approach to school reform and fiscal management was severely damaged when Republican Gov. Corbett succeeded former Philly mayor-turned-governor Rendell and made enormous cuts to public education budgets. By September 2011, Ackerman's contract was bought out for almost $1 million, and she left her post (Owens, 2011). The buyout of her contract raised many concerns, not just because of how much it was while educators lost their jobs, but initially, there was the belief that anonymous private sources would contribute just over $400,000 to Ackerman's buyout. These donors had money to buy out her contract but not to save the jobs of SDP teachers.

One benefit of outsiders may have been the ability to see what District insiders could not see. Perhaps it was because of this benefit, that Hornbeck, Vallas, and Ackerman chose to hire many outsiders to assist them in leading the District (Royal, 2012). However, this choice to value outsiders over District insiders called into question the merit and value of the educators who were already in Philadelphia. This then exacerbated the insider-outsider tension, as veteran SDP educators felt disrespected by the unspoken reality of lack of promotions for themselves.

This insider-outsider tension existed at other levels within SDP. Both Rotan Lee (Board of Education Chair, 1992–1994) and James Nevels (School Reform Commission Chair, 2001–2007) were Black men and therefore, racial insiders in SDP. However, they were both also outsiders: Lee was educated in Bryn Mawr (a wealthy suburb outside Philadelphia), and Nevels was educated in Indiana and was also a political outsider as a Republican. Both Lee and Nevels demonstrated a lack of reverence for what already existed in Philadelphia; Lee, through the contentious relationship he developed with Clayton; Nevels, through his insistence that sweeping, symbolic changes must be made to the school system (such as selling the historic District headquarters building) (Goss, 2001; Leary, 1994).

As previously mentioned, there is a long-standing history of contention between Philadelphia and state lawmakers in Harrisburg. The Philadelphia *Citypaper* attributes the city-state relationship and its subsequent handling of SDP to "decades of underfunding and mismanagement at the hands of shortsighted Philadelphians and mean-spirited politicians in Harrisburg" (Denvir, 2012).

Recently, more district outsiders have taken even greater interest in education in Philadelphia. The Philadelphia School Partnership (PSP) started in 2010 "to accelerate the pace of education reform in Philadelphia by increasing the number of great school options available to children in our city," as per its website. PSP supports conversions from traditional public schools to charters, as well as parochial schools. It has not, as of yet, given money to SDP, though its website states "PSP invests in all types of schools—public, public charter, and private." Its Board of Directors and leadership team comprises mostly businessmen and nonprofiteers with limited experience working with SDP (http://www.philaschoolpartnership.org/). The PSP has committed itself to raising $100 million to support schools in Philadelphia. As of late August 2012, it had $52 million committed from foundations, businesses, and high net worth individuals. The corporations with the most charter schools in Philadelphia—Mastery, Universal, and Aspira—have all received grants from PSP to assist with their conversion of traditional public schools into charters. PSP has also given grants to stand-alone charter schools and to Catholic schools in the area (Mezzacappa, 2012).

Concern continues to mount over the PSP, its purse strings, and the Boston Consulting Group, the organization responsible for urging that 60 SDP schools be closed by 2017. One retired SDP administrator with 43 years of education leadership in Philly and the surrounding area has referred to this current moment in SDP as the most turbulent in its recent history. Concerned about the current state of SDP and Philadelphia's charter schools, he posed these questions in a blog post for *The Philadelphia Public School Notebook:*

> The large and looming question behind the drive for charters in Philadelphia and nationally is, "Who will profit from this shift in the provision of education in inner cities?" Why is it that Gates/Microsoft and Walton/Walmart are proponents of charters, portfolio management, and market-based approaches? Why is it that rich White folks are leading the conversation about what poor Black and Latino kids need? Why is so much campaign money being used to support charter and voucher proponents? Where is the evidence that charter schools do a better job than traditional public schools? And what does Boston Consulting Group know about urban schooling that School District teachers and principals don't? (Lytle, 2012)

SDP and the Philadelphia Federation of Teachers

SDP and the Philadelphia Federation of Teachers (PFT) have had a complicated but improved relationship over time. Tense negotiations, financial constraints, and constant budget shortfalls led to threats of strikes and at least six strikes in the 10-year period that included the Shedd, Costanzo, and Marcase administrations. Some were short while others lasted four weeks to eight weeks. There was one after which union leaders were arrested and jailed for not directing their members to return to work and another in 1981 when school did not begin until November. With Clayton at SDP's helm, though there were disputes and threats of strikes, no strikes occurred.[4] *The Philadelphia Tribune* credited her with shifting the tone of the 1985 contract negotiations. In years previous, contract sticking points were always economic, not instructional or academic. Clayton maintained her stance that SDP was for children, and though she did not get the educational reforms she sought, an agreement was reached and the school year started on time (Cornish, 1985, August 20, August 27; St. Hill & Wilson, 1985; Wilson, 1985). From her leadership through that of Hornbeck, Vallas, and Ackerman, there have been no teacher strikes in Philadelphia, though the relationship between the PFT and SDP has been tense at times. Whereas Clayton and Vallas worked well with the unions, Hornbeck and Ackerman did not (Royal, 2012).

With the looming $600 million projected budget deficit of 2011, the SRC expected $75 million in give backs from its labor unions, including the PFT. But the relationship between the PFT and Ackerman became irreparably damaged because of how she handled the layoffs, her approach to instructional reform, and how she disciplined a teacher. Thus, Jerry Jordan, head of the PFT, would not discuss concessions with Ackerman as superintendent and he began to urge her dismissal, which soon followed (Graham, 2011; MacDonald & McDonald, 2011).

Further complicating the significance of the PFT, as the number of charter schools continually increase in Philadelphia, there is the concern that most charter school teachers are nonunionized, at-will employees who work extended hours without the benefits and protections of collective bargaining and advocacy. As teachers have been laid off and charters teach more students and employ more teachers, the PFT's membership has declined. As of summer 2010, teachers at three Philadelphia charter schools had opted to unionize (Whitehorn, 2010). Unionizing charter school-teachers face challenges, such as high turnover yearly and retribution from school administration (Whitehorn, 2010).

Philadelphia is an interesting case study in large part because of its history as the "canary" (Guinier & Torres, 2003) of the modern era of school reform that has opted to disenfranchise communities by shrinking its locally elected school board, closing schools it deems as failing, and expanding school choice options. Chicago, historically a "leader" in urban school reform, has also been a site for the recent neoliberal education reform policies of closing schools, expanding choice through charter schools, and wresting control of public schools from elected school boards.

Chicago School Re-Forms

The notion of reform often connotes a change of some type of deviant or self-destructive behavior, policy, or institution toward a more idealized and hoped-for future. The prefix *re,* however, etymologically, also means a returning to a previous state or configuration. *Form,* on the other hand, suggests the structure, shape, arrangement, or mold of something. So, when taken together both *re* and *form* may invoke a return to a previous arrangement. Therefore, when thinking about "reform," one must continually question, with the lenses of equity and justice, the direction of and interests in said reform effort. The field of education has undergone a dizzying series of reforms, some of which have had positive impacts, while others have had deleterious impacts, but all have been contested (see Darling-Hammond, 1997; Kliebard, 2004; Tyack & Cuban, 1995; Watkins, 2001). Educational reforms in Chicago are no exception. Education reform in Chicago, not unlike those in most cities, cannot be sufficiently understood or accurately illustrated without taking into account the totality of circumstances that produce and inform iterations of restructuring at particular historical junctures. This section charts the three major reform efforts that have evolved over the past quarter of a century in Chicago—the 1988 Chicago School Reform Act, the 1995 Chicago School Reform Act, and the 2004 Renaissance 2010 reform. These reforms efforts can be categorized as the *tripartite reforms,* for the purposes of this section.

Historical Antecedents to the Tripartite Reforms

Before moving to the somewhat more recent educational reform efforts that have occurred over the past quarter of a century in Chicago, an articulation of that which came before may have some utility. This will be kept brief, given the space limitations of this chapter.[5]

Chicago schools have often served as testing grounds of educational reform since the early 20th century with individuals such as John Dewey, Ella Flag Young, and Francis Parker creating space for progressive education approaches (Herrick, 1971). Reform efforts aligned with progressive methods of education often sought to create innovative curricula and attempted to forge stronger connective programs between communities and schools (Herrick, 1971). However, as Michael Homel (1976) points out during the period of 1910–1940, for African Americans in Chicago, efforts of progressive education seemed rather elusive and both educational as well as housing patterns overlapped and coagulated to constrain African Americans. While there were some White supporters, overall, the struggle for quality education remained an arduous, politically intricate task (Homel, 1976). During this period there remained a steadfast effort against a recalcitrant educational system informed by political machines, economic elites, and overarching racial stratification (Homel, 1976; Shipps, 2006). African Americans mobilized and strategically contended for improved classroom accommodations, integration, and representation on the city's Board of Education—to little avail (Homel, 1976).

The struggle for quality education persisted in spite of the setbacks experienced by African Americans. The Civil Rights and Black Power Movements helped in providing the ideological invigoration and the mobilizing impetus for a large-scale social movement that would propel change in Chicago schools and impact future policy directions (Danns, 2002). African American parents and students were fed up with the subpar, overcrowded facilities, curricular erasure, and segregated schools (Lipman, 2004). Danns (2002) noted that according to a Chicago activist, "the city benefited from the maintenance of segregation because businessmen warned Mayor Richard M. Daley that desegregation would increase white flight and would decrease the middle class buying power. Therefore, in an effort to maintain the city's economy, all students suffered" (pp. 636–637). This segregation was particularly egregious, as then Superintendent of Schools, Benjamin Willis, set up trailers for African American students in overcrowded schools, while there was ample space in White neighborhoods (Lipman, 2004; Shipps, 2006). This continued segregation and cavalier disregard for the desires of African American students and parents led to a student boycott of their schools in which nearly 225,000 African American students and 20,000 parents protested and called for Willis's resignation (Lipman, 2004). Student demands in the late 1960s, buoyed by boycotts, protests, and other mechanisms such as conferences and sit-ins, called for more robust reform efforts that entailed the inclusion of African American history in the curriculum, community control of schools, more African American administrators and teachers, increased funding, and restructuring of schools (Danns, 2002; Lipman, 2004). Following the African American movement in education, increased articulation of inequities within Chicago Public Schools (CPS) came to the fore. Issues such as high Latino/a dropout rates as well as inadequate teacher pay, which culminated in teacher strikes, helped inform the 1988 reform effort.

1988 Chicago School Reform

In 1987 former Secretary of Education William Bennett proclaimed that Chicago had the worst school system in the nation. His statement came after decades of racialized urban disinvestment, White flight, housing segregation to say nothing of inequitable school resources, tracking, and culturally irrelevant curriculum and teaching. Nevertheless, later that year, the public shaming of Chicago Public Schools and a group of devoted citizens prompted the Illinois legislature to pass a reform bill that significantly altered the terrain of education in Chicago (Hess, 1991; Wong, 1992). The 1988 Chicago School Reform Act seemed to usher in many of the hopes from years past regarding community control of schools.

One of the key provisions of the act was the establishment of local school councils (LSCs). These local school councils were a critical shift away from central office authority to a decentralized governance structure (Shipps, Kahne, & Smiley, 1999). This reform reconstituted power in the hands of democratically elected, community-accountable groups. The LSCs, which comprised parents, community members, and educators (and a student at the high school level), had the ability to "hire and fire principals, approve annual school improvement plans, and allocate the school's discretionary budget (Federal Title I and State Chapter 1 funds)" as well as set curricular imperatives (Lipman, 2004, p. 35; Wong, 2000). This is significant because LSCs opened critical space for civic participation and changed institutional cultures at some schools. For instance, Wong (2000) highlights the demographic shift in principals between 1989 and 1994. According to Wong, the number of African American principals increased from 37% to 50% and there was an increase from 7% to 11% of Latino principals, while White principals declined from 56% to 39% (Wong, 2000).

In many ways, this reform is resultant of the converging of interests of the African American community's mobilization and Chicago's business elite (Bell, 1980; Chambers, 2002/2003). African American communities were not the only groups to benefit from the 1998 reform. Authority was vested in the mayor to appoint an Interim School Board, and the School Finance Authority, who oversaw CPS finances, was awarded greater oversight of both the central office and the Board (Lipman, 2004). The Interim School Board as well as the School Finance Authority were significantly connected to or made up of major Chicago business leaders (Lipman, 2004). The emphasis on grassroots governance by way of decentralization connected well with the rising efforts of businesses to recreate the city and privatize various sectors, due to their alleged inefficiency. This convergence allowed, for a short time, the engaging of communities of color in being active agents in their schools. Communities felt their LSCs genuinely had an interest and stake in improving the educational outcomes of the students, providing flexibility during meetings to truly hear the concerns of parents (Chambers, 2002/2003). However, what became more apparent were the glaring differences among schools and LSCs (Rubenstein, 1998). While parents and community members had access to the resources that were allotted to them, there seemed just to be a shifting of the actors and not the terrain of reform. That is to say, as Lipman (2004) highlights, "no additional resources were provided, despite differential existing resources within school communities, including ability to obtain grants, expertise in managing budgets, and levels of community organization" (p. 35). With mixed results in terms of improvement, Mayor Daley feeling constrained, the school board still suffering from a deficit of over $100 million, and growing loss of "public" confidence in the LSCs, the Illinois legislature in July 1995 passed the Chicago School Reform Amendatory Act (Wong, 2000).

1995 Chicago School Reform

The 1995 reform represented a striking departure from the 1988 reform, which aimed to increase community and parental participation in schools. The new reform, while not eliminating the LSCs, significantly aided in diminishing their importance. Control was reconfigured, centralizing it within the mayor's office. As Chambers (2002/2003) highlighted, the business community was able to "make the case that the fiscal situation was so bad that only strong and *centralized* management could correct the dilemma of the schools and possibly reduce further white flight from the city" (p. 665). The mayor now had unparalleled influence and control over the public schools. The new reform afforded the mayor power to select the Chief Executive Officer (CEO) and the Board of Trustees to run public schools (Lipman, 2002, 2004; Shipps, 1997; Wong, 2000). Additionally, the new reform placed heavy emphasis on accountability and thus standardized testing, configuring a test regime that would only be complemented by elements of Renaissance 2010. The 1995 reform allowed for a host of expanded powers such as "dissolv[ing] Local School Councils when deemed necessary, and [to] cancel union contracts and outsource and privatize work done by unionized school district employees" (Lipman, 2004, p. 36).

While the tacit weakening of LSCs by shifting resources, maintaining true authority of the purse in the hands of the mayor, as well as top-down governing and the rather well-articulated moratorium on teacher's ability to strike and to collectively bargain during this period are troublesome, the true hallmark of this reform laid in efforts to "reengineer" institutional confidence, if there ever was any, in the CPS by way of high-stakes testing under the guise of accountability (Shipps et al., 1999). Gery Chico, Mayor Daley's chief of staff, orchestrated the reform. Chico was appointed to head the CPS Board of Trustees and his former budget director, Paul Vallas, who was appointed CEO of CPS, later became Superintendent of the Recovery School District in New Orleans post-Katrina (Lipman, 2004).

The accountability reforms resonated with some communities, given the historic disinterest and pernicious disinvestment CPS had toward their students and communities; it, at the very least, now *appeared* that CPS was not giving students permission to fail (Chambers, 2002/2003; Lipman, 2002, 2004; Lipman & Haines, 2007). Vallas's tough on education approach was more of a relabeling and reconstituting of certain schools, students, and teachers as "good," or "bad," "successes" or "failures"—all of which was established by how one performed or prepared students to perform on a standardized test, whose validity was never questioned by Vallas and his team. As Lipman and Haines (2007) comment,

> CPS responded with an accountability system that institutionalized a simplistic, one-size-fits-all practice of demarcating students, teachers, and schools into those deemed "failing" or "successful" and then meted out penalties without regard for inequities in resources, opportunities to learn, teacher's ideologies, cultural disconnections in curriculum and instruction, social contexts of the school, or strengths children bring to the school setting. (p. 480)

The iteration of reform seemed more interested in proving its legitimacy than dealing with the inequities that undergird CPS and the city of Chicago. While Vallas did provide after-school and summer remedial programs for students who were "at-risk" of or had already failed, the policy effectively reconstructed (or, perhaps, reconfirmed in some Chicagoans' eyes) many students as "failures," teachers as ineffective and undetermined, and schools as unproductive. This led to a test-driven pedagogy in many schools, with some low-scoring schools using scripted direct instruction (Lipman, 2004).

Renaissance 2010

Shipps et al. (1999) has commented, "if the slogan of the 1988 reform had been parent power, the watchword of the 1995 reform became accountability" (p. 519). One could then add that the unspoken word for the 2004 Renaissance 2010 reform is *retrenchment*. The Renaissance 2010 (Ren2010) reform takes a decidedly explicit pro-market approach to education reform, restructuring *public* schooling as a pseudo-laissez-faire terrain in which markets, "choice," competition, and efficiency become ad hoc synonymous with improving the educational achievement of underresourced, frequently abjected low-income students of color. Three facets can, perhaps, best categorize Ren2010: school closings, nonunion teachers, and proliferation of charter schools (Lipman, 2011b).

The 1995 reform with its emphasis on high-stakes testing and accountability as well as its weakening of LSCs provided fertile ground for the new reform enacted by then CEO of Chicago Public Schools, Arne Duncan, now the current Secretary of Education. Ren2010 specifically aims to target underperforming schools, offering the guise of accountability but the reality of limited resource redistribution (Lipman, 2011a; Saltman, 2007). By 2004 when Renaissance 2010 was announced, No Child Left Behind (2001) had already become the order of the day in terms of education reform. Indeed, Chicago was, in many ways, ahead of the game with pervasive testing and an accountability regime that set in place a destructive labeling system for students, teachers, and schools. Ren2010 articulated a mission of closing *at least* 60 of the lowest-performing schools and offering more choice to parents by creating alternatives to traditional public schools (Ayers & Klonsky, 2006; Lipman, 2011a, 2011b; Saltman, 2007).

Underpinning the reform is the idea that offering parents more choices somehow equates to better choices or choices parents actually want. Riddled with the notion that public in essence is bad, alternatives to traditional public education, such as charter schools, contract schools, and performance schools, often give the impression of inherent difference vis-à-vis academic success for students (Lipman, 2011a; Saltman, 2007). Incidentally, access to high-quality alternative forms of education often is limited and selective; students and families, in educational limbo, after their schools have been closed and they are kicked out, find themselves relying on lotteries for admission into schools with limited enrollment (Gwynne & de la Torre, 2009). Unfortunately, these "choices" for displaced students and families have afforded them no better opportunities. As Lipman (2011a) notes, "most displaced students from public housing units were reassigned to schools academically and demographically similar to those they left, with 84% attending schools with well below the average district test scores and 44% in schools on probation for low test scores" (p. 54). Lauen's (2009) study corroborated with Lipman, finding that exercising "choice" actually benefits high-achieving students as well as students in low-poverty neighborhoods. This seems to suggest that the discourse of choice, materially, has a more profound positive impact for students and families who already have many choices available to them, that is to say, students with whom the policy was neither targeted for nor geared toward.

With the closing of traditional public schools, Ren2010 set ambitious goals to establish more nontraditional schools in the form of charter, contract, and performance schools. These alternative schools, while touted as solutions to the ineffectiveness and inefficiency of traditional public schools, often are not held any more accountable than their traditional counterparts (Saltman, 2007). Indeed, CPS has a long-standing issue with capriciously holding some schools accountable, particularly those in areas being gentrified, while allowing lower-performing schools to remain open (Ayers & Klonsky, 2006; Lipman, 2011a).

Particularly troubling within charter schools in Chicago is the fact that schools are not required to hire and adhere to the teacher's union collective bargaining agreement (Christianakis & Mora, 2011). Lipman (2011b) noted that conditions within these schools for educators often entail long hours at relatively low pay, panoptic surveillance of teachers with almost cult-like enforcement of high-stakes accountability, narrowing both definer and definitions of excellence and effectiveness, performing tasks often outside of the role of educator, and the constant threat of being fired at will. Lipman (2011b) goes further in saying, "teachers at a charter school chain in Chicago reported they had no breaks and were required to work extra hours and clean floors and classrooms with no additional pay. They were afraid to protest because they could be fired at will" (p. 131).

When It's Not Just Education Reform

Educational reform is never solely endogenously set. That is to say, particular historical events, bound by very narrow ideology about "successful schools," "effective teaching," and "academic achievement," provide the foundation for the reforms that have been proscribed for public education since the dawning of the Common School. The aforementioned reforms paint a disturbing picture of the way ideology is embedded within so-called neutral, apolitical reforms that are, indeed, socially constructed and effects of power (Leonardo, 2003; Popkewitz, 2000). These reforms challenge notions of "democratic localism" and usurp the language of "effectiveness," "accountability," "choice," and "citizen," creating discursive veneers of justice and equity, with little attention to actual equity and justice.

An interesting commonality between Philadelphia, Chicago, and New Orleans, particularly in the reform movement of the late 1990s through 2005, has been the leadership of Paul Vallas, a Chicago businessman who morphed into school leader and education reformer. That Vallas used

Philadelphia and Chicago as test runs for his complete dismantling of public education in New Orleans is obvious.

Do You Know What It Means to Miss New Orleans?[6]

Norman Rockwell's famous portrait, "The Problem We All Live With," that depicted U.S. Marshals walking a young Black girl into a school building poignantly captured the context of race and public education in New Orleans in the 1960s. The girl in Rockwell's portrait was not an image conjured by his imagination but rather was Ruby Bridges, a 6-year-old girl who bravely integrated William Franz Elementary School on November 14, 1960.[7] Although Franz School and McDonogh 19[8] were integrated, it was not until the 1969–1970 school year that Orleans Parish School Board (OPSB) was fully desegregated through the 12th grade (Cowen Institute, 2010). While the district experienced fluctuations in its enrollment among Black and White students from the 1970s through the 1980s, by the 2004–2005 school year, the district had a Black enrollment of 94%. In addition, 77% of the students enrolled in OPSB were also eligible for free/reduced lunch.

As the student enrollment in New Orleans integrated racially, so did the teaching force. In 1937, Black teachers formed their own union as an affiliate of the American Federation of Teachers (AFT). They established Local 527. The local chapter of the National Education Association was segregated and only open to Whites. Establishing Local 527 was the only way Black teachers could organize and protest the disparity in pay between themselves and their White counterparts.[9] In 1972, the two unions combined and formed the United Teachers of New Orleans (UTNO) and represented nearly 5,000 teachers in the city. By 2005, UTNO represented 7,500 teachers and other school staff. The racial demographics of the OPSB teaching force were 90% African American representing nearly 4,000 teachers. After Katrina, those numbers shifted most dramatically in the Recovery School District (RSD) schools where Teach For America teachers (see Table 25.1) constituted the majority of teachers (Cowen Institute, 2010).

Authored by a bipartisan group of 16 state senators and representatives, Louisiana Legislative Act 35 (LA 35) was signed into law by Governor Kathleen Babineaux Blanco during a special session of the Louisiana Legislature on November 22, 2005. Eleven of the 20 representatives from Orleans Parish voted against the legislation. LA 35 was a revision of Louisiana Legislative Act 9 (LA 9) passed in 2003. Act 9 was authored by six of the same state senators and representatives who authored LA 35. LA 9 allowed for the establishment and governance of the RSD,

Table 25.1 New Orleans Teachers by Years of Experience Before and After Katrina

	0–1 Years	*2–3Years*	*4–10 Years*	*11–14 Years*	*15–19 Years*	*20–24 Years*	*25+ Years*
2004–2005	9.7%	7.3%	24.7%	9.0%	8.9%	10.9%	29.5%
2007–2008	36.7%	17.2%	19.3%	4.8%	5.5%	4.9%	11.6%
Change (2004–2005 and 2007–2008)	27.0%	9.9%	–5.4%	–4.2%	–3.4%	–6.0%	–17.9%

Source: Cowen Institute (2009).

a state-run school district that would take over failed school(s). LA 9 identifies four criteria for determining a failed school:

(a) fails to present a plan to reconstitute the failed school to the state board, as required pursuant to such an accountability program, or
(b) presents a reconstitution plan that is unacceptable to the state board, or
(c) fails at any time to comply with the terms of the reconstitution plan approved by the state board, or
(d) the school has been labeled an academically unacceptable school for four consecutive years.

In Louisiana, the primary state accountability program is the Louisiana Educational Assessment Program (LEAP), the standardized testing program designed to measure students' academic achievement.[10] LEAP was part of the composite that made up the School Performance Score (SPS).[11] LA 9 allowed the RSD to take over "academically unacceptable" (AU) schools with an SPS of 45 for four years. In 2004, the state legislature raised the SPS score to 60. The average SPS for the State of Louisiana was 86.2 in the 2004–2005 school year. By July 2004, the RSD had taken over one school run by the Orleans Parish School Board (OPSB). As late as May 2005, just three months before Hurricane Katrina and six months before Governor Blanco signed LA 35 into law, the RSD had only taken over four OPSBs (Cowen Institute, 2010).

Among other issues relative to accountability, funding, and oversight of public elementary and secondary schools, LA 9 was also an entre for charter schools in Louisiana. The specific language in the legislation is, "to establish and provide for a Type 5 charter school; to eliminate the termination of the authority for certain chartering authorities to enter into certain types of charters; to provide for an effective date; and to provide for related matters."

With the passage of LA 35, the minimum SPS was raised to "below" the state average of 87.4. Indeed, OPSB schools were above the SPS cutoff of 60 yet still taken over by the RSD. In fact, LA 35 not only allowed the RSD to take over individual schools but also expanded its jurisdiction to entire school districts that had 30 or more schools that were academically unsuccessful (AU). OPSB was one of the 14 school districts in the state that had at least 30 AU schools. According to Dr. Barbara Ferguson, founder of the Center of Action Research on New Orleans School Reform, the Board of Elementary and Secondary Education (BESE) only applied the SPS score cutoff to schools in Orleans Parish (Ferguson, 2010). Both Ferguson's 2010 report on what she describes as the "double standard" of the SPS scores (see Table 25.2) and a 2010 report by the Cowen Institute at Tulane University show that no other schools in the state that had been taken over by the RSD had SPS scores above 60 (see Table 25.3).

Prior to Hurricane Katrina, OPSB operated 128 schools and was the only district in the state with that many schools. As a result of LA 35, RSD was able to take over 112 of the 128 schools run by OPSB. The law was changed such that schools did not have to be AU for four consecutive years before RSD could take them over. In addition, Blanco signed two executive orders that expanded chartering options. The first executive order removed timelines with respect to when the RSD could take over a school. The second executive order lifted the requirement that parents and teachers approve of the charter. For many stakeholders, especially teachers and UTNO, it appeared that LA 35 was designed to target OPSB and create the conditions that led to the firing of the entire teaching force in OPSB and effectively dismantled the teachers' union (UTNO, 2007). This maneuvering created the "system of systems" currently in place for public education in New Orleans (see Figure 25.1).

According to a 2007 report by UTNO, teachers in New Orleans, whether in an RSD school (charter/noncharter) or OPSB school (charter/noncharter), unlike their colleagues in neighboring

Table 25.2 School Performance Scores in Louisiana

No.	*Code*	*Name*	*Grades*	*Baseline SPS 2004–2005*
1	036003	Henry W. Allen Elem	Pk-7	*65.6*
2	036007	Thurgood Marshall	7-8	*77.6*
3	036014	Stuart R. Bradley Elem	Pk-6	*78.5*
4	036019	Parkview Fundamental Magnet	Pk-6	*85.7*
5	036021	Mary D. Coghill	Pk-6	*76.6*
6	036032	John Dibert Elem	Pk-6	*65.8*
7	036038	Dwight D. Eisenhower Elem	Pk-6	*67.6*
8	036040	William J. Fischer Elem	Pk-6	*73.8*
9	036048	Gentilly Terrace Elem	Pk-6	*65.5*
10	036052	William J. Guste Elem	Pk-6	*66.2*
11	036053	Paul B. Habans Elem	k-6	*64.2*
12	036068	Thomy Lafon	Pk-6	*61.5*
13	036073	Ronald G. McNair Elem	Pk-6	*70.6*
14	036082	McDonogh15 Creative Arts Magnet	Pk-6	*63.5*
15	036094	McDonogh #07 Elem	Pk-6	*64.6*
16	03097	Harriet Tubman Elem	Pk-6	*73.3*
17	036104	Mildred Osborne	Pk-8	*62.6*
18	036110	Rabouin Career Magnet HS	8-12	*61.1*
19	036114	H.C. Schaumburg Elem	Pk-8	*72.1*
20	036117	Sherwood Forest Elem	Pk-6	*64.5*
21	036135	N.O. Free School	k-8	*63.6*
22	036164	Dr.MLKElemSchForSciAndTech	Pk-6	*81.8*
23	036167	N.O. Charter Middle	6-8	*70.5*
24	036176	Lake Area Middle	7-8	*63.0*
25	036178	N.O. Technology High	9	*61.7*

Source: Ferguson (2010).

parishes, have no collective bargaining agreement with their employers and their work conditions are often more stringent—longer workdays and larger class sizes. They also have no job security because of the absence of a tenure system and working on an "at-will" contract from year to year. In some charter schools, teachers are forbidden from discussing their salaries because they are negotiated on an individual basis. Discussing and/or disclosing their salary can be grounds for dismissal (UTNO, 2007). These conditions are in stark contrast to pre-Katrina conditions for teachers in OPSB. Teachers who were not dues-paying members of UTNO were covered by the benefits of the collective bargaining agreements. However, one veteran teacher we interviewed who worked in OPSB pre-Katrina and has returned to an RSD charter believes that working in the charter is in many ways better than under the old system.[12] For this teacher, a 20-year veteran, native New Orleanian and graduate of a teacher education program at a local historically Black college, teaching in a charter school affords her more autonomy and control over the curriculum. Moreover, she appreciated that school administrators were responsive to her requests for curricular and teaching materials. She also appreciated the fact that she did not have to navigate the bureaucracy of a central office to get what she believed she needed to effectively teach her students. It is important to note, however, her school is one of the few schools, within the current schooling context in New Orleans, where most of the teachers in her school, with the exception of two new teachers, are veteran OPSB teachers (Cowen Institute, 2010; Royal, 2012; UTNO, 2007). Both the principal and assistant principal taught in OPSB. The principal led a school for nearly 10 years before Hurricane Katrina. Thus, while this teacher enjoys control, she also enjoys working in a school with a stable and experienced faculty, which in many ways allows her to focus on her instruction rather than on climate and discipline issues. This teacher's preference for her charter school over OPSB supports the finding by the AFT that teachers value stable and positive working conditions, supportive administrators, and feeling comfortable working with particular groups of students over higher salaries and benefits (American Federation of Teachers, 2006.).

Implications

Despite the representation of education reform, particularly education reform since the late 1990s, as being "successful" and "effective," by mainstream media outlets, research on charters versus public schools is relatively inconclusive as to which type of school is "better" or "worse" in terms of academic achievement (CREDO, 2009; Henig, 2009). What appears to be a more salient concern as it relates to urban schools and the current iteration of school reform is the dislocation of elected school boards and the governance model of public schools. One has to wonder how urban school districts, particularly in light of the financial challenges facing not only the nation on a federal level, but also, at the state and municipal levels, can continue to fund reforms that have been initially underwritten by particular foundations and other philanthropic organizations. That is, as funders move on to the next great idea, how will these reforms be sustainable in contexts where funding has historically been a chronic issue and concern? Moreover, how sustainable are reforms that presume to redress racial inequity when they are premised on the disenfranchisement of the communities they aim to serve? Although Chicago is the only district of the three we analyzed that is under mayoral control, it behooves city leaders of all three contexts to seriously consider the ramifications of reform models that effectively disempower entire communities and render them powerless in the decision-making process. As we are seeing in all three contexts, community members, parents, students, and teachers are fighting back against reform policies that they believe further exacerbate racial inequity and economic disparities rather than resolve them.

Our analysis also suggests that teachers' unions strategize around issues that resonate with the communities they serve. Given the high concentration of poverty in all three school districts we analyzed, calling for higher wages and job security in a context with disproportionate and chronic unemployment and poverty often fall flat and in fact get used against teachers who chose to strike and/or protest the reforms. The unions in all three cities have had to rethink their efforts to galvanize support for teachers by framing their concerns within what is best for students in general but also for students of color who live in poverty. We argue that while teachers who are adequately compensated and feel secure in their employment are in the best interest of students, framing demands that also attend to the needs of students in terms of structural inequalities and supports for struggling students will have more purchase power and garner more support. The CTU strike demonstrated the support that teachers and unions still enjoy despite the antiteacher and anti-union perspective of far too many of the high-profile reformers.

Table 25.3 New Orleans Schools with SPS Scores Above 60 Taken Over by BESE in 2005

No.	*Parish*	*Name*	*Baseline SPS 2008–2009*
1	Caddo	Linear Middle School	52.9
2	Caddo	Linwood Middle School	51.1
3	EBR*	Banks Elementary	52.4
4	EBR	Capitol Middle School	54.6
5	EBR	Crestworth Middle	49.5
6	EBR	Dalton Elementary	54.4
7	EBR	Kenilworth Middle School	55
8	EBR	Lanier Elementary	56.6
9	EBR	Parker Elementary	49.4
		Takeover School Average	52.8
		LA SPS Average	86.2

Note: *EBR is East Baton Rouge Parish.

Source: Cowen Institute (2010).

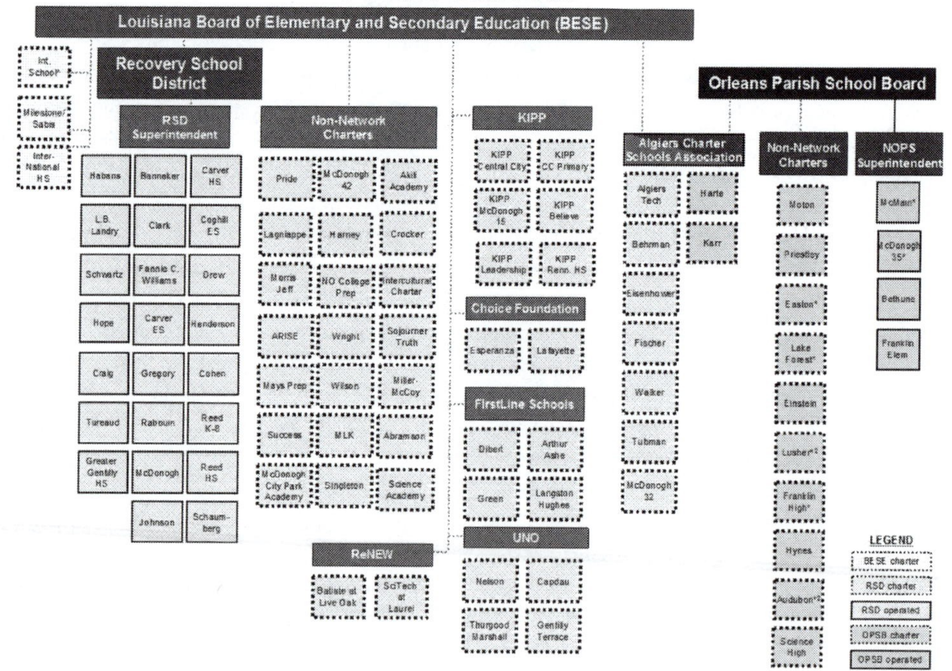

Figure 25.1 School Governance in New Orleans

Note: An asterisk (*) next to a school name indicates a selective admissions school. A number two (2) next to a school name indicates two campuses. Each independent (non-networked) charter school has its own board of directors to which it reports.

Source: Cowen Institute (2010).

Conclusion

This chapter highlighted three separate school districts that have faced and are facing similar reform efforts. While the scale for each district is different, the impact on communities, families, and teachers has been frighteningly similar. That these reforms are highly politicized and often introduced by "outsiders" to the local community is not a coincidence. As we argued in earlier sections of this chapter, the reforms we see emerging since the mid-1980s have been part of a much larger neoliberal project aimed at defunding and dismantling perhaps the nation's largest public works program: public education.

Public education in each context is radically different from its founding. For some, that is good news. For others, it represents a loss of voice, influence, and participation. The dismantling of duly elected school officials and school boards in all three contexts has allowed outside Charter Management Organizations (CMO) to set the educational agenda for cities with which they have no history, and some would argue, no vested interested in its sustainability. The encouraging news for all of us is that, although community members across all three contexts have been formally locked out of the decision-making process, they have created opportunities to be heard. This organic organizing against hegemonic educational policies is not a new occurrence in the history of urban public education. Indeed, communities who feel disenfranchised and locked out of public education have often fought back against educational policies they perceived to be inequitable and not in the best interests of their children. The impact of these protests is yet to be fully realized but they are important. In this regard, despite the challenges community members face in having their voices heard, we are reminded of the importance of public education to how we practice and understand democracy.

Notes

1. In this instance one can think of the actual "natural" disaster that decimated the city of New Orleans or the symbolic disaster understood in the reform discourse as public schools. Charter schools are considered a salvivic remedy to both.
2. Pew Charitable Trusts gave $9.8 million for SDP school reform, specifically, "Children Achieving" (Pew Grants, 1995). Most of the money would go toward creating new academic standards for students; William Penn Foundation gave $13.8 million to "Children Achieving" (Dabney, 1996, March 15). Gov. Ridge proposed freezing basic education funding for all 501 school districts in Pennsylvania. SDP is the largest district in the state. The District was expecting to get $606 million in basic funding but instead would only get $594 million. SDP was also expecting $85 million for special education but would only receive $83 million (Dabney, 1996, February 9).
3. Pennsylvania House Speaker John Perzel called Vallas a friend and said he was successful (Toomer, 2006, July 11); Pennsylvania House Speaker John Perzel, State Sen. Vincent Fumo, and State Rep. Dwight Evans worked together to get $12 million in additional funds from the state (Toomer, 2006, July 14).
4. Cornish (1985); Editorial: Clayton Continues (1989); Editorial: Clayton's Tenure (1993); School District's First Balanced Budget (1984); Smith (1993); Weldon (1988); Wilson (1991). In announcing her retirement, Lee and Ed Rendell lauded Clayton for bringing financial stability to SDP; Boyd & Christman (2003); Royal (2012).
5. For a more thorough discussion of reform efforts prior to 1980, see Herrick (1971); Lyons (2008); or Shipps (2006).
6. Portions of this section were previously published as Adrienne D. Dixson, "Whose Choice?: A Critical Race Perspective on Charter Schools," in Cedric Johnson (Ed.), The Neo-Liberal Deluge: Hurricane Katrina, Late Capitalism and the Remaking of New Orleans (pp. 130–151) (Minneapolis: University of Minnesota Press, 2011).
7. Bridges (1999).
8. In the late 1870s, John McDonogh was a wealthy businessman and trader of enslaved Africans who left his entire estate to the city of New Orleans to open public schools. There were originally over 30

schools named after John McDonogh and they were numbered. Through a series of closings for various reasons, by 1970, only 20 schools remained open. McDonogh 35 opened in 1917 as the only Black high school in the city. Until Katrina, McDonogh 35 was one of the premier high schools in the city. Booker T. Washington opened in 1940 as a career training high school and was also a premier all-Black high school in the city. Prior to Katrina, its reputation had declined significantly. Both schools have reopened as charters with McDonogh 35 as an OPSB charter school servicing grades 7 through 12.

9. In the 1937–1938 school year, the annual salary for White teachers was $1,193 compared to $504 for Black teachers.
10. In response to the No Child Left Behind legislation (NCLB), Louisiana revised its statewide, high-stakes testing program. LEAP is a criterion-referenced, high-stakes examination that schools administer to students in 4th and 8th grades. LEAP measures students' achievement in English/Language Arts (ELA), mathematics, science, and social studies. LEAP has five achievement ratings: advanced, mastery, basic, approaching basic, and unsatisfactory. Students who do not score "basic" or higher on ELA and mathematics will not be promoted to the next grade level (5th or 9th grade).
11. Students in grades 3, 5, 6, 7, and 9 take the Integrated Louisiana Educational Assessment Program, or iLEAP, in ELA and mathematics. The iLEAP has both a norm-referenced component and a criterion-referenced component. Louisiana is the only state in the United States that uses a norm-referenced examination as part of its SPS component to be compliant with NCLB (Ferguson, 2010).
    The criterion for promotion to the next grade level is somewhat complicated in that students must score a "basic" or higher on one test and be "approaching basic" or higher on the other in order to be promoted to the next grade. For example, a 4th- or 8th-grade student who scored "basic" on mathematics but "approaching basic" on ELA would be promoted to the next grade level. A student who scored "approaching basic" on both mathematics and ELA would be retained.
12. Included in the SPS are school attendance and dropout rates.

References

A fine legacy from Hornbeck. (2000, August 15). *The Philadelphia Tribune*, p. *6A*.

American Federation of Teachers. (2006). *"National model" or flawed approach? The Post-Katrina New Orleans public schools.* Washington, DC: Author. Retrieved from http://www.coweninstitute.com/our-work/applied-research/education-archive/education-transformation-archive/national-model-or-flawed-approach

Anderson, J. (1988). *The education of Blacks in the South, 1860–1935*. Chapel Hill, NC: University of North Carolina Press.

Anyon, J. (2005). *Radical possibilities*. New York, NY: Routledge.

Argue, K., Honeyman, S., & Shlay, A.B. (2006). *Separate and unequal: The distribution of instructional resources in the school district of Philadelphia, 2001–2005*. Philadelphia, PA: Research for Democracy.

Ayers, W., & Klonsky, M. (2006). Chicago's renaissance 2010: The small schools movement meets the ownership society. *Phi Delta Kappan, 87*(6), 453–457.

Baer, J.M. (1997, June 12). Lawmakers ok charter schools. *Philadelphia Daily News*, p. 5.

Ball, A. (2002). Three decades of research on classroom Life: Illuminating the classroom communicative lives of America's at risk students. *Review of Research in Education*, 26, 71–111.

Barton, P.E. (2004). Why does the gap persist? *Educational Leadership, 62*(3), 8–13.

Bell, D.A. (1980). *Brown v. Board of Education* and the interest convergence dilemma. *Harvard Law Review, 93*(3), 518–533.

Birger, J. (1996). Race, reaction, and reform: The three Rs of Philadelphia school politics, 1965–1971. *The Pennsylvania Magazine of History and Biography, 120*(3), 163–216.

Boyd, W.L., & Christman, J.B. (2003). A tall order for Philadelphia's new approach to school governance: Heal the political rifts, close the budget gap, *and* improve the schools. In Larry Cuban & Michael Usdan (Eds.), *Powerful reforms with shallow roots: Improving America's urban schools* (pp. 96–124). New York, NY: Teachers College Press.

Bridges, R. (1999). Through my eyes. New York, NY: Scholastic Press.

Brooks, M. (2002, December 13). Nevels optimistic on schools' future, Rendell relations. *The Philadelphia Tribune p. 5A.*

Buras, K.L. (2009). "We have to tell our story": Neo-griots, racial resistance, and schooling in the other south. *Race Ethnicity and Education, 12*(4), 427–453.

Center for Research on Education Outcomes. (2009). Multiple choice: Charter school performance in 16 states. Stanford, CA: Stanford University.

Chambers, S. (2002/2003). Urban education reform and minority political empowerment. *Political Science Quarterly, 117*(4), 643–665.

Charter School Performance in Pennsylvania. (2011, April). Retrieved from credo.stanford.edu

Christianakis, M., & Mora, R. (2011). Charting a new course for public education through charter schools: Where is Obama taking us? In P.A. Carr (Ed.), *The phenomenon of Obama and the agenda for education: Can hope audaciously trump neoliberalism?* (pp. 97–119). Charlotte, NC: Information Age.

Cornish, L. (1985, August 20). Fattah urges school talks. *The Philadelphia Tribune,* p. 1A.

Cornish, L. (1985, August 27). Teachers, board must be committed to kids. *The Philadelphia Tribune,* p. 1A.

Cornish, L. (1985, September 10). Clayton toughens graduation requirements. *The Philadelphia Tribune,* p. 1A.

Countryman, M.J. (2006). *Up South.* Philadelphia, PA: University of Pennsylvania Press.

Cowen Institute. (2009). State of public education in New Orleans report. Retrieved July 11, 2013 from http://www.coweninstitute.com/wp-content/uploads/2009/08/Addendum-Full-January-2009-Part-II.pdf

Cowen Institute. (2010). *Recovery School District of Louisiana.* New Orleans, LA: Cowen Institute, Tulane University.

Cuban, L., & Usdan, M. (Eds.). (2003). *Powerful reforms with shallow roots: Improving America's urban schools.* New York, NY: Teachers College Press.

Dabney, M. (1996, February 9). Gov's proposed budget will come as heavy blow to Philadelphia schools. *The Philadelphia Tribune,* p. 1A.

Dabney, M. (1996, March 15). Foundation gives $13 million for "Children Achieving." *The Philadelphia Tribune,* p. 1A.

Danns, D. (2002). Black student empowerment in Chicago: School reform efforts in 1968. *Urban Education, 37*(5), 631–655.

Darling-Hammond, L. (1997). *The right to learn: A blueprint for creating schools that work.* San Francisco, CA: Jossey-Bass.

Denvir, D. (2012, April 24). *Philadelphia School District announces its dissolution.* Retrieved from http://www.citypaper.net/blogs/nakedcity/Philadelphia-School-District-announces-its-dissolution-.html?ref=facebook.com

Dixson, A.D. (2011). Whose choice: A critical race perspective on charter schools. In C. Johnson (Ed.), *The neoliberal deluge: Hurricane Katrina, late capitalism, and the remaking of New Orleans* (pp. 130–151). Minneapolis, MN: University of Minnesota Press.

Du Four, R. (2004). What is a professional learning community? *Educational Leadership, 61*(8), 6–11.

Du Four, R., Eaker, R., & Karhanek, G. (2004). *Whatever it takes: How professional learning communities respond when kids don't learn.* Bloomington, IN: National Education Service.

Editorial: Charter schools not a case of either or. (2000, May 9). *Philadelphia Daily News.* p. 15.

Editorial: Clayton continues standard of excellence. (1989, November 28). *The Philadelphia Tribune,* p. 8A.

Editorial: Clayton's tenure restored confidence in school system. (1993, August 20). *The Philadelphia Tribune,* p. 6A.

Editorial: Let's see what Hornbeck can do for our schools. (1994, August 19). *The Philadelphia Tribune,* p. 6A.

Editorials & Comment: Children's education should not be used as a political football. (1971, November 23). *The Philadelphia Tribune,* p. 8.

Editorials & Comment: Dr. Mark Shedd is doing a commendable job as school superintendent. (1971, March 27). *The Philadelphia Tribune,* p. 8.

Editorials & Comment: Parents and city leaders are asleep while school board is being appointed. (1971, November 16). *The Philadelphia Tribune,* p. 8.

Enderlin-Lampe, S. (2002). Empowerment: Teacher perceptions, aspirations and efficacy. *Journal of Instructional Psychology, 29*(3), 139–146.

Etheridge, S. (1979, October). Impact of the 1954 *Brown v. Topeka Board of Education* decision on Black educators. *Negro Educational Review, 30*(4), 217–232.

Ferguson, B. (2010). *New Orleans schools decline following state's "double standard" takeover.* New Orleans, LA: Center for Action Research on New Orleans School Reform.

Fine, M. (1991). *Framing dropouts: Notes on the politics of an urban public high school.* Albany, NY: State University of New York Press.

Foster, M. (1990). The politics of race: Through the eyes of African-American teachers. *Journal of Education, 172*(3), 123–141.

Frankenberg, E., & Lee, C. (2002). *Race in American public schools: Rapidly resegregating school districts.* Cambridge, MA: The Civil Rights Project, Harvard University.

Franklin, V.P. (1979). *The education of Black Philadelphia: The social and educational history of a minority community, 1900–1950.* Philadelphia, PA: University of Pennsylvania Press.

Freire, P. (1970/2000). *Pedagogy of the oppressed.* New York, NY: Continuum.

Gamoran, A. (1996). Student achievement in public magnet, public comprehensive, and private city high schools. *Educational Evaluation and Analysis, 18*(1), 1–18.

Gold, E., Christman, J.B., & Herold, B. (2007). Blurring the boundaries: A case study of private sector involvement in Philadelphia Public Schools. *American Journal of Education, 113*(2), 181–213.

Goss, S. (2001, November 30). Takeover tonight? Investment advisor targeted to run Philadelphia schools. *The Philadelphia Tribune,* p. 1A.

Graham, K.A. (2011, August 3). *Wild SRC meeting; Jordan calls for Ackerman's ouster.* Retrieved from http://www.philly.com/philly/blogs/school_files/Special-SRC-meeting-Budget-update-and-more.html

Graham, K.A., & Woodall, M. (2010, January 28). 14 schools put on city reform list. *The Philadelphia Inquirer.*

Guiner, L., & Torres, G. (2003). The mine's canary: Enlisting race, resisting power, transforming democracy. Cambridge, MA: Harvard University Press.

Gwynne, J., & de la Torre, M. (2009). When schools close: Effects on displaced students in Chicago Public Schools. *Consortium on Chicago School Research.* Retrieved from http://ccsr.uchicago.edu/publications?type=All&year[value]&keyword=&author=&page=1

Henig, J. (2009). *Spin cycle: How research is used in policy debates: The case of charter schools.* New York, NY: Russell Sage Foundation/The Century Foundation.

Herrick, M. (1971). *The Chicago schools: A social and political history.* Thousand Oaks, CA: Sage Publications.

Hess, F.M. (1998). *Spinning wheels: The politics of urban school reform.* Washington, DC: Brookings Institution Press.

Hess, G.A. (1991). *School restructuring, Chicago style.* Newbury Park, CA: Corwin Press.

Hilliard, A.G. (2003). No mystery: Closing the achievement gap between Africans and excellence. In T. Perry, C. Steele, & A. Hilliard (Eds.), *Young, gifted, and Black: Prompting high achievement among African-American students* (pp. 131–165). Boston, MA: Beacon Press.

Homel, M. (1976). The politics of public education in Black Chicago, 1910–1941. *Journal of Negro Education, 45*(2), 179–191.

Hornbeck, D.W. (1994, November 11). Our city's children can—and will—achieve. *The Philadelphia Tribune,* p. 7A.

Hornbeck, D.W., & Conner, K. (2009). *Choosing excellence in public schools: Where there's a will, there's a way.* New York, NY: Rowman and Littlefield Education.

Ingersoll, R. (2003). *Who controls teachers' work?: Power and accountability in America's schools.* Cambridge, MA: Harvard University Press.

Jones, B.A. (2005). Forces for failure and genocide: The plantation model of urban educational policy making in St. Louis. *Educational Studies, 37*(1), 6–24.

Kantor, H. (1991). Education, social reform, and the state: ESEA and federal education policy in the 1960s. *American Journal of Education, 100*(1), 47–83.

Kantor, H., & Lowe, R. (1995). Class, race, and the emergence of federal education policy: From the new deal to the great society. *Educational Researcher, 24*(4), 4–11, 21.

Kantor, H., & Lowe, R. (2004). Reflections on history and quality education. *Educational Researcher, 33*(6), 6–10.

Kliebard, H.M. (2004). *The struggle for the American curriculum: 1893–1958*. New York, NY: RoutledgeFalmer.

Kozol, J. (1991). *Savage inequalities*. New York, NY: Harper Perennial.

Ladson-Billings, G. (2004). Landing on the wrong note: The price we paid for *Brown*. *Educational Researcher, 33*(7), 3–13.

Ladson-Billings, G. (2006). From the achievement gap to the education debt: Understanding achievement in U.S. schools. *Educational Researcher, 35(7)*, 3–12.

Lauen, D.L. (2009). To choose or not to choose: High school choice and graduation in Chicago. *Educational Evaluation and Policy Analysis, 31*(3), 179–199.

Leary, R. (1994, September 2). Rotan Lee: Point man for the Philadelphia School District. *The Philadelphia Tribune*, p. 12.

Lee, J. (2008). Is test driven external accountability effective? Synthesizing the evidence from cross-state causal-comparative and correlational studies. *Review of Educational Research, 78*(3), 608–644.

Leonardo, Z. (2003). *Ideology, discourse, and school reform*. Westport, CT: Praeger.

Lipman, P. (2002). Making the global city, making inequality: The political economy and cultural politics of Chicago school policy. *American Educational Research Journal, 39*(2), 379–419.

Lipman, P. (2004). *High stakes education: Inequality, globalization, and urban school reform*. New York, NY: RoutledgeFalmer.

Lipman, P. (2011a). Contesting the city: Neoliberal urbanism and the cultural politics of education reform in Chicago. *Discourse: Studies in the Cultural Politics of Education, 32*(2), 217–234.

Lipman, P. (2011b). *The new political economy of urban education: Neoliberalism, race, and the right to the city*. New York, NY: Routledge.

Lipman, P., & Haines, N. (2007). From accountability to privatization and African American exclusion: Chicago's renaissance 2010. *Educational Policy, 21*(3), 471–502.

Lyons, J. (2008). *Teachers and reform: Chicago public education, 1929–1970*. Champaign, IL: University of Illinois Press.

Lytle, J. (2012, August 28). Commentary: Making sense of what's happening in the school district. *The Philadelphia Public School Notebook*. http://thenotebook.org/blog/125096/commentary-making-sense-whats-happening-school-district

MacDonald, T., & McDonald, S. (2011, August 22). Ackerman out, with Nunery taking the helm. Retrieved from http://www.newsworks.org/index.php/local//the-feed-feature/25293-report-ackerman-out-with-nunery-taking-the-helm

Mac Iver, M. A. and Vaughn, E. S. (2007). "But how long will they stay?" Alternative certification and new teacher retention in an urban district. *Educational Research Service Spectrum, 25*(2), 33–44.

Matthews, J. (2009). *Work hard. Be nice: How two teachers created the most promising schools in America*. Chapel Hill, NC: Algonquin Books.

Mezzacappa, D. (2012, August 23). Partnership has raised more than $50 million to give to "great" schools. *The Philadelphia Public School Notebook*. http://thenotebook.org/blog/125090/partnership-raises-more-50-million-give-great-schools

Morgan, K. (2000, June 13). District plans national search for superintendent. *The Philadelphia Tribune*, p. 1A.

Neild, R.C., Useem, E., & Farley, E. (2005). *The quest for quality: Recruiting and retaining teachers in Philadelphia*. Philadelphia, PA: Research for Action.

Neild, R.C., Useem, E., Travers, E.F., & Lesnick, J. (2003). *Once and for all: Placing a highly qualified teacher in every Philadelphia classroom*. Philadelphia, PA: Research for Action.

New Charter School Scandal: Not Surprising. (2010, April 1). *Philadelphia Daily News*.

News In Brief. (2008, Winter). *The Philadelphia Public School Notebook*, p. 8.

Nieto, S. (2003). *What keeps teachers going?* New York, NY: Teachers College Press.

Noguera, P. (2003). *City schools and the American dream*. New York, NY: Teachers College Press.

Orfield, G., & Lee, C. (2007). *Historic reversals, accelerating resegregation, and the need for new integration strategies.* Los Angeles, CA: The Civil Rights Project.

Our Opinion: What happens when Mayor Green wipes out school board, Marcase? (1981, January 30). *The Philadelphia Tribune.*

Owens, E. (2011, October). Ackerman's tenure in Philadelphia: 2008–11 key events. *The Philadelphia Public School Notebook, 19*(2), n.p.

Pew Grants Will Help "Children Achieving" Program. (1995, November 3). *The Philadelphia Tribune,* p. 8A.

PFT Teachers' Unit Urges Shedd Retention. (1971, February 23). *The Philadelphia Tribune,* p. 4.

Phillips, A.E. (2005). A history of the struggle for school desegregation in Philadelphia, 1955–1967. *Pennsylvania History: A Journal of Mid-Atlantic Studies, 72*(1), 49–76.

Popkewitz, T.S. (2000). The denial of change in educational change: Systems of ideas in the construction of national policy and evaluation. *Educational Researcher, 29*(1), 17–29.

Ramanathan, A. (2008). Paved with good intentions: The Federal role in the oversight and enforcement of the Individuals with Disabilities Education Act (IDEA) and the No Child Left Behind Act (NCLB). *Teachers College Record, 110*(2), 278–321.

Rorrer, A.K., Skrla, L., & Scheurich, J.J. (2008). Districts as institutional actors in educational reform. *Educational Administration Quarterly, 44*(3), 307–358.

Royal, C. (2012). *Policies, politics, and protests: The shifting landscape of Philadelphia's school reforms, 1967–2007* (Unpublished doctoral dissertation). Temple University, Philadelphia, PA.

Rubenstein, R. (1998). Resource equity in the Chicago Public Schools: A school-level approach. *Journal of Education Finance, 23*(4), 468–489.

Rury, J.L. (Ed.) (2005). Urban education in the United States: A historical reader. New York, NY: Palgrave Macmillan.

Saltman, K.J. (2007). *Capitalizing on disaster: Taking and breaking public schools.* Boulder, CO: Paradigm.

Saporito, S. (2003). Private choices, public consequences: Magnet school choice and segregation by race and poverty. *Social Problems, 50*(2), 181–203.

Schneider, M., & Buckley, J. (2003). Comparing DC charter schools to other DC public schools. *Educational Evaluation and Policy Analysis, 25*(3), 203–215.

School District of Philadelphia. (n.d.) Accessed August 28, 2012 from www.philasd.org

School District's first balanced budget in 18 years pays off. (1984, August 14). *The Philadelphia Tribune,* p. 2.

Schools Students Deserve Report. (2012).

Shedd Administration counts its (own) blessings; but remains cursed with crowding, violence, and segregation. (1971, February 16). *The Philadelphia Tribune,* p. 6.

Shipps, D. (1997). The invisible hand: Big business and Chicago school reform. *Teachers College Record, 99*(1), 73–116.

Shipps, D. (2006). *School reform, corporate style: Chicago, 1880–2000.* Lawrence, KS: University Press of Kansas.

Shipps, D., Kahne, J., & Smiley, M.A. (1999). The politics of urban school reform: Legitimacy, city growth, and school improvement in Chicago. *Educational Policy, 13*(4), 518–545.

Smith, J. (1993, July 23). A man concerned: Did Clayton really have to retire? *The Philadelphia Tribune,* p. 5A.

State Might Take Over City Schools, Hornbeck Predicts. (1998, November 17). *The Philadelphia Tribune,* p. 2A.

St. Hill, T., & Wilson, K. (1985, September 6). School's open, but were students biggest victors? *The Philadelphia Tribune,* p. 1A.

Sutton, J. (1994, June 28). Having your say. *The Philadelphia Tribune,* p. 6A.

Tatum, B.D. (2007). Can we talk about race? And other conversations in an era of school resegregation. Boston, MA: Beacon Press.

Toomer, R. (2006, July 11). Vallas grateful: Contract support. *The Philadelphia Tribune,* p. 1A.

Toomer, R. (2006, July 14). Vallas waits on $10M from city. *The Philadelphia Tribune,* p. 8A.

Tyack, D. (1974). *The one best system: A history of American urban education.* Cambridge, MA: Harvard University Press.

Tyack, D., & Cuban, L. (1995). *Tinkering toward utopia: A century of public school reform.* Cambridge, MA: Harvard University Press.

United Teachers of New Orleans [UTNO], Louisiana Federation of Teachers & American Federation of Teachers. (2007, June). No experience necessary: How the New Orleans school takeover experiment devalues experienced teachers [report]. New Orleans, LA: Author.

United Teachers of New Orleans [UTNO]. (2010, March). The New Orleans model: Shortchanging poor and minority students by over-relying on new teachers [Report]. New Orleans, LA: Author.

Useem, E. (2005, September). *Learning from Philadelphia's school reform: What do the research findings show so far?* Paper presented at No Child Left Behind Conference sponsored by the Sociology of Education section of the American Sociological Association, Philadelphia, PA.

Useem, E., Christman, J.B., & Boyd, W.L. (2006). *The role of district leadership in radical reform: Philadelphia's experience under the state takeover, 2001–2006.* Philadelphia, PA: Research for Action.

Useem, E., Offenberg, R., & Farley, E. (2007). *Closing the teacher quality gap in Philadelphia: New hope and old hurdles.* Philadelphia, PA: Research for Action.

Vergari, S. (2007). Federalism and market-based education policy: The supplemental educational services mandate. *American Journal of Education, 113*(2), 311–339.

Watkins, W.H. (2001). *The white architects of black education: Ideology and power in America, 1865–1954.* New York, NY: Teachers College Press.

Weiner, L. (1999). To teach or not to teach in an urban school? *English Journal, 88*(5), 21–25.

Weldon, O. (1988, September 16). Don't Blame Dr. Clayton. *The Philadelphia Tribune*, p. 6A.

Wellisch, J.B., MacQueen, A.H., Carriere, R.A., & Duck, G.A. (1978). School management and organization in successful schools (ESAA In-Depth Study School). *Sociology of Education, 51*(3), 211–226.

Wells, A.S., Lopez, A., Scott J., & Holme, J.J. (1999 Summer). Charter schools as postmodern paradox: Rethinking social stratification in an age of derugulated school choice. *Harvard Educational Review, 69*(2), 172–204.

Whitehorn, R. (2010, Summer). Alliance seeks to unionize Philly charters. *The Philadelphia Public School Notebook, 17*(6). Retrieved from http://thenotebook.org/summer-2010/102556/alliance-seeks-unionize-philly-charters?page=3

Wilms, W.W. (2003). Altering the structure and culture of American public schools. *Phi Delta Kappan*, April, 606–615.

Wilson, F. (1985, October 8). The PFT-School District settlement: Who really won? *The Philadelphia Tribune,* p. 16A.

Wilson, K. (1991, March 15). School district marked triple B in fund management. *The Philadelphia Tribune,* p. 2A.

Wong, K. (1992). The politics of urban education as a field of study: An interperative analysis. In R.R.J. Cibulka (Ed.), *The politics of urban education in the United States* (pp. 3–26). Washington, DC: Falmer Press.

Wong, K. (2000). Big change questions: Chicago school reform: From decentralization to integrated governance. *Journal of Educational Change, 1,* 97–105.

Wong, K.K., & Shen, F.X. (2003). Big city mayors and school governance reform: The case of school district takeover. *Peabody Journal of Education, 78*(1), 5–32.

Woodall, M. (2008, December 29). Charter schools' problems surfacing. *The Philadelphia Inquirer,* p. A1.

26

Charter Schools and Urban Education Reform

Thandeka K. Chapman

Introduction

The charter school movement will soon celebrate its 20-year anniversary as a nationwide school reform. Since 1992, when Minnesota opened the first charter school, the number of charter schools across the United States has increased exponentially. In 1994, as part of the reauthorization of the Elementary and Secondary Education Act (ESEA), Congress created and funded the Public Charter School Program (PCSP) to promote the growth of charter schools (Gleason, Clark, Tuttle, Dwoyer, 2010). Since that time, researchers have struggled to decisively ascertain the overall impact of charter schools on student achievement. Large- and small-scale research studies have shown varied results with regard to the success or failure of charter schools in fulfilling the promise of creating better, more successful schools for children in the United States.

Although critics of education worry about America's global standing in education, and have posed charter schools as a means to boost the nation's ability to remain competitive, the need to create stronger schooling opportunities strikes at the heart of social justice calls for equitable schooling primarily for students in urban areas. In 2009–2010, there were 2,574 charter schools, or 52.3% of all charters schools, in metropolitan areas; whereas only 24.5% of traditional public schools are found in metropolitan areas (see Table 26.1). These charter schools serve a student population with approximately 570,866 students (63.3%) who are eligible for free or reduced lunch. While traditional public schools located in urban areas host 28.5% of all traditional students, 55.4% of charter school students are hosted in urban areas (National Alliance for Public Charter Schools, 2011–2012).

However, a review of current research on charter schools demonstrates that charters are as varied in academic achievement as their traditional public school counterparts. Moreover, the frames of reference used by researchers to label charter schools as successful or failing are called into question due to the limited scope of research focusing on achievement scores (Frankenberg, Siegel-Hawley, & Wang, 2010) and the comparison of low-income students of color to their traditional public school(s) (TPS) peers. Missing from these conversations are questions concerning charter school students' abilities to be competitive with White middle-class students who make up the bulk of college-bound students, the resource gap between traditional public schools and charter schools, and the educational divide between suburban and urban districts.

Table 26.1 Charter School Enrollment

2009–2010	*# of Students Enrolled*	*% Students Enrolled*	*# of Schools*	*% of Schools*
Urban Charter Schools	901,662	52.3	2,574	52.3
Traditional Public Schools (TPS)	13,572,890	28.5	22,817	28.5

Source: National Alliance for Public Charter Schools (2012).

The limited definition of success, the consistent comparison to students in failing schools, and the silenced conversation concerning the differences between urban charter schools and suburban schools that produce college-bound students, begs the question: "Are charter schools a red-herring to prevent larger conversations concerning education equity between urban and suburban districts?"

Charter School Growth

Regardless of the mixed research on charter schools, they have become a popular reform in the United States. Charter schools expanded 7.2% between 2009–2010 and 2010–2011 (Gross, Bowen, & Martin, 2011). Begun under the Clinton administration, the charter school movement has enjoyed bipartisan support from Congress and the full support of three presidents. In 2009, President Obama urged states to remove the caps limiting the numbers of charter schools, and tied federal funding Race to the Top grant monies as an incentive to create more charter schools (Witte, Wolf, Dean, & Carlson, 2011). States such as Tennessee, which received Race to the Top funds, recently removed its cap on charter schools. To date, only 10 states and Washington, DC, continue to cap the number of charter schools. Since 2008–2009, 16 states expanded the number of charter schools or charter school students (Lake & Gross, 2012). Even though some states slowed the progression of new charter schools in response to poor test scores, no state has repealed their laws creating charter schools.

Charter schools constitute 5.4% of public schools in the United States (Lake & Gross, 2012). Currently, 41 states and the District of Columbia host 1.8 million students in 5,275 charter schools (Gross, Bowen, & Martin, 2012). Charter schools host almost 4% of the K–12 school population. The percentage of students in charter schools significantly varies between the states. Arkansas, Arizona, California, Colorado, Florida, Georgia, Illinois, Louisiana, Minnesota, Missouri, New Mexico, North Carolina, Ohio, and Texas, and the District of Columbia "educate over one half the K–12 students in the United States and more than 70% of the nation's charter school students" (CREDO, 2009, p. 9). Four states, California, Arizona, Texas, and Florida, contain 49% of the 959 new charter schools that opened between 2009 and 2011. In some cities, a substantial percentage of students attend charter schools. Sixteen of the 40 states and the District of Columbia have 50% or more charter schools in urban areas, while several other states have 40% or more charter schools in urban areas (Table 26.2). Several of the states with high percentages of urban charter schools, such as California and New York, are also the most populated states in the United States.

Charter School Demographics. While the demographics of charter schools vary widely by state, the majority of states have an overrepresentation of African American students in charter

Table 26.2 States With 50% or More Charter Schools in Urban Areas

States	*% Charter Schools in Urban Areas*
Arizona	57.1
California	51.1
Connecticut	83.3
District of Columbia	100
Delaware	50
Indiana	74.1
Louisiana	87
Maryland	77.8
Missouri	66.7
New Mexico	52.8
New York	93.6
Ohio	72
Oklahoma	94.4
Pennsylvania	63.7
Tennessee	72.7
Texas	69.8
Virginia	66.7

Source: National Alliance for Public Charter Schools (2012).

schools, particularly in urban areas. In 2009–2010, White students represented 37% charter and 53% Traditional Public School (TPS), Blacks represent 30% charter and 15% TPS, Latinos represent 26% charter and 23% TPS, Asians represent 4% charter and 4% TPS, and Native Americans are 1% for both charter and TPS (Aud et al., 2012) (Table 26.3).

For a more accurate picture of charter school demographics, a state-by-state analysis is useful (see Frankenberg et al., 2010). In general, charter schools in urban areas enroll larger percentages of Black and Latino students, and suburban, rural, and towns enroll larger percentages of White students (see Table 26.4). In the western region of the United States, Arizona, Hawaii, California, New Mexico, Nevada, Colorado, Oregon, Utah, and Idaho have the highest percentages of White students in their charter schools. These numbers are alarming, considering the high numbers of Latino students in the states who are underrepresented in charter schools. Similarly, North Carolina is "the only non-western state to have a higher percentage of white students in charter schools than traditional public schools" (Frankenberg et al., 2010, p. 31). The fact that

Table 26.3 Charter and Traditional Public School Demographics in the United States

% Students	*White*	*Black*	*Latino*	*Asian*	*Native American*
Charter Schools	37%	30%	26%	4%	1%
Traditional Public Schools (TPS)	53%	15%	23%	4%	>1%

Source: National Center for Education Statistics (2012).

Table 26.4 Racial Demographics of Urban Charter Schools in the United States

Student Race/ Ethnicity	*# of Students*	*% of Students*
White	211,004	23.5
Black	366,063	40.7
Latino	266,399	29.6
Asian	27,226	3.0
Other	27,819	3.1

Source: National Alliance for Public Charter Schools (2012).

North Carolina's charter schools are more widely dispersed between urban, suburban, rural, and town areas may explain the higher percentage of White students while maintaining a significant percentage of Black and Latino students as well.

Purpose and Goals

The original intent of charter schools entailed four primary goals: (1) to provide more schooling options for low-income families, (2) to invite middle-income and affluent families into urban settings, (3) to provide nontraditional learning spaces for all children, and (4) to host laboratories for good practice. Historically, low-income parents have had the least number of schooling options because they are less likely to leave urban areas for better suburban schools and often cannot afford private school tuition. Alternatively, the second goal of charter schools speaks to the schooling needs of middle- and upper-income families. Charter schools are a means to invite these families back into the inner-city by giving them high-achieving schools, similar to the environments found at private schools, without the price tag of private tuition. White middle-class flight from urban areas remains a concern for urban planners and educators. Without middle- and upper-income families purchasing homes in metropolitan areas, the economic base of the city becomes impossible to sustain and education and social programming suffer. The third goal of charter schools was to give parents the option to find specialized curriculum and nontraditional learning environments where their children's unique learning styles and social needs can be optimized. The unique features of charter schools range from schools catering to LGBT students, online schools, project-based academies, and Montessori schools to schools with a focus on the arts, sciences, technology, and other professions. Lastly, President Obama calls charter schools "laboratories of excellence" (Obama, 2010), where teachers and students are exposed to new and rigorous educational curricular designs. The fourth goal of charter schools was to create education laboratories where new curricular reforms, modes of instructions, and leadership structures could be tested and evaluated.

Recent Reports on Charter Schools

The published scholarship on charter schools is substantial and diverse. Scholars have examined the curricula, organizational structures, parental involvement, student mobility, and other elements of schooling to mark the success and failure of charter school reform. The studies included in this chapter were chosen because they are large-scale research designs conducted by nonpartisan, bipartisan, nonprofit researchers who are not aligned with a particular political entity to promote or dismantle charter schools (see Table 26.5). These studies represent the most recent and cutting-edge information on the success of charter schools across the nation and

Table 26.5 Reviewed Studies

Studies Conducted From 2007–2011	*Type of study*	*Location*	*Number of Charter Schools*	*Average Impact*	*Impact by Student Subgroups*
Hanushek et al. 2007	Nonexperimental	Texas	248	Negative	No impact by income or race/ethnicity
Ballou et al. 2008	Nonexperimental	Idaho	28	Positive for elementary; non for middle schools	N/A
Abdulkadiroglu et al. 2009	Nonexperimental and experimental	Boston	28	Positive for middle and high school	N/A
CREDO 2009	Nonexperimental	14 states and DC	2,403	Negative	More positive for lower-income students More negative impacts for Black/ Latino students
Hoxby et al. 2009	Experimental	New York	42	Positive	No impact by race/ethnicity or gender More positive impact for students in higher grades
Zimmer et al. 2009	Nonexperimental	7 states and DC	231	None/negative	No impacts by race/ ethnicity Some positive postsecondary predictions for Chicago and Florida high school students
Gleason et al. 2010	Experimental	15 states	36	None	Less negative for schools with: – lower enrollment – use of ability grouping – larger proportion of lower-income students – larger proposition of lower-achieving students
Witte et al. 2011	Nonexperimental	Milwaukee	10	Positive	Positive change in middle grades No significant change for 10th graders

Primary source: Gleason, Clark, Tuttle, and Dwoyer (2010), pp. 83–85.

in large metropolitan areas in the United States. The studies attempt to provide readers with a more comprehensive look at charter school education in a single state or across multiple states. Earlier studies often compared charter schools in their first few years with well-established TPS. Although the newer studies include new charter schools, enough charter schools have been serving students for five or more years and can be viewed as having established their curriculum, their student population, and the leadership styles. Few researchers would debate the existence of high-quality charter schools; however, given the call to increase the numbers of charter schools, and the monies that would be extracted from traditional schools to fund these initiatives, an expansive lens is necessary to assess the charter school movement as a large-scale federal policy initiative. If politicians and government officials continue to speak of charter schools as a monolithic entity, then they should be judged by the same measure.

The reviewed studies fall into three categories: two experimental designs, five nonexperimental designs, and one combined experimental and nonexperimental design. The experimental design studies use charter schools that are considered "oversubscribed" because they have more applicants than available seats. Charter students apply to the schools and are accepted or denied. The sample for the experimental studies is students who have entered "oversubscribed" charter schools through a lottery system and students who applied for the lottery, but were not accepted into a charter school. The nonexperimental designs used convenience samples of achievement data from students across the United States. They utilize students who are currently attending charter schools and students from similar demographics who attend nearby, demographically similar traditional public schools. Additionally, the eight studies compare charter school students to their traditional public school peers.

Similarities Within the Research

These studies share several similarities that will be discussed following the review of research. First, they seek to compare "apples to apples"— meaning that demographic data such as race, socioeconomic status, and gender are controlled in the studies. In three of the eight studies, low-income students of color are directly compared with their middle-income White counterparts who constitute the majority of college-bound students in the United States.

Second, each study attempts to control for "selection bias." Selection bias occurs when parental and/or student agency is not removed from the statistical equation. Thus, parents who actively seek different options for their children's education and possibly expend significant resources to secure nontraditional education programs are seen as "skewing the data" and must be statistically controlled. These studies seek to lessen or remove the impact that social capital has on the student achievement data. "Social capital refers to the social relations between persons that provide resources for achieving certain goals (such as improvements in student learning)," according to Berends and Zottola (2009, p. 43). However, it is difficult to ascertain to what extent parental impact and peer culture can be lessened through statistical reasoning (Berends, Cannata, & Goldring, 2011).

Third, the studies primarily are informed by achievement data to demonstrate the success or challenges of charter schools. Resources provided by charter schools and the TPS are rarely discussed as contributing to a child's potential for success beyond K–12 schooling. One study explores the number of music programs; but no study discussed extracurricular activities or opportunities for leadership that are factored into college admissions (Gleason et al., 2010). Additionally, only the study from the National Center for Education Evaluation and Regional Assistance (Gleason, et al., 2010) details the types of physical plant resources such as gymnasiums, counselors, and medical care found in charter schools.

Fourth, there is a dearth of information on high school student achievement in general. Although several of the studies include student achievement data from high school students, the bulk of the research is focused on elementary schools. Data on college admissions, attendance, and retention for students attending charter schools is relatively absent.

These four similarities will be discussed in more depth after the studies have been reviewed. The review provides an overall picture of the charter school movement by highlighting what elements of the movement are working, the challenges to assessing the success of the movement, and what questions are not being asked nor answered. In the next section, the three studies focusing on single urban centers will be presented first. The two studies evaluating the reform as a statewide entity will be next; and last will be the three national comprehensive reports.

Studies of Urban Centers

"How New York City's Charter Schools Affect Student Achievement." Interestingly, the studies focused on urban areas had the most positive results of the eight studies in the review. The New York City Charter School Evaluation Project is an experimental design study that focuses on 93% of the charter school students enrolled in grades 3–12 in New York City from 2001 through 2007 using a lottery-based analysis (Hoxby, Murarka, & Kang, 2009). The study provides results in aggregate form for the 78 charter schools in New York City, but does not give an overall number for charter school students who participated in the study. The percentage breakdown for the grade levels has substantial differentiation, with grades 3–5 representing 26.9%, grades 6–8 representing 10.3%, and grades 9–12 representing only 4.9% of the students being evaluated. In fact, only four high schools are included in the analysis. Given the longitudinal time span of the study, there are challenges with participant attrition as students grow older. Arguably, how a student completes his or her K–12 academic career is just as important and telling as the data from other grades.

The New York Charter School Evaluation Project (Hoxby et al., 2009) is one of the studies that compares students of color to their White, middle-class peers. In addition to evaluating student achievement growth, Hoxby et al. evaluated how much of the "Scarsdale-Harlem achievement gap" closes for charter schools versus traditional school students. The Scarsdale-Harlem achievement gap is the 35–40 point gap between traditional public school students in Harlem and traditional public school students in the upper-middle-class, predominately White suburb of Scarsdale, New York. Because Black students are 61.8% and Latino students are 31% of the New York City charter school population (National Alliance for Public Charter Schools, 2012), this type of analysis speaks directly to the achievement gap between White students in affluent suburbs and students of color in urban settings.

The results from the study indicate that students in grades 3–8 make significantly larger gains than their TPS peers each year. These gains are compounded each year a student remains in a charter school. Based on the data from 3rd and 6th grades, the researchers estimate that when a charter school student reaches the 8th grade, he or she is estimated to score 30 points higher in math than a comparable student who matriculated through the TPS. This would mean that charter school students close 86% of the gap between Harlem students and Scarsdale students (Hoxby et al. 2009). In reading, charter school students would make up 66% of the Scarsdale-Harlem achievement gap. At the high school level, charter school students taking the Regents Exam, the statewide proficiency test to receive a Regents diploma in New York, score 3 points higher for every year he or she matriculates through a charter school in grades 9–12 than his or her traditional public school counterpart. However, the low sample number of high school students in the study who took the Regents Exam provides only statistical predictions that favor charter school students passing the exam at higher rates than students in the TPS.

"Informing the Debate: Comparing Boston's Charter, Pilot, and Traditional Public Schools." Researchers in Boston also found positive results for charter school students when evaluating Boston's two sets of charter schools (Abdulkadiroglu et al., 2009). "Pilot" schools are connected to the Boston Public School (BPS) district and the Boston's Teacher's Union, and "charter" schools are independent schools run by autonomous groups. Approximately 17% of the 10th graders and 21% of middle school students in Boston attend charter or pilot schools. Data were provided from 2001–2007. Charter and pilot schools in Boston serve smaller percentages of English Language Learners, free/reduced-lunch students, and students with special needs, but higher percentages of Black and Latino students than TPS.

Using experimental and nonexperimental designs, the researchers evaluated the success of both the charter and pilot schools in Boston (Abdulkadiroglu et al., 2009). Data from all charter school and pilot school students were compared with that of TPS student counterparts; additionally, students from oversubscribed charter and pilot schools were paired with TPS students for a more rigorous study. To reduce the bias introduced by students leaving charters and returning to a TPS mid-year, and to counter claims that charter and pilot schools push out the lowest-achieving students, students who left during the study were still counted as part of the charter and pilot school sample. However, since students who left charter and pilot schools had overall lower baseline scores, the charter and pilot schools may benefit from these students returning to TPS.

Researchers reported mixed findings for the two types of schools. For both sets of evaluations, charter school students outperformed their TPS counterparts in English language arts (ELA) and math. The results state that the students in charter schools made gains "equal to roughly half the black-white achievement gap" (p. 29). The results for the pilot schools were not positive; pilot students did not make significant gains in ELA or math when compared to TPS students.

"The Performance of Charter Schools in Wisconsin." Even though Witte, Wolf, Dean, and Carlson (2011) ended their five-year nonexperimental longitudinal study of 10 independent charter schools with 1,559 students in Milwaukee, Wisconsin, with mixed results, they provided several positive results favoring charter schools. These charter schools are defined as "independent" because they are chartered through organizations outside of Milwaukee Public Schools (MPS), and therefore, are not beholden to MPS policies or accountability criteria. However, the researchers paired the charter school student participants, or sample, with their MPS peers to evaluate the success of the 10 charter schools. The researchers collected state test scores from students in grades 3–8 for their baseline data, and collected the students' achievement data on an annual basis. The final set of test scores is completed in the 10th grade because no state tests are given beyond this grade. Therefore, there are no measurable indicators of student success being collected in any uniform fashion for charter high school or TPS success. Interestingly enough, measures could not be provided for English Language Learners, or for other racial ethnic groups besides Black students. Although White, Latino, Asian American students, and English-language learners exist in significant numbers in MPS, the independent charter schools are overwhelmingly Black.

Although charter school students experienced spurts of growth in reading and math in the 7th and 8th grades, the researchers concluded that there were no overall areas of significant growth for charter school students compared to their TPS peers. However, charter school students who remained in the same charter school for the four years of the study exhibited significant gains in math and reading when compared to the TPS students. Black students with higher baseline data experienced more growth than students with low baseline data, and students with exceptional needs experienced lower growth than other students. If these urban charter schools cannot definitely excel when compared to their TPS counterparts, it poses a dire comparison between urban charter schools and their suburban school counterparts.

State Studies of Charter Schools

"Charter School Quality and Parental Decision Making With School Choice." The two state studies of charter schools yielded more negative results than the studies in specific urban areas. Researchers explored student achievement gains, rates of student mobility, and parental satisfaction in this evaluation of over 200 Texas charter schools (Hanushek, Kain, Rivkin, & Branch, 2007). Urban charter schools constitute 70% of Texas charter schools, with 78% of charter school students located in urban areas (National Alliance for Public Charter Schools, 2012). Black students tend to be overrepresented in Texas charter schools, Latino students appear to have a balanced representation in TPS and charter schools, and White students are underrepresented in charter schools. The study does not provide a number of schools or students sampled for the research, nor does it provide percentages for subgroups. After an extended discussion of statistical measures, the researchers state,

> Our results indicate that, although charter schools have difficult start-up periods, they settle down within roughly four years and are not significantly different than traditional public schools on average in terms of value added to reading and mathematics achievement. Although there is little or no evidence of differential effects by race, ethnicity, or income, the charter school deficit appears to be smaller for students with higher initial achievement. (Hanushek, et al., 2007, p. 825)

Although charter school students are not achieving at higher rates, the researchers found that students who remain in charter schools progress more quickly in achievement (Hanushek et al., 2007). Hanushek et al. also found that mobility rates are higher among charter school students than those of their TPS peers. Additionally, students in the lowest quartile of baseline achievement tend to achieve the least of any group.

"Charter Schools in Idaho." Using a nonexperimental design, researchers in Idaho had mixed results (Ballou, Teasley, & Zeidner, 2008). Although urban areas in Idaho, such as Boise, host significant charter school populations, charter schools in Idaho have a more unique population than the majority of charter schools across the country. Only one out of the 28 charter schools dips below 85.89% for average White enrollment, with the rest of the charter schools posting White enrollment percentages significantly higher than their districts. Idaho charter schools also have low enrollments of Latino and Native American students, even though these students constitute significant state and district enrollment percentages. With the exception of the Boise District Schools, the charters do not service English Language Learners, and few Idaho charters service students receiving free and reduced lunch. Yet, the charters equally service students with special needs in the various districts (Ballou et al., 2008).

The results showed that charter school students in the elementary grades outscore their TPS peers, but do not outscore their TPS peers at the middle or high school levels. Perhaps a rationale that is not provided by the researchers is the number of charter school students who reenter TPS after middle school due to the lack of charter high schools; however, this rationale does not resolve the lower gains made by middle school students since the majority of charter elementary schools are K–8. Ironically, there is an extensive waiting list to enter charter schools in Idaho, regardless of how their performance contrasts with the performance of students in TPS.

Comprehensive Studies of Charter Schools

"Charter Schools in Eight States: Effects on Achievement, Attainment, Integration, and Competition." The results from three comprehensive studies provide several nuances to the findings, but support the conclusion that overall charter schools are not living up to the goal to create schools of excellence. Zimmer, Gill, Booker, Lavertu, Sass, and Witte (2009) studied charter schools in the cities of Chicago, San Diego, Philadelphia, Denver, Milwaukee, and the states of Ohio, Texas, and Florida. Based on availability, reading and math achievement data from each location were collected in various longitudinal time frames that ranged from 10 years in San Diego (1997–2007) and Texas (1994–2004) to five years in Denver (2001–2006) and four years in Ohio (2004–2008). The study focused on middle and high school, "nonprimary" grades, achievement. Through their analysis, the researchers also reported postsecondary projections for charter middle school students who continued in charter high schools.

Researchers state, "In five out of seven locales, these nonprimary charter schools are producing achievement gains that are, on average, neither substantially better or worse than those of local TPS" (Zimmer et al., 2009, p. xiii). Moreover, in Ohio and Texas, the results are significantly negative for reading and math. Only in Chicago did the estimates shift from negative to positive as the charter schools remained open. Additionally, the results from Chicago and Florida showed that charter middle school students who graduated from charter high schools were 7–15% more likely to graduate and 8–10% more likely to enroll in college than TPS students who attended traditional high schools. Unfortunately, Illinois and Florida are two of the only states that track postsecondary data.

"Multiple Choice: Charter School Performance in 16 States." To widen the scope of the literature, the report by the Center for Research on Education Outcomes (CREDO, 2009) employed a nonexperimental design to evaluate student achievement in charter K–12 schools in 15 states and the District of Columbia. The 15 states and DC were chosen because they represent over 70% of the students in U.S. charter schools. The states included were Arkansas, Arizona, California, Colorado (Denver), the District of Columbia, Florida, Georgia, Illinois (Chicago), Louisiana, Minnesota, Missouri, New Mexico, North Carolina, Ohio, and Texas. The study used various standardized test scores in both reading and math from the states and DC; researchers controlled for standardized test scores, race/ethnicity, eligibility for free/reduced lunch, and special education. More than 2,400 charter schools and 1.7 million records from these charter schools are included in the data analysis (CREDO, 2009).

They provided an aggregated picture of the results, as well as disaggregated results for individual states. In addition to state achievement tests, the researchers utilized National Assessment of Educational Progress (NAEP) scores to examine the charter schools in their specific communities. The CREDO study compares students of color to their White middle-class counterparts as part of the analysis. The CREDO researchers recognize the importance of closing the achievement gap between White middle-class students and students of color, and not just increasing achievement in charter schools above the low bar of many TPS counterparts. Researchers state, "Realistically, the relative standard of performance—whether charter schools are producing student outcomes that are at least as good as the schools in their community—is a fairly low threshold" (CREDO, 2009, p. 46).

Table 26.6 Aggregated State Gains in Reading and Math

	AZ	*AR*	*CA*	*CO*	*DC*	*FL*	*GA*	*IL*	*LA*	*MA*	*MN*	*MO*	*NM*	*NC*	*OH*	*TX*
Reading	NS	PS	PS	PS	–	NS	–	–	PS	N/A	NS	PS	NS	PS	–	NS
Math	NS	PS	NS	PS	–	NS	NS	PS	PS	N/A	NS	PS	NS	NS	NS	NS

NS = Negative Significant; PS = Positive Significant; — = no effect; N/A = no data

The results yielded a number of positive and negative results that further demonstrate the difficulty of evaluating the reform across the country. However, the researchers posted some results depicting a national landscape of charter school achievement. For example, when evaluating the academic growth of students in math, 46% of the charter school students had "statistically indistinguishable" (CREDO, 2009, p. 3) gains from the average student in the TPS. Although 17% of the charter schools exceeded their TPS equivalents in math growth, 37% of the charter schools were significantly below the growth students would have made in TPS.

Variations in the data are evident when looking at the different grade levels. In reading, charter elementary school students experience a small gain when compared to their TPS peers, but did not surpass their TPS peers in math. At the middle school level, charter school students also demonstrated gains above their TPS peers for both math and reading. Unfortunately, charter high school students' gains were lower for both math and reading. The negative gains made by high school charter students are particularly troubling at this juncture of students' academic careers and certainly would impact their ability to make future plans.

The state-by-state level data may be less unsettling, if one lives in a state with successful charter schools. Table 26.6 shows the states' overall growth for charter school students in reading and math. The level of significance ranges for each state, with some states being closer to their TPS than others (CREDO, 2009). The table shows the numerous areas where the results in charter schools were not different, negatively or positively, from those of their TPS peers. Given the goals of charter schools, no significant difference is almost as much a failure as negative significant difference. However, the students may receive other benefits that are not easily acknowledged in this design.

Data disaggregated by subgroups show a different set of challenges (Tables 26.7 & 26.8). According to CREDO, students of color and special education students are not surpassing their TPS counterparts. Also, students in poverty and English Language Learners have larger gains in charter schools than do those in traditional public schools; but students who are not in poverty and are not English Language Learners make larger gains in traditional public schools. In urban areas, 67% of all charter school students are eligible for free/reduced lunch, so charter schools are more successful with this population. However, for the 33% who are not designated as poor, charter schools may not be working for them. This 33% comprises middle- and working-class families who may be compelled to live in the city limits due to policies concerning district and city workers, such as police and teachers, as well as other families who actively choose to live in urban areas for a variety of reasons.

"The Evaluation of Charter School Impacts." The Evaluation of Charter School Impacts is the second large-scale multistate study (Gleason et al., 2010). National Center for Education Evaluation and Regional Assistance contracted with Mathematica Policy Research to study the effectiveness of charter schools (2010). They evaluated 36 charter middle schools across 15 states to assess achievement outcomes from oversubscribed charter schools that were least two years old. Interestingly, there were 130 charter schools eligible for participation in the study, but 63

Table 26.7 State Reading Gains by Subgroup

	AR	*AZ*	*CA*	*CO*	*DC*	*FL*	*GA*	*IL*	*LA*	*MA*	*MN*	*MO*	*NM*	*NC*	*OH*	*TX*
Special Education	—	—	—	—	—	—	—	—	—	—	—	—	—	—	—	—
Black Students	—	—	PS	—	—	NS	NS	NS	PS	—	PS	PS	—	—	—	NS
Latino Students	—	—	—	—	—	—	NS	NS	—	—	—	PS	NS	—	NS	NS
English Language Learners	—	PS	CA	—	—	—	—	—	—	—	—	—	PS	—	—	PS
Students Living in Poverty	PS	—	PS	—	—	—	PS	PS	NS	—	—	NS	—	PS	PS	PS

NS = Negative Significant; PS = Positive Significant; — no effect

Table 26.8 State Math Gains by Subgroup

	AR	*AZ*	*CA*	*CO*	*DC*	*FL*	*GA*	*IL*	*LA*	*MA*	*MN*	*MO*	*NM*	*NC*	*OH*	*TX*
Special Education	—	PS	PS	—	—	—	—	—	—	—	—	—	—	—	—	—
Black Students	PS	NS	—	—	—	NS	NS	—	PS	—	PS	PS	—	NS	—	NS
Latino Students	PS	NS	NS	PS	—	—	NS	NS	PS	—	—	PS	NS	—	NS	NS
English Language Learners	—	—	PS	—	—	—	PS	—	—	—	—	NS	—	—	—	—
Students Living in Poverty	PS	NS	PS	—	—	—	PS	PS	NS	—	—	NS	—	—	PS	PS

NS = Negative Significant; PS = Positive Significant; — no effect

declined the invitation. Charter school administrators are often overwhelmed with their responsibilities and likely hesitant to increase the workload required to participate in research. However, as "laboratories of excellence," it is part of their obligation to the public to be open for study and evaluation. Moreover, the question lingers as to why a high-performing charter would not enthusiastically accept an invitation to demonstrate its success.

The researchers caution that the study is not meant for generalizability to all charter middle schools because the lottery system format is not indicative of the majority of charter middle schools. The sample included 2,330 students who were admitted to the charter school through the lottery system (1,400) and who were not admitted (930) and were forced to return to a TPS. There were some interesting differences between the TPS and charter schools. Charter schools in the study had fewer gifted and talented programs, certified teachers, ESL programs, and students who were eligible for free/reduced lunch. The charter schools had fewer English Language Learners and students with suspension problems. These students were followed for a two-year period to document their achievement, behavior, attitudes, parental involvement, and school satisfaction. State performance tests, student and parent surveys, a charter school authorizer survey, and administrative records also were collected to evaluate the charter schools (Gleason et al., 2010). For each of these surveys, the researchers received significant response rates that ranged from 80% of charter school authorizers to 86% of student respondents.

The researchers presented the following conclusions concerning the overall impact of charter schools serving grades 6–8:

- On average, charter schools did not statistically significantly impact student achievement.
- Charter schools had a positive effect on parental and student satisfaction.
- Charter schools did not significantly affect most other outcomes examined. Other outcomes examined included absences, suspensions, student behavior and attitudes, student work ethic, and parental involvement.
- Charter schools had an inverse relationship between student achievement and student income level. Students who were not eligible for free/reduced lunch were negatively impacted for reading and math test scores. Students eligible for free and/or reduce lunch were positively impacted in Year 2 on their math scores.
- There was evidence of an inverse relationship between students' baseline achievement levels and charter school impacts on achievement. The higher the student's baseline assessment score, the more negative the impacts were from charter schools.
- No significant differences for race/ethnicity or gender existed. (Gleason et al., 2010, pp. xxii–xxiv)

The more nuanced explanation of the result bears reporting. For example, 10 of the 28 charter schools scored statistically significantly higher than their TPS counterparts on both reading and math test scores. Charter schools with the highest proportions of disadvantaged students and charter schools located in large urban areas had positive impacts of Year 2 test scores.

Unfortunately, the findings from the study are more troubling than positive when other factors are also considered. Interestingly, the study charter schools started with a higher-achieving population, with fewer English Language Learners, fewer disadvantaged students, and more autonomy, but could not significantly increase achievement. The students in the study charter schools had longer school days than students at the TPS and were less likely to be in a school with a library, gym, or cafeteria. Yet, parents and students were more likely to praise the school and consider it successful.

Discussion

While the results from the studies of individual cities show more positive gains, the studies across cities show the larger percentages of underachieving charter schools. According to the National Alliance for Public Charter Schools, 42% of urban charter schools did not make Annual Yearly Progress (AYP) in 2009–2012. Since 2005, charter schools have consistently posted a 40% rate of charter schools not making AYP (National Alliance for Public Charter Schools, 2012). CREDO reported that 46% of the 2,403 charter schools were not significantly different from the TPS peers in math, and 37% had significantly negative growth relative to their traditional school peers (CREDO, 2009). Given the dire achievement gains in many of the urban areas in the 16 states, these results are very disheartening. While there are a few hopeful results for charter schools, the research overwhelmingly shows that charter schools are struggling to meet the needs of their students, and are not fulfilling the goals of the charter reform.

The studies also remind the reader that the research is conducted in aggregate form and obfuscates distinctions between high-performing and low-performing charter schools. However, when high and lows are averaged, and the results paint a dismal picture of charter schools, that means there are some significant lows in the sample pool. As the reform grows older, some researchers are calling for policy reforms to protect students in failing charter schools (Zimmer et al. 2009; CREDO, 2009). CREDO states that, "When schools consistently fail, they should be closed" (2009, p. 7). Conversely, while the White House has encouraged districts to raise caps on charter schools, no outcry has been made to close charter schools that are not performing. Given the fact that charter schools underperform in the first few years, President Obama is calling for the creation of more charter schools, without eliminating of the current under-performing charter schools.

Moreover, because charter schools are most present in urban districts, those policy makers who propose lifting caps without a sincere conversation on closing schools are relegating urban schools to a newly created second- or third-rate education system. Thus, researchers focused on urban areas celebrate their limited triumphs over the TPS (Hoxby et al., 2009; Abdulkadiroglu et al., 2009) while acknowledging that these charter students remain far behind their suburban counterparts, are resigning urban students to second-class school status. Additionally, other ways in which the conversations concerning charter schools have been constructed seem to relegate charter school students to a second- or third-tier education.

The push for charter schools does not appear to be waning in debates over public school reform; rather, policy makers are fervently pushing to uncritically expand the scope of charter schools with little regard for students matriculating through unsuccessful charter schools. Therefore, researchers, educators, and community activists must work at the local levels of schooling to reduce the numbers of students in failing schools, increase the visibility and replication of high-performing traditional and charter schools, and continue to press for viable reforms that will produce equitable school options for all children in the United States.

"Apples to Apples"

Although the research demonstrates the extreme variability of charter school success, they have several similarities that were previously mentioned. For methodological purpose the researchers strive to compare "apples to apples" or similar students from traditional public schools. These comparisons control for race and socioeconomic background to demonstrate how students are competing within subgroups and geographic areas. If the traditional public schools in urban areas used for comparisons were not highly problematic, there would be little need for charter schools.

While comparing like groups from similar nearby schools presents the public with information about local school district dynamics, it does not address the achievement gap. Only three studies make any reference to the achievement gap between racial subgroups and their White counterparts, and in all three comparisons, the students of color remain far behind their White peers. Given recent court decisions denying the use of race as a significant consideration for undergraduate college admissions (*Gratz v. Bollinger,* 2003), the charter school students remain less competitive for admissions to elite colleges. This means students from urban charter schools will be relegated to community colleges and second-tier state schools. In the long run, it may limit their ability to secure employment or compete with students from top-tier universities.

Selection Bias

Each of the studies delegates a significant portion of its reporting to a discussion of controls for "selection bias." For statisticians, the removal of "unobservable indicators" to provide results that can solely be attributed to the independent variable, the charter school, is sound reasoning. "However, students don't go to school in a vacuum. Instead their achievement is shaped not only by instruction and family background factors, but also by achievement, attitudes, and aspirations of their schoolmates" (Weitzel & Lubienski, 2010a, p. 224). For the policy maker, the education administrator, the teacher, and the parents, the issue of "selection bias" is a key component in the charter school debate. These "unobservable characteristics" such as social capital, parental motivation, and student history in other schools were part of the original, and must remain central to, conversations around the charter school reform.

Reformers against charter schools feared the "cream" of students would be skimmed from TPS into charter schools. While many interpreted "cream" to be students with high test scores, others saw "cream" as including knowledgeable, motivated parents as well. If charter schools attract more motivated parents with greater social capital, or if parents use charter schools to flee traditional public schools because their children have behavior problems, then researchers need to know more about these dynamics, not try to erase them. Abdulkadiroglu et al. state,

> Precisely because of this volunteer status, there are strong reasons to believe that Pilot and Charter students are not representative of the typical public school students. One possibility is that the volunteers are refugees, those least well-served by the traditional public school system and the most desperate to escape. On the other hand, those parents who are willing to volunteer could be the most engaged in their children's education, willing to drive long distances to help their children achieve. (2009, p. 8)

Furthermore, many charter schools such as the Knowledge is Power Program (KIPP) schools require parents and students to sign a "school contract" that defines parental participation (Hoxby et al., 2009; Weitzel & Lubienski, 2010b). The parent willing to commit to a set number of participation hours may be a different parent than parents who cannot or will not make that choice; and perhaps this type of consistent parental involvement leads to strong achievement. Conversely, "If expanded school choice is primarily utilized by more motivated or affluent subsets of urban populations, this suggests inequitable access" (Miron, 2010, p. 31). Addressing these scenarios helps reformers to replicate the successful factors of charter schools, while dismissing them as "unobservable" continues to provide few answers into the workings of successful charter schools.

Quality Education

Trying to determine the success of a national reform requires data that can be amassed and processed through measurable indices that are collected by schools, districts, states, and federal agencies. Using state assessments from various states requires researchers to produce complex research designs in order to compare data across states and districts. However, even a uniform assessment, such as NAEP, shows that charter school students score lower than students in public schools in grades 4, 8, and 12 in math and reading (Aud et al., 2012). Furthermore, the studies do not provide other measures of academic achievement. Using NAEP scores, Aud et al. found that charter school students score equal to or above the TPS students in history, geography, and civics at grades 4 and 8, but they fall below TPS students in the 12th grade.

Yet, the best of standardized tests are constantly challenged as being poor measures of intelligence because the assessments do not represent the full spectrum of student learning and achievement. Unfortunately, state and federal databases do not consistently collect other necessary measures of success that are used in college admissions or citizenship beyond standardized tests. Nor do charter schools report other indicators of quality schools such as extracurricular activities, arts curriculum, college counseling, and opportunities for leadership. Zimmer et al. suggest that, "researchers and policy makers need to look beyond test scores to fully assess charter schools' performance" (2009, p. xv). Truly, no one is debating the need for grade school students to be able to write, read, and do math; but there are other components beyond basic content instruction that make a great school. While many traditional urban schools also may struggle to provide various resources and components, traditional schools in suburbs and towns are able to equip their schools with ample resources that contribute to students receiving a quality education that are not found in traditional urban or charter schools.

For example, when compared to TPS, charter school students are less likely to have a library (64% vs. 88%), a gym (54% vs. 81%), cafeterias (54% vs. 86%), counselors (82% vs. 89%, or nurse's office (69% vs. 88%) (Gleason et al., 2010). Charter schools are less likely to serve English Language Learners and students with special needs, particularly in Southwest cities with high populations of students who benefit from English as a second-language curriculum (Gleason et al., 2010). In the area of curriculum, although the percentage of students taking algebra, geometry, and algebra II in charter schools appears similar to traditional public schools, not enough charter schools provided courses in statistics or calculus to report findings (Aud et al., 2012). Charter schools also have significantly fewer students taking biology and chemistry (55.7% vs. 66.9%) (Aud et al., 2012).

Goals of Charter Schools Revisited

Efforts to achieve the goals of charter schools—to create more schooling options, to meet the needs of upper- and middle-income families, to create nontraditional schooling options, to create laboratories of excellence, and to privatize public education—have been met with varied success. In this section, how these goals have and have not been met is discussed.

In regard to offering longer school days and years, more team-teaching, and diverse leadership practices, charter schools are considered innovative (Hoxby et al., 2009, Gleason et al., 2010; Weitzel & Lubienski, 2010b). In particular states, charter school teachers do not have the same certification requirements (Aud et al., 2012). Some schools require parents to commit specific amounts of their time to their children and the school. Yet, it remains unclear if these changes lead to academic growth for charter school students (Hoxby et al., 2009).

In several studies reviewed, researchers found the same types of curriculum in charter schools that are found in traditional public schools (Ballou et al., 2008; Hoxby et al., 2009; Gleason et al., 2010), thus calling into question the "innovative" nature of charter schools. Researchers report that, as a whole, charter schools are not sites of new and groundbreaking curriculum (Loveless & Field, 2009). As pressure comes to bear on charter schools to produce high achievement, they utilize the same types of curriculum found in traditional public schools. Additionally, charter schools have less curricular options because they have fewer teachers to cover a wider array of curriculum.

Furthermore, it is uncertain if charter schools have met the needs of middle-class families by providing high-achieving schools for children in urban areas. Several studies show that students who are not receiving free/or reduced lunch and are not second-language learners are not achieving beyond their TPS peers (Gleason et al., 2010; CREDO, 2009; Abdulkadiroglu et al., 2009). Gleason et al. state,

> Among charter schools popular enough to hold lotteries, overall, our results suggest that they are no more successful than nearby traditional public schools, in boosting student achievement. However, those located in large urban areas and serving disadvantaged students are the most successful in doing so, a finding consistent with other recent lottery-based studies on charter schools in urban areas. (Gleason et al., 2010, p. xxix)

Middle-income parents may find that charter schools are not the answer to their education concerns regarding high achievement, and they are willing to move their children in/out of charter schools (Hanushek et al., 2007; Ballou et al., 2008). However, as in the previous discussion on the limited scope of charter school evaluation, researchers recognize that parents are concerned with a host of schooling factors beyond academic achievement.

The goal that appears to have had the most success is the privatization of public schools. Over the past two decades, research on charter schools has reported mixed, but substantially poor, results for charter schools (Weitzel & Lubienski, 2010b). However, charter school proponents continue to push for more charter schools rather than close existing failing schools to make room for new schools. Weitzel and Lubienski explain,

> In an age where policy makers require "data-driven decision making," a focus on "what works," and the use of "scientifically-based research" in advancing school reform, one would expect that policy makers drew on evidence of charter school effects in advancing the movement. However, a retrospective analysis of the evidence available at the time indicates that information on program effectiveness did not seem to be the primary driver of charter school expansion. Instead, policy makers appear to have drawn on other justifications regarding the theoretical potential of charter schools in embracing this model—and still do today. (2010b, p. 26)

Not only does the number of charter schools grow despite the body of research, charter schools grew exponentially before there was research to demonstrate their effectiveness (Lubienski & Weitzel, 2010). One example of continued growth is the charter schools in Ohio run by Imagine Inc., in which the six schools have received "D" ratings since 2005. The company is not allowed to open more schools until *one* school receives a "C" rating (van Lier, 2010). *One* school out of *six* must receive a "C" rating, and the corporation is back in business? Really?

Yet, parents and policy makers appear very much in line with each other. Regardless of the research that continues to challenge the success of the charter school movement, there are extensive waiting lists for charter schools across the country. For example, Ballou et al. reported a waiting list of 4,671 students, despite the overall poor academic performance of Idaho charter schools (2008). The 365,000 students who are on waiting lists for charter schools across the country demonstrate that parents remain excited about charter schools despite their poor performance (Lubienski & Weitzel, 2010; Stein, Goldring, & Cravens, 2011; Weil, 2009).

Conclusion

Issues of parental and community goals for schooling and the absence of academics in many charter schools complicates the primary goal of charter schools to create schools of excellence. An overwhelming percentage of charter schools are placed in urban areas and serve urban families. The conversations around "choice" and charter schools obfuscate the realities of future schooling options for parents seeking safe and rigorous schools. In essence, most charter school students are matriculating through schools not unlike their original failing traditional public school counterparts. Moreover, they are in charter schools with less resources than their traditional public schools, and are far less able to access the same sort of resources found in their suburban counterparts. When urban charter school students are compared to White suburban students, charter schools continue to propagate the achievement gap. Yet, where is the conversation about charter schools and the Black/ White and Latino/White achievement gap? Where is the conversation about other unmeasured skill sets students need to be competitive beyond standardized test scores? If a child cannot read or compute math or if a high school student needs remedial courses as a college freshman, no amount of new curriculum and instructional designs, warm fuzzy school culture, and leadership model counts for success. Appositionally, if a child can read and compute math, but cannot think conceptually and in imaginative ways, and if a high school student has not had opportunities to explore his or her other talents and leadership capabilities, it is doubtful that the student will have the skills to be successful in postsecondary school or work capacities that lead to employment opportunities with room for growth or civic leadership.

In urban schools plagued by low test scores, dwindling resources, and top-down curricular mandates, the promise of charter schools becomes extremely important. Families looking for ways to give their children the best opportunities for success with limited means rely on public education. Charter schools are supposed to not only be different learning spaces, but academically successful as well. Charter schools were created to raise the bar of American education for the nation's families with limited options for good schools. Given the large numbers of urban families seeking good schools in the United States, these options are invaluable. Importantly, the measure of success cannot be different for schools in urban areas. They must not be "good enough for them" schools in which urban charter school students remain academically underachieving and underexposed to environments that enrich their intellect, cultivate their social and emotional growth, and prepare them to compete in the real world.

References

Abdulkadiroglu, A., Angrist, J., Cohodes, S., Dynarski, S., Fullerton, J., Kane, T., & Pathak, P. (2009). *Informing the debate: Comparing Boston's charter, pilot and traditional public schools.* Boston, MA: Boston Foundation.

Aud, S., Hussar, W., Johnson, F., Kena, G., Roth, E., Manning, E., Wang, X., & Zhang, J. (2012). *The condition of education 2012* (NCES 2012–045). Washington, DC: U.S. Department of Education, National Center for Education Statistics. Retrieved from http://nces.ed.gov/pubsearch

Ballou, D., Teasley, B., & Zeidner, T. (2008). Charter schools in Idaho. In M. Berends, M.G. Springer, & H.J. Walberg (Eds.), *Charter school outcomes* (pp. 228–241). Mahwah, NJ: Lawrence Erlbaum Associates.

Berends, M., Cannata, M., & Goldring E., (2011). *School choice and school improvement.* Cambridge, MA: Harvard Education Press.

Berends, M., & Zottola, G.C. (2009). Social perspectives on school choice. In M. Berends, M.G. Springer, D. Ballou, & H.J. Walberg (Eds.), *Handbook of research on school choice* (pp. 35–53). New York, NY: Routledge.

Center for Research on Education Outcomes [CREDO]. (2009). *Multiple choice: Charter school performance in 16 states.* Stanford, CA: Stanford University Press.

Frankenberg, E., Siegel-Hawley, G., & Wang, J. (2010). *Choice without equity: Charter school segregation and the need for civil rights standards.* Los Angeles, CA: The Civil Rights Project/Proyecto Derechos Civiles at UCLA. http://www.civilrightsproject.ucla.edu

Gleason, P., Clark, M., Tuttle, C.C., & Dwoyer, E. (2010). *The evaluation of charter school impacts: Final report (NCEE 2010–4029).* Washington, DC: National Center for Education Evaluation and Regional Assistance, Institute of Education Sciences, U.S. Department of Education. http://ies.ed.gov/ncee/pubs/20104029/pdf/20104029.pdf

Gratz v. Bollinger, 539 US 244 (2003).

Gross, B., Bowen, M. Martin, K. (2012) Accessing the charter school landscape. In R. Lake, & B. Gross, (Eds.). *Hopes, fears, & reality: A balanced look at American charter schools in 2011* (pp. 9–22). Seattle, WA: National Charter School Resource Center. Retrieved from http://www.ncsrp.org/downloads/hfr06/hfrdec1_web.pdf

Hanushek, E., Kain, J.F., Rivkin, S.G., & Branch, G.F. (2007). Charter school quality and parental decision making with school choice. *Journal of Public Economics, 91*(5–6), 823–848.

Hoxby, C.M., Murarka, S., & Kang, J. (2009). *How New York City's charter schools affect student achievement: August 2009 report*. Second report in series. Cambridge, MA: New York City Charter Schools Evaluation Project.

Lake, R.J., & Gross, B. Eds. (2012). *Hopes, fears, and reality: A balanced look at American charter schools in 2011*. Seattle, WA: National Charter School Resource Center. Retrieved from http://www.ncsrp.org/downloads/hfr06/hfrdec1_web.pdf

Loveless, T., & Field, K. (2009). Perspectives on charter schools. In M. Berends, M.G. Springer, D. Ballou, & H.J. Walberg (Eds.), *Handbook of research on school choice* (pp. 99–114). New York, NY: Routledge.

Lubienski, C.A., & Weitzel, P.C. (2010). Information use and epidemics in charter school policy. In C.A. Lubienski & P.C. Weitzel (Eds.), *The charter school experiment: Expectations, evidence, implications* (pp. 197–218). Cambridge, MA: Harvard Education Press.

Miron, G. (2010). Performance of charter schools and implications for policy makers. In C.A. Lubienski & P.C. Weitzel (Eds.), *The charter school experiment: Expectations, evidence, implications* (pp. 73–92). Cambridge, MA: Harvard Education Press.

National Alliance for Public Charter Schools. (2012). *Dashboard: A comprehensive data source from the National Alliance for Public Charter Schools.* Accessed June 30, 2013 from http://dashboard.publiccharters.org/dashboard/reports

National Center for Education Statistics. (2012). Data tools. http://nces.ed.gov/datatools/

Obama, B (2010). Today Show interview with Matt Lauer. http://www.today.com/id/39378576/ns/today-parenting_and_family/t/obama-money-without-reform-wont-fix-school-system/#.UdDfwhaTP-Y

Stein, M.L., Goldring, E.B., & Cravens, X. (2011). Do parents do as they say? In M. Berends, M. Cannata, & E. Goldring (Eds.), *School choice and school improvement* (pp. 105–123). Cambridge, MA: Harvard Education Press.

van Lier, P. (2010). *Public good vs. private profit.* Cleveland, OH: Policy Matters Ohio. Retrieved from http://www.policymattersohio.org/public-good-vs-private-profit-imagine-schools-inc-in-ohio

Weil, D. (2009). *Charter school movement. History, politics, policies, economics, and effectiveness* (2nd ed.). Amenia, NY: Grey House.

Weitzel, P.C., & C.A. Lubienski. (2010a). Assessing the charter school experiment. In C.A. Lubienski & P.C. Weitzel (Eds.), *The charter school experiment: Expectations, evidence, implications* (pp. 219–230). Cambridge, MA: Harvard Education Press.

Weitzel, P.C., & C.A. Lubienski. (2010b). Grading charter schools. In C.A. Lubienski & P.C. Weitzel (Eds.), *The charter school experiment: Expectations, evidence, implications* (pp. 15–32). Cambridge, MA: Harvard Education Press.

Witte, G, Wolf, P., Dean, A., & Carlson, D. (2011). Milwaukee Independent Charter Schools Study: Report on Two- and Three-Year Achievement Gains. SCDP Milwaukee Evaluation. Report #25. School Choice Demonstration Project. http://www.eric.ed.gov/PDFS/ED518594.pdf

Zimmer, R., & Buddin, R. (2007). Getting inside the black box: Examining how the operation of charter schools affects performance. *Peabody Journal of Education, 82*(2/3), 231–273.

Zimmer, R., Gill, B., Booker, K., Lavertu, S., Sass, T.R., & Witte, J. (2009). *Charter schools in eight states: Effects on achievement, attainment, integration, and competition*. Santa Monica, CA: RAND Corporation.

27

High-Stake Reforms and Urban Education

Julian Vasquez Heilig, Muhammad Khalifa & Linda C. Tillman

The United States has exhibited long-standing achievement gaps between Whites and Latina/os, African Americans, and Native Americans in urban schools. These gaps are not coincidence. Whether it was *Plessy v. Ferguson*[1] (1896) or Arizona's House Bill 2281 (2010),[2] a long history of legislative, executive, and judicial enactments have relegated many students of color to the periphery of society. Despite an interest in educating students of color spurred by the Civil Rights Movement, they still constitute a large sector of urban students vulnerable to poor school performance, as many of these youth continue to receive uneven instruction (Vasquez Heilig, Cole, & Springel, 2011). As a result, a significant number of urban students of color exhibit low academic achievement, poor performance on standardized exams, low graduation rates, and high dropout rates (Vasquez Heilig & Darling-Hammond, 2008).

In 1983, *A Nation at Risk* made the case that the U.S. school system was not globally competitive and that student achievement was in decline (National Commission on Excellence in Education, 1983). In the late 1980s and early 1990s, systemic reform arose in the literature as a purported panacea for long-standing gaps in student performance and a decline in perceived academic achievement relative to other countries (Smith & O'Day, 1991). Those in the professoriate who advocate systemic reform wrote that rigorous academic goals and the measurement of student progress against those standards would be important components of new reform efforts (Cohen, 1996). Students and educators would then be held accountable to the raised bar of academic expectations (Vasquez Heilig & Darling-Hammond, 2008). The systemic reform movement supposed that once academic standards are established and aligned with high-stakes testing, schools held accountable to these measures will automatically increase students' educational achievement, decreasing the long-standing achievement gap (Vasquez Heilig,, Young, & Williams, 2012).

Reformers from the professoriate supported systemic reform because they believed it would build capacity in schools (Scheurich, Skrla, & Johnson, 2000), while reformers who focused on the efficiency of the educational system saw systemic reform as an opportunity to build school reform in the model of Frederick Taylor-like schemas (Salinas & Reidel, 2007). The history of Texas school reform is a salient example of the integration of the efficiency paradigm into school systemic reform efforts. Starting in the early 1980s, Ross Perot and his allies were "influential actors" and proponents of accountability and testing in Texas (Carnoy & Loeb, 2003). The Perot Commission, and later the Texas Business-Education Coalition (TBEC), united corporate leaders in Texas in an effort to promote a business perspective in education reform (Vasquez Heilig, Young, & Williams, 2012). Codified in this reform effort was a determination to inculcate reform measures into the public consciousness that increased efficiency, quality, and accountability in a push for schools to perform more like businesses (Grubb, 1985). As a result, Texas was one of the earlier states in the 1980s to develop a statewide data system and high-stakes competency testing (Vasquez Heilig, 2011).

A third reform group saw systemic reform as a means to achieve equal education for all students (Ravitch, 2011). This group, the social justice systemic reformers, including Senator Edward Kennedy, saw systemic reform as a primary role of the state and federal government. Social justice systemic reformers acknowledged that students of color still faced a plethora of contextual factors, and these factors were problematic for public schools in their attempts to educate children who continued to be marginalized in U.S. society. As popular films such as *Waiting for Superman* have highlighted, the social justice reformers attribute the achievement gaps to myriad problems facing students of color including poverty (i.e., increased levels of homelessness among students and their families), serial underfunding, school safety issues, and shortages of highly qualified leaders and teachers in hard-to-staff areas. The social justice reformers acknowledge high-stakes testing and accountability as vehicles for identifying and publicizing achievement gaps in schools.

Considering the promise with which NCLB came to prominence as a panacea to improve education as systemic reform, it is an important exercise to contextualize the impact of the reform on urban education over the past decade. We then use postcolonial theory to conceptualize why NCLB failed to close the achievement gaps in urban schools due to its hegemonic approach to educational policy. Approaches to reform that find their origins in postcolonial educational apparatuses were never meant to *serve* vanquished, marginalized populations, rather only to *exploit* them. As alternative to NCLB for urban education, we then revisit structural issues that have been largely ignored during the NCLB era and also pose a new community-based direction for accountability that is counterhegemonic.

Birth and Growth of Systemic Reform in the United States

Here we highlight Texas as a way to explore how postcolonial structures intersect with urban educational reforms in the United States. In 1993, each of the systemic reform camps first came together in Texas to create legislation addressing long-standing achievement gaps between students of color and White students in the Lone Star State. The Texas Legislature enacted Texas Senate Bill (SB) 7 (1993), the incipient statute for the creation of the Texas public school accountability system to rate school districts and evaluate campuses. SB 7 modified the existing public school accountability system from a diagnostic to a performance-based system. Signed into law by Democratic Governor Ann Richards in 1993, SB 7 represented a bipartisan solution to the state's educational woes, as it was passed by a wide margin in both the Texas House and Senate (Vasquez Heilig, Young, & Williams, 2012). As test-based accountability commenced in Texas, publicly reported achievement gains across grade levels, coupled with increases in high school graduation rates and decreases in dropout rates, brought nationwide acclaim to the Texas accountability "miracle" (Haney, 2000).

Due to its purported success in the Lone Star State and urban areas such as Houston and Dallas, Texas-style systemic reform was brought to Washington, DC. The alliance between Senator

Edward Kennedy (social justice systemic reformer) and George W. Bush (efficiency systemic reformer), combined with support from academics such as Diane Ravitch (professoriate systemic reformer), demonstrated systemic reform camps coming together again to create a new wide-ranging systemic federal educational policy. McNeil (2005) related that Texas-style high-stakes testing and accountability policy, by force of federal law, has become the driving education policy for the entire nation with the No Child Left Behind Act (NCLB) of 2001 (2002) passing in early 2002.

NCLB replicated the Texas model of accountability by injecting public rewards and sanctions into national education policy, ushering in an era where states and localities are required to build accountability systems based on high-stakes assessments. The centerpiece of NCLB requires that schools and districts meet a federally established, Adequate Yearly Progress (AYP) goal, currently associated with minimum levels of improvement on high-stakes assessments for demographic subgroups. Schools and districts that fail to meet AYP then face federal sanctions and penalties—a measurement approach that reproduces the Texas mixture of efficiency and social justice approaches to educational policy reform. These policies were especially designed to address long-standing achievement gaps in urban schools—as they had apparently been shown to be successful in the Houston Independent School District, a large, urban area (Vasquez Heilig, 2011). Did high-stakes testing and accountability deliver on their promise to improve urban education?

Rethinking High-Stakes Testing and Accountability

Ten years post-NCLB, achievement gaps between students of color and their White peers stubbornly persist in urban schools. A recent study by Reardon, et al. (2012) suggested that, at the glacial pace in which achievement gaps are closing in the current high-stakes testing and accountability environment, it will take roughly 80 more years to equalize national testing results. Thus, a continuing question in the literature is whether high-stakes testing that rewards or sanctions schools based on AYP and other cross-sectional student scores is the most effective or valid form of educational reform for the United States. In fact, accountability's theory of action anchored to high-stakes testing and accountability intuitively seemed plausible to each of the systemic reformer groups during the time of NCLB's implementation, ultimately resulting in the "Texas Miracle"[3] being the primary source of evidence of accountability fostering the long-term success of low-performing students and the schools that served them (Nichols, Glass, & Berliner, 2006).

Elsewhere, Vasquez Heilig along with Nichols (2013) posited that a review of the literature indicates limited improvement in student outcomes after a decade of national high-stakes testing and accountability (and almost two decades in Texas). In fact, emerging research actually suggests that high-stakes testing policies are having a negative effect on the educational outcomes of students of color due to their interaction with low-quality pedagogy, low levels of teacher quality, and inequitable education funding (McNeil, 2000; Vasquez Heilig et al., 2011; Vasquez Heilig, Williams, & Jez, 2010). Considering these aforementioned constraints, schools (and entire districts) have in desperation sought to manipulate the accountability system by excluding low-scoring students of color and special populations from testing through the use of exemptions and other gaming actions, resulting in the appearance of overall increased educational achievement (Cullen & Reback, 2006; Jacob, 2005; Jennings & Beveridge, 2009). Such manipulation leads to persisting high rates of grade retention, and dropout and depressed high school completion despite a decade of NCLB and national high-stakes testing and accountability (Vasquez Heilig & Nichols, 2013).

African Americans, Latina/os, and High-Stakes Testing and Accountability

High-stakes testing and accountability has been shown to negatively impact African American and Latina/o students in urban school contexts (Vasquez Heilig & Darling-Hammond, 2008). First, while there is an assumption that these policies are neutral, requiring *all* urban students to achieve the same level of proficiency, high-stakes tests are often punitive because they do not take into account a student's prior educational experiences or scores on other types of assessments. Thus, being placed in a subgroup can be disadvantageous for African American and Latina/o students. As Tillman (2006a) noted,

> Factors such as the high-poverty status of the school and a lack of social and cultural capital can affect students' opportunities to access high quality education, both in an out of school, as well as their ability to master key subject matter content, and to ultimately consistently score at a level of proficiency on the mandated tests. (p. 198)

Second, under NCLB, when a school received the label "good"—a label based on test scores—the school may become inaccessible to many African American and Latina/o students in urban districts. Ryan (2004) argued that using test performance data to distinguish between and label higher- and lower-performing schools may lead to their resegregation. Labeling schools as high- or low-performing is likely to be more beneficial for middle- and upper-class parents, as they have the financial ability to move to school districts that have a record of demonstrating proficiency in reading and math on standardized tests. However, the opportunity to choose a high-performing school is more often an unlikely scenario for students of color and low-income parents, as parents in this category are more likely to be limited in their ability to access high-performing schools because of their racial/ethnic and socioeconomic background. School labels can also negatively impact the ability to recruit and retain "highly qualified" teachers, as defined by NCLB. While policy makers have argued that highly qualified teachers are needed in core content subject areas in all schools, Darling-Hammond (2005) argued that students of color and low-income students are less likely than their White peers to have access to a "highly qualified" teacher. She wrote,

> Unfortunately, policy makers have nearly always been willing to fill vacancies by lowering standards so that people who have had little or no preparation for teaching can be hired, especially if their clients are "minority" and low-income students. Although this practice is often excused by the presumption that virtually anyone can figure out how to teach, a number of reviews of research have concluded that fully prepared and certified teachers are more highly rated and more successful with students than teachers without full preparation. (p. 207)

One would assume that a requirement for "highly qualified" teachers in all schools, regardless of performance level and label, should be the norm rather than the exception. But the reality of public school arrangements today is that the majority of "highly qualified" teachers usually choose to work in high-performing, low-poverty schools. Also, NCLB specifically mandates that schools must raise test scores generally, and particularly the test scores of students in identified subgroups. However, while teachers may be considered "highly qualified," they may lack urban school experience and access to a systematic mentoring program for novice teachers, contributing to a shortage of teachers who are highly qualified to teach in an urban school context (Vasquez Heilig et al., 2011).

As discussed above, the requirements of NCLB (2002) contribute to increased dropout rates for African American and Latina/o students in urban schools (Vasquez Heilig & Darling-Hammond, 2008). Ryan (2004) noted that,

> An even more serious threat to disadvantaged students is the problem of student exclusion, which the NCLBA threatens to exacerbate. . . . This is why schools, to the extent they can, will work to avoid enrolling those students who are at risk of failing the exams. . . . This temptation presumably will be strongest at the high school level, both because students most typically drop out at this stage and because low-performing high school students are most likely to be farthest behind. Given the connection between performance on tests, socio-economic status, and race, the students most likely to be targeted for exclusion will be poor and/or racial minorities. Just as these students will suffer from any incentive to segregate created by the NCLBA, they will also suffer, even more dramatically, from any incentive to exclude them from school altogether. (p. 969)

Consequently, a significant number of African American and Latina/o students, particularly at the high school level, are at great risk of dropping out of school and entering society under-served and undereducated. Thus, in this chapter, we proffer that a reanalysis of the approaches inherent to NCLB need to be revisited. In fact, despite themes of equity being prominent in any discussion (especially for African Americans and Latina/os) regarding accountability, high-stakes testing and accountability is educational policy that is reminiscent of prior historical eras that emphasized a colonial approach, hegemonic educational policy with its locus of control external to local communities. NCLB, despite being consistently framed as social justice–oriented, was destined for failure due to its punitive and paternal approach to educational reform. Moreover, the reforms were constructed and enforced largely outside of the communities they sought to effect, while purposely ignoring the aforementioned structural issues in the educational system. This, along with the stubbornly persistent failures of the children they purport to help, all are suggestive of a postcolonial educational structure.

Understanding No Child Left Behind: Visiting Postcolonial Theory

When examining high-stakes educational reforms, postcolonial theory is useful because of the striking similarities between schools predominated by academically poor-performing students and the educational regimes of the uncivilized masses in colonized nations. For one, education was used as a hegemonic form to monitor, sanction, and control civilized people. The colonizers adhered strictly to data-driven Western ways of learning and knowing, as do American reformers who oversee urban schooling. Interestingly enough, both the Third World colonizers and the architects of modern educational reforms tend to be White, and Western. And perhaps more pertinent to our discussion, there was *always* a "high-stakes" element to colonial and postcolonial educational apparatus.

Thus, postcolonial theory (Fanon, 1952, 1961; Memmi, 1965; Said, 1978) offers a critical framework through which urban educational policy and practice—including NCLB—can be understood and critiqued (DeLeon, 2012; Shahjahan, 2011). At base, theorists interrogate the relationship between the legitimized, conquering power and the vanquished subaltern, and ask questions about who defines subjectivities, such as knowledge, resistance, space, voice, or even thought. It is important to note that colonial apparatuses occurred not only in the psyche of the subaltern and in public social contexts but have always had a strong relationship with physical space. Essentially, colonizers delegitimize the knowledge, experience, and cultures of the colonized, and establish policy and practice that will always confirm the colonial status quo. On this construction, this review of the literature looks at the role of high-stakes testing and accountability on the reproduction and reification of power relationships (Foucault, 1972) in urban spaces.

Postcolonial domination occurs in multiple ways, including through hegemonic control (Alexander, M., 2010; Alexander, J., 2010), discursive reproductions of power and knowledge (Foucault, 1980), and policy (Shahajahan, 2011). A number of postcolonial theorists focus on multiple ways that oppressors dominate their subjects and maintain power over them. For example, Freire (1970) and Carnoy (1974) argued that education is a central way in which people were oppressed and a primary means for liberation. They posited that colonizers not only defined knowledge in hegemonic ways, but also structured education in a way that allowed for the maximal economic usage of the conquered subjects. Similarly in today's high-stakes educational environments, knowledge is strictly defined by educationalists at the very top of society, and seems to most often punish urban people of color. No Child Left Behind's narrative of equity cloaked in high-stakes testing and accountability is the paradigm that has been pressed by policy makers for the last decade. District, school, and student success (and with growth models, even teacher success) have been very narrowly defined as to how a student performs on a standardized test on a single given day, instead of, for example, how much students go on to volunteer or otherwise contribute to their neighborhood communities. Opposition from districts and communities to this limited paradigm has drawn terse responses from Western reformers that are determined to press forward (Scheurich, Skrla, & Johnson, 2000).

On first blush, high-stakes educational reforms may seem to be unbiased, equitable reforms that actually help marginalized bodies. However, earlier scholars have been particularly sagacious and quite nuanced in how they identified and named multiple ways in which oppression has been enacted on the oppressed "other." Foucault (1972, 1980) argued that power is maintained through discourses that are defined by those in control. How marginalized bodies are ordered, associated with meaning, and discursively subjugated to oppressive societal norms must be considered when reflecting on the utility of modern educational reforms. Fanon (1952), relying on his training in psychoanalysis and psychiatry, emphasized the psychological attachment of the subaltern to the norms, understandings, and subjectivities of the oppressors. Perhaps most influential in the field of postcolonial studies, Edward Said (1978) focused on discourse, and specifically literature, as a way that orientalist (i.e., Western scholars and authors who write about "Eastern" peoples and cultures) define Asia and the exotic bodies within. To Said (1978), the European imagination and literary contributions of Arab-Islamic (i.e., "Oriental") peoples simply reified stereotypes and subtly casted them into an inferior status. Despite the variance in method and emphasis, these writings all highlight the diverse ways that the powerful elite can arrange power, reproduce social structures, and normalize their own hegemonic positionalities while concurrently promoting equity in educational policy.

Postcolonial Power and Knowledge: From the Colony to Urban Spaces

Postcolonial theoretical underpinnings are useful for urban school reformers because of the similarities of postcolonial contexts and urban spaces (DeLeon, 2012; Paperson, 2010). The subjugation of the urban *other* and normalization of dominant group subjectivities (Fanon, 1952; Gandhi, 1998; Said, 1978), the validation and delegitimization of knowledge (Foucault, 1980), surveillances of urban spaces (DeLeon, 2012; Wood, 2007), and the modern control-oriented policies—such as school turnaround and emergency takeover laws—(Shahjahan, 2011) all indicate a shared historical legacy of postcolonial empires and America's urban spaces. Indeed, the colonizers of Asiatic and African lands and those of the American territories represented the same European interests, and thus it is easy to see why Fanon and others argued that slavery and American racism are distinctly postcolonial: "Colonial racism is no different from any other racism" (Fanon, 1961, p. 88).

Moreover, there are striking similarities between the strong European economic interests in African and Asian natural and human resources and the economic resourcefulness, first of slaves, and then of an urban industrial proletariat. These racist postcolonial urban contexts had not exclusively existed in urban spaces, but the large majority of Black, Latina/o, and Native American public school students have consistently received a worse quality education than their White peers despite the existing educational policy (Orfield, 2001; Trent, 2008). Given the very dismal progress and benefit of NCLB and other high-stakes reforms—and indeed, even the harms that these reforms have caused—one must begin to look at the global, historical, and theoretical origins of such policy.

In other words, it is important to note that postcolonial studies, though often thought of as relegated to a particular period, are actually also a reference to thoughts, practices, policies, and laws that impact bodies of the current educational policy era. Essentially, colonialism is when one population (most often represented by a government or monarchy) seeks to conquer a different geographical area, and all of the resources of that area, for an economic benefit to the conquering power (Gandhi, 1998). These spaces should not be viewed as static, however. In fact, the colonial practices would not only extend across *time* into a period after the colonialists left, but also across *space,* as new techniques and technologies of control, exploitation, and domination would be imported for usage within the homelands of colonizing powers on their local subjects. It is where these worlds cross that we interrogate an American postcolonial experience and its impact in schools. As Crossley and Tikly (2004) pointed out, education systems have remnants of a colonial past:

> Many existing education systems still bear the hallmarks of the colonial encounter in that they remain elitist, lack relevance to local realities and are often at variance with indigenous knowledge systems, values and beliefs. (p. 149)

It is not surprising that this colonial impulse to dominate and control would have an impact on urban educational policy. Fanon (1961) argued, "Colonialism wants everything to come from it. But the dominant psychological feature of the colonised is to withdraw before any invitation of the conquerors" (p. 63). Controlling policies that regulate urban schools are often legislated at state or federal levels.

The very impetus for such policies are often "low-performing" urban and rural schools. Though scholars like Antrop-Gonzalez (2011) argued that schools should be largely informed by epistemologies and realities of youth of color and their educators, U.S. school districts are pressured to respond to the demands and mandates of state and federal policies that require a standardized curriculum that is measured in culturally-specific and exclusionary ways (Shahjahan, 2011).

Colonial Apparatuses in Western Urban Education

Since African Americans, Latinas/os, Indigenous Native Americans, and other racialized minorities are more likely to have been segregated and confined to urban (and rural) spaces (Iceland, 2004; Sugrue, 2005), and since the quality of urban education is typically less than suburban education, scholars have been keen to explore the relationship between urban education and a postcolonial past. Definitions of good or bad education, content of education, movement of bodies (i.e., who goes to what schools), policies of reform, measures of success, and even the very structures and purposes of schooling are often defined by people outside of urban spaces. Scholars like Lipman (2003), Tillman (2004), and Hursh (2007) demonstrated that national policies such as NCLB (2002) were written for and directed at—and overwhelmingly punish—urban families and educators, most of whom had no say in the policies. The link between urban space and colonialism is intractable and might be measured through understandings of knowledge, administration and surveillance, and descriptions of urban teachers, parents, and children.

Validation of Knowledge

Defining, controlling, and regulating knowledge has been one of the primary ways NCLB, as a postcolonial apparatus, continues to exist in urban educational contexts. Scholars and urban educators have often called for alternative ways of validating knowledge and success, such as consideration of community involvement (Khalifa, 2012; Siddle Walker, 1993), mentoring (Tillman, 2004), community service (Youniss & Yates, 1997), and postsecondary community involvement and success. Yet, as Vasquez Heilig and Darling-Hammond (2008) reported, the primary means of measuring success in Texas and the nation has been essentially a single focus: standardized testing—even while research has shown that the AYP requirement of NCLB as a single indicator of student achievement is unlikely to raise the achievement levels of African American students (Tillman, 2004).

The value of standardized testing (Ravitch, 2011) is often obfuscated as districts pull full-steam ahead in attempts to boost their scores. But this very history is most explanatory for postcolonial urban schools. Indeed, in much the same way that colonizers would determine and measure success of colonial boarding schools throughout conquered nations, governmental educational authorities have full discretion to determine what knowledge, and what testing of this knowledge, is acceptable in urban settings. Perhaps Foucault (1978) notated this well as he reflects on the power of those who define knowledge:

> Power is not an institution, and not a structure; neither is it a certain strength we are endowed with; it is the name that one attributes to a complex strategical situation in a particular society. (p. 93)

The privilege to define success or failure in urban school contexts represents a "power over" dynamic. This power has not historically been in the hands of urban educators and citizens. As Tikly (2001) noted, "First, it (colonial education) provided a key mechanism and template for the spread of contemporary forms of education" (p. 157). In short, the early architects of urban education—and by extension, the education of minorities (Watkins, 2001)—did not validate any indigenous knowledge (Khalifa, 2010). In other words, the fact that success is being measured by only standardized test scores is not only invisibly rooted in a very particular, unique educational tradition, but it is also marginalizing to other historical traditions. Certainly, there are other epistemologies and bodies of knowledge in urban areas to foment learning and gauge success, but that they are not accepted as knowledge.

Surveillance and Urban Spaces

Indeed, one of the primary methods in which urban schools exist in the postcolonial era is through constant surveillances and gazes. This gaze, which is always conjoined with meanings, definitions, and relationships of power and of subjugation, at root, is a mechanism of control. It allows the state apparatus to cast an overseer's gaze and penalize urban educators and students for low-test score performance and dangerous environments. Foucault (1980) mentioned that "an inspecting gaze, a gaze which each individual under its weight will end by interiorizing to the point that he is his own overseer, each individual thus exercising this surveillance over, and against, himself" (p. 155).

In places with long histories of racial discord, like Detroit or Los Angeles, the gaze on schools is often coterminous with deficit constructions and punitive policies that respond to school performance. But in his analysis of discourses around school shootings, DeLeon (2012) noted that this imperialist gaze is tightly associated with widespread stereotypes that are present in society. For example, he posited that since urban areas are already popularly constructed as dangerous places, urban school shootings are described as normal (DeLeon, 2012). Yet, he critiques constructions of suburban/White school shootings, described as aberrations, as carried out by lone gunmen who were misfits in their safe and secure, nonurban environments. These "dangerous" and "beastly" descriptions of urban areas are an overlay on previous characterizations of the colonial exotic other. We find similarities in how high-stakes testing and accountability policy is utilized. Students of color in urban spaces (also suburban and rural areas) are constantly under the overseer's gaze as they are pressed to increase their standardized test scores—scores that innumerable scholars have described as *racially biased,* and as *destructive* when the entire purpose of "education" becomes to "pass" the test (McNeil, 2005).

Not only do a number of scholars note the problems with relying on test scores (Tillman, 2006b; Vasquez Heilig & Darling-Hammond, 2008), but many even show the detrimental impact that reforms based on scores have on urban students (Lipman, 2003; Noddings, 2004). Yet, much like colonial schools that disparaged the indigenous "native" cultures and superimposed a "civilizing" education in the colonized world, governmental agencies have the job of correcting those perpetually failing urban schools. Urban educational policies and practices often have postcolonial origins, but this origin has been invisibilized and couched in the discourses of urban educational reforms for America's most needy people.

Old and New Directions

In this chapter we reexamined the success of NCLB-inspired high-stakes testing and accountability as a hegemonic policy via the lens of postcolonial theory. We challenged the narratives of efficacy and social justice that are prominent in the public discourse framing high-stakes testing and accountability as solutions to the challenges of educating students of color. Considering the failure of NCLB to close the achievement gap in urban schools by 2014, we will now discuss in more depth the structural issues that have been largely ignored in the NCLB era, but still must be addressed so to effect change in the process of schooling: school leadership, teacher quality, and school finance. In addition to the structural issues that should be addressed, we conclude our chapter by proposing community-based accountability, a counterhegemonic approach to educational policy as a substitute to the current colonial form of accountability. We argue that this new direction for urban education and public policy will likely yield better results by refocusing the process of education beyond high-stakes testing. These new directions, we believe, will confront the postcolonial educational apparatus and empower urban communities.

School Leadership. Principals of color continue to be underrepresented in K–12 public schools. According to the most recent data from the National Center for Educational Statistics (2009), Latina/o principals represent 5.9% of all public school principals who primarily work in urban school districts. Additionally, African Americans represent 9.6% of all public school principals working primarily in urban school districts. Latina/o and African American principals are rarely seen as experts on the education of students with whom they may identify racially and culturally and with whom they more often have direct and personal experiences (Tillman, 2004, 2006b). It is still the case that the work of principals of color is seen as less important than that of White principals, thus setting up a Eurocentric preference for what school leadership is, how it is defined, and who should be school leaders (Tillman, 2004, 2006b).

Clearly the work of Latina/o and African American principals continues to be underinvestigated and undertheorized in the educational leadership and policy literature (Khalifa, 2011). Yet many Latina/o and African American principals who lead in urban school districts face significant challenges in their attempts to educate all students, particularly low-income students of color. Many of these challenges are familiar to us: educating and caring for students who live at or below the poverty level and who come to school undernourished and with physical and mental health issues; a shortage of highly qualified teachers in key subject matter areas; and chronic underfunding of urban school districts. Tillman (2006b), in her study of African American principals in a large urban school district, found that many of these principals struggled to educate their students in the face of high teacher turnover and the mandates of standardized testing. These challenges directly influenced the principals' capacity to lead in ways that placed student success at the center of their work.

Teacher Quality. Despite the persistent assault on teacher certification and training, the most successful countries in the world are focused on placing highly qualified and expertly trained teachers into the classroom (Darling-Hammond, 2010). In the United States, the current policy reform movement is pressing to find alternative routes to the classroom for teachers who lack training and certification. Vasquez Heilig et al. (2011) argued that teacher training and experience can never be replaced with short-term, Band-Aid solutions such as alternative certification programs and Teach For America. Teachers trained at selective and highly ranked teacher education programs are effective teachers (Clotfelter, Ladd, & Vigdor, 2007). Teachers who stay in the profession for more than five years have better pedagogical skills, and are able to develop and maintain effective classroom management and discipline than teachers with less time in the classroom (Darling-Hammond, Holtzman, Gatlin, & Vasquez Heilig, 2005). We know who good teachers are, and we know something about how to train them to be effective (Darling-Hammond, 2010). Unfortunately, we are not using that knowledge in our current school reform efforts. Instead, a strong push of the current reform era is a political push to remove standards, and the loosening of requirements and definitions is only likely to exacerbate the inconsistencies within the profession (Vasquez Heilig et al., 2011).

Funding Equity. In the United States, it is not uncommon to hear the refrain that "money doesn't matter" for student and school success when states trot out the usual suspects in state education funding lawsuits (Holme & Vasquez Heilig, in press). Despite how inconvenient it is for states and policy makers when communities continue to raise the issue in the courts, large disparities in the distribution of school expenditures are evident in many states. For example, Darling-Hammond (2007) reported that U.S. public schools spend $3,000 to $30,000 per pupil—with urban schools tending to be on the lower end of this spectrum—leaving inadequate resources for schools that serve large numbers of students of color. Reformers have long sought to create equalization schemes anchored at the state level to create more equality of funding between districts (Vasquez Heilig et al., 2010). For example, Texas has a codified, statewide school-funding equalization scheme created after decades of battles in state and federal courts. Many reformers argued that a statewide finance scheme would create greater equality in school finance (Reschovsky, 1994). However, in the 82nd legislative session, Republican policy makers wielded their political power to cut billions of dollars from schools (Weber, 2011). So the unintended consequence (or perhaps intended outcome) of statewide equalization in Texas and elsewhere is that it gives politicians legislative power to create even *more* inequity and divestment in school funding and resources.

Community-Based Accountability

High-stakes testing and accountability continues as the dominant paradigm despite vocal dissatisfaction in urban communities across the nation. Despite mounting opposition, clearly Tayloristic efficiency models of systemic reform are ruling the day—such as data-driven schooling, education models derived from economic paradigms, and hierarchical administrative structures, to name just a few—and are institutionalized in U.S. schools (Labaree, 2005). In terms of efficiency, the source and operationalization of modern educational theory has not only been invisibilized, but has been casted as impartial, ahistorical, and normal. This serves to permanently ostracize indigenous and empowerment-based educational models that are counterepistemic to the dominant Western European "survival of the fittest" schooling approach—an approach that currently permeates accountability and high-stakes testing. In her use of Nandy's work, Gandhi has captured this well:

> This colonialism colonises minds in addition to bodies and it releases forces within colonised societies to alter their cultural priorities once and for all. In the process, it helps to generalise the concept of the modern West from a geographical and temporal entity to a psychological category. The West is now everywhere, within the West and outside, in structures and in minds. (1983, as quoted in Ghandi, 1998, p. 15)

What is the alternative to the dominant colonial paradigm? The answer is a community empowered to be accountable to themselves and to the nation—an "indigenous" educational policy approach where communities democratically set achievement and outcome goals. For some communities, maybe high-stakes test scores derived by the Pearson test score development company is the goal; or perhaps a community will choose to focus on a new, more valuable set of outcomes.

In the current era, most states have reams of data that can be disaggregated in ways previously unthinkable. We can follow students from pre-kindergarten to any number of outcomes such as higher education, workforce, and incarceration. Thus, community-based accountability could involve a process where superintendents, school boards, school staff, parents, students, and community stakeholders set short-term and long-term goals based on their priorities. Maybe those goals are higher ACT and SAT scores. Or a community may choose to focus on increasing the percentage of students enrolled and completing higher education. Perhaps the local priorities are employment and salary gains for their students. Each of these goal statements would serve as an alternative to the intense focus on state-sponsored test scores. This new form of accountability would allow a district to drive locally based approaches that focus on the *process* of education for one-year, five-year, and ten-year terms.

One example of the focus on the process of education instead of on high-stakes testing outcomes is in San Antonio's Café College resource centers. Mayor Julian Castro funded these college-knowledge information centers in response to the community making higher education enrollment and graduation a priority. As a result, the city has placed both its resources and its will behind that goal. This focus on the process rather than the outcomes is a stark contrast to the current approaches observed in urban Texas high schools. Due to the current high-stakes testing regime, high schools are spending their resources on double-blocking students in test-prep courses to focus on multiple choice worksheets for high-stakes exit exams instead of on the arts, band, PE, and other important courses that build 21st-century skills (Vasquez Heilig, 2011; Vasquez Heilig, Cole & Aguilar, 2010).

Notably, community-based accountability should appeal to political conservatives that espouse the ideals of local control and liberals that support community empowerment. The state and federal government role would be relegated to calculating baselines for a set of 10–15 goals that communities set in a democratic process relative to the current levels of those particular outcomes. This accountability goal-setting would seek to influence the process of schooling choices in each community and would then motivate policy makers from communities to lobby state and federal governments for the resources to achieve its accountability goals rather than focusing on high-stakes testing results. This turn of events in the frame of accountability would be novel because politicians (local, state, and federal) would also be held accountable—they could be shamed and sanctioned—if resources to meet the community goals do not materialize. Accountability would become a two-way street.

Community-based accountability may also usher in a turn in community involvement in schools. In the United States, our communities, our parents, our educators must see themselves as the solution rather than the problem. In conjunction with the aforementioned structural reforms that our nation continues to avoid by using Band-Aids (such as vouchers, charters schools, and Teach For America), this return to a community-based schooling approach would foment a multiple measures approach to community education outcomes—outcomes derived by the community—driven by a desire to see their children succeed, rather than a continuing focus on failed high-stakes testing and accountability policies persistently promoted in state capitols and Washington, DC.

As discussed above, our society is aware of the structural issues in education; however, policy makers continuously fail to address them because of the costs involved. Politicians in the United States are often focused on looking for "efficiency" in education, also known as inexpensive and/or free policy solutions that can be "brought to scale." Charter schools and vouchers are the primary poster children of this inanity—an approach to educational policy that just "moves around the chairs." Considering that other countries such as Singapore, China, and Finland are investing heavily in their K–12 and Higher Education systems, our democracy now depends on communities holding policy makers accountable for the current colonial form of accountability. Extended divestment in education and a continued colonial approach to policy will perpetuate what the last 10 years of high-stakes testing and accountability has yielded—more disappointment.

Notes

1. *Plessy v. Ferguson* was a United States Supreme Court decision upholding the constitutionality of state laws requiring racial segregation in public facilities under the doctrine of "separate but equal."
2. Arizona's House Bill 2281 prohibits schools from teaching ethnic studies.
3. The Texas Miracle was a narrative in the Lone Star State that dropout rates had reportedly plummeted and test scores and graduation rates skyrocketed.

References

Alexander, J. (2010). The political imaginaries of social lives and political prisoners in post-2000 Zimbabwe. *Journal of Southern African Studies, 36*(2), 483–503.

Alexander, M. (2010). *The new Jim Crow. Mass incarceration in the age of colorblindness.* New York, NY: New Press.

Antrop-Gonzalez, R. (2011). *Schools as radical sanctuaries: Decolonizing urban youth through the eyes of youth of color and their teachers.* Charlotte, NC: Information Age.

Carnoy, M. (1974). *Education as cultural imperialism*. London, UK: Longman.

Carnoy, M., & Loeb, S. (2003). Does external accountability affect student outcomes? A cross-state analysis. *Educational Evaluation and Policy Analysis, 24*(4), 305–331.

Clotfelter, C., Ladd, H. F., Vigdor, J. L., & Wheeler, J. (2007). *High poverty schools and the distribution of teachers and principals* (No. CALDER Working Paper 1). Washington, DC: National Center for Analysis of Longitudinal Data in Education Research. Retrieved from http://www.urban.org/url.cfm?ID=1001057

Cohen, D. (1996). Standards-based school reform: Policy, practice, and performance. In H.F. Ladd (Ed.), *Holding schools accountable* (pp. 99–127). Washington, DC: Brookings Institution.

Crossley, M., & Tikly, L. (2004). Postcolonial perspectives and comparative and international research in education: A critical introduction. *Comparative Education, 40*(2), 147–156.

Cullen, J., & Reback, R. (2006). Tinkering toward accolades: School gaming under a performance accountability system. Cambridge, MA: National Bureau of Economic Research. Working Paper No. 12286.

Darling-Hammond, L. (2005). New standards and old reform inequalities: School reform and the education of African American students. In J. King (Ed)., *Black education: A transformative research and action agenda for a new century* (pp. 197–223). Mahwah, NJ: Lawrence Erlbaum Associates for the American Educational Research Association.

Darling-Hammond, L. (2007, September). Race, inequality and educational accountability: the irony of 'No Child Left Behind.' *Race Ethnicity and Education, 10*(3), 245–260.

Darling-Hammond, L. (2010). *The flat world and education: How America's commitment to equity will determine our future.* New York, NY: Teachers College Press.

Darling-Hammond, L., Holtzman, D.J., Gatlin, S.J., & Vasquez Heilig, J. (2005). Does teacher preparation matter? Evidence about teacher certification, Teach for America, and teacher effectiveness. *Education Policy Analysis Archives, 13*(42). Retrieved from http://epaa.asu.edu/epaa/v13n42/

DeLeon, A. (2012). "A perverse kind of sense": Urban spaces, ghetto places, and the discourse of school shootings. *Urban Review, 44*(1), 152–169.

Fanon, F. (1952). *Black skin, white masks.* New York, NY: Grove Press.

Fanon, F. (1961). *The wretched of the earth.* New York, NY: Grove Weidenfeld.

Foucault, M. (1972). *The archeology of knowledge.* London, UK: Routledge.

Foucault, M. (1978). *The history of sexuality, Vol. 1: An introduction.* New York, NY: Random House.

Foucault, M. (1980). *Power/knowledge: Selected interviews and other writings 1972–77.* Brighton, UK: Harvester Press.

Freire, P. (1970). *Pedagogy of the oppressed.* New York, NY: Continuum.

Gandhi, L. (1998). *Post-colonial theory: A critical introduction.* New York, NY: Columbia University Press.

Gordon, M. & Reinhart, M. (2011, January 1). Arizona ethnic studies ban goes into effect. *Arizona Republic.* Retrieved from http://www.azcentral.com/arizonarepublic/local/articles/2011/01/01/20110101arizona-ethnic-studies-ban.html

Grubb, N. (1985). *The initial effects of House Bill 72 on Texas public schools: The challenges of equity and effectiveness.* Austin, TX: Lyndon B. Johnson School of Public Affairs.

Haney, W. (2000). The myth of the Texas miracle in education. *Education Policy Analysis Archives, 8*(41). Retrieved from http://epaa.asu.edu/epaa/v8n41

Hargreaves, A. (2005). Leadership succession. *The Educational Forum, 69*(2), 163–173.

Holme, J. J., & Vasquez Heilig, J. (2012). High-stakes decisions: The legal landscape of high school exit exams and the implications for schools and leaders. *Journal of School Leadership, 22*(6), 1177–1197.

Hursh, D. (2007). Assessing No Child Left Behind and the rise of neoliberal education policies. *American Educational Research Journal, 44*(3), 493–518.

Iceland, J. (2004). Beyond Black and White: Metropolitan residential segregation in multi-ethnic America. *Social Science Research, 33*(2), 248–271.

Jacob, B. (2005). Accountability, incentives and behavior: The impact of high-stakes testing in the Chicago Public Schools. *Journal of Public Economics, 89*(5–6), 761–796.

Jennings, J., & Beveridge, A. (2009). How does test exemption affect schools' and students' academic performance? *Educational Evaluation and Policy Analysis, 31*(2), 153–175.

Khalifa, M. (2010). Validating social and cultural capital of hyperghettoized at-risk students. *Education and Urban Society, 42*(5), 620–646.

Khalifa, M. (2011). Principal expectations and principal behavior: Responding to teacher acquiescence. *The Urban Review, 43*(5), 702–727.

Khalifa, M. (2012). A re-new-ed paradigm in successful urban school leadership. Principal as community leader. *Educational Administration Quarterly, 48*(3), 424–467.

Labaree, D.F. (2005). Progressivism, schools and schools of education: An American romance. *Paedagogica Historica, 41,* 275–288.

Lipman, P. (2003). *High stakes education: Inequality, globalization, and urban school reform.* New York, NY: Routledge.

McNeil, L. (2000). *Contradictions of school reform: Educational costs of standardized testing.* New York, NY: Routledge.

McNeil, L. (2005). Faking equity: High-stakes testing and the education of Latino youth. In A. Valenzuela (Ed.), *Leaving children behind: How "Texas-style" accountability fails Latino youth* (pp. 57–111). Albany, NY: State University of New York Press.

Memmi, A. (1965). *The colonizer and the colonized.* Boston, MA: Beacon Press.

National Commission on Excellence in Education. (1983). *A nation at risk: The imperative for educational reform.* Washington, DC: U.S. Government Printing Office.

Nichols, S.L., Glass, G.V., & Berliner, D.C. (2006). High-stakes testing and student achievement: Does accountability pressure increase student learning? *Education Policy Analysis Archives, 14*(1). Retrieved from http://epaa.asu.edu/epaa/v14n1/

No Child Left Behind (NCLB) Act of 2001. (2002). Pub. L. No. 107–110, § 115, Stat. 1425.

Noddings, N. (2004). High stakes testing. Why? *Theory and Research in Education, 2*(3), 263–269.

Orfield, G. (2001). *Schools more separate: Consequences of a decade of resegregation.* Cambridge, MA: Civil Rights Project.

Paperson, L. (2010). The postcolonial ghetto: Seeing her shape and his hand. *Berkeley Review of Education, 1*(1), 5–34.

Plessy v. Ferguson, 163 U.S. 537 (1896).

Ravitch, D. (2011). *The death and life of the great American school system: How testing and choice are undermining education.* New York, NY: Basic Books.

Reardon, S., Greenberg, E., Kalogrides, D., Shores, K., & Valentino, R. (2012). *Left Behind? The Effect of No Child Left Behind on Academic Achievement Gaps Working Paper.* Stanford, CA: Stanford University Press.

Reschovsky, A. (1994). Fiscal equalization and school finance. *National Tax Journal, 47,* 185–197.

Ryan, J.E. (2004, June). The perverse incentives of the No Child Left Behind Act. *New York University Law Review, 79,* 932–989.

Said, E. (1978). *Orientalism.* New York, NY: Vintage.

Salinas, C., & Reidel, M. (2007). The cultural politics of the Texas' educational agenda: Examining who gets what, when and how. *Anthropology and Education Quarterly, 38*(1), 42–56.

Scheurich, J.J., Skrla, L., & Johnson, J.F. (2000). Thinking carefully about equity and accountability. In L. Skrla & J.J. Scheurich (Eds.), *Educational equity and accountability* (pp. 293–299). New York, NY: Routledge.

Shahjahan, R. (2011). Decolonizing the evidence-based education and policy movement: Revealing the colonial vestiges in educational policy, research, and neoliberal reform. *Journal of Educational Policy, 26*(2), 181–206.

Siddle Walker, V. (1993). Caswell County Training School, 1933–1969. Relationships between community and school. *Harvard Educational Review, 63*(2), 161–181.

Smith, M., & O'Day, J. (1991). Systemic school reform. In S. Fuhrman & B. Malen (Eds.), *The politics of curriculum and testing* (pp. 233–267). New York, NY: Falmer.

Sugrue, T. (2005). *Origins of urban crisis: Race and inequality in postwar Detroit.* Princeton, NJ: Princeton University Press.

Tikly, L. (2001). Globalization and education in the postcolonial world: Towards a conceptual framework. *Comparative Education, 37*(2), 151–171.

Tillman, L.C. (2004). African American principals and the legacy of *Brown. Review of Research in Education, 28,* 101–146.

Tillman, L.C. (2006a). Accountability, high stakes testing and No Child Left Behind. In F. Brown & R. Hunter (Eds.), *No Child Left Behind and other federal programs for urban school districts* (pp.189–200). Oxford, UK: Elsevier Science.

Tillman, L.C. (2006b, May/June). Researching and writing from an African American perspective: Reflective notes on three research studies. *International Journal of Qualitative Studies in Education, 19*(3), 265–287.

Trent, W. (2008). *Resources, assets, and strengths among successful diverse students: Understanding the contributions of the Gates Millennium Scholars Program, Vol. 23.* New York, NY: AMS Press.

Vasquez Heilig, J. (2011). Understanding the interaction between high-stakes graduation tests and English language learners. *Teachers College Record, 113*(12), 2633–2669.

Vasquez Heilig, J., Cole, H., & Aguilar, A. (2010). From Dewey to No Child Left Behind: The evolution and devolution of public arts education. *Arts Education Policy Review, 111*(4), 136–145.

Vasquez Heilig, J., Cole, H., & Springel, M. (2011). Alternative certification and Teach For America: The search for high quality teachers. *Kansas Journal of Law and Public Policy, 20*(3), 388–412.

Vasquez Heilig, J., & Darling-Hammond, L. (2008). Accountability Texas-style: The progress and learning of urban minority students in a high-stakes testing context. *Educational Evaluation and Policy Analysis, 30*(2), 75–110.

Vasquez Heilig, J. & Nichols, S. (2013). A quandary for school leaders: Equity, high-stakes testing and accountability. In L. C. Tillman & J. J. Scheurich (Eds.), *Handbook of Research on Educational Leadership for Diversity and Equity* (pp. 409–435). New York, NY: Routledge.

Vasquez Heilig, J., Williams, A., & Jez, S. (2010). Inputs and student achievement: An analysis of Latina/o-serving urban elementary schools. *Association of Mexican American Educators Journal, 10*(1), 48–58.

Vasquez Heilig, J., Young, M., & Williams, A. (2012). At-risk student averse: Risk management and accountability. *Journal of Educational Administration, 50*(5), 562–585.

Watkins, W. (2001). *The white architects of black education: Ideology and power in America, 1865–1954.* New York, NY: Teachers College Press.

Weber, P. (2011). Texas school budget cuts, teacher layoffs add to unemployment. *Huffington Post.* Retrieved from http://www.huffingtonpost.com/2011/09/29/shrinking-texas-school-pa_0_n_986909.html

Wood, D. (2007). Beyond the Panopticon. Foucault and surveillance studies. In J. Crampton & S. Elden (Eds.), *Space, knowledge and power: Foucault and geography* (pp. 245–264). Hampshire, UK: Ashgate.

Youniss, J., & Yates, M. (1997). *Community service and social responsibility in youth.* Chicago, IL: University of Chicago Press.

Afterword

Sonia Nieto

Although we are accustomed to speaking of urban schools as if they had been invented only recently, urban education, with all its dilemmas and challenges, is not new. Even as far back as the mid-19th century, schools in urban areas began feeling the pressure to educate (and "Americanize," to use the lexicon of the time) hundreds of thousands of immigrant children, most of whom were poor and whose families were unschooled. The heady rhetoric of public education as "the great equalizer" was in vogue at the time, as was the growing realization among a small number of educators that the problems of urban schools had far more to do with societal inequality than with schooling. John Dewey, writing about a hundred years ago, could easily have been speaking of urban education today when he reflected on the glaring inequalities that existed at the time, adding that nevertheless, "It is the aim of progressive education to take part in correcting unfair privilege and unfair deprivation, not to perpetuate them" (Dewey, 1916, pp. 119–120). These noble words, unfortunately, have resulted neither in equality nor in correcting "unfair privilege and unfair deprivation." On the contrary, harsh inequalities continue today, and nowhere is this more evident than in our urban schools.

In spite of some similarities between urban schools of the past and those of the present, there are also enormous differences. While Dewey was concerned with inequalities of social class in the early 1900s—a time of unprecedented immigration from Europe—it is mainly Latinos and African Americans, some of whom have been in this nation for hundreds of years, who populate today's urban schools. Inequality today persists not only because of social class differences but also because of the endurance of racism, a legacy that goes back as far as the founding of the nation. Nowadays, many urban neighborhoods are still riddled with poverty and deprivation, and *urban* has become a code word primarily for African Americans and Latinos as well as, in smaller numbers, other immigrants and refugees from Latin America, Asia, and Africa. In addition, cities are now more segregated than ever, with housing patterns and zip codes determining the quality of education that students receive. Even when urban schools are surrounded by neighborhoods of privilege and power (commonplace in "gentrifying" urban areas), many of the middle-class residents of these communities choose to send their children to private or charter schools. The term *urban schools,* then, has become shorthand for schools populated by poor students of color and, sadly, it has also come to signify the miseducation of those students. The "pedagogy of poverty" so fittingly described by Martin Haberman (1991) over two decades ago—a pedagogy defined by low expectations and mindless rote activities that lead neither to the development of significant life skills nor to genuine learning—is still evident in too many schools serving students in urban schools.

The *Handbook of Urban Education* recognizes how *urban* is defined today but also challenges the taken-for-granted vision of the term as simply an oppressive and debilitating place and state of mind, while also recognizing the richness and possibility of urban schools and communities and the students who inhabit them. The editors and authors of this volume define *urban* in more complex ways as context, place, and space. This inclusive and broad-based perspective opens up the opportunity to view urban areas not as simply framed by poverty, crime, and hopelessness, but also as places of hope and possibility.

In the remainder of this Afterword, I highlight three salient insights to be gleaned from the wide-ranging research and resources in this volume, insights that can be helpful to teachers, researchers, policy makers, and others interested in the future of urban schools.

No Easy Answers

The first lesson to be learned is that there are no easy answers, no one-shot solutions, to fixing the deep-seated problems of urban schools. Regardless of the newest fads and reforms, gross disparities continue to exist between urban schools and their suburban and rural counterparts. For example, whereas over the past several decades, policy makers have viewed various privatization approaches as the remedy to failing schools, Mark Berends points out in his chapter on school choice that the research is inconclusive at best. In fact, because charter schools have proliferated in urban areas, children in urban schools are once again the guinea pigs for whether they might be effective or not. As Thandeka K. Chapman concludes in her wide-ranging review of the research literature on charter schools, "While there are a few hopeful results for charter schools, the research overwhelmingly shows that charter schools are struggling to meet the needs of their students, and are not fulfilling the goals of the charter reform." Even more alarming, according to Chapman, in spite of the success of a minority of charter schools, the ongoing and bipartisan pressure for more of these schools may lead to permanently relegating children in urban schools to a second- or third-rate education.

Similarly, in writing about special education, Wanda J. Blanchett points out that the positive effects of special education are not universal but rather based on students' race and social class. Her conclusion is a disheartening one for proponents who view special education as one of the cornerstones of the improvement of urban schools. Although special education has allowed many young people to receive the services they may need, it has brought up other dilemmas such as whether inclusion or resegregation work best, and whether regular classroom teachers will ever be sufficiently prepared to deal with all the challenges of students with special needs.

Broadening the Conversation

This *Handbook* does an admirable job of broadening the conversation about urban schools to include topics that may not have been included in the past. Paramount among these is moving beyond a one-dimensional view of students in urban schools, and of the schools themselves. Although students attending urban schools are predominantly Latino and African American, like all human beings, they have multiple and complex identities and they participate in diverse networks. Several of the chapters point out how crucial community networks are in the lives of students, in the process challenging the notion that the families and communities of urban students have nothing to contribute to the education of their children.

Issues such as language diversity, social class, and LGBTQ identities, among others, are also part of the diversity of students in urban schools. In this context, Molly V. Blackburn and Lance T. McCready present a thorough review of the issue of LGBTQQ identity in urban schools, effectively making the case that although these issues are often invisible in discussions about urban schools, they are another example of how students from urban schools, including LGBTQQ youths, face innumerable odds, and not just those related to race, ethnicity, and social class. For example, in their chapter, Samuel R. Hodge and Alexander Vigo-Valentín tackle the triple issues of health, nutrition, and physical education, topics rarely discussed in the context of urban schools. Yet given the lack of adequate health care in urban communities, the paucity of healthy food venues and information, and the growing obesity rate, these are significant and timely topics related to physical and mental health and learning. These issues particularly affect children and families living in poverty, and schools too have a hand in creating some of these conditions. As an example, given the press for improving test scores, many schools have eliminated physical education and even recess; this is especially true of urban schools. In addition, the high teen pregnancy rate in some urban areas is alarming, yet appropriate sex education is often unavailable.

For their part, Adai Tefera, Kathleen King Thorius, and Alfredo J. Artiles consider the thorny issue of teacher influences on the racialization of students, contending that recent efforts to evaluate teachers based largely on student test scores have a disproportionately negative impact on students in urban schools. To help offset this growing trend, these authors argue for the systematic study of the contextual factors that help create and maintain disproportionality in the assignment of students to special education.

For many years the discourse around the "achievement gap" has been widespread and until recently, relatively unchallenged. Then in 2006 Gloria Ladson-Billings reframed the conversation by calling this gap "the education debt," suggesting that a long-standing debt was due to students of color who have been marginalized by an educational system that has largely abandoned them (Ladson-Billings, 2006). Julian Vasquez Heilig, Muhammad Khalifa, and Linda C. Tillman likewise challenge the so-called reforms based on rigid forms of accountability that include high-stakes testing for students, penalties for teachers and schools not achieving AYP, redefining "highly qualified teachers" based on students' test scores, the labeling of schools as "underperforming," and even closing entire schools. The most oppressive of these "reforms" have been inflicted on students in urban schools and Vasquez Heilig, Khalifa, and Tillman describe these approaches as hegemonic practices that have little to do with learning and more with control and power. Noting that these accountability schemes have not yet resulted in appreciable achievement gains for students in urban schools, these authors propose instead community-based accountability practices that might yield better results than simply punishing students and schools for not living up to some arbitrary standards.

Pedro A. Noguera also critiques the negative ways that urban schools have defined Black male students rather than recognizing that schools themselves, as well as conditions in the neighborhoods in which they are located, have historically offered few opportunities for these students to excel. In his chapter, he also reviews the results of promising research that may help school systems redefine the problem so that school policies and practices from elementary through high school can become more proactive.

Emerging Ecological, Sociocultural, and Sociopolitical Perspectives

In spite of the sobering lessons provided by this *Handbook,* there are many exciting and heartening possibilities as well. For one, the authors refuse to accept the one-dimensional portrait of urban students and schools prevalent in both the literature and the popular imagination. Instead, they present students and their families as multidimensional and complex human beings who—in spite of the many challenges they may face on a daily basis—attempt to lead productive and dignified lives. The editors as well as all of the chapter authors also insist on the urgency to tackle and eradicate the deficit perspective so common in the urban education discourse.

What is particularly noteworthy about this *Handbook* is how urban education has been reframed. Rather than follow the traditional view that the problems of urban schools are caused by individuals—usually students, but also their families and teachers—the authors consider sociocultural and sociopolitical contexts as essential in understanding the ecology of urban schools and communities. This approach is clearly evident in many of the chapters. For instance, the chapter by Carla O'Connor, Jennifer Mueller, and Alaina Neal makes the case that resilience is a complex issue. Rather than view resilience as something inherent only in individuals, these scholars point to the context of urban schools and communities as significant factors in creating and perpetuating risk, or alternatively, in nurturing resilience. That is, according to O'Connor and her co-authors, more than simply a psychological construct, resilience is also a process that is contextualized in societal conditions, in this case, in urban schools and communities, with both positive and negative influences on children's well-being. William F. Tate IV and his co-authors, writing about how urban contexts impact mental health, juvenile justice, and special education, follow a similar approach, arguing that an ecological framework is a better way to understand how youths in urban contexts can best be supported. For these authors, as well as for others in this volume, environmental and school-related factors (i.e., school disciplinary policies, the lack of mental health support in the community, and so on) are as consequential as are youths' individual and psychological factors. Resilience, then, is not simply a question of individual personality, ambition, and drive, but rather a complicated set of individual and contextual factors.

Rethinking parent involvement is another hallmark of the volume. How families are invited to participate in their children's education tends to be quite different in suburban schools and urban schools, particularly those populated by children living in poverty. Traditional perceptions about families living in poverty focus on their lack of support for the education of their children. It is not unusual, for example, to hear teachers and administrators bemoan the lack of involvement of the families in their schools, even suggesting that these families simply do not place a high value on education. The authors of a number of the chapters debunk this perception, emphasizing the importance of outreach, sensitivity, and knowledge about families and all that they have to offer (see, for example, the chapters by William Jeynes, and Gloria Swindler Boutte and George L. Johnson, Jr.). The authors of these chapters suggest that rather than change the parents and families—the typical approach in many parent involvement efforts—what needs changing are the perspectives, policies, and practices of schools. Specifically, the chapter by Ana Christina DaSilva Iddings, Mary Carol Combs, and Luis C. Moll proposes an ecological framework for both challenging deficit perspectives and for educating language minority students. Their "funds of knowledge" framework offers exciting possibilities for changing negative perceptions of students, their families, and their identities.

Consistent with the need to dismantle negative discourses and deficit perspectives is the need to recruit and retain a more diverse professional staff in urban schools. There are implications here not only for teacher preparation, but also for policy at the local, state, and national levels. Tyrone C. Howard and H. Richard Milner IV tackle the dilemma of teacher preparation head-on by suggesting some of the subject matter knowledge, pedagogical knowledge, and cultural and racial knowledge that teachers and other educators need if they are to be to effective with students of diverse backgrounds in urban schools. Another recent fruitful direction is the effort to recruit and retain teachers and other educators from urban communities, thus accomplishing the dual goals of diversifying the teaching force while also providing urban schools with teachers who know the community intimately because they have gone to the same schools, lived similar lives, and continue to live in the same communities where they will teach. In his chapter, Eric Toshalis presents a thorough description of some of these "Grow Your Own" (GYO) initiatives, focusing on those that recruit future teachers at middle and high schools in urban areas.

In a related vein, ethnic-matching, that is, matching the ethnicity, race, and culture of students with those of teachers, is growing in significance as a strategy to positively affect student learning. In his chapter, Donald Easton-Brooks presents evidence from a small but growing group of studies on the positive impact of ethnic-matching on student learning. Although ethnic-matching is no guarantee that students will learn more effectively in all cases, hiring a more diverse teaching and professional staff can nonetheless change the culture and climate of schools by providing a more diverse pool of professionals available to all students. New and innovative approaches to preparing teachers, as suggested by several of the chapter authors here—if taken seriously by policy makers—could help change the course of urban education. These include having teachers learn not only their subject matter and pedagogy, but just as important, learn about their students and the communities in which they live.

The field of culturally responsive pedagogy, quite new just two decades ago, emerged from the multicultural education movement of the 1980s and 1990s. Geneva Gay, one of the pioneers in the field of multicultural education, is also one of the foremost proponents of culturally responsive pedagogy. In her chapter, she defines this approach, reviewing the important research in the field and its achievements, and also documents through concrete examples how culturally responsive pedagogy is providing practitioners and researchers with a promising approach to working with students of diverse backgrounds. It is not only teachers, however, who have the responsibility to be culturally responsive educators. Kofi Lomotey and Kendra Lowery, in their chapter, discuss the prominent role that principals and other African American leaders can play in ensuring a quality education for students in urban schools. In their chapter, Gary M. Crow and Samantha Paredes Scribner focus not on the technocratic skills that principals in urban schools need, but rather on their values, beliefs, and identities. Both chapters reconceptualize the role of the principal as more than an administrator and instead as a mentor to teachers, an example to students, and a visionary leader for the community.

Joyce E. King and her co-authors build on the idea of culturally responsive pedagogy for African American students by suggesting that urban education can indeed become education for liberation. They argue that academic excellence cannot exist without cultural excellence, that is, unless students are given the opportunity to learn about and appreciate their histories and identities and understand the important role they can play in helping their communities thrive. In a related vein, the insistence that subject matter must be more than rote learning and instead build on students' knowledge and expertise is evident throughout the volume. David E. Kirkland describes this perspective in his chapter on urban literacies, while Danny Bernard Martin and Gregory V. Larnell do it through the research on mathematics education, and Jon Yasin uses Hip Hop culture to explore how it can resonate with students in urban schools. These strategies open up possibilities for empowerment and mental health, not to mention for learning opportunities frequently unavailable to urban students. In all these chapters, education for students of color in urban schools is defined primarily as consciousness raising and liberation, a far cry from what is prevalent today.

Critical Race Theory (CRT), originally developed in the field of law, was taken up by scholars in education beginning two decades ago with the Gloria Ladson-Billings and William Tate article on the subject (1995). This framework has been enormously influential as a powerful tool to understand how racism and structural inequality have limited both the education and the life chances of students of color. In her chapter in this volume, Ladson-Billings explains the basic tenets of CRT and reviews recent legislation and court cases to determine how they have either curtailed or opened up possibilities for children in urban schools.

Another way to confront hegemonic policies that place students in urban schools at a disadvantage is to include students' voices in research. In the past several years, Participatory Action

Research (PAR), an innovative approach to educating students in urban schools, has emerged as an important research tool. This methodology uses students as researchers of their own experiences and contexts, in the process often changing not only their knowledge and insights but also their futures. Jason G. Irizarry and Anjale Welton's chapter defines this approach while also presenting Irizarry's research with high school students, as well as other examples of PAR in various contexts. What is clear from this research is that it can provide a powerful way for students to understand how their schooling has hindered their progress. PAR, as well as other creative methodologies, is an antidote to urban education as it is typically conceptualized. It is only through such innovations that urban schools can become transformative spaces of learning.

Conclusion

From considerations of culturally responsive education to discussions of school choice and descriptions of successful family outreach efforts, this *Handbook* provides as comprehensive a landscape of urban education as has ever been available. The authors' perspectives are varied and nuanced, but what they all have in common is the insistence that students in urban schools are multidimensional human beings whose identities and experiences cannot be essentialized or stereotyped. Vast differences exist even within the same race or ethnic group, and issues of home language, gender, sexual orientation, social class, and individual differences provide yet more nuances that help define the tremendous diversity among students who are often painted with broad strokes.

In the final analysis, urban education should be about equality and liberation, a liberation that can only happen through the combined efforts of students, families, teachers, administrators, researchers, policy makers, and the general public. *The Handbook of Urban Education* has come along at a pivotal time in conversations about the hope and the promise of our cities and our increasingly diverse population. This volume provides us with a holistic and hopeful vision of what urban schools and communities can become. Given the many negative portraits of both the people and the communities in which they live, this volume can help shape the discourse of urban education for many years to come.

References

Dewey, J. (1916). *Democracy and education.* New York, NY: Free Press.

Haberman, M. (1991). The pedagogy of poverty versus good teaching. *Phi Delta Kappan, 73*(4), 290–294.

Ladson-Billings, G. (2006). From the achievement gap to the education debt: Understanding achievement in U.S. schools. *Educational Researcher, 35*(7), 3–12.

Ladson-Billings, G., & Tate, W. (1995). Toward a critical race theory of education. *Teachers College Record, 9*(1), 47–67.

Index

Note: Page numbers in *italics* indicate figures and tables.